# Japan

## THE ROUGH GUIDE

There are more than one hundred Rough Guide titles
covering destinations from Amsterdam to Zimbabwe

**Forthcoming titles include**
Chile • Indonesia • New Orleans • Toronto

**Rough Guide Reference Series**
Classical Music • European Football • The Internet • Jazz
Opera • Reggae • Rock Music • World Music

**Rough Guide Phrasebooks**
Czech • French • German • Greek • Hindi & Urdu • Hungarian • Indonesian
Italian • Japanese • Mandarin Chinese • Mexican Spanish • Polish
Portuguese • Russian • Spanish • Thai • Turkish • Vietnamese

**Rough Guides on the Internet**
www.roughguides.com

# ROUGH GUIDE CREDITS

**..t editors:** Sarah Dallas, Jo Mead & Amanda Tomlin
**.eries editor:** Mark Ellingham
**Production:** Susanne Hillen, Link Hall, Julia Bovis, Michelle Draycott
**Cartography:** Maxine Burke, Nichola Goodliffe
**Picture research:** Eleanor Hill
**Finance:** John Fisher, Celia Crowley, Neeta Mistry, Katy Miesiaczek
**Marketing & Publicity:** Richard Trillo, Simon Carloss, Niki Smith (UK); Jean-Marie Kelly, SoRelle Braun (US)
**Administration:** Tania Hummel

...................................................................................................................................................................

## ACKNOWLEDGEMENTS

The authors would like to thank the staff of JNTO in Tokyo and London, especially Patrick Wilson, Higashimoto Takenobu and Oishi Nozomi who went beyond the call of duty in checking facts and giving general assistance; members of the Japanese Inn Group, particularly Sawa Isao; the Japan Youth Hostels Association; New Ōtani Hotels, Kodansha Europe Ltd; Helen Durrant of JET. A big thanks also to everyone at Rough Guides, including Sarah Dallas, Jo Mead, Amanda Tomlin, Link Hall, Maxine Burke and Nichola Goodliffe, and to The Map Studio, Romsey, Hants, for cartography, Elaine Pollard for proofreading, Sean Harvey and Alison Cowan for additional Basics research, and Yamamoto Yuka and Sophie Branscombe for their assistance with the Japanese language boxes; *domo arigatō gozaimasu.*

**Jan**: Many thanks to all the people who helped with this guide. In Tokyo and Yokohama, special thanks to Neil & Cathy Richards & family, Chris and Tako, Herb Donovan, Sally Hanamura, Sekiwa Tomioka, Karen Fraser, Sue McParland, Chie, Paul Sands, Rob Schwartz and Tada Rumiko. In Tōno, to Tada Shizuko, and in Kyoto, to Inuishi Tomoko at JNTO, Corbett Daly, Ed Guertierrez and David Waddell. In Kyūshū, to John Derlega in Kita-Kyūshū, Henk Boer at Huis ten Bosch, Dominic Thomas in Nagasaki; David Yates, Takebayashi Yuko, Shimadzu Yoshihide and Nakazano-san in Kagoshima; and Chris Doyle in Miyazaki. In Okinawa, to Carolyn Kerr and Amy Landa. In Britain and elsewhere, many thanks to Ron Clough, Peter Grimshaw, Marie Conte-Helm, Anne Hemingway, Mike & Julie Jeremy, Dr Richard Sims and the staff of SOAS, Hugh Canaway, Tim George, Rose Carnegie, Elise Hagensen and Tara Dempsey. Finally, heartfelt thanks to my long-suffering family and friends, and to Steve for his unstinting support and boundless patience.

**Simon**: In Tokyo, I'm heavily indebted to Herb and Keiko Donovan, Paul and Karen Fisher, and Chris and Tako Matthews – all treasured friends and Japanese *sensei*. Also, past colleagues and friends from *Tokyo Journal* and *Nikkei News Bureau* including Abigail Haworth, Greg Starr, Dave McCombs, Funayama Mutsumi, Takamoto Yoshiharu and Matthew Smith. Thanks also to Tajima Noriyuki and Catherine Powell. For invaluable assistance during my travels around Japan I'd like to thank Alison Knowles, Gavin Anderson, Phred Kaufman and Miyazawa-san in Sapporo, John Longphre in Nagoya, Dominic Al-Badri and David Jack at *Kansai Time Out*, Tachibana-san in Takarazuka, Ray Smith and Charlie Pimm in Hiroshima, Will Stapely in Okayama, Erik Nielson in Kōchi and Peter Lenhardt in Tokushima. JET scheme teachers and CIRs who also lent a hand along the way include Michelle Damian, Matthew Lambourne, Liza Fletcher, Lynn Russell and Katherine Hemmingway. In London, many thanks to Rebecca Moore for giving me the chance to return to Hokkaidō and for cutting out my waffle. For their unwaivering support and encouraging me to keep going in the toughest times, my love to Alex and Bradd and my best pal Donna.

The extract from *Letters from the End of the World* by Ogura Toyofumi, translated by Kisaburo Murakami and Shigeru Fujii, on p.553, is reprinted by permission of Kodansha International Ltd. English translation copyright © 1997. All rights reserved.

The extract from Donald Richie's *The Inland Sea* on p.519 is reprinted by kind permission of the author.

......................................................................................................

## PUBLISHING INFORMATION

This first edition published March 1999 by
 Rough Guides Ltd, 62–70 Shorts Gardens,
 London WC2H 9AB.
Distributed by the Penguin Group:
Penguin Books Ltd, 27 Wrights Lane, London W8 5TZ
Penguin Books USA Inc., 375 Hudson Street, New York
 10014, USA
Penguin Books Australia Ltd, 487 Maroondah Highway, PO
 Box 257, Ringwood, Victoria 3134, Australia
Penguin Books Canada Ltd, 10 Alcorn Avenue, Toronto,
 Ontario, Canada M4V 1E4
Penguin Books (NZ) Ltd, 182–190 Wairau Road, Auckland 10,
 New Zealand
Typeset in Linotron Univers and Century Old Style to an
 original design by Andrew Oliver.
Printed in England by Clays Ltd, St Ives PLC.
Illustrations in Part One and Part Three by Edward Briant.

Illustrations on p.1 & p.767 by Henry Iles
© Jan Dodd and Simon Richmond 1999
No part of this book may be reproduced in any form without
 permission from the publisher except for the quotation of
 brief passages in reviews.
864pp – Includes index
A catalogue record for this book is available from the British
 Library
ISBN 1-85828-340-X

..........................................................

The publishers and authors have done their best to ensure
 the accuracy and currency of all the information in *The
 Rough Guide to Japan*, however, they can accept no
 responsibility for any loss, injury or inconvenience
 sustained by any traveller as a result of information or
 advice contained in the guide.

# Japan

## THE ROUGH GUIDE

written and researched by

## Jan Dodd
## and Simon Richmond

with additional research by
Ron Clough, Marie Conte-Helm
and Peter Grimshaw

THE ROUGH GUIDES

# THE ROUGH GUIDES

## TRAVEL GUIDES • PHRASEBOOKS • MUSIC AND REFERENCE GUIDES

 We set out to do something different when the first Rough Guide was published in 1982. Mark Ellingham, just out of university, was travelling in Greece. He brought along the popular guides of the day, but found they were all lacking in some way. They were either strong on ruins and museums but went on for pages without mentioning a beach or taverna. Or they were so conscious of the need to save money that they lost sight of Greece's cultural and historical significance. Also, none of the books told him anything about Greece's contemporary life – its politics, its culture, its people, and how they lived.

So with no job in prospect, Mark decided to write his own guidebook, one which aimed to provide practical information that was second to none, detailing the best beaches and the hottest clubs and restaurants, while also giving hard-hitting accounts of every sight, both famous and obscure, and providing up-to-the-minute information on contemporary culture. It was a guide that encouraged independent travellers to find the best of Greece, and was a great success, getting shortlisted for the Thomas Cook travel guide award,

and encouraging Mark, along with three friends, to expand the series.

The Rough Guide list grew rapidly and the letters flooded in, indicating a much broader readership than had been anticipated, but one which uniformly appreciated the Rough Guide mix of practical detail and humour, irreverence and enthusiasm. Things haven't changed. The same four friends who began the series are still the caretakers of the Rough Guide mission today: to provide the most reliable, up-to-date and entertaining information to independent-minded travellers of all ages, on all budgets.

We now publish more than 100 titles and have offices in London and New York. The travel guides are written and researched by a dedicated team of more than 100 authors, based in Britain, Europe, the USA and Australia. We have also created a unique series of phrasebooks to accompany the travel series, along with an acclaimed series of music guides, and a best-selling pocket guide to the Internet and World Wide Web. We also publish comprehensive travel information on our Web site:

www.roughguides.com

## HELP US UPDATE

A lot of effort has gone in to ensure that *The Rough Guide to Japan* is up-to-date and accurate. However, things change – places get "discovered", opening hours are notoriously fickle, restaurants and rooms raise prices or lower standards. If you feel we've got it wrong or left something out, we'd like to know, and if you can remember the address, the price, the time, the phone number, so much the better.

We'll credit all contributions, and send a copy of the next edition (or any other Rough Guide if you prefer) for the best letters. Please mark letters: "Rough Guide Japan Update" and send to:
Rough Guides, 62–70 Shorts Gardens, London WC2H 9AB, or Rough Guides, 375 Hudson St, 9th floor, New York NY 10014.
Or send email to: mail@roughguides.co.uk
Online updates about this book can be found on Rough Guides' Web site at www.roughguides.com

# THE AUTHORS

On discovering onsen in the early 1990s, **Jan Dodd** decided to investigate further. She spent a couple of years studying Japanese language and searching for the ultimate *rotemburo*, before settling in France to work on this book. Jan is also co-author of *The Rough Guide to Vietnam* and *The Rough Guide to Tokyo*.

In 1991 **Simon Richmond** headed east to work as an editor and journalist in Tokyo. Two and a half years later he traded in his treasured shoe-box apartment for an itinerant life as a freelance travel writer. Now based in Sydney, he has had features published in many major national newspapers and had reports broadcast on BBC Radio 4. As well as contributing to *The Rough Guide to Malaysia, Singapore and Brunei*, Simon is co-author of *The Rough Guide to Tokyo*.

# CONTENTS

## • CHAPTER 3: NORTHERN HONSHŪ 224–294

## • CHAPTER 4: HOKKAIDŌ 295–343

## • CHAPTER 5: CENTRAL HONSHŪ 344–401

## • CHAPTER 6: KANSAI 402–518

# PART THREE CONTEXTS 767

# LIST OF MAPS

## MAP SYMBOLS

| | | | |
|---|---|---|---|
| ═══ Major road | ▬ ▬ Prefecture boundary | ∴ Ruins | |
| ═══ Minor road | ◉ Hotel | 🌲 Pagoda | |
| ----- Path | ▣ Restaurant | ⊓ Temple | |
| ++++++ Private Railway | ⌂ Refuge | ♥ Museum | |
| ▬══ JR Line | ▲ Campground | 🕯 Lighthouse | |
| ▬▬ Shinkansen Line | ✕ Airport | ⓘ Information centre | |
| --★-- Tram line | ★ Bus stop | ⊠ Post office | |
| —★— Astram | ◆ Site of interest | ⊞ Hospital | |
| -Ⓢ- Subway line | ⌂ Cave | ▨ Building | |
| — Ferry route | ⌣ Cliff | ╬ Church | |
| River | ▲ Mountain peak | ░ Park | |
| ▬▬ International Boundary | 🔺 View point | ╬ Cemetery | |
| —▬— Chapter division boundary | ♟ Castle | | |

# INTRODUCTION

For a country that lived in self-imposed isolation until 150 years ago, **Japan** has not hesitated in making up for lost time since the world came calling. Anyone who's eaten sushi or used a Sony Walkman feels they know something about this slinky archipelago of some 6800 volcanic islands tucked away off the far eastern coast of Asia, and yet, from the moment of arrival in this oddly familiar, quintessentially Oriental land it's almost as if you've touched down on another planet.

Japan is a place of ancient gods and customs, but is also the cutting edge of cool modernity. High-speed trains whisk you from one end of the country to another with frightening punctuality. You can catch sight of a farmer tending his paddy field, then turn the corner and find yourself next to a neon-festooned electronic games parlour in the suburb of a sprawling metropolis. One day you could be picking through the fashions in the biggest department store on earth, the next relaxing in an outdoor hot-spring pool, watching cherry blossom or snow flakes fall, depending on the season.

Few other countries have, in the space of mere generations, experienced so much or made such an impact. Industrialized at lightning speed, Japan shed its feudal trappings to become the most powerful and outwardly aggressive country in Asia in a matter of decades. After defeat in World War II, it transformed itself from atom bomb victim to wonder economy, the envy of the globe. Currently facing up to recession and rising unemployment after years of conspicuous consumption, Japan still remains fabulously wealthy and intent on reinvention for the twenty-first century, when, together with South Korea, it will become the first Asian nation to host soccer's World Cup in 2002.

You don't want to wait until then to visit, though. Given the devalued yen and lower prices, Japan is now more attractive than ever to anyone keen to see just what makes this extraordinary country tick. It's never going to be a cheap place to travel, but there's no reason why it should be wildly expensive either. Some of the most atmospheric and traditionally Japanese places to stay and eat are often those that are the best value.

In the cities you'll first be struck by the mass of people. In this mountainous country, one and a half times the size of Britain, the vast majority of the 126 million population live on the crowded coastal plains of the main island of **Honshū**. The three other main islands, running north to south, are **Hokkaidō**, **Shikoku** and **Kyūshū**, and all are linked to Honshū by bridges and tunnels that are part of one of Japan's modern wonders – its efficient transport network of trains and highways.

If you're after the latest buzz, the hippest fashions and technologies, and a worldwide selection of food, head for the exciting, overwhelming metropolises of Tokyo and Ōsaka. The cities are also the best places in which to sample Japan's traditional performance arts, such as Kabuki and Nō plays, to catch the titanic clash of sumo wrestlers, and track down the wealth of Japanese visual arts in the major museums.

Outside the cities, from the wide open spaces and deep volcanic lakes of Hokkaidō, blanketed by snow every winter, to the balmy sub-tropical islands of Okinawa, there's a vast range of other holiday options, including hiking, skiing, scuba diving and surfing. You'll seldom have to travel far to catch sight of a lofty castle, ancient temple or shrine, or locals celebrating at a colourful street festival. The Japanese are inveterate travellers within their own country and there's hardly a town or village, no matter how small or plain, that doesn't boast some unique attraction.

It's not all perfect, though. Experts on focusing on detail (the exquisite wrapping of gifts and the tantalizing presentation of food are just two examples), the Japanese often miss the broader picture. Rampant development and sometimes appalling pollution is

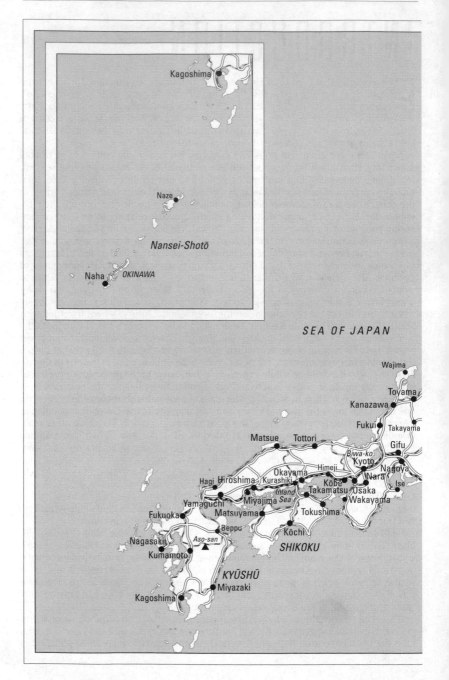

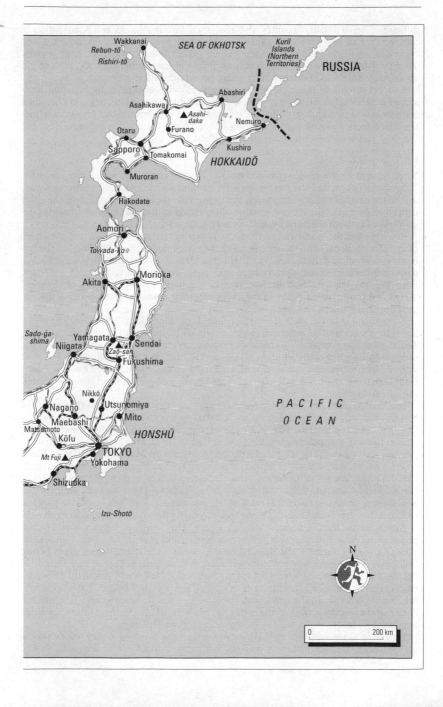

difficult to square with a country also renowned for cleanliness and appreciation of nature. Part of the problem is that natural cataclysms, such as earthquakes and typhoons, regularly hit Japan, so few people expect things to last for long anyway. There's also a blindness to the pernicious impact of mass tourism, with ranks of gift shops, ugly hotels and crowds often ruining potentially idyllic spots.

And yet, time and again, Japan redeems itself with unexpectedly beautiful landscapes, charmingly courteous people, and its tangible sense of history and cherished traditions. Most intriguing of all is the opaqueness at the heart of this mysterious "hidden" culture that stems from a blurring of traditional boundaries between East and West – Japan is neither wholly one nor the other.

## Where to go

You'll need at least a couple of weeks just to skim the surface of what Japan can offer. The capital Tokyo, and the former imperial city and thriving cultural centre of Kyoto, will be top of most visitors' itineraries, and deservedly so, but you could avoid the cities entirely and head to the mountains or smaller islands to discover a different side of the country, away from the most heavily beaten tourist tracks.

Few cities in the world can compare to **Tokyo** in terms of its scale and the sheer range of attractions, from the serene calm of the premier shrine Meiji-jingū to the frenetic, eye-boggling fish market Tsukiji. Here you'll find some of the world's most ambitious architecture, most stylish shops and most outrageous restaurants and bars. Frequent tragedies, both natural and manmade, have destroyed much of historical Tokyo and yet the past lingers, in the alleys around the temple Sensō-ji and in the elegant imperial gardens now open to the public.

Even on the shortest trip to Tokyo you should consider taking in surrounding attractions, in particular the historical towns of **Nikkō** to the north, where the amazing Tōshō-gū shrine complex is set amid glorious mountain forests, and **Kamakura** to the south with its giant statue of the Buddha and tranquil woodland walks. To the west stands Japan's eternal symbol **Mount Fuji**, best visited during the climbing season from June to September, and the beautiful hot-spring (onsen) resort of **Hakone** around the lake Ashi-no-ko.

Mountains, lakes and hot-spring resorts continue north from Tokyo to the very tip of Honshū island. This district, known as Tōhoku, sees surprisingly few visitors, but its sleepy villages and nicely laid-back cities deserve greater attention. While the region has little in the way of top-tier sights, the Golden Hall of **Hiraizumi** more than justifies the journey, and can easily be combined with the islet-sprinkled **Matsushima Bay** or **Tōno**, where a more traditional way of life survives among the fields and farmhouses. Northern Honshū is also known for its vibrant **summer festivals**, notably those of Sendai, Aomori, Hirosaki and Akita, and for its sacred mountains. Of these, **Dewa-sanzan**, on the Japan Sea coast, is home to a colourful sect of ascetic mountain priests, while souls in purgatory haunt the eerie wastelands of **Osore-zan**, way up on the rugged Shimokita Peninsula.

North across the Tsugaru Straits from here, **Hokkaidō** is Japan's final frontier, home to the Ainu, the country's indigenous people, and popular for its outdoor sports. **Daisetsu-zan National Park**, dominating the centre of the island has excellent hiking trails over mountain peaks and through soaring rock gorges carved into incredible shapes. For remoteness it's hard to beat the **Shiretoko National Park** in the far northeast, covering the spindly peninsula of volcanoes and primeval forests that juts out into the Sea of Okhotsk. To the northwest, the lovely islands **Rebun-tō** and **Rishiri-tō** are ideal summer escapes, while in the south, the **Shikotsu-Toya National Park**, includes two beautiful lakes, onsen and the baby volcano Shōwa Shin-zan.

Hokkaido's most historic city is **Hakodate**, with its turn-of-the-century wooden houses, churches of expat traders and lively fish market. Most of the appealing capital

**Sapporo** is thoroughly modern, particularly the raging nightlife centre Suskino, but two older attractions are worth catching: the original Sapporo Brewery and the Historical Village of Hokkaidō, a park with over sixty buildings from the island's frontier days. Winter is also a fantastic time to visit Hokkaidō to catch Sapporo's amazing Snow Festival (*Yuki Matsuri*) in February, ski at top resorts or take a boat through the drift ice off the port of Abashiri.

Skiing, mountaineering and soaking in hot springs are part of the culture of Central Honshū (Chubu), an area dominated by the magnificent **Japan Alps**. Either the old castle town of **Matsumoto** or **Nagano**, with its atmospheric temple of pilgrimage, Zenkō-ji, can be used as a starting point for exploring this region. Highlights include the tiny mountain resort of **Kamikōchi**, accessible only from April to November, and the immaculately preserved Edo-era villages of **Tsumago** and **Magome**, linked by a short hike along the remains of a three-hundred-year-old stone-paved road. On the Gifu-ken side of the mountains, **Takayama** deservedly draws many visitors to its handsome streets lined with merchant houses and temples built by generations of skilled carpenters. In the remote neighbouring valleys you'll find the rare A-frame thatched houses of **Ogimachi**, **Suganuma** and **Ainokura**, remnants of a fast disappearing rural Japan and all designated World Heritage Sites.

On the Japan Sea coast, the historic city of **Kanazawa** is home to Kenroku-en, one of Japan's best gardens, and is the departure point for the charming fishing villages along the wild coastline of the **Noto-hantō**, a peninsula to the northeast. Also accessible from Kanazawa, you can join a working community of Zen Buddhist monks at **Eihci-ji**, a beautiful temple in total harmony with its wooded surroundings. Chubu's southern coast is heavily industrialized, although the major city of **Nagoya** has a few minor points of interest, including the Tokugawa Art Museum, and the pretty castle-town of Inuyama, which holds summer displays of the ancient skill of *ukai*, or cormorant fishing. Also worth visiting is Meiji Mura, a vast outdoor museum of turn-of-the-century architecture.

South of the Japan Alps, the Kansai plains are scattered with ancient temples, shrines and the remnants of imperial cities. The most famous of these former capitals is **Kyoto**, where at first the sheer wealth of sights can be overwhelming. The city's prime attractions are its magnificent temples and palaces, filled with superb statuary or exquisite painted screens, and surrounded by the most glorious gardens. Kyoto is also Japan's premier cultural centre, home to its most refined cuisine and most classy ryokan, while the city's hidden corners make casual wandering a delight. Nearby, **Nara** is a more manageable size but no slouch when it comes to venerable monuments, notably the great bronze Buddha of Tōdai-ji and Hōryū-ji's unrivalled collection of early Japanese statuary. The surrounding region contains a number of still-thriving religious foundations, such as the highly atmospheric temples of **Hiei-zan** and **Kōya-san**. Over on the east coast, Japan's most revered Shinto shrine, **Ise-jingū**, consists of a collection of austere buildings shaded by towering cryptomeria trees.

Not all Kansai is quite so rarefied, however. The opening of Kansai International airport has given a boost to the fast-moving, slightly unconventional metropolis of **Ōsaka**. Apart from its easy-going atmosphere and boisterous nightlife, the city's main attractions are its fabulous aquarium, a superbly restored castle and a hard-hitting civil rights museum. Further west, the port of **Kōbe**, now with 1995's earthquake firmly set behind it, offers a gentler cosmopolitan atmosphere, but is no match for **Himeji**, home of Japan's must-see castle as well as some impressive modern gardens and buildings.

History hangs heavy on Western Honshū (Chūgoku) and not just in its most visited city, the reborn **Hiroshima**. The Kanmon Straits separating Honshū from Kyūshū witnessed one of Japan's most crucial naval battles, Dannoura, in the twelfth century, while in the northern coastal town of Hagi disgruntled *samurai* sparked the Meiji Restoration some 600 years later. The most rewarding sights are on the area's southern San-yō and northern San-in coasts.

After Hiroshima, on the southern coast, it's worth pausing at **Okayama** to stroll around one of Japan's top three gardens, Kōraku-en, and the appealingly preserved Edo-era town of **Kurashiki**. The beauty of the Inland Sea, dotted with thousands of islands, is best appreciated from spots such as the idyllic fishing village of **Tomo-no-Ura**, or the port of **Onomichi**. If you have time, don't miss out on the islands themselves, especially Shōdo-shima, Ikuchi-jima and Miya-jima – home to one of the country's most famous symbols, the waterbound red *torii* gate at the ancient shrine of Itsukushima-jinja. All have a relaxed atmosphere, a world apart from the metropolitan bustle of mainland Japan.

Crossing to the San-in coast, the castle town of **Hagi**, retains some handsome *samurai* houses and atmospheric temples, only surpassed by the even more enchanting **Tsuwano**, further inland. Home to the pantheon of Shinto dieties, one of Japan's most venerable shrines, Izumo Taisha, lies roughly mid-point along the coast, near the watery capital of **Matsue**, which has the region's only original castle. The pine-forested sand spit at **Amanohashidate**, one of Japan's top scenic spots, extends at the far eastern end of the region, and is easily accessible from both Kyoto and Ōsaka.

You don't need to visit all 88 temples on Japan's most famous pilgrimage to enjoy the best of **Shikoku**, the country's fourth largest island. Apart from dramatic scenery in the Iya valley and along the often rugged coastline, the places to aim for are **Matsuyama**, with its imperious castle and splendidly ornate Dōgo Onsen Honkan – one of Japan's best hot springs; the lovely garden Ritsurin-kōen in **Takamatsu**; and the ancient shrine at **Kotohira**, one of the most important in the Shinto religion. Japanese tourists know these places well, but you're unlikely to run into many other *gaijin* on Shikoku.

The southernmost of Japan's four main islands, **Kyūshū** is probably best known as the target for the second atomic bomb, which exploded over **Nagasaki** in 1945. This surprisingly attractive, cosmopolitan city quite rightly acts as Kyūshū's prime tourist focus, but it's worth devoting a few extra days to exploring the island's more far-flung sights. Hikers and onsen enthusiasts should head up into the central highlands, where **Aso-san**'s smouldering peak dominates the world's largest volcanic crater, or to the more southerly meadows of **Ebino Kōgen**. So much hot water gushes out of the ground in **Beppu**, on the east coast, that it's known as Japan's hot-spring capital, complete with jungle baths, sand baths and wonderfully tacky amusement centres. Major cities such as **Kagoshima** and **Kumamoto** offer more conventional castles, museums and craft centres, while **Fukuoka** takes pride in its innovative modern architecture and an exceptionally lively entertainment district.

Last but not least, **Okinawa** comprises more than a hundred smaller islands stretching in a great arc from southern Kyūshū to within sight of Taiwan. Okinawa was an independent kingdom until the early seventeenth century and traces of its distinctive culture still survive. The beautifully reconstructed former royal palace dominates the capital city, **Naha**, but to really appreciate the region you need to make for the remoter islands. Though not undiscovered, this is where you'll find Japan's most stunning, white sand beaches and its best diving, particularly around the sub-tropical islands of Miyako, Ishigaki and Iriomote.

## When to go

In an archipelago stretching over 3000km from north to south you'd expect the average temperature and weather patterns to vary greatly. The main influences on the climate on Honshū are the mountains and surrounding warm seas, bringing plenty of rain and snow. **Winter** weather differs greatly, however, between the western Sea of Japan and the Pacific coasts, the former suffering cold winds and heavy snow while the latter tends towards dry, clear winter days. Regular heavy snowfalls in the mountains provide ideal conditions for skiers.

Despite frequent showers, **spring** is one of the most pleasant times during which to visit Japan, when the weather reports chart the steady progress of the cherry blossom from warm Kyūshū in March to colder Hokkaidō around May. A rainy season (*tsuyu*) during June ushers in the swamp-like heat of **summer**; if you don't like tropical conditions, head for the cooler hills or the northern reaches of the country. A bout of typhoons and more rain in September precede **autumn**, which lasts from October through to late November and is Japan's most spectacular season, when the maple trees explode into a range of brilliant colours.

Also worth bearing in mind when planning your visit are Japan's **national holidays**. During such periods as the days around New Year, the "Golden Week" break of April 28 to May 6 and the Obon holiday of mid-August, the nation is on the move making it difficult to secure last-minute transport and hotel bookings. Avoid travelling during these dates, or make your arrangements well in advance.

## AVERAGE TEMPERATURES AND MONTHLY RAINFALL

Average daily temperatures (°C, max and min) and monthly rainfall (mm)

| | Jan | Feb | Mar | Apr | May | June | July | Aug | Sept | Oct | Nov | Dec |
|---|---|---|---|---|---|---|---|---|---|---|---|---|
| **Akita** | | | | | | | | | | | | |
| max °C | 2 | 3 | 6 | 13 | 18 | 23 | 26 | 28 | 24 | 18 | 11 | 4 |
| min °C | -5 | -5 | -2 | 4 | 8 | 14 | 18 | 19 | 15 | 8 | 3 | -2 |
| rainfall mm | 142 | 104 | 104 | 109 | 112 | 127 | 198 | 188 | 211 | 188 | 191 | 178 |
| **Kōchi** | | | | | | | | | | | | |
| max °C | 12 | 12 | 15 | 19 | 22 | 24 | 28 | 29 | 28 | 23 | 19 | 14 |
| min °C | 4 | 4 | 7 | 12 | 17 | 19 | 24 | 25 | 22 | 17 | 12 | 7 |
| rainfall mm | 64 | 142 | 160 | 188 | 244 | 323 | 257 | 213 | 323 | 279 | 175 | 107 |
| **Nagasaki** | | | | | | | | | | | | |
| max °C | 9 | 10 | 14 | 19 | 23 | 26 | 29 | 31 | 27 | 22 | 17 | 12 |
| min °C | 2 | 2 | 5 | 10 | 14 | 18 | 23 | 23 | 20 | 14 | 9 | 4 |
| rainfall mm | 71 | 84 | 125 | 185 | 170 | 312 | 257 | 175 | 249 | 114 | 94 | 81 |
| **Sapporo** | | | | | | | | | | | | |
| max °C | 2 | 2 | 6 | 13 | 18 | 21 | 24 | 26 | 22 | 17 | 11 | 5 |
| min °C | -10 | -10 | -7 | -1 | 3 | 10 | 16 | 18 | 12 | 6 | -1 | -6 |
| rainfall mm | 25 | 43 | 61 | 84 | 102 | 160 | 188 | 155 | 160 | 147 | 56 | 38 |
| **Tokyo** | | | | | | | | | | | | |
| max °C | 10 | 10 | 13 | 18 | 23 | 25 | 29 | 31 | 27 | 21 | 17 | 12 |
| min °C | 1 | 1 | 4 | 10 | 15 | 18 | 22 | 24 | 20 | 14 | 8 | 3 |
| rainfall mm | 110 | 155 | 228 | 254 | 244 | 305 | 254 | 203 | 279 | 228 | 162 | 96 |

# PART ONE

# THE
# BASICS

## GETTING THERE FROM BRITAIN AND IRELAND

Japan's two main international air gateways from Britain are Tokyo and Ōsaka. Four airlines (All Nippon Airways, British Airways, Japan Airlines and Virgin) fly non-stop from London into New Tokyo International airport (better known as Narita), while ANA and JAL also fly non-stop to Kansai International airport, built on an artificial island in Ōsaka Bay. In addition, JAL flies directly to Nagoya airport, in Western Honshū, twice a week. There are plenty of airlines with indirect flights (eg via Paris or Bangkok) to Narita and Kansai – some also offer connecting services to major regional airports, such as Nagoya and Fukuoka. Direct flights from London take around twelve hours.

There are no direct flights **from Ireland** – you'll need to stop over in Europe en route, with the cheapest deals usually being via London. For details of travelling overland and by ferry to Japan, see p.12.

### BUYING A TICKET

To find out the best deals on **fares** to Japan, contact a flight agent – see the box on overleaf for a list of dependable ones. You should also check the ads in the travel pages of the weekend newspapers, regional listings magazines, Teletext and Ceefax for special deals and the latest prices. Whoever you

### AIRLINES

**Aeroflot** ☎0171/355 2233. *Four flights a week to Tokyo via Moscow.*
**Air France** ☎0181/742 6600. *Daily flights to Tokyo, six times weekly to Ōsaka, and twice weekly to Nagoya, all via Paris.*
**All Nippon Airways (ANA)** ☎0171/355 1155. *Daily direct services to both Tokyo and Ōsaka.*
**Alitalia** ☎0171/602 7111. *Five weekly flights to Tokyo and three to Ōsaka, both via Rome.*
**British Airways** ☎0345/222111. *Direct flights to Tokyo twice daily. Flights to Ōsaka and Nagoya may be re-instated in the future.*
**Cathay Pacific** ☎0171/747 8888. *Daily flights to both Tokyo and Ōsaka, via Hong Kong.*
**Finnair** ☎0171/408 1222. *Twice weekly to Tokyo and three times weekly to Ōsaka, via Helsinki.*
**Garuda Indonesia** ☎0171/486 3011. *Daily flights to Tokyo via Jakarta.*
**Japan Airlines (JAL)** ☎0345/747700. *Daily to Tokyo, six times weekly to Ōsaka and twice weekly to Nagoya.*
**KLM Royal Dutch Airlines** ☎0990/750 900. *Daily services to Ōsaka, five times weekly to Tokyo, twice weekly to both Sapporo and Nagoya, all via Amsterdam.*
**Korean Air** ☎0171/495 8641. *Daily to Tokyo, Fukuoka, Nagoya, Ōsaka and Sapporo, six times weekly to Okayama, four times weekly to Niigata, three times weekly to Aomori and Kagoshima and twice weekly to Ōita, all via Seoul.*
**Lufthansa German Airlines** ☎0345/737747. *Twice weekly flights to Tokyo and three times weekly to Ōsaka via Frankfurt.*
**Malaysia Airlines (MAS)** ☎0171/341 2020. *Daily to Tokyo via Kuala Lumpur.*
**Singapore Airlines** ☎0181/747 0007. *Daily to Tokyo, Ōsaka and Nagoya, four times weekly to Sendai and Hiroshima, all via Singapore.*
**Swissair** ☎0171/434 7300. *Five times weekly to Tokyo and six times weekly to Ōsaka, via Geneva.*
**Thai International** ☎0171/499 9113. *Daily to both Tokyo and Ōsaka via Bangkok.*
**Virgin Atlantic Airways** ☎01293/747747. *Twice daily to Tokyo.*

## FLIGHT AGENTS

**Bridge the World**, 47 Chalk Farm Rd, London NW1 8AN (worldwide ☎0171/911 0900). *Specialists in round-the-world tickets, with good deals aimed at backpackers.*

**Council Travel**, 28a Poland St, London W1V 3DB (☎0171/437 7767). *Flights and student discounts.*

**Far East Travel Centre**, 3 Lower John St, London W1A 4XE (☎0171/734 9318). *Specialists in good-value Korean Air tickets to Japan, via Seoul.*

**Flightbookers**, 177–178 Tottenham Court Rd, London W1P 0LX (☎0171/757 2444); 34 Argyle Arcade, off Buchanan St, Glasgow G1 1RS (☎0141/204 1919). *Low fares on a wide range of scheduled flights.*

**The London Flight Centre**, 131 Earls Court Rd, London SW5 9RH (☎0171/244 6411); 47 Notting Hill Gate, London W11 3JS (☎0171/727 4290); Shop 33, The Broadway Centre, Hammersmith tube, London W6 9YE (☎0181/748 6777). *Long-established agent dealing in discount flights.*

**Japan Travel Centre**, 212 Piccadilly, London W1V 9LD (☎0171/287 1388). *Offers discount fares for all the major carriers to Japan, as well as organizing Jaltour packages. and rail passes. In the same building is the excellent Japan bookshop and food mini-market.*

**Joe Walsh Tours**, 8–11 Baggot St, Dublin (☎01/671 8751) and Cork (☎021/277959). *General budget fares agent.*

**Quest Worldwide**, 10 Richmond Rd, Kingston, Surrey, KT2 5HL (☎0181/547 3322). *Specialists in round-the-world and Australasian discount fares.*

**STA Travel**, 86 Old Brompton Rd, London SW7 3LH; 117 Euston Rd, London NW1 2SX; 38 Store St, London WC1E 7BZ (☎0171/ 361 6262); 25 Queens Rd, Bristol BS8 1QE (☎0117/929 4399); 38 Sidney St, Cambridge CB2 3HX (☎01223/366966); 75 Deansgate, Manchester M3 2BW (☎0161/834 0668); 88 Vicar Lane, Leeds LS1 7JH (☎0113/244 9212); 36 George St, Oxford OX1 2OJ (☎01865/792800); plus other branches throughout the UK. *Worldwide specialists in low-cost flights and tours for students and under-26s, though other customers welcome. Also has offices in Japan.*

**Trailfinders**, 42–50 Earls Court Rd, London W8 6FT (☎0171/938 3366); 194 Kensington High St, London, W8 7RG (☎0171/938 3939); 58 Deansgate, Manchester M3 2FF (☎0161/839 6969); 254–284 Sauchiehall St, Glasgow G2 3EH (☎0141/353 2224); 22–24 The Priory Queensway, Birmingham B4 6BS (☎0121/236 1234); 48 Corn St, Bristol BS1 1HQ (☎0117/929 9000). *One of the best-informed and most efficient agents for independent travellers.*

**The Travel Bug**, 125A Gloucester Rd, London, SW7 4SF (☎0171/835 2000); 597 Cheetham Hill Rd, Manchester M8 5EJ (☎0161/721 4000). *Large range of discounted tickets.*

**Usit**, Fountain Centre, Belfast BT1 (☎01232/324073), Aston Quay, Dublin 2 (☎01/679 8833) and branches in Cork, Derry, Galway, Limerick and Waterford. *Student and youth flight specialist.*

**Usit CAMPUS**, 52 Grosvenor Gardens, London SW1W 0AG (☎0171/730 8111); 541 Bristol Rd, Selly Oak, Birmingham B29 6AU (☎0121/414 1848); 61 Ditchling Rd, Brighton BN1 4SD (☎01273/570226); 37–39 Queen's Rd, Clifton, Bristol BS8 1QE (☎0117/929 2494); 5 Emmanuel St, Cambridge CB1 1NE (☎01223/324283); 53 Forest Rd, Edinburgh EH1 2QP (☎0131/225 6111); 122 George St, Glasgow G1 1RS (☎0141/5531818); 166 Deansgate, Manchester M3 3FE (☎0161/833 2046); 105–106 St Aldates, Oxford OX1 1DD (☎01865/242067). *Student/youth travel specialists, with branches also in YHA shops and on university campuses all over Britain.*

buy your ticket through, check that they belong to the travel industry bodies ABTA or IATA, so that you'll be covered if the agency goes bust before you receive your ticket. **Students** and people **under 26** can often get discounts through specialist agents such as Campus and STA (see above).

**Seasons** differ from airline to airline, but generally July, August and December are the costliest months to travel. If you're not tied to particular dates, check the changeover dates between seasons; you might make a substantial saving by travelling a few days sooner or later. **Fares** to Tokyo from London start from around £500 and rise to roughly £1000 at peak times. However, you can find occasional special deals from as low as £300, so it pays to shop around. Due to the current financial situation in southeast Asia, the airlines are constantly revising their schedules and fares, so it is worth keeping an eye out for last-minute bargains.

Another way to cut the cost of a flight – although you'll be limited on your luggage – is to apply for a **courier flight**, where in exchange for a lower fare you have to carry documents or pacels from airport to airport. For details, contact British Airways Travel Shop, World Cargo Centre, Export Cargo Terminal, Heathrow airport, Middlesex TW6 2JS (☎0181/562 6213).

## STOPOVERS, OPEN-JAWS AND ROUND-THE-WORLD TICKETS

If you have time, you might think about breaking your journey with a **stopover** en route to Japan, for example in Malaysia or Thailand. Not all air-lines charge extra for this option, and with some you'll have to stop over anyway while waiting for a connecting flight. It's also worth noting that some bargain fares to Australia from London can include stopovers in Tokyo or Ōsaka.

On airlines that serve more than one interna-tional airport in Japan, it's possible to buy **open-jaw tickets**, usually for no extra cost, making it possible, say, to fly into Tokyo and out of Ōsaka. These tickets are well worth considering as a way of saving the time and money involved in back-tracking on a journey around the country. Both JAL and ANA offer open-jaw tickets for the same price as a simple return.

## SPECIALIST PACKAGE AND TOUR OPERATORS

**Airwaves** ☎0181/875 1199. *The Japan Sunrise tour offers four nights each in Tokyo and Kyoto, with a side trip to Nikkō, from £1725. Also offers flight- and hotel-only packages to Tokyo and combined Tokyo and Hong Kong packages.*

**Birdquest** ☎01254/826317. *Offers unusual tours to see Japan's winter bird gatherings, including the famous dancing cranes of Hokkaidō. Prices for a two-week tour including flights, accommodation, all meals, transport and specialist guides start at £3150.*

**Creative Tours** ☎0171/495 1775. *Agent for Jaltour, offering five-night packages starting at around £900 for Tokyo and £800 for Kyoto. Longer packages taking in most of Japan's top sights, rail passes and individual itineraries also arranged, including Southeast Asian stopovers.*

**Dream Journeys** ☎01784/449832. *Three-night packages stopping in either Tokyo, Ōsaka or a combination of the two start at around £700. Tours taking in Kyoto, Hiroshima and Kurashiki, or Hakone, Toba and Kyoto are also available.*

**Exodus** ☎0181/675 5550. *Thirteen-night trip, starting at £1900, offered three times a year, taking in Kyoto, Nara, Hiroshima, Takayama, Matsumoto and Tokyo. Accommodation includes four nights in a ryokan.*

**Explore Worldwide** ☎01252/319448. *Offers an imaginative walking tour, starting and finish-ing in Kyoto, which follows part of the ancient Nakasendō through the picturesque Kiso Valley, and is one of the best packages to Japan. Prices start from £1895 including flights, or £1560 land-only.*

**The Imaginative Traveller** ☎0181/742 8612. *Two-week packages to Japan and on the Trans-Siberian to and from Vladivostok or Beijing. Can arrange stopovers and tours at a range of places en route, including Lake Baikal, Mongolia and St Petersburg.*

**The Japan Experience** ☎01703/730 830. *Wide variety of packages offered, including the "Taste of Tokyo" tour at £900 for six days; the National Parks of Japan tour, an eight-day trip round Tokyo, Nikkō, Kyoto and the Ise-Shima National Park area; and the South Japan Tour which concen-trates on Kyūshū. Stopovers in Hong Kong, Singapore and Thailand are also available along with tailor-made itineraries and Japan Rail Passes.*

**Kuoni Worldwide** ☎01306/740500. *Japan and the Orient tour combines four nights in Hong Kong with six nights split between Kyoto and Tokyo, starting at £900.*

**Nippon Travel Agency** ☎0171/437 2424. *Offers tours to some of Japan's less famous sights, as well as a seven-day tour of Tokyo and surrounding attactions for £600 excluding flight. Also offers Japan Rail passes, a hotel pass for pre-paid accommodation and individual itineraries.*

**Oriental Magic** ☎01253/791100. *Flight and top-class hotel packages available to both Tokyo and Ōsaka, starting at under £900 for five nights accommodation in the ANA Hotel, Ōsaka.*

**Regent Holidays** ☎0117/921 1711. *Offers interesting Trans-Siberian packages with a range of stopover options. The basic Moscow–Vladivostok package costs £552 and they can make bookings on the ferry to Niigata, Japan (June–September only).*

**Westminster Travel** ☎01483/728989. *Will put together individual flight, hotel and day-trip packages in Tokyo, Kyoto, Nagoya and Ōsaka.*

A further option is a **round-the-world ticket**, although you may have to hunt around flight agents for those who include Tokyo on their global itineraries. Prices start at around £800 for a one-year open ticket.

## PACKAGES AND TOURS

Japan isn't a difficult country for the independent traveller to negotiate, nor need it be expensive. However, if you're worried about the cost or the potential language problems, a **package tour** is worth considering. Packages tend to come into their own if you want to stay in upmarket hotels – these usually offer cheaper rates for group bookings. All tours use scheduled airline flights, so it's usually no problem extending your stay beyond the basic package. If you want to venture off the beaten track, however, package tours will not be for you.

For a return flight, five nights' accommodation at a three- to four-star hotel, airport transfers and a sightseeing tour, prices begin around £800, based on double occupancy. You'll pay more if you're on a package that combines Tokyo with other areas of Japan or a specialized tour, such as Explore Worldwide's hiking tour along the Kiso Valley (see box on p.5). All the tour prices quoted include flights unless otherwise stated.

# GETTING THERE FROM THE USA AND CANADA

**There are a number of airlines serving Tokyo International airport (Narita) and – less often – other Japanese international airports non-stop from North America, with connections from virtually everywhere in Canada and the United States. The recent Asian financial turmoil has led to a sharp decline in inter-Asian tourism, and the airlines are trying to make up the slack by increasing volume from North America. As a result, many flights are offered at up to half-price, so keep a sharp eye out for special offers. It's also possible to reach Japan via Europe, though this can be a lot more expensive.**

## SHOPPING FOR TICKETS

Barring special offers, the cheapest of the airlines' published fares is usually an **Apex** ticket, although this will carry certain restrictions: you have to book – and pay – at least 21 days before departure, spend at least seven days abroad (maximum stay three months), and you tend to get penalized if you change your schedule. Some airlines also issue **Special Apex** tickets to people younger than 24, often extending the maximum stay to a year. Many airlines offer youth or student fares to **under 26s**; a passport or driving license are sufficient proof of age, though these tickets are subject to availability and can have eccentric booking conditions. It's worth remembering that most cheap return fares involve spending at least one Saturday night away and that many will only give a percentage refund if you need to cancel or alter your journey, so make sure you check the restrictions carefully before buying a ticket.

You can normally cut costs further by going through a **specialist flight agent** – either a **consolidator**, who buys up blocks of tickets from the airlines and sells them at a discount, or a **discount agent**, who in addition to dealing with discounted flights may also offer special student and youth fares and a range of other travel-related services such as travel insurance, rail passes, car rentals, tours and the like. Bear in mind, though, that penalties for changing your plans can be stiff. Remember too that these companies make their money by dealing in bulk – don't expect them to answer a lot of questions. If you travel a lot, **discount travel clubs** are another option – the annual membership fee may be worth it for benefits such as cut-price air tickets and car rental.

Don't automatically assume that tickets purchased through a travel specialist will be cheapest – once you get a quote, check with the airlines and you may turn up an even better deal. Be advised also that the pool of travel companies is swimming with sharks – exercise caution and *never* deal with a company that demands cash up front or refuses to accept payment by credit card.

## ROUTES AND FARES

Airlines running **direct non-stop** flights from North America to Narita and Ōsaka's Kansai airport include All Nippon, American, Delta, Korean,

Northwest and United. Flying time is fifteen hours from New York, thirteen hours from Chicago and ten hours from Los Angeles and Seattle. Returning to North America from Japan requires one hour less due to favourable wind currents. Many European and Asian airlines, such as Air France, Cathay Pacific and Malaysia Airlines, offer **indirect** flights (often with a stopover in their home city included in the price) to Narita and Kansai, as well as to Fukuoka, Hiroshima, Nagoya, Okinawa, Sapporo and Sendai. It's also possible to get to other points in Japan by flying non-stop to Narita and transferring in Tokyo, though you should bear in mind that most domes-

## AIRLINES

**All Nippon Airways (ANA)** ☎1-800/235-9262. *Daily non-stop flights to Narita from New York, Los Angeles and Washington DC.*

**Air Canada** US ☎1-800/776-3000; Canada call ☎1-800/555-1212 for local toll-free number. *Daily non-stop to Ōsaka's Kansai airport from Vancouver, with connections possible from Montreal, Toronto, Winnipeg and Calgary.*

**Air France** US ☎1-800/237-2747; Canada ☎1-800/667-2747. *Flights from several US cities, as well as Montréal and Toronto, to Narita via Paris.*

**Air New Zealand** US ☎1-800/262-1234; Canada ☎1-800/563-5494. *Flights to Narita and Kansai twice weekly via Sidney.*

**American Airlines** ☎1-800/433-7300. *Non-stop flights from San José CA to Narita six times weekly. Daily non-stops to Narita from Boston, Chicago, Dallas and Seattle.*

**Asiana Airlines** ☎1-800/227-4262. *Flights from New York, Los Angeles, San Francisco and Seattle – all via Seoul – to Fukuoka, Hiroshima, Kansai, Nagoya, Narita, Okinawa and Sendai.*

**British Airways** US ☎1-800/2471-9297; Canada ☎1-800/668-1059. *Flights to Tokyo's Narita airport from several US and Canadian cities, via London. Best value of the routes via Europe.*

**Cathay Pacific** ☎1-800/233-2742. *Daily flights to Fukuoka, Kansai, Nagoya, Narita and Sapporo, all with stopovers. Also sells the good-value All Asia Pass ($999–1399) valid for a round-trip flight to any Asian city they serve from North America.*

**Continental Airlines** ☎1-800/231-0856. *Daily east and west coast flights to Fukuoka, Kansai,*

*Nagoya, Narita, Sapporo and Sendai via Honolulu and Guam.*

**Delta Airlines** ☎1-800/221-1212. *Daily non-stop flights to Nagoya and Narita from Portland, Oregon, with connections across the US.*

**Japan Airlines (JAL)** ☎1-800/525-3663. *Daily non-stop flights to Narita from New York, Chicago, Los Angeles and San Francisco. Non-stop flights to Narita from Atlanta via Honolulu three times weekly. Daily non-stop flights to Kansai from Los Angeles.*

**Korean Airlines** ☎1-800/438-5000. *Daily non-stop flights to Narita from Los Angeles. Flights to Narita via Seoul from New York and San Francisco (daily), Chicago (five times a week), Atlanta and Boston (three times a week).*

**Malaysia Airlines** ☎1-800/552-9264. *Non-stop flights to Narita from Los Angeles three times weekly, flights to Ōsaka's Kansai airport and Nagoya from Los Angeles via Kuala Lumpur three times weekly.*

**Northwest Airlines** ☎1-800/447-4747. *Daily non-stop flights to Narita and Ōsaka's Kansai airport from Chicago, Los Angeles, San Francisco and Seattle, with extensive connections from other American cities.*

**Singapore Airlines** ☎1-800/742-3333. *Daily non-stop flights to Narita from Los Angeles.*

**Swissair** ☎1-800/221-4750. *Expensive flights to Narita via Zurich or Geneva five times weekly.*

**United Airlines** ☎1-800/538-2929. *Daily non-stop flights to Ōsaka's Kansai airport and Narita from Los Angeles and San Francisco, with numerous connections from other American cities.*

## DISCOUNT TRAVEL COMPANIES IN NORTH AMERICA

**Air Brokers International**, 150 Post St, Suite 620, San Francisco, CA 94108 (☎1-800/883-3273 or ☎415/397-1383). *Consolidator and specialist in RTW and Circle Pacific tickets.*

**Air Couriers Association**, 191 University Blvd, Suite 300, Denver, CO 80206 (☎1-800/282-1202 or ☎303/215-9000). *Courier flight broker. Annual fee $28.*

**Cheap Tickets, Inc.** 115 E 57th St, Suite 1510, NYC 10017 (☎1-800/377-1000). *Consolidator.*

**Council Travel**, 205 E. 42nd St, New York, NY 10017 (☎1-800/226-8624), *and branches in many other US cities. Student/budget travel agency.*

**Discount Airfares Worldwide On-Line** *www.etn.nl/discount.htm*
*A hub of consolidator and discount agent web links, maintained by the nonprofit European Travel Network.*

**Education Travel Centre**, 438 N Frances St, Madison, WI 53703 (☎1-800/747-5551 or ☎608-256-5551). *Student/youth and consolidator fares.*

**High Adventure Travel**, 353 Sacramento St, Suite 600, San Francisco, CA 94111 (☎1-800/350-0612 or ☎415/912-5600). *Specialists in round-the-world and Circle Pacific tickets.*

**International Association of Air Travel Couriers**, 8 South J St, PO Box 1349, Lake Worth, FL 33460 (☎561/582-8320). *Courier flights; annual membership $45.*

**Last Minute Travel Club**, 132 Brookline Ave, Boston, MA 02215 (☎1-800/LAST MIN). *Travel club specializing in standby deals.*

**Mr. Cheaps** 9123 SE St. Helena St. #280 Clackamas, OR 97015 (☎1-800/672-4327). *Consolidator.*

**Now Voyager**, 74 Varick St, Suite 307, New York, NY 10013 (☎212/431-1616). *Gay and lesbian-run courier flight broker and consolidator.*

**Skylink**, 265 Madison Ave, 5th Fl, New York, NY 10016 (☎1-800/AIR-ONLY or ☎212/573-8980) *with branches in Chicago, Los Angeles, Montréal, Toronto and Washington DC. Consolidator.*

**STA Travel**, Head office: 48 E 11th St, New York, NY 10003 (☎1-800/781-4040 or ☎212/627-3111), and other branches in the Los Angeles, San Francisco and Boston areas. *Worldwide discount travel firm specializing in student/youth fares; also student IDs, travel insurance, car rental, etc.*

**Student Flights**, 5010 E Shea Blvd, Suite 104A, Scottsdale, AZ 85254 (☎1-800/255-8000 or ☎602/951-1177). *Student/youth fares, student IDs.*

**Travel Avenue**, 10 S Riverside, Suite 1404, Chicago, IL 60606 (☎1-800/333-3335 or ☎312/876-6866). *Full service travel agent that offers discounts in the form of rebates.*

**Travel Cuts**, 187 College St, Toronto, ON M5T 1P7 (☎1-800/667-2887 Canada only or ☎416/979-2406), *and branches all over Canada. Organization specializing in student fares, IDs and other travel services.*

**Travelocity** *www.travelocity.com Online consolidator.*

tic flights will leave Tokyo from Haneda airport, a two-hour bus ride from Narita.

The price of your ticket, of course, will depend on when you are travelling and where you are travelling from. Fares are highest in July and August, and at Christmas and New Year when seats are at a premium; prices drop during the shoulder **seasons** – April through June and September through October – and you'll get the best deals in the low season, January through March and November through December (excluding Christmas and New Year). Note also that flying on weekends ordinarily adds $200–250 to the round-trip fare.

The **fares** quoted below give rough idea of what you can expect to pay for a round-trip ticket to Tokyo bought direct from the airlines (midweek low season–weekend high season); they are exclusive of

airport tax, which is an extra $20. From Chicago tickets cost $930–1600; from Los Angeles $675–1600; from Vancouver CAN$900–1400; from New York $960–1800; from San Francisco $675–1450; from Seattle $830–1400; and from Toronto CAN$1215–1650. However, unless you need to travel at very short notice, you are likely to get a much better deal through a specialist flight agent or consolidator (see Shopping for Tickets, p.6)

## ROUND-THE-WORLD-TICKETS, CIRCLE PACIFIC DEALS AND COURIER FLIGHTS

If Japan is only one stop on a longer journey, you might want to consider buying a **round-the-world (RTW) ticket**. Some travel agents can sell you an "off-the-shelf" RTW ticket that will have you touching down in about half a dozen cities (Tokyo is on many itineraries); others will have to assemble one for you, which can be tailored to your needs but is apt to be more expensive. Figure on $3000 to $5000 for a RTW ticket including Japan. It may also be worth checking out the **Circle Pacific** deals offered by many of the major airlines; these allow four stopovers at no extra charge, if tickets are bought fourteen to thirty days in advance.

A further possibility is to see if you can arrange a **courier flight**, although the hit-or-miss nature of these makes them most suitable for the single traveller who travels light and has a very flexible schedule. In return for shepherding a parcel through customs and possibly giving up your bag-gage allowance, you can expect to get a deeply discounted ticket. You'll probably also be restrict-ed in the duration of your stay. A couple of couri-er-flight brokers are listed in the box opposite.

## PACKAGES

A number of tour operators in the US and Canada offer tours in Japan. Most focus on Tokyo, Kyoto or trekking in the Japan Alps, but there are sever-al tours available of the traditional countryside as well as a few specializing in cultural aspects, such as traditional cuisine, artisans or folk art. Before booking, confirm exactly what expenses are included, what class of hotel you'll be offered and how large a group you'll be joining.

## NORTH AMERICAN TOUR OPERATORS

**Abercrombie & Kent**, 1520 Kensington Rd, Oak Brook, IL, 60521 (☎1 800/323-7308). *High-end tailor-made tours, including transfer and sight seeing with private local guides.*

**Adventure Center**, 1311 63rd St, Suite 200, Emeryville, CA 94608 (☎1-800/227-8747). *Twelve-day rural tour starting in Kyoto with visits to temples and medieval villages.*

**Asia Transpacific Journeys**, P.O. Box 1279, Boulder, CO 80306 (☎303/443-6789). *Japan mountain trekking experts.*

**Cross-Culture**, 52 High Point Dr, Amherst, MA 01002-1224 (☎413/256-6303). *Cultural tours of cities and countryside.*

**Geographic Expeditions**, 2627 Lombard St, San Francisco, CA 94123 (☎1-800/777-8183 or ☎415/922-0448). *City, village and mountain trekking tours, along with one focusing on Japanese cuisine and arts.*

**Guides for All Seasons**, 202 County Rd, Calpine, CA 96124 (☎1-800/457-4574 or 916/994-3613). *Japan specialists with two trekking expeditions, cultural walking tours and exploration of Kyoto's traditional artisans.*

**Japan & Orient Tours**, 3131 Camino del Rio North, Suite 1080, San Diego, CA 92108-5789 (☎1-800/377-1080). *Several "modules" from which to select and combine, including Tokyo, bullet train to Kyoto, Ōsaka, Hakone, and stays in traditional ryokan.*

**Japan Travel Bureau**, 810 Seventh Ave, 34th Floor, New York, NY 10019 (☎1-800/223-6104 or ☎212/698-4919). *Day-trips across the country,* including Tokyo, Tokyo Disneyland, Kyoto, Kamakura, Nikkō and Mount Fuji.

**Journeys East**, PO Box 1161-B, Middletown, CA 95461 (☎1-800/527-2612 or ☎707/279-9539). *Tours focusing on art and architecture.*

**Kintetsu International Express**, 1325 Ave of the Americas, Suite 2002, New York, NY 10019 (☎1-800/422-3481 or ☎212/259-9710). *Package and day tour operator.*

**Northwest World Vacation**, Northwest Airlines (☎1-800/800-1504 or ☎612/470-3062). *Standard package tours.*

**Orient Flexi-Pax Tours**, 630 Third Ave, New York, NY 10017 (☎1-800/545-5540 or ☎212/692-9550). *Tour "modules" from which to select, including Tokyo, Ōsaka, Buddhist temples and Mount Fuji.*

**Pacific Holidays**, 2 W 45th St, Suite 1102, New York, NY 10036-4212 (☎1-800/355-8025 or ☎212/764-1977). *Solid package tour operator.*

**TBI Tours**, 53 Summer St, Keene, NH 03431 (☎1-800/223-0266). *Wide selection of tours and authorized Japan Rail Pass agent.*

**Tour East**, 1033 Bay St, Suite 302, Toronto, Ontario M5S 3A5 (☎416/929-0888). *Culture tours combining modern and medieval Japan.*

**Vantage Travel**, 111 Cypress St, Brookline, MA 02146 (☎1-800/322-6677). *Tours of Asia, includ-ing Japan, for the more mature (55-plus) traveller.*

**Worldwide Adventures**, 36 Finch Ave W, North York, Ontario, M2N 2G9 (☎1-800/387-1483). *Operator focusing on mountain trekking with a culture tour as well.*

# GETTING THERE FROM AUSTRALIA AND NEW ZEALAND

There's plenty of choice of flights to Japan from Australia and New Zealand, with both Australasian, Japanese and other regional airlines regularly serving Tokyo (Narita airport) and Ōsaka (Kansai airport). In addition, there are a limited number of flights to the regional airports of Nagoya, Fukuoka and Sapporo.

Increased competition, particularly on services from Eastern Australia (Sydney, Brisbane and Cairns) to Tokyo and Ōsaka, means that fares on these routes are generally the cheapest. It is worth noting, however, that as airlines absorb the impact of the fluctuating economic situation in the Far East, they are likely to adjust their services

## AIRLINES

**Air New Zealand** Australia ☎13 2476; New Zealand ☎09/357 3000.

**ANA** (All Nippon Airways) ☎02/9367 6700.

**Ansett** Australia ☎13 1414; New Zealand ☎09/302 2146.

**Garuda** Australia ☎02/9334 9944 or 1300/365 330; New Zealand ☎09/366 1855.

**JAL** (Japan Airlines) Australia ☎02/9272 1111; New Zealand ☎09/379 9906.

**Korean Air** Australia ☎02/9262 6000; New Zealand ☎09/307 3687.

**Malaysian Airlines** Australia ☎13 2627; New Zealand ☎09/373 2741.

**Philippine Airlines** ☎02/9262 3333 or 1800/112 458.

**Qantas** Australia ☎13 1211; New Zealand ☎09/357 8900 or 0800/808 767.

**Singapore Airlines** Australia ☎13 1011; New Zealand ☎09/379 3209.

## TRAVEL AGENTS

**Anywhere Travel**, 345 Anzac Parade, Kingsford, Sydney (☎02/9663 0411).

**Brisbane Discount Travel**, 260 Queen St, Brisbane (☎07/3229 9211).

**Budget Travel**, 16 Fort St, Auckland, plus branches around the city (☎09/366 0061 or 0800/808 040).

**Destinations Unlimited**, 3 Milford Rd, Auckland (☎09/373 4033).

**Flight Centres** Australia: 82 Elizabeth St, Sydney, plus branches nationwide (☎13 1600); New Zealand: 205 Queen St, Auckland (☎09/309 6171), plus branches nationwide.

**Northern Gateway**, 22 Cavenagh St, Darwin (☎08/8941 1394).

**STA Travel**, Australia: 702 Harris St, Ultimo, Sydney; 256 Flinders St, Melbourne; other offices in state capitals and major universities (nearest branch ☎13 1776, fastfare telesales ☎1300/360 960). New Zealand: 10 High St, Auckland (☎09/309 0458, fastfare telesales ☎09/366 6673), plus branches in Wellington, Christchurch, Dunedin, Palmerston North, Hamilton and at major universities.

**Thomas Cook**, 175 Pitt St, Sydney; 257 Collins St, Melbourne (☎1800/063 913); for branches in other state capitals, call ☎13 1771; 96 Anzac Ave, Auckland (☎09/379 3920).

**Trailfinders**, 8 Spring St, Sydney (☎02/9247 7666).

**The Travel Specialists**, 80 Clarence St, Sydney (☎02/9290 1500).

**Tymtro Travel**, Level 8, 130 Pitt St, Sydney (☎02/9223 2211 or 1300 652 969).

more than usual in the near future. You'd be well advised, therefore, to check the latest situation with a travel agent.

All the **fares** quoted below are for travel during low or shoulder seasons, and exclude airport taxes; flying at peak times (primarily mid-Dec to mid-Jan) can add substantially to these prices. Whatever kind of ticket you're after, first call should be one of the **specialist travel agents** listed in the box below, which can fill you in on all the latest fares and any special offers. If you're a **student** or **under 26**, you may be able to undercut some of the prices given here; STA is a good place to start.

## FARES

All Nippon Airways, Ansett, Garuda Indonesia, JAL, Korean Airlines, Malaysian Airlines, Philippine Airlines, Qantas and Singapore Airlines all offer regular services **from Australia** to Japan: prices for a return flight (with a maximum stay of six months) **to Tokyo** or **Ōsaka** from Sydney, Cairns or Brisbane are around A$1399; fares from Melbourne or Adelaide range from A$1499 to A$1699. Return fares with Garuda, Philippine or Korean can be as low as A$1105, but these generally restrict stays to ninety days and tend to involve longer flight times or overnight stops en route.

Tickets valid for stays of up to a year start at A$1847, though special fares are sometimes available to holders of working holiday visas, which can bring prices down to nearer the A$1380 mark.

From Western Australia, only Qantas flies direct from Perth to Japan, with fares starting at A$1760, but other regional carriers, including Malaysian and Singapore, offer cheaper fares for flights via Kuala Lumpur and Singapore respectively, with prices from A$1460.

**From New Zealand**, Air New Zealand, Ansett New Zealand, Garuda, Qantas and Singapore Airlines, among others, operate regular or code-share services to Japan, with fares starting at NZ$1479, though the most direct routings will cost at least NZ$1799.

## OPEN-JAW AND ROUND-THE-WORLD TICKETS

An **open-jaw ticket**, which enables you to fly into one Japanese city and out of another, saves on backtracking and doesn't add hugely to the cost – count on around A$1599 out of Sydney, flying with JAL or Qantas.

Given enough time to make the most of them, **round-the-world** tickets offer greater flexibility and represent good value compared to straightforward return flights. Virtually any combination of stops is possible, as more and more airlines enter into partnerships to increase their global coverage. A sample itinerary from Melbourne to Tokyo, followed by New York, Montréal, Paris, London, Prague, and back to Melbourne costs from A$2669, but ultimately your choice will depend on where you want to travel before or after Japan – again, a good travel agent is your best ally in planning a route to suit your preferences.

## PACKAGE HOLIDAYS AND SPECIALIST TOURS

If you can only manage a short visit and are happy to base yourself in one city or region, package

## SPECIALIST AGENTS AND TOUR OPERATORS

Note: most travel agents offer a range of holidays and tours, so check out those listed in the box opposite as well as the following:

**Adventure World**, 73 Walker St, North Sydney (☎02/9956 7766 or 1800/221 931), plus branches in Brisbane and Perth; 101 Great South Rd, Remuera, Auckland (☎09/524 5118).

**Asia and World Travel**, cnr George St & Adelaide St, Brisbane (☎07/3229 3511).

**Asian Travel Centre**, 126 Russell St, Melbourne (☎03/9654 8277).

**Jaltour**, Level 14, Darling Park, 201 Sussex St, Sydney (☎02/9285 6666), plus branches in Adelaide, Brisbane, Cairns, Melbourne and Perth.

**Japan Travel Bureau**, Level 24, 1 Market St, Sydney (☎02/9510 0101).

**Japan Experience Tours**, Australia Square Tower, Sydney (☎02/9247 3086).

**Nippon Travel Agency**, 135 King St, Sydney (☎02/9221 8433); 25/151 Queen St, Auckland (☎09/309 5750).

deals can be an economical and hassle-free way of getting a taste for Japan. Five-night **packages** in Tokyo or Kyoto from eastern Australia start at A$1399 (NZ$1700 from Auckland) with Air New Zealand, Ansett Australia or Qantas (book through travel agents), including return airfare, transfers, twin-share accommodation and breakfast. A few specialist agents and operators, such as Jaltour and Japan Experience (and others listed in the box on the previous page), offer more comprehensive **tours**; most can also arrange Japan Rail passes and book accommodation in regional Japan – either in business-style hotels or at more traditional minshuku and ryokan through consortia, such as the Japanese Inn Group. Prices start at A$1799 for five nights' accommodation in tra-

ditional inns, including international flights and a seven-day Japan Rail Pass.

Tours catering to **special interests** tend to be expensive. Explore Worldwide (book though Adventure World – see box on p.11), for example, runs a thirteen-day walking trip along the old Nakasendō Highway from Kyoto, staying at hotels, traditional inns and monasteries, with prices starting at A$3595/NZ$4135 (including some meals, but excluding international airfare). From Eastern Australia (Adelaide, Brisbane, Melbourne or Sydney), Japan Experience Tours also offers fifteen-night **language programmes**, incuding airfares, accommodation in Tokyo and tuition, for A$3235–3485, as well as itineraries combining three nights in Tokyo with three nights in either Beijing or Shanghai (from A$2650).

## LAND AND SEA ROUTES TO JAPAN

Adventurous travellers can take advantage of a number of alternative routes to Japan from Europe and Asia combining **rail and ferry** transport. There are three long-distance train rides – the Trans-Siberian, Trans-Mongolian and Trans-Manchurian – all of which will put you on the right side of Asia for a hop across to Japan. The shortest ferry route is on the hydrofoil between Pusan in South Korea and Fukuoka (Hakata port) on Japan's southern island of Kyūshū. Advance reservations for all ferries are recommended.

### THE TRANS-SIBERIAN AND FERRIES FROM RUSSIA

The classic overland adventure route to or from Japan is via the **Trans-Siberian train**, an eight-night journey between Moscow and Vladivostok on Russia's far eastern coast. The cost of a one-way ticket in a four-berth sleeper compartment is around £400 and can be booked through several agents in the UK (see box, p.5) and Japan (see box, opposite). The same agents can arrange tickets on the Trans-Manchurian train which heads down through northern China to terminate in Beijing, and the Trans-Mongolian via Mongolia to Beijing. You can then take a train to Shanghai to pick up a ferry to Japan. Although purists will want to do the whole train journey at one stretch, one of the best points for a break is Irkutsk, the jumping-

off point for Lake Baikal, which contains around one fifth of the world's freshwater supplies.

The charmingly decrepit Russian port of **Vladivostok** is connected **to Niigata** (see p.281) year-round by Aeroflot's twice-weekly **flights**, every Sunday and Thursday (around ¥46,000/ £200 one-way), and from July to September by a twice-monthy **ferry** service on M/V Antonina Nezhdanova. Between July and the first week of October, the same ferry sails twice a month **to Fushiki**, near Toyama (see p.378) and back. The ferry departs Vladivostok at 3pm and arrives in Niigata and Fushiki at 9am, two days later. Return journeys to Russia from both ports leave at 4pm. The cheapest one-way ticket for a place in a four-berth cabin is ¥43,700 (£190).

Making your own travel arrangements for this route in Russia is now possible, but can be a big hassle – booking a package is well-worth considering. For those planning to return to Europe from Japan, it's worth noting that if you can afford to wait two weeks and have all the correct paperwork, arranging a visa for Russia at the Russian Embassy in Tokyo (2-1-1 Azabudai, Minato-ku, Tokyo 106 ☎03/3583-5982) or the consulate (1-2-2 Nishimidorigaoka, Toyonaka-shi, Ōsaka ☎06/848-3452), is a simpler and cheaper (¥1000) process than in the UK.

The shortest journey from Russia to Japan is on the weekly service (late-April to early

September) **from Korsakov** on the Siberian island of Sakhalin **to Wakkanai** in Hokkaidō (see p.329). The journey takes six hours and thirty minutes and costs ¥40,000 (£170) one-way, ¥57,000 (£250) return. In August, ferry services also run from Korsakov **to Otaru** (see p.309) close to Sapporo, costing ¥48,000 (£210) one-way.

## FERRIES FROM CHINA AND TAIWAN

If you want to take the slow boat **from China** to Japan, you can board a **ferry** from Shanghai to Ōsaka or Kōbe. The China Ferry Company (known as the Japan Ferry Company in Japan; ☎06/536-6541) sails to Kōbe and Ōsaka, while the Shanghai Ferry sails only to Ōsaka (☎06/243-6345 in Japan). The frequency of the services varies with the seasons, but there are usually a couple of departures a week, taking 48 hours and costing around ¥20,000 (£87). Conditions on board are good, the berths are clean and comfortable, and facilities include swimming pools, restaurants, and even discos. Similar services, run by China Express Line (☎078/321-5791 in Kōbe), leave Tanggu, the port 50km east of Tianjin, for Kōbe every Monday, returning on Thursdays. The journey also takes about 48 hours and costs around ¥25,000 (£110).

From the **Taiwanese** port of Keelung you can reach Japan's southern islands of Okinawa in twenty hours. This is a great way to arrive or leave Japan, as the ferry stops at the Miyako and Ishigaki islands en route. There are weekly sailings to Shinkō port in Naha, Okinawa's main town (see p.746), with prices starting from around ¥15,600 (£70). Tickets are available in Taipei from Yeong An Maritime Co (☎02/771-5911) and Keelung (☎02/424-8151). In Naha, tickets can be bought from the ferry company Arimura Sangyō (see box, below) and it's also possible from here to arrange onward connections to Ōsaka by ferry for ¥15,750 (£70).

## FERRIES FROM SOUTH KOREA

The most popular and fastest sea route to Japan is from the South Korean port of Pusan, some 200km north of Kyūshū, across the Korea Strait. There are daily services from Pusan to Fukuoka (see p.657) in Kyūshū and Shimonoseki (p.568) at the western tip of Honshū.

From **Pusan to Fukuoka**, there is a choice of two services. The hydrofoil Beetle 2 operated by JR Kyūshū takes two hours and fifty-five minutes and leaves Pusan daily at 2pm (10am from Fukuoka). The fare is ¥12,400 (£50) one way, ¥22,500 (£100) return. Reservations can be made in Pusan (☎051/465-7799), through major travel agencies in Japan, such as JTB, or in Fukuoka (☎092/281-2315). The slower (15hr 40min) and cheaper service on the ferry Camellia leaves Pusan on Tuesday, Thursday and Sunday (the return trip from Fukuoka leaves on Monday, Wednesday and Friday). The cheapest fare is ¥9000 (£40) for a *tatami* room rising to ¥12,000 (£50) for a first-class berth in a two to three-

---

## FERRY BOOKING AND TOUR AGENTS IN JAPAN

**Arimura Sangyō Co**, Echo Kyobashi Bldg, 3-12-1 Kyōbashi, Chūō-ku, Tokyo (☎03/3562-2091); New Okazakibashi Bldg, 2-5-19 Nishimoto-cho, Nishi-ku, Ōsaka (☎06/531-9267); Naha (☎098/860-1980). *Main agent for ferry tickets from Okinawa to Taiwan, via the Miyako and Ishigaki islands.*

**Euras Tours**, 1-7-3 Azabudai, Minato-ku, Tokyo 106 (☎03/5562-3380). *Can arrange rail journeys to Europe and ferry tickets to Russia and China as well as tour packages.*

**Fushiki Kairiku Unsu Co**, 5-1 Fushiki-minato-machi, Takaoka-shi, Toyama (☎0766/45-1175). *Agent for Fushiki–Vladivostok ferry.*

**Japan-China International Ferry Co (JIFCO)**, 10-14 Sarugakuchō, Shibuya-ku, Tokyo 150 (☎03/5489-4800), and Sa-ai Bldg, 1-8-6, Shinmachi, Nishi-ku, Ōsaka (☎06/536-6541). *Booking agent for ferry services from Ōsaka and Kōbe and Shanghai.*

**Kampu Ferry Co**, 1-10-60 Higashi-yamatochō, Shimonoseki, Yamaguchi-ken (☎0832/24-3000). *Agent for the Shimonoseki–Pusan ferry.*

**Rinkō Air Service**, 5-11-20 Bandai, Niigata (☎025/274-5181). *Agent for Niigata–Vladivostok ferry.*

**United Orient Shipping Agency**, 7F Rikkokai-sogo Bldg, 2-32-2 Kita-Shinagawa, Shinagawa-ku, Tokyo (☎03/3740-2061). *General agent for Niigata/Fushiki–Vladivostok ferry tickets.*

person cabin. Reservations can be made in Fukuoka (☎092/262-2323).

Ferries from **Pusan to Shimonoseki**, operated by Kampu Ferry Co (see box on previous page), leave daily at 6pm and arrive in Shimonoseki at 8.30am. The return from Shimonoseki leaves at 4pm. The lowest regular fare is ¥8500 (£35), rising to ¥14,000 (£60) for a first-class berth in a two-person cabin, with an extra ¥600 (£2.60) charge to pay at Shimonoseki. If you are doing a return trip from Shimonseki, it's cheaper to buy separate one-way tickets rather than a return from Japan, since the fares in Pusan are cheaper.

# VISAS AND RED TAPE

All visitors to Japan must have a valid passport for the duration of their stay, but only residents of certain countries need apply for a visa in advance. Citizens of Austria, Germany, Ireland, Liechtenstein, Mexico, Switzerland and the UK can stay in Japan for up to nintey days without a visa provided they are visiting for tourism or business purposes. This stay can be extended for another three months (see below).

Citizens of Argentina, the Bahamas, Barbados, Belgium, Canada, Chile, Colombia, Costa Rica, Croatia, Cyprus, Denmark, Dominica, El Salvador, Finland, France, Greece, Guatemala, Honduras, Iceland, Israel, Italy, Lesotho, Luxembourg, Malta, Mauritius, the Netherlands, New Zealand, Norway, Portugal, San Marino, Singapore, Slovenia, Spain, Surinam, Sweden, Tunisia, Turkey, Uruguay and the USA can also stay for up to ninety days without a visa, though this is unextendable. Anyone wishing to stay longer will have to leave the country, then re-enter.

All other nationalities, including Australians, must apply for a visa in advance from the Japanese embassy or consulate in their own country. These are usually free, though in certain circumstances, you may be charged a small fee. The rules on visas do change from time to time, so check first with your embassy or consulate, or on the Japanese embassy Web site (*www.embjapan.org.uk*), for the current situation.

## VISA EXTENSIONS

To get a **visa extension** you'll need to fill in two copies of an Application for Extension of Stay, available from local immigration bureaux (see the listing sections of major city accounts). These must then be returned along with passport photos, a letter explaining your reasons for wanting to extend your stay, and a processing fee of ¥4000. In addition, you may be asked to show proof of sufficient funds, and a valid onward ticket out of the country. If you're not a national of one of the few countries with six-month reciprocal visa exemptions (ie: Austria, Germany, Ireland, Liechtenstein, Mexico, Switzerland and the UK), expect a thorough grilling from the immigration officials. An easier option – and the only alternative available to nationals of those countries who are not eligible for an extension – may be a short trip out of the country, say to South Korea or Hong Kong, though you'll still have to run the gauntlet of immigration officials on your return.

## WORKING HOLIDAY VISAS

Citizens of Australia, Canada and New Zealand, aged between 18 and 25 (and in certain circumstances 30), can apply for a **working holiday visa**, which grants a six-month stay and two possible six-month extensions. This entitles the holder to work for a maximum of twenty hours a week, and is intended primarily to subsidize bona fide

## JAPANESE EMBASSIES AND CONSULATES

**Australia**, 112 Empire Circuit, Yarralumla, Canberra ACT 2600 (☎02/6273 3244); 17th Floor, Comalco Place, 12 Creek St, Brisbane, Queensland, 4000 (☎07/3221-5188); 45th Floor, Melbourne Central Tower, 360 Elizabeth St, Melbourne, Victoria, 3000 (☎03/9639-3244); 21st Floor, The Forrest Centre, 221 St. George St, Perth, WA 6000, Australia (☎08/9321 7816); Level 34, Colonial Centre, 52 Martin Place, Sydney, NSW 2000 (☎02/9231-3455).

**Canada**, 255 Sussex Drive, Ottawa, Ontario KIN 9E6 (☎613/241-8541); 2480 ManuLife Place, 10180-101 St, Edmonton, Alberta, T5J 3S4 (☎403/422-3752); 600 Rue de la Gauchetière Ouest, Suite 2120, Montréal, Québec, H3B 4L8, (☎514/866-3429); Suite 2702, Toronto Dominion Bank Tower, PO Box 10 Toronto-Dominion Centre, Toronto, Ontario, M5K 1A1 (☎416/363-7038); 900-1177 West Hastings St, Vancouver, BC, V6E 2K9, (☎604/684-5868).

**China**, 7 Ri Tan Rd, Jian Guo Men Wai, Beijing (☎10/532-2361).

**France**, 7 Ave Hoche, 75008 Paris (☎01/48-08-62-00)

**Ireland**, Nutley Bldg, Merrion Centre, Nutley Lane, Dublin 4 (☎01/269-4033).

**New Zealand**, 7th Floor Norwich Insurance House, 3-11 Hunter St, Wellington 1 (☎04/473 1540); 6th Floor, National Mutual Centre Bldg, 37-45 Shortland St, Auckland 1 (☎09/303-4106); Level 5 Forsyth Barr House, 764 Colombo St, Christchurch 1 (☎03/366-5680).

**Singapore**, 80 Anson Rd, #34-00, #35-00, IBM Tower, Singapore, 079907 (☎2358855).

**South Korea**, 18-11 Choonghak-dong, Chongro-ku, Seoul (☎02/733-5626).

**Thailand**, 1674 New Petchburi Rd, Bangkok 10310 (☎02/252 6151).

**UK**, 101-104, Piccadilly, London, W1V 9FN (☎0171/465-6500); 2 Melville Crescent, Edinburgh EH3 7HW (☎0131/225-4777).

**USA**, 2520 Massachusetts Ave NW, Washington DC, 20008-2869 (☎202/238-6700); 550 West 7th Ave, Sutie 701, Anchorage, Alaska 99501 (☎907/279-8428); Suite 2000, 100 Colony Square Bldg, 1175 Peachtree St N.E., Atlanta, GA 30361 (☎404/892-2700); Federal Reserve Plaza, 14th Floor, 600 Atlantic Ave, Boston, Massachusetts 02210 (☎617/973-9772); Olympia Centre, Suite 1100, 737 North Michigan Ave, Chicago, Illinois 60611 (☎312/280-0400); 200 Renaissance Center, Suite 3450, Detroit, Michigan 48243 (☎313/ 567-0120); 1742 Nuuanu Ave, Honolulu, Hawaii 96817-3294 (☎808/536-2226); First Interstate Bank Plaza, Suite 5300, 1000 Louisiana St, Houston, Texas 77002 (☎713/652-2977); 2519 Commerce Tower, 911 Main St, Kansas City, Missouri 64105-2076 (☎816/471-0111); 350 South Grand Ave, Suite 1700, Los Angeles, California 90071 (☎213/617-6700); World Trade Center Bldg, Suite 3200, 80 SW 8th St, Miami, Florida 33130 (☎305/530-9090); Suite 2050, One Poydras Plaza, 639 Loyola Ave, New Orleans, Louisiana 70113 (☎504/529-2101); 299 Park Ave, New York, NY 10171 (☎212/371-8222); 2400 First Interstate Tower, 1300 SW, 5th Ave, Portland, Oregon 97201 (☎503/221-1811); 50 Fremont St, Suite 2300, San Francisco, California 94105 (☎415/777-3533); 601 Union St, Suite 500, Seattle, Washington 98101 (☎206/682-9107).

travellers. You need to apply at least three weeks before leaving your home country, and must be able to show evidence of sufficient funds. Contact your local embassy or consulate to check the current details of the scheme.

## CUSTOMS

The **duty free allowance** for bringing goods into Japan is 400 cigarettes or 100 cigars or 500 grammes of tobacco; three 760cc bottles of alcohol; two ounces of perfume; and gifts and souvenirs up to a value of ¥200,000. As well as firearms and drugs, Japanese customs officials are particularly strict about the import of pornographic material, which will be confiscated if your bags are searched.

On the plane you'll be given an immigration form and a **customs declaration** to fill out; if you're within the allowances outlined above, you can ignore the customs form. If you're arriving from a third-world country you will also have to fill out a yellow health form, detailing any illness you may have suffered in the previous fourteen days. If you've been well, you can ignore this form, too.

There is no limit on the amount of foreign or Japanese **currency** that you can bring into the country, but ¥5 million is the maximum that you can take out of Japan.

## INSURANCE

Most people will find it essential to take out a good travel insurance policy, particularly one with comprehensive medical coverage, due to the high cost of hospital treatment in Japan. Bank and credit cards (such as American Express or Barclaycard) often include certain levels of medical or other insurance, especially if you use them to pay for your trip. This can be quite comprehensive, covering anything from lost or stolen baggage to missed connections, though certain policies will only cover medical costs, in which case it is advisable to take out extra insurance.

Travel insurance **policies** vary widely: some are comprehensive while others cover only certain risks (accidents, illnesses, delayed or lost luggage, cancelled flights, etc). In particular, ask whether the policy pays medical costs up front and reimburses you later, and whether it provides for medical evacuation to your home country. For policies that include lost or stolen luggage, check exactly what is and isn't covered, and make sure the per-article limit will cover your most valuable possession. If you plan to do any diving, mountaineering, skiing, or other **adventurous sport**, you'll usually have to pay an extra premium; check carefully that any insurance policy you are considering will cover you in case of an accident.

Very few insurers will arrange on-the-spot payments in the event of a major expense or loss; you will usually be reimbursed only after going home. In all cases of loss or **theft** of goods, you will have to get a report from the local **police**, in order to make a claim. For medical purposes, you'll also

need copies of the bills paid for treatment and medicines.

### BRITISH AND IRISH COVER

It's almost always cheaper to arrange your travel insurance independently in Britain and Ireland than through a travel agent or tour operator; if an agent insists that you take its insurance as part of the flight or package deal, you should think about shopping elsewhere. Whichever policy you go for, always check the small print.

You should also check your existing **home insurance policy**, as it may well cover your possessions against loss or theft when overseas. If not, you may find it cheaper to extend your household cover to include overseas and medical costs. Many private **medical schemes** also cover you when abroad – make sure you know the procedure and the helpline number.

Failing all these options, both Usit CAMPUS and STA (see p.4 for addresses) can provide good-value policies, as can any of the insurance companies listed below. For full medical and possessions cover in Japan, excluding adventurous sports, you should expect to pay around £30 for two weeks, £40 for a month and £100 for three months.

### UK TRAVEL INSURANCE COMPANIES

**Columbus Travel Insurance**, 17 Devonshire Square, London EC2M 4SQ (☎0171/375 0011).

**Endsleigh Insurance**, 97-107 Southhampton Row, London, WC1B 4AG (☎0171/436 4451).

**Frizzell Insurance**, Frizzell House, County Gates, Bournemouth, Dorset BH1 2NF (☎01202/292333).

### NORTH AMERICAN COVER

Before buying an insurance policy, check that you're not already covered. **Canadian provincial health plans** typically provide some overseas medical coverage, although they are unlikely to pick up the full tab in the event of a mishap. Holders of official **student/teacher/youth cards** are entitled to accident coverage and hospital in-patient benefits – the annual membership is far

## TRAVEL INSURANCE COMPANIES IN NORTH AMERICA

**Access America** ☎1-800/284-8300.

**Carefree Travel Insurance** ☎1-800/323-3149.

**Desjardins Travel Insurance** Canada only ☎1-800/463-7830.

**STA Travel Insurance** ☎1-800/781-4040.

**Travel Assistance International** ☎1-800/821-2828.

**Travel Guard** ☎1-800/826-1300.

**Travel Insurance Services** ☎1-800/937-1387.

*All the above numbers apply in the US and Canada, unless otherwise stated.*

less than the cost of comparable insurance. **Students** may also find that their student health coverage extends during the vacations and for one term beyond the date of last enrollment. Bank and credit cards (particularly American Express) often provide certain levels of medical or other insurance, and travel insurance may also be included if you use a major credit or charge card to pay for your trip. **Homeowners' or renters'** insurance often covers theft or loss of documents, money and valuables while overseas.

After exhausting the possibilities above, you might want to contact a specialist **travel insurance** company; your travel agent can usually recommend one, or see the box below. The best **premiums** are often to be had through student/youth travel agencies – STA, for example, offers policies costing US$48–69 for fifteen days (depending on level of coverage), US$80–105 for a month, US$149–207 for two months, and US$510–700 for a year.

## AUSTRALIAN AND NEW ZEALAND COVER

In Australia and New Zealand, travel insurance is available from most **travel agents** (see p.10) or direct from **insurance companies** (see box below), for periods ranging from a few days to a year or even longer. Most policies are similar in premium and coverage – but if you plan to indulge in high-risk activities such as mountaineering or diving check the policy carefully to make sure you'll be covered.

A typical **policy** to cover you for travel in Japan will cost A$130/NZ$145 for two weeks, A$190/NZ$210 for one month, and A$280/NZ$310 for two months.

## TRAVEL INSURANCE COMPANIES

**Cover More**, 9/32 Walker St, North Sydney (☎02/9202 8000 or 1800/251 881).

**Ready Plan**, 141 Walker St, Dandenong, Melbourne (☎03/9791 5077 or 1800/337 462); 10/ 63 Albert St, Auckland (☎09/379 3208).

# HEALTH

**Japan has high standards of health and hygiene, and there are no significant diseases worth worrying about. No compulsory immunizations or health certificates are needed to enter the country.**

Medical treatment and drugs are of a high quality, but can be expensive, so, if possible, you should bring any medicines you might need with you, especially prescription drugs. Also bring a copy of your prescription and make sure you know what the generic name of the drug is, rather than its brand name. Some common drugs widely available throughout the US and Europe, such as the contraceptive pill, are generally not available in Japan.

Although mosquitoes buzz across Japan in the warmer months, **malaria** is not endemic so there's no need to take any tablets. It's a good idea to pack mosquito repellent, however, and to burn coils in your room at night, or to use a plug-in repellent.

Tap **water** is safe to drink throughout Japan, but you should avoid drinking directly from streams or rivers. It's also not a good idea to walk barefoot through flooded paddy fields, due to the danger of water-borne parasites. Foodwise, you should have

## MEDICAL RESOURCES FOR TRAVELLERS

### AUSTRALIA AND NEW ZEALAND

**Travellers' Medical and Vaccination Centres**, 27–29 Gilbert Place, Adelaide (☎08/8212 7522); 1/170 Queen St, Auckland (☎09/373 3531); 6/247 Adelaide St, Brisbane (☎07/3221 9066); Mezzanine Level, City Walk Arcade, 2 Mort St, Canberra (☎02/6257 7156); 5 Westralia St Darwin (☎08/8981 2907); 6 Washington Way, Christchurch (☎03/379 4000); 270 Sandy Bay Rd,

Sandy Bay, Hobart (☎03/6223 7577); 2/393 Little Bourke St, Melbourne (☎03/9602 5788); 5 Mill St (☎08/9321 1977), Perth; 7/428 George St (☎02/9221 7133), Sydney. The Web site *www.tmvc.com.au* has a list of all the Travellers' Medical and Vaccination Centres throughout Australia, New Zealand and Southeast Asia, as well as general information on travel health.

### NORTH AMERICA

**Centers for Disease Control**, 1600 Clifton Rd NE, Atlanta, GA 30333 (☎404/639-3311; *www.cdc.gov/travel/travel.html*). Publishes outbreak warnings, suggested inoculations, precautions and other background information for travellers, and has a very useful Web site.

**International Association for Medical Assistance to Travellers (IAMAT)**, 417 Center St, Lewiston, NY 14092 (☎716/754-4883; *www.*

*sentex.net/~iamat*) and 40 Regal Rd, Guelph, ON N1K 1B5 (☎519/836-0102). A non-profit organization supported by donations, it can provide a list of English-speaking doctors in Japan, climate charts and leaflets on various diseases and inoculations.

**Travel Medicine**, 351 Pleasant St, Suite 312, Northampton, MA 01060 (☎1-800/872-8633). Sells first-aid kits, mosquito netting, water filters and other health-related travel products.

### UK

**British Airways Travel Clinics**. There are around forty regional clinics throughout the country including airport locations at Gatwick and Heathrow (call ☎01276/685040 for the one nearest to you or consult *www.britishairways.com*). The clincs provide information about health care in the country you are travelling to and can give up-to-the-minute advice on any recommended health precautions and vaccinations.

**Hospital for Tropical Diseases Travel Clinic**, St Pancras Hospital, 4 St Pancras Way, London

NW1 0PE (Mon–Fri 9am–5pm by appointment only; ☎0171/388 9600; a consultation costs £15 which is waived if you have your injections here). A recorded Health Line (☎0839/337733; 49p per min) gives hints on hygiene and illness prevention.

**MASTA (Medical Advisory Service for Travellers Abroad)**, London School of Hygiene and Tropical Medicine. Operates a pre-recorded 24-hour Travellers' Health Line (☎0891/224100; 50p per min), giving written information tailored to your journey by return of post.

no fears about eating raw seafood or seafish, including the notorious *fugu* (globe fish). However, raw meat and river fish are best avoided.

### GETTING MEDICAL HELP IN JAPAN

In the case of an **emergency**, the first port of call should be to ask your hotel to phone for a doctor or ambulance. You could also head for or call the nearest tourist information office or international centre (in major cities only), which should be able to provide a list of local doctors and hospitals with English-speaking staff. Alternatively, you could call the toll-free 24hr Japan Helpline (☎0120-46 1997).

If you need to call an **ambulance** on your own, dial ☎119 and speak slowly when you're asked to give an address. Ambulance staff are not trained paramedics, but will take you to the nearest appropriate hospital. Unless you're dangerously ill when you go to hospital, you'll have to wait your turn in a clinic before you see a doctor, and you'll need to be persistent if you want to get full details of your condition: some doctors are notorious for witholding information from patients.

For minor ailments and advice, you can go to a **pharmacy**, which you'll find in most shopping areas. There are also numerous smaller private **clinics**, where you'll pay in the region of ¥10,000 to see a doctor. You could also try **Asian medical remedies**, such as accupuncture (*hari*) and pressure point massage (*shiatsu*), though it's worth trying to get a personal recommendation to find a reputable practitioner.

## TRAVELLERS WITH DISABILITIES

**Japan is not an easy place to travel around for anyone using a wheelchair, or for those who find it difficult to negotiate stairs or walk long distances. Most train and subway sta-** tions have seemingly endless corridors, and few have escalators or lifts; the sheer crush of people can also be a problem at times. It's sometimes possible to organize assistance at

### CONTACTS FOR TRAVELLERS WITH DISABILITIES

#### AUSTRALIA AND NEW ZEALAND

**ACROD** (Australian Council for Rehabilitation of the Disabled), PO Box 60, Curtin, ACT 2605 (☎02/6282 4333). Provides lists of useful organizations, as well as offering information and advice on specialist travel agencies and tour operators.

**Disabled Persons Assembly**, 173–175 Victoria St, Wellington (☎04/811 9100). Referral organization dealing with access and mobility for the disabled overseas.

#### BRITAIN AND IRELAND

**Disability Action Group**, 2 Annadale Ave, Belfast BT7 3JH (☎01232/491 011). Can provide a list of accommodation suitable for disabled travellers and a holiday fact sheet, as well as a wide range of useful publications.

**Holiday Care Service**, 2nd floor, Imperial Bldg, Victoria Rd, Horley, Surrey RH6 7PZ (☎01293/774535, fax 784647; Minicom ☎01293/776943). Provides free lists of accessible accommodation abroad. Information on financial help for holidays is also available.

**RADAR (Royal Association for Disability and Rehabilitation)**, 12 City Forum, 250 City Rd, London EC1V 8AF (☎0171/250 3222; Minicom ☎0171/250 4119). A good source of advice on holidays and travel abroad. They produce a biennial holiday guide in association with Holiday Care Service for long-haul holidays (£5 inc. p&p).

**Tripscope**, The Courtyard, Evelyn Rd, London W4 5JL (☎0181/994 9294, fax 994 3618). This registered charity provides a national telephone information service offering free advice on UK and international transport for those with a mobility problem.

**continued overleaf**

## CONTACTS FOR TRAVELLERS WITH DISABILITIES contd

### JAPAN

**Japanese Red Cross Language Service Volunteers**, 1-1-3 Shiba-Daimon, Minato-ku, Tokyo 105 (☎03/3438-1311, fax 3432-5507; *jwindow.net/LWT/TOKYO/REDCROSS/ redcross_index.html* Publishes the English-language guide *Accessible Tokyo*, with detailed information on hotels, restaurants and attractions in the Tokyo area. Send an international reply coupon with your order.

**The Japanese Society for Rehabilitation of Disabled Persons**, 1-22-1 Toyama, Shinjuku-ku, Tokyo 162 (☎03/5723-0601, fax 5273-1523). As well as providing a general information service, the JSRD runs a Tokyo centre for disabled persons (including limited accommodation) and a lift bus.

### NORTH AMERICA

**Directions Unlimited**, 720 N Bedford Rd, Bedford Hills, NY 10507 (☎1-800/533-5343). Tour operator specializing in custom-made tours for people with disabilities.

**Mobility International USA**, PO Box 10767, Eugene, OR 97440 (Voice and TDD 503/343-1284). Information and referral services, access guides, tours and exchange programmes. Annual membership $20 (includes quarterly newsletter).

**Society for the Advancement of Travel for the Handicapped**, 347 Fifth Ave, New York, NY 10016 (☎212/447-7294). Non-profit travel-industry referral service that passes queries on to its

members as appropriate; allow plenty of time for a response.

**Travel Information Service**, Moss Rehabilitation Hospital, 1200 West Tabor Rd, Philadelphia, PA 19141 (☎215/456-9600). Telephone information and referral service.

**Twin Peaks Press**, Box 129, Vancouver, WA 98666 (☎206/694-2462 or 1-800/637-2256). Publisher of the *Directory of Travel Agencies for the Disabled*, listing more than 370 agencies worldwide; *Travel for the Disabled*; the *Directory of Accessible Van Rentals*, and *Wheelchair Vagabond*, loaded with personal tips.

stations, but you'll need a Japanese-speaker to make the arrangements. That said, most Shinkansen trains and a few of the other services, such as the Narita Express from Narita International airport into Tokyo, have spaces for wheelchair users, but you'll need to make reservations well in advance. For travelling short distances, taxis are an obvious solution, though few drivers will offer help getting in or out of the car.

When it comes to **accommodation**, the international chains or modern Western-style hotels, as well as some of the newer youth hostels, are most likely to provide facilities such as fully adapted rooms and lifts. Similarly, most modern shopping complexes, museums and other public buildings are equipped with ramps, wide doors and special toilets. For further information, including details of specialist tour companies, contact the organizations listed in the box.

# INFORMATION AND MAPS

The Japan National Tourist Organization (JNTO) maintains a number of overseas offices (see box), which are stocked with a wealth of free maps and leaflets, varying from general tips on Japanese culture to detailed area guides, lists of accommodation and practical information about local transport. If you can't get to a JNTO office, you'll find much of the same material avail-

## JAPAN NATIONAL TOURIST ORGANIZATION OFFICES

**Australia** Level 33, The Chifley Tower, 2 Chifley Square, Sydney, NSW 2000 (☎02/9232-4522).

**Canada** 165 University Ave, Toronto, Ontario, M5H 3B8 (☎416/366-7140).

**Hong Kong** Suite 3704-05, 37F, Dorset House, Taikoo Place, Quarry Bay (☎2968-5688).

**South Korea** 10F, Press Centre Bldg, 25 Taepyongno 1-ga, Chung-gu, Seoul (☎02/732-7525).

**Thailand** Wall Street Tower Bldg, 33/61, Suriwong Rd, Bangkok 10500 (☎02/233-5108).

**UK** Heathcoat House, 20 Savile Row, London W1X 1AE (☎0171/734-9638).

**USA** One Rockefeller Plaza, Suite 1250, New York, NY 10020 (☎212/757-5640); 401 North Michigan Ave, Suite 770, Chicago, IL 60611 (☎312/222-0874); 360 Post St, Suite 601, San Francisco, CA 94108 (☎415/989-7140); 515 Figueroa St, Suite 1470, Los Angeles, California, 90071 (☎213/623-1952).

## JAPANESE ADDRESSES

Japanese **addresses** are described by a hierarchy of areas, rather than numbers running consecutively along named roads. A typical address starts with the largest administrative district, the *ken* (prefecture) accompanied by a three-digit postal code; for example, Nagasaki-ken 850. However, there are four exceptions: Tokyo-*to* (metropolis), Kyoto-*fu* and Ōsaka-*fu* (urban prefectures) and Hokkaidō are all independent administrative areas at the same level as the *ken*. Next comes the *shi* (city) or, in the country, the *gun* (county) or *mura* (village). The largest cities are then subdivided into *ku* (wards), followed by *chō* (districts), then *chōme* (local neighbourhoods), blocks and, finally, individual buildings.

Japanese addresses are therefore written in reverse order from the Western system. However, if it is written in English, it usually follows the Western order; this is the system we adopt in the guide. For example, the address 2-12-7 Kitano-chō, Chūō-ku, Kōbe-shi identifies building number 7, somewhere on block 12 of number 2 *chōme* in Kitano district, in Chūō ward of Kobe city. Most buildings bear a small metal tag with their number (eg 2-12-7, or just 12-7), while lamp-posts often have a bigger plaque with the district name in *kanji* and the block reference (eg 2-12). Note that the same address can also be written 12-7 Kitano-chō 2-chōme, Chūō-ku.

Though the system's not too difficult in theory, actually **locating an address** on the ground can be frustrating. The consolation is that even Japanese people find it tough. The best strategy is to have the address written down, preferably in Japanese, and then get to the nearest train or bus station. Once in the neighbourhood, start asking; local police boxes (*kōban*) are a good bet and have detailed maps of their own areas. If all else fails, don't be afraid to telephone – often someone will come to meet you.

able on their Web site; see box below, for details of this and other recommended information sources on the Internet.

Within Japan, JNTO operates four **Tourist Information Centres** (TIC), all of which have English-speaking staff. These offices are located in central Tokyo, Tokyo's Narita airport, Kansai International airport and Kyoto (see individual city accounts for details). They provide a similar range of information as JNTO's overseas offices, covering the whole of Japan as well as their local area, and can usually answer all sorts of individual queries. Not surprisingly, you may have to queue at busy times. The offices in Narita, Kyoto and Kansai Airport provide accommodation booking services (no commission), while the Tokyo TIC is located next door to the Welcome Inn Reservation Centre (see p.39 for details). Though the staff will help sort out routes and timetables, they can't make travel reservations, nor usually sell tickets to theatres, cinemas and so on (some occasionally have discounted tickets on offer); instead,

they'll direct you to the nearest appropriate outlet. It's worth noting that much of their printed information isn't always available in the regions, so stock up while you can.

**Local tourist offices** with English-speaking staff are called **"i" centres**, of which there are now over ninety in nearly sixty cities, usually located in or close to the main railway station. In practice, the amount of English information available – whether written or spoken – is a bit hit or miss, but at least the staff should be able to assist with local maps, hotel reservations (some charge a small commission) and simple queries. Next level down are the ordinary tourist information offices where there's little chance of getting English-language assistance. Nevertheless, they can usually supply maps, transport information and, sometimes, help with accommodation.

If you're stuck, JNTO runs the excellent **Japan Travel-Phone** (daily 9am–5pm; toll-free ☎0120–444800 or ☎0088–224800), which provides English-language information and assis-

---

## JAPAN ON THE INTERNET

Although Japan has been surprisingly slow to make its presence felt on the Internet, there are now a growing number of Web sites out there, many of them in both English and Japanese. Yahoo's directory (see below) is a good jumping-off point for a general overview of Japan-related sites, of which some of the more useful and well-established are detailed below. (See p.55 for information about getting connected while in Japan.)

### Airports
Both Narita and Kansai International airports run their own Web sites, complete with flight information, floor plans and the low-down on local access. They're at *www.narita-airport.or.jp* and *www.kansai-airport.or.jp* respectively.

### Discussion forums
To post a question or browse for interesting messages, the best newsgroups are *soc.culture.japan* (also *soc.culture.japan.moderated*) and *fj.life.in-japan*

### Japan National Tourist Organization
JNTO's Japan Travel Updates at *www.jnto.go.jp* is probably the best single place to look for general, travel-related information. It's well-designed, updated reasonably regularly and posts useful guides to events, galleries, budget travel and accommodation. Also includes a selected list of links.

### Links
Yahoo at *www.yahoo.com* is a good place to start, while Stanford University's JGuide, at

*fuji.stanford.edu/jguide* has a large, well-organized list of links. Otherwise, try Japan Web Guide, at *www.gol.com/jguide* or *www.ifnet.or.jp/~daruma/Home.html* for more selective, annotated listings.

### News and media
The digital version of the *Japan Times* at *www.japantimes.co.jp* is the most comprehensive and accessible of the Web sites run by Japan's English-language newspapers. For economic and financial news, however, the *Nihon Keizai Shimbun* site, at *www.nikkei.co.jp/enews* wins hands down.

### Tokyo
Without doubt, Tokyo's biggest and best site to date is Tokyo Q at *www.so-net.or.jp/tokyoq* It contains a weekly round-up of current news and upcoming arts events, as well as the latest restaurant listings and links to some of the city's more quirky sites.

tance, not only on travel-related topics. You can call from any grey or green public phone – insert a phone card or ¥10 piece to get the dial tone – except within Tokyo and Kyoto, where you should phone the appropriate TIC at a local call rate (¥10 per minute).

Another useful source of English-language information is the **Goodwill Guides**, groups of volunteer guides located in nearly thirty cities mostly in central and western Japan. The guides' services are free – although you're expected to pay for their transport, entry tickets and any meals you have together – and the language ability obviously varies. But they provide a great opportunity to learn more about Japanese culture and to visit local restaurants, shops and so forth

with a Japanese speaker. The TICs have a list of groups and their contact details, or the local information office should be able to help with arrangements; try and give at least two days' notice.

A number of cities also operate a **Home Visit System**, where English-speaking Japanese families welcome foreigners into their homes for a couple of hours, usually after the evening meal. Again, arrangements can be made through the local "i" centre or TIC a few days in advance.

## MAPS

The Japan National Tourist Organization publishes four tourist **maps** covering Japan, Tokyo, Kansai and Kyoto. These are available free at JNTO

---

## MAP OUTLETS

### AUSTRALIA AND NEW ZEALAND

**The Map Shop**, 16a Peel St, Adelaide (☎08/8231 2033).

**Specialty Maps**, 58 Albert St, Auckland (☎09/307 2217).

**Worldwide Maps and Guides**, 187 George St, Brisbane (☎07/3221 4330).

**Bowyangs**, 372 Little Bourke St, Melbourne (☎03/9670 4383).

**Perth Map Centre**, 891 Hay St, Perth (☎08/9322 5733).

**Travel Bookshop**, Shop 3, 175 Liverpool St, Sydney (☎02/9261 8200).

### BRITAIN AND IRELAND

**Blackwell's Map and Travel Shop**, 53 Broad St, Oxford OX1 3BQ (☎01865/792792; *www.bookshop.blackwell.co.uk*).

**Daunt Books**, 83 Marylebone High St, London W1M 3DF (☎0171/224 2295); 193 Haverstock Hill, London NW3 4QL (☎0171/794 4006).

**Easons Bookshop**, 40 O'Connell St, Dublin 1 (☎01/873 3811).

**Fred Hanna's Bookshop**, 27–29 Nassau St, Dublin 2 (☎01/677 1255).

**Heffers Map Shop**, 3rd Floor, in Heffers Stationery Department, 19 Sidney St, Cambridge, CB2 3HL (☎01223/568467; *www.heffers.co.uk*). Mail order available.

**James Thin Melven's Bookshop**, 29 Union St, Inverness, IV1 1QA (☎01463/233500; *www.jthin.co.uk*). Mail order available.

**John Smith and Sons**, 57–61 St Vincent St, Glasgow, G2 5TB (☎0141/221 7472; *www.johnsmith.co.uk*). Mail order service.

**The Map Shop**, 30a Belvoir St, Leicester, LE1 6QH (☎0116/2471400). Mail order available.

**National Map Centre**, 22–24 Caxton St, London SW1H 0QU (☎0171/222 2466; *www.mapsworld.com*).

**Newcastle Map Centre**, 55 Grey St, Newcastle upon Tyne, NE1 6EF (☎0191/261 5622).

**Stanfords**, 12–14 Long Acre, WC2E 9LP (☎0171/836 1321; email *sales@stanfords.co.uk*); within Usit CAMPUS at 52 Grosvenor Gardens, SW1W 0AG (☎0171/730 1314); within the British Airways offices at 156 Regent St, W1R 5TA (☎0171/434 4744); and 29 Corn St, Bristol BS1 1HT (☎0117/929 9966).Mail order available.

**The Travel Bookshop**, 13–15 Blenheim Crescent, W11 2EE (☎0171/229 5260; *www.thetravelbookshop.co.uk*).

**Waterstone's**, Queens Bldg, 8 Royal Ave, Belfast BT1 1DA; 69 Patrick St, Cork (☎021/276 522); 91 Deansgate, Manchester, M3 2BW (☎0161/832 1992; *www.waterstones.co.uk*); and branches throughout the UK. Mail order available.

**continued oveleaf**

## MAP OUTLETS contd

### NORTH AMERICA

**Adventurous Traveler Bookstore**, PO Box 1468, Williston, VT 05495 (☎1-800/282-3963; *adventuroustraveler.com*).

**Book Passage**, 51 Tamal Vista Blvd, Corte Madera, CA 94925 (☎415/927-0960).

**The Complete Traveller Bookstore**, 199 Madison Ave, New York, NY 10016 (☎212/685-9007).

**Map Link**, 30 S La Petera Lane, Unit #5, Santa Barbara, CA 93117 (☎805/692-6777).

**The Map Store Inc.**, 1636 1st St, Washington, DC 20006 (☎202/628-2608).

**Open Air Books and Maps**, 25 Toronto St, Toronto, ON M5R 2C1 (☎416/363-0719).

**Phileas Fogg's Books & Maps**, #87 Stanford Shopping Center, Palo Alto, CA 94304 (☎1-800/533-FOGG).

**Rand McNally**, 444 N Michigan Ave, Chicago, IL 60611 (☎312/321-1751); 150 E 52nd St, New York, NY 10022 (☎212/758-7488); 595 Market St, San Francisco, CA 94105 (☎415/777-3131); call 1-800/333-0136 ext 2111 for other locations, or for maps by mail order.

**Sierra Club Bookstore**, 6014 College Ave, Oakland, CA 94618 (☎510/658-7470).

**Travel Books & Language Center**, 4931 Cordell Ave, Bethesda, MD 20814 (☎1-800/220-2665).

**Traveler's Bookstore**, 22 W 52nd St, New York, NY 10019 (☎212/664-0995).

**Ulysses Travel Bookshop**, 4176 St-Denis, Montreal (☎514/843-9447).

**World Wide Books and Maps**, 736 Granville St, Vancouver, BC V6Z 1E4 (☎604/687-3320).

---

offices abroad and at the TICs in Japan, and are perfectly adequate for most purposes. Tourist offices in other areas usually provide local maps, which are of varying quality, and often only in Japanese, but generally adequate. If you need anything more detailed, most bookshops sell maps, though you'll only find English-language maps in the big cities (see individual city Listings for details). By far the most useful are the **bilingual maps** published by Kodansha or Shōbunsha, which are available from specialist shops outside Japan (see box above for suggested outlets). Kodansha's

*New Tokyo Bilingual Atlas* is a must for anyone spending more than a few days in the capital, while Shōbunsha's *Japan Road Atlas* is the best available map for exploring by car. If you're **hiking**, an excellent guide is the relevent *Area Map*, published by Shōbunsha in Japanese only.

Note that **maps on signboards** in Japan, such as a map of footpaths in a national park, are usually oriented the way you are facing. So, if you're facing southeast, for example, as you look at the map, the top will be southeast and the bottom northwest.

# COSTS, MONEY AND BANKS

Whilst being bad news for Japan, the recent economic recession and the subsequent devaluation of the yen have meant good news for travellers. Despite its reputation as a prohibitively expensive place to visit, prices in Japan are now on a par with other developed countries and, with some careful planning, it's a manageable destination for even those on a modest budget. The key is to do what the majority of Japanese do: eat in local restaurants, stay in Japanese-style inns and take advantage of any available discounts. That said, if you make the wrong choice of bar or take a longish taxi ride, it can be prohibitively expensive.

The **Japanese currency** is the yen (¥), of which there are no subdivisions. Notes are available in denominations of ¥1000, ¥5000 and ¥10,000, while coins come in values of ¥1, ¥5, ¥10, ¥50, ¥100 and ¥500. Apart from the ¥5 piece, a copper-coloured coin with a hole in the centre, all other notes and coins indicate their value in Western numerals. At the time of writing, the **exchange rate** was approximately ¥230 to £1, ¥140 to US$1, and ¥85 to AUS$1. Japan's rate of inflation currently stands at around one percent per annum.

## COSTS

By far your biggest outlays are likely to be accommodation and transport. In the case of **accommodation**, you can keep costs down by staying in hostels or cheap Japanese inns and by sharing a room with two or more people (see Accommodation on p.36 for details). As a rough guide, the average price of staying in a youth hostel dorm is ¥2600 (£11/US$19); for a double room in a basic Japanese inn, expect to pay around ¥5000 (£22/US$36) per person; while a similar room in a moderately comfortable business hotel will set you back upwards of ¥6000 per person (£26/US$43).

As regards **transport**, the best strategy for most travellers is to buy a Japan Rail Pass before departure, though it's also worth investigating special deals on internal flights. Within the country, all sorts of discount fares and excursion tickets are available, while overnight ferries and buses are an economical, if not always comfortable, way of getting around; see Getting Around on p.27 for more details.

By staying in youth hostels and eating in the cheapest local restaurants, the absolute minimum **daily budget** for food and accommodation alone is ¥5000 (£22/US$36). By the time you've added in some transport costs, a few entry tickets, meals in better class restaurants and one or two nights in a ryokan or business hotel, you'll be reaching a more realistic expenditure of at least ¥8000–¥10,000 (approximately £35–£45/US$60–US$70) per day.

Holders of **international student cards** are eligible for discounts on transport and some admission fees. If you're planning to stay in hostels, it's worth buying a **Youth Hostel card** in your home country; not only does the card qualify for slight reductions at some hostels (see p.40), but you can also take advantage of discount tour packages offered by the Japan Youth Hostel association (see

| MONEY AND INFORMATION | | |
|---|---|---|
| Bank | *ginkō* | 銀行 |
| Foreign exchange desk | *Gaikoku kawase mado-guchi/ryōgae jo* | 外国為替窓口／両替所 |
| Yen | *yen* (or *en*) | 円 |
| Tourist information office | *kankō annaijo* | 観光案内所 |

## CONSUMPTION TAX AND LOCAL TAX

A **consumption tax** (*shōhizei*) of five percent is levied on virtually all goods and services in Japan, including restaurant meals and accommodation. Sometimes this tax will be included in the advertised price, sometimes not, so, for large amounts, check first.

In addition, a **local tax** of three percent is added to hotel and restaurant bills in certain instances: in the case of hotels, the local tax is added if the bill exceeds ¥15,000 per person per night; in restaurants, it applies to amounts more than ¥7500 per person. If you're eating in your hotel, therefore, it might help to pay for your room and meals separately.

Note that any service charges will be calculated *after* these two taxes have been added.

box p.42 for details). Before setting off, it's also worth reading JNTO's *Your Travel Companion* and *Japan for the Budget Traveller*, both full of useful information and tips on how to save money.

### CHANGING MONEY

Though credit cards are gaining in popularity, Japan is still very much a **cash society**; even in major cities you'll be settling most bills in ready money. Thanks to the country's low crime levels and a surprisingly undeveloped banking system, most Japanese carry around relatively large amounts of yen, and it's fine for you to follow suit. That said, it's always safest to carry the bulk of your money in **travellers' cheques**, with the added advantage that in Japan they attract a slightly better exchange rate than notes. The most widely accepted cheques are American Express, Visa and Thomas Cook. You'll have no problem changing dollar or sterling travellers' cheques in major towns and cities, but it would be wise to carry a small amount of yen travellers' cheques or dollars cash, if you plan to visit more remote areas.

When exchanging either cash or travellers' cheques, look for **banks** announcing "Authorized Foreign Exchange Bank" in English outside the front door; banks usually offer the best rates, with little variation between them and no commission fees. Remember to take your passport along, and allow plenty of time, since even a simple transaction can take thirty minutes or more. Note that, while all foreign exchange banks accept dollars and the vast majority will take sterling, other currencies can be a problem even in Tokyo; if you're stuck, Tokyo Mitsubishi Bank handles the widest range of currencies and has branches in most large cities.

Main **post offices** often have an exchange counter where you can change cash or travellers' cheques in seven major currencies, including American, Canadian and Australian dollars and sterling; their rates are usually close to the banks' and they have slightly longer opening hours (Mon–Fri 9am–4pm). When changing money, ask for a few ¥10,000 notes to be broken into ¥5000 and ¥1000 denominations; these come in handy for ticket machines and small purchases.

If you need to change money at any other time, the big **department stores** often have an exchange desk, though they might charge a small fee. Alternatively, you could try a major **hotel**; whilst hotels are only supposed to change money for their guests, some might be persuaded to help in an emergency. In rural areas, however, you'll be lucky to find a bank or anywhere else offering exchange services, so make sure you've got plenty of cash before heading into the sticks.

### CREDIT CARDS AND WIRING MONEY

**Credit cards** are far more widely accepted in Japan than they were a few years ago. The most useful cards to carry are American Express and Visa, followed by Mastercard and then Diners Club, which you should be able to use in big-city hotels, restaurants, shops and travel agencies where they're used to serving foreigners. However, many retailers only accept locally issued cards, so it's never safe to assume you'll be able to use your foreign plastic.

It's the same situation with **cash advances**. You'll find **ATM**s in city-centre shopping malls and department stores, but relatively few accept non-Japanese cards. The other problem with

### BANKING HOURS

**Banks** open Monday–Friday 9am–3pm, though some don't open their exchange desks until 10.30am or 11am. All banks close on Saturdays, Sundays and public holidays.

## 24HR CREDIT CARD EMERGENCY NUMBERS

If you lose your credit card, call:

**American Express** ☎0120–020120.

**Mastercard** ☎03/3256-6271; dial ☎0051 first for a collect call.

**Visa** ☎0120–1331363.

ATMs is that they generally close around 8pm on weekday and Saturday evenings, and are closed all day Sunday. Some Citibank machines, however, are now open 24hr and allow international access for cards in the Cirrus or PLUS networks (including Visa and Mastercard); Citibank is well-represented in Tokyo and is expanding gradually

to other major cities (see individual city Listings for details). Alternatively, try local ATMs operated by JCB, UC, DC, Sumitomo or Million, which are the most likely to accept foreign cards; they usually have instructions in English and a helpline which may have English-speaking staff.

In an emergency, **wiring money** is the quickest option. You'll need to contact one of the major Japanese banks to find which overseas banks they're associated with, and then instruct the associated bank in your home country where to send the money; the whole process can take several days and hefty charges are levied at both ends. Alternatively, you can use MoneyGram, whereby you receive the money at a MoneyGram agent, such as American Express in Tokyo (see the relevant city Listings for details); the charges vary according to the amount, but can be up to ten percent.

# GETTING AROUND

**Birthplace of the Shinkansen or "Bullet Train", Japan is one of the world's great railway countries, though you shouldn't automatically assume that the train is always the best way to get around the country. Although tunnels and bridges now link all four of the main islands, to reach hundreds of others you have no choice but to board a ferry or a plane. The length of the country also makes flying say from Tokyo to Sapporo in the north or Kagoshima in the south well worth considering, especially since the difference in cost with the fastest trains is negligable. It's**

**also worth considering flying into one airport and home from another (see pp.5 & 11).**

The time of year is an important factor to consider when arranging your transport around Japan. **Peak travelling seasons** are a few days either side of New Year, the Golden Week holidays of late April and early May, and the mid-August Obon holidays (see p.57–58 for further details of public holidays). During these times the whole of Japan can seem on the move, with trains, planes and ferries packed to the gills and roads clogged with traffic. If you want to be assured of a seat, book well in advance and be prepared to pay higher fares on flights, as all discounts are suspended during peak periods.

The main domestic **travel agencies** – JTB and NTA (see relevant city Listings sections for details) – can handle bookings for all types of transport and are also useful sources for checking travel schedules. The assistants there have access to the monthly-updated timetable bible (*jikokuhyō*), an incredible source of information on virtually every form of public transport in Japan. There's always a *jikokuhyō* available for consultation at stations and most accommodation has a copy too. If you're going to travel around Japan a lot, and especially if you're planning an adventurous trek through rural areas, having your own timetable can be invaluable. Pocket versions are

## USEFUL TRAVEL PHRASES

| | | |
|---|---|---|
| Shinkansen | *Shinkansen* | 新幹線 |
| Limited express train | *tokkyū* | 特急 |
| Express train | *kyūkō* | 急行 |
| Rapid train | *kaisoku* | 快速 |
| Ordinary train | *futsū* | 普通 |
| Reserved seat | *shitei-seki* | 指定席 |
| Unreserved seat | *jiyū-seki* | 自由席 |
| Non-smoking seat | *kin'en-seki* | 禁煙席 |
| Green Car | *guriin-sha* | グリーン車 |
| | | |
| **Tickets** | | |
| One-way | *katamichi* | 片道 |
| Return | *ōfuku* | 往復 |
| Seishun Jūhachi-kippu | *Seishun Jūhachi-kippu* | 青春十八切符 |
| shūyūken | *shūyūken* | 周遊券 |
| Multiple purchase ticket | *kaisūken* | 回数券 |
| Discount ticket shop | *kinken shoppu* | 金券ショップ |

available cheaply from most bookstores, and train stations often give out free mini train timetables for the areas they serve. Although they're all in Japanese, once you've decoded the relevant *kanji* characters, they're simple to use.

## BY TRAIN

Japan has the world's most efficient and frequent **trains,** with services running to all regions of the country and varying from the highspeed Shinkansen to the chugging steam locomotives maintained as tourist attractions. The vast majority of services are operated by **JR**, which split into seven regional networks when it was privatized in 1987 but still runs as a single company as far as buying tickets is concerned. In addition, there are fourteen smaller rail companies, including Hankyū, Odakyū and Tōbu, which are based in the major cities and surrounding areas, but in the vast majority of Japan it's JR services that you'll be using.

Individual **tickets** are expensive, especially for the fastest trains, but there are a range of discount tickets and **rail passes** available to cut the cost, with JR Rail Passes providing the best deal (see p.30). If you have lots of time, and are travelling during the main student holiday periods, the **Seishun Jūhachi-kippu** (see p.31) is also an excellent buy.

### SHINKANSEN

The Shinkansen speeding past snow-capped Fuji-san is one of the most famous images of Japan and, for many, a trip on the **Bullet Train** (so-called because of the smooth, rounded design of the earliest locomotives) is an eagerly anticipated part of a trip to the country. So smooth-running are these trains that you'll barely notice the

## EATING AND DRINKING ON TRAINS AND AT STATIONS

Buffet cars are not a common feature of Japanese trains, but a **trolley** laden with overpriced drinks and snacks certainly is. You're generally better off both financially and in culinary terms packing your own picnic for the train, but useful fallbacks are the **station noodle stands** and the **ekiben**, a contraction of *eki* (station) and *bentō* (boxed meal). At the station noodle stalls, you can get warming bowls of freshly-made hot noodles, usually soba or the thicker udon, for under ¥500 which can be slurped up in minutes. *Ekiben*, often featuring local speciality foods, are sold both on and off the trains and come in a wide range of permutations. Although some *ekiben* are famous for their quality, few are worth the ¥1000-plus often charged; if you have time, pop into a convenience or department store close to the station for better quality and a more keenly priced selection of *bentō*.

## TRAIN CLASSES AND RESERVATIONS

On Shinkasen, JR *tokkyū* (limited express) and *kyūkō* (express) services, there is a choice of **ordinary** (*futsū-sha*) carriages, or the more expensive first-class **Green car** (*guriin-sha*) carriages, though the extra leg room and plusher seats of the Green car are not worth the extra money. You also have a choice between smoking and non-smoking cars.

Each train also has both **reserved** (*shitei-seki*) and **unreserved** (*jiyū-seki*) sections. Seat reservations cost ¥500 (free if you have a rail pass) and are always worth making, particularly if you plan to travel at peak times. You cannot sit in the reserved section of a train without a reservation, even if it is empty and the unreserved section full. If you don't have a reservation, aim to get to the station with thirty minutes to spare, locate your platform and stand in line at the marked section for the unreserved carriages; ask the platform attendants for *jiyū-seki*, and they'll point the way. If you have a reservation, platform signs will also direct you where to stand, so that you're beside the right door when the train pulls in.

speed, which on the top-of-the-range *Nozomi*-503 averages 261.8km/h, making it the fastest train in the world. They are also frighteningly punctual – ten seconds late on the platform and you'll be waving goodbye to the back end of the train – and reliable: only the severest weather conditions or earthquakes stop the Shinkansen.

There are six Shinkansen lines, all starting at either Tokyo or Ueno stations in Tokyo. The busiest route is the **Tōkaidō-Sanyō** line running south along the coast of Honshū through Nagoya, Kyoto, Ōsaka and Hiroshima, terminating at Fukuoka (Hakata Station). The Tōkaidō line runs from Tokyo to Shin-Ōsaka Station, with the Sanyō line continuing from there to Fukuoka. Three types of Shinkansen services are available; the *Kodoma* which stops at all stations, the *Hikari* which stops only at major stations and the *Nozomi*, the fastest service for which you'll have to pay an extra fee (and which you're not allowed to take if you're travelling on most types of rail pass). If you're travelling from Tokyo to Fukuoka, the *Nozomi* shaves an hour off the six-hour journey on the *Hikari*, but for shorter hops to Nagoya, Kyoto or Ōsaka, the time saved isn't worth the extra expense of the ticket.

The **Tōhoku line** is the main northern route passing through Sendai and terminating at Morioka. The fastest service stopping only at major stations is the *Yamabiko*, while the *Aoba* service stops at all stations. At Morioka, you can change to the **Akita line**, which continues on to Akita on the north coast, while the **Yamagata line** to Yamagata in the middle of the Tōhoku region, splits off west from the Tōhoku line at Fukushima.

The **Jōetsu line** heads north from Tokyo, tunnelling through the mountains to Niigata on the Japan Sea coast, with the **Hokuriku line**, built for the 1998 Winter Olympics, branching off west at Takasaki to end at Nagano.

To travel by Shinkansen you'll pay a hefty **surcharge** on top of the basic fare, and you may be issued with two tickets when you book a seat. When you pass through the ticket barrier to the Shinkansen section of a station, the attendant will either stamp or retain one portion of your ticket, depending on the type you have. On the train there are announcements and electronic signs in English telling you which stations are coming up. Get to the door in good time before the train arrives as you'll generally only have a few seconds in which to disembark before the train shoots off again. A range of **refreshments** (see box opposite) are always available from the attendants who regularly hawk their wares up and and down the aisles. Some of the Shinkansen trains also have dining cars, but these are nothing special. The newer models have vending machines for drinks, and telephones.

### OTHER TRAINS

Aside from the Shinkansen, the fastest services are **limited express** (*tokkyū*) trains, so-called because they make a limited number of stops. Like Shinkansen, you have to pay a surcharge to travel on *tokkyū* and there are separate classes of reserved and non-reserved seats (see box above). Less common are the **express** (*kyūkō*) trains, which also only stop at larger stations, but impose a lower surcharge. Despite their name, the **rapid** (*kaisoku*) trains are slower still, making more stops than a *kyūkō*, but with no surcharge. Finally, the **ordinary** (*futsū*) trains are local services stopping at all stations and usually limited to routes under 100km.

The above categories of train and surcharges apply to all JR services, and some, but not all, of the private rail routes. To further confuse matters, you may find that if you're travelling on a JR train on one of the more remote branch lines, you may be charged an additional fare due to part of the old JR network having been sold off to another operating company.

For long-distance journeys between major cities, such as from Tokyo to Sapporo or from Ōsaka to Nagasaki and Kyoto, you can catch an overnight **sleeper train**, which will be either *tokkyū* or *kyūkō*. If you have a JR Rail Pass (see below) and want a berth for the night, you'll have to pay the berth charge, plus the surcharge for the express or limited express service. Some overnight trains have reclining seats or carriages without seats where you can sleep on the floor, which cost no extra, though it's a good idea to make a reservation.

Even though JR last ran a regular **steam train** service in the mid-1970s, a few routes still offer occasional SL (for "steam locomotive") services from spring through to autumn, mainly on weekends and holidays. These leisurely trains, with lovingly restored engines and carriages, have proved a huge hit with tourists and you'd be well advised to book in advance. Some of the more popular routes are the Yamaguchi line between Ogōri and Tsuwano (see p.564) in Western Honshū; and the Mōka line from Shimodate to Mashiko in Tochigi-ken (see p.179).

## BUYING TICKETS

JR tickets can be bought at any JR station and at many travel agencies, though agents may charge a handling fee. At most stations there are both **ticket counters** and **vending machines**; you can use the latter to buy all local (*futsū*) and some *kyūkō* train tickets. Only at major city stations will there be a fare map in English beside the vending machine, and you'll probably feel more comfortable going to the ticket counter. It's a good idea to have written down on a piece of paper the date and time you wish to travel, your destination, the number of tickets you want and whether you'll need smoking or non-smoking seats. This will hopefully overcome any language difficulties you may have with the station staff. If you're still not sure, just buy the minimum fare ticket from the vending machine, and pay any surcharges on the train.

To make **advance reservations** for *tokkyū* and Shinkansen trains or to buy special types of tickets, you'll generally need to go to the green window (*midori-no-madoguchi*) sales counters, marked by a green logo. In order to swap your exchange voucher for a JR Rail Pass (see below), you'll have to go to one of the much less common **JR Travel Service Centres** (see opposite). It's worth noting that few train stations accept credit cards and if you wish to pay this way, you should buy your ticket from a major travel agent, most of which accept cards.

## JAPAN RAIL PASSES

Japan Rail Passes can only be bought outside Japan (with one exception), but are not really worth the money if you only plan to make just one long-distance train journey, such as Tokyo to Kyoto. In this case, an alternative rail pass or discount ticket may offer a better overall deal. However if you're planning longer and more frequent journeys (say a return journey from Tokyo to Kyoto plus several side trips) or want unfettered flexibility, then the Japan Rail Passes really come into their own. The new regional Japan Rail Passes (of which there are currently three) are the best deal if you want to concentrate on any particular area of the country. All four types of Japan Rail Pass are available in ordinary or the more expensive Green car versions, though the latter are not really worth the extra money; all the prices quoted below are for the ordinary version.

The traditional **Japan Rail Pass** allows travel on virtually all JR services throughout Japan, including buses and ferries, and is valid for seven (¥28,300), fourteen (¥45,100) or twenty-one (¥57,000) consecutive days. The major service for which it is not valid is the *Nozomi* Shinkansen; if you're caught on one of these, even unwittingly, you'll be liable for the full Shinkansen fare for the trip. This pass is the best if you plan, say, to fly into Tokyo and head down to Kyūshū by train stopping off along the way. As with all JR tickets, children between six and eleven inclusive pay half price, while those under six travel free.

If you plan to explore a less extensive area of Japan, the regional versions of the pass are likely to be better buys. The **JR East Pass** is valid on all services operated by JR East, including the Shinkansen, and covers the northern half of Honshū from Nagano-ken up to Aomori-ken. This pass is particularly good value if you're aged between twelve and twenty five. For five days' consecutive use the price is ¥20,000 (¥16,000 for 12–25 year-olds), while a ten-day pass is ¥32,000

(¥25,000 for 12–25 year-olds). Even better value is the flexible four-day pass (¥20,000/¥16,000), which is valid for any four days within a month from the date that the pass is issued.

In a similar vein, the **JR-West Rail Pass**, can be used for trips along both the Sanyō Shinkansen and regular lines running west from Ōsaka to Fukuoka in Kyūshū, as well as on the super-fast *Nozomi* Shinkansen. It's valid for four (¥20,000) or eight (¥30,000) consecutive days, and children aged six to eleven inclusive travel for half price, though there's no youth fare. The pass also gives a discount on car rental at Eki Rent-a-car offices (see Listings sections of relevent city accounts). This is the only pass that can be bought in Japan as well as abroad, although you must have a foreign passport with a temporary visitor's stamp in it and a valid ticket out of Japan.You can buy the pass from Green Ticket windows in JR-West Stations, TIS travel agents in JR stations, or from other travel agents such as JTB or NTA.

The **JR-Kyūshū Rail Pass** is valid on all JR trains (except the Shinkansen) within Japan's southern island of Kyūshū, and costs ¥15,000 for five days and ¥20,000 for seven days. It also gives a discount on car rental with Eki Rent-a-car.

The cost of all these passes in your own currency will depend on the exchange rate at the time of purchase. When you buy any of the passes in your country, you'll be given an exchange voucher which must be swapped for a pass in Japan within **three months**. Once issued, the dates on the pass cannot be changed. Exchanges can only be made at **JR Travel Service Centres** at major stations; you'll be issued with a list of locations when you buy your pass. It's important also to note that passes can only be issued if you're travelling

on a **temporary visitor visa**; JR are very strict about this and you'll be asked to show your passport when you present your exchange voucher for the pass. Also if you lose your pass, it will not be replaced, so take good care of it.

## OTHER DISCOUNT TICKETS

If you don't have a JR Rail Pass, you can still get a wide range of discount tickets and other rail passes. It's also worth hunting out some of the specialist discount agencies (see overleaf) for cheaper Shinkansen tickets.

At the budget end of the range is the **Seishun Jūhachi-kippu** (Youth 18 ticket), available to everyone regardless of age, but only valid during school vacations. These are roughly March 1–April 10, July 20–September 10 and December 10–January 20, with tickets being on sale ten days prior to the validity period and stopping ten days before the end. For a total cost of ¥11,500 you get five day-tickets that can be used to travel anywhere in Japan as long as you take only the slow *futsū* and *kaisoku* trains. The tickets can also be split and used by up to four other people. If you're in no hurry, this ticket can be the biggest bargain on the whole of Japan's rail system, allowing you for example to go from Tokyo to Hiroshima for ¥2300, as long as you don't mind being on a slow train all day and much of the night. The tickets are also handy for touring a local area in a day, since you can get on and off trains as many times as you wish within twenty four hours.

If two or more of you are travelling together, you should check out the **kaisūken** (multiple purchase ticket) deal. *Kaisūken* are usually four or more one-way tickets to the same destination. These work out substantially cheaper than buying the tickets individually and, among other places, are available on the limited express services from Tokyo to Matsumoto (p.357) and Nagano-ken (p.346).

There are also many types of **shūyūken** and **furii kippu** (excursion tickets) available for various areas of Japan, which combine return travel – typically by Shinkansen – with unlimited use of local transport for a specified period of time. **Waido** (wide) **shūyūken**, for example, are available for Hokkaidō and Kyūshū, and the latter is especially worth considering since it allows you to travel part or all of one way by ferry. Despite their name, *furii kippu* (meaning free ticket) always cost money, but allow unlimited travel

---

### TRAVEL INFORMATION SERVICES

The English-language service **Japan Travel-Phone** gives information about bus, train and ferry schedules, and can be contacted daily 9am–5pm. The service is available toll-free outside Tokyo and Kyoto on ☎0088–224800 or 0120–444800. Within Tokyo or Kyoto city limits, you'll have to contact the local TIC offices (see p.22).

JR East Infoline (Mon–Fri 10am–6pm; ☎03/3423-0111) is an English-language information service dealing with all train enquiries nationwide.

## DISCOUNT TICKET SHOPS

In most big cities, usually in the main shopping areas near stations, you can find **discount ticket shops** (*kinken shoppu*) which sell, among other things, cheap airline and Shinkansen tickets. These shops (usually identified by a window full of hand-written signs indicating the cost of tickets to different destinations) buy up discount group tickets and sell them on individually, usually at around twenty percent cheaper than the regular prices. These are legitimate operations but you'll need to be able to read and speak some Japanese to be sure you've got the ticket you need, and there may be some days when travel isn't allowed. With the Shinkansen tickets you can't make seat reservations at a discount shop, so you'll need to go to a JR ticket office as well to arrange these.

within a certain area over a set amount of time. One of the best value is the **Hakone Furii Pass**, offered by the Odakyū railway company, which covers routes from Tokyo to the lakeland area of Hakone (see p.184). If you plan to travel in one area, it's always worth asking the JR Infoline or the tourist information offices if there are any other special tickets that could be of use.

Older married couples whose combined ages total at least 88, are eligible for the **Full Moon Pass**, which costs ¥79,000 for five days, ¥98,000 for seven days and ¥122,000 for twelve days. These prices cover both people for travel in Green cars on all trains (except the *Nozomi*), including sleeper trains. Although this pass is very pricey, it may be worth considering if you're planning a lot of travel and want to do it in comfort.

If you're thinking of renting a car (see opposite) to explore more off-the-beaten track areas, it's worth looking into the **Eki Rent-a-car-kippu** tickets which you can buy if your total journey is more than 200km. These provide a twenty percent discount on the cost of the train fare and car rental.

## BY AIR

Since the deregulation of the airline industry in 1996, **domestic flights** in Japan have come down in price, and more competition is on the way with the imminent introduction of Skymark, a new airline owned by discount flight agent HIS.

However, the big three domestic airlines – All Nippon Airways (ANA), Japan Airlines (JAL) and Japan Air System (JAS) – still have the market pretty much carved up between them and there's little competition on even the busiest routes as far as prices and quality of service are concerned; you're best off choosing whichever airline offers the most convenient flight time. Of the smaller domestic airlines, Air Nippon Koku (ANK) and South-West Airlines (SWAL) offer the widest choice of routes.

If you **book in advance**, you can make substantial savings on the regular fares with all the major airlines. Tickets booked two months to 28 days in advance qualify for a forty-five to fifty percent discount; if you book 21 days in advance, you can get a thirty percent discount, and fourteen days in advance gives a twenty percent reduction. There's also sometimes thirty-five to forty percent off early morning (generally before 7am) departures. If you're not using a rail pass (see p.30), the discounted plane fares are well worth considering in comparison to train fares. For example, to travel by train to Sapporo from Tokyo costs ¥23,000 and takes the better part of a day, compared to a ¥25,000 discount plane fare from Tokyo to Shin-Chitose airport, near Sapporo, taking ninety minutes. Note that none of these discounts are available during the peak travelling season of the April/May Golden Week holidays (see p.57), most of August and over New Year.

If you plan to fly long distances in Japan or want to make several plane trips, it's worth considering JAL's **Welcome to Japan** fare system. You don't need to fly JAL to Japan to take advantage of this ticket which offers two flights anywhere in the country for ¥25,200, three flights for ¥37,800, four for ¥50,400 and five for ¥63,000.

## CONTACTING THE AIRLINES

ANA, JAL and JAS all have English-speaking **reservation** agents who can be contacted on the toll-free numbers below from anywhere in Japan. They also all have English-language Web sites, of which JAS and ANA's are the most useful, both offering flight schedules, seat availability, fares and airport access information.

**ANA** ☎0120–029222; *www.ana.co.jp*
**JAL** ☎0120–255971; *www.jal.co.jp*
**JAS** ☎0120–511283; *www.jas.co.jp*

This fare is particularly good value if you plan to visit far-flung destinations, such as the islands of Okinawa, where the standard one-way fares are over ¥30,000. Again, Welcome to Japan fares are not available during peak travelling seasons.

## BY BUS

Japan has a comprehensive system of long-distance **buses** (*chokyori basu*), including night buses between major cities, such as Tokyo, Kyoto and Ōsaka. Fares are always cheaper than on the train, but the buses are much slower and can get caught up in traffic, even on the expressways, Japan's fastest roads, especially during peak travel periods. Most bus journeys start and finish next to or near the main train station. For journeys over two hours there is usually at least one rest stop along the way.

There's little in the way of pleasant scenery along the highways, so if you have a long journey to make, it's worth considering a **night bus** (*yakō basu*), if that option is available. You'll save on a night's accommodation, and the seats recline (unlike those on overnight trains), making sleep possible. To compare costs, the overnight bus from Tokyo to Kyoto, for example, costs ¥8030 and takes eight hours, while the Shinkansen costs ¥12,970 and takes two hours and forty minutes. There are hundreds of small bus companies operating different routes, so for full details of current services, timetables and costs make enquiries with local tourist information offices.

In all Japan's major cities and tourist areas, you'll find **escorted bus tours**, though these are generally expensive, and, outside of Tokyo and Kyoto, you're unlikely to find any with English-speaking guides.

## BY FERRY

One of the most pleasant ways of travelling around the island nation of Japan is by **ferry**. If you have the time, the overnight journeys to and from the main island Honshū to Hokkaidō in the north, and Kyūshū and Shikoku, in the south, are highly recommended. A particularly good-value service is between Niigata on Honshū and Otaru on Hokkaidō, a relaxing 18-hour cruise costing as little as ¥5250. Also memorable are the cruises across the beautiful Inland Sea, or from Kyūshū to the Southwest Islands and Okinawa. If you only have a little time, try a short hop, say to one of the islands of the Inland Sea, or from Niigata to Sado-ga-shima.

There's little reason to shell out extra for the first class sections of ferries, which provide more luxurious accommodation and facilities, as second class is fine. On the **overnight ferries**, in particular, the cheapest fares, which entitle you to a sleeping space on the floor of a large room with up to a hundred other passengers, are a bargain compared to train and plane fares to the same destinations. For example, the overnight ferry from Tokyo to Tomakomai, around an hour south of Sapporo on Hokkaidō, costs ¥11,840 compared to ¥21,980 for the Tokyo to Sapporo train ticket. Even if you pay extra for a bed in a shared or private berth, it's still cheaper than the train and you'll have a very comfortable cruise into the bargain. Ferries are also an excellent way of transporting a bicycle or motorbike (though you'll pay a small supplement for these) and many also take cars.

Ferry **schedules** are subject to seasonal changes and also vary according to the weather, so for current details of times and prices it's best to consult the local tourist information office. The Japan Long Distance Ferry Association, Iino Bldg, 2-1-1 Uchisaiwaichō Chiyoda-ku, Tokyo (☎03/3501-0889) also publishes a free annual English-language brochure, detailing current schedules and fares.

## BY CAR

While it would be foolhardy to rent a car to get around Japan's cities, **driving** is often the best way to tour the country's less populated and off-the-beaten-track areas, such as Hokkaidō or the San-in coast of Western Honshū. Japanese roads are generally of a good standard, with the vast majority of signs on main routes being in *romaji* as well as Japanese script. Although you'll have to pay pricey tolls to travel on the expressways, many other perfectly good roads are free and petrol is cheaper than in Europe, averaging ¥90 a litre. If you team up with a group of people, hiring a car to tour a rural area over a couple of days can work out much better value than taking infrequent and expensive buses. It's often possible to hire cars for less than a day, too, for short trips.

There are **car rental** counters at all the major airports and train stations in cities and towns, with the main local companies being Nippon Rent-a-car, Toyota Rent-a-car, Mazda Rent-a-car, Japaren and the JR-run Eki Rent-a-car. Budget and Hertz also have rental operations across

---

Japan (although not as widely spread). For car rental firms' contact numbers, see the Listings sections in the relevant major cities. Rates, which vary little between companies and usually include unlimited mileage, start from around ¥6500 for the first 24 hours for the smallest type of car (a subcompact Minica, seating four people), plus ¥1000 insurance. It's possible to pay much more for flashier cars and during the peak seasons of Golden Week, Obon and New Year, rates for all cars tend to increase.

Since you're unlikely to want to drive in any of the cities, often the best rental **deals** are through Eki Rent-a-car, which gives a discounted rate by combining the rental with a train ticket to the most convenient station for the area you wish to explore (see p.32). With any rental company, it's also worth thinking about making a return trip since one-way charges are high.

To rent a car you must have an **international driver's licence** as well as your national licence; if you've been in Japan for more than six months you'll need to apply for a Japanese licence. Driving is on the left, the same as in Britain, Ireland, Australia and most of southeast Asia and international traffic signals are used. It's a good idea to buy a copy of the bilingual *Japan Road Atlas* (¥2890) published by Shōbunsha, which includes many helpful notes, such as the dates that some roads close during winter. If you're a member of an automobile association at home, the chances are that you'll qualify for reciprocal rights with the Japan Auto Federation, 3-5-8 Shiba-kōen, Minato-ku, Tokyo 105 (☎03/3436-2811), which publishes the English-language *Rules of the Road* book, detailing Japan's driving code.

The top **speed limit** in Japan is 80km/h, which applies only on expressways, though drivers frequently exceed this and are rarely stopped by police. In cities, the limit is 40km/h, though you'll usually be lucky to be travelling at anything close to this rate, let alone speeding. To use the expressways you have to pay a **toll**, typically around ¥30 per kilometre, which can mount up to make the overall cost more expensive than taking a bus or train. On the Tokyo–Ōsaka route, for example, you'll shell out around ¥10,000 in tolls; for ¥3500 extra you could take the Shinkansen instead.

You shouldn't forget **parking** charges for towns and cities, either, where free roadside parking is virtually unheard of. There are always car parks close to main railway stations; at some your vehicle will be loaded onto a rotating conveyor belt and whisked off to its parking spot. Reckon on ¥500 per hour for a central city car park and ¥300 per hour elsewhere. If you manage to locate a parking meter, take great care not to overstay the time paid for (usually around ¥200 per hour); some have mechanisms to trap cars, which will only be released once the fine has been paid directly into the meter. In rural areas, parking is not so much of a problem and rarely attracts a charge.

If you've drunk any **alcohol** at all, even the smallest amount, don't drive; it's illegal and if you're stopped by the police and breathalized you'll be in big trouble.

## BY BIKE

Although you're unlikely to want **to cycle** around the grimy, traffic-clogged streets of Japan's main cities, in the smaller towns and countryside a bike is a great way to get from A to B while seeing plenty en route. Outside of the main island, Honshū, cycle touring is a very popular activity over the long summer vacation with students. Hokkaidō, in particular, is a cyclist's dream with excellent roads through often stunning scenery and a network of ultra-cheap (but basic) cyclist's accommodation.

In many tourist towns you can **rent bikes** from outlets beside or near the train station. Youth hostels often rent out bikes, too, usually at the most competitive rates. You can buy a brand-new bike in Japan for under ¥20,000 but you wouldn't want to use it for anything more than getting around town; for sturdy touring and mountain bikes, hunt out a specialist bike shop or bring your own. Although repair shops are nationwide, for foreign models it's best to bring essential spare parts with you. And despite Japan's low crime rate, a small but significant section of the Japanese public treats bikes as common property; if you don't want to lose it, make sure your bike is well chained whenever you leave it.

If you plan to take your bike on a train or bus, make sure you have a bike bag in which to parcel it up; on trains you're also supposed pay a special **bike transport supplement** of ¥270 (ask for a *temawarihin kippu*), although ticket inspectors may not always check.

If you are planning a serious cycling tour of Japan, an excellent investment is *Cycling Japan* (¥2200; Kodansha), a handy practical guide detailing many touring routes around the country. The book is edited by Brian Harrell, a local cyclist who also edits the *Oikaze* cycling newsletter, available from 2-24-3 Tomigaya, Shibuya-ku, Tokyo.

## HITCHING

There's always a risk associated with **hitching**, and if you have a choice it's best to err on the side of caution. That said, Japan is one of the safest and easiest places in the world to hitch a ride, and in some rural areas it's just about the only way of getting around without your own transport. It's also a fantastic way to meet locals, who are often only too happy to go miles out of their way to give you a lift just for the novelty value (impecunious students apart, hitching is very rare in Japan), or the opportunity it provides to practise English.

As long as you don't look too scruffy you'll seldom stand around long waiting for a ride. It's a

### CABLE CARS AND ROPEWAYS

It's worth noting a linguistic distinction that applies to the transport at several of Japan's mountain resorts. What is known as a cable car in the West (for example, a capsule suspended from a cable going up a mountain) is called a **ropeway** in Japan, while the term **cable car** is used to refer to what we know as a funicular or rack and pinion railway.

good idea to write your intended destination in large *kanji* characters on a piece of card to hold up. Also carry a stock of small gifts you can leave as thank yous.

## CITY TRANSPORT

All Japanese cities are served by buses and trains, but only the largest have subway systems. Some towns and cities have retained their trams, although in Tokyo, Ōsaka and Sapporo, they've all but disappeared. Taxis are always a useful stand-by and need not be that pricey if used over short distances or by a group of people.

### SUBWAYS AND TRAINS

The easiest and fastest way of getting around the major cities is to use the efficient **subways** and local **trains**. Stations almost always have English signs and trains are often colour coded to match the transport maps.

You need to buy a **ticket** before getting on an overground or subway train, usually from a ticket machine. Some machines take yen bills and all will give change if you don't have the exact fare. If you're not sure what the fare is, buy the cheapest ticket and sort out the difference either on the train or with the guard at the ticket gate when you get off. You can also buy **stored value cards**, which work out slightly cheaper than buying individual tickets (the JR pre-paid card is called the Orange Card). Another deal to look out for are **kaisūken** tickets, a carnet-type deal of, say, eleven ¥200 tickets for ¥2000. Generally, to make it worth buying any of the unlimited-use **day tickets** (available, for example, in Tokyo, Ōsaka and Sapporo), you'll have to travel long-distances on the trains and subways and get on and off frequently.

If you don't relish being squashed in a tight spot, avoid travelling on subways and trains during the morning rush hour which generally lasts between 8am and 9.30am. The evening rush hour is not so much of a problem since workers tend to go home at different times, but it's worth remembering that virtually all public transport systems close down shortly after midnight and don't reopen until around 5am.

## BUSES AND TRAMS

**Buses** tend not to be that useful for non-Japanese speakers, since their signs are seldom translated into English. However you may need to use them for getting about towns or parts of the cities not covered by subways or trains. On some city buses you'll pay a flat fare on entering the bus; if you don't have the correct change, there's always a machine to convert large coins and ¥1000 bills beside the slot where you deposit the fare. If you pay the fare on leaving the bus, you'll usually need to pick up a small ticket with a zone number on, when you enter the bus – if in doubt, watch what the other passengers do. There will be a fare chart at the front of the bus which tells you how much to pay according to where you got on.

It's generally the smaller, more characterful cities, such as Matsuyama, Kōchi, Nagasaki and Hakodate, that have retained extensive **tram** systems, although you'll find the odd route still in Tokyo and Ōsaka. Unlike the buses, it's fairly easy to work out where you're going on a tram by looking at local transport maps, even if the signs are written in Japanese. Fares usually work in a similar way to the buses, with payment of either a flat fee, or different amounts depending on where you got on.

## TAXIS

**Taxis** can be flagged down on the streets of all towns and cities; even in quiet country villages you'll probably find one hanging around outside the train station. However, because of the cost, you are only likely to take a taxi on very short journeys. They work out a better deal if shared by a group of people, but it's worth noting that there's a limit of four people in most taxis.

The minimum **rate**, posted on the driver's window, is generally around ¥600 for the first 2km, rising by around ¥100 per 350m thereafter. If you get stuck in traffic you'll also pay a time charge and rates also rise by about twenty percent between 11pm and 5am. Tipping is not expected.

An empty taxi will show a red light. There's never any need to open or close the passenger doors since they are operated automatically by the taxi driver. It's also a good idea to have the name and address of your destination clearly written on a piece of paper to hand to the driver. Don't expect the driver to know where he's going, either; a stop at a local policebox may be necessary to locate the exact address.

# ACCOMMODATION

Although prices have tumbled in recent months, accommodation in Japan still takes a large portion of your budget. However, with a bit of planning it's possible to keep costs within reasonable limits. Though some places offer a mix of rooms, accommodation tends to divide broadly into various permutations of Western-style hotels and Japanese ryokan, or the more downmarket minshuku. In all cases rooms tend to be small but, as a general rule, Japanese *tatami* rooms represent slightly better value for money – they at least feel more spacious. Youth hostels offer some of the cheapest accommodation options, particularly for people travelling alone, while camping is a possibility in certain areas, though not always particularly cheap.

Before arriving in Japan, it's wise to **reserve** at least your first few nights' accommodation, especially in Tokyo and Kyoto where budget places are particularly scarce. During peak holiday seasons, however, reservations are essential throughout the country as rooms get booked up

## ACCOMMODATION PRICE CODES

All accommodation in this book has been graded according to the following price codes, which refer to the cheapest double or twin room available for most of the year, and include taxes. Note that rates may increase during peak holiday periods, in particular around Christmas and New Year, the Golden Week (April 28–May 6) and Obon (the week around August 15), when accommodation is very difficult to get without an advance reservation. In the case of hostels providing dormitory accommodation, the code refers to the charge per bed.

| | | |
|---|---|---|
| ① under ¥3000 | ④ ¥7000–10,000 | ⑦ ¥20,000–30,000 |
| ② ¥3000–5000 | ⑤ ¥10,000–15,000 | ⑧ ¥30,000–40,000 |
| ③ ¥5000–7000 | ⑥ ¥15,000–20,000 | ⑨ over ¥40,000 |

months in advance. You can get lists of accommodation from JNTO offices abroad (see p.21) and make your own arrangements or, alternatively, ask your travel agent to help. Both the Welcome Inn Group and Japanese Inn Group (see p.39) offer inexpensive accommodation which can be booked before departure, while some of the bigger hotel chains, such as Tōkyū, Prince, New Ōtani and ANA hotels, have overseas offices and may offer discounts on bookings made outside Japan. You can also find details of major hotels through the Japan Hotel Association Web site (*www.j-hotel.or.jp/english.html*), some of which offer on-line booking. If you do arrive without a reservation, make use of the free hotel booking services in Narita and Kansai International airports (see p.84 and p.406).

Within Japan, it pays to book one or two days ahead to ensure that you're not left with the most expensive rooms. Outside the peak season, however, you'll rarely be stuck for somewhere to stay. The best bet is to head for the nearest **train station**, where there's usually a clutch of cheap business hotels and a **tourist information desk** – most will make a booking for you, sometimes for a small fee, or at least provide a list of phone numbers.

Most large- and medium-sized hotels in big cities have English-speaking receptionists who'll take a booking over the phone. The cheaper and more rural the place, however, the more likely you are to have to speak in Japanese, or a mix of Japanese and English. Don't be put off: armed with the right phrases (see Language on p.827), and speaking slowly and clearly, you should be able to make yourself understood – many of the terms you'll need are actually English words pronounced in a Japanese way. If time allows, booking by fax is another option, with the advantage that written English is easier for people to understand. Otherwise, ask the local tourist information office or the staff at your current accommodation for help.

Almost without exception, **security** is not a problem, though it's never sensible to leave valuables lying around in your room. In youth hostels it's advisable to use the lockers, if provided, or leave important items at the reception desk. Standards of **service** and **cleanliness** vary according to the type of establishment, but are usually more than adequate. When **checking in**, the registration form won't necessarily be in English but the details are fairly obvious: name, age, passport number, dates of arrival and departure. Check-in is generally between 5pm and 7pm, and check-out by 10am.

While credit cards are becoming more widely accepted, in the majority of cases **payment** will be in cash, but it's always wise to check beforehand. In youth hostels and many cheaper business hotels, you'll be expected to pay when you check in. It is always worth asking beforehand whether the advertised rates include **tax** (see box on p.26) and **service charges**, as these can bump up your bill considerably. In general, only top and middle range hotels or ryokan levy a service charge, typically between ten and twenty percent. In hot-spring resorts, there's a small **onsen tax** (usually ¥150), though again this may already be included in the rates. Note that **tipping** is not necessary in Japan.

## HOTELS

Most **hotel** rooms in Japan come with en-suite bathrooms, TV, phone and air-conditioning as standard – as well as a numbing lack of character, though things are beginning to improve at the upper end. **Rates** for a double or twin room range from an average of ¥30,000 at a top-flight hotel, to ¥15,000–20,000 for a smartish establishment, probably with its own restaurant, room service and other refinements. At the lowest level, a room in a basic hotel with minimal amenities will cost around ¥7,000–10,000. Charges are almost always on a per room basis and usually exclude meals, though breakfast may occasionally be provided.

**Top hotels** provide the full range of services – a choice of restaurants and bars, a swimming pool or fitness centre, shopping arcade, business centre and so forth. However, most visitors to Japan are likely to be staying in the more modest **business hotels** that constitute the middle and lower price brackets. As the name suggests, these places are primarily designed for travelling businessmen (rarely women) and are usually clustered around train stations. They are generally clean, efficient, offer a minimum level of service and are perfect if all you want is a place to crash out. The majority of business hotel rooms are single, but most places have a few doubles or "semi-doubles" – a large single bed which takes two at a squeeze. They are functional and perfectly adequate, though at the cheapest places you may find smoky boxes with tiny beds, a desk and a chair squeezed into the smallest possible space. Squeeze is also the operative word for the aptly named "unit baths" which business hotels specialize in; these moulded plastic units contain a shower, bath tub, toilet and wash-basin but leave little space for an occupant. That said, some business hotels are relatively smart and there are a number of reliable chains. Among the biggest, Washington hotels are consistently good, as are Sunroute, Tōkyū Inn and Dai-ichi Inn, while the Green, Alpha and Hokke Club hotels are cheap and usually very basic.

Japan's unique contribution to the hotel scene is the **capsule hotel**, which originated in the early 1970s to cater for office workers who've missed their last train home – you'll find them mostly near major stations. Inside, ranks of plastic or fibreglass cubicles, roughly two metres by one metre, contain everything the stranded, often inebriated, salaryman could want: bedding, *yukata* (a cotton dressing-gown), towel, phone, alarm and TV with porn pay-channels. Each cubicle is "sealed" with a flimsy curtain, so noisy neighbours can be a problem, and they are definitely not designed for claustrophics. However, they're

relatively cheap (averaging around ¥3800 per night) and fun to try at least once, though the majority are for men only. You can't stay in the hotel during the day – not that you'd want to – but you can leave luggage in their lockers. Check-in usually starts around 4.30pm and often involves buying a ticket from a vending machine in the lobby.

**Love hotels** are another, wonderful hybrid which can be a source of cheap accommodation for the adventurous. Generally located in entertainment districts, they are immediately recognizable from their ornate exteriors, incorporating cupids, crenellations or, most incongruously, the Statue of Liberty, and a sign quoting prices for "rest" or "stay". They're not as sleazy as they sound and the main market is young people or married couples taking a break from crowded apartments. You usually choose your room from a back-lit display showing which are still available – the best contain moving beds, lurid murals and even swimming pools – and then negotiate with a cashier lurking behind a tiny window. Though daytime rates are high (from about ¥4000 for two hours), the price of an overnight stay costs a little less than a basic business hotel (roughly ¥5000–7000). The main drawback is that you can't check-in until around 10pm.

## JAPANESE-STYLE ACCOMMODATION

A night in a traditional Japanese inn, or **ryokan**, is one of the highlights of a visit to Japan. The best can be unbelievably expensive, but there are plenty where you can enjoy the full experience at affordable prices. At the cheaper end, ryokan merge into **minshuku**, family-run guesthouses, and the larger government-owned **kokumin-shukusha** (People's Lodges) located in national parks and resort areas. In addition, some **temples** and **shrines** offer simple accommodation, or you can arrange to stay with a Japanese family through the **homestay** programme.

Unlike at hotels, it's essential to **reserve** at least a day ahead if you want to stay in Japanese-style accommodation. Though a few don't take foreigners, mainly through fear of language problems and cultural faux pas, you'll find plenty that do listed in the Guide. JNTO also publishes useful lists of ryokan, minshuku and pensions, and distributes brochures for the two following organizations which specialize in inexpensive, foreigner-friendly accommodation.

The government-run **Welcome Inn Group**, B1, Tokyo International Forum, 3-5-1 Marunouchi, Chiyoda-ku, Tokyo 100 (☎03/3211-4201, fax 3211-9009; *www.jnto.go.jp*) has around 700 members, and covers a wide range of mostly Japanese-style accommodation, as well as hotels, pensions and youth hostels. You can make up to three reservations from abroad using their free, centralized booking system (by mail, fax or email), as long as you apply at least three weeks before departure. However, once in Japan, it's possible to make further bookings at their Tokyo office, the Kyoto Tourist Information Centre and in Narita and Kansai airports.

The **Japanese Inn Group** (c/o Ryokan Shigetsu, 1-31-11 Asakusa, Taitō-ku, Tokyo 111; or Kyoto Liaison Office, c/o Hiraiwa Ryokan, 314, Hayao-chō, Kaminokuchi-agaru, Ninomiya-chō-dōri, Kyoto 600) is a private association of about eighty budget ryokan and minshuku, with rates varying between ¥4000 and ¥10,000 per person excluding meals. Most also belong to the Welcome Inn Group, but tend to be the smaller, more homely places. If they're not within the Welcome Inn system, you can book direct with each member by mail, phone or fax. Some may ask for a deposit, but they all take American Express cards and most accept Visa. Once in Japan, one member will help make onward reservations for the cost of the phone call.

Alternatively, you can contact the **Japan Minshuku Centre**, B1, Kōtsū Kaikan, 2-10-1 Yūrakuchō, Tokyo 100 (Mon–Sat 10am–7pm; ☎03/3216-6556), which claims some 3000 members throughout Japan. They don't issue lists of minshuku, but will make reservations on your behalf. If you book from abroad they charge a ¥6000 handling fee plus fifty percent deposit. Once in Japan, however, you can make reservations in person at the Centre's Tokyo office (¥500–1000 commission per minshuku), or ask local tourist offices for recommendations in their area.

### RYOKAN

Accommodation in a typical **ryokan** consists of a bare room, with just a low table sitting on pale-green *tatami* (rice-straw matting) and a hanging scroll – nowadays joined by a TV and phone – decorating the alcove (*tokonoma*) on one wall. Though you'll increasingly find a toilet and wash-basin in the room, baths are generally communal. The rules of ryokan etiquette (see box below) can seem daunting at first, but they're really not complicated and, once you've got the hang of it, these are great places to stay.

**Rates** are usually quoted per person and almost always include breakfast and an evening meal; in the Guide, however, we give the appropriate rate for two people, including taxes. Prices

---

## STAYING IN JAPANESE-STYLE ACCOMMODATION

Whenever you're staying in Japanese-style accommodation, you'll be expected to check-in early – between 4pm and 6pm – and to follow local custom from the moment you arrive.

Just inside the front door, there's usually a row of **slippers** for you to change into, but remember to slip them off when walking on the *tatami* (see p.61 for more on footwear). The **bedding** is stored behind sliding doors during the day and only laid out in the evening. In top-class ryokan this is done for you, but elsewhere be prepared to tackle your own. There'll be a mattress (which goes straight on the *tatami*) with a sheet to put over it, a soft quilt to sleep under and a pillow stuffed with rice husks.

Most places provide a **yukata**, a loose cotton robe tied with a belt, and a short jacket (*tanzen*) in cold weather. The *yukata* can be worn in bed, during meals, when going to the bathroom and even outside – in resort areas many Japanese holiday-makers take an evening stroll in their *yukata* and wooden sandals (*geta*), also supplied by the ryokan. Whether male or female, you should always wrap the left side of the *yukata* over the right; the opposite is used to dress the dead.

The traditional Japanese bath (*furo*) is a luxurious experience with its own set of rules (see p.61). In ryokan there are usually separate bathrooms for men and women, but elsewhere there will either be designated times for males and females, or guests take it in turns – it's perfectly acceptable for couples and families to bathe together, though there's not usually a lot of space.

Evening **meals** tend to be early, at 6pm or 7pm. Smarter ryokan generally serve meals in your room, while communal dining is the norm in cheaper places. **At night**, the doors are locked pretty early, so check before going out – they may let you have a key.

vary according to the season, the grade of room, the quality of meal you opt for and the number of people in a room; rates are calculated on the basis of double occupancy, so one person staying in a room will pay slightly more than the advertised price and three people slightly less per person. However, on average, a night in a basic ryokan will cost between ¥8000 and ¥10,000 per head, while a more classy establishment, perhaps with meals served in the room, will set you back between ¥10,000 and ¥20,000. If money is no object, a top-class ryokan with exquisite meals and the most attentive service imaginable can be upwards of ¥50,000 per person.

At cheaper ryokan it's possible to ask for a room without **meals**, though this is frowned on at the more traditional places and, anyway, the meals are often very good value. If you're offered the choice of Japanese or Western food, Japanese meals are invariably better. However, many Westerners find miso soup, cold fish and rice a bit hard to tackle in the morning, so you might want to opt for a Western breakfast.

## MINSHUKU AND KOKUMINSHUKUSHA

There's a fine line between the cheapest ryokan and a **minshuku**, the mainstay of accommodation outside big cities. In general, minshuku are smaller and less formal than ryokan, more like staying in a private home, with varying degrees of comfort and cleanliness. All rooms will be Japanese-style, with communal bathrooms and dining areas, and few minshuku provide towels or *yukata*. At the most basic level, a night in a minshuku will cost from ¥4000 per person excluding meals, or between ¥6000 and ¥10,000 with two meals; rates are calculated in the same way as for ryokan.

In the national parks, onsen resorts and other popular tourist spots, minshuku are supplemented by large, government-run **Kokuminshukusha** (People's Lodges), which cater to family groups and tour parties. Though some might be on a bus route, they're often quite isolated and difficult to get to without your own transport. The average cost of a night's accommodation is around ¥6500 per person, including two meals.

In country areas and popular resorts, you'll also find homely guesthouses called **pensions** – a word borrowed from the French. Though the accommodation and meals are Western-style, these are really minshuku in disguise. They're family-run – generally by young couples escaping city life – and specialize in hearty home-cooking.

Pensions seem to appeal mostly to young Japanese and can be pretty remote, though someone will usually collect you from the nearest station. Rates average around ¥8000 per head including dinner and breakfast.

## TEMPLES AND SHRINES

Traditionally reserved for pilgrims, a number of Buddhist **temples** and Shinto **shrines** now take in regular guests for a small fee, and some belong to the Japanese Inn Group (see previous page) or the Japan Youth Hostels association (see below). By far the best places to experience temple life are at the Buddhist retreat of Kōya-san (p.493), and in Kyoto's temple lodges (see p.432).

Though the accommodation is inevitably basic, the food can be superb, especially in temple lodgings (*shukubō*), where the monks serve up delicious vegetarian cuisine (*shōjin ryōri*). In many temples you'll also be welcome to attend the early morning prayer ceremonies. Prices vary between ¥3000 and ¥9000 per person including meals.

## HOMESTAY PROGRAMMES

Through EIL (the Experiment in International Living) you can apply to **stay with a Japanese family** for a period of one to four weeks. At £285 per person for one week, up to £537 for four weeks, it's not a particularly cheap option, but this is one of the best ways to get a real feel for the country. Details are available from the EIL office in Britain at 287 Worcester Rd, Malvern WR14 1AB (☎01684/562577, fax 562212; www.experiment.org), or in Australia from PO Box 355, Curtin 2605 (☎02/6282 5171, fax 6285 3247, infor@experimentaust.org.au). Applications take at least two months to process.

## YOUTH HOSTELS

Japan has more than four hundred **youth hostels** spread throughout the country, offering some of the cheapest accommodation, especially for people travelling alone. However, for two people or more, a night at a hostel may work out only slightly less expensive than staying at an ordinary minshuku. There's no upper age limit, although children under four years are not accepted, and, with some notable exceptions, the majority of hostels are well-run, clean and welcoming. The best are housed in wonderful old farmhouses or temples, often in great locations, while you'll also find hostels in most big cities. The main drawbacks are a raft of regulations, an evening curfew and a maximum stay of three nights.

The average **price** of hostel accommodation is ¥2800 per person, with meals (optional) costing around ¥600 for breakfast and ¥1000 for dinner; occasionally a five percent consumption tax (see p.26) is added to the bill. Rates at some hostels increase during peak holiday periods, while a few offer reductions of up to ¥500 per night to foreigners with full membership cards (see below).

Hostels are either run by the government or by Japan Youth Hostels (JYH), which is affiliated to Hostelling International (HI), or are privately owned. **Membership** cards are not required at government hostels, though they will want ID, but all other hostels ask for a current Youth Hostel card. It's easiest and cheapest to get one at home, provided your national Youth Hostel Association is a full member of HI. Alternatively, you can buy a Hostelling International card (¥2800) in Tokyo at the main JYH office (Mon–Sat 10am–5pm, closed Sun and every other Sat; see box overleaf for details) or at a branch office in basement two of Sogō department store in Yūrakuchō. Otherwise, non-members have to buy a "welcome stamp" (¥600) each time they stay at a JYH or private hostel; six stamps within a twelve month period entitles you to the Hostelling International card. Note that a few hostels only accept people with a fully paid-up membership card.

JNTO offices stock copies of the free **map** giving contact details of all youth hostels, but it's also worth investing in the *Youth Hostel Handbook* (¥300). Though nearly all in Japanese, it gives useful location maps (by no means to scale, so beware) for each hostel together with an English-language key; with a bit of patience it's possible to work out the essentials. The Handbook comes free with JYH/Hostelling International membership, or you can buy it at JYH in Tokyo or from larger hostels.

It's essential to make **reservations** well in advance for the big-city hostels and anywhere during school vacations: namely, New Year, March, around Golden Week (late April through mid-May), and in July and August. At other times, it's a good idea to book ahead since hostels in prime tourist spots are always busy, and some close for a day or two off-season. If you want an evening meal, you also need to let them know a day in advance. Before arriving in Japan you can book direct with the hostels in writing (send an International Postal Coupon for the reply) or

through the International Booking Network (IBN), a computerized system covering around thirty Japanese hostels, for which you have to pay a small fee. Once in Japan, the simplest thing is to reserve by phone – staff often speak a little English and will help you make onward bookings. In Tokyo, all JYH hostels can be booked through the head office (see box overleaf) or the branch office in Sogō (see above).

Hostel accommodation consists of either dormitory bunks or Japanese-style *tatami* rooms, with communal bathrooms and dining areas. A few also have private or family rooms but these tend to fill up quickly. **Bedding** is provided, though in some hostels you have to pay an extra ¥100 or so for sheets; since many hostels only issue one sheet, you may want to carry a sheet sleeping-bag. The majority of hostels have **laundry** facilities.

Though hostel **meals** vary in quality, they are often pretty good value. Dinner will generally be Japanese style, while breakfast frequently includes bread, jam and coffee, sometimes as part of a buffet. Some hostels have a basic "members' kitchen" which you can use for a small fee, or you can picnic in the dining room. Note that one or two hostels don't provide evening meals and there may not be any restaurants close by, so ask when you book.

**Check-in** is generally between 3pm and 8pm (by 6pm if you're having the evening meal), and you have to vacate the building during the day (usually by 10am). **In the evening**, doors are locked around 9.30pm or 10pm – maybe as late as 10.30pm if you're lucky – while loudspeakers announce when it's time to bath, eat, turn the lights out and get up; there's even an approved way to fold hostel blankets. Some people find this boarding school atmosphere totally offputting, but you'll come across plenty of hostels with a more laidback attitude. And you won't be expected to do any chores, beyond clearing the table after meals and taking your sheets down to reception when you leave.

Hostel managers, tellingly known as "parents", traditionally hold an **evening meeting** to talk about the area and encourage people to mix. Nowadays it's likely to be a fairly informal gathering and, though not compulsory, your participation will be appreciated.

## CAMPING AND MOUNTAIN HUTS

There are hundreds of **campsites** (*kyampu-jō*) scattered throughout Japan, with prices ranging from nothing up to ¥3000 to pitch a tent. In some

## YOUTH HOSTEL ASSOCIATION

### AUSTRALIA AND NEW ZEALAND

422 Kent St, Sydney (☎02/9261 1111); 205 King St, Melbourne (☎03/9670 9611); 38 Stuart St, Adelaide (☎08/8231 5583); 154 Roma St, Brisbane (☎07/3236 1680); 236 William St, Perth (☎08/9227 5122); 69a Mitchell St, Darwin (☎08/8981 2560); 28 Criterion St, Hobart (☎03/6234 9617); and PO Box 436, Christchurch (☎03/379 9970).

### BRITAIN AND IRELAND

**Youth Hostel Association** (YHA), Trevelyan House, 8 St Stephen's Hill, St Albans, Herts AL1 2DY (☎01727/855215). London membership desk and booking office: 14 Southampton St, London WC2 7HY (☎0171/836 8541; www.yha.org.uk).

**Youth Hostel Association of Northern Ireland**, 22 Donegall Rd, Belfast BT12 5JN (☎01232/324 733).

**An Oige**, 61 Mountjoy St, Dublin 7 (☎01/830 4555; www.irelandyha.org).

**Scottish Youth Hostel Association**, 7 Glebe Crescent, Stirling, FK8 2JA (☎01786/451181; www.syha.org.uk).

### JAPAN

**Japan Youth Hostels**, 5F, Suidōbashi Nishiguchi Kaikan Bldg, 2-20-7 Misaki-chō, Tokyo 101 (☎03/3288-1417; www1.999.com/JYH/JYH-English/jyh.html).

### USA AND CANADA

**Hostelling International-American Youth Hostels** (HI-AYH), 733 15th St NW, Suite 840, PO Box 37613, Washington, DC 20005 (☎202/783-6161; www.hiayh.org).

**Hostelling International/Canadian Hostelling Association**, Room 400, 205 Catherine St, Ottawa, ON K2P 1C3 (☎1-800/663-5777 or 613/237-7884).

---

places you'll also pay an entry fee of a few hundred yen per person, plus charges for cooking gas and water, making it a fairly pricey option. In general, facilities are pretty basic compared to American or European sites; many have no hot water, for example, and the camp shop may stock nothing but pot-noodles. Most sites only open during the summer months, when they're packed out with students and school parties.

If you do fancy a spot of fresh air, however, JNTO publishes a short list of campsites, or you can ask at local tourist offices. If you haven't got your own tent, you can often hire everything on site or rent simple cabins from around ¥2500 – check before you get there. Camping is a better prospect if you've got your own transport, since the best sites are in national parks and can be both time-consuming and costly to get to. You're not supposed to sleep rough in national parks, but elsewhere in the countryside **camping wild** is tolerated. However, it's advisable to choose an inconspicuous spot, don't put your tent up till dusk and leave early in the morning.

In the main hiking areas, you'll find a good network of **mountain huts**. These range from basic shelters to much fancier places with wardens and meals. Again, the huts get pretty crowded in summer and during student holidays, and aren't particularly cheap; count on at least ¥5000 per head including two meals. You can get information about mountain huts from local tourist offices or, if you're going to be spending a lot of time in the mountains, invest in Kodansha's *Hiking in Japan*, which includes details of accommodation along recommended hiking trails.

## LONG-TERM ACCOMMODATION

Finding reasonably priced **long-term accommodation** is a perennial problem for foreigners (*gaijin*) working in Japan. Not only is it prohibitively expensive but many landlords simply won't rent apartments to non-Japanese. If possible, make sure accommodation is covered in your contract, or be prepared for a long haul.

Most newcomers start off in what's known as **gaijin houses**. Located in Tokyo, Kyoto and other cities with large foreign populations, these privately owned houses or apartments consist of shared and private rooms with communal cooking and washing facilities. They're usually rented by the month, though if there's space, weekly or even nightly rates may be available. Many are not entirely legal and are very unhygienic, while the best ones are nearly always full. But ask around and scan the English-language press or notice boards and you may be lucky. Monthly rates start from ¥30,000–40,000 per person for a shared room and ¥50,000 for a single (a deposit may be required), while a night's accommodation costs from around ¥2000 per person.

To find your own **apartment**, it helps enormously to have a Japanese friend or colleague to act as an intermediary; alternatively, you could try a housing agent. Once you've found somewhere,

you'll have to fork out for "key money" (one to two months' rent), a refundable deposit (one to three months' rent), and the first month's rent in advance, plus a month's rent in commission for the agent. Rentals in Tokyo start at ¥50,000–60,000 per month for a one-room box. After all that, the "management fee", normally a few thousand yen a month, hardly seems worth mentioning.

## EATING AND DRINKING

One of the great pleasures of a trip to Japan is exploring the full and exotic range of Japanese food. Whilst dishes such as sushi and tempura are well-known the world over these days, there are hundreds of other types of local cuisine that will be new discoveries to all but the most sophisticated of Western palates. Many Japanese recipes embody a subtlety of flavour and mixture of texture rarely found in Western cuisine, and the presentation is often so exquisite that it feels an insult to the chef to eat what has been so beautifully crafted.

Picking at delicate morsels with chopsticks is only one small part of the dining experience, though. Robust and cheap dishes such as hearty bowls of ramen noodles or the comforting concoction *kare raisu* (curry rice) are staples of the Japanese diet, along with burgers and fried chicken from ubiquitous Western-style fast-food outlets. All the major cities have an extensive range of restaurants serving Western and other Asian

dishes, with Tokyo and Ōsaka in particular being major league destinations for foodies.

With a little planning, eating out need not be too expensive. Lunch is always the best-value meal of the day, seldom costing more than ¥2000. If you fuel up earlier in the day, a cheap bowl of noodles for dinner could carry you through the night, especially if you're planning on drinking, which is never a cheap affair.

### MEALS

**Breakfast** is generally served early (from around 7am to 9am) at most hotels, ryokan and minshuku, with a traditional meal consisting of a gut-busting combination of miso soup, fish, pickles and rice. Western-style breakfasts, when available, seldom resemble what you might eat at home, and usually involve wedges of thick white tasteless bread, and some form of eggs and salad. Away from home and hotels, many Japanese prefer a quick *kōhii* and *tōsuto* (coffee and toast) to start the day, which is served at most cafés on the "morning service" menu.

Restaurants generally open for **lunch** around 11.30am and finish serving at 2pm. Try to avoid the rush hour from noon to 1pm when most office workers eat. Lacklustre sandwiches are best passed over in favour of a full meal at a restaurant, all of which offer **set menus** (called *teishoku*), usually around ¥1000 for a couple of courses, plus a drink, and rarely topping ¥2000 per person. At any time of day you can snack in stand-up noodle bars – often found around train stations – and beside the revolving conveyor belts at cheap sushi shops.

**Dinner**, the main meal of the day, can be eaten as early as 6pm with many places taking

## BENTŌ: THE PACKED LUNCH

Every day millions of Japanese trot off to school or their workplace with a **bentō** stashed in their satchel or briefcase. *Bentō* are boxed lunches which can be made at home or bought from shops all over Japan. Traditional *bentō* include rice, pickles, grilled fish or meat and vegetables. There are thousands of permutations depending on the season and the location in Japan (see box on railway food, p.28), with some of the best being available from department stores – there's always a model or picture to show you what's inside the box. At their most elaborate, *bentō* served in classy Japanese restaurants will come in beautiful multi-layered lacquered boxes, each compartment containing some exquisite culinary creation. It's also worth searching out empty *bentō* boxes in the household section of department stores since they make unusual souvenirs.

last orders around 9pm. The major cities are about the only option for late-night dining. In a traditional Japanese meal (see pp.46–51 for a description of the main dishes) you'll usually be served all your courses at the same time, but at more formal places, rice and soup are always served last. Heavy **puddings** are almost unheard of in traditional Japanese restaurants, and you are most likely to finish your meal with a piece of seasonal **fruit**, such as melon, orange, persimmon, or *nashi* (a crisp type of pear), or an or ice cream (if it's green, it will be flavoured with *matcha* tea).

At **tea ceremonies** (see p.52), small intensely sweet *wagashi* cakes are served, which are prettily decorated sweetmeats, usually made of pounded rice, red adzuki beans or chestnuts. *Wagashi* can also be bought from specialist shops and department stores and make lovely gifts. Western-style cakes available in *kissaten* are often disappointingly synthetic, although there are pastry shops (not to mention the fab doughnut cafés, *Mister Donut*) across Japan which specialize in tasty nibbles.

## WHERE TO EAT AND DRINK

One of the most common types of Japanese restaurant is the **shokudō** (eating place), which serves a range of traditional and generally inexpensive dishes. Usually found near train and subway stations and in busy shopping districts, *shokudō* can be identified by the displays of plastic meals in their windows. Other restaurants (*resutoran*) usually serve just one type of food, for example sushi and sashimi (*sushi-ya*), or *yakitori* (*yakitori-ya*), or specialize in a particular style of cooking, such as *kaiseki* (haute cuisine) or *teppanyaki*, where food is prepared on a steel griddle, either by yourself or a chef.

All over Japan, but particularly in the city suburbs, you'll find bright and breezy **family restaurants**, such as *Royal Host* and *Dennys*, specifically geared to family dining. These American-style operations serve Western and Japanese food which can be on the bland side, but are invariably keenly priced. They also have menus illustrated with photographs to make ordering easy. If you can't decide what to eat, head for the restaurant floors of major **department stores**, where you'll find a collection of Japanese and Western operations, often outlets of reputable local restaurants. Many will have plastic food displays in their front windows and daily special menus.

Western and other ethnic food restaurants proliferate in the cities, and it's seldom a problem finding popular **foreign cuisines** such as Italian (*Itarira-ryōri*), French (*Furansu-ryōri*), Korean (*Kankoku-ryōri*), Chinese (*Chūgoku-* or *Chūka-ryōri*) or Thai (*Tai-ryōri*) food. However, the recipes are often adapted to suit Japanese tastes, so be prepared for the dishes to be less spicy than you may be used to.

**Coffee shops** (*kissaten*) are something of an institution in Japan, often designed to act as an alternative lounge or business meeting place for patrons starved of space at home or the office. Others have weird designs or specialize in, say, jazz or comic books. For this reason, in many of the old-style *kissaten*, a speciality coffee or tea will usually set you back a pricey ¥500 or more. In recent years a caffeine-fuelled revolution has taken place, with cheap and cheerful operations like *Doutor* and *Mister Donut* springing up across the country, serving drinks and nibbles at reasonable prices; search these places out for a cheap breakfast or snack.

The best-value and liveliest places **to drink** are the **izakaya** pub-type restaurants, which also serve an extensive menu of small dishes. The major breweries run reliable *izakaya* chains, such as Sapporo's *Lions Beer Hall* and Kirin's *Kirin City*, which are generally large with a boozy atmosphere. The traditional *izakaya* are rather rustic looking, although in the cities you'll come across more modern, trendy operations aimed at the youth market. One type of traditional *izakaya* is an *aka-chōchin*, named after the red lanterns hanging outside, with another variation being the *robatayaki*, which serves food grilled over charcoal. Most *izakaya* open around 6pm and shut down around midnight. From mid-June to late August, outdoor **beer gardens** flourish across Japan's main cities and towns; look out for the fairy lights on the roofs of buildings, or in street-level gardens and plazas.

Regular bars, or **nomiya**, often consist of little more than a short counter and a table, and are usually run by a *mama-san* (or sometimes a *papa-san*), a unique breed who both charm and terrorize their customers. Prices at *nomiya* are high and although you're less likely to be ripped off if you speak some Japanese, it's no guarantee. All such bars operate a **bottle keep** system for regulars to stash a bottle of drink with their name on it behind the bar. It's generally best to go to such bars with a regular, since they tend to operate like mini-clubs, with non-regulars being given the cold shoulder. *Nomiya* will stay open to the early hours, provided there are customers.

If there's live music in a bar you'll pay for it through higher drinks prices or a **cover charge**. Some regular bars also have cover charges, although there's plenty of choice among those that don't, so always check before buying your drink. Bars specializing in **karaoke** are not difficult to spot; if you decide to join in, there's usually a small fee to pay and at least a couple of songs with English lyrics to choose from, typically *Yesterday* and *My Way*.

## ORDERING AND ETIQUETTE

On walking into most restaurants in Japan you'll be greeted by the word *Irasshaimase* (welcome), often shouted out with brio by the entire staff. In response, you should indicate with your fingers how many places are needed. After being seated you'll be handed an *oshibori*, a damp, folded hand towel, usually steaming hot, but sometimes offered refreshingly cold in summer. A chilled glass of water (*mizu*) will also usually be brought automatically.

The most daunting aspect of eating out in Japan comes next – deciphering the menu. We've included a basic glossary of essential words and

### KAISEKI-RYŌRI: JAPANESE HAUTE CUISINE

At the top end of the eating spectrum is Japan's finest and most expensive style of cooking, **kaiseki-ryōri**, which began as an accompaniment to the tea ceremony and still retains the meticulous design of that simple, elegant ritual. At the best *kaiseki-ryōri* restaurants the atmosphere of the room in which the meal – a series of small, carefully balanced and expertly presented dishes – is served is just as important as the food; you'll sit on *tatami*, a scroll decorated with calligraphy will hang in the *tokonoma* (alcove); a waitress in kimono will serve each course on beautiful china and lacquerware. For such a sublime experience you should expect to pay around ¥10,000 or more for dinner, although a lunchtime *kaiseki bentō* (see box, opposite) is a more affordable option.

phrases in this section; for more detail, try *Japanese: a Rough Guide Phrasebook*, or the comprehensive *What's What in Japanese Restaurants* by Robb Satterwhite (¥1200; Kodansha). In addition, it's always worth asking if an English menu is available (*eigo no menyū o onegai shimasu*). If a restaurant has a plastic food window display, use it to point to what you want. If all else fails, look round at what your fellow diners are eating and point out what you fancy. Remember that the *teishoku* (set meal) or *kōsu* (course) meals offer the best value and look out for the word Viking (*Baikingu*), which means a help-yourself buffet.

**Chopsticks** (*hashi*) come with their own etiquette; don't stick them upright in your rice, or use them to pass food to another diner – both allusions to death. If you're taking food from a shared plate, turn the chopsticks round and use the other end to pick up the food. Also never cross your chopsticks when you put them on the table or use them to point at things. When it comes to eating soupy noodles you can relax and enjoy a good slurp; it's also fine to bring the bowl to your lips and drink directly from it.

When you want **the bill**, say *okanjō kudasai* (bill please); the usual form is to pay at the till on the way out, not to leave the money on the table. There's no need to leave a tip, but it's polite to say *gochisō-sama deshita* (that was delicous) to the waiter or chef. Apart from the five percent consumption tax added to all meals (sometimes included in the advertised price, sometimes not), an additional three percent tax is added if the bill exceeds ¥7500 per person. Only the most upmarket Western restaurants and top hotels will add a service charge (typically ten percent).

## SUSHI, SASHIMI AND SEAFOOD

Many *gaijin* falsely assume that all **sushi** is fish, but the name actually refers to the way the rice is prepared with vinegar, and you can also get sushi dishes with egg or vegetables. Fish and seafood are, of course, essential and traditional elements of Japanese cuisine, and range from the seaweed used in *miso-shiru* (soup) to the slices of tuna, salmon and squid laid across the slabs of sushi rice. Slices of raw fish and seafood on their own are generally called **sashimi**.

In a traditional **sushi-ya** each plate is freshly made by a team of chefs working in full view of the customers. If you're not sure of the different types to order, point at the trays on show in the glass chiller cabinets at the counter, or go for the *nigiri-zushi mori-awase*, a slab of perhaps six or seven different types of fish and seafood on fingers of sushi rice. Other types of sushi include *maki-zushi*, rolled in a sheet of crisp seaweed, and *chirashi-zushi*, a layer of rice topped with fish, vegetables and cooked egg.

While a meal at a *sushi-ya* averages ¥5000 (or much more at high class joint) at **kaiten-zushi** shops, where you choose whatever sushi dish you want from the continually replenished conveyor belt, the bill will rarely stretch beyond ¥1500 per person. In *kaiten-zushi*, plates are colour-coded according to how much each one costs, and are totted up at the end for the total cost of the meal. If you can't see what you want, you can ask the chefs to make it for you. Green tea is free, and you can usually order beer or sake.

If you want to try the infamous **fugu**, or blow-fish, you'll generally need to go to a specialist fish restaurant, which can be easily identified by the picture or model of a balloon-like fish outside. *Fugu*'s reputation derives from its potentially fatally poisonous nature rather than it's bland, rubbery taste. The actual risk of dropping dead at the counter is virtually nil – at least from *fugu* poisoning – and you're more likely to keel over at the bill, which (cheaper cultivated *fugu* apart) will be in the ¥10,000 per person bracket.

A more affordable and tasty seafood speciality is **unagi**, or eel, typically basted with a thick sauce

of soy and sake, sizzled over charcoal and served on a bed of rice. This dish is particularly popular in summer, when it's believed to provide strength in the face of sweltering heat. Restaurants specializing in **crab** (*kani*) dishes are also popular and are easily identified by the models of giant crabs with wiggling pincers over the doorways.

## NOODLES

One of Japan's most popular and best-value meals is a bowl of **noodles**, the three main types being soba, udon and ramen. **Soba** are thin noodles made of brown buckwheat flour and are particularly ubiquitous in the central Honshū prefectures of Gifu and Nagano, though available all over Japan. If the noodles are green, they've been made with green tea powder.

There are two main styles of serving soba – hot and cold. *Kake-soba* is served in a clear hot broth, often with added ingredients such as tofu, vegetables and chicken. Cold noodles piled on a bamboo screen bed, with a cold sauce for dipping (which can be flavoured with chopped spring onions, seaweed flakes and *wasabi* – grated green horseradish paste) is called *zaru-soba* or *mori-soba*. In more traditional restaurants you'll also be served a flask of the hot water used to cook the noodles, which is added to the dipping sauce to make a soup drink once you've finished the soba.

In most soba restaurants, **udon** will also be on the menu. These chunkier noodles are made with plain wheat flour and are served in the same hot or cold styles as soba. In Nagoya, a variation on udon is *kishimen*, flattened white noodles, while the Shikoku and Okayama-ken version is known as *sanuki-udon*. For **yakisoba** and **yakiudon** dishes the noodles are fried, often in a thick soy sauce along with seaweed flakes, meat and other vegetables.

**Ramen**, or stringy yellow noodles, were originally imported from China but have now become part and parcel of Japanese cuisine. They're usually served in big bowls in a steaming oily soup, which typically comes in three varieties: *miso* (flavoured with fermented bean paste), *shio* (a salty soup) or *shōyu* (a broth made with soy sauce). A range of garnishes, including seaweed, bamboo shoots, pink and white swirls of fish paste, and pork slices, often finish off the dish, which you can spice up with added garlic or a red pepper mixture. As with the other types of noodle, many regions of Japan have their own local ver-

## FOOD AND DRINK

### Places to eat and drink

| | | |
|---|---|---|
| Bar | *nomiya* | 飲み屋 |
| Café/coffee shop | *kissaten* | 喫茶店 |
| Cafeteria | *shokudō* | 食堂 |
| Pub | *pabu* | パブ |
| Pub-style restaurant | *izakaya* | 居酒屋 |
| Restaurant | *resutoran* | レストラン |
| Restaurant specializing in charcoal-grilled foods | *robatayaki* | 炉端焼 |

### Ordering

| | | |
|---|---|---|
| Breakfast | *asa-gohan* | 朝ご飯 |
| Lunch | *hiru-gohan* | 昼ご飯 |
| Dinner | *ban-gohan* | 晩ご飯 |
| Boxed meal | *bentō* | 弁当 |
| Chopsticks | *hashi* | はし |
| Fork | *fōku* | フォーク |
| Knife | *naifu* | ナイフ |
| Spoon | *supūn* | スプーン |
| Set meal | *teishoku* | 定食 |
| Daily special set meal | *higawari-teishoku* | 日変わり定食 |
| Menu | *menyū* | メニュー |
| How much is that? | *ikura desu ka* | いくらですか？ |
| I would like (a) | *(a) o onegai shimasu* | （ａ）をお願いします |
| May I have the bill? | *okanjō o onegai shimasu* | お勘定をお願いします |

### Staple foods

| | | |
|---|---|---|
| Bean curd | *tōfu* | 豆腐 |
| Butter | *batā* | バター |
| Bread | *pan* | パン |
| Dried seaweed | *nori* | のり |
| Egg | *tamago* | 卵 |
| Fermented soybean paste | *miso* | 味噌 |
| Garlic | *ninniku* | にんにく |
| Oil | *abura* | 油 |
| Pepper | *koshō* | こしょう |
| Rice | *gohan* | ご飯 |
| Salt | *shio* | 塩 |
| Soy sauce | *shōyu* | しょうゆ |
| Sugar | *satō* | 砂糖 |

### Fish and seafood dishes

| | | |
|---|---|---|
| Fish | *sakana* | 魚 |
| Shellfish | *kai* | 貝 |
| Raw fish | *sashimi* | さしみ |
| Sushi | *sushi* | 寿司 |
| Sushi mixed selection | *nigiri-zushi* | にぎり寿司 |
| Sushi rolled in crisp seaweed | *maki-zushi* | まき寿司 |
| Sushi topped with fish and vegetables | *chirashi-zushi* | ちらし寿司 |
| Abalone | *awabi* | あわび |
| Blowfish | *fugu* | ふぐ |
| Cod | *tara* | たら |
| Crab | *kani* | かに |
| Eel | *unagi* | うなぎ |

**continued overleaf**

## Fish and seafood dishes cont.

| | | |
|---|---|---|
| Herring | *nishin* | にしん |
| Horse mackerel | *aji* | あじ |
| Lobster | *ise-ebi* | 伊勢海老 |
| Octopus | *tako* | たこ |
| Oyster | *kaki* | かき |
| Prawn | *ebi* | えび |
| Sea bream | *tai* | たい |
| Sea urchin | *uni* | うに |
| Squid | *ika* | いか |
| Sweet smelt | *ayu* | あゆ |
| Tuna | *maguro* | まぐろ |
| Yellowtail | *buri* | ぶり |

## Fruit

| | | |
|---|---|---|
| Fruit | *kudamono* | 果物 |
| Apple | *ringo* | りんご |
| Banana | *banana* | バナナ |
| Grapefruit | *gurēpufurūtsu* | グレープフルーツ |
| Grapes | *budō* | ぶどう |
| Japanese plum | *ume* | うめ |
| Lemon | *remon* | レモン |
| Melon | *meron* | メロン |
| Orange | *orenji* | オレンジ |
| Peach | *momo* | 桃 |
| Pear | *nashi* | なし |
| Persimmon | *kaki* | 柿 |
| Pineapple | *painappuru* | パイナップル |
| Strawberry | *ichigo* | いちご |
| Tangerine | *mikan* | みかん |
| Watermelon | *suika* | すいか |

## Vegetables & salads

| | | |
|---|---|---|
| Vegetables | *yasai* | 野菜 |
| Salad | *sarada* | サラダ |
| Aubergine | *nasu* | なす |
| Beans | *mame* | 豆 |
| Bean sprouts | *moyashi* | もやし |
| Carrot | *ninjin* | にんじん |
| Cauliflower | *karifurawā* | カリフラワー |
| Green pepper | *piiman* | ピーマン |
| Green horseradish | *wasabi* | わさび |
| Leek | *negi* | ねぎ |
| Mushroom | *kinoko* | きのこ |
| Onion | *tamanegi* | たまねぎ |
| Potato | *poteto* | ポテト |
| Radish | *daikon* | だいこん |
| Sweetcorn | *kōn* | コーン |
| Tomato | *tomato* | トマト |

## Meat and meat dishes

| | | |
|---|---|---|
| Meat | *niku* | 肉 |
| Beef | *gyūniku* | 牛肉 |
| Chicken | *toriniku* | 鳥肉 |
| Lamb | *ramu* | ラム |
| Pork | *butaniku* | 豚肉 |

| Breaded, deep-fried slice of pork | *tonkatsu* | とんかつ |
| Chicken, other meat and vegetables grilled on skewers | *yakitori* | 焼き鳥 |
| Skewers of food dipped in breadcrumbs and deep fried | *kushiage* | 串揚げ |
| Stew including meat (or seafood), vegetables and noodles | *nabe* | 鍋 |
| Thin beef slices cooked in broth | *shabu-shabu* | しゃぶしゃぶ |
| Thin beef slices braised in a sauce | *sukiyaki* | すきやき |

## Vegetarian and noodle dishes

| Buddhist-style vegetarian cuisine | *shōjin-ryōri* | 精進料理 |
| Chinese-style noodles | *rāmen* | ラーメン |
| Chinese-style dumplings | *gyōza* | ぎょうざ |
| Fried noodles | *yakisoba/udon* | 焼そば／うどん |
| Stewed chunks of tofu, vegetables and fish on skewers | *oden* | おでん |
| Thin buckwheat noodles | *soba* | そば |
| Soba in a hot soup | *kake-soba* | かけそば |
| Cold soba for dipping in a sauce | *zaru-soba/mori-soba* | ざるそば／もりそば |
| Thick wheat noodles | *udon* | うどん |

## Other dishes

| Fried rice | *chāhan* | チャーハン |
| Lightly battered seafood and vegetables | *tempura* | 大ぷら |
| Meat, vegetable and fish cooked in soy sauce and sweet sake | *teriyaki* | 照り焼き |
| Mild curry served with rice | *karē raisu* | カレーライス |
| Octopus in balls of batter | *takoyaki* | たこやき |
| Pounded rice cakes | *mochi* | もち |
| Rice topped with fish, meat or vegetable | *donburi* | どんぶり |
| Rice triangles wrapped in crisp seaweed | *onigiri* | おにぎり |
| Savoury pancakes | *okonomiyaki* | お好み焼 |
| Chinese food | *Chūka/Chūgoku-ryōri* | 中華／中国料理 |
| French food | *Furansu-ryōri* | フランス料理 |
| Italian food | *Itaria-ryōri* | イタリア料理 |
| Japanese-style food | *washoku* | 和食 |
| Japanese haute cuisine | *kaiseki-ryōri* | 懐石料理 |
| Korean food | *Kankoku-ryōri* | 韓国料理 |
| No-nationality food | *mukokuseki-ryōri* | 無国籍料理 |
| Thai food | *Tai-ryōri* | タイ料理 |
| Western-style food | *yōshoku* | 洋食 |

## Drinks

| Beer | *biiru* | ビール |
| Black tea | *kōcha* | 紅茶 |
| Coffee | *kōhii* | コーヒー |
| Fruit juice | *jūsu* | ジュース |
| Green tea | *sencha* | 煎茶 |
| Milk | *miruku* | ミルク |
| Oolong tea | *ūron-cha* | ウーロン茶 |
| Powdered green tea | *matcha* | 抹茶 |
| Water | *mizu* | 水 |
| Whisky | *uisukii* | ウイスキー |
| Whisky and water | *mizu-wari* | 水割り |
| Sake (rice wine) | *sake/nihon-shu* | 酒／日本酒 |
| Wine | *wain* | ワイン |

sions of the dish, such as Sapporo which specializes in the rich *batā-kōn* (butter and corn flavoured) ramen. Wherever you eat ramen, though, you can usually get **gyōza**, fried half-moon-shaped dumplings filled with pork or seafood, to accompany them.

## RICE DISHES

Although fluffy white, tasteless bread is becoming more and more popular in Japan, it will never replace the ever present bowl of **rice** as the staple food. Rice also forms the basis of both the alcoholic drink sake and **mochi**, a chewy dough made from pounded glutinous rice, usually prepared and eaten during festivals such as New Year.

A traditional meal isn't considered finished until a bowl of rice has been eaten, and the grain is an integral part of several cheap snack-type dishes. **Onigiri** are palm-sized triangles of rice with a filling of soy, tuna, salmon roe, or sour *umeboshi* (pickled plum), all wrapped up in a sheet of crisp *nori* (seaweed). They can be bought at convenience stores for around ¥150 each and are ingeniously packaged so that the *nori* stays crisp until the *onigiri* is unwrapped. **Donburi** is a bowl of rice with various toppings, such as chicken and egg (*oyako-don*, literally parent and child), strips of stewed beef (*gyū-don*) or *katsu-don*, which come with a *tonkatsu* (see below) pork cutlet.

Finally, the Japanese equivalent of beans on toast is **curry rice**, which bears little relation to the Indian dish. What goes into the sludgy brown sauce that makes up the curry is a mystery and you'll probably search in vain for evidence of any beef or chicken in the so-called *bifu karē* and *chikin karē*. However, the dish most definitely qualifies as a top comfort food and cheap snack.

## MEAT DISHES

Meat is alien to traditional Japanese cuisine, but in the last century dishes using beef, pork and chicken have become a major part of the national diet. Beefburger and fried chicken (*kara-age*) fast-food outlets are just as common these days as noodle bars. The more expensive steak restaurants serving up dishes like **sukiyaki** (thin beef slices cooked in a soy, sugar and sake broth) and **shabu-shabu** (beef and vegetable slices cooked at the table in a light broth and dipped in various sauces) are popular treats.

Like *sukiyaki* and *shabu-shabu*, **nabe** (the name refers to the cooking pot) stews are prepared at the table over a gas or charcoal burner by diners who throw a range of raw ingredients (meat or fish along with vegetables) into the pot to cook. As things cook they're fished out, and the last thing to be immersed is usually some kind of noodles. *Chanko-nabe* is the famous chuck-it-all in stew used to beef up sumo wrestlers.

Other popular meat dishes include **tonkatsu**, breadcrumb-covered slabs of pork, crisply fried and usually served on a bed of shredded cabbage with a brown semi-sweet sauce; and **yakitori**, delicious skewers of grilled chicken and sometimes other meats and vegetables. At the cheapest *yakitori-ya*, you'll pay for each skewer individually. **Kushiage** is a combination of *tonkatsu* and *yakitori* dishes, where skewers of meat, seafood and vegetables are coated in breadcrumbs and deep fried.

## VEGETARIAN DISHES

Despite being the home of macrobiotic cooking, vegetarianism isn't a widely practised or fully understood concept in Japan. You might ask for a vegetarian (*saishoku*) dish in a restaurant and still be served something with meat or fish in it. That said, Japan has bequeathed some marvellous vegetarian foods to the world. Top of the list is **tofu**, compacted cakes of soybean curd, which comes in two main varieties, *momengoshi-dōfu* (cotton tofu), so called because of its fluffy texture, and the smoother, more fragile *kinugoshi-dōfu* (silk tofu). The most popular tofu dish you'll come across is *hiya yakko*, a small slab of chilled tofu topped with grated ginger, spring onions, dried bonito flakes and soy sauce. Buddhist cuisine, *shōjin-ryōri*, concocts whole menus based around different types of tofu dishes; although they can be expensive it's worth searching out the specialist restaurants serving this type of food, particularly in major temple cities, such as Kyoto, Nara and Nagano.

**Miso** (fermented bean paste) is another crucial ingredient of Japanese cooking, used in virtually every meal, if only in the soup *miso-shiru*. It often serves as a flavouring in fish and vegetable dishes and comes in two main varieties, the light *shiro-miso* and the darker, stronger tasting *aka-miso*. One of the most delicious ways of eating the gooey paste is *hoba miso*, where the miso is mixed with vegetables, roasted over a charcoal brazier, and served on a large magnolia leaf. This dish is a speciality of Takayama, where vegetarians should also sample the *sansai* (mountain vegetable) dishes.

One question all foreigners in Japan are asked is "can you eat **nattō?**". This sticky, stringy fermented bean paste has a strong taste and unfamiliar texture which can be off-putting to Western palates. It's worth trying at least once, though, and is usually served in little tubs at breakfast, to be mixed with mustard and soy sauce and eaten with rice.

Scraping into the vegetarian catagory as long as you avoid the fish versions is **oden**, a warming winter dish that tastes much more delicious than it looks. Oden is large chunks of food, usually on skewers, simmered in a thin broth, and often served from portable carts (*yatai*) on street corners. The main ingredients are blocks of tofu, *daikon* (a giant radish), *konnyaku* (a hard jelly made from a root vegetable), *konbu* (seaweed), hard-boiled eggs and fish cakes, and all are best eaten with a smear of fiery English-style mustard.

## OTHER CUISINES

Said to have to been introduced to Japan in the sixteenth century by Portuguese traders, **tempura** are lightly battered pieces of seafood and vegetables. Best eaten piping hot from the fryer, tempura are dipped in a bowl of light sauce (*tentsuyu*) mixed with grated *daikon* radish and sometimes ginger. At specialist tempura restaurants, you'll generally order the *teishoku* set meal, which includes whole prawns, squid, aubergines, mushrooms and the aromatic leaf *shiso*.

Japan's equivalent of the pizza is **okonomiyaki**, a fun, cheap meal which you can often assemble yourself. A pancake batter is used to bind shredded cabbage and other vegetables, with either seafood or meat. If it's a DIY restaurant, you'll mix the individual ingredients and cook them on a griddle in the middle of the table. Otherwise, you can sit at the kitchen counter watching the chefs at work. Once cooked, *okonomiyaki* is coated in a sweet brown sauce and/or mayonnaise and dusted off with dried seaweed and flakes of bonito fish, which twist and curl in the rising heat. At most *okonomiyaki* restaurants you can also get fried noodles (*yakisoba*). In addition, *okonomiyaki* along with its near cousin **takoyaki** (battered balls of octopus) are often served from *yatai* carts at street festivals.

Authentic Western restaurants are now commonplace across Japan, but there is also a hybrid style of cooking known as **yōshoku** (Western food) that developed during the Meiji era at the turn of the century. Often served in *shokudō*, *yōshoku* dishes include omelettes with rice (*omu-rāisu*), deep-fried potato croquettes (*korokke*) and hamburger steaks doused in a thick sauce (*hanbāgu*). The contemporary version of *yōshoku* is **mukokuseki** or "no-nationality" cuisine, a mish-mash of world cooking styles usually found in trendy *izakaya*.

## DRINKS

The Japanese are enthusiastic social drinkers, several shared bottles of beer or flasks of sake being the preferred way for salarymen and women to wind down after work. It's not uncommon to see totally inebriated people slumped in the street, though on the whole drunkeness rarely leads to violence.

If you want a **non-alcoholic** drink, you'll never be far from a coffee shop (*kissaten*), or a *jidohanbaiki* (vending machine), where you can get a vast range of canned soft drinks, teas and coffees, both hot and cold, though canned tea and coffee is often very sweet. Cans from machines typically cost ¥110 and hot drinks are identified by a red stripe under the display. It's worth noting that vending machines selling beer, sake and other alcoholic drinks shut down at 11pm, the same time as liquor stores.

### SAKE

Legend has it that the ancient deities brewed **sake** – Japan's most famous alcoholic beverage – from the first rice of the new year. Although the twentieth century newcomer, beer, is now Japan's most popular tipple, thousands of different brands of the clean-tasting rice wine are still produced throughout the country in sweet (*amakuchi*) and dry (*karakuchi*) varieties. Some 2500 local sake breweries make *ji-zaké* (regional sake); these can be identified by the ball of cedar leaves hanging over the shop door.

Although sake is graded as *tokkyū* (superior), *ikkyū* (first) and *nikkyū* (second), this is mainly for tax purposes; if you're after the best quality, *tsū* (connoisseurs) recommend going for *gingō-zukuri* (or *ginjō-zō*), the most expensive and rare of the *junmai-shu* pure rice sake. Some types of sake are cloudier and less refined than others, and there's also the very sweet milky *amezaké*, often served at temple festivals and at shrines over New Year.

In restaurants and *izakaya*, you'll have a choice of drinking your sake warm (*atsukan*) in a small flask (*tokkuri*), or cold (*reishō*), when it'll probably be served in a small wooden box with a smidgen of salt on the rim to counter the sweet taste. The cups are small because at 15–16.5 percent alcohol content (or more), sake is a strong drink, which goes to your head even more quickly if drunk warm. Delicious as it can be, sake can leave you with a raging hangover, so is best drunk in moderation.

## BEER

When beer was first brewed in Japan in Sapporo during the late-nineteenth-century colonization period of Hokkaidō, the locals had to be bribed to drink it. These days, they need no such encouragement knocking back a whopping seven million kilolitres a year. Beer in Japan generally means lager, produced by the big four brewers Asahi, Kirin, Sapporo and Suntory, who also turn out a range of ale-type beers (often called black beer), as well as half-and-half concoctions, which are mixture of the two. The current best seller is Asahi Superdry, a dry-tasting lager.

Standard size cans of beer cost around ¥200 from a shop or vending machine, while bottles (*bin-biiru*) served in restaurants and bars usually start at ¥500. Draft beer (*nama-biiru*) is also sometimes available and, in beer halls, will be served in a *jōkki*, which comes in three different sizes: *dai* (big), *chūō* (medium) and *shō* (small).

In recent years, the big four have seen their monopoly on domestic sales eroded by cheap foreign imports and deregulation of the industry, which has encouraged local **microbreweries** to expand their operations. In Japanese, the new brews are called *ji-biiru* (regional beer), and although few have got their act together to pro-

duce really fine beers, their drinks are always worth sampling as an alternative to the bland brews of the big four.

## OTHER ALCOHOLIC DRINKS

Much stronger and cheaper than sake is the distilled grain alcohol, **shōchū**, usually mixed with a soft drink into a *sawā* (as in lemon-sour) or a *chōhai* highball cocktail. At best *shōchū* is like vodka, and very drinkable; at worst it tastes like diesel, and is reputed to leave the worst hangovers in Japan.

The Japanese love **whisky**, with the top brewers producing several of their own respectable brands, often served with water and ice and called *mizu-wari*. In contrast, Japanese **wine**, often very sweet, is a less successful product, at least to hardened Western palates. Imported wines, however, are available and are becoming cheaper in both shops and restaurants.

---

### DRINKING ETIQUETTE

If you're out drinking with Japanese friends, always pour your colleagues' drinks, but never your own; they'll take care of that. In fact, you'll find your glass being topped up after every couple of sips making it difficult to judge how much you've imbibed.

In many bars you'll be served a small snack or a plate of nuts with your first drink, whether you've asked for it or not; this is often a flimsy excuse for a cover charge to be added to the bill. It's fine to get blinding drunk and misbehave with your colleauges at night, but it's very bad form to talk about it in the cold light of day. The usual way to make a **toast** in Japanese is *kampai*.

---

### THE TEA CEREMONY

Tea was introduced to Japan from China in the ninth century and was popularized by Zen Buddhist monks who appreciated its caffeine kick during their long meditation sessions. Gradually, tea-drinking developed into a formal ritual known as *cha-no-yu*, the **tea ceremony**, whose purpose is to heighten the senses within a contemplative atmosphere. In its simplest form the ceremony takes place in a *tatami* room, undecorated save for a hanging scroll or display of *ikebana* (tradi-

tional flower arrangement). Using beautifully crafted utensils of bamboo, iron and rustic pottery, your host will whisk *matcha* (powdered green tea) into a thick, frothy brew and present it to each guest in turn. Take the bowl in both hands, turn it clockwise a couple of inches and drink it down in three slow sips. It's then customary to admire the bowl while nibbling on a dainty sweetmeat (*wagashi*), which counteracts the tea's bitter taste.

## TEA, COFFEE AND SOFT DRINKS

Other than in the new coffee shops, such as *Doutor* and *Pronto*, **coffee** tends to be expensive in Japan, averaging ¥400–500 a cup. Most of the time you'll be served blend (*burendo*), a medium-strength coffee which is generally black and comes in a choice of hot (*hotto*) or iced (*aisu*). American coffee is a weaker version. If you want milk ask for *miruku-kōhii* (milky coffee) or *kafe-ōre* (café au lait). Treat cappuccino on the menu with caution; whilst some *kissaten* take great care over their gourmet coffees, on the whole a really frothy cup is a rarity.

You can also get regular **black tea** in all coffee shops, served either with milk, lemon or iced. If you want the Japanese slightly bitter **green tea**, *ocha* (honourable tea), you'll usually have to go to a traditional teahouse, or be invited into a Japanese home. Green teas, which are always served in small cups and drunk plain, are graded according to their quality. *Bancha*, the cheapest, is for everyday drinking and, in its roasted form, is used to make the smoky *hōjicha*, or mixed with popped brown rice for the nutty *genmaicha*. Medium-grade *sencha* is served in upmarket restaurants or to favoured guests, while top-ranking, slightly sweet *gyokuro* (dewdrop) is reserved for special occasions. Other types of tea you may come across are *ūron-cha*, a refreshing Chinese-style tea, and *mugicha* made from roasted barley.

As well as the international brand-name **soft drinks** and fruit juices, there are some sports or isotonic drinks that are unique to Japan. You'll probably want to try *Pocari Sweat*, *Post Water* or *Calpis* for the name on the can alone.

# COMMUNICATIONS AND THE MEDIA

The Japanese are masters in the art of keeping in touch, but for a supposedly high-tech nation their communications infrastructure can at times seem rather old fashioned. It's not unusual, for example, to see post office staff counting on an abacus. Public telephones are available in the most unlikely of places, including on top of Mount. Fuji during the climbing season, but few allow you to make international calls. Email is slowly catching on, but remains unknown outside the main urban centres. At least every convenience store has a fax machine for public use, and at all the major stations and top

| MAIL AND TELEPHONE GLOSSARY | | |
|---|---|---|
| **Post** | *yūbin* | 郵便 |
| Post office | *yūbin-kyoku* | 郵便局 |
| Stamp | *kitte* | 切手 |
| Postcard | *hagaki* | はがき |
| Courier delivery service | *takkyūbin* | 宅急便 |
| poste restante | *tomeoki yūbin* | 留置郵便 |
| **Telephones** | | |
| Telephone | *denwa* | 電話 |
| Mobile phone | *keitai-denwa* | 携帯電話 |
| Phonecard | *terefon kādo* | テレフォンカード |

**bookstores in the cities you can buy English-language newspapers and magazines.**

## MAIL

Japan's **mail** service is highly efficient and fast, with post offices (*yūbin-kyoku*) all over the country, easily identified by their red and white signs of a T with a parallel bar across the top, the same symbol that you'll find on the red letter boxes. Letters posted within Japan should get to their destination in under two days, and all post can be addressed in Western script (*romaji*) provided it is clearly printed.

Inside urban post offices there are separate counters, with English signs, for postal and banking services; in central post offices you can also exchange money, at rates comparable to those in banks. Within Japan, a stamp (*kitte*) for a letter up to 25g costs ¥80 and for a postcard (*hagaki*) ¥50. For **overseas post** to anywhere in the world, it costs ¥70 to send a postcard and ¥90 for an aerogram. Letters up to 25g cost ¥90 to Asian destinations, ¥110 to North America, Australasia, Europe and the Middle East, and ¥130 to Africa and South America. Each extra 25g costs ¥50, ¥80 and ¥100 respectively. Stamps are also sold at convenience stores, shops displaying the post office sign, and at larger hotels.

If you need to send bulkier items or **parcels** back home, all post offices sell reasonably priced special envelopes and boxes for packaging, with the maximum weight for an overseas parcel being 20kg. A good compromise between expensive air mail and lengthy sea mail is Surface Air Lifted (SAL) mail, which takes around three weeks to reach most destinations, and costs between the two.

Central **post offices** generally open Monday–Friday 9am–7pm, Saturday 9am–5pm and Sunday 9am–12.30pm, with most other branches opening Monday–Friday 9am–5pm only. A few larger branches may also open on a Saturday from 9am–3pm, and may operate after-hours services for parcels and express mail. The Tokyo International Post Office, next to Tokyo Station, is open daily 24 hours for both domestic and international mail.

**Poste restante** (*tomeoki* or *kyoku dome yūbin*) is available at the larger central post offices in the big cities, but mail will only be held for thirty days before being returned. The same goes for American Express offices (which only accepts mail for card holders), unless it's marked "please hold for arrival". American Express has offices in Tokyo (see relevant city Listings section for details).

For sending parcels and baggage around Japan, take advantage of the excellent, inexpensive *takkyūbin* or **courier delivery services**, which can be arranged at most convenience stores, hotels and some youth hostels. These services – which typically cost under ¥2000 – are especially handy if you want to send luggage (usually up to 20kg) on to places where you'll be staying later in your journey or to the airport to be picked up prior to your departure.

## PHONES

You're rarely far from a payphone in Japan, but only from certain ones – usually grey or metallic silver and bronze colour with a sign in English – can you make **international calls**. In some restaurants and coffee shops you'll find the antique-looking dial phones that only accept ¥10 coins (which will get you 90 seconds of local talk time), but the vast majority of payphones take both coins (¥10 and ¥100), as well as **phonecards** (*terefon kādo*). The latter come in ¥500 (50 units) and ¥1000 (105 units) versions and can be bought in department and convenience stores and at station kiosks. Virtually every tourist attraction sells specially decorated phonecards, which come in a vast range of designs, though you'll pay a premium for these, with a ¥1000 card only giving ¥500-worth of calls.

For local calls, you should use ¥10 rather than ¥100 coins in payphones; that way you'll get back any unused money. For international calls, it's best to use a phonecard, and to call between 7pm and 8am Monday to Friday, or at any time on weekends or holidays when the rates are cheaper. All toll-free numbers begin with either ☎0120 or ☎0088; for operator assistance for overseas calls, dial ☎0051.

**Mobile phones** (*keitai-denwa*, sometimes just shortened to *keitai*) have become wildly popular since the deregulation of the telecommunications market a few years ago, and it's not unusual to see trendy young things in the cities carrying a couple of the sleek fashion accessory-style phones. Announcements are now common on trains and in cinemas asking customers to refrain from using their mobile phones, though they're often ignored. You can rent a mobile phone while you're in Japan (call NTT Mover

## PHONING JAPAN FROM ABROAD

To call Japan from abroad, dial your international access code (UK☎00; US☎011; Canada☎011; Australia ☎0011; New Zealand ☎00), plus the country code (☎81), plus the area code minus the initial zero, plus the number.

## PHONING ABROAD FROM JAPAN

To call abroad from Japan you can use the services of three operators, although there's little to choose between them – they are all expensive. First dial ☎001 for KDD, ☎0041 for ITJ or ☎0061 for IDC, followed by the country code (UK☎44; US☎1; Canada ☎1; Australia ☎61; New Zealand ☎64), plus the area code minus the initial zero, plus the number.

Alternatively, you could use a **charge card**, which will automatically debit the cost of any calls from your domestic phone account or credit card. To use these, dial the relevant access code (see below), followed by your account and PIN number, then the number you want to call.

**AUSTRALIA AND NEW ZEALAND** Optus Calling Card ☎0039 612; New Zealand Telecom's Calling Card ☎0039 641; Telstra Telecard ☎00539 611.
**UK** BT ☎0031004410; Cable & Wireless Calling ☎006655444 for calls made within Japan and abroad, and ☎0039444 for calls to the UK.
**US AND CANADA** AT&T ☎0039111; MCI ☎0039121; Sprint ☎0039131.

**INTERNATIONAL OPERATOR ASSISTED CALLS**

You can use the **Home Country Direct Call** service to speak with an operator in your home country.
UK ☎0039/441; US ☎0031-111; Canada ☎0039-161; Australia ☎0039-611; New Zealand ☎0039-641

## PHONING WITHIN JAPAN

Everywhere in Japan has an area code which must be dialled in full if you're making a long-distance call and is omitted if the call is a local one. Area codes are given for all telephone numbers throughout the book.

Rental Centre on ☎0120–680200; Mon–Fri 9am–6pm), but the high rental fees and deposit make it uneconomical for all but a few high-flying business-types.

### FAXES, EMAIL AND THE INTERNET

Most hotels and youth hostels will allow you to send a **fax** for a small charge, while receiving a fax is usually free if you're a guest. Alternatively, most central post office or convenience stores (often open 24 hours) have public fax machines.

Surprisingly **email** and the **Internet** have had a slow start in Japan, but are catching up fast. Most major cities now have at least one cyber-café, while the giant domestic telecoms company, NTT, offers free Internet access in their main offices. This means that sending emails and browsing the Web are not a problem. If you want to receive emails, however, and you're not carrying your own computer, you might want to set up an account with a Web-based email service, such as Hotmail (*www.hotmail.com*) or Yahoo!

Mail (*www.yahoo.com*), before leaving home. This enables you to pick up emails from any computer connected to the Web. The alternative is to arrange a POP3 email account with your Internet Service Provider (ISP), which allows you to access your account from any computer on the Internet. **Cybercafés** come and go fairly swiftly, but you'll find up-to-date lists on the Web at *www.netcafeguide.com/japan.htm* and *www.sfc.keio.ac.jp/index.html*.

If you're travelling with **your own computer**, before setting off ask your domestic ISP for details of any associated providers in Japan; both CompuServe and AOL have local nodes. Japanese phones use the standard American RJ11 plug, and you can access the phone system in your hotel or via your own cellphone. It's also possible to plug your laptop into the increasingly widespread grey, international public phones – they have a display screen and are fitted with both analogue and ISDN jacks, but only permit local access.

## THE MEDIA

If you read Japanese, Japan is a news-junkie heaven with 166 daily national and local **newspaper** companies printing some 70 million papers a day, more than triple the amount for the UK and even topping the US and China, despite both having much larger populations. Japan's top paper, the *Yomiuri Shimbun*, sells over 14 million copies daily, making it the most widely read newspaper in the world. Lagging behind by about two million copies a day is the *Asahi Shimbun*, with the other three national dailies, the *Mainichi Shimbun*, the *Sankei Shimbun* and the business paper the *Nihon Keizai Shimbun*, also selling respectable numbers.

The only one of these five papers not to publish a daily **English-language** version is the *Sankei Shimbun*, with the most widely available English-language daily throughout Japan being the independent *Japan Times* (¥160). Although far from sparkling, the *Japan Times* has the most comprehensive coverage of national and international news, carries a major situations vacant section every Monday, and has occasionally interesting features, some culled from the world's media. Doing a better job on the features front is the *Daily Yomiuri* (¥120), with specially compiled sections from the *Los Angeles Times* on Saturdays, and Britain's *Independent* newspaper on Sundays, as well as a decent arts and entertainment supplement on Thursdays. Also worth a look is the *Asahi Evening News*, the only English-language evening newspaper, and Japan editions of the *International Herald Tribune* and the *Financial Times*. Outside of the major cities, however, you'll be hard pushed to find anything but the *Japan Times*, if that. The best places to hunt out copies are the main stations and local international centres, which will often have reference copies of foreign newspapers.

The most widely available English-language **magazines** are *Time* and *Newsweek*. Bookstores such as Kinokuniya and Maruzen stock extensive (and expensive) ranges of imported and local magazines; in Tokyo and Ōsaka, Tower Records is the cheapest place to buy magazines. Local titles to look out for include *Tokyo Journal* (¥600) and *Kansai Time Out* (¥300), well-written listings and features magazines for their respective areas. With

more a fanzine feel, *The Alien* and *The Outsider* are published in Nagoya and Hiroshima respectively. If you're studying Japanese, or even just trying to pick up a bit of the language during your vacation, the bi-lingual magazines *Nihongo Journal* and *Hiragana Times* are worth searching out.

Japanese **television's** notorious reputation for silly game shows and samurai dramas is well earned. If you speak no Japanese, you're likely to find all TV shows, bar the frequent weather forecasts, totally baffling and only a little less so once you have picked up the lingo. However, watching some TV during your stay is recommended if only because of the fascinating insight it gives into Japanese society.

NHK, the main state broadcaster, has two channels (NHK on channel one and NHK Educational on channel three) that are roughly equal to BBC1 and BBC2 in the UK, although much less adventurous. If you have access to a bi-lingual TV, it's possible to tune into the English language commentary for NHK's nightly 7pm news. Films and imported TV shows on both NHK and the commercial channels are also sometimes broadcast with an alternative English soundtrack. In Tokyo, the other main channels are Nihon TV (four), TBS (six), Fuji TV (eight), TV Asahi (ten) and TV Tokyo (twelve), all flagship channels of the nationwide networks, with little to choose between them.

The one bright spark on Japan's TV horizon is the increasing inroads made by **satellite** and **cable** channels. As well as the ubiquitous CNN and MTV, BBC World is now available in most major cities and is often part of the room package at the top-end hotels. Perfect TV is a satellite operation offering a wide range of channels, including several devoted to sport and movies.

**Radio** is nowhere near as popular in Japan as TV, with most young people prefering to listen to CDs and tapes. In Tokyo the main FM stations broadcasting bi-lingual programmes are J-WAVE (81.3MHz) and Inter FM (76.1MHz), although both tend towards the bland end of the music spectrum. In the Kansai area, bi-lingual broadcasts are available on CO-CO-LO (76.5MHz). In other areas of the country the only alternative is likely to be the US armed services Far East Network (FEN), worth enduring just once for its bizarre public service announcements.

## OPENING HOURS, PUBLIC HOLIDAYS AND FESTIVALS

**Business hours are generally Mon–Fri 9am–5pm, though private companies often close much later in the evening and may also open on Saturday mornings. Department stores and bigger shops tend to open around 10am and shut at 7pm or 8pm, with no break for lunch. Local shops, however, will generally stay open later, while many convenience stores are open 24 hours. Most shops will take one day off a week, not necessarily on a Sunday.**

**Banks** open on weekdays from 9am–3pm, and close on Saturdays, Sundays and public holidays. **Post offices** tend to work 9am–5pm on weekdays, closing at weekends and also on national holidays, though a few open on Saturdays from 9am to 3am. Central post offices, on the other hand, stay open till 7pm in the evening, open on Saturdays from 9am–5pm and on Sundays and holidays from 9am–12.30pm. Larger offices are also likely to operate an after-hours service for parcels and express mail, sometimes up to 24hrs at major post offices.

The majority of **museums** close on a Monday, but stay open on Sundays and public holidays; last entry is normally thirty minutes before closing. There's almost invariably an **admission charge** to museums and other tourist sights. In the Guide we give the cost of an adult entry ticket; school-age children and students usually get reduced rates, which may be up to half the adult price.

While most museums and department stores stay open on **public holidays**, they usually take the following day off instead. However, during the

New Year festival (January 1–4), Golden Week (April 28–May 6) and Obon (the week around August 15) almost everything shuts down. Around these periods every form of transport and accommodation will be booked out weeks in advance, and all major tourist spots will be besieged.

### FESTIVALS

**Festivals** (*matsuri*) still play a central role in many Japanese communities. Most are Shinto in origin and mark important occasions in the agricultural cycle, re-enact historic events or honour elements of the local economy, such as sewing needles or silk-worms. Since every shrine and temple observes its own festivals, in addition to national celebrations, the chances are you'll stumble across a *matsuri* at some stage during your visit. However, if you get the chance, it's worth trying to take in one of the major festivals, some of which are described below.

*Matsuri* (meaning both festival and worship) can take many forms, from stately processions in period costume to sacred dances, fire rituals, archery contests, phallus worship or poetry-writing competitions. The best are riotous occasions where *mikoshi* (portable shrines) are shouldered by a seething, chanting crowd, usually fortified with quantities of sake and driven on by resonating drums. Don't stand back – anyone prepared to enter into the spirit of things will be welcome. However, if you are heading for any of the famous festivals, make sure you've got your transport and accommodation sorted out well in advance.

Though not such a lively affair, by far the most important event in the Japanese festive calendar is the **New Year** festival of renewal, *Oshōgatsu* (see overleaf). It's mainly a time for family reunions, and most of the country – bar public transport – closes down for at least the first three days of the year, with many people taking the whole week off work (roughly December 28 to January 4). Whilst Japanese used to celebrate the lunar New Year, since the Meiji government adopted the Western calendar in 1873, the festivities have been moved to January 1. According to the Japanese system of numbering years, starting afresh with each change of emperor, 1999 is the 11th year of Heisei – Heisei being the official name of Emperor Akihito's reign.

In recent years, several non-Japanese festivals have been catching-on, with a few adaptations for local tastes. Only women give men gifts on **Valentine's Day** (February 14), usually chocolates, while on **White Day** (March 14) men get their turn to give their loved ones more chocolates (white, of course), perfume or racy underwear. Another import is **Christmas**, celebrated in Japan as an almost totally commercial event, with carols, plastic holly and tinsel in profusion and, for some reason, endless recitals of Beethoven's Ninth Symphony. **Christmas Eve**, rather than New Year, is *the* time to party and a big occasion for romance – you'll be hard-pressed to find a table at any restaurant or a room in the top hotels.

## OSHŌGATSU

In the days leading up to New Year, generally known as **Oshōgatsu**, Japan succumbs to a frenzy of cleaning as last year's bad luck is swept away. People decorate their rooms, doorways and even car radiators with bamboo and pine sprigs, and visit temple fairs to buy lucky charms such as rakes, arrows and Daruma dolls – the chubby little red fellow with staring white eyes; the idea is to make a wish while drawing in one eye and complete the other when it comes true. Shops also do well as everyone gets a new haircut or a new kimono, buys bundles of the obligatory New Year cards and generally lays in food to tide them over the coming festivities. Fortunately, traditional

---

## JAPAN'S MAJOR FESTIVALS AND PUBLIC HOLIDAYS

### JANUARY
**Ganjitsu** (or *Gantan*): January 1. On the first day of the year everyone heads for the shrines to pray for good fortune (public holiday).
**Yamayaki**: January 15. The slopes of Wakakasuyama, Nara, are set alight during a grass-burning ceremony.
**Seijin-no-hi** (Adults' Day): January 15. Twenty-year-olds celebrate their entry into adulthood by visiting their local shrine. Many women dress in sumptuous kimono (public holiday).

### FEBRUARY
**Setsubun**: February 3 or 4. On the last day of winter (by the lunar calendar), people scatter lucky beans round their homes and at shrines or temples to drive out evil and welcome in the year's good luck.
**Yuki Matsuri**: February 5–11. Sapporo's famous snow festival features giant snow-sculptures.
**National Foundation Day**: Feb 11 (public holiday).

### MARCH
**Hina Matsuri** (Doll Festival): March 3. Families with young girls display sets of fifteen dolls (*hina ningyō*) representing the Emperor, Empress and their courtiers dressed in ancient costume. Department stores, hotels and museums put on special exhibitions of antique dolls.
**Spring Equinox**: March 21 or 20 (public holiday).
**Cherry-Blossom festivals**: late March to early May.
With the arrival of spring in late March, a pink tide of cherry blossom washes north from

Kyūshū, travels up Honshū during the month of April and peters out in Hokkaidō in early May. There are cherry-blossom festivals, and the sake flows at blossom-viewing parties. Though every area has its own favoured cherry blossom spots, the most celebrated are the mountains around Yoshino (near Kyoto), Tokyo's Ueno Kōen and Hirosaki on the tip of northern Honshū.

### APRIL
**Hana Matsuri**: April 8. Buddha's birthday is celebrated at all temples with parades, and a small statue of the infant Buddha is sprinkled with sweet tea.
**Takayama Matsuri**: April 14–15. Parade of ornate festival floats (*yatai*), some with acrobatic marionettes.
**Greenery Day**: April 29 (public holiday).

### MAY
**Constitution Memorial Day**: May 3 (public holiday).
**Kodomo-no-hi** (Children's Day): May 5. The original Boys' Day now includes all children as families fly carp banners, symbolizing strength and perseverance, outside their homes (public holiday).
**Aoi Matsuri** (Hollyhock Festival): May 15. Costume parade through the streets of Kyoto, with ceremonies to ward off storms and earthquakes.
**Sennin Gyōretsu** (Thousand Man Parade): May 17–18. Procession of 1000 armour-clad warriors escorting three *mikoshi*, to commemorate the burial of Shogun Tokugawa Ieyasu in Nikkō in 1617.

year-end bonuses help cover the costs, but often less welcome are the interminable rounds of aptly named "forget the year" parties (*bonenkai*) when groups of colleagues, club-members and friends consume enough alcohol to wipe out any bad memories or ill-luck from the previous year.

By the time **New Year's Eve** arrives, everyone's exhausted. So nowadays, at 9pm, the whole nation flops down to watch a three-hour TV extravaganza of the best – and less memorable – pop groups from the previous year. Those with only mild hangovers might slurp a bowl of *toshi-koshi soba*, extra-long noodles symbolizing longevity which traditionally form the last meal of the year, and then hurry off to the nearest shrine or temple to join the crowds waiting to make their first offerings of the new year. Temple bells ring out 108 times to cast out the 108 human frailties; the last chime heralds the New Year and a clean slate.

The first shrine-visit (*hatsumode*), the first meal, the first drive – each activity in the new year must be performed properly and safely to ensure good luck. On the first day, families share a **celebratory meal**, prepared earlier since no-one's supposed to work for the first three days, consisting of symbolic foods. It starts with a toast of sweet sake mixed with medicinal herbs, designed to confer long-life, followed by a feast including herring roe (prosperity and fertility), black beans (good health), chestnuts (success)

---

**Sanja Matsuri**: Around May 18. Tokyo's biggest festival takes place in Asakusa. Over 100 *mikoshi* are jostled through the streets, accompanied by lion dancers, *geisha* and musicians.

### JULY
**Hakata Yamagasa**. July 1–15. Fukuoka's main festival culminates in a 5km race carrying heavy *mikoshi*, while spectators douse them with water.
**Tanabata Matsuri** (Star Festival): July 7. According to legend, the only day in the year when the astral lovers, Vega and Altair, can meet across the Milky Way. Poems and prayers are hung on bamboo poles outside houses.
**Gion Matsuri**: July 16–17. Kyoto's largest festival climaxes in a parade of huge floats hung with rich silks and paper lanterns.
**Hanabi taikai**: last Saturday in July. The most spectacular of the many summer firework displays takes place in Tokyo, on the Sumida River near Asakusa.

### AUGUST
**Nebuta** and **Neputa Matsuri**: August 1–7. Aomori and Hirosaki hold competing summer festivals, with a parade of illuminated paper-covered figures, like huge lanterns.
**Tanabata Matsuri**: August 6–8. Sendai holds its famous Star Festival a month after everyone else, so the lovers get another chance.
**Obon** (Festival of Souls): August 13–15, or July 13–15 in some areas. Families gather around the ancestral graves to welcome back the spirits of the dead and honour them with special *Bon-odori* dances on the final night.

**Awa Odori**: August 12–15. The most famous *Bon-odori* takes place in Tokushima, when up to 80,000 dancers take to the streets.

### SEPTEMBER
**Respect-for-the-Aged Day**: September 15 (public holiday).
**Autumn Equinox**: Sept 23 or 24 (public holiday).

### OCTOBER
**Kunchi Matsuri**: October 7–9. Shinto rites mingle with Chinese- and European-inspired festivities to create Nagasaki's premier celebration, incorporating dragon dances and floats in the shape of Chinese and Dutch ships.
**Sports Day**: October 10 (public holiday).
**Jidai Matsuri**: October 22. Kyoto's famous, if rather sedate, costume parade vies with the more exciting **Kurama Matsuri**, a night-time fire festival which takes place in a village near Kyoto.

### NOVEMBER
**Culture Day**: November 3 (public holiday).
**Shichi-go-san** (Seven-five-three): November 15. Children of the appropriate ages don mini-kimono and *hakama* (loose trousers) to visit their local shrine.
**Labour Thanksgiving Day**: November 23 (public holiday).

### DECEMBER
**Emperor's Birthday**: Dec 23 (public holiday).
**Omisoka**: December 31. Just before midnight on the last day of the year, temple bells ring out 108 times to cast out each of man's earthly desires and start the year afresh.

Note that if any of the above public holidays fall on a Sunday, then the following Monday is also a public holiday.

and *mochi*. These sticky-rice cakes are usually served with vegetables in a special soup (*ozoni*); they may not look – or taste – much, but *mochi* are said to ensure strength, stamina and, again, longevity.

The traditional **New Year's greeting** is *akemashite omedetō gozaimasu*, and it's customary for adults to give the children of friends and family envelopes containing a few thousand yen in crisp notes.

# SOCIAL CONVENTIONS AND ETIQUETTE

**Japan is famous for its complex web of social conventions and rules of behaviour, which only someone who's grown up in the society could hope to master. Fortunately, allowances are made for befuddled foreigners but it will be greatly appreciated – even draw gasps of astonishment – if you show a grasp of the basic principles. The two main danger areas are shoes and bathing, which, if you get them wrong, can cause great offence.**

The Japanese treat most foreigners with incredible, even embarrassing, kindness. There are endless stories of people going miles out of their way to help, or paying for drinks or even meals after the briefest of encounters. That said, foreigners will always remain "outsiders" (*gaijin*), no matter how long they've lived in Japan or how proficient they are in the language and social niceties. On the positive side this can be wonderfully liberating; you're expected to make mistakes, so don't get too hung up about it. The important thing is to be seen to be trying. As a general rule, when in doubt, simply follow what everyone else is doing.

## MEETINGS AND GREETINGS

Some visitors to Japan complain that it's difficult to meet local people. It's certainly true that many Japanese are shy of foreigners, mainly through a fear of being unable to communicate. A few words of Japanese will help enormously, and there are various opportunities for fairly formal contact, such as through the Home Visit System and Goodwill Guides (see p.23). Otherwise, youth hostels are great places to meet people of all ages, or try popping into a local bar, *yakitori* joint or such like; emboldened by alcohol, the chances are someone will strike up a conversation.

Japanese people tend to **dress** smartly, especially in cities. Though as a tourist you don't have to go overboard, you'll be better received if you

look neat and tidy, and for anyone hoping to do business in Japan, a snappy suit is de rigeur. It's also important to be punctual for social and business **appointments**.

Whenever Japanese meet, express thanks or say goodbye, there's a flurry of **bowing**. The precise depth of the bow and the length of time it's held for depend on the relative status of the two individuals – receptionists are sent on courses to learn the precise angles required. Again, foreigners aren't expected to bow, but it's terribly infectious and you'll soon find yourself bobbing with the best of them. The usual compromise is a slight nod or a quick, half bow. Japanese more familiar with Western customs might offer you a hand to shake, in which case treat it gently – they won't be expecting a firm grip.

Japanese **names** are traditionally written with the family name first, followed by a given name, which is the practice used throughout this book (except where the Western version has become famous, such as Issey Miyake). When dealing with foreigners, however, they may well write their name the other way round. Check if you're not sure because, when **addressing people**, it's normal to use the family name plus *-san;* for example, Suzuki-san. *San* is an honorific term used in the same way as Mr or Mrs, so remember not to use it when introducing yourself, or talking about your friends or family. As a foreigner, you can choose whichever of your names you feel comfortable with; inevitably they'll tack a *-san* on the end. You'll also often hear *-chan* as a form of address; this is a diminutive reserved for very good friends, young children and pets.

An essential part of any business meeting is the swapping of *meishi*, or **name cards**. Always carry a copious supply since you'll be expected to exchange a card with everyone present. It's useful to have them printed in Japanese as well as English; if necessary, you can get this done at major hotels. *Meishi* are offered with both hands, facing so that the recipient can read the writing. It's polite to read the card and then place it on the table beside you, face up. Never write on a *meishi*, at least not in the owner's presence, and never shove it in a pocket – put it in your wallet or somewhere suitably respectful. Business meetings invariably go on much longer than you'd expect and rarely result in decisions. They are partly for building up the all-important feeling of trust between the two parties, as is the after-hours entertainment in a restaurant or karaoke bar.

## HOSPITALITY, GIFTS AND TIPS

**Entertaining**, whether it's business or purely social, usually takes place in bars and restaurants. The host generally orders and, if it's a Japanese-style meal, will keep passing you different things to try. You'll also find your glass continually topped up. It's polite to return the gesture but, if you don't drink, or don't want any more, leave it full. See p.45 and p.52 for more on eating and drinking

It's a rare honour to be invited to someone's home in Japan and you should always take a small **gift**. Fruit, flowers, chocolates or alcohol (wine, whisky or brandy) are safe bets, as is anything from your home country, especially if it's a famous brand-name. The gift should always be wrapped, using plenty of fancy paper and ribbon if possible. If you buy something locally, most shops gift-wrap purchases automatically and anything swathed in paper from Mitsukoshi or one of the other big department stores has extra caché.

Japanese people love giving gifts, and you should never refuse one if offered, though it's good manners to protest at their generosity first. Again it's polite to give and receive with both hands, and to belittle your humble donation while giving profuse thanks for the gift you receive. However, it's not the custom to open gifts in front of the donor, thus avoiding potential embarrassment.

If you're fortunate enough to be invited to a **wedding**, it's normal to give money to the happy couple. This helps defray the costs, including, somewhat bizarrely, the present you'll receive at the end of the meal. How much you give depends on your relationship with the couple, so ask a mutual friend what would be appropriate. Make sure to get crisp new notes and put them in a special red envelope available at stationers. Write your name clearly on the front and hand it over as you enter the reception.

**Tipping** is not expected in Japan, and if you press money on a taxi driver, porter or bell-boy it can cause offence. So, if someone's been particularly helpful, the best approach is to give a small gift, or present the money discretely in an envelope.

## SHOES AND SLIPPERS

It's customary to change into **slippers** when entering a Japanese home or a ryokan, and not uncommon in traditional restaurants, temples or, occasionally, in museums and art galleries. In general, if you come across a slightly raised floor and a row of slippers, then use them; either leave your shoes on the lower floor (the *genkan*) or on the shelves (sometimes lockers) provided. Slip-on shoes are much easier to cope with than lace-ups and, tricky though it is, try not to step on the *genkan* with bare or stockinged feet.

Once inside, remove your slippers before stepping onto *tatami*, the rice-straw flooring, and remember to change into the special **toilet slippers** lurking by the bathroom door when you go to the toilet. (See below for more on toilet etiquette.)

## BATHING

Taking a traditional Japanese **bath**, whether in a ryokan, hot spring (onsen), or public bath-house (*sentō*), is a ritual that's definitely worth mastering. Nowdays most baths are segregated, so memorize the *kanji* for male and female (see box overleaf). It's customary to bathe in the evening, and in small ryokan or family homes there may well be only one bathroom. In this case you'll either be given a designated time or simply wait till it's vacant.

Key points to remember are that everyone uses the same water and the bath tub is only for soaking. It's therefore essential to wash then rinse the soap off thoroughly – showers and bowls are provided, as well as soap and shampoo in many cases – *before* stepping into the bath. Ryokan and the more upmarket public bathhouses provide small towels, though no-one minds full nudity. Lastly, the bath in a ryokan and family home is filled once each evening, so never pull the plug out.

## TOILETS

Traditional Japanese **toilets** (*toire* or *ōtearai*) are of the Asian squat variety. Though these are still quite common in homes, old-style restaurants and many public buildings, Western toilets are gradually becoming the norm. Look out for nifty enhancements such as a heated seat – glorious in winter – and those that flush automatically as you walk away. Another handy device plays the sound of flushing water to cover embarrassing noises. These are either automatic or are activated with a button and were invented because so much water was wasted by constant flushing. In some places toilets are still communal, so don't be alarmed to see a urinal in what you thought was the women's room, and note that public toilets rarely provide paper.

Increasingly, you'll be confronted by a high-tech Western model, known as a Washlet, with a control panel to one side. It's usually impossible to find the flush button, and instead, you'll hit the temperature control, hot-air drier or, worst of all, the bidet nozzle, resulting in a long metal arm extending out of the toilet bowl and spraying you with warm water.

| toilet | *toire* or *otearai* | トイレ／お手洗い |
| male | *otoko* | 男 |
| female | *onna* | 女 |

## SOME GENERAL POINTERS

It's quite normal to see men urinating in the streets in Japan, but **blowing your nose** in pub-

lic is considered extremely rude – just keep sniffing until you find somewhere private. In this very male, strictly hierarchical society, men always take precedence over women; don't expect **doors** to be held open for you or **seats** vacated. Although meticulously polite within their own social group, the Japanese relish **pushing and shoving** on trains or buses. However, you should never respond by getting angry or showing **aggression**, as this is considered a complete loss of face. By the same token, don't make your **opinions** too forcefully or contradict people outright; it's more polite to say maybe than a direct no.

The meaning of "yes" and "no" can in themselves be a problem, particularly when **asking questions**. For example, if you say "don't you like it?", a positive answer means "yes, I agree with you, I don't like it", and no means "no, I don't agree with you, I *do* like it". To avoid confusion, try not to ask negative questions – stick to "do you like it?". And if someone seems to be giving vague answers, don't push too hard, unless it's important. There's a good chance they don't want to offend you by disagreeing or revealing a problem.

Finally, you'll be excused for not **sitting** on your knees, Japan-style, on the *tatami* mats. It's agony for people who aren't used to it, and many young Japanese now find it uncomfortable. If you're wearing trousers, sitting cross-legged is fine; otherwise, tuck your legs to one side.

## SHOPPING AND SOUVENIRS

**Even if you're not an inveterate shopper, cruising Japan's gargantuan department stores or rummaging around its vibrant discount outlets is an integral part of local life that shouldn't be missed. Japan also has some of the most enticing crafts souvenirs in the world, from lacquered chopsticks and luxurious, handmade paper to a wealth of wacky electronic gadgets.**

Historically, the epicentre of commercial frenzy is Tokyo's Ginza, to such an extent that the name has become synonymous with shopping street; you'll find "little Ginzas" all over Japan. However, the mechanics of shopping are the same throughout: all prices are fixed, except in fleamarkets and some discount electrical stores where bargaining is acceptable. Few shops take **credit cards** and fewer still accept cards issued abroad, so make sure you have plenty of cash. All except the smallest purchases will be meticulously wrapped.

In general, shop **opening hours** are from 10am to 7pm, or 8pm. Most close one day a week, not always on Sunday, and smaller places tend to shut on public holidays. Nearly all shops close for at least three days over New Year. If you need anything **after hours**, you'll find 24-hour convenience stores in most towns and cities, often near the train station. These sell a basic range of toiletries, stationery and foodstuffs, at slightly inflated prices; Lawson, AM/PM and Seven-Eleven are the most common.

### TAXES, DUTY-FREE AND DISCOUNT STORES

A five percent **consumption tax** is levied on virtually all goods sold in Japan. Sometimes this tax will be included in the advertised price, and sometimes it will be added at the time of payment, so you should check first for large purchases.

Foreigners can buy **duty-free** items (that is, without consumption tax), but only in certain tourist shops and the larger department stores. Perishable goods, such as food, drinks, tobacco, cosmetics and film, are exempt from the scheme, and most stores only offer duty-free if the total bill exceeds ¥10,000. The shop will either give you a duty-free price immediately or, in department stores especially, you pay the full price first and then apply for a refund at their "tax-exemption" counter. The shop will attach a copy of the customs document (*warrin*) to your passport, to be removed by customs officers when you leave Japan. Note that regulations vary for foreign residents, and also that you can often find the same goods elsewhere at a better price, including tax, so shop around first.

Some of the best places to look for cut-price goods are the **discount stores**, which have mushroomed since the Japanese economy began to falter. You'll find them mainly around train stations (the "¥100" shops are easy to spot), selling mostly household items and unusual souvenirs. But perhaps the most interesting discount stores are those offering electrical goods and cameras (see p.65), which you'll find in nearly all major cities.

### DEPARTMENT STORES

Japan's most prestigious **department stores** are Mitsukoshi and Takashimaya, followed by the cheaper, more workaday Matsuya, Matsuzakaya,

---

### AUTOMATED SHOPPING

Japan boasts an estimated 5.4 million **vending machines** – roughly one for every twenty people. Nearly all essentials, and many non-essentials, can be bought from a machine: pot noodles, drinks, films, batteries, shampoo, razors, CDs, flowers and so on. Their prime attraction is obviously convenience, but vending machines also allow people in this highly self-conscious society to buy things surreptitiously. Condoms and alcohol are obvious examples, as Japanese law prohibits the sale of alcohol to anyone under twenty years old.

As a logical extension to vending machines, Japan recently introduced the world's first "**RoboShops**", staffed entirely by robots. On receiving the customers' order – in the form of codes punched into a key-pad – and payment, the robot scoots along the shelves filling its bucket, which it then empties out through a trap-door. They sell a similar range of items to convenience stores but, with no salaries to pay, can offer them at much reduced prices.

Seibu and Tōbu. All these big names have branches throughout Japan, and sell almost everything, from impressive food-halls through fashion, crafts and household items, to stationery and toys. One floor is usually devoted to restaurants, and somewhere near the top of the store you'll generally find a section specializing in discount items. Bigger stores may also have an art gallery, travel bureau, ticket agent and a currency-exchange desk, as well as English-speaking staff and a duty-free service. It's also worth looking out for the excellent bargain sales in January, July and August.

## ART, CRAFTS AND SOUVENIRS

Japan is famous for its wealth of **arts** and **crafts**, many dating back thousands of years, and handed down from generation to generation (see Contexts, p.790, for more on the arts). Though the best are phenomenally expensive, there are plenty at more manageable prices which make wonderful **souvenirs**. Most department stores have a reasonable crafts section, but it's far more enjoyable to trawl Japan's specialist shops, even if you do pay a little extra for the pleasure. Kyoto is renowned for its traditional crafts, and even in Tokyo you'll find a number of artisans still plying their trade, while most regions have a vibrant local crafts industry turning out products for the tourists.

Tokyo and Kyoto are also well-known for their regular **flea markets**, usually held at shrines and temples (see individual city accounts for details). You need to get there early for the best deals, but you might come across some gorgeous secondhand kimono, satin-smooth lacquerware or rustic pottery among a good deal of tat. Keep an eye out, too, for unusual items in the discount stores, which can yield amazing gizmos for next to nothing.

Japan's most famous craft is its **ceramics** (*tōjiki*). Of several distinct regional styles, Imari-ware (from Arita in Kyūshū) is best known for its colourful, ornate designs, while the iron-brown unglazed Bizen-ware (from near Okayama) and Mashiko's simple folk-pottery are satisfyingly rustic. Other famous names include Satsuma-yaki (from Kagoshima), Kasama-yaki (from Ibaraki) and Kyoto's Kyō-yaki. Any decent department store will stock a full range of styles, or you can visit local showrooms. Traditional tea bowls, sake sets and vases make popular souvenirs.

Originally devised as a means of making everyday utensils more durable, **lacquerware** (*shikki*) has developed over the centuries into a unique artform. Items such as trays, tables, boxes, chopsticks and bowls are typically covered with reddish-brown or black lacquer and either left plain or decorated with paintings, carvings, sprinkled with eggshell or given a dusting of gold or silver leaf. Though top-quality lacquer can be hideously expensive, you'll find a whole range of lesser pieces at more reasonable prices. Lacquer needs a humid atmosphere, especially the cheaper pieces made on a base of low-quality wood which cracks in dry conditions; inexpensive plastic bases won't be affected.

Some of Japan's most beautiful traditional products stem from **folkcrafts** (*mingei*), ranging from elegant, inexpensive **bamboo-ware** to **wood-carvings**, **toys**, **masks**, **kites** and a whole host of delightful **dolls** (*ningyō*). Peg-shaped *kokeshi* dolls from northern Honshū are among the most appealing, with their bright colours and sweet, simple faces. But look out also for the rotund, round-eyed *daruma* dolls, made of papier-mâché, and fine, clay *Hakata-ningyō* dolls from Kyūshū.

Traditional Japanese **paper** (*washi*), made from mulberry or other natural fibres, is fashioned into any number of tempting souvenirs. You can buy purses, boxes, fans, oiled umbrellas, light shades and toys all made from paper, as well as beautiful stationery. Indeed, some *washi* is so beautifully patterned and textured, that a few sheets alone make a great gift.

Original **woodblock prints**, *ukiyo-e*, by world-famous artists such as Utamaro, Hokusai and Hiroshige have long been collectors' items fetching thousands of pounds. However, you can buy copies of these "pictures of the floating world", often depicting Mount Fuji, willowy *geisha* or lusty heroes of the Kabuki stage, at tourist shops for more modest sums. Alternatively, some art shops specialize in originals, both modern and antique.

**Kimono**, the traditional Japanese dress, are still worn for special occasions and every department store has a corner devoted to ready-made or tailored kimono. However, it's far more economical to look for secondhand or antique versions at tourist shops or in the kimono sales held by department stores usually in the spring and autumn. Sumptuous wedding kimono make striking wall hangings, as do **obi**, the broad, silk sash worn with a kimono. A cheaper, more practical alternative is the light, cotton kimono, **yukata**, which are popular as dressing gowns; you'll find them in all department stores. To complete the outfit, you could pick up a pair of *zōri*, traditional straw **sandals**, or their wooden counterpart, *geta*.

Other attractive textiles include **noren**, a split curtain hanging in the entrance to a restaurant or bar; cotton **tenugui** (small hand towels), decorated with cute designs; and the large, square, versatile wrapping cloth, **furoshiki**.

Whilst the chunky, iron kettles, a speciality of Morioka in northern Honshū, are rather unwieldy momentos, the area also produces delicate *furin*, or **wind-chimes**, in a variety of designs. **Damascene** is also more portable, though a bit fussy for some tastes. This metal inlay-work, with gold and silver threads on black steel, was originally used to fix the family crest on sword hilts and helmets, though nowadays you can buy all sorts of jewellery and trinket boxes decorated with birds, flowers and other intricate designs. However, **pearls** are undoubtedly Japan's most famous jewellery item, since Mikimoto Kokichi first succeeded in growing cultured pearls in Toba in 1893. Toba is still the centre of production, though you'll find specialist shops in all major cities selling pearls at fairly competitive prices.

Finally, there are a host of **edible souvenirs**. Items that might tempt you include **rice-crackers** (*sembei*), vacuum-packed bags of **pickles** (*tsukemono*), and Japanese **sweets** (*okashi*), such as the eye-catching *wagashi*. Made of sweet, red-bean paste in various colours and designs, *wagashi* are the traditional accompaniment to the tea ceremony. **Tea** itself (*ocha*) comes in a variety of grades, often in attractive canisters, while **sake** is another inexpensive gift option, which occasionally comes in interesting-shaped bottles.

## ELECTRICAL GOODS AND CAMERAS

Japan is well-known as a producer of high-quality, innovative **electrical** and **electronic goods**. New designs are tested on the local market before going into export production, so this is the best place to check out the latest technological advances. The majority of high-tech goods are sold in discount stores, where prices may be up to forty percent cheaper than at a conventional store. Akihabara, in north Tokyo, is the country's foremost area for discount electronic goods, but in every major city you can buy audio equipment, computers, software and any number of wacky gadgets, at low prices.

Before buying, make sure that the goods are compatible with your domestic electricity system; the Japanese power supply is 100v, but export goods usually have a voltage switch that can adapt the appliance to your own system. If English-language instructions, after-sales service and guarantees are important, stick to export models which are sold mostly in the stores' duty-free sections. It's worth shopping around first and, though you may not get it, always ask for a discount.

Similarly, Japanese **cameras** and other photographic equipment are among the best in the world. Shinjuku, in Tokyo, is the main centre, where you can pick up discontinued and second-hand cameras at decent prices.

## BOOKS AND MUSIC

Imported foreign-language **books** are expensive in Japan, and only available in major cities. However, some locally produced English-language books are cheaper here than at home, if you can find them at all outside Japan. The best bookstores are Kinokuniya, Tower Books (part of Tower Records), Maruzen and Yurindo, all of which stock imported newspapers and magazines as well as a variable selection of foreign-language books. Alternatively, most top-class hotels have a small bookstore with a range of titles on Japan and a limited choice of imported fiction and journals.

Foreign-label **records**, **cassettes** and **CDs** are generally cheaper than their local counterparts, and may well cost less than you would pay at home. Furthermore, major record stores, such as Tower Records, HMV, Virgin Megastore and the home-grown Wave, have a tremendous selection – everything from Japanese classical and folk music to world music, rock, dance and techno.

## CLOTHES

All Japan's big **department stores** have several floors devoted to fashion, from haute-couture to more modest wear at affordable prices. Elsewhere, you'll find trendy **boutiques** catering to a younger, less affluent crowd, and selling cut-price clothes and the latest in recycled grunge gear. The centre of high-fashion is Tokyo's Omotesandō, where you'll find the likes of Issey Miyake, Comme des Garçons and Yohji Yamamoto, whose showrooms make for great window shopping, even if you don't have the money to buy.

Finding clothes and, especially, **shoes** that fit can be a problem. Some stores do now stock larger sizes, of which *Washington* shoe shops are usually a good bet, though the women's selection is pretty limited.

# SPORTS AND OUTDOOR ACTIVITIES

**Big believers in team spirit, the Japanese embrace many sports with almost religious fervour. It's not uncommon for parts of the country to come to a complete standstill during crucial moments of major baseball matches and sumo *basho* (tournaments), as fans gather round television screens in homes, offices, shops, bars, and even on the street. Baseball is actually more popular than the home-grown sumo, and hot on the heels of both sports is soccer, which since the launch of the professional J League in 1993 has enjoyed phenomenal popularity.**

**Martial arts**, such as aikido, judo and karate, all traditionally associated with Japan, have a much lower profile than you might expect. Tokyo with its many *dōjō* (practice halls) is the best place in the country in which to view or learn these ancient sports. The TIC at Yūrakuchō (see p.86) in Tokyo has a full list of *dōjō* which allow visitors to watch practice sessions for free.

If you're interested in attending any sporting event, check the local media, such as *The Japan Times* and *Tokyo Journal*, for details. To get tickets it's best, in the first instance, to approach one of the major advance ticket agencies. Ticket Saison, in most Seibu-affiliated department stores, and Ticket Pia can be found in most main cities. In Tokyo, Ticket Pia also has an English-launguage telephone booking line (☎03/5237-9999). Major games and events sell out quickly, so a second approach is to go directly to the venue on the day and see if you can get a ticket from the box office or a tout outside; expect to pay well over the odds, though, if it's a popular game.

In terms of participation sports, **golf** is the most popular, with some fourteen million golfers in Japan, and more courses and driving ranges than you can swing a club at. The current recession has taken the shine off the sport being used for business meetings and as a status symbol, but fees for playing a round remain out of the reach of all but the most dedicated visiting golf fan.

More accessible outdoor activities in this mountainous, volcanic country are **skiing** during the winter and **hiking** and **mountain climbing** during the summer. If you're interested in outdoor pursuits, it's worth getting in touch with the Tokyo-based **International Adventurers Club** (IAC) or its sister club for the Kansai region, the **International Outdoor Club** (IOC), both of which provide informal opportunities to explore the Japanese countryside and mountains in the company of likeminded people. For details check the IAC Web site on *www2.gol.com/users/adventur/*

## BASEBALL

**Baseball** first came to Japan in the 1870s, but it wasn't until 1934 that the first professional teams were formed. Now Japan is *yakyū* (the Japanese word for baseball) crazy and if you're in the country from April to the end of October during the baseball season, think about taking in a professional match. Even if you're not a fan, the buzzing atmosphere and audience enthusiasm can be infectious.

In addition to the two professional leagues, Central and Pacific, each with six teams, there's the equally, if not more, popular All-Japan High School Baseball Championship. You might be able to catch one of the local play-offs before the main tournament which is held each summer at Koushien Stadium near Ōsaka; check with the tourist office for details.

In the professional leagues, the teams are sponsored by big businesses, immediately apparent from their names such as the Yakult (a food company) Swallows and Yomiuri (a newspaper conglomerate) Giants. The victors from the Central and Pacific leagues go on to battle it out for the supreme title in the seven-match Japan Series every autumn. **Tickets** for all games are available from the stadia or at advance ticket booths. They start at ¥1000 and go on sale on the Friday, two weeks prior to a game. For more information on

Japan's pro-baseball leagues, check out the Web site on *www.inter.co.jp/Baseball/*

## SUMO

There's something fascinating about Japan's national sport **sumo**, even though the titanic clashes between the enormous, near-naked wrestlers, some weighing well over 1000kg, can be blindingly brief. However, the age-old pomp and ceremony that surrounds sumo – from the design of the *dohyō* (the ring in which the bouts take place), to the wrestler's hair slicked back into a topknot – give the sport a gravitas completely absent from Western wrestling.

Despite their formidable girth, top *rishiki* (wrestlers) such as Takanohana and his brother Wakanohana enjoy the media status of supermodels. But in a neat reversal of Japan's appropriation of baseball and export of pro-players to the US league, two of sumo's most revered stars – the top-ranked *yokuzuna* Akebono and Konishiki (aka the "dump truck"), who retired in 1998 – were both born in Hawaii.

Accounts of sumo bouts are related in Japan's oldest annals of history when it was a Shinto rite connected with praying for a good harvest. By the Edo period, sumo had developed into a spectator sport and really hit its stride in the post-World War II period when *basho* started to be televised. The old religious trappings remain, though; the *gyoji* (referee) wears robes not disimilar to those of a Shinto priest and above the *dohyō* hangs a thatched roof like those found at shrines.

At the start of a bout the two *rishiki* wade into the ring, wearing only *mawashi* aprons, which look like giant nappies. Salt is tossed to purify the ring, the *rishiki* hunker down and indulge in the time-honoured ritual of psyching each other out with menacing stares. When ready, each *rishiki* attempts to throw his opponent to the ground or out of the ring using one or more of 48 legitimate techniques. The first to touch the ground with any part of his body other than his feet, or to step out of the *dohyō*, loses.

When not fighting in tournaments, groups of *rishiki* live and train together at their *heya* (stables), the youngest wrestlers acting pretty much as the menial slaves of their elder, more experienced colleagues. If you make an advance appointment, it's possible to visit some *heya* to observe the early morning practice sessions; contact the TIC in Tokyo (see p.86) for details.

## SOCCER

The J-League, Japan's first professional **soccer** league launched amid a multi-billion-yen promotional drive in 1993, has captured the public's imagination and wallet with its full range of associated merchandise. The game is going from strength to strength, with the league having ten teams at its inception, seventeen currently, and soon to rise to nineteen. Top footballers have been bought in from around the world (Gary Linekar was the star draw of the initial season) and with the World Cup scheduled to be held in Japan and Korea in 2002, the game's continued popularity is assured. For full details of the J-League in English, including match reports check out the Web site at *www.j-league.or.jp*

## AIKIDO

Half sport, half religion, **aikido** translates as "the way of harmonious spirit," and blends elements of judo, karate and kendo into a form of non-body-con-

---

## THE ANNUAL SUMO TOURNAMENTS

The must-see **Annual Sumo Tournaments** are held at the following locations, always starting on the Sunday closest to the tenth of the month and lasting for two weeks: **Tokyo** at Kokugikan Hall in January, May and September; **Ōsaka** at Ōsaka Furitsu Taiiku Kaikan in March; **Nagoya** at Aichi-kenTaiiku-kan in July; and **Fukuoka** at Fukuoka Kokusai Centre in November.

It's virtually impossible to book the prime ringside **seats** in advance, but quite feasible to bag reserved seats in the balconies (they cost around ¥7000, for which you'll also get a bag of souvenirs) or the cheapest unreserved seats (¥1500), which go on sale on the door on the day of the tournament at 9am. To be assured of a ticket you'll need to line up well before that, especially towards the end of a *basho*. Matches start for the lower ranked wrestlers at 10am and at this time it's OK to sneak into any vacant ringside seats to watch the action close up; when the rightful owners turn up, just return to your own seat. The sumo superstars come on around 4pm and tournaments finish at around 6pm.

If you can't get a ticket, NHK televises each *basho* daily from 3.30pm, and you can tune into FEN on 810 KHz for a simultaneous English commentary.

tact self defence. It's one of the newer martial arts having only been created in Japan earlier this century and, as a rule, is performed without weapons.

The **International Aikido Federation**, 17-18 Wakamatsuchō, Shinjuku-ku (☎03/3203-9236), is around ten minutes by bus from the west exit of Shinjuku Station in Tokyo. You'll also find the *Aikikai Hombu Dōjō* at the same address and telephone number, where visitors are welcome to watch practice sessions.

## JUDO

Probably the martial art most closely associated with Japan, **judo** is a self-defence technique that developed out of the Edo-era fighting schools of Jujutsu. All judo activities in Japan are controlled by the **All-Japan Judo Federation**, at the Kodokan Dōjō, 1-16-30 Kasuga, Bunkyō-ku (☎03/3818-4199), reached from either Kasuga or Kōrakuen subway stations in Tokyo. The *dōjō* has a spectators' gallery open to visitors free of charge (Mon–Fri 6–7.30pm and Sat 4–5.30pm). There's also a hostel here where you can stay if you have an introduction from an authorized judo body or an approved Japanese sponsor. Judo is also taught at the Nippon Budōkan Budō Gakuen, 2-3 Kitanomaru-kōen, Chiyoda-ku (☎03/3216-5143), near Kudanshita subway station in Tokyo.

## KARATE

**Karate** has its roots in China and was only introduced into Japan via the southern islands of Okinawa in 1922. Since then the sport has developed many different styles, all with governing bodies and federations based in Tokyo. At one of the main overseeing bodies, the **Japan Karate Association**, 2F Kowa Bldg, 2-9-6 Shiroganedai, Minato-ku (☎03/3440-1415), you can watch the classes (usually held Mon–Sat 10.30–11.30am & 5–8pm), but it's best to call first. To reach the *dōjō*, take Exit 2A from Takanawadai station, turn left and walk along the main street for five minutes.

The umbrella organization, **Japan Karatedo Federation**, 6F, 2 Senpaku Shinko Bldg, 1-11-2 Toranomon, Minato-ku, Tokyo (Mon–Fri 9am–5pm; ☎03/3503-6640), can advise on the main styles of karate and where you can best see practice sessions or take lessons. The closest subway station is Toranomon.

## KENDO

Meaning "the way of the sword", **kendo** is Japanese fencing using either a long bamboo

weapon, the *shinai*, or a lethal metal *katana* blade. This fighting skill has the longest pedigree in Japan, dating from the Muromachi period (1392–1573), then developed as a sport during the Edo-period, and is now watched over by the All-Japan Kendo Federation, Nippon Budōkan, 2–3 Kitanomaru-kōen, Chiyoda-ku, Tokyo (☎03/3211-5804), near Kudanshita subway station. Practice sessions are not generally open to the public, but you might be fortunate enough to catch the All-Japan Championships held in Tokyo each December at the Budōkan.

## SKIING

Every winter so many Japanese head for the slopes to perfect their **ski** technique, or just to hang out in the latest designer gear, that if you don't join them you'll feel left out. It's easy enough to arrange a ski day-trip, especially since many of the major resorts on Honshū are within a couple of hours' train ride of Tokyo, Nagoya or Ōsaka. Serious skiers will want to take more time to head to the northern island of Hokkaidō, which has some of the country's best ski resorts.

The **cost** of a ski trip need not be too expensive. Lift passes are typically ¥4000 per day, or less if you ski for several days in a row; equipment rental averages around ¥4000 for the skis, boots and poles; whilst accommodation at a family-run minshuku compares favourably to that of many European and American resorts.

**Transport** to the slopes is fast and efficient; at one resort (Gala Yuzawa in Niigata) you can step straight off the Shinkansen onto the ski lifts. Ski maps and signs are often in English, and you're sure to find some English speakers, and at the major resorts, *gaijin* staff, if you run into difficulties.

The main drawback of skiing in Japan is that top resorts can get very crowded, especially at weekends and holidays; if you don't want to ski in rush-hour conditions, plan your trip for mid-week. In addition, the runs are, on the whole, much shorter than in Europe and US. Compensating factors, however, are fast ski lifts, beautiful scenery – especially in the Japan Alps area of Nagano – and the opportunity to soak in onsen hot springs at night. **Snowboarding** is currently very fashionable, especially among younger skiers, and is now allowed at most major resorts, although it's best to check with local tourist offices first.

Recommended resorts for beginners include **Gala Yuzawa** and trendy **Naeba**, both reached in under two hours from Tokyo by Shinkansen.

**Nozawa Onsen** (p.354) also has good beginners' runs, but its off-the-beaten track location makes it a better bet for more experienced skiers. **Appi Kōgen** and **Zao** in northern Honshū and **Hakuba** in Nagano (p.356) are considered the Holy Trinity of Japanese ski-resorts. **Shiga Kōgen** (p.356) is another mammoth resort in Nagano, parts of which were used for competitions during the 1998 Winter Olympics. If you're after the best powder snow skiing without the crowds, head north to Hokkaidō, to the world-class resorts of **Furano** (p.329) and **Niseko** (p.309). There are also many slopes easily accessible on a day-trip from Sapporo.

All the major travel agents offer **ski packages**, which are worth looking into, with Tokyo's Beltop Travel (☎03/3211-6555; *www.beltop.com/*) having plenty of experience setting up deals for the ex-pat community. **Youth hostels** near to ski areas often have excellent-value packages, too, including accommodation, meals and lift passes, and can arrange competative equipment rental; see Furano and Niseko in Hokkaidō and Togakushi (p.352) and Norikura Kōgen Onsen (p.364) in Nagano-ken.

There are several comprehensive annual **guides** in Japanese listing all resorts, providing detailed maps of the runs and lists of all the facilities; one of the best is *Ski Mapple* published by Shōbunsha. For English-language information, invest in the spot-on *Ski Japan!* by TR Reid (¥2300; Kodansha).

## MOUNTAINEERING AND HIKING

Until the turn of the century few Japanese would have considered climbing one of their often sacred mountains for anything other than religious reasons. These days, prime highland beauty spots such as Kamikōchi (p.362), are widely popular with day **hikers** and serious **mountaineers**, so much so that they run risk of being overrun. In addition, there are 28 national parks (see box below) and exploring them and other picturesque areas of the countryside on foot is one of the great pleasures of a trip to Japan.

**Hiking trails**, especially in the national parks, are well marked. Campsites and mountain huts open during the climbing season which runs from June to the end of August. The efficient train network means that even from sprawling conurbations like Tokyo you can be in beautiful countryside in just over an hour. Top hiking destinations from the capital include the lakes, mountains and rugged coastline of the Fuji-Hakone-Izu National Park (pp.180–201) to the southwest and Nikkō (p.170) to the north. Also west of the capital is the Chichibu-Tama National Park and the sacred mountain Takao-san, particularly lovely when the leaves change colour each autumn; for details of hiking in these areas and 31 others across Japan, pick up a copy of the excellent *Hiking in Japan* by Paul Hunt (¥2000; Kodansha).

## BEACHES, SURFING AND DIVING

As Japan is an archipelago of islands, you'd be forgiven for thinking that it is blessed with some pleasant beaches. The truth is that industrialization has blighted much of the coastline and that many of the decent beaches are covered with litter and/or pollution. The best **beaches** are those furthest away from the main island of Honshū, which means those on the islands of Okinawa south of Kyūshū, or the Izu and Ogasawara islands south of Tokyo.

Incredibly, Japan's market for **surf** goods is the world's largest and when the surfers aren't haul-

---

### JAPAN'S NATIONAL PARKS

It can come as a surprise to find that more than sixty percent of Japan is natural or planted forest, and that the country has as many as 28 **national parks** (*kokuritsu kōen*), often including volcanos and onsen and covering islands such as Rishiri-tō and Rebun-tō north of Hokkaidō. The national park system was created in 1931 as a response to the threat to the environment posed by rapid industrialization, and the parks are now largely managed by central government.

In addition to the national parks are the 54 quasi-national parks (*kokutei kōen*), which are jointly managed by both national and local government. As well as these, prefectures can appoint smaller areas as partly protected parks (*todōfuken shizen kōen*). All these areas are popular countryside escapes for urbanites and it's as well to bear this in mind at weekends and holidays, when parks close to cities can get very busy. If you can, visit the parks mid-week and out of season when you'll find the trails less crowded.

ing their boards off to Hawaii and Australia, they can be found braving the waves at various home locations. Top spots include the southern coasts of Shikoku and Kyūshū. Closer to Tokyo, pros head for the rocky east Kujikuri coast of the Chiba peninsula, while the beaches around Shonan, near Kamakura, are fine for perfecting your style and hanging out with the trendiest surfers.

**Diving** in Japan is expensive, but if you want to explore under the oceans, the best places to head are Okinawa, around the island of Sado-ga-shima, near Niigata, and off the Izu Peninsula, close to Tokyo.

## POLICE, TROUBLE AND EMERGENCIES

**Japan boasts one of the lowest crime rates in the world, and personal safety is rarely a worry. On the whole, the Japanese are honest and law-abiding, there's little theft, and drug-related crimes are relatively rare. The main exception is bicycle theft, which is rife, so make sure yours is securely locked whenever you leave it. In addition, it always pays to be careful in crowded areas and to keep money and important documents stowed in an inside pocket or money-belt, or in your hotel safe.**

In theory, you should carry your **passport** or ID at all times and the police have the right to arrest anyone who fails to do so. In practice, however, they rarely stop foreigners, though car drivers are more likely to be checked. If you're found without your ID, the usual procedure is to escort you back to your hotel or apartment to collect it. Anyone found **taking drugs** will be treated less leniently; if you're lucky, you'll simply be fined and deported, rather than sent to prison.

The presence of **police boxes** (*kōban*) in every neighbourhood helps discourage petty crime, and the local police seem to spend the majority of their time dealing with stolen bikes, and helping bemused visitors – Japanese and foreigners – to

find addresses. This benevolent image is misleading, however, as the Japanese police are notorious for forcing confessions and holding suspects for weeks without access to a lawyer, and recent Amnesty International reports have criticized Japan for its brutal treatment of illegal immigrants and other foreigners held in jail.

**Racial discrimination** can be a problem in Japan, especially for non-Whites, though it is mainly directed at immigrant workers rather than tourists. **Sexual discrimination** is widespread, and foreign women working in Japan can find the predominantly male business culture hard-going. The generally low status of women is reflected in the amount of groping that goes on in crowded commuter trains – there are even pornographic films and comics aimed at gropers. If you do have the misfortune to be groped, the best solution is to grab the offending hand, yank it high in the air and embarrass the guy as much as possible. Fortunately, more violent **sexual abuse** is rare, though rape is seriously under reported and may be up to ten times higher than the current statistics suggest (under 2000 cases per year).

If you need **emergency help**, phone ☎110 for the **police**, and ☎119 for an **ambulance** or **fire engine**. You can call free from any public phone by pressing the red button before dialling, though with the old-style pink or red phones you need to put a coin in first to get the dialling tone. Better still, ask someone to call for you, since few police speak English. If you get really stuck, Tokyo Metropolitan Police operates a 24hr English-language hotline on ☎03/3501-0110, while the 24hr Japan Helpline (☎0120–461997) handles emergencies as well general enquires.

### EARTHQUAKES

**Earthquakes** are a part of life in Japan, with at least one quake recorded every day somewhere in the country. It is home to one tenth of the world's active volcanoes and one tenth of its major earthquakes (over force 7 on the Richter scale), with the most recent major quake being at Kōbe in January 1995. More than 6000 people died, many of them in fires that raged through the old wooden houses, though most of the newer structures – built since the 1980s when tighter regulations were introduced – survived. Fortunately, the vast majority of Japan's seismic activity consists of minor tremors which you probably won't even notice.

Prior to Kōbe, the last really big quake was the Great Kantō Earthquake which devastated Tokyo in 1923, killing an estimated 140,000 people. There's a sequence of major quakes in Tokyo every 70-odd years, and everyone's been talking about the next "Big One" for at least a decade.

Whilst scientists argue about the likelihood of another serious earthquake, Tokyo is equipped with some of the world's most sophisticated censors which are monitored round the clock, and architects employ mind-boggling techniques to ensure the city's new high-rises remain upright.

Nevertheless, earthquakes are notoriously difficult to predict and it's worth taking note of a few basic **safety procedures** (see box below). You should beware of aftershocks which may go on for a long time, and can topple structures that are already weakened, and note that most casualties are caused by fire and traffic accidents, rather than collapsing buildings. In the aftermath of a major earthquake, it may be impossible to contact friends and relatives for a while, since the phone lines are likely to be down or reserved for emergency services.

## EARTHQUAKE SAFETY PROCEDURES

- Extinguish any fires and turn off electrical appliances (TV, air-conditioners, kettles, etc).
- Open any doors leading out of the room, as they often get jammed shut, preventing your exit later.
- Stay away from windows because of splintering glass. If you have time, draw the curtains to contain the glass.
- Don't rush outside (many people are injured by falling masonry), but get under something solid, such as a ground floor doorway, or a desk.

- If the earthquake occurs at night, make sure you've got a torch (all hotels, ryokan, etc, provide torches in the rooms).
- When the tremors have died down, go to the nearest park, playing field or open space, taking your documents and other valuables with you. It's also a good idea to take a cushion or pillow to protect your head against falling glass.
- Eventually, make your way to the designated neighbourhood emergency centre for information, food and shelter.
- Ultimately, get in touch with your embassy.

# WORKING AND STUDYING IN JAPAN

Since the Japanese economy took a nose-dive, the days of *gaijin* flying into Japan and immediately being hired on a lucrative salary for a few hours' work (typically teaching English) are well and truly over. With the exception of the government-sponsored JET program (see below), employment opportunities for foreigners have shrunk, while the number of well-qualified, Japanese-speaking *gaijin* in Japan has increased. That said, finding employment is far from impossible, especially if you have the right qualifications (a degree is essential) and appropriate visa.

With the exception of Australian, New Zealand and Canadian citizens aged between 18 and 30 who qualify for a working holiday visa (see p.14), all foreigners working in Japan, must apply for a **work visa** *outside* the country, for which the proper sponsorship papers from your prospective employer will be necessary. A few employers may be willing to hire you in Japan before the proper papers are sorted, but you shouldn't rely on this and if you arrive in the country without a job make sure you have plenty of funds to live on until you find one. Working visas do not need to be obtained in your home country, so if you do get offered a job in Japan, it's possible to sort out the paperwork in South Korea, for example.

The main places to look for job adverts are Monday's edition of *The Japan Times*, the free weekly magazine *Tokyo Classified* and, in the Kansai area, *Kansai Time Out*. You'll quickly see that the most common job available to foreigners

is **teaching English**. Some of the largest English-language schools, such as NOVA, also have recruiting offices in the UK and US, so you can try and arrange a job before arriving. However, some of the conversation schools are far from professional operations, so before signing any contract, it's a good idea to attend a class and find out what will be expected from you. If you have a professional teaching qualification, plus experience, your chances of getting one of the better jobs will be higher, as will they if you also speak another language such as French or Italian.

A much more limited job option for *gaijin* is rewriting or editing translations of Japanese for technical documents, manuals, magazines, etc, so that they make grammatical sense and read well in English. For such jobs, it will be a great help if you have at least a little Japanese. Other options include modelling, for which it will be an asset to have a professional portfolio of photographs. Whatever work you're looking for – or if you're doing any sort of business in Japan – a smart set of clothes will give you an advantage, as will following other general rules of social etiquette (see p.60).

## THE JET PROGRAMME

One of the best ways to work in Japan is to get a place on the **Japan Exchange and Teaching (JET) programme**, started by the government in 1987 in an attempt to improve foreign-language teaching in schools and promote international understanding. The benefits, which include a generous salary and help with accommodation, return air travel to Japan and paid holidays, have led to the programme being a huge success and there are now more than 5000 graduates taking part each year from some eighteen different countries. The scheme is only open to those aged between eighteen and thirty-five, though in certain circumstances, people over the age limit will be considered.

Around ninety per cent of applicants are employed as Assistant Language Teachers (ALTs) in secondary schools, their duties being primarily to team-teach with Japanese instructors of English and other foreign languages, and also to act as ambassadors for their country. Other applicants opt for one of the local government posts as Coordinator for International Relations (CIRs), though a functional command of Japanese is essential. CIR duties include assisting in a range of international exchange projects and tasks, such as interpreting, editing and producing bi-lingual pamphlets and receiving guests from abroad.

Applying for the JET programme is a lengthy process for which you need to be well prepared. Application forms for the following year's quota are available from late September, with the deadline for submission being early December. Interviews are held in January and February with decisions made in March. After health checks and orientation meetings, ALTs and CIRs head off to their posts in Japan in late July on year-long contracts. These contracts can be renewed for up to two more years by mutual consent.

For further details of the scheme and **application forms**, UK citizens should contact the JET Programme Desk, Council on International Educational Exchange, 52 Poland St, London W1V 4QJ, UK (☎0171/478-2010), whilst residents of the US, Canada, Australia and New Zealand should contact their nearest Japanese consulate or embassy (see p.15).

## STUDYING JAPANESE LANGUAGE AND CULTURE

If you're thinking about **studying Japanese** in Japan, consider picking a school away from the main urban centres. Regional cities such as Sapporo and Kanazawa are cheaper places to live and you're much more likely to find yourself having to use Japanese on an everyday basis than you would be in Tokyo or Ōsaka. That said, the range of courses and institutions on offer in the big cities is much wider.

As well as the language, there are opportunities to study other aspects of Japanese culture,

from pottery to playing the *sakuhachi* (a traditional flute). In order to get a **cultural visa**, you'll need documents from the institutions where you plan to study, including one stating that all tuition fees have been paid, and a letter of guarantee from a private sponsor, preferably Japanese. Full-time courses are expensive, but once you have your visa you may be allowed to undertake paid work to support yourself.

The monthly bi-lingual language magazines *Nihongo Journal* and *Hiragana Times*, and the listings magazines *Tokyo Journal* and *Kansai Time Out* all carry adverts for Japanese language schools. Also check out the Association of International Education Japan, 4-5-29 Komaba, Meguro-ku, Tokyo 153 (☎03/5454-5216, fax 5454-5236; *www.aiej.or.jp*) whose Web site lists details of accredited institutions and has other useful information for those considering studying in Japan.

### CERTIFICATE OF ALIEN REGISTRATION

Whether you're on holiday, working or studying, if your stay in Japan is over three months, you must apply for a **certificate of alien registration** from the local government office closest to the area in which you live. This small identification card includes your photograph and finger print and must be carried at all times; if you're stopped by the police on the street (even for innocuous activities such as riding a bike late at night through the city) you'll have to produce this card, or your passport. If you have neither, expect a trip to the local police station to do some explaining.

## GAY AND LESBIAN JAPAN

Despite there being an honourable tradition of male homosexuality in Japan, with some ancient Buddhist sects believing that love among men was preferable to love between the sexes, modern gay life in Japan is very low-key compared to that in similar industrialized countries. There is still a huge amount of pressure put on men and women to marry, this being an almost essential step along the career ladder at many corporations. Such expectations keep many Japanese gays in the closet and outside of the main cities, such as Tokyo and Ōsaka, the gay scene is all but invisible.

However, in recent times homosexuality has come to be seen as trendy, particularly in the major cities and among the all-important, cash-rich group of young working women known as OLs or "office ladies". Comic books and movies with homosexual characters have been a huge success with OLs who swoon over the gay romances. Gay and transves-tite celebrities are the in thing on TV and there are even bars in Tokyo staffed by cross-dressing women, who flatter and fawn over their female customers in only a slightly more macho way than bona fide hostesses do over salarymen (see p.157 for gay bars in Tokyo). Whilst you're highly unlikely to encounter any problems as a gay traveller in Japan, you may find it difficult to break into any local gay scene without having some contacts.

### INFORMATION SERVICES

**International Gay Friends** is a networking group for gays which organizes support groups for men and women. To contact them, write to if/Passport, CPO 180, Tokyo 100-91 or call ☎03/5693-4569. Alternatively, the useful **GayNet Japan** Web site (*www.gnj.or.jp/gaynet/*), covers most aspects of gay life in the country.

## DIRECTORY

**CIGARETTES** One of Japan's bargain buys, cigarettes are available in a vast range of brands – usually from 24-hour vending machines – at around ¥250 a pack.

**CHILDREN** The Japanese love children and, with standards of health and hygiene so high, there is no real reason not to bring your kids here. All the products you need – such as nappies and baby food – are easily available at shops and department stores, though taking a pram on subways and trains is problematic, since there are often no elevators at stations. Children under six ride free on trains, subways and buses, while those aged six to eleven pay half fare (this applies to the Japan Rail Pass, too). On domestic flights, children under three fly free but have to share a parent's seat, while kids aged three to eleven are charged half-price. Unless they're very young, reduced accommodation rates for children are rare, although the large Western chain hotels, such as the Hilton and Holiday Inn, don't charge extra if children share rooms with their parents. Only at upmarket hotels will you be able to arrange babysitting. Virtually all tourist attractions have a set of reduced charges for children, depending on their age.

**CONTRACEPTIVES** The Pill is not generally available in Japan, so you'll need to bring your own supply. Local brand condoms are widely sold in pharmacies and vending machines.

**ELECTRICITY** The electrical current is 100v, 50Hz AC in eastern Japan including Tokyo, and 100v, 60Hz AC in western Japan including Nagoya, Kyoto and Ōsaka. Japanese plugs have two flat pins and although they are identical to North American plugs, you'll need a transformer to safely use any foreign appliances.

**EMERGENCIES** In order to get a quick response from the national police emergency number (☎110) or the ambulance and fire services (☎119), you'll need to speak some Japanese. The Japan Helpline (☎0120–461997) is a 24-hour English-language toll-free service, while the Tokyo English Lifeline (TELL; ☎03/3403-7106) is open for calls daily 9am–4pm and 7–11pm.

**LAUNDRIES** A laundry service is available in all types of accommodation, with most cheaper hotels and hostels having coin-operated washing machines and dryers. All Japanese neighbourhoods also have coin laundries (*koin rōndori*), often open long hours, which charge between ¥200–300 per wash and ¥100 for around ten minutes of drying time. Virtually all Japanese washing machines use cold water.

**LEFT LUGGAGE** Usually only at the largest train stations in big cities will you find left luggage rooms, though all train stations, many subway stations and some department stores and shopping centres have coin lockers where you can stash your luggage. These come in a range of sizes, charging around ¥500 for a day's storage.

**PHOTOGRAPHY** All major brands of film are available across Japan, at relatively cheap prices especially if bought in bulk from the discount camera shops in the big cities. If you want special types of film, it's best to stock up here, too, before setting off to Japan's more remote areas where the choice is more limited. Worth considering are disposable cameras, which come in a vast range of sizes and types (with or without flash; panoramic; sepia-tinted or black and white images; advance photo system), cost from as little as ¥700 and make great souvenirs and presents.

**PUBLIC TOILETS** All trains and subway stations, parks, department stores and large hotels have public lavatories; ask for the *otearai* or *toire*, pronounced "toy-ray". Note that, hotels and department stores excepted, there is rarely toilet paper, so carry around some tissues; the small packs carrying advertising that are dished out free at busy stations and shopping districts are ideal. See p.61 for more on toilets.

**STUDENT CARDS** It's a good idea to bring along an International Student Identity Card (ISIC) since many museums and other tourist facilities charge lower prices to students.

**TAXES** A departure tax (known locally as a "passenger service facility charge") of ¥2650 is levied on all adults leaving from Kansai International airport (children aged 2–11 years pay ¥1330). For details of consumption and local taxes, see p.26.

**TIME ZONES** The whole of Japan is nine hours ahead of Greenwich Mean Time, so at noon in London, it's 9pm in Tokyo. Japan is fourteen hours ahead of Eastern Standard Time in the US. There is no daylight-saving, so during British Summer Time, for example, the difference drops to eight hours.

**TIPS** Tipping is not a Japanese custom and nobody expects it. The only exception is at high-class Japanese inns where it's good form to leave ¥2000 for the room attendant, but only if the money is put in an envelope and handed over discreetly.

**WEIGHTS AND MEASURES** The only exception to Japan's use of the metric system is its measurement of rooms, usually quoted in *jō*, the size of one *tatami*. It's worth noting that *tatami* size varies around the country, Tokyo having the smallest size at 1.76m by 0.88m.

# PART TWO

## THE

# GUIDE

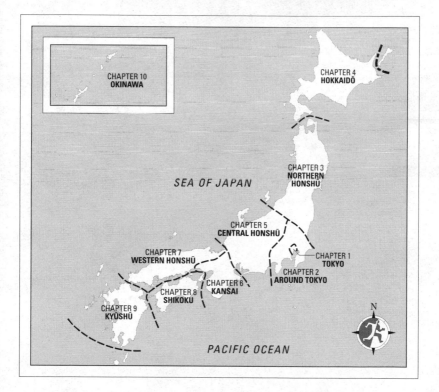

CHAPTER 10
**OKINAWA**

CHAPTER 4
**HOKKAIDŌ**

*SEA OF JAPAN*

CHAPTER 3
**NORTHERN
HONSHŪ**

CHAPTER 5
**CENTRAL HONSHŪ**

CHAPTER 7
**WESTERN HONSHŪ**

CHAPTER 1
**TOKYO**

CHAPTER 2
**AROUND TOKYO**

CHAPTER 6
**KANSAI**

CHAPTER 8
**SHIKOKU**

CHAPTER 9
**KYŪSHŪ**

N

*PACIFIC OCEAN*

# CHAPTER ONE

# TOKYO

On the edge of the Orient, **TOKYO** – the last great conurbation before the yawning chasm of the Pacific Ocean – is one of the world's most perplexing cities. On the one hand, gaudily hung about with eyeball-searing neon and messy overhead cables, plagued by seemingly incessant noise, often clogged with bumper-to-bumper traffic, and packed with twelve million people squashed into minute apartments, it can seem like the stereotypical urban nightmare. Yet behind the barely ordered chaos lie remnants of a very different past. Step back from the frenetic main roads and chances are you'll find yourself in a world of tranquil backstreets, where wooden houses are fronted by neatly clipped bonsai trees; wander beyond the high-tech department stores, and you'll find ancient temples and shrines. In this city of twenty-four-hour shops and vending machines a festival is held virtually every day of the year, people regularly visit their local shrine or temple and scrupulously observe the passing seasons. And, at the centre of it all, is the mysterious green void of the **Imperial Palace** – home to the emperor and a tangible link to the past.

In many ways Tokyo is also something of a modern-day utopia. Trains run on time; the crime rate is hardly worth worrying about; shops and vending machines provide everything you could need (and many things you never thought you needed) 24 hours a day; the people wear the coolest fashions, eat in fabulous restaurants and party in the hippest clubs. It's almost impossible to be bored here and first time visitors should be prepared for a massive assault on the senses – just walking the streets of this hyperactive city can be an energizing experience. You'll also be surprised how affordable many things are. Cheap and cheerful *izakaya* (bars that serve food) and noodle shacks far outnumber the big-ticket French restaurants and high-class *ryōtei*, where *geisha* serve minimalist Japanese cuisine, while day tickets for a sumo tournament or a Kabuki play can be bought for the price of a few drinks. Many of the city's highlights are even free: a stroll through the evocative **Shitamachi** (low city) area around Asakusa and the major Buddhist temple **Sensō-ji**; a visit to the tranquil wooded grounds of **Meiji-jingū**, the city's most venerable Shinto shrine, and the nearby teenage shopping mecca of **Harajuku**; the frenetic fish market at **Tsukiji**; the crackling, neon-saturated atmosphere of the mini-city **Shinjuku** – you don't need to part with lots of cash to explore this city.

Even if you don't arrive in Tokyo, chances are you will end up here or pass through on your way to other parts of Japan, since the capital is the major **transport hub**. Every day, scores of Shinkansen (bullet trains) speed up to the far north of Honshū or south to Kyūshū, while flights, buses and ferries connect Tokyo to the far-flung corners and islands of the Japanese archipelago.

The only time Tokyo is best avoided is during the steamy height of summer in August and early September, when the city's humidity sees its citizens scurrying from one air-conditioned haven to another. October and November, by contrast, are great months to take in the spectacular fireburst of autumn leaves in Tokyo's parks and gardens. Temperatures dip to freezing in the winter months, though the crisp blue skies are rarely disturbed by rain or snow showers. April is the month when Tokyoites love to party beneath the flurries of falling cherry blossoms – one of the

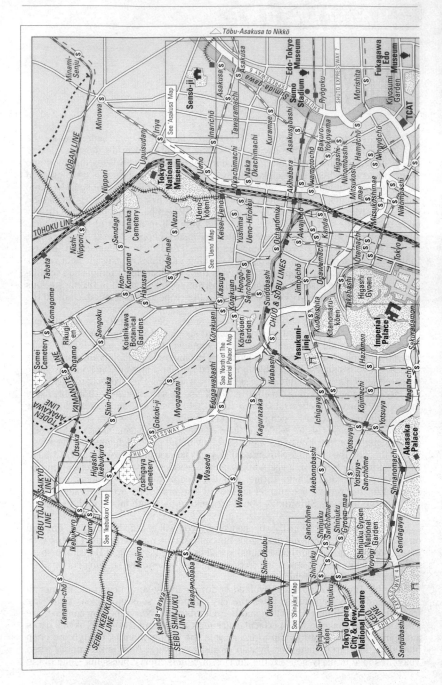

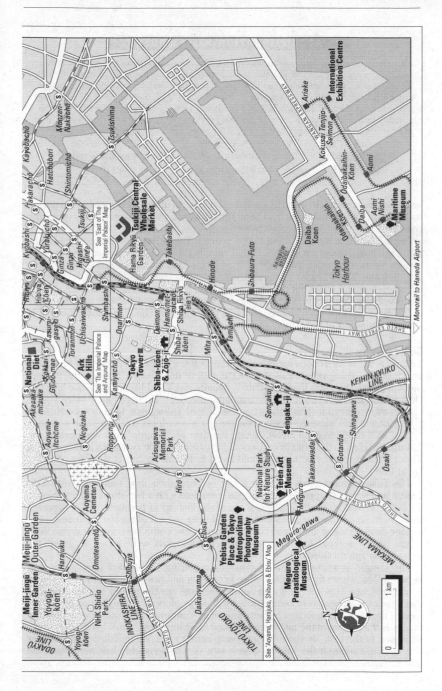

Monzen-
Nakachō

Kayabachō

Takarachō

Hatchobori

Kyōbashi Ⓢ
Ⓢ Yūrakuchō
Ⓢ Shintomichō
Ginza Ⓢ Tsukiji
Ⓢ Higashi-
Ginza

Ⓢ Tsukishima

Tsukiji Central
Wholesale
Market

Hama Rikyū
Garden

Hama Rikyū
Garden

See *East of The
Imperial Palace* Map

Ⓢ Tsukishima

Ⓢ Takebashi

Ariake

International
Exhibition Centre

WANGAN EXPRESSWAY

Ⓢ Kokusai Tenijo-
Seimon

Odaibakaihin-
kōen

Aomi

Daiba

Aomi
Nishi

Maritime
Museum

Hibiya Ⓢ
Ⓢ Hibiya
kōen
Ⓢ Kasumi-
gaseki
Ⓢ Uchisaiwaichō

Ⓢ Shimbashi Ⓢ

Onarimon

Daimon Ⓢ
Ⓢ Hamamatsu-
chō

Shiba-
kōen Shiba Rikyū
Garden

Hinode

Shibaura-Futo

Odaiba

Daiba
Kōen

Tokyo
Harbour

National
Diet

Ark
Hills

Tokyo
Tower

Shiba-kōen
& Zōjō-ji

See *The Imperial Palace
and Around* Map

Toranmon Ⓢ
Ⓢ Ginko-mae
Kamiyachō Ⓢ

Shiba-
kōen

Mita Ⓢ

Tamachi Ⓢ

Tamachi

RAINBOW BRIDGE

Akasaka Ⓢ
mitsuke

Akasaka Ⓢ

Ⓢ Roppongi

Sengaku-
ji

Sengaku-ji

Shinagawa

KEIHIN KYŪKO
LINE

SHUTO EXPRESSWAY 1

Ⓢ Aoyama-
Itchōme

Ⓢ Negizaka

Arisugawa
Memorial
Park

Hirō Ⓢ

National Park
for Nature Study

Teien Art
Museum

Takanawadai Ⓢ

Ⓢ Gotanda

Ōsaki

SHUTO EXPRESSWAY 2

MEGAMA LINE

Aoyama
Cemetery

Meiji-jingū
Outer Garden

Ⓢ Omotesandō

Ⓢ Ebisu

Yebisu Garden
Place & Tokyo
Metropolitan
Photography
Museum

Meguro

Meguro-gawa

Meguro
Parasitological
Museum

Meiji-jingū
Inner Garden

Yoyogi-
kōen

Harajuku Ⓢ

Ⓢ Shibuya

NHK Studio
Park

INOKASHIRA
LINE

SHUTO EXPRESSWAY 3

Daikanyama

TŌKYŪ TŌYOKO LINE

MEKAMA LINE

See *Aoyama, Harajuku, Shibuya & Ebisu* Map

ODAKYŪ
LINE

Yoyogi
kōen Ⓢ

N

1 km

0

Monorail to Haneda Airport

**ACCOMMODATION PRICE CODES**

All accommodation in this book has been graded according to the following price codes, which refer to the cheapest double or twin room available for most of the year, and include taxes. Note that rates may increase during peak holiday periods, in particular around Christmas and New Year, the Golden Week (April 28–May 6) and Obon (the week around August 15), when accommodation is very difficult to get without an advance reservation. In the case of hostels providing dormitory accommodation, the code refers to the charge per bed. See p.36 for more details on accommodation.

| | | |
|---|---|---|
| ① under ¥3000 | ④ ¥7000–10,000 | ⑦ ¥20,000–30,000 |
| ② ¥3000–5000 | ⑤ ¥10,000–15,000 | ⑧ ¥30,000–40,000 |
| ③ ¥5000–7000 | ⑥ ¥15,000–20,000 | ⑨ over ¥40,000 |

best seasons in which to visit the capital. Carrying an umbrella is a good idea during *tsuyu*, the rainy season in June and September, when typhoons occasionally strike the coast.

Legend says that a giant catfish sleeps beneath Tokyo Bay, and its wriggling can be felt in the hundreds of small tremors that rumble the capital each year. Around every seventy years, the catfish awakes, resulting in the kind of major **earthquake** seen in 1995 in Kōbe. There is a long-running, half-hearted debate about moving the Diet and main government offices out of Tokyo, away from danger. Yet, despite the fact that the city is well overdue for the Big One, talk of relocating the capital always comes to nothing. Now, more than ever before, Tokyo is the centre of Japan and nobody wants to leave and miss any of the action.

## Some history

Today's restless metropolis sprawling on the western shores of Tokyo Bay began life as a humble fishing village called **Edo** ("mouth of the estuary") beside the marshy Sumida-gawa. The city's founding date is usually given as 1457, when minor lord Ōta Dōkan built his castle on a bluff overlooking the river. However, a far more significant event occurred in 1590 when the feudal lord **Tokugawa Ieyasu** (see History, p.772) chose this obscure castle-town for his power-base. In little over a decade Ieyasu had conquered all rivals, taken the title of "shogun" and established the **Tokugawa clan** as the effective rulers of Japan for the next two and a half centuries. Though the emperor continued to hold court in Kyoto, Japan's real centre of power lay in Edo.

The Tokugawa set about creating a city befitting their new status. By 1640 **Edo Castle** was the most imposing in all Japan, complete with a five-storey central keep, a double moat and a spiralling network of canals. Instead of perimeter walls, however, there were simple barrier gates and a bewildering warren of narrow, tortuous lanes, sudden dead-ends and unbridged canals to snare unwelcome intruders. Drainage work began on the surrounding marshes, and embankments were raised to guard the nascent city against floods.

The shogun protected himself further by requiring the *daimyō* to split the year between Edo, where their families were kept as virtual hostages, and their provincial feudal holdings. This left them with neither the time nor the money to raise a serious threat, but the *daimyō* were compensated with large plots on the higher ground to the west of the castle, an area that became known as **Yamanote**. Artisans, merchants and others at the bottom of the pile were confined to **Shitamachi**, a low-lying, overcrowded region to the east. By the mid-eighteenth century Edo's population was well over one million, making it the world's largest city, of whom roughly half were squeezed into Shitamachi at an astonishing 70,000 people per square kilometre. Though growing less distinct, this division between the "high" and "low" city is still apparent today.

During the long period of peace, the shogunate and its beneficiaries grew ever more conservative, but life down in the Shitamachi buzzed with a wealthy merchant class and a vigorous, often bawdy subculture. This is the world most closely associated with Edo, the world of *geisha* and Kabuki, of summer days on the Sumida-gawa, moon-viewing parties and picnics under the spring blossom – fleeting moments captured in *ukiyo-e*, pictures of the floating world. Inevitably, there was also squalor, poverty and violence, as well as frequent fires; in January 1657, the **Fire of the Long Sleeves** laid waste to three-quarters of the city's buildings and killed an estimated 100,000 people.

By the early nineteenth century the Tokugawa regime had become increasingly weak and isolated. When they failed to confront Commodore Perry, the American who insolently sailed his Black Ships into Edo Bay in 1853, the shoguns' days were numbered, and ended with the **Meiji Restoration** in 1868. The following year Emperor Meiji took up permanent residence in the city, now renamed **Tokyo** (Eastern Capital) in recognition of its proper status.

As Meiji Japan embraced the new, Western technologies, the face of Tokyo gradually changed: the castle lost its outer gates and much of its grounds; canals were filled in or built over; the commercial focus shifted south into Ginza, and Shitamachi's wealthier merchants decamped to more desirable Yamanote. However, the city was still disaster-prone; the **Great Kantō Earthquake** of 1923 devastated half of Tokyo, and another 100,000 people lost their lives.

More trauma was to come during **World War II**. In just three days of sustained incendiary bombing in March 1945 hundreds of thousands were killed and great swathes of the city burnt down, including Meiji-jingū, Sensō-ji, Edo Castle and most of Shitamachi. From a pre-war population of nearly seven million, Tokyo was reduced to around three million people in a state of near-starvation. This time regeneration was fuelled by an influx of American dollars and food aid under the Allied Occupation, and a manufacturing boom sparked by the Korean War in 1950.

Political tensions erupted in the capital in **May 1960** when rioting broke out over ratification of the revised Security Pact (see p.777). The crisis passed, though student discontent continued to rumble for a long time and riot police became a familiar sight on the streets. On October 10, 1964, however, Emperor Hirohito opened the Tokyo **Olympic Games**, and visitors were wowed by the stunning new Shinkansen trains running south to Ōsaka.

The booming economy of the late **1980s** saw Tokyo land prices reach dizzying heights, matched by excesses of every conceivable sort, from gold-wrapped sushi to mink toilet-seat covers. The heady optimism was reflected in the building projects of the time – the Metropolitan Government offices in Shinjuku, the Ōdaiba reclamation and the vast new development of Makuhari Messe. Then, in 1991, the bubble burst. This, along with revelations of political corruption, financial mismanagement and the release of deadly Sarin gas on Tokyo commuter trains by the AUM cult in 1995 – a particularly shocking event in what is one of the world's safest cities – has led to the more sober Tokyo of the late 1990s.

# Arrival, information and orientation

If you're **arriving** in Tokyo from abroad, you'll almost certainly touch down at New Tokyo International Airport. Otherwise, if you're coming to the capital from elsewhere in Japan, your arrival points will be one of the main train stations (Tokyo, Ueno or Shinjuku), the ferry port at Ariake on Tokyo Bay, or the long-distance bus terminals, mainly at Tokyo and Shinjuku stations.

| TOKYO: ARRIVAL | | |
|---|---|---|
| Haneda Airport | *Haneda Kūkō* | 羽田空港 |
| New Tokyo International Airport (Narita) | *Shin-Tōkyō Kokusai Kūkō (Narita)* | 新東京国際空港（成田） |
| **BUS, FERRY AND TRAIN STATIONS** | | |
| Ikebukuro | *Ikebukuro-eki* | 池袋駅 |
| Shibuya | *Shibuya-eki* | 渋谷駅 |
| Shinagawa | *Shinagawa-eki* | 品川駅 |
| Shinjuku | *Shinjuku-eki* | 新宿駅 |
| Tokyo | *Tōkyō-eki* | 東京駅 |
| Tokyo Ferry Port | *Tōkyō Ferii Noriba* | 東京フェリー乗り場 |
| Ueno | *Ueno-eki* | 上野駅 |

## By plane

Some 66km east of the city centre, **New Tokyo International Airport** (better known as Narita) has two terminals (flight arrivals and departures ☎0476/34-5000 or 0476/32-2802); which one you arrive at depends on the airline you fly. Be prepared for immigration delays and baggage searches; strict security procedures have been enforced ever since the airport's construction back in the 1960s was disrupted by violent protests by local farmers and students.

There are **bureau de change** outlets at both terminals (Terminal 1: 6.30am–11pm; Terminal 2: 7am–10pm) which offer the same rates as city banks. The main **tourist information centre** (daily 9am–8pm; ☎0476/34-6251) is at the newer Terminal Two; staff here can provide maps and leaflets for across Japan. There's a separate counter for making hotel bookings, free of charge. Terminal One has a smaller information centre (daily 9am–8pm), providing much the same service. If you have a JR Rail Pass exchange order, you can arrange your pass for use immediately or at a later date at the JR travel agencies (not the ticket offices) in the basement; English signs indicate where these are. There are direct bus and train connections from Narita to Haneda airport for transfers to domestic flights; the bus (1hr 20min; ¥2900) is more frequent than the train (1hr 10min; ¥1500).

Most domestic flights touch down at **Haneda Airport** (flight information ☎03/5757-8111), located on a spit of land jutting into Tokyo Bay, 20km south of the Imperial Palace. The only international connection at Haneda is provided by Taiwan's China Airlines. There is no tourist office here, but the airport information desk can provide you with an English-language map of Tokyo.

## By train

If you're coming into Tokyo by Shinkansen **JR train** from Ōsaka, Kyoto and other points south, you'll pull in to **Tokyo Station**, close to the Imperial Palace. Most Shinkansen services from the north (the Hokuriku line from Nagano, the Jōetsu line from Niigata and the Tōhoku lines from Yamagata and Morioka) also arrive here, though a few services only go as far as **Ueno**, northeast of the Imperial Palace. Both Tokyo and Ueno stations are on the Yamanote line and are connected to several subway lines, putting them in reach of most of the capital. Long-distance JR train services from the west stop at a few city stations; Tokyo and Ueno stations, Shinjuku Station on Tokyo's west side and Ikebukuro Station in the city's northwest corner.

Private rail lines not run by JR terminate at different stations: the Tōkyū Tōyoko line from Yokohama terminates at Shibuya Station, southwest of the Imperial Palace; the Tōbu Nikkō line runs from Nikkō to Asakusa Station, east of Ueno; and the Odakyū line

## TRANSPORT BETWEEN THE CITY AND AIRPORTS

The fastest way into Tokyo **from Narita** is on one of the frequent JR or Keisei **trains** which depart from the basements of both terminals. Keisei, located on the left side of the basements, offers the cheapest connection into town: the no-frills *tokkyū* (limited express) service, which costs ¥1000 to Ueno (every 30min; 1hr 10min). This service stops at Nishi Nippori, a few minutes north of Ueno, where an easy transfer can be made to the Yamanote or the Keihin Tōhoku lines. If you're staying around Ueno, or you're not carrying much luggage, this – or the slightly faster and fancier Skyliner (¥1920) – is the best option.

JR, who operate on the righthand side of the basements, run the more luxurious red and silver **Narita Express** (N'EX) to several city stations. The cheapest fare is ¥2890 to Tokyo Station (every 30min; 1hr), and there are frequent direct N'EX services to Shinjuku (hourly; 1hr 20min) for ¥3110. The N'EX services to Ikebukuro, Shinagawa (both ¥3110) and Yokohama (¥4180) are much less frequent; you're better off going to Shinjuku and changing on to the Yamanote line for Ikebukuro, while there are plenty of trains to Shinagawa and Yokohama from Tokyo Station. Cheaper than the N'EX are JR's *kaisoku* (rapid) trains, which despite their name, chug slowly into Tokyo Station (hourly; 1hr 20 min) for ¥1280.

**Limousine buses** are useful if you're weighed down by luggage, but they are pricey and prone to delays in traffic. You buy tickets from the limousine bus counters in each of the arrival lobbies; the buses depart directly outside (check which platform you need) and stop at a wide range of places around the city, including all the major hotels and train stations. The journey to hotels in Shinjuku and Ikebukuro costs around ¥2900 and takes a minimum of one hour, thirty minutes. **Taxis** to the city centre can be caught from stand 9 outside the arrivals hall of Terminal One and stand 30 outside the arrival hall of Terminal Two; note that a taxi journey will set you back around ¥20,000, and is no faster than by bus.

**From Haneda Airport** you can take a twenty-minute monorail journey to Hamamatsuchō Station on the Yamanote line (every 5–10min; daily 5.20am–11.15pm) for ¥460. A **taxi** from the Haneda to central Tokyo costs ¥6000, while a **limousine bus** to Tokyo Station is ¥900.

If you're **leaving** Tokyo from Narita airport, it's important to set off around four hours before your flight. **International departure tax** from Narita is no longer levied as a separate payment, but is included in the price of your ticket. During peak holiday periods, queues at the baggage check-in and immigration desks can be lengthy.

from Hakone finishes at Shinjuku Station, the terminus also for the Seibu Shinjuku line from Kawagoe – all these stations have subway connections, and only Asakusa is off the Yamanote rail line.

## By bus

Long-distance **buses** pull in at several major stations around the city, making transport connections straightforward. The main overnight services from Kyoto and Ōsaka terminate at the bus station beside the eastern Yaesu exit of Tokyo Station – other arrival stations for buses are Ikebukuro, Shibuya, Shinagawa and Shinjuku.

## By boat

The most memorable way to arrive in the capital is by long-distance **ferry**, sailing past the suspended roads and monorail on the Rainbow Bridge and the harbour wharfs to dock at **Tokyo Ferry Port** at Ariake on the man-made island of Ōdaiba (see p.140) in Tokyo Bay. There are ferry connections to Tokyo from Kita-Kyūshū in Kyūshū,

Kushiro and Tomakomai in Hokkaidō, and Kōchi and Tokushima on Shikoku. Buses run from the port to Shin-Kiba Station both on the subway and the JR Keiyō line and ten minutes' ride from Tokyo Station. A taxi from the port to central Tokyo shouldn't cost more than ¥2000.

## Information

Tokyo has plenty of English-language information sources and it's as well to take advantage of them before heading off to other regions. There are two **Tourist Information Centres** (TIC), one at Narita airport (see p.84), and the other in central Tokyo, in the basement of Tokyo International Forum (Mon–Fri 9am–5pm, Sat 9am–noon; ☎03/3201-3331), close to Yūrakuchō Station. To find the latter, take the Forum exit from the JR station, or exit A4b from the subway – avoid coming here at noon, when there's often only a skeleton staff.

There are also information desks at Tokyo and Shinjuku stations. The Tokyo Station desk (Mon–Sat 9am–6pm) occupies the corner of a JR booking office in the station's central hall on the east (Yaesu) side. Staff here mainly dispense train timetables and excursion tickets and answer general queries. There are two booths in Shinjuku Station: one is on the Nishi-guchi (west exit) side of the station, near the entrance to the Keiō train lines, and partially obscured by the cardboard city of the homeless; the other is in the lobby above the train lines under the Luminé department store at the northern end of the station.

You can pick up free **maps** of the city from any of the tourist centres; look out for the handy, one-page map of central Tokyo (within the Yamanote line), with detailed area maps on the back. If you plan to be here for more than just a few days or want to wander off the normal routes, it's worth buying Kodansha's *Tokyo Bilingual Atlas* (¥2000), which gives more detail and, importantly, includes the *chōme* numbers to help pin down addresses (see box, p.21).

By far the best **English-language magazine** is the free weekly *Tokyo Classified*, packed with ads, listings and features, and available at bars, restaurants and shops frequented by *gaijin*. Also worth a look is *Tokyo Journal* (¥600), with reviews and listings covering everything from arts events to food and nightlife. *Tokyo Finder* (¥300) is more touristy, but have a look at its free sister-publication, *Tokyo Day & Night*. The other freebies, *City Life News* and *Tokyo Weekender*, carry useful articles, reviews and snippets of practical information. You'll find most of these at the Tokyo TIC, larger hotels and shops.

If all else fails, you can always phone **Teletourist** (☎03/3201-2911), which provides 24-hour pre-recorded information in English on events in and around the capital, though you'll be hanging on the phone while they reel through a long list.

## Orientation: along the Yamanote line

The best way to think of Tokyo is not as one city with a central heart, but as several mini-cities, linked by the arteries of the railway and the veins of the subway system. It's a vast place, spreading from the mountains in the north and west to tropical islands some 1300km to the south, but as a visitor you're unlikely to stray beyond its most central wards. The most useful reference point is the **Yamanote line**, an elongated overland train loop which connects and encloses central Tokyo and virtually everything of interest to visitors. Sightseeing destinations that fall outside of the loop are mainly within what was once called Shitamachi, or the "low city", east of the Imperial Palace, including Asakusa and Ryōgoku, and on Tokyo Bay to the south, including the nascent 21st century metropolis of Ōdaiba.

The best way of getting your bearings is to trace the Yamanote route on a map, starting at the mini-city of **Shinjuku**, on the west side of Tokyo, where a cluster of skyscrapers provides a permanent directional marker wherever you are in the city. From Shinjuku, the line heads north towards the mini-city of **Ikebukuro**, where the sixty-floor Sunshine Building, east of the station, is another landmark. The Yamanote then veers east towards **Ueno**, the jumping-off point for the park and national museums. Further east of Ueno, at Asakusa, is Sensō-ji, Tokyo's major Buddhist temple.

From Ueno the Yamanote runs south to **Akihabara**, the electronic discount shop district. Bisecting Akihabara station is the Sōbu line which, together with the Chūō line from Tokyo station, flows directly westwards, providing the shortest rail route back to Shinjuku. Handy stations along these two lines include Suidōbashi for Tokyo Dome and Kōrakuen garden, Iidabashi for the Tokyo International Youth Hostel, and Sendagaya for the Metropolitan Gymnasium and the gardens of Shinjuku Gyoen. East of Akihabara, on the other hand, the Sōbu line runs across the Sumida-gawa to the sumo centre of Ryōgoku.

From Akihabara the Yamanote continues south through **Tokyo Station**, with the Imperial Palace and business districts of Ōtemachi and Maranouchi immediately to the west. Further south lie the entertainment districts of **Ginza** (closest stop Yūrakuchō) and **Shimbashi**, after which the line passes **Hamamatsuchō** (connected by monorail to Haneda airport), where you'll be able to see, to the east, the gardens of Hama Rikyū, next to the market at Tsukiji, on the edge of Tokyo Bay. On the west side is Tokyo Tower, just beyond which is the party district of Roppongi.

The Rainbow Bridge across to the man-made island of Ōdaiba is clearly visible as the Yamanote veers down to **Shinagawa**, a hub of upmarket hotels, with rail connections through to Kawasaki and Yokohama. Just beyond here, the line turns sharply north and heads up towards fashionable **Shibuya**, another mini-city. On the western flank of **Harajuku**, the next stop after Shibuya, are the wooded grounds of Meiji-jingū, the city's most important shrine, and Yoyogi Park. Yoyogi, the station after Harajuku, is also on the Sōbu line, and is just one stop from the start of your journey at Shinjuku.

# City transport

The whole of Tokyo's public transport system is efficient, clean and safe, but as a visitor, you'll probably find the **trains and subways** the best way of getting around; the simple colour-coding on trains and maps, as well as clear signposts (many in English) and directional arrows make this by far the most *gaijin*-friendly form of transport. And while during rush hour (7.30–9am & 5.30–7.30pm), you may find yourself crushed between someone's armpit and another person's back, only rarely do the infamous white-gloved platform attendants shove commuters into carriages.

Lack of any signs in English make the **bus system** a lot more challenging. However, once you've got a feel for the city, buses can be a good way of cutting across the few areas of Tokyo not served by a subway or train line, and as long as you have a map, fellow passengers should be able to help you get to where you want to be. For short, crosstown journeys, **taxis** are handy and, if shared by a group of people, not that expensive.

Once you've chosen the area you wish to explore, **walking** is the best way to get yourself from one sight to another; you're almost guaranteed to see something interesting on the way. **Cycling**, if you stick to the quiet back streets, can also be a good way of zipping around (see Listings, p.165 for rental places).

Given the excellent public transport facilities, the often appalling road traffic, the high cost of parking (if you're lucky enough to find a space) and Tokyo's confusing street layout, you'd need a very good reason to want to **rent a car** to get around the city, but we've listed some rental companies on p.165.

## The subway

Its colourful map may look like a messy plate of *yakisoba* (fried noodles), but Tokyo's **subway** is relatively easy to negotiate. There are two systems, the eight-line TRTA (which stands for Teito Rapid Transit Authority, but is also referred to as the Eidan) and the four-line Toei, run by the city authority, which also manages the buses and the tram line. The systems share some of the same stations, but unless you buy a special ticket from the vending machines that specifies your route from one system to the other, you cannot switch mid-journey between the two sets of lines. Subways have connecting passageways to overland train lines, such as the Yamanote. See the colour insert for a plan of the Tokyo subway.

You'll generally pay for your **ticket** at the vending machines beside the electronic ticket gates – apart from major stations (marked with a triangle on the subway map, there are no ticket sales windows. If fazed by the wide range of price buttons you can choose from, buy the cheapest ticket and sort out the difference with the gatekeeper at the other end. You must always buy separate tickets for subways and overland trains.

Trains run daily from around 5am to just after midnight, and during peak daytime hours as frequently as every five minutes. Leaving a station can be complicated by the number of exits (sixty in Shinjuku, for example), but there are maps close to the ticket barriers and on the platforms indicating where the exits emerge, and strips of yellow tiles on the floor mark the routes to the ticket barriers.

Most journeys across central Tokyo cost no more than ¥180 – this means that few of the **travel passes** on offer are good value for short-stay visitors. However, if you're going to be travelling around a lot, it makes sense to buy *kaisūken,* carnet-type tickets where you get eleven tickets for the price of ten – look for the special buttons on the automated ticket machines at the stations. Also handy is the SF Metro Card, which saves you no money, but can be used directly in the subway wickets, which deduct the fare from the card's stored value; these cards can be bought from ticket offices and machines. If you're here for a month or more and will be travelling the same route most days, you might buy a *teiki* season ticket, which runs for one, three or six months and cover your specified route and stations in between.

## Trains and trams

Spend any length of time in Tokyo and you'll become very familiar with the JR **Yamanote train line** that loops around the city centre (see pp.86–7 for a summary of its route). Other useful JR train routes include the **Chūō line** (orange), which starts at Tokyo Station and runs west to Shinjuku and the suburbs beyond to terminate beside the mountains at Takao – the rapid services (look for the red *kanji* characters on the side of the train) miss out on some stations. The yellow Sōbu line goes from Chiba in the east to to Mitaka in the west, and runs parallel to the Chūō line in the centre of Tokyo, doubling as a local service stopping at all stations. The **Keihin Tōhoku line**, with blue trains, runs from Ōmiya in the north, through Tokyo Station, to Yokohama and beyond. It's fine to transfer between JR lines on the same ticket, but you must buy a new ticket if you transfer to a subway line. Trains run daily from around 5am to just after midnight.

As on the subway, **tickets** are bought from vending machines. The lowest fare on JR lines is ¥140. Like the subways, JR offers prepaid cards and *kaisūken* (carnet) deals on tickets. The pre-paid Orange Card (not always orange, just to confuse things), comes in denominations of ¥1000, ¥3000, ¥5000 (worth ¥5300) and ¥10,000 (worth ¥10,700), and is available from station vending machines. The card must be re-inserted into the same vending machines to pay for individual tickets (the price is deducted from the value of the card), but can be used on the JR system anywhere in Japan.

Central Tokyo's last remaining **tram** service, the Toden Arakawa line, loops round from Waseda in the northwest to Minowa, above Asakusa, on the northeast. Though not a particularly useful route for visitors, it passes through some interesting back streets, especially between Higashi-Ikebukuro and Kōshinzuka. There's a flat-fare of ¥160, paid on entry, and stations are announced in English. Trams run from around 6am to 10pm.

## Buses

Although Tokyo's **buses** are handy for crossing the few areas without convenient subway and train stations, none of the buses or routes are labelled in English, so you'll have to get used to recognizing the *kanji* names of places or memorizing the numbers of useful bus routes. The final destination is on the front of the bus, along with the route number. You pay on entry, by dropping the flat rate of ¥200 into the fare box by the driver. There is a machine in the box for changing notes. A recorded voice announces the next stop in advance, as well as issuing constant warnings about not forgetting your belongings when you get off the bus. If you're not sure when your stop is, ask your fellow passengers.

## Ferries

Double-decker **ferries**, known as *suijō basu* (water buses), ply the 35-minute route between the Sumida-gawa River Cruise stations at Asakusa, northeast of the city centre and Hinode Sanbashi, on Tokyo Bay (every 40min; daily to 6.15pm; ¥660). The large picture windows, which give a completely different view of the city than you'll get from the streets, are reason enough for hopping aboard one, especially if you want to visit both Asakusa and the gardens at Hama Rikyū on the same day, and then walk into Ginza. The ferries stop at the gardens en route, and you can buy a combination ticket for the ferry and park entrance for around ¥720.

Hinode Sanbashi (close by Hinode Station on the Yurikamome monorail line or a ten-minute walk from Hamamatsuchō Station on the Yamanote line) is also the jumping-off point for several good cruises around Tokyo Bay and to various points around the island of Ōdaiba (see p.140), or across to Kasai Rinkai-kōen (see p.142) on the east side of the bay. In bad weather the ferries are best avoided, especially if you're prone to sea sickness.

## Taxis

For short hops around the centre of Tokyo, **taxis** are often the best option, though heavy traffic can slow them down. The basic rate is ¥660 for the first 2km, after which the meter racks up ¥80 every 274m, plus a time charge when the taxi is moving at less than 10km per hour. Between 11pm and 5am rates are about 20 percent higher.

You can flag down a taxi on most roads – a red light next to the driver means the cab is free; green means occupied – and there are designated stands in the busiest parts of town. When the taxi stops, the driver will press an automatic door-opening button. Try to have your destination written down (preferably in Japanese) and don't be surprised if the driver draws a blank; locating addresses in Tokyo is a skill that even cabbies are not always expert in, and a stop at a *kōban* (local police box) may be necessary to locate your destination. No tip need be paid on leaving the taxi. After the trains stop at night, be prepared for long queues at taxi stands, especially in areas such as Roppongi and Shinjuku. Some drivers are reluctant to pick up foreigners because they assume they are only going a short distance; it makes better sense to ferry drunken salarymen to their suburban homes.

# Accommodation

Tokyo offers a whole range of **places to stay**, from first-class hotels to bottom-end dormitory bunks. The main difficulty is finding somewhere affordable, since rates are governed more by square-footage than by quality of service. We've concentrated on hotels in the middle and lower price categories but have also included a representative sample

## TOKYO: ACCOMMODATION

| | | |
|---|---|---|
| Hotel Alcyone | *Hoteru Arushiyon* | ホテルアルシヨン |
| ANA Hotel Tokyo | *ANA Hoteru Tōkyō* | ANAホテル東京 |
| Hotel Asakusa & Capsules | *Hoteru Asakusa to Kapuseru* | ホテル浅草とカプセル |
| Asakusa View Hotel | *Asakusa Byū Hoteru* | 浅草ビューホテル |
| Asia Centre of Japan | *Ajia Kaikan* | アジア会館 |
| Capitol Tōkyū Hotel | *Kyapitoru Tōkyū Hoteru* | キャピトル東急ホテル |
| Capsule Hotel Riverside | *Kapuseru Hoteru Ribāsaido* | カプセルホテルリバーサイド |
| Hotel Clarion | *Hoteru Kurerion* | ホテルクレリオン |
| Dai-ichi Hotel | *Dai-ichi Hoteru* | 第一ホテル |
| Diamond Hotel | *Daiyamondo Hoteru* | ダイヤモンドホテル |
| Fairmont Hotel | *Ferumonto Hoteru* | フェルモントホテル |
| Hotel Florasian | *Hoteru Furorashion* | ホテルフロラシオン |
| Gajōen Kankō Hotel | *Gajōen Kankō Hoteru* | 雅叙園観光ホテル |
| Harajuku Trimm | *Harajuku Torimu* | 原宿トリム |
| Hilltop Hotel | *Yama-no-Ue Hoteru* | 山の上ホテル |
| Hotel Ibis | *Hoteru Aibisu* | ホテルアイビス |
| Ryokan Katsutaro | *Ryokan Katsutaro* | 旅館勝太郎 |
| Keihin Hotel | *Keihin Hoteru* | 京浜ホテル |
| Kimi Ryokan | *Kimi Ryokan* | 貴美旅館 |
| Marroad Inn Akasaka | *Maroudo In Akasaka* | マロウドイン赤坂 |
| Hotel Metropolitan | *Hoteru Metoroporitan* | ホテルメトロポリタン |
| New Ōtani | *Nyū Ōtani* | ニューオータニ |
| New Ōtani Inn Tokyo | *Nyū Ōtani In Tōkyō* | ニューオータニイン東京 |
| New Takanawa Prince Hotel | *Shin Takanawa Purinsu Hoteru* | 新高輪プリンスホテル |
| Hotel Nikkō Tokyo | *Hoteru Nikkō Tōkyō* | ホテル日光東京 |
| Hotel Ōkura | *Hoteru Ōkura* | ホテルオークラ |
| Park Hyatt Tokyo | *Pāku Haiatto Tōkyō* | パークハイアット東京 |
| Hotel Pine Hill | *Hoteru Pain Hiru* | ホテルパインヒル |
| Ryokan Sansuisō | *Ryokan Sansuisō* | 旅館山水荘 |
| Sawanoya Ryokan | *Sawanoya Ryokan* | 澤の屋旅館 |
| Shibuya Tōbu Hotel | *Shibuya Tōbu Hoteru* | 渋谷東武ホテル |
| Shibuya Tōkyū Inn | *Shibuya Tōkyū In* | 渋谷東急イン |
| Ryokan Shigetsu | *Ryokan Shigetsu* | 旅館指月 |
| Suigetsu Hotel Ohgaisō | *Suigetsu Hoteru Ohgaisō* | 水月ホテル鴎外荘 |
| Hotel Theatre | *Hoteru Teatoru* | ホテルテアトル |
| Tokyo Hilton Hotel | *Tōkyō Hiruton Hoteru* | 東京ヒルトンホテル |
| Tokyo International Youth Hostel | *Tōkyō Kokusai Yūsu Hosuteru* | 東京国際ユースホステル |
| Tokyo Koma Ryokō Kaikan. | *Tōkyō Koma Ryokō Kaikan* | 東京コマ旅行会館 |
| Tokyo YMCA Hotel | *Tōkyō YMCA Hoteru* | 東京ＹＭＣＡホテル |
| Tokyo Yoyogi Youth Hostel | *Tōkyō Yoyogi Yūsu Hosuteru* | 東京代々木ユースホステル |
| Tokyo YWCA Sadohara | *Tōkyō YWCA Sadohara* | 東京ＹＷＣＡ砂土原 |
| Hotel Tōkyū Kankō | *Hoteru Tōkyū Kankō* | ホテル東急観光 |
| Hotel Top Asakusa | *Hoteru Toppu Asakusa* | ホテルトップ浅草 |
| Washington Hotel | *Washinton Hoteru* | ワシントンホテル |
| Hotel Watson | *Hoteru Watoson* | ホテルワトソン |
| YMCA Asia Youth Centre | *YMCA Ajia Yūsu Sentā* | ＹＭＣＡアジアユースセンター |

at the higher end. At all levels, security and cleanliness are top-notch, and you'll nearly always find someone who speaks some English.

Most **hotels** are Western-style and seriously lacking in character; you'll find better value and a more authentic atmosphere at the family-run **ryokan** in Tokyo's less central districts. Moving down the scale, there's a clutch of YMCAs and hostels, though these aren't much cheaper than ryokan, and the relatively inexpensive **capsule hotels**, clustered around major train stations, which are fun to try at least once. Otherwise, the only real alternatives for budget travellers are Tokyo's two city-centre **youth hostels**, which have the usual proviso of a three-day maximum stay and an evening curfew.

If you're staying in Tokyo for more than a week, and need to keep costs down, you'll probably have to start looking at the so-called **gaijin houses**. These provide cheap, rented rooms for foreigners (*gaijin*) in a shared house or apartment, and usually operate on a weekly or monthly basis, though some offer daily rates. They are privately owned and not always legal; the best are nearly always full and the worst are the stuff of nightmares. Check the English press, particularly *Tokyo Journal* and *Tokyo Classified*. Kimi Information Centre, 8F, Oscar Building, 2-42-3 Ikebukuro, (☎03/3986-1604, fax 3986-3037; *www.gsquare.or.jp/kimi*) runs a useful letting agency.

Whatever your budget, it's wise to **reserve** your first few nights' accommodation before arrival. This is especially true of the cheaper places, which tend to go quickly, particularly over national holidays and in late February when thousands of students descend on Tokyo for the university entrance exams. If you do arrive without a reservation, head for Narita airport's tourist information desk, which handles hotel bookings (see Arrival, p.84), or the Welcome Inn Reservation Centre (Mon–Fri 9am–noon & 1–5pm; ☎03/3211-4201, fax 3211-9009, email *wirc@www.jnto.go.jp*), next door to Tokyo TIC (see p.86).

Bear in mind that trains stop running around midnight; if you're a night animal, opt for somewhere within walking distance of one of the entertainment districts to avoid unecessary taxi fares.

## Akasaka and Roppongi

**ANA Hotel Tokyo**, 1-12-33 Akasaka, Minato-ku (☎03/3505-1111, fax 3505-1155). Stylish hotel conveniently located midway between Akasaka and Roppongi. The rooms are luxurious and have good views in any direction, but especially towards Tokyo Tower. Akasaka Station. ⑦.

**Asia Centre of Japan**, 8-10-32 Akasaka, Minato-ku (☎03/3402-6111, fax 3402-0738). A bargain for this area, so it fills up quickly, especially during the holiday seasons. The small, neat rooms are Western style, and cheaper if you forgo en-suite bathrooms. Also has an inexpensive café and pleasant garden restaurant. Singles start from ¥5100. Nogizaka Station. ③–④.

**Capitol Tōkyū Hotel**, 2-10-3 Nagatachō, Chiyoda-ku (☎03/3581-4511, fax 3581-5882). Adjacent to Hie-jinja, Tōkyū's flagship hotel mixes Japanese and Western styles successfully, although some might find the overall ambience a little dark. Facilities include a small traditional garden, an outdoor pool in the summer and several restaurants and bars. Kokkaigijidō-mae Station. ⑦.

**Hotel Ibis**, 7-14-4 Roppongi, Minato-ku (☎03/3403-4411, fax 3479-0609). A stone's throw from Roppongi crossing, the cheapest doubles are small but bright and have TV and fridge. The lobby is on the fifth floor. Roppongi Station. ⑥.

**Marroad Inn Akasaka**, 6-15-17 Akasaka, Minato-ku (☎03/3585-7611, fax 3585-7191). Good-value business hotel offering rooms with desk and TV. Cheaper rooms have one double bed rather than two singles. The on-site Chinese restaurant does a ¥1000 dinner. Akasaka Station. ④.

**New Ōtani**, 4-1 Kioichō, Chiyoda-ku (☎03/3265-1111, fax 3221-2619). The original star-shaped main building is now dwarfed by the adjacent 40-storey tower block. Inside, the rooms are beautifully designed, and facilities include a staggering 37 restaurants and bars, a tea ceremony room, an art gallery (see p.109), sports centre, traditional garden, swimming pools and tennis courts, a well-stocked bookshop and a post office. Akasaka Mitsuke Station. ⑦.

**Hotel Ōkura**, 2-10-4 Toranomon, Minato-ku (☎03/3582-0111, fax 3582-3707). One of Tokyo's most prestigious hotels, close to the US Embassy, and favoured by diplomats and celebrities. Has a classic 1950s style, especially in the spacious lobby with its low chairs and garden view. Has its own oriental art museum, tea ceremony rooms and several restaurants. Kamiyachō Station. ⑦.

**Tokyo Koma Ryoko Kaiken**. 1-7-30 Roppongi, Minato-ku (☎03/3585-1046, fax 3583-0689). Opposite the raised Shuto Expressway from IBM Japan's headquarters, within walking distance of the main Roppongi drag. The huge *tatami* rooms have en-suite toilets and separate bathrooms. Roppongi Station. ④.

**Hotel Tōkyū Kankō**, 2-21-6 Akasaka, Minato-ku (☎03/3582-0451, fax 3583-4023). Slightly faded 1960s hotel in a quiet location between Akasaka and Roppongi. The staff are pleasant and the rooms are large and at the low end of this price range. The cheapest singles (¥8,500) have no windows. Akasaka Station. ④.

## Asakusa and Ueno

*The following hotels are marked on the maps on p.113 and p.116.*

**Hotel Asakusa & Capsules**, 4-14-9 Kotobuki (☎03/3847-4477). Big, old capsule hotel on the south edge of Asakusa which accepts women, and has a few cheap single rooms with bath attached. Asakusa or Tawaramachi stations. Capsule ①, room ②.

**Asakusa View Hotel**, 3-17-1 Nishi-Asakusa, Taitō-ku (☎03/3847-1111, fax 3842-2117). Though it sticks out like a sore thumb, this is Asakusa's grandest hotel – all sparkling marble and chandeliers. The rooms are more ordinary, but have great views from the higher floors. There's a top-floor bar, which also does a reasonable buffet lunch, plus a shopping arcade and swimming pool (¥3000). Tawaramachi Station. ⑥.

**Capsule Hotel Riverside**, 2-20-4 Kaminarimon (☎03/3844-1155). Smart, friendly capsule hotel for men and just 15 women in the thick of Asakusa. Asakusa Station. ②.

**Ryokan Katsutaro**, 4-16-8 Ikenohata, Taitō-ku (☎03/3821-9808, fax 3821-4789). A good alternative if *Sawanoya* is full (see below), handily located within walking distance of Ueno Park. It's a homely place with just seven, slightly faded *tatami* rooms, some with bath, and laundry facilities. Nezu Station. ③.

**Hotel Pine Hill**, 2-3-4 Ueno, Taitō-ku (☎03/3836-5111, fax 3837-0080). Best-value among the clutch of ordinary, mid-range business hotels in central Ueno. Rooms are small but adequate. Ueno-Hirokōji Station. ⑤.

**Sawanoya Ryoken**, 2-3-11 Yanaka, Taitō-ku (☎03/3822-2251, fax 3822-2252). Welcoming ryokan with good-value, traditional *tatami* rooms, all with wash basin, TV, telephone and air-conditioning, though only three have en-suite baths. The owner, Sawa-san, is something of a local character, and his son performs lion-dances for guests. While not an ideal location, the surrounding streets are worth exploring and Ueno Park is within walking distance. Nezu Station. ③.

**Ryokan Shigetsu**, 1-31-11 Asakusa, Taitō-ku (☎03/3843-2345, fax 3843-2348). Elegant ryokan which is definitely *the* place to stay in Asakusa. Just off bustling Nakamise-dōri, inside is a world of kimono-clad receptionists and tinkling *shamisen* music. It's surprisingly affordable, with a choice of smallish Western- or Japanese-style rooms, all en suite. There's also a Japanese bath on the top floor with views over temple roofs. The only downside is an 11pm curfew. Asakusa Station. ④.

**Suigetsu Hotel Ohgaisou**, 3-3-21 Ikenohata, Taitō-ku (☎03/3822-4611, fax 3823-4340). One of very few mid-range hotels with a Japanese atmosphere. Its three wings, containing a mix of Western and *tatami* rooms, are built around the Meiji-period house and traditional garden of novelist Ogai Mori. Prices are reasonable, especially for the Japanese-style rooms, as long as you specify no meals. Nezu Station. ④.

**Hotel Top Asakusa**, 1-5-3 Asakusa, Taitō-ku (☎03/3847-2222, fax 3847-3074). Modest business hotel that's a cut above the competition for its location on Asakusa's main street, English-speaking staff and its small but well-appointed rooms, all with TV and telephone. Asakusa Station. ④.

## Ginza and around the Imperial Palace

*The following hotels are marked on the maps on p.97, p.101 and p.106.*

**Hotel Alcyone**, 4-14-3 Ginza, Chūō-ku (☎03/3541-3621, fax 3541-3263). In a prime location just round the corner from the Kabuki-za and five-minutes' walk from Tsukiji. Ignore the gawdy Seventies decor in the lobby and head straight for the smart *tatami* rooms, which are good-value at ¥8000 per person. There's a communal bath in the basement and an attached Swiss restaurant. Higashi-Ginza Station. ⑥.

**Dai-ichi Hotel**, 1–2–6 Shimbashi (☎03/3501-4411, fax 3595-2634). Luxury hotel exuding European-style opulence. Rooms are an adequate size and are all beautifully decked out in pale creams. There are ten restaurants and all the usual services, though no pool. Shimbashi Station. ⑧–⑨.

**Diamond Hotel**, 25 Ichibanchō, Chiyoda-ku (☎03/3263-2211, fax 3263-2222). Top-range hotel that maintains a personal touch. While its rooms don't quite live up to the plush, red-velvet lobby, they're comfortable and well-furnished. Hanzōmon Station. ⑦.

**Fairmont Hotel**, 2-1-17 Kudan-Minami, Chiyoda-ku (☎03/3262-1151, fax 3264-2476). Relaxed hotel on a quiet side street overlooking the Imperial Palace moat, within easy reach of Yasukuni Shrine. Bedrooms are plain, but light and airy – the best have views. Kudanshita Station. ⑦.

**Hilltop Hotel**, 1-1 Kanda-Surugadai, Chiyoda-ku (☎03/3293-2311, fax 3233-4567). Small, 1930s hotel near Meiji University which makes up for a rather inconvenient location with its Art Deco touches and friendly welcome. Rooms in the main building have plush chocolate and green, period furnishings. Ochanomizu Station. ⑤.

**Tokyo International Youth Hostel**, 18F Central Plaza Building, 1-1 Kaguragashi, Shinjuku-ku (☎03/3235-1107). On a clear winter's day, you can see Fuji from this smart hostel above Iidabashi Station. Each bunk has its own curtains and locker, and there are international phones, a members' kitchen and laundry facilities. The reception is open 3–9pm and there's a 10.30pm curfew. To find the hostel, exit B2 from the subway brings you straight up into the lift lobby; or, from the JR station's west exit, turn right into the Ramla Centre and keep straight ahead. Iidabashi Station. ①–②.

**Tokyo YMCA Hotel**, 7 Kanda-Mitoshirochō, Chiyoda-ku (☎03/3293-1911, fax 3293-1926). Surprisingly smart accommodation at reasonable prices. Rooms are functional but comfortable and guests can use the YMCA pool (¥1500). In a handy location, on the fringes of central Tokyo. Ogawamachi Station. ⑥.

**YMCA Asia Youth Centre**, 2-5-5 Sarugakuchō, Chiyoda-ku (☎03/3233-0611, fax 3233-0633). Both men and women can stay at this hostel, with a small discount for YMCA members. The rooms, mostly single, are a bit worn but all come with bathroom and TV, and there's a 25m swimming pool in the basement which guests can use at restricted times (¥1000). Suidōbashi Station. ④.

## Harajuku and Shibuya

*The following hotels are marked on the map on p.133.*

**Hotel Florasian**, 4-17-58 Minami-Aoyama, Minato-ku (☎03/3403-1541, fax 3403-5450). Given the high standard of the Western-style rooms and the convenient location, five-minutes from Omotesandō, in a quiet residential area, this mid-range hotel is excellent value. Omotesandō Station. ⑤.

**Harajuku Trimm**, 6-28-6 Jingū-mae, Shibuya-ku (☎03/3498-2101, fax 3498-1777). In the yellow brick building five minutes' walk along Meiji-dōri towards Shibuya from the crossing with Omotesandō. Good-value business hotel with slightly larger beds than usual and a bit more room space. Also has a fitness centre. Singles start at ¥7700. Meiji-jingū-mae Station. ④.

**Shibuya Tōbu Hotel**, 3-1 Udagawachō, Shibuya-ku (☎03/3476-0111, fax 3476-0903). Pleasant chain hotel, well-located near Shibuya's department stores, with friendly service and a good range of restaurants on the premises. One of the few hotels where the single rooms are brighter than the doubles. Shibuya Station. ⑤.

**Shibuya Tōkyū Inn**, 1-24-10 Shibuya, Shibuya-ku (☎03/3498-0109, fax 3498-0189). Less than a minute from the station, this hotel is not quite as grand as other in the Tōkyū group, but it does have a couple of restaurants and bars and a lively atmosphere. Shibuya Station. ⑥.

## Ikebukuro

*The following hotels are marked on the map on p.122.*

**Hotel Clarion**, 2-3-1 Ikebukuro, Toshima-ku (☎03/5396-0111, fax 5396-9815). International-class hotel in a good location on the west side of Ikebukuro Station. It's well-priced and has more character than its local rivals. ⑤.

**Kimi Ryokan**, 2-36-8 Ikebukuro, Toshima-ku (☎03/3971-3766). Great-value institution on Tokyo's budget scene and a good place to meet fellow travellers. It's tricky to find, in the backstreets of west Ikebukuro. Book well ahead. Ikebukuro Station. ③.

**Hotel Metropolitan**, 1-6-1 Nishi-Ikebukuro, Toshima-ku (☎03/3980-1111, fax 3980-5600). Ikebukuro's plushest hotel is part of the *Holiday Inn* group, and has all the facilities you'd expect, including limousine bus connections to Narita airport. The rooms are comfortable and well-priced. Located on the more interesting, west side of Ikebukuro. Ikebukuro Station. ⑥.

**Hotel Theatre**, 1-21-4 Higashi-Ikebukuro, Toshima-ku (☎03/3988-2251). Small, pleasant hotel with English-speaking staff. The rooms are nothing special, but a touch better than average for the price. Ikebukuro Station. ④.

## Meguro, Shinagawa and Tokyo Bay

**Gajōen Kankō Hotel**, 1-8-1 Shimo-Meguro, Meguro-ku (☎03/3491-0111, fax 3495-2450). The unassuming facade of this hotel opposite Meguro's famous wedding hall hides one of the few Tokyo hotels with its own style. Much of the interior decoration is Art Deco, and the rooms are a good size at a fair price for all the facilities, including CNN on the TV. Meguro Station. ⑤.

**Keihin Hotel**, 4-10-20 Takanawa, Minato-ku (☎03/3449-5711, fax 3441-7230). Small, old-fashioned hotel directly opposite Shinagawa Station. The cheaper rates mean you have to pay to use the TVs in the room and the bathrooms are tiny. There are some Japanese-style rooms, and the cheapest singles are ¥9200. Shinagawa Station. ④.

**New Ōtani Inn Tokyo**, 1-6-2 Ōsaki, Shinagawa-ku (☎03/3779-9111, fax 3779-9181). Upmarket business hotel with efficient service and some rooms exclusively for non-smokers and women. Conveniently located right beside the Yamanote line and above a large shopping and restaurant complex. Ōsaki Station. ⑥–⑦.

**New Takanawa Prince Hotel**, 3-13-1 Takanawa, Minato-ku (☎03/3442-1111, fax 3444-1234). Best of the three *Prince* hotels in Shinagawa. The sedate lobby overlooks the elegant gardens created for Prince Takeda and there's a swimming pool in summer. Shinagawa Station. ⑦.

**Hotel Nikkō Tokyo**, 1-9-1 Daiba, Minato-ku (☎03/5500-5500, fax 5500-2525). Beautiful modern works of art adorn the walls, and there are great views of the Rainbow Bridge and the city across Tokyo Bay. Rooms are spacious and have small balconies. Search out the shoe-shine girl, who has elevated cleaning footwear to a performance art. Daiba Station. ⑦.

**Ryokan Sansuisō**, 2-9-5 Higashi-Gotanda, Shinagawa-ku (☎03/3441-7475, fax 3449-1944). Simple, homely Japanese-style accommodation at this spotless ryokan, which is part of the Japanese Inn Group. Most of the *tatami* rooms are without en-suite bath and there is no food available. A five-minute walk from the station, near the Gotanda Bowling Centre. Gotanda Station. ③–④.

**Hotel Watson**, 2-26-5 Kami-Ōsaki, Shinagawa-ku (☎03/3490-5566). Decent-sized rooms, with TV and mini-bar, at this sleek business hotel with friendly management. Near the *Blues Alley* club and *tonkatsu* restaurant, *Tonki*. Meguro Station. ⑤.

## Shinjuku

*The following hotels are marked on the maps on p.126 and p.133.*

**Park Hyatt Tokyo**, 3-7-1-2 Nishi-Shinjuku, Shinjuku-ku (☎03/5322-1234, fax 5322-1288). Among the largest hotel rooms in Tokyo, with huge grey marble baths, and laser and CD players. The restaurants and health and fitness centre, all occupying the pinnacles of Tange Kenzō's tower, have breathtaking views on all sides. Shinjuku Station. ⑦.

**Tokyo Hilton Hotel**, 6-6-2 Nishi-Shinjuku, Shinjuku-ku (☎03/3344-5111, fax 3342-6094). In the slinky, wave-like building behind the more traditional skyscrapers of Nishi-Shinjuku, the *Hilton's* rooms have nice Japanese design touches, such as *shōji* (paper screens) on the windows. Renowned for its buffet breakfast (¥3200), lunch (¥2500) and afternoon tea spreads (¥1700). Shinjuku Station. ⑦.

**Tokyo Yoyogi Youth Hostel**, 3-1 Kamizonochō, Shibuya-ku (☎03/3467-9163, fax 3467-9417). Single rooms only at this comfortable, good-value hostel which is part of the Olympic Youth Centre, and in a new complex of buildings at the top of the hill. Guests must be out between 9am and 4pm, and there's a vague 10pm curfew. Book well in advance. Sangūbashi Station. ①.

**Tokyo YWCA Sadohara**, 3-1-1 Ichigaya-Sadoharachō, Shinjuku-ku (☎03/3268-7313, fax 3268-4452). Women and married couples only can stay in this hostel, with sixteen single rooms, all with toilet (but no bathrooms), and just four twins. There's a shared kitchen, while two twins have their own cooking facilities. Reservations can be made up to one month before. Outside the busy periods (January through February, July and August), special monthly rates may be available on request. Ichigaya Station. ④.

**Washington Hotel**, 3-2-9 Nishi-Shinjuku, Shinjuku-ku (☎03/3343-3111, fax 3340-1804). Upmarket business hotel in the building with the port-hole windows. The lobby is on the third floor, where there are automated check-in machines (as well as humans) dishing out the electronic key cards for the compact, well-equipped, good-value rooms. Shinjuku Station. [5].

# THE CITY

Tokyo's size and confusing layout can make it a bit of a headache for straightforward sightseeing. To keep things simple, we've divided the city into four areas; central Tokyo, northern Tokyo, southern and western Tokyo and bayside Tokyo, each of which can take several days to explore thoroughly.

## Central Tokyo

A vast chunk of **central Tokyo** is occupied by a swathe of green at the core of which sits the **Imperial Palace**, inaccessible, wrapped round with moats and broad avenues. The surrounding public gardens, however, provide a gentle introduction to the city with a glance back to its origins as a castle town. More recent history continues to stir debate at Yasukuni-jinja, north of the palace, where the nation's war dead are remembered at a solemn shrine.

East of the palace, the city really gets into its stride. **Yūrakuchō**, **Ginza** and **Nihombashi** may be lacking in aesthetic appeal but these districts form the heart of downtown Tokyo, with the city's biggest concentration of department stores, theatres and cinemas, its financial centre and major train station, let alone enough bars and restaurants to last a lifetime. The best approach is simply to wander, but there are several specific sights, notably a clutch of art museums and the new Tokyo International Forum with its soaring, glass atrium.

North of the palace, **Kanda**'s historic shrines, and the nearby bookshop district of **Jimbōchō** or the gardens of **Suidōbashi**, won't be on anyone's must-see list, though they all merit a quick look in passing. However, neighbouring **Akihabara**, dubbed Tokyo's silicon city, is a much livelier place, crammed with cut-price electronic goodies. And from Akihabara it's a short hop east across the Sumida-gawa to **Ryōgoku**, not only the Mecca of sumo but also home to the ultra-modern, highly informative **Edo–Tokyo Museum** which celebrates the city's history since the seventeenth century.

After a hard day's work, the bureaucrats and politicians from Kasumigaseki and Nagatachō head for **Akasaka**, the glitzy entertainment district south of the Imperial Palace, and home to many of Tokyo's luxury hotels, while a younger generation of Japanese and *gaijin* party down in **Roppongi**, to the west. Both these areas also have their day-time attractions, although none deserve more than second billing on any tour of the city. **Tokyo Tower** has long since been out-done on the height stakes, but on a clear day it still commands an impressive view of the bay area. Nearby **Zōjō-ji**, once the temple of the Tokugawa clan, has a long history, as does Akasaka's premier shrine **Hie-jinja**, with its attractive avenue of red *torii*.

### Imperial Palace and around

The natural place to start exploring Tokyo is the **Imperial Palace**, home to the Emperor and his family, and the city's geographical and spiritual heart. Well-hidden behind the old castle's massive, stone ramparts and a wall of trees, the palace itself is off-limits, but parts of its grounds have been hived off as public parks, providing a

## CENTRAL TOKYO

| | | |
|---|---|---|
| **Imperial Palace** | *Kōkyo* | 皇居 |
| Higashi Gyoen | *Higashi Gyoen* | 東御苑 |
| Kitanomaru-kōen | *Kitanomaru-kōen* | 北の丸公園 |
| National Museum of Modern Art | *Kokuritsu Kindai Bijutsukan* | 国立近代美術館 |
| Yasukuni Jinja | *Yasukuni-jinja* | 靖国神社 |
| | | |
| **Hibiya** | *Hibiya* | 日比谷 |
| Idemitsu Museum of Arts | *Idemitsu Bijutsukan* | 出光美術館 |
| Tokyo International Forum | *Tōkyō Kokusai Fōramu* | 東京国際フォーラム |
| Yūrakuchō | *Yūrakuchō* | 有楽町 |
| | | |
| **Ginza** | *Ginza* | 銀座 |
| Bridgestone Museum of Art | *Burijisuton Bijutsukan* | ブリジストン美術館 |
| Kabuki-za | *Kabuki-za* | 歌舞伎座 |
| Nihon-shu Centre | *Nihon-shu Sentā* | 日本州センター |
| Sony Building | *Sonii Biru* | ソニービル |
| | | |
| **Nihombashi** | *Nihombashi* | 日本橋 |
| Kite Museum | *Tako no Hakubutsukan* | 凧の博物館 |
| Mitsukoshi | *Mitsukoshi* | 三越 |
| Tokyo Stock Exchange | *Tōkyō Shōken Torihikijo* | 東京証券取引所 |
| Yamatane Museum of Art | *Yamatane Bijutsukan* | 山種美術館 |
| | | |
| **North of the Imperial Palace** | | |
| Akihabara | *Akihabara* | 秋葉原 |
| Jimbōchō | *Jimbōchō* | 神保町 |
| Kanda | *Kanda* | 神田 |
| Kanda Myōjin | *Kanda Myōjin* | 神田明神 |
| Koishikawa-Kōrakuen | *Koishikawa-Kōrakuen* | 小石川後楽園 |
| Nikolai Cathedral | *Nikorai-dō* | ニコライ堂 |
| Ochanomizu | *Ochanomizu* | 御茶の水 |
| Suidōbashi | *Suidōbashi* | 水道橋 |
| Tokyo Dome | *Tōkyō Dōmu* | 東京ドーム |
| Yushima Seidō | *Yushima Seidō* | 湯島聖堂 |
| | | |
| **Akasaka** | *Akasaka* | 赤坂 |
| Akasaka Detached Palace | *Geihinkan* | 迎賓館 |
| Hie-jinja | *Hie-jinja* | 日枝神社 |
| Suntory Museum of Art | *Santorii Bijutsukan* | サントリー美術館 |
| Toyokawa Inari shrine | *Toyokawa Inari-jinja* | 豊川稲荷神社 |
| | | |
| **Roppongi** | *Roppongi* | 六本木 |
| Ark Hills | *Āku Hiruzu* | アークヒルズ |
| Nogi-jinja | *Nogi-jinja* | 乃木神社 |
| Tokyo Tower | *Tōkyō Tawā* | 東京タワー |
| Zōjō-ji | *Zōjō-ji* | 増上寺 |
| | | |
| **Ryōgoku** | *Ryōgoku* | 両国 |
| Edo–Tokyo Museum | *Edo–Tōkyō Hakubutsukan* | 江戸東京博物館 |
| National Sumo Stadium | *Kokugikan* | 国技館 |

green lung for the city centre. Most attractive of these is **Higashi Gyoen**, site of the castle's main keep, while to its north **Kitanomaru-kōen** has a mixed collection of museums and makes a pleasant approach to Japan's most controversial shrine, **Yasukuni-jinja**.

## The Imperial Plaza

Vast and windswept, the **Imperial Plaza** forms a protective island in front of the modern royal palace. In earlier times the shoguns' most trusted followers were allowed to build their mansions here, but after 1899 the area was razed to make way for today's austere expanse of spruce lawns and manicured pine trees. The primary reason to follow the groups of local tourists straggling across the broad avenues is to view one of the palace's most photogenic corners, where two bridges span the moat and a jaunty little watchtower perches on its grey stone pedestal beyond; if you're lucky, you'll catch the scene framed in a fringe of fresh green willow while swans glide majestically by. Though this double bridge, **Nijūbashi**, is a late-nineteenth-century embellishment, the

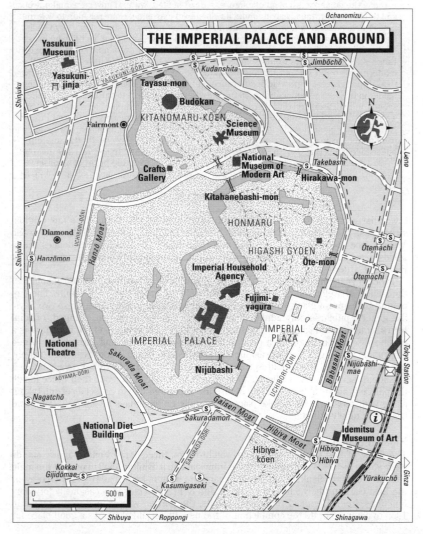

## DESCENDANTS OF THE SUN GODDESS

Japan's imperial family is the world's longest reigning dynasty; Emperor Akihito, the 125th incumbent of the Chrysanthemum throne, officially traces his ancestry back to 660 BC and Emperor Jimmu, great-great-grandson of the Sun Goddess Amaterasu (see Religion p.781). Until this century, emperors – there have been few empresses – were regarded as living deities whom ordinary folk were forbidden to set eyes on, or even hear. But on 15 August 1945, a stunned nation listened to the radio as Emperor Hirohito's quavering voice announced Japan's surrender to the allies, and a few months later he declared that emperors no longer held divine status.

Today the emperor is a symbolic figure, a head of state with no governmental power, and the family is gradually abandoning its cloistered existence. Emperor Akihito was the first to benefit: as crown prince, he had an American tutor and studied at Tokyo's elite Gakushuin University, followed by a stint at Oxford University; then, in 1959, he broke further with tradition by marrying a commoner he met on the tennis court – though Empress Michiko comes from an impeccable family. Their children have continued the modernizing trend without denting the public's deep respect for the imperial family, though polls reveal a growing indifference and the more radical papers are becoming bolder in their scandal-mongering. In the most serious incident to date, Prince Akishino, second in line, was forced to deny allegations of being on "intimate" terms with a Thai woman. And Princess Masako, a gifted former diplomat now married to Crown Prince Naruhito, has been the subject of unusually severe criticism – for impudently walking in front of her husband and for speaking too much at a press conference. Pretty tame stuff, but the feeling is that there's a power struggle going on behind the scenes and that the royal wives, rather than the Emperor or his sons, are bearing the brunt of a conservative backlash against the albeit very gentle moves to modernize Japan's imperial institution.

tower dates back to the seventeenth century and is one of the castle's few original structures. The present palace is a long, sleek, 1960s structure, built to replace the Meiji palace burnt down in the 1945 bombing raids. The imperial residences themselves are tucked away beyond another moat in the thickly wooded, westernmost Fukiage Garden.

Twice a year (on December 23, the Emperor's official birthday, and on January 2) thousands of well-wishers file across Nijūbashi to greet the royal family, lined-up behind bullet-proof glass, with a rousing cheer of *Banzai*. Apart from these two days, the general public is only admitted to the palace grounds on pre-arranged, **official tours**, conducted in Japanese. The tours are a bit of a hassle to get on, but there is a certain fascination in taking a peek inside this secret world, and the pre-tour video shows tantalizing glimpses of vast function rooms and esoteric court rituals. To apply, phone the Imperial Household Agency (☎03/3213-1111 ext 485; Mon–Fri 9am–noon & 1–4.30pm) several days in advance to make a reservation, then go to their office inside the palace grounds at least one day before the appointed day to collect a permit, taking along your passport. Tours take place twice daily on weekdays (10am & 1.30pm) and last about ninety minutes.

### Higashi Gyoen

The finest of Edo Castle's remaining watchtowers, three-tiered Fujimi-yagura, stands clear above the trees to the north of the Imperial Plaza. Built in 1659 to protect the main citadel's southern flank, these days it ornaments what is known as **Higashi Gyoen**, or the East Garden (daily 9am–4pm except Mon & Fri; also closed occasionally for court functions; free). Hemmed round with moats, the garden was opened to the public in 1968 to commemorate the completion of the new Imperial Palace. It's a good place for a stroll, though there's little to evoke the former glory of the shoguns' castle beyond several formidable gates and the towering, granite walls.

The main gate to the garden, and formerly to Edo Castle itself, is **Ōte-mon**; from the Imperial Plaza follow the moat northwards, joining the stream of joggers circling the palace's five-kilometre perimeter, to the first bridge on your left. Two other gates are also in use – **Hirakawa-mon** and **Kitahanebashi-mon**, both to the north; on entry you'll be given a numbered token to hand in again as you leave. These gates were all built in the highly effective *masu-gata* design; a narrow outer gate and wider inner gate are set at right angles to each other, creating a square enclosure within which the invaders could be held and picked off at leisure from the containing walls.

Inside Ōte-mon, don't be put off by the violent screams carrying over the fence (next door is the Imperial Guards' martial arts hall), but press on to the first building ahead on the right. This small **museum** (free) exhibiting just a tiny fraction of the 6000 artworks in the imperial collection is worth a quick look. Just beyond it, you might also want to pop into the shop for a **map** of the garden (¥150).

From here a path winds gently up, beneath the walls of the main citadel, and then climbs more steeply towards **Shiomizaka**, the Tide-Viewing Slope, from where it was once possible to gaze out over Edo Bay rather than the concrete blocks of Ōtemachi. You emerge on a flat grassy area, empty apart from the stone foundations of **Honmaru** (the "inner citadel"), with fine views from the top, and a scattering of modern edifices, among them the bizarre, mosaic-clad **Imperial Music Hall**. Designed by Imai Kenji, the hall commemorates the sixtieth birthday of the then empress in 1963 and is used for occasional performances of court music.

## Kitanomaru-kōen

The northern citadel of Edo Castle is now occupied by **Kitanomaru-kōen**, a park worth checking out for its two museums. On the main road to the right of the park entrance, the **National Museum of Modern Art** (Tues–Sun 10am–5pm; ¥420) kicks off with an impressive display of twentieth-century Japanese art. Its top floors show works from the permanent collection, rotated regularly, while temporary exhibitions are held downstairs. More interesting is the museum's annexe, the **Crafts Gallery** (same hours), included in the ticket price, which lies about five minutes' walk to the west. Housed in a neo-gothic, red-brick pile, the gallery exhibits a selection of top quality, traditional Japanese crafts, many of them by modern masters. Erected in 1910 as headquarters of the Imperial Guards, this is one of very few Tokyo buildings dating from before the Great Earthquake of 1923.

Back beside the entrance to Kitanomaru-kōen, a white concrete lattice-work building houses the **Science Museum** (daily 9.30am–4.50pm; ¥600). Aimed at kids in their early teens or younger, it's often inundated with school parties, but some of the interactive displays are a lot of fun, and worth exploring if you can afford the hefty entry fee. It's best to start with the newer exhibits on the fifth floor and work your way down, stopping to step inside a giant bubble or chat on a video phone. Most things are self-explanatory and there's a fairly decent English guidebook.

The park's last major building is the **Budōkan** martial arts hall, built in 1964 to host Olympic judo events. The design, with its graceful, curving roof and gold top-knot, pays homage to a famous octagonal hall in Nara's Hōryū-ji temple, though supposedly there's a strong hint of Fuji as well. Today the huge arena is used for sports meetings, graduation ceremonies and, most famously, big-name rock concerts – The Beatles played here in 1966.

## Yasukuni-jinja

Across the road from the lighthouse an over-sized, grey steel *torii*, claiming to be Japan's tallest, marks the entrance to **Yasukuni-jinja**. This **shrine**, whose name means "for the repose of the country", was founded in 1869 to worship supporters of the emperor killed in the run up to the Meiji Restoration. Since then it has expanded to include the legions sacrificed in subsequent wars, in total nearly 2.5 million souls, of whom some two million died in the Pacific War alone; the parting words of kamikaze pilots (see p.722) were said to be "see you at Yasukuni".

Not surprisingly, all sorts of tensions and protests revolve around Yasukuni-jinja. To start with, its foundation was part of a Shinto revival promoting the new emperor and so it became a natural focus for the increasingly aggressive nationalism that ultimately took Japan to war in 1941. Then in 1979, General Tōjō and a number of other Class A war criminals (see History, p.777) were enshrined here, to be honoured along with all the other military dead. Equally controversial are the visits made to Yasukuni by prime ministers on the anniversary of Japan's defeat (August 15) in World War II. Because Japan's post-war Constitution requires the separation of State and religion, ministers have usually maintained they attend as private individuals but in 1985 Nakasone, in typically uncompromising mood, caused an uproar when he signed the visitors' book as Prime Minister.

For many ordinary Japanese, Yasukuni is simply a place to remember family and friends who died in the last, troubled century. Its surprisingly unassuming Worship Hall stands at the end of a long avenue lined with cherry and gingko trees, and through a simple wooden gate. The architecture is classic Shinto styling, solid and unadorned except for two gold imperial chrysanthemums embossed on the main doors.

Since 1882 the land immediately north of the shrine has been occupied by a **military museum** (daily: Mar–Oct 9am–5pm; Jan, Feb, Nov & Dec 9am–4.30pm; ¥300). Most exhibits consist of sad personal possessions – blood-stained uniforms, letters, faded photographs. The most disturbing displays concern the kamikaze pilots and other suicide squads active during the Pacific War. It's hard to miss them: the museum's central hall is dominated by a replica glider, its nose elongated to carry a 1200 kilo bomb, while a spine-chilling, black *kaiten* (manned torpedo) lours to one side.

As an antidote, take a walk through the little Japanese **garden** lying behind the shrine buildings. Just beyond, the sunken enclosure is the venue for a sumo tournament during the shrine's spring festival, when top wrestlers perform under trees laden with cherry blossom. At both the spring and autumn festivals (April 21–23 & Oct 17–19) an imperial messenger presents offerings to the deities at Yasukuni on behalf of the Emperor.

## East of the Imperial Palace

Walk east from the Imperial Palace, across Babasaki Moat, and you're straight into the hurly-burly of downtown Tokyo, among grey-faced office blocks, swanky department stores and streets full of rush-hour crowds, transformed at dusk into neon-lit canyons. It's a compact district, with no dramatic sights, but one where you can happily spend an hour exploring a single high-rise stacked with boutiques and cafés, or rummaging in the backstreets. Even the most anonymous building can yield a speciality store or avant-garde gallery, while some wonderfully atmospheric eating and drinking places lurk under the railway tracks which split the area from north to south.

West of the tracks, **Yūrakuchō** and **Hibiya** are theatre-land, and also where you'll find airline offices and major banks. From here it's a short walk east into **Ginza**, home to some of Tokyo's most exclusive shops and restaurants. Ginza spills northwards along Chūō-dōri, a road lined with department stores culminating in the venerable Mitsukoshi. To the north, Ginza merges with the high-finance district of **Nihombashi**, once the heart of boisterous, low-town Edo, and now the preserve of blue-suited bankers. In the midst of all this **Tokyo Station** turns its old red-brick frontage away from the city to face the Imperial Palace across the ranks of corporate headquarters that populate Marunouchi district.

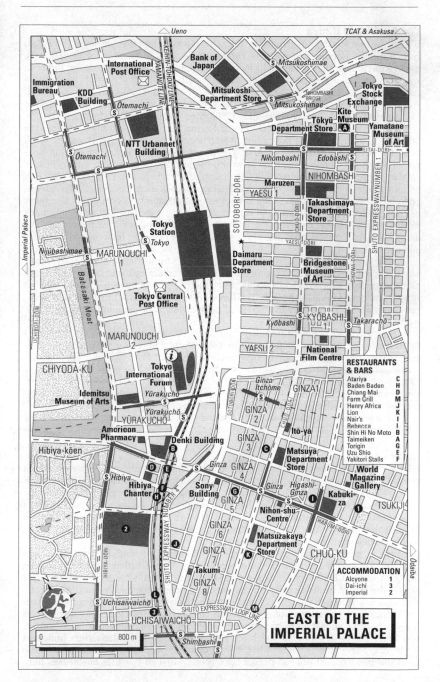

△ Ueno

TCAT & Asakusa △

Immigration Bureau

International Post Office

Bank of Japan

s Mitsukoshimae

KDD Building

Ōtemachi

Mitsukoshi Department Store

Mitsukoshimae

NIHOMBASHI BRIDGE

Tokyo Stock Exchange

Ōtemachi

NTT Urbannet Building

Tōkyū Department Store

Kite Museum

Yamatane Museum of Art

EITAI-DŌRI

Nihombashi

Edobashi s

NIHOMBASHI

Imperial Palace △

Batasaki Moat

Nijūbashimae

MARUNOUCHI 1

Tokyo Station

Tokyo

SOTOBORI-DŌRI

Maruzen

YAESU 1

Takashimaya Department Store

YAESU-DŌRI

SHUTO EXPRESSWAY NUMBER 1

SHOWA-DŌRI

CHUO-DŌRI

Daimaru Department Store

Bridgestone Museum of Art

UCHIBORI-DŌRI

Tokyo Central Post Office

MARUNOUCHI 2

Kyōbashi

S KYŌBASHI

Takaracho

CHIYODA-KU

Tokyo International Forum

YAESU 2

National Film Centre

Idemitsu Museum of Arts

Yūrakuchō

Yūrakuchō

YŪRAKUCHŌ

American Pharmacy

Hibiya-kōen

Denki Building

B

Ginza Itchōme

GINZA 1

Ginza 2

GINZA 3

Ito-ya

C

Matsuya Department Store

## RESTAURANTS & BARS

| | |
|---|---|
| Atariya | C |
| Baden Baden | H |
| Chiang Mai | D |
| Farm Grill | M |
| Henry Africa | J |
| Lion | K |
| Nair's | I |
| Rebecca | B |
| Shin Hi No Moto | A |
| Taimeiken | G |
| Torigin | E |
| Uzu Shio | F |
| Yakitori Stalls | F |

World Magazine Gallery

Hibiya

D

S Hibiya

Hibiya Chanter

E

F

H

Sony Building

G

GINZA 4

Ginza

Higashi-Ginza

Nihon-shu Centre

Kabuki-za

I

TSUKIJI

SHUTO EXPRESSWAY NUMBER 1

HIBIYA-DŌRI

2

GINZA 5

GINZA 6

Matsuzakaya Department Store

K

HARUMI-DŌRI

CHŪ-KU

△ Odaiba

J

GINZA 7

Takumi

GINZA 8

S Uchisaiwaichō

L

## ACCOMMODATION

| | |
|---|---|
| Alcyone | 1 |
| Dai-ichi | 3 |
| Imperial | 2 |

M

UCHISAIWAICHŌ

SHUTO EXPRESSWAY LOOP LINE

3

UCHISAIWAICHŌ 1

0 ——— 800 m

Shimbashi

# EAST OF THE IMPERIAL PALACE

### Yūrakuchō and Hibiya

Within the first few days of arriving in Tokyo most people find themselves in the **Tokyo International Forum**, just north of Yūrakuchō JR Station, heading for the TIC (see p.86). American architect Raphael Viñoly's remarkable building is stunning; the boat-shaped main hall is a sixty-metre-high atrium sheathed in 2600 sheets of "earthquake-resistant" glass, with a ceiling ribbed like a ship's hull, and looks magical at night. If you've got an hour to spare, head for the ground-floor audio-visual hall, where the "Tokyo Multiscope" (hourly 11am–4pm; ¥300) gives a snap-shot introduction to the city.

From the south exit of the International Forum, head west two blocks to find the Imperial Theatre, showing big-budget Western musicals, and above it, on the ninth floor, the **Idemitsu Museum of Arts**. The magnificent collection of mostly Japanese art, of which only a tiny proportion is on show at any one time, includes many historically important pieces, ranging from fine examples of early Jōmon (10,000 BC–300 BC) pottery to Zen Buddhist calligraphy, hand-painted scrolls, richly gilded folding screens and elegant *ukiyo-e* paintings of the late-seventeenth century. The museum also owns valuable collections of Chinese and Korean ceramics, as well as slightly incongruous works by French painter Georges Rouault and American artist Sam Francis. The lounge area is a comfortable place to rest, with views over the Imperial Palace moats and gardens.

Well before the theatres and art galleries, the area immediately south of the castle was occupied by the Tokugawa shoguns' less-favoured *daimyō*, and before that was a muddy inlet of Edo Bay. The land was cleared after 1868, but was too waterlogged to support modern buildings, so in 1903 **Hibiya-kōen**, Tokyo's first European-style park, came into being. These days the tree-filled **park** is a popular lunchtime spot for office-workers and courting couples.

Across the road is the **Imperial**, Tokyo's first Western-style **hotel**. On August 31 1923, the eve of the Great Earthquake, the hotel celebrated the formal opening of their magnificent new building by American architect Frank Lloyd Wright. This famously withstood both the earthquake and the war but eventually fell victim to the 1960s property development boom. Today, just a hint of Wright's style exists in the Old Imperial Bar, with some old tiles and furniture; the original facade and main lobby have been reconstructed in Meiji Mura, near Nagoya (see p.398).

Walk from here onto the main road, Harumi-dōri, and you're immediately into the bright lights of Ginza.

### Ginza

**Ginza**, the "place where silver is minted", took its name after Shogun Tokugawa Ieyasu started making coins here in the early 1600s. It was a happy association – Ginza's Chūō-dōri grew to become Tokyo's most stylish shopping street. Though some of its shine has faded, and cutting-edge fashion has moved elsewhere, Ginza still retains much of its elegance and its undoubted snob appeal. Here you'll find the greatest concentration of exclusive shops, clubs and restaurants in the city, the most theatres and cinemas, and branches of all the major department stores.

Ginza is packed into a mere half-square-kilometre rectangular grid of streets bounded on four sides by the Shuto expressway. Three broad avenues run from north to south, **Chūō-dōri** being the main shopping street, while **Harumi-dōri** cuts across the centre from the east. This unusually regular pattern is due to British architect Thomas Waters, whose task was to create a less combustible city after a fire in 1872 destroyed virtually all of old, wooden Ginza. His "Bricktown", as it was soon known, became an instant tourist attraction, with its rows of two-storey, brick houses, tree-lined avenues, gaslights and brick pavements. But since the airless buildings were totally unsuited to Tokyo's hot, humid climate, people were reluctant to settle until the government offered pepper-corn rents. Most of the first businesses here dealt in foreign wares, and in no time Ginza had become the centre of all that was modern, Western and therefore fashionable – Western dress and hairstyles, watches, cafés and beerhalls.

Bricktown itself didn't survive the Great Earthquake, but Ginza's status was by then well-established. The height of sophistication in the 1930s was simply to stroll around Ginza. The practice still continues, particularly on Sunday afternoons when Chūō-dōri is closed to traffic and everyone turns out for a spot of window-shopping.

In the west, Ginza proper begins at the Sukiyabashi crossing, where Sotobori-dōri and Harumi-dōri intersect. The **Sony Building** (daily 11am–7pm), one of several Ginza landmarks and a popular meeting place, occupying the crossing's southeast corner, is a must for techno-freaks, with six of its eleven stories showcasing the latest Sony gadgets. Continuing east along Harumi-dōri, past Jena bookstore, you'll reach the intersection with Chūō-dōri known as **Ginza Yon-chōme crossing**, which marks the heart of Ginza. Awesome at rush-hour, this spot often features in films and documentaries as the epitome of this overcrowded yet totally efficient city. A number of venerable emporia cluster round the junction. **Wakō**, now an exclusive department store, started life roughly a century ago as the stall of a young, enterprising watch-maker who developed a line called Seiko ("precision"); its clock tower, built in 1894, is one of Ginza's most enduring landmarks. Immediately north of Wakō on Chūō-dōri, Kimuraya bakery was founded in 1874, while Mikimoto Pearl opened next door a couple of decades later. South of the crossing, just beyond the cylindrical, glass San'ai Building, Kyūkyodō is filled with the dusty smell of *sumi-e* ink; this shop has been selling traditional paper, calligraphy brushes and inkstones since 1800.

Heading on east down Harumi-dori, the **Nihon-shu Centre** (daily except Thurs 10.30am–6.30pm; free) provides an interesting diversion with its three floors dedicated to the serious business of making sake (also known as "Nihon-shu"). You can learn about the brewing process, consult a databank covering the thousands of individual producers and, best of all, sample a few varieties, either at the third-floor tasting corner or in the shop downstairs.

From the Centre it's a short hop, depending on your sake consumption, to the **Kabuki-za**, which has been the city's principal Kabuki theatre since its inauguration in 1889. Up until then Kabuki had belonged firmly to the low-brow world of Edo's Shitamachi, but under Meiji it was cleaned-up and relocated to this more respectable district. The original, European-style Kabuki-za made way in 1925 for a Japanese design, of which the present building is a 1950s replica. Performances take place daily during the first three weeks of the month, and a visit is highly recommended; for those who don't want to sit through the whole programme, (which may last up to four hours) one-act tickets are available on the door (see p.160 for details).

If you're looking for somewhere to kill time before the Kabuki, or simply to chill out for a while, head for **World Magazine Gallery** (Mon–Fri 11am–7pm), one block north of the Kabuki-za in Magazine House. The gallery subscribes to 900 magazines from 53 different countries, including a few of the major news weeklies (though no daily papers). You can't take magazines out, but there's a seating area and a small coffee shop on the mezzanine floor

Back on **Chūō-dōri**, heading north, there's little to hold your interest until you reach the **Bridgestone Museum of Art** (Tues–Sun 10am–6pm; Jan–March, Nov & Dec until 5.30pm; ¥500; entrance from Yaesu-dōri). This superb collection focuses on the Impressionists and continues through all the great names of early-twentieth-century European art, plus a highly rated sampler of Meiji-era, Japanese paintings in Western-style. It's not an extensive display, but a rare opportunity to view famous artists such as Renoir, Picasso and Van Gogh close-up and often with hardly anyone else around.

In front of the museum, Yaesu-dōri heads west towards Daimaru department store and the east entrance to **Tokyo Station**, known as the Yaesu entrance. Here you'll find the information desk (see p.86) and Shinkansen tracks, as well as the JR Express Bus ticket office, while limousine buses for Narita and Haneda airports stop across the road outside Daiwa Bank.

Continuing north on Chūō-dōri, a row of cheerful, red awnings on the right-hand side announces another of Tokyo's grand old stores, **Takashimaya**, which dates back to a seventeenth-century kimono shop and is worth popping into for its fabulous old-fashioned lifts. Across the street, **Maruzen** bookstore is a relative upstart, founded in 1869 to import Western texts as part of Japan's drive to modernize and still a good source of foreign-language books.

## Nihombashi

On the northern fringes of central Tokyo, **Nihombashi** ("Bridge of Japan") grew from a cluster of riverside markets in the early seventeenth century to become the city's chief financial district. Once the heart of Edo's teeming Shitamachi (see p.79), the earlier warehouses and money-lenders have evolved into the banks, brokers and trading companies that line the streets today. For most people the prime attraction is Mitsukoshi, one of Tokyo's great department stores, but there are also a couple of interesting museums tucked among the office blocks.

Since 1603, the centre of Nihombashi, and effectively of all Japan, was an arched **bridge** – a favourite of *ukiyo-e* artists – which marked the start of the Tōkaidō, the great road running between Edo and Kyoto. The original wooden bridge has long gone, but distances from Tokyo are still measured from a bronze marker at the halfway point of the present double-span of stone. Prior to the 1964 Olympics the government needed a quick solution to Tokyo's notorious traffic problems; wherever possible they built the new Shuto Expressway over the old waterways still conveniently threading the city and in the process smothered the historic bridge under looming flyovers.

To see what's driving all those salarymen pounding the streets of Tokyo, head east along the river's south bank to the **Tokyo Stock Exchange**. If you visit during trading hours (9–11am & 12.30–3pm), you should see some of the ingenious hand signals used to relay orders – for example, a clerk holding his nose is dealing in Tokyo Gas. There's also a huge amount of information on display, including interactive terminals explaining the stock markets – look out for the silver robot, who obligingly demonstrates a number of hand signals.

Of the dozens of securities companies clustering round the exchange, one of the largest contains the **Yamatane Museum of Art** (Tues–Sun 10am–5pm; ¥700), with a fine collection of post-1868 paintings in the traditional Japanese style, known as *Nihonga*. Selected works, some designated Important Cultural Properties, are beautifully presented in a restful setting of *shōji* screens and soft lighting.

On the way back to central Nihombashi, it's worth tracking down the lively little **Kite Museum** (Mon–Sat 11am–5pm; ¥200) on a backstreet behind Tōkyū department store, above *Taimeiken* restaurant. Since 1977 the restaurant's owner has amassed over two thousand kites of every conceivable shape and size, from no bigger than a postage stamp to a record-breaking monster (14m by 19m).

Back at Nihombashi bridge, head north on Chūō-dōri to find the most traditional of Japan's department stores, **Mitsukoshi**. The shop traces its ancestry back to a dry goods store, opened in 1673 by Mitsui Takatoshi, who revolutionized retailing in Edo and went on to found the Mitsui empire. His methods were simple: fixed prices, goods on display, no credit and continuous innovation. This was the first store in Japan to offer a delivery service, the first to sell imported goods, and the first with an escalator, though until 1923 customers were still required to take off their shoes and don Mitsukoshi slippers. The most interesting part of today's store is the north building, which dates from 1914.

# North of the Imperial Palace

**Kanda**, the region immediately north and west of Nihombashi, straddles Tokyo's crowded eastern lowlands – the former Shitamachi – and the more expansive western hills. The area's scattered sights reflect these contrasting styles, kicking off at **Ochanomizu** with historic Kanda Myōjin, a lively Shinto shrine, and an austere monument to Confucius at Yushima Seidō. Below them lie the frenetic, neon-lit streets of **Akihabara**, the "Electric City" dedicated to technological wizardry. Akihabara is also the jumping-off point for **Ryōgoku**, the heartland of sumo and home to one of the city's most enjoyable museums, over on the east bank of the Sumida-gawa. Heading back westwards, **Suidōbashi** has a couple of minor attractions in Tokyo's foremost baseball stadium and a classic seventeenth-century garden, while a studious hush prevails among the secondhand bookshops of **Jimbōchō**, just to the south.

## Ochanomizu to Akihabara

Kanda's two great shrines lie on the north bank of the Kanda-gawa and are within easy reach of either **Ochanomizu**'s JR or Marunouchi line stations. If you're here in the afternoon, take a quick detour south along Hongō-dōri, to visit the Russian Orthodox **Nikolai Cathedral** (Tues–Sat 1–4pm; free). It's not a large building but its Byzantine flourishes stand out well against the characterless blocks around and the recently refurbished interior positively glows in the soft light. Founded by Archbishop Nikolai Kassatkin, who came to Japan as a missionary in 1861, the cathedral took seven years to complete (1884–1891); the plans were sent from Russia but the British architect Josiah Condor supervised the project and gets most of the credit.

Back at the river, some woods on the north bank hide the distinctive shrine of **Yushima Seidō** (Sat, Sun & hols 10am–5pm, closed 4pm in winter; free), dedicated to the Chinese sage, Confucius. The Seidō (Sacred Hall) was founded in 1632 as an academy for the study of the ancient classics at a time when the Tokugawa were promoting Confucianism as the State's ethical foundation. In 1691 the hall was moved to its present location, where it became an elite school for the sons of *samurai* and high-ranking officials, though most of these buildings were lost in the fires of 1923. Today, the quiet compound contains an eighteenth-century wooden gate and, at the top of broad steps, the Taisen-den, or "Hall of Accomplishments", where Confucius is enshrined. This imposing, black-lacquered building on the far side of a stone-flagged courtyard was rebuilt in 1935 to the original design, whose only adornment is the four tiger-like guardians poised on the roof tiles. Inside, the hall is empty save for a small statue of Confucius.

Follow the road round to the north of Yushima Seidō to find a large, copper *torii* and a cluster of traditional shops, including the famous Amanoya, selling sweet, ginger-laced sake (*amazaké*). Beyond, a vermilion gate marks the entrance to **Kanda Myōjin** (9am–5pm; free), one the city's oldest shrines and host to one of its top three **festivals**, the Kanda Matsuri, which takes place in mid-May every even-numbered year (see p.161). Founded in 730 AD, the shrine originally stood in front of Edo Castle, where it was dedicated to the gods of farming and fishing (Daikoku and Ebisu). Later, the tenth-century rebel Taira no Masakado – who was beheaded after declaring himself emperor – was also enshrined here; according to legend, his head "flew" to Edo where it was honoured as something of a local hero. When Shogun Tokugawa Ieyasu was strengthening the castle's fortifications in 1616, he took the opportunity to move the shrine but mollified Masakado's supporters by declaring him a guardian deity of the city.

Some 500m southeast of Kanda Myōjin, following a road that drops steeply downhill, a blaze of adverts and a cacophony of competing audio-systems announces **Akihabara**. This is Tokyo's foremost discount shopping area for electrical and electronic goods of all kinds, from computers, cameras and car stereos to "washlets" – electronically

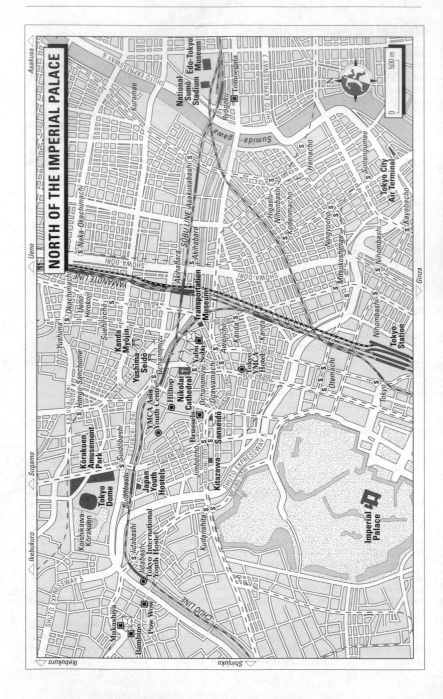

# NORTH OF THE IMPERIAL PALACE

controlled toilet-cum-bidets with an optional medical analysis function. Today's high-tech stores are direct descendants of a post-war blackmarket in radios and radio parts which took place beneath the train tracks around Akihabara Station. You can recapture some of the atmosphere in three narrow passages just southwest of the station, or among the tiny, specialist stalls of **Tokyo Radio Depāto**, three floors stuffed with plugs, wires, boards and tools for making or repairing radios; follow the Sōbu line tracks west from Akihabara Station to find the store just west of Chūō-dōri.

## Ryōgoku

From Akihabara, hop on a Sōbu-line train two stops west across the Sumida-gawa, to **Ryōgoku**, a sort of sumo-town where shops selling outsize clothes and restaurants serve flavourful tureens of *chanko-nabe*, the wrestlers' traditional body-building stew. Three times each year major sumo tournaments fill the **National Sumo Stadium**, outside Ryōgoku Station's west exit, with a two-week pageant of thigh slapping, foot stamping and arcane ritual (see p.67 for more on sumo). If you're in Tokyo at the time – usually the middle fortnight of January, May and September – it's well-worth trying to see a few bouts. At other times of year, you can get a taster at the small, historical **museum** (Mon–Fri 10am–4.30pm; free) beside the stadium or, better still, wander the streets immediately south of the train tracks. Until recently, this area housed many of the major "stables" where wrestlers live and train, but rising land prices have forced most of them out. Nevertheless, there's still a good chance of bumping into some junior wrestlers, in their *yukata* and wooden *geta* with slicked-back hair, popping out to a store or for a quick snack of *chanko-nabe*. If you're feeling peckish yourself, one of the best places to sample this traditional sumo hot-pot packed with tofu and vegetables is *Tomoegata* restaurant (see p.148 for details).

You'll need plenty of stamina for the next stop, the **Edo–Tokyo Museum** (Tues–Sun 10am–6pm, closes 8pm Thurs & Fri; ¥600) in its colossal building plonked behind the Sumo Stadium; the ticket lasts a whole day, so you can come and go. The museum tells the history of Tokyo from the days of the Tokugawa shoguns to post-war reconstruction, using life-size replicas, cut-away models and holograms as well as more conventional screen paintings, ancient maps and documents, with plenty of information in English. Things kick off with a bang on the sixth floor, where a soaring Nihombashi, the "Bridge of Japan" (see p.104), takes you over the roofs of famous Edo landmarks – a Kabuki theatre, *daimyō* residence and Western-style office – on the main exhibition floor below. The displays then run roughly chronologically and are particularly strong on both life in Edo's Shitamachi, with its pleasure quarters, festivals and vibrant popular culture, and on the giddy days after 1868 when Japan opened up to the outside world (see p.82 for more on Tokyo history).

## Suidōbashi

Take the Sōbu line back into central Tokyo, past Akihabara to **Suidōbashi,** where the slides and rides of "Big Egg City" punctuate the skyline. The name comes from its centre-piece, the plump, white roofed **Tokyo Dome**, which is Tokyo's major baseball venue and home ground for both the Yomiuri Giants and Nippon Ham Fighters (see p.166). The Dome's **Baseball Museum** (Tues–Sun 10am–6pm; Jan–March & Oct–Dec closes 5pm; ¥400) is for diehard fans only, who'll appreciate the footage of early games and all sorts of baseball memorabilia, including one of Babe Ruth's jackets.

Tokyo Dome is surrounded by an old-fashioned entertainment complex, plus the inevitable baseball souvenir shops and fast-food outlets. On its west side, **Koishikawa-Kōrakuen** (daily 9am–5pm; ¥300) is a fine example of an early-seventeenth-century stroll-**garden**. Winding paths take you past waterfalls, ponds and stone lanterns down to the shores of a small lake draped with gnarled pines and over daintily humped bridges, where each view replicates a famous beauty spot. Zhu Shun Shui, a refugee scholar from Ming China, advised on the design, so Chinese as well as Japanese landscapes feature, the most obvious being Small Lu-shan, represented by rounded hills of bamboo grass. The garden attracts few visitors but intrusive announcements from Tokyo Dome, looming over the trees, means it's not totally peaceful. The entrance gate lies in the garden's southwest corner, midway between Suidōbashi and Iidabashi stations.

### Jimbōchō

From Suidōbashi hop on the Toei Mita subway one stop, or walk 1km south down Hakusan-dōri to **Jimbōchō**, a lively student centre which is also home to dozens of secondhand **bookshops** around the intersection of Yasukuni-dōri and Hakusan-dōri. You'll find the best ones along the south side of Yasukuni-dōri, in the two main blocks either side of Jimbōchō subway station, where racks of dog-eared novels and textbooks sit outside shops stacked high with dusty tomes. Most of these are in Japanese, but some dealers specialize in English-language books – both new and old – while a bit of rooting around might turn up a volume of old photographs or cartoons in one of the more upmarket antiquarian dealers. Note that many shops close on either Sunday or Monday.

A good place to start is Kitazawa, a smart, English-language bookstore, with an unusually broad selection, to the west of Hakusan-dōri. A few doors further along, Haga – always packed with men pouring over its "adult porn" – marks the end of the district, but it's worth continuing over the next junction to peek in the martial arts specialist, Yomeido, full of bamboo staves, black masks and padded armour. Back at the Hakusan crossing, head east along Yasukuni-dōri to find Matsumura, a small shop selling mostly secondhand foreign art books, and then a rather disappointing Tuttle outlet just where the road begins to curve. Finally, look out for Ōhya Shobō, with a good range of old illustrated books, prints and maps, before reaching the big Sanseidō store with foreign-language books on its fifth floor.

## South and west of the Imperial Palace

To the west of the Imperial Palace, beside the government areas of Kasumigaseki and Nagatachō, where you'll find the **National Diet**, Japan's parliament, is **Akasaka**. This was once an agricultural area (*akane*, plants that produce a red dye were farmed here, hence the area's name, which means "red slope"). It developed as an entertainment district in the late nineteenth century, when *ryōtei* restaurants, complete with performing *geisha*, started opening to cater for the modern breed of politicians and bureaucrats. The area still has its fair share of exclusive establishments, shielded from the hoi poloi by high walls and even higher prices. Their presence, along with the headquarters of the TBS TV station and some of Tokyo's top hotels, lend the area a degree more glamour than it perhaps deserves. Don't be put off exploring Akasaka's colourful streets at night, since the prices at many of the restaurants and bars are no worse than elsewhere in Tokyo.

### National Diet Building

Physically raised above the civil servants of Kasumigaseki, on a hill in neighbouring Nagatachō, are the politicians in the **National Diet Building**. This squat, three-story affair, dominated by a central tower block decorated with pillars and a pyramid-shaped roof, is supposedly based on the Senate Building in Washington DC – though Japan's style of government has more in common with the British parliamentary system. On the left stands the House of Representatives, the main body of government, while on the right is the House of Councillors, which approximates to the UK's House of Lords.

Forty-minute **tours** of this side of the Diet are available free (Mon–Fri, 9.30am–4pm, except when the House of Councillors is in session; call ☎03/3581-3100 to check). Some of the guides speak English and in the actual chamber a taped English commentary is played explaining what you can see. There's an Edwardian-style grandeur to the Diet's interior, especially in the carved-wood debating chamber and the central reception hall, decorated with paintings reflecting the seasons and bronze statues of significant statesmen. You'll have to observe the room the Emperor waits in when he visits the Diet through a glass panel: it's decorated in real gold.

## Akasaka

The main thoroughfare of Akasaka is **Sotobori-dōri**. At its southern end stands a huge stone *torii* gate, beyond which is a picturesque avenue of red *torii* leading up the hill to the **Hie-jinja**, a **shrine** dedicated to the god Oyamakui-no-kami, who is believed to protect against evil. Although the ferroconcrete buildings date from 1967, Hie-jinja's history stretches back to 830, when it was first established on the outskirts of what would become Edo. The shrine's location shifted a couple more times before it came to rest on its current hill-top site. Shogun Tokugawa Ietsuna placed it here in the seventeenth century as a source of protection for his castle (now the site of the Imperial Palace). Today, Hie-jinja hosts the Sanno Matsuri, one of Tokyo's most important **festivals**, every June (June 10–16). The highlight is a parade on June 15 involving four hundred participants dressed in Heian period costume and carrying fifty sacred *mikoshi* (portable shrines).

The front entrance to the shrine is actually through the large stone *torii* on the east side of the hill, beside the *Capitol Tōkyū Hotel*. Fifty-one steps lead up to a large enclosed courtyard, in which roosters roam freely and salarymen bunk off work to idle on benches. To the left of the main shrine, look for the carving of a female monkey cradling its baby, a symbol that has come to signify protection for pregnant women.

Heading north from the shrine along Sotobori-dōri and across Benkei-bashi, the bridge that spans what was once the outer moat of the shogun's castle, you'll soon reach the **New Ōtani** hotel. Within its grounds is a beautiful traditional Japanese **garden**, originally designed for the *daimyō* Kato Kiyomasa, lord of Kumamoto in Kyūshū, over four hundred years ago. You can stroll freely through the garden or admire it while sipping tea in the *New Ōtani's* lounge. The hotel also has its own small **art gallery** (Tues–Sun 10am–6pm; ¥500, free to guests), with works from Japanese and European artists, including Chagall and Modigliani, and a tea ceremony room, where tea (¥1,050) is served in the traditional way from Thursday to Saturday between 11am and 4pm. The top-floor bars and restaurants of this hotel and the neighbouring *Akasaka Prince* and *ANA* have spectacular views of the city, especially at night with the explosion of neon and the twisting ribbon of the Shuto Expressway, flowing like a yellow river.

Returning across the Benkei-bashi, beside the Akasaka Mitsuke intersection, is the Suntory Building, which houses the elegant **Suntory Museum of Art** on the eleventh floor (Tues–Sun 10am–5pm, Fri 10am–7pm; ¥500 or more depending on exhibition). As well as changing exhibitions of ceramics, lacquerware, paintings and textiles, the museum has a traditional tea ceremony room, where tea and sweets are served for around ¥300.

Walking from the museum up Aoyama-dōri you'll soon encounter the colourful **Toyokawa Inari** (also known as Myogon-ji), an example of a combined temple and shrine, which was much more common across Japan before the Meiji government forcibly separated Shinto and Buddhist places of worship. The temple's compact precincts are decked with red lanterns and banners and the main hall is guarded by statues of pointy-eared foxes – the messengers of the Shinto god Inari, found at all Inari shrines – wearing red bibs.

Toyokawa Inari borders the extensive grounds of the grand, European-style **Akasaka Detached Palace** (Geihinkan), which serves as the official State Guest House. When it was completed in 1909, this vast building, modelled after Buckingham Palace on the outside and Versailles on the inside, only had one bathroom in the basement and the empress's apartments were in a separate wing from her husband's; this was fine by the emperor since he was in the habit of taking his nightly pick from the ladies-in-waiting. Some members of the imperial family, including the Crown Prince, still live within the grounds of the palace, which, unfortunately, puts it off limits to humble visitors.

## Roppongi

Roppongi's rather minor daytime attractions lie at its outer edges. Beside the Roppongi exit of the Nogizaka subway station is **Nogi-jinja**, a small **shrine** honouring the Meiji-era General Nogi Maresuke, a hero in both the Sino-Japanese and Russo-Japanese wars. When the Emperor Meiji died, Nogi and his wife followed the *samurai* tradition and committed suicide in his house within the shrine grounds. The best time to visit the shrine is on the second Sunday of every month, when it hosts an antique flea market.

Around 1km southeast of Nogi-jinja is the **Ark Hills** complex, which houses the *ANA hotel* and the classical music venue **Suntory Hall**, reputed to have the best accoustics in the city. Behind Ark Hills and next to the *Hotel Ōkura*, is the **Ōkura Shūkokan** (Tues–Sun 10am–4.30pm; ¥500, free to hotel guests), an **art museum** established in 1917 by the self-styled Baron Ōkura Tsuruhiko. This Chinese-style building is looking a little worse for wear, but inside, its two floors display intriguing oriental ceramics, paintings prints and sculptures from a collection of over 1700 traditional works of art.

Heading down from the *Hotel Ōkura* to Sakurada-dōri, past Kamiyachō subway station and up the hill will bring you to **Tokyo Tower** (daily: March–Nov 9am–8pm, except Aug until 9pm; Jan, Feb & Dec 9am–6pm; main observatory ¥800; top observatory ¥1400). Built during an era when Japan was becoming famous for producing cheap copies of foreign goods, the 333-metre vermilion tower opened in 1958, and managed to top its Parisienne role model by several metres. The top observation deck is, at 250m, still the highest viewpoint in Tokyo and is reputed to attract 10,000 visitors a day – impressive given that Tokyo is now littered with skyscrapers, many of which provide their views for free (or at least for the price of a drink). More attractions have been added over the years, including an aquarium (¥1000), a wax works (¥850) and a holographic "Mystery Zone" (¥400), as well as the usual souvenir shops – to the point where the place feels more like an amusement arcade than the Eiffel Tower. Unless it's an exceptionally clear day, you're better off saving your cash.

## On to Zōjō-ji

Tokyo Tower stands on the eastern flank of Shiba-kōen, a park whose main point of interest is **Zōjō-ji**, the family **temple** of the Tokugawa clan. Zōjō-ji dates from 1393 and was moved to this site in 1598 by Tokugawa Ieyasu (the first Tokugawa shogun) in order to spiritually protect southeast Edo and provide a way-station for pilgrims approaching the capital from the Tōkaidō road. This was once the city's largest holy site, with 48 sub-temples and over a 100 other buildings. Since the fall of the Tokugawa, however, Zōjō-ji has been raised to the ground by fire three times, and virtually all of the current buildings date from the mid-1970s. The main remnant of the past is the imposing **San-gadetsu-mon**, a 21-metre-high gateway dating from 1612 and the oldest wooden structure in Tokyo. The name translates as "Three Deliverences Gate"

(Buddhism is supposed to save believers from the evils of anger, greed and stupidity) and the gate is one of the nation's Important Cultural Properties. Ahead lies the Taiden (Great Main Hall), the temple building often in the foreground of many postcard images of Tokyo Tower. To the right are ranks of Jizō statues, capped with red bonnets and decorated with plastic flowers and colourful windmills that twirl in the breeze. Amid this army of mini-guardians lie the remains of six shoguns, behind a wrought-iron gate decorated with dragons.

# Northern Tokyo

The northern districts of Tokyo are where you'll find the city at its most traditional, harking back to a world before the bright lights and high-tech commercialism of Ginza and Shinjuku. Nowhere is this more obvious than among the craftshops and neighbourhood restaurants of **Asakusa**, a must on any visit to Tokyo, and in the constant festival atmosphere around its magnificent temple, **Sensō-ji**.

| NORTHERN TOKYO | | |
|---|---|---|
| **Asakusa** | *Asakusa* | 浅草 |
| Asakusa-jinja | *Asakusa-jinja* | 浅草神社 |
| Dembō-in | *Dembō-in* | 伝法院 |
| Kappabashi-dōgu-gai | *Kappabashi dōgu-gai* | かっぱ橋道具街 |
| Sensō-ji | *Sensō-ji* | 浅草寺 |
| Sumida-kōen | *Sumida-kōen* | 隅田公園 |
| | | |
| **Ueno** | *Ueno* | 上野 |
| Ameyoko-chō | *Ameyoko-chō* | アメ横丁 |
| National Museum of Western Art | *Kokuritsu Seiyō Bijutsukan* | 国立西洋美術館 |
| National Science Museum | *Kokuritsu Kagaku Hakubutsukan* | 国立科学博物館 |
| Shitamachi Museum | *Shitamachi Fūzoku Shiryōkan* | 下町風俗資料館 |
| Tokudai-ji | *Tokudai-ji* | 徳大寺 |
| Tokyo Bunka Kaikan | *Tōkyō Bunka Kaikan* | 東京文化会館 |
| Tokyo National Museum | *Tōkyō Kokuritsu Hakubutsukan* | 東京国立博物館 |
| Tōshō-gū | *Tōshō-gū* | 東照宮 |
| Ueno Park | *Ueno-kōen* | 上野公園 |
| Ueno Zoo | *Ueno Dōbutsuen* | 上野動物園 |
| | | |
| **Along the Yamanote line** | | |
| Kōgan-ji | *Kōgan-ji* | 高岩寺 |
| Kōshinzuka Station | *Kōshinzuka-eki* | 庚申塚 |
| Rikugi-en | *Rikugi-en* | 六義園 |
| Sugamo | *Sugamo* | 巣鴨 |
| Toden Arakawa Line | *Toden Arakawa sen* | 都電荒川線 |
| | | |
| **Ikebukuro** | *Ikebukuro* | 池袋 |
| Amlux | *Amurakkusu* | アムラックス |
| Metropolitan Art Space | *Tōkyō Geijutsu Gekijō* | 東京芸術劇場 |
| Rikkyō University | *Rikkyō Daigaku* | 立教大学 |
| Sezon Museum of Art | *Sezon Bijutsukan* | セゾン美術館 |

East of Asakusa, **Ueno** is best known for its park and museums, including the flagship Tokyo National Museum offering a comprehensive romp through Japanese art history. The Yamanote line loops east from Ueno past Rikugi-en, a serene classical garden, and Sugamo, famous for its quirky, old-peoples' shopping street, before grinding into **Ikebukuro**. With its huge department stores and entertainment district, Ikebukuro is a downmarket version of Shinjuku and Shibuya. Despite its lack of sophistication, it's an area worth exploring – if only for its cheap accommodation (see p.93) and discount shops.

## Asakusa

Last stop on the Ginza line heading north, **Asakusa** is best-known as the site of Tokyo's most venerable Buddhist temple, **Sensō-ji**, whose towering worship hall is a continual throng of petitioners and holiday-makers. Stalls before the temple cater to the crowds, peddling trinkets and keepsakes as they have done for centuries, while old-fashioned craftshops display exquisite hair combs, paper fans and calligraphy brushes, and all around are the inevitable array of restaurants, drinking places and fast-food stands. It's this infectious, carnival atmosphere that makes Asakusa so appealing; this is the area of Tokyo where you'll find most vivid reminders of Edo's Shitamachi and the popular culture it spawned, and one which seems to be constantly in the throes of some celebration or other. The biggest bash is the Sanja Matsuri (see p.114), but there are numerous smaller festivals, so it's worth asking at the tourist information if there's anything in the offing.

One of the best ways to get to Asakusa is by **riverboat**, following the Sumida-gawa north from Hama Rikyū Teien or Hinode Pier (see p.89 for details) to dock under Azuma Bridge, across the river from Phillipe Starck's eye-catching Asahi Brewery Building, its rooftop flame looking more like a golden turd. Leaving Asakusa by river, boats depart roughly every forty minutes from the same landing stage (daily 9.50am–6.15pm, Sat & Sun last boat 6.55pm; ¥620 to Hama Rikyū Teien, ¥660 to Hinode Pier), though note that 2.45pm is the last departure stopping at Hama Rikyū Teien.

### Sensō-ji

Walking west from the river or the Ginza line subway station, you can't miss the solid, red-lacquer gate with its monstrous paper lantern that marks the southern entrance to **Sensō-ji**. This magnificent **temple**, also known as Asakusa Kannon, was founded in the mid-seventh century to enshrine a tiny golden image of Kannon, the Goddess of Mercy, caught in the nets of two local fishermen. Though most of the present buildings are post-war, concrete reconstructions, there's a great sense of atmosphere as you draw near the main hall with its sweeping, tiled roofs. Before heading into the temple grounds, cross over to the helpful **Asakusa Information Centre** (daily 9.30am–8pm) to see if there are any special events going on.

A colourful parade of small shops lines the main approach to the shrine, through the great **Kaminari-mon** or "Thunder Gate", named for its two vigorous guardian gods of Thunder and Wind (Raijin and Fūjin). Every spare inch of Nakamise-dōri is packed with merchandise, whether it's gaudy souvenirs, tiny traditional dolls, kimono accessories, or *sembei* rice crackers in sweet-scented piles. Street vendors gather round the temple, especially at weekends and during the Hagoita-ichi fair (Dec 17–19), when dozens of stalls selling *hagoita* – battledores decorated with the plump, appliquéd torsos of Kabuki stars – make a dramatic display.

At the north end of the approach, a double-storied treasure gate, **Hōzō-mon**, stands astride the entrance to the main temple complex; the treasures, fourteenth-century Chinese sutras, are locked away on the upper floor. Its two protective gods – *Niō*, the traditional guardians of Buddhist temples – are even more imposing than those at

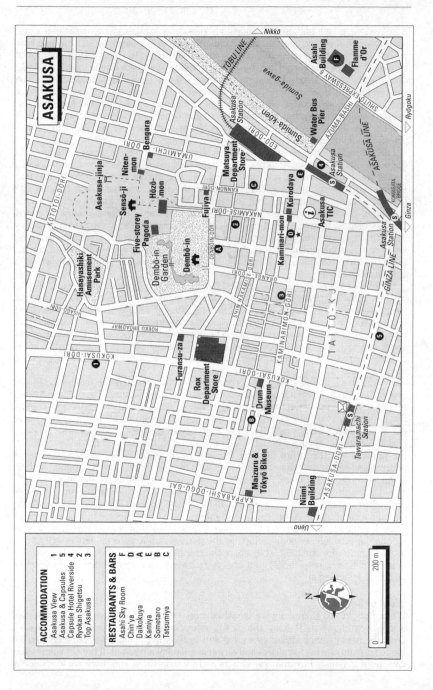

**ASAKUSA**

0    200 m

Kaminari-mon; look out for their enormous rice-straw sandals slung on the gate's rear wall. Beyond, there's a constant crowd clustered around a large, bronze incense bowl where people waft the pungent smoke – breath of the gods – over themselves for its supposed curative powers. There's nothing much to see inside the temple itself, since the little Kannon – said to be just three inches tall – is a *hibutsu*, a hidden image considered too holy to be on view. The hall however is full of life: the rattle of coins tossed into a huge wooden coffer, swirling plumes of incense smoke, the constant bustle of people coming to pray, buy charms and fortune papers or to attend a service. Three times a day (6am, 10am & 2pm) drums echo through the hall into the courtyard as priests chant sutras beneath the altar's gilded canopy.

Like many Buddhist temples, Sensō-ji accommodates Shinto shrines in its grounds, the most important being **Asakusa-jinja**, dedicated to the two fishermen brothers who netted the Kannon image, and their overlord. The shrine was founded in the mid-seventeenth century by Tokugawa Iemitsu and this is the original building, though it's hard to tell under all the restored paintwork. More popularly known as Sanja-sama, "shrine of the three guardians", this is the focus of the tumultuous **Sanja Matsuri**, Tokyo's biggest **festival**, which takes place every year on the third weekend in May. The climax comes on the second day when over one hundred *mikoshi* (portable shrines) are manhandled through the streets of Asakusa by a seething crowd, among them the three *mikoshi* of Asakusa-jinja, each weighing around 1000kg and carried by at least seventy men.

Sensō-ji's eastern entrance is guarded by the attractively aged **Niten-mon**, its plain wooden pillars spattered with votive papers traditionally left by Shinto pilgrims. Originally built in 1618, this gate is all that remains of a shrine honouring Tokugawa Ieyasu which was relocated to Ueno in 1651 after a series of fires. Niten-mon has since been rededicated and now houses two seventeenth-century Buddhist guardians of the south and east. The road heading east leads to a narrow strip of park, **Sumida-kōen**; the river here provides the stage for one of the great summer firework displays (*han-abi taikai*) held in late July or early August.

Walking back across the temple grounds from Niten-mon, make for the five-storey pagoda on the far western side of the courtyard. The reconstructed pagoda, which shelters bone fragments of the Buddha, is now part of the Chief Abbot's residence. Though the monastery is usually closed to the public, you can go as far as the ground floor office to obtain an entry-pass for **Dembō-in garden** (daily 10am–3pm; occasionally closed for special events; free). The office is through the door on the left as you face the pagoda, and then third door on the left; you'll be asked to register your name, address and signature before being issued with the pass. The garden entrance is about 200m away, through a large, black gate on the garden's south side. Inside, go straight ahead through a second gate and hand in your pass at the office facing you – it's often difficult to attract someone's attention. All this effort is rewarded with a secluded garden and a classic view of the pagoda and monastery roofs reflected in its central pond.

On leaving Dembō-in, turn right to take a quick look at a little **shrine** dedicated to racoon dogs, which are oddly deified as the gods of public entertainers as well as protecting against fire and theft. They share the compound with a Jizō statue, the guardian deity of children, resplendent in a cherry-red beret and surrounded by a cluster of infants in matching attire.

## West of Sensō-ji

When Kabuki and Bunraku were banished from central Edo in the 1840s they settled in the area known as **Rokku**, (Block 6), between Sensō-ji and today's Kokusai-dōri. Over the next century almost every fad and fashion in popular entertainment started life here, from cinema to cabaret and striptease. Today a handful of the old venues survive, most famously **Furansu-za**, with its nightly strip-show, and there are loads of cinemas, *pachinko* parlours and drinking dives. It's not all low-brow though; next door to Furansu-za they still perform *rakugo*, a centuries-old form of comic monologue where familiar jokes and stories are mixed with modern satire.

A wide avenue called Kokusai-dōri forms the western boundary of Rokku. Near its southerly junction with Kaminarimon-dōri, across from the Rox department store, **Miyamato Unosuke Shōten** (daily except Tues 9am–6pm) is easily identifiable from the elaborate *mikoshi* in the window. The shop is an Aladdin's cave of traditional Japanese percussion instruments and festival paraphernalia: masks, happi coats, flutes, cymbals and, of course, all kinds of *mikoshi*, the largest with a price tag over ¥3 million. Since 1861, however, the family passion has been drums, resulting in an impressive collection from around the world which now fills the fourth floor **Drum Museum** (Wed–Sun 10am–5pm; ¥300). Wood, clay, metal, hide, there's every type of percussion material and, best of all, you are allowed to have a go on some: a red dot on the name card indicates those not to be touched; blue dots you can tap lightly, just with your hands; and the rest have the appropriate drumsticks ready waiting.

Continuing westwards from this corner after a few blocks you hit another main road, Kappabashi-dōgu-gai. This is **"Kitchenware Town"**, the best-known of several wholesale markets in northeast Tokyo, where you can kit out a whole restaurant in approximately five hundred metres. You don't have to be a bulk-buyer, however, and this is a great place to pick up unusual souvenirs, such as the plastic food displayed outside restaurants to tempt the customer. This practice dates from the last century, originally using wax, but came into its own about thirty years ago when foreign foods were being introduced to a puzzled Japanese market. The best examples are absolutely realistic; try Maizuru or Tokyo Biken for a particularly mouth-watering show. Note that most shops along here close on Sunday.

## Ueno

Most people visit **Ueno** for its **park**, which is one of Tokyo's largest open spaces, and contains a host of museums, including the prestigious **Tokyo National Museum**, plus a few relics from a vast temple complex that once occupied this hilltop. But Ueno also has proletarian, Shitamachi roots and much of its eastern district has a rough and ready feel, especially around the station and the slightly shady markets extending south beside the tracks.

Ueno is well-served by trains and subways, but if you're coming from Asakusa, a novel way of getting here is on a thirty-minute ride by **double-decker tourist bus** (departs every 30min on weekdays; ¥250; see area maps for bus stops). It's slower and more expensive than the Ginza line, but at least you're above ground. However, avoid the bus at weekends and when rush-hour traffic clogs the roads.

### Some history

In 1624 the second shogun, Tokugawa Hidetada, chose Ueno hill for a magnificent temple, rivalling Kyoto's Enryaku-ji (see p.469), to protect his castle's northeast quarter, traditionally the direction of evil forces. **Kan'ei-ji** became the city's prime Buddhist centre, with 36 subtemples extending over nearly 120 hectares. It incorporated the Tokugawa's mortuary temple and a major shrine dedicated to Ieyasu, first of the line, as well as the tombs of six subsequent shōguns. When the Shōgunate collapsed early in 1868, this was the natural place for Tokugawa loyalists to make their last stand, in what became the **battle of Ueno**. Though the shogun had already resigned and the castle surrendered peacefully, roughly two thousand rebel *samurai* occupied Kan'ei-ji until the emperor's army finally attacked. Whether it was fires caused by the shelling or deliberate arson on either side, nearly all the temple buildings were destroyed; ironically Ieyasu's shrine was spared.

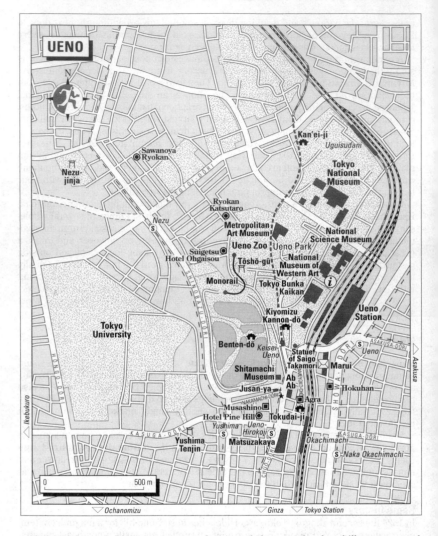

In 1873 the new Meiji government designated the now desolate hilltop as one of Tokyo's first five **public parks**. Ten years later, a station was built nearby and for many years Ueno was the terminus for northbound trains, bringing in migrants from the poor, northern provinces in search of jobs. The station was flooded with even more desperate people in 1945, when firebombs destroyed huge swathes of the city, and thousands lived in its underground passages or made makeshift homes in the park. For several years a black-market flourished under the railway arches, reaching its peak as the economy boomed in the early 1950s; though the market has largely been cleaned up and the *yakuza* are less obvious these days, this is still one of the cheapest places to shop in the city, and is a world away from genteel Ginza.

## Ueno Park

**Ueno Park** was designed by the Meiji government primarily as a place for self-improvement – Tokyo's first national exhibition was held here in 1877, quickly followed by its first zoo and museum – rather than somewhere to relax in the open air. Nevertheless, its wide tarmac avenues are among the city's most popular spots for **cherry-blossom** viewing (late March to mid-April). According to local tradition, saplings were brought here from the famous cherries of Yoshino near Kyoto and there are now said to be 1200 in Ueno, but, with an annual crowd of over one million, that's still eight hundred people per tree. It's best to visit during the evening, when hanging lanterns light the blossoms, though this also the noisiest time, as groups of office workers, lubricated with quantities of sake, croon to competing karaoke machines.

From Ueno Station there are two routes into the park: "Park Exit" takes you to the main, west gate where you'll also find an **information desk** (daily 9am–6pm); while the "Shinobazu Exit" brings you out closer to the southern entrance, above Keisei-Ueno Station where trains depart for Narita airport. Taking the southerly option, at the top of the steps stands a bronze statue of **Saigō Takamori**, out walking his dog. Despite his casual appearance, this is the "Great Saigō", leader of the Restoration army, who helped bring Emperor Meiji to power but then committed ritual suicide in 1877 after his ill-fated Satsuma Rebellion (see p.711). General Saigō's popularity was such, however, that he was rehabilitated in 1891 and his statue unveiled a few years later, though a military uniform was deemed inappropriate.

Following the main path northwards, the recently renovated, red-lacquered **Kiyomizu Kannon-dō** comes into view on the left. Built out over the hillside, this **temple** is a smaller, less impressive version of Kyoto's Kiyomizu-dera (see p.445), but it has the rare distinction of being one of Kan'ei-ji's few existing remnants, dating from 1631. The temple is dedicated to Senjū Kannon (the 1000-armed Kannon), whose image is displayed only in February, although the second-rank Kosodate Kannon receives more visitors as the bodhisattva in charge of conception. Hopeful women leave dolls at the altar during the year, following which they're all burnt at a rather sad memorial service on September 25.

The temple faces westwards across a broad avenue lined with ancient cherry trees towards Shinobazu Pond. Once an inlet of Tokyo Bay, the pond is now a wildlife protection area and, unlikely as it may seem in the midst of a city, hosts a permanent colony of wild black cormorants as well as temporary populations of migrating waterfowl. A causeway leads out across its reeds and lotus beds to a small, leafy island occupied by an octagonal-roofed **temple**, **Benten-dō**, dedicated to the goddess of good fortune, water and music among other things. Inside the half-lit worship hall, you can just make out Benten's eight arms, each clutching a holy weapon, while the ceiling sports a snarling dragon.

Head back into the park on the tree-lined avenue which marks the approach to Tokugawa Ieyasu's **shrine**, **Tōshō-gū**. Ieyasu died in 1616 and is buried in Nikkō (see p.170), but this was his main shrine located in the city, founded in 1627, rebuilt on a grander scale in 1651 and now listed as a National Treasure. For once it's possible to penetrate beyond the screened entrance and enclosing walls to take a closer look inside (daily 9am–5pm, summer to 6pm; ¥200), though you have to contend with high-volume broadcasts of court music and Japanese commentary. A path leads from the left-hand ticket-gate round the gilded halls, and into the worship hall whose faded decorative work contrasts sharply with the gleaming black-lacquer and gold of Ieyasu's shrine room behind. Before leaving, take a look at the ornate, Chinese-style front gate, where two golden dragons carved in 1651 by Hidari Jingoro – he of Nikkō's sleeping cat (see p.175) – attract much attention; so realistic is the carving that, according to local tradition, the pair sneak off at midnight to drink in Shinobazu Pond.

The seventeenth-century, five-storey pagoda rising above the trees to the north of Toshō-gū is actually marooned inside **Ueno Zoo** (Tues–Sun 9.30am–4.30pm; ¥500). Considering this zoo is over a century old and in the middle of a crowded city, it's less depressing than might be feared. In recent years they've been upgrading the pens – though they're still small and predominantly concrete – and there's plenty of vegetation around, including some magnificent, corkscrewing lianas. The main attraction is the pandas, who snooze away on their concrete platform, blithely unaware they're supposed to be performing for the hoards of excited school children. As ever, weekends are the worst time, and it's a good idea to bring a picnic since prices inside the zoo are expensive.

## Ueno's museums

The best reason to visit Ueno is for its wealth of **museums** and galleries around the north and eastern edges of the park. First stop has to be Japan's oldest and most important, the **Tokyo National Museum** (Tues–Sun 9am–4.30pm; April–Sept to 8pm on Fridays; ¥400), where three galleries contain the world's largest collection of Japanese art, from ancient archeology to the modern day, plus an extensive collection of oriental antiquities. Displays are rotated every few months, from a collection of 89,000 pieces, and the special exhibitions are usually also worth seeing if you can stand the crowds. The museum style tends to old-fashioned reverential dryness, but among such a vast collection there's something to excite everyone's imagination. Two new galleries are scheduled for 1999: one will re-house the priceless Hōryū-ji treasures from Nara's famous temple (see p.490), while the Heisei-kan will host special exhibitions and ease congestion elsewhere.

It's best to start with the **Hon-kan**, the central building, where you'll find English-language booklets at the lobby information desk and a good museum shop in the basement. The Hon-kan presents the sweep of Japanese art, from Jōmon-period pots (pre-fourth century BC) to early-twentieth-century painting, via theatrical costume for Kabuki, Nō and Bunraku, colourful Buddhist mandalas, *ukiyo-e* prints, exquisite lacquerware and even seventeenth-century Christian art from southern Japan.

On the west side of the coutyard, the copper-domed **Hyōkei-kan**, built in 1908 and now an Important Cultural Property in its own right, covers some of the same ground with its collection of Japanese archeological relics up to the late twelfth century. After the refinement of the Hon-kan, many of the objects here are refreshingly simple and bursting with energy. Highlights are the bug-eyed, curvaceous clay figures (*dogū*) of the Jōmon-period, and the funerary *haniwa* from the fifth and sixth centuries AD; terra-cotta representations of houses, animals, suits of armour and stocky little warriors placed on the burial mounds to protect the deceased lord in the afterlife.

The third and final gallery is the **Tōyō-kan,** housing a delightful hotch-potch of oriental antiquities where Javanese textiles and nineteenth-century Indian prints rub shoulders with Egyptian mummies and a wonderful collection of Southeast Asian bronze buddhas. The Chinese and, particularly, Korean collections are also interesting for their obvious parallels with the Japanese art seen earlier. Built in 1968, the gallery's low lighting and open design provide a better setting and, if you've got the energy, it's well-worth taking a quick walk through, though there's frustratingly little English labelling.

In the park's northeast corner, the **National Science Museum** (Tues–Sun 9am–4.30pm; ¥400) is easily identified by a life-size statue of a blue whale romping outside. Compared with Tokyo's other science museum (see p.99), this one has fewer interactive exhibits but a great deal more information, some of it in English, covering natural history as well as science and technology. The "discovery" floors of the Purple Hall probably offer most for younger children, while the traditional technology displays in the last hall take a look at Japanese crafts, such as lacquer and paper-making.

Next stop south is the **National Museum of Western Art** (Tues–Sun 9am–5pm; ¥420) recently re-opened after extensive renovation. Around fifty Rodin sculptures populate the courtyard in front of Le Corbusier's gallery, which was erected in 1959 to house the mostly French Impressionist paintings left to the nation by Kawasaki shipping magnate Matsukata Kōjirō. Since then works by Rubens, Tintoretto, Max Ernst and Jackson Pollock have broadened the scope of the collection.

The long, low building next door, beside the main exit to Ueno Station, is Tokyo **Bunka Kaikan**, a major venue for classical concerts (see p.160). Further south again the **Royal Museum** (daily 10am–5pm; variable prices) hosts temporary exhibitions of Japanese and Western art, and may have something that appeals.

Last but by no means least comes the **Shitamachi Museum** (Tues–Sun 9.30am–4.30pm; ¥200), a few minutes' walk away in a distinctive, partly traditional-style building beside Shinobazu Pond. The museum opened in 1980 to preserve something of the Shitamachi while it was still within living memory. A reconstructed merchant's shop-house and a 1920s tenement row, complete with sweet shop and coppersmith's workroom, fill the ground floor. Upstairs is devoted to rotating exhibitions focusing on articles of daily life; old photos, toys, advertisements and artisans' tools. All the museum's exhibits have been donated by local residents; you can take your shoes off to explore the shop interiors and can handle most items. There's plenty of information in English, plus a well-produced museum booklet (¥400).

## South of Ueno Park

Ueno town centre lies to the south of the park and is a lively mix of discount outlets, market streets, drinking clubs, a sprinkling of upmarket stores and craftshops, "soaplands" (a euphemism for brothels) and restaurants. While it's not strong on sophistication or culture, there's a great sense of vitality and rawness here which you won't find elsewhere in Tokyo.

The biggest draw for both bargain-hunters and sightseers is the bustling **market** area south of Ueno Station, **Ameyoko-chō**, which extends nearly half a kilometre along the west side of the elevated JR train lines down to Okachimachi Station, spilling down side-alleys and under the tracks. The name is an abbreviation of Ameya Yoko-chō, or "candy sellers' alley", dating from the immediate post-war days when sweets were a luxury and hundreds of stalls here peddled mostly sweet potatoes coated in sugar-syrup. Since rationing was in force, black-marketeers joined the candy sellers, dealing in rice and other foodstuffs, household goods, personal possessions – whatever was available. Later, American imports also found their way from the army stores onto the streets, especially during the early-1950s Korean War.

By then the market had been legalized and over the years the worst crime has been cleaned up, but Ameyoko-chō still retains a flavour of those early days: gruff men with sandpaper voices shout out their wares; stalls selling bulk tea and coffee, cheap shoes, clothes, jewellery and fish are all jumbled up, cheek-by-jowl; and under the arches a clutch of *yakitori* bars still tempt the market crowds. In the thick of all this it's not surprising to stumble across a temple, **Tokudai-ji**, dedicated to a goddess offering prosperity and abundant harvests. Look out for the temple's colourful banners, up on the second floor two blocks before the southern limit of Ameyoko-chō.

The west side of central Ueno is dominated by a seedy nightlife area, in the midst of which Nakamachi-dōri still boasts a number of traditional **craft shops**, specializing in woven cords, *obi* sashes and calligraphy supplies. Jūsan-ya, on Shinobazu-dōri opposite the Shitamachi Museum, is probably the most famous; a craftsman sits in the window working on beautiful boxwood combs as successive generations have done since 1736. This tiny shop also has a rare collection of antique combs.

## West along the Yamanote line

Travelling **west** from Ueno to Ikebukuro on the Yamanote line there are a couple of sights to stop for, and a possible diversion along Tokyo's last remaining **tram-line**. **Rikugi-en**, near Komagome Station, is one of the city's most attractive Edo-period gardens, while **Sugamo** boasts the silver generation's very own shopping street and a temple with an interesting statue. From Sugamo it's a short walk to Kōshinzuka Station on the Toden Arakawa line, where you can pick up a tram for Higashi-Ikebukuro.

### Rikugi-en

Rikugi-en is Tokyo's best surviving example of a classical, **Edo-period stroll-garden**, (daily 9am–5pm; ¥300) and it's also large enough to be relatively undisturbed by surrounding buildings and traffic noise. The entrance lies ten-minutes' walk south of Komagome Station on Hongō-dōri, taking a right turn just before the next major junction, beside a 7-Eleven store.

In 1695 the fifth shogun granted one of his high-ranking feudal lords, Yanagisawa Yoshiyasu, a tract of farmland to the north of Edo. Yanagisawa was both a perfectionist and a literary scholar: he took seven years to design his celebrated garden – with its 88 allusions to famous scenes, real or imaginary, from ancient Japanese poetry – and then named it Rikugi-en, "garden of the six principles of poetry", in reference to the rules for composing *waka* (poems of 31 syllables). After Yanagisawa's death, Rikugi-en fell into disrepair until Iwasaki Yatarō, founder of Mitsubishi, bought the land in 1877 and restored it as part of his luxury villa. The family donated the garden to Tokyo city authorities in 1938, since when it has been a public park.

Not surprisingly, few of the 88 landscapes have survived – the guide map issued at the entrance identifies a mere eighteen. Nevertheless, Rikugi-en still retains its rhythm and beauty, kicking off with an ancient, spreading cherry tree, then slowly unfolding along paths that meander past secluded arbours and around the indented shoreline of an islet-speckled lake. In contrast, there are also areas of more natural woodland and a hillock for admiring the whole scene.

### Sugamo

From Rikugi-en you can walk to **Sugamo** in fifteen minutes, or go back to Komagome and hop on the Yamanote line for one stop. On the northern side of Sugamo JR Station, a shopping street branches left off the main road, marked by an arch with orange characters – ask for Sugamo Jizō-dōri. Its alternative, unofficial name is "obāchan no Harajuku" or old ladies' Harajuku, in ironic reference to Tokyo's epicentre of young fashion (see p.134). Sugamo's Jizō-dōri is, of course, anything but fashionable; shops here sell floral aprons, sensible shoes, walking sticks and shopping trolleys, interspersed with speciality food stores and pharmacies selling both traditional and Western medicines.

This all arose because of the popularity of its local temple, **Kogan-ji**, one hundred metres up on the right, dedicated to "thorn-removing" Togenuki Jizō who provides relief from both physical pain and the metaphorical suffering of the soul. In case a prayer doesn't work, people also queue up in front of a small Kannon statue, known as the "migawari Kannon", tucked into a corner of the temple forecourt. Each person in turn pours water over the statue and wipes whatever part of its anatomy corresponds to their own ailment, thus transferring it to the Kannon – until recently people used brushes but now it's hand-towels only as the poor goddess was being scrubbed away. It's not just pensioners who are attracted to the temple and its promise of a cure, but they are definitely in the majority and, despite the sad undertones, there's a fairly buzzing atmosphere, enlivened by quack doctors and other hucksters who set up stalls outside.

Although Kogan-ji is the centre of activity, shops continue northwards as far as the tram lines and Kōshinzuka Station, less than ten minutes' walk from the temple.

### Along the Toden Arakawa tram line

Early-twentieth-century Tokyo boasted a number of tram lines, of which only the twelve-kilometre **Toden Arakawa line** remains, running north from Waseda to Asukayama and then looping southeast to the suburbs above Ueno. The most interesting section lies along a short stretch from Kōshinzuka Station westwards towards Higashi-Ikebukuro, rocking and rolling along narrow streets and through Tokyo backyards. All tickets cost ¥160, however far you go, and it's pay as you enter, with station signs and announcements in English.

Most of the original tram lines were private enterprises – the Arakawa line was built purely to take people to the spring blossoms in Asukayama Park – and were gradually replaced with subways. However, it seems that these *chin chin densha* ("ding ding trains"), as they're known from the sound of their bells, may be staging a comeback, as they are environmentally friendly and cheap to build. The Metropolitan Government is considering electric trams for their new LRT (Light Rail Transit) system due to be completed early next century.

# Ikebukuro

Northwest of central Tokyo, **Ikebukuro** is dominated by two vast department stores glaring at each other from opposite sides of its equally confusing station. The district west of the train tracks, **Nishi-Ikebukuro**, is the more interesting to explore, particularly the wedge of streets going out towards the attractive Rikkyō University campus, if only for its plethora of bars and restaurants. Across the tracks, **Higashi-Ikebukuro** is the main shopping centre, and has a good reputation for its discount stores with cameras and electronic goods at prices rivalling Akihabara (see p.105). Apart from a pretty tacky entertainment district, Higashi-Ikebukuro's only other draw is the monstrous Sunshine City, a sixty-storey building whose prime attraction is a museum of ancient oriental art.

Marsh and farmland until a hundred years ago, Ikebukuro is a product of the railway age. Its first station was completed in 1903 and now six lines connect the area with central Tokyo and the low-cost dormitory suburbs to the north and east. Cheap accommodation and good transport have attracted an increasing number of resident expatriates, typically Chinese and Taiwanese, but covering a broad sweep of nationalities, which lends Ikebukuro a faintly cosmopolitan air.

### West Ikebukuro

Ikebukuro Station handles around one million passengers per day – second only to Shinjuku – and its warren of connecting passages, shopping arcades and countless exits are notoriously difficult to negotiate. It's even worse on the west side when the helpfully colour-coded signs mutate to blue, indicating you are now in Tōbu territory. **Tōbu** is Japan's largest department store, with over 80,000 square metres of floor space in three interconnected buildings, including the glass-fronted Metropolitan Plaza. It's got a sports club, an art museum, six floors of restaurants in the main building, plus five more in its Spice 2 annex, a recommended food department, and the usual range of goods – if you can ever find what you want. Both the nearby *Metropolitan Hotel* and **Metropolitan Art Space** also belong to the Tōbu empire. The latter, facing Tōbu store across an open square, hosts regular concerts and theatre performances, plus occasionally rewarding exhibitions on the first floor. But its main claim to fame is its long escalator, best on the way down for a dizzying, ninety-second descent beneath the glass atrium.

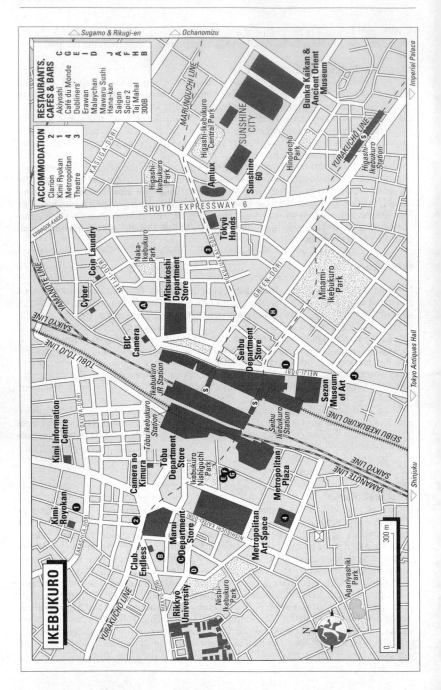

## IKEBUKURO

△ Sugamo & Rikugi-en  △ Ochanomizu

▷ Imperial Palace

**RESTAURANTS, CAFÉS & BARS**

| | |
|---|---|
| Akiyoshi | C |
| Café du Monde | G |
| Dubliners' | E |
| Erawan | D |
| Malaychan | J |
| Mawaru Sushi | A |
| Hana-kan | F |
| Saigon | H |
| Spice 2 | B |
| Taj Mahal | |
| 300B | |

**ACCOMMODATION**

| | |
|---|---|
| Clarion | 2 |
| Kimi Ryokan | 1 |
| Metropolitan | 4 |
| Theatre | 3 |

Bunka Kaikan & Ancient Orient Museum

MARUNOUCHI LINE

Higashi-Ikebukuro Central Park

SUNSHINE CITY

Hinodechō Park

YURAKUCHO LINE

Higashi-Ikebukuro Station

KASUGA-DORI

Higashi-Ikebukuro Park

Amlux

Sunshine 60

SHUTO EXPRESSWAY 6

KAWAGOE-KAIDO

Coin Laundry

Naka-Ikebukuro Park

Tōkyū Hands

RIKKYO-DORI

Minami-Ikebukuro Park

Cyber

MEIJI-DORI

Mitsukoshi Department Store

GREEN-DORI

SAIKYO LINE

BIC Camera

Seibu Department Store

TOBU TOJO LINE

Ikebukuro JR Station

Tobu Ikebukuro Station

Sezon Museum of Art

Seibu Ikebukuro Station

MEIJI-DORI

SEIBU IKEBUKURO LINE

▷ Tokyo Antiques Hall

Kimi Information Centre

TOKIWA-DORI

Camera no Kimura

Tobu Department Store

Ikebukuro Nishiguchi Park

YAMANOTE LINE

▷ Shinjuku

SAKASHITA-DORI

Kimi Ryokan

Metropolitan Plaza

Club Endless

Marui Department Store

Metropolitan Art Space

NISHIGUCHI KAISEI-DORI

YURAKUCHO LINE

RIKKYO-DORI

Rikkyō University

Nishi-Ikebukuro Park

Agariyashiki Park

300 m

N

0

△ Sugamo & Rikugi-en

## BLOOD FEUD

Ikebukuro's two huge department stores, **Tōbu** and **Seibu**, vie constantly to be the biggest and best: if one adds extra floor-space then the other follows soon after and each spurns the rival's credit card. Owned by two half-brothers, this is **sibling rivalry** on a grand scale, but their simmering hatred for each other is not altogether surprising. Tsutsumi Yoshiaki, the younger brother, is the brusque, famously stingy son of a successful post-war property developer and politician. Despite being illegitimate, Yoshiaki was also the favourite and inherited most of the family business, building it into one of Japan's biggest empires, with over sixty hotels, thirty ski resorts and thirty golf courses, let alone the Tōbu department stores and railway companies. Though profits have dipped in recent years, Yoshiaki still stands high among the world's wealthiest business tycoons.

The legitimate son, Tsutsumi Seiji, on the other hand, inherited the trading name, Seibu, and a few lacklustre department stores from his father, but little else. It's not clear exactly why he was disinherited, but the end-result was a cold determination to give his brother some serious competition. A cultured man, who is a prize-winning poet and generous sponsor of the arts, Seiji fought back with the upmarket Seibu stores and the Saison Group, a hotel, railway and finance empire which hasn't quite managed to outshine Tōbu – yet.

If you want to know more, pick up a copy of Lesley Downer's *Brothers*, in which the whole gripping tale is revealed (see Books, p.815).

Behind the Art Space, take any of the small roads heading west through an area of lanes rich in restaurants and bars, until you hit tree-lined Rikkyō-dōri. Turn left, in front of a white clapboard wedding hall, and continue for just over a hundred metres until you see a square, red-brick gateway on the left. This is the main entrance to **Rikkyō University**, founded as St Paul's School in 1874 by an American Episcopalian missionary, Bishop Channing Moore Williams. Through the gateway the old university courtyard has an Ivy League touch in its vine-covered halls, white windows and grassy quadrangle. Originally located in Tsukiji, it moved to Ikebukuro in 1918 and weathered the 1923 earthquake with minimal damage except for one toppled gate tower; the lopsided look was left, so it's said, as a memorial to those who died, but a deciding factor was perhaps the sheer lack of bricks. Other original buildings include the congregation hall, now a nicotine-stained refectory opposite the main entrance, All Saint's Chapel and a couple of wooden missionary houses.

### East Ikebukuro

Over on the east side of Ikebukuro Station, **Seibu** rules. This is the company's flagship store, the largest in the country until Tōbu outgrew it a few years back as part of a bitter rivalry between the two brother owners (see box above). Though the group has been retrenching in recent years, Seibu has a history of innovation and spotting new trends, being the first to target "office ladies" and other young women with money to burn. Apart from the main store, there's also Parco and Wave, Seibu offshoots specializing in fashion and music respectively, and the **Sezon Museum of Art** (daily 10am–8pm; varying prices) which hosts modern art exhibitions.

Heading east from Ikebukuro Station, you can't miss the monstrous 60 stories of **Sunshine 60**, which at 240m was Japan's tallest building until it was pipped by Yokohama's Landmark Tower. Just in front of it lurks the much smaller but equally distinctive, metallic blue **Amlux** showroom, Toyota's very own, non-stop motor-show. It's hard to imagine anyone actually buying a car here; there's too much else to do – you can design your own car with the help of a computer, visit the sensorama theatre to enjoy its "aroma system emitting fragrance according to the scene", and – last but not least – sit inside the cars.

An underground passage leads from Amlux basement into the **Sunshine 60** tower, just one of four buildings comprising the Sunshine City complex of shops, offices, exhibition space, hotel and cultural centres. The most interesting aspect of this much vaunted "city within a city" is that it stands on the site of old Tokyo Prison, where Japan's war criminals were incarcerated after 1945 and where the seven Class A criminals were hanged. The tower's sixtieth-floor observatory (10am–8.30pm; ¥620) may be a shade higher than Shinjuku's rivals, but you have to pay, and unless it's a really clear day there's not a lot to see anyway. However, if you're into high-speed lifts, you can ride the express elevator – one of the world's fastest at 230m in 35 seconds – for free; it leaves from basement floor B/1.

Sunshine City's most easterly building, Bunka Kaikan, houses the **Ancient Orient Museum** (daily 10am–5pm; ¥500) on its seventh floor, displaying archeological finds from the Middle East and Syria in particular. While there are the inevitable bits of old pot, the collection focuses on more accessible items such as statues, jewellery, icons and other works of art, including some superb Gandhara Buddhist art from Pakistan and a charming, wide-eyed Mother Goddess made in Syria around 2000 BC.

# Southern and western Tokyo

The **southern and western districts** of Tokyo are where you should head if you're looking for the younger, hipper side of the city. The mini-city of **Shinjuku**, with its skyscrapers, department stores and red-light district, buzzes with life, and includes one of the city's most beautiful parks, **Shinjuku Gyoen**, a spacious combination of Japanese, English and French landscape gardens.

South of Shinjuku are the desirable residential, shopping and entertainment districts of **Aoyama**, **Harajuku** and **Shibuya**, a collective showcase of contemporary Tokyo fashion and style. Consumer culture is not the only thing on offer; the verdant grounds of the city's most venerable shrine, **Meiji-jingū**, stretch from Aoyama to Harajuku. **Yoyogi-kōen**, also in Harajuku, was the focus of the 1964 Olympics and several of the stadia surrounding it are a legacy of that event, as is the cosmopolitan atmosphere that pervades the designer shops and cafés along the super-chic **Omotesandō**, a tree-lined boulevard often referred to as Tokyo's Champs Elysées. The transport hub of **Shibuya**, further south, is another youth-orientated enclave of trendy department stores, cinemas and restaurants.

**Ebisu** is an up-and-coming area for bars and clubs, and also has the excellent **Tokyo Metropolitan Photography Museum**, while **Meguro** further south has a couple of interesting museums as well as the tranquil **National Park for Nature Study**. Heading eastwards from here towards Tokyo Bay will bring you to the transport and hotel hub of **Shinagawa**, one of the original checkpoints for entry to the old capital of Edo. The area's highlight is the temple **Sengaku-ji**, a key location in one of city's bloodiest true-life samurai sagas.

## Shinjuku

Some 4km due west of the Imperial Palace, **Shinjuku** is the modern heart of Tokyo. From the love hotels and hostess bars of Kabukichō, on the east side, together with the tiny, no-frills bars of the Golden Gai and Shomben Yokochō (Piss Alley) to the shop-till-you-drop department stores and high-tech towers, a day and evening spent in this area will show you Tokyo at its best and worst.

Shinjuku is split in two by a thick band of railway tracks. The western half, **Nishi-Shinjuku**, with its soaring skyscrapers, is a showcase for contemporary architecture;

## SOUTHERN AND WESTERN TOKYO

| | | |
|---|---|---|
| **Shinjuku** | *Shinjuku* | 新宿 |
| Golden Gai | *Gōruden Gai* | ゴールデン街 |
| Hanazono shrine | *Hanazono-jinja* | 花園神社 |
| Kabukichō | *Kabukichō* | 歌舞伎町 |
| Kinokuniya | *Kinokuniya* | 紀伊国屋 |
| New National Theatre | *Shin Kokuritsu Gekijō* | 新国立劇場 |
| Piss Alley | *Shomben Yokochō* | しょんべん横丁 |
| Shinjuku Gyoen | *Shinjuku Gyoen* | 新宿公園 |
| Shinjuku-Nichōme | *Shinjuku-Nichōme* | 新宿二丁目 |
| Shinjuku Park Tower | *Shinjuku Pāku Tawā* | 新宿パークタワー |
| Taisō-ji | *Taisō-ji* | 大宗寺 |
| Tokyo Metropolitan Government Building | *Tōkyō Tochō* | 東京都庁 |
| Tokyo Opera City | *Tōkyō Opera Shitii* | 東京オペラシティー |
| | | |
| **Aoyama** | *Aoyama* | 青山 |
| Aoyama Cemetery | *Aoyama Reien* | 青山霊園 |
| Japan Traditional Crafts Centre | *Zenkoku Dentōteki Kōgeihin Sentā* | 全国伝統的工芸品センター |
| | | |
| **Harajuku** | *Harajuku* | 原宿 |
| Meiji-jingū | *Meiji-jingū* | 明治神宮 |
| Meiji Memorial Picture Gallery | *Meiji Kaigakan* | 明治絵画館 |
| National Nō Theatre | *Kokuritsu Nō Gekijō* | 国立能劇場 |
| Nezu Museum of Art | *Nezu Bijutsukan* | 根津美術館 |
| Omotesandō | *Omotesandō* | 表参道 |
| Ōta Memorial Museum of Art | *Ōta Kinen Bijutsukan* | 太田記念美術館 |
| Takeshita-dōri | *Takeshita-dōri* | 竹下通り |
| Tōgō-jinja | *Tōgō-jinja* | 東郷神社 |
| Yoyogi-kōen | *Yoyogi-kōen* | 代々木公園 |
| | | |
| **Shibuya** | *Shibuya* | 渋谷 |
| Bunkamura | *Bunkamura* | 文化村 |
| Dōgenzaka | *Dōgenzaka* | 道玄坂 |
| Hachikō | *Hachikō* | ハチコウ |
| NHK Studio Park | *NHK Sutajio Pāku* | NHKスタジオパーク |
| Tobacco and Salt Museum | *Tabako-to-Shio-no-Hakubutsukan* | たばこと塩の博物館 |
| | | |
| **Ebisu** | *Ebisu* | 恵比寿 |
| Tokyo Metropolitan Photography Museum | *Tōkyō-to Shashin Bijutsukan* | 東京都写真美術館 |
| Yebisu Garden Place | *Yebisu Gāden Pureisu* | 恵比寿ガーデンプレイス |
| | | |
| **Meguro** | *Meguro* | 目黒 |
| Meguro Parasitological Museum | *Meguro Kiseichū-kan* | 目黒寄生虫館 |
| National Park for Nature Study | *Kokuritsu Shizen Kyōikuen* | 国立自然教育園 |
| Tokyo Metropolitan Teien Art Museum | *Tōkyō-to Teien Bijutsukan* | 東京都庭園美術館 |
| | | |
| **Shinagawa** | *Shinagawa* | 品川 |
| Sengaku-ji | *Sengaku-ji* | 泉岳寺 |

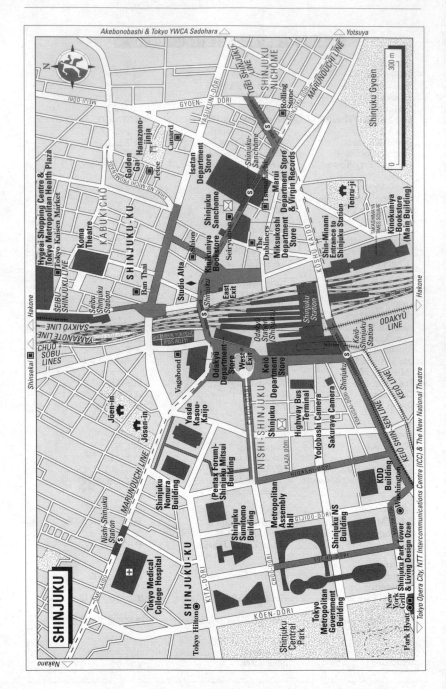

**SHINJUKU**

Tokyo at night

Tokyo Tower, Roppongi

Tokyo Metropolitan Government Building, Shinjuku

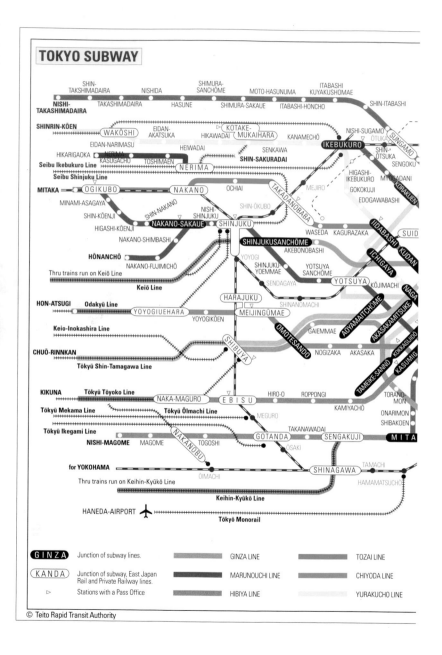

# TOKYO SUBWAY

| | | GINZA | Junction of subway lines. | GINZA LINE | TOZAI LINE |
| KANDA | Junction of subway, East Japan Rail and Private Railway lines. | MARUNOUCHI LINE | CHIYODA LINE |
| ▷ | Stations with a Pass Office | HIBIYA LINE | YURAKUCHO LINE |

© Teito Rapid Transit Authority

the raunchier eastern side, **Higashi-Shinjuku**, is a non-stop red-light and shopping district, and the inspiration for Ridley Scott's *Bladerunner*. Also on the east is one of Tokyo's most attractive parks, **Shinjuku Gyoen**.

**Shinjuku Station** is a messy combination of three terminals (the main JR station and the Keiō and Odakyū stations beside their respective department stores on the west side), plus connecting subway lines. There's also the separate Seibu Shinjuku Station, northeast of the JR station. At least two million commuters are fed into these stations every day and spun out of sixty exits. The rivers of people constantly flowing along the station's many underground passages, only add to the confusion and it's easy to get hopelessly lost. The best advice is to head for street level and get your bearings from the skyscrapers to the west.

## Some history

In the late 1600s, several "new lodgings" (the meaning of Shinjuku), were set up west of the city centre for travellers en route to Edo, but were promptly shut down in 1718 after a fracas in a brothel involving an influential *samurai*. It took sixty years for Shinjuku to recover, by which time it had become one of Edo's six **licensed quarters**, catering mainly to the lower classes. By the late 1800s, the area had been nicknamed "Tokyo's anus", due to the transportation of human waste through its streets to the countryside – and had the most prostitutes of any area in the city.

A turning – point came in 1885, when the opening of the railway encouraged people to move out of the city to the increasingly fashionable western suburbs. The area was further boosted by the 1923 earthquake, which left Shinjuku relatively undamaged and the ideal location for department stores servicing the hoards of daily commuters. After the air raids of 1945 most of Shinjuku had to be rebuilt and there were plans to relocate Tokyo's Kabuki theatre to the east side of the station. But such sophisticated entertainment was not really Shinjuku's style, so although the area adopted the name Kabukichō, the black market stayed put, the red-light trade resumed and the Kabuki theatre was rebuilt in Ginza.

Shinjuku's seediness attracted a bohemian population of writers, students and radical intellectuals, who hung out in its jazz bars and coffee shops. In October 1968 passions bubbled over into **riots** and paving stones were ripped up and hurled at the police in an anti-Vietnam demo. On the western side of the station, another type of revolution was underway. The area's first skyscraper, the 47-storey Keiō Plaza Hotel opened in 1971 and was swiftly followed by several more earthquake-defying tower blocks. Tange Kenzō's Tokyo Metropolitan Government Building set the modernist seal on the area in 1991. It has since been joined by his Shinjuku Park Tower on the south side of Shinjuku Chūō-kōen and, further west, the arty performance halls of Tokyo Opera City and the New National Theatre, the latest attempt to bring respectability to the area.

## Nishi-Shinjuku

If there is one area of Tokyo in which you can fully appreciate Japan's monumental wealth and economic power it is among the soaring skyscrapers of **Nishi** (west) **Shinjuku**. In themselves, few of these towers of glass, concrete and steel are worth spending much time exploring, though most of them have free observation rooms on their upper floors, and a wide selection of restaurants and bars with good views. Collectively, however, their impact is awesome, mainly because their scale, coupled with the spaciousness of their surroundings, is so unusual for Tokyo.

Head for the west exit at Shinjuku Station and the pedestrian tunnel beyond the two fountains in the sunken plaza in front of the Odakyū department store. On the way you'll pass Tokyo's largest cardboard city of homeless – as permanent a fixture of Shinjuku as the billion-yen skyscrapers. Protest art, some of it very imagi decorates the sides of many of these makeshift dwellings, outside of which you'll notice the occupants' shoes neatly laid out.

On the left-hand side of Chūō-dōri as you emerge at the end of the tunnel, you won't be able to miss the monumental **Tokyo Metropolitan Government Building** (TMGB), a 400,000-square-metre complex designed by top Tokyo architect, Tange Kenzō. Thirteen thousand city bureaucrats go to work each day at the TMGB and the entire complex – which includes twin 48-storey towers, an adjacent tower block, the Metropolitan Assembly Hall (where the city's councillors meet) and a sweeping, statue-lined and collanaded plaza – feels like Gotham City. Tange was actually aiming to evoke Paris's Notre Dame, and there's certainly something of that grand cathedral's design present in the shape of the twin towers. But the building's real triumph is that it is unmistakably Japanese; the dense criss-cross pattern of its glass and granite facade is reminiscent of both traditional architecture and the circuitry of an enormous computer chip. Both of the twin towers have identical free observation rooms on their forty-fifth floors. It's worth timing your visit for dusk, so you can see the multicoloured lights of Shinjuku spark and fizzle into action as the setting sun turns the sky a deep photo-chemical orange. The TMGB also has inexpensive cafés on the thirty-second floor and the ground floor of the Metropolitan Assembly Hall.

Just behind the TMGB is Shinjuku Chūō-kōen, a dusty park on the south side of which is **Shinjuku Park Tower**, another building across which Tange's modernist style is confidently written. The trendy credentials of this complex of three linked tow-

## MODERN ARCHITECTURE IN TOKYO

The most enduring legacy of the bubble years of the late 1980s is Tokyo's astonishing array of **modern architecture**. **Tange Kenzō** is the city's most prominent architect – his monumental Tokyo Metropolitan Government Building (see above) in Shinjuku has been described as the last great edifice of post modernism, though some would argue that he has gone one step further with the other-worldly Fuji TV building in Ōdaiba (see p.142). Although better associated with his hometown of Ōsaka, **Andō Tadao**, former boxer, self-taught architect and recipient of the UK Royal Gold Medal for architecture in 1997, also has buildings in Tokyo; the Collezione building, close to Omotesandō in Harajuku (see p.134), is a good example of his liking for rough concrete and bold structural forms.

Other notable Japanese architects who made their mark in the 1980s are **Maki Fumihiko**, whose designs include the futuristic Tokyo Metropolitan Gymnasium in Sendagaya, and the Spiral Building near Omotesandō, with its deliberately fragmented facade; **Arata Isozaki**'s Ochanomizu Square Building, just north of the Imperial Palace, is a good example of how old and new architecture can be successfully combined, and visibly taking its inspiration from traditional Japanese art – in this case, paintings of over-lapping mountains fading into the mists – is **Rokkaku Kijo**'s Tokyo Budōkan, the martial arts mecca.

Many top foreign architects have used Tokyo as a canvas on which to work out their most extravagant designs: in Asakusa, look for **Philippe Starck**'s Super Dry Hall, with its enigmatic "golden turd" on the roof; **Nigel Coates**'s Wall in Nishi-Azabu, a similar fish-out-of-water construction, and **Sir Norman Foster**'s Century Tower at Ochanomizu, which incorporates the vernacular design of the *torii*, ten of which appear to be piled on top of each other on the building's facade. **Rafael Viñoly**'s Tokyo International Forum in Yūrakuchō – the highlight of which is the soaring glass hall – has plenty of space to show off its sleek design, unlike **Sir Richard Rogers**' Kabukichō Building, swathed in a framework of stainless-steel rods and squashed on a Shinjuku side street.

For an excellent insight into the city's modern architecture, pick up a copy of Noriyuki Tajima's *Tokyo: A Guide to Recent Architecture*, an illustrated pocket-sized guidebook.

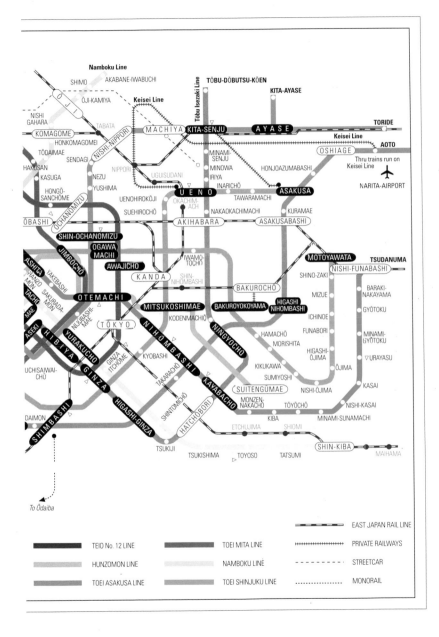

Namboku Line

SHIMO  AKABANE-IWABUCHI  TŌBU-DŌBUTSU-KŌEN

KITA-AYASE

ŌJI-KAMIYA  Keisei Line

NISHI GAHARA
ŌJI-KAMIYA
TABATA
TORIDE

KOMAGOME
HONKOMAGOMEI
MACHIYA  KITA-SENJU  AYASE

TŌDAIMAE
SENDAGI
NISHI-NIPPORI
Keisei Line
AOTO

HAKUSAN
NEZU
NIPPORI
MINAMI-SENJU
OSHIAGE
Thru trains run on
Keisei Line

KASUGA
UGUISUDANI
MINOWA
HONJOAZUMABASHI

HONGŌ-SANCHŌME
YUSHIMA
IRIYA
NARITA-AIRPORT

UENOHIROKŌJI
INARICHŌ

ŌBASHI
OCHANOMIZU
UENO  TAWARAMACHI  ASAKUSA

SUEHIROCHŌ
OKACHIM-ACH
NAKAOKACHIMACHI
KURAMAE

SHIN-OCHANOMIZU
AKIHABARA  ASAKUSABASHI

OGAWA MACHI

JIMBOCHŌ
AWAJICHŌ
IWAMŌ-TOCHŌ
MOTOYAWATA  TSUDANUMA

ASHITA
YAKEBASHI
KANDA
SHIN-NIHOMBASHI
NISHI-FUNABASHI

SHINO-ZAKI
BARAKI-NAKAYAMA

TACHI
SAKURADA-MON
OTEMACHI
BAKUROCHŌ
MIZUE

ASEKI
NIJŪBASHI-MAE
MITSUKOSHIMAE  BAKUROYOKOYAMA  HIGASHI-NIHOMBASHI
GYŌTOKU

HIBIYA
YURAKUCHO
TŌKYO
KODENMACHIŌ
ICHINOE

HAMACHŌ
FUNABORI
MINAMI-GYŌTOKU

GINZA-ITCHŌME
KYOBASHI
MORISHITA

UCHISAIWAI-CHŪ
GINZA
TAKARACHŌ
KIKUKAWA
HIGASHI-ŌJIMA
URAYASU

SUMIYOSHI
ŌJIMA
KASAI

DAIMON
HIGASHI-GINZA
SHINTOMICHŌ
SUITENGŪMAE
MONZEN-NAKACHO
NISHI-ŌJIMA

SHIMBASHI
HATCHŌBORI
KIBA
TŌYŌCHŌ
NISHI-KASAI

ETCHUJIMA
SHIOMI
MINAMI-SUNAMACHI

TSUKIJI
SHIN-KIBA
MAIHAMA

TSUKISHIMA  TOYOSO  TATSUMI

To Ōdaiba

============ EAST JAPAN RAIL LINE

| | | |
|---|---|---|
| TEIO No. 12 LINE | TOEI MITA LINE | ++++++++++ PRIVATE RAILWAYS |
| HUNZOMON LINE | NAMBOKU LINE | - - - - - - - STREETCAR |
| TOEI ASAKUSA LINE | TOEI SHINJUKU LINE | ............ MONORAIL |

Noodle stall, Shibuya

Cherry blossom, Ueno Park

Sensō-ji, Asakusa

ers, all topped with glass pyramids, are vouched by the presence of the luxurious *Park Hyatt Hotel* (which occupies the building's loftiest floors), the Conran Shop, and the **Living Design Centre Ozae** (Thurs–Tues 10am–5pm; entrance fee varies with exhibition), a spacious museum specializing in interior design, with regularly changing exhibitions by both Japanese and Western designers that are worth checking out. There's a regular free shuttle bus that runs from beside Sanwa Bank opposite the Odakyū department store to the south side of the Tower.

A ten-minute walk west of the tower, and connected to Hatsudai Station on the Keiō line, is **Tokyo Opera City**, with 54 floors of offices, shops and restaurants. The 234-metre-high tower also has a state-of-the-art concert hall and, on the fourth floor, the **NTT Intercommunication Centre** (ICC) (Tues–Sun 10am–6pm, Fri 10am–9pm; ¥800), the most innovative interactive exhibition space in Tokyo. The permanent displays of "high-tech art" include a soundproof room where you listen to your own heart beat, light-sensitive robots you can control with your brain waves, and an installation of juggling wire figures, which look like 3-D computer images. There's also an electronic library, with Internet terminals, and an Internet café. Directly behind Tokyo Opera City is the **New National Theatre**, an ambitious complex of three performing arts auditoria which opened in October 1997 (see Entertainment, p.160).

Returning to the east side of Shinjuku station, squashed up against the railway tracks running north from the Odakyū department store are the narrow alleyways of the **Shomben Yokochō**. The name of this a cramped, four-block neighbourhood of ramshackle mini-bars and restaurants translates as "Piss Alley", don't be put off exploring this atmospheric quarter – you're less likely to be ripped off for a drink here than in the similar Golden Gai district of Kabukichō. A pedestrian tunnel at the southern end of the alleys, just to the right of the cheap clothes outlets, provides a short cut to the east side of Shinjuku station and Studio Alta.

## Higashi-Shinjuku

Some days it seems as if all of Tokyo is waiting at Shinjuku's favourite meeting spot, beneath the huge TV screen on the **Studio Alta** building on the east (*higashi*) side of the JR station. It's worth bearing this in mind if you arrange to meet anyone there – a better option is at the plaza opposite Studio Alta from where you can fully soak up the super-charged atmosphere, especially at night, when the district is ablaze with neon. To the southeast of here is **Shinjuku-dōri**, along which you'll find some of the classier department stores and shops, such as Mitsukoshi and **Isetan**, which has excellent food halls in its basement, a good range of restaurants on the top floor and an art gallery which frequently holds notable exhibitions (check local English-language newspapers and magazines for details).

Directly to the east of Studio Alta, across the wide boulevard of Yasakuni-dōri, lie the exotic delights of **Kabukichō**, which are by no means all sexual. A sharp contrast is provided by the sleek new shopping and entertainment complex of **Takashimaya Times Square**, close by the Shin-Minami ("new south") entrance to Shinjuku Station, while further south is the green oasis of **Shinjuku Gyoen**. You need never come out on the streets to see any of this. Beneath the pounding feet of pedestrians on Yasakuni-dōri, lies an extensive subterranean shopping complex, Shinjuku Subnade, while a tunnel with exits to all the major shops runs the length of Shinjuku-dōri from the main JR station to the Shinjuku Sanchōme subway station.

### KABUKICHŌ AND AROUND

To the north of Yasakuni-dōri, five minutes' walk from Studio Alta, is the red-light district **Kabukichō**, at the heart of which is the Koma Theatre, where modern musicals and samurai dramas are performed. The tatty plaza in front of the theatre is lined with cinemas, many showing the latest Hollywood blockbusters, and the streets radiating around it contain a wide range of bars and restaurants. Stray a block or so further north and you're in the raunchier side of Kabukichō, with soaplands, hostess bars and girly shows lining the narrow streets. You stand a good chance of spotting members of the *yakuza* crime syndicates at work (the tight perm hairdos and 1970s-style clobber are giveaway signs) around here, but the overall atmosphere is not unlike London's Soho, where the porn industry and illicit goings-on nestle unthreateningly beside less salacious entertainment.

Local shopkeepers come to pray for business success at Kabukichō's attractive **Hanazono-jinja**. This **shrine** predates the founding of Edo by the Tokugawa, but the current granite and vermilion buildings are modern recreations. It's worth paying a visit at night, when spotlights give the shrine a special ambience. From here, you're well poised to take a stroll through the **Golden Gai**, the low-rent drinking quarter where intellectuals and artists have rubbed shoulders with Kabukichō's *demi monde* since the war. In this compact grid of streets there are around two hundred bars, virtually all no larger than broom cupboards and universally presided over by no-nonsense *mama-san*. You probably won't want to stop for a drink; most of the bars operate like mini-clubs where only regulars are welcome, while the others – usually the ones which a dubious-looking woman is urging you to enter – will fleece you rotten. In recent years, the cinderblock buildings have been under threat from both property redevelopers and their own fifty-year-old collapse-by date. However, the recession and its hip notoriety has given the Golden Gai a reprieve; catch it while it lasts, since it is among Tokyo's fast disappearing links with its raffish past.

By contrast, the city's squeaky clean future is on display at **Takashimaya Times Square**, which is shifting Shinjuku's focus to immediately south of the station, away from Kabukichō to the east. The sleek new shopping and entertainment complex is connected to the southern (Shin-Minami) entrance of Shinjuku Station by a broad wooden promenade, and includes branches of the Takashimaya department store, interior design and handcrafts superstore Tōkyū Hands, and the vast seven-floor Kinokuniya bookstore. Inside the mall are also **Shinjuku Joypolis** (daily 10am–11.15pm; ¥300), a high-tech amusement park of virtual reality rides produced by Sega, and **Tokyo IMAX Theatre** (daily except Wed 11am–11pm; ¥1300) which screens 3-D films on its six-storey-high cinema screen – both good places to keep the kids occupied if you want to go shopping.

### SHINJUKU GYOEN AND AROUND

Five minutes' walk southeast of Takashimaya Times Square, close by the Shinjuku-Gyoen-mae subway station is the main entrance to **Shinjuku Gyoen** (Tues–Sun 9am–4.30pm, last entry 4pm; ¥200), the largest and possibly most beautiful gardens in Tokyo. The grounds, which once held the mansion of Lord Naito, the *daimyō* of Tsuruga on the Japan Sea coast, became the property of the Imperial Household in 1868. After World War II, the 150-acre park was opened to the public. Apart from their spaciousness, the gardens' main feature is their variety of design. The southern half is traditionally Japanese, with winding paths, stone lanterns, artificial hills, islands in ponds linked by zig-zag bridges and a delightful teahouse (Tues–Sun 10am–4pm; ¥700). At the northern end of the park are formal, French-style gardens, with neat rows of tall birch trees and hedge-lined flower beds. Finally, the middle of the park is modelled on English landscape design, and on the eastern flank there is a large greenhouse (Tues–Sun 11am–3.30pm), packed with sub-tropical vegetation – particularly cosy on a chilly winter's day. In spring, the whole park bursts with pink and white cherry blossoms while in early November, kaleidoscopic chrysanthenum displays and golden autumn leaves are the main attractions. There are several cafés within the gardens where you can grab a reasonable lunch for around ¥900, but it's much nicer to bring a picnic and relax in the tranquil surroundings. An alternative entrance to the gardens is through the western gate, a five–minute walk under and alongside the railway tracks from Sendagaya Station.

Walking back towards Shinjuku Station will take you past the **gay district** of Shinjuku Nichōme. During the day the area is inconspicuous, but come nightfall the numerous bars spring into action, catering to every imaginable sexual orientation. Close by is **Taiso-ji**, a temple founded in 1668, which has the city's largest wooden statue of Yama, the King of Hell. The statue is in the temple building next to a large copper Buddha dressed in a red bib and cap. You have to press a button to illuminate the 5.5-metre Yama, whose fiercesome expression is difficult to take seriously once you've spotted the offerings of a couple of tins of pineapple and such like.

## Meiji-jingū

Covering parts of both Aoyama and Harajuku, the areas immediately south of Shinjuku, is **Meiji-jingū**, Tokyo's premier Shinto **shrine**, a memorial to Emperor Meiji, who died in 1912, and his Empress Shōken, who died in 1914. The shrine is split into two sections; the **Outer Garden**, between Sendagaya and Shinanomachi stations, contains the Meiji Memorial Picture Gallery and several sporting arenas, including the National Stadium and Jingū Baseball Stadium, while the more important **Inner Garden**, beside Harajuku Station, includes the emperor's shrine, the empress's iris gardens, the imperial couple's Treasure House and extensive wooded grounds.

Together with the neighbouring shrines to General Nogi and Admiral Tōgō (see p.134), Meiji-jingū was created as a symbol of imperial power and Japanese racial superiority. Rebuilt in 1958 after being destroyed during World War II, the shrine remains the focus of several **festivals** during the year. The most important of these, **hatsumode** (first visit of the year to a shrine), is held on January 1 and attracts three million visitors – traffic lights have to be operated within the shrine grounds to control the crowds on the day. But more entertaining is **Seijin-no-hi** (Adults' Day) on January 15: on this day, twenty-year-olds attend the shrine, the women often dressed in elaborate long-sleeved kimono, fur stoles wrapped around their necks. Meiji-jingū's gravel approach is lined with ice sculptures and there is a colourful display of traditional *momoteshiki* archery by costumed archers. Between April 29 and May 3 and on November 1 and 3, *bugaku* (court music and dances) are performed on a stage erected in the shrine's main courtyard, while *Shichi-go-san-hi* (Seven-five-three Day) on November 15, provides an opportunity to see children of these ages dressed in delightful mini-kimono. Apart from the festivals, Meiji-jingū is best visited mid-week when its calm serenity can be appreciated without the crowds.

### The Outer Garden and around

The closest subway to the entrance to Meiji-jingū's Outer Garden is Aoyama Itchōme. The **Meiji Memorial Picture Gallery** (daily 9am–5pm; ¥300), at the northern end of a long gingko-tree lined approaching road, which runs beside the rugby and baseball stadiums, has a stern, European-style exterior, similar to the Diet building (see p.108). The entrance hall, liberally decorated with marble, soars up to a central dome on either side of which are halls containing forty paintings which tell the life story of the Emperor Meiji. These are more interesting for the depiction of Japan emerging from its feudal past, than for their artistic merits.

To the side of the gallery looms the 75,000-seater **National Stadium**, Japan's largest sporting arena, built for the 1964 Olympics. Today it regularly plays host to J-League soccer games and will be one of the venues for the 2002 World Cup. On the western side of the stadium and best viewed from outside Sendagaya Station is the outer garden's most striking feature; the **Tokyo Metropolitan Gymnasium**. At first glance the building looks like a giant alien spacecraft, but on closer examination it becomes obvious that the inspiration is a traditional *samurai* helmet. The corrugated stainless-steel-roofed building houses the main arena, while in the block to the right are public swimming pools and a subterranean gym, the latter crowned with a glass pyramid roof (entrance to the swimming pool, which includes a heated deck, is ¥400).

Follow the railway line and road west will lead to a sign pointing to the **National Nō Theatre**, set back from the street in a walled compound. Only built in 1983, the theatre incorporates traditional Japanese architectural motifs, particularly in the design of its slightly-sloping roofs. Although Nō, Japan's oldest and most stylized form of theatre, is something of an acquired taste, this is one of the best places in which to see a production. Return to the main road and follow the raised expressway as it crosses over the railway lines. You'll go under the tracks and veer off left up the hill to Meiji-jingū's Inner Garden eastern entrance.

### The Inner Garden

The most impressive way to approach the **Inner Garden** is through the southern gate next to Harajuku's toy-town-style station building, complete with mock-Tudor clock tower. From here a wide gravel path runs through densely forested grounds to the twelve-metre-high **Ō-torii**, made from 1500-year-old cypress pine trees from Taiwan, the largest Myōjin-style gate in Japan. Just to left of the gate is the entrance to the **Jingū Neien** (daily 8.30am–5pm; ¥500), a traditional garden said to have been designed by the Emperor Meiji for his wife, and which is at its most beautiful in June when over one hundred varieties of **irises**, the empress's favourite flowers, pepper the lush greenery with their purple and white blooms.

Returning to the garden's entrance, the gravel path turns right and passes through a second wooden *torii*, Kita-mon (north gate). There are several shrine buildings in the stone-flagged precinct. Before the gateway to the main *honden* (central hall), you'll pass an extension of the **Treasure House** (daily: April–Nov 8.30am–4pm; Jan–March & Dec 9.30am–3.30pm; ¥500 entry to both buildings), whose display of kimono and Western-style military uniforms of the imperial couple can be safely passed over in favour of checking out the central halls. With their Japanese cypress wood and green copper roofs, the buildings are a fine example of how Shinto architecture can blend seamlessly with nature. There are exits from the courtyard on its eastern and western flanks; follow either of the paths northwards through the woods to arrive at the pleasant grassy slopes and pond before the main Treasure House (same hours as extension). Don't bother going in – the contents of the museum are no more thrilling than the lumpen grey concrete building that houses them.

## Harajuku

Apart from the wooded grounds of Meiji-jingū, **Harajuku** is also blessed with Tokyo's largest park, **Yoyogi-kōen**, a favourite spot for joggers and bonneted groups of kindergarten kids with their minders. Once an imperial army training ground, the park was dubbed "Washington Heights" after World War II, when it was used to house US military personnel. In 1964, the land was used for the Olympic athletes' village, after which it became Yoyogi-kōen. Two of the stadia, built for the Olympics, remain the area's most famous architectural features. The main building of Tange Kenzō's **Yoyogi National Stadium** is a dead ringer for Noah's ark, and its steel suspension roof was a structural engineering marvel at the time. Inside are a swimming pool and skating rink (Mon–Sat noon–8pm, Sun 10am–6pm; ¥900). The smaller stadium, used for basket ball, is like the sharp end of a giant swirling seashell.

The road that separates the stadia from Yoyogi-kōen, Inokashira-dōri, used to be closed every Sunday to allow bands to play and people to dance in the street. It became

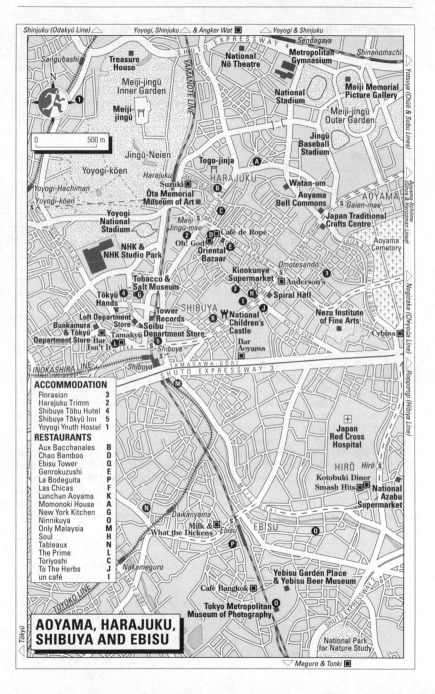

△ *Shinjuku (Odakyū Line)* △   *Yoyogi, Shinjuku* △ *& Angkor Wat* ◼   △ *Yoyogi & Shinjuku*

SHUTO EXPRESSWAY 4

*Sangubashi*

*Treasure House*

*National Nō Theatre*

*Metropolitan Gymnasium*   *Sendagaya*

*Shinanomachi*

*Meiji-jingū Inner Garden*

YAMANOTE LINE

*National Stadium*

*Meiji Memorial Picture Gallery*

*Meiji-jingū*

*Meiji-jingū Outer Garden*

◁ *Yotsuya (Chūō & Sobu Lines)*

0    500 m

*Jingū-Neien*

*Yoyogi-kōen*

*Harajuku*

*Togo-jinja*

Ⓐ

*Jingū Baseball Stadium*

*Yoyogi-Hachiman*

*Suzuki* ◼

Ⓑ

*HARAJUKU*

*Watan-um*

*AOYAMA*

◁ *Aoyama-itchome (Ginza & Hanzōmon Lines)*

*Yoyogi-kōen*

Ⓢ

*Ōta Memorial Museum of Art* ◼

*Aoyama Bell Commons*

Ⓢ *Gaien-mae*

*Yoyogi National Stadium*

Ⓒ

*Meiji-jingū-mae*

Ⓐ

*Japan Traditional Crafts Centre*

Ⓓ

*Café de Ropé*

GAIEN

*Aoyama Cemetery*

*Oh! God*

Ⓔ

*Oriental Bazaar*

◁ *Nogizaka (Chiyōda Line)*

*NHK & NHK Studio Park*

*Tobacco & Salt Museum*

*Kinokuniya Supermarket*

*Omotesandō*

Ⓒ

*Anderson's*

Ⓕ

Ⓗ

*Spiral Hall*

*Tōkyū Hands*

Ⓓ   Ⓖ

*SHIBUYA*

Ⓘ

Ⓙ

*Nezu Institute of Fine Arts*

*Loft Department Store*

*Tower Records*

Ⓚ

*National Children's Castle*

*Cybina* ◼

◁ *Roppongi (Hibiya Line)*

*Bunkamura & Tōkyū Department Store*

*Seibu Department Store*

*Tamakyū*

*Bar Isn't It*

Ⓛ

Ⓢ *Shibuya*

Ⓢ

*Bar Aoyama*

INOKASHIRA LINE

*Shibuya*

TAMAGAWA-DŌRI

SHUTO EXPRESSWAY 3

Ⓜ

*Japan Red Cross Hospital*

**ACCOMMODATION**

| | |
|---|---|
| Florasian | 3 |
| Harajuku Trimm | 2 |
| Shibuya Tōbu Hotel | 4 |
| Shibuya Tōkyū Inn | 5 |
| Yoyogi Youth Hostel | 1 |

**RESTAURANTS**

| | |
|---|---|
| Aux Bacchanales | B |
| Chao Bamboo | D |
| Ebisu Tower | Q |
| Genrokuzushi | E |
| La Bodeguita | P |
| Las Chicas | F |
| Lunchan Aoyama | K |
| Momonoki House | A |
| New York Kitchen | G |
| Ninnikuya | O |
| Only Malaysia | M |
| Soul | H |
| Tableaux | N |
| The Prime | L |
| Toriyoshi | C |
| To The Herbs | J |
| un café | I |

*HIRŌ*   *Hirō* Ⓢ

*Kotobuki Diner*

*Smash Hits* ◼

*National Azabu Supermarket*

Ⓝ

*Daikanyama*

*Milk & What the Dickens*

Ⓢ

*Ebisu*

*EBISU*

Ⓞ

Ⓟ

*Nakameguro*

*Yebisu Garden Place & Yebisu Beer Museum*

*Café Bangkok* ◼

**AOYAMA, HARAJUKU, SHIBUYA AND EBISU**

TOYOKO LINE

◁ *Tōkyū*

YAMANOTE LINE

*Tokyo Metropolitan Museum of Photography*

Ⓠ

SHUTO EXPRESSWAY 2

*National Park for Nature Study*

▽ *Meguro & Tonki* ◼

known as **"Din Alley"**, and was one of Tokyo's highlights, a raucous and invigorating display of youth culture and general joi de vivre by a colourful cast of hippies, punks, rockabillies, grunge artists and plain weirdos. However, in 1996 the local authorities stopped the bands and re-opened the road to Sunday traffic (although connecting Omotesandō remains a pedestrian-only thoroughfare from 1 to 5pm). Clusters of punky teenagers, dressed as their favourite pop idols, still hang out in groups beside the station, but the quiff-haired bikers jitterbugging around their Harley Davidsons at the entrance to Yoyogi-kōen, and a couple of guitarists on the bridge over the railway tracks, are the lone guardians of the anarchic flame.

## Omotesandō

Harajuku's most elegant boulevard, the elm-lined **Omotesandō**, leads from the entrance to Meiji-jingū to the cluster of contemporary designer boutiques on the other side of Aoyama-dōri. On either side are dense networks of streets, packed with funky little shops, restaurants and bars. One of the most famous roads is **Takeshita-dōri**, whose hungry mouth gobbles up teenage fashion victims as they swarm out of the north exit of Harajuku station, and spits them out the other end on Meiji-dōri minus their cash. The shops sell every kind of tat imaginable, are hugely enjoyable to root around and provide a window on Japanese teen fashion. On Sundays the crush of bodies on the street is akin to that on the Yamanote line at rush hour.

Serious bargain hunters never miss out on the outdoor antiques market held on the first and fourth Sundays of each month in the precincts of the neighbouring **Tōgō-jinja**. The market sells everything from fine *tansu* (traditional Japanese chests) to old kimono and crockery, but you need to get there early in the morning to snag any bargains. The **shrine** itself is dedicated to Admiral Tōgō Heihachiro, who led the victorious Japanese fleet against the Russians in the Russo-Japanese War of 1904–5, and has a pretty pond and garden fronting onto Meiji-dōri. Walking back towards the crossing with Omotesandō, look out for Laforet, a trendy boutique complex, behind which is the excellent **Ōta Memorial Museum of Art** (Tues–Sun 10.30am–5pm; ¥500), well worth stepping into. You'll have to leave your shoes in the lockers and put on slippers to wander the small galleries on two levels featuring *ukiyo-e* paintings and prints from the private collection of the late Ōta Seizo, the former chairman of the Toho Life Insurance Company. The art displayed comes from a collection which numbers 12,000 pieces, including masterpieces by Utamaro, Hokusai and Hiroshige.

Returning to Omotesandō and heading east, shops to keep an eye open for include Kiddy Land, Harajuku's premier toy store where kids line up well before the opening hours to purchase the latest gimmick, and the green and red Oriental Bazaar, a Chinese-style building packed with all manner of souvenirs. Opposite you'll notice the ivy-covered Aoyama Apartments, built in 1925 as an experiment in modern living, but currently being taken over by young fashion designers and artists, adding a bohemian flavour to the road.

As it crosses Aoyama-dōri Omotesandō narrows and develops into a street of swanky designer-label boutiques such as Comme des Garçons, Issey Miyake, Yohji Yamamoto and Calvin Klein. At the T-junction, just beyond the Andō Tadao-designed Collezione building (see box, p.128), turn right for the entrances to the **Nezu Museum of Art** (Tues–Sun 9.30am–4.30pm; ¥1000). The rather steep entrance charge makes this small museum a bit of a luxury, but it does have a classy collection of oriental arts, including many national treasures. The best time to visit is the ten-day period at the end of April and beginning of May, when Ōgata Kōrin's exquisite screen paintings of irises are displayed. Otherwise, the museum's nicest feature is its garden, which slopes gently away around an ornamental pond and features several traditional teahouses.

## Aoyama Reien and around

Turning left at the end of Omotesandō, the road leads round into Tokyo's most important graveyard, officially entitled Aoyama Reien, but generally known as **Aoyama Botchi**. Everyone who was anyone, including Hachikō the faithful dog (see p.136), is buried here, and the graves, many decorated with elaborate calligraphy, are interesting in their own right. Look out for the section where foreigners are buried; their tombstones provide a history of early *gaijin* involvement in Japan. That such an extensive slice of prime central Tokyo real estate, graveyard or not, has survived the developers' clutches for so long is nothing short of a miracle – perhaps it is because of the fantastic avenues of cherry trees, which many locals enjoy partying under during the *hanami* season.

Returning to Aoyama-dōri from the main entrance to the graveyard, walk west for five minutes to the **Japan Traditional Crafts Centre** (daily except Thurs 10am–6pm; free), in the Plaza 246 building on the corner of Gaien-nishi-dōri. This extensive display of arts and crafts from all over the country includes lacquerware, ceramics, dolls and hand-made paper. Many of the items are for sale, there's an information desk where the attendants speak English, and a small library with English-language books on the traditional arts. Continuing west along Aoyama-dōri, past the crossing with Omotesandō, you'll pass, on your left, the **Spiral Building**, which includes a gallery, a couple of restaurants and a trendy cards shop. The interior, with its sweeping, seemingly freestanding ramp walkway, is worth a look. On the opposite side of the street is Kinokuniya, supermarket to the smart set, and closer to Shibuya, the funky **National Children's Castle** (Tues–Fri 12.30–5.30pm; Sat, Sun & holidays 10am–5pm; ¥500), a large kids' playground featuring a small hotel.

# Shibuya

The glitzy entertainment district of **Shibuya**, immediately south of Harajuku, is primarily an after-dark destination – at night its restaurants, cinemas and signs create an invigorating neon-light display. Most of the action is on the west side; the plaza here is the famous waiting spot of **Hachikō the dog** (see box, p.136), and the best place from which to take in the evening buzz. Opposite, to the west, the 109 Building stands at the apex of **Dōgenzaka** and Bunkamura-dōri, the former leading up to one of Tokyo's most famous love hotel districts.

If you walk through Dōgenzaka, over the crest of the hill and past the On Air live music venues, you'll end up next to the main entrance to the **Bunkamura**, a complex with an excellent art gallery (with temporary exhibitions of mainly Western art), a couple of cinemas, the 2000-seater Orchard Hall, home of the Tokyo Philharmonic Orchestra, and the Theatre Cocoon, which hosts some of the city's more avant garde productions. The Bunkamura is also the base for the Tokyo International Film Festival, held every September. The ticket counter is on the first floor (daily 10am–7.30pm; ☎03/3477-3244 for programme information).

Emerging from the Tōkyū department store next to the Bunkamura and passing through the opposite couple of blocks of streets, a favourite stomping ground of Tokyo's trendier youths, you'll emerge in the Seibu stronghold. The main branch of the department store is at the base of Kōen-dori, close to the station, with the fashionable Loft, Seed and Parco complexes further up the hill. Slipping down the hill behind Parco are the steps of Spain-zaka, a close-runner to Harajuku's Takeshita-dōri, with its emporia of the ephemeral. At the top of this narrow street is Cinema Rise, an imaginatively designed movie theatre which shows mainly art-house foreign films.

Walking back towards the upper slope of Kōen-dōri will bring you to the **Tobacco and Salt Museum** (Tues–Sun 10am–5.30pm; ¥100). With the rest of the world

---

### HACHIKŌ – THE TRUE STORY

The true story of **Hachikō** the dog proves that fame in Japan comes to those who wait. Every morning, the Akita pup faithfully accompanied his master Ueda Eisaburō, a professor in the department of agriculture at the Imperial University, to Shibuya Station, and would be back at the station in the evening to greet him.

In May 1925, Professor Ueda died while at work, but Hachikō continued to turn up every day at the station. By 1934, Hachikō had waited paitiently for nine years and locals were so touched by the dog's devotion that a bronze statue was cast of him. In 1935, Hachikō was finally united in death with his master when he was buried with Ueda in Aoyama cemetry. The stuffed skin of the dog created a doppleganger Hachikō, which can be viewed at the National Science Museum (see p.118). During World War II, the original Hachikō statue was melted down for weapons, but was quickly reinstated beside the station in 1948. Today, this is the most famous **rendezvous** in all of Tokyo, though the throngs of people around the small statue and the rats that rummage through the rubbish in the surrounding bushes do not make it a particularly relaxing place to hang out in.

---

shunning the possibly dodgy salt and certainly lethal tobacco, only in Japan could you find a museum devoted to these products, which until the 1980s, were national monopolies. Take the lift at the side of the entrance desk to the fourth floor, which has temporary exhibitions, and work your way down past displays on the third, which focus on the harvesting of salt from the sea and other sources of sodium. The second floor has the tobacco exhibits, including two thousand packets from around the world, and dioramas showing how the leaves were prepared for smoking in the past. It's all in Japanese, and only on the ground floor are you allowed to spark up your fags.

At the top of Kōen-dōri, opposite the Shibuya Ward Office and Public Hall, is the NHK Broadcasting Centre, housing Japan's equivalent of the BBC. You can take an entertaining tour around part of the complex by visiting the **NHK Studio Park** (daily 10am–6pm; closed second Mon of the month; ¥200). Although it's all in Japanese, much of the exhibition is interactive, including opportunities to become a news reader and weather presenter and to mess around on multimedia products. If you try out the 3-D screen TV (not one of NHK's better inventions), make sure you read the English instructions on how contort your body first to get the desired effect.

## Ebisu

Up-and-coming **Ebisu**, just south of Shibuya, is currently bubbling with life, as new shops, bars and clubs open their doors along the narrow sidestreets. Day-time attractions include a couple of good museums in **Yebisu Garden Place**, a huge shopping, office and entertainment complex connected to Ebisu Station by a long moving walkway, and on the site of the nineteenth-century Sapporo brewery that once was the source of the area's fortunes.

You can find out more about the history of beer in Japan – and of the brewery that used to be here – at the lively **Yebisu Beer Museum** (Tues–Sun 10am–6pm; free), on the western side of the complex, behind the Mitsukoshi department store. Look out for the touch-screen video displays and a computer simulation, where one of the participants is chosen to be the leader of a virtual-reality tour around different aspects of the brewing process. There's also an opportunity to sample some of Sapporo's beers, at ¥200 for a small glass. On the eastern side of the complex, and equally absorbing, is the **Tokyo Metropolitan Photography Museum** (Tues–Sun 10am-6pm; Thurs & Fri until 8pm; ¥800), with excellent exhibits of major Japanese and Western photographers, along with study rooms and an experimental photography and imaging room. The museum's policy of concentrating on one photographer at a time in its frequently changing exhibitions allows you to see the artist's work develop and gain an understanding of the motivations behind it.

If you have time, head for the restaurants on the 38th and 39th floors the **Yebisu Tower** next to the photography museum; you don't need to eat or drink here to enjoy the spectacular free views of the city.

## Meguro and Shinagawa

South of Ebisu, stylish **Meguro**, home to many local celebrities, is mainly a residential area, but there are some sightseeing surprises to be found here, including the infamous **love hotel**, *Meguro Club Sekitei*, a fairy-tale castle whose green turrets and balconies are easily spotted to the west of the station, and which, allegedly, has rooms where guests can cavort amid artificial cloudbursts.

Even more curious is the **Meguro Parasitological Museum** (Tues–Sun 10am–5pm; free), across the Meguro-gawa and up the hill just beyond Yamate-dōri, and the only museum in the world specializing in parasites. Any vision you had of Japan being a healthy place to live in will be quickly dispelled by these two floors of exhibits, which emphasize the dangers of creepy crawlies in uncooked food. Record-breaking tapeworms (onc 8.8 metres long) are on display, pickled in jars, along with some gruesome photographs of past victims, including one poor fellow whose swollen testicles scrape the ground. The museum does a lively trade in souvenir T-shirts, books and jewellry.

Returning to Meguro Station and continuing for five minutes down Meguro-dōri, past the raised Shuto Expressway, you'll come to the elegant **Tokyo Metropolitan Teien Art Museum** (10am–6pm; closed 2nd and 4th Wed of the month; entrance fee depends on the exhibition). This Art Deco building is the former home of Prince Asaka Yasuhiko, Emperor Hirohito's uncle, who lived in Paris for three years during the 1920s, where he developed a taste for the European style. It's worth popping into for the gorgeous interior decoration and landscaped grounds with Japanese gardens, pond and tea ceremony house (entry to gardens only is ¥200).

Next to the museum's grounds is the **National Park for Nature Study** (Tues–Sun 9am–4pm; May–Aug until 5pm; ¥200). Covering about 200,000 square metres, the park is an attempt to preserve the original natural features of the countryside before Edo was settled and developed into Tokyo. It partially succeeeds – among the 8000 trees in the park there are some that have been growing for 500 years; frogs can be heard croaking amid the grass beside the marshy ponds; and the whole place is a bird-spotter's paradise. The best thing about the park is that entry at any one time is limited to 300 people, making it one of the few public areas in Tokyo where you can really escape the crowds.

Heading a couple of kilometres east from Meguro, you'll hit a clump of railway lines flowing through the transport and hotel hub of **Shinagawa**, the location of one of the original checkpoints on the Tōkaidō, the major highway into Edo during the reign of the shoguns. One of the highlights here is **Sengaku-ji**, the local **temple** where the graves of Asano Takumi and his 47 *rōnin* (see box overleaf) can be found. Most of the temple was destroyed during the war and has since been rebuilt, but a striking gate dating from 1836 and decorated with a metalwork dragon remains. The statue and grave of Oishi Kuranosuke, the avenging leader of the 47 *rōnin*, are in the temple grounds. A **museum** (daily 9am–4pm; ¥200) to the left of the main building contains the personal belongings of the *rōnin* and their master Asano, as well as a receipt for the severed head of Kira.

## THE 47 RŌNIN

Celebrated in Kabuki and Bunraku plays, as well as on film, *Chushingura* is a true story of honour, revenge and loyalty. In 1701, a young *daimyō*, Asano Takumi, became embroiled in a fatal argument in the shogun's court with his teacher and fellow lord Kira Yoshinaka. Asano had lost face in his performance of court rituals, and, blaming his mentor for his lax tuition, drew his sword within the castle walls and attacked Kira. Although Kira survived, the shogun, on hearing of this breach of etiquette, ordered Asano to commit *seppuku*, the traditional form of suicide, which he did.

Their lord having been disgraced, Asano's loyal retainers, the **rōnin** – or masterless *samurai* – vowed revenge. On December 14, 1702, the 47 *rōnin*, lead by Oishi Kuranosuke, stormed Kira's villa (the remains of which are in Ryōguku), cut off his head and paraded it through Edo in triumph before placing it on Asano's grave in Sengaku-ji. Although their actions were in line with the *samurai* creed, the shogun had no option but to order the *rōnin*s' deaths. All 47 committed *seppuku* on February 14, 1703, including Oishi's fifteen-year-old son. They were buried with Asano in Sengaku-ji and, today their graves are still wreathed in the smoke from the bundles of incense placed by their gravestones.

# Bayside Tokyo

It comes as something of a shock to many visitors (and some residents) that Tokyo is actually beside the sea. Yet many of the *ukiyo-e* masterpieces of Hokusai and Hiroshige depict waterside scenes of **Tokyo Bay**, and several of the city's prime attractions are to be found here. The teeming fish market of **Tsukiji** provides a rowdy early-morning antidote to the serenity of the nearby traditional gardens, **Hama Rikyū Teien**. East of the market is **Tsukudashima**, a pocket of traditional wooden homes and shops dating from the Edo period, while, to the south, across the Rainbow Bridge, lie the modern waterfront city and pleasure parks of **Ōdaiba**, built on vast islands of reclaimed land.

Beyond Ōdaiba on the north side of Tokyo Bay, some of the city's older recreational facilities still pull the crowds. The open spaces of **Kasai Rinkai-kōen** make a good place to catch the sea breeze, but the park's greatest attraction is its aquarium and particularly the doughnut-shaped tuna tank where silver shoals race round you at dizzying speeds. From the park, the Cinderella-spires of **Tokyo Disneyland** are clearly visible

## BAYSIDE TOKYO

| | | |
|---|---|---|
| **Tokyo Bay** | *Tōkyō-wan* | 東京湾 |
| Central Wholesale Market | *Chūō Oroshiuri Ichiba* | 中央卸売市場 |
| Decks Tokyo Beach | *Dekkusu Tōkyō Biichi* | デックス東京ビーチ |
| Hama Rikyū garden | *Hama Rikyū Teien* | 浜離宮庭園 |
| Kasai Rinkai-kōen | *Kasai Rinkai-kōen* | かさい臨海公園 |
| Museum of Maritime Science | *Fune no Kagakukan* | 船の科学館 |
| Ōdaiba Seaside Park | *Ōdaiba Kaihin-kōen* | お台場海浜公園 |
| Sengaku-ji | *Sengaku-ji* | 泉岳寺 |
| Sumiyoshi-jinja | *Sumiyoshi-jinja* | 住吉神社 |
| Tsukiji Hongan-ji | *Tsukiji Hongan-ji* | 築地本癌字 |
| Tsukudashima | *Tsukudashima* | 佃島 |
| Tokyo Disneyland | *Tōkyō Dizuniirando* | 東京ディズニーランド |

to the west. Though not everyone's cup of tea, this little bit of America can make a hugely entertaining day out, even if you're not travelling with kids.

## Tsukiji

A dawn visit to the vast **Tokyo Central Wholesale Market**, on the edge of Tokyo Bay, some 2km southeast of the Imperial Palace, is one of the highlights of any trip to Tokyo and is a must for raw-fish fans, who can breakfast afterwards on the freshest slices of sashimi and sushi.

Covering 56 acres of reclaimed land south of Ginza, the market is popularly known as **Tsukiji** (reclaimed land), and has been here since 1923. The area it stands on was created in the wake of the disastrous Furisode (Long Sleeves) Fire of 1657. Tokugawa Ieyasu had the debris shovelled into the marshes at the edge of Ginza, thus providing his lords with space for their mansions and gardens. In the early years of the Meiji Era, after the *daimyō* had been kicked out of the city, the city authorities built a special residential area for Western expats here. The market relocated to this area from Nihombashi after the 1923 earthquake.

Emerging from Tsukiji subway, you'll first notice the **Tsukiji Hongan-ji**, one of the largest and most Indian-looking of Tokyo's Buddhist temples. Pop inside to see the intricately carved golden altar and cavernous interior with room for one thousand worshippers. From the temple, the most direct route to the **market** is to continue along Shin-Ōhashi-dōri, crossing Harumi-dōri (the route from Ginza) and past the row of grocers and noodle bars. On the next block lies the sprawling bulk of the market. Every day, bar Sundays and public holidays, five million pounds of fish are delivered here from far-flung corners of the earth. Over four hundred different types of seafood come under the hammer, including eels from Taiwan, salmon from Santiago and tuna from Tasmania. But as its official title indicates, fish is not the only item on sale at Tsukiji, which also deals in meat, fruit and vegetables.

The auctions, held at the back of the market, aren't officially open to the public, but no one will stop you slipping in quietly to watch the buyers and sellers gesticulating wildly over polystyrene crates of squid, sea-urchins, crab and the like. The highlight is the sale of rock-solid frozen tuna, looking like steel torpedos, all labelled with yellow stickers indicating their weight and country of origin. Depending on their quality, each tuna sells for between ¥600,000 to ¥1 million. At around 7am, Tokyo's restauranteurs and food retailers pick their way through the day's catch on sale at 1600 different wholesalers' stalls under the crescent-shaped hanger's roof.

Sloshing through the water-cleansed pathways, dodging the *ta-ray* mini-motorized trucks which shift the produce around, and being surrounded by piled crates of seafood – some of it still alive – is what a visit to Tsukiji is all about. If you get peckish, head for the outer market area (Jogai Ichiba), which is crammed with sushi stalls and noodle bars servicing the 60,000 people who pass through here each day. Good choices include *Daiwa Zushi*, open from 5.30am, which is actually within the market, while *Tatsuzushi* and the more expensive *Sushisei* are in the block of shops between the market and Tsukiji Hongan-ji. Expect to pay around ¥2000 for a set course.

The closest **subway station** to the market is Tsukiji (on the Hibiya line), but if you want to witness the frantic auctions that start at 5am you'll have to catch a taxi or walk to the market. If you can't make it that early, it's still worth coming here; the action in the outer markets continues through to midday.

## Hama Rikyū Teien and Tsukudashima

The contrast between bustling Tsukiji and the traditional garden of **Hama Rikyū Teien** (Tues–Sun 9am–4.30pm; ¥300), less than a ten-minute walk east couldn't be more acute. This beautifully designed park once belonged to the shoguns, who hunted ducks here. These days the ducks, protected inside the garden's nature reserve, are no longer used for target practice and only have to watch out for the large number of cats that wander the idly twisting pathways. There are three ponds, the largest spanned by a trellis-covered bridge that leads to a floating teahouse. Next to the entrance is a sprawling, three-hundred-year-old pine tree and a manicured lawn dotted with sculpted, stunted trees. One of the best times of year to come here is in early spring, when lilac wisteria hangs in fluffy bunches from the trellises around the central pond. From the Tokyo Bay side of the garden, you'll get a view across to the Rainbow Bridge, and can see the floodgate which regulates how much sea water flows in and out of this pond with the tides. By far the nicest way of approaching the gardens is to take a ferry from Asakusa, down the Sumida-gawa (see p.112 for details).

Another rewarding diversion from Tsukiji, across the Sumida-gawa, is **Tsukudashima**, a tiny enclave of Edo-period houses and shops, clustered around a backwater spanned by a dinky red bridge. Sheltering in the shadow of the modern River City 21 tower blocks, the area has a history stretching back to 1613, when a group of Ōsaka fishermen were settled on the island by the shogun. In addition to providing food for the castle, the fishermen were expected to report on any suspicious comings and goings in the bay. For their spiritual protection, they built themselves the delightful **Sumiyoshi-jinja**, dedicated to the god of the sea, like the related shrine in Ōsaka (see p.417). The water well beside the shrine's *torii* has a roof with eves decorated with exquisite carvings of scenes from the fishermen's lives. Every three years, on the first weekend in August, the shrine hosts the Sumiyoshi Matsuri **festival**, during which a special *mikoshi* (portable shrine) is dowsed in water as it is paraded through the streets; this is symbolic of the real dunking it would once have had in the river.

The Tsukudashima community is also famous for **tsukudani**, delicious morsels of seaweed and fish preserved in a mixture of soy sauce, salt or sugar. You'll find eighteen different types of this speciality served up at *Tenyasu Honten* (daily 9am–6pm), a weather-worn wooden shop typical of the area, outside of which hangs a tattered *noren* (cloth shop sign). Ask nicely and the white-aproned ladies, who sit cross-legged on the *tatami* platform from which customers are served, will allow you to take a peep behind the scenes to see how this delicacy is made. A wooden box set of six types of *tsukudani* costs around ¥2000.

To reach Tsukudashima on foot, head for the Tsukuda-Ōhashi bridge, a ten-minute walk from Tsukiji subway station, past St Luke's Hospital. The area is easily spotted on the left side of the island as you leave the bridge and shouldn't take you more than thirty minutes to explore. The closest **subway station** is Tsukishima, on the Yūrakuchō line.

## Ōdaiba

Returning to Tsukiji and heading west towards the raised Shuto Expressway will bring you to Shimbashi Station and the start of the Yurikamome monorail line out to an **island** of reclaimed land in Tokyo Bay. Popularly known as **Ōdaiba**, the island takes its name from the cannon emplacements set up by the shogun in 1853 in the bay to protect the city from Commodore Perry's threatening Black Ships (see History, p.774), but is now better known as the site of an illfated construction project of the late 1980s, which proved to be the downfall of the city's former governor, Suzuki Shunichi. The remains of the two cannon emplacements are now dwarfed by the huge landfill site – Rinkai Fukutoshin, of which Ōdaiba is a part – on which the Metropolitan Government set about constructing a 21st-century city in 1988. The economic slump and spiralling development costs slowed the project down, and when the Rainbow Bridge linking

Ōdaiba to the city opened in 1993, the area was still a series of empty lots. Suzuki's plan to spend more public money on an International City Exposition here in 1996 was the last straw for Tokyo's citizens: the governor was kicked out in the 1995 elections.

Today, Ōdaiba is beginning to blossom; futuristic buildings linked by the space-age monorail, a man-made beach, parks, sunny shopping plazas and architectural wonders have turned the island into such a local hit that on weekends the monorail is often swamped with day-trippers. In the evenings, the illuminated Rainbow Bridge and twinkling towers of the Tokyo skyline make Ōdaiba a romantic spot – you'll see plenty of canoodling couples staring wistfully at the glittering panorama.

The easiest way of reaching Ōdaiba is on the **Yurikamome monorail**, which arcs up to the Rainbow Bridge on a splendid circular line and stops at all of the area's major sites, terminating at Ariake Station. An ¥800 one-day ticket is best if you intend to see all of the island – walking across Ōdaiba is a long slog. **Buses** from Shinagawa Station, southwest of the bay, cross the Rainbow Bridge and run as far as the Maritime Museum, stopping at Ōdaiba Kaihin-kōen on the way. Alternatively, you can take a ferry from Hinode Sanbashi to either Ariake or the Maritime Museum via Harumi and Ōdaiba Kaihin-kōen – a journey which costs no more than ¥520, doubling as a quick and cheap cruise of Tokyo Bay.

The following description of the island starts at the far south side of Rinkai Fukutoshin (to be renamed Rainbow Town) and ends with a walk back across the Rainbow Bridge – easily the highlight of any trip out to this modern world.

## Tokyo Big Sight and around

One stop from the monorail terminus at Ariake is the enormous and striking Tokyo International Exhibition Centre, better known as the **Tokyo Big Sight**. Its entrance is composed of four huge inverted pyramids, and in front stands a 15.5-metre sculpture of a red-handled saw, sticking out of the ground as if left behind by some absent-minded giant. West of the Big Sight is a fat finger of reclaimed land partly covered by Tokyo's container port and overlooked by the Telecom Centre, a wanna-be clone of Paris's Grande Arche at La Défense. The centre has a viewing platform on its twenty-first floor (¥600), which can be safely skipped in favour of the observatory at the top of the excellent **Museum of Maritime Science** (daily 10am–5pm), housed in a concrete reproduction of a 60,000-ton, white cruise ship. The exhibits include many detailed model boats and the engines of a giant ship. Docked outside are a couple of real boats: the *Soya*, which undertook scientific missions to the South Pole, and the *Yotei Marine*, a liner refitted as an exhibition space, which includes an evocative recreation of the 1920s Tokyo waterfront. Admission to the two ships only is ¥600; for the museum and the Yotei Marine ¥700 and for everything ¥1000. Within the museum ground are also a couple of lighthouses, submarines, a flying boat and two open-air swimming pools (open July 18–Aug 31; ¥2800 including admission to the museum).

Heading around the waterfront from the museum, past the curiously shaped triangular tower (an air vent for the road tunnel that goes under Tokyo Bay), is a park, **Ōdaiba Kaihin-kōen**. Across the bay, the lines of red cranes at the container port look like giraffes at feeding time.

## The beach and around

As you turn the corner of the island, and the Rainbow Bridge comes into view, Ōdaiba's man-made **beach** begins. As Japanese beaches go, it's not bad, but you'd be wise to avoid it on sunny weekends, when you'll see more raw flesh than sand. Fronting on to the beach is Decks Tokyo Beach shopping mall, which as well as trendy shops and restaurants, houses its own brewery and **Joypolis** (daily 10am–11.30pm; ¥500 admission only), a multi-storey arcade filled with Sega's interactive entertainment technology.

Next to the mall, a surreal aura hangs over Tange Kenzō's **Fuji TV Building**, a futuristic block with a huge metal sphere suspended in its middle, that looks like it has been made from a giant Mecano set. Demand for the neighbouring apartment blocks, with their views and proximity to the beach, was so high that allocation was decided by a lottery.

From the Sunset Beach row of restaurants beside the Decks Mall you can walk across on to one of the shogun's gun emplacement islands, now a public park, or continue on for an exhilarating walk along the **Rainbow Bridge**. This 918-metre-long single-span suspension bridge has two levels, the lower for the waterfront road and the monorail, and the upper for the Metropolitan Expressway. On both sides is a pedestrian promenade linking the observation rooms (daily: April–Oct 10am–9pm; Jan–March, Nov & Dec 10am–6pm; ¥300) in the anchorages at either end of the bridge. The walk along the bridge takes about forty minutes and provides magnificent views across the bay, even as far as Mount Fuji, if the sky is clear. One minute's walk from the exit from the shore-side observation room is the station for the monorail back to Shimbashi.

# Beyond Ōdaiba

West of Ōdaiba, older blocks of reclaimed land, sporting dormitory towns, golf links and other recreational facilities, jut out into Tokyo Bay. The prime attractions are **Kasai Rinkai-kōen**, a seaside **park** boasting one of Tokyo's biggest aquariums and a bird-watching centre, and the enormously popular **Tokyo Disneyland**. Though you probably won't have time to visit both in one day, these places are at adjacent stops on the JR Keiyō line from Tokyo Station. Coming from Ōdaiba, you can pick up the Keiyō line at Shin-Kiba Station.

### Kasai Rinkai-kōen

Lying between its JR Station and the sea, the flat expanse of **Kasai Rinkai-kōen** (open 24hr; free) isn't the most attractive of landscapes, but there's more to it than first appears. For many Tokyo families this is a favourite weekend spot – for picnicking, cycling or summer-swimming in its small, crescent-shaped beach – while bird enthusiasts ogle water-birds and waders in the well-designed bird sanctuary. The park's biggest draw, however, is its large aquarium, **Tokyo Sea Life Park** (Tues–Sun 9.30am–5pm; last entry 4pm; ¥800), under a glass and steel dome overlooking the sea. The first thing you meet coming down the escalators are two vast tanks of tuna and sharks, the aquarium's highlight; go down again and you stand in the middle of this fishy world, surrounded by 2,200 tons of water. Smaller tanks showcase sea life from around the world, from flashy tropical butterfly fish and paper-thin seahorses to the lumpy mudskippers of Tokyo Bay. Not everyone is here to admire the beauty of the fish – as you walk round, listen out for murmurs of *oishii* (the Japanese equivalent of "delicious!"). In the 3-D theatre the short videos on show are in Japanese only, but worth catching for the visuals.

If you're heading back into central Tokyo from here, one of the nicest ways is to hop on the **Sea Bus ferry** for the 45-minute ride (¥800) via Ariake to Hinode Sanbashi near Hamamatsuchō. Boats leave hourly from the park's western pier, with the last departure at 5pm. See p.89 for further details.

### Tokyo Disneyland

The big-daddy of Tokyo's theme parks, **Tokyo Disneyland** is a pretty close copy of the Californian original, plonked in commuter land, fifteen-minutes' train ride east of the city centre. Its theme-lands, parades and zany extravaganzas follow the well-honed Disney formula and, whatever your preconceptions, it's pretty hard not to have a good time.

You'll probably want to devote a whole day to Disneyland to get your money's worth; tickets start at ¥3670 for general admission, but the best deal is the ¥5200 "passport" covering all attractions except the "Shootin' Gallery". Opening times vary according to the season – from 10am to 7.30pm in mid-winter, up to a summer maximum of 8am to 10pm – but the park is occasionally closed for special events, so it's best to check beforehand. There's an information hot line (☎047/354-0001) and a Web page (*www.tokyodisneyland.co.jp*), but the best option is to visit the **Tokyo Disneyland Ticket Centre** (Mon–Sat 10am–6.30pm; ☎03/3201-3511) in Yūrakuchō, where you can pick up an English leaflet and buy your tickets at the same time; find the office on the first floor of the Denki Building near Hibiya subway station (see map on p.101).

The gates to Disneyland sit right in front of Maihama Station (on the JR Keiyō line; ¥210 from Tokyo Station). Inside, you'll find World Bazaar, with its shops and general services (stroller rentals, bank, lockers and information), followed by the central plaza in front of Cinderella's castle, from where the six theme-lands radiate. Toon Town is the latest addition, but Tomorrowland's Star Tours and Space Mountain offer the most heart-stopping rides. The park attracts over 30,000 visitors per day on average, which means that queues are inevitable – from thirty minutes up to one hour for the more popular attractions and at peak times such as weekends and holidays.

# EATING, DRINKING AND ENTERTAINMENT

Deciding what to **eat** in Tokyo can be a bewildering experience, and not just because you might be at a loss working out what's on the menu, or even on your plate. The problem is that with at least 80,000 restaurants in central Tokyo (compared to New York's 15,000 and London's mere 6000), you're swamped with choice. Virtually every type of cuisine is on offer, from African to Vietnamese, not to mention endless permutations of Japanese favourites such as sushi, ramen, tempura and *yakitori*. With so much choice there's no need to panic about prices: for every mega-expensive restaurant there's a cheap noodle bar or *shokudō* (eating place) dishing up curry rice, the Japanese equivalent of beans on toast.

Tokyo's **nightlife** and **entertainment** options similarly run the full gamut, from grand Kabuki theatres and cinemas to broom-cupboard bars and live music venues, (known as "live houses"). Additionally, cruising the **boutiques** and **fashion-malls**, toting a couple of designer-label carrier bags is such a part of Tokyo life that it's hard not to be caught up in the general enthusiasm. There are shops to suit every taste and budget, from swanky department stores to rag-bag flea markets.

# Eating

Tokyo periodically becomes gripped by **food crazes**. Currently, *mukokuseki* (no-nationality) food, whereby menus are an eclectic mish-mash of world cuisines, is being pushed in the *izakaya*. Another trend is for authentic foreign food – soggy pizza is out, genuine Italian cooking is in. Don't expect much from the *tabehodai/nomihodai* (eat-and-drink-all-you-can for a set price) restaurants; they might seem good value but are rarely carried off with much style or taste. What can always be relied upon are the **noodle bars**, **shokudō** and **chain restaurants**, where the Japanese go when they need to fill up without fear of the cost. Tokyo has a plethora of such places, with many clustering around and inside the train stations. **Bentō shops**, serving set boxes of food, are also good and plentiful, especially at lunchtime in shopping areas.

For Japanese **fast food**, head for *Yoshinoya*, which serves reasonably tasty *gyūdon* (stewed strips of beef on rice), and *Tenya*, which offers a similar low-cost deal for tempura and rice dishes. You'll find plenty of *McDonald's* and *KFC*s around town; a good local chain is *Mos Burger*, serving up rice burgers, carrot juice and green *konyaku* jelly (a root vegetable). It's worth noting that the ubiquitous *Mr Donut*'s menu includes Chinese dim sum snacks (known in Japan as *yum cha*) as well as coffee and doughnuts.

At any time of the day or night, **convenience stores** such as Seven-Eleven, AM/PM and Lawsons, sell a wide range of snacks and meals which can be heated up in the shop's microwave or reconstituted with hot water. For more upmarket goodies, make your way to the basement food halls of the major department stores.

## Restaurants

Tokyo has several **restaurant chains** worth checking out. For **Indian** food, *Moti*, with a outlets in Roppongi and Akasaka, is a long-time local favourite. For good **Italian** food, head for *Capricciosa*, with branches all over the city – its sign is in elongated *katakana* on a green, red and white background. You'll find the all-**American** *Tony Roma's*, specializing in spare ribs, and *Victoria Station*, good for inexpensive steak dishes, at various locations, including Roppongi, Akasaka and Aoyama. The *Seiryumon* chain of Chinese restaurants are notable for their outlandish decor rather than the authenticity of their food. Among the **Japanese chains** to look out for are *Tapa*, a lively **izakaya** specializing in *ōzara* (big plate) cuisine; *Sushisei*, a classy sushi restaurant with branches in Tsukiji, Akasaka and Roppongi, and *Tsunahachi*, which has forty branches around Japan, and is *the* place for tempura.

Hasegawa Kozo, Tokyo's cut-price Terence Conran, is the man behind the *La Bohème, Zest* and *Monsoon* chains, as well as the upmarket *Tableaux*. These restaurants serve mainly Western dishes, but can be relied on for value and late-night dining in chic settings.

If you can't decide what to go for, make your way to the restaurant floors of the major **department stores**, where you'll generally find a wide choice of cuisines and dining atmospheres under one roof, often with plastic food displays in the windows and daily specials.

To keep abreast of the latest restaurants, browse through the weekly freesheet *Tokyo Classified* or the monthly *Tokyo Journal*'s cityscope listings. The *Tokyo Q* Web site (*www.so-net.or.jp/tokyoq/*) has a great database of restaurants, plus weekly reviews and *izakaya* recommendations. Where we give telephone numbers for the restaurants listed, it's advisable to **book ahead**. The listings give the closest subway or train station to the restaurant.

---

### RESTAURANT PRICES

**Restaurants** in Tokyo have been graded as **inexpensive** (under ¥1000 for a meal without alcohol); **moderate** (¥1000–4000); **expensive** (¥4000–6000) and **very expensive** (over ¥6000). The cheapest time to eat out is lunchtime, when even the priciest places offer good-value set meals, and you'd be hard pressed to spend over ¥2000. **Tipping** is not expected, but **consumption tax** (5 percent) and local tax (3 percent, payable only if the bill exceeds ¥7500 per person) can significantly push up the total cost. Some restaurants and bars serving food, especially those in hotels, add on a **service charge** (typically ten percent). Make sure you have cash to hand; payment by **credit card** is becoming more common, but is generally restricted to upmarket restaurants and hotels.

## TOKYO: RESTAURANTS

| | | |
|---|---|---|
| Agra | *Āgurā* | アーグラー |
| Akiyoshi | *Akiyoshi* | 秋吉 |
| Angkor Wat | *Ankōru Watto* | アンコールワット |
| Atariya | *Atariya* | 当リヤ |
| Aux Bacchanales | *Ō Bakunaru* | オーバクナル |
| Ban Thai | *Ban Tai* | バンタイ |
| Bikkuri Sushi | *Bikkuri Sushi* | びっくり寿司 |
| Chiang Mai | *Chen Mai* | チェンマイ |
| Chin'ya | *Chinya* | ちんや |
| Daikokuya | *Daikokuya* | 大黒家 |
| Ebisu Tower | *Ebisu Tawā* | 恵比寿タワー |
| El Mocambo | *Eru Mokambo* | エルモカンボ |
| Erawan | *Erawan* | エラワン |
| Farm Grill | *Fāmu Guriru* | ファームグリル |
| Genrokuzushi | *Genrokuzushi* | 元禄寿司 |
| Hokuhan | *Hokuhan* | 北畔 |
| Ichioku | *Ichioku* | 一億 |
| Inakaya | *Inakaya* | 田舎家 |
| Jangara | *Jangara* | じゃんがら |
| Kakiniku Karubiya | *Kakiniku Karubiya* | かきにくカルビヤ |
| La Bodeguita | *Bodegiita* | ボデギータ |
| Las Chicas | *Rasu Chikasu* | ラスチカス |
| Lunchan Bar and Grill | *Ranchan Bā ando Guriru* | ランチャンバーアンドグリル |
| Malaychan | *Marēchan* | マレーチャン |
| Mawaru Sushi Hana-kan | *Mawaru Sushi Hana-kan* | まわる寿し花館 |
| Momonoki House | *Momonoki Hausu* | モモノキハウス |
| Musashino | *Musashino* | 武蔵野 |
| Nair's | *Nairu Resutoran* | ナイルレストラン |
| New York Kitchen | *Nyū Yōku Kitchin* | ニューヨークキッチン |
| Ninnikuya | *Ninnikuya* | ニンニク屋 |
| Only Malaysia | *Onrii Mareishia* | オンリーマレイシア |
| Oz Café | *Ozu Kafe* | オズカフェ |
| Rebecca | *Rebekka* | レベッカ |
| Saigon | *Saigon* | サイゴン |
| Salty Box Grill | *Sorutii Bokkusu Guriru* | ソルティーボックスグリル |
| Seiryūmon | *Seiryūmon* | 青龍門 |
| Shimauta Paradise | *Shimauta Paradaisu* | 島歌パラダイス |
| Shinsekai | *Shinsekai* | 新世界 |
| Shion | *Shion* | シオン |
| Sometarō | *Sometarō* | 染太郎 |
| Soul | *Souru* | ソール (魂) |
| Sushisei | *Sushisei* | 寿司清 |
| Taimeiken | *Taimeiken* | たいめいけん |
| Tatsumiya | *Tatsumiya* | 辰巳屋 |
| Tokyo Kaisen Market | *Tōkyō Kaisen Ichiba* | 東京海鮮市場 |
| Tomoegata | *Tomoegata* | 巴潟 |
| Tonki | *Tonki* | とんき |
| Torigin | *Torigin* | 鳥ぎん |
| Toriyoshi | *Toriyoshi* | 鳥良 |
| Tsunahachi | *Tsunahachi* | つな八 |
| Uzu Shio | *Uzu Shio* | うず潮 |
| Volga | *Boruga* | ボルガ |
| Yabu Soba | *Yabu Soba* | やぶそば |
| Yama no Chaya | *Yama no Chaya* | 山の茶屋 |

## Akasaka

**Blue Sky**, 17th floor, *New Ōtani Hotel*, 4-1 Kiochō, Chiyoda-ku (☎03/3238-0028). Revolving restaurant at the top of one of the hotel's towers providing a range of cuisines, including a Chinese buffet, as well as Japanese and Italian dishes. Best at night when the neon-lit skyline provides as romantic backdrop as you could wish for. Akasaka Mitsuke Station. Moderate to expensive.

**Jangara**, Sotobori-dōri, near the entrance to the Hie-jinja. Funky noodle bar serving up large bowls of ramen (chinese noodles), in three types of soup: fish, mild and light, and greasy garlic, from ¥550 and beer at ¥450. Open Mon–Fri 11am–3pm, 5pm–12.30am. Also in Akihabara, Ginza and two branches in Harajuku, both close by Omotesandō. Akasaka Station. Inexpensive.

**Kakiniku Karubiya**, 3-12-7 Akasaka, Minato-ku. Korean barbecue run by a friendly English-speaking manager. There's a picture menu and an all-you-can-eat lunch deal for ¥800. Dinner courses including soup, rice, salad, pickles as well as beef are ¥2000. Akasaka Station. Moderate.

**Sushisei**, 3-11-4 Akasaka, Minato-ku. One of the city's most famous sushi restaurant chains, which means you may have to wait to be served at peak meal times. You're guaranteed a hearty selection of fish slices at a fraction of the cost charged by some à-la-carte *sushi-ya*. You can expect to spend around ¥3000 (less for lunch). Closed Sunday. Branches also in Tsukiji, close to the market, and Roppongi on TV Asahi-dōri. Akasaka Station. Moderate.

**Yama no Chaya**, 2-10-6 Nagatachō, Chiyoda-ku (☎03/3581-0656). If you're going to splash out on traditional Japanese cuisine, this teahouse restaurant set in a wooded glade next to the Hie-jinja is a fine choice. It's been serving a delicatedly prepared set menu (¥15,000 for lunch, ¥17,000 for dinner) based around *unagi* (eel) for the last seventy years. Akasaka Station. Very expensive.

## Aoyama and Harajuku

*All the following restaurants are marked on the map on p.133.*

**Angkor Wat**, 1-38-13 Yoyogi, Shibuya-ku (☎03/3370-3019). The best Cambodian restaurant in Tokyo. Tell the waiters your price limit and let them bring you a selection of dishes (¥3000 per head is more than enough). The sweetly spicy salads, soups and vegetable rolls are all excellent. 5min walk west of Yoyogi station; look for the pottery elephant outside the entrance on a sidestreet. Yoyogi Station. Moderate.

**Aux Bacchanales**, 1-6-1 Jingū-mae, Shibuya-ku. Nicest of the French-style bistros that are currently taking over Harajuku. The tables spills on to the pavement, and there are even surly French waiters to compliment the authentic Parisienne sidewalk furniture and steak frites. Cheaper prices for drinks at the bar, just as in Paris, but who would want to miss out on the passing parade on Meiji-dōri. Meiji-jingū-mae Station. Moderate.

**Chao Bamboo**, 6-1-5 Jingū-mae, Shibuya-ku. Same management as the larger and inferior *Bamboo* further up Omotesandō, but this one specializes in cheap and tasty South East Asian street food, served at rickety outdoor tables. There's a photo menu and you'd be hard pressed to spend more than ¥2000. Meiji-jingū-mae Station. Moderate.

**Genrokuzushi**, 5-8-5 Jingū-mae, Shibuya-ku. Not the cheapest *kaitenzushi* (conveyor-belt sushi) restaurant you will come across, with plates starting at ¥150 each. But its prime position on Omotesandō, just beyond the Oriental Bazaar, means a fast turnover of clients, ensuring freshly prepared sushi on the conveyor belt. Also does take-out *bentō* – ideal for picnics in Yoyogi-kōen or Meiji-jingū. Meiji-jingū-mae Station. Inexpensive.

**Las Chicas**, 5-47-6 Jingū-mae, Shibuya-ku (☎03/3407-6865). On a summer's night there are few nicer places to dine than in *Las Chicas'* enchanting courtyard, where fairylights twinkle in the trees. The Australian-esque cuisine is supported by some fine Antipodean wines. There's also a spacious indoor restaurant, a lively bar (with Internet terminals) and a hair salon in the complex hidden away on Harajuku's quiet backstreets. Omotesandō Station. Moderate.

**Mominoki House**, 2-18-5 Jingū-mae, Shibuya-ku (☎03/3405-9144). Lots of natural ingredients used at this macrobiotic restaurant on the quiet side of Harajuku. Plants, paintings, and jazz add to the vibe. A good lunch can be had for around ¥1500. Closed Sun. Meiji-jingū-mae Station. Moderate.

**Soul**, Kita-Aoyama, Minato-ku. On the road beside the Kinokuniya supermarket – look for the big red lantern. Popular with young Japanese, and specializing in *mukokuseki*. The menu is in Japanese, but you can point to the large plates of food on the counter. Around ¥3000 per person. Dishes tend to be spicy, so order lots of beer. Omotesandō Station. Moderate.

**Toriyoshi**, 4-28-21 Jingū-mae (☎03/3470-3901). Ultra-modern chicken restaurant that serves the bird in all manner of ways, from stew to *yakitori* and raw as sashimi. *Tori sembei* crackers, made out of deep-fried chicken skin, are worth trying. Lots of other restaurants worth checking out on the same backstreet running parallel to Meiji-dōri. Meiji-jingū-mae Station. Moderate.

**To the Herbs**, 5-10-1 Minami-Aoyama, Minato-ku. Decent Italian food (crispy pizza, flavoursome pasta sauces) at this second-floor mini-chain. The emphasis is on the use of authentic ingredients and traditional recipes. The Nishi-Azabu branch is in a stand-alone wooden building near the crossing and stays open until 5am, while the Mejiro outlet, west of the station, specializes in spaghetti. ¥3000 per head. Omotesandō Station. Moderate.

**un café**, Cosmos Aoyama Bldg, 5-53-67 Jingū-mae, Shibuya-ku (☎03/5469-0275). Tucked away in the sunken plaza behind the UN University building this sleek operation has a hip, post-modern ambience. The menu ranges from spaghetti and salads to beef carpaccio on savoury couscous and seared tuna steaks. Tables spill out into the plaza, making this an ideal al fresco dining spot in summer. Around ¥4000 per person for dinner. Omotesandō Station. Moderate.

## Ebisu and Meguro
*All the following restaurants are marked on the map on p.133.*

**Ebisu Tower**, Yebisu Garden City. Two floors of restaurants with great views across the city. Try *Torigin* on the 39th floor, a classy *yakitori-ya* with sets for around ¥1000. Ebisu Station. Moderate to expensive.

**La Bodeguita**, 2F, 1-7-3 Ebisu-Minami, Shibuya-ku (☎03/3715-7721). Tokyo's premier Cuban restaurant serving top-class *arroz con frijoles* (rice and beans), on the western side of the station, a block down from a *Doutor* café. Despite the lack of dancing space, it also qualifies as the city's longest-running salsa club. Open 6pm to midnight, with last orders at 11.30pm. Closed Sun. Ebisu Station. Moderate.

**Ninnikuya**, 1-26-12 Ebisu, Shibuya-ku (☎03/3446-5887). Tokyo's original garlic restaurant is still one of the best. Virtually everything on the menu is cooked with the pungent bulb, and the buzzing atmosphere in the long dining room with large shared wooden tables can't be beat. Around ¥4000 a head. Ebisu Station. Moderate to expensive.

**Tableaux**, Sunroser Daikenyama Bldg, 11-6 Sarugakuchō (☎03/5489-2201). Chandeliers, velvet upholstery and lots of mirrors at this trendy restaurant. The menu takes its inspiration from all corners of the globe – it's best to ask what the recommended dishes are. Expect to pay ¥5000 per head. 5min from the station. Daikenyama Station. Expensive.

**Tonki**, 1-1-2 Shimo-Meguro, Meguro-ku. Tokyo's most famous *tonkatsu* restaurant, where a seemingly telepathic team make order of chaos. Queue outside the main branch, west of the station, and try the *teishoku*, which comes with soup, rice, cabbage, pickles and tea for ¥1500. Closed on the third Monday of the month, when you could try the annexe on the east side of the station, across the plaza on the second floor of the corner building. Meguro Station. Moderate.

## Roppongi, Nishi Azabu and Hirō

**Bikkuri Sushi**, 3-14-9 Roppongi, Minato-ku. Conveyor-belt sushi shop on the corner of Gaien Higashi-dōri, opposite the Roi Building. Open long hours (11am–5am), helping clubbers keep their energy levels topped up. Dishes start at ¥130. Roppongi Station. Inexpensive.

**El Mocambo**, 1-4-38 Nishi-Azabu, Minato-ku. South American restaurant which is a long-running favourite for those in the mood for a fiesta. Across the road from the US Army's *Star & Stripes* newspaper offices on Seijōki-dōri. Pitchers of margaritas will get you into the swing of things. Occasional live salsa music. Roppongi Station. Moderate to expensive.

**Hard Rock Café**, 5-4-20 Roppongi, Minato-ku. It's hard to miss the giant gorilla clamped on to the side of this rock'n'roll burger joint that needs no introduction. Very noisy, very lively, very Roppongi. Open until 4am at the weekend. Roppongi Station. Moderate to expensive.

**Homework's**, 5-1-20 Hirō, Shibuya-ku. Decent burgers – the chunky home-made variety – at this popular pitstop at the end of Hirō's main shopping street. The french fries are well up to scratch, too. Also at 1-5-8 Azabu-Jūban, Minato-ku. Hirō Station. Moderate.

**Ichioku**, 4-4-5 Roppongi, Minato-ku. At the Nogizaka end of Roppongi, look for the green, yellow and red front of this funky *mukokuseki* restaurant. Many swear by their cheese *gyōza* and tofu steaks, but there's plenty of other options to choose from the picture menu on the table top. Dishes are made from organically grown vegetables. Roppongi Station. Moderate.

**Inakaya**, 7-8-4 Roppongi, Minato-ku (☎03/3405-9866). Food preparation as theatre at this famous *robatayaki*. The chefs kneel on a raised dias amid a carnival of raw ingredients, screaming out the names of the cooked dishes that they gleefully pass over to customers on oar-like wooden spatulas. A meal can easily clock up at ¥10,000 per person, but you'll have had memorable night. Also at 3-12-7 Akasaka, Minato-ku (☎03/3586 3054). Roppongi Station. Very expensive.

**Oz Café**, 1-8-13 Nishi-Azabu, Minato-ku. Crocodile, emu and kangaroo are on the menu, and there's an Aussie flag and giant toy Skippy outside just in case you have trouble locating this place. All the potted palms and hanging baskets make for a greenhouse atmosphere and there's a pleasant street-side patio. Roppongi Station. Moderate to expensive.

**Salty Box Grill**, 1-11-6 Nishi-Azabu, Minato-ku (☎03/3403-6631). Relaxed Canadian restaurant with a tantalizing menu (imported smoked salmon, Atlantic fish broth, huge prawns in brandy and vermouth). Take a friend and go for one of the combination plates. Expect to pay ¥3000 per head. Their Sunday brunch is popular so book ahead. Roppongi Station. Moderate to expensive.

**Shimauta Paradise**, 4F Seishidō Bldg, 7-14-10 Roppongi. Birdsong greets you as you push through the door to this lively restaurant, close by Roppongi Crossing, serving Okinawan cuisine, such as pickled sea cucumber, stewed pigs' trotters, and fermented squid with tofu. Wash it down with a flask of *shōchū* (distilled grain alcohol) diluted with warm water or Orion beer. When there's live music, there's a ¥1000 cover charge. Roppongi Station. Moderate to expensive.

**Volga**, 3-5-14 Shiba-kōen, Minato-ku (☎03/3433-1766). Like entering a set from *Dr Zhivago*. Outside is a camp onion-domed confection, inside the decor is heavy on velvet and gilt. Has live jazz each evening, 25 different types of vodka, and a menu that embraces standard Russian dishes such as borsch and piroshki. Lunch from ¥1200, dinner ¥4500. Kamiyachō Station. Expensive.

## Ginza, Kanda and Ryōgoku

*All the following restaurants are marked on the maps on p.101 and p.106.*

**Atariya**, 3-5-17 Ginza. One of the more reasonable places to eat in Ginza, this small, workaday restaurant, with its fulsome English menu, is a good introduction to *yakitori* bars. Mon–Sat 4.30–11pm. Ginza Station. Inexpensive to moderate.

**Chiang Mai**, 1-6-10 Yūrakuchō (☎03/3580-0456). Cosy, relaxed Thai restaurant with excellent-value set lunches and a wicked tom yam soup. If this place is full try the more formal *Siam* round the corner. Closed Sat. Hibiya Station. Inexpensive to moderate.

**Farm Grill**, 2F, Ginza Nine Sango-kan, 8-5 Ginza (☎03/5568-6156). Hugely popular with the expat crowd for its good prices and mega portions, though service can be slow. Wooden floors and rattan chairs make for a nice vibe. The food is Nineties Americana; rotisserie chicken, Pasta Malibu and Delirium Fudge Brownie. Reservations are recommended for the Sunday brunch buffet (3–10pm), a two-hour eat-and-drink-all-you-can blow-out for around ¥4000. They also claim 93 types of wine and 29 beers from 15 countries. Open 11am–11pm. Shimbashi Station. Moderate.

**Nair's**, 4-10-7 Ginza. A Tokyo institution since the 1950s, now offering Kerala home-cooking. Maybe not the best Indian around, but the food's tasty and reasonably cheap for Ginza – count on ¥2000–3000 per head. The Murghi lunch at ¥1300 is a better deal. Closed Tues. Higashi-Ginza Station. Moderate.

**Rebecca**, 1-7-8 Uchisaiwaichō. Sanitized *Bladerunner* feel to this huge, under-the-tracks beer restaurant. It's best at night when neon graffiti signs splatter colour over the grungy backstreet, though in the evening you pay ¥4000 on entry, which covers four dishes from the mostly Chinese buffet and limitless beer, wine or soft drinks. There's a cheaper deal at lunchtime (¥1000). Shimbashi Station. Moderate to expensive.

**Taimeiken**, 1-2-10 Nihombashi. One of Tokyo's original Western-style restaurants, whose "*omuraisu*" (rice-stuffed omelette) featured in the movie *Tampopo* (see p.804). Downstairs is a cheap and cheerful cafeteria serving large portions of curry rice, *tonkatsu* and noodles, with a more expensive restaurant above. Open Mon–Sat 11am–9pm. Nihombashi Station. Inexpensive to moderate.

**Tomoegata**. 1-7-11 Ryōgoku. In the heart of sumo territory, this is one of the best places to sample the wrestlers' protein-packed stew, *chanko-nabe*. For under ¥3000 you can have the full-blown meal cooked at your table, though most people will find the smaller, ready-made version (¥800) more than enough. This mini *chanko* is only available for lunch and is slightly more expensive on week-ends and holidays. *Tomeogata* is easy to spot from its parade of colourful flags, two blocks south of the station; there's a new annexe on the north side of the street. Open 11.30am–10pm. Ryōgoku Station. Inexpensive to moderate.

**Torigin**, 5-5-7 Ginza. Bright, upmarket restaurant serving *yakitori* and *kamameshi* (kettle-cooked rice with various toppings), tucked down an alley two blocks east of Ginza's Sony Building (New Torigin next door is a cheeky rival). Good for a snack or a full meal: courses start from ¥740 for five *yakitori* sticks, or ¥800 for *kamameshi*. The English menu makes it a lot easier. Ginza Station. Inexpensive to moderate.

**Uzu Shio**, 1-1-13 Yūrakuchō. Hone your *kaitenzushi* (conveyor-belt sushi) skills in this friendly sushi bar under the train tracks. If you look lost, they'll give you English guidelines on how it all works. Prices start at ¥150 per plate. Open 11am–10pm. Hibiya Station. Inexpensive.

**Yabu Soba**, 2-10 Kanda-Awajichō. Connoisseurs travel a long way to slurp their noodles and listen to the distinctive sing-song cries of *Yabu Soba*'s cheerful waiting staff. You might have to wait at busy times, but it doesn't take long, and there's an attractive garden to look out on. Prices start at ¥600. Open 11.30am–7pm. Awajichō Station. Inexpensive to moderate.

## Asakusa and Ueno
*All the following restaurants are marked on the maps on p.113 or p.116.*

**Agra**, 2F 4-7-2 Ueno. Squeeze round a few tables or up at the counter at this tiny Indian behind Ab-Ab department store. Curries come in five strengths and include generous amounts of meat, fish or vegetable. Dishes start at around ¥1000 (including rice or bread), or there's a choice of good-value lunch and dinner sets. They also have a quieter annex the other side of the train tracks. Okachimachi Station. Moderate.

**Chin'ya**, 1-3-4 Asakusa. Founded in 1880, this famous, traditional *shabu-shabu* and *sukiyaki* restaurant offers well-priced set menus (from ¥1900) on seven floors, with casual dining in the basement. Open 11.30am–9pm. Closed Wed. Asakusa Station. Moderate to expensive.

**Daikokuya**, 1-38-10 Asakusa. Avoid the lunchtime rush at this Meiji-era tempura restaurant, in an attractive old building opposite Dembō-in garden. The speciality is *tendon*, a satisfying bowl of shrimp, fish and prawn fritters on a bed of rice (from ¥1400). The *tatami* room upstairs tends to be less hectic. Open 11.30am–8.30pm. Closed Thurs. Asakusa Station. Moderate.

**Hokuhan**, 6-7-10 Ueno. Duck under the curtain and enter the congenial world of *Hokuhan*, presided over by a lady with a smattering of English. Tell her how much you'd like to spend (¥2500–3000 for a basic meal), and wait for a feast of mountain vegetables and grilled fish in the no-nonsense flavours of north Japan. Open 5–10pm. Ueno Station. Moderate.

**Musashino**, 2-8-11 Ueno. Ueno is famed for its *tonkatsu* (breaded pork cutlets). Prices are reasonable for a big thick slab that melts in the mouth. Choose between standard "rose" or fillet, at around ¥1500 including soup, rice and pickles. Ueno-Hirokōji Station. Moderate.

**Sometaro**, 2-2-2 Nishi-Asakusa. Homely restaurant specializing in *okonomiyaki*, cheap and filling savoury pancakes cooked on a hotplate. One good-size bowl costs from ¥400, depending on your ingredients. There's a book of English instructions and plenty of people to offer advice. Avoid the queues at peak mealtimes (noon–2pm and 6pm–8pm). There's no sign outside; look for a bamboo-fenced garden and lantern. Noon–10pm. Tawaramachi Station. Inexpensive.

**Tatsumiya**, 1-33-5 Asakusa. This cluttered, country-style establishment offers a range of traditional Japanese dishes (and a welcome English menu). The best options are a lunchtime bentō (under ¥1000) or the sets from ¥1300, though in winter the more expensive *nabe* (wholesome stews) are tempting. A modest evening meal will set you back around ¥3000 per head. Closed Mon. Asakusa Station. Inexpensive to moderate.

## Ikebukuro
*All the following restaurants are marked on the map on p.122.*

**Akiyoshi**, 3-30-4 Nishi-Ikebukuro. Unusually large *yakitori* bar with a good atmosphere and a helpful picture-menu. You might have to queue at peak times for the tables, but there's generally space at the counter. Mon–Sat 5pm–midnight. Ikebukuro Station. Inexpensive.

**Erawan**, 3F, 1-21-2 Minami-Ikebukuro. Large, glitzy place that's best-known for its lunchtime buffets (¥1000 including soft drinks; 11.30am–2.30pm). Ikebukuro Station. Moderate.

**Malaychan**, 3-22-6 Nishi-Ikebukuro. Popular, unpretentious Malay restaurant dishing up decent food, from Malay grilled fish and *nasi lemak* (rice cooked in coconut milk, with various toppings) to shark's fin soup. The beer pitchers are good-value, or throw in a Singapore Sling and you can still eat well for under ¥2000. Ikebukuro Station. Moderate.

**Mawaru Sushi Hana-kan**. 3-13-10 Minami-Ikebukuro. Smart, big *kaitenzushi* with stools and family tables at the counter. Plates cost from ¥120 to ¥500, and they also do take-out sushi *bentō*. Open 11am–11pm. Ikebukuro Station. Inexpensive to moderate.

**Saigon**, 3F, 1-7-10 Higashi-Ikebukuro. Friendly place serving authentic Vietnamese food, even down to the *333* beer. *Banh xeo* (sizzling pancake with a spicy sauce) or *bun bo* (beef noodle soup) are recommended, with a side-dish of *nem* (spring rolls) if you're really hungry. Lunchtime sets are well under ¥1000. Ikebukuro Station. Inexpensive to moderate.

**Taj Mahal**, 2F, 2-27-5 Minami-Ikebukuro. Unfussy Indian restaurant charging moderate prices. The set menus aren't the cheapest around, but the portions are generous. If you're here in the evening, a *thali* is recommended (vegetarian version available). Ikebukuro Station. Moderate.

## Shibuya

*All the following restaurants are marked on the map on p.133.*

**Lunchan Aoyama**, 1-2-5 Shibuya (☎03/5466-1398). Rather glitzy restaurant with car-showroom windows that is a bit overblown for this quiet corner of Shibuya. Large servings of California-style cuisine, including Caesar salad, ribs and cheesecakes. Sunday brunches are great. Expect to pay around ¥4000 per person. Shibuya Station. Expensive.

**New York Kitchen**, Mulbery Bldg, Shibuya-ku. Stylish deli-café, just off Kōen-dōri around the corner from the Tobacco and Salt Museum, has a good-value self-service food bar for about ¥480 per plate. Also does bagel sandwiches for ¥290 and has an outdoor terrace opposite. Daily 11am–11pm. Shibuya Station. Inexpensive.

**Only Malaysia**, 3-17-3 Shibuya and 109 Bldg, 26-5 Udagawachō, Shibuya-ku. No longer the "only" Malaysian restaurant in town, but still one of the most reliable. There's a branch on either side of Shibuya station. Plenty of the dishes are suitable for vegetarians. Shibuya Station. Moderate.

**The Prime**, 2-29-5 Dōgenzaka, Shibuya-ku. A restaurant supermarket on the second floor of this building; sit where you like and pick from a range of outlets around the edge of the floor. Everything from curries and bagels to sushi and noodles. Shibuya Station. Moderate.

## Shinjuku and around

*All the following restaurants are marked on the map on p.126.*

**Ban Thai**, 1-23-14 Kabukichō, Shinjuku-ku. Shinjuku's most famous Thai restaurant serves authentic dishes at moderate prices. On the third floor of a building surrounded by the screaming neon strip joints of Kabukichō. For a quieter atmosphere, journey out to their other branch (1-15-1 Tamagawa, Setagaya-ku ☎03/5716-3771), housed in a Thai wooden palace by the Tamagawa river. Both venues have live music. Shinjuku Station. Moderate.

**Canard**, B1 Sankocho Haimu, 5-17-6 Shinjuku (☎03/3200-0706). Sublime French cooking in this cramped basement down an alley opposite the Marui Interior department store on Meiji-dōri. Set menus of ¥2500 and ¥3800 at night. Arrive early for the set lunch. Shinjuku-Sanchōme Station. Moderate to expensive.

**New York Grill**, Park Hyatt Tower, 3-7-1-2 Nishi-Shinjuku (☎03/5323-3458). Stylish 52nd-floor restaurant where great views, huge portions and a bustling vibe make for a sublime eating experience. The ¥4200 lunch is worth splurging on. You'll need to book, especially for evenings and weekends. Shinjuku Station. Expensive.

**Seiryumon**, 3/4F Shinjuku Remina Bldg, 3-17-4 Shinjuku, Shinjuku-ku (☎03/3355-0717). The theme at this branch of the Chinese-café chain is Shanghai opium den circa 1840; you dine inside cages and there's a mock secret entrance to the restaurant. Shinjuku Station. Moderate to expensive.

**Shinsekai**, 1-16-19 Ōkubo, Shinjuku-ku. Malaysian and Singaporean food, such as *char kuay teow* (flat fried noodles), at foodstall prices, served 24 hours a day. Only a couple of minutes' walk west of the station, along the main shopping street. Shin-Ōkubo Station. Moderate.

**Shion**. Round the corner from *Kirin City* on the west side of Shinjuku, this is one of the city's best conveyor-belt sushi operations. There's often a queue, but it moves quickly. Plates are a cheap ¥100 or ¥200 each and you can order beer and sake. Shinjuku Station. Inexpensive.

**Tokyo Kaisen Market**, 2-36-1 Kabukichō, Shinjuku-ku (☎03/5273-8301). Choose your seafood from the giant pools on the ground floor and have it served as you wish (sashimi, sushi or cooked) at the second floor warehouse-like space. The market is just north of the plaza surrounded by cinemas. Shinjuku Station. Moderate to expensive.

**Tsunahachi**, 3-31-8 Shinjuku. The main branch of the famous tempura restaurant almost always has a queue outside. You're likely to sit down quickly if you settle for the upstairs rooms away from the frying action. Everything is freshly made and even with the ¥1100 set – including soup, rice and pickles – you'll be full. Shinjuku Station. Moderate.

# Cafés and teahouses

Tokyo's **café scene** was revolutionized in the early 1990s with the arrival of a new breed of chain coffee shop. In contrast to the **kissaten**, old-style cafés where customers idle their afternoons away over expensive blended and speciality coffees, these modern places are slick, convenient and cheap and have proved an instant hit with locals. You can now find branches of *Café Veloce, Doutor,* and *Mr Donut,* all over Tokyo, serving straight-forward "blend" (medium strength) coffee and tea from as little as ¥180, and a decent range of snacks; they're ideal for breakfast or a quick break. The chain cafés *Giraffe* and *Pronto* transform into bars in the evening, serving reasonably-priced alcoholic drinks and nibbles.

For all the convenience of these operations, you shouldn't miss sampling at least one of Tokyo's old-style cafés, where the emphasis is on service and creating an interesting, relaxing space. You'll pay more, but many of these places, such as Roppongi's *Almond,* have become city institutions. Another famous caffeine hotspot is Harajuku, where the main boulevard Omotesandō's faint Parisienne quality has been pushed to the limit with a rush of fake **French cafés**. These ersatz bistros charge outrageous prices, but if you want to people-watch with the beautiful people they are the places to hang out. Just remember to take your time, since you've rented the table rather than paid for a quick pick-me-up.

**Teahouses** are much thinner on the ground, though Japanese green tea and sweets are undergoing something of a revival, as a low-calorie, traditional alternative to coffee and cake. For a traditional Japanese tea ceremony, the best places to head are the *New Ōtani* and the *Ōkura* hotels (see Accommodation, p.91). It's worth noting that while cafés keep late hours, teahouses are strictly a daytime affair. The listings below give the nearest subway or train station.

## Cafés
**Almond**. Old-style chain of coffee shops, serving sickly synthetic cream cakes. None of the other branches dotted around the city has quite the same retro chic as the Roppongi outlet, now a famed meeting place. Roppongi Station.

**Andersons**, 5-1-26 Aoyama, Minato-ku. Tokyo outpost of the famous Swedish-style bakery in Hiroshima (see p.554). Good location on the corner of Omotesandō and Aoyama-dōri, an excellent range of pastries and sandwiches and a reasonably-priced sit-down café good for breakfast and lunch. Omotesandō Station.

**Café de Ropé**, 6-1-8 Jingū-mae, Shibuya-ku. Eternally popular Omotesandō hang-out, also serving alcohol and snack food, that somehow manages to hold its head above local Frenchified upstarts. The floor to ceiling glass windows are ideal for people-watching. Meiji-jingū-mae Station.

**Café du Monde**, Spice 2 Building, 1–10–10 Nishi-Ikebukuro. Bright, modern New Orleans coffee shop specializing in chicory coffee and beignets (doughnuts fried in cotton-seed oil) to eat with various dipping sauces. Ikebukuro Station.

**Cyberia**, 1-14-17 Nishi-Azabu, Minato-ku. Hook up to the Web at the Tokyo outpost of the London-based Internet café chain. Internet access costs ¥500 for 30 minutes – a pot of tea or coffee ¥620. A five-minute walk towards Aoyama Botchi from the Nishi-Azabu crossing. Email address: *cyberia@cyberia.co.jp*. Roppongi Station.

**Doutor**. Branches all over the city. The café-au-lait is the closest you'll get to a cappuccino at this ubiquitous cheap chain coffee shop. Also does toast, hot dogs, sandwiches and some cakes. Most outlets are small and are often crowded.

**Kōbe Bell**. Branches all over the city. Chain pastry shop, but the Akasaka branch has a nice sit-down café at the back and wins the prize for the city's cheapest cuppa; ¥120 for a coffee, almost the same as a can from a vending machine. Akasaka station.

**Mr Donut**. Branches all over the city. Drinks at the Tokyo branches of this huge chain operation are more expensive than in other parts of the country (¥300, rather than ¥250 for a coffee or tea), but you get free coffee refills, if you ask. The range of doughnuts, muffins, pastries and savoury treats is unsurpassed.

**Pow Wow**, 2-7 Kagurazaka. The most atmospheric of several cafés along Kagurazaka. It's dark and rustic, with a brick floor and big wooden tables, though upstairs is more high-tech. There are a few snacks, including home-made cakes and cookies, and a wide range of coffees. Iidabashi station.

### Teahouses

**Mariage Frères**, 2nd floor, In the Room, 1-12-13 Jinnan, Shibuya-ku. Around four hundred different varieties of tea to choose from at this pricey no-smoking tearoom in the interior design department store, a seven-minute walk towards Harajuku from the station. Shibuya station.

**Suzuki**. An oasis of calm in the midst of Harajuku, a minute's walk from the station. Tucked behind teeming Takeshita-dōri, but a million miles away in atmosphere, this traditional Japanese tea shop has *tatami* rooms, *fusuma* screens and manicured gardens to gaze upon. A frothy *matcha* (powdered green tea) and one pick from a wide choice of Japanese sweets costs ¥1000. Harajuku station.

# Nightlife and entertainment

The distinction between restaurants, **bars and clubs** in the city's *sakariba* (lively places), such as Ginza, Shibuya or Shinjuku, is a hazy one, with many places offering a range of entertainment depending on the evening or customers' spirits.

On the cultural side, you can sample all Japan's major **performance arts** in Tokyo, from stately **Nō**, the oldest in its theatrical repertoire, to **Butō**, the country's unique contribution to contemporary dance. However, if you only have the energy, or budget, for one such cultural experience, then save it for **Kabuki** with its larger-than-life heroes, flamboyant costumes and dramatic finales. Information about these and other performances is available in the English-language press, notably *Tokyo Journal*, and from Tokyo TIC (see p.86). Alternatively, ring Teletourist (☎03/3201-2911; 24hr) for recorded details of what's on. Tickets are available from theatres and ticket agencies (see Listings, p.166).

## Bars and izakaya

The authentic Japanese **bar** – smoky, cramped, exclusively male and always expensive – is the **nomiya**, often containing nothing more than a short counter bar, run by a *mama-san*, a unique breed who both charm and terrorize their customers, and who are less likely to rip you off if you speak some Japanese (but that's no guarantee). If you're game, try the *nomiya* under the tracks at Yūrakuchō, along Shinjuku's Shomben Yokochō (Piss Alley) and Golden Gai, and on the alley running along side the JR rail tracks just north of Shibuya Station.

The major breweries have their own more reliable chains of **izakaya** (Japanese pubs) which are generally quite large, serve a good range of drinks and bar snacks and often have a lively atmosphere. There are branches of *Kirin City*, in Ginza, Harajuku and Shinjuku, *Suntory Shot Bar* (in Roppongi) and Sapporo's *Lions Beer Hall* in Ebisu, Ginza, Ikebukuro and Shinjuku among other places. These *izakaya* open at around 6pm and shut down around midnight, while the *mama-san* will keep their bars open to the early hours, as long as there are customers. If there's live music you'll often be paying for it through higher drinks prices or a cover charge. Some regular bars also have cover charges, although there's plenty of choice among those that don't, so always check the deal before buying your drink.

For **bars with a view**, the major hotels are hard to beat, though you'll need to dress up not to feel out of place amid the gold-card crowd. Try the top-floor bars in the *New Ōtani* and the *Akasaka Prince* for views across the centre of the city, or the *Intercontinental* and *Nikkō* for stunning panoramas of the Rainbow Bridge. From mid-June through to late August, **outdoor beer gardens** flourish around Tokyo – look for the red lanterns and fairy lights on the roofs of buildings or in street-level gardens and plazas. You'll find particularly nice beer gardens at the *Prince Hotel* near Tokyo Tower and *Hanezawa Gardens*, 3-12-15 Hirō, Shibuya-ku.

## Ginza and Yūrakuchō

**Baden Baden**, 2-1-8 Yūrakuchō. Best of several German beer restaurants, selling Hofbrauhaus on draft and a decent selection of schnapps. The food's not bad either – serious platters of franks, cheese and potatoes – and they do special food and drink deals for groups of four or more. Yūrakuchō Station.

**Henry Africa**, 7-2-17 Ginza. African "concept bar" where moose and buffalo heads pose uncomfortably among tiffany lamps, potted palms and gleaming brass; you'll need that drink. There's a long list of cocktails, and an eclectic range of snack foods. Ginza Station.

**Lion**, 7-9-20 Ginza. Opened in 1934, this baronial, ground-floor beer hall, flagship of the Sapporo chain, harks back to the days of Lloyd Wright (see the *Imperial Hotel*, p.102), with its dark tiles and mock wood-panelling. There are snacks on offer, and a restaurant upstairs. Ginza Station.

**Shin Hi No Moto**, Yūrakuchō 1-chōme. Lively traditional *izakaya* under the tracks just south of Yūrakuchō Station. One of the few places to try the excellent Sapporo Red Star beer, or cheap, strong *shōchū* (grain liquor). The manager's English, so tell him what you like to eat and your budget. The fish comes fresh from Tsukiji. Yūrakuchō or Hibiya stations.

## North Tokyo

**Asahi Sky Room**, 22F Asahi Building, 1-23-1 Azumabashi. The famous Flamme d'Or building next door has own its modernistic beer hall, but the top-floor Sky Room wins out for its night views over Asakusa. It's not expensive, but the uncomfortable seats and uninspiring food mean you won't want to linger. Asakusa Station.

**Bambino**, 5-32 Kagurazaka. Jazz-playing basement shot bar open until 5am (midnight on Sundays). This being a student area, prices are reasonable and there lots of other decent bars nearby – like *Bronx* across the road. Iidabashi Station.

**Brussels**, 3-16-1 Kanda-Ogawamachi. Fifty varieties of Belgian beer to work your way through, either wedged in at the counter or sitting in more spacious surroundings upstairs. Lively, studenty atmosphere. Closed Sun. Jimbōchō Station.

**Dubliners'**, 1-10-8 Nishi-Ikebukuro. Plenty of elbow-room in this relaxed basement Irish pub, part of the Sapporo chain. There's Guinness and Kilkenny on draft, and dishes such as Colcannon (mushy cabbage and potato stew) or Beef and Guinness pie. Ikebukuro Station.

**Kamiya**, 1-1-1 Asakusa. Popular drinking hole that's been a feature of Asakusa since 1880. This was Tokyo's first Western-style "bar", and the haunt of literary figures such as Nagai Kafū and Tanizaki Junichirō. It's also famous for its Denkibran ("electric brandy"), first brewed in 1883 when electricity was all the rage. A small shot of gin, wine, curaçao and brandy, it's a potent tipple, though they also make a weaker version (¥260 a glass; souvenir bottles available). The ground floor's the liveliest and most informal; pay at the cash desk as you enter for your first round of food and drinks. Closed Tues. Asakusa Station.

**Mukashiya**, 5-12 Kagurazaka. Big, old-style *izakaya* with a rustic flavour. *Yakitori* is the speciality – try their *Mukashiyaki*, made of soya bean skins. There's also an English menu to choose from. Closed Sun. Iidabashi Station.

**300B** (*Sanbyaku B*), 3-30-11 Nishi-Ikebukuro. There are two *300B*s on opposite sides of the road but make sure you get this one (no.1) for the dried whale's penis hanging in the entrance. These are big, bubbling *izakaya*, popular with a young crowd for the cheap prices and good food. Ikebukuro Station.

## Tokyo Bay

**T.Y. Harbor Brewery**, Bond St, 2-1-3 Higashi-Shinagawa, Shinagawa-ku. Rave reviews for this new microbrewery, with attached Californian-cuisine restaurant, in a converted Bayside warehouse. The freshly made real ales include Amber Ale, Porter, Wheat Beer and California Pale Ale. Take the monorail from Hamamatsuchō to Tennoz Isle Station.

**Sunset Beach Brewing Company**, 1-6-1 Decks Tokyo Beach, Ōdaiba. The beer is actually made within the California-style mall. For glasses of the two types of beer on offer it's ¥600 at the stand-up bar; inside the large, colourful beer hall, a so-so all-you-can-eat buffet is ¥1380 for lunch, ¥2980 for dinner. The real attraction is the view across Tokyo Bay of the Rainbow Bridge. Ōdaiba Kaihin-kōen Station.

## Ebisu and Hirō

**Billy Barew's Beer Bar Ebisu**, 3-1-26 Minami-Ebisu. On Komazawa-dōri, this convivial bar boasts a menu of 120 different beers from around the world, at around ¥1000 a bottle. There's also a branch in Takadanobaba, near the *Mean Fiddler* (see Live Music, p.158). Ebisu Station.

**Café Bangkok**, 3F America Bldg, 1-23-5 Minami-Ebisu. Rooftop bar, with drinks and Thai nibbles served from street vendor carts (*yatai*), overlooking the train tracks and Yebisu Garden Place. Ideal place to while away steamy summer nights over Singha beer (¥600). Ebisu Station.

**Kotobuki Diner**, Hirō. Lively, modern *izakaya* on two floors with ground-floor bar open to the street in the summer. An English menu details a wide range of keenly priced dishes. It's popular with the local expat community. Hirō Station.

**Smash Hits**, B1, M2 Hirō Bldg, 5-6-26 Hirō. Karaoke for exhibitionists in this basement bar designed as a mini-amphitheatre. With 10,000 Japanese and 8000 English songs to choose from you'll never be stuck for a tune. On the 21st of each month entry is free, the first beer ¥1000 and ¥500 thereafter. Mon–Sat 8pm–3am, Sun hols 7pm–midnight. ¥3000 cover charge includes unlimited karaoke and one drink. Hirō Station.

**What the Dickens**, 4F, Roob 6 Bldg, 1-13-3 Ebisu-Nishi. The AUM cult once had its offices in this building, which has been transformed into Olde England with beams and candle-lit nooks. Guinness and Bass Pale Ale are on tap at ¥950 a pint, ¥600 a half. The food – a range of hearty pies served with potatoes, veggies and bread, all for ¥1500 – is excellent and there's occasional live music. Very much a *gaijin* scene, it can become raucous at weekends. Ebisu Station.

**Yebisu Beer Station**, Yebisu Garden Place. Several bars and *izakaya* spread across Sapporo's office and shopping development, and including a spacious beer garden. Ebisu Station.

## Harajuku and Shibuya

**Bar Aoyama**, Daikyo Bldg, 4-5-9 Shibuya. Garage-sale chic at this arty bar which gets going around midnight. Drinks from ¥700. Every Saturday there's a ¥1000 cover charge for the techno/jungle club. The bar's entrance, a grimy black metal door in the wall beside thundering Roppongi-dōri, is easily missed. Shibuya Station.

**Bar Isn't It?**, Opposite Shibuya's performing arts centre Bunkamura is the second Tokyo outpost of the pack 'em in, serve 'em cheap bar operation. All drinks are ¥500 and, needless to say, it's usually heaving. Shibuya.

**Oh! God**, 6-7-18 Jingū-mae (☎03/3406 3206). Standard Western snacks on offer at this basement bar in the same complex as restaurants *La Boheme* and *Zest*. The real attraction are the free movies screened nightly. Nothing up-to-date (call for the programme), but worth checking out. Drinks start at around ¥700 and there are two pool tables. Good post-club venue since it's open till around 6am. Meiji-jingū-mae Station.

**Tamakyū**, 2-30-4 Dōgenzaka, Shibuya-ku. You have to admire this old-fashioned *izakaya* in a shabby wooden shack for refusing to sell out to Tōkyū when they developed the 109 Building. The speciality is grilled fish and a little Japanese ability will help make you a honoured guest. Shibuya Station.

## Roppongi

**Acarajé Tropicana**, B2F Edge Bldg, 1-1-1 Nishi-Azabu. Large and popular Latin-American-style basement bar/restaurant just off Roppongi-dōri, which turns into a dance club on the weekend (¥1000 cover charge). Closed Mon. Roppongi Station.

**Bar Isn't It**, 3F, MT Bldg, 3-8-18 Roppongi, Minato-ku. Part of a large chain, *Bar Isn't It*'s concept of big space, small prices (well, ¥500 for most drinks) has found a natural home in Roppongi. There are beer-vending machines for when it's too crowded to get to the bar. There are high ceilings and dramatic window views of Roppongi Cemetery, but things can get steamy on Friday and Saturday nights, when there's a ¥1000 cover charge. Roppongi Station.

**Déjà vu**, 3-15-24 Roppongi, Minato-ku. Long-running *gaijin* dive still packing them in at the weekends. The open front stops it getting too sweaty. Overshadowed these days by the *Gas Panic* collection of bars that have moved next door. Roppongi Station.

**Gas Panic Miller Bar**, 50 Togensha Bldg, 3-15-24 Roppongi. The lastest outpost for Roppongi's most consistently popular and grungy bar. Although it's just about the last word on Roppongi sleaze (drunken *gaijin* males groping scantily-clad Japanese girls), virtually everyone passes through here at least once. Get ripped and enjoy. Happy Hour 5–8pm, when all drinks are ¥300. On Thurdays, all drinks cost ¥300 all night. Downstairs is *Club 99 Gas Panic* (see p.156). Roppongi Station.

**Ginga Kogen Beer**, 3-8-15 Roppongi. One of the larger regional breweries, which began in Sawa Uchi Mura in Iwate-ken, has opened this *izakaya* to promote its three types of beer: Weizen, Pilsner and Stout. The usual snack-type food (squid pizza, seaweed-topped spaghetti) is the on the menu. Roppongi Station.

**Paddy O'Folleys**, B1, Roi Bldg, 5-5-1 Roppongi. Popular Irish bar in the heart of Roppongi. All the usual beers, plus a range of cocktails at ¥1000 a pop. *The Celt*, next door, serves food and has live music every night from 8pm. Roppongi Station.

**Pints Sports Bar**, 3F Second Reine Bldg, 5-3-1 Roppongi. A long bar lines one side of this all-American, clubby establishment where you can leaf through sports magazines, watch a game (usually American football) on the big-screen TV or indulge in bar sports. Pool is ¥1000 for 30 minutes, Foozball ¥200 a game, darts free. Pints (Ebisu, Bass, Guinness and Miller on tap) are ¥1000. Roppongi Station.

## Shinjuku and around

**The Dubliners'**, 2F, Shinjuku Lion Hall, 3-28-9 Shinjuku. Sapporo has latched on to the Irish-bar concept with all its corporate might. The interior decoration is mock-Victorian, all polished mahogany, padded chairs and brass. The menu includes decent fish and chips, Irish stew and several other dishes. And, of course, there's Guinness and creamy Kilkenny bitter on tap. As good a bet for a quiet lunch or coffee as well as a rowdy night's drinking. Shinjuku Station.

**Jetee**, 2F, 1-1-8, Kabukichō, Shinjuku-ku. Run by Kawai-san, a francophile *mama-san* whose passion for films and jazz are combined in this quintessential Golden Gai bar. Room for eight people maximum in this second floor cubbyhole decorated with movie posters and hand-painted *bottle keeps* (regulars' own bottles of booze). Don't bother turning up during May when she decamps to the Cannes Film Festival. Closed Sun. Cover charge ¥1000. Shinjuku-Sanchōme Station.

**Pousse Café**, B1 Masukura Bldg, 3-9-4 Shinjuku. Cosy basement wine bar run by the French guy behind the excellent *Canard* (see p.150). Serves food and is open till sunrise, providing a relaxed post-club bolthole. Closed Mon. Shinjuku-Sanchōme Station.

**Pub Elvis**, 2F Tack Eleven Bldg, 2-19-7 Takadanobaba. Mementos of the King decorate Tokyo's own Elvis karaoke bar, where you can croon your favourite Presley number for ¥200 a shot. In the building directly opposite the JR exit, virtually under the tracks. On Tues there's a house band (¥300 extra). ¥800 cover charge, 20 percent service charge after midnight. Closed Sun. Takadanobaba Station.

**Rolling Stone**, B1, Ebichu Bldg, 3-2-7 Shinjuku. Conversation is out, ear-splitting rock music in at this long-running rock'n'roll Shinjuku bar. You can slip a note to the DJ for your favourite tracks. Every weekend it becomes a sweaty hell hole for those who can't think of anything better to do than mosh their way to the bar. From Monday to Thursday a ¥200 table charge is added to the bill (¥500 after midnight). On Fridays and Saturdays, expect to pay ¥2000 cover charge including two drinks. Shinjuku-Sanchōme Station.

**Vagabond**, 2F, 1-4-20 Nishi-Shinjuku. Local institution where Matsuoka-san plays the genial host to perfection, greeting guests and sometimes accompanying the jazz pianists who play every night from 7pm. There's a ¥500 cover charge for table snacks, but the drinks are good value and the atmosphere is priceless. Shinjuku Station.

# Clubs and discos

The chameleon-like nature of the city's nightlife, fuelled by an insatiable appetite for new trends, means that Tokyo is one of the most exciting, but also unpredictable places in the world to party. While some **clubs** weather the vagueries of fashion, it pays to check the media before heading out. *Tokyo Journal*'s monthly listings and Web site are good, and the weekly free magazine *Tokyo Classified* has listings on the latest bars and nightspots. *Tokyo Q*'s Web site (*www.so-net.or.jp/tokyoq/*) also has weekly recommendations and a link to listings from *Tokyo Night City*, a rundown of the city's hippest bars and clubs.

At all clubs, there'll be a **cover charge**, typically around ¥2500, which usually includes tickets for your first couple of drinks. With the exception of *Velfare* (see opposite), most clubs don't really get going until after 11pm, especially at weekends, and most stay open until around 4am.

**Blue**, 6-2-9 Minami-Aoyama. A hazy blue glow over the door halfway down Kotto-dōri, next to a classy jewellers, is the only give-away to this acid-jazz joint, imbued with the spirit of the swinging sixties. Two levels – one for chilling, one for dancing – and sessions from the renowned acid-jazz/drum and bass UFO (United Future Organization) DJs. ¥2500 cover charge includes two drinks. Omotesandō Station.

**Cave**, 34-6 Udagawachō, Shibuya-ku. A young crowd packs into this subterrenean collection of pitch-black rooms with two main dance areas and a better-lit bar. Opposite the Tōkyū Honten department store. Usual ¥2500 entrance plus two drinks deal. Shibuya Station.

**Club Asia**, 1-8 Maruyamachō, Shibuya-ku. Individual club events, including the popular gay/straight theme parties by *The Ring*, are held at this dance club in the heart of the Dōgenzaka love hotel district. Internet terminals provide something for the danced-out to fiddle with. The ¥2500 cover charge includes two drinks. Shibuya Station.

**Club Endless**, B1, Umemoto Building, 3-29-3 Nishi-Ikebukuro. Hip-hop music, cheap drinks and chilled vibes keep this place jumping until 5am. No cover charge. Ikebukuro Station.

**Club 99 Gas Panic**, 50 Togensha Bldg, 3-15-24 Roppongi. Beneath the *Gas Panic Miller Bar* and so-named because its open 9pm–9am. Has a ¥1000 entry charge after midnight and doesn't get going until at least 3am, when the *gaijin* who work at other bars get off work. Roppongi Station.

**Fai**, B2, 5-10-1 Minami-Aoyama, Minato-ku. Deep in the basement of the same building as the restaurant *To the Herbs*, on the corner of Aoyama-dōri and Kotto-dōri. Cosy easy-listening lounge bar where the kids go wild to everything from Abba to Japan-pop classics. Food available and no entrance charge before 11pm; ¥2000 with two drinks after 11pm. Omotesandō Station.

**Gas Panic Club**, 3F Marina Bldg, 3-10-5 Roppongi. Plumbs the same depths as its sister establishment bar, yet somehow manages at times to sink even lower. The stainless steel decor (easily hosed down) just about sums it up. Drinks ¥300 all Thursday night. No cover, except on Friday and Saturday when it's ¥1000. Roppongi Station.

**JMens**, Wall Bldg, 4-2-4 Nishi-Azabu (☎03/3409-7607). Hunky *gaijin* guys get their kit off for the girls and normally demure Japanese women go wild. Shows at 7, 8.30 and 10pm. ¥4000 including one drink. Reservations required. Roppongi Station.

**Liquid Room**, 7F Shinjuku HUMAX Pavillion, 1-20-1 Kabukichō. Different music genres on the decks at this trendy live house and club in the heart of Shinjuku; check local media and flyers since it also hosts one-off club events. Expect to pay at least ¥2000 entrance charge. Shinjuku Station.

**Maniac Love**, 5-10-6 Minami-Aoyama. Small but happening basement club just off Kotto-dōri. Everything from ambient and acid jazz to hard house and garage depending on the night of the week. Hardcore clubbers adore its early morning raves. Cover charge ¥2000 weekdays, ¥2500 Friday and Saturday, ¥1000 Sunday from 5am, plus unlimited coffee. Omotesandō Station.

**Milk**, B1 Roob 6 Bldg, 1-13-3 Ebisu-Nishi. Cross between a club and a live house, *Milk* packs in a lively crowd. If you get bored of the live thrash rock bands, check out the dildos and other sex toys in the cabinet in the kitchen. The regular Brit-pop nights are worth watching out for. ¥3000 entrance charge with two drinks. Ebisu Station.

**Mix**, 3-6-19 Kita-Aoyama. This long narrow basement space on Aoyama-dōri hosts an arty crowd at weekends who don't seem to mind being squashed in like sardines. Perhaps it's got something to do with the music, an infectious mix of soul and reggae. Cover charge is ¥2000 with two drinks; free on Sunday. Omotesandō Station.

**Pylon,** 4/5F, Dr Jeekan's Bldg, 4-6 Maruyama-chō, Shibuya. Only open Friday and Saturday, the DJs at this club play a pleasing mix of dance anthems, moving smoothly from Brit-pop to hip-hop via jazz funk. Although on the spacious side, usually heaves with a sparkling crowd. ¥2500 gets you in and a couple of drinks. Shibuya Station.

**328 (San-nippa),** 3-24-20 Nishi-Azabu. Popular, long-standing DJ bar in a basement right on the Hirō side of the Nish-Azabu crossing, next to the police box. More laid back than many other late-night Roppongi options. Roppongi Station.

**Velfare,** 7-14-22 Roppongi. This monolithic club cost its sponsors ¥4 billion, and the expense is obvious from the moment you mount the wide marble staircase to the entrance and part with ¥5000 (¥4000 for women, ¥500 extra for men on Fri & Sat). For this you get as many as three drinks and food depending on the night and time you arrive. Come early since it's packed by 9pm and you'll be leaving, like Cinderella, at midnight when the club shuts. Roppongi Station.

**Yellow,** 1-10-11 Nishi-Azabu. Look for the blank yellow neon sign and go down to the basement to discover one of Tokyo's most enduring and trendy clubs, offering a range of music on different nights. Mainly techno and house at the weekends when cover charges (including two drinks) can rise to ¥4000. Roppongi Station.

# Gay bars and clubs

Take advantage of the relatively open **gay and lesbian** scene in Tokyo; in the rest of Japan (even in big cities like Ōsaka), things are a lot more cliquey and closeted. Even so, compared to London, San Francisco or Sydney, Tokyo's scene is a low-key affair. The first gay pride march was held in Tokyo in 1995, and it's now an annual event (in May) with over two thousand participants – the first spin-off lesbian march happened in October 1997. Every May there's also the Tokyo International Lesbian and Gay Video and Film Festival and more films, comic books and television programmes are featuring gay characters as homosexuality has become trendy among the all important metropolitan OL ("office-lady") market.

Shinjuku-Nichōme, bulging with bars and clubs, is the epicentre of Tokyo's gay world, and is as cruisey as it gets for Japan. Apart from the venues listed below, all in Nichōme (the closest subway station is Shinjuku-Sanchōme), there are several gay events held at clubs around the city. The Ring and Too Much are usually held at *Club Asia* in Shibuya, while Roppongi's *Yellow* also has a regular gay night (see above); *Tokyo Journal* has details in its Cityscope listings. The US gay and lesbian magazine *Out*, on sale at Tower Records, has a useful insert, *Out in Japan*, which provides information on the local scene.

**Arty Farty,** 2-4-17 Shinjuku. Tokyo's bright young gays shine in this bar with decor that is a cross between New Mexico adobe chic and a tacky Christmas grotto. Open until 5am and from 2pm on Sunday for gay/straight events.

**Delight,** B1 Dai-ni Hayakawaya Bldg, 2-14-6 Shinjuku. House and garage rule at this basement club just next to the cruising park in Nichōme. Women-only third Thursday of the month.

**Fuji Bar,** 2-12-16 Shinjuku. Cosy karaoke bar in the basement of the building around the corner from *GB* (see below) has a wide selection of English songs, in case you're in the singing mood. The crowd is a gay/straight mix. ¥100 per song. 7.30pm–2.30am, Fri & Sat closes at 4am.

**GB,** B1 Business Hotel T Bldg, 2-12-3 Shinjuku. Only for the boys, this basement gay bar has a friendly atmosphere and a good mix of Japanese and foreigners. Most gay *gaijin* come here first before exploring the more exotic corners of Nichōme.

**Kinsman,** 2F, 2-18-5 Shinjuku, Shinjuk-ku. Long-running *gaijin*-friendly gay/straight bar, behind the BYGS Building and famous for its easy-going atmosphere and eye-catching *ikebana* (Japanese flower arrangments). Daily 9pm–5am.

**Kinswomyn,** 3F Dai-ichi Tenka Bldg, 2-15-10 Shinjuku. Tara is the master of this women-only bar, which has a more relaxed ambience (and lower prices) than many of Nichōme's other lesbian bars.

# Live music, film and cultural events

There's always plenty going on culturally in Tokyo, though language can be a problem when it comes to performance arts. Colourful extravaganzas like **Takarazuka** or the more traditional **Kabuki** are the easiest to enjoy, but even the notoriously difficult **Nō** or **Butō** are worth seeing just once. Tokyo may not seem the obvious place to seek out a classical concert or Shakespearean play – tickets are expensive and often hard to get hold of. However, major international **orchestras** and **theatre** groups often pass through on their tours and the city now boasts several top-class performance halls.

## Live music

Tokyo has a wide range of **live music venues** offering everything from the most mellow jazz to the hardest of rock and indie. "Live houses" are little more than a pub with a small stage, but the city also has several prestigious venues, such as the Tokyo Dome (affectionately known as the "Big Egg"), where the likes of U2 and Madonna play when they're in town.

**Birdland**, Square Bldg, 3-10-3 Roppongi (☎03/3478-3456). Candles light this traditional jazz joint in the basement of a building that also offers far rowdier clubs. Sun–Thurs 6pm–midnight, Fri, Sat until 1am. ¥1500 cover charge, ¥1500 minimum drink order, plus service charge of 10 percent. Roppongi Station.

**Blue Note**, 5-13-3 Minami-Aoyama (☎03/3407-5781). Tokyo's premier live jazz venue attracts world-class performers like Tony Bennett and Sarah Vaughan. Mon–Sat 6pm–1am. Shows at 7.30 and 10pm. Entry starts at ¥7000 (including one drink) depending on the acts. Omotesandō Station.

**Blues Alley Japan**, B1 Meguro Station Hotel, 1-3-14 Meguro (☎03/5496-4381). This offshoot of the Washington DC blues and jazz club occupies a small basement space near the station. Admission cost depends on the acts. Food is also available. Meguro Station.

**Cavern Club**, 5-3-2 Roppongi. No prizes for guessing what kind of music is played here. A meticulous recreation of the Beatles' Liverpool venue, with pretty decent Beatle cover bands providing the entertainment. Roppongi Station.

**Club Citta**, Ogawachō 4-chōme, Kawasaki (☎044/246-8888). One of Tokyo's major live music venues, in the suburb-city of Kawasaki. If you're a real enthusiast, it's usually worth checking who's on. Five-minutes' walk south of Kawasaki Station. Varying ticket prices.

**Club Quattro**, 5F Quattro Bldg, 32-13 Udagawachō, Shibuya-ku (☎03/3477-8750). Intimate rock music venue in a loft-like space, which hosts both well-known local and international acts. Tends to showcase up-and-coming bands and artists. Shibuya Station.

**Crocodile**, 6-18-8 Jingū-mae (☎03/3499-5205). Everything from samba to blues and reggae at this long-running basement space on Meiji-dōri between Harajuku and Shibuya. Also broadcasts gigs live on the Internet (check them out on *www.music.co.jp/~croc/*). Cover charge ¥2000-3000, shows start at around 8pm. Meiji-jingū-mae.

**Cyber**, B1, 1-43-14 Higashi-Ikebukuro. Dark, throbbing rock dive among the soaplands and love hotels north of Ikebukuro Station. Though the bands are variable, there's not a lot else on offer in Ikebukuro. Cyber also runs a record label, magazine and Web site (*www.music.co.jp*). Entry ¥2000 up, depending on the band. Ikebukuro Station.

**Kento's**, B1 Dai 2 Renu Bldg, 5-3-1 Roppongi, Minato-ku (☎03/3401-5775). Nostalgic rock'n'roll tracks from the 1950s and 60s played by the house band. The concept has proved so popular that there are now *Kento's* in most of Japan's major cities. Roppongi Station.

**Mean Fiddler**, B1F, 2-1-2, Takadanobaba, Shinjuku-ku. British pub with rock and blues bands playing most nights. Also serves fish and chips, shepherd's pie, and pints of Guinness and Bass go for ¥900. Attracts students from nearby Waseda University. At the intersection of Waseda-dōri and Meiji-dōri. No cover charge. Takadanobaba Station.

**New York Bar**, *Park Hyatt Hotel*, 3-7-1-2 Nishi-Shinjuku. Top-class live jazz music plus the glittering night view of Shinjuku are the not inconsiderable attractions of this sophisticated bar attached to the *Park Hyatt's New York Grill*. Shinjuku Station.

**On Air West**, 2-3 Maruyamachō, Shibuya-ku (☎03/5458-4646). Pop concert venue in a spacious hangar-like building slap in the middle of Shibuya's love hotel district. Often attracts top international acts. Shibuya Station.

**Shinjuku Pit Inn**, B1 Accord Shinjuku Bldg, 2-12-4 Shinjuku (☎03/3354-2024). Long-standing serious jazz club, which has been the launch platform for many top Japanese performers. Also attracts overseas acts. Shinjuku Station.

## Cinema

**Cinemas** aren't cheap; average ticket prices are around ¥1800 (¥2500 for *shitei-seki* – reserved seats). You can cut the cost by buying discount tickets in advance from a **ticket agency**, such as Ticket Saison and Pia (see Listings, p.166). On Cinema Day, generally the first day of the month, tickets at all cinemas cost only ¥1000. Hollywood blockbusters predominate, and movies are generally subtitled in Japanese, not dubbed. The last show is usually at 7pm. Listings are published sporadically throughout the week in *The Japan Times* and on Thursday in the *Daily Yomiuri*. *Tokyo Journal* and *Tokyo Classified* both carry listings reviews, but no times, and have good maps locating all the major cinemas.

For art-house and **independent** releases, head for Roppongi to the Haiyu-za Talkie Night (☎03/3470-2880), near the crossing, or Ciné Vivant (☎03/3403-6061) in the Wave Building on Roppongi-dōri; both have late-night shows. The Hibiya Chanter (☎03/3591-1551), near Yūrakuchō Station and Cinema Rise (☎03/3464-0052) at the top of Spain-zaka in Shibuya, carve up between themselves most of the independent movies coming out of Europe and the USA. Cine Saison Shibuya (☎03/3770-1721), in the Prime Building also showcases a fine range of films, including classic revivals. Shibuya's Bunkamura (☎03/3477-9111) has two screens and provides one of the few opportunities you'll have to see Japanese films with English sub-titles at the Tokyo International Film Festival, held each autumn at these and other local cinemas. Namiki-za, Ginza (☎03/3561-3034) screens Japanese classics. The National Film Centre (☎03/3272-8600), near Kyōbashi Subway Station, is a real treasure-trove for film lovers, with a gallery showing film-related exhibitions (¥300) and two small cinemas screening retrospectives from their 17,000 archived movies (mostly Japanese classics).

## Contemporary theatre

Tokyo has a flourishing contemporary **theatre** scene, and though most events take place in Japanese, the more accessible forms are definitely worth checking out. Perhaps the most famous is **Takarazuka**, the all-singing, all-dancing, all-female revue which originated near Ōsaka in the early 1900s (see p.422). It's a great spectacle in which mostly Hollywood musicals are sugar-coated and punched out by a huge cast in fabulous costumes in front of an audience comprised mainly of middle-aged housewives and star-struck teenage girls. Regular performances alternate with ordinary dramas in the Takarazuka Theatre (☎03/3201-7777), opposite the *Imperial Hotel* (see p.102); ask at the theatre or look in the English-language press for details of the current schedule.

Keep an eye out as well for **Butō** performances. This unique, highly expressive dance-form developed in the early 1950s, inspired by contemporary American dance, and until recently was more popular abroad than in Japan (see p.797 for more). It's not to everyone's taste – minimalist, introspective, and often violent or sexually explicit – but shouldn't be missed if you're interested in Japanese performance arts. There are six established Butō groups in Tokyo; you'll find major performances listed in the English-language press, or ask at the TIC (see p.86).

Both Takarazuka and Butō have entered the mainstream arts' world, but there's plenty happening on the fringes as well, as a glance at *Tokyo Journal*'s listings will confirm. Theatre Cocoon (☎03/3477-9999), in Shibuya's Bunkamura, or Jean-Jean (☎03/3462-0641), next to Seed department store, are prime places to catch the most accessible of Tokyo's **avant garde theatre**, while every September Ikebukuro's Tokyo International Festival of Performing Arts showcases the best on the current scene.

## Traditional theatre

Of the traditional performance arts, **Kabuki** is by far the most accessible for both Japanese and foreign spectators; it's dramatic, colourful and the plots are easy to follow even if you don't understand a word of Japanese, while shouts of appreciation from the audience add to the sense of occasion. The one draw-back is that performances tend to be lengthy, often lasting three or four hours. However, these days you can buy single-act tickets for the **Kabuki-za** (☎03/5565-6000), the main theatre in Ginza (see p.103), where they hold performances during the first three weeks of every month. There are two daily programmes, starting at around 11am and 4pm, for which you can buy tickets at the theatre or an agency. Prices start at ¥2500 for the full programme, while one-act tickets usually cost under ¥1000, depending on the length – note that one-act tickets are only on sale at the theatre itself. The theatre produces a brief English summary of the programme (free at the TIC and hotels), or you can rent an earphone guide (¥600, plus ¥1000 deposit) for background information about Kabuki as well as the plot. If you have a pair of binoculars, remember to bring them – all the cheapest seats are way up at the back.

The other main venue for Kabuki is **Kokuritsu Gekijō** (☎03/3265-7411), the National Theatre west of the Imperial Palace near Hanzōmon Station, which holds a varied programme of traditional theatre and music. Three or four times a year, **Bunraku**, a form of puppet theatre predating Kabuki, which shares many of the same plots, is performed here. It's less dramatic – the puppets need three people to manipulate them – but the artistry of the puppeteers is astounding. Again, English-language programmes and earphones are available, and tickets start at ¥1500 for Kabuki and ¥4300 for Bunraku.

**Nō** is Japan's oldest and least accessible form of theatre. Even most Japanese find it unfathomable, and its esoteric, highly stylized, painfully slow movements and ancient form of language certainly don't make for a rip-roaring theatrical experience. That said, it's not all tedious: during the intervals *kyōgen*, short satirical plays with an earthy humour and simple plots, provide light relief. There are several schools of Nō in Tokyo, each with their own theatre, including Shibuya's **Kanze Nō-gakudō** (☎03/3469-5241), in addition to the **National Nō Theatre** (☎03/3423-1331), five minutes' walk from Sendagaya Station (see p.132). Tickets cost upwards of ¥2000 and can be bought from agencies or the theatre itself. It's also worth asking at the TIC (see p.86) about free performances by amateur groups.

## International performance arts

Tokyo is on the circuit for many international **theatre companies**, who usually get a tremendous reception, with seats selling out months in advance, though a few are often reserved for sale on the day. Both the New National Theatre (tickets ☎03/5352-9999, information ☎03/5352-5745), in Shinjuku, and the Panasonic Globe (☎03/3360-1151), a covered recreation of the original London Globe Theatre near Shin-Ōkubo Station, host high profile theatre troupes, including the Royal Shakespeare Company and Cheek by Jowl; Shibuya's Theatre Cocoon (see p.135) is another popular venue for international groups.

There are usually at least one or two concerts of Western **classical music** on every week, either by one of Tokyo's several resident orchestras (notably the Tokyo City Philharmonic or Japan Philharmonic) or a visiting group, as well as occasional performances of opera and ballet. 1997 saw the opening of several major performance halls: Tokyo Opera City (☎03/5353-0799) and the New National Theatre (see above), both in Shinjuku, and another four halls in Yūrakuchō's Tokyo International Forum (☎03/5221-9000). Among the older auditoria, Suntory Hall (☎03/3584-9999) in Akasaka's Ark Hills, NHK Hall (☎03/3465-1751), south of Meiji-kōen, and the Orchard Hall (tickets ☎03/3477-9999, information ☎03/3477-3244) in Shibuya's Bunkamura are the main venues. Tickets, which tend to be expensive (¥3000 and above), are available from the box offices or a ticket agency.

## MAJOR TOKYO FESTIVALS

Whenever you visit Tokyo, the chances are there'll be a **festival** (*matsuri*) taking place somewhere in the city. The TIC (see p.86) has comprehensive lists of events in and around Tokyo, or check in the English press for what's on. Below is a review of the city's biggest festivals (see p.57 for more about nationwide celebrations). Note that dates may change, so be sure to doublecheck before setting out.

**Jan 1–3: Ganjitsu (or Gantan).** The first shrine-visit of the year (Hatsumode) draws the crowds to Meiji-jingū, Hie-jinja, Kanda Myōjin and other city shrines. Performances of traditional dance and music take place at Yasukuni-jinja.

**Jan 6: Dezomeshiki** Tokyo firemen in Edo-period costume pull off dazzling stunts atop long, bamboo ladders. In Harumi, Tokyo Bay.

**Jan 15: Momoteshiki** Archery ritual at Meiji-jingū to celebrate "Coming-of-Age Day". A good time to spot colourful kimono, here and at other shrines.

**Feb 3 or 4: Setsubun** The last day of winter is celebrated with a bean-scattering ceremony to drive away evil. The liveliest festivities take place at Sensō-ji, Kanda Myōjin, Zōjō-ji, and Hie-jinja.

**Early April: Hanami** Cherry-blossom-viewing parties get into their stride. The best displays are at Chidorigafuchi Park and nearby Yasukuni-jinja, Ueno-kōen, Aoyoma Cemetery and Sumida-kōen.

**Mid-May: Kanda Matsuri** One of Tokyo's top three festivals, occurring in even-numbered years at Kanda Myōjin. People in Heian-period costume escort eighty gilded *mikoshi* through the streets.

**Mid-May: Sanja Matsuri** Tokyo's most rumbustuous annual bash focuses on Asakusa-jinja. Music, dance and a costume parade, with over one hundred *mikoshi*.

**June 10–16: Sanno Matsuri** The last of the big three festivals takes place in odd-numbered years at Hie-jinja. Fifty *mikoshi* are paraded through Akasaka.

**Late July & Aug: Hanabi Taikai** Summer skies explode with thousands of fireworks, harking back to traditional "river-opening" ceremonies. The Sumida-gawa display is the most spectacular (view it from river-boats or Asakusa's Sumida-kōen), but those in Edogawa, Tamagawa, Arakawa and Harumi come close.

**Mid-Aug: Fukagawa Matsuri** Every three years Tomioka Hachiman-gū (Monzen-nakachō Station) hosts the city's wettest festival, when spectators throw buckets of water over 54 *mikoshi* being shouldered through the streets. Next event in 1999.

**Nov: Tori-no-ichi** Fairs selling *kumade*, bamboo rakes decorated with lucky charms, are held at shrines on "rooster days" according to the zodiacal calendar. The main fair is at Ōtori-jinja (Iriya Station).

**Nov 15: Shichi-go-san** Kids aged seven, five and three in traditional garb, and their doting grandparents are out in force at Meiji-jingū, Yasukuni, Hie-jinja and other shrines to celebrate their health and pray for future happiness.

**Dec 17–19: Hagoita-ichi** The build-up to New Year begins with a battledore fair outside Asakusa's Sensō-ji (see p.112) . Stalls stay open all night.

# Shopping

Tokyo is a prime hunting ground for the latest electronic gadgets, and also for certain types of electrical equipment and cameras. CDs are slightly cheaper than at home, and the selection of world music, jazz and techno in particular takes some beating. Foreign-language books and magazines are less well-represented and very pricey, though Tokyo is the place to stock up before heading off to other regions.

**Ginza** is the preserve of conservative chic and still regarded as the capital's foremost shopping centre. However, **Shinjuku** has recently begun to stage a challenge, with its shiny new malls offering everything under one roof. Young and funky, **Shibuya** and **Harajuku** are probably the most enjoyable places to shop; even if you don't want to buy, the passing fashion parade doesn't get much better. The haute-couture boutiques of nearby **Omotesandō** and **Aoyama** provide a more rarefied shopping experience, while, of the northern districts, only **Asakusa** figures highly for its crafts shops, while **Ikebukuro** has a plethora of discount stores.

Tokyo also has a number wholesale districts which can be fun to poke around. The most famous are **Tsukiji fish market** (see p.139), **Kappabashi** "Kitchenware Town" (see p.115), the book stores of **Jimbōchō** (see p.108) and **Akihabara's** electrical emporia (see below). North of Asakusabashi Station, **Edo-dōri** and its backstreets specialize in traditional Japanese dolls, while further north again, the area called **Kuramae** is "Toy Town", where shops sell fireworks, fancy goods and decorations as well as toys of every description. Between Ueno's mainline station and the Shuto Expressway, slick-haired guys in leathers stalk the rows of sleek machines in **"Motorbike Town"**.

## Department stores

The most obvious place to start shopping is in one of Tokyo's massive **department stores**: they're convenient, usually have English-speaking staff and are more likely to accept foreign-registered credit cards or offer duty free prices. You could spend a whole day exploring just one store, from its basement food hall, through fashion and furnishings to the roof-top garden-centre, eat on the restaurant floor and then see what's on at the in-store art gallery. The main draw-backs are the sheer size of these places – grab a floor guide on the way in – and the fact that they also tend to be more expensive than the competition. However, they often hold excellent bargain sales several times a year – the kimono sales are most famous – which you'll find advertised in the English-language press, and among their top floors most stores have an area promoting a variety of discount items.

**Chūō-dōri**, from Ginza north, is the epicentre of Tokyo department stores. Here you'll find the city's most prestigious establishments, **Mitsukoshi**, represented by its flagship Nihombashi store (with branches in Shibuya, Ikebukuro and Ebisu), and nearby **Takashimaya** (recently expanded into Shinjuku). Elegant and spacious, these two stores are renowned for their quality, and also stock a good range of traditional household items, as well as kimono, *obi* and other accessories. **Matsuya** (Ginza and Asakusa) and **Matsuzakaya** (Ginza and Ueno) are more workaday places which appeal to similarly conservative tastes but at lower prices.

For younger fashion, head for Shibuya, where Parco, Seed and Loft are famous trend-setters, not only in designer-clothes but also general merchandise, and their racks and shelves groan with state-of-the art ephemera. These three stores belong to the **Seibu** group, whose sprawling Ikebukuro headquarters competes with neighbouring **Tōbu** to be Tokyo's most confusing store; better to shop in Seibu's smaller outlet in Shibuya. Also worth checking out are the main Tōkyū department store in Shibuya and its fantastic DIY Tōkyū Hands (there are also branches in Ikebukuro and Shinjuku). **Isetan** is Higashi-Shinjuku's top department store, offering well-designed local produce at reasonable prices, while **Marui** (with branches in Shibuya and Ikebukuro) consists of several self-explanatory buildings called Fashion, Young and Men's.

## Arts, crafts and souvenirs

While most department stores have a fair selection of **arts and crafts**, it's more enjoyable to rummage around Tokyo's specialist shops. Asakusa offers the largest concentration of traditional crafts among all its touristy souvenirs, as well as the most attractive environment. A few gems from the Edo-era still survive in the thick of Ginza and Nihombashi, while, if money is no object, arcades in the big hotels, such as the

*Imperial, Ōkura* and *New Ōtani*, provide luxury gifts from Mikimoto pearls to Arita porcelain. Below are a few suggestions of the more interesting places to head for; the listings indicate the nearest subway or JR station.

**Bengara**, 2-35-11 Asakusa. This shop to the west of Sensō-ji is *the* place to look for *noren*, the split curtain hanging outside every traditional shop or restaurant. There's a whole range of patterns, sizes and prices, or you can order your own design. Closed Thurs. Asakusa Station.

**Beniya**, 2-6-8 Shibuya. Broad range of folk-crafts (*mingei*) from around the country, on four floors. Closed Thurs. Shibuya Station.

**Bingoya**, 10-16 Wakamatsuchō. Tokyo's best *mingei* shop, located northeast of Shinjuku. Expensive. Closed Mon. Akebonobashi Station.

**Fujiya**, 2-2-15 Asakusa. Hand-printed cotton towels, *tenugui*, make a packable souvenir, and you won't find a better selection than this. Some Fujiya towels are now collectors' items. Closed Thurs. Asakusa Station.

**Itō-ya**, 2-7-15 Ginza. This wonderful stationery store, with nine floors and two annexes, is great for a whole range of packable souvenirs. *Itō-ya 3* specializes in traditional *washi* paper, calligraphy brushes, inks and so on. Also in Shibuya. Ginza Station.

**Kurodaya**, 1-2-5 Asakusa. For over one hundred years Kurodaya has been selling hand-made *washi* paper and anything that can be made from it – boxes, fans, kites and all types of stationery, as well as wood-block prints and wrapping papers. Closed Mon. Asakusa Station.

**Oriental Bazaar**, 5-9-13 Jingū-mae. Popular, one-stop souvenir emporium, selling everything from second-hand kimono to origami paper, all at reasonable prices. Closed Thurs. Meiji-jingū-mae Station.

**Takumi**, 8-4-2 Ginza. Folk-craft shop chock-a-block with bags, baskets, pots, toys and fabrics. Closed Sun. Shimbashi Station.

**Okome Gallery**, 5-11-4 Ginza. Dedicated to rice, this gallery-cum-shop yields some novel souvenirs, including rice-powder lotions, rice cosmetics, rice shampoo and, naturally, rice. Closed Mon. Higashi-Ginza Station.

**Washikobo**, 1-8-10 Nishi-Azabu. Delightful shop crammed to the rafters with *washi* products. Closed Sun. Roppongi Station.

## Antique and flea markets

There's at least one **flea market** in Tokyo every weekend, though you'll need to arrive early for any bargains. Among the regular markets, stalls at Hanazono-jinja (see p.130) spring into life every Sunday, while Tōgō-jinja (see p.134) hosts a market on the first and fourth Sundays of the month.

Alternatively, try one of the two upmarket **antique halls**, which are permanent fixtures consisting of several dealers gathered under one roof. Among a good deal of tat, you'll come across original *ukiyo-e*, magnificent painted screens or *samurai* armour – but don't expect any particular bargains. Tokyo Antiques Hall, 3-9-5 Minami-Ikebukuro (11am–6pm, closed Thurs), has more than thirty stalls, while the smaller Antique Market, in the basement of the Hanae Mori Building, 3-6-1 Kita-Aoyama, (Mon–Sat 10.30am–7pm), is somewhat less interesting. Several times a year about two hundred dealers get together for the **Heiwajima Antiques Fair**, held over three days at the Ryūtsū Centre (10am–6pm), a stop on the monorail from Hamamatsuchō to Haneda. If you're in town, it's well worth the journey; get the current schedule from Tokyo TIC.

## Books and music

Tokyo's best selection of foreign-language **books and magazines** is to be found in Shinjuku's new, seven-storey Kinokuniya bookstore behind Takeshimaya Times Square, though Tower Records, in Shibuya with branches in Shinjuku and Ikebukuro, has cheaper prices for imported journals and newspapers. In Nihombashi, Maruzen stocks a wide range of imported and locally produced books, with a strong showing in art and design, while Ginza's Jena is distinguished by its helpful and knowledgeable staff as well as a decent section for Japanese-language students. Though small, Wise

Owl Bookshop deserves a special mention for its select choice of titles; you'll find it on the fourth floor of Shin'eidō bookstore, Higashi-Ikebukuro. Finally, it's always worth popping into the luxury hotels, most of which run midget bookstores with an array of books on Japan.

Shibuya's Tower Records currently runs the biggest **music** store in Tokyo, with six floors of CDs, records and related paraphernalia, including videos and games. Wave used to figure highly, particularly its main Roppongi store, but has faded slightly in recent years – the one exception is its twelfth-floor outlet in Ikebukuro's Seibu department store; dance, rock, Japanese and world music are all well represented and there's a great techno section covering labels that you won't find anywhere else. Virgin concentrates its energies in its large Shinjuku store (in the Marui Building), with a smaller outlet in Marui Ikebukuro, while HMV signs are spattered over central Tokyo, from Shibuya's 109 Building to AbAb department store in Ueno.

## Cameras and electronic equipment

Shinjuku is Tokyo's prime centre for **cameras**; Yodobashi Camera in Nishi-Shinjuku usually offers decent reductions and stocks the broadest range, and claims to be the world's largest camera shop. It's also worth taking a look round Ikebukuro, where BIC Camera, renowned for cheap prices, dominates the market; you'll find BIC shops all over Higashi-Ikebukuro, but their main store lies immediately north of the station on Meiji-dōri. Alternatively, over on the west side of Ikebukuro Station, Camera no Kimura has a solid reputation for new and used cameras, while in the south of Tokyo, Matsuzakaya boasts Tokyo's largest selection of secondhand cameras – though it's more of a trek to get to, in Takanawa near Sengakuji Station. Professional photographers, meanwhile, swear by Shimizu Camera in the backstreets of Ginza, northeast of the Sukiyabashi crossing.

You'll find the biggest concentration of **electronic goods** in Akihabara. It can be a bewildering place at first, with the big stores split into several outlets – each one a megastore of up to seven floors apiece – selling overlapping product ranges. Fortunately, they're mostly concentrated along a small stretch of Chūō-dōri and its sidestreets, all within walking-distance of Akihabara Station. Of the big stores, Laox is the best place to start: prices are reasonable, they have a well-established duty-free section with English-speaking staff, and their nine stores sell everything from pocket-calculators to computers. Both Yamagiwa and Hirose Munsen are also worth trying, and Onoden has a good reputation for the latest audio-equipment. Further north on Chūō-dōri, T-Zone Minami carries a good range of English-language software, while games enthusiasts should head for Furijia and Sofmap. Whatever you're buying, it's important to compare prices first and, though you might not get it, always ask for a discount.

# Listings

**Airlines** Aeroflot (☎03/343-9671); Air Canada (☎03/3586-3891); Air China (☎03/5251-0711); Air France (☎03/3475-1511); Air India (☎03/3214-1981); Air Lanka (☎03/3573-4261); Air New Zealand (☎03/3287-1641); Air Nippon (☎0120–029003); Air Pacific (☎03/3435-1371); Alitalia (☎03/3580-2181); All Nippon Airways (☎0120–029333); American Airlines (☎03/3214-2111); Asiana Airlines (☎03/3582-6600); British Airways (☎03/3593-8811); Canadian Airlines (☎03/3281-7426); Cathay Pacific (☎03/3504-1531); China Airlines (☎03/3436-1661); Delta (☎03/5257-7000); Dragonair (☎03/3506-8361); Egyptair (☎03/3211-4521); Garuda Indonesia (☎03/3593-1181); Iberia (☎03/3578-3555); Japan Airlines (international ☎0120–255931); Japan Air System (☎0120–711283); KLM (☎03/3216-0771); Korean Air (☎03/5443-3311); Lufthansa (☎03/3578-6777); Malaysia Airlines (☎03/3503-5961); Northwest (☎03/3533-6000); Pakistan International (☎03/3216-6511); Philippine Airlines (☎03/3593-2421); Qantas (☎03/3593-7000); Sabena (☎03/3585-6151); SAS Scandinavian Airlines (☎03/3503-8101); Singapore Airlines (☎03/3213-3431); South African Airways (☎03/3470-

1910); Swissair (☎03/3212-1016); Thai International (☎03/3503-3311); United Airlines (☎0120–114466); Varig (☎03/3211-6751); Virgin Atlantic (☎03/3499-8811).

**American Express** 4-30-16 Ōgikubo, Suginami-ku (☎0120–020666). Travel service centre (Mon–Fri 9am–4pm) with a 24hr ATM for card members only.

**Banks and exchange** You'll find dozens of "Authorized Foreign Exchange Banks" all over central Tokyo; Tokyo Mitsubishi Bank generally handles the broadest range of currencies. If you need money outside normal banking hours (see p.26), department stores often have exchange desks, or try the World Currency Shop with branches in Ikebukuro (8F, Metropolitan Plaza; Mon–Sat noon–7pm), Jimbōchō (just north of Yasukuni-dōri opposite Sanseidō bookstore; noon–6pm) and Shibuya (on Bunkamura-dōri; Mon–Sat noon–6pm). The American Express office in Suginami-ku, west of Shinjuku (4-30-16 Ōgikubo; ☎0120–020666) has a 24hr ATM (American Express cards only), while many of the Citibank ATMs popping up all over Tokyo provide a 24hr cash facility for Citibank, Mastercard and Visa card holders. Call the following numbers for further information in English: Citibank (☎0120–110330 for account holders; ☎0120–504189 for general enquiries, 24hr); Mastercard (☎03/5350-8051); Visa (☎03/5251-0633).

**Bike rental** Try Rental Acom at Shinjuku (☎03/3350-5081), Ikebukuro (☎03/3988-2841) or Shimbashi (☎03/3432-8522), all open daily 10am–7pm, which also rents just about anything else you could need. For a minimum of two days an ordinary bike is ¥2000 and a mountain bike ¥5000. You'll need to present your passport and make an advance booking in Japanese.

**Car rental** The main rental companies are Budget (☎03/3263-6321); Hertz ☎0120–388002; Nippon (☎03/3485-7196); Nissan (☎03/3587-4123); Orix (☎03/3779-0543) and Toyota (☎03/3246-0100). All have branches around the city and at Narita and Haneda airports, and English-speaking staff. Expect to pay between ¥8000–9000 per day for a compact 1000–1300cc car.

**Credit cards** for lost credit cards call: American Express ☎0120–020120 (24hr); Mastercard ☎03/3256 6271 (24hr; dial ☎0051 first for a collect call); Visa International ☎0120–133163 (24hr).

**Embassies** Australia, 2-1-14 Mita, Minato-ku (☎03/5232-4111); Canada, 7-3-38 Akasaka, Minato-ku (☎03/3408-2101); China, 3-4-33 Moto-Azabu, Minato-ku (☎03/3403-3380); France, 4-11-44 Minami-Azabu, Minato-ku (☎03/5420-8800); Germany, 4-5-10 Minami-Azabu, Minato-ku (☎03/3473-0151); Ireland, 2 10 7 Kojimachi, Chiyoda-ku (☎03/3263-0695); Israel, 3 Nibanchō, Chiyoda-ku (☎03/3264-0911); Italy, 2-5-4 Mita, Minato-ku (☎03/3453-5291); Netherlands, 3-6-3 Shiba-kōen, Minato-ku (☎03/5401-0411); New Zealand, 20-40 Kamiyamachō, Shibuya-ku (☎03/3467-2271); South Africa 2-7-9 Hirakawachō, Chiyoda-ku (☎03/3265-3366); United Kingdom, 1 Ichibachō, Chiyoda-ku (☎03/3265-5511); USA, 1-10-5 Akasaka, Minato-ku (☎03/3224-5000).

**Emergencies** Tokyo Metropolitan Police run a 24hr helpline to provide foreign-language assistance in an emergency; call them on ☎03/3501-0110. Alternatively, try Japan Helpline (☎0120–461997), a 24hr English-language toll-free service. Tokyo English Life Line (TELL) provides telephone counselling on their helpline (☎03/3968-4099; daily 9am–4pm & 7–11pm). Numbers for the emergency services are listed in Basics on p.70.

**Hospitals and clinics** To find an English-speaking doctor and the hospital or clinic best suited to your needs, phone the Tokyo Medical Information Service (☎03/5285-8181; Mon–Fri 9am–8pm); they also provide emergency medical translation services (Mon–Fri 5–10pm, Sat & Sun 9am–10pm). Otherwise, two major hospitals with English-speaking doctors are St Luke's International Hospital, 9-1 Akashichō, Chūō-ku (☎03/3541-5151) and Tokyo Adventist Hospital, 3-17-3 Amanuma, Suginami-ku (☎03/3392-6151); their reception desks are open Mon–Fri 8.30–11am for non-emergency cases. Among several private clinics with English-speaking staff, try Tokyo Medical and Surgical Clinic, 32 Mori Building, 3-4-30 Shiba-kōen, Minato-ku (☎03/3436–3208, by appointment only) or the International Clinic, 1-5-9 Azabudai, Minato-ku (☎03/3582–2646).

**Immigration** To renew your tourist or student visa, apply to the Tokyo Regional Immigration Bureau (Mon–Fri 9am–noon & 1–4pm; ☎03/3213-8523; 1-3-1 Ōtemachi, Chūō-ku), signed from Ōtemachi Station.

**Internet access** You can surf the Net for free at the following places: 4F, Sony Building (Ginza); the KDD Building and NTT Urbannet Building, both near Ōtemachi subway station. Or try one of the cyber cafés: *Cyberia* (1-14-17 Nishi-Azabu); *T-Zone Minami* (7F, 4-3-3 Soto-Kanda); *Nets* (1-39-2 Higashi-Ikebukuro); *The News* (2-17-4 Asakusa). The going rate is about ¥500 for 30min.

**Left luggage** Most hotels will keep luggage for a few days. If not, baggage rooms at Tokyo and Ueno stations take bags for up to fifteen days, on a sliding scale of charges from ¥500 per day. Note that coin lockers can only be used for a maximum of three days.

**Lost property** If you've lost something, try the local police box (*kōban*). Alternatively, ask your hotel to help call the following Japanese-speaking offices to reclaim lost property : Taxis (☎03/3648-0300);

JR trains (☎03/3231-1880); Eidan subways (☎03/3834-5577); Toei buses and subways (☎03/3815-7229). If all else fails, contact the Metropolitan Police Lost and Found Office (☎03/3814-4151).

**Pharmacies** The American Pharmacy (Hibiya Park Building, 1-8-1 Yūrakuchō; daily 9.30am–7pm, hols 11am–7pm) has English-speaking pharmacists and a good range of drugs and general medical supplies. Alternatively, there's a pharmacy above the National Azabu supermarket (nearest subway station is Hiro), while major hotels usually have a limited array of common medicines.

**Post offices** Tokyo Central Post Office is on the west side of Tokyo Station (Mon–Fri 9am–7pm, Sat 9am–5pm, Sun & hols 9am–12.30pm; 24hr service for stamps and parcels). The International Post Office (2-3-3 Ōtemachi; same times) is a bit less convenient, but usually quieter. For English-language information about the postal services, call ☎03/5472-5851. Poste restante can be collected from the basement counter of Tokyo Central Post Office (Mon–Fri 8am–8pm, Sat 8am–5pm, Sun & hols 9am–12.30pm). The postal address is 2-7-2 Marunouchi, Chiyoda-ku, Tokyo 100.

**Sports** The baseball season runs from April to the end of October. The Nippon Ham Fighters and Yomiuri Giants both play at Tokyo Dome (☎03/3811-2111) at Suidōbashi, while the Yakult Swallows are based at Jingū Stadium (☎03/3404-8999) near Gaienmae Station. Tickets start from ¥1000. If you're keen to see some martial arts action, the TIC at Yūrakuchō (see p.86) has a full list of *dōjō* which allow visitors to watch practice sessions for free. Of the sixteen teams in the J-League, the professional soccer league, the nearest one to Tokyo is Verdi Kawasaki, based near Musashikōsugi Station on the JR Nambu or Tōkyū Tōyoko lines. Tickets cost from ¥2000.

**Taxis** The major taxi firms are Daiwa (☎03/3563-5151); Hinomaru (☎03/3814-1111); Kokusai (☎03/3491-6001); and Nihon Kōtsū (☎03/3586-2151).

**Ticket agencies** To get tickets for theatre performances, films, concerts and sporting events, it's best, in the first instance, to approach one of the major advance ticket agencies. Ticket Saison, in most Seibu-affiliated department stores, and Ticket Pia can be found in the main city areas, such as Ginza, Ikebukuro, Shibuya and Shinjuku. Ticket Pia also has an English-language telephone booking line (☎03/5237-9999) Major events sell out quickly, but you can go directly to the venue on the day and see if you can get a ticket from the box office or a tout outside; expect to pay well over the odds.

**Tours** Japan Travel Bureau (Sunrise Tours, ☎03/5620-9500) and Japan Gray Line (☎03/3436-6881) offer all-inclusive bus tours of Tokyo and nearby attractions, including Kamakura, Nikkō and Hakone, with English-speaking guides. Prices start at around ¥4500 for a half-day tour of the main sights, to ¥10,000 for a full day's excursion including lunch and dinner – well over double what a similar DIY tour would cost. Tours can be booked at the TIC in Yūrakuchō and at all major hotels. For a walking tour, Mr Oka Nobuō (☎0422/51-7673) runs half-day Sunday walks, generally in the Shitamachi area, usually for ¥2000.

**Trains** For English-language information on JR's services, including train times and ticket prices, call the JR East-Infoline on ☎03/3423-0111 (Mon–Fri 10am–6pm).

**Travel agents** For international tickets try one of the following English-speaking agents. In each case just the head-office number is given, though they all have several branches – see their adverts in the English press. A'cross Travellers Bureau (Shinjuku ☎03/3340-6471); Hit Travel (Ebisu ☎03/3473-9040); No.1 Travel (Shinjuku ☎03/3200-8871); STA (Ikebukuro ☎03/5391-2922). The main domestic travel agents are Japan Travel Bureau (JTB) (☎03/5620-9500), with dozens of branches all over Tokyo, Nippon Travel Agency (☎03/3572-8744) and Kinki Nippon Tourist (☎03/3253-6131); the contact numbers are for their foreign tourist departments.

# travel details

You can **leave Tokyo** by land, air or sea, on a multitude of daily services. For international destinations you'll almost certainly be catching a plane from Narita. For domestic travel, the **train** – either Shinkansen or *tokkyū* (limited express) – will generally be the best way to move on. If you're happy to spend a night on a bus, **long-distance buses** are a slightly cheaper than trains. Only if you're heading out to the more far-flung corners of the archipelago will catching a **plane** be the best option. Virtually all domestic flights leave from Haneda. **Ferries** are worth considering for leisurely, long-distance trips to Hokkaidō or south to Shikoku and Kyūshū.

### Trains

**Tokyo Station** to: Fukuoka (Hakata Station) (25 daily; 6hr 12min); Hiroshima (at least 25 daily; 4hr 51min); Kamakura (at least 30 daily; 55min); Kyoto (at least 80 daily; 2hr 37min); Morioka (at least 25 daily; 2hr 50min); Nagano (15 daily; 1hr); Nagoya (at least 80 daily; 1hr 52min); Niigata (30 daily; 1hr 40min); Okayama (at least 25 daily; 3hr 53min); Sendai (55 daily; 1hr 44min); Shin-Kōbe (at least 25 daily; 3hr 13min); Shin-Ōsaka (at least 80 daily; 2hr 53min); Yokohama (at least 80 daily; 44min).

**Asakusa Station** to: Nikkō (14 daily; 1hr 55min).

**Shinjuku Station** to: Hakone (23 daily; 1hr 30min); Kofu (27 daily; 1hr 30min); Matsumoto (18 daily; 2hr 38min).

**Ueno Station** to: Kanazawa (daily; 6hr 6min); Karuizawa (20 daily; 2hr 2min).

## Buses

**Tokyo Station** to: Aomori (1 daily; 9hr 30min); Fuji (30 daily; 2hr 30min); Fukui (daily; 8hr); Hiroshima (daily; 12hr); Kōbe (daily; 8hr 45min); Kōchi (daily; 11hr 45min); Kyoto (2 daily; 8hr); Matsuyama (daily; 12hr 5min); Morioka (daily; 7hr 30min); Nagano (daily; 6hr 34min); Nagoya (14 daily; 6hr); Nara (daily; 9hr 30min); Ōsaka (3 daily; 8hr 50min); Sendai (2 daily; 5hr 15min); Shimoda (6 daily; 2hr 50min); Takamatsu (daily; 10hr 25min); Yamagata (2 daily; 5hr 35min).

**Ikebukuro Station** to: Ise (2 daily; 8hr); Kanazawa (4 daily; 7hr 30min); Niigata (6 daily; 5hr).

**Shibuya Station** to: Himeji (daily; 9hr); Wakayama (daily 8hr 20min).

**Shinagawa Station** to: Hirosaki (daily; 9hr 15min); Imabari (daily; 12hr 20min); Kurashiki (daily; 11hr); Tokushima (daily; 10hr 40min).

**Shinjuku Station** to: Akita (daily; 9hr 40min); Fuji Go-gōme (at least 3 daily; 3hr); Fukuoka (Hakata Station) (2 daily; 14hr 20min); Hakone-Togendai (13 daily; 2hr 11min); Kawaguchi-ko (at least 14 daily; 1hr 45min); Matsumoto (12 daily; 3hr 10min); Okayama (2 daily; 10hr 20min); Shin-Gifu (daily; 6hr 20min).

## Ferries

There are regular ferry connections between Tokyo Ferry Port, at Ariake on the area of reclaimed land in Tokyo Bay, and Kushiro and Tomakomai in Hokkaidō, Kōchi and Tokushima on Shikoku. From Shin-Kiba subway and train station on the east side of Tokyo Bay you can take a bus to the ferry port.

**Tokyo Ferry Terminal** to: Kōchi (4 weekly; 21hr 20min); Kushiro (weekly; 31hr 35min); Naha (1–2 weekly; 45hr); Tokushima (4 weekly; 19hr 40min); Tomakomai (4 weekly; 30hr)

## Flights

**Haneda** to: Akita (6 daily; 1hr); Asahikawa (7 daily; 1hr 35min); Fukuoka (29 daily; 1hr 45min); Hakodate (8 daily; 1hr 15min); Hiroshima (10 daily; 1hr 25min); Kagoshima (10 daily; 1hr 50min); Kansai International (9 daily; 1hr 15min); Kōchi (5 daily; 1hr 50min); Komatsu (for Kanazawa; 8 daily; 1hr); Kumamoto (8 daily; 1hr 50min); Kushiro (5 daily; 1hr 35min); Matsuyama (8 daily; 1hr 25min); Misawa (4 daily; 1hr 10min); Miyazaki (9 daily; 1hr 45min); Nagasaki (9 daily; 1hr 55min); Obihiro (4 daily; 1hr 35min); Oita (8 daily; 1hr 30min); Okayama (4 daily; 1hr 20min); Okinawa (Naha; 10 daily; 2hr 30min); Ōsaka (Itami; 9 daily; 1hr); Sapporo (Chitose; 34 daily; 1hr 30min); Takamatsu (7 daily; 1hr 10min); Tokushima (6 daily; 1hr 15min); Toyama (6 daily; 1hr); Yamagata (3 daily; 55min).

**Narita** to: Nagoya (daily; 1hr).

CHAPTER TWO

# AROUND TOKYO

Tokyo is hemmed into its coastal location on the Kantō plain by a ring of mountains and volcanoes, featuring temples, parks and a couple of bustling towns and cities. It doesn't take long to get out of the capital – two hours at most – and it's well worth doing, though if time is short take care to prioritize. The single best reason for venturing out lies to the north, at **Nikkō**, where the incredible shrine complex of **Tōshō-gū**, built to deify the Tokugawa shoguns, is a riotous feast for the senses – you might dislike its ostentatiousness, but you won't regret making the journey to see it. The surrounding mountains – fantastic walking country – are beautiful throughout the year, but particularly so when decked out in autumn colours. If you can, make time to check out the spectacular waterfalls nearby, up at the lakes by Chūzenji and Yumoto, another excellent area for walking and cross-country skiing.

The temple complex of **Naritasan Shinshō-ji**, with a lovely pagoda, extensive gardens, woods and ornamental ponds, is the highlight of the pilgrim town of **Narita**, some 60km northeast of Tokyo, and is certainly the best way of passing time before catching a flight at the nearby international airport. Ceramics lovers should not miss out on **Mashiko**, north of Tokyo in Tochigi-ken, a pottery town with over three hundred kilns and associated with the famed craftsman Hamada Shōji and British potter Bernard Leach.

Also within easy reach of the city is Japan's most famous landmark, the venerable **Mount Fuji**, where you might choose to make the tough ascent up the volcano, or simply relax in the surrounding countryside. Nearby, the inviting landscapes of the Fuji-Hakone-Izu National Park, particularly around **Hakone** and south through **Izu Hantō**, warrant at least two or three days' exploration.

Closer to Tokyo, the deceptively unassuming town of **Kamakura** is one of Japan's major historical sights, home to several imposing Zen temples and the country's second-largest bronze Buddha, the magnificent **Daibutsu**. There are also hiking trails through the surrounding hills, and an enjoyable train-ride further along the coast to the sacred island of Enoshima. Just north of Kamakura you're back into the urban sprawl where Tokyo merges with **Yokohama**, Japan's second largest and most cosmopolitan city with a smattering of attractions, not least the gourmet restaurants of Chinatown.

### ACCOMMODATION PRICE CODES

All accommodation in this book has been graded according to the following price codes, which refer to the cheapest double or twin room available for most of the year, and include taxes. Note that rates may increase during peak holiday periods, in particular around Christmas and New Year, the Golden Week (April 28–May 6) and Obon (the week around August 15), when accommodation is very difficult to get without an advance reservation. In the case of hostels providing dormitory accommodation, the code refers to the charge per bed. See p.36 for more details on accommodation.

| | | |
|---|---|---|
| ① under ¥3000 | ④ ¥7000–10,000 | ⑦ ¥20,000–30,000 |
| ② ¥3000–5000 | ⑤ ¥10,000–15,000 | ⑧ ¥30,000–40,000 |
| ③ ¥5000–7000 | ⑥ ¥15,000–20,000 | ⑨ over ¥40,000 |

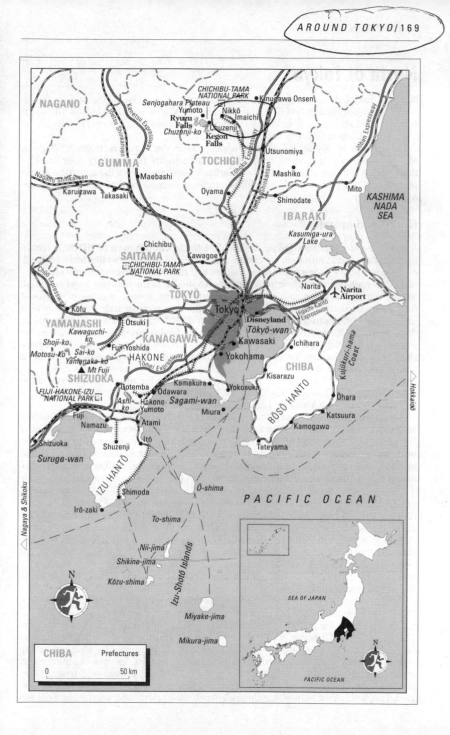

CHICHIBU-TAMA
NATIONAL PARK

NAGANO

Senjogahara Plateau
Yumoto
**Ryuzu
Falls**
*Chuzenji-ko*
Nikkō
Imaichi
Chuzenji
**Kegon
Falls**

Kinugawa Onsen

GUMMA

Maebashi

Karuizawa  Takasaki

TOCHIGI

Oyama

Utsunomiya

Mashiko

Mito

KASHIMA
NADA
SEA

Shimodate

IBARAKI

Chichibu

Kawagoe

SAITAMA

CHICHIBU-TAMA
NATIONAL PARK

Kasumiga-ura
Lake

Kōfu

Otsuki

TŌKYŌ

Narita

**Narita
Airport**

Tokyo

KANAGAWA

YAMANASHI
*Kawaguchi-
ko*
*Shoji-ko*
*Sai-ko*
*Motosu-ko*
*Yamanaka-ko*
▲ Mt Fuji

HAKONE

**Disneyland**
*Tōkyō-wan*
Kawasaki
Yokohama

Ichihara

Kisarazu

CHIBA

Gotemba
Odawara

SHIZUOKA

FUJI-HAKONE-IZU
NATIONAL PARK

*Ashi-
ko*
Hakone
Yumoto

Kamakura
Yokosuka

*Sagami-wan*

Miura

BŌSŌ HANTŌ

Ōhara

Katsuura

Fuji
Namazu

Atami

Kamogawa

Shizuoka

Shuzenji

Itō

*Suruga-wan*

IZU HANTŌ

Tateyama

Shimoda

Ō-shima

Irō-zaki

*PACIFIC OCEAN*

To-shima

Nii-jima

Shikine-jima

Kōzu-shima

Izu-Shotō Islands

Miyake-jima

Mikura-jima

N

△ Nagaya & Shikoku

△ Hokkaidō

Chūō Expressway
Kan-etsu Expressway
Jōetsu Shinkansen
Nagano Shinkansen
Tōhoku Shinkansen
Tōhoku Expressway
Tōmei Shinkansen
Jōban Expressway
Higashi-Kantō
Expressway
Kujūkuri-hama
Coast
Tōmei Expressway

SEA OF JAPAN

PACIFIC OCEAN

CHIBA    Prefectures

0          50 km

# North of Tokyo

North of Tokyo, the urban sprawl starts to disappear as you rise up the densely forested mountains of Tochigi-ken. The highlight here is **Nikkō**, with its fabulous **Tōshō-gū** complex of multi-coloured shrines and temples and national park scenery, crowned by the pristine lakes at Chūzenji and Yumoto.

On the way to Nikkō, it's worth stopping off in the attractive pottery village of **Mashiko**, where you can pick up traditional earthenware pieces or try your hand on the wheel. Northeast of the capital lies **Narita**, where, apart from the international airport, stands a large and striking Buddhist temple, a long-established and popular place of pilgrimage.

## Nikkō and around

If you make one trip from Tokyo, it should be to the pilgrim town of **NIKKŌ**, 128km north of the capital, with a shrine complex set amid splendid mountains and surrounded by outstanding hiking trails. The antithesis of the usually austere Shinto shrines – and often considered overbearingly gaudy – **Tōshō-gū** is the dazzling jewel of Nikkō, which, appropriately enough, means "sunlight". Year round, masses of Japanese tourists tramp dutifully around Tōshō-gū and the surrounding holy buildings, which include the **Futarasan-jinja** shrine and the Buddhist temple of **Rinnō-ji**. After you've done the same, it's worth investigating the **Nikkō Tōshō-gū Museum of Art**, in the woods behind Tōshō-gū, and then escaping the crowds by crossing the Daiya-gawa river to explore the dramatically named **Ganman-ga-fuchi abyss**, which is in fact a tranquil riverside walk.

If it's the great outdoors you're after, don't miss out on the most beautiful part of the Nikkō National Park around **Chūzenji-ko**, some 17km from Nikkō, or the quieter and less touristy resort of **Yumoto**, higher in the mountains.

Although with an early start it's possible to see both Tōshō-gū and Chūzenji-ko in a long day-trip from Tokyo, you're far better off making an overnight stay in or around Nikkō to get the most out of the area. Cramming both places into one day during the peak summer and autumn seasons is impossible; far better to concentrate on Nikkō alone. A final tip: pack some warm clothes since Nikkō is cooler than lowland Tokyo, and in winter you can expect plenty of snow.

### SOME HISTORY

Although Nikkō has been a holy place in both the Buddhist and Shinto religions for over a thousand years – a hermitage was built here in the eighth century – its fortunes only took off big time with the death of **Tokugawa Ieyasu** in 1616; in his will, the shogun requested that a shrine be built here in his honour. The shrine, which deified Ieyasu, was completed in 1617, but was deemed not nearly impressive enough by Ieyasu's grandson, **Tokugawa Iemitsu**, who ordered work to begin on the elaborate decorative mausoleum seen today.

Iemitsu's dazzling vision was driven by practical as well as aesthetic considerations. The shogun wanted to stop rival lords amassing money of their own, so he ordered the *daimyō* to supply the materials for the shrine, and to pay the thousands of craftsmen. The mausoleum, Tōshō-gū, was completed in 1634 and the jury has been out on its over-the-top design ever since. Whatever you make of its grandiosity, Tōshō-gū, along with the slightly more restrained Daiyūin-byō mausoleum of Iemitsu, is entirely successful at conveying the immense power and wealth of the Tokugawa dynasty. Every year, on May 17, the **Grand Festival** restages the spectacular interment of Ieyasu at Tōshō-gū, with a cast of over one thousand costumed priests and warriors in a colour-

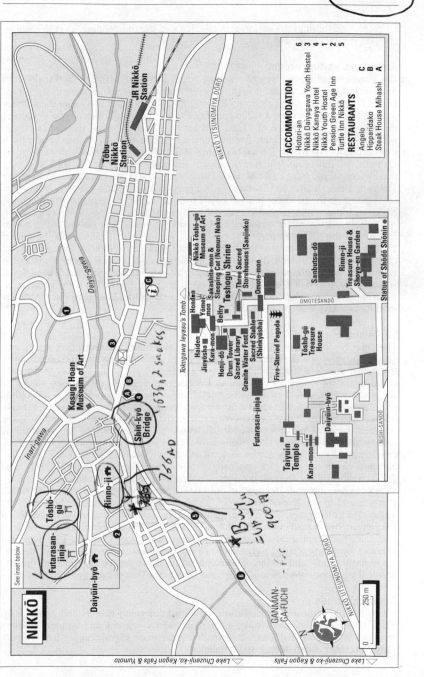

# NIKKŌ

See inset below

Futarasan-jinja ⛩

Tōshō-gū ⛩

Daiyūin-byō

Kosugi Hoan Museum of Art

Rinno-ji 卍

Shin-kyō Bridge

Inari-gawa

Daiya-gawa

Tōbu Nikkō Station

JR Nikkō Station

NIKKŌ UTSUNOMIYA DŌRO

GANMAN-GA-FUCHI

◁ Lake Chuzenji-ko, Kegon Falls & Yumoto

◁ Lake Chuzenji-ko & Kegon Falls

0    250 m

**ACCOMMODATION**
Hotori-an                        6
Nikkō Daiyagawa Youth Hostel     3
Nikkō Kanaya Hotel               4
Nikkō Youth Hostel               1
Pension Green Age Inn            2
Turtle Inn Nikkō                 5

**RESTAURANTS**
Angelo                           C
Hipparidako                      B
Steak House Mihashi              A

Tokugawa Ieyasu's Tomb ◁

Nikkō Tōshō-gū Museum of Art

Sakashita-mon & Sleeping Cat (Nemuri Neko)

Three Sacred Storehouses (Sanjinko)

Honden
Yōmei-mon
Kara-mon
Haiden
Jinyōsha
Belfry
Honji-dō
Drum Tower
Sacred Library
Granite Water Font
Sacred Stable (Shinkyūsha)

Omote-mon

**Teshogu Shrine**

Futarasen-jinja

Five-Storied Pagoda

OMOTESANDŌ

Tōshō-gū Treasure House

Sanbutsu-dō

Rinno-ji Treasure House & Shoyo-en Garden

Taiyuin Temple

Kara-mon

Daiyūin-byō

NISH-SANDŌ

Statue of Shōdō Shonin ●

ful procession through the shrine grounds. It's well worth attending, as is the almost identical festival of October 17.

## Arrival and getting around

The cheapest and easiest way of reaching Nikkō is to take a Tōbu-Nikkō **train** from Asakusa in Tokyo (the station is in the basement of the Matsuya department store, connected by tunnel to Asakusa subway station). *Kaisoku* (rapid) trains make the journey in around two hours and cost ¥1330 one way. For the marginally faster *kyūkō* (express) trains you pay a surcharge of ¥1220, and for the "Kegon" *tokkyū* (limited express), which takes one hour and forty five minutes, a total fare of ¥2750. Unless your train is a direct one for Nikkō, you'll need to change at Shimo-Imaichi. Nikkō is also served by JR trains, but this route, which takes longer and costs more than the Tōbu line, only makes sense if you have a JR rail pass. The fastest route is by Shinkansen from either Tokyo or Ueno stations to Utsunomiya Station, a journey of fifty minutes, where you must change to the JR Nikkō line for a local train taking forty five minutes to reach the Nikkō terminus, a minute's walk east of the Tōbu station.

The Tōbu railway offers various **travel passes**, known as "free passes", for travel to and around the Nikkō area from Tokyo. These tickets, which can only be bought at Tokyo's Tōbu stations, include the train fare from Asakusa to Nikkō (express train surcharges still apply), unlimited use of local buses, and discounts on entrance charges at many of the area's attractions, including the cable cars and boat trips at Chūzenji-ko. If you only intend to visit Tōshō-gū, it's not worth buying the pass, but if you're planning a trip out to Chūzenji-ko, the most useful ticket is the Nikkō Mini Free Pass, which is valid for two days and costs ¥4960.

## Information

The **Tōbu Nikkō station**, designed like a giant Swiss chalet, is fronted by a square surrounded by gift shops, the main road in the western corner running up to Tōshō-gū. Inside the station there's a cloakroom where you can leave luggage for the day (¥300–¥500 depending on the size of the bag) and an **information desk** (daily 9am–5pm; ☎0288/53-4511), where the assistant speaks some English and can provide you with maps and leaflets on the area. The town's main **tourist information centre** is the Nikkō Kyōdo Centre (daily 8.30am–5pm; ☎0288/54-2496), on the main road from the station to the Tōshō-gū complex; assistants here can make accommodation bookings. The centre also has an attached **gallery** (daily 8.30am–7pm) showcasing local art and an area where you can watch short videos, with English commentaries, on local attractions, history and culture. If you're planning on hiking in the area, pick up a copy of the excellent English-language *Hiking Guide* (¥150), which is illustrated with good maps and pictures of local flora and fauna.

You can save money if you buy the right **ticket** for the temples and shrines in Nikkō. If you intend to see Rinnō-ji, Tōshō-gū and Futarasan-jinja you should buy the ¥900 *nisha-ichiji* (two-shrines, one-temple) **combination ticket**, which includes entrance to the Daiyūin-byō mausoleum, but not the roaring dragon hall (*Honji-dō*) nor the area containing the sleeping cat (*Nemuri neko*) carving and Ieyasu's tomb at Tōshō-gū. Pay the extra for these excluded sights, as you'll still be better off than buying separate tickets at each temple and shrine. The combination ticket can be bought from booths beside the Sanbutsu-dō hall in Rinnō-ji and outside the Omote-mon gate to Tōshō-gū.

## Accommodation

Nikkō has plenty of **accommodation**, ranging from youth hostels and pensions to plush hotels and ryokans. However, in peak holiday seasons and autumn advance reservations are essential. Rates at virtually all places are slightly higher from August 21 to November 3, and during major holidays.

## NIKKŌ AND AROUND

| | | |
|---|---|---|
| **Nikkō** | *Nikkō* | 日光 |
| Daiyūin-byō | *Daiyūin-byō* | 大猷院廟 |
| Futarasan-jinja | *Futarasan-jinja* | 二荒山神社 |
| Ganman-ga-fuchi abyss | *Ganman-ga-fuchi* | 含満ヶ淵 |
| Kosugi Hōan Museum of Art | *Kosugi Hōan Bijutsukan* | 小杉放庵美術館 |
| Nikkō Tōshō-gū Museum of Art | *Nikkō Tōshō-gū Bijutsukan* | 日光東照宮美術館 |
| Rinnō-ji | *Rinnō-ji* | 輪王寺 |
| Shin-kyō bridge | *Shin-kyō* | 神橋 |
| Tōshō-gū | *Tōshō-gū* | 東照宮 |
| *AROUND NIKKŌ* | | |
| Chūzenji-ko lake | *Chūzenji-ko* | 中禅寺湖 |
| Kegon Falls | *Kegon-no-taki* | 華厳の滝 |
| Kinugawa Onsen | *Kinugawa Onsen* | 鬼怒川温泉 |
| Nikkō Edo Village | *Nikkō Edo-mura* | 日光江戸村 |
| Nikkō Natural Science Museum | *Nikkō Shizen Kagaku Hakubutsukan* | 日光自然科学博物館 |
| Yumoto | *Yumoto* | 湯元 |
| *ACCOMMODATION* | | |
| Chūzenji Kanaya Hotel | *Chūzenji Kanaya Hoteru* | 中禅寺金谷ホテル |
| Hotori-an | *Hotori-an* | ほとり庵 |
| Nikkō Daiyagawa Youth Hostel | *Nikkō Daiyagawa Yūsu Hosuteru* | 日光大谷川ユースホステル |
| Nikkō Kanaya Hotel | *Nikkō Kanaya Hoteru* | 日光金谷ホテル |
| Nikkō Lakeside Hotel | *Nikkō Rēkusaido Hoteru* | 日光レークサイドホテル |
| Nikkō Youth Hostel | *Nikkō Yūsu Hosuteru* | 日光ユースホステル |
| Pension Green Age Inn | *Penshon Guriin Eiji In* | ペンショングリーンエイジイン |
| Petit Pension Friendly | *Puchi Penshon Furendorii* | プチペンションフレンドリー |
| Turtle Inn Nikkō | *Tātoru In Nikkō* | タートルイン日光 |
| Yumoto Hillside Inn | *Yumoto Hirusaido In* | 湯元ヒルサイドイン |
| Yunoka | *Yunoka* | ゆの香 |
| *EATING* | | |
| Angelo | *Angero* | アンジェロ |
| Chez Hoshino | *Shé Hoshino* | シェホシノ |
| Hippari Dako | *Hippari Dako* | ひっぱり凧 |
| Steak House Mihashi | *Sutēki Hausu Mihashi* | ステーキハウスみはし |
| Suzuya | *Suzuya* | 鈴家 |
| Tsugaya | *Tsugaya* | つがや |
| Yumoto Rest House | *Yumoto Resuto Hausu* | 湯元レストハウス |

**Hotori-an**, 8-28 Takumi-chō (☎0288/53-3663, fax 53-3883). In a tranquil location beside the path to the Ganman-ga-fuchi abyss, this is the modern annexe of the *Turtle Inn* (see below) and has good-value *tatami* rooms with en-suite bathrooms. There's a pottery shop and café, and dinner is served over at the *Turtle Inn*. ⑤.

**Nikkō Daiyagawa Youth Hostel**, 1075 Naka-Hatsuishi-machi (☎0288/54-1974). English signposts lead to this cosy hostel near the river. It may not be the grandest place, but it's run by a very hospitable family and deservedly gets rave reviews from former guests. Dorms have bunkbeds and the meals are excellent. ①.

**Nikkō Kanaya Hotel**, 1300 Kami-Hatsuishi-machi (☎0288/54-0001, fax 53-2487) Nikkō's top western-style hotel harks back to the glamour of early twentieth-century travel. There are some cheaper rooms with en-suite shower or just a toilet (the hotel has a communal bath), but most rooms are pricey and rates skyrocket during peak holiday seasons. ⑦.

**Nikkō Youth Hostel**, 2854 Tokorono (☎0288/54-1013). On the far side of the Daiya-gawa from the town, this medium-sized hostel has a secluded location behind the high school. Bunk bedrooms, hearty meals, real log fire and English newspaper are available. From November to March, guests pay ¥200 extra for heating. ①.

**Pension Green Age Inn**, 10-9 Nishi-sandō (☎0288/53-3636). Eccentric decorations such as an organ, stained-glass windows and mock-Tudor facade, enliven this small Western-style hotel close by Tōshō-gū. The comfy rooms are excellent value and there's a communal onsen bath made from pine. ④.

**Turtle Inn Nikkō**, 2-16 Takumi-chō (☎0288/53-3168, fax 53-3883). Popular pension run by an English-speaking family, in a quiet location next to the Daiya-gawa river and five minutes' walk from the main shrines, with small, plain *tatami* rooms, common bathrooms and a cosy lounge. The evening meal at ¥2000 is a good deal, but breakfast is pricey at ¥1000 per person. ③.

## The approach to Tōshō-gū

Frequent buses head towards the main approach to Tōshō-gū from in front of both of Nikkō's train stations, but the walk uphill to the shrine complex along the town's main street takes only fifteen minutes. At the top of the gently sloping road you'll pass one of Nikkō's most famous landmarks, the red **Shin-kyō bridge**, a 1907 replica of the original arched wooden structure built in 1636. Legend has it that when the Buddhist priest Shōdō Shōnin first visited Nikkō in the eighth century he was helped across the Daiya-gawa river at this very spot by the timely appearance of two snakes who formed a bridge and then vanished.

If you have time, it's worth turning right at the bridge and walking up to the modern terracotta-coloured **Kosugi Hoan Museum of Art** (Tues–Sun 9.30am–5pm; ¥700), which displays the dreamily beautiful figurative and landscape paintings of local artist Hoan (1920–1964). The main shrine and temple complex are in the opposite direction; take the left-hand uphill path across from the bridge and you'll emerge in front of the main compound of **Rinnō-ji**, a Tendai Buddhist temple founded in 766 by Shōdō Shōnin, whose statue stands on a rock at the entrance. The large, red-painted hall, Sanbutsu-dō, houses three giant gilded statues; the thousand-handed Kannon, the Amida Buddha and the fiercesome horse-headed Kannon. It's worth paying to view these awe-inspiring figures from directly beneath their lotus flower perches – entry is included in the combination ticket (see p.172), which you can buy at the booth outside. Rinnō-ji's **Treasure House** (daily 8am–5pm; ¥300), opposite the Sanbutsu-dō, has some interesting items on display, but its nicest feature is the attached Shōyō-en, an elegant garden with a strolling route around a small pond.

## Tōshō-gū and Nikkō Tōshō-gū Museum of Art

The broad, tree-lined Omotesan-dō leads up to the main entrance to Tōshō-gū, just to the east of Rinnō-ji. You'll pass under a giant stone *torii* gate (one of the few remaining features of the original 1617 shrine) and will see on the left an impressive red and green five-storey pagoda, an 1819 reconstruction of the 1650 original which burned down. Ahead is the Omote-mon gate, the entrance to the main shrine precincts, where you'll need to hand over a section of your combination ticket or Tōshō-gū-only ticket (¥1250), either of which can be bought from the booth in front of the gate.

Inside the precincts, turning to the left will take you past the **Three Sacred Storehouses** (*Sanjinko*) on the right and the **Sacred Stables** (*Shinkyūsha*) on the left. In front of the stables there is usually a crowd of amateur photographers jostling to capture one of the many famous painted wood carvings within Tōshō-gū – the "hear no evil, see no evil, speak no evil" **monkeys**, which represent the three major principles of

Tendai Buddhism. The route leads to the steps up to the dazzling **Yōmei-mon** (Sun Blaze Gate), with wildly ornate carvings, gilt and intricate decoration. Impressive as it is, the gate has less dramatic impact than the detailed panels on the flanking walls, which are adorned with fantastic flowers and birds. A belfry and drum tower stand alone amid pools of pebbles in front of the gate. Behind the drum tower is the **Honji-dō** (¥50), a small hall which is part of Rinnō-ji temple and inside of which is the ceiling painting of a "roaring dragon". A priest will demonstrate how to make the dragon roar by standing beneath its head and clapping to create an echo.

It's better to pay the small charge to see the roaring dragon rather than fork out ¥430 for the less impressive sleeping cat (*nemuri neko*), just above the Sakashita-mon gate to right of the inner precinct beyond the Yōmei-mon – you'd easily miss this minute carving if it wasn't for the gawping crowd. Two hundred stone steps lead uphill from the gate to the surprisingly unostentatious **tomb of Ieyasu**, amid a glade of pines, and about the only corner of the shrine where the crowds are generally absent.

Directly in front of the Yōmei-mon is the serene, white and gold gate of **Kara-mon**, beyond which is the **Haiden**, or hall of worship. The side entrance to the hall is to the right of the gate and you'll need to remove your shoes and stop taking photographs. Inside, you can walk down into the Honden, the shrine's central hall, still decorated with its beautiful original paintwork. On the way back out through the Yōmei-mon, you'll pass the Jinyōsha, a building where the *mikoshi* (portable shrines) used during Tōshō-gū's spring and autumn festivals are hidden away.

Before rushing off, don't miss the **Nikkō Tōshō-gū Museum of Art** (daily: April–Oct 9am–5pm; Jan–March, Nov & Dec 9am–4pm; ¥800), at the back of the shrine complex, to the left as you walk out of the Omote-mon gate. The traditional wooden mansion, dating from 1928 and impressive in its simplicity, is the former head office of the shrine. Inside, the sliding doors and screens were decorated by the top Japanese painters of the day and together constitute one of the most beautiful collections of this type of art that you'll see anywhere in the country.

## Futarasan-jinja, Daiyūin-byō and the Ganman-ga-fuchi abyss.

A trip around Tōshō-gū is likely to leave you visually, if not physically exhausted, but it's worth pressing on to some of the other temples and shrines in the surrounding woods. At the end of the right-hand path next to Tōshō-gū's pagoda, the simple red colour scheme of the **Futarasan-jinja** comes as a relief to the senses. This shrine, originally established by the priest Shōdō Shōnin in 782, is the main one dedicated to the deity of Nantai-san, the volcano whose eruption created nearby Chūzenji-ko. The middle shrine is beside the lake and the innermost shrine stands on the top of the mountain. There are some good paintings of animals and birds on votive plaques in the shrine's main hall, while the attached garden (¥200) is a quiet retreat with a small tea-house serving *matcha* green tea and sweets for ¥350. You can also inspect the *bake-mono tōrō*, a "phantom lantern" made of bronze in 1292 and said to be possessed by demons.

Just beyond Futarasan-jinja, and by-passed by the tourist mélée is the charming **Daiyūin-byō**, which contains the mausoleum of the third shogun, Tokugawa Iemitsu, who died in 1651. This complex – part of Rinnō-ji and hidden away on a hillside, surrounded by lofty pines – was deliberately designed to be less ostentatious than Tōshō-gū. Look out for the green god of wind and the red god of thunder in the alcoves behind the Niten-mon gate and the beautiful Kara-mon (Chinese-style gate) and fence surrounding the gold and black lacquer inner precincts.

If the relative peacefulness of Daiyūin-byō has left you wary of Nikkō's ever-present tourist scrum, make for another nearby tranquil escape. From the temple area, head for the Nishi-sandō main road (where the bus to and from Nikkō's stations stops), cross over and continue down to the Daiya-gawa river – five minutes' walk west is the

Ganman-bashi, a small bridge across from which begins the riverside pathway through the **Ganman-ga-fuchi abyss**. Part of this restful walk, along the attractive and rocky river valley, is lined by the *Narabi-jizō*, some fifty decaying stone statues of Jizō, the Buddhist saint of travellers and children.

## Eating

Avoid the bland tourist restaurants clustered around Nikkō's train and bus stations and chances are you'll **eat** pretty well. This area's speciality is *yuba-ryōri*, thin, tasty strips of tofu made from soya beans, usually rolled into tubes and cooked in various stews. You're likely to be served this at your hotel or pension, the best place to eat if you stay overnight since most restaurants shut down around 8pm.

**Angelo**, on Route 119 running up to Tōshō-gū. Bright Italian pizza parlour with a counter bar and a few tables. This is one of the few places in Nikkō serving something other than Japanese food. Pasta dishes are also on offer, and there's an English menu.

**Hippari Dako**, at the top of the main drag up to Tōshō-gū. Inexpensive *yakitori* and noodle café – look for the giant kite outside – popular with just about every *gaijin* who has ever set foot in the place, as the written recommendations that plaster the walls testify. Beer and sake are also served. Open daily 11am–7pm.

**Nikkō Kanaya Hotel**, 1300 Kami-Hatsuishi-machi. Several eating options at this hotel: a meal in the elegant second-floor dining room will set you back at least ¥3500 for lunch, ¥6000 for dinner, while the first-floor *Maple Leaf* coffee shop is cheaper, but less glamorous. Best bet is is the *Yashio* Japanese restaurant, behind the coffee shop, which has set lunches for under ¥2000.

**Steak House Mihashi**, on the slope up to the *Kanaya Hotel* (look for the English sign). Fill up on set steak meals, which are fairly good value at ¥2800 per person.

**Suzuya**. Stand-alone restaurant just before you cross over the bridge up the slope from the Kosugi Hoan Museum of Art. This is a good place to sample *yuba-ryōri*; the set lunch is ¥1300 and includes tempura, rice, noodles and rolled tofu. Open daily 11am–3pm.

## Chūzenji-ko and the Kegon Falls

Some 10km west of Nikkō lie **Chūzenji-ko** and the dramatic **Kegon Falls** that flow from it. Local buses usually take less than an hour to get here, running east along Route 120 and up the twisting, one-way road to reach Chūzenji, the lakeside resort, though travelling times can easily be doubled – even tripled – during *kōyō* in mid-October, the prime time for viewing the changing autumn leaves, when it's bumper-to-bumper traffic.

Both the lake and the waterfalls were created thousands of years ago, when nearby Mount Nantai erupted, its lava plugging the valley. The best way of seeing the evidence of this geological event is to hop off the bus at Akechi-daira, the stop before Chūzenji, where a **cable car** (daily 9am–4pm; ¥390 one way, ¥710 return) will whisk you up to a viewing platform. From here it's a 1.5km walk uphill and across the Chanoki-daira plateau. From the plateau there are sweeping views of Chūzenji-ko, Mount Nantai and the famous waterfalls and you can either walk down to the lake or take another cable car (daily: April–Nov 8.30am–4.30pm; ¥440) to just behind Chūzenji bus station. An even better view of the falls can be had from the viewing platform at their base (daily: May–Sept 7.30am–6pm; Oct 7.30am–5pm; March, April & Nov 8am–5pm; Jan, Feb & Dec 9am–4.30pm; ¥530). The lift to this vantage point lies east across the car park behind the Chūzenji bus station; don't be put off by the queues of tour groups – a shorter line is reserved for independent travellers. The lift drops 100m through the rock to the base of the falls, where you can see over a ton of water per second cascading from the Ojiri river which flows from the lake.

Walking west along the shore for around 1km will bring you to the second Futarasan-jinja of the Nikkō area. This colourful **shrine**, which once bore the name Chūzenji now adopted by the town, has a pretty view of the lake, but is nothing extraordinary. To reach the third Futarasan-jinja, you'll have to part with ¥500 for being allowed to climb the sacred volcano Nantai-san, which is owned by the shrine. The hike up to the 2484-metre peak takes around four hours and should only be attempted in good weather.

*PRACTICALITIES*
Chūzenji's **hotels** and tourist facilities are clustered around the northeastern corner of the lake. The most luxurious place to stay is the *Chūzenji Kanaya*, 2482 Chugushi (☎0288/51-0001, fax 51-0011; ⑧), on the way to the Ryūzu falls (see below), and specially designed to blend in with its woodland surroundings. Near the bus station and set back from the lake, the *Nikkō Lakeside Hotel*, 2482 Chūzenji (☎0288/55-0321, fax 55-0771; ⑦), offers Western-style rooms at reasonable prices and has a couple of in-house restaurants. For a more homely feel, head for *Petit Pension Friendly*, Chūzenji (☎0288/55-0027, fax 55-0549; ⑥), five minutes' walk from the bus station. This family-run hotel and café, overlooking the lake, has both Western and Japanese-style rooms – the cheaper ones have no en-suite bathroom.

As far as **eating** goes, a good choice is the stylish, European-style *Chez Hoshino*, on the main row of hotels and giftshops facing Chūzenji-ko (a set three-course lunch with coffee is around ¥2500 per person) – the restaurant has a real log fire in winter. A good selection of set Japanese meals is on offer at *Tsugaya*, a laid-back restaurant with English-speaking staff opposite the Chūzenji bus station. The Nikkō Natural Science Museum, next to the bus station, has a good restaurant serving cheap snacks and noodles, as well as the excellent "Kegon" set meal, which includes soup, fish, salad and coffee for ¥1200. You buy food coupons from the machines outside the restaurant; the plastic food displays will help you choose. For light lunches and snacks, such as burgers and tacos, head for the *Coffee House Yukon* (closed Jan–March & Dec), a log house next to the *Chūzenji Kanaya Hotel*, where you must order at the counter before sitting down (give your table number).

## Yumoto

Before exploring Chūzenji, a rewarding day can be spent by continuing on the bus to the end of the line and getting off at the onsen village of **YUMOTO**, which nestles cosily at the base of the mountains on the northern shore of lake Yuno-ko. Five minutes' walk from the bus terminal at the back of the village is the **Yu-no-daira**, a field where bubbling water breaks through the ground, and the source of the sulphur smell that hangs so pungently in air. Nearby is **Onsen-ji**, a small temple notable for its onsen bath which you can bathe in. At the *Yumoto Rest House*, next to a miniature lake, you can rent row boats (50min; ¥1000) from May to the end of October – a lovely way to take in the surrounding scenery.

To walk around the lake takes around an hour. If you're feeling energetic, it's worth embarking on the easy and enjoyable ten-kilometre (or three-hour) **hike** from Yumoto across the Senjōgahara marshland plateau, past two spectacular waterfalls and back to Chūzenji-ko. First, follow the west bank of Yuno-ko around to the steps down to the picturesque Yudaki Falls, where you might stop off at the lodge serving delicious grilled **fish** and rice cakes (*mochi*) dipped in sweet miso paste. The trail continues along the Yu-gawa through shady woods, before emerging beside the Izumiyado, a large pond and the start of a two-hour tramp across the raised walkways above the Senjōgahara marshland, which blooms with many wildflowers during the summer.

Roughly one hour further on, at the Akanuma junction, you can branch off back to the main road, or continue along the riverside path for thirty minutes to the main road and bridge overlooking the spectacular **Ryūzu Falls** and giving clear views of Chūzenji-ko. At the base of the falls you'll find several giftshops and noodle bars, one of which is superbly located, overlooking the water as it gushes into the lake. A lakeside path continues back to Chūzenji, finally emerging on the main road around 1km before Furatasan-jinja. A more relaxing way of completing this last section is to board a boat at Shobugahama, the jetty near the base of the Ryūzu Falls, and cruise for twenty minutes back to Chūzenji.

*PRACTICALITIES*

The two most attractive **places to stay** in Yumoto are the *Yumoto Hillside Inn* (☎0288/62-2434, fax 62-2519; ⑦), a Western-style hotel in a wooden chalet with an outdoor deck, English-speaking owners, a small heated swimming pool and indoor and outdoor onsen. Also good is the nearby *Yunoka* (☎0288/62-2326, fax 62-2347; ⑦), a small minshuku above a giftshop, a few minutes' walk east of the bus terminus, and offering *tatami* and Western-style rooms. The *Yumoto Rest House*, beside Yuno-ko, with a lovely view of the lake, is a large **café** with a good selection of set meals from around ¥850 per person; pay first at the cash desk, where a photo menu will help you choose your food.

## Nikkō Edo Village

Several onsen resorts are dotted along the Kinu-gawa river, which flows through the mountains northeast of Nikkō. Avoid the touristy Kinugawa Onsen, where multi-storey concrete hotels line the river bank, and head instead for **Nikkō Edo Village** (daily: April–Nov 9am–5pm; Jan–March & Dec 9am–4pm; ¥4500), a fantasy recreation of eighteenth-century life complete with bewigged *samurai* guides and entertaining shows, many great for kids. Light-hearted Japanese costume dramas are played out year round at this theme park, where you can easily spend half a day, though to get the jokes in the *geisha* and comedy shows you'll need to know some Japanese. The live ninja aerial action display is a real hoot, as is "Hell Temple", a Buddhist take on a house of horrors. To get here from Tōbu Nikkō Station, go one stop to Tōbu Shimo-Imaichi, and change to a train on the Tōbu Kinugawa line (¥290), getting off at Shin-Takatoku station (a five-minute walk from Western Village, a cowboy theme park) and crossing the road to catch the shuttle bus to Nikkō Edo Village, five minutes' ride away.

# Mashiko

Some 30km south of Nikkō, the village of **MASHIKO**, with its major pottery museum, numerous pottery shops and over three hundred working kilns spread out around the surrounding paddy fields, makes a rewarding half-day trip en route to Nikkō. Although **Mashiko-yaki**, the distinctive country-style earthenware **pottery**, has been made in this area since the Nara period (710–784), the village only achieved nationwide fame in the 1930s, when the potter and "living national treasure" Hamada Shōji built a kiln here and promoted the pottery throughout Japan. Hamada's former residence has since been restored and relocated – along with his traditional-style kiln – to the impressive **Togei Messe** complex (daily except Wed 9am–4pm). The building contains a pottery studio where you can take lessons for around ¥1200 for two hours (bookings essential on ☎0285/72-7555) and a **museum** featuring works by Hamada and Bernard Leach, the renowned English potter who lived for a short time in this village. To reach the complex, you can walk from Mashiko Station along the main street, Jōnaizaka, which takes roughly twenty minutes – or longer if you browse the many pottery shops along the way. Alternatively, hop on a bus from Utsunomiya or Mashiko stations (see below); an announcement in English will let you know when to get off for the complex, which is a ten-minute walk to the east of the bus stop.

## Practicalities

The easiest way to get to Mashiko is to take the **Shinkansen** (50min; ¥4510) to Utsunomiya, where you'll need to transfer to a **bus** (1hr; ¥1100) which leaves to the left of the Miyano-hashi, the bridge on the west side of the station. Taking a **train** is marginally cheaper; first take the JR Tōhoku line to Oyama (1hr), then change to the Mito line and change again at Shimodate to the private Mōka line, from where it's a forty-minute journey to Mashiko. On weekends and holidays, between March and December, you can travel for ¥500 extra on a restored **steam train** on the Mōka line – tickets can be booked at JR stations (ask for a ticket on the "SL").

English maps and leaflets on Mashiko are available at the **tourist information booths** in Utsunomiya Station (daily 9.30am–6pm; ☎0286/36-2177) and next to Mashiko Station (daily 8.30am–5pm; ☎0285/72-8846), though the staff don't speak English. If you want to tour around the kilns you'll need to rent a car in Tokyo (see Listings, p.165) since they're spread over a wide area. There are several ryokan and minshuku around the village, but once you've checked out the pottery, there's little reason to stay.

## Narita and around

The rambling temple complex of Naritasan Shinshō-ji is the main attraction at the pilgrim town of **NARITA**, some 60km northeast of Tokyo, and a great place to stop off on your way to or from Narita airport. Every year millions of people visit this one-thousand-year-old temple, which is an important landmark in the Shingon sect of Buddhism, but it's such a vast place that as long as you're not here on one of the main festival days (New Year and Setsubun on February 3 or 4), you won't notice the crowds.

To find **Naritasan Shinshō-ji**, follow the central shopping street, Omotesandō, north for ten minutes, turning downhill when it forks beside a small triangular paved island and you'll reach the souvenir stalls lining the approach to the temple's ornate Niō-mon gate. Many of the buildings inside the complex are modern reproductions, but in front of the Great Main Hall is a colourful, three-storey pagoda, dating from the eighteenth century and decorated with fiercesome gilded dragon heads snarling from under brightly painted rafters. Behind the main hall, the temple's gardens include small forests and ornamental ponds and rivers.

While you're in this area, it's worth checking out the **National Museum of Japanese History** (Tues–Sun 9.30am–4.30pm; ¥420), in **Sakura**, a town four stops before Narita on the Keisei line. Set in wooded grounds, a ten-minute walk east from Keisei Sakura Station, this huge museum houses a great collection of Japanese arts and crafts, including 10,000BC Jōmon pottery figurines (which look as though they could be sculptures by Picasso), detailed models of temples, towns and settlements through the ages, and an extensive range of colourful cultural artefacts. An English pamphlet and taped commentary will help guide you around.

| NARITA AND MASHIKO | | |
|---|---|---|
| **Narita** | *Narita* | 成田 |
| Naritasan Shinshō-ji | *Naritasan Shinshō-ji* | 成田山しんしょう寺 |
| National Museum of Japanese History | *Kokuritsu Rekishi Minzoku Hakubutsukan* | 国立歴史民族博物館 |
| Keisei Sakura Station | *Keisei Sakura-eki* | 京成佐倉駅 |
| | | |
| *ACCOMMODATION* | | |
| Kirinoya Ryokan | *Kirinoya Ryokan* | きりのや旅館 |
| Ohgiya Ryokan | *Ohgiya Ryokan* | 扇屋旅館 |
| | | |
| **Mashiko** | *Mashiko* | 益子 |
| Togei Messe | *Togei Messe* | 陶芸メッセ |
| Utsunomiya Station | *Utsunomiya-eki* | 宇都宮駅 |

### Practicalities

Frequent JR **trains** go to Narita from Tokyo Station, leaving from underground platforms 2, 3 and 4. Keisei trains depart from Ueno and Nishi Nippori stations. The journey takes around an hour and fifteen minutes. From the airport, both JR and Keisei trains take less than ten minutes to reach the town, pulling in at separate stations on Omotesandō.

On the same street, closer to the temple, is the **Narita Tourist Pavilion** (Tues–Sun: June–Sept 10am–6pm; Jan–May & Oct–Dec 9am–5pm), where staff can provide information on the area. Narita has plenty of **accommodation** to cater for the groups of pilgrims. Upmarket choices include the *ANA* (☎0476/33-1311; ⑥) and *Holiday Inn* (☎0476/32-1234; ⑥), while good-value *tatami* rooms are on offer at the friendly *Ohgiya Ryokan* (☎0476/22-1161, fax 24-1663; ④), a ten-minute walk from the railway stations towards the temple, with single rooms priced from ¥6500. Meals and en-suite rooms cost extra, but you pay nothing more for the rooms overlooking the lovely garden with a carp pond. The best budget option is *Kirinoya Ryokan* (☎0476/22-0724; ③), five minutes' east of the main entrance to Naritasan Shinshō-ji. This spotless Japanese-style establishment is described by its English-speaking owner Katsumata-san as a "museum hotel", and is crammed with his *samurai* family's heirlooms, including gold-plated suits of armour, swords, muskets, and even a palaquin. Singles cost around ¥5000 and there's a café and a small carp pond to gaze at from the communal bathroom.

You'll find plenty of decent **restaurants**, particularly along Omotesandō. *Kikuya*, opposite the Tourist Pavilion and *World Cook*, an Indian restaurant, closer to the stations, are both reasonably priced and have English menus.

# Fuji Five Lakes

The best reason for heading 100km west from Tokyo towards the area known as **Fuji Five Lakes** is to climb **Mount Fuji**, Japan's most sacred volcano and at 3776m, its highest mountain. At its most beautiful from October to May, when the summit is crowned with snow, Fuji-san, as it's respectfully known by the Japanese, has long been worshipped for its latent power (it last erupted in 1707) and near-perfect symmetry. The

**FUJI FIVE LAKES**

| | | |
|---|---|---|
| **Fuji Five Lakes** | *Fuji Go-ko* | 富士五湖 |
| Fuji Sengen-jinja | *Fuji Sengen-jinja* | 富士浅間神社 |
| Fuji-Yoshida | *Fuji-Yoshida* | 富士吉田 |
| Fujikyū Highland | *Fujikyū Hairando* | 富士急ハイランド |
| Kubota Itchiku Art Museum | *Kubota Itchiku Bijutsukan* | 久保田一竹美術館 |
| Kawaguchi-ko | *Kawaguchi-ko* | 河口湖 |
| Motosu-ko | *Motosu-ko* | 本栖湖 |
| Mount Fuji | *Fuji-san* | 富士山 |
| Sai-ko | *Sai-ko* | 西湖 |
| Shōji-ko | *Shōji-ko* | 精進湖 |
| Yamanaka-ko | *Yamanaka-ko* | 山中湖 |
| *ACCOMMODATION* | | |
| Fuji-Yoshida Youth Hostel | *Fuji-Yoshida Yūsu Hosuteru* | 富士吉田ユースホステル |
| Kawaguchi-ko Youth Hostel | *Kawaguchi-ko Yūsu Hosuteru* | 河口湖ユースホステル |
| Petit Hotel Ebisuya | *Puchi Hoteru Ebisuya* | プチホテルエビスヤ |
| Taikoku-ya | *Taikoku-ya* | たいこくや |

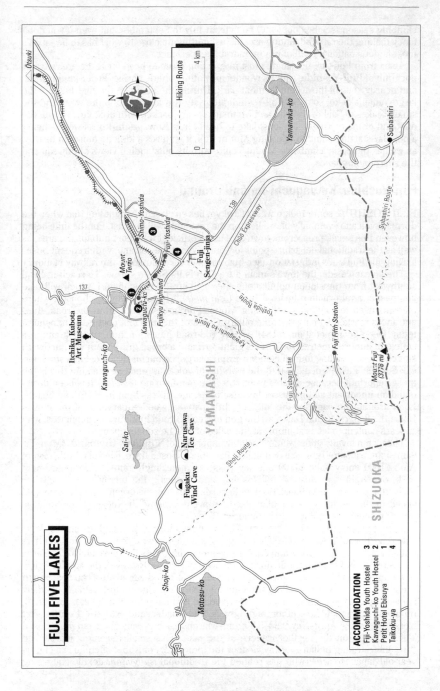

climbing season (see box opposite) runs from July to September, but even if you don't fancy making the rather daunting ascent, just getting up close to what has to be Japan's most famous national symbol is a memorable experience.

Apart from Fuji-san, the single most interesting place to head for is the area's transport hub of **Fuji-Yoshida**, with its wonderfully atmospheric shrine, **Fuji Sengen-jinja**, and nearby state-of-the-art amusement park. During the summer, the **five lakes** – the large Yamanaka-ko, south of Fuji-Yoshida, touristy Kawaguchi-ko to the west, and the smaller lakes of Sai-ko, Shōji-ko and Motosu-ko – are packed with urbanites fleeing the dust and grime of Tokyo. The best lake to head for is **Kawaguchi-ko**; as well as being a popular starting point for climbing Mount Fuji, it features a kimono museum nearby, as well as the easily climbable Mount Tenjō, with its outstanding views of Fuji-san and the surrounding lakes.

## Fuji-Yoshida, Kawaguchi-ko and around

**FUJI-YOSHIDA**, some 100km west of Tokyo, lies so close to Mount Fuji that when the dormant volcano eventually blows her top the residents will be toast. For the time being however, this small, prosperous town acts as an efficient transport hub for the area, as well as the traditional departure point for journeys up the volcano, with frequent buses leaving for Fuji-san's fifth station (see box opposite) from outside the railway station.

The volcano aside, the town's main attraction is its Shinto shrine. To reach it, head southwest from the station uphill along the main street, Honchō-dōri, which will take you past several ornate **pilgrims' inns** (*oshi-no-ie*). These old lodging houses, where pilgrims used to stay before climbing Mount Fuji, are set back from the road, their entrances marked by narrow stone pillars. Some of the inns still operate as minshuku today (see Accommodation, p.184). Where the road hits a junction, turn left and in a couple of hundred metres you'll see a giant *torii* and a broad gravel pathway lined with stone lanterns leading to **Fuji Sengen-jinja**, a large, colourful shrine set in a small forest. Sengen shrines, dedicated to the worship of volcanos, encircle Fuji, but this is the most important because it dates from 788. The main shrine (*honden*) has been designated an important cultural asset because of its age (it was built in 1615) and beauty. Look around the back for the jolly, brightly painted wooden carvings of the deities Ebisu the fisherman and Daikoku, the god of wealth, good humour and happiness, who appears content to let a rat nibble at the bales of rice he squats upon.

These fun-loving gods would certainly approve of **Fujikyū Highland** (Mon–Fri 9am–5pm, Sat 9am–7pm, Sun & holidays 9am–6pm; closed third Tues of month, except Aug; ¥1000 entry only; ¥4300 one-day pass) an appealingly ramshackle amusement park, one train stop west of Fuji-Yoshida, and featuring the terrifying rollercoaster Fujiyama, listed in the Guiness Book of Records as having the greatest height, drop and speed in the world. It's a popular place, so avoid coming on weekends or holidays unless you enjoy standing in long queues.

At first glance, there doesn't seem to be a whole lot to recommend the shabby lakeside resort of **KAWAGUCHI-KO**, a couple of kilometres west of Fuji-Yoshida. With its dolphin-shaped cruise boats and crass souvenir shops, this is the tourist hub of the area and is often choked with traffic during the holiday season. However, the fabulous view of Mount Fuji and lake Kawaguchi-ko from the top of **Tenjō-zan** make a trip here worth the effort. You can either take a three-minute cable car ride up to the look-out (daily 9am–5.20pm; ¥700 return), or get some exercise by hiking up, which takes around 45 minutes. Kawaguchi-ko's other highlight is the Guadi-esque **Kubota Itchiku Art Museum** (daily: April–Nov 9.30–5.30; Jan–March & Dec 10am–5pm; Jan–Feb closed Tues; ¥1000), on the northern shore of the lake. This small museum, approached through a striking Indian gateway, houses the kimono art of Kubota Itchiku , an eighty-year-old Japanese artist who has refined the traditional *tsujigahana* textile patterning

## CLIMBING MOUNT FUJI

"A wise man climbs Fuji once. A fool climbs it twice" – so goes the Japanese proverb. Don't let the sight of children and grannies trudging up lull you into a false sense of security; this is a tough climb.

There are several **routes** up the volcano, with the ascent divided into sections known as **stations**. Most people take a bus to the Kawaguchi-ko fifth station (*go-gōme*), where a Swiss chalet-style giftshop marks the end of the road about halfway up the volcano. The traditional hike, though, begins at Fuji-Yoshida; walking from here to the fifth station takes around five hours, and another six hours to reach the summit. Many choose to climb at night to reach the summit by dawn; during the season the lights of climbers' torches resemble a line of fireflies trailing up the volcanic scree.

Essential items to carry include at least one litre of water and some food, a torch and batteries, a raincoat and extra clothes; however hot it might be at the start of the climb, the closer you get to the summit the colder it becomes, with temperatures dropping to well below freezing and sudden rain and lightening strikes not uncommon. You can rest en route at any of seventeen **huts**, most of which provide dorm accommodation from around ¥5000 per night for just a bed (no need for a sleeping bag), and ¥7000 with dinner. It's essential to book in advance (☎0555/22-1948). Once at the summit, it will take you around an hour to make a circuit of the crater. Otherwise you can take part in the time-honoured tradition of making a phone call or mailing a letter from the post office.

Mount Fuji's official **climbing season**, when all the facilities on the mountain are open, including lodging huts and pay phones at the summit, runs from July 1 to August 27. For more details, pick up a free copy of the *Mt Fuji Climber's Guide Book*, published by the Fuji-Yoshida city hall and available at the local tourist information office (see below) and Tokyo TIC (see p.86).

technique. Inside the pyramid-shaped building are works from the artist's *Symphony of Light* series, a continuous mountain landscape through the seasons, formed when the kimono are placed side by side. The museum, some 4km west of the town, can be reached by bus from both Fuji-Yoshida and Kawaguchi-ko.

Of the other four lakes, the smallest, **Shōji-ko**, 2km west of Kawaguchi-ko, shaped like a horse-shoe, is by far the prettiest. The largest lake, **Yamanaka**, south of Fuji-Yoshida is just as developed as Kawaguchi-ko and has fewer attractions, while **Motosu-ko** and **Sai-ko** are marginally less touristy, but not worth the touble of visiting.

## Practicalities

The easiest way to reach the Fuji Five Lakes area is to take the **bus** (¥1700) from the Shinjuku bus terminal in Tokyo, on the west side of the train station; in good traffic, the trip takes around one hour and 45 minutes and during the climbing season there are frequent services, including at least three a day that run directly to the fifth station. The **train** journey from Shinjuku Station involves transferring from the JR Chūō line to the Fuji Kyūkō line at Ōtsuki, from where a local train chugs first to Fuji-Yoshida and then on to Kawaguchi-ko. On Sundays and public holidays an early-morning train from Shinjuku does the trip in just over two hours.

The best place for **tourist information** is the Fuji-Yoshida Tourist Information Service (daily 9am–5.30pm; ☎0555/22-7000), to the left as you exit Fuji-Yoshida Station. The helpful English-speaking staff will shower you with leaflets and can help with accommodation. In Kawaguchi-ko, the Fuji Information Centre (daily 7am–7pm; ☎0555/72-2121), provides a similar service and is located five minutes' walk west of the station, on the way to the youth hostel.

A comprehensive system of buses will help you **get around** once you've arrived at either Fuji-Yoshida or Kawaguchi-ko. Individual bus fares are high so if you're going to be touring the area, it's worthing buying the Fuji Kyūkō Wide Free Pass (¥4760) at Shinjuku or as soon as you arrive at Ōtsuki: this is valid for three days and covers all rail travel and buses around the five lakes, plus tickets for the cable car and lake cruise at Kawaguchi-ko.

## Accommodation

Fuji-Yoshida and Kawaguchi-ko have plenty of good **places to stay**, including youth hostels and hotels. Fuji climbers could consider overnighting in one of the mountain huts, but the claustrophobic should stick to the roomier accommodation at the base of the mountain. There are also several campsites around the lakes.

**Fuji-Yoshida Youth Hostel**, 2-339 Shimo Yoshida Hon-chō, Fuji-Yoshida-shi (☎0555/22-0533). Small, basic hostel in a family home twenty minutes' walk from Fuji-Yoshida station, or a seven-minute walk from Shimo-Yoshida the preceding station. English is spoken and you can also get meals. ①.

**Kawaguchi-ko Youth Hostel**, 2128 Funatsu, Kawaguchi-ko-machi (☎0555/72-1431, fax 72-0630). Run by a friendly manager who speaks a little English, this large hostel, a five-minute walk southwest of Kawaguchi-ko station, has *tatami* rooms and bunks. Bicycles can be rented at ¥800 per day. ①

**Petit Hotel Ebisuya**, 3647 Funatsu, Kawaguchi-ko-machi (☎0555/72-0165). Not much to look at from the outside, this family-run hotel is conveniently located next to Kawaguchi-ko Station and has splendid views of Mount Fuji from some of its *tatami* rooms. The café downstairs serves hearty set meals. ⑤.

**Taikoku-ya**, Honchō-dōri, Fuji-Yoshida (☎0555/22-3778). This original pilgrim's inn on the main road still takes guests in its very traditional and beautifully decorated *tatami* rooms. There's a pretty ornamental garden in front of the guesthouse. ⑥.

## Eating

The best place to **eat** is Fuji-Yoshida, enowned for its thick *teuchi udon* (handmade) noodles, prepared and served in people's homes at lunchtime only – the tourist information office can provide a list and map of the best places (in Japanese). One of the easiest to locate is the convivial *Hanaya*, towards the top of Honchō-dōri, which serves just three types of dishes: *yumori* noodles in a soup; *zaru* cold noodles and *sara* warm noodles dipped in hot soup – simple stuff, but manna from heaven compared to the dreary, over-priced tourist cafés in **Kawaguchi-ko**, where the best option is a picnic lunch from the lakeside Seven Eleven convenience store. During the climbing season, you can buy snacks and stamina-building dishes, such as curry rice, from the huts on Mount Fuji – but the prices, needless to say, are high.

# Hakone

South of Mount Fuji and 90km west of Tokyo is the lakeland and mountain area known as **Hakone**. Even though there's nothing here that you absolutely must see while in Japan, you're bound to enjoy a trip to this region, especially if you follow the well-established day-trip route which combines rides on several trains or buses, a funicular, cable car and pirate ship. You can also take in the lake, **Ashino-ko**, numerous **onsen**, some excellent walks, several art museums, and – weather permitting – great views of nearby Mount Fuji. There's so much to do that an overnight stop is best, especially if you want to unwind at one of Hakone's top-notch hotels and ryokan, all with their own hot-spring baths. Be aware, though, that the region is always busy on weekends and holidays; if you want to avoid the crowds, aim to visit during the week. Excellent transport links mean that you can stay pretty much anywhere and go where you want within the day.

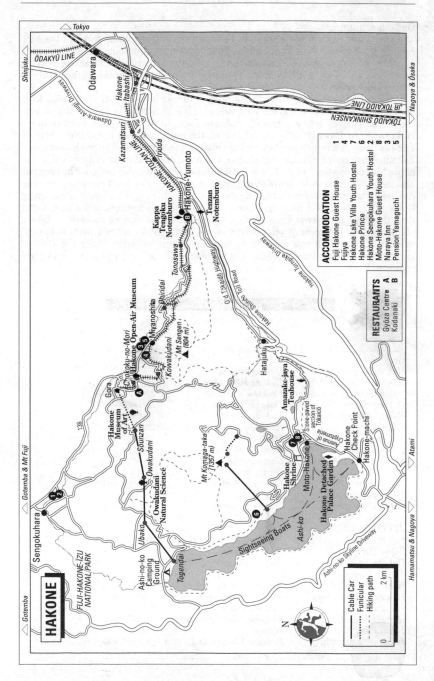

HAKONE

FUJI-HAKONE-IZU
NATIONAL PARK

ŌDAKYŪ LINE

△ Tokyo

△ Shinjuku

Odawara

Hakone Itabashi

Kazamatsuri

Iryuda

TŌKAIDŌ SHINKANSEN

JR TŌKAIDŌ LINE

△ Nagoya & Ōsaka

HAKONE-TOZAN LINE

Kappa
Tengoku
Notemburo

Hakone-Yumoto

Tenzan
Notemburo

Tonosawa

Hakone Turnpike Driveway

Dōridai

Miyanoshita

Chōkoku-no-Mori
Hakone Open-Air Museum

Kowakudani

Mt Sengen
(804 m)

Old Tōkaidō Highway

Hakone Shindo Toll Road

Hatajuku

Gora

Hakone
Museum
of Art

Sōunzan

Amazake-jaya
Teahouse

Stone-paved
section of
Tōkaidō

Owakudani

Owakudani
Natural Science

Avenue of
Cryptomeria

Hakone
Check Point

Mt Komaga-take
(1357 m)

Hakone-machi

Ubako

Hakone
Shrine

Moto-Hakone

Hakone Detached
Palace Garden

Ashi-ko

Togendai

Ashi-no-ko
Camping
Ground

Sightseeing Boats

Ashi-no-ko Skyline Driveway

△ Sengokuhara

△ Gotemba & Mt Fuji

△ Gotemba

△ Hamamatsu & Nagoya

△ Atami

138

Odawara-Atsugi Driveway

Cable Car
Funicular
Hiking path

0        2 km

N

## Getting around

The traditional day-trip route through Hakone runs anti-clockwise through the Fuji-Hakone-Izu National Park from Hakone-Yumoto, over Mount Sōun, across the length of Ashino-ko lake to Moto-Hakone and back to the start. Approaching Hakone from the west, you can follow a similar route clockwise from Hakone-machi on the southern shore of Ashino-ko to Hakone-Yumoto.

The most enjoyable way of getting around is to take a combination of **trains** from Shinjuku Odakyū Station, (on the west side of Shinjuku Station in Tokyo), thus breaking up the journey into a series of mad-cap rides. To do this, you'll need to buy a **Hakone Free Pass** (¥5400), available from the ticket office at the Odakyū Station. The pass covers a return journey on the Odakyū line from Shinjuku to Odawara, and unlimited use of the Hakone-Tōzan line, Hakone-Tōzan funicular railway, cable car, pirate boat across the lake and most local buses over a three-day period. The pass will also get you discounts at many of Hakone's attractions. For ¥800 extra one-way you can take the more comfortable "Romance Car", which goes directly through to Hakone-Yumoto in one hour and thirty minutes, around twenty-five minutes faster than the regular express train. With a JR rail pass, the fastest route is to take a Shinkansen to Odawara, from where you can catch either a train or bus into the national park area. If you don't fancy hopping on and off trains, take the Odakyū express **bus** (¥1830) from Shinjuku bus terminal – this will get you to Ashino-ko in a couple of hours.

| HAKONE | | |
|---|---|---|
| **Hakone** | *Hakone* | 箱根 |
| Ashino-ko lake | *Ashino-ko* | 芦の湖 |
| Amazake-jaya teahouse | *Amazake-jaya* | 甘酒茶屋 |
| Gōra | *Gōra* | 強羅 |
| Hakone Barrier | *Hakone Sekisho* | 箱根関所 |
| Hakone Museum of Art | *Hakone Bijutsukan* | 箱根美術館 |
| Hakone Open-Air Museum | *Chōkoku-no-Mori* | 彫刻の森美術館 |
| Hakone Shrine | *Hakone Gongen* | 箱根神社 |
| Hakone-Yumoto | *Hakone-Yumoto* | 箱根湯元 |
| Hatajuku | *Hatajuku* | 畑宿 |
| Miyanoshita | *Miyanoshita* | 宮ノ下 |
| Moto-Hakone | *Moto-Hakone* | 元箱根 |
| Mount Komaga-take | *Komaga-take* | 駒ヶ岳 |
| Ōwakudani | *Ōwakudani* | 大湧谷 |
| Ōwakudani Natural History Museum | *Ōwakudani Shizen Kagakukan* | 大湧谷自然科学館 |
| Tenzan Notemburo | *Tenzan Notemburo* | 天山野天風呂 |
| | | |
| *ACCOMMODATION* | | |
| Fuji Hakone Guest House | *Fuji Hakone Gesuto Hausu* | 富士箱根ゲストハウス |
| Fujiya Hotel | *Fujiya Hoteru* | 富士屋ホテル |
| Hakone Lake Villa Youth Hostel | *Hakone Reiku Vira Yūsu Hosuteru* | 箱根レイクヴィラユースホステル |
| Hakone Prince Hotel | *Hakone Purinsu Hoteru* | 箱根プリンスホテル |
| Hakone Sengokuhara Youth Hostel | *Hakone Sengokuhara Yūsu Hosuteru* | 箱根仙石原ユースホステル |
| Moto-Hakone Guest House | *Moto-Hakone Gesuto Hausu* | 元箱根ゲストハウス |
| Naraya Inn | *Naraya* | 奈良屋 |
| Pension Yamaguchi | *Penshon Yamaguchi* | ペンション山口 |

## Odawara and Hakone-Yumoto

Travelling from Tokyo to Hakone, you'll pass through the historic castle town of **ODAWARA**, some 75km west of the capital. The castle (daily 9am–10am; ¥250) looks pretty impressive, especially in spring when the cherry trees in the grounds explode in pink blossom, but it is a recent reconstruction and a visit here is soured by the appalling conditions of the zoo just next door. Better to press on to **HAKONE-YUMOTO**, the small town nestling in the valley at the gateway to the national park. Despite being marred by scores of concrete-block hotels and *bessō* (vacation lodges for company workers), not to mention the usual cacophony of souvenir shops, the town has some good **onsen**, ideal for unwinding after a day's sightseeing around the park. You can also pick up a **map** of the area at the Hakone Tourist Information Office (daily 8.30am–5pm), two minutes' walk from Hakone-Yumoto Station along the main road. Up the hill from the station is the **Kappa Tengoku Notemburo** (daily 10am–10pm; ¥700) a small, traditional outdoor onsen, which can get crowded. More stylish is **Tenzan Notemburo** (daily 9am–11pm; ¥900) a luxurious public onsen complex at Oku-Yumoto, 2km southwest of town. The main building has separate male and female outdoor baths, including waterfalls and jacuzzi baths, in a series of rocky pools. Men also have a clay hut sauna, and for ¥200 extra on weekdays (¥900 on weekends) both men and women can use the wooden baths in the building across the parking lot. A free shuttle bus runs to the baths from the bridge just north of Hakone-Yumoto Station.

While you probably won't want to stay in Hakone-Yumoto, it's a good place to **eat**; try *Kodanaki*, along the main road south from the station, which specializes in udon noodles. There are also three good-value restaurants at the Tenzan Notemburo, serving rice, *shabu-shabu* (sautéed beef) and *yakiniku* (grilled meat) dishes.

## Miyanoshita and around

Rising up into the mountains, the Hakone-Tōzan switchback railway zig-zags for nearly 9km alongside a ravine from Hakone-Yumoto to the village of Gōra. There are small traditional inns and temples at several of the stations along the way, but the single best place to alight – and even stay overnight – is the village onsen resort of **MIYANOSHITA**. As well as hot springs, the village has decent antique shops along its main road, and several hiking routes up 804-metre **Mount Sengen** on the eastern flank of the railway – one path begins just beside the station. At the top, you'll get a great view of the gorge below.

Miyanoshita's real draw is its handful of splendid **hotels**. The *Naraya Inn* (☎0460/2-2411, fax 7-6231; ⑦), is a fabulous traditional ryokan founded in the sixteenth century, and hardly looks as if it has changed since. Guests sleep in mini-villas and there are several onsen baths dotted around the compound, which includes twelve acres of gardens. Also worth popping in – if only to peek at the handsome wooden interior – is the *Fujiya Hotel* (☎0460/2-2211, fax 2-2210; ⑥), which opened for business in 1878 and is a living monument to a more glamorous era of travel. Despite being the first Western-style hotel in Japan, the *Fujiya* has lots of Japanese touches, including traditional gardens and temple-like decorative gables. The plush, 1950s-style decor is fantastic and the rooms are good value, especially from Sunday to Friday, when foreign guests qualify for a cheaper rate. There's also the delightful, European-style *Pension Yamaguchi* (☎0460/2-3158; ⑥), roughly a five-minute walk downhill from the train station, and tucked away off the main road behind the post office – the rates here include Western-style meals.

As far as **eating** goes, the *Fujiya*'s Orchid Lounge is great for afternoon tea, while its ornate French restaurant is an excellent, if pricey, choice for lunch or dinner. The *Picot Bakery* on the main road outside the *Fujiya* is a good place to pick up bread and cakes for breakfast or lunch.

Moving on, two more stops on the Hakone-Tōzan railway will bring you to Chōkoku-no-Mori Station, where the nearby **Hakone Open-Air Museum** (daily: March–Oct 9am–5pm; Jan, Feb, Nov & Dec 9am–4pm; ¥1500) is well worth making time for. This wide-ranging museum, spread across 70,000 square metres, is packed with sculptures; works from Rodin and Giacometti to Michelangelo reproductions and bizarre modern formations are scattered across the landscaped grounds, which have lovely views across the mountains to the sea. There's an enclave of 26 pieces by Henry Moore, a "Picasso Pavilion", which houses 230 paintings, lithographs, ceramics and sculptures by the Spanish artist and four galleries featuring works by Chagall, Miro and Renoir and modern Japanese artists such as Umehara Ryuzaburo and Takeshi Hayashi. You can rest between galleries at several restaurants or cafés – there's also a traditional Japanese teahouse.

### Gōra, Kōen-ue and Ōwakudani

There's little reason to stop at **GŌRA** except to have lunch (see below) or to transfer from the Hakone Tōzan railway to a funicular tram (¥400), which takes only ten minutes to cover the short but steep distance to **Sōunzan**, the start of the cable car across Mount Sōun. On the way, you might want to stop at **KŌEN-UE**, a couple of stops from Gōra, where the **Hakone Museum of Art** (daily except Thurs 9am–4pm; ¥800), and its collection of ancient ceramics is likely to appeal to experts only, but the delicate moss gardens and the view from the traditional teahouse across the verdant hills is captivating.

From Sōunzan, the **cable car** (¥1300 one way) floats like a balloon on its thirty-minute journey high above the mountain to the Tōgendai terminal, beside the lake Ashino-ko, stopping at a couple of points along the way. The first stop, **ŌWAKUDANI**, is the site of a constantly bubbling and steaming valley formed by a volcanic eruption three thousand years ago. You can learn more about this at the informative **Ōwakudani Natural History Museum** (daily 9am–4.30pm; ¥400), downhill from the cable car station, with an entertaining diorama model of a volcano that flashes, rumbles and glows red at the point of eruption. To see the real thing, hike up the valley through the lava formations to the bubbling pools, where eggs are boiled until they are black and scoffed religiously by every Japanese tourist, for no better reason than it's the done thing to do when visiting Ōwakudani.

There are a couple of good **places to stay** on this side of Hakone. The quiet *Fuji Hakone Guesthouse* (☎0460/4-6577, fax 4-6578; ④), best reached by bus #4 from the east exit of Odawara Station, is run by the friendly, English-speaking Takahashi-san, and has *tatami* rooms, and onsen water piped into a communal bath – only breakfast is available. Directly behind, in a lovely wooden building, is the *Hakone Sengokuhara Youth Hostel* (☎0460/4-8966, fax 4-6578; ②), run by the same family and offering Japanese-style rooms, with private rooms available for ¥5000 per person.

You shouldn't miss out on the *Gyōza Centre* (daily 11.30am–2.30pm & 5–8.30pm) on the main road between Gōra and the Hakone Open-Air Museum. This two-floor **restaurant** usually has a long line of customers waiting to sample the thirteen types of delicious home-made dumplings (*gyōza*), including ones stuffed with prawns (*ebi*) and fermented beans (*nattō*). A set meal with rice and soup costs ¥1000. At Ōwakudani the best eating choice is one of the noodle bars beside the entrance to the volcanic area. Also good for lunch is the café downstairs at the Tōgendai cable car terminal, which is reasonably priced and has pleasant views across the lake.

### Ashino-ko and around

Emerging from the cable car at Tōgendai you'll find yourself at the northern end of the bone-shaped lake, **Ashino-ko**, from where, weather permitting, you'll get fantastic views of **Mount Fuji**. If it's cloudy though, you'll have to make do with the less impressive 1357-metre Komaga-take on the eastern shore. A walk around the shoreline trails along the western side of the lake to the small resort of Hakone-machi, some 8km south, takes around three hours. It's more fun to board one of the colourful, cartoon-like "pirate ships" (¥1000) that regularly sail the length of the lake in around thirty minutes. This area of Hakone, part of the *Prince* empire of hotels and resorts, is not covered by the Hakone Free Pass and so is somewhat marginalized from the rest of the national park's attractions – and all the more peaceful for it. Boats run from Tōgendai to the *Prince* hotel resort at Hakone-en, midway down the east side of the lake, where there's also a large outdoor skating rink and a cable car up to Komaga-take's summit, from where there's a fabulous view. The summit can also be reached by bus from the tourist village of Moto-Hakane.

There's a cluster of upmarket hotels and ryokan at **HAKONE-MACHI**, where the "pirate ships" dock. This is also the location of the **Hakone Barrier** (daily 8.30am–4.30pm; ¥200) through which all traffic on the Tōkaidō, the ancient road linking Kyoto and Edo, once had to pass (see box overleaf). What stands here today is a reproduction, enlivened by wax-work displays which provide the historical background. There's nothing much to keep you here though; instead, stroll north of the barrier around the wooded promontory, past the bland reconstruction of the Emperor Meiji's Hakone Detached Palace, and take in the views of the lake.

Running for around 1km beside the road leading from the Hakone Barrier to the lakeside village of **MOTO-HAKONE** is part of the Tōkaidō road, shaded by 420 lofty cryptomeria trees, planted in 1618 and now designated "Natural Treasures". Across the lake, you'll spot a vermilion *torii* gate, standing in the water just north of Moto-Hakane – a scene celebrated in many a *ukiyo-e* print and modern postcard. The gate belongs to the **Hakone Gongen** and is the best thing about this small Shinto **shrine**, set back in the trees, where *samurai* once came to pray.

Though it's fairly touristy, you'll find some decent **accommodation** at Moto-Hakone. At the bottom of the price range is the *Hakone Lake Villa Youth Hostel* (☎0460/3-1610; ②), in a secluded spot above Ashino-ko lake. The hostel has *tatami* and bunk-bed dorms, a lounge with a large outdoor deck surrounded by woods, a bath filled with onsen water and good-value meals. A lot more upmarket is the *Hakone Prince Hotel* (☎0460/3-1111, fax 3-7616; ⑦), with a prime location on the Komaga-take side of Ashino-ko and a multitude of facilities – the nicest rooms are in the Japanese-style annexes. A short bus ride or stiff ten-minute walk uphill from the village lies the *Moto-Hakone Guest House*, (☎0460/3-7880, fax 0460/4-6578; ④), offering spotless, Japanese-style rooms, with singles at ¥5000, and serving breakfast only.

## Back to Hakone-Yumoto

From either Moto-Hakone or Hakone-machi you can take a **bus** back to Hakone-Yumoto. Far more rewarding however, is the eleven-kilometre **hike** along part of the Tōkaidō road, which after the first couple of kilometres is all downhill and takes around four hours. The route begins five minutes up the hill from the Hakone Tōzan bus station in Moto-Hakone, where large paving stones are laid through the shady forests. When the path comes out of the trees and hits the main road, you'll see the **Amazake-jaya teahouse**, where you can rest, just as travellers did hundreds of years ago, and sip a restorative cup of the milky, sweet and alcoholic rice drink *amazake*, with some pickles for ¥400.

From the teahouse, the path shadows the main road to the small village of **Hatajuku**, where since the ninth century craftsmen have perfected the art of *yosegi-zaiku*, or marquetry. The wooden boxes, toys and other objects inlaid with elaborate mosaic patterns make great souvenirs and there are workshops throughout the village, including one

---

### THE HAKONE BARRIER

In 1618, the second shogun, Tokugawa Hidetada, put up the **Hakone Barrier** (Sekisho), which was actually more of a large compound than a single gate, and it stood at Hakone-machi until 1869. The shogun decreed that all his lords' wives and their families live in Edo (now Tokyo) and the lords themselves make expensive formal visits to the capital every other year – a strategy designed to ensure no-one attempted a rebellion. The Tōkaidō, on which the barrier stands, was one of the major routes in and out of the capital, and it was here that travellers were carefully checked to see how many guns they were taking into the Edo area and that the lords' hostage families were stopped from escaping. Any man caught trying to dodge the barrier was crucified and then beheaded, while accompanying women had their heads shaved and were, according to statute, "given to anyone who wants them".

---

right where the path emerges onto the main road. Hatajuku is a good place to pick up the bus for the rest of the way to Hakone-Yumoto if you don't fancy hiking any further. From here the path descends to the **Sukumo-gawa** and past several old temples, as well as the Tenzan Notemburo (see p.187), before ending up in the centre of **Hakone-Yumoto**.

# Izu Hantō

Formed by Mount Fuji's ancient lava-flows, **Izu Hantō** protrudes like an arrowhead into the ocean west of Tokyo, a mountainous spine whose tortured coastline features some superb scenery and a couple of decent beaches. It takes at least two days to make a complete circuit of this region, taking in some intriguing historical sights and stopping at a few of the peninsula's estimated 2300 hot springs.

Direct train services from Tokyo run down Izu's more developed east coast, passing through **Atami**, with its stylish art museum, to the harbour town of **Shimoda**, one of the places Commodore Perry parked his "Black Ships" in 1854, and the site of Japan's first American consulate. Shimoda makes a good base for exploring southern Izu, including the Rendaiji hot spring, and the striking coastal scenery around Irō-zaki at its most southerly tip.

Over on west Izu, **Dōgashima** is another famous beauty spot with a crop of picturesque islands set in clear, tropical-blue water. Most of this coast still belongs to traditional fishing communities and the central uplands are also sparsely populated, with only a few roads cutting through the maple and beech forests to give sweeping views over the peninsula and north to Fuji. The only settlement of any size in central Izu is **Shuzenji**, whose nearby **onsen** resort has long been associated with novelists such as Kawabata and Sōseki Natsume (see p.818). Local history also inspired a popular Kabuki play based on the twelfth-century murder of a former Kamakura Shogun. The town's few sights revolve around these events and it's a reasonable place to stay before taking the train north out of Izu.

Izu's mild climate makes it a possible excursion even in winter, though it's close enough to Tokyo to be crowded at weekends and is best avoided during the summer holidays. If you haven't got a JR pass and want to explore the whole peninsula, check out the various discount tickets available, such as JR's "*Izu Free Kippu*" which covers the Shinkansen from Tokyo as well as local transport by train and bus. Renting a car is a good idea, as public transport is slow and only really covers the main coastal settlements; you'll find rental companies in Atami (Eki *Rent-a-car*, ☎0557/82-1382), Shimoda and Shuzenji (see individual accounts for details).

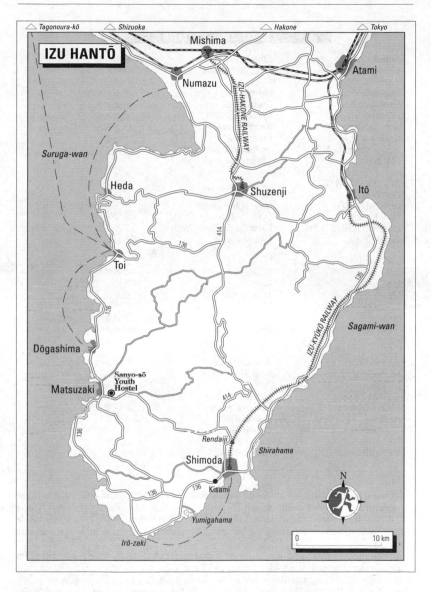

## Atami

Situated on the Shinkansen line between Tokyo and Ōsaka, the hot spring resort of **ATAMI** serves as the eastern gateway to Izu. It's an expensive, sometimes garish place but is home to the outstanding **MOA Museum of Art** (9.30am–5pm; closed Thurs; ¥1600), which is carved into a hillside above the town. Though the steep

## ATAMI AND SHIMODA

| | | |
|---|---|---|
| **Atami** | *Atami* | 熱海 |
| MOA Museum of Art | *MOA Bijutsukan* | ＭＯＡ美術館 |
| | | |
| **Shimoda** | *Shimoda* | 下田 |
| Gyokusen-ji | *Gyokusen-ji* | 玉泉寺 |
| Hōfuku-ji | *Hōfuku-ji* | 宝福寺 |
| Nesugata-yama | *Nesugata-yama* | 寝姿山 |
| Ryōsen-ji | *Ryōsen-ji* | 了仙寺 |
| Zushu Shimoda Folk Museum | *Zushu Shimoda Kyōdo Shiryōkan* | 豆州下田郷土資料館 |
| | | |
| *ACCOMMODATION* | | |
| Hōraikan | *Hōraikan* | 蓬莱館 |
| Hotel Marseille | *Hoteru Maruseiyu* | ホテルマルセイユ |
| Ōizu Ryokan | *Ōizu Ryokan* | 大伊豆旅館 |
| Shimoda Station Hotel | *Shimoda Sutēshon Hoteru* | 下田ステーションホテル |
| Hotel Uraga | *Hoteru Uraga* | ホテルウラガ |
| | | |
| *RESTAURANTS* | | |
| Gorosaya | *Gorosaya* | ごろさや |
| Kiyū | *Kiyū* | 亀遊 |
| Matsu-zushi | *Matsu-zushi* | 松寿司 |
| Musashi | *Musashi* | むさし |
| Seikoen | *Seikoen* | 米青香 |
| Sushi Izutarō | *Izutarō* | 伊豆太郎 |
| | | |
| *AROUND SHIMODA* | | |
| Ernest House | *Ānesuto Hausu* | アーネストハウス |
| Ishibashi Ryokan | *Ishibashi Ryokan* | 石橋旅館 |
| Irō-zaki | *Irō-zaki* | 石廊崎 |
| Kanaya Ryokan | *Kanaya Ryokan* | 金谷旅館 |
| Kisami-Ōhama | *Kisami-Ōhama* | 吉佐美大浜 |
| Rendai-ji | *Rendai-ji* | 蓮台寺 |
| Rendai-ji-sō | *Rendai-ji-sō* | 蓮台寺荘 |
| Seiryū-sō | *Seiryū-sō* | 清流荘 |
| Yumigahama | *Yumigahama* | 弓ヶ浜 |

admission is offputting, the museum's remarkable architecture and collection of mostly ancient oriental art justify a visit. Note that you can buy slightly reduced tickets (¥1400) at the **tourist information desk** (daily 9.30am–6pm; ☎0557/81-6002) inside Atami Station, before hopping on a bus from the station concourse up to the museum (5min; ¥160).

Buses drop you outside the museum's lower entrance, from where you ride four escalators cut through the rock – taking in a laser show on the way – to the main exhibition halls. Each room contains just a few pieces from this magnificent private collection, of which the most famous is a dramatic folding screen entitled "Red and White Plum Blossoms" by the innovative Ōgata Kōrin (1658–1716). But the most eye-catching exhibit is a full-size replica of a golden tea room, lined with gold-leaf and equipped with utensils made of gold, built in 1586 for when the warlord Toyotomi Hideyoshi invited Emperor Ogimachi for a cuppa. The museum's well-tended gardens contain teahouses serving *matcha* and sweet cakes (¥600).

## WILL ADAMS

In 1600, before Japan closed its doors to the world, a Dutch ship washed up on east Kyūshū. It was the lone survivor of five vessels that had set sail from Europe two years previously; three quarters of the crew had perished from starvation and the remaining twenty five were close to death.

One of those rescued by Japanese fishermen was the navigator, an English man called **Will Adams** (1564–1620). He was summoned by Tokugawa Ieyasu, the future shogun, who quizzed Adams about European affairs, religion and various scientific matters. Ieyasu liked what he heard – at the time there was growing distrust of merchants from Catholic countries (see History, p.787) – and made Adams his personal advisor on mathematics, navigation and guns. Eventually Adams, known locally as Anjin (pilot), also served as the shogun's interpreter and as a diplomat, brokering trade treaties for both Holland and Britain. In return he was granted *samurai* status, the first and last foreigner to be so honoured, along with a Japanese wife and an estate near Yokosuka on the Miura Peninsula.

Adams' main task, however, was to oversee the construction of Japan's first Western-style sailing ships. In 1605 he set up a shipyard at **Itō**, on the east coast of Izu, where he built at least two ocean-going vessels over the next five years. One of these apparently made it to Mexico, while Adams himself took to the seas on diplomatic missions to the Philippines and China.

By the end of his career, the government had grown increasingly opposed to foreign intervention and after Ieyasu died in 1616 Adams retired to his Miura estate, where he was buried in 1620. His fascinating lifestory forms the basis for James Clavell's novel, *Shogun* (see Books, p.819), and he is still remembered in Itō each August with his own festival, the *Anjin Matsuri*.

## Shimoda

At Atami trains peel off down the east coast of Izu, cutting through craggy headlands and high above bays ringed with fishing villages or resort hotels. Nearly halfway down the peninsula, **ITŌ** port was where Will Adams launched Japan's first Western-style sailing ships (see box above), but there's nothing really to stop for until you reach **SHIMODA**. Off-season, this small, amiable town, with its attractive scenery and sprinkling of temples and museums, makes a good base for a couple of days. Its sights revolve around Shimoda's moment of glory, when Commodore Perry sailed his Black Ships (*Kurofune*) into the harbour in 1854 and it became one of Japan's first ports to open to foreign trade (see below). Shimoda people are immensely proud of their part in Japanese history and you'll find Black Ships everywhere, from a replica outside the train station to a customized tourist bus; there's even a **Black Ships Festival** (May 16–18), when American and Japanese naval bands parade through the streets, followed by the inevitable fireworks.

Express trains, known as *Odoriko-gō* (the "dancing girl") after Kawabata's novel (see p.818), run direct from Tokyo Station to Shimoda several times a day. However, some trains divide at Atami for Shuzenji, so check you're on the right section, and note also that JR Rail Passes are only valid for the journey as far as Itō; beyond Itō it's a private line down to Shimoda. Some seats on the *Odoriko-gō* face the windows, in which case it's best to sit on the left side heading south – though you're often staring at a tunnel wall.

*SOME HISTORY*

Following his first, brief sally into Tokyo Bay in 1853, American **Commodore Perry** returned the next year to begin the negotiations which ultimately prized Japan out of its isolation (see History, p.774). Having signed an initial treaty in Yokohama, which granted America trading rights in Shimoda and Hakodate (on Hokkaidō) and consular representation, Perry sailed his Black Ships down to Izu. Here, in Shimoda's Ryōsen-ji temple, he concluded a supplementary **"Treaty of Friendship"** in 1854. Soon after, Russian, British and Dutch merchants were granted similar rights and then, in 1856, **Townsend Harris** arrived in Shimoda as the first American Consul – a controversial figure thanks to his relationship with his Japanese servant, Okichi (see box below). By now, however, it was obvious that Shimoda was too isolated as a trading post and Harris began negotiating for a revised treaty which was eventually signed, again in Shimoda, in July 1858. According to this new agreement, Kanagawa replaced Shimoda as an open port, so the burgeoning foreign community decamped north to Yokohama.

## The Town
Central Shimoda lies on the northwestern shore of a well-sheltered harbour, surrounded by steep hills. Most of its sights are in the older, southerly district, where you'll find a number of attractive, grey and white latticed walls near the original fishing harbour; this style of architecture, found throughout Izu, is resistant to fire, earthquakes and corrosive sea air. Your first stop should be **Ryōsen-ji**, the temple where Perry signed the Treaty of Friendship in May 1854. In fact, the small but elaborate temple, founded in 1635, is less interesting than its attached **museum** (daily 8.30am–5pm; ¥500; closed Aug 1–3 & Dec 24–26) which is full of fascinating historical documents from the 1850s. Delightful portraits of Perry and his devilish crew, penned by Japanese artists, contrast with the European view of Japan – embellished with Chinese touches – from contemporary editions of the *Illustrated London News*. Many exhibits relate to the tragic Okichi, the servant of Consul Harris (see box), while a room downstairs contains an odd display of sex in religious art – including some beautiful pieces from India, Nepal and Japan's Shinto shrines.

---

### TŌJIN OKICHI AND TOWNSEND HARRIS

It's impossible to get to the absolute truth about **Tōjin Okichi**, a seventeen-year-old maidservant to Consul Townsend Harris, but according to popular sentiment she was sacrificed on the altar of friendly relations between Japan and America. As far as is known, in 1854 local officials ordered the reluctant Okichi to abandon her fiancé, Tsurumatsu, and to work for Harris, a puritanical bachelor in his mid-fifties who suffered from stomach ulcers. Whether Okichi was sent as a concubine, perhaps at Harris's request, or simply as a nurse or maidservant in unclear, but her beauty fueled endless gossip.

Whatever the truth, Okichi was tainted by association with a foreigner. After Harris was posted back to America, she wandered aimlessly until she bumped into Tsurumatsu in Yokohama. The two settled for a while, but by now she had started drinking and eventually he divorced her. Okichi then returned to Shimoda, where she opened a restaurant, but it wasn't a success and before long she was forced to sell. Not long after, aged 47, she was partially paralysed by an alcohol-induced stroke but survived another three years before finally drowning herself in a local river.

---

From Ryōsen-ji, **Perry Road** leads along a small river lined with picturesque old houses and dancing willows, east to **Shimoda-kōen**. This extensive, hill-top park has good views over the town and harbour but little else to recommend it outside the hydrangea season (June) when over one million blooms colour the slopes. Instead, walk back past Ryōsen-ji to the nearby **Zushu Shimoda Folk Museum** (daily 8.30am–5.30pm; ¥1000), housed in a traditional, latticework building. Alongside caricatures of big-nosed foreigners, Harris and Okichi are again much in evidence: there's Harris's kimono, decorated with the American eagle, and a portrait of a beautiful young woman which is commonly held to be Okichi. But the museum also has more information, much of it in English, about local life, including the area's distinctive architecture and its festivals.

Heading north again, the last sight in central Shimoda is Okichi's grave. She's buried behind **Hōfuku-ji**, another fairly unremarkable temple which has a small museum (daily 8am–5pm; ¥300) dedicated to her memory. The exhibits are much the same, though this time it's the original, sepia-tinted photo of Okichi on display alongside stills from some of the many films made about her – one of them is usually running on video.

The east side of Shimoda is dominated by a 200m-high peak called **Nesugata-yama**. On a clear day it's worth taking the ropeway (daily 9am–5pm; ¥1000 return ticket; departures every 10–15min) from beside the train station up to the summit for dramatic views of the harbour and out to the Izu islands on the eastern horizon. Nesugata-yama's south face drops steeply to the harbour, where there's a string of resort hotels and a tourist wharf, from where a "Black Ship" makes short, expensive **harbour cruises** (¥920 for 20min).

On the far, eastern side of the bay, **Gyokusen-ji** is where Townsend Harris established Japan's first American consulate in 1856 – it's a bit of a hike but an interesting diversion if time allows. A monument in front of the temple records Harris's misgivings, noted later in his diary, as he raised the flag here at 2.30pm on September 4: "Grave reflections. Ominous of change. Undoubted beginning of the end. Query, – if for the real good of Japan?" Nearby, a black-stone slab scrawled with US President Carter's signature, commemorating his visit in 1979, stands next to a strange memorial donated by Tokyo butchers; it supposedly marks where the first cow was slaughtered in Japan for human consumption, at Harris's request.

Townsend Harris lived and worked in Gyokusen-ji for about fifteen months, accompanied by his Dutch interpreter, Chinese servants and, possibly, Okichi. The **Townsend Harris Memorial Hall** (daily 8am–5pm; ¥300), to the right of the temple, actually devotes more space to Jimmy Carter and other famous visitors, but follow the path behind the hall and you'll find the graves of three Russians who died off Shimoda in 1854 when their ship was wrecked by a tidal wave. On the opposite side of the temple, in the main part of the cemetery, five Americans are buried, including three of Perry's young sailors. To reach Gyokusen-ji, take a bus from Shimoda Station (see Practicalities, below) to Kakisaki (4min), from where it's a two-minute walk; alternatively, it's a rather tedious hike along the busy main road.

## Practicalities

Shimoda's **train station** lies on the north side of town. There's an **information** desk inside the front exit (daily 9am–5pm; ☎0558/22-3200), or try the helpful Shimoda Tourist Association (daily 9am–5pm; ☎0558/22-1531), to the left of the station in a traditional-style building beside the main crossroads. Both places can help with town maps and accommodation, though neither has English-speaking staff.

Local **buses** depart from in front of the station: Shimoda Bus operates within the town boundaries, including Rendaiji (see p.197), while Tōkai Bus (marked TB) serves the more useful long-distance routes to Dōgashima and Irō-zaki (see pp.199 & 197). If you're exploring the local area, it's worth buying Tōkai Bus's two-day "Minami Izu Free Pass" (¥2790); you'll make a saving on these two day-trips alone, and their buses also serve Gyokusen-ji (see above) and Rendaiji. The Tōkai Bus office lies across the bus terminal from the station. Alternatively, **car rental** is available from Izu Rent-a-car (☎0558/27-4800) inside the station, or across the road at Nissan (☎0558/23-4123).

### *ACCOMMODATION*

Although dominated by pricey resort **hotels** on the harbour front, Shimoda's most appealing options, listed below, are around the station and among the older streets to the south. Other possibilities in the area include Rendaiji's upmarket ryokan or the beach-side hotels at Kisami-Ōhama (see p.197).

**Hōraikan**, 4-6-9 Shimoda-shi (☎0558/22-2175, fax 27-2480). Attractive, well-located ryokan, ten minutes' walk south of the station. It offers fairly basic accommodation in a handful of *tatami* rooms, with three communal onsen baths – with taps but no showers. Meals are available. [5].

**Hotel Marseille**, 1-1-5 Higashi-Hongo (☎0558/23-8000, fax 23-8001). New hotel just east of the station with a cheerful, Mediterranean theme. Rooms are nicely decorated with TV, phone and en-suite bathrooms. Prices increase up to 35 percent during August and at New Year. [5].

**Ōizu Ryokan**, 3-3-25 Shimoda-shi (☎0558/22-0123). This homely ryokan is a very slightly cheaper version of the *Hōraikan*, just round the corner. Again, there's an option of rooms with or without meals. [4]–[5].

**Shimoda Station Hotel**, 1-1-3 Nishi-Hongo (☎0558/22-8885, fax 22-3693). Dowdy, but fairly cheap hotel immediately outside the station. The small rooms, in Western or Japanese-style, come with enormous TVs and tiny bathrooms. [4].

**Hotel Uraga**, 3-3-10 Shimoda-shi (☎0558/23-6600, fax 23-6603). Clean, bright business hotel in the south part of town, with 24-hour check in. Its worth paying a little extra for the larger, twin rooms, but they're all comfortable, with TV, phone and bathroom. [4].

### *EATING AND DRINKING*

Shimoda has a number of affordable *izakaya* and sushi **restaurants**, as well as straightforward soba joints, and several Korean places serving *yakiniku*. For breakfast or a quick bite, there are a few **coffee shops** around the station – try *Naka*, immediately across the road.

**Gorosaya**, 1-5-25 Shimoda-shi (☎0120–155638). Popular, relaxed fish restaurant where it's best to book ahead. Prices are surprisingly reasonable if you keep to the set meals – their standard *teishoku* (¥1500) give a choice of sashimi, tempura or fried fish (*yaki-sakana*). Open daily 11.30am–2pm & 5–9pm.

**Kiyū**, 1-10-18 Shimoda-shi. Spacious and lively fish restaurant with a choice of set meals from ¥1300. Open 11am–10pm. Closed one day a week.

**Matsu-zushi**, 1-2-21 Shimoda-shi. Reasonable sushi place with a few tables as well as the standard counter. Their plastic window display makes ordering less painful; dishes start at ¥800 for a small sampler. Winter open 11am–8pm, closed Wed; summer open daily to 11pm.

**Musashi**, 1-13-1 Shin-shi. Casual, cosy soba restaurant with wooden tables. Its extensive menu also offers sashimi and standard rice dishes, such as *tendon* (rice with tempura) and *katsudon* (with breaded pork fillet), all for ¥1000 or less. Open 11am–8pm. Closed first and third Tues of the month.

**Seikoen**, 3-2-10 Shimoda-shi. Tiny Korean restaurant opposite *Ōizu Ryokan*; look for the yellow sign. No English is spoken, so the simplest strategy is to order a plate of marinated "*rōsu*" beef, liver (*rebā*) or the more expensive *karubi* (rib) which you then grill at your table. They also have various salads, soup and rice to fill up on. For a decent meal, count on spending ¥2000 per head, excluding drinks.

**Shōya**, 2F, 1-8-7 Higashi-Hongo. Modern *yakiniku* restaurant with an English menu which is more expensive than the *Seikoen* – around ¥3000 per person. Pep up your meal with a spicy tofu or *kimchi* side-dish. Open 5–10.30pm. Closed Wed.

**Spice Dog**, 2F, 3-13-10 Shimoda-shi. This cluttered, laid-back bar makes a good pit-stop on Perry Road, either for an afternoon coffee or an aperitif. They can also rustle-up light meals, such as curry or chorriso sausage, for around ¥1000. At weekends it fills up with expats. Noon–10pm. Closed Wed.

**Sushi Izutarō**, 1-2-1 Higashi-Hongo. Spruce *kaitenzushi* place near the station with a couple of tables or seats at the revolving counter. Plates containing two sushi are priced at ¥110–310, and they also offer soup, fruits and deserts. Open 11.15am–2pm & 4.30–8.30pm; closed Thurs & occasionally Wed.

## Around Shimoda

Though Shimoda is a popular hotspring resort, onsen connoisseurs will find better bathing a little further north at **Rendaiji**. This village, accessible by train or bus, has a collection of classy ryokan, several of which open their *rotemburo* to the public.

Heading in the opposite direction, south Izu's rocky, indented coastline shelters some of the peninsula's best **beaches** and has stretches of dramatic scenery around **Irō-zaki**, its southernmost tip. Though a car is the ideal way of getting around, all the places mentioned below are covered by local buses; if you're travelling by bus and combining this area with Dōgashima (see p.199), it's worth investing in a "Minami Izu Free Pass" (see Practicalities, p.195, for more about transport around Shimoda).

## Rendaiji

Set in a narrow valley just west of National Highway 414, this quiet, one-street village consists mostly of exclusive ryokan which tap into the area's abundant supply of hot water. It's these onsen baths that make **RENDAIJI** worth a visit, though afterwards there are a few meandering back lanes to explore, and some people might want to splash out on a night of luxury. Two or three **trains** an hour (¥160; 3–4min) run between Shimoda – roughly 3km to the south – and Rendaiji Station, from where the village is a short walk west across the river and the Highway. Local **buses** are slightly less frequent, but most drop you right on the main street; both Shimoda and Tōkai buses ply this route (¥250; 10min).

The most appealing of Rendaiji's **onsen** is the big public bath (¥1000) at *Kanaya Ryokan* (☎0558/22-0325, fax 23-6078; [5]–[7]), a traditional place with several pools, including a *rotemburo*, where many of your fellow-bathers will be local families. You'll find the ryokan on the main highway, just north of the village turning; there's a bus stop right outside or it's a couple of minutes' walk to the station. Walking south, peek in at the immaculate entrance to *Seiryū-sō* (☎0558/22-1361; fax 23-2066; [9]) on the left before the bridge; this elegant ryokan is where President Carter stayed in 1979 when he visited Gyokusen-ji (see p.195 above) – unfortunately the baths here are for residents only.

Opposite *Seiryū-sō*, a road heads west into Rendaiji proper. Among several marginally more affordable ryokan in this part of town, the beautiful old *Ishibashi Ryokan* (☎0558/22-2222, fax 22-2121; [7]) has the best bathing facilities, with *rotemburo*, jacuzzi and sauna (¥1000). The ryokan is tucked under a small hill on the right as you walk from the highway. Continue past it for few hundred metres and you'll find a neat bamboo fence, also on the right, belonging to *Rendaiji-sō* (☎0558/22-3501, fax 23-0373; [9]), a rambling ryokan whose jungle baths – one hosting a twenty-five-year-old hibiscus – make a steamy finale (noon–9pm; ¥800).

## South to Irō-zaki

In summer Izu's beaches are packed with surfers and sun-worshippers, but out of season they're usually fairly deserted. The major resort is just north of Shimoda, at Shirahama, but there are a couple of smaller, more attractive bays southwest of the town on the Tōkai Bus route to Izu's southern cape, **IRŌ-ZAKI**. From Shimoda Station **buses** depart for Irō-zaki roughly every thirty minutes, but check before boarding as some buses skip certain stops. If you want to continue round the coast, hop on one of the four daily buses which leave from Irō-zaki for the picturesque ride to Matsuzaki (see p.199), from where you can loop back to Shimoda, and Dōgashima; alternatively, take one of the **tourist boats** plying between Irō-zaki port and Shimoda for the return journey (see overleaf).

Nearly 4km southwest of Shimoda, Highway 136 passes through the village of **KISAMI**, where a road forks left across a river towards the coast. **Ōhama**, the name of Kisami's sandy bay, is one of south Izu's more attractive beaches – marred slightly by a factory on the far horizon – and a popular surfing spot. Along the road there's a handful of small **hotels**, the nicest of which is *Ernest House* (☎0558/22-5880, fax 23-3906; [5]–[6]); its fresh, bright rooms get booked up at weekends and in season, so it pays to phone ahead. They offer **meals** – including great picnic breakfasts – otherwise, try one of the laid-back cafés closer to the beach. If you're travelling by bus, ask the driver to drop you on the main road at Ōhama-iriguchi, from where it's a ten-minute walk.

A little further along the coast, **YUMIGAHAMA** is a larger, more developed resort but has the advantage that buses from here take you all the way down to the wide horseshoe bay, ringed with pines and casuarina. Continuing southwards, Highway 136 climbs through lush vegetation to emerge in an expanse of carparks that cap the headland. Fortunately, **Irō-zaki** improves dramatically as you walk out along the promontory for about 500m, past a missable "Jungle Park", souvenir shops and lighthouse, to a minuscule **shrine** balanced on the cliff edge. The views here are superb: on either side the sea has cut deep, blue gashes into the coastline, leaving behind a sprinkling of rocky islets between which colourful **tourist boats** bob and weave. The boats leave from Irō-zaki port – a tiny fishing village sheltering in the northern bay; from the headland it's a pleasant, five-minute stroll downhill, or get off the bus at Irōzaki-kō iriguchi on the main highway, a short walk from the village. Depending on the weather and the season, there are one or two trips per hour around the headland (¥1120 for 25min), or three daily sailings all the way back to Shimoda (¥1530; 40min).

## West Izu

Despite its rugged coastal scenery and occasionally spectacular views of Mount Fuji, **West Izu** remains far less developed than the eastern side – with the exception of **Dōgashima**, whose pitted, pine-tufted islands draw the coach parties in droves. This lack of development is largely due to the difficulties of access, since public transport is limited to slow bus routes between the main settlements and infrequent ferry services.

| WEST IZU AND SHUZENJI | | |
|---|---|---|
| **Dōgashima** | *Dōgashima* | 堂ヶ島 |
| New Ginsui-sō | *Nyū Ginsui-sō* | ニュー銀水荘 |
| Minshuku Koharu-sō | *Minshuku Koharu-sō* | 民宿小春荘 |
| Sebama-zushi | *Sebama-zushi* | 瀬浜寿し |
| **Matsuzaki** | *Matsuzaki* | 松崎 |
| Hamamiya | *Hamamiya* | 浜宮 |
| Izu-Matsuzaki-sō | *Izu-Matsuzaki-sō* | 伊豆松崎荘 |
| Sanyo-sō Youth Hostel | *Sanyo-sō Yūsu Hosuteru* | 山余荘ユースホステル |
| Sunset Hill Matsuzaki | *Sansetto Hiru Matsuzaki* | サンセットヒル松崎 |
| Tontsū | *Tontsū* | とん通 |
| **Shuzenji** | *Shuzenji* | 修善寺 |
| Minshuku Fukui | *Minshuku Fukui* | 民宿福井 |
| Goyōkan | *Goyōkan* | 五葉館 |
| Kikuya | *Kikuya* | 菊屋 |
| Nanaban | *Nanaban* | なな番 |
| Shigetsu-den | *Shigetsu-den* | 指月殿 |
| Shuzen-ji Temple | *Shuzen-ji* | 修善寺 |
| Shuzenji Onsen | *Shuzenji Onsen* | 修善寺温泉 |
| Shuzenji Youth Hostel | *Shuzenji Yūsu Hosuteru* | 修善寺ユースホステル |
| **Toi** | *Toi* | 土肥 |
| Heda | *Heda* | 戸田 |
| Takasagoya Ryokan | *Takasagoya Ryokan* | 高砂屋旅館 |

If you've got time to spare, it's worth taking a couple of days to meander between the traditional fishing ports that punctuate the journey north.

## Matsuzaki

Travelling from Shimoda, the main road cuts across Izu's upland spine to **MATSUZA-KI** on the west coast. Though spoilt by the high-rise *Prince Hotel* plonked in its midst, this modest town hides some attractive streets of traditional lattice-work buildings along the riverfront and down by its busy harbour. The town is also an onsen resort, but its main attraction is good-value **accommodation**. For budget travellers, there's the appealingly aged *Sanyo-sō Youth Hostel* (☎ & fax 0558/42-0408; ①), set in a traditional garden among rice-fields 3km east of town; Shimoda–Matsuzaki buses stop right outside and you can rent bikes to explore the surrounding area. Otherwise, the best option is *Izu-Matsuzaki-sō* (☎0558/42-0450; ④), at the north end of Matsuzaki's rather grungy beach, which offers a choice of comfortable Western or Japanese rooms and communal onsen baths but no private bathrooms. Finally, *Sunset Hill Matsuzaki* (☎0558/42-1515, fax 42-2688; ⑤), sits perched on a hill at the north end of town, ten minutes' walk from the bus station, or phone for a free shuttle bus. This is another onsen hotel, with great views over the bay from its large *rotemburo* (¥1000 for non-residents). All the above places serve food, but if you're looking for somewhere to **eat** in Matsuzaki, try *Hamamiya* (closed Wed), a moderately expensive fish restaurant on the beach just south of the *Prince Hotel*, or *Tonstū*, a homely *tonkatsu* restaurant three blocks further inland.

## Dōgashima

Just 5km up the road from Matsuzaki, **DŌGASHIMA** is west Izu's prime tourist trap, where hotels, souvenir shops and cafeterias cater to a steady stream of punters. The focus of all this activity is a collection of picturesque limestone outcrops lying serenely offshore. You can admire these islands from various viewpoints around the bay or, better still, from one of the **tour boats** puttering among their caves and tunnels; boats depart every five-to-ten minutes (daily 8.15am–4.30/5pm; ¥920) from a jetty in front of the main car park. The highlight of the twenty-minute ride is a cave with a large cavity in its roof; afterwards, walk up onto the hill immediately north of the jetty to watch the boats sail through from above.

The old part of Dōgashima, a traditional fishing village known as **Sawada**, occupies the bay's south side. It's sheltered by a rocky promontory with a **rotemburo** (¥500; closed Tues) in a spectacular location halfway up the cliff-face on the seaward side; skippers on the tourist boats take pleasure in sailing slowly by the apparently unconcerned bathers. This area is also the best place for affordable accommodation, but otherwise there's no reason to linger.

With an hour to spare, Dōgashima's **Orchid Sanctuary** (daily 8am–5pm; ¥1600) is surprisingly interesting, though a little expensive; to reach the ticket gate walk through the "Vivi Coast" souvenir shop. The Sanctuary grows more than 8000 types of orchid, from cosseted miniatures to hardier varieties growing wild in the woods. A well-marked route leads through the extensive park to lookout points over the bay, and then out through the inevitable souvenir shop where you can stock up on orchid essences, perfumes and even orchid ice-cream.

The centre of Dōgashima is a large car park which also doubles as the **bus terminal**. The **information office** is in a hut across the main road, north of the tourist jetty (Mon–Fri 8.30am–5pm; July & Aug daily; ☎0558/52-1268), where you can get local maps (in Japanese only) and help with hotel bookings; if they're closed, try the Tōkai Bus office, opposite. Both these places provide information about **onward transport**. There are hourly buses northeast through Toi to Shuzenji, or ferries which hop up the lovely coast via Toi and Heda to Numazu on the JR Tōkaidō Line.

Dōgashima is dominated by big, expensive resort **hotels**, most of which have stunning views and luxurious onsen baths. Pick of the bunch is the *New Ginsui-sō* (☎0558/52-2211, fax 52-1210; [9]), located on its own beach, five minutes' drive north of town. Prices are more affordable in Sawada fishing village at the southern end of Dōgashima, where you'll find dozens of minshuku, such as the cheerful *Koharu-sō* (☎ & fax 0558/52-0181; [5]), one block in from the main road. There's no shortage of **places to eat** if you don't mind the cafeteria-style dining rooms of the souvenir shops. For somewhere less hectic – despite its location on the central car park – *Sebama-zushi* serves sushi sets from around ¥1500, as well as soba and other staples.

## Inland to Shuzenji

Travelling north from Dōgashima the road hugs the coast, climbing over headlands and then zigzagging down to fishing villages squeezed into sheltered bays. At **Toi**, the largest settlement in west Izu, the main road turns inland, but a few buses continue on up the coast to **Heda**, a very picturesque village, with onward bus connections to Shuzenji; these buses are few and far between, so check the timetables before setting off. Both Toi and Heda lie on the ferry-route from Dōgashima to Numazu, while Toi also has regular sailings to Tagonoura-kō (near Shin-Fuji Station on the Shinkansen line) on the north coast of Suruga Bay. The only other reason to stop in Toi is for its **youth hostel**: *Takasagoya Ryokan* (☎0558/98-0200; [1]) is located in the centre of town, three minutes' walk from the *Bamba* bus stop and fifteen minutes from the ferry port.

### Shuzenji

Beyond Toi, Highway 136 climbs eastward through pine-clad mountains before dropping down into the wide valley of **SHUZENJI**. The modern town holds no interest beyond its transport connections, but the original settlement of **Shuzenji Onsen**, some 3km southeast, has a couple of historical sights that are worth exploring. To get there, you can take a bus from outside Shuzenji Station to a tiny terminal on the east side of the village.

Shuzenji Onsen consists of little more than one road and a string of riverside hotels on a narrow valley. Follow the main street west and you'll soon reach an open area with some pleasing older buildings and a succession of red-lacquered bridges over the tumbling Katsura-gawa. Here, on a rocky outcrop beside the river, a very skimpy palisade surrounds Shuzenji's first and most famous **onsen**, *Tokko-no-yu* (24hr; free; unsegregated); not surprisingly, dawn and dusk are more popular among women bathers. According to legend, the onsen was "created" by Kōbō Daishi, the founder of Shingon Buddhism (see p.784), in 807 AD when he found a boy washing his ailing father in the river; the priest struck the rock with his *tokko* (the short, metal rod carried by Shingon priests), and out gushed hot water with curative powers.

Kōbō Daishi is also credited with founding the nearby **temple**, **Shuzen-ji**, from which the town gets its name. Standing at the top of the steps on the river's north bank, the present temple was rebuilt roughly a century ago and its now quiet halls belie a violent history. During the Kamakura period (1185–1333), Shuzen-ji was a favourite place of exile for the shoguns' potential rivals. In 1193 Minamoto Noriyori, the younger brother of Shogun Yoritomo, committed suicide – some say he was murdered – after being banished here on suspicion of treason. A more famous death occurred soon after when **Minamoto Yoriie** was murdered in the bath. Yoriie was the son of Yoritomo and succeeded to the title of Shogun in 1199, aged only eighteen. Four years later his mother, Hōjō Masako, and grandfather seized power and sent Yoriie packing to Shuzen-ji, where he started planning his revenge. The plot was discovered, however, in 1204 and not long after Yoriie was found dead, supposedly killed by bathing in poisoned water.

Opposite the temple office you'll find a small **museum** (daily 8.30am–4.30/5pm; ¥300) full of temple treasures, including possessions allegedly belonging to Kōbō Daishi. But its main interest is the wealth of information in English about Shuzen-ji's eventful history.

Minamoto Yoriie's grave lies on the hillside directly across the valley from Shuzen-ji, beside a smaller temple, **Shigetsu-den**, which a repentant Hōjō Masako built to appease the soul of her son. Though not a dramatic building, it's the oldest in Shuzenji and has some fine Buddhist statues inside.

Returning to the bridge beside *Tokko-no-yu*, take a stroll west along the river. The path meanders across pretty bridges and through a bamboo grove to emerge near a modern onsen bath, *Yu-no-sato* (daily 9am–10pm; ¥1000 for 2hr), with a more secluded *rotemburo*. The bathhouse marks the western outskirts of Shuzenji village; turn right and you're back on the main street.

### *PRACTICALITIES*

Travelling to Shuzenji from Tokyo, the best option is an *Odoriko-gō* express **train** direct from Tokyo Station; these divide at Atami, so make sure you're in the right carriage. Alternatively, hop on any of the regular JR services to Mishima, from where the private Izu-Hakone Railway runs south to Shuzenji (¥500). There's an **information office** inside the station (daily 5am–11.30pm; ☎ & fax 0558/72-0667), while **buses** for Shuzenji Onsen, Dōgashima and other destinations around Izu depart from a terminal outside. If you want to **rent a car**, you could try Nissan (☎0558/72-2332) or Toyota (☎0558/72-9200) – both have branches near Shuzenji Station.

It's best to **stay** in Shuzenji Onsen, where one of the nicest options is the elegant *Kikuya Ryokan* (☎0558/72-2000, fax 72-2002; [8]), under a high-peaked roof immediately opposite the bus terminal, and featuring traditional gardens. A few doors down the road to the east, behind a lattice-work facade, *Goyōkan* (☎0558/72-2066, fax 72-8212; [5]), is a comfortable ryokan with large onsen baths but no en-suite facilities. Prices get cheaper as you walk away from the river. Among a group of minshuku on the northern hillside, *Fukui* (☎0558/72-0558, fax 72-3529; [4]), is a decent choice – none of the rooms have their own bathrooms, but it's got a small *rotemburo* with views across the valley. The **Shuzenji Youth Hostel** (☎0558/72-1222, fax 72-1771; [1]), is on the west side of town; take a bus bound for "New Town" or "Niji-no-sato" from Shuzenji Station and get off fifteen minutes later at "New Town iriguchi", from where the hostel is a three-minute walk uphill.

When it comes to **eating**, you'll find plenty of atmosphere at *Nanaban* (10am–4.30pm; closed Thurs), a rustic-looking soba restaurant east of Shuzenji Onsen's bus terminal. Though they serve good-value rice and noodle dishes, their speciality is *Zen-dera* soba, in which you dip cold soba in an eye-watering sauce of sesame and freshly grated horseradish – it's said to bring you the blessings of Buddha, so is surely well worth the ¥2000 price tag.

## Kamakura and around

A small, relaxed town trapped between the sea and a circle of wooded hills one hour's train ride south of Tokyo, **KAMAKURA** is steeped in history. Many of its 65 temples and 19 shrines were founded some eight centuries ago when, for a brief and tumultuous period, this was Japan's political and military centre. Its most famous sight is the **Daibutsu**, a glorious bronze Buddha surrounded by trees, but the town's ancient **Zen temples** are equally compelling.

Kamakura's prime sights can be covered on a day-trip from Tokyo, starting with the temples of **Kita-Kamakura**, the town's northern suburb, and then walking south to the

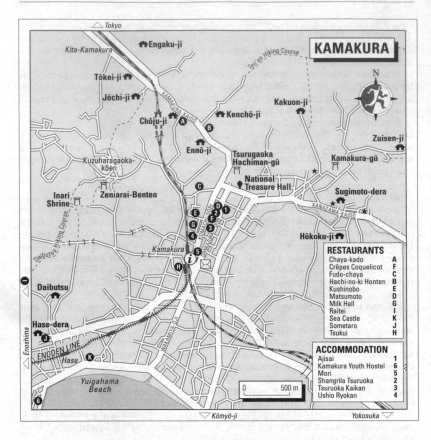

Tokyo

Kita-Kamakura

Engaku-ji

Tōkei-ji

Jōchi-ji

Chōju-ji Ⓐ Ⓑ Kenchō-ji

Kakuon-ji

Zuisen-ji

Kamakura-gū

Ennō-ji

Tsurugaoka
Hachiman-gū

Kuzuharagaoka-
kōen

Inari
Shrine

Zeniarai-Benten

Ⓒ

National
Treasure Hall

Sugimoto-dera

Hōkoku-ji

Ⓔ Ⓓ Ⓘ
Ⓖ Ⓕ
Ⓗ

Kamakura

Ⓘ

Daibutsu

Hase-dera

Ⓙ

ENODEN LINE

Hase

Ⓚ

Yuigahama
Beach

Ⓖ

0    500 m

Kōmyō-ji

Yokosuka

**RESTAURANTS**

| | |
|---|---|
| Chaya-kado | A |
| Crêpes Coquelicot | F |
| Fudo-chaya | C |
| Hachi-no-ki Honten | B |
| Kushinobo | E |
| Matsumoto | D |
| Milk Hall | G |
| Raitei | I |
| Sea Castle | K |
| Sometaro | J |
| Tsukui | H |

**ACCOMMODATION**

| | |
|---|---|
| Ajisai | 1 |
| Kamakura Youth Hostel | 6 |
| Mori | 5 |
| Shangrila Tsuruoka | 2 |
| Tsuruoka Kaikan | 3 |
| Ushio Ryokan | 4 |

sights of **central Kamakura**, before finishing up at the Great Buddha in **Hase** on its western outskirts. If you can only spare a day, make sure you get an early start: most sights close early (generally 4.30pm in winter and only a little later in summer). However, the town more than justifies a two-day stopover, allowing time for the enchanting temples of **east Kamakura** and to follow one of the gentle "hiking cours-es" up into the hills, or to ride the Enoden line west to tiny **Enoshima** island.

Kamakura's biggest **festivals** take place in early April and mid-September, including displays of horseback archery and costume parades, though the summer fireworks dis-play (August 10) over Sugami Bay is its most spectacular event. The town is also well-known for its spring blossoms and autumn colours, while many temple gardens are famous for a particular flower – for example, Japanese apricot at Zuisen-ji and Tōkei-ji (February) and Hydrangea at Meigetsu-in (mid-June).

The easiest way of **getting to Kamakura** is on the JR Yokosuka line from Tokyo Station via Yokohama. Trains stop in Kita-Kamakura before pulling into the main Kamakura Station three minutes later; make sure you board a Yokosuka- or Kurihama-bound train to avoid changing at Ōfuna. For a two-day outing, it's worth considering the Kamakura–Enoshima Free Kippu (¥1930), a discount ticket covering both the Yokosuka and Enoden lines.

## Some history

When the epic power-struggle between the Taira and Minamoto clans (see History, p.771) ended in 1185, the warlord **Minamoto Yoritomo** became the first permanent shogun and the effective ruler of Japan. Seven years later he established his military government – known as the *Bakufu*, or "tent government" – in Kamakura. Over the next century dozens of grand monuments were built here, notably the great Zen temples founded by monks fleeing Song-dynasty China. Zen Buddhism flourished under

| KAMAKURA AND AROUND | | |
|---|---|---|
| **Kamakura** | *Kamakura* | 鎌倉 |
| | | |
| Daibutsu | *Daibutsu* | 大仏 |
| Daibutsu Hiking Course | *Daibutsu Haikingu Kōsu* | 大仏ハイキングコース |
| Engaku-ji | *Engaku-ji* | 円覚寺 |
| Ennō-ji | *Ennō-ji* | 円応寺 |
| Hase | *Hase* | 長谷 |
| Hase-dera | *Hase-dera* | 長谷寺 |
| Hōkoku-ji | *Hōkoku-ji* | 報国寺 |
| Jōchi-ji | *Jōchi-ji* | 浄智寺 |
| Kakuon-ji | *Kakuon-ji* | 覚園寺 |
| Kamakura-gū | *Kamakura-gū* | 鎌倉宮 |
| Kamakura National Treasure Hall | *Kamakura Kokuhō-kan* | 鎌倉国宝館 |
| Kenchō ji | *Kenchō-ji* | 健長寺 |
| Kita-Kamakura | *Kita-Kamakura* | 北鎌倉 |
| Sugimoto-dera | *Sugimoto-dera* | 杉本寺 |
| Ten'en Hiking Course | *Ten'en Haikingu Kōsu* | 天園ハイキングコース |
| Tōkei-ji | *Tōkei-ji* | 東慶寺 |
| Tsurugaoka Hachiman-gū | *Tsurugaoka Hachiman-gū* | 鶴が岡八幡宮 |
| Zeniarai Benten | *Zeniarai Benten* | 銭洗弁天 |
| Zuisen-ji | *Zuisen-ji* | 瑞泉寺 |
| | | |
| *ACCOMMODATION* | | |
| Hotel Ajisai | *Hoteru Ajisai* | ホテルあじさい |
| Kamakura Kagetsuen Youth Hostel | *Kamakura Kagetsuen Yūsu Hosuteru* | 鎌倉花月園ユースホステル |
| Hotel Mori | *Hoteru Mori* | 小テルモリ |
| Shangrila Tsuruoka | *Shangurira Tsuruoka* | シャングリラ鶴岡 |
| Hotel Tsurugaoka Kaikan | *Hoteru Tsurugaoka Kaikan* | ホテル鶴が岡会館 |
| Ushio Ryokan | *Ushio Ryokan* | 潮旅館 |
| | | |
| *RESTAURANTS* | | |
| Chaya-kado | *Chaya-kado* | 茶屋かど |
| Chōju-ji | *Chōju-ji* | 長寿寺 |
| Fudō-chaya | *Fudō-chaya* | 不動茶屋 |
| Hachi-no-ki Honten | *Hachi-no-ki Honten* | 鉢の木本店 |
| Kōmyō-ji | *Kōmyō-ji* | 光明寺 |
| Matsumoto | *Matsumoto* | まつ本 |
| Raitei | *Raitei* | らい亭 |
| Sometarō | *Sometarō* | 染太郎 |
| Tsukui | *Tsukui* | つくい |
| | | |
| *AROUND KAMAKURA* | | |
| Enoshima | *Enoshima* | 江の島 |

the patronage of a warrior class who shared similar ideals of single-minded devotion to duty and rigorous self-discipline.

The Minamoto rule was brief and violent. Almost immediately, Yoritomo turned against his valiant younger brother, Yoshitsune, who had led the clan's armies, and hounded him until Yoshitsune committed ritual suicide – a favourite tale of Kabuki theatre. Both the second and third Minamoto shoguns were murdered and in 1219 power passed to the Hōjō clan, who ruled as fairly able regents behind puppet shoguns. Their downfall followed the Mongol invasions in the late thirteenth century and in 1333 Emperor Go-Daigo wrested power back to Kyoto; as the imperial armies approached Kamakura, the last Hōjō regent and an estimated eight hundred retainers committed *seppuku*. Kamakura remained an important military centre before fading into obscurity in the late-fifteenth century. Its temples, however, continued to attract religious pilgrims until Kamakura was "rediscovered" in the last century as a tourist destination and a desirable residential area within commuting distance of Tokyo.

## Arrival, information and getting around

**Trains** from Tokyo pass through Kita-Kamakura before arriving at the central Kamakura Station. At the rear of the station, you'll find ticket machines and platforms for the private Enoden line to Hase (see p.208) and Enoshima (see p.211), with trains running from roughly 7am to 11pm. Outside the station's main, eastern exit, and immediately to the right, there's a small **tourist information** window (daily 9am–5/6pm; ☎0467/22-3350) with English-speaking staff, though they're a bit reluctant to hand out maps and brochures – call in at the Tokyo TIC before you set off for their useful *Tourist Map of Kanagawa* which includes Kamakura, Yokohama and Hakone. Alternatively, you can buy rather sketchy Japanese-language maps (¥200) at major tourist spots round town.

Local **buses** depart from the main station concourse. Given the narrow roads and amount of traffic, however, it's usually quicker to use the trains as far as possible and then walk. The only time a bus might come in handy is for a couple of the more far-flung restaurants or out to the eastern sights; in the latter case you want either bus #24 or #36 from stand 4 (¥160 minimum fare). A better, but more expensive, option is to rent a **bike** from the outfit up the slope beyond the tourist office; rates are on a sliding scale from ¥500 for the first hour to ¥1500 for a day (daily 8.30am–5pm).

## Kita-Kamakura

As the Tokyo train nears Kita-Kamakura Station, urban sprawl gradually gives way to gentle, forested hills which provide the backdrop for some of Kamakura's greatest Zen temples. Chief among these are **Kenchō-ji** and the wonderfully atmospheric **Engaku-ji**. It takes over an hour to cover the prime sights, walking south along the main road, the Kamakura-kaidō, to the edge of central Kamakura. With more time, follow the Daibutsu Hiking Course up into the western hills to wash your yen at an alluring temple dedicated to **Zeniarai Benten**.

### Engaku-ji

The second most important but most satisfying of Kamakura's major Zen temples, **Engaku-ji** (daily 8am–4/5.30pm; ¥200) lies buried among ancient cedars just two minutes' walk south of Kita-Kamakura Station. It was founded in 1282 by a Chinese Zen monk, at the request of Regent Hōjō Tokumine, to honour victims (on both sides) of the ultimately unsuccessful Mongolian invasions in 1274 and 1281 (see History, p.771). The layout follows a traditional Chinese Zen formula – a pond and bridge (now cut off by the railway tracks), followed by a succession of somewhat austere buildings – but the encroaching trees and secretive gardens add a gentler touch.

Engaku-ji's two-storied main gate, **San-mon**, rebuilt in 1783, is a magnificent structure, beneath which the well-worn flagstones bear witness to generations of pilgrims. Beyond, the modern **Butsu-den** (Buddha Hall) houses the temple's primary Buddha image, haloed in soft light, while behind it the charming **Shari-den** lies tucked off to the left past an oblong pond. This small reliquary, usually closed to visitors, is said to contain a tooth of the Buddha brought here from China in the early thirteenth century. It's also considered Japan's finest example of Song-dynasty Zen architecture, albeit a sixteenth-century replica. The main path continues gently uphill to another pretty, thatched building, **Butsunichi-an** (¥100), where regent Hōjō Tokimune was buried in 1284; in fine weather they serve green tea (¥500) in its attractive garden. Finally, tiny **Ōbai-in** enshrines a pale yellow Kannon statue but its best attribute is a nicely informal garden with a grove of February-flowering Japanese apricot.

On the way out, follow signs up a steep flight of steps to the left of San-mon, to find Kamakura's biggest bell, **Ōgane**, forged in 1301 and an impressive 2.5m tall. From its wooden platform you get a fine view across the valley to Tōkei-ji, the next stop.

## Tōkei-ji and Jōchi-ji

Two minutes' walk along the main road from Engaku-ji, **Tōkei-ji** (daily 8.30am–4/5pm; ¥50; English leaflet ¥100) was founded as a nunnery in 1285 by the young widow of Hōjō Tokimune. It's an intimate temple, with a pleasing cluster of buildings and a profusion of flowers at almost any time of year: Japanese apricot in February, magnolia and peach in late March, followed by peonies and then irises in early June; September is the season for cascades of bush clover.

Tōkei-ji is more popularly known as the "Divorce Temple". Up until the mid-nineteenth century, when women were given the legal right to seek divorce, this was one of the few places where wives could escape domestic ill-treatment. If they reached the sanctuary, which many didn't, they automatically received a divorce after three years according to traditional, temple-law. Husbands could be summoned to resolve the dispute or, ultimately, sign the divorce papers. Some of these documents are preserved, along with other temple treasures, in the newly-built Treasure House (¥300), including two books detailing the women's reasons for seeking sanctuary – unfortunately, not translated. At the back of the temple, take a walk round the peaceful, mossy cemetery hidden among stately cryptomeria trees where many famous and forgotten nuns lie buried.

Continuing along the main valley almost as far as the train tracks, a sign to the right indicates **Jōchi-ji** (daily 9am–4.30pm; ¥100). The fourth of Kamakura's great Zen temples, founded by the nephew of Hōjō Tokumine in 1283, Jōchi-ji was almost completely levelled by the 1923 earthquake. Nevertheless, it's worth walking up the lane to see its beautifully proportioned Chinese-style gate which doubles as a bell-tower. The small worship hall contains a trinity of Buddhas while, at the back, there's another graveyard, this time sheltered by a bamboo grove.

## Zeniarai Benten and the Daibutsu Hiking Course

Follow the lane running north beside Jōchi-ji and you'll find some steps which mark the start of the **Daibutsu Hiking Course**. This meandering ridge-path (2.2km) makes an enjoyable approach to Hase's Great Buddha (see p.209), but in any case, it's well worth taking a diversion as far as the captivating cave-shrine dedicated to the goddess **Zeniarai Benten** ("Money-Washing Benten"). From Jōchi-ji follow signs for Daibutsu along a trail heading southeast through Kuzuharagaoka-kōen to a road junction, where the main trail turns right. Instead, take the steps straight ahead and duck under the shrine's tunnel-entrance to emerge in a natural amphitheatre filled with a forest of *torii* wreathed in incense and candle-smoke.

Despite being so hidden, there's a constant stream of hopeful punters come to test the goddess's powers. According to tradition, money washed in the spring, gushing out of a cave on the opposite side from entrance, is guaranteed to double at the very least – though not immediately. It's worth a shot; your notes won't dissolve, but let the money dry naturally to retain the beneficial effects.

If you're following the hiking trail **to Hase**, rather than retracing your steps, take a path downhill from the shrine's southern exit under a tunnel of tightly-packed *torii*, then turn right at a T-junction to find another avenue of vermilion *torii* leading deep into the cryptomeria forest. At the end lies a simple shrine dating from before the twelfth century, which is dedicated to Inari, the god of harvests. His messenger is the fox; as you head up the steep path behind, climbing over tangled roots, you'll find fox statues of all shapes and sizes peering out of the surrounding gloom. At the top, turn right and then left at a white sign board to pick up the hiking course for the final kilometre to the Daibutsu.

## South to Kenchō-ji and Ennō-ji

Back at the main road near Jōchi-ji, walk southwest for another five minutes to find the greatest of Kamakura's Zen temples, **Kenchō-ji** (8.30am–4.30pm; ¥300). Headquarters of the Rinzai sect and Japan's oldest Zen training monastery, Kenchō-ji is more formal than Engaku-ji and a lot busier, partly because of the neighbouring high-school and some major construction work. It contains several important buildings, most of which have been relocated here from Tokyo and Kyoto to replace those lost since the temple's foundation in 1253. Again, the layout shows a strong Chinese influence; the founding abbot was another Song Chinese émigré, in this case working under the patronage of Hōjō Tokiyori, the devout fifth Regent and father of Engaku-ji's Tokumine.

The main complex begins with the towering, copper-roofed San-mon, an eighteenth-century reconstruction, to the right of which hangs the original temple bell, cast in 1255 and considered one of Japan's most beautiful. Beyond San-mon, a grove of gnarled and twisted juniper trees hides the dainty, nicely dilapidated Butsu-den. The main image is, unusually, of Jizō seated on a lotus throne, his bright, half-closed eyes piercing the gloom. Though the Hattō, or lecture hall, numbers among Japan's largest wooden, Buddhist buildings, the curvaceous Chinese-style gate, Kara-mon, and the Hōjō hall beyond are much more attractive structures. Walk round the latter's balcony to find a surprisingly neglected garden; it's generally attributed to a thirteenth-century monk, making it Japan's oldest-surviving Zen garden.

The track heading northeast from the Hōjō, up steep steps and past a temple packed with statues of long-nosed, mythical *tengu*, is the start of the **Ten'en Hiking Course**. It takes roughly two hours to complete the trail from Kenchō-ji, which loops round the town's northeast outskirts before dropping down to Kamakura-gū (see p.208).

Sticking to the main road, though, there's one last temple to visit before you hit central Kamakura. **Ennō-ji** (daily 9am–3.30/4pm; ¥200) looks fairly insignificant, but

---

### ZAZEN

**Zazen**, or sitting meditation, is a crucial aspect of Zen Buddhist training, particularly among followers of the Rinzai sect. Several temples in Kamakura hold public *zazen* sessions at various levels, of which the most accessible are those at Engaku-ji and Kenchō-ji, as detailed below. These hour-long sessions are free and no reservations are required, though check the current schedule at the temple, or Kamakura information office (see p.204).

| | |
|---|---|
| Engaku-ji | Kenchō-ji |
| ☎0467/22-0478 (Japanese language only) | ☎0467/22-0981 (Japanese language only) |
| April–Oct daily 5.30am; Nov–March daily 6am. | Every Sat and Sun 5pm. |

inside its hall reside the red-faced King of Hell, *Enma*, and his ten cohorts. This ferocious crew are charged with deciding the appropriate level of reincarnation in your next life and their wonderfully realistic expressions are meant to scare you into better ways. In fact the original statues are in safe-keeping in the National Treasure Hall, but usually only one is on display, whereas here you get to see the whole gang.

From Ennō-ji it's only another five minutes through the tunnel and downhill to the side entrance of Tsurugaoka Hachiman-gū (see below).

# Central Kamakura

Modern Kamakura revolves around its central **train station** and a couple of touristy streets leading to the town's most important shrine, Tsurugaoka Hachiman-gū. The traditional approach to this grand edifice lies along **Wakamiya-ōji**, also known as Dankazura-dōri at its northern end, which runs straight from the sea to the shrine entrance. Shops here peddle a motley collection of souvenirs and crafts, the most famous of which is *Kamakura-bori*, a 700-year-old method of laying lacquer over carved wood. More popular, however, is the more recent *Hato*, a pigeon-shaped, French-style biscuit first made by Toshimaya bakers a century ago – follow the trail of yellow and white bags to find their shop (9am–7pm; closed Wed) at the south end of Dankazura-dōri. Shadowing Wakamiya-ōji to the west, **Komachi-dōri** is a narrow, pedestrian-only shopping street, packed with more souvenir shops, restaurants and a few fairly smart boutiques.

## Tsurugaoka Hachiman-gū

A majestic, vermilion-lacquered *torii* marks the front entrance to **Tsurugaoka Hachiman-gū**, the Minamoto clan's guardian shrine since 1063. Hachiman-gū, as it's popularly known, was moved to its present site in 1191, since when it has witnessed some of the more unsavoury episodes of Kamakura history. Most of the present buildings, however, date from the early nineteenth century, and their striking, red paintwork, combined with the parade of souvenir stalls and the constant bustle of people, create a festive atmosphere in sharp contrast to Kamakura's more secluded Zen temples.

Three hump-backed bridges lead into the shrine compound between two connected ponds known as **Genpei-ike**. These were designed by Minamoto Yoritomo's wife, Hōjō Masako, and are full of heavy, complicated symbolism, anticipating the longed-for victory of her husband's clan over their bitter enemies, the Taira (see p.771 for the history of this feud); strangely, the bloodthirsty Masako was of Taira stock. Moving hurriedly on, the **Mai-den**, an open-sided stage at the end of a broad avenue, was the scene of another unhappy event in 1186, when Yoritomo forced his brother's mistress to dance for the assembled *samurai*. Yoritomo wanted his popular brother, Yoshitsune, killed and was holding Shizuka prisoner in the hope of discovering his whereabouts; instead, she made a defiant declaration of love and only narrowly escaped death herself, though her newborn son was murdered soon after. Her bravery is commemorated with classical dances and Nō plays during the shrine **festival** (Sept 14–16), which also features demonstrations of horseback archery.

Beyond the Mai-den, a long flight of steps leads up beside a knobbly, ancient gingko tree, reputedly one thousand years old and scene of the third shogun's murder by his vengeful nephew, to the **main shrine**. It's an attractive collection of buildings set among trees, though, like all Shinto shrines, you can only peer in. Appropriately, the principal deity, Hachiman is the God of War.

The **Hōmotsu-den** (daily 8.30am–4.15pm; ¥100), in a corridor immediately left of the shrine, contains a missable exhibition of shrine treasures – although its ticket desk sells informative maps of Hachiman-gū (¥100). Instead, head back down the steps and left past the beautifully restrained, black-lacquered **Shirahata-jinja**, dedicated to the first and third Kamakura shoguns, to find the modern **Kamakura National Treasure Hall** (Tues–Sun

9am–4pm; ¥300; English-language leaflet ¥250). This one-room museum is noted for its collection of Kamakura- and Muromachi-period art (1192–1573), mostly gathered from local Zen temples, though only a few of the priceless pieces are on display at any one time.

## East Kamakura

The eastern side of Kamakura contains a scattering of less-visited shrines and temples, including two of the town's most enchanting corners. Though it's possible to cover the area on foot in a half day, or less if you hop on a bus for the return journey, by far the best option for these scattered locations is to rent a bicycle (see p.204 for information on buses and bikes).

From Hachiman-gū work your way eastwards through a quiet, suburban area north of the main highway, the Kanazawa-kaidō, until you find signs indicating an optional left turn for **Kamakura-gū**. Mainly of interest for its history and torchlight Nō dramas (21–22 September; tickets by postal lottery in early September), this shrine was founded by Emperor Meiji in 1869 to encourage support for his new imperial regime. It is dedicated to Prince Morinaga, a forgotten fourteenth-century hero who helped restore his father, Emperor Go-Daigo, briefly to the throne. The prince was soon denounced, however, by power-hungry rivals and held for nine months in a Kamakura cave before being executed. The small cave and a desultory treasure house (daily 9am–4.30pm; ¥300) lie to the rear of the classically styled shrine, but don't really justify the entry fee.

Kamakura-gū marks the eastern access point to the Ten'en Hiking Course (see p.206); the main trail starts 900 metres further east, near dilapidated **Zuisen-ji** (daily 9am–5pm; ¥100), while a short cut takes you north to join the trail above **Kakuon-ji** (by appointment only). The nearest bus stop is at "Daito-no-miya", from where it's a ten-minute walk northeast to Kamakura-gū.

You have to join the main road for the last short stretch to Kamakura's oldest temple, **Sugimoto-dera** (daily 8am–4.30pm; ¥200), at the top of a steep, foot-worn staircase lined with fluttering white flags. Standing in a woodland clearing, the small, thatched temple, founded in 734, exudes a real sense of history. Inside its smoke-blackened hall, spattered with pilgrims' prayer stickers, you can slip off your shoes and take a look behind the altar at the three wooden statues of *Jūichimen Kannon*, the Eleven-faced Goddess of Mercy. The images were carved at different times by famous monks, but all three are at least one thousand years old. According to legend, they survived a devastating fire in 1189 by taking shelter – all by themselves – behind a giant tree; since then the temple has been known as Sugimoto, "under the cedar".

Just a few minutes further east along Kanazawa-kaidō, turn right over a small bridge to reach the entrance to **Hōkoku-ji** (daily 9am–4pm; ¥200), or *Take-dera*, the "Bamboo Temple". The well-tended gardens and simple wooden buildings are attractive in themselves, but the temple is best-known for a grove of evergreen bamboo protected by the encircling cliffs. This dappled forest of thick, gently curved stems, where tinkling water spouts and the soft creaking of the wind-rocked canes muffle the outside world, would seem the perfect place for the monks' meditation. Too soon, though, the path emerges beside the manicured rear garden, which was created by the temple's founding priest in the thirteenth century.

To return to central Kamakura, you can catch a bus for the 2km ride from opposite Sugimoto-dera. Alternatively, take the small lane left in front of Hōkoku-ji and follow it west through an attractive residential area, which cuts off at least a chunk of the highway.

## Hase-dera and the Daibutsu

The west side of Kamakura, an area known as **Hase**, is home to the town's most famous sight, the Daibutsu (Great Buddha), who was cast in bronze nearly 750 years ago. On the way, it's worth visiting Hase-dera to see an image of Kannon, the Goddess of Mercy, which pre-dates the Daibutsu by at least five hundred years, and is said to be Japan's largest wooden statue. Both these sights are within walking distance of Hase Station, three stops from Kamakura Station (¥190) on the private Enoden line.

**Hase-dera** (daily 8am–4.30/5pm; ¥300) stands high on the hillside a few minutes' walk north of Hase Station, with good views of Kamakura and across Yuigahama beach to the Miura peninsula beyond. Though the temple's present layout dates from the mid-thirteenth century, according to legend it was founded in 736 when a wooden Eleven-faced Kannon washed ashore nearby. The statue is supposedly one of a pair carved from a single camphor tree in 721 by a monk in the original Hase, near Nara; he placed one Kannon in a local temple and pushed the other out to sea.

Nowdays the Kamakura Kannon – just over 9m tall and gleaming with gold leaf, a thir-teenth-century embellishment – resides in an attractive, chocolate-brown and cream building at the top of the temple steps. This central hall is flanked by two smaller build-ings: the right hall houses a large Amidha Buddha carved in 1188 for Minamoto Yoritomo's forty-second birthday, to ward off the bad luck traditionally associated with that age; while on the left is a small treasure hall (closed Mon), whose most prized exhibits are the original temple bell, cast in 1264, and an early-fifteenth-century statue of Daikoku-ten, the cheerful God of Wealth. Beside the viewing platform, the Sutra Repository contains a revolving drum with a complete set of Buddhist scriptures inside – one turn of the wheel is equivalent to reading the whole lot. Ranks of Jizō statues are a common sight in Hase-dera, some clutching sweets or "windmills" and wrapped in tiny, woollen mufflers; these sad little figures commemorate stillborn or aborted children.

From Hase-dera turn left at the main road and follow the crowds north for a few hun-dred metres to find the **Daibutsu** (daily 7am–5.30/6pm; ¥200) in the grounds of Kōtoku-in temple. After all the hype, the Great Buddha can seem a little disappointing, but as you approach and his serene, rather aloof face comes into focus, the magic begins to take hold. He sits on a stone pedestal, a broad-shouldered figure lost in deep meditation, with his head slightly bowed, his face and robes streaked grey-green by centuries of sun, wind and rain.

The eleven-metre-tall image represents Amida Nyorai, the future Buddha who receives souls into the Western Paradise, and was built under the orders of Minamoto Yoritomo to rival the larger Nara Buddha (see p.485). Completed in 1252, the statue is constructed of bronze plates bolted together around a hollow frame – you can climb inside for ¥20 – and evidence suggests that, at some time, it was covered in gold leaf. Amazingly, it has withstood fires, typhoons, tidal waves and even the Great Earthquake of 1923. Its predecessor, however, was less successful: the wooden statue was unveiled in 1243 only to be destroyed in a violent storm just five years later. And various attempts to build a shelter suffered similar fates until, happily, they gave up after 1495 and left the Daibutsu framed by trees and an expanse of sky.

## Accommodation

Central Kamakura offers little budget **accommodation**, but a fair choice of mid-range hotels. Many places charge higher rates at weekends and during peak holiday periods – generally over New Year, Golden Week and the summer months of July and August – when it's hard to get a room in any case.

**Hotel Ajisai**, 1-12-4 Yukinoshita (☎0467/22-3492, fax 22-3530). A handful of bright, simple Western-style rooms above a confectionery shop at the north end of Dankazura. TV, phone, air-conditioning and small en-suite bathroom. Prices include breakfast. English spoken. ⑤–⑥.

**Kamakura Kagetsuen Youth Hostel**, 27-9 Sakanoshita (☎0467/25-1234). Well-organized hostel, located in a rather aged hotel on the seafront ten minutes' walk from Hase Station. Reception is open from 3.30pm to 8pm, and there's an 11pm curfew. Meals are available. Be warned that the hotel rooms are not good value. Dorm ①–②. Room ⑤–⑥.

**Hotel Mori**, 3F, 1-5-21 Komachi (☎0467/22-5868). Round the corner from the station on Dankazura, offering comfortable, decent-sized rooms with TV and en-suite bathrooms. ⑥.

**Shangrila Tsuruoka**, 3F, 1-9-29 Yukinoshita (☎0467/25-6363, fax 25-6456). A good alternative if the *Ajisai* is full, though a little hard to find on the third floor of a shopping mall. The rooms are a bit fussy and a little worn, but perfectly adequate. ⑤.

**Hotel Tsurugaoka Kaikan**, 2-12-27 Komachi (☎0467/24-1111). Big, old-fashioned hotel on Dankazura with glitzy chandeliers and expanses of floral wallpaper. The *tatami* rooms are more restrained, though all rooms are comfortably furnished, with en-suite bathroom. Meals are usually included, so specify if you want cheaper, room-only rates. English spoken. ⑥.

**Ushio Ryokan**, 2-3-9 Komachi (☎0467/22-7016). Four no-frills rooms in this welcoming ryokan tucked down a quiet backstreet, and the cheapest option available in central Kamakura. English spoken. 10.30pm curfew. ④–⑤.

## Eating and drinking

Kamakura is famous for its beautifully-presented vegetarian cuisine, known as **shōjin ryōri**, traditionally eaten for lunch at the Zen temples. You'll need to book in advance – ask the tourist offices in Tokyo or Kamakura for help. Two well-known temples to try are Chōju-ji (☎0467/22-2147), south of Kita-Kamakura Station, and Kōmyō-ji (☎0467/22-0603), on the southeast edge of Kamakura (take bus #40 or #41 from Kamakura Station, stand 1). Meals start at noon and cost around ¥3700 per person. Alternatively, you can eat *shōjin ryōri* at a few ordinary **restaurants**. For a **picnic**, Kinokuniya has a good food-hall on the west side of Kamakura Station, or try Union Store on Dankazura.

**Chaya-kado**, 1518 Yamanouchi. This homely soba restaurant, on the opposite side of the main road just north of Kenchō-ji, makes a good pit stop on the temple trail. Try *chikara udon* with a couple of filling *mochi* (steamed rice cakes). Prices start at ¥950. Open daily 10am–5pm.

**Crêpes Coquelicot**. Cheerful little crêperie on Komachi-dōri with a small coffee shop or a take-away counter. ¥500 for a scrumptious crêpe and a drink. Daily 10.30am–6pm.

**Fudo-chaya**, 2-2-21 Yukinoshita. Delightfully quirky restaurant serving good-value soba and ramen dishes (from ¥550; picture menu) next to a tiny cave-shrine – you eat outside under red umbrellas or in the cave itself. It's worth the trek, down a lane of picturesque houses to the west of Hachiman-gū; look for a red lantern by its entrance gate. 11am–5pm. Closed Thurs.

**Hachi-no-ki Honten**, 7 Yamanouchi (☎0120–28719). Eating at this famous old *shōjin ryōri* restaurant near Kenchō-ji, requires booking several weeks in advance and prices start at ¥4600 (closed Mon). However, reservations aren't necessary at the two new branches, up the road opposite Tōkei-ji, where prices range from around ¥3500 for a lunchtime *bentō*.

**Kushinobo**, 1-2-4 Komachi. Lively, modern *izakaya* where you need to arrive early for a seat. You can eat well for around ¥2000 – choose from a range of daily specials on the counter. Open daily 5.30–11.30pm.

**Matsumoto**, B2, 1-8-36 Yukinoshita. Recommended sushi restaurant tucked at the end of the corridor. A meal will cost around ¥2000 but their English-language picture menu is a plus point. Closed Mon.

**Milk Hall**, 2-3-8 Komachi. Relaxed, jazz-playing coffee-house-cum-antique shop buried in the back-streets west of Komachi-dōri. Best for a coffee and cake, or an evening beer, rather than a place to eat. Daily 11am–10.30pm; bar from 6pm.

**Raitei**, Takasago (☎0467/32-5656). Atmospheric soba restaurant in an old farmhouse set in beautiful gardens among the hills west of Kamakura, with views to Enoshima and Fuji – if you're lucky. Basic dishes start at ¥850, or you can reserve *kaiseki* meals (from ¥6000); the garden entry fee is discounted from your bill. It's a bit off the beaten track but well-worth the effort; take bus #4 or #6 from stand 2 outside Kamakura Station (20min).

**Sea Castle**, 2-7-15 Hase (☎0467/25-4335). Since 1957, this cosy, seafront German restaurant has been serving hearty home-made fare, such as sausages, sauerkraut and goulash, with German beer to wash it down and delicious cakes to follow. There's a reasonable-value course menu for ¥2200 and daily specials. Noon–9pm. Closed Wed and occasionally for private functions, so ring first.

**Sometaro**, 2F, 3-12-11 Hase. Traditional, *okonomiyaki* (do-it-yourself savoury pancakes) restaurant in front of Hase-dera. ¥850 for a bowl of ingredients, or opt for the more expensive *teppanyaki*. Daily 11.30am–10pm.

**Tsukui**, 11-7 Onarimachi. Cheap option in the centre of Kamakura, this is a relaxed *okonomiyaki* and *yakisoba* joint. Find it on the west side of Kamakura Station and right down the first alley at the north end of Onari-dōri. Mon–Fri 5–10pm; Sat & Sun noon–10pm. Closed Tues.

# Around Kamakura

With so much to see in Kamakura, there's little time left for exploring the surrounding area. However, one possibility is the tiny, sacred island of **ENOSHIMA**, twenty minutes west of Kamakura Station on the private Enoden line (¥250). Tied to the mainland by a six-hundred-metre-long bridge, Enoshima has a few sights – some shrines, a botanical garden and a missable cave – but its prime attraction is as a pleasant place to walk away from motor-traffic. The island's best appreciated on weekdays in the off-season; during summer and on holiday weekends it seems liable to sink under the weight of visitors.

As the Enoden-line train rattles into Enoshima Station from Kamakura, look out on the right for the copper-clad roofs of **Ryūkō-ji**. This temple was built on the spot where the monk Nichiren, founder of the eponymous Buddhist sect (see p.785), was nearly beheaded in 1271 for his persistent criticisms of the government and rival sects. According to legend, as the executioner's sword was about to fall, a fortuitous bolt of lightening split the blade in two, just in time for the shogun's messenger to arrive with a reprieve. Ryūkō-ji was founded a few years later and the main hall, its Buddha image surrounded by a sea of gold, is a good example of the sect's striking decorative style. To the left of the hall there's a statue of Nichiren in the cave where he was imprisoned and a staircase leading up to a smaller temple. Turn right here and follow the path round to where a magnificent five-storey pagoda, erected in 1910, seems part of the surrounding forest.

From Enoshima Station it's roughly fifteen minutes' walk southwest to **the island**, via a bridge constructed over the original sand-spit. Enoshima's eastern side shelters a yacht harbour and car parks, but otherwise the knuckle of rock – less than one kilometre from end to end – is largely covered with woods and a network of well-marked paths. Where the bridge ends, walk straight ahead under the bronze *torii* and uphill past restaurants and souvenir shops (the first on the left stocks informative, English **maps**), to where the steps begin; though the climb's easy enough, there are three escalators tunnelled through the hillside (¥300, or pay for each separately).

Enoshima is mostly famous for a naked **statue of Benten**, the goddess of fortune and the arts, which is housed in an octagonal hall (daily 9am–5pm; ¥150) halfway up the hill. In fact there are three Benten statues enshrined here, but the pale-skinned, voluptuous beauty clutching her lute, said to be 600 years old, is ranked among Japan's top three Benten images. On the way up you'll pass several other shrine buildings belonging to Enoshima-jinja, founded in the thirteenth century and dedicated to the guardian of sailors and fisherfolk, before emerging beside a nicely laid-out **botanical garden** (daily 9am–5pm; ¥200). If it's clear, you'll get good views south to Ōshima's smoking volcano and across to Fuji in the west from the lighthouse (an extra ¥250), inside the garden. The path then drops down steeply to the island's rocky west shore and two caves known as **Iwaya** (daily 9am–4pm, or 6pm in summer; ¥500). Though it's an attractive walk, you might want to give these very artificial grottoes, with their piped music and roaring dragons, a miss.

If you're heading back to **central Tokyo** from Enoshima, the easiest route is the Odakyū-Enoshima line direct to Shinjuku, though note that these trains depart from a different station; from the island causeway, turn left across the river and then immediately right to find Katase-Enoshima Station. Alternatively, walk back to Enoshima Station and take the Enoden line west to its terminal in Fujisawa, where you have to change stations for Tōkaidō-line trains to Tokyo Station via Yokohama and Shinagawa.

# Yokohama and around

Thanks to its open harbour-frontage and low-rise skyline, **YOKOHAMA** feels far more spacious and airy than neighbouring Tokyo. Locals are proud of their city's international heritage, and there's definitely a cosmopolitan flavour to the place, with its scattering of Western-style buildings, Chinese temples and world-cuisines, and its sizeable foreign community.

| YOKOHAMA AND AROUND | | |
|---|---|---|
| **Yokohama** | *Yokohama* | 横浜 |
| Chinatown | *Chūka-gai* | 中華街 |
| Doll Museum | *Ningyō no Ie* | 人形の家 |
| Foreigners' Cemetery | *Gaikokujin Bochi* | 外国人墓地 |
| Ishikawachō | *Ishikawachō* | 石川町 |
| Kannai | *Kannai* | 関内 |
| Kantei-byō | *Kantei-byō* | 関帝廟 |
| Minato Mirai 21 | *Minato Mirai 21* | みなとみらい２１ |
| Mitsubishi Minato Mirai Industrial Museum | *Mitsubishi Minato Mirai Gijutsukan* | 三菱みなとみらい技術館 |
| Motomachi | *Motomachi* | 元町 |
| Ōsanbashi | *Ōsanbashi* | 大さん橋 |
| Sakuragichō | *Sakuragichō* | 桜木町 |
| Sanbo Centre | *Sanbo Sentā* | サンボセンター |
| Silk Museum | *Shiruku Hakubutsukan* | シルク博物館 |
| Yamate | *Yamate* | 山手 |
| Yokohama Archives of History | *Yokohama Kaikō Shiryōkan* | 横浜開港資料館 |
| Yokohama Museum of Art | *Yokohama Bijutsukan* | 横浜美術館 |
| *ACCOMMODATION* | | |
| Echigoya Ryokan | *Echigoya Ryokan* | エチゴヤ旅館 |
| Kanagawa Youth Hostel | *Kanagawa Yūsu Hosuteru* | 神奈川ユースホステル |
| Hotel New Grand | *Hoteru Nyū Gurando* | ホテルニューグランド |
| Pan Pacific Hotel | *Pan Pashifikku Hoteru* | パンパシフィックホテル |
| Royal Park Hotel Nikkō | *Roiyaru Pāku Hoteru Nikkō* | ロイヤルパークホテルニッコー |
| San-ai Yokohama Hotel | *San-ai Yokohama Hoteru* | 三愛ヨコハマホテル |
| Star Hotel | *Sutā Hoteru* | スターホテル |
| Washington Hotel | *Washinton Hoteru* | ワシントンホテル |
| *RESTAURANTS* | | |
| Manchinrou | *Manchinrou* | 萬珍楼 |
| Peking Hanten | *Pekin Hanten* | 北京飯店 |
| Rikyūan | *Rikyūan* | 利久庵 |
| Shei Shei | *Shei Shei* | 謝謝 |
| Yamate Jūbankan | *Yamate Jūbankan* | 山手十番館 |
| *AROUND YOKOHAMA* | | |
| Negishi | *Negishi* | 根岸 |
| Rāmen Museum | *Rāmen Hakubutsukan* | ラーメン博物館 |
| Sankei-en | *Sankei-en* | 三渓園 |
| Shin-Yokohama | *Shin-Yokohama* | 新横浜 |

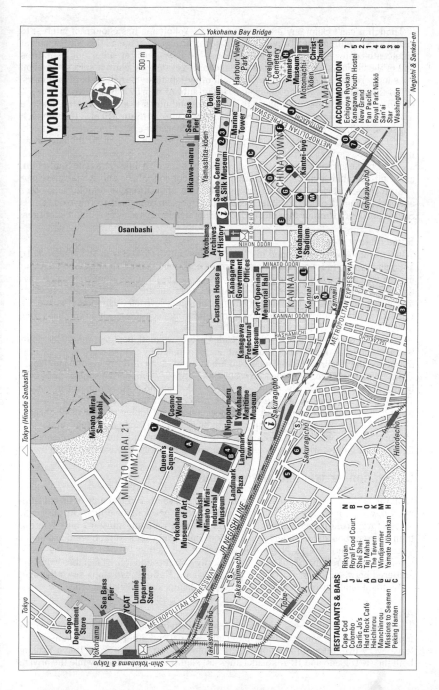

△ *Yokohama Bay Bridge*

▷ *Negishi & Sankei-en*

# YOKOHAMA

0     500 m

Yokohama Bay Bridge

Harbour View Park

Foreigner's Cemetery

Yamate Museum

Motomachi Christ
Church

YAMATE

Kōen

## ACCOMMODATION

| | |
|---|---|
| Echigoya Ryokan | 7 |
| Kanagawa Youth Hostel | 5 |
| New Grand | 2 |
| Pan Pacific | 1 |
| Royal Park Nikkō | 4 |
| San'ai | 6 |
| Star | 3 |
| Washington | 8 |

Doll
Museum

Sea Bass
Pier

Hikawa-maru

Yamashita-kōen

Marine
Tower

2 3

Sanbo Centre
& Silk Museum

Kantei-byō

CHINATOWN

Ishikawachō

Osanbashi

Yokohama
Archives
of History

Customs House

Kanagawa
Government
Offices

NIHON ŌDŌRI

HON-CHŌ DŌRI

Yokohama
Stadium

Port Opening
Memorial Hall

MINATO ŌDŌRI

KANNAI

Kannai

Kannai

METROPOLITAN EXPRESSWAY

Kanagawa
Prefectural
Museum

KANNAI ŌDŌRI

BASHAMICHI

Minato Mirai
San'bashi

Cosmo
World

Nippon-maru

Yokohama
Maritime
Museum

Sakuragichō

Sakuragichō

Queen's
Square

MINATO MIRAI 21
(MM21)

Landmark
Tower

Landmark
Plaza

Hinodechō

Yokohama
Museum of Art

Mitsubishi
Minato Mirai
Industrial
Museum

JR NEGISHI LINE

Takashimachō

Tōbe

Sea Bass
Pier

YCAT

Luminé
Department
Store

Sōgo
Department
Store

METROPOLITAN EXPRESSWAY

Takashimachō

△ *Tokyo*

△ *Yokohama*

▽ *Shin-Yokohama & Tokyo*

◁ *Tokyo (Hinode Sanbashi)*

## RESTAURANTS & BARS

| | | | |
|---|---|---|---|
| Cape Cod | N | Rikyuan | L |
| Colombo | B | Royal Food Court | J |
| Garlic Jo's | I | Shei Shei | F |
| Hard Rock Café | O | Taj Mahal | D |
| Heichinrou | A | The Tavern | G |
| Manchinrou | K | Windjammer | E |
| Missions to Seamen | M | Yamate Jūbankan | C |
| Peking Hanten | H | | |

Though it can't claim any outstanding sights, Yokohama has enough of interest to justify a day's outing from Tokyo. It might seem strange to come all this way to look at nineteenth-century European-style buildings, but the upmarket suburb of **Yamate** is one of the city's highlights, an area of handsome residences, church spires and bijou tea shops. Yamate's "exotic" attractions still draw Japanese tourists in large numbers, as do the vibrant alleys and speciality restaurants of nearby **Chinatown**. There's a clutch of assorted **museums** along the sea-front and north to where **Kannai** boasts a few grand old Western edifices, in complete contrast to **Minato Mirai 21**'s high-tech sky-scrapers in the distance. This half-completed "harbour-city of the twenty-first century" forms the focus of Yokohama's ambitious plans to grab some of the initiative away from Tokyo.

A tour of these central sights will easily fill a day, but with a little extra time **Sankei-en**, just south of Yokohama, makes a good, half-day excursion. This extensive Japanese garden provides a perfect backdrop for its collection of picturesque temples and other ancient buildings. If modern culture's more your thing, en route back to Tokyo don't miss Shin-Yokohama's **Ramen Museum** which celebrates Japan's answer to the hamburger.

## Some history

When Commodore Perry sailed his "Black Ships" into Tokyo Bay in 1853 (see p.774), Yokohama was a mere fishing village of some eighty houses on the distant shore. But it was this harbour, well out of harm's way as far as the Japanese were concerned, that the shogun designated one of the five **treaty ports** open to foreign trade in 1858. At first foreign merchants were limited to a small, semi-restricted compound in today's Kannai – allegedly for their protection from anti-foreign sentiment – but eventually they moved up onto the more favourable southern hills.

From the early 1860s until the first decades of the twentieth century, Yokohama flourished on the back of raw silk exports, a trade dominated by British merchants. During this period the city provided the main conduit for **new ideas and inventions** into Japan: the first bakery, photographers, ice cream shop, brewery and, perhaps most importantly, the first railway line which linked today's Sakuragichō with Shimbashi in central Tokyo in 1872. Soon established as Japan's major international port, Yokohama held pole-position until the **Great Earthquake** levelled the city, killing more than 40,000 people, in 1923. It was eventually rebuilt, only to be devastated again in air raids at the end of World War II. By this time Kōbe was in the ascendancy and, though Yokohama still figures among the world's largest ports, it never regained its hold over Japanese trade.

# Orientation, arrival and getting around

With the harbour bounding its east side, hills to the south and a couple of useful landmark towers, Yokohama is an easy enough place to get your bearings. On the north side of town, **Yokohama Station** functions as the city's main transport hub, offering train, subway, bus and even ferry connections, and featuring several huge department stores. From here the JR Negishi line, part of the Keihin-Tōhoku line, runs south through central Yokohama, passing the majority of sights and tourist facilities which lie scattered between the train tracks and the harbour. **Kannai**, two stops down the line, is the traditional downtown area and a focus for banks and prefectural offices.

## Arrival

The best way to get to Yokohama **from central Tokyo** is on a JR Keihin-Tōhoku **train** from Tokyo Station, which calls at Yokohama, Kannai and other central stations; trains leave every five to ten minutes on the forty-minute journey. Also from Tokyo Station, both the JR Tōkaidō and JR Yokosuka lines are slightly faster (30min), while the private

Tōyoko line from Shibuya is cheaper (¥270, as opposed to ¥450), but these three routes only serve Yokohama Station. An interesting alternative is to hop on a **cruise boat** from Tokyo's Hinode Sanbashi (see p.89) to Ōsanbashi (1hr 25min) and Minato Mirai Sanbashi (1hr 40min) in Yokohama. There are two departures each afternoon and tickets cost ¥2600; for more information contact Coast Ways (☎045/212-5431).

Coming straight **from Narita Airport**, services on JR's **Narita Express** (N'EX) depart roughly every hour for Yokohama Station and take ninety minutes (¥4180); note that not all N'EX trains go to Yokohama and some separate at Tokyo Station, so check before you get on. Otherwise, get on the cheaper rapid train (JR "Airport Narita"), which takes two hours to reach Yokohama Station (¥1890). From **Haneda Airport** a limousine bus is the best option, with frequent departures and only a forty-minute ride into town; the bus drops you at **YCAT** (Yokohama City Air Terminal), in the Sky Building just east of Yokohama Station. Alternatively, take the monorail from Haneda to Hamamatsuchō (see p.85 for details) and then a Keihin-Tōhoku train, a total journey-time of at least one hour.

**Shinkansen** trains from Kyoto, Ōsaka and points south pause briefly at **Shin-Yokohama**, 5km north of the centre. From here there's a subway link to the main Yokohama Station and Kannai, but it's usually quicker to get the first passing JR Yokohama line train – the journey takes between ten and fifteen minutes, depending if you have to change at Higashi-Kanagawa Station.

## Information

Yokohama has five English-speaking "i" **information** centres; the most convenient, but also the busiest, is in the underground concourse of **Yokohama Station** (daily 10am–6pm; ☎045/41-7300). Otherwise, try the booth immediately outside **Sakuragichō Station**'s east entrance (Mon–Thurs & Sun 9am–6pm, Fri, Sat & hols 9am–8pm; ☎045/211-0111), or the harbour-front **Sanbo Centre** east of Kannai Station (Mon–Sat 10am–6pm; ☎045/641-4759). If you're stuck in **Shin-Yokohama Station**, there's an office under the Shinkansen tracks on the northwest side of the main concourse (daily 10am–6pm; ☎045/473-2895), while **YCAT** has English-speaking staff at its arrivals hall desk (daily 9am–5pm; ☎045/459-4880). All these places provide free **city maps** and brochures, including the useful *Yokohama City Guide*, and can help with hotel reservations.

## Getting around

**Getting around** central Yokohama is best done on the JR Negishi line (the local name for Keihin-Tōhoku trains). **Trains** run every five or ten minutes (minimum fare ¥130) between Yokohama, Sakuragichō, Kannai and southerly Ishikawachō stations, each within walking distance of selected sights. A single **subway** line connects Kannai with stations north to Shin-Yokohama, but it's more expensive and usually slower than regular trains; services run every five to fifteen minutes and the minimum fare is ¥180. The most enjoyable way of moving about the city, and sightseeing at the same time, is on one of the *Sea-Bass* **ferries** which shuttle between Yokohama Station (from beside Sogō department store) and southerly Yamashita-kōen via Minato Mirai 21. There are departures every twenty minutes (10am–7pm), with one-way tickets costing ¥600 for the full fifteen-minute journey, or ¥340 to MM21. From Yamashita-kōen you can also join the *Marine Shuttle* for a variety of **sightseeing cruises** round the harbour; prices start at ¥900 for forty minutes.

# Accommodation

Yokohama's new luxury **hotels**, all located in MM21, are a tourist attraction in their own right. Facilities at this level are on a par with Tokyo and, if you've got the money to spend, you'll need a reservation at the weekend, though weekdays should be no problem. Lower down the scale, there a few reasonable business hotels scattered round the city centre, but very little in the way budget accommodation.

**Echigoya Ryokan**, 1-14 Ishikawachō, Naka-ku (☎045/641-4700, fax 641-8815). Conveniently located on the chic Motomachi shopping street, east of Ishikawachō Station, this homely ryokan is one of the few budget places in central Yokohama. The fourteen *tatami* rooms are basic and a bit worn, but the friendly landlord can speak a little English. Look out for an inconspicuous sign on the second floor, next to *Vie de France* bakery. No meals are served. ④.

**Kanagawa Youth Hostel**, 1 Momijigaoka, Nishi-ku (☎045/241-6503). Aged and overpriced, this isn't the most appealing youth hostel, but its dormitory beds are the cheapest option in town. From the west exit of Sakuragichō Station walk north along the tracks, past graffiti-spattered wall, and take the first left after the Jomo gas stand, over a small bridge and uphill. ①.

**Hotel New Grand**, 10 Yamashitachō, Naka-ku (☎045/681-1841, fax 681-1895). Built in the late 1920s in European style, the main building retains some of its original elegance and rooms are slightly cheaper than in the new tower. All come with satellite TV and en-suite bath, and many have harbour views. There's a small roof-top pool and a choice of restaurants. ⑧.

**Pan Pacific Hotel**, 2-3-7 Minato Mirai, Nishi-ku (☎045/682-2222, toll free ☎0120–884522, fax 045/682-2223). The new *Pan Pacific* has caused quite a stir with its bold interior decoration, from the lobby's startling fresco to a palm-tree-filled Italian restaurant. The rooms are less dazzling, but nicely done, some with tiny balconies and night-time views. There's a fitness centre, with indoor pool, a child care centre and good restaurants. Ask about special weekday rates. ⑧.

**Royal Park Hotel Nikkō** (or the *Nikkō Hotel*), 2-2-1-3 Minato Mirai, Nishi-ku (☎045/221-1133, fax 224-5153). The gargantuan Landmark Tower houses the *Nikkō*'s guestrooms on its 52nd to 67th floors, so spectacular views are guaranteed. The rooms are spacious and elegant, with a separate bath and shower cubicle. As well as a fitness club (¥5000) and swimming pool on the 49th floor, facilities include a tea ceremony room (¥1000), Sky Lounge bar (70F) and French, Chinese or Japanese restaurants. The hotel's lobby entrance is opposite the Nippon-maru training ship. Again, weekday packages are often available. ⑨.

**San-ai Yokohama Hotel**, 3-95 Hanasakichō, Naka-ku (☎045/242-4411, fax 242-7485). Popular mid-range business hotel, to the west of Sakuragichō Station, where reservations are a must. The rooms – in Japanese or Western style – are a bit dowdy but a decent size, all with en-suite bathrooms. The hotel's located one block before the Youth Hostel (see above), and English is spoken. ⑤.

**Star Hotel**, 11 Yamashitachō, Naka-ku (☎045/651-3111, fax 651-3119). Right on the seafront, this revamped hotel offers good value for money in Yokohama terms. The bright, fresh décor compensates for smallish rooms at the cheaper end, though all have bathrooms, fridge, TV and phone. Or upgrade for extra space and harbour views. ⑤.

**Washington Hotel**, 5-53 Chōjamachi, Naka-ku (☎045/243-7111, fax 253-7731). A recent addition to the *Washington* chain, with rooms a touch more spacious than usual. Five minutes' walk west of Kannai Station, or take the subway to Isezaki-Chōjamachi Station. ⑤–⑥.

# The City

Though much of Yokohama was destroyed in the 1923 earthquake and again in bombing raids during World War II, it retains a few European-style buildings from its days as a treaty port, some of which lie scattered around **Kannai**, the traditional city centre. For a more evocative atmosphere, climb up to **Yamate** (or the Bluff), a genteel residential area of clapboard houses, tennis clubs and church spires on the southern hills. **Chinatown**, back down on the levels, makes for a lively contrast with its hoards of colourful trinket shops and bustling restaurants. From here it's a short stroll down to **the harbour-front** Marine Tower and a couple of nearby museums, or a train ride north to where the aptly named **Landmark Tower**, Japan's tallest building, pinpoints the futuristic **Minato Mirai 21** (MM21) development. Among its gleaming hotels, shopping malls and conference centres, there are a couple of specific sights, notably a modern art museum and an incongruous four-masted barque, the Nippon-maru. All these central sights can be covered in an easy day's outing; in the account below we start with Yokohama's southern districts and head north.

## Motomachi and Yamate

South of central Yokohama, the JR Negishi line stops at **Ishikawachō Station** before plunging into a series of tunnels beneath Yamate hill. Take the station's southeastern exit to find **Motomachi**, a fashionable shopping street from pre-war days which used to serve the city's expatriate community and still exudes a distinctively European flavour – albeit of the mock-Tudor variety. Today the narrow lane of small shops, selling foreign brand names, imported books and exotic foodstuffs, still draws the punters, particularly on Sundays and holidays when it's turned over to pedestrians; note that many stores close on Monday.

At the east end of Motomachi a wooded promontory marks the beginning of **Harbour View Park**; take any of the paths going uphill to find the lookout point where the British and French barracks once stood – the panoramic view of the harbour and its graceful Bay Bridge is particularly beautiful at night. Turning inland and walking through the park will bring you to the **Foreigners' Cemetery** on the western hillside. Over 4500 people from more than forty countries are buried here, the vast majority either British or American. Wandering among the crosses and sculpted angels, look out for Edward Morel, chief engineer on the Yokohama–Tokyo railway who died of TB at the age of thirty, and Charles Richardson, a British merchant whose murder in 1862 provoked a war between Britain and the Satsuma clan (see p.710). You'll also find more modern tombstones – an average of twenty foreigners a year are still buried on Yamate.

Heading south along the cemetery's eastern perimeter, you'll pass a handsome row of houses, including the turreted *Yamate Jūbankan* – a French restaurant (see p.221) – and the city's oldest wooden building, next door. The latter, erected in 1909 for a wealthy Japanese family, now houses the **Yamate Museum** (daily 11am–4pm; ¥200), most interesting for its collection of cartoons from *Japan Punch*, a satirical magazine published in Yokohama for a while in the late nineteenth century. Just beyond, the square tower of **Christ Church**, founded in 1862 but rebuilt most recently in 1947, adds a village-green touch to the neighbourhood, which is still a popular residential district for Yokohama's expatriate community.

## Down to the harbour

From the cemetery, drop down through Motomachi-kōen and cross Motomachi shopping street to find one of the several entrance gates to **Chinatown**. Founded in 1863, Yokohama's Chinatown is the largest in Japan; its streets contain roughly two hundred restaurants and over 350 shops, while some thirteen million tourists pass through its narrow byways every year to browse among stores peddling Chinese herbs or cooking utensils, and grocers, silk shops and jewellers with windows full of flashy gold. Few leave without tasting what's on offer, from steaming savoury dumplings to a full-blown meal in one of the famous speciality restaurants (see Eating, p.220).

The fortunes of the Chinese community based here (around 2500 ethnic Chinese) have followed the vagaries of mainland history: during the late nineteenth and early twentieth centuries hundreds of radicals – most famously Sun Yat-sen and Chiang Kai-shek – sought refuge here, while Communist and Nationalist factions polarized Chinatown in the 1940s and later during the Cultural Revolution. The focus of community life is **Kantei-byō** (daily 10am–8pm; free), a shrine dedicated to Guan Yu, the God of War and guardian deity of Chinatown. The building is a bit cramped but impressive nonetheless, with a colourful ornamental gateway and writhing dragons wherever you look. Inside, a long-haired Guan Yu sits on the main altar, gazing over the heads of supplicants petitioning for health and prosperity. The best times to visit are during the major festivities surrounding Chinese New Year (late January or early February) and Chinese National Day (October 1).

From the eastern edge of Chinatown it's a short hop down to the harbour – aim for the pink-grey **Marine Tower** (daily 10am–9pm; Jan & Dec 10am–7pm; ¥700; joint ticket with Hikawa-maru ¥1300, or ¥1550 including the Doll Museum). The 106-metre-high tower, built in 1961 to celebrate the port's centenary, is supposedly the world's tallest lighthouse, but better to save your money for the Landmark's observation deck. In front of the tower there's a seafront park, an expanse of concrete interspersed with flower beds, known as **Yamashita-kōen** which was created as a memorial to victims of the Great Earthquake. Here you can pick up a *Sea Bass* ferry (see p.215) or take a harbour cruise from the pier beside the **Hikawa-maru** (Mon–Thurs 9.30am–9pm; Fri, Sat & Sun 9.30am–8/9pm; ¥800), a retired passenger liner. The vessel, also known as the "Queen of the Pacific" was built in 1930 for the NYK Line Yokohama–Seattle service, though it was commandeered as a hospital ship during the war. It now serves as a "floating amusement ship" whose best feature is a small museum full of nostalgic memorabilia from the days of the great ocean-going liners.

At the south end of Yamashita-kōen, the **Doll Museum** (Tues–Sun 10am–5pm; July & Aug 10am–7pm; ¥300) offers a more diverting display of dolls from around the world. Unfortunately there's little information in English, but the vast collection of Japanese folk and classical dolls is worth a look. Don't miss the exquisite, ceremonial *hina* dolls which are traditionally displayed on March 3 during the *Hina Matsuri*, or Doll Festival.

## North to Sakuragichū

Yokohama's rapid growth in the late nineteenth century was underpinned by a flourishing export trade in raw silk. You can check out the practical aspects of silk production, from mulberry leaves to gorgeously coloured kimono at the **Silk Museum**, at the north end of Yamashita-kōen (Tues–Sun 9am–4.30pm; ¥300).

Continuing north across a leafy square, you'll come to a modern, windowless building which houses the **Yokohama Archives of History** (Tues–Sun 9.30–5pm; ¥200). This is the best of the city's historical museums, thanks to an unusual amount of English translation. The museum itself details the opening of Yokohama, and Japan, after 1853 through an impressive collection of photos, artefacts and documents, including contemporary newspaper reports from London.

You're now in the thick of Yokohama's administrative district, where several European-style facades still survive. Kanagawa Government offices occupy the next block north, while the biscuit-coloured **Customs House**, opposite, is a more attractive structure topped by a distinguished, copper-clad dome. Or follow the road heading inland, Minato Ōdōri, to find the graceful **Port Opening Memorial Hall**; erected in 1918, this red-brick Neo-Renaissance building now serves as public function rooms. In front of the hall, turn north again, onto Honchō-dōri, to reach the last and most ornate of Yokohama's Western-style facades. The building was completed in 1904 as the headquarters of a Yokohama Bank, and then later converted into the **Kanagawa Prefectural Museum** (Tues–Sun 9.30am–5pm; ¥300). Unfortunately, the exhibition itself is a missable affair, dealing primarily with local archeology and natural history.

The museum sits near the junction of Honchō-dōri and **Bashamichi**. This tree-lined shopping street, once the showcase of Yokohama and much vaunted in the tourist literature for its old-fashioned street lamps and red-brick paving, is somewhat disappointing. Bashamichi heads west across the train tracks near Kannai Station and then continues as a pedestrianized shopping mall called **Isezakichō**. Otherwise, follow Honchō-dōri north over a bridge for five hundred meters to **Sakuragichō Station**.

## Minato Mirai 21 (MM21)

In a bid to beat Tokyo at its own game, Yokohama now boasts Japan's tallest building and is in the process of creating a non-stop, high-tech international city of the twenty-first century. **Minato Mirai 21**, or MM21 as the development is better known, is rapidly changing the face of Yokohama. A mini-city of hotels, apartment blocks, offices and cultural facilities will eventually occupy nearly two hundred hectares of reclaimed land and disused dockyards, with its own subway line and state-of-the-art waste disposal and heating systems. Most of the hotels and some of the conference facilities, shopping malls and museums are already in place, but the unfilled building plots behind suggest that it won't meet its millennium deadline.

At present access to MM21 is via Sakuragichō train and subway station, from where a covered moving walkway whisks you towards the awesome, 296-metre-tall **Landmark Tower**. Inside, take the world's fastest lift for an ear-popping, forty-second ride up to the 69th-floor **Sky Garden** (Mon–Fri & Sun 10am–9pm, Sat & July–Sept 10am–10pm; ¥1000). On clear days when Fuji is flaunting her beauty, superb views more than justify the observatory's steep entry fee. Alternatively, if you don't mind missing the thrill of the elevator, you can enjoy an all-inclusive set tea – cake and tea or coffee, plus views (daily 11.30am–5pm; ¥1300) – for only a little more in the opulent *Sirius Sky Lounge* on the 70th floor of the *Nikkō Hotel*, or splash out on an early evening cocktail as the city lights spread their magic.

Next door, the **Landmark Plaza** consists of a swanky shopping mall around a five-storey-high atrium. Here you'll find flash boutiques, Yurindo bookstore – with an excellent foreign language section – and plenty of restaurants and coffee shops, some of which are built into the stone walls of an old dry dock.

Another, water-filled dock in front of Landmark Tower, is now home to the sleek **Nippon-maru** sail training ship, part of the enjoyable **Yokohama Maritime Museum** (Tues–Sun 10am–4.30/5pm, July & Aug 10am–6.30pm; ¥600). The *Nippon-maru* was built in 1930 and served up until 1984, during which time she sailed the equivalent of 45 times round the world; when her pristine white sails are hoisted twice monthly, it's clear why she's more familiarly known as the "Swan of the Pacific". You can explore the entire vessel, from the engine room to the captain's wood-panelled cabin. There's copious English labelling and alternating Japanese and English commentary over the loud-speakers.

The museum's main exhibition rooms occupy a purpose-built, underground hall beside the ship. In addition to well-designed coverage of Yokohama's historical development, there's also a lot about the modern port and the technical side of sailing, though little in English. Nevertheless, you can still test your navigational skills at a mock-up bridge with a simulator, or have a bash at unloading a container vessel.

Landmark Tower stands in the extreme south of MM21. Off to the east, the stepped towers of **Queen's Square**, another huge complex, and the sail-shaped Intercontinental Hotel fill the skyline. More inviting is the slowly revolving **Cosmo Clock 21** (¥600) standing in the foreground. At 105m this is the world's tallest Ferris wheel; one circuit takes fifteen minutes, allowing plenty of time to admire the view. It's inside a small amusement park called **Cosmo World** (Tues–Fri 1–9pm, Sat, Sun hols 11am–10pm; separate tickets for each attraction).

Two of MM21's projected museums are already open for business in the blocks immediately north of Landmark Tower. Head first for the splendid **Yokohama Museum of Art** (daily except Thurs 10am–6pm; ¥500; varying prices for special exhibitions) in which mostly twentieth-century Japanese and Western art is set off to fine effect by designer Tange Kenzō's cool, grey space. In fact, the architecture – particularly the magnificent central atrium – grabs your attention as much as the exhibits. The photography galleries are always worth checking out, while other highlights include the Art Library, containing international art and design publications, and the delightful Children's Workshop, unfortunately only for those under twelve years old.

Kids will also be in their element at the **Mitsubishi Minato Mirai Industrial Museum** (Tues–Sun 10am–5.30pm; ¥600) in the neighbouring block. The museum's five well-laid-out zones illustrate technological developments, from today's power generators, oil platforms and deep-sea probes to the space stations of tomorrow. There are plenty of models and interactive displays, with English-speaking staff on hand if needed, but the biggest draw is the Sky-Walk Adventure up on the second floor. At one time kids were queuing round the block to have a ride in this helicopter simulator, though on weekdays it's now usually pretty clear. After a two-minute flying lesson, you get to take the "real" chopper swooping and soaring over Fuji or down into the Grand Canyon for a stomach-wrenching fifteen-minute ride.

### Around Yokohama Station

Apart from one small but important art museum, there's not a great deal to see around **Yokohama Station**. However, this is the city's prime centre for department stores: Mitsukoshi, Takashimaya and Joinus vie for shoppers on the station's west side, above a warren of underground arcades known as "The Diamond"; over to the east, on the other hand, the Sogō and Luminè stores lord it over "Porta" underground mall. This east side is also home to the city's Central Post Office and to Yokohama City Air Terminal, while *Sea Bass* ferries for MM21 and Yamashita-kōen depart from a pier behind Sogō (see p.215 for details).

If you're not here to shop or catch a train, the area's only real attraction is located on Sogō's sixth floor. Though it may seem an expensive option, the one room **Hiraki Ukiyo-e Museum** (daily except Tues 10am–5.30pm; ¥500) houses one of Japan's most highly rated collections of woodblock prints. Unfortunately, only a small portion of the museum's 8000 *ukiyo-e* can be displayed during each month-long exhibition. Nevertheless, all the great woodblock artists are represented and there's usually something to capture the imagination of any art enthusiast.

## Eating and drinking

Most visitors to Yokohama head straight for Chinatown to eat, but there are also Indian, French, Sri Lankan and American **restaurants** to choose from, as well as plenty of Japanese. All the major department stores have a restaurant floor, of which Sogo's has the best choice, while shopping malls such as Landmark Plaza and Porta are also happy hunting grounds. Though less boisterous than when the American GIs were passing through town on their way to the Vietnam War in the 1960s, Yokohama has no shortage of lively drinking holes. The area around Chinatown and across to Kannai Station is a good place to trawl for **bars**. Summer brings the **beer gardens**: both Luminè department store (near Yokohama Station) and the *Star Hotel* (see Accommodation p.216) sport the rooftop variety, or there's a real garden outside Yamate Jūbankan (see opposite).

### Eating

**Colombo**, 2F, 2-88-1 Motomachi. Watch the world go by from this breezy, café-style Sri Lankan restaurant just off Motomachi shopping street. Weekday lunches represent the best deal; otherwise reckon on at least ¥2000 per head for a good feast. 11.30am–10/11pm. Closed Thurs.

**Garlic Jo's**, 107 Yamashitachō. Cheerful restaurant festooned with garlic and peppers – no guesses as to the favoured ingredients. The food is mainly Western style, from pizza to chorrizo fondue, and there's a good choice of vegetarian dishes. Closed Mon.

**Hard Rock Café**, Queen's Tower A, 1F, 2-3-1 Minato Mirai. The rock and burger chain has hit Yokohama with its lively cross between a bar and a restaurant. Also does salads, sandwiches and daily lunchtime specials. Mon–Thurs 11.30am–2am, Fri & Sat till 4am, Sun & hols till 11.30pm.

**Heichinrou**, 149 Yamashitachō (☎045/681-3001). It's best to book at this large, popular Cantonese institution which has good-value, weekday lunch deals for under ¥2000, and does *dim sum* sets from ¥600 per plate (up to 4.30pm). Evening menus start at ¥5500. Open daily 10am–10pm.

**Manchinrou**, 153 Yamashitachō (☎0120–284004). Another famous old name, this time serving Guangdong cuisine. Choose carefully and eating here need not break the bank, with noodle and fried rice dishes starting at around ¥1000, though course menus (from ¥4500) are less affordable. English spoken. Open daily 11am–10pm.

**Peking Hanten**, 79-5 Yamashitachō. Right beside Chinatown's eastern gate, this highly decorated Beijing restaurant is unmissable. However, it's fairly low-key inside, and has well-priced lunchtime menus (¥1500). Their late opening hours and English menu are also plus points. Open daily 11.30am–2pm.

**Rikyuan**, 2-17 Masago-chō. Traditional soba joint tucked down a backstreet, two blocks east of Kannai Station. Dishes include tempura as well as the standard varieties of soba and udon; prices start at around ¥800. Open 11am–8.30pm, closed Sun.

**Royal Food Court**, 5F, Landmark Tower, 2-2-1-3 Minato Mirai. A selection of self-service fast-food restaurants – Italian, Chinese, salad bars, curry rice – around a central seating area. It's better than it sounds, and perfect for a group with different tastes. Open daily 8.30am–10pm.

**Shei Shei**, 138 Yamashitachō. Casual Szechuan restaurant serving an excellent-value set lunch (¥500) or choose from their picture menu. There are only a handful of tables, so at busy times you'll be asked to share.

**Taj Mahal**, 3F, 1-15 Ishikawachō. Unpretentious Indian serving a great buffet lunch on weekdays for around ¥1000, or a slightly more expensive thali lunch at weekends. In the evening there's a reasonable dinner set (¥2500). Open daily 11.30am–3pm & 5–10pm.

**Yamate Jūbankan**, 247 Yamatechō. Pleasant French restaurant in a pretty clapboard house opposite the Foreigners' Cemetery. There's a proper restaurant upstairs and a less formal dining area on the ground floor, where you can snack on a sandwich or croque, or have the set lunch (¥3000). In July and August they run a popular beer garden. Open daily 11am–9pm.

## Drinking

**Cape Cod**, 1-4-2 Tokiwachō. Relaxed, spit-and-sawdust bar with an international crowd and reasonable prices, especially for big beer drinkers (a 1.8-litre pitcher costs ¥2000). They can rustle up cheapish bar snacks and there's also a darts board. 5pm–1am, closes midnight on Sun.

**Missions to Seamen**, 3F, New Port Building, 194 Yamashitachō. Though catering primarily to visiting sailors, everyone is welcome to sup on some of Yokohama's cheapest beer or take a turn at one of Japan's oldest-surviving snooker tables (¥300 for 30min); naturally, things can get nicely rowdy at times. Mon–Sat 11am–11pm, Sun from 5pm.

**The Tavern**, 4F, 214 Yamashitachō. Traditional English pub with British beers, darts and home-made food, including a popular Sunday roast. Open 6pm–late.

**Windjammer**, 215 Yamashitachō. Another expat haunt which crosses between cocktail lounge (with a list as long as your arm) and restaurant serving a mix of Japanese and Western dishes. Occasional live jazz. Mon–Sat 7pm–5am, Sun 6pm–midnight.

## Listings

**Banks and exchange** The area east of Kannai Station is where you'll find branches of major banks with foreign exchange facilities; try along Kannai Ōdōri and Honchō-dōri. The World Currency Shop (10am–7pm; closed 2nd Sun & 3rd Fri of the month) can change travellers' cheques and cash outside normal banking hours; find it in B2 of Sogō department store, near the exit to Yokohama Station.

**Buses** Most long-distance and night buses leave from two terminals either side of Yokohama Station. Nearby, YCAT is the departure point for limousine buses for Haneda and Narita airports.

**Emergencies** For information about emergency medical care, call the 24-hour helpline on ☎045/201-1199, but have a Japanese speaker on hand. For more advice on what to do in an emergency, see Basics, p.70.

**Festivals** The lunar new year (late Jan or early Feb) and China's National Day (Oct 1) are celebrated in style with lion dances around the streets of Chinatown. On July 20 the city puts on a dramatic fireworks display (*hanabi taikai*) over the harbour, while late September sees a huge lantern parade as part of Yokohama Carnival. For music lovers, jazz fills the air in mid-October and in recent Augusts the WOMAD festival has brought World Music to MM21, though it's not yet a permanent event.

**Post offices** The city's Central Post Office is located on the east side of Yokohama Station. However, the main office for international mail, including a poste restante service, is Yokohama Port Post Office (5-3 Nihon-Ōdōri, Naka-ku) near Kannai Station.

# Around Yokohama

A short bus ride south from Yokohama will bring you to Negishi, and the traditionally Japanese lakes and winding pathways of **Sankei-en**. It's well worth devoting half a day to exploring this large stroll-garden with its historic tea arbours, aristocratic residences and farmhouses. Heading north towards Tokyo, make some time for **Shin-Yokohama**, with its delightfully quirky museum dedicated to noodles.

## Sankei-en

In the late-nineteenth century a wealthy silk merchant, Hara Tomitaro, established his residence in sculptured parkland on Yokohama's southern hills and filled it with rare and beautiful buildings from Kamakura and the Kansai region. Today **Sankei-en** (daily: outer garden 9am–5pm, inner garden 9am–4.30pm; ¥300 each) is divided into an outer garden and a smaller inner core, where most of the famous structures are located. To reach Sankei-en, take bus #8 from Yokohama or Sakuragichō stations to Honmoku Sankeien-mae, from where the garden is a three-minute walk, or hop on a JR Negishi-line train to Negishi Station and then a bus as far as the Honmoku stop, 600m north of the main gate.

From the gate follow the well-marked route to the **inner garden**, where Rinshunkaku, an elegant, lakeside mansion built for one of the Tokugawa lords in 1649, is the only structure of its kind still in existence. Another Tokugawa legacy, dating from 1623, sits beside a picturesque stream a few minutes further on; named Choshukaku, it originally served as a tea ceremony house in the grounds of Kyoto's Nijō Castle (see p.437). Tenju-in may not be as famous, but it's worth walking up beside the stream to see its fine carving. This little seventeenth-century temple dedicated to Jizō, the guardian deity of children, hails from Kamakura.

In the less formal **outer garden**, thatched farm roofs blend with bamboo thickets and groves of twisted plum trees, above which rises a graceful three-tiered pagoda. The most interesting building here is Old Yanohara House (¥100), the former home of a wealthy farmer, where you can take a close look at the vast roof built in *gassho* style – no nails but plenty of rope. Don't bother climbing up the hill to Shofukaku: the concrete viewing platform has great views of billowing chimney stacks and industrial dockyards.

## Shin-Yokohama

Even if you're not a noodle fan, it's worth making the trek to Shin-Yokohama – on the subway or JR Yokohama line – to visit the **Ramen Museum** (daily except Tues 11am–11pm; restaurant to 9.45pm; ¥300). This well-designed museum-cum-restaurant is devoted to Japan's most popular fast food, in its most basic form a noodle soup garnished with roast pork, bamboo shoots and dried seaweed. It's five minutes' walk northeast of Shin-Yokohama Station; walk straight ahead, to the left of the NTT Building, to the second set of traffic lights, then turn right and first left.

The museum's first-floor hall delves into the roots of ramen, tracing them back to southern China, and then chronicles the moment in 1958 when instant ramen – chicken flavoured – was launched on the world, followed in 1971 by cup noodles. There are some mind-boggling statistics: as a taster, in 1993 the world consumed an estimated 22.1 billion bowls of ramen.

Once you've digested all of that, head for the basement, where you're transported into 1950s downtown Japan. Below you lies a city square at dusk: lights are coming in the shops and *pachinko* parlours, as vendors call out their wares under grimy film posters. Walk round the mezzanine's dingy alley, complete with bars and an old-fashioned sweet-shop, before heading down into the courtyard where each storefront hides a restaurant from Japan's most famous ramen regions. The local variety are available in the Beauty Salon, while other stalls specialize in ramen from Fukuoka, Sapporo, Kumamoto or Tokyo; buy a ticket (from around ¥800) at the machine – ask for help as it's all in Japanese – and then join the slurping throng at tables in the courtyard. Note that there's no smoking except in the bars on the mezzanine floor, and it's best to avoid the crowds at lunchtimes and weekends.

## travel details

### Trains

The trains between the major cities listed below are the fastest, direct services. There are also frequent slower services, run by JR and several private companies, covering the same destinations. It is usually possible, especially on long-distance routes, to get there faster by changing between services.

**Atami** to: Kyoto (15 daily; 2hr 20min–3hr 20min); Shimoda (every 30min; 1hr 30min); Tokyo (every 10min; 35min–2hr 10min).

**Enoshima** to: Tokyo (Shinjuku Station) (every 30min; 1hr 15min).

**Hakone-Yumoto** to: Shinjuku (23 daily; 1hr 30min)

**Kamakura** to Enoshima (every 10–15min; 20min); Tokyo (every 10–20min; 55min).

**Narita** to: Tokyo (every 30min; 1hr); Ueno (every 30min; 1hr).

**Nikkō** to: Asakusa (14 daily; 1hr 50min).

**Shimoda** to: Rendaiji (every 20min; 4min); Tokyo (every 20min; 2hr 40min–3hr 30min).

**Shuzenji** to: Mishima (every 20min; 25min–30min); Tokyo (3 daily; 2hr 10min).

**Yokohama** to: Tokyo (every 5–10min; 30–40min); Tokyo (Shibuya Station) (every 5min; 40min); Kamakura (every 10–20min; 25min).

### Buses

The buses listed below are mainly long-distance services – often travelling overnight – between the major cities, and local services where there is no alternative means of transport. For shorter journeys, however, trains are almost invariably quicker and often no more expensive.

**Dōgashima** to: Irō-zaki (3 daily; 1hr 30min–1hr 50min); Matsuzaki (every 20min; 10min), Shuzenji (every 30min; 1hr 35min); Toi (every 30min; 40min).

**Fuji Go-gōme** to: Shinjuku (3 daily; 2hr 25min).

**Fuji-Yoshida** to: Fuji Go-gōme (at least 4 daily; 55min), Shinjuku (16 daily; 1hr 45min)

**Heda** to: Shuzenji (5 daily; 1hr).

**Kawaguchi-ko** to: Shinjuku (16 daily; 2hr).

**Shimoda** to: Dōgashima (hourly; 1hr); Irō-zaki (every 30min; 35–50min); Matsuzaki (hourly; 50min); Shuzenji (1 daily; 2hr).

**Toi** to: Heda (6 daily; 35min); Shuzenji (hourly; 50min).

**Yokohama** to: Hirosaki (daily; 10hr); Hiroshima (1 daily; 12hr); Ōsaka (2 daily; 8hr); Nagoya (daily; 5hr 30min).

### Ferries

**Dōgashima** to: Numazu (3–5 daily; 1hr 5min–1hr 25min).

**Toi** to: Tagonoura-kō (3–7 daily; 1hr 20min).

CHAPTER THREE

# NORTHERN HONSHŪ

When the famous poet Matsuo Bashō set out on his travels along the "narrow road to the deep north" in 1689 he commented, somewhat despondently, "I might as well be going to the ends of the earth". Even today many urban Japanese regard the harsh, mountainous provinces of **NORTHERN HONSHŪ** as irredeemably backward. Not that it's all thatched farmhouses and timeless agricultural vistas, but certainly the rural traditions have survived here longer than in most other parts of the country. However, it doesn't take long to discover the region's particularly vibrant **crafts** industry and huge array of **festivals**. Nor do you have to delve much deeper to find the rich heritage of folktales and evidence of ancient religious practices which give parts of north Honshū a deliciously mysterious tang.

Northern Honshū, or Tōhoku as it's often called (encompassing the six prefectures covered here with the exception of Niigata), was the last part of Japan's main island to be brought under central control. As such, it boasts more in the way of military sights – ruined castles, *samurai* towns and aristocratic tombs – than great temples or religious foundations. The one glorious exception is **Hiraizumi**, a seemingly insignificant town north of Sendai, whose opulent Golden Hall (Konjiki-dō) is the highlight of any tour round this region. By way of contrast, perhaps the archetypal north-country town lies not far away, at **Tōno**. It's often referred to as the birthplace of Japanese folklore, where goblin-like *kappa* inhabit local rivers and fairy-children scamper through old farmhouses. Much of this is heavily commercialized, but it's still worth devoting a couple of days to exploring Tōno's more secretive shrines with their references to primitive cults. Darker forces are also at work much further north where souls in purgatory haunt **Osore-zan**'s volcanic wasteland on the hammer-head Shimokita Hantō. In summer, pilgrims come here to consult blind mediums, while over on the west coast, the holy mountain of **Dewa-sanzan** is home to *yamabushi*, ascetic priests who are similarly endowed with mystical powers.

The region is also defined by its splendid **scenery**, ranging from prolific rice-fields and cosseted orchards to the wild, rugged coastline, and the pine-crusted islands of **Matsushima Bay**. The central spine of magnificent, empty mountains provides excellent opportunities for hiking and skiing, notably around **Bandai-san** in the south and

## ACCOMMODATION PRICE CODES

All accommodation in this book has been graded according to the following price codes, which refer to the cheapest double or twin room available for most of the year, and include taxes. Note that rates may increase during peak holiday periods, in particular around Christmas and New Year, the Golden Week (April 28–May 6) and Obon (the week around August 15), when accommodation is very difficult to get without an advance reservation. In the case of hostels providing dormitory accommodation, the code refers to the charge per bed. See p.36 for more details on accommodation.

| | | |
|---|---|---|
| ① under ¥3000 | ④ ¥7000–10,000 | ⑦ ¥20,000–30,000 |
| ② ¥3000–5000 | ⑤ ¥10,000–15,000 | ⑧ ¥30,000–40,000 |
| ③ ¥5000–7000 | ⑥ ¥15,000–20,000 | ⑨ over ¥40,000 |

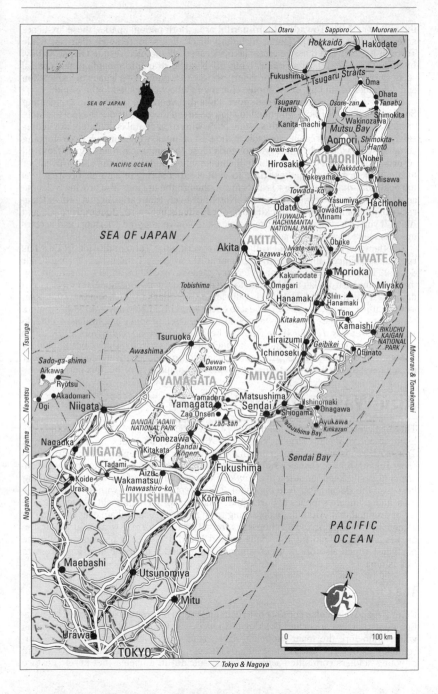

the more northerly **Towada–Hachimantai** area. Both national parks, these areas are noted for their flora and fauna, including black bears in remoter districts, while **Towada-ko** itself is a massive crater-lake accessed via the picturesque **Oirase valley**. In **Sado-ga-shima**, a large island lying off Niigata, dramatic mountain and coastal scenery provides the backdrop for a surprisingly rich culture – a legacy of its isolation and a number of famous, or infamous, characters who were exiled to the island.

Although there are good **transport** links between the main cities, including Shinkansen lines to Tokyo, you need to allow plenty of time to explore the more remote corners of northern Honshū – this is one place where car rental is definitely worth considering. Public buses can be sporadic at the best of times, with many services stopping completely in winter when **heavy snowfalls** close the mountain roads. Apart from ski resorts, many tourist facilities outside the major cities shut down from early November to late April. In general, the **best time to visit** is either spring or autumn, before it gets too busy and while the scenery is at its finest, though the uplands also provide welcome relief from summer's sweltering heat. Note, however, that early August brings thousands of people flocking to Tōhoku's big four **festivals** in Sendai, Aomori, Hirosaki and Akita. If you're travelling at this time, make sure you've got your transport and accommodation sorted out well in advance.

JR offers a variety of **special rail tickets** covering the Tōhoku district. JR East has recently introduced three schemes similar to the regular JR Rail Pass (see p.30 for details). Their four-day, five-day and ten-day passes are valid on all JR trains, including the Shinkansen, from Izu and Nagano to the northern tip of Honshū. Of these, the four-day pass is the most useful since it is valid for any four days within a month, rather than a consecutive period, so you can save it to cover longer train journeys within the region. Note that these passes are only available to tourists and must be purchased outside Japan. The ten-day *Tōhoku Wide Pass* can be bought in Japan and covers all JR trains and buses within the Tōhoku region, including travel from Tokyo but excluding Shinkansen trains. However, the ten days must run consecutively and to get your money's worth you'll have to take a number of long journeys within this period.

# Aizu-Wakamatsu and around

The small, relaxed but rather featureless city of **AIZU-WAKAMATSU** sits in a wide valley near one of Japan's largest lakes, some two and a half hours' train ride north of Tokyo. An important castle-town on what was once the main trunk road north from Edo (now Tokyo), the area's major sights revolve around its warrior past, including a reconstructed castle keep, an attractive *samurai* house and the graves of nineteen young heroes of the Bōshin War (see opposite). The surrounding area, with its mountain climate and abundant supplies of pure water, is famous for its high-quality **sake**. The centre of production is **Kitakata**, a sprawling town north of Aizu-Wakamatsu, where a collection of traditional sake storehouses, *kura*, attest to its former wealth. In winter, the area is popular for **skiing**, especially around **Bandai Kōgen**, a plateau rising to the northeast which also offers great summer hiking and a dramatic bus ride across to Fukushima.

## The City

Central Aizu-Wakamatsu consists of a rectangular grid of streets with the main train station on its northwest corner. Byakko-dōri heads east from the station to Iimori-yama, while Chūō-dōri, the main shopping street, runs south 3km to the castle and surrounding sights. The town's most famous attraction is the **Iimori-yama** where a band of young soldiers committed *seppuku* (ritual suicide) in a useless but heroic gesture

AIZU-WAKAMATSU
& BANDAI KŌGEN

during one of the last battles of the Meiji Restoration. After a brief visit to their graves, head for the southern district where you'll find a beautiful replica of a *samurai* house, **Buké-yashiki**, and the reconstructed castle keep, **Tsuruga-jō**. Nearby, there's also a herb garden, an old sake brewery and a moderately interesting museum. Though it's possible to cover all these sights on foot in a long day, it's worth taking a few bus rides or renting a bike (see p.229 for details).

### Iimori-yama

A quick climb up **Iimori-yama** is a good way to get your bearings, taking in views of the town as you scale the hill's steep staircases or ride the handy escalator (Mar–Nov daily 8am–5pm; ¥250). At the top, an imperial eagle – a gift of the Italian Fascist Party in 1928 – dominates the small clearing and underlines some of the more disturbing aspects of local history, whose main focus is the line of **Byakkotai graves** over to the left. During the **Bōshin War**, a series of skirmishes surrounding the Meiji Restoration in 1868, the warriors of Aizu-Wakamatsu were among the few clans to put up serious opposition to the imperial armies. The Byakkotai (White Tigers) were one of several bands of young fanatics who joined the fighting and, in one of the final battles, a group of twenty Byakkotai, aged 16 and 17 years old, were cut off from their comrades. Trying to reach the safety of the castle, they climbed Iimori-yama, only to see Tsuruga-jō apparently in flames. Assuming the battle was lost, they did what all good *samurai* should do and killed themselves by ritual disembowelment, though one boy was saved

| AIZU-WAKAMATSU AND AROUND | | |
|---|---|---|
| **Aizu-Wakamatsu** | *Aizu-Wakamatsu* | 会津若松 |
| Aizu Sake History Museum | *Aizu Shuzō Rekishikan* | 会津酒造歴史館 |
| Buké-yashiki | *Buké-yashiki* | 武家屋敷 |
| Fukushima Museum | *Fukushima Kenritsu Hakubutsukan* | 福島県立博物館 |
| Iimori-yama | *Iimori-yama* | 飯盛山 |
| Sazae-dō | *Sazae-dō* | さざえ堂 |
| Tsuruga-jō | *Tsuruga-jō* | 鶴ヶ城 |

*ACCOMMODATION AND RESTAURANTS*

| | | |
|---|---|---|
| Aizuno Youth Hostel | *Aizuno Yūsu Hosuteru* | 会津のユースホステル |
| Aizu-no-sato Youth Hostel | *Aizu-no-sato Yūsu Hosuteru* | 会津の里ユースホステル |
| Hotel Alpha One | *Hoteru Arufā Wan* | ホテルアルファーワン |
| Fuji Grand Hotel | *Fuji Gurando Hoteru* | フジグランドホテル |
| Green Hotel Aizu | *Guriin Hoteru Aizu* | グリーンホテル会津 |
| Sasa-no-an | *Sasa-no-an* | 笹乃庵 |
| Takino | *Takino* | 田季野 |
| Washington Hotel | *Washinton Hoteru* | ワシントンホテル |

| | | |
|---|---|---|
| **Kitakata** | *Kitakata* | 喜多方 |
| Genrai-ken | *Genrai-ken* | 源来軒 |
| Mokoto Shokudō | *Mokoto Shokudō* | もこと食堂 |
| Sasaya Ryokan | *Sasaya Ryokan* | 笹屋旅館 |
| Yamatogawa Sake Brewing Museum | *Yamatogawa Shuzō Kitakata Fūdokan* | 大和川酒造北方風土館 |

| | | |
|---|---|---|
| **Bandai Kōgen** | *Bandai Kōgen* | 磐梯高原 |
| Bandai-kōgen-eki | *Bandai-kōgen-eki* | 磐梯高原駅 |
| Goshikinuma-iriguchi | *Goshikinuma-iriguchi* | 五色沼入口 |
| Hotel Goshiki-sō | *Hoteru Goshiki-sō* | ホテル五色荘 |
| Inawashiro | *Inawashiro* | 猪苗代 |
| Urabandai Royal Hotel | *Urabandai Roiyaru Hoteru* | 裏磐梯ロイヤルホテル |
| Urabandai Youth Hostel | *Urabandai Yūsu Hosuteru* | 裏磐梯ユースホステル |

before he bled to death. Although the castle was not burning and the boys' deaths were completely unnecessary, the Byakkotai are revered as heroic role models. Twice a year (April 24 and Sept 24) proud parents watch as local school boys of the same age re-enact the suicides.

Further down the hill, **Sazae-dō** (daily 8.30am–5pm; ¥300) is an attractive antidote. This elegant, octagonal building, erected in 1796 as part of a larger temple complex, is a unique structure, containing two ramps spiralling round a central pillar. Sealed inside the pillar are 33 statues of Kannon, the Goddess of Mercy. At the bottom of the hill, turn left and you'll find a distinctive, white building housing the **Byakkotai Memorial Hall** (April–Nov daily 8am–5pm; Jan–March & Dec daily 8.30am–4.30pm; ¥400), of interest mostly for its portraits of the young soldiers and videos of related television dramas and documentaries.

## Buké-yashiki, Oyaku-en and Tsuruga-jō

From Iimori-yama, follow the by-pass south for 2km and then turn left for **Buké-yashiki** (April–Nov daily 8.30am–5pm; Jan–March & Dec daily 9am–4.30pm; ¥850), a magnificent reproduction of a nineteenth-century *samurai* residence belonging to Saigō

Tanomo, a chief retainer of the Aizu clan. Its 38 rooms range from a sand-box toilet and cypress bath tub to a "classy reception room" reserved for the Lord of Aizu. In 1868 Saigō went off to fight in the Bōshin War, leaving his wife and daughters, aged between 2 and 16 years, at home. As the imperial army closed in, the family decided to commit suicide rather than be taken prisoner; the 16-year-old failed to die immediately but was killed soon after by an enemy soldier, and the house was set on fire. The complex also includes a number of original buildings such as a rice mill and thatched shrine brought from surrounding villages.

Two kilometres west of Buké-yashiki lie the imposing walls of Aizu's castle, but on the way it's worth taking a stroll round **Oyaku-en** (daily 8.30am–5pm; ¥310), a garden famed for its medicinal herbs. Oyaku-en was laid out in 1670 by one of the Aizu lords as a tea-ceremony garden, with rustic arbours and a shallow lake patrolled by ducks and slow, fat carp. Unusually, he devoted a part of the garden to neat rows of around 300 different herbs, such as angelica, lycoris and gentian. You can buy dried herbs and remedies in the garden's gift shop, or take a cup of *matcha* (¥500) in the teahouse.

The north gate of **Tsuruga-jō** stands fifteen minutes' walk southwest of Oyaku-en. Its imposing entrance lies over a moat, between massive stone ramparts, inside which the dainty white keep (daily 8.3am–5pm; closed first week in July & first week in Dec; ¥400) seems rather dwarfed. Originally built in 1384, the castle was besieged by Meiji troops for several months in 1868 before the Aizu clan finally surrendered. After the new government ordered it to be demolished, it lay in ruins until 1965 when the central keep was rebuilt – now housing an uninteresting local history museum – and the gardens were landscaped. The castle is the focus of the city's main **festival** (Sept 22–24) which includes a procession of *samurai* and ceremonies for the Byakkotai (see p.227).

Outside Tsuruga-jō's east gate lies the ultra-modern **Fukushima Museum** (Tues–Sun 9.30am–5pm; ¥260), covering local history from mock-ups of Jōmon-period huts (2000 BC) to a charcoal-driven bus from the 1930s. The displays are well presented, with sufficient English to get the gist of what's going on. Equally interesting is the **Aizu Sake History Museum** (daily 8.30am–5pm; ¥300), five minutes' walk north of the castle gates, in an old wooden building where the Yamaguchi family has been brewing sake for 350 years.

## Practicalities

**From Tokyo**, the quickest way to reach Aizu-Wakamatsu is to take a Shinkansen on the Tōhoku line from either Tokyo or Ueno stations as far as Kōriyama, where you change onto the JR Ban-etsu line. It's a pleasant ride up from Kōriyama, but if you have time a more attractive approach is via the private Tōbu and Aizu lines from Asakusa Station, changing trains at Aizu-Tajima; this route has the added advantage of allowing you to visit Nikkō (see p.170) on the way. If you're coming **from Niigata**, or heading on to the west coast, you have a choice of direct JR Ban-etsu line services, or very slow local trains on the JR Tadami line via Koide and Urasa. This latter option is especially recommended in October when the autumn colours are at their peak.

Aizu-Wakamatsu has two helpful **tourist information centres** with English-speaking staff, one in the train station (daily 10am–5/6pm; ☎0242/32-0688) and the other inside the castle's north gate (daily 8.30am–5.30pm; ☎0242/29-1151).

**City buses** depart from outside the train station every twenty minutes for Buké-yashiki (stand #4), or you can catch loop-line buses (going clockwise or anti-clockwise) from stand #6 to Tsuruga-jō, Buké-yashiki and Iimori-yama. Alternatively, **bike rental** is available at Takahashi Rent-a-cycle, south of the *Washington Hotel* (March–Nov 8am–5pm; ¥1000 per day). If you want to **rent a car**, try Eki Rent-a-car (☎0242/24-5171) or Nissan (☎0242/25-4123), both near the station. You'll find foreign exchange facilities at **banks** on Chūō-dōri, including Fukushima Bank, located about half-way down.

## Accommodation

**Aizuno Youth Hostel**, 88 Kakiyashiki, Terasaki Aizu-Takada-chō (☎ & fax 0242/55-1020). Small, spick and span hostel set among rice-fields, offering bunks, good food and bike rental. You'll find it twenty minutes' walk northwest of Aizu-Takada Station, on the JR Tadami line (20min from Aizu-Wakamatsu Station); walk straight ahead from the station, take the second right and keep going. (Note that services on this line are infrequent.) ②.

**Aizu-no-sato Youth Hostel**, 36 Kofune-hatakata, Aizu-Shiokawa-chō (☎ & fax 0241/27-2054). Homely, slightly aged youth hostel with three *tatami* rooms, run by the genial, English-speaking owner of the next-door liquor store. It's located ten minutes' walk northeast of Shiokawa Station, third stop on the JR Ban-etsu line towards Kitakata (10min from Aizu-Wakamatsu Station). No meals. ①.

**Hotel Alpha One**, 5-8 Ekimae-machi (☎0242/32-6868, fax 32-6822). Smartish business hotel near the station (behind the *Fuji Grand*), offering reasonably sized rooms with TV, phone and a mini bathroom. ⑤.

**Fuji Grand Hotel**, 5-25 Ekimae-machi (☎0242/24-1111, fax 24-3112). The older rooms in this big, busy business hotel are a bit worn, but a touch cheaper than the *Alpha One*. Located right outside the station. ④.

**Green Hotel Aizu**, 3-7-23 Chūō (☎0242/24-5181, fax 24-5182). This small, spruce hotel has a choice of Western or better-value *tatami* rooms. Find it in the backstreets, just south of the *Washington Hotel*. ④.

**Washington Hotel**, 201 Byakko-machi (☎0242/22-6111, fax 24-7535). New hotel on Byakko-dōri, three minutes' walk east of the station. All the standard *Washington* services, including a coffee lounge, bar and restaurants. ⑤.

## Eating

Aizu-Wakamatsu is not that well off for **restaurants**. The best area to head for is along Chūō-dōri and Nanokomachi-dōri, which cuts across it halfway down, or try *Takino* (daily 11am–10pm), tucked into the backstreets southeast of this junction. It's a little tricky to find, but worth it for the beautiful old building and tasty food. The house speciality is *wappa-meshi*, a wooden box of steamed rice with various toppings such as flowering fern (*zenmai*), fish or mushrooms (*kinoko*) depending on the season (from ¥1300, including pickles and soup). Closer to the station, the cheerful *Sasa-no-an* (Tues–Sun 11am–2pm & 5–8pm) serves some of Aizu-Wakamatsu's renowned handmade soba noodles.

# Around Aizu-Wakamatsu

Twenty kilometres north of Aizu-Wakamatsu, the town of **Kitakata** is famed for its sake and for more than two thousand *kura* (traditional storehouses), built in a variety of styles. Some of these once housed a sake brewery is now a museum. Further afield, the lake-spattered plateau of **Bandai Kōgen** is worth exploring, for its gentle nature strolls or a more strenuous hike up Bandai-san, its highest peak.

## Kitakata

In contrast to Aizu-Wakamatsu, **KITAKATA** was always an important commercial centre, producing sake, miso paste, rice and charcoal. At some point, a craze for building **kura** swept through the town until almost everyone had one of these fire-proof storehouses encased in thick, mud walls. Later, they started building brick versions, and today even the post office and other public offices hide behind *kura* facades. It's best to concentrate on the central district where you can visit a **sake brewery** and take in several *kura* on route, but there's no need to devote more than a couple of hours to Kitakata, since the storehouses are now swamped by an otherwise uninteresting, sprawling town.

Trains from Aizu-Wakamatsu (on the JR Ban-etsu line) arrive on the south side of Kitakata, from where it's a twenty-minute walk to the central shopping street, **Chūō-**

**dōri**, where you'll see your first *kura*. Two blocks beyond the *Sasaya Ryokan* (see below), a left turn leads to the **Yamatogawa Sake Brewing Museum** (daily 9am–4.30pm; free). The museum occupies an attractive collection of seven *kura*, where sake was made from 1790 to 1990 before production moved to a new, automated plant. You'll be given a guided tour – a brief English pamphlet should be available – and the opportunity to taste a few samples, though there's no obligation to buy. As you go round, note the globe of cedar fronds hanging in the entrance hall. Traditionally, breweries hang a green cedar ball outside in March when the freshly brewed sake is put in vats to age; by September the browned fronds indicate that it's ready to drink.

*PRACTICALITIES*

You can pick up English-language **maps** of Kitakata at the **tourist office** (daily 8.30am–5pm; ☎0241/24-2633) outside the train station, though the staff don't speak English. **Bike rental** (daily 8am–6pm) is available at the laundry on the northeast side of the station concourse; prices start at ¥250 for an hour, up to ¥1000 per day. Alternatively, in summer you can take a relaxed **tour** of the town in a *kura*-shaped horse-drawn cart which leaves every couple of hours from outside the station (April–Nov; ¥1300).

You're unlikely to want **to stay** in Kitakata, but if you need to, head for the *Sasaya Ryokan* on Chūō-dōri (☎0241/22-0008, fax 22-0238; ④–⑥), in a beautiful old Meiji-era building with its own *kura*. As for food, Kitakata is known for its ramen, with nearly one hundred ramen **restaurants** to choose from. The first to open was the café-style *Genrai-ken* (daily except Tues 10am–8pm), beside the traffic lights at the south end of Chuo-dori. However, *Mokoto Shokudō*, in the backstreets east of Chūō-dōri (Tues–Sun 7.30am–7pm), packs more atmosphere in its old, *tatami* rooms, and also serves other, inexpensive dishes; take a right turn at the brewery museum junction.

## Bandai Kōgen

Northeast of Aizu-Wakamatsu **Bandai-san** rises steeply above Lake Inawashiro, it's wooded flanks shaved here and there for **ski slopes**. In 1888 this previously dormant volcano erupted, blowing a huge hole in its north face and triggering mud flows which dammed the local rivers. In the process, the plateau now known as **Bandai Kōgen** was created. This beautiful area of some 300 lakes and marshes scattered among beech forests is an easy day-trip by bus or car from Aizu-Wakamatsu, or makes a pleasant stop on the spectacular Bandai-Azuma Skyline road (see below) north to Fukushima.

The most popular walk on Bandai-kōgen is the 3.7-kilometre-long **Goshikinuma nature trail**, an easy, woodland romp past a series of lakes tinged various shades of cobalt blue, white and red according to their mineral content. The trail starts at Goshikinuma-iriguchi bus stop, where you can buy maps (¥200) at the **Visitors' Centre** (daily except Wed 8.40am–4pm; ☎0241/32-2850), and then heads roughly west to emerge about an hour later at the bus stop near **Bandai-kōgen-eki**. This hamlet – little more than a collection of hotels and restaurants – lies at the south end of the plateau's largest lake, **Hibara-ko**, and is the starting point for another recommended walk (3.2km) along the lake's eastern shore. It's also the jumping-off point for one of the longer routes up **Bandai-san** (allow around four hours to reach the summit; 1819m), giving spectacular views as you skirt round the red-coloured lake which fills the still-steaming crater. In winter (mid-Dec–March), Bandai-san's deep snow cover provides some excellent **skiing**, and there are numerous resorts in the area. One of the more accessible is *Inawashiro Ski-jō* (☎0242/62-2111), perched above Inawashiro town, with regular bus services from Inawashiro Station (20min).

Several scenic toll roads cut across the Bandai plateau. You'll need your own transport to explore most of these, but between late April and early November public buses run northeast along the **Bandai-Azuma Skyline**. There are two to three buses a day from Bandai-kōgen-eki via Goshikinuma-iriguchi (3hr; ¥2780), and one tour bus from Aizu-Wakamatsu which also includes a cruise on Hibara-ko (7hr 30min; ¥7970). From Bandai Kōgen the road climbs steeply through forests, giving stunning views back to Bandai-san or down to crinkle-cut lakes, before reaching **Jōdodaira**, a high, volcanic wasteland. The buses pause here for thirty minutes, allowing plenty of time to scramble up the tiny, perfect cone of Azuma-Kofuji (Little Fuji). Journey's end is **Fukushima**, from where you can catch a train back to Tokyo or head on north to Yamagata or Sendai.

*PRACTICALITIES*

From Aizu-Wakamatsu the quickest route to Bandai Kōgen is by **train** to Inawashiro Station and then over the road to pick up a **local bus** via Goshikinuma-iriguchi to Bandai-kōgen-eki. Note that the last departure from Inawashiro is 6.10pm, and the last bus down leaves Goshikinuma-iriguchi at around 7.30pm. After that, call ☎0242/32-2950 for a **taxi**.

If you decide to **stay** on the plateau, the best options are all located around Goshikinuma-iriguchi. The slightly dilapidated *Urabandai Youth Hostel* (March–Nov; ☎0241/32-2811, fax 32-2813; [1]) is nicely situated in woodland at the start of the nature trail; to find it turn right by the Red Cross monument. Across the other side of the main road, the new *Resort In* (☎ & fax 0241/32-2155; [5] including meals) is another cheapish option, while two smarter places, both with onsen baths, are the homely *Hotel Goshiki-sō* (☎0241/32-2011, fax 32-2027; [7] including meals), overlooking the first Goshikinuma lake, and the more upmarket *Urabandai Royal* (☎0241/32-3121, fax 32-3130; [7]) across the main road.

# Yamagata and around

Few tourists make it to **YAMAGATA**, a large, workaday city ringed by high mountains, and those that do are usually just passing through. Apart from a couple of engaging museums, Yamagata's prime attraction is as a base for the atmospheric temples of **Yamadera** and **Zaō Onsen**. Zaō-san provides excellent summer hiking, while winter transforms these mountains into one of Japan's top three ski resorts, known for its deep snow and beguiling "snow monsters" – fir trees engulfed in wind-sculpted ice and snow.

## The City

Central Yamagata occupies a grid of streets lying northeast of the train station. Its southern boundary is Ekimae-dōri, a broad avenue leading straight from the station as far as the *Hotel Castle*, from where the main shopping street, Nanokamachi-dōri, strikes north to the former Prefectural Office, one of the city's main sights. The district's west side is bounded by the train tracks and Kajō-kōen, an area of gardens and sports facilities created on the site of Yamagata castle, where there's a moderately interesting Municipal Museum. Pottery enthusiasts might like to wander the picturesque lanes of Hirashimizu village, on Yamagata's southeastern outskirts, and visit some of the workshops clustered in the narrow valley. In early August (5–7) the city turns out for its major **festival**, the *Hanagasa Matsuri*, during which *yukata*-clad women wielding flowery hats perform a slow, graceful dance.

An imposing, European-style building of stone and ornate stucco dominates the north end of Nanokamachi-dōri, some twenty minutes' walk from the station. Originally built in 1911, the interior of this **former Prefectural Office** (Tues–Sun 9am–4.30pm; free) has been magnificently restored, particularly the third floor with its parquet-floored dining room and elegant Assembly Hall. As you walk through, don't forget to

| | | |
|---|---|---|
| **YAMAGATA AND AROUND** | | |
| **Yamagata** | *Yamagata* | 山形 |
| City Museum | *Kyōdokan* | 郷土館 |
| Former Prefectural Office | *Bunshōkan* | 文翔館 |
| Kajō-kōen | *Kajō-kōen* | 霞城公園 |
| Yamakō Building | *Yamakō Biru* | 山交ビル |
| | | |
| *ACCOMMODATION AND EATING* | | |
| Benibana-tei | *Benibana-tei* | べにばな亭 |
| Hotel Castle | *Hoteru Kyassuru* | ホテルキャッスル |
| Green Hotel | *Guriin Hoteru* | グリーンホテル |
| Hotel Metropolitan | *Hoteru Metoroporitan* | ホテルメトロポリタン |
| Sagorō | *Sagorō* | 佐五郎 |
| Sakaeya | *Sakaeya* | さかえや |
| Shiraume | *Shiraume* | 志ら梅 |
| Hotel Yamagata | *Hoteru Yamagata* | ホテル山形 |
| Washington Hotel | *Washinton Hoteru* | ワシントンホテル |
| Yamashiroya Ryokan | *Yamashiroya Ryokan* | 山城屋旅館 |
| | | |
| **Hirashimizu** | *Hirashimizu* | 平清水 |
| Bun'emon-gama | *Bun'emon-gama* | 文右衛門窯 |
| Hcikichi-gama | *Heikichi-gama* | 平吉窯 |
| Seiryūdō | *Seiryūdō* | 清竜堂 |
| Shichiemon-gama | *Shichiemon-gama* | 七右衛門窯 |
| | | |
| **Yamadera** | *Yamadera* | 山寺 |
| | | |
| **Zaō Onsen** | *Zaō Onsen* | 蔵王温泉 |
| Okama | *Okama* | お釜 |
| Zaō Sanroku Ropeway | *Zaō Sanroku Rōpu-uei* | 蔵王山麓ロープウエイ |

look up at the ceilings' spectacular plasterwork – it was all handcrafted by one man at the rate of 15cm per day.

From the Prefectural Office, head southwest to the **Yamagata Art Museum** (Tues–Sun 10am–5pm; ¥500–1000 according to the exhibition) beside the castle walls. This modern museum boasts a small collection of big European names, such as Picasso, Chagall, Renoir and Monet, but unless there's a special exhibition of interest it's not really worth the entrance fee. Instead, cross the train tracks to the entrance to **Kajō-kōen** by its beautifully restored East Gate, the only remnant of the former castle. Inside the park, turn left and you'll come to the **City Museum** (Tues–Sun 9am–4.30pm; ¥200), occupying a delightful, multi-coloured clapboard building. Erected in 1878, the museum originally served as the town's main hospital and its exhibits include a fearsome array of early medical equipment and anatomical drawings, including a guide to pregnancy rendered as woodblock prints. There's also a room devoted to an Austrian, Dr Albert von Roretz, who came here in 1880 and spent two years instructing local doctors in the ways of Western medicine.

Though **Hirashimizu** lies on the city's southeastern outskirts, this pretty little pottery village has a surprisingly rural atmosphere. There's just one main street and a small river running down from the hills which provides local potters with their distinctive, speckled clay. If you poke about a bit, you'll find several family **potteries** with showrooms (daily 9am–5/6pm), such as Shichiemon-gama on the left at the top of the main street, just before the road splits. On the way, you'll pass Bun'emon-gama and the attractive Heikichi-gama, all of which offer the chance to throw a pot or two (daily 9am–3pm; ¥1500–1800 plus postage), while the more refined Seiryūdō occupies a thatched building down the lane opposite Heikichi-gama. To reach Hirashimizu, take a bus from Yamagata Station (8 daily; 30min) or the Yamakō Building bus terminal (hourly; 20min). Alternatively, a taxi will cost around ¥2000 one way.

## Practicalities

Yamagata is the terminus for a spur of the Tōhoku Shinkansen from Tokyo via Fukushima. Dominating the west side of town, the **train station** houses the city's main **tourist information office** (daily 10am–5/6pm; ☎0236/31-7865), opposite the ticket gates. The office has English-speaking staff, plentiful English-language information, including city maps, and can help with accommodation. There's also an information office in **Yamagata airport** (☎0237/47-3111), which is located 23km north of the city. Limousine buses (40min; ¥650) run between the airport and central Yamagata, stopping outside the station and at the central **bus terminal** in the Yamakō Building, behind Ekimae-dōri's Daiei department store. All long-distance buses use this terminal, while most city buses depart from outside the station's east exit. If you'd rather be independent, there are several **car rental** companies in town; try Eki Rent-a-car (☎0236/31-6746) or Toyota (☎0236/25-0100).

To change money, both Yamagata Bank, marked by a cherry logo, and 77 Bank are located close to the station on Ekimae-dōri. Nanokamachi-dōri boasts a mixture of traditional **shops** and big stores such as AZ (pronounced Azu), while at its north end the Merchandise Exhibition Plaza (daily 9am–5.30pm; Jan–March, Nov & Dec closed Mon & hols) sells a range of local souvenirs. The most famous Yamagata products are *Sasano ittōbori* (single-blade carvings of hawks or roosters with flamboyant, curling tail feathers), cast-iron kettles and chunky, wooden Japanese chess pieces, *shōgi*.

### Accommodation

Yamagata has a reasonable choice of **accommodation** within easy walking distance of the train station. At the cheaper end, *Yamashiroya Ryokan* (☎0236/22-3007; ④ excluding meals) has a few basic but perfectly adequate *tatami* rooms with shared washing facilities; it's located in the backstreets just to the north of the station. Ekimae-dōri boasts a number of more comfortable alternatives, such as the *Hotel Yamagata* (☎0236/42-2111, fax 42-2119; ④) and the slightly overpriced *Green Hotel* (☎0236/22-2636, fax 42-8005; ⑤), both offering Western-style rooms with en-suite bathrooms. Further along Ekimae-dōri, about seven minutes' walk from the station, *Hotel Castle* (☎0236/31-3311, fax 31-3373; ⑤) has a range of well-priced rooms and used to be the smartest place in town until the *Metropolitan* (☎0236/28-1111, fax 28-1166; ⑥) opened above the station. Lastly, there's a reliable *Washington Hotel* (☎0236/25-1111, fax 24-1512; ⑤) towards the north end of Nanokamachi-dōri, roughly fifteen minutes from the station.

### Eating

Yamagata's **speciality foods** include marbled Yonezawa beef, similar to the more famous Matsuzaka variety, and *Imoni*, a warming winter stew of taro, meat, *konnyaku* (devil's tongue) and onions served in slightly sweet sauce. If you fancy a splurge, *Sagorō* (Mon–Sat 10.30am–9pm; ☎0236/31-3560) is one of the city's best **restaurants** for beef, dished up as *sukiyaki*, *shabu-shabu* (from ¥4000) or straightforward steaks (from ¥7000); it's on the third floor above a butcher's shop on Ōtemon-dōri, to the north of Ekimae-dōri. Opposite *Sagorō*, locals fill the few tables of *Shiraume* (Mon–Sat 11.30am–11pm) which has no menu but serves a range of well-priced *teishoku* (from

¥700) as well as *imoni* in season (¥600). If you're looking for a pit stop near Nanokamachi-dōri, take the sidestreet opposite the AZ store for the rustic *Sakaeya* (11.30am–7pm, closed Wed) serving an unusual selection of ramen in generous portions – in summer, you can even feast on cold ramen, served on a bed of ice with an attractive salad of corn, tomato, beef, shrimp and egg. Above the station, there's a small parade of restaurants at the north end of the second-floor Metro Plaza shopping mall. The cheap and friendly *Benibana-tei* (daily 11am–10.30pm) offers reasonable *izakaya*-style food and set meals.

## Zaō Onsen

Roughly 20km southeast of Yamagata city, **ZAŌ ONSEN** is the main focus of activity in the Zaō Quasi National Park, an attractive region of volcanoes, crater lakes and hot springs. In winter (Dec–late March), the resort offers some of Japan's best **skiing** (with fourteen runs to choose from), night skiing and onsen baths to soak away the aches and pains. Non-skiers can enjoy the cable-car ride over **Juhyō Kōgen**, where a thick covering of snow and hoar frost transforms the plateau's fir trees into giant "snow monsters" (*juhyō*).

**Buses** run approximately every hour from Yamagata Station to the Zaō Onsen bus terminal (45min; ¥770), at the bottom of the village, where you'll also find the **tourist information office** (☎0236/94-9328). From here it's a ten-minute walk southeast to the **Zaō Sanroku Ropeway** (every 15min, 8am–5pm; ¥1200 one way) which whisks you up to Juhyō Kōgen. The snow monsters are at their best in February though you can see photos of them at other times of year in the **Juhyō Museum** (daily 9am–4pm; free), located in the terminal building. A second ropeway (same times and ticket) then continues up to Zaō Jizō Sanchō Station at 1661m. This top station lies between Sanpokojin-san (1703m) and Jizō-san (1736m), just two of the peaks which make up the ragged profile of **Zaō-san**. In the summer hiking season (May–Oct), you can follow the right-hand (southeasterly) path over Jizō-san and Kumano dake (1841m) for spectacular views and a fairly rugged hour's walk to the desolate, chemical-blue **Okama crater lake**.

## Yamadera

The temple complex of Risshaku-ji, or **YAMADERA** as it's more popularly known, is one of Tōhoku's most holy places. It was founded in 860 AD by a Zen priest of the Tendai sect and reached its peak in the Kamakura period (1185–1333). Today around forty temple buildings still stand scattered among the ancient cedars on a steep, rocky hillside. The temple lies close by Yamadera Station on the JR Senzan line between Yamagata and Sendai.

From the station follow the crowds across the river and right, past shops selling walking sticks, snacks and souvenirs, to where you can see the temple roofs on the slopes of Hōju-san. Ignore the first two flights of steps to your left and take the third staircase up to the temple's main hall, **Konpon Chūdō**. This impressive building, dating from 1356, shelters a flame that was brought from Enryaku-ji, the centre of Tendai Buddhism near Kyoto (see p.469), 1100 years ago and has supposedly been burning ever since – as you peer inside, it's the left-hand one of the two hanging lanterns. Walking back west along the hillside, you pass a small shrine and a solemn statue of Bashō who, travelling before the days of coach parties, penned a characteristically pithy ode to Yamadera: "In the utter silence of a temple, a cicada's voice alone penetrates the rocks." He sits across from the modern **Hihōkan** (daily 8.30am–4.30pm; closed Jan–Mar & Dec; ¥200) which houses a fine collection of temple treasures, including a beautiful, 3D mandala and a large painting of Buddha in repose sporting a tight perm.

A few steps further on, San-mon marks the entrance to the **mountain** (daily 6am–6pm; ¥300), from where over 1100 steps meander past moss-covered Jizō statues, lanterns and prayer wheels, and squeeze between rocks carved with prayers and pitted with caves. It takes about forty minutes to reach the highest temple, **Okuno-in**, where breathless pilgrims tie prayer papers round a mammoth lantern. Before setting off downhill, don't miss the views over Yamadera from the terrace of **Godai-dō** perched on the cliff face just beyond the distinctive, red **Nōkyō-dō** pavilion.

Yamadera village consists mainly of souvenir shops and expensive ryokan. However, if you need **accommodation**, *Yamadera Pension* (☎0236/95-2134, fax 95-2240; [5]–[6]) is the most attractive option. It's in a half-timbered building right in front of the station, with a decent **restaurant** downstairs.

# Sendai

The largest city in the Tōhoku region, **SENDAI** is a sprawling but pleasant place, with broad, tree-lined avenues and a lively downtown district. Though often just regarded as a staging post on the way to Matsushima Bay (see p.241), the city's **castle ruins**, with their local history museum, and the ornate mausoleum of Sendai's revered founder, the *daimyō* **Daté Masamune**, are worth a brief stop. During the **Star Festival**, the *Tanabata Matsuri* (Aug 6–8), the city centre is awash with thousands of bamboo poles festooned with colourful paper tassels, poems and prayers, celebrating the only day in the year – weather permitting – when the two astral lovers, Vega the weaver and Altair the cowherd, can meet.

**SENDAI**

| | | |
|---|---|---|
| **Sendai** | *Sendai* | 仙台 |
| Aoba-jō | *Aoba-jō* | 青葉城 |
| Aoba-jō Exhibition Hall | *Aoba-jō Shiryōtenjikan* | 青葉城資料展示館 |
| Sendai City Museum | *Sendai-shi Hakubutsukan* | 仙台市博物館 |
| Zuihō-den | *Zuihō-den* | 瑞鳳殿 |
| *ACCOMMODATION* | | |
| Aisaki Ryokan | *Aisaki Ryokan* | 相崎旅館 |
| Dōchūan Youth Hostel | *Dōchūan Yūsu Hosuteru* | 道中庵ユースホステル |
| Dormy Inn | *Dōmii In* | ドーミーイン |
| Intercity Hotel | *Intāshitii Hoteru* | インターシティーホテル |
| Kōyō Grand Hotel | *Kōyō Gurando Hoteru* | 江陽グランドホテル |
| Hotel Metropolitan | *Hoteru Metoroporitan* | ホテルメトロポリタン |
| Hotel Universe | *Hoteru Yunibāsu* | ホテルユニバース |
| *RESTAURANTS* | | |
| Dayū | *Dayū* | ダユウ |
| Heiroku-zushi | *Heiroku-zushi* | 平禄寿司 |
| Kaki Toku | *Kaki Toku* | かき徳 |
| Kazu | *Kazu* | 和 |
| Saboten | *Saboten* | さぼてん |
| Santake | *Santake* | さん竹 |
| Tasuke | *Tasuke* | 太助 |
| Zeami | *Zeami* | ゼアミ |

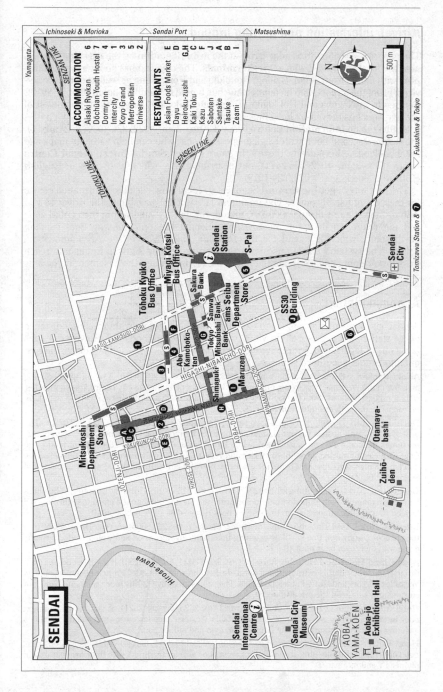

SENDAI

**ACCOMMODATION**
Aisaki Ryokan 6
Dōchūan Youth Hostel 7
Dormy Inn 4
Intercity 1
Koyo Grand 3
Metropolitan 5
Universe 2

**RESTAURANTS**
Asian Foods Market E
Dayu D
Heiroku-zushi G,H
Kaki Toku C
Kazu F
Saboten J
Santake A
Tasuke B
Zeami I

Ichinoseki & Morioka
Sendai Port
Matsushima
Yamagata
Fukushima & Tokyo
Tomizawa Station & 7
Sendai City
Sendai Station
S-Pal
Miyagi Kōtsū Bus Office
Tōhoku Kyūkō Bus Office
Sakura Bank
Sanwa Bank
Tokyo Mitsubishi Bank
Seibu Department Store
ims
SS30 Building
Abe Kamaboko-ten
Maruzen
Mitsukoshi Department Store
Otamaya-bashi
Zuihō-den
Sendai International Centre
Sendai City Museum
Aoba-jō Exhibition Hall
AOBA-YAMA-KŌEN

SENZAN LINE
SENSEKI LINE
TŌHOKU LINE
ATAGO-KAMISUGI-DŌRI
HIGASHI-NIBANCHŌ-DŌRI
MINAMIMACHI-DŌRI
AOBA-DŌRI
HIROSE-DŌRI
KOKUBUNCHŌ-DŌRI
JŌZENJI-DŌRI
Hirose-gawa

N
0 500 m

## Arrival, information and getting around

The majority of visitors to Sendai arrive at the main JR **station** on the east side of town, near the local and long-distance **bus terminals**. The city also has an international **airport** with flights from Seoul, Beijing, Honolulu and Hong Kong as well as domestic services. From the airport, hop on a limousine bus bound for Sendai Station (40min; ¥910). **Ferries** from Nagoya and Hokkaidō (Tomakomai) dock at Sendai Port, northwest of the city, which is served by local buses (40min; ¥490).

Sendai's main **information centre** (daily 8.30am–8pm; ☎022/222-4069) is located on the station's second floor, with English-speaking staff who can help with city maps and hotel bookings. Alternatively, there's the more relaxed **Sendai International Centre** (daily 10am–8pm; ☎022/265-2471), out near the castle, which also runs an **English Hotline** (same hours; ☎022/224-1919).

The best way of **getting around** Sendai is by **local bus** – ask the information centre for their list of useful routes. The minimum fare is ¥150, payable to the driver as you exit, or there's a one-day pass (¥620), though this is only valid within the central zone and not really worth it for most visitors. Sendai has one **subway** line, running north–south, which is useful for the *Dōchūan Youth Hostel* (see Accommodation, below). The system's easy to use, with announcements and signs in English; to reach the subway from Sendai's JR station follow the signs through the basement of the ams Seibu store.

## Accommodation

Sendai has plenty of mid-range and expensive business **hotels** within walking distance of the station, but is less well provided with budget accommodation. However, it does boast one of Japan's most attractive city youth hostels, which more than repays the trek out into Sendai's southern suburbs.

**Aisaki Ryokan**, 5-6 Kitame-machi, Aoba-ku (☎022/264-0700, fax 227-6067). A rather disappointing member of the Welcome Inn group, but one of the cheaper places in the city centre, fifteen minutes' walk southeast of the station. The facilities are old and basic, with a choice between Western or *tatami* rooms, some with en-suite bathrooms. ④.

**Dōchūan Youth Hostel**, 31 Onoda-Kitayashiki, Taihaku-ku (☎022/247-0511, fax 247-0759). The best of three youth hostels in Sendai, built among trees in traditional farmhouse style. Shared *tatami* rooms include a TV and wash basin, while there's also a cedar bath and excellent food – the English-speaking warden grows his own rice and vegetables. The only downside is the hostel's location ten minutes' walk due east from Tomizawa Station and fifteen minutes by subway from central Sendai (¥290). ②.

**Dormy Inn**, 2-10-17 Chūō, Aoba-ku (☎022/715-7077, fax 715-7078). This new, bottom-end business hotel has a range of boxy but adequate rooms, with satellite TV, minibar and en-suite bathroom. It's located roughly five minutes' from the station, near Hirose-dōri subway station. ⑤.

**Intercity Hotel**, 2-9-4 Hon-chō, Aoba-ku (☎022/222-4647, fax 222-5006). Across Hirose-dōri from the cheaper *Dormy Inn*, this small, welcoming hotel is nicely decorated and well priced. All rooms come with their own bathroom. ⑤.

**Kōyo Grand Hotel**, 2-3-1 Hon-chō, Aoba-ku (☎022/267-5111, fax 265-2252). It's worth taking a walk through the lobby of this extraordinary hotel, decked out with "antique" French furniture, cupids, Versailles mirrors and stuffed antelope heads. The rooms are only slightly more restrained and, not surprisingly, a little on the pricey side. ⑥.

**Hotel Metropolitan**, 1-1-1 Chūō, Aoba-ku (☎022/268-2525, fax 268-2521). Smart, new hotel next door to Sendai Station with a range of comfortable Western- and Japanese-style rooms. Facilities include a choice of restaurants, Sky Lounge bar, gym and indoor pool. ⑥–⑦.

**Hotel Universe**, 3F, 4-3-22 Ichiban-chō, Aoba-ku (☎022/261-7711, fax 261-7745). Simple business hotel on Ichiban-chō shopping street. Rooms are a good size for the price, with their own bathroom, phone, TV and minibar. ⑤.

## The City

Though central Sendai had to be rebuilt after World War II, its streets follow the original grid pattern laid out by Daté Masamune in the seventeenth century. The main downtown area, a high-rise district of offices, banks and shopping malls, lies on the east bank of the Hirose-gawa. Its principal thoroughfare, Aoba-dōri, runs west from the train station to where the city's few sights are located on the far side of the river. After an initial bus ride, the area is best tackled on foot.

The natural place to start exploring is the wooded hilltop park, **Aobayama-kōen**, which was once the site of the magnificent Sendai Castle, popularly known as Aoba-jō. Only a few stretches of wall and a reconstructed gateway remain, but the site is impeccable, protected by the river to the east and a deep ravine on its south side. Buses run from Sendai Station (stand #9) to Aobajōshi-mae (20min), from where it's a short walk to the **statue of Masamune**, astride his horse, surveying the city below. A fearsome warrior, Masamune was nicknamed the "One-eyed Dragon" thanks to a childhood attack of smallpox. He had been granted the fiefdom in return for helping bring Tokugawa Ieyasu to power in 1603, and the Daté clan continued to rule Sendai for the next 270 years. Their castle was constructed in highly ornate Momoyama style, with painted ceilings and huge rooms divided by glorious screens, more like a luxurious palace than a fortress. Though it's a bit gimmicky, you can get an idea of its former glory in the small **Aoba-jō Exhibition Hall** (daily 9am–5pm; ¥700), located above the park's souvenir shops, where a short, computer-generated film takes you "inside" the castle; the red seats are equipped with foreign-language earphone sets.

Ten minutes' walk down the north side of the hill brings you to the more interesting **Sendai City Museum** (Tues–Sun 9am–4.45pm; ¥400, extra for special exhibitions). This modern, well-laid out installation traces the city's history from the early Stone Age to the present day, though the main emphasis is on the glory days under Masamune and his successors. On the second floor you'll find displays of his armour, with the distinctive crescent moon on the helmet, his sword and various portraits – always with two eyes.

When Daté Masamune died in 1636, aged 70, he was buried in the **Zuihō-den** on a wooded hillside just along the river from Aoba-jō. Eventually his two successors joined him and their three **mausoleums** (daily 9am–4/4.30pm; ¥550) now stand at the top of broad, stone steps, all in the same opulent Momoyama style, their polychrome carvings glittering against the plain, dark wood and overhanging eaves. In fact, the mausoleums are fairly recent reconstructions – during the five-year project the graves were opened and you can see the treasures they unearthed, as well as a fascinating video of the excavations, in a one-room **museum** beside the Zuihō-den. Though the mausoleums are only a short distance from Aoba-jō as the crow flies, getting here is either a good twenty-minute walk, or you have to take a bus back to Sendai Station and out again (stand #11) to the Otamaya-bashi stop. If you're walking from the castle, cross the river by the City Museum and take the first right, heading southeast to cross again at the next bridge, then look out on the right for the main approach road.

## Eating and drinking

Sendai's **speciality foods** include *gyū-tan* (broiled, smoked or salted calf's tongue) or oysters from Matsushima Bay in winter (Dec–March). *Sasa-kamaboko*, a leaf-shaped cake of rather rubbery white-fish paste, is a popular local snack which you can sample in Abe Kamaboko-ten, a famous outlet on the Chūō-dōri shopping mall. Chūō-dōri and the connecting Ichiban-chō arcades are good places to look for **restaurants and cafés**, while S-Pal, at the south end of Sendai Station, and the top two floors of the SS30 Building also have a decent selection. **Kokubun-chō**, just west of the Ichiban-chō shopping mall, is Sendai's main entertainment district.

**Asian Foods Market**, 2-5-1 Kokubun-chō. Cheerful, noisy *izakaya* serving a mix of Korean, Chinese and local foods at good prices. Expect to pay around ¥2000 for an evening meal, and note that after 5pm there's a drink-all-you-want deal (¥1000 for 100min). Open till 4am Mon–Sat, midnight on Sun.

**Dayu**, 2F, 4-2-13 Ichiban-chō. A casual restaurant on the Ichiban-chō arcade specializing in garlic cuisine and a variety of Indonesian, Thai and Italian foods. Prices are reasonable, though there's an annoying table charge. English menu. Daily 1.30am–2pm & 5.30–11.30pm.

**Heiroku-zushi**, Chūō-dōri & Ichiban-chō. Two spick and span sushi outlets on the shopping arcades, with a take-away service or conveyor-belt counter. Prices start at ¥120 for two pieces. Daily 11am–2pm.

**Kaki Toku**, 2F, 4-9-1 Ichiban-chō. Elegant oyster and seafood restaurant with a choice of tables or *tatami* seating. Set menus cost from ¥6000, though there are plenty of cheaper options, including rice and tempura dishes from ¥1000. Mon–Fri 11am–2pm & 5–9pm; Sat, Sun & hols noon–9pm.

**Kazu**, B1, 2-11-11 Chūō. Small, friendly *okonomiyaki* joint that's worth seeking out in the backstreets north of Chūō-dōri. They cook the pancake for you, from a choice of ingredients and regional styles. English spoken. Tues–Sun 11.30am–9pm.

**Saboten**, 28F, SS30 Building, 4-6 Chūō. This well-rated, café-style *tonkatsu* restaurant at the top of Sendai's tallest building is surprisingly good value, with individual dishes from ¥1000 or various set meals. *Saboten* also has a branch in the S-Pal building, but you don't get the views. Daily 11.30am–10pm.

**Santake**, 4-9-24 Ichiban-chō. Casual soba shop opposite Mitsukoshi department store on the Ichiban-chō arcade. Individual dishes from ¥570, or ¥1300 plus for a set meal. Tues–Sun 11am–8pm.

**Tasuke**, 2-11-11, Kokubun-chō. One of Sendai's best-known *gyū-tan* restaurants, where you can eat tongue in all its forms. If it's full, try the cheaper outlets in the alleys opposite. Tues–Sun 11.30am–10pm.

**Zeami**, 1-6-15 Kokubun-chō. Another large, lively *izakaya* serving hearty portions of "assorted foods", from Californian nuggets to *yakisoba*. Count on ¥2000 per head for a decent meal. Mon–Sat 5pm–3/5am, Sun & hols till midnight.

## Listings

**Airlines** Air China (☎022/221-2025); ANA (☎0120–029222 for domestic flights; ☎0120–029333, international); Asiana Airlines (☎022/265-0022); Cathay Pacific (☎022/227-8681); Dragon Air (☎022/227-8681); JAL (☎0120–255971 domestic; ☎0210–255931 international); Japan Air System (☎0120–511283 domestic; ☎0120–711283 international); Northwest Airlines (☎022/268-5871); Singapore Airlines (☎022/215-7571).

**Airport information** ☎022/224-5111.

**Banks and exchange** There are branches of major foreign-exchange banks, such as Sanwa, Sakura and Tokyo Mitsubishi, at the east end of Aoba-dōri, near Sendai Station.

**Buses** Long-distance JR Buses (☎022/256-6646) for Niigata, Tokyo (Shinjuku) and Akita leave from the east side of Sendai Station. Express buses go to Kyoto, Ōsaka, Nagoya and destinations around Tōhoku from outside the Miyagi Kōtsū (☎022/261-5333) office at the west end of Hirose-dōri. On the opposite side of the road, Tōhoku Kyūkō (☎022/262-7031) buses leave for Tokyo Station.

**Car rental** Central car rental outlets include Eki Rent-a-car (☎022/227-8335), Mazda (☎022/267-0123) and Nippon (☎022/297-1919).

**Ferries** Overnight ferries to Hokkaidō (Tomakomai) and Nagoya leave from Sendai Port, accessible by bus from Sendai Station (stand #34; 40min; ¥490). For Hokkaidō, Higashi-Nihon Ferry (☎022/256-7221) and Taiheiyō Ferry (☎022/263-9877) run services on alternate days. Taiheiyō Ferry also operates the daily service to Nagoya.

**Hospitals** Sendai City Hospital (3-1 Shimizu-kōji; ☎022/263-9900) has a 24hr emergency clinic, or otherwise ring the English Hotline (daily 10am–8pm; ☎022/224-1919) for advice on clinics with English-speaking doctors.

**Post office** Sendai Central Post Office (1-7 Kitame-machi, Aoba-ku) has a 24hr service for stamps and international mail (Mon–Sat), and also poste restante. There's a useful sub-post office inside Sendai Station.

**Shopping** The main shopping streets are the covered malls of Chūō-dōri and Ichiban-chō. For traditional crafts, try Shimanuki, towards the west end of Chūō-dōri, which sells a good range of *kokeshi* dolls, wooden toys, *ittabōri* carved birds, fabrics, ironware and lacquer goods. Maruzen is the best place in town for foreign-language books and magazines; you'll find it on the southern extension of Ichiban-chō, across Aoba-dōri.

**Taxis** Plenty of taxis cruise the streets of Sendai and wait outside the station. If you need to call one, the two biggest firms are Kankō (☎022/236-1221) and Nikkō (☎022/241-4061).

# Matsushima Bay

The jumble of wooded islands decorating **Matsushima Bay**, a short train ride northeast of Sendai, is officially designated one of Japan's top three scenic areas, along with Miyajima and Amanohashidate (see p.556 & p.593 respectively). Roughly 12km by 14km, the bay contains over 260 islands of every conceivable shape and size. The smaller islets are cut through with tunnels and sculpted by wind and waves into fanciful likenesses of tortoises, whales, or even human profiles with a scraggy fringe of contorted pine trees – or so the guides would have you believe. In between, the shallower parts of the bay have been used for farming oysters for around three hundred years.

Bashō, travelling through in 1689, commented that "much praise had already been lavished upon the wonders of the islands of Matsushima", and many visitors today find the bay slightly disappointing. Nevertheless, a **boat trip** among the white, ribbed islands makes an enjoyable outing, though it's best to avoid weekends and holidays. **Matsushima** town itself has a couple of less-frequented picturesque spots, and a venerable temple, **Zuigan-ji**, with an impressive collection of art treasures. Most people visit Matsushima on a day-trip from Sendai, but there are some reasonable accommodation options in the area if you're heading on up the coast to Kinkazan (see p.244).

## Touring the bay

The best approach to Matsushima is via **SHIOGAMA**, from where you can travel on across the bay **by boat**. A busy industrial and fishing port with a large tuna fleet, Shiogama lies on the JR Senseki line which runs from the basement of Sendai Station through

| MATSUSHIMA BAY | | |
|---|---|---|
| **Matsushima** | *Matsushima* | 松島 |
| Century Hotel | *Senchurii Hoteru* | センチュリーホテル |
| Donjiki Chaya | *Donjiki Chaya* | どんじき茶屋 |
| Godai-dō | *Godai-dō* | 五大堂 |
| Fukūra-jima | *Fukura-jima* | 福浦島 |
| Ryokan Matsushima-jō | *Ryokan Matsushima-jō* | 旅館松島城 |
| Oshima | *Oshima* | 雄島 |
| Saigyō Modoshi-no-matsu | *Saigyō Modoshi-no-matsu* | 西行戻しの松 |
| Santori Chaya | *Santori Chaya* | さんとり茶屋 |
| Shintomi-yama | *Shintomi-yama* | 新富山 |
| Sōkanzan | *Sōkanzan* | 双観山 |
| Zuigan-ji | *Zuigan-ji* | 瑞巌寺 |
| | | |
| **Shiogama** | *Shiogama* | 塩釜 |
| Hon-Shiogama | *Hon-Shiogama* | 本塩釜 |
| Marine Gate | *Marin Gēto* | マリンゲート |
| | | |
| **Nobiru** | *Nobiru* | 野蒜 |
| Boyō-sō | *Boyō-sō* | 望洋荘 |
| Ōtakamori | *Ōtakamori* | おおたかもり |
| Pi-La Matsushima Youth Hostel | *Pai-Ra Matsushima Yūsu Hosuteru* | パイラ松島ユースホステル |

**Hon-Shiogama** (25–40min; ¥400) to Matsushima and beyond. The station's **tourist infor-mation office** (daily 10am–4pm) can give you timetables and point you to the Marine Gate ferry pier, ten minutes' walk to the east; turn right outside the station and right again under the train tracks and you'll see the modern terminal building straight ahead.

The **Marine Gate pier** is the departure point for both local **ferries** serving the inhabited islands and **tourist boats** which take a leisurely womble through Matsushima Bay before dropping you in Matsushima town. In high season (April–Nov) boats run every thirty minutes (8am–4pm; 50min; ¥1420, or ¥2220 for the upper deck), and there's also the option of a longer voyage into the northern reaches of the bay (11.10am; 1hr 50min; ¥2950). From December through March there are sailings every hour only on the shorter course.

It's also possible to take a cruise round the bay **from Matsushima** tourist pier (roughly every hour 8am–4pm; 45min; ¥1400), though they tend to be more crowded than the boats from Shiogama. Another, more interesting route goes north from Matsushima to Miyato-jima (see p.243), with the possibility of catching a later boat back (May–Oct; 9am & noon; 1hr; ¥1220). Alternatively, hire your own four-person motor-boat from Matsushima's two smaller piers; rates start at ¥4000 for a twenty-minute ride.

## Matsushima

The modern town of **MATSUSHIMA** is little more than a strip of resort hotels and sou-venir shops, but its origins go back to 828 when Zen priests founded a temple over-looking the bay. Though **Zuigan-ji** has been rebuilt many times since then, it still retains a compelling sense of history and boasts some magnificent works of art, many of which are stored in the temple museum. Other religious buildings followed Zuigan-ji, such as a much-photographed **Godai-dō**, a tiny pavilion accessed by three red-lac-quer bridges, while the nearby island of **Ōshima** is pitted with caves and carvings left by Buddhist monks.

All Matsushima's main sights lie within easy walking distance of both the central tourist pier, where boats from Shiogama dock, and the train station (Matsushima-kaigan) ten minutes' walk to the southwest. Halfway between the two, a grove of 400-year-old cedar trees makes a suitably grand approach to **Zuigan-ji** (daily 8am–5pm; Jan–March & Oct–Dec closes 3.30/4.30pm; ¥600). Though deceptively plain from the outside, Zuigan-ji's main hall bears the unmistakable stamp of Daté Masamune, the first lord of Sendai (see p.239), who oversaw its reconstruction in the early seventeenth cen-tury. He employed the best craftsmen and the highest quality materials to create a splendid monument of intricately carved doors and transoms, wood-panelled ceilings and gilded screens lavishly painted with hawks, chrysanthemums, peacocks and pines.

A number of these screens and other items on display are replicas, but you can see some of the originals in the modern **Seiryū-den** (included in the ticket), to the left as you exit Zuigan-ji's inner compound. Alongside the normal array of temple treasures, there are statues of the one-eyed Masamune, in full armour and an uncompromising mood, and his angelic-looking wife and eldest daughter. Note that his daughter, dressed in black, is clutching a rosary; she was a firm Christian who refused to renounce her faith at a time when it was strictly prohibited in Japan.

In front of Zuigan-ji, just north of the ferry pier, two tiny islands are threaded togeth-er with arched, vermilion bridges. No one knows why the bridges were built with pre-carious gaps between the planks, but one suggestion is that it kept women, in their awk-ward kimono, from despoiling the sacred ground. The object of their curiosity was the **Godai-dō**, a picturesque pavilion built by order of Masamune in the early 1600s. It hous-es statues of five Buddhist deities which can only be viewed every 33 years – so come back in 2006. Meanwhile, you'll have to make do with the charming carvings of the twelve animals of the zodiac decorating the eaves, starting with the rat on the north side.

If time allows, there are a couple of larger, less-frequented islands along the seafront of which **Ōshima**, five minutes' walk south, is the more interesting. On the way you'll pass **Karantei**, (daily 8.30am–4.30/5pm; ¥200) a famous teahouse with a beautiful name – "place to view the ripples on the water" – but little else to recommend it. Instead, press on to where another red-lacquered bridge leads to Oshima. Once a retreat for Buddhist priests, the island's soft rock is pocked with caves, tablets, and monuments; from its east side you get attractive views of Matsushima Bay. The second island, **Fukūra-jima** (daily 8am–4/6pm; ¥150), lies north of Godai-dō across a 250-metre-long bridge. A natural botanical garden, it's inhabited by more than 250 native plant species, and makes a good picnic spot.

The hills around Matsushima town provide plenty of opportunities for panoramic views of the bay. Of the four main **lookout points**, southerly Sōkanzan is reckoned to offer the best all-round views, including both Shiogama and Matsushima itself; take a taxi (¥2000 return fare) to avoid the long, thirty-minute climb on a busy road. Otherwise, Saigyō Modoshi-no-matsu is a more pleasant, fifteen-minute scramble west of the station, or allow a few minutes more for Shintomi-yama, on the northwest edge of town above Fukūra-jima.

### Practicalities

Apart from the sea route via Shiogama (see pp.241–2), you can travel directly to Matsushima from Sendai on the JR Senseki line (15–30min; ¥320), getting off at Matsushima-kaigan Station. There's a **tourist information office** outside the station (Mon–Fri 10am–4pm; Sat, Sun & hols 10.30am–3.30pm; ☎022/354-2263), with English-speaking staff, and a second beside the boat pier (daily 8.30am–5pm; ☎022/354-2618).

Matsushima has a number of smart but expensive **hotels**, where prices are more reasonable on weekdays and in winter (Dec–early April); if you're looking for budget accommodation, then head on up the coast to Nobiru (see below). Matsushima's most appealing hotel is the old *Ryokan Matsushima-jō*, also known as the *Matsushima Kankō Hotel*, (☎022/354-2121, fax 344-2883; [5]–[6]), in an imitation castle inland from the Fukūra-jima bridge. Its *tatami* rooms are all nicely decorated with antiques and offer bay views; some have en-suite bathrooms, or there's an onsen bath. In front of the *Matsushima-jō*, the modern *Century Hotel* (☎022/354-4111, fax 354-4191; [5]–[6]) has a choice of Western or *tatami* rooms, all en suite, plus seafront balconies at the higher end and a huge onsen bath with picture windows over the bay.

Most of Matsushima's **restaurants** lining the main road cater to tour parties, but there a couple of attractive alternatives. *Santori Chaya* (11.30am–3pm & 5.30–10pm, closed Wed), a small, simple place on the seafront north of the Godai-dō, serves a range of reasonable *teishoku* as well as sashimi, sushi and rice dishes; go upstairs for sea views over the kitchen roof. For a snack or light lunch, try the thatched *Donjiki Chaya* surrounded by gardens in the woods south of Zuigan-ji, which offers soba, *dango* (rice dumplings) and drinks.

## Oku-Matsushima

The eastern side of Matsushima Bay, an area known as **Oku-Matsushima**, is protected by a large, ragged island, **Miyato-jima**, linked to the mainland by a road bridge. Apart from a number of sandy beaches, the island's main draw is a low hill, **Ōtakamori**, from where you get more panoramic views over the bay.

The gateway to Oku-Matsushima is the small town of **NOBIRU**, fifteen minutes north on the JR Senseki line from Matsushima, which also provides some of the area's cheapest accommodation. The station **information office** (daily 8.30am–5.30pm; ☎0225/88-2611) provides maps and can help with reservations, though the staff don't speak English. One of the nicest **places to stay** around here is the smart *Pi-La*

*Matsushima Youth Hostel* (☎0225/88-2220, fax 88-3797; ②), with a choice of dormitories or Western-style family rooms, and hearty meals. The hostel lies roughly fifteen minutes' walk from Nobiru Station; cross the bridge and keep heading south towards the sea until you find a right turn signed to the hostel. On the way, you'll pass the *Boyō-sō* (☎0225/88-2159; ⑤) including two meals), the newest of several minshuku scattered in the pine woods south of Nobiru Station.

The pine trees stretch all along Nobiru beach, a wide expanse of dark sand which gets packed in summer, but there are better coves further south on **Miyato-jima**. The best way to explore the island is by bicycle – the youth hostel has **bikes for rent** (¥500 for 3hr, ¥800 per day) and the manager can advise on the best routes. It takes three to four hours to cycle round the whole island, plus an extra half hour to walk up to the viewpoint on top of Ōtakamori.

# Oshika Hantō

North of Sendai, Honshū's coastal plain gives way to a fractured shoreline of deep bays and knobbly peninsulas. The first of these is the **Oshika Hantō**, a rugged spine on the eastern edge of Sendai Bay, whose broken tip forms **Kinkazan**. This tiny island has been a sacred place since ancient times but its prime attractions these days are its isolation and hiking trails through forests inhabited by semi-wild deer and monkeys. The main gateway to the area is **Ishinomaki**, from where buses run down the peninsula to **Ayukawa**, a former whaling port with a moderately interesting museum and connecting ferries to Kinkazan. Many tourist facilities close in winter (Nov–March), so check the schedules first at the information offices in Sendai or Matsushima and ask them to help with booking accommodation.

## Kinkazan

The first inhabitants of **KINKAZAN** (Mountain of the Gold Flowers), a conical-shaped island lying 1km off the tip of Oshika Hantō, were gold prospectors. Though the seams dried up long ago, Kinkazan is still associated with wealth and good fortune, and its prime sight, the shrine of **Koganeyama-jinja**, is dedicated to the twin gods of prosperity, Ebisu and Daikoku. The shrine stands in a deer-cropped clearing on the west slope

| OSHIKA HANTŌ | | |
|---|---|---|
| **Ayukawa** | *Ayukawa* | 鮎川 |
| Atami-sō | *Atami-sō* | あたみ荘 |
| Caravan | *Kyaraban* | キャラバン |
| Minami-sō | *Minami-sō* | みなみ荘 |
| Misaki-ya | *Misaki-ya* | みさき屋 |
| Ojika Ryokan | *Ojika Ryokan* | おじか旅館 |
| | | |
| **Ishinomaki** | *Ishinomaki* | 石巻 |
| | | |
| **Kinkazan** | *Kinkazan* | 金華山 |
| Anbe Ryokan | *Anbe Ryokan* | 阿部旅館 |
| Koganeyama-jinja | *Koganeyama-jinja* | 黄金山神社 |
| Shiokaze | *Shiokaze* | 潮風 |
| | | |
| **Onagawa** | *Onagawa* | 女川 |

of Kinka-san, a good twenty minutes' walk above the ferry pier – turn left from the pier and follow the road steeply uphill. From behind the shrine buildings a rough path leads on a stiff two-kilometre hike up Kinka-zan (445m) where the effort is rewarded with truly magnificent views along the peninsula and west towards distant Matsushima.

Various other **hiking trails** are indicated on a small, green map you'll be given on the ferry or by Ayukawa tourist office (see below). However, be aware that the paths themselves are poorly signed and may well be overgrown, so check the route before setting out. Remember also to take plenty of food and water. If you do get lost, head down to the rough track circumnavigating the island; the whole place is less than 25km around, so you can't go too far wrong.

### Practicalities

The best way of getting to Kinkazan is via the JR Senseki line from Sendai (or Matsushima) to **Ishinomaki** and then hop on a bus for the scenic ride south to **Ayukawa** (1hr 30min; ¥1460). Buses depart from outside Ishinomaki Station, where there is also a small **tourist office** (daily 9.30am–5.30/6pm; Jan–March, Nov & Dec closed Mon; ☎0225/93-6448), and **car rental** is available through Eki Rent-a-car (☎0225/93-1665). In summer there are hourly **ferries** from Ayukawa to Kinkazan (April–early Nov; 25min; ¥900), with only three boats per day during the winter season. Alternatively, high-speed boats also depart for Kinkazan from **Onagawa**, at the end of the JR Ishinomaki line on the peninsula's northeast coast, but only in summer, and reservations are essential (30min; ¥1600, or ¥3040 return; ☎0225/53-3121).

The most atmospheric **accommodation** on Kinkazan is the pilgrims' lodge at Koganeyama-jinja (☎0225/45-2264; [6]), where you can attend the shrine's early-morning prayer sessions. There are also a number of minshuku around the ferry pier, of which *Anbe Ryokan* (☎0225/45-3082 or eve 53-4674; [5]) and *Shiokaze* (☎0225/45-2666 or eve 45-2244; [5]) are recommended. Note that these places may close in the off-season, so it's essential to phone ahead, and though there are a few **restaurants** by the pier, it's a better idea to eat in your lodgings; all the above prices include two meals.

## Ayukawa

The sleepy town of **AYUKAWA**, on the southwest tip of Oshika Hantō, makes an alternative base for Kinkazan. A thriving port until commercial **whaling** was banned in 1987, Ayukawa now depends on tourism and its only sight is a smart new whaling museum beside the ferry pier. Despite the moratorium, Japan still hunts whales for "scientific purposes" and the residents of Ayukawa continue to receive whale-meat rations. You can even eat whale (*kujira*) in local restaurants and buy whale products in the souvenir shops.

Though it's a little pricey, the well-designed **Oshika Whale Land museum** (daily 9am–5pm, Jan–March & Dec closed Tues; ¥1000), pushes a more conservationist line while also tracing the history of Ayukawa's whaling fleet. The first exhibition hall takes you through the stylized rib-cage of a whale, accompanied by recordings of their eerie, underwater chatter. There are various films and interactive displays concerning the life of whales, many aimed at children, though you might want to miss the section full of pickled organs and embryos.

The museum, Kinkazan **ferry pier** and **bus terminal** are all grouped together at the south end of Ayukawa. You can buy ferry tickets in an office next to the bus stop (daily 8am–4.30/5pm; ☎0225/45-2181), while the **tourist information office** (daily 8.30am–5pm; Jan–March, Nov & Dec closed Sun; ☎0225/45-3456) is a few doors further north. Staff here can provide maps and make bookings for accommodation in both Ayukawa and Kinkazan.

If you're looking for **accommodation** in Ayukawa, the *Minami-sō minshuku* (☎0225/45-2501; ⑤) is close to the ferry pier and the most likely to be open all year. It's in a grey, iron building on the hill above the pier but, despite appearances, is perfectly adequate and turns out pretty good food. Smarter options are the new *Atami-sō* (☎0225/45-2227; ⑤), on the main road coming into town, or the more upmarket *Ojika Ryokan* (☎0225/45-3068; ⑤–⑥) in the backstreets two minutes' walk north of the pier.

A cluster of **restaurants** along the road behind the information office sell ultra-fresh seafood. Try *Misaki-ya* (closed Thurs), on the crossroads towards Whale Land, which serves moderately priced sushi, sashimi and a range of standard dishes, or the soba joint next door. Most places close at 5pm in the off-season, but at the north end of town *Caravan* coffee shop serves curry-rice, spaghetti and other Western dishes till a touch later (10am–8pm, closed Thurs). Opposite *Caravan*, you'll find Ayukawa **post office**, while the **bank** on the main road in the middle of town has a foreign exchange desk.

# Hiraizumi and around

For a brief period in the eleventh century the temples of **Hiraizumi**, now a quiet backwater around 120km north of Sendai, rivalled even Kyoto in their magnificence. Though the majority of monasteries and palaces have since been lost, the gloriously extravagant **Konjiki-dō**, the "Golden Hall", and the other treasures of **Chūson-ji** temple bear witness to the area's former wealth and level of artistic accomplishment. Hiraizumi's **Mōtsū-ji** also boasts one of Japan's best-preserved Heian-period gardens, while a boat ride along the nearby Satetsu-gawa, between the towering cliffs of **Geibikei gorge**, provides a break from the cultural refinement.

Travelling north **to Hiraizumi** by train – whether on the Tōhoku Shinkansen or the Tōhoku main line – it's necessary to change at **ICHINOSEKI**, a small town 8km further south. From Ichinoseki you can either hop on the next stopping train, or pick up one of the more frequent local buses which depart from outside the station, though note that the last Hiraizumi bus leaves at around 7pm (6.30pm Sun & hols). Ichinoseki is also the terminal for Geibikei trains, and you might find it more convenient to visit the gorge (see p.248) before travelling on to Hiraizumi. In Ichinoseki it's worth visiting the useful **information office** (Mon–Sat 10am–5.30pm; ☎0191/23-8640) in Ichinoseki Station's "View Plaza", which has English-speaking staff. Nearby, there are also a couple of **car rental** outlets – Orix (☎0191/21-3272) and Eki Rent-a-car (☎0191/21-5570) –

| HIRAIZUMI AND AROUND | | |
|---|---|---|
| **Hiraizumi** | *Hiraizumi* | 平泉 |
| Bashō-kan | *Bashō-kan* | 芭蕉館 |
| Chūson-ji | *Chūson-ji* | 中尊寺 |
| Izumi Soba-ya | *Izumi Soba-ya* | 泉そば屋 |
| Konjiki-dō | *Konjiki-dō* | 金色堂 |
| Mōtsū-ji | *Mōtsū-ji* | 毛越寺 |
| Sankōzō | *Sankōzō* | 讃衡蔵 |
| Shirayama Ryokan | *Shirayama Ryokan* | 志羅山旅館 |
| | | |
| **Ichinoseki** | *Ichinoseki* | 一関 |
| City Hotel | *Shitii Hoteru* | シティーホテル |
| Geibikei Gorge | *Geibikei* | げいび渓 |
| Hotel Sunroute | *Hoteru Sanrūto* | ホテルサンルート |

and several reasonable business **hotels**, notably *City Hotel* (☎0191/23-7799, fax 23-2299; [5]), or the more upmarket *Hotel Sunroute* (☎0191/26-4311, fax 26-4317; [6]).

## Hiraizumi

Nowdays it's hard to imagine **HIRAIZUMI** as the resplendent capital of the **Fujiwara** clan, who chose this spot on the banks of the Kitakami-gawa for their "paradise on earth". At first sight it's a rather dull little town on a busy main road, but the low, western hills conceal one of the most important sights in northern Honshū, where the gilded Konjiki-dō has somehow survived war, fire and natural decay for nearly nine hundred years. You can easily cover this and the nearby gardens of Mōtsū-ji in a day, with the option of staying in Hiraizumi itself or Ichinoseki.

In the early twelfth century Fujiwara Kiyohara, the clan's first lord, began building a vast complex of Buddhist temples and palaces, lavishly decorated with gold from the local mines, in what is now Hiraizumi. Eventually, the Fujiwara's wealth and military might started to worry the southern warlord Minamoto Yoritomo (see p.771) who was in the throes of establishing the Kamakura Shogunate. Earlier, Yoritomo's valiant brother, **Yoshitsune**, had trained with the warrior monks of Hiraizumi, so when Yoritomo turned against him (see p.203), Yoshitsune fled north with his loyal servant Benkei. Though at first he was protected by the Fujiwara, they soon betrayed him on the promise of a sizeable reward and in 1189 Benkei – peppered with arrows and spears – held off the attackers while Yoshitsune committed suicide. According to one legend, however, Yoshitsune escaped to Mongolia where he resurfaced as Genghis Khan. Meanwhile, Yoritomo rewarded the Fujiwara by annihilating them, destroying their temples and leaving the town to crumble into ruin. Bashō, passing through Hiraizumi five hundred years after Yoshitsune's death, caught the mood in one of his famous haiku: "The summer grass, 'tis all that's left of ancient warriors' dreams."

The flight of Yoshitsune to Hiraizumi is commemorated with a costume parade during the town's main spring **festival** (May 1–5), which also features open-air Nō performances at Chūson-ji. Other important events include an ancient sacred dance, *Ennen-no-Mai*, held by torch light at Mōtsū-ji on January 20 and during the autumn festival (Nov 1–3).

### Chūson-ji

The Fujiwara's first building projects concentrated on **Chūson-ji** (daily 8am–5pm; Jan–March, Nov & Dec 8.30am–4.30pm; ¥800 including Konjiki-dō, Kyōzō and the Sankōzō), which had been founded by a Tendai priest from Kyoto in the mid ninth century. Of the temple's original forty buildings, only two remain: Konjiki-dō (the Golden Hall) and the nearby sutra repository, Kyōzō. They sit on a forested hilltop, alongside a number of more recent structures, on the main bus route north from Ichinoseki and Hiraizumi stations (20min and 4min respectively).

From the main road, a broad avenue leads uphill past minor temples sheltering under towering cryptomeria trees, until you reach the first building of any size, the Hon-dō, at the top on the right-hand side. A few minutes further on, set back on the left, a concrete hall shelters Chūson-ji's greatest treasure. The **Konjiki-dō** is tiny – only 5.5 square metres – and protected behind plate glass, but it's still an extraordinary sight. The whole structure, bar the roof tiles, gleams with thick gold leaf, while the altar inside is smothered in mother-of-pearl inlay and delicate, gilded copper friezes set against dark, burnished lacquer. The altar's central image is of Amida Nyorai, flanked by a host of buddhas, bodhisattvas and guardian kings, all swathed in gold. This extravagant gesture of faith, and power, took fifteen years to complete and was unveiled in 1124; later, the mummified bodies of the four Fujiwara lords were buried under its altar.

Behind the Konjiki-dō, the second of Chūson-ji's original buildings, the **Kyōzō** is not nearly so dramatic. This small, plain hall, erected in 1108, used to house more than 5000 Buddhist sutras written in gold or silver characters on rich, indigo paper. The next-door hall was built in 1288 to shelter the Konjiki-dō – you can still see the old foundation stones – while across the way, there's a much more recent Nō stage where outdoor performances are held in summer by firelight (Aug 14), and during Haraizumi's two major spring and autumn festivals. Finally, the road beside the entrance to the Konjiki-dō leads to the modern **Sankōzō**, a museum containing what remains of Chūson-ji's treasures. The most valuable items are a statue of the Senjū Kannon (Thousand-armed Goddess of Mercy), a number of sutra scrolls and a unique collection of lacy metal-work decorations (*kalavinkas*) which originally hung in the Konjiki-dō.

### Mōtsū-ji

Hiraizumi's other main sight, the Heian-period gardens of **Mōtsū-ji** (daily 8.30am-5pm; ¥500), lie eight minutes' walk west from Hiraizumi Station. In the twelfth century the Fujiwara added to this temple, originally founded in 850, until it was the largest in northern Honshū. Sadly, nothing remains now save a few foundation stones and an earthly paradise which is Japan's best-preserved Heian garden, the **Jōdo-teien**. The garden's main feature is a large lake, speckled with symbolic islands, in the midst of velvet lawns. There are a few, simple buildings among the trees and ancient foundation stones, but otherwise the garden is simply a pleasant place to stroll. You'll find flowers in bloom at almost every season, including cherry, lotus, bush clover and azaleas, but the most spectacular display is in late June when 30,000 irises burst into colour. As you leave the temple gate, pop into the small **museum** on the left, which is most of interest for its photos of Mōtsū-ji's colourful festivals, including the sacred *Ennen-no-Mai* dance (see previous page) and a poetry-writing contest in Heian-period dress which takes place on the last Sunday in May.

### Practicalities

Hiraizumi has its own **information** booth (daily 8.30am–4.30/5pm; ☎0191/46-2110), to the right as you exit the station. Buses for Chūson-ji and Ichinoseki also depart from this concourse, and you can **rent bikes** (April–Nov daily 8am–5pm; ¥1000 per day) from beside the information office. Despite its size, Hiraizumi merits both a **post office** and foreign-exchange **bank**; both located in the backstreets to the west of the station.

The best place to **stay** in Hiraizumi is *Motsu-ji Youth Hostel* (☎0191/46-2331, fax 46-4184; dorm ①; rooms ④), in the grounds of Mōtsū-ji temple and run by the monks. The hostel also doubles as a *shukubō* (temple lodging) with private *tatami* rooms overlooking the gardens, though all washing facilities and meals are shared. In summer (July 20–Sept 10) there are free *zazen* meditation sessions, and at any time of year you can attend prayers in the temple (daily 6.30–7am). Another possibility is the clean and comfortable *Shirayama Ryokan* (☎0191/46-2883, fax 46-3914; ⑤–⑥ including meals), located in the sidestreets west of the station.

Hiraizumi has a couple of **coffee shops** and small **restaurants** outside the station, though none of them stay open in the evening. On the north side of the concourse, just before the crossroads, *Bashō-kan* (daily 9am–3.30pm; Jan–April, Nov & Dec closed Wed) serves a range of tempura and soba dishes, or try the good-value *soba teishoku* in *Izumi Soba-ya* (daily 9am–6pm) on the opposite side of the road. If you fancy a picnic, there's an A-Coop supermarket on the road to Mōtsū-ji.

## Around Hiraizumi

The Hiraizumi area boasts two river **gorges** with confusingly similar names. **Geibikei** (as opposed to Gembikei) is the more impressive of the two, a narrow defile best viewed by boat, which lies some 20km east of Hiraizumi. Unless you've got your own transport, however, the easiest way to get there is by train from Ichinoseki Station. It's an attractive ride on the JR Ōfunato line to Geibikei Station (30min) marred at the end by a huge cement works. From the station, turn right and walk along the lane for five minutes, then follow the road under the tracks to find the boat dock.

Though not cheap, the Geibikei **boat trip** (hourly 8.30/9am–3/4.30pm; 90min; ¥1500) is a lot of fun. Despite poling fairly sizeable wooden punts upstream for 2km, the boatmen still find breath to regale their passengers with local legends, details of the passing flora and endless statistics about the gorge. It's all in Japanese of course, but the general mirth is infectious and, on the way downstream, he'll break into song – getting a great echo off the hundred-metre-high cliffs. At the halfway point, everyone gets out on a shingle beach to throw stones into a small hollow in the opposite cliff, for luck, and to buy bags of fish food for the river's huge, brightly coloured carp.

# The Tōno valley

Set in a bowl of low mountains in the heart of one of Japan's poorest regions, **Tōno** takes pride in its living legacy of farming and folk traditions. The district's main sights consist of several **magariya** – large, L-shaped farmhouses – and a number of museums devoted to the old ways, but the area is perhaps most famous for its wealth of **folk-tales** known as *Tōno Monogatari* (see box overleaf). There are references to these legends

| TŌNO | | |
|---|---|---|
| **Tōno** | *Tōno* | 遠野 |
| Chiba Family Magariya | *Chiba-ke Magariya* | 千葉家曲り家 |
| Dan-no-hana | *Dan-no-hana* | ダンノハナ |
| Denderano | *Denderano* | デンデラ野 |
| Denshō-en | *Denshō-en* | 伝承園 |
| Fukusen-ji | *Fukusen-ji* | 福泉寺 |
| Furusato-mura | *Furusato-mura* | ふるさと村 |
| Gohyaku Rakan | *Gohyaku Rakan* | 五百羅漢 |
| Jōken-ji | *Jōken-ji* | 常堅寺 |
| Sui-kōen | *Sui-kōen* | 水公園 |
| Tōno Folk Village | *Tōno Mukashi Banashi Mura* | 遠野昔話村 |
| Tōno Municipal Museum | *Tōno Shiritsu Hakubutsukan* | 遠野市立博物館 |
| Tsuzuki Stone | *Tsuzuki-ishi* | 続石 |
| Watermill | *Suisha* | 水車 |
| Unedori-jinja | *Unedori-jinja* | 卯子酉神社 |
| *ACCOMMODATION AND EATING* | | |
| Folklore Tōno | *Forukurōro Tōno* | フォルクローロ遠野 |
| Ichi-riki | *Ichi-riki* | 一力 |
| Minshuku Magariya | *Minshuku Magariya* | 民宿曲り家 |
| Mizumoto | *Mizumoto* | みず本 |
| Momiji-an | *Momiji-an* | もみじ庵 |
| Minshuku Rindō | *Minshuku Rindō* | 民宿りんどう |
| Sakae Ryokan | *Sakae Ryokan* | さかえ旅館 |
| Taigetsu | *Taigetsu* | 待月 |
| Minshuku Tōno | *Minshuku Tōno* | 民宿とおの |
| Tōno Youth Hostel | *Tōno Yūsu Hosuteru* | 遠野ユースホステル |
| Ume-no-ya | *Ume-no-ya* | うめのや |

## THE LEGENDS OF TŌNO

When the far-sighted folklorist **Kunio Yanagita** visited Tōno in 1909 he found a world still populated with the shadowy figures of demons and other usually malevolent spirits which the farmers strove to placate with ancient rituals. The following year he published **Tōno Monogatari** (published in English as *The Legends of Tōno*), the first book to tap the rich oral tradition of rural Japan. The 118 tales were told to him by Kyōseki (or Kizen) Sasaki, the educated son of a Tōno peasant, to whom the goblins, ghosts and gods were part of everyday life.

People in Tōno still talk about **Zashiki Warashi**, a mischievous child spirit (either male or female) who can be heard running at night, or might put your pillow under your feet while you sleep, but also brings prosperity to the household. Another popular tale tells of a farmer's beautiful daughter who fell in love with their horse. When he heard that she'd married the horse, he hung it from a mulberry tree, but his grieving daughter was whisked off to heaven clinging to her lover.

Probably the most popular character from the legends, however, is the **kappa**, an ugly water creature that isn't unique to Tōno but seems to exist here in large numbers. You'll find *kappa* images everywhere in town – on post boxes, outside the station, and even the police box is *kappa*-esque. The "real" *kappa* has long skinny limbs, webbed hands and feet, a sharp beak and a hollow on the top of his head which must be kept full of water. He's usually green, sometimes with a red face, and his main pastime seems to be pulling young children into ponds and rivers – though many malformed babies were attributed to being fathered by a *kappa*. In the legends, one local *kappa* got a fright when he grabbed a horse's tail, hoping to drag it into the river, but was carried back to the stable instead. He hid under a bucket until he was discovered, and was then sent packing after promising never to cause trouble again. If you do meet a *kappa*, remember to bow – on returning your bow the water will run out of the hollow on his head and he'll have to hurry off to replenish it.

all around the valley, alongside ancient shrines, rock carvings and traces of primitive cults which help create Tōno's slightly mysterious undercurrent.

Today Tōno is connected to the modern world by train, an attractive journey east on the JR Kamaishi line from Hanamaki, or Shin-Hanamaki for the Shinkansen. Once in Tōno, it's best to hire a bike or taxi to explore the valley's far-flung sights, though in summer there are also tour buses (see Practicalities, p.252). Allow at least two days to do the area justice.

## Tōno

**TŌNO** itself is a small town set among flat rice-lands, with orchards and pine forests clothing the surrounding hills. Although it's mainly of interest for its hotels, banks and other facilities, there are a couple of museums to see before setting off round the valley. From Tōno Station it's an eight-minute walk straight across town and over the river to the **Tōno Municipal Museum** (daily 9am–5pm, closed last day of the month & hols; Jan–March, Nov & Dec also closed Mon; ¥300, or ¥500 with Tōno Folk Village), at the back of a red-brick building which doubles as the library. This entertaining museum gives a good overview of life in Tōno – its festivals, crafts and agricultural traditions – and you can watch beautifully presented cartoon versions of the most famous legends; though narrated in Japanese, these simple tales are easy to follow.

Walking back towards the station, turn left just across the river for **Tōno Folk Village** (daily 9am–5pm, closed last day of the month & Sept 20–30; Jan–March & Dec also closed Mon; ¥300). The "village" consists of several buildings, including the ryokan where Yanagita stayed while researching his legends, and an old storehouse containing more dramatizations of the stories. Look out for the translations of Japanese fairy tales by Lafcadio Hearn (see p.588), compiled in the late nineteenth century; his interest in these stories helped keep them alive.

## Practicalities

Tōno's **information office** (daily 8am–6/6.30pm; ☎0198/62-3030) is on the right as you exit the station. Though the staff don't speak English, they have English-language maps and brochures, and a larger-scale Japanese map which is useful for navigating around the valley. The attached shop stocks copies of *The Legends of Tōno* (¥2000); you might also find it at the Municipal Museum or Denshō-en (see p.253).

*GETTING AROUND*

To make the most of the Tōno valley you really need your own transport. There's a **car-rental** place inside the station, Tōno Kankō Rent-a-car (☎0198/62-1375), and Eki Rent-a-car (☎0198/62-3200) nearby. However, most people opt to cycle. You can **rent bikes** from the information office and other outlets on the station concourse (¥1000 per day), or from the Youth Hostel (see Accommodation overleaf) for ¥800. Tōno maps show three recommended cycling routes (also possible by car), of around four hours each which cover the main sights – they're reasonably well sign-posted, though not always in English. You can also hire **taxis** outside Tōno Station: Tōno Kōtsū Taxi (☎0198/62-3355), for example, offers a range of tours from ¥5500 for an hour up to ¥37,500 for a full day.

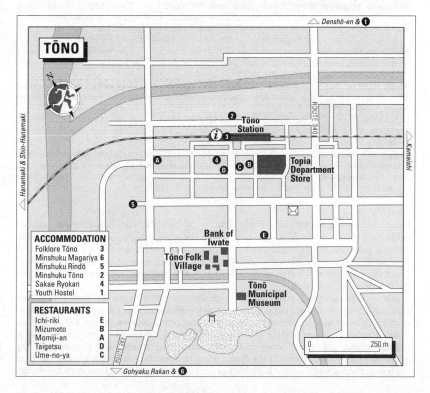

△ *Denshō-en &* ❶

**TŌNO**

◁ *Hanamaki & Shin-Hanamaki*

▷ *Kamaishi*

ROUTE 340

❷ Tōno Station
ℹ️ ❸

Ⓐ ❹ Ⓒ Ⓑ
Ⓓ

Topia Department Store

❺

🏤

Bank of Iwate
Tōno Folk Village
Ⓔ

Tōno Municipal Museum

ROUTE 283

| ACCOMMODATION | |
|---|---|
| Folklore Tōno | 3 |
| Minshuku Magariya | 6 |
| Minshuku Rindō | 5 |
| Minshuku Tōno | 2 |
| Sakae Ryokan | 4 |
| Youth Hostel | 1 |

| RESTAURANTS | |
|---|---|
| Ichi-riki | E |
| Mizumoto | B |
| Momiji-an | A |
| Taigetsu | D |
| Ume-no-ya | C |

| 0 | 250 m |

▽ *Gohyaku Rakan &* ❻

In addition there are **organized tours**, the most comprehensive of which are run by JR Bus; unfortunately, rail passes aren't valid on these. They operate two tours daily on weekends and holidays from late-April to late-October, and every day throughout August. The longer A-course (5hr; ¥4500) includes Tōno's two museums, Fukusen-ji, Denshō-en, the Chiba Magariya and Gohyaku Rakan, while the B-course (3hr 30min; ¥3900) omits the two museums. Both tours depart from outside the station and include lunch. Alternatively, "Shuttle Taxis" (nine-person minibuses) depart three times a day (8.30am, 10.25am & 12.40pm; 3hr; ¥1200) for Denshō-en and Furusato-mura from outside the tourist office. This is a transport-only service (no guide) and is also restricted to summer weekends and holidays (April–early Nov), depending on demand.

**Local buses** also stop outside the station, but the only really useful routes are those heading northeast to Denshō-en and Furusato-mura (see p.254 for details). These buses also stop near *Tōno Youth Hostel* (see below).

## ACCOMMODATION

Tōno has a reasonable selection of **accommodation** within walking distance of the station. If you want more atmosphere, however, you can stay in a real *magariya* farmhouse on the west side of town, while Tōno's excellent youth hostel is located about 4km northeast.

**Folklore Tōno**, 5-7 Shinkoku-chō (☎0198/62-0700, fax 62-0800). A new, JR-owned hotel built inside the station building. Its rooms are Western-style, with TV, phone and bathroom, and the price includes a simple breakfast. ④–⑤.

**Minshuku Magariya**, 30-58-3 Niisato, Ayaori-chō (☎0198/62-4564). This traditional farmhouse is located 3km southwest of the station (around ¥1000 by taxi). The rooms are all Japanese-style, with shared facilities, and excellent meals are served round a big open hearth. Apart from being a little inconvenient, the downsides are that no one speaks English and they don't accept children. ⑦.

**Minshuku Rindō**, 2-34 Daiku-chō (☎0198/62-5726, fax 62-4636). Simple, homely minshuku on an attractive street, roughly five minutes' walk west from the station. The owner speaks a little English, and offers rooms with or without meals. ④–⑤.

**Sakae Ryokan**, 3-14 Shinkoku-chō (☎0198/62-2407, fax 62-0483). More refined ryokan opposite the station, with nine well-kept *tatami* rooms, though none with en-suite facilities. Rooms available with or without meals. ⑤–⑥.

**Minshuku Tōno**, 2-17 Zaimoku-chō (☎ & fax 0198/62-4395). Small, friendly minshuku with an English-speaking owner, on the north side of the tracks. Rates available with or without meals. ④–⑤.

**Tōno Youth Hostel**, 13-39-5 Tsuchibuchi-chō (☎ & fax 0198/62-8736). Delightful, modern hostel with dorms and family rooms, laundry facilities and excellent-value meals. It's set among rice-fields about fifteen-minutes' walk from the Denshō-en or Ashiarai-gawa bus stops (see opposite). The nicely offbeat manager speaks a little English and can advise on local cycling routes. Bike rental available. ②.

## EATING

Local speciality foods include *hitsuko soba*, small bowls of rough, handmade noodles eaten with a mix of chicken, raw egg, onion and mushrooms, and the regional dish *Nambu hitssumi* (or *suiton*), which is a soup laced with seasonal vegetables and dumplings. You can sample these and other local delicacies, such as *ayu* (river fish) and *Jingis Kan* (barbecued lamb), at the folk-village **restaurants**, or try one of the following places in central Tōno.

For a coffee or quick snack, walk down the main road from the station to where *Taigetsu* (10am–11pm) serves staples such as cheese toast, curry-rice and ramen dishes till relatively late. On the opposite side of the road, *Ume-no-ya* (daily except Tues 11am–8pm) is another simple place, offering good portions of curry-rice, *ebi*-fry, omelettes and set meals from ¥500. For something a little more upmarket, try *Mizumoto* (daily except Wed 11am–8pm), a bright cheerful place with a broad range of dishes on the back of this block, or *Momiji-an* (daily except Wed 11am–2pm & 4–8pm), a welcoming soba joint west of the station, where bowls of noodles start at ¥500. Finally, *Ichi-riki* (daily 11am–2pm & 5–8pm), down towards the river, is an attractive place with a reputation for its fresh fish, though they also serve *tonkatsu*, tempura and warming, winter stews.

## West of Tōno

West of Tōno the main valley narrows, funnelling the road and railway along beside the Sarukaishi-gawa. The wooded southern hillside hides some unusual shrines and an appealing group of Buddha images, which make one of the best short trips out of Tōno. Further up the valley, an imposing *magariya* farmhouse attracts a lot of attention, but it's better to save your energy for more accessible examples on the east side of town.

Heading out of Tōno on the south side of the river (on the old Route 283), look out after 2.5km for a stone staircase on the left. At the bottom of the steps, past the house, you'll find a tree festooned with red and white ribbons and, behind it, **Unedori-jinja**. This little shrine is dedicated to the god in charge of matrimonial affairs; if you want to get married, tie a red ribbon onto the tree with your left hand. Having wowed the god with your skill, go back and climb the stone steps, cross a lane and follow the path into a narrow, wooded valley filled with mossy stones. Keep looking closely at these stones; at first you won't see anything, but gradually faint outlines appear, then full faces and rounded bodies, until you're seeing little figures everywhere. Known as the **Gohyaku Rakan**, there are supposed to be five hundred of these Buddhist "disciples", which were carved by a local monk in the late eighteenth century to commemorate victims of a terrible famine in 1754.

Before heading back down to the main road, turn right (east) along the lane and continue for 700m until you come to a *torii* on the right and a steep path leading up through the pine woods. At the top of a short, stiff climb there's a larger shrine building (usually locked) and two small shrines with a collection of phallic and female symbols made of stone or wood. Though rather dilapidated nowdays, this is one of the few remaining shrines dedicated to **Konsei-sama**, the local god of fertility and an interesting vestige of an ancient cult.

The thatch-roofed **Chiba Family Magariya** (daily 8.30am–5pm; Jan–March, Nov & Dec 9am–4pm; ¥350) stands high above the valley some 11km west of Tōno, north of the main valley up a steep side road. This two-hundred-year-old farmhouse was selected for restoration as an important example of a *magariya*, an L-shaped building with the stables in the shorter wing. It once housed the Chiba family plus fifteen labourers and twenty horses, but today it's rather empty and neglected. If you do venture out this way, take a look at the **Tsuzuki Stone**, 500m before the farmhouse and set back in the woods. Though it's said to be natural, the enormous, rounded boulder balanced on a smaller stone looks like a dolmen.

## Northeast of Tōno

The broad valley northeast of Tōno is home to a number of somewhat touristy "folk villages" aimed at preserving the old crafts. It's worth visiting one of these, of which the new Furusato-mura is probably the best, though the smaller Denshō-en and Sui-kōen are slightly more accessible. Other sights to aim for include a *kappa* pool, an old water mill and a temple housing Japan's tallest Kannon statue. However, the area's chief highlight is the scenery dotted with the occasional thatched farmhouse – it's best to get a bike and just follow the country lanes.

The main road northeast of Tōno (Route 340) leads past **Denshō-en** (daily 9am–4.30pm; ¥300), located about 4km out of town. This village-museum contains various buildings relocated from around Tōno, including a waterwheel, storehouses and a *magariya*, where local folk demonstrate weaving, rope-making and other crafts. Inside the *magariya*, follow the narrow corridor at the back to a small shrine room filled with brightly dressed dolls. These are images of Oshira-sama, an agricultural deity worshipped throughout northern Honshū. They're stick-like figures, their faces either drawn on or simply carved, and are made from mulberry; according to the legends, Tōno's original Oshira-sama came from the same tree on which the horse-husband died (see box, p.250). The deities, often used by blind mediums, are also supposed to predict the future – hence all the prayer papers tied around the shrine. Denshō-en is one of the few places which is feasible by local bus. Services depart every hour or so from Tōno Station and drop you either at the village or 100m further back at the Ashiaraigawa stop (15–20min; ¥290).

A short distance east along the main road from Denshō-en, a sign-posted right turn leads to **Jōken-ji**. Founded in 1490, the temple is mainly of interest for its statue of Obinzuru-sama, a little figure in a cloak and hat with a very shiny anatomy – the deity is supposed to cure illnesses if rubbed in the appropriate place. Behind the temple there's a **kappa pool** with a particularly helpful *kappa* who is credited with dousing a fire in Jōken-ji. An eccentric local has built a small shrine to himself beside the pool and may well regale you with incomprehensible but good-natured stories.

### Fukusen-ji and Furusato-mura

Just before Denshō-en, a road branches north, following the main valley for another 2km to **Fukusen-ji** (daily 8.15am–5pm; Jan–March & Dec Sat & Sun only; ¥300). This fairly modern temple, founded in 1912, is famous for its seventeen-metre-tall image of Kannon, the Goddess of Mercy. The slender, gilded statue with a blue hair-do is carved from a single tree trunk and took the craftsman twelve years before it was finally unveiled in 1963. It stands in an attractive temple at the top of the hill, where the artist's tools and photos of the huge tree being brought to Tōno by train are also on display.

Continue on this road another 3km and you'll reach **Furusato-mura** (daily 9am–5pm, last entry 4pm; ¥500). The biggest and most attractive of Tōno's folk-museums, Furusato-mura resembles a working village, with its own rice-fields, vegetable plots and duck ponds. There are five refurbished *magariya* on the hillside, where pensioners sit beside smoking hearths, busily making souvenirs such as straw slippers, wooden *kappa* and bamboo baskets – if you want to have a go, they'll be only too pleased to show you. You can buy their handiwork in the museum shop, where there's also a small restaurant. Some Denshō-en buses continue up the valley to Furusato-mura though they're fairly sporadic (every 1–2 hours; 30min; ¥490).

### East of Denshō-en: Sui-kōen

The most beautiful part of the Tōno valley lies **east of Denshō-en**, though to appreciate it you'll have to get off onto the side roads. One attractive ride takes you out to an old watermill and then loops back past the third folk-village. To find the turning, follow Route 340 for 3km east from Denshō-en and then fork right immediately after crossing a red-lacquered bridge. The lane climbs gently up hill, past a number of old farms to a small, thatched **watermill**. On the way you pass the **house of Kyōseki Sasaki** (of Tōno Legends fame; see p.250), opposite which there's a path signed to **Dan-no-hana**. Again, there's not a great deal to see, but the small hill of Dan-no-hana is another of Tōno's slightly eerie places. In the not so distant past, old people were sent to places called Dan-no-hana to die, however, in this case the old folk got bored waiting, so they came down to work the fields during the day and returned to their hill at night.

Heading back down to the main road, look out on the left for a turning signed to "Denderano". Follow this lane west for nearly 2km and you'll come to the last of the folk-villages, **Sui-kōen** (daily 10am–5pm; ¥200), with a *magariya*, a *kappa* pool and displays of antique farm implements. From here you can drop down to the main road, or continue west along country lanes.

# Morioka and around

A former castle-town on the confluence of three rivers, the small, congenial city of **MORIOKA** is the terminus of the Tōhoku Shinkansen. It has no outstanding sights, but the attractive setting, range of accommodation and interesting local cuisine make Morioka a good overnight stop on the journey through Northern Honshū. With a couple of hours to spare, you could stretch your legs around the castle ruins and some of the older neighbourhoods, or take a bus out to a rather bizarre art museum. Additionally, Morioka is one of the main access points for hikes around the nearby **Hachimantai plateau**.

The city has two major summer **festivals**. At the end of the rice-planting season the *Chagu-Chagu Umakko* (June 15) features a fifteen-kilometre procession of richly caparisoned horses ending at the city's Hachiman-gū shrine. Then, in early August (2–4), thousands of dancers parade through town during the *Sansa Odori* accompanied by flutes and drums, followed by a general knees-up.

## The City

The **Nakatsu-gawa** cuts through the centre of Morioka, flowing south beneath the old castle walls and under a seventeenth-century bridge which is the pride of the city. From the station, located on the far west side of town, it takes about twenty minutes to walk along Saien-dōri, one of Morioka's two major shopping streets, straight to the castle. If you turn right in front of the castle park, **Iwate-kōen**, and walk down to the Nakatsu-

| MORIOKA AND AROUND | | |
|---|---|---|
| **Morioka** | *Morioka* | 盛岡 |
| Gozaku | *Gozaku* | ござく |
| Hashimoto Art Museum | *Hashimoto Bijutsukan* | 橋本美術館 |
| Ishiwari-sakura | *Ishiwari-sakura* | 石割桜 |
| Iwate-kōen | *Iwate-kōen* | 岩手公園 |
| Kami-no-hashi | *Kami-no-hashi* | 上ノ橋 |
| Kōgensha | *Kōgensha* | 光原社 |
| Naka-no-hashi | *Naka-no-hashi* | 中ノ橋 |
| | | |
| *ACCOMMODATION AND RESTAURANTS* | | |
| Hotel Ace | *Hoteru Ēsu* | ホテルエース |
| Azuma-ya | *Azuma-ya* | 東家 |
| Kumagi Ryokan | *Kumagi Ryokan* | 熊ヶ井旅館 |
| Morioka Youth Hostel | *Morioka Yūsu Hosuteru* | 盛岡ユースホステル |
| Hotel Rich | *Hoteru Ritchi* | ホテルリッチ |
| Sansa Odori | *Sansa Odori* | さんさ踊り |
| Seirōkaku | *Seirōkaku* | 盛楼閣 |
| Taishōkan | *Taishōkan* | 大正館 |
| | | |
| **Hachimantai** | *Hachimantai* | 八幡平 |
| | | |
| **Iwate-san** | *Iwate-san* | 岩手山 |

gawa, you can pick up a pleasant riverside path to the east of the old walls. Once the seat of the Nambu lords, Morioka castle took 36 years to complete (1597–1633), only to be destroyed in the battles surrounding the Meiji Restoration. From here, a right turn on **Ōdōri**, the city's foremost shopping street, and across the river via the **Naka-no-hashi** bridge will lead you towards to a remnant of the older city.

Immediately over the river, you can't miss the ornate red-brick and grey-slate facade of **Iwate Bank** which dates from 1911. Inside, clerks still bustle around the original banking hall with its high, plastered ceiling, elaborate woodwork and stone-flagged floor. Turn left beside the bank and you'll come to a row of traditional, Meiji-era buildings known as **Gozaku**, whose centrepiece is a shop selling brushes, straw and wicker goods. Stores opposite specialize in the region's most famous **crafts** – heavy iron kettles and eye-catching cotton textiles dyed with intricate patterns – while appetizing odours greet you at the top of the street where a *sembei* shop turns out local-style rice crackers sprinkled with sesame seeds or nuts; walk round the side and you can see the bakers hard at work. The pale-blue clapboard building with a slender watch tower across the road from the bakery was built at the beginning of the nineteenth century and still functions as a **fire station**. Continuing north to the next T-junction, to the right you'll find an old, blackened **kura**, a traditional storehouse, with a relaxed coffee-shop, *Issaryō*, upstairs; turn left, however, and you reach the renowned seventeenth-century bridge, **Kami-no-hashi**. In fact, the supports are all concrete nowdays, and you'd be forgiven for missing the bridge's most important feature: eighteen bronze, bulb-shaped top-knots forged in the early 1600s which ornament the railings.

Heading south along the river from Kami-no-hashi the next major avenue is Chūō-dōri, lined with civic offices. About 400m west of the river, a 300-year-old cherry tree bulges out of a fifteen-centimetre-wide fissure in a rounded granite boulder. Known as the **ishiwari-sakura**, or "rock-splitting cherry", no-one knows whether the tree really split the rock, but it's a startling sight. If you follow Chūō-dōri west to the Kitakami-gawa, you'll reach a small neighbourhood known as **Zaimoku-chō** whose main feature is a traditional shopping street running parallel to the river. Among smart modern boutiques there are a number of craftshops, notably **Kōgensha** (daily 10am–6pm, closed 15th of each month), with two outlets on opposite sides of the street. They sell a good range of modern and more traditional designs of ironware, paper, bamboo work and so on, while at the back of their southerly, larger outlet you'll find a coffee shop in an attractive alley leading down to the river.

The last of Morioka's central sights requires a bus ride out to the rather eccentric **Hashimoto Art Museum** (daily 10am–5pm; ¥700) on the town's eastern outskirts. Buses, which depart from Morioka Station, don't run in winter (Dec–mid-March) and are infrequent at the best of times (4–7 daily; 22min; ¥270), but are timed to give you about an hour in the museum. Hashimoto Yaoji (1903–79), who designed the museum, was a man of eclectic tastes: works by Courbet and Daubigny are followed by local artists and Hashimoto's own dark, bold canvases. Other nooks and crannies are stuffed with priceless ceramics, folk art, antique Western furniture, festival gear and a wonderful collection of Nambu ironware kettles. And to cap it all, there's a complete *magariya* farmhouse perched on the roof.

## Practicalities

Morioka's excellent **"i" information centre** (daily 9am–7pm; ☎019/625-2090) is located on the train station's second floor, near the southern entrance to the Shinkansen tracks. The English-speaking staff can provide maps and information about the region, and there's also a JR information desk next door. For news of local **events**, look out for *Trailblazer*, the International Association's newsletter (see Listings for details).

Local and long-distance **buses** depart from the east side of Morioka Station, with services running to Tokyo, the Hachimantai plateau and Towada-ko. Apart from the

Hashimoto Art Museum, central Morioka can easily be covered on foot, but from May to late-November there's also the option of city **bus tours**, with a half-day tour starting at ¥4500, including lunch; ask at the information centre for details.

## Accommodation

The cheapest **accommodation** in town is the friendly *Morioka Youth Hostel* (☎019/662-2220; ①), though it's rather inconveniently located in the northwestern suburbs; to get there take a bus from Morioka Station to Takamatsu-no-ikeguchi (20min; ¥210) and then walk east for five minutes. Closer to the centre, the best option is the welcoming *Ryokan Kumagai* (☎0196/51-3020, fax 626-0096; ④), where the owners speak a little English, located south of Saien-dōri and about eight minutes' walk from the station. If they're full, *Taishōkan* (☎019/622-4436; ④), opposite, is more basic but perfectly adequate. In front of the station, *Hotel Rich* (☎019/625-2611, fax 625-2673) is a standard, mid-range business hotel with a choice of Western- or Japanese-style rooms and in-house restaurants. If you'd rather be in the downtown area, *Hotel Ace* (☎019/654-3811, fax 654-3815; ④–⑤), just north of Ōdōri, also has English-speaking staff and comfortable rooms, though it's worth paying a little extra to stay in their new wing.

## Eating

Morioka's famous **speciality food** is named *Wanko-soba*, after the small bowls that the thin, flat buckwheat noodles are served in. They're now usually eaten as a contest during which diners don an apron and shovel and down as many bowls as possible while a waitress relentlessly dishes up more; to stop, you have to get the top on to your emptied bowl – easier said than done. It's not the most relaxed dining experience, but lots of fun with a large enough group. The meal includes side-dishes, such as sashimi, chicken or mushrooms, but true *Wanko-soba* eaters stick to the noodles; the record is a staggering 350 bowls or so. If you fancy having a go, the best-known **restaurant** is *Azuma-ya* (daily except Tues 11am–8pm), in the streets east of Gozaku (see opposite) with another branch near Morioka Station. Expect to pay between ¥2000 and ¥3000 for *Wanko-soba*, though both places also serve standard noodle dishes at reasonable prices.

Another rather odd Morioka concoction, rēmen consists of a large bowl of cold, semi-transparent, slightly chewy egg noodles eaten with spicy Korean *kimchi*, and a variety of garnishes which might include boiled egg, sesame seeds and slices of apple or cold meat. This delight is only consumed in summer (May–Oct) and can be sampled at *Seirokaku* (daily 11am–2am), opposite the station, on the second floor above a *pachinko* parlour; they also serve more conventional *yakiniku* and other meat dishes.

In the town centre, Ōdōri and the entertainment district immediately to its north have a broad selection of more traditional eating and drinking places, from hamburger joints to top-class establishments. Despite its unpromising entrance above another *pachinko* parlour, *Sansa Odōri* (Mon–Sat 5pm–midnight) is a bustling, modern-style *izakaya* where you can eat for around ¥2000 per head; it's about halfway along Ōdōri, opposite the Daiei department store.

# Listings

**Banks** Iwate Bank, Tōhoku Bank and 77 Bank all have branches on Ōdōri with foreign exchange desks. Iwate Bank also has a branch outside the train station.

**Car rental** Nippon Rent-a-car (☎019/622-0100), Nissan (☎019/654-5825) Toyota (☎019/652-0100) and Eki Rent-a-car (☎019/624-5212) all have offices in or near the station.

**Hospitals** The two main central hospitals are Iwate Medical University Hospital, 19-1 Uchi-maru (☎019/651-5111) and the Prefectural Hospital, 1-4-1 Ueda (☎019/653-1151).

**International Association**, 2-4-20 Ōsakawara (☎019/654-8900, fax 654-8922). The local forum for international exchange will also offer help and advice to any foreigner in difficulties.

**Post office** The Central Post Office (Morioka Chūō Yūbin-kyoku, Morioka-shi), just north of Chūō-dōri, has a poste restante service. There's also a more convenient sub-post office in the blocks in front of the station.

**Shopping** Nambu ironware, dyed cotton textiles and plain wooden *kokeshi* dolls are the representative crafts of this region. The best crafts shop is Kōgensha (see p.256), but you'll also find local souvenirs in the station's basement and in Park Avenue, Morioka's main department store on Saien-dōri. Or, try the more modern Cube II, next door.

**Taxi** For a taxi call the station's central booking office on ☎019/622-5240.

## Around Morioka

Tōhoku's highest peak, **Iwate-san** (2041m), dominates Morioka's northern horizon and marks the eastern edge of the **Hachimantai plateau**, a beautiful area for hiking among marshes and pine forests. At present, the volcanic peak is off-limits, but you can spend a day walking around the plateau to the north of Iwate-san, from where it's an easy stroll to the less daunting summit of **Hachimantai** (1613m). From the Hachimantai Chōjō bus stop, a well-marked path leads to the summit (around 40min), across Hachiman-numa marshes. Afterwards you can follow a variety of tracks wandering across the plateau with views south to the barren slopes of Iwate-san.

**Buses** from Morioka, or the slightly closer Ōbuke Station, run up to the plateau on the "Aspete line" toll road from late May to late October (5 daily; 1hr 25min–1hr 50min; ¥1320), after which these roads are closed by snow. Alternatively, you can combine this with a bus along the new "Jyukai line" road which loops south through Matsukawa-onsen before joining the Aspete line at Hachimantai Chōjō bus stop. Since there are only three buses a day on this route (July & Aug only 8.02am & 11.52am going up; 2.10pm on the return journey; 2hr 20min; ¥1320), it's best to travel up on the early morning Jyukai line bus and return to Morioka on the Aspete line. There are also three buses each day from Hachimantai Chōjō for Towada-ko (see p.270), again in summer only.

# Aomori and around

Honshū's most northerly city, **AOMORI**, sits at the bottom of Mutsu Bay, sheltered by the two claws of the Tsugaru and Shimokita peninsulas. It's a spacious, but rather characterless, city which has lost a good deal of its Hokkaidō-bound visitors now that trains run straight through to Hakodate via the Seikan Tunnel (see box on p.313). However, the crowds still turn up for Aomori's **Nebuta Matsuri** (Aug 2–7), one of Japan's biggest and rowdiest **festivals**, featuring giant, illuminated floats and energetic dancing. It takes less than a day to cover Aomori's main sights, of which the most appealing is a park displaying *nebuta* floats, followed by a couple of decent museums of history and folkcraft.

Southwest of Aomori, the small town of **Hirosaki** has a number of interesting historical sights around its once magnificent castle which can be covered on a day-trip. Allow at least two days, however, to explore the **Shimokita Hantō**, the axe-head peninsula lowering over Aomori from the east. Shimokita is dominated by the sacred Osorezan, an eerie wasteland where souls hover between life and death, but the region also has some excellent coastal scenery and a hardy wildlife population, including the world's most northerly population of wild monkeys.

## Orientation, arrival, information and city transport

The striking Bay Bridge and a sleek, glass pyramid known as ASPAM dominate Aomori's **harbour skyline**. Inland, the city centre is a functional place with nothing to detain you beyond an unusually well-designed prefectural museum, the **Kyōdokan**, covering local history and culture. Afterwards, hop on a bus out to the southern

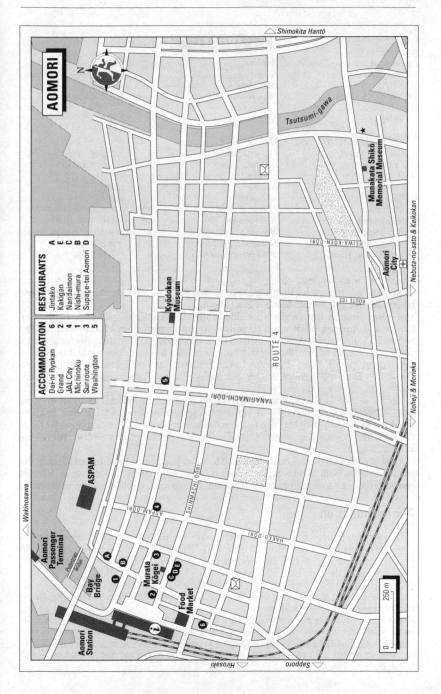

△ *Shimokita Hantō*

# AOMORI

N

*Tsutsumi-gawa*

Munakata Shikō Memorial Museum

HEIWA-KŌEN-DŌRI

Aomori City ✚

▷ *Nebuta-no-sato & Keikokan*

ROUTE 103

RESTAURANTS
Jintako              A
Kakigin             E
Nandaimon      C
Nishi-mura        B
Supage-tei Aomori  D

ACCOMMODATION
Dai-ni Ryokan    6
Grand                2
JAL City            4
Michinoku         1
Surroute            3
Washington       5

Kyōdokan Museum

ROUTE 4

5

YANAGIMACHI-DŌRI

▷ *Noheji & Morioka*

ASPAM

SHINMACHI-DŌRI

ASPAM-DŌRI

HAKKŌ-DŌRI

Aomori Passenger Terminal

Pedestrian Bridge

△ *Wakinosawa*

Bay Bridge

A
B
1
Murata Kōgei
2
3
C D E
4
Food Market
6

Aomori Station

ℹ

250 m

0

▷ *Sapporo*

▷ *Hirosaki*

| | | |
|---|---|---|
| **AOMORI** | | |
| Aomori | *Aomori* | 青森 |
| Keikokan | *Keikokan* | 稽古館 |
| Kyōdokan | *Kyōdokan* | 郷土館 |
| Munakata Shikō | *Munakata Shikō* | 棟方志功記念館 |
| Memorial Museum | *Kinenkan* | |
| Nebuta-no-sato | *Nebuta-no-sato* | ねぶたの里 |
| | | |
| *ACCOMMODATION AND EATING* | | |
| Dai-ni Ryokan | *Dai-ni Ryokan* | 大二旅館 |
| Grand Hotel | *Gurando Hoteru* | グランドホテル |
| Hotel JAL City | *Hoteru JAL Shitii* | ホテルJALシティー |
| Jintako | *Jintako* | 甚太古 |
| Kakigen | *Kakigen* | 柿源 |
| Michinoku | *Michinoku* | みちのく |
| Nishi-mura | *Nishi-mura* | 西むら |
| Hotel Sunroute | *Hoteru Sanrūto* | ホテルサンルート |
| Supage-tei Aomori | *Supage-tei Aomori* | すぱげ亭青森 |
| Washington Hotel | *Washinton Hoteru* | ワシントンホテル |

suburbs where the spectacular display of festival floats at **Nebuta-no-sato** gives some inkling of what the *Nebuta Matsuri* is all about.

**Aomori Station** lies on the west side of the city centre, just inland from the Bay Bridge and **Aomori passenger terminal**, where **ferries** from Wakinosawa (on the Shimokita Hantō) dock. Arriving by boat from Hokkaidō's Hakodate or Muroran ports, you'll pull up at a wharf further west, from where it's a ten-minute taxi ride into the centre (around ¥1000). **Long-distance buses** terminate at Aomori Station, while limousine buses from the **airport** drop you outside either the station or ASPAM (40min; ¥560).

The most useful **information centre** is the City Tourism Office (daily 8.30am–5pm; ☎0177/39-4670), located inside the station, towards its south end, which has English-speaking staff. Alternatively, there are information desks in the first-floor lobby of ASPAM (daily 9am–6pm; ☎0177/34-2500) and in Aomori airport (daily 9am–6pm; ☎0177/39-4561).

Most of central Aomori is manageable on foot, but you'll need **local buses** to reach the southern sights. Both the green Shiei buses and the less-frequent blue-and-white JR buses run out to Nebuta-no-sato from Aomori Station; rail passes are valid on these JR services.

## Accommodation

It's a good idea to book **accommodation** in advance in Aomori at any time of year, but essential during the *Nebuta Matsuri* (Aug 2–7). Though there's a decent range of business hotels in the city centre, it's short on budget places – at this level you might consider staying in Hirosaki instead (see p.265).

**Dai-ni Ryokan**, 1-7-8 Furukawa (☎ & fax 0177/22-3037). Basic but well-kept *tatami*-room accommodation a couple of minutes' walk southeast of the station, behind the Sunfriend Building. No ensuite bathrooms and no meals. ③–④.

**Grand Hotel**, 1-1-23 Shin-machi (☎0120–231011, fax 0177/34-0505). This smart, old-fashioned hotel on the main street offers a range of comfortable, well-furnished rooms, some with sea views. ⑤.

**Hotel JAL City**, 2-4-12 Yasukata (☎0177/32-2580). Popular new hotel with an upmarket feel. Rooms are nicely decorated and well priced, and there's an in-house restaurant. About six minutes' walk east from the station. ⑤.

**Michinoku**, 1-2-15 Yasukata (☎ & fax 0177/23-1735). Slightly aged, bottom-end business hotel in a good location just northeast of the station. Western- and Japanese-style rooms are available, some with en-suite bathrooms. ④.

**Hotel Sunroute**, 1-9-8 Shin-machi (☎0177/75-2321, fax 75-2329). Good-value business hotel with largish, Western-style rooms, all with en-suite bathrooms, TV and minibar, and a choice of restaurants. Three minutes' walk east of the station. ⑤.

**Washington Hotel**, 2-1-26 Honchō (☎0177/75-7111, fax 75-7181). A new member of the *Washington* chain, on the eastern edge of town. It's fifteen minutes from the station but close to the Airport Limousine bus route (get off at Shin-machi 2-chōme). ⑤.

## The City

The distinctive, harbour-front **ASPAM** (Aomori Prefectural Centre for Tourism and Industry; daily 9am–6pm) building, about ten minutes' walk northeast of the station, is a good place to start exploring the city. There's usually a video of the *Aomori Nebuta Matsuri* playing in the entrance hall, but the highlight is a twenty-minute panoramic slide show of the region including its festivals and scenery (hourly 9.30/10am–5pm; 20min; ¥600). It's not really worth forking out for the top-floor observation lounge (daily 9am–10pm; ¥400, or ¥800 with the Panorama Theatre), but take a look at the fourth floor where they occasionally have demonstrations of local crafts.

Roughly fifteen minutes' walk southeast of ASPAM, the **Kyōdokan** (Tues–Sun 9.30am–4/4.30pm; closed hols; ¥310) takes a look at the region's history, culture and natural environment. Recent archeological digs have revealed evidence of human occupation since at least 3000 BC, and the museum kicks off with Jōmon-period earthenware pots, replica thatched huts and the beautiful, insect-eyed *dogū* figurines whose ritualistic purpose is still unclear. The most immediately interesting displays, however, are in the top-floor gallery devoted to local folk culture, where vine-woven baskets and rice-straw raincoats rub shoulders with fertility dolls and the distinctive agricultural deity Oshira-sama (see p.254).

Returning to Aomori Station from the Kyōdokan, you pass down Aomori's main shopping street, Shinmachi-dori, with its banks, craftshops and department stores. At the west end, in front of the station, turn left and head for the Sunfriend Building, beneath which you'll find a good old-fashioned **food market** (Mon–Sat 5am–6.30pm). Not surprisingly, a large proportion of stalls are loaded with iridescent fish, hairy crabs, scallops and squids, but among them you'll find neat pyramids of Aomori's other staple product – oversized, paper-wrapped apples.

### Out of the centre

The city's remaining sights are all in the southern suburbs, of which by far the most rewarding is an exhibition of festival floats at **Nebuta-no-sato** (daily 9am–6pm, June–mid Sept till 8pm; ¥630). JR and Shiei buses (1–2 hourly; 30min; ¥450) drop you on the main road, from where it's a short walk to the ticket gate. One of Japan's great summer festivals, the *Nebuta Matsuri* is named after the gigantic, bamboo-framed paper lanterns (*nebuta*) which take the form of Kabuki actors, *samurai* or even sumo wrestlers in dramatic poses. The features are painted by well-known local artists, and the lanterns – lit nowdays by electricity rather than candles – are mounted on wheeled carts and paraded through the night-time streets of Aomori. According to the most popular local legend, the lanterns originated in 800 AD when local rebels were lured out of hiding by an imaginative general who had his men construct an eye-catching lantern and play festive music. You can see several of today's magnificent *nebuta* in a darkened hall, on the hillside to the left as you walk through the park, alongside photos of early festivals and of the construction techniques. On the way out take a look in a smaller hall, just before the river, which contains a fan-shaped float from the rival Hirosaki festival, known as the *Neputa Matsuri* (see pp.266–7).

On the way back into central Aomori, ask to get off at the Kami-Tamagawa bus stop. This rather unpromising area of *pachinko* parlours and drive-ins is also home to an interesting folk museum, the **Keikokan** (daily except Thurs 9.30am–4.30pm; ¥600), dedicated to documenting the daily life of the "snow country" – Japan's mountainous interior. The museum has a valuable collection of local crafts, from fine lacquerware to heavily embroidered textiles and sturdy wooden furniture. If you're not going to Hokkaidō, the small display of Ainu clothes and jewellery is also worth a look.

One of Aomori's most famous citizens, a woodblock artist inspired by Van Gogh, is honoured in the **Munakata Shikō Memorial Museum** (Tues–Sun 9am–4/4.30pm; ¥300). The small museum shows rotating exhibitions of his bold, almost abstract scenes of local festivals and Aomori people. Though best known for his black-and-white prints, Shikō also dabbled in oils, painted screens and calligraphy. To reach the museum, take a bus from Aomori Station bound for Koyanagi and get off at the Munakata Shikō Kinenkan-dōri-mae stop (15min; ¥190), from where it's a four-minute walk west, in front of the NTT building.

## Eating, drinking and entertainment

Seafood, apples and apple products fill Aomori's food halls and souvenir shops. Among the more appetizing **speciality foods**, *hotate kai-yaki*, fresh scallops from Mutsu Bay grilled in their shell and served with a dash of miso sauce, and *jappa-jiru*, a winter codfish stew, are both worth a try. Shinmachi-dōri, the main shopping street, and around the station, are good places to look for **restaurants**, though ASPAM also has a number of reasonable options. In the evenings, some of Aomori's famous **shamisen** (a traditional stringed instrument) players give dinner-concerts at *Jintako*.

**Jintako**, 1-6 Yasukata (☎0177/22-7727). A cosy restaurant where you can hear a concert of *shamisen* music after the meal. Reservations are essential and it's not cheap: ¥5000 or ¥6000 including food. Daily 6.30–11.30pm, closed 1st and 3rd Sun of the month.

**Kakigen**, Shin-machi 1-chōme. Small, casual restaurant specializing in *hotate* and other seafood, though also serving *tonkatsu*, *donburi* and noodle dishes at reasonable prices. Look for its mossgreen *noren* (hanging curtain) just east of the *Sunrise Hotel* on Shinmachi-dōri. Daily 10.30am–8pm.

**Nandaimon**, Shin-machi 1-chōme. This cheap and cheerful Chinese-Korean eatery serves goodvalue *yakiniku*, grilled *hotate* and other seafoods. Lunch sets start at ¥750. Daily 11am–10pm.

**Nishi-mura**, 1-5 Yasukata (☎0177/73-2880). Choose from a broad range of inexpensive local cuisine including *hotate* and *Jappa-jiru*, or set meals from ¥1300. There's a picture menu and some staff speak a little English. Reservations recommended in the evening. Mon–Sat 11am–2pm & 4.30–10pm.

**Supage-tei Aomori**, 1-8-8 Shin-machi. A café-style spaghetti house in the basement next to *Kakigen*. Their handy English menu lists an unusual range of tasty pasta dishes – cod's roe, sea urchin, *kimchi* and ginger-flavoured soy sauce – mostly around ¥1000. Tues–Sun 11am–8.30pm.

## Listings

**Airlines** ANA (☎0120–029222); Japan Air System (☎0120–511283); Korean Air (☎0177/29-0511).

**Airport information** For flight information, phone ☎0177/73-2135.

**Banks** Dai-ichi Kangyō, Michinoku and Aomori banks are all located on Shinmachi-dōri, around the junction with ASPAM-dōri.

**Buses** Limousine buses to Aomori airport leave from ASPAM and call at the station en route (40min; ¥560). Long-distance buses for Tokyo, Sendai and Morioka depart from the station terminal.

**Car rental** Eki Rent-a-car (☎0177/22-3930), Toyota (☎0177/34-0100, Nippon (☎0177/22-2369) and Nissan (☎0177/22-4625) all have branches near the station.

**Ferries** Higashi-Nihon Ferry Co (☎0177/82-3631) operates daily ferries and a high-speed *Unicorn* service to Hokkaidō (Hakkodate and Murora) from the car ferry wharf, only accessible by taxi

(¥1000). Passenger ferries for Wakinosawa and the coast of Shimokita Hantō (Shimokita Kisen; ☎0177/22-4545) leave from the passenger terminal beside Bay Bridge.

**Hospital** Aomori City Hospital, 1-14-20 Katsuda (☎0177/34-2171).

**Post office** Aomori Central Post Office has a poste restante service but it's inconveniently located on the west side of town, at 1-7-24 Tsutsumi-machi. There's a more handy sub-post office in the backstreets southeast of the train station.

**Shopping** Apart from ASPAM's souvenir and craftshops, browse along Shinmachi-dōri, where Murata Kōgei stocks a good range of local kites, embroidery, lacquerware, brightly painted horses and Tsugaru *kokeshi* dolls. Further east you'll also find Narita Books, with a small selection of English-language titles.

**Taxis** Aomori Taxi (☎0177/41-6000); Miyago Kankō Taxi (☎0177/43-0385).

# Shimokita Hantō

The **Shimokita Hantō** protrudes into the ocean northeast of Aomori like a great axe-head. Its jagged blade is covered with low, forested peaks, of which the most notorious is **Osore-zan**, the "terrible mountain" where spirits of the dead are believed to linger on their way to a Buddhist paradise. Despite its growing commercialization, Osore-zan's bleak crater lake surrounded by a sulphurous desert, where pathetic statues huddle against the bitter winds, is a compelling, slightly spine-tingling place. On the way to or from Osore-zan it's worth visiting **Wakinosawa**, a port on the southwest tip with ferry connections to Aomori, and taking a boat trip along this wild coastline. With a bit of patience, you might also see some of Japan's hardy macaque monkeys or the sure-footed serow, a distant relative of the goat, which still inhabit the forests north of Wakinosawa.

## Osore-zan

The main focus of **Osore-zan**, an extinct volcano consisting of several peaks, lies about halfway up its eastern slopes, where **Osorezan-Bodaiji** (May 1–Oct 31 daily 6am–6pm; ¥500) sits on the shore of a silvery crater lake. Though the temple was founded in the ninth century, Osore-zan was already revered in ancient folk religion as a place where dead souls gather, and it's easy to see why – the desolate volcanic landscape, with its yellow- and red-stained soil, multi-coloured pools and bubbling, malodorous streams, is a truly unearthly scene. The temple also receives a steady trickle of non-spectral visitors, but during the summer **festival** (July 20–24) people arrive in force to contact their

| | SHIMOKITA HANTŌ | |
|---|---|---|
| **Mutsu** | *Mutsu* | むつ |
| Masakari Plaza | *Masakari Puraza* | まさかりプラザ |
| Murai Ryokan | *Murai Ryokan* | 村井旅館 |
| Hotel New Green | *Hoteru Nyū Guriin* | ホテルニューグリーン |
| Nankō | *Nankō* | 楠こう |
| Noheji | *Noheji* | 野辺地 |
| Osore-zan | *Osore-zan* | 恐山 |
| Shimokita Station | *Shimokita-eki* | 下北駅 |
| Tanabu Station | *Tanabu-eki* | 田名部駅 |
| | | |
| **Wakinosawa** | *Wakinosawa* | 脇野沢 |
| Dome Minshuku | *Dōmu Minshuku* | ドーム民宿 |
| Sai-mura | *Sai-mura* | 佐井村 |
| Wakinosawa Youth Hostel | *Wakinosawa Yūsu Hosuteru* | 脇野沢ユースホステル |

ancestors or the recently deceased through the mediation of *itako*, usually blind, elderly women who turn a profitable trade. During the open season (May–Oct) six **buses** a day run up to the temple from Mutsu (see below; 35min; ¥750); note that the last bus leaves Osore-zan at 4.45pm.

From Mutsu, the road to Osorezan-Bodaiji winds through pine forests, past a succession of stone monuments and a spring where it's customary to stop for a sip of purifying water. At the top you emerge by a large lake beside which a small, humped bridge represents the journey souls make between this world and the next; it's said that those who led an evil life will find it impossible to cross over. After a quick look round the temple, take any path leading over the hummock towards the lake's barren foreshore. The little heaps of stones all around are said to be the work of children who died before their parents. They have to wait here, building stupas, which demons gleefully knock over during the night – most people add a pebble or two in passing. **Jizō**, the guardian deity of children and the bodhisattva charged with leading people to the Buddhist Western Paradise, also comes along to scare away the demons, though it seems with less success. Sad little statues, touchingly wrapped in towels and bibs, add an even more melancholy note to the scene. Many have offerings piled in front of them: bunches of flowers, furry toys – faded and rain-sodden at the end of summer – and plastic windmills whispering to each other in the wind.

Three times a day (6.30am, 11am & 2pm) the sound of chanting from **services** at Bodaiji echoes over the rocks, and the temple also offers **accommodation** (☎0175/22-3825; ⑤ including meals). For most visitors, however, it's something of a relief to be heading back down to Mutsu, leaving Osore-zan to its wandering souls.

## Mutsu

A workaday town on the southern edge of Shimokita Hantō, **MUTSU** is the main base for Osore-zan. The easiest **access** route is a JR train from Noheji, on the main Tōhoku line, to Shimokita Station in Mutsu's southern suburbs. To reach the centre either take a taxi (around ¥1000) or change to the private Shimokita-kōtsu Ohata line to Tanabu Station, two stops up the line (7min; ¥200), on the east side of Mutsu town centre.

Mutsu's **information desk** (daily 10am–6pm; ☎0175/22-0909) is in the ground-floor lobby of Masakari Plaza, a modern, pink building immediately northwest of Tanabu Station. Staff can provide English-language maps and bus timetables and will help with accommodation, though they don't speak English. You can catch **local buses** for Osore-zan and Wakinosawa (see below) outside the station: this latter route is served by blue-and-white JR buses, for which rail passes are valid.

One of the nicest **places to stay** in Mutsu is the new *Murai Ryokan* (☎0175/22-4755, fax 23-4572; ④–⑤), just in front of Masakari Plaza. None of the *tatami* rooms is en suite, but everything's spanking clean and the food is excellent value, though they do offer rooms without meals. A good alternative is the *Hotel New Green* (☎0175/22-6121, fax 22-5180; ④–⑤), with a choice of Western- or Japanese-style rooms about five minutes' walk from the station; follow the road straight ahead (west) from the station, then left at the T-junction.

Though it's the smartest **restaurant** in town, prices at *Nankō* (daily 11.30am–9.30pm), located down the side street on the left just before the *Hotel New Green*, are surprisingly affordable. The best deals are their *teishoku* (from ¥1100), but you can also choose from a picture menu of seafood, steaks and stews for around ¥2000 per head. Alternatively, the second-floor **restaurant** in the Masakari Plaza (daily 11.30am–8pm) serves a decent range of mostly Western-style meals for under ¥1000.

## Wakinosawa and around

Rather than back-tracking to Noheji, you can leave the Shimokita Hantō by ferry from **WAKINOSAWA** direct to Aomori. Though it's possible to do this journey in a day, it's worth staying the night in Wakinosawa to take a boat trip along the attractive stretch of coast and see some of the local wildlife. The peninsula is home to an estimated four hundred macaques, the world's most northerly colony of wild monkeys, and a growing population of red-haired, goat-like serow, both of which are a protected species. There's more chance of seeing them in winter, when the animals move closer to human habitation in search of food, often within an hour's walk of the port.

Arriving **by bus** from Mutsu (1hr 35min; ¥1790), you come into Wakinosawa from the northeast, beside the **ferry pier** and a red-roofed, octagonal building where you can get **information** and tickets (daily 7.30am–4.30/5.30pm; ☎0175/44-3371). The most interesting **boat trip** takes you north along the coast to Sai-mura (1hr 25min; ¥2640), past a small area of much-photographed needle-shaped cliffs; the 10.35am sailing from Wakinosawa will bring you back in the early afternoon. These **ferries** also run across Mutsu Bay to Aomori (50min; ¥2540), or there's a car ferry to Kanita-machi on the Tsugaru Peninsula (1hr 10min; ¥1120), where you can pick up JR trains for Aomori or Hokkaidō.

Wakinosawa has a small, homely **youth hostel** (☎ & fax 0175/44-2341; [1]), offering basic dormitory accommodation about five minutes' walk from the bus terminal on the west side of town; follow the road over a small headland and you'll find the hostel signed to the right. It's run by a couple with a passion for the local wildlife – they'll recommend the most likely places to find anything, and even lend you maps and binoculars. If the hostel's full try *Dome Minshuku* (☎0175/44-3216; [5] including meals) in a three-storey building on the seafront.

## Hirosaki

Behind its modern facade **HIROSAKI**, former seat of the Tsugaru clan, still retains a few reminders of its feudal past. Most of its sights lie around **Hirosaki-kōen**, on the west side of the Tsuchibuchi-gawa, where one picturesque turret marks the site of Hirosaki-jō. Nearby there's a well-preserved Japanese garden and a collection of Meiji-era Western-style buildings, contrasting with a street of traditional *samurai* houses on the north side of the castle grounds. Hirosaki's summer lantern **festival**, the *Neputa Matsuri* (Aug 1–7), has its own museum attached to a craft centre, and there's also a district of dignified Zen temples out on the west side of town. Though these sights can be covered in a full day's outing from Aomori, Hirosaki is a pleasant place to stay and is even worth considering as an alternative base for the area.

### The City

The older, more interesting, part of Hirosaki lies around Hirosaki-kōen to the west of the modern town; take a bus from the station for the twenty-minute ride (¥170) to Shiyakusho-mae on the south side of the park. A little way west of the park entrance are the gates of a beautiful but unusually varied Japanese garden, **Fujita Kinen Teien** (April 13–Nov 23 Tues–Sun 9am–5pm; ¥300). Designed in 1919 for a successful local businessman, the garden consists of three distinct sections flowing over a steep hillside. At the top, beside Fujita's elegant residence, dark pines frame the distant peak of Iwaki-san – a classic example of "borrowed scenery" – from where paths lead down, beside a tumbling waterfall and over a perfect, red-lacquer bridge, to another flat area of lawns and lakes at the bottom.

Back at the main park gates, the modern **Sightseeing Information Centre** (daily 9am–6pm), houses an information desk (see Practicalities, p.267), crafts displays and a **float pavilion** (same hours, free) in the hall behind. These floats, which mostly carry tableaux depicting historical scenes, originated in the late seventeenth century when merchants would parade them round the streets as part of a local shrine festival. Beyond the float pavilion, two colourful Western-style buildings stand out against the

| HIROSAKI | | |
|---|---|---|
| Hirosaki | *Hirosaki* | 弘前 |
| Chōshō-ji | *Chōshō-ji* | 長勝寺 |
| Fujita Kinen Teien | *Fujita Kinen Teien* | 藤田記念庭園 |
| Hirosaki-kōen | *Hirosaki-kōen* | 弘前公園 |
| Itō House | *Itō-ke* | 伊藤家 |
| Iwate House | *Iwate-ke* | 岩手家 |
| Neputa Mura | *Neputa Mura* | ねぷた村 |
| Sightseeing Information Centre | *Kankōkan* | 観光館 |

*ACCOMMODATION*

| Akira | *Akira* | 晃荘 |
|---|---|---|
| City Hirosaki Hotel | *Shitii Hirosaki Hoteru* | シティー弘前ホテル |
| Hirosaki Grand Hotel; | *Hirosaki Gurando Hoteru* | 弘前グランドホテル |
| Hirosaki Youth Hostel | *Hirosaki Yūsu Hosuteru* | 弘前ユースホステル |
| Hotel Hokke Club | *Hoteru Hokke Kurabu* | ホテル法華クラブ |
| Kobori Ryokan | *Kobori Ryokan* | 小堀旅館 |
| Hotel New Rest | *Hoteru Nyū Resuto* | ホテルニューレスト |

*RESTAURANTS*

| Anzu | *Anzu* | 杏 |
|---|---|---|
| Iso-zushi | *Iso-zushi* | 磯寿し |
| Kikufuji Honten | *Kikufuji Honten* | 菊富士本店 |
| Live House Yamauta | *Raibu Hausu Yamauta* | ライブハウス山唄 |
| Takasago | *Takasago* | 高砂 |

sleek concrete and steel. The **Former City Library** and **Missionaries' House** (daily 9am–4.30pm; ¥320) both date from the early 1900s and are nicely preserved, though there's no particular reason to go inside.

Ōte-mon, the main entrance to **Hirosaki-kōen** lies across the road from the Sightseeing Centre. It takes ten minutes to walk from this gate, zig-zagging between the moats and containing walls of **Hirosaki-jō**, to reach the inner keep where a tiny, three-storied tower (April 1–Nov 23 daily 9am–5pm; ¥200) guards the southern approach. There's nothing left of the original castle, constructed by the Tsugaru lords in 1611, but the tower was rebuilt in 1810 using traditional techniques. In late April the little white turret, floodlit and framed in pink blossom, is the focus of a cherry blossom festival (April 23–May 5) as the park's five thousand trees signal the end of the harsh northern winter.

Leaving the park by its northern gate (Kita-mon), you emerge opposite the old **Ishiba shop** (daily 9am–5pm, closed 1st & 3rd Sun of the month; ¥100) which was built 250 years ago to sell rice baskets and other household goods to the Tsugaru lords. Since the family, now selling sake, still live here, you only get a glimpse into the warehouse behind. However, there are several more houses from this era in a smart residential street behind the Ishiba shop, some of which are open to the public (April–Oct daily 10am–4pm; Jan–March, Nov & Dec Sat & Sun only; free). At the west end of the street, the **Itō House** was once the home of the *daimyō*'s official doctor, while the next-door **Umeda House** was the residence of a minor *samurai*, as was the **Iwate House**, 500m further east.

**Neputa Mura** (daily 9am–4/5pm; ¥500), a museum focusing on Hirosaki's lantern festival, lies at the northeast corner of Hirosaki-kōen. The *Neputa Matsuri* (Aug 1–7) is similar in style to Aomori's *Nebuta* festival (see p.261), but in this case the giant lanterns are fan-shaped and painted with scenes from ancient Chinese scrolls or with the faces of scowling *samurai*. Like the festival itself, the museum gets off to a rousing start with a demonstration of energetic drumming which you can try afterwards. Then there's a collection of floats, from a seven-metre-tall monster to child-size versions, followed by a display of local crafts – this is a good place to pick up souvenirs, such as ingenious spinning tops, cotton embroideries or the stylish, black-and-white Tsugaru pottery.

Hirosaki's final sight is a "temple town", around fifteen minutes' walk southwest of the castle park or twenty minutes by bus from the station – take bus #3 for Shigemori and get off at the Chōshō-ji Iriguchi stop. In the seventeenth century around thirty temples were relocated to this spot, of which the most interesting is **Chōshō-ji** (daily: April–Oct 8am–5pm; Jan–March, Nov & Dec 9am–4pm; ¥300). It stands at the end of a tree-lined road through a large, two-storey gate, dating from 1629, which barely contains the two guardian gods peering out of the gloom. Inside, ring the bell outside the thatched building on the right and someone will show you into the **main sanctuary** and the mortuary rooms behind. Chōshō-ji was the family temple and burial place of the Tsugaru clan and in 1954 excavations revealed the mummified body of Prince Tsugutomi, son of the eleventh lord, who had died about a century before – his death was variously blamed on assassination, poisoning or eating peaches with imported sugar. During the cherry-blossom festival (see opposite) the mummy is on display but usually you'll have to make do with a photo in the mortuary room behind the main altar where it's rather overshadowed by a life-like statue of Tsugaru Tamenobu, the founder of the clan. As you leave the building, take a closer look at the glass cabinets near the kitchen. These contain some of Prince Tsugutomi's prized possessions, including his telescope, watch and portraits of his favourite actresses.

## Practicalities

Central Hirosaki is bracketed by the station to the east and by the castle park roughly 1500m away on the northwest side of town. One main road runs northwest from the station, past banks and the central post office, while the prime shopping street, Dotemachi, parallels it about 300m above. Hirosaki has two **information offices**: there's a small one in the station (daily 8.45am–5/6pm; ☎0172/32-0524) plus the main Sightseeing Information Centre (daily 9am–6pm; ☎0172/37-5501) beside the southern entrance to Hirosaki-kōen. Both of these have English-speaking staff and can supply town guides in English. Local **buses** stop outside the station for destinations around town, while long-distance buses go from a terminal behind Daiei department store, immediately west of the **station**, served by trains on the JR Ōu line between Aomori and Akita.

### ACCOMMODATION

**Akira**, 1-10-20 Ōmachi (☎0172/33-1101, fax 33-5035). Slightly spartan but well-kept ryokan three minutes' walk south of the station – just follow the tracks until you reach a modern, grey building on the right. Rooms available without meals. ⑤.

**City Hirosaki Hotel**, 1-1-2 Ōmachi (☎0172/37-0109, fax 37-1229). Big, new business hotel right outside the station with sizeable, en-suite rooms. There's also a choice of restaurants, a bar and a swimming pool (¥1600). ⑥.

**Hirosaki Grand Hotel**, 1 Ichiban-chō (☎0172/32-1515, fax 32-1810). Despite its name, an ordinary, rather basic Western-style hotel at the west end of Dotemachi. ⑤.

**Hirosaki Youth Hostel**, 11 Mori-machi (☎ & fax 0172/33-7066). Old but welcoming hostel in a prime location for exploring the castle area – the owners will set you up with a hearty breakfast. Take a bus from the station to Daigaku Byōin-mae (20min; ¥170), from where it's a five-minute walk further west. ①.

**Hotel Hokke Club**, 126 Dotemachi (☎0120–123489, fax 0172/32-0589). Western- and Japanese-style en-suite rooms that are a touch above *Hokke Club*'s normal, basic standard. In a good location, halfway up Dotemachi. ④.

**Kobori Ryokan**, 89 Hon-chō (☎0172/32-5111, fax 34-8273). This old, wooden ryokan near the castle has been recently renovated and offers a choice of *tatami* or Western-style rooms, some with bath. Meals are optional. ⑤–⑦.

**New Rest Hotel**, 8-25 Ekimae-chō (☎0172/33-5300). A basic business hotel opposite the train station, with bright, simple rooms. ⑤.

### EATING AND ENTERTAINMENT

Like Aomori, Hirosaki has a fine tradition of folk **music**, played on the *Tsugaru Jamisen*, which has a thicker neck than the ordinary *shamisen* stringed instrument and is struck harder. You can hear dinner concerts at a couple of the **restaurants** listed below.

**Anzu**, 1-44 Oyakata-machi (☎0172/32-6684). Named after an apricot, this cosy restaurant behind Hi Rosa department store, at the west end of Dotemachi, holds evening *shamisen* concerts according to demand – it's best to reserve. Set meals start at around ¥3000. Mon–Sat 5–11pm.

**Gloria Jean's**, Dotemachi. Relaxed coffee shop across the river from Nakasan department store, with a great range of coffees and some luscious home-made cakes. Daily 10am–8pm.

**Iso-zushi**, Wakaba Bldg, 11 Okeya-machi. This tiny sushi bar's worth searching out in the entertainment district southeast of the *Kobori Ryokan*. There's a choice of three set meals (¥1100, ¥1600 and ¥2000), so ordering is manageable even for non-Japanese speakers. Mon–Sat 6pm–1am.

**Kikufuji Honten**, 1 Sakamoto-chō. A clean, bright restaurant with a good range of Japanese foods, including well-priced sets (from ¥880 at lunchtime). Choose from their picture menu or window display. Daily 11am–10pm.

**Live House Yamauta**, 2F, 1-2-7 Ōmachi (☎0172/36-1835). Well-known restaurant where you can hear local *shamisen* music most evenings. The food is inexpensive *izakaya*-style. Reservations advised. Daily 5–11pm, closed one day a month.

**Takasago**, 1-2 Oyakata-machi. Inexpensive soba restaurant in an old wooden house southeast of the castle grounds. The limited menu includes tempura soba, *saru* soba and even curry soba. Prices start at ¥650. Tues–Sun 11am–6pm.

# South to Towada-ko

Japan's third largest lake, **Towada-ko**, fills a three-hundred-metre-deep volcanic crater in the northern portion of the Towada-Hachimantai National Park. The steep-sided, crystal clear lake rates as one of northern Honshū's top tourist attractions, but for many visitors the real highlight is the approach over high passes and along deep, wooded valleys. Though there are four main access roads, the most attractive route is south from Aomori via the Hakkōda mountains, Sukayu Onsen and the picturesque **Oirase valley**. For this last stretch it's the done thing to walk the final few kilometres beside the tumbling Oirase-gawa, and then hop on a cruise boat across to the lake's main tourist centre, **Yasumiya**.

Many roads around Towada-ko are closed in winter, and public **buses** only operate from April to November. During the open season, however, there are regular services to the lake from Aomori, Morioka, Hirosaki and southerly Towada-minami, a station on the line between Ōdate and Morioka. Though it's best to buy tickets in advance on all these routes, reservations are required on the JR buses from Aomori; tickets can be bought at any JR Green Window and rail passes are valid but you still need a booking.

## Hakkōda-san and the Oirase valley

Leaving the dreary outskirts of Aomori behind, Route 103 climbs steeply on to the Kayano plateau and round the flanks of **Hakkōda-san**. Every winter cold, wet winds dump snow up to 8m deep over these mountains, transforming the fir trees into "snow monsters" (see p.235) and maintaining a flourishing ski industry. This was also the site of the ill-fated **"snow march"** in January 1902 when Corporal Gotō and 210 soldiers on

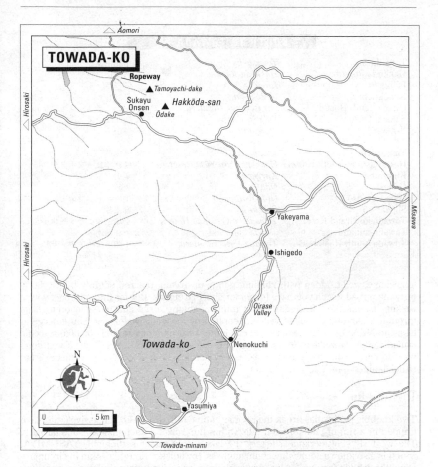

a training exercise in the run-up to the Russo-Japanese War (see History, p.775) were caught in a blizzard. It took four days before rescuers found the half-frozen Corporal Gotō and only ten other survivors, most of whom lost at least one limb from frostbite.

In summer, however, it's a beautiful spot with excellent walking among Hakkōda-san's old volcanic peaks, of which the tallest is Ōdake (1584m). To ease the climb you can whisk to the top of nearby Tamoyachi-dake (1326m) on the **Hakkōda Ropeway** (daily 9am–4/4.45pm; closed for a few days mid-Nov; ¥1050) and then walk down to **Sukayu Onsen**, both of which are stops on the Aomori–Towada-ko bus route. The most famous of several onsen resorts in the area, Sukayu consists of just one **ryokan** (☎0177/38-6400, fax 38-6677; ⑨) with a "thousand-person" cedar-wood bath (7am–7.30pm; ¥420). Sukayu's healing waters have been popular since the late seventeenth century and this is one of very few onsen left in Japan which is not segregated.

South of Sukayu the road crosses another pass and then starts descending through pretty, deciduous woodlands – spectacular in autumn – to **YAKEYAMA** village where you'll find the *Oirase Youth Hostel* (☎0176/74-2031, fax 74-2032; ③). Yakeyama is also the start of the **Oirase valley** walk, but it's better to join the path 5km further down the road at **ISHIGEDO**. From here it takes less than three hours to Towada-ko (9km)

| SOUTH TO TOWADA-KO | | |
|---|---|---|
| Towada-ko | *Towada-ko* | 十和田湖 |
| Hakkōda Ropeway | *Hakkōda Rōpu-uei* | 八甲田ロープウエイ |
| Ishigedo | *Ishigedo* | 石ヶ戸 |
| Nenokuchi | *Nenokuchi* | 子ノ口 |
| Oirase Youth Hostel | *Oirase Yūsu Hosuteru* | おいらせユースホステル |
| Sukayu Onsen | *Sukayu Onsen* | 酸ヶ湯温泉 |
| Yakeyama | *Yakeyama* | 焼山 |
| | | |
| **Yasumiya** | *Yasumiya* | 休屋 |
| Hakubutsukan Youth Hostel | *Hakubutsukan Yūsu Hosuteru* | 博物館ユースホステル |
| Kuriyama | *Kuriyama* | 栗山 |
| Ōdate | *Ōdate* | 大館 |
| Oide Camp-jō | *Oide Kyanpu-jō* | 生出キャンプ場 |
| Shuzan-sō | *Shuzan-sō* | 春山荘 |
| Towada-ko Grand Hotel | *Towada-ko Gurando Hoteru* | 十和田湖グランドホテル |
| Towada-minami | *Towada-minami* | 十和田南 |
| Towada Youth Hostel | *Towada Yūsu Hosuteru* | 十和田ユースホステル |

following a well-trodden path running gently upstream, marred slightly by the fairly busy main road which you have to join for short stretches. But for the most part you're walking beside the Oirase-gawa as it tumbles among ferns and moss-covered rocks through a narrow, tree-filled valley decorated by ice-white waterfalls. You emerge at lakeside **NENOKUCHI**, where you can either pick up a passing bus or take a scenic cruise across Towada-ko to Yasumiya (see below for details). Note that, if you don't want to carry your bags, there's a delivery service (May–Oct; ¥400 per piece) from either Ishigedo, or Yakeyama to Nenokuchi.

## Towada-ko

Two knobbly peninsulas break the regular outline of **Towada-ko**, a massive crater lake trapped in a rim of pine-forested hills within the Towada-Hachimantai National Park. The westerly protuberance shelters the lake's only major settlement, **YASUMIYA**, which is also known somewhat confusingly as Towada-ko. Roughly 44km in circumference, the lake is famous for its spectacularly clear water, with visibility down to 17m, which is best appreciated from one of several **boat trips** which run from early April to the end of January, though sailings are fairly limited in winter. The most interesting route is from Yasumiya to Nenokuchi (April–early Nov; 1hr; ¥1320) at the southern end of the Oirase valley (see above), or there's a one-hour circuit between the two peninsulas from Yasumiya (Jan & mid-April–Dec; ¥1320). Once you've navigated the lake, the only other thing to do in Towada-ko is pay a visit to the famous statue of the "**Maidens by the Lake**", which stands on the shore fifteen minutes' walk north of central Yasumiya. The two identical bronze women, naked and rough cast, seem to be circling each other with hands almost touching. They were created in 1953 by the poet and sculptor Kōtarō Takamura, then 70 years old, and are said to be of his wife, a native of Tōhoku, who suffered from schizophrenia and died tragically young.

### Practicalities
Though the small town of Yasumiya consists almost entirely of hotels and souvenir shops, its shady, lakeside setting makes it a pleasant overnight stop. Its centre is dominated by two **bus terminals** opposite each other on a T-junction just inland

from the boat pier; the more northerly one serves JR buses only. The **information office** (daily 8am–5pm; ☎0176/75-2506) is in a separate building immediately right (north) of the JR bus terminal, where you can get town maps and help with **accommodation**. Be aware, however, that it's advisable to book rooms in advance from July right through to October, when people come for the autumn leaves. The lakeside *Towada-ko Grand Hotel* (☎0176/75-1111, fax 78-1118; ⑥–⑦), to the south of the ferry pier, offers a choice of Western or *tatami* rooms and also lets out some of its older rooms as the *Hakubutsukan Youth Hostel* (☎0176/75-2002; ②). If this is full, try the cheaper *Towada Youth Hostel* (☎0176/75-2603; May–Oct only; ①) in a big new building on the bus route south to Towada-minami. Among a number of minshuku near the centre of Yasumiya, try the *Kuriyama* (☎ & fax 0176/75-2932; ⑤ including meals) or the older *Shuzan-sō* (☎0176/75-2607; ⑤ including meals), both a few minutes' walk inland from the pier. In summer, the patches of flat land around Towada-ko fill with tents; the closest **campsite** to Yasumiya is 4km southwest at *Oide Camp-jō* (☎0176/75-2079; late April–Oct).

**Moving on** from Yasumiya, buses to Towada-minami, Aomori and some Morioka services leave from the JR bus terminal, while other services for Morioka, Hirosaki and Hachimantai use the Towada-ko Terminal, opposite. If you're heading to Akita, take a bus south to Towada-minami and then a local train to Ōdate on the main JR line, or catch the daily bus (not JR) direct to Ōdate (April–early Nov 3.40pm).

# Akita and around

One of the few big cities on the northwest coast of Japan, modern **AKITA** is an important port and industrial centre with access to some of the country's only domestic oil reserves. Though it was founded in the eighth century, almost nothing of the old city remains and Akita's few central sites – three contrasting museums – can easily be covered on foot in half a day. With its airport and Shinkansen services, however, Akita makes a convenient base for the region. The small town of **Kakunodate**, a short train ride to the east, preserves a street of two-hundred-year-old *samurai* houses, while nearby Tazawa-ko, Japan's deepest lake, offers boat rides and some attractive scenery, though it's generally outclassed by its northern rival, Towada-ko (see opposite).

The city of Akita is also home to the last of the great Tōhoku summer **festivals**, albeit a pleasantly low-key affair compared to events in Sendai (p.236) and Aomori (p.258). In the *Kantō Matsuri* (Aug 4–7) men parade through the streets balancing tall bamboo poles strung with paper lanterns, which they transfer from their hip, to head, hand or shoulder while somehow managing to keep the swaying, top-heavy structure upright.

## The City

The centre of modern-day Akita is bounded to the east by its smart, new train station and to the north by the willow-lined moats of its former **castle**, Kubota-jō. This was Akita's second castle, founded in 1604 by the Satake clan who, unusually for northerners, backed the emperor rather than the shogun during the Meiji Restoration. Nevertheless, they still lost their castle after 1868 and the site is now a park, **Senshū-kōen**.

Walking straight ahead from Akita Station on the city's central avenue, Hiro-koji, the **Atorion**'s twelfth-floor observatory is a good place to get the lie of the land. Atorion also houses a crafts hall, bookstore, concert hall and restaurants around its classy atrium. A little further on, cross the moat into Senshū-kōen and you'll find the **Hirano Masakichi Art Museum** (Tues–Sun 10am–5/5.30pm; ¥610) on the second floor of the otherwise uninteresting Prefectural Art Museum. Though the Hirano museum has a

| AKITA AND AROUND | | |
|---|---|---|
| **Akita** | *Akita* | 秋田 |
| Akarenga-kan | *Akarenga-kan* | 赤れんが館 |
| Atorion | *Atorion* | アトリオン |
| Hirano Masakichi Art Museum | *Hirano Masakichi Bijutsukan* | 平野政吉美術館 |
| Kantō Festival Centre | *Neburi-Nagashi-kan* | ねぶり流し館 |
| Senshū-kōen | *Senshū-kōen* | 千秋公園 |
| | | |
| *ACCOMMODATION & RESTAURANTS* | | |
| Akita View Hotel | *Akita Byū Hoteru* | 秋田ビューホテル |
| Hamanoya Bekkan | *Hamanoya Bekkan* | 濱乃家別館 |
| Hotel Hawaii Eki-mae | *Hoteru Hawai Eki-mae* | ホテルハワイ駅前 |
| Kamada Kaikan | *Kamada Kaikan* | 鎌田会館 |
| Kohama Ryokan | *Kohama Ryokan* | 小浜旅館 |
| Hotel Metropolitan | *Hoteru Metoroporitan* | ホテルメトロポリタン |
| Suginoya | *Suginoya* | 杉のや |
| Washington Hotel | *Washinton Hoteru* | ワシントンホテル |
| | | |
| **Kakunodate** | *Kakunodate* | 角館 |
| Aoyagi-ke | *Aoyagi-ke* | 青柳家 |
| Denshōkan | *Denshōkan* | 伝承館 |
| Folklore Hotel | *Forukurōro Hoteru* | フォルクローロホテル |
| Minshuku Hyakusui-en | *Minshuku Hyakusui-en* | 民宿百穂苑 |
| Inaho | *Inaho* | 稲穂 |
| Ishiguro-ke | *Ishiguro-ke* | 石黒家 |
| Ishikawa Ryokan | *Ishikawa Ryokan* | 石川旅館 |
| Murasaki | *Murasaki* | むら咲 |

valuable collection of Western artists, including Goya, Picasso, Reubens and Rembrandt, it's more memorable for an enormous canvas (3.65m by 20.5m) by the local artist Tsuguji Fujita (1886–1968). He completed the painting, entitled *Events in Akita*, in an incredible fifteen days in 1937, after which the wall of his studio had to be knocked down to extract it. The panel, which takes up one wall of the museum, depicts Akita's annual festivals.

You can learn more about local celebrations in the **Kantō Festival Centre** (daily 9.30am–4.30pm; ¥100, or ¥250 with Akarenga-kan, below), located to the west of Senshū-kōen and across a small river. There are videos of recent *Kantō Matsuri* and sample *kantō* to try out. The *kantō* is a bamboo pole, up to 10m tall and weighing perhaps 60kg, to which dozens of paper lanterns are attached on crossbars. During the festival (Aug 4–7), as many as two hundred poles are carried through the streets in celebration of the coming harvest, as teams of men and young boys show their skill in balancing and manipulating the hefty poles. The festival was originally a pre-harvest ritual and, as the line of *kantō* sway in the dark, the yellow lanterns look like so many heads of golden rice.

From the Festival Centre, turn right and head south down this street for about 500m to the unmistakable, red-and-white-brick **Akarenga-kan** (daily 9.30am–4.30pm; ¥200). This Western-style building was erected in 1912 as the headquarters of Akita Bank, and its well-preserved banking hall and offices are worth a quick look. Don't miss the woodcuts by local artist Katsuhira Tokushi in a modern extension behind. The self-taught Tokushi won recognition for his appealingly bold, colourful portrayals of local farmers and scenes of rural life.

## Practicalities

Most visitors to Akita arrive at the JR **station**, located on the east side of town, though the city also has its own **airport** some forty minutes to the south by limousine bus (¥890). The city's **information office** (daily 9am–7pm; ☎ 0188/32-7941) is inside the JR station, with a Prefectural Information Centre on the first floor of the Atorion Building (daily except Wed 9am–7pm; ☎0188/36-7835); they both stock English-language maps and other printed information, but in general the staff don't speak English.

Among a good choice of **accommodation**, *Kohama Ryokan* (☎0188/32-5739, fax 32-5845; ④–⑤), is recommended for local atmosphere and a friendly welcome. None of the Japanese-style rooms is en suite, but everything's squeaky clean, the food's excellent and the ryokan is located on the main road only five minutes' walk south of the station. If they're full, try *Hotel Hawaii Eki-mae* (☎ & fax 0188/33-1111; ③–⑤), on Hiro-koji beside the southeast corner of Senshū-kōen; its rooms are small but spruce, though with only a washbasin in the cheaper rooms. Opposite the *Hawaii*, the *Akita View Hotel* (☎0188/32-1111, fax 32-0037; ⑥), offers the best rooms in town, plus a range of restaurants and even a pool in the fitness centre (¥3500). For something more modest, try the *Hotel Metropolitan* (☎0188/31-222, fax 31-2290; ⑥), immediately outside the station, or the lowlier *Washington Hotel* (☎0188/65-7111, fax 21-8133; ⑤), at the far end of Hiro-koji about fifteen minutes' walk away.

The region's most famous **speciality food** is *kiritampo*. It's a substantial stew of chicken, mushrooms, onions, glass noodles, seasonal vegetables and the key ingredient, *mochi* (rice cakes), made of pounded new rice and shaped round a cedar-wood stick before grilling over a charcoal fire. *Shottsuru* is more of an acquired taste; this strong-tasting stew is made with a broth of fermented, salted fish. The most famous **restaurant** at which to sample these and other local dishes is *Hamanoya Bekkan*, 4-2-11 Ōmachi (daily 11.30am–10pm; ☎0188/62-6611), located one block southeast of the Akarenga-kan museum, or in its branch in the *Hotel Metropolitan*; prices aren't too outrageous, but note that reservations are advisable on weekend evenings in the main restaurant. *Suginoya*, 4-1-15 Naka-dōri (daily 11am–9pm), is less refined but has a helpful window display and serves a wider range of foods at cheaper prices, including *kiritampo*, *shottsuru* and set meals from ¥1300. It's on the corner of Chūō-dōri, two blocks south of the Atorion. As ever, the station and surrounding streets provide a whole variety of eating choices, such as the *Kamada Kaikan*, 4-16-4 Naka-dōri, on a corner southwest of the station, opposite Eki Rent-a-car. This popular second-floor restaurant (daily 11am–10pm) offers excellent-value set meals, particularly at lunchtime, as well as local speciality foods.

### Listings

**Airlines** ANA (☎0120–029222); JAL (☎0120–255971); JAS (☎0188/33-0271).

**Airport information** ☎0188/86-3366.

**Banks and exchange** For foreign exchange, try Akita Bank or Hokuto Bank on Chūō-dōri, running parallel to Hiro-koji two blocks further south.

**Buses** Long-distance buses to Tokyo and Sendai stop outside Akita Station.

**Car rental** Eki Rent-a-car (☎0188/33-9308), Nippon Rent-a-car (☎0188/32-5798) and Toyota Rentals (☎0188/33-0100) are all located near Akita's JR Station.

**Hospitals** The biggest central hospital is the Red Cross Hospital, 1-4-36 Naka-dōri (☎0881/34-3361), or there's the University Hospital, 1-1-1 Hondō (☎0881/34-1111), out on the east side of town.

**Post office** The central post office (5 Hodōno Teppo-machi, Akita-shi) has a poste restante service.

## Kakunodate

While Akita City has lost nearly all its historical relics, nearby **KAKUNODATE** still has the air of a feudal town with its strictly delineated *samurai* and merchants' quarters. It's an atmospheric place, and although you can visit on a day-trip from either Akita or Morioka, it merits an overnight stay.

In 1620 the lords of Akita established a military outpost at Kakunodate consisting of a castle, on a hill to the north, a *samurai* town of around eighty residences, and 350 merchants' homes in a cramped district to the south. This basic layout and a handful of the *samurai* houses have survived the years, as have several hundred of the weeping cherry trees brought from Kyoto three centuries ago.

Pick up a town map from the tourist information centre (see Practicalities below) before setting off for the *samurai* quarter, roughly fifteen minutes' walk northwest. You can't miss the division between the packed streets of the commercial town – now mostly modern and rather run-down – and the wide avenues where the *samurai* lived in their spacious mansions among neatly fenced gardens. The most interesting of the *samurai* houses is the **Aoyagi-ke** (April–Nov daily 8.30am–5pm, Jan–March & Dec 9am–4pm; ¥500), a large, thatched house towards the north end of the *samurai* street, which is easily identified by an unusually grand entrance gate. Aoyagi-ke was lived in up to 1985 but now contains an odd mix of museums, including *samurai* armour, agricultural implements, memorabilia from the Sino-Japanese and Pacific wars, and a wonderful display of antique gramophones and cameras.

A little further up the street, the impressive **Ishiguro-ke** (May–Nov daily 9am–5pm; ¥300, or ¥720 with the Art Museum and Denshōkan) is one of the oldest of Kakunodate's *samurai* houses. It was built in 1809 for the *daimyō*'s financial advisor and its main feature are two large *kura*, fireproof warehouses used for storing rice, miso and other valuables. Despite its extraordinary green concrete exterior, the **Hirafuku Memorial Art Museum** (April–Nov daily 9am–4.30pm, Jan–March & Dec closed Thurs; ¥300), at the top end of the street, houses a small but decent collection of traditional Japanese art. Heading south again, the **Denshōkan** (daily 9am–4.30/5pm, Jan–March & Dec closed Thurs; ¥300) occupies a more attractive, red-brick building. This museum of Satake-clan treasures also doubles as a training school for *kaba-zaiku*, the local craft in which boxes, tables and tea caddies are coated with a thin veneer of cherry bark. Developed in the late eighteenth century to supplement the income of impoverished *samurai*, *kaba-zaiku* is now Kakunodate's trademark souvenir. If you prefer your bark still on the trees, turn right outside the Denshōkan where there's a two-kilometre tunnel of cherries along the Hinokinai-gawa embankment.

## Practicalities

Kakunodate is best reached by train from either Akita or Morioka. The **station** lies on the southeast side of town, where you will also find the **tourist information** centre (daily 9am–5.30/6pm; ☎0187/54-2700) in a *kura*-style building to the right as you exit the station. If you're short of time, you can **rent bikes** at the Hanaba Taxi office on the road into town (¥300 per hour).

It's best to **stay** in one of Kakunodate's traditional ryokan. The hundred-year-old *Hyakusui-en* (☎0187/55-5715, fax 55-2767; [4]–[6]), is popular for its English-speaking owner and hearty meals served around an open hearth, though the accommodation is fairly basic and cheaper rooms have only partition walls. The ryokan is less than ten minutes' walk from the station in the old merchants' quarter: walk straight ahead to the T-junction and turn left – it's in a black *kura* just past the post office. The more upmarket *Ishikawa Ryokan* (☎0187/54-2030, fax 54-2031; [6] including meals) lies in the next street east and offers comfortable *tatami* rooms with the option of en-suite facilities. If you'd rather have Western-style accommodation, the new *Folklore Hotel* (☎0187/53-2070, fax 53-2118; [5]) is right beside the station; rates include a basic breakfast.

In the *samurai* quarter, the Aoyagi house has a decent **restaurant** serving *inaniwa udon*, a long, slippery noodle in a thin soup of mushrooms, onion and bamboo shoots (daily 9am–2pm). In the centre of town, *Inaho* (daily 11.30am–4pm) and the more casual *Murasaki* (daily 11am–2pm & 5–10pm) offer daily set menus at reasonable prices; they're both down a side street to the north of the main station road, one block before the Akita Bank.

# Dewa-sanzan and around

For more than one thousand years, pilgrims have been trekking up the slopes of **Dewa-sanzan** (or simply, Dewa-san), one of Japan's most sacred mountains. It's an arduous rather than difficult climb, which takes in ancient cedar woods, alpine meadows and three intriguing shrines where *yamabushi* (mountain ascetics) continue to practise their secret rites. It's best to visit Dewa-san in summer (July–late-Sept) when all three shrines are open, but at any time of year you'll find white-clothed pilgrims climbing the well-worn steps to the outer shrine on the summit of **Haguro-san**. From here the path follows the ridge to **Gas-san**, the highest peak, before finally descending to the outer shrine, **Yudono-jinja**, which is in fact a surprising, ochre-yellow rock washed by a hot spring. Though it's possible to complete the circuit in a long day, it's more enjoyable to spread it over two or three days and spend a couple of nights in the *shukubō* (temple lodgings) scattered over the mountain or in the village of **Haguro-machi**, the

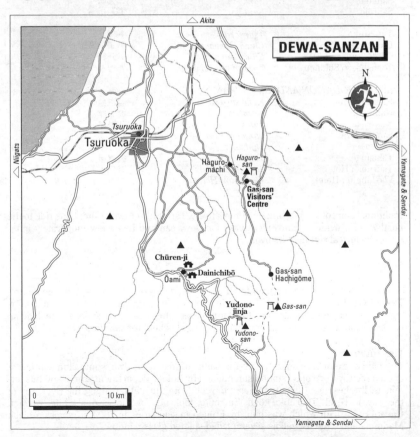

| DEWA-SANZAN AND AROUND | | |
|---|---|---|
| **Dewa-sanzan** | *Dewa-sanzan* | 出羽三山 |
| Chūren-ji | *Chūren-ji* | 注連寺 |
| Dainichibō | *Dainichibō* | 大日坊 |
| Gas-san | *Gas-san* | 月山 |
| Haguro Centre | *Haguro Sentā* | 羽黒センター |
| Haguro-san | *Haguro-san* | 羽黒山 |
| Haguro-machi | *Haguro-machi* | 羽黒町 |
| Ideha Bunka Kinenkan | *Ideha Bunka Kinenkan* | いでは文化記念館 |
| Ōami | *Ōami* | 大網 |
| Yudono-jinja | *Yudono-jinja* | 湯殿神社 |
| Yudono-san | *Yudono-san* | 湯殿山 |
| | | |
| *ACCOMMODATION* | | |
| Okuibō | *Okuibō* | 奥井坊 |
| Orinbō | *Orinbō* | 桜林坊 |
| Saikan | *Saikan* | 斎館 |
| Sankō-in | *Sankō-in* | 三光院 |
| Sanrōjo | *Sanrōjo* | 参籠所 |
| | | |
| **Tsuruoka** | *Tsuruoka* | 鶴岡 |
| Chidō Hakubutsukan | *Chidō Hakubutsukan* | 致道博物館 |
| Chidō-kan | *Chidō-kan* | 致道館 |
| Togashi-erō Sokuten | *Togashi-erō Sokuten* | 富樫ろうそく店 |
| | | |
| *ACCOMMODATION AND RESTAURANTS* | | |
| Kanazawa-ya | *Kanazawa-ya* | 金沢屋 |
| Narakan | *Narakan* | 奈良館 |
| Sanmai-an | *Sanmai-an* | 山昧庵 |
| Sannō Plaza | *Sannō Puraza* | 山王プラザ |
| Shuku-tei | *Shuku-tei* | しゅく亭 |
| Takisui-tei | *Takisui-tei* | 滝水亭 |
| Tsuruoka Hotel | *Tsuruoka Hoteru* | 鶴岡ホテル |
| Washington Hotel | *Washinton Hoteru* | ワシントンホテル |

traditional start of the pilgrimage. Alternatively, **Tsuruoka** town, a short bus ride to the northwest, provides a convenient base for Dewa-san and has a few moderately interesting historical sights of its own.

# Tsuruoka

A former castle-town with a handful of attractive, willow-lined streets in its old centre, **TSURUOKA** is mainly useful as a staging post on the pilgrimage to Dewa-san. Its few sights are located in and around **Tsuruoka-kōen**, the site of the castle, and include an eclectic local museum and an unusual Edo-period school for *samurai*.

## The Town
The old centre of Tsuruoka lies on the banks of the Uchi-gawa, some 2km southwest of the recently developed station surrounded by hotels, department stores and bus terminals. It takes about twenty minutes to walk from the station, along the river part of the way, to reach Tsuruoka-kōen. En route, look out for the virginal-white, wooden **Catholic Church** which was built by French missionaries in 1903; it houses a black Madonna and child as well as several faded stained-glass windows.

Tsuruoka's prime sight, the **Chidō Hakubutsukan** (Tues–Sun 9am–5pm; ¥620), lies on the southwest corner of the park in what was once a retirement home for lords of the ruling Sakai clan; buses from the station drop you right outside at the Chidō Hakubutsukan-mae stop. The compound now contains a number of striking buildings, kicking off with the Nishitagawa District Office, built in 1881 in Western style. The Goinden, the lords' residence, was constructed only two decades earlier but to a classic Japanese design, and now houses a few Sakai family heirlooms as well as a beautiful collection of bamboo fishing rods made by trainee *samurai*. Local folk culture is well-represented in a massive thatched farmhouse and in a new building packed with old fishing tackle, sake barrels, lacquerware and huge wooden mortars. Look out, as well, for the intricate *bandori* backpacks used to cushion heavy loads; when worn these woven, straw pads with their protruding shoulder straps are said to resemble flying squirrels (*bandori*).

Walking back along the south side of Tsuruoka-kōen, you'll pass another beautifully preserved Western-style building, the **Taishōkan**, built in 1915 as an assembly hall. It now houses a missable museum of local luminaries, but the **Chidō-kan** (Tues–Sun 9am–5pm; free), a little further along on the right-hand side, is worth a quick stop. This Confucian school was founded in 1805 by the ninth Sakai lord who wanted to restore order among his restless clan and educate young *samurai*. They progressed to the next grade on merit alone; some students were 30 years old. Inside, there are still a few of the original buildings, including a shrine to Confucius and the main auditorium, where you can see the old textbooks and printing blocks as well as some marvellous photos of the school still in use earlier this century.

In the next block east, the **Tsuruoka-shi Bussan-kan** (daily 9am–6pm) showcases a range of local produce, from eggplant pickles and Gas-san wine to painted candles and other crafts. You can see more of these somewhat expensive, tapering candles at a 300-year-old shop, **Togashi-erō Sokuten** (closed first and third Sun), on the way back to the station. Alternatively, try painting one (¥1500) on the second floor of the **Shōnai Centre** opposite the station, where you'll also find a crafts centre and souvenir shops.

## Practicalities

Tsuruoka's **train station** is located on the northeast side of town, while the Shōkō Mall **bus centre** lies a few minutes' walk west along the tracks under the *Daiichi Hotel*. Most buses also stop outside the station, including limousine buses serving the local **Shōnai Airport** (30min; ¥700). However, note that some long-distance buses start from outside the *Daiichi Hotel*. The town's **information office** (daily 10am–5/6pm; ☎ 0235/25-7678) is to the right as you exit the station building, while you can **rent bikes** at JR's green ticket window (10am–6pm; ¥500 per day). **Car rental** is available at Eki Rent-a-car (☎0235/24-2670), next to the information office, or at the airport's Nissan Rentals (☎0234/92-3894).

For somewhere convenient to **stay** near the station, the *Washington Hotel* (☎0235/25-0111, fax 25-0110; ⑤), right opposite, has cheerful rooms with bathroom, TV and phone, though it fills up quickly midweek. The friendly *Narakan* (☎0235/22-1202, fax 24-3548; ④–⑤), provides good-value *tatami* rooms, with an option on meals; it's a five-minute walk south from the station along the main road, just after the second set of lights. If they're full, try the basic *Sannō Plaza* (☎0235/22-6501; ④), a white, seven-storey building tucked in the backstreets another five minutes further into town. Finally, there's the Meiji-era *Tsuruoka Hotel* (☎0235/22-1135; ⑤–⑥), a bit worn at the edges but offering lots of atmosphere; the hotel is near the Uchikawa-dōri bus stop, just across the river from Tsuruoka-kōen.

One of the nicest **places to eat** in Tsuruoka is the refined *Shyuku-tei* (Tues–Sun 11.30am–2pm & 5.30–9.30pm) which serves reasonably priced *kaiseki bentō* and *teishoku* (from ¥2000–¥3000) as well as more expensive menus; the restaurant is located a short distance south of the Chidō-kan. There's a decent soba restaurant, the *Sanmai-an*, beside the Chidō Hakubutsukan, or try the rustic *Kanazawa-ya* (daily except Wed 11am–3pm & 5–8pm) which serves handmade soba and udon. A traditional-style building surrounded by low bushes, the *Kanazawa-ya* is in an unpromising location about five minutes from Tsuruoka Station – turn left in front of the Jusco department store and you'll eventually see it on the far side of a busy crossroads. Closer to the station, the *Takisui-tei* (daily 10.30am–9pm), on the second floor of the Shōnai Centre, is a simple place with a plastic-food display and a good range of meals from ¥1000 up.

## Dewa-sanzan

A lumpy, extinct volcano, **Dewa-sanzan** faces the Sea of Japan across the famously prolific rice-fields of the Shōnai plain. Many people take the road up its first peak, **Haguro-san** (414m), but it's well-worth slogging up the 2446 stone steps, among venerable cedars, to reach the impressive, thatch-roofed **Gosaiden** which enshrines the mountain's three deities. Dewa-san's middle shrine perches atop **Gas-san** (1984m), with spectacular views in clear weather, though otherwise it's the least interesting of the three. So if time's short, you might want to skip round by road to **Yudono-jinja**, visiting a couple of rather grisly, mummified monks en route.

Today Dewa-san and its three shrines fall under the Shinto banner, but the mountain was originally home to one of the colourful offshoots of Esoteric Buddhism later unified as **Shugendō** (see Contexts, p.786). The worship of Dewa-san dates from the seventh century when an imperial prince fled to this area following the death of his father. In a vision, a three-legged crow led him to Haguro-san (Black Wing Mountain) where he lived to the ripe old age of 90, developing his unique blend of Shinto, Buddhism and ancient folk-religion. Later the **yamabushi**, the sect's itinerant mountain priests, became famous for their mystic powers and their extreme asceticism – their route to enlightenment consisted of living in caves off a diet of nuts and wild garlic, and meditating under icy waterfalls. Though once fairly widespread, the sect dwindled after the mid-nineteenth century when Shinto reclaimed Japanese mountains for its own. Nevertheless, you'll still find a few *yamabushi* around Dewa-san, kitted-out in their natty checked jacket, white knickerbockers and tiny, black pill-box hat. They also carry a huge conch-shell horn whose haunting cry summons the gods.

The best time to see *yamabushi* in action is in Haguro-machi's *shukubō* (see opposite) and during the various **festivals**. The biggest annual bash is the *Hassaku Matsuri* (Aug 24–31) when pilgrims take part in a fire festival on Haguro-san to ensure a bountiful harvest. At New Year Haguro-san is also the venue for a festival of purification, known as the *Shōreisai*, which combines fire and acrobatic dancing with ascetic rituals.

### Mountain practicalities

There are various ways of tackling Dewa-san, depending on the time of year and how much walking you want to do. The recommended **route** is described on pp.279–80, climbing Haguro-san on the first day and then continuing via Gas-san to Yudono-jinja on the second. From there you can either head straight back to Tsuruoka or overnight in a *shukubō* and visit the Ōami temples the next day. However, note that Gassan-jinja and Yudono-jinja are only open in summer (July–mid-Sept and April–Nov respectively); the path itself stays open longer, depending on the weather.

Two **bus services** run from Tsuruoka: one via Haguro-machi to the Haguro-sanchō stop at the top of Haguro-san, with onward services to Gas-san Hachigōme (see p.280) in summer only (July–Sept); the second operates between May and early November, looping round from Tsuruoka to Yudono-jinja. These services are few and far between, so make sure you pick up a map and timetable at Tsuruoka's **information centre** (see p.277 for details), where they can also help book accommodation. In Haguro-machi, the Haguro Centre (24hr; ☎0235/62-2260) is primarily a **taxi** service, but they also stock some English-language information and will assist in finding accommodation.

If possible, try to spend at least one night at a **shukubō** (temple lodgings) while visiting Dewa-san. There are about thirty in Haguro-machi's Tōge district, including a number of traditional, thatched-roof inns. Prices don't vary much and they all serve the exquisite *shōjin-ryōri* (Buddhist vegetarian cuisine) favoured by *yamabushi*. In fact, many *shukubō* are run by *yamabushi* and you may well be invited to attend a prayer service, involving a lot of conch-blowing and a ritual fire. In Haguro-machi, *Sankō-in* (☎0235/62-2302; [5]) is a lovely, old thatched place near the Haguro Centre, or try nearby *Orinbō* (☎0235/62-2322; [5]), also thatched, or the newer *Okuibō* (☎0235/62-2283; [5]) further down the road. If you have problems booking direct, the Haguro Town Office (☎0235/62-2111, fax 62-3755) may be able to assist.

There are also a couple of useful *shukubō* on Haguro-san itself and near Yudono-jinja. The former, *Saikan* (☎0235/62-2357, fax 62-2352; [5] including meals), is an impressive old building with great views over the Shōnai plain, while the newer *Sanrōjo* (June–Oct only; ☎0235/54-6131, fax 54-6134; [5] including meals) occupies a wonderful setting beside the Yudono-jinja bus terminal. Both these places also serve excellent vegetarian lunches to non-residents (from ¥1500; reservations recommended).

## Haguro-san

Regular buses from from Tsuruoka (17–19 daily; 40min; ¥660) serve the village of **HAGURO-MACHI** at the beginning of the mountain trail; get off at the Haguro Centre stop, just where the road kinks left to the start of the path up the mountain. Before heading off along the track, **Ideha Bunka Kineikan** (daily except Tues 8.30am–5pm; ¥400; ☎0235/62-4727, fax 62-4729), a little further along the main road, is worth a look if you're interested in the *yamabushi*. This oddly high-tech museum contains examples of *yamabushi* clothes and foodstuffs, as well as holograms of various rituals. The Ideha centre also runs three-day courses (¥26,000) for would-be *yamabushi*, in which you get to stand under waterfalls, leap over fires and take part in a pilgrimage – these aren't for the faint-hearted.

A weather-beaten red-lacquered gate marks the start of the **Haguro-san trail** (1.7km; roughly 1hr) which consists of three long staircases built by a monk in the early seventeenth century. The first stretch is a deceptively gentle amble beside a river, where pilgrims purify themselves, among stately cedar trees. Most of these cedars are between 300 and 500 years old but the oldest, a massive tree girded by a sacred rope, is reputed to be at least 1400 years old. After passing a magnificent five-storey pagoda, which was last rebuilt in the fourteenth century, it's uphill all the way, past a little **tea shop** (late April–early Nov daily 8.30am–5pm) with superb views, until a large red *torii* indicates you've made it. If you're staying at the *Saikan shukubō* (see above), it's on the left at the end of a mossy path just before you duck under the *torii*.

The shrine compound contains a collection of unmistakably Buddhist buildings. At the centre stands a monumental, vermilion hall, the **Gosaiden**, where the mountain's three deities are enshrined behind gilded doors under an immaculate thatch. In front of the hall, the lily-covered **Kagami-ike** is said to mirror the spirits of the gods. However, it's probably more famous for its treasure-trove of more than five hundred antique polished-metal hand mirrors; in the days before women were allowed onto Dewa-san, their male relatives would consign one of their mirrors into the pond. The best of these are now on display in the shrine **museum** (daily 9am–4/4.30pm; ¥200). There's also a useful relief map of Dewa-san here.

Follow the paved road exiting the compound's south side and you'll find the Haguro-sanchō bus stop among restaurants and souvenir shops. Buses depart from here for

Tsuruoka (6–12 daily; 50min) via Haguro-machi (10min), and also to Gas-san Hachigōme (see below); alternatively, it's a forty-minute walk further south – take the footpath rather than the road – to the Kyuka-mura stop beside Gas-san Visitors' Centre where you can also pick up buses to Gas-san (see below).

## Gas-san and Yudono-jinja

It's a long, twenty-kilometre hike along the ridge from Haguro-san to **Gas-san**, so it really is worth taking a bus as far as the "Eighth Station", Gas-san Hachigōme. In summer (July–Sept) there are buses from Tsuruoka (2–3 daily; 1hr 30min) via Haguro-machi and Kyuka-mura, or you can take a bus from Haguro-sanchō (see p.278; 1–2 daily; 50min). Even from the Eighth Station it takes over two hours to cover the final 5km along the ridge to Gas-san (1900m), though it's a beautiful walk across the marshy Mida-ga-hara meadows, renowned for their profusion of rare alpine plants in late June.

The final few metres are a bit of a scramble onto the rocky peak, where **Gassan-jinja** (July 1–Sept 15 daily 6am–5pm; ¥500) huddles behind stout stone walls. There's not a lot to the shrine, but you need to be purified before venturing inside; bow your head while a priest waves his paper wand over you and chants a quick prayer; then rub the paper cut-out person, which he gives you, over your head and shoulders before placing it in the water.

From Gas-san, the trail drops more steeply to **Yudono-jinja** (April–Nov daily 6am–5pm; ¥500), located in a narrow valley on the mountain's west flank (9km). For the final descent you have to negotiate a series of iron ladders strapped to the valleyside where the path has been washed away. Once at the river it's only a short distance to the inner sanctum of Dewa-san, which occupies another walled area. Inside, take off your shoes and socks before receiving another purification, and then enter the second compound; note that photography is forbidden. Having bowed to the steaming, orange boulder you can then haul yourself over it using ropes to another little shrine on the far side. It's then just a quick ten-minute trot down the road to the Yudono-san bus stop, where the *Sanrōjo shukubō* occupies a black-and-white building beside the *torii* (see previous page for details).

If you're arriving at Yudono-san by road, shuttle buses wait by the *torii* to take you up to Yudono-jinja (5min; ¥100), or it's a steepish, twenty-minute walk. From May to early November you can get here by local bus from Tsuruoka (2–4 daily; 1hr 20min; ¥1480).

## Dainichibō and Chūren-ji

On the way back to Tsuruoka from Yudono-jinja, the hamlet of **ŌAMI** is worth a stop for its two "living Buddhas", the naturally mummified bodies of ascetic Buddhist monks who starved themselves to death. The mummies, or *mira*, are on display in two competing temples on either side of Ōami, each a few minutes' walk from where the bus drops you next to the village store; all buses from Yudono-san to Tsuruoka (see above) stop at Ōami (30min; ¥780).

**Dainichibō** (daily 8am–5pm; ¥500) is the more accessible of the two temples on the east side of the village; from the bus stop follow red signs of a little, bowing monk left in front of the post office and past a school and you'll see its colourful flags after about ten minutes. The temple was supposedly founded in 807 AD by Kōbō Daishi – after a brief purification ceremony and introductory talk the head priest will show you the hard-working saint's staff, a handprint of Tokugawa Ieyasu and other temple treasures before taking you to the mummy. The tiny figure sits slumped on an altar, dressed in rich, red brocades from which his hands and skull protrude, sheathed in a dark, glossy, parchment-thin layer of skin. He's said to have died in 1782 at the age of 96, which is quite extraordinary when you learn that he lived on a diet of nuts, seeds and water. As the end drew closer, the monk took himself off to a cave to meditate and eventually stopped eating all together. Finally he was buried alive with a breathing straw until he expired completely. Apparently this road to enlightenment was not uncommon prior to the nineteenth century when the practice was banned.

Though it's a bit further to walk (2km), **Chūren-ji** (daily 8am–5pm; ¥500) is slightly less commercialized and more atmospheric. To reach the temple, head generally north from the bus stop on a country road. There are signs at every junction except one, where you need to take the left fork past a graveyard. Again, you receive a short talk and a purification ceremony, before entering the side hall where the *mira* rests in a glass case. Another grimacing, walnut-brown figure swathed in red and gold, this little fellow reached Buddha-hood in 1829, aged 62 years.

# Niigata

Most visitors to **NIIGATA**, the largest port-city on the Japan Sea coast, are either on their way to Sado-ga-shima (see p.285) or making use of the ferry and air connections to Korea, China and Russia. It's a likeable but unexciting city, sitting on the banks of Shinano-gawa, with few specific sights beyond a well-presented local history museum. In 1964 a tidal wave devastated much of east Niigata, while the area on the west side of the river retains some attractive streets of older houses.

NIIGATA

RESTAURANTS & BARS

| | |
|---|---|
| Aiueo | E |
| Choen | G |
| Genki-zushi | H |
| Ginza Lion | B |
| Hon-chō Lunch Centre | C |
| Inakaya | F |
| Kirin Bandaibashi Hall | D |
| La Barcarola | A |

ACCOMMODATION

| | |
|---|---|
| Green | 5 |
| Kinsu | 1 |
| Maruko Inn | 2 |
| Shinoda Ryokan | 3 |
| Single Inn 3 | 6 |
| Tōkyū Inn | 4 |

| NIIGATA | | |
|---|---|---|
| **Niigata** | *Niigata* | 新潟 |
| Furumachi | *Furumachi* | 古町 |
| Hakusan-kōen | *Hakusan-kōen* | 白山公園 |
| Hon-chō Market | *Hon-chō Ichiba* | 本町市場 |
| Northern Cultural Museum | *Kitakata Bunka Hakubutsukan* | 北方文化博物館 |
| | | |
| *ACCOMMODATION* | | |
| Green Hotel | *Guriin Hoteru* | グリーンホテル |
| Hotel Kinsu | *Hoteru Kinsu* | ホテル金寿 |
| Marukō Inn | *Marukō In* | マルコーイン |
| Shinoda Ryokan | *Shinoda Ryokan* | 篠田旅館 |
| Single Inn 3 | *Shinguru In 3* | シングルイン3 |
| Tōkyū Inn | *Tōkyū In* | 東急イン |
| | | |
| *RESTAURANTS* | | |
| Aiueo | *Aiueo* | あいうえお |
| Chōen | *Chōen* | 張園 |
| Genki-zushi | *Genki-zushi* | 元気寿司 |
| Ginza Lion | *Ginza Raion* | 銀座ライオン |
| Hon-chō Lunch Centre | *Ranchi Sentā Hon-chō* | ランチセンター本町 |
| Inaka-ya | *Inaka-ya* | 田舎家 |
| Kirin Bandaibashi Hall | *Kirin Bandaibashi Hōru* | キリン万代橋ホール |
| La Barcarola | *Ra Barukarōra* | ラバルカローラ |

If you're travelling by Shinkansen from Tokyo, make sure you appreciate the journey. Completed in only 1982, this line took eleven years to build at a cost of 1.7 trillion yen – a staggering ¥6 billion per kilometre – making it the most expensive line in the world and throwing the whole of Japan's national railways into debt. More than one-third of the journey is through tunnels and the train takes a most bizarre route, stopping in one-eyed villages where the station is the biggest thing around. All this was thanks to Tanaka Kakuei, the MP for Niigata who served briefly as prime minister (1972–74) and who almost single-handedly transformed Niigata from a backwater into a major industrial city – while also garnering a few votes and a substantial personal fortune along the way. For more about the notorious Tanaka and his role in Japanese politics, read *Shadow Shoguns* (see Books, p.814).

## Arrival, information and city transport

All Niigata's transport facilities are centred around the new developments on the east side of the Shinano-gawa. The JR station and the Eki-mae bus terminal lie at the east end of Higashi-Ōdōri, the city's central spine which leads to Bandai City, with its distinctive Rainbow Tower and Bandai City Bus Centre. Continue northwest on this road, across the Bandai Bridge and along Masaya-koji Street, and you come to Furumachi, Niigata's downtown area focused around the mammoth Next 21 building.

Limousine buses connect the city's **airport** with the station bus terminal (1–2 hourly; 30min; ¥320), while ferries dock at one of three **ferry terminals** on the east bank of Shinano-gawa. All three terminals are linked by local bus (20–30min; ¥170) to Niigata Station, or a taxi will cost around ¥1300. Most **express buses** use the Bandai City Bus Centre, though some also stop outside the station.

Niigata is well provided with English-language maps and information which you can pick up at the **"i" information centre** (daily 8.30am–7pm; ☎025/241-7914) outside the station's central (Bandai) exit. The English-speaking staff can also help with same-day hotel reservations and ferry tickets to Sado. If you have more complicated language problems, the International Exchange Foundation, 6-1211-5 Kamiōkawamae-dōri (☎025/225-2777), should be able to assist; they're located three blocks west of the Bandai Bridge.

**Local buses** depart from the station terminal and may stop outside Bandai City depending on the route. Within the central district there's a flat fare of ¥170 which you pay on exit; in most buses you need to take a ticket as you enter.

## Accommodation

**Green Hotel**, 1-4-9 Hanazono (☎025/246-0341, fax 246-0345). Bright, clean bottom-end business hotel to the right as you exit Niigata Station. Rooms in the new building are slightly better, though most are singles. ④.

**Hotel Kinsu**, 1429-8 Higashibori-dōri (☎025/229-1695, fax 229-1393). Simple but fair-sized rooms with bathrooms, mini-bar and TV. One of the best choices in downtown Niigata, in an interesting area of old streets. ⑤.

**Marukō Inn**, 2-3-35 Benten (☎025/247-0505, fax 243-3341). This smart, mid-range business hotel is located halfway between the station and Bandai City. Its bright rooms come with TV, phone and bathroom, some with kitchenette. ⑤.

**Shinoda Ryokan**, 2-3-37 Benten (☎025/245-5501, fax 244-0902). A nice old ryokan next to the *Marukō Inn*. More expensive rooms have their own bathroom, and meals are optional. Five minutes from the station. ⑥–⑦.

**Single Inn 3**, 2-2-23 Hanazono (☎ & fax 025/243-3900). The cheapest of four *Single Inn* business hotels northwest of the station. The rooms are boxy but nicely done, all with TV and en-suite bathroom. ③–④.

**Tōkyū Inn**, 1-2-4 Benten (☎025/243-0109, fax 243-0401). This big hotel opposite the station has a range of good-size en-suite rooms, with TV, mini-bar and phone as standard. ⑤.

## The City

With its old Assembly Hall, lively market and classy shopping malls, Niigata's western district is an interesting area to explore if you've got a couple of hours to spare. Given more time, however, it's worth trekking out to Yokogoshi village, on the banks of the easterly Agano-gawa, to see the beautifully preserved mansion of a wealthy landowner which is now part of a cultural museum.

For the central sights, take a bus bound for Irefune-chō from in front of Niigata Station, to the Hakusan-kōen-mae stop (15min; ¥170), just across the Shinano-gawa. The gingerbread building beside the park, the **Former Prefectural Assembly Hall** (Tues–Sun 9am–4.30pm; free), was built in 1883. Local representatives continued to meet here until 1932 in an impressive hall which is the building's main attraction – sepia photos show Japan's new democracy in action. Walking back to the bus stop, stroll through **Hakusan-kōen** which contains a shrine to the god of marriage and various stone monuments, including one to the happiness of pine trees.

From here, either get back on a passing Irefune-chō bus or walk northwest along Nishibori-dōri for 1km, heading for the landmark **Next 21** building – and up to the nineteenth floor observation lounge for a free view of the city. Though Bandai City is putting up some competition, this area, known as **Furumachi**, is Niigata's foremost shopping district, though you'll still find some older buildings hidden away in the backstreets. Another relic of the past is the bustling **Hon-chō Market** (daily 10am–5pm, closed three days per month) which spreads over a few streets to the south of Masayo-koji. This fresh produce market, where you can still bargain, is a prime place to look for cheap places to eat (see Eating and drinking, overleaf).

The fertile plains around Niigata supported a number of wealthy landowners who lived in considerable luxury until the Land Reform Act of 1946 forced them to sell all rice land above three hectares per household. One such was the Itō family, whose superb mansion, now the centrepiece of the **Northern Cultural Museum** (daily 9am–5pm; ¥700), is the largest and most accessible of several such houses around Niigata. It's located in Yokogoshi village, 12km southeast of today's city centre, and can be reached by special express bus from Bandai City or the Eki-mae terminal (4 daily; 45min; ¥500 one way, or ¥1570 return including entry ticket); the last bus back leaves at 3.40pm. The huge house was erected in 1887 and comprises sixty rooms containing family heirlooms, but the classic garden steals the show – viewed from inside it forms a magnificent frieze along one side of the principal guest room.

## Eating and drinking

If you're going to be in Niigata for some time, get hold of the English-language booklet *Out & About in Niigata City*, available free from the tourist office or the International Exchange Foundation (see p.283 for details). Not surprisingly, the city is famous for its fresh fish and fragrant rice, which means excellent sushi. Glutinous rice is used to make *sasa-dango*, a sweet snack of bean paste and rice wrapped in bamboo leaves, while in wintertime *noppe* combines taro root, gingko nuts, salmon roe and vegetables in a colourful stew. There are numerous **restaurants** and bars in the streets near the station and around Furumachi.

**Aiueo**, 4F, Bandai Ciné Mall, 1-3-1 Bandai. Popular, rustic *izakaya* where English speakers are usually on hand to help out with the menu. Reasonable prices. Daily 4.30pm–midnight.

**Choen** (also know as *Harbin*), 1-6-2 Higashi-ōdōri. Cheap and cheerful Chinese restaurant serving good-value lunch sets from ¥700 and menus from ¥2000. Open 11am–3pm & 5–11pm, closed third Mon of the month.

**Genki-zushi**, Hanazono. This spick and span sushi bar has a picture menu and prices from ¥105 per plate (two pieces). Look for the scowling-face logo. Daily 11.30am–9.30pm.

**Ginza Lion**, NTT Plaza, 7-1017 Higashibori-dōri. A branch of the famous Tokyo beer hall serving standard bar food, including sausages, fries and salads. Daily 11.30am–10pm.

**Hon-chō Lunch Centre**, 5-248 Honchō-dōri. In the midst of Hon-chō street market, this friendly little Cafeteria offers a huge range of staple dishes, including sushi, curry-rice, ramen and soba dishes. Some English spoken. Mon–Fri 7.30am–8pm, Sat 9am–4pm, Sun & hols 11am–4pm.

**Inaka-ya**, B1, 1-2-23 Higashi-dōri. *Wappa-meshi* (steamed rice with various toppings) is the order of the day at this unpretentious, locals' restaurant. From ¥600, or ¥1100 for set meals. Mon–Sat 11.30am–2pm & 4.30–10pm, closed hols.

**Kirin Bandaibashi Hall**, 2-4-28 Bandai. Be prepared to queue at this big, imaginatively designed beer hall overlooking the Bandai Bridge. Eclectic menu. Daily 5–10/11pm.

**La Barcarola**, 7-920 Nishiborimae-dōri. It's hard to resist the smell of pizzas cooking at this relaxed Italian in the Furumachi district. Excellent lunchtime deals (Mon–Sat 11.30am–1.30pm) with a choice of pasta, pizza or paella, salad and free coffee refills for ¥720. Open daily except Wed 10am–9/10pm.

## Listings

**Airlines** ANA (☎0120–029222); Aeroflot (☎025/275-5000); JAL & J Air (☎0120–255971); JAS (☎0120–511283); Korean Air (☎025/241-2991); Kyokushin Air (☎025/273-0312); New China Airlines (☎025/275-4352).

**Airport information** ☎025/275-2633.

**Banks and exchange** You'll find foreign exchange banks near the station on Akashi-dōri and along Masaya-koji on the west side of the river.

**Bookshops** Kinokuniya, on the 2nd floor of Bandai City's Mitsukoshi department store, has Niigata's best selection of foreign-language books.

**Car rental** Around the station, try Eki Rent-a-car (☎025/245-4292), Nippon (☎025/245-3221), Nissan (☎025/243-5523) or Toyota (☎025/245-0100).

**Ferries** Sado Kisen (☎025/245-1234) operates ferries and jet-foil services to Ryōtsu (Sado) from the Sado Kisen Terminal, reached by local bus from Niigata Station (15min). Ferries to Otaru (Hokkaidō) are run by Shin-Nihonkai Ferry (☎025/273-2171) and leave from the Shin-Nihonkai Ferry Terminal; take a bus from the station for Rinkō Nichōme and get off at the Suehiro-bashi stop (20min). In summer Vladivostock boats (Rinkō Air Service; ☎025/244-5671) depart from Niigata's International Passenger Terminal; get off the Rinkō Nichōme bus at the Chūō-futō stop (25min).

**Hospitals** The two largest city-centre hospitals are Niigata University Hospital, 1-757 Asahimachi-dōri (☎025/223-6161), and Niigata City General Hospital, 2-6-1 Shichikuyama (☎025/241-5151).

**Post office** Niigata Central Post Office, 2-6-26 Higashi-ōdōri, is located a few minutes' walk north of the station and has a poste restante service.

**Taxi** Fuji (☎025/244-5166); Hato (☎025/287-1121); Miyakō (☎025/222-0611); Tōshin Taxi (☎025/245-6131).

# Sado-ga-shima

For centuries this rugged, S-shaped island lying off the coast of northwest Honshū was a place of exile for criminals and the politically undesirable. Even today **Sado-ga-shima** has a unique atmosphere, born of its isolation and distinct cultural heritage encompassing haunting folk songs, Nō theatre and puppetry, as well as the more recently established Kodo drummers. It's a deceptively large island, consisting of two parallel mountain chains linked by a fertile central plain which shelters most of Sado's historical relics. These include several important **temples**, such as Konpon-ji, founded by the exiled Buddhist monk Nichiren, and a couple of bizarre, high-tech **museums** where robots perform Nō plays and narrate local history. The Edo-period **gold mines** of Aikawa, on Sado's northwest coast, make another interesting excursion, but the island's greatest attractions are really its scenery and glimpses of an older, less-developed Japan. Travelling by public bus it takes at least three days just to cover the main areas, so it's well worth considering car rental or an organized tour round the more inaccessible regions.

Sado has a packed calendar of **festivals** from April to November. Many of these involve *okesa* folk songs and the devil-drumming known as *ondeko* (or *oni-daiko*), both of which are also performed nightly during the tourist season in Ryōtsu, Ogi and Aikawa (see individual accounts for details). Throughout June, Nō groups perform in

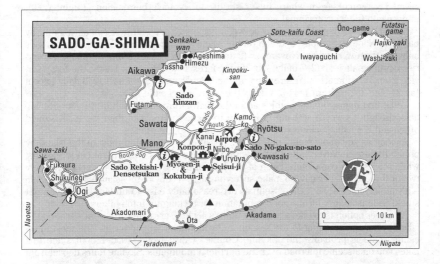

shrines around the central plain, while the island's biggest event nowadays is probably the Kodo drummers' international "Earth Celebration", held in Ogi (see box, p.291). If you're spending much time on the island, take a copy of Angus Waycott's affectionate and informative travelogue, *Sado; Japan's Island in Exile*.

## Some history

Since before the twelfth century Sado was viewed as a suitably remote place for former emperors, outspoken monks and out-of-favour actors, as well as more ordinary criminals. The most illustrious exile was the ex-Emperor Juntoku (reigned 1211–1221), who tried to wrest power back from the Kamakura and spent the last twenty years of his life on Sado. A few decades later, Nichiren, the founder of the eponymous Buddhist sect (see p.785), found himself on the island for a couple of years after 1271, where he wasted no time in erecting temples and converting the local populace. Finally, Zeami, a famous actor and playwright credited with formalizing Nō theatre, died here in 1443 after eight years in exile; though he had certainly fallen out of favour at court, the exact reasons for his banishment aren't clear.

In 1601 rich seams of gold and silver were discovered in the mountains above Aikawa. From then on, criminals were sent to work in the mines, supplemented by "homeless" workers from Edo (Tokyo), who dug some 400km of tunnels down to 600m below sea level – all by hand. In 1896 Mitsubishi took the mines over from the imperial household and today they're owned by the Sado Gold Mining Co, who continued to extract small quantities of gold up until 1989.

## Island practicalities

The main gateway to Sado is **Ryōtsu** town, on the east coast, which has ferry and air connections with Niigata. Sado Kisen (Niigata ☎025/245-1234; Ryōtsu ☎0259/27-5111) operates car **ferries** (6–8 daily; 2hr 20min; from ¥2060) and jet-foil services (3–11 daily; 1hr; ¥5960 one way, or ¥10,730 five-day return ticket) from Niigata's Sado Kisen Terminal (see p.285 for details). Reservations are required for the jet-foil and recommended for all crossings in the high summer season. Light **airplanes** operated by Kyokushin Air (Niigata ☎025/273-0312; Ryōtsu ☎0259/23-5005) make the crossing from Niigata to Ryōtsu airport in 25 minutes (2–5 daily; ¥7350 one way, or ¥11,020 seven-day return), from where buses shuttle to Ryōtsu's bus station (15min; ¥220), underneath the ferry terminal.

Sado Kisen ferries also operate between Naoetsu port, south of Niigata (20min by bus from Naoetsu Station), and **Ogi** on the island's south coast. In this case the jet-foils only run from April to late November (2 daily; 1hr; fares as for Ryōtsu), though car ferries continue all year (2–7 daily; 2hr 30min; fares as for Ryōtsu). Lastly, the ferry service from Teradomari to **Akadomari** on the island's southeast coast (2–3 daily except Jan 21–Feb 7; 2hr; from ¥1410) follows the old route of exile.

You'll find maps, bus timetables and other **information** at each of the ferry terminals, though it's worth arriving in Ryōtsu to make the most of their well-provisioned office and English-speaking staff before heading into the wilds.

As long as you allow plenty of time, it's possible to get around most of the island by public **buses**. However, note that in winter some services only operate at weekends, while others stop completely. Even at the best of times, a number of routes have only two or three buses per day, so make sure you carry a copy of the island's bus timetable – it's all in Japanese, but the essentials are reasonably easy to understand. If you get stuck, Sado islanders have a good reputation for picking up hitch-hikers.

An easier option is to take a tour and there's a whole array of **tour buses** around the island, varying according to the season and which port you arrive at. The most interesting route is probably the "Skyline Course" (April–Nov; ¥4000–¥8000) since this takes you on a scenic toll road over the northern mountains. Skyline tours depart from

## SADO-GA-SHIMA

| | | |
|---|---|---|
| **Sado-ga-shima** | *Sado-ga-shima* | 佐渡ヶ島 |
| | | |
| **Ryōtsu** | *Ryōtsu* | 両津 |
| Ajisai | *Ajisai* | 味彩 |
| Kagetsu Hotel | *Kagetsu Hoteru* | 花月ホテル |
| Ryōtsu ferry terminal | *Ryōtsu futō* | 両津埠頭 |
| Ryōtsu Kaikan | *Ryōtsu Kaikan* | 両津会館 |
| Sado Nō-gaku-no-sato | *Sado Nō-gaku-no-sato* | 佐渡能楽の里 |
| Sado Seaside Hotel | *Sado Shiisaido Hoteru* | 佐渡シーサイドホテル |
| Tenkuni | *Tenkuni* | 天国 |
| Tōkyō-an | *Tōkyō-an* | 東京庵 |
| Yoshidaya | *Yoshidaya* | 吉田家 |
| | | |
| **Sawata** | *Sawata* | 佐和田 |
| Green Village Youth Hostel | *Guriin Virejji Yūsu Hosuteru* | グリーンヴィレッヂユースホステル |
| Kokubun-ji | *Kokubun-ji* | 国分寺 |
| Konpon-ji | *Konpon-ji* | 根本寺 |
| Mano | *Mano* | 真野 |
| Myosen-ji | *Myosen-ji* | 妙宣寺 |
| Niibo | *Niibo* | 新穂 |
| Sado Rekishi-Densetsukan | *Sado Rekishi-Densetsukan* | 佐渡歴史伝説館 |
| Seisui-ji | *Seisui-ji* | 清水寺 |
| Silver Village | *Shirubā Birejji* | シルバービレッジ |
| Urashima Ryokan | *Urashima Ryokan* | うらしま旅館 |
| | | |
| **Ogi** | *Ogi* | 小木 |
| Gonzaya Ryokan | *Gonzaya Ryokan* | ごんざや旅館 |
| Iwaseya | *Iwaseya* | 岩屋 |
| Hotel New Kihachiya | *Hoteru Nyū Kihachiya* | ホテルニュー喜八屋 |
| Ogi Sakuma-sō Youth Hostel | *Ogi Sakuma-sō Yūsu Hosuteru* | 小木佐久間荘ユースホステル |
| Sakae-zushi | *Sakae-zushi* | 栄寿司 |
| Minshuku Sakaya | *Minshuku Sakaya* | 民宿さかや |
| Sawa-zaki | *Sawa-zaki* | 沢崎 |
| Shukunegi | *Shukunegi* | 宿根木 |
| Sitiuemon | *Sitiuemon* | 七右門 |
| | | |
| **Aikawa** | *Aikawa* | 相川 |
| Ageshima-yūen | *Ageshima-yūen* | 揚島遊園 |
| Dōyū Ryokan | *Dōyū Ryokan* | 道遊旅館 |
| Iwayaguchi | *Iwayaguchi* | 岩谷口 |
| Kokuminshukusha Senkaku-sō | *Kokuminshukusha Senkaku-sō* | 国民宿舎尖閣荘 |
| Hotel Ōsado | *Hoteru Ōsado* | ホテル大佐渡 |
| Sado Kinzan | *Sado Kinzan* | 佐渡金山 |
| Sado Belle Mer Youth Hostel | *Sado Beru Mēru Yūsu Hosuteru* | 佐渡ベルメールユースホステル |
| Sado Royal Hotel Manchō | *Sado Roiyaru Hoteru Manchō* | 佐渡ロイヤルホテル万長 |
| Soto-kaifu Youth Hostel | *Soto-kaifu Yūsu Hosuteru* | 外海府ユースホステル |
| Tassha | *Tassha* | 達者 |
| | | |
| **Akadomari** | *Akadomari* | 赤泊 |

both Ryōtsu and Ogi. Tickets are available from travel agents, in the ferry terminals or at the relevant bus stations; in summer it's a good idea to buy tickets in advance.

By far the most flexible option for exploring Sado is to **rent a car**. You'll find Sado Kisen Rent-a-car (☎0259/27-5195) at all three ferry terminals, while Nippon Rent-a-car

(☎0259/23-4020) and Watanabe Sanshō Rent-a-car (☎0259/27-5705) also have offices on the island. A day's rental costs around ¥6000 for the smallest vehicle, but prices go up roughly ten percent in July and August. Sado Kisen also rents out **motorbikes** and **bicycles**, which are a good alternative for the central plain and some of the quieter coast roads. You can also rent bikes in Mano and at some youth hostels (see individual accounts for details).

## Ryōtsu and around

Sitting on a huge, horseshoe bay with the mountains of Sado rising behind, **RYŌTSU** is an appealing little place which makes a good base for a night or two. The town revolves around its modern ferry pier and bus terminal, at the south end, while there's still a flavour of the original fishing community in the older backstreets to the north, among the rickety wooden houses with their coiled nets and fishy odours. Much of the town occupies a thin strip of land between the sea and a large salt-water lake, Kamo-ko, which is now used for oyster farming. Once you've wandered the old streets, taken a look at the lake and seen an *okesa* dance, there's not much else to do in Ryōtsu except plan your onward journey.

Given its history it's not surprising that Sado's theme music, **okesa**, focuses on anguished songs of exile accompanied by mournful, hypnotic dances. There are nightly **performances** of *okesa*, and the more lively *ondeko*, every evening from April to October (8pm; ¥800, ¥700 if booked at your hotel) in the Ryōtsu Kaikan, located in the old part of town. Still in the theatrical vein, the **Sado Nō-gaku-no-sato** (daily 8.30am–5pm; ¥800), around the south shore of Kamo-ko lake, is a new museum celebrating Sado's long association with Nō. Unfortunately there's nothing in English, but the masks and costumes are enjoyable, as is the short performance by remarkably lifelike robots who are admirably suited to Nō's studied movements. To reach the museum, take a bus on the Minami-sen route (line #2) for Sawata and get off after ten minutes at the Nō-gaku no sato-mae stop.

### Practicalities

The main Sado-ga-shima **tourist office** (daily 8.30am–6/7pm; Jan–April, Nov & Dec closed Sat pm, Sun & hols; ☎0259/23-3300) is located in a row of shops opposite the ferry terminal building. Since this is the one place on Sado where you can obtain English-language assistance, it's a good idea to check your planned route and bus timetables while you can. Local buses and tours depart from the bus terminal under the ferry building, where you'll also find car-rental agencies and taxis. There's a **post office** on the north side of the channel leading from the lake, near the middle bridge, and foreign exchange **banks** further along this highstreet.

Though Ryōtsu has plenty of expensive resort **hotels**, there's little in the way of more affordable accommodation. Your best bet is the friendly *Sado Seaside Hotel* (☎0259/27-7211, fax 27-7213; [5]), which offers rather worn *tatami* rooms – some en suite – but a warm welcome, good food and an onsen bath. The hotel is located on a pebbly strip of beach at the very southern end of Ryōtsu, 1.6km from the pier; if you phone from Niigata, they'll meet you off the ferry. In the centre of Ryōtsu, about ten minutes' walk north from the pier, the *Kagetsu Hotel* (☎0259/27-3131, fax 23-4446; [6]–[7]), is a much smarter place with elegant *tatami* rooms and a garden running down to the lake, or try the larger *Yoshidaya* (☎0259/27-2151, fax 23-4488; [6]–[7]), nearby. All these places have English-speaking staff and offer full-board deals.

Ryōtsu has a better choice of **restaurants**. One of the nicest is *Ajisai* (daily except Wed 11am–2pm & 4–10pm), overlooking the lake one block south of the *Yoshidaya*, which serves good-quality but not overly expensive beef, noodle and rice dishes. The friendly *Tōkyō-an* (daily 10am–9pm), on the main street two blocks north of the river, specializes in handmade soba, while *Tenkumi* (daily 11am–1.30pm & 5–10pm) dishes up moderately priced sashimi, tempura and *donburi* dishes – it's south of the river on the main road, then down the right fork between a school and a temple.

# Central Sado

Sado's **central plain** is the most heavily populated part of the island and home to a number of impressive temples, some dating back to the eighth century. Two routes cross this plain linking Ryōtsu to towns on the west coast: the main highway cuts north of Kamo-ko and Sado airport to **Sawata**, served by buses on the Hon-sen route (line #1), while the quieter, southerly route takes you through **Niibo**, **Hatano** and **Mano** along the Minami-sen bus route (line #2). The majority of historical sights lie scattered across this southern district – for many of them you'll need your own transport or be prepared to walk a fair amount. One solution is to **rent a bike** either in Mano's information office or at the *Green Village Youth Hostel* (see overleaf).

Sado's most accessible and important temple, **Konpon-ji** (daily 8am–4/5.30pm; ¥300) is located a few kilometres south of Niibo village; buses from Ryōtsu run roughly every hour up to 2pm, then every thirty minutes. Konpon-ji marks the spot where the exiled Nichiren lived in 1271, though the temple itself was founded some years later. If you can get there before the coach parties, it's a pleasant stroll round the mossy garden with its thatched temple buildings filled with elaborate gilded canopies, presided over by a statue of Nichiren in his characteristic monk's robes.

Backtracking a little way east from Konpon-ji along the main road, take the turning southeast signed to Onogawa Dam and follow the lane up a gentle valley. After about 2km you'll see, to your right, the crumbling steps of **Seisui-ji**. Founded in 808, this faded temple surrounded by cryptomeria trees and dancing dragon-flies receives few visitors. Though it seems abandoned, its wooden terrace, built in imitation of Kyoto's famous Kiyomizu-dera (see p.445), has recently been repaired.

On the eastern outskirts of **MANO**, **Myōsen-ji** was founded by one of Nichiren's first disciples and includes a graceful five-storey pagoda. Nearby **Kokubun-ji** dates from 741 though the temple's present buildings were erected in the late seventeenth century. If you follow this side road south, skirting round the back of Mano town, you come to a simple shrine dedicated to Emperor Juntoku. He's actually buried about 800m further up the valley, but the next-door **Sado Rekishi-Densetsukan** (daily 8am–5.30pm; ¥700) is more interesting. This museum, also known as Toki-no-sato, is similar in style to Ryōtsu's Nō museum (see opposite), though in this case the robots and holograms represent Juntoku, Nichiren and other characters from local history or folk tales. Each scene only lasts a couple of minutes and, on the whole, they're easy enough to follow. The museum lies about thirty minutes' walk southeast from central Mano and about ten minutes from the nearest bus stop, Mano goryō-iriguchi, on the route from Sawata south to Ogi (line #10).

A few kilometres north along the coast from Mano, **SAWATA** now serves as Sado's main administrative centre, though here too, there's no particular reason to stop unless you're changing buses or need accommodation. If you happen to be passing through around lunchtime, pop along to the **Silver Village** resort, on the town's northern outskirts, to see a brief display of *bunya*, a form of seventeenth-century **puppetry** performed by a master puppeteer (April–Nov daily except Wed 12.45pm & 1.30pm; ¥350).

## Practicalities

**Sawata**'s bus terminal is located on the north side of town, not far from the *Silver Village*. You can rent **bikes** at *Silver Village* (9am–6pm; ¥2000 per day), or in Mano's tourist **information** office (May–Oct daily 8.30am–5pm; Jan–April, Nov & Dec

Mon–Fri 8.30am–5pm; ☎0259/55-3589) for only ¥1100 a day; the office is located a few doors south of the main junction between Route 350 and the Niibo road.

One of the nicest **places to stay** in central Sado is the homely *Green Village Youth Hostel*, 750-4 Uryūya (☎0259/22-2719, fax 22-3302; [1]), to the east of Niibo village – ask the bus driver to let you off at the turning. As well as good-value meals, they have bikes for rent and can suggest cycling routes. For a more upmarket alternative, Sawata's *Silver Village* (☎0259/52-3961, fax 52-3963; [5]) offers comfortable Western-style en-suite rooms with sea views. Though the next-door *Urashima Ryokan* (☎0259/57-3751; [5]) is currently being rebuilt, it might provide a slightly cheaper option.

## Ogi and around

Sado's second port is tiny **OGI** situated near the island's southern tip. This sleepy fishing town is best known for its tub boats, which now bob around in the harbour for tourists, and the annual "Earth Celebration" hosted by the locally-based Kodo drummers (see box). But the area's principal attraction is its picturesque, indented coastline to the west of town. You can take boat trips round the headland, or cycle over the top to **Shukunegi**, a traditional fishing village huddled behind a wooden palisade.

The **tub boats**, or *tarai-bune*, were originally used for collecting seaweed, abalone and other shellfish from the rocky coves. Today they're fibreglass but still resemble the cut-away, wooden barrels from which they were traditionally made. If you fancy a shot at rowing one of these awkward vessels, go to the small jetty west of the ferry pier where the women will take you out for a ten-minute spin round the harbour (daily 8/9am–4/5pm; ¥450 per person). This jetty is also the departure point for **sightseeing boats** (April–Nov; 6–18 daily; 40min; ¥1400 return-trip) which sail along the coast past caves and dainty islets as far as Sawa-zaki Lighthouse. Tickets for both the *tarai-bune* and tour boats are available from the Marine Terminal building beside the jetty.

Buses run west along the coast as far as Fukaura (5 daily; 20min), but the ideal way to explore the **headland** is to rent a bicycle (see Practicalities, below). After climbing out of Ogi on the road to Shukunegi, turn right towards a concrete Jizō standing above the trees. The statue itself isn't worth stopping for but continue another 300m along this side road and you'll find a short flight of steps leading up to the **Iwaseya cave** – the old trees and tiny, crumbling temple surrounded by Jizō statues make a good place to catch your breath. Further along the Shukunegi road, next to a still-functioning boat yard, the **Sadokoku Ogi Folk Museum** (daily 8.30am–5pm; Jan, Feb, Nov & Dec closed Sat, Sun & hols; ¥400) is worth a brief stop. It contains a delightful, dusty jumble of old photos, paper-cuts, tofu presses, straw raincoats and other remnants of local life. Behind, in a new building, there's a relief map of the area and beautiful examples of the ingenious traps used by Ogi fisherfolk.

From here the road drops down steeply to **SHUKUNEGI** fishing village, tucked in a fold of the hills beside a little harbour full of jagged black rocks. The village itself is hardly visible behind its high wooden fence – protection against the fierce winds – where its old wooden houses are all jumbled together with odd-shaped corners and narrow, stone-flagged alleys. Two of the houses are open to the public (April–Oct daily 8.30am–5pm; ¥400, including village map), though they're not wildly interesting; tickets and refreshments are available at the soba restaurant (daily 8am–4/5pm, Jan–March & Oct–Dec closed Wed) beside the village car park.

### Practicalities

Ogi is split in two by a small headland, with the original fishing harbour to the west and the new **ferry terminal** on its east side. **Tour buses** depart from the ferry building, while **local buses** use the station behind Ogi **post office**, just inland from the tourist-boat pier. The town's **information centre** (daily 9.30am–5/6pm; ☎0259/86-3200) occupies the

**CHILDREN OF THE DRUM**

In the early 1970s a group of musicians came to the seclusion of Sado-ga-shima to pursue their study of traditional *taiko* drumming and to experiment with its potent music. A decade later the **Kodo Drummers** unleashed their primal rhythms on the world, since when they have continued to stun audiences with their electrifying performances. The name Kodo can mean both "heartbeat" and "children" – despite its crashing sound, the beat of their trademark, giant *Ōtaiko* is said to resemble the heart heard from inside the womb.

The drummers are now based in Kodo Village, a few kilometres north of Ogi, where they recently set up the **Kodo Cultural Foundation**. Apart from a two-year apprenticeship programme, the drummers hold occasional workshops (*Kodo juku*) which are open to anyone with a basic knowledge of Japanese. Each year, usually the third week of August, they also host the three-day "**Earth Celebration**" arts festival when percussionists from all over the world stir up the sleepy air of Ogi. Details of Kodo's scheduled tours and the next Earth Celebration are posted on their Web site at *www.sme.co.jp/Music/Info/KODO/index.html* or you can contact them at Kodo Village, 148-1 Kaneta-shinden, Ogi; ☎0259/86-3630, fax 86-3631.

ground floor of the Marine Plaza building, one block west of the post office, where you can get maps, book accommodation and arrange car rental. This building is also used for evening performances of *okesa odori* (March–Nov; ¥800, ¥700 if booked at your hotel). For **bike rental**, walk inland from the ferry terminal, in front of the *Hotel New Kihachiya* to the Seaside Villa shop which has bikes for ¥1500 per day (daily 7am–7pm).

It's a good idea to book **accommodation** well ahead in summer, but during the rest of the year you shouldn't have any problem. The cheapest option is the basic *Ogi Sakuma-sō Youth Hostel* (April–Nov; ☎0259/86-2565; ①), located a good twenty minutes' walk uphill from the ferry; take the road heading west for Shukunegi, then turn right beside the Shell fuel station. For something more central, the sea-front *Minshuku Sakaya* (☎0259/86-2535, fax 86-2145; ⑤ including meals) offers smart *tatami* rooms and tasty food about five minutes' walk east of the ferry terminal – unfortunately its sea views are blocked by the harbour wall. The more traditional *Gonzaya Ryokan* (☎0259/86-3161, fax 86-3162; ⑤–⑥) has the option of rooms with en-suite facilities and without meals, and is located inland from the local bus terminal. Finally, despite its looks, the classiest place in town is the *Hotel New Kihachiya* (☎0259/86-3131, fax 86-3141; ⑦) with Western and *tatami* rooms, some with harbour views.

For **food**, try *Sakae-zushi* (daily 11.30am–10pm) in the block behind the Marine Plaza, where they serve sea-fresh sushi and sashimi at reasonable prices. Or, at lunchtime, head for *Sitiuemon* (11am–2pm), at the top of the shopping street curving behind the western harbour, which dishes up just one variety of delicious, handmade soba (¥480).

## North Sado

Sado's northern promontory contains the island's highest mountains and some of its best coastal scenery. **Aikawa**, the only settlement of any size in this area, was once a lively mining town whose gold and silver ores filled the shoguns' coffers. The mines are no longer working, but a section of tunnel has been converted into a museum, **Kinzan**, where more computerized robots show how things were done in olden times. North of Aikawa there's the rather over-rated **Senkaku-wan**, a small stretch of picturesque cliffs; it's better to head on up the wild **Soto-kaifu** coast to Hajiki-zaki on the island's northern tip. Not surprisingly, this area isn't well-served by public transport, particularly in winter when snow blocks the mountain passes.

## Aikawa

After gold and silver were discovered in 1601, the population of **AIKAWA** rocketed from a hamlet of just ten families to 100,000 people, of whom many were convict labourers. Now a mere tenth of that size, there's nothing specific to see in Aikawa beyond the mine museum a few kilometres out of town. Nevertheless, it's not an unattractive place for an overnight stay once you get off the main road and delve among the temples, shrines and wooden houses pressed up against the hillside.

The road from Sawata enters Aikawa from the southeast beside the *Sado Royal Hotel Mancho* and then turns north along the seafront, past the bus terminal and skirts round the main town centre. Just beyond the municipal playing fields, at the north end of Aikawa, a right turn leads up a steep, narrow valley to the old gold mines of **Sado Kinzan** (April–Oct 8am–5pm, Jan–March, Nov & Dec 8.30am–4.30pm; ¥600). The Sōdayū tunnel, one of the mine's richest veins, is now a museum showing working conditions during the Edo period, complete with sound effects and life-size mechanical models, followed by a small exhibition with equally imaginative dioramas of the miners at work. You can reach Sado Kinzan by local bus (line #21) from Ryōtsu (4 daily; 1hr 20min) and Aikawa (8 daily; 15min), though for most of the year these only run on weekends and national holidays. Alternatively, several tour buses include Kinzan on their itineraries, along with the "**Skyline**" road which climbs east to Kinpoku-san (1173m). From here you get fine views over the whole island.

### *PRACTICALITIES*

Aikawa's **information office** (April–Oct daily except Tues 9am–5.30/6pm; ☎0259/74-3773) is located outside the bus terminal's seaward side, though the bus company staff can also provide maps and help with accommodation. From April to mid-November, evening **performances** of *okesa* are held in the Sado Kaikan, above the terminal building (¥800, or ¥700 if booked at your hotel).

If you're looking for somewhere to **stay** in Aikawa, head straight for *Dōyū Ryokan* (☎0259/74-3381, fax 74-3783; [5]) on a quiet street one block inland from the bus terminal. *Sado Royal Hotel Mancho* (☎0259/74-3221, fax 74-3738; [6]) is a less attractive possibility on the main road, while onsen addicts should walk south along the seafront to the large, luxurious *Hotel Ōsado* (☎0259/74-3300, fax 74-3219; [8]) to indulge in its glorious *rotemburo*.

The best place to look for somewhere to **eat** is in the main shopping street north of Dōyū Ryokan. For snacks, stock up on *dango*, *manjū* and other traditional sweets at the little Kisuke Kashi-ten bakery, on the main road northeast of town, opposite the turning for Sado Kinzan.

## The northern cape

Five kilometres north of Aikawa the road skirts round the edge of a bay where jagged cliffs crumble away into clusters of little islands. You get a pretty good view of **Senkaku-wan** from the road itself or from the observatory in Ageshima-yūen (daily 8am–5pm; ¥400), a park on the bay's north side. However, if you want to get closer, during the summer season a variety of **tour boats** set sail from Tassha village, 2km further south. The choice is between glass-bottomed "shark" boats (April–Oct every 30min according to demand; 30min; ¥850) and ordinary sightseeing (*Yūransen*) boats (April–mid-Nov; 30min; ¥700) which wait to fill up with at least ten people. There are also four scheduled sailings every day from Tassha to Ageshima-yūen (April–mid-Nov; ¥720 one way, including entry to the park).

Tassha and Ageshima-yūen are both stops on the Kaifu-sen bus route (line #9) from Aikawa to Iwayaguchi, with services roughly every hour. On the hilltop, near Ageshima-yūen, there's a good **youth hostel**, the *Sado Belle Mer* (☎0259/75-2011, fax 75-2071; [2]), and the government-run *Kokuminshukusha Senkaku-sō* (☎0259/75-2226; [5] including meals). They're both a few minutes' walk from the Himezu bus stop.

Continuing north, the settlements gradually peter out and the scenery becomes wilder as you approach Hajiki-zaki, where you can walk out along a narrow, pebble causeway to two islands, **Futatsu-game**. In summer this area's popular for swimming and camping, but it's worth doing at any time of year for the journey alone. Between late April and early November it's possible to take a bus all the way round the peninsula from Aikawa to Ryōtsu (3hr 30min), with changes at Iwayaguchi, Ōno-game and Washi-zaki depending on the schedule. During the rest of the year, however, services terminate at **Iwayaguchi**, where you'll find the *Soto-kaifu Youth Hostel* (☎ & fax 0259/78-2111; ①), handy if you need somewhere to stay before heading back south.

## travel details

### Trains

**Aizu-Wakamatsu** to: Aizu-Takada (8 daily; 20min); Inawashiro (hourly; 30min); Kitakata (16 daily; 15–25min); Koide (3 daily; 4hr); Kōriyama (hourly; 1hr–1hr 15min); Niigata (6 daily; 2hr 15min–3hr); Sendai (hourly; 2hr 30min); Shiokawa (16 daily; 10min); Tokyo via Kōriyama (2hr 30mins–3hr); Tokyovia Aizu-Tajima (12 daily; 4hr 15min–5hr); Yamagata (hourly; 3hr).

**Akita** to: Aomori (10 daily; 2hr 30min–3hr 40min); Kakunodate (12 daily; 45min); Morioka (hourly; 1hr 40min); Niigata (6 daily; 4hr); Tokyo (hourly; 4hr–4hr 30min); Tsuruoka (6 daily; 2hr).

**Aomori** to: Akita (10 daily; 2hr 30min–3hr 40min); Hakodate (hourly; 2hr–2hr 30min); Hirosaki (hourly; 30min–1hr); Morioka (1–2 hourly; 2hr–2hr 15min); Noheji (1–2 hourly; 30–45min), Sapporo (daily; 7hr 10min); Sendai (1–2 hourly; 4hr); Tokyo (2daily; 9hr 30min).

**Fukushima** to: Sendai (every 10min; 25min–1hr 30min); Yamagata (1–2 hourly; 1hr–1hr 40min); Tokyo (every 10–20min; 1hr 25min–2hr).

**Hiraizumi** to: Hanamaki (hourly; 50min); Kitakami (hourly; 30min); Morioka (hourly; 1hr 20min); Sendai (hourly; 45min–1hr).

**Ichinoseki** to: Geibikei (11 daily; 30min); Hiraizumi (hourly; 8min); Kogota (hourly; 50min); Morioka (hourly; 1hr 30min); Sendai (hourly; 30min–45min); Shin-Hanamaki (1–2 hourly; 20–30min).

**Ishinomaki** to: Kogota (11 daily; 40min); Onogawa (12 daily; 30min); Sendai (every 30min; 55min–1hr 20min).

**Matsushima-kaigan** to: Hon-Shiogama (every 30min; 10min); Ishinomaki (every 30min; 30–45min); Nobiru (every 30min; 12–18min); Sendai (every 30min; 25–35min).

**Morioka** to: Akita (hourly; 1hr 40min); Aomori (1–2 hourly; 2hr–2hr 15min); Hanamaki (every 30min; 20min–35min); Kakunodate (hourly; 50min–2hr 25min); Kitakami (every 30min; 50min); Noheji (hourly; 1hr 45min); Shin-Hanamaki (1–2 hourly; 13min); Tokyo (every 15–30min; 2hr 20min–3hr 30min); Towada-minami (7 daily; 1hr 45min–2hr 15min).

**Mutsu** (Tanabu) to: Shimokita (10 daily; 6min).

**Niigata** to: Aizu-Wakamatsu (6 daily; 2hr 15min–3hr); Kanazawa (3 daily; 3hr 40min); Kyoto (3 daily; 6hr); Nagano (2 daily; 3hr); Ōsaka (3 daily; 6hr 30min); Tokyo (1–3 hourly; 1hr 50min–5hr 30min); Tsuruoka (8 daily; 1hr 45min).

**Noheji** to: Aomori (1–2 hourly; 30–45min); Morioka (hourly; 1hr 45min); Shimokita (10 daily; 45min–1hr).

**Sendai** to: Fukushima (every 10min; 25min–1hr 30min); Hon-Shiogama (every 30min; 15–30min); Matsushima-kaigan (every 30min; 25–40min); Ichinoseki (hourly; 30min–45min), Ishinomaki (every 30min; 55min–1hr 20min); Morioka (1–3 hourly; 45min–1hr 20min); Tokyo (every 15–20min; 1hr 35min–2hr 30min); Yamadera (hourly; 50min–1hr 5min).

**Tōno** to: Hanamaki (12 daily; 50min–1hr 10min); Morioka (5 daily; 1hr 20min–2hr); Shin-Hanamaki (12 daily; 40min–1hr).

**Towada-minami** to: Morioka (7 daily; 1hr 45min–2hr 15min); Ōdate (10 daily; 30–40min).

**Tsuruoka** to: Akita (6 daily; 2hr); Niigata (8 daily; 1hr 45min).

**Yamagata** to: Sendai (hourly; 1hr 10min–1hr 30min); Tokyo (hourly; 2hr 30min–3hr); Yamadera (hourly; 20min).

### Buses

**Akita** to: Sendai (4 daily; 3hr 30min); Tokyo (2 daily; 8hr 30min–9hr 30min).

**Aomori** to: Morioka (6 daily; 3hr 15min); Tokyo (1 daily; 9hr 30min); Towada-ko (April–mid-Nov 4–8 daily; 3hr 10min); Sendai (4 daily; 5hr).

**Hirosaki** to: Morioka (hourly; 2hr 20min); Sendai (3 daily; 4hr 20min); Tokyo (2 daily; 9hr); Towada-ko (April–late Oct 3–4 daily; 2hr 15min).

**Ichinoseki** to: Chūson-ji (every 15–20min; 25min); Geibikei (9–11 daily; 30–40min); Hiraizumi (every 15–20min; 20min).

**Inawashiro** to: Bandai-kōgen-eki (hourly; 30min); Goshikinuma-iriguchi (hourly; 25min).

**Ishinomaki** to: Ayukawa (7daily; 1hr 30min).

**Morioka** to: Aomori (6 daily; 3hr 15min); Hirosaki (hourly; 2hr 20min); Sendai (hourly; 2hr 40min); Tokyo (1 daily; 7hr 30min); Towada-ko (April–early Nov 5–6 daily; 2hr 15min).

**Mutsu** (Tanabu) to: Wakinosawa (8 daily; 1hr 35min).

**Niigata** to: Kanazawa (2 daily; 4hr 40min); Kyoto (daily; 8hr 20min); Nagano (2 daily; 3hr 50min); Ōsaka (daily; 9hr 20min); Sendai (4 daily; 4hr–6hr 15min); Tokyo (6 daily; 5hr); Yamagata (2 daily; 3hr 45min).

**Ryōtsu** to: Aikawa (1–2 hourly; 1hr); Mano (1–2 hourly; 45min); Sawata (every 30min; 45min).

**Sawata** to: Aikawa (1–2 hourly; 20min); Ogi (hourly; 1hr 5min).

**Sendai** to: Akita (4 daily; 3hr 30min); Aomori (4 daily; 4hr 50min); Hirosaki (3 daily; 4hr 20min); Kyoto (1 daily; 10hr 40min); Morioka (hourly; 2hr 40min); Nagoya (1 daily; 10hr 30min); Niigata (4 daily; 4hr–6hr 15min); Ōsaka (1 daily; 12hr 20min); Tokyo (2 daily; 5hr 30min–8hr); Tokyo (Shinjuku) (3 daily; 5hr 30min); Tsuruoka (7 daily; 3hr); Yamagata (every 30min; 1hr).

**Towada-ko** to: Aomori (April–mid-Nov 4–8 daily; 3hr 10min); Hirosaki (April–late Oct 3–4 daily; 2hr 15min); Hachimantai (late-April–Nov 2 daily; 2hr 30min); Morioka (April–early Nov 5–6 daily; 2hr 15min); Ōdate (April–early-Nov 1 daily;1hr 30min); Towada-minami (April–early-Nov 4 daily; 1hr).

**Tsuruoka** to: Sendai (7 daily; 3hr); Tokyo (2daily; 8–9hr); Yamagata (10 daily; 2hr 15min).

**Yamagata** to: Niigata (2 daily; 3hr 45min); Sendai (every 30min; 1hr); Tokyo (2 daily; 5hr 40min–8hr 30min); Tsuruoka (10 daily; 2hr 15min).

### Ferries

**Aomori** to: Hakodate (11–13 daily; 2hr–3hr 40min); Murora (2 daily; 7hr); Wakinosawa (2 daily; 50min).

**Kinkazan** to: Ayukawa (3–10 daily; 25min); Onogawa (April–early Nov 4 daily; 30min).

**Niigata** to: Otaru (Hokkaidō; 1–2 daily; 17hr 30min); Ryōtsu (9–19 daily; 1hr–2hr 20min); Vladivostok (Russia; July-Oct 2 weekly; 42hr).

**Ogi** to: Naoetsu (2–9 daily; 1hr 5min–2hr 30min).

**Sendai** to: Nagoya (daily; 21hr); Tomakomai (Hokkaidō) (1 daily; 15hr).

**Wakinosawa** to: Kanita-machi (2–3 daily;1hr 10min); Sai-mura (1–2 daily;1hr 25min).

### Flights

From Northern Honshū there are some interesting international connections, mainly to Russia, Korea and China.

**Akita** to: Fukuoka (3–4 weekly; 1hr 45min); Kansai International (daily; 1hr 30min); Nagoya (2 daily; 1hr 10min); Ōsaka (Itami; 1 daily; 1hr 20min); Sapporo (2 daily; 55min); Tokyo (6 daily; 1hr).

**Aomori** to: Fukuoka (2 weekly; 2hr); Hiroshima (3 weekly; 1hr 35min); Khabarovsk (Russia; 2 weekly; 4hr 25min); Kansai International (daily; 1hr 35min); Nagoya (2–3 daily; 1hr 20min); Ōsaka (Itami; 2 daily; 1hr 30min); Sapporo (2–3 daily; 45min); Seoul (South Korea; 3 weekly; 2hr 50min); Tokyo (6 daily; 1hr 10min).

**Niigata** to: Fukuoka (1 daily; 1hr 45min); Hiroshima (1–2 daily; 2hr 10min); Irkutsk (Russia; weekly; 4hr 30min); Khabarovsk (Russia; 2 weekly; 1hr 55min); Kansai International (3 daily; 1hr 30min); Nagoya (2 daily; 55min); Ōsaka (Itami; 3 daily; 1hr 10min); Ryōtsu (Sado) (2–5 daily; 25min); Sapporo (2–3 daily; 1hr 15min); Seoul (South Korea; 4 weekly; 2hr); Shanghai (2 weekly; 3hr 45min); Vladivostock (Russia; 2 weekly; 1hr 20min); Xi'an (2 weekly; 4hr 30min).

**Sendai** to: Beijing (China; 4 weekly; 5–7hr); Fukuoka (3 daily; 2hr); Hiroshima (1 daily; 1hr 35min); Hong Kong (4 weekly; 5hr 30min); Honolulu (Hawaii; 6 weekly; 6hr 30min); Kansai International (1–2 daily; 1hr 40min); Nagoya (5 daily; 1hr 10min); Naha (Okinawa; 1 daily; 2hr 55min); Ōsaka (Itami; 6 daily; 1hr 20min); Sapporo (9 daily; 1hr 10min); Seoul (South Korea; 7 weekly; 2hr 45min); Shanghai (China; 2 weekly; 3hr 30min).

**Tsuruoka** (Shōnai) to: Kansai International (daily 1hr 30min); Sapporo (daily; 1hr); Tokyo (3 daily; 1hr).

**Yamagata** to: Fukuoka (3 weekly; 1hr 55min); Kansai International (1 daily; 1hr 35min); Nagoya (1 daily; 1hr 5min); Ōsaka (Itami; 2 daily; 1hr 20min); Sapporo (2 daily; 1hr 5min); Tokyo (3 daily; 1hr).

CHAPTER FOUR

# HOKKAIDŌ

Many Japanese see **HOKKAIDŌ** as an idyllic, unspoilt frontier – the perfect place to escape from industrialized Japan and get back in touch with nature. Although this vision is rose-tinted, there is something remote and wild about the country's northernmost main island. In spite of the fact that in many places you'll find the same ugly factories and buildings as on Honshū, and that, far from being a hick town, **Sapporo**, the island's capital, is the fastest-growing city in Japan, Hokkaidō can feel worlds apart from the rest of the country. Over seventy percent of the island is still covered by forest, and its enormous national parks, snow-covered slopes, rugged coastline and active volcanoes attract millions of nature-lovers every summer. Fortunately, Hokkaidō can cope with such crowds; this is Japan's second largest island, yet a mere five percent of the country's population lives here.

With five national parks to explore, your main problem will be time. If you're here for a week, aim to see **Daisetsu-zan National Park**, in central Hokkaidō, which features the island's highest mountain and many hiking trails and onsen resorts. In southern Hokkaidō, the **Shikotsu-Tōya National Park** has two beautiful lakes, and a volcano that broke out of the ground as recently as 1943. Highlights in the north include the lovely islands of **Rebun-tō** and **Rishiri-tō** and the dramatic **Shiretoko peninsula**, where you can bathe under thermally heated waterfalls and climb still-steaming volcanoes. In winter, Hokkaidō is Japan's prime **skiiing** destination; the long and uncrowded slopes at **Niseko** in the south and **Furano** towards the centre of the island are among the best skiing spots in the country. Festivals are another highlight of this season – if you're here in February, don't miss Sapporo's fabulous snow and ice sculpture festival, the **Yuki Matsuri**.

Camping or hiking around the island may bring you into contact with some of Hokkaidō's unique **wildlife,** which includes the *tancho* (a red-crowned crane), sable, Blakiston's fish-owl and the Hokkaidō brown bear (*ezo higuma*). There are believed to be around two thousand brown bears in the woods and locals are careful to warn you about the potential dangers of an encounter with one – the bears can grow to a height of 2m and weigh up to 300kg.

### ACCOMMODATION PRICE CODES

All accommodation in this book has been graded according to the following price codes, which refer to the cheapest double or twin room available for most of the year, and include taxes. Note that rates may increase during peak holiday periods, in particular around Christmas and New Year, the Golden Week (April 28–May 6) and Obon (the week around August 15), when accommodation is very difficult to get without an advance reservation. In the case of hostels providing dormitory accommodation, the code refers to the charge per bed. See p.36 for more details on accommodation.

| | | |
|---|---|---|
| ① under ¥3000 | ④ ¥7000–10,000 | ⑦ ¥20,000–30,000 |
| ② ¥3000–5000 | ⑤ ¥10,000–15,000 | ⑧ ¥30,000–40,000 |
| ③ ¥5000–7000 | ⑥ ¥15,000–20,000 | ⑨ over ¥40,000 |

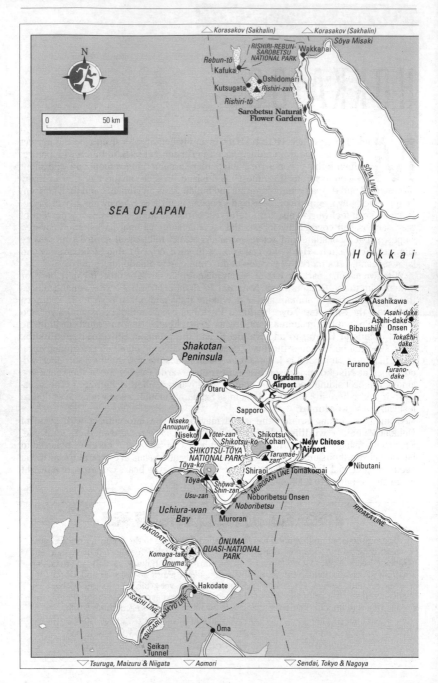

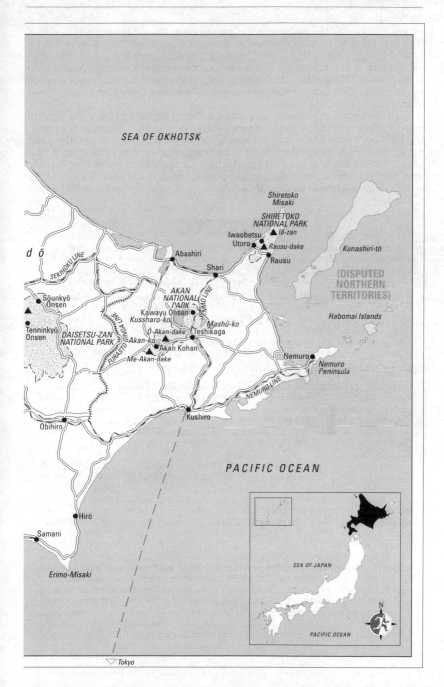

SEA OF OKHOTSK

Shiretoko
Misaki

SHIRETOKO
NATIONAL PARK

▲ Iō-zan

Iwaobetsu
Utoro ▲ Rausu-dake

Rausu

Kunashiri-tō

(DISPUTED
NORTHERN
TERRITORIES)

Abashiri

Shari

d ō

SEKIHOKU LINE

Sōunkyō
Onsen

▲

Tenninkyō
Onsen

DAISETSU-ZAN
NATIONAL PARK

FURANO LINE
SENMO LINE

AKAN
NATIONAL
PARK

Kawayu Onsen
Kussharo-ko

Mashū-ko

Ō-Akan-dake
Akan-ko
▲ Akan Kohan
Me-Akan-dake
▲

Teshikaga

Habomai Islands

Nemuro

Nemuro
Peninsula

NEMURO LINE

Obihiro

Kushiro

PACIFIC OCEAN

Hirō

Samani

Erimo-Misaki

SEA OF JAPAN

PACIFIC OCEAN

N

▽ Tokyo

Only colonized by the Japanese in the last 150 years, Hokkaidō is entirely devoid of ancient temples, shrines and historical monuments. What it does have is an intriguing cultural history, defined by its dwindling **Ainu** population (see box below). This aboriginal group of uncertain origin nearly disappeared completely after Japan opened up to the West in 1868 and large-scale immigration to Hokkaidō started. Today the best way to explore their ancient traditions is to visit an Ainu museum or spend time in some rather touristy, recreated villages.

The fastest route to Hokkaidō is by **plane** to New Chitose Airport, 40km south of Sapporo, where you can pick up connecting flights to most other places on the island. You'll get good value out of a JR rail pass by taking the Shinkansen to Morioka and transferring to a limited express **train** to Sapporo, via Aomori and Hakodate, a total journey time of eleven hours from Tokyo. There are also nightly direct sleeper trains from Tokyo to Sapporo, via Hakodate, and several a week from Osaka, but you'll have to pay a hefty supplement for these if you're using a rail pass. The most relaxing way of

---

## THE AINU

*"... they are uncivilizable and altogether irreclaimable savages, yet they are attractive and ... I hope I shall never forget the music of their low sweet voices, the soft light of their mild, brown eyes and the wonderful sweetness of their smile."*

Isabella Bird, *Unbeaten Tracks in Japan*, 1880.

Victorian traveller Isabella Bird had some misconceived notions about the **Ainu**, but anyone who has ever listened to their hauntingly beautiful music will agree that they are a people not easily forgotten. The Ainu's roots are uncertain – some believe they come from Siberia or Central Asia, and they are thought to have lived on Hokkaidō and northern Honshū since the seventh century. The early Ainu were hairy, wide-eyed and lived a hunter-gatherer existence, but their culture – revolving around powerful animist beliefs – was sophisticated, as shown by their unique clothing and epic songs and stories in a language quite unlike Japanese.

Like Bird, the Japanese also considered the Ainu savages. As their control of the archipelago increased, the Ainu were forced to retreat to undeveloped Hokkaidō, then called Ezochi. But even here they were not safe once the Japanese began to fully colonize the island from the late 1860s. The new immigrants kicked them off their lands, cleared the forests where they used to hunt, brought new diseases and suppressed their culture. The Ainu had little choice but to assimilate and their way of life went into seemingly terminal decline.

Today there are reckoned to be around 25,000 full and part-blooded Ainu in Hokkaidō and in recent years there has been more interest in and sensitivity towards the ethnic group. The United Nations Year of Indigenous People in 1993 helped promote the Ainu's cause, and Ainu activist Kayano Shigeru was elected to the House of Councillors – the second house of Japan's parliament – in 1994. A landmark legal verdict in 1997 recognized Ainu rights over the land (see p.322) and, although controversial, the New Ainu Law of 1997 aims to protect what is left of Ainu culture and ensure that it is passed on to generations to come.

There are several recreated **Ainu villages** around Hokkaidō, including Poroto Kotan in Shiraoi and Akan-kohan, but the best place to get an accurate idea of how the people live today is at **Nibutani** (see p.322), which has two excellent museums and is the only place in Japan where the Ainu form a majority of the community. Also worth seeking out for a broader understanding of the Ainu and their relationship to similar ethnic groups are the Museums of Northern Peoples in Hakodate (see p.315) and Abashiri (see p.336).

Despite her presumptions, Bird's account of the Ainu in *Unbeaten Tracks in Japan* (see Books, p.816) is still one of the best you can read, while for an excellent insight into contemporary Ainu issues, cast your eye over *The Japan We Never Knew* by David Suzuki and Keibo Oiwa (see Books p.816).

arriving in Hokkaidō is by **ferry**, and there are several overnight services from Honshū to various ports around the island (see Travel details, p.343).

As far as **accommodation** goes, Hokkaidō has a wide range of places to stay, including the good-value Toho network of minshuku and many lively youth hostels which are renowned for their delicious home cooking and nightly sing-a-long sessions. In the winter, most places add on a **heating charge**, typically ¥300 per person, while between June and early September, and particularly during Obon in mid-August, it's vital to make advance bookings. In the unlikely event that you get stuck, you'll find that many towns and villages have a basic **biker house**, providing no-frills dorms, in the same locations as youth hostels, and you don't have to be a biker to stay at one.

**Getting around** most of Hokkaidō is easy enough on trains and buses, but to reach some of the more remote corners of the island you'll need your own transport. This is a good place to consider renting a car or motorbike – cycling is also very popular. Hokkaidō is also one area of Japan where you may find yourself **hitching** – especially if you want to explore the Shiretoko peninsula and Akan National Park in northeastern Hokkaidō, where public transport is patchy. Locals are only too keen to give rides to foreigners so they can practice their English, if you take the necessary precautions (see Basics, p.35), safety shouldn't be a problem.

If you're planning on a slow journey around the island, it may be worth investing in one of several **special rail tickets**. The best value by far is the five one-day ticket package *Sei-shun Jūhachi-kippu* (see Basics p.31), which is valid on slow trains only from March 1 to April 10, from July 20 to September 10 and from December 10 to January 20. This package can be great value, since it's possible to travel from one end of Hokkaidō to the other in one day, and the tickets can also be used on overnight services, as long as you don't go in the sleeping cars. To get the most out of the *Hokkaidō Wide Shu-yu-ken*, valid for fourteen days on all trains and including return local train travel from Honshū, you'll need to make several long journeys across the island. The same goes for the *Hokkaidō New Wide Pass*, which is for unlimited travel within Hokkaidō only over a ten-day period.

# Sapporo and around

With a population of some 1.75 million, Hokkaidō's booming capital of **SAPPORO** is the fifth largest city in Japan, and as it's the transport hub of the island, you're almost bound to pass through it. Despite its size and bustle, this is a pleasant and vibrant city, overlooked to the south by the mountains that served as the location for the 1972 Winter Olympics and less than thirty minutes from the coast. It's also generously endowed with parks and gardens and is laid out in an easy-to-follow grid plan.

Sapporo is perhaps best known for the beer brewed here since 1891 and a visit to the handsome, late-nineteenth-century **Sapporo Brewery** is a must, as is a stroll through the gardens and museums of the **Botanical Gardens**, which date from the same era. After dark, the bars and restaurants of **Suskino** spark to life and you'll be hard pressed to find a livelier nightlife district outside of Tokyo.

Pleasantly cool temperatures tempt many visitors to Sapporo's **Summer Festival** (July 21–Aug 20), which features outdoor beer gardens and other events in Ōdōri-kōen, the swathe of parkland that cuts through the city centre. This park is also the focus of activity during the fabulous **Yuki Matsuri**, a "snow festival" held every February (see box p.301), which draws over two million visitors to the city.

There are some good day-trip possibilities around Sapporo; top of the list is the **Historical Village of Hokkaidō**, a huge, landscaped park featuring over sixty restored buildings from the island's frontier days. The nearby port of **Otaru**, one of the entry points into Hokkaidō, has some appealing nineteenth-century architecture and can be easily

SAPPORO

Hokkaidō University Campus

Sapporo Station

Sapporo Station Bus Terminal & Sogō Department Store

*Sapporo*

Gobankan Seibu Department Store

Miyabe Hall

Botanical Garden

Ainu Museum

Natural History Museum

Old Hokkaidō Government Building

Greenhouse

Bus Stop for Sapporo Beer Garden, Museum & Sapporo Factory

American Express

Sapporo International Communication Plaza

Tokeidai Clocktower

City Hall

Chūō Bus Terminal

TV Tower

Ōdori Kōen

*Ōdori*

*TŌZAI LINE*

*Nishi-Yon-Chōme*

Gaijin Bar

Tanuki Koji Shopping Arcade

Miss Jamaica & Havana

*Suskino*

Electric Sheep Bar

Rad Brothers 2

SUSKINO

*Hosui-Suskino*

Rad Brothers 1

King Xhmu

Mugishutei

Nakajima-kōen

Nakajima-kōen

**RESTAURANTS**

| | |
|---|---|
| Aburiya | D |
| Aji-no-Tokeidai | A |
| Chanko Kitanofuji | J |
| City Hall | B |
| Daruma | F |
| F45 Biru | I |
| Janbo | G |
| Kirin Beer Garden | K |
| Ramen Yōkochō | H |
| Shaberitai Shaberitai | E |
| Taj Mahal | C |

0        200 m

**ACCOMMODATION**

| | |
|---|---|
| Clubby Sapporo | 7 |
| Keio Plaza Hotel Sapporo | 3 |
| Lions Youth Hostel | 8 |
| Marks Inn Sapporo | 11 |
| Nakamuraya Ryokan | 5 |
| New Ōtani Sapporo | 6 |
| Sapporo House Youth Hostel | 2 |
| Sapporo International Inn NADA | 9 |
| Sapporo Washington Hotel I | 4 |
| Sauna Hokuo Club | 10 |
| Yuguri Ryokan | 1 |

Asabu Station   Sakaemachi Station

Otaru & Hakodate

Kotoni Station

Hokkaidō Museum of Modern Art &

Sapporo Beer Garden & Museum

Historical Village of Hokkaidō & Asahikawa

Sapporo Factory Shopping Mall &

Shin-Sapporo Station

Fukuzumi Station

Makomanai Station

## THE YUKI MATSURI

Sapporo's famous **snow festival**, the **Yuki Matsuri**, has its origins in the winter of 1950, when six small snow statues were created by high-school children in Ōdōri-kōen, the city's main park. The idea caught on and by 1955, the Japanese army, known as the Self Defense Force (SDF), was pitching in to help build the gigantic snow sculptures, which included intricately detailed copies of world landmarks such as the Taj Mahal.

Running from February 5 to 11 every year and spread across three sites (the Suskino entertainment district, Makomanai, south of the city centre, and Ōdōri-kōen), the festival now includes an international snow sculpture competition and many other events, such as co-ordinated ski jumping and nightly music performances in the park. Arrive one week in advance and you'll be able to see the statues being made, and even take part in the construction, since at least one giant statue in Ōdōri-kōen is a community effort – all you need do is turn up and offer your services. Be aware of the need to **book** transport and accomodation well ahead of time. With two million visitors flooding into Sapporo during the *matsuri*, finding last-minute accommodation in the city centre, and even arranging a flight or train to the city, can very difficult.

visited in a half a day from the capital. Just about possible as a day-trip, but better experienced over a longer stay, are the ski slopes of **Niseko**, some 100km south of the city.

Sapporo's name comes from the Ainu word for the area, *Sari-poro-betsu*, meaning "a river which runs along a plain filled with reeds". The city's layout was designed in the 1870s by a team of European and American experts engaged by the government to advise on the development of the island. Statues of these advisers can be found around the Sapporo; the most famous is the one of the American **Dr William S. Clark**, who set up Hokkaidō University and whose invocation to his pupils – "Boys, be ambitious!" – has been adopted as the city's motto.

## Arrival, information, orientation and city transport

**New Chitose airport** (☎0123/23-1111), 40km southeast of Sapporo, is the main gateway into Hokkaidō and the connecting point for flights to other destinations on the island. From the airport, the fastest way to Sapporo is on the frequent JR train (¥1030), which runs from Shin-Chitose Kūkō Station in the basement of the airport to Sapporo Station in around thirty-five minutes. The bus is cheaper (¥820), but takes at least twice as long to arrive at the Chūō Bus Terminal, one block north of the TV Tower at the eastern end of Ōdōri-kōen. **Okadama airport** (☎011/781-4161), 8km northeast of Sapporo, is only for flights within Hokkaidō, and a regular bus (¥300) runs from here to opposite the Chūō Bus Terminal.

Arriving by **train**, you'll pull in at busy Sapporo Station, six blocks north of Ōdōri-kōen. Long-distance **buses** terminate at the Chūō Bus Terminal and the Sapporo Station Bus Terminal on the south side of the railway station beneath the Sogō department store. The closest port to Sapporo is Otaru, served by **ferries** from Honshū and also with a service to the Russian island of Sakhalin.

### Information

Sapporo has several excellent **tourist information** facilities, all staffed by English-speakers. A useful first stop is the International Information Corner (daily 9am–5pm; Jan, Mar–June & Oct–Dec closed 2nd & 4th Wed of month; ☎011/213 5062), inside the Lilac Paseo arcade, on the western side of Sapporo Station, where you can pick up an English pamphlet and map of the city, and information on accommodation (but not bookings). More leaflets, along with camping, skiing and youth hostel guidebooks in

English, are available at the Sapporo International Communications Plaza i (daily 9am–5.30pm; ☎011/211-3678), on the first floor of the MN Building, opposite the city's famous clocktower. There's also a good jobs and events noticeboard here, plus a lounge on the third floor where you can read English newspapers and magazines, and may meet Japanese people eager to practise their English.

The free monthly English newsletter *What's on in Sapporo?* gives **listings** of the city's entertainment and events and is available from all tourist offices, as is the free bilingual magazine *Zene*, which is also worth a browse, especially for nightlife.

## Orientation

Finding your way around Sapporo is easy compared to many other Japanese cities because every address has a precise location within the city's **gridplan**. The city blocks are named and numbered according to the compass points, the apex being the TV Tower in **Ōdōri-kōen**, the **park** that bisects Sapporo from east to west – Sapporo Station, for example, is six blocks' north of the TV Tower and three blocks' west, so its address is North Six, West Three. Between the station and Ōdori-kōen lies the commercial district, with its department stores, banks and government offices. To the west of here are the old Hokkaidō Government Building and the Botanical Gardens, while to the east stands the old Sapporo Factory, now a trendy shopping and entertainment mall. Northeast of the station, beer is still brewed at the Sapporo Beer Garden and Museum, while to the west you'll find the extensive grounds of Hokkaidō University. The entertainment district of **Suskino** lies directly south of Ōdori-kōen and further south is another park, Nakajima-kōen.

## City transport

Most of Sapporo's sights are within easy **walking** distance of each other, but the efficient network of subways and buses can be useful if you get tired. There are three **subway** lines: the green Nanboku line and the blue Toho line run from north to south through Sapporo Station, while the orange Tozai line intersects them both, running east to west under Ōdōri-kōen. The lowest fare is ¥200 which covers all the stops in the city centre. There's also one **tram** line (in purple on the tourist map), which for a flat fare of ¥170 runs from Nishi-Yon-Chōme (West Four), just south of Ōdōri-kōen, out to Mount Moiwa, south of the city, and back to Suskino. If you're going to be in the city for a while, it's worth investing in the pre-paid travel card "Withyou", which gives ten percent extra travel for free, so that, for example, ¥1000 buys you ¥1100 worth of travel on all types of transport.

City **buses** depart from around the JR station. The most useful service is the Factory bus (look for the word in stylish English lettering on the side of the white bus), which runs to the Sapporo Museum and Beer Garden via the Factory shopping centre. Bus fares start at ¥200.

Public transport stops running at around 11.30pm, after which you'll probably be glad of the many **taxis** that roam Sapporo's streets.

## Accommodation

Even though Sapporo has plenty of **accommodation**, many places get booked up well in advance of the summer season and the Snow Festival in February. The bulk of hotels are clustered around Sapporo Station, but if it's nightlife you're after, you're better off staying in Suskino. If you can't find a room in town, consider staying at nearby Otaru, some 40km northwest of the capital (see p.309).

**Hotel Clubby Sapporo** Kita 2, Higashi 3 (☎011/242-1111, fax 242-3339). This smart hotel is part of the redevelopment of the Sapporo Factory on the east side of the city. Leather and wood fittings

## SAPPORO AND AROUND

| **Sapporo** | *Sapporo* | 札幌 |
| Botanical Gardens | *Shokubutsu-en* | 植物園 |
| Historical Village of Hokkaidō | *Hokkaidō Kaitaku-no Mura* | 北海道開拓の村 |
| Hokkaidō Museum of Modern Art | *Hokkaidō Ritsu Kindai Bijutsukan* | 北海道立近代美術館 |
| Nakajima-kōen | *Nakajima-kōen* | 中島公園 |
| Ōdōri-kōen | *Ōdōri-kōen* | 大通公園 |
| Sapporo Beer Garden and Museum | *Sapporo Biiru Hakubutsukan* | サッポロビール博物館 |
| Susukino | *Susukino* | すすきの |

*ACCOMMODATION*

| Hotel Clubby Sapporo | *Hoteru Kurabii Sapporo* | ホテルクラビーサッポロ |
| Keio Plaza Hotel Sapporo | *Keio Puraza Hoteru Sapporo* | 京王プラザホテル札幌 |
| Marks Inn Sapporo | *Mākusu In Sapporo* | マークスイン札幌 |
| Nakamuraya Ryokan | *Nakamuraya Ryokan* | 中村屋旅館 |
| Hotel New Ōtani Sapporo | *Hoteru Nyū Ōtani Sapporo* | ホテルニューオータニ札幌 |
| Sapporo House Youth Hostel | *Sapporo Hausu Yūsu Hosuteru* | 札幌ハウスユースホステル |
| Sapporo Inn NADA | *Sapporo In NADA* | 札幌インNADA |
| Sapporo Lions Youth Hostel | *Sapporo Raionzu Yūsu Hosuteru* | 札幌ライオンズユースホステル |
| Sapporo Washington Hotel 1 | *Sapporo Wushinton Hoteru 1* | 札幌ワシントンホテル I |
| Sauna Hokuo Club | *Sauna Hokuo Kurabu* | サウナ北欧クラブ |
| Yugiri Ryokan | *Yugiri Ryokan* | 夕霧旅館 |

*EATING*

| Aburiya | *Aburiya* | あぶりや |
| Aji-no-Tokeidai | *Aji-no-Tokedai* | 味の時計台 |
| Chanko Kitanofuji | *Chanko Kitanofuji* | ちゃんこ北の富士 |
| Daruma | *Daruma* | だるま |
| Kirin Beer Garden | *Kirin Biiru-en* | キリンビール園 |
| Rāmen Yokochō | *Rāmen Yokochō* | ラーメン横丁 |
| Sapporo Bier Garten | *Sapporo Biiru-en* | サッポロビール園 |
| Sapporo City Hall Shokudō | *Shiyakusho Shokudō* | 市役所食堂 |
| Shaberitai Shaberitai | *Shaberitai Shaberitai* | しゃべりたいしゃべりたい |
| Taj Mahal | *Tāji Mahāru* | タージマハール |

*AROUND SAPPORO*

| New Chitose Airport | *Shin-Chitose Kūkō* | 新千歳空港 |

| **Otaru** | *Otaru* | 小樽 |
| Otaru Green Hotel | *Otaru Guriin Hoteru* | 小樽グリーンホテル |
| Otaru Tengu-yama Youth Hostel | *Otaru Tengu-yama Yūsu Hosuteru* | 小樽天狗山ユースホステル |
| Pon Pon | *Pon Pon* | ポンポン |

| **Niseko** | *Niseko* | ニセコ |
| Niseko Annupuri Youth Hostel | *Niseko Annupuri Yūsu Hosuteru* | ニセコアンヌプリユースホステル |
| Niseko Kōgen Youth Hostel | *Niseko Kōgen Yūsu Hosuteru* | ニセコ高原ユースホステル |
| Niseko Prince Hotel | *Niseko Purinsu Hoteru* | ニセコプリンスホテル |
| Pension Asauta | *Penshon Asauta* | ペンションあさうた |

lend an old-fashioned air to the lobby and restaurant, but the rooms are modern, spacious and elegantly decorated. Rates include breakfast, making this a good-value choice. ⑦.

**Keio Plaza Hotel Sapporo**, Kita 5, Nishi 7 (☎011/271-0111, fax 221-5450). Huge, upmarket hotel, a few blocks west of the JR station. Rooms are conservatively decorated, and there is a wide range of restaurants, plus a swimming pool, gym and sauna. Worth considering between November and April, when rates drop significantly. ⑦.

**Marks Inn Sapporo**, Nishi 3, Minami 8 (☎011/512-5001, fax 512-3999). Single rooms only at this good-value business hotel conveniently located on the southern side of Suskino. ④.

**Nakamuraya Ryokan**, Nishi 7, Kita 3 (241-2111, fax 241-2118). Stylish Japanese inn in a modern block, seven minutes' walk from Sapporo Station and near the Botanical Gardens. The *tatami* rooms are spacious, the maids wear kimono, there's a large communal bath and a pleasant café in the lobby. ⑤.

**Hotel New Ōtani Sapporo**, Kita 2, Nishi 1 (☎011/222-1111, fax 222-5521). One of Sapporo's most luxurious hotels, and within walking distance of both the JR station and Ōdōri-kōen. Rooms have all the conveniences you'd expect in this price range. Check out the striking fresco of Hokkaidō cranes by French artist Bernard Buffet in the ground-floor café. ⑧.

**Sapporo House Youth Hostel**, 3-1 Nishi 6, Kita (☎011/726-4235). Spartan hostel with a strict timetable, but an excellent location, a couple of minutes' walk west of Sapporo Station. ①.

**Sapporo Inn NADA**, Minami 5, Nishi 9 (☎011/551-5882). Dorm accommodation in *tatami* rooms in a quiet neighbourhood ten minutes' walk west of Suskino. The atmosphere is relaxed, and there's no curfew, though the manager likes to be notified if you plan to check in after 6pm. Western-style breakfast costs ¥600. Part of the Toho group. ②.

**Sapporo Lions Youth Hostel**, 18-4-15 Miyanomori (☎011/611-4709, fax 613-2141). The nicest of Sapporo's hostels, but the least convenient to reach; it's near the Olympic ski jump, 4km from the city centre. Getting here involves taking a subway, followed by an infrequent bus and then a seven-minute uphill hike. ②.

**Sapporo Washington Hotel 1**. Kita 4, Nishi 4 (☎011/251-3211, fax 241-8238). The cheaper of the city's two *Washington* hotels, and opposite the south exit of Sapporo Station. Rooms are bland but functional – the singles for ¥6300 are very small. ⑥.

**Sauna Hokuo Club**, Minami 6, Nishi 5 (☎011/531-2233). Amazingly luxurious and excellent value capsule hotel in the heart of Suskino. Facilities include a swimming pool, ornamental baths, a gym and a mini-cinema. There are also capsules for women. Check in from 5pm. ③.

**Yugiri Ryokan**, Kita 7, Nishi 5 (☎011/716-5482). Despite the welcome sign in English outside, the management don't speak the language at this small and slightly shabby ryokan on the quieter north side of Sapporo Station. A cotton *yukata* and green tea are provided in the basic *tatami* rooms, but no meals are served. ④.

## The City

Although there isn't much to see in central Sapporo, it's a pleasant place simply to stroll around. The single best attraction is the compact and pretty **Botanical Gardens** (April 29–Nov 3 Tues–Sun 9am–4pm; Oct 1–Nov 3 closes at 3.30pm; ¥400), at North Three, West Eight, a ten-minute walk southwest of Sapporo Station. Immediately to the right as you enter is the small but interesting **Ainu Museum**, which is also known as the "Batchelor Kinenkan" in memory of Reverend John Batchelor, a British priest and author of *The Ainu of Japan*, considered to be the definitive work on Hokkaidō's aborigines. The museum has a collection of around 2500 Ainu artifacts (though only a fraction are displayed at any time), ranging from clothes made of bird skins from the Kuril islands (see p.339) to a sacred altar for performing the ritual slaughter of a bear cub – there are English-language explanations.

Following the red-gravel pathway around to the right of the museum will lead you to **Miyabe Hall**, with its intriguing displays of letters and journals belonging to Professor Miyabe Kingo, the first director of Hokkaidō University, who established the gardens in 1886. Miyabe's descriptions of his travels abroad, written in English and illustrated with photographs, make fascinating reading.

The gardens themselves are very attractive, with a long pond, a greenhouse, a rockery, shaded forest walks and neat flower gardens, including a collection which shows the plants and flowers used by the Ainu in their daily lives. In the centre of it all stands a **natural history museum**, housed in a pale green wooden building dating from 1882. Inside you'll find a staggering collection of stuffed animals, paintings and other bizarre objects, including snarling wolves, huge sea lions, and a dog sled from Sakahalin.

On the way to or from the gardens, check out the **Old Hokkaidō Government Building**, at North Three, West Six. This palatial red-brick building is a fine example of the Sapporo-style of architecture that fused the late-nineteenth-century European and New World influences flooding into Japan. You'll see the same style on the campus of Hokkaidō University at North Eight, West Seven, and at Sapporo Brewery (see below). Directly in front of the Sapporo International Communication Plaza is the **Tokeidai**, a wooden clock tower which attracts hordes of Japanese tourists. You'd be right in thinking that this newly renovated building, which is a symbol of the city, would look more at home in somewhere like Boston, because that's where it was made in 1880. One block south lies Ōdōri-kōen and the contrasting 147-metre red steel **TV Tower**. There's no need to fork out ¥600 to go up to the viewing platform; the vista from the nineteenth floor of Sapporo City Hall opposite is free and just as good.

The neon-illuminated excess of **Suskino**, the largest area of bars, restaurants and nightclubs north of Tokyo, begins on the southern side of Ōdōri-kōen, and is best explored at night. If you've not yet had your fill of parks, **Nakajima-kōen**, at West Four, South Nine, is the third of central Sapporo's large-scale green spots and is only worth visiting to see the Hasso-an, an early Edo-period teahouse, virtually the only traditional Japanese building in the city. A better use of time is to head to West Seventeen, North One, to the large, white **Hokkaido Museum of Modern Art** (Tues–Sun 10am–5pm; ¥250 for permanent exhibition), which holds a modest but absorbing collection of paintings and sculptures, some by Japanese artists. The nearest subway station to the museum is Nishi Juhatchichōme, on the Tozai line.

## Sapporo Beer Garden and Museum

It was an American advisor to Hokkaidō who noted the hops growing locally and realized that with its abundant winter ice Sapporo was the ideal location for a commercial brewery. When the first brewery opened in 1876, locals didn't touch beer, so for years Sapporo exported to the foreign community in Tokyo – today the Japanese knock back around seven million kilolitres a year.

The hugely popular **Sapporo Beer Garden and Museum** (daily 9am–5pm; free) stands just east of the city centre. Beer is still brewed in this grand red-brick building, which dates from 1891, but it's now the company's smallest brewery since much of the building has been turned over to a large, modern exhibition on the brewing process and the history of the company, not to mention several restaurants, pubs and souvenir shops. It's worth going on the free, one-hour tour, as you can pick up a recorded English-language commentary at the beginning, though this often gets drowned out by the guide's enthusiatic use of her mini megaphone. The best tactic is to lag behind the tour group and catch up at the end, when free samples of the main product can be enjoyed. Look out for the ingenious combined model and video display where a fairy emerges from a glass of beer.

The beer garden (see Eating, overleaf) and museum are roughly a twenty-minute walk east of Sapporo Station. The easiest way to get here is to hop on the Factory bus which departs every ten minutes or so from in front of the Seibu department store at West Three, North Four. The bus goes via the Sapporo Factory, the first of Sapporo's breweries in the city, converted in 1993 into a shopping and entertainment complex.

## Historical Village of Hokkaidō

The brewery may pull the biggest crowds, but the best of the attractions around Sapporo – indeed, one of the most impressive sights on the entire island – is the **Historical Village of Hokkaidō** (Tues–Sun 9.30am–4.30pm; ¥610), some 14km east of the city centre. This impressive museum, laid out across a spacious park, gathers together some sixty buildings constructed around Hokkaidō between the mid-nineteenth and twentieth centuries, as large-scale immigration from Honshū cranked up. Wandering around the village's four main areas, representing town, farm, mountain and fishing communities, will give you a strong picture of what Hokkaidō looked like before pre-fabricated buildings and concrete expressways became the norm.

The buildings have been restored as beautifully inside as out and spruced up with displays related to their former use, be it a sweet shop, a silkworm house or a woodcutters' shanty. There are guides in some houses (explaining in Japanese only) and written English explanations in all. It's a good idea to wear slip-on shoes, as you'll be taking them off a lot to explore the interiors. In summer, you can hop aboard the horsedrawn trolley car (¥200) which plies the main street – in winter this is replaced by a sleigh. Some of the houses are shut from December to April, but the village is worth visiting even then for its special atmosphere when blanketed in snow.

To cover the whole site will take you a good half day and it's a good place to bring a picnic. Otherwise, there are a couple of inexpensive **restaurants** and refreshment stops within the village. You can extend your visit by exploring the neighbouring grounds of **Nopporo Forest Park**, created to commemorate Hokkaidō's centennial and containing the mildly interesting **Historical Museum of Hokkaidō** (Tues–Sun 9.30am–4.30pm; ¥300) and the **Centennial Memorial Tower**, a one-hundred-metre-tall metal spike which you can ascend for a free view of the city.

Three JR buses run directly from Sapporo Station each morning to the Historical Village in around one hour. There are more frequent buses from platform 10 at the terminus beneath Shin Sapporo Station, connected to the city centre by both train and subway. The bus journey from Shin Sapporo Station takes only fifteen minutes, but note that the last bus departs at 1.50pm (2.10pm between July 26 and August 16). A taxi to or from the park to Shin Sapporo will cost you around ¥1000.

# Eating

As you'd expect from a capital city, Sapporo has the best range of **restaurants** in Hokkaidō, and many of them are very good value, if not downright cheap. There are also plenty of cafés, including branches of the ever-reliable *Mr Donut* and *Doutor*. The pick of the restaurants are clustered around the **Suskino** area, but there's also a good range of places above and beneath Sapporo Station, within the major department stores and at the Factory shopping mall, east of the city centre.

Sapporo is reknowned for its **ramen** noodles; try the version called *batā-kōn* – a noodle broth of butter and corn. A more expensive local speciality is the *jingisukan*, or "Genghis Khan" barbecue, a delicious feast of flame-grilled lamb and vegetables available at many restaurants and at all the beer gardens. At the beer gardens you'll be provided with a plastic bib to protect against dribbles from the dipping sauce, but it's still best to dress down since the smell of sizzled mutton lingers long after you've left. At both the Sapporo and Kirin beer gardens you can pig out on as much barbecue and beer as you can get down you within one hundred minutes for a set price, but you'll find the quality of mutton much better at the smaller Suskino *jingisukan* joints. It's best to book ahead at the restaurants where we give a telephone number.

## Restaurants and cafés

**Aburiya**, Minami 3, Nishi 2. Downstairs at the end of the shopping arcade, this spacious and stylish *izakaya* specializes in fish dishes, which you can see being prepared at the open kitchen. Other branches around the city are at Minami 2, Nishi; Minami 2, Nishi 5 and Kita 4, Nishi 5 in the Asutei building opposite Sapporo Station. Daily 5–11.30pm.

**Aji-no-Tokeidai**, Kita 1, Nishi 3. One of a chain of lively noodle shops, serving large bowls of *batā-kōn ramen* for ¥1000. You'll be asked whether you want your soup flavoured with miso (fermented bean paste), *shōyu* (soy sauce) or *shio* (salt). Downstairs you can sit at the bar and watch the white-aproned chefs at work.

**Chanko Kitanofuji**, Minami 7, Nishi 4. Atmospheric restaurant, complete with a mock sumo ring, serving a chuck-it-all-in stew dish used to fatten up sumo fighters. You can either sit on *tatami* or at tables, and meals start at around ¥2500 per person. Daily 4–11pm.

**Daruma**, Minami 5, Nishi 4. Run by a couple of crusty old ladies, this cosy *jingisukan* joint is on a narrow street in the midst of Suskino; look for the red lantern and scowling bald Genghis on the sign outside. The cuts of meat are much juicier than at the beer gardens, with one plate costing ¥700. Mon–Sat 5.30pm–2am, Sun 4.30pm–1am.

**F45 Biru**, Minami 4, Nishi 5. Look for the giant cracked golden egg outside this fourteen-storey building in Suskino, housing a good range of restaurants and *izakaya*, including the garlic-cuisine restaurant *Ninikuya* on the fourth floor, and *Mama Sabrosso*, an Italian place with a ¥1000-all-you-can-drink (of wine) deal.

**Kirin Beer Garden**, Minami 10, Nishi 1 (☎011/533-3000). The first floor houses the intimate *Bierhalle*, with regular accoustic live music, while the second and third floors form a vast, high-tech amphitheatre, called *SpaceCraft*. The all-you-can-eat-and-drink *jingisukan* and beer is ¥4000 per person for one hundred minutes. Daily 11.30am–10pm.

**Rāmen Yōkochō**, Minami 5, Nishi 3. Although no self-respecting local would be caught dead here, this narrow alley in the heart of Suskino is crammed with scores of ramen joints and big on atmosphere. A huge bowl of freshly cooked noodles costs around ¥1000.

**Sapporo Bier Garten**, Kita 7, Higashi 9 (☎011/742-1531). Germanic atmosphere in this airy restaurant in the old Sapporo brewery, with an outdoor area where you can down a cooling beer in the summer. The all-you-can-eat-and-drink deal is good value. Daily 11.30am–9pm.

**Sapporo City Hall Shokudō**, Kita 1, Nishi 2. Around ¥600 gets you a decent meal at this self service canteen in the basement. Plastic food displays show what's on the menu. Pay for the appropriate ticket from the vending machine (look for a matching *kanji* label), present it at the counter, and then take your food and eat with the shirt-sleeved civil servants. Picture windows look onto a pleasant ornamental garden. On the nineteenth floor there's a café and a good outdoor-viewing platform.

**Shaberitai Shaberitai**, Minami 3, Nishi 6. Inexpensive coffee and a good range of spaghetti dishes are the only things on the menu at this delightful café in a real log cabin, decorated with back packs, ropes and other climbing gear. Mon–Sat noon–10.30pm.

**Taj Mahal**, Minami 1, Nishi 2. This basement restaurant is the main branch of an Indian chain which serves hearty curries and freshly baked *nan*. The lunch set courses starting at ¥1020 are the best value. Also at Kita 2, West, 3 on the second floor, and in the Sapporo Factory shopping mall. Daily 11am–10pm.

# Drinking and nightlife

Apart from the beer gardens, the best place to head for a **drink** in Sapporo is bustling, neon-drenched Suskino. This area is notorious for its "soaplands" – brothels so thinly disguised it's unlikely you'll wander into one by accident. The **nightlife** here is as subject to the whims of fashion as any other of Japan's big cities. If only the hippest place will do, check first with the clued-up assistants at the International Communications Plaza i (see p.302) or leaf through the free magazine *Zene*. Several of the bars listed below also serve good food.

**Bar Isn't It?**, Minami 3, Nishi 2, next to *Hotel Attache*. The Ōsaka chain bar phenomenon – loud music, all drinks ¥500, beer machines for when you don't want to wait at the bar – has made it north to Sapporo. Not the place for a quiet drink, but fun if you're up for it. There's a ¥1000 cover charge at weekends.

**Bazoku**, Minami 2, Nishi 5, Sanyu Bldg. Friendly basement bar with occasional live music. Beers start at ¥300 and the Mexican food comes in generous portions.

**Electric Sheep Bar**, Minami 4, Nishi 2, Watanabe Bldg. Cool name and even cooler view of the Suskino nightscape from this laid-back, ninth-floor bar which has a ¥2500 drink-all-you-can-in-two-hours deal. In the same building is the *69 Diner*, which serves huge portions of California-style cuisine.

**Gaijin Bar**, Minami 2, Nishi 7. The sign outside translates as "nest of delinquent *gaijin*" but everyone knows this friendly second-floor joint by its shorter name. Serves a similar range of beers as *Mugishutei* (see below), but at cheaper prices and with no cover charge. Mon–Thurs 7–11pm, Fri & Sat 7pm–3am.

**Janbo**, Minami 5, Nishi 4. Across the street from *Daruma* (see Restaurants and cafés, p.307), this tiny *yakitori* bar has a friendly, rock-loving owner who serves up succulent sticks of grilled chicken to nibble with your beer. Mon–Sat 8pm–3am.

**King Xhmu**, Minami 7, Nishi 4. The exterior of this club (pronounced "King Mu") resembles a misplaced Mayan colussus, while the interior is a high-tech Indiana Jones adventure. The music is generally grinding techno and entry hovers around ¥4000, although it's only ¥1000 on Mon, Thurs and Fri if you're 23 or over. Entrance charge includes two drinks.

**Miss Jamaica**, Minami 3, Nishi 6. Drinks are around ¥600 each at this funky Caribbean bar with great music and 150 different kinds of rum. The menu includes Jamaican curry and rice for ¥900. Continuing the sultry theme, check out *Havana*, a Cuban bar and restaurant on the second floor of the same building, which occasionally holds salsa parties.

**Mugishutei**, Minami 9, Nishi 5, Onda Bldg, B1. Convivial basement bar at the quiet end of Suskino, decorated with 5000 beer cans and bottles from around the world. Over 250 different types of ale are served – plus food (including fish and chips). Show this *Rough Guide* and tell the bartender that owner Phred says you don't need to pay the ¥900 "charm charge".

**Rad Brothers 1**, Minami 7, Nishi 3, Mitsuwa Bldg. Beers are ¥600 each at this uncluttered bar on the corner of a block in Suskino. Fights have been known to break out, but this is far a better bet than *Rad Brothers 2*, at Minami 5, Nishi 5. Both branches are open daily 6pm–6am.

**Suskino Reien**, Minami 4, Nishi 3. On the eighth floor of the Green Building, Sapporo's most bizarre bar takes the graveyard as its theme. Shrunken heads dangle from the ceiling and the staff perform conjuring tricks.

## Listings

**Airlines** ANA & ANK, Kita 4, Nishi 4 (☎0120–029333); Cathay Pacific, Kita 4, Nishi 4 (☎0120–355747); Continental Micronesia Airlines, Kita 1, Nishi 3 (☎011/221-4091); JAL, Kita 2, Nishi 4 (domestic flights ☎0120-255971; international ☎0120–255931); JAS , Kita 2, West 4 (☎0120–511283); Korean Air, Kita 4, Nishi 5 (☎011/210-3311); Qantas, Kita 4, Nishi 4 (☎011/242-4151).

**Banks** Bank of Tokyo Mitsubishi, Ōdōri, Nishi 3, changes all major currencies, as does the Ōdōri post office one block west, and the central post office east of Sapporo Station. Mitsukoshi, Marui and Gobankan Seibu department stores all have foreign exchange counters, though only Mitsukoshi changes sterling.

**Bookshops** Maruzen, Minami 1, Nishi 4 (Tues–Sun 10am–7pm), with a wide range of English-language books and magazines on its fourth floor, has the edge over Kinokuniya (daily expect Wed 10am–7pm), opposite the TV tower on Ōdōri, Nishi 1.

**Car rental** Eki Rent-a-car (☎011/241-0931); Nippon Rent-a-car (☎011/746-0919); Orix Rent-a-car (☎011/241-0543).

**Consulates** Australia, Kita 1, Nishi 3 (☎011/242-4381); China, Minami 13, Nishi 23 (☎011/563-5563); Russia, Minami 14, Nishi 12 (☎011/561-3171); USA, Kita 1, Nish 28 (☎011/641-1115).

**Hospital** Sapporo City General Hospital, Kita 11, Nishi 13 (☎011/726-2211).

**Internet access** There's an Internet café on the sixth floor of HAL, a computer shop at Minami 3, Nishi 2 (daily 10am–8pm). The charge is ¥700 for thirty minutes, including a drink.

**Laundry** Motoi Yasunobu coin laundry, open daily 8am–10pm, is at Minami 2, Higashi 4.

**Police** The main police station is at Kita 1, Nishi 5 (☎011/241-3201). Emergency numbers are listed in Basics on p.70.

**Post office** The central post office is at Kita 6, Higashi 1, two blocks east of the JR station (Mon–Fri 9am–7pm, Sat 9am–5pm, Sun 9am–12.30pm). There's also a branch at Ōdōri, Nishi 2 (Mon–Fri 9am–6pm).

**Shopping** Sapporo has branches of all of Japan's top department stores, including Mitsukoshi, Seibu, Sogō and Tōkyū. The huge Robinsons in Suskino is worth rooting around, as is the Tanuki Koji, the covered shopping arcade that stretches for six blocks across Minami 3, which was once the city's main shopping street.

**Taxis** The main rank is at the south exit of Sapporo Station. To book a taxi (¥100 extra charge) call the Taxi Association on ☎011/892-6000.

**Travel agency** The main JTB office where you'll find English-speakers is in the Nissei Building at Kita 3, Nishi 4 (☎011/241-6201).

# Otaru

One of the most relaxing ways of arriving at or leaving Hokkaidō is on a ferry to or from the port of **OTARU**, some 40km northwest of Sapporo. Though the town itself has no major attractions, save for an area of restored Meiji-era buildings along a canal, and Mount Tengu, where there's skiing in winter, its cluster of good-value **hotels** make this a possible base if you can't find anywhere to stay in Sapporo.

To find the nineteenth-century canal quarter, head towards the sea from Otaru Station down Chūō-dōri, the town's main street. The canal is at its most attractive for a very short stretch to the right of Chūō-dōri, especially at dusk, when the gas lamps flicker to life. Facing the canal, to the left of Chūō-dōri, is the **Otaru Museum** (daily 9.30am–5pm; ¥100), with an average collection of historical and nature displays in a converted 1893 warehouse. In one of the warehouses to the right of the main road you'll find the *jibiiru* (microbrewery) **Otaru Biiru**, where gleaming copper stills dominate the wooden beer hall. The brewery serves three regular German-style **beers** (a crisp Alt, the darker Dunkel and the cloudy, "banana flavoured" Weissbier) at ¥500 a glass, as well as special seasonal beers and snacks. If they're around, the German masterbrewer and his American assistant Brian can give you a tour of the brewery.

Limited express **trains** (¥610) from Sapporo take around thirty minutes to reach Otaru – **buses** and local trains are slower and cheaper. **Ferries** from Niigata (see p.285) in northern Honshū and Maizaru and Tsuruga, just north of Kyoto, dock at the ferry terminal, some 5km east of the train station. There are also ferries in August serving Korsakov on the Russian island of Sakhalin (¥48,000). Regular buses run between the ferry terminal and Otaru Station – a taxi will cost around ¥1000. You can pick up an English map at the **tourist information office** in the wooden hut outside the station (daily 9am–6pm; ☎0134/29-1333).

Of the cluster of **hotels** near Otaru Station, one of the cheapest is the *Green Hotel* (☎0134/33-0333; ④), five minutes' walk down Chūō-dōri, offering singles for under ¥4000. The *Otaru Tengu-yama Youth Hostel* (☎0134/34-1474, fax 24-0422; ①) is 5km south of the station, near the cable car which goes up Mount Tengu and is convenient for the ski slope on the mountain. To reach the hostel, take the bus from platform 3 outside the station. *Pon Pon* (☎0134/27-0866; ②) is a homely minshuku with good views, a ten-minute walk up the Funami-zaka slope behind Otaru Station. More upmarket is *Hotel Nord Otaru* (☎0134/24-0500, fax 24-1085; ⑦), with Western-style rooms in an elegant stone building overlooking the canal.

For **eating**, head for *Pane e Cacio*, which overlooks the Asakusa-bashi bridge over the canal, serves inexpensive sandwiches and cakes and has outdoor seating. Otaru is also renowned for its sushi and sashimi restaurants, none of which are cheap – you'll find them at the end of the Sun Mall Ichiban-gai shopping arcade, to the east of the station.

# Niseko

Some 100km west of Sapporo, between the dormant volcano Mount Yōtei-san (also known as the Ezo Fuji for its resemblance to its famous southern cousin) and Mount Niseko Annupuri, lies **NISEKO**, one of the best **ski resorts** in Japan. This widely spread-out town is also within the Niseko-Shakotan-Otaru Quasi National Park and makes a good summer base if you want to take advantage of the many adventure sports activities on offer in the area.

The **ski slopes** are a couple of kilometres north of Niseko Station, at the foot of Mount Niseko Annupuri. Ski lifts are run by three separate **resorts**: *Hirafu Kōgen*, *Higashiyama* (part of the *Prince* hotel empire) and *Annupuri Kokusai*. You can buy individual lift tickets from each of the resorts, but the best deal is to go for the "Free Passport", which allows you to use all lifts, and thus ski the whole mountain. A one-day pass costs around ¥4800 and is issued as an electronic tag – you'll need to wave it at the barrier at each of the lifts. If you only buy a pass for one resort, take care not to ski beyond their lifts, otherwise you'll find yourself wasting precious skiing time making your way back to the right resort from the mountain base.

In summer the same mountain becomes the focus for **adventure sports**, including white-water rafting, mountain-biking and kayaking. The Niseko Adventure Centre (☎0136/23-2093) offers all these activities most days between mid-April and November. All-inclusive packages can be arranged through the Niseko Annupuri Youth Hostel (see Practicalities).

## Practicalities

Niseko is not an easy area to visit without your own car, except for in winter, when **buses** run directly to the ski slopes from Sapporo and New Chitose Airport; the Chūō bus goes straight to Annupuri, while the Donan service stops first at Hirafu and Higashiyama. Buy your ticket from the booths on the second floor of the bus station under Sogō department store, next to Sapporo Station. Alternatively, there are infrequent **trains** to Niseko Station, from where you'll have to take a bus or a taxi to the slopes. Combined lift-pass and bus or train ticket packages will save you money; details are available from the TIC in Sapporo (see p.301). **Ski maps** can be picked up at the accommodation listed below and from the ticket offices at the three resorts. There are no information centres at the ski resorts.

With an early start it's possible to ski for most of the day at Niseko and return to Sapporo the same evening. If you stay overnight, you're best off **eating** breakfast or dinner at your pension or hostel since there are few alternative options. There are plenty of places for lunch on the slopes – the *Rāmen Corner* hut at the Higashiyama resort is worth checking out, and there's a *KFC* at Hirafu.

### *ACCOMMODATION*

Most of Niseko's **hotels** and **pensions** are at the Annupuri and Hirafu resorts – Higashiyama is the preserve of the *Prince Hotel* chain. Of the two youth hostels, the *Niseko Annupuri* is the most convenient for the slopes and has the nicest atmosphere.

**Niseko Annupuri Youth Hostel**, 479-4 Niseko (☎0136/58-2084). Charming, European-style log-cabin pension, with a roaring fire, a couple of minutes' walk from the Annupuri Kokusai resort. Mitsura-san, the friendly manager, can sort out ski rental and he and his wife are excellent cooks. ②.

**Niseko Kōgen Youth Hostel**, 336 Niseko (☎0136/44-1171). This former schoolhouse is rather isolated, but offers ski-break packages, and the managers will run you out to the slopes. Guests are entertained every night with an accordian concert. ①.

**Niseko Prince Hotel**, Higashiyama (☎0136/44-1111, fax 44-3224). Upmarket hotel with comfortable rooms, several restaurants, an onsen bath and ski lifts close at hand. There are fantastic views of Mount Yōtei-zan, especially from the newer Annex building. ⑦.

**Pension Asauta**, 35 Higashiyama (☎0136/44-2943, fax 44-1332). Excellent Western-style family-run accommodation in this pale green wooden chalet close to the Higashiyama ski area at Niseko. The meals are delicious and Sato-san, the owner, speaks good English. ⑤.

# Hakodate and around

If you travel to Hokkaidō by train, the first major city you'll come to after emerging from the Seikan Tunnel (see box, p.313) is the attractive port of **HAKODATE**, 260km southwest of Sapporo. Along with Shimoda on the Izu Hantō (see p.193), this was one

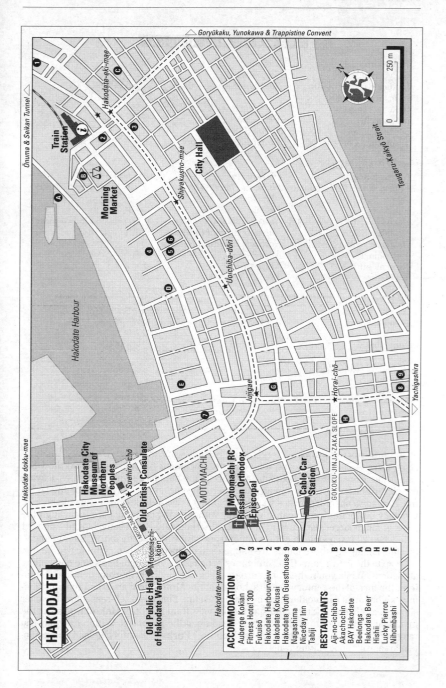

△ *Goryūkaku, Yunokawa & Trappistine Convent*

250 m

Hakodate-eki-mae

Train Station

Ōnuma & Seikan Tunnel △

Hakodate dokku-mae △

i

City Hall

Morning Market

Shiyakusho-mae

Uoichiba-dōri

Hakodate Harbour

Tsugaru-Kaikyō Strait

Yachigashira △

Horai-chō

Jujigae

GOKOKU-JINJA-ZAKA SLOPE

Cable Car Station

Russian Orthodox
Motomachi RC
Episcopal

MOTOMACHI

Old British Consulate

Hakodate City Museum of Northern Peoples

Suehiro-chō

MOTOI-ZAKA SLOPE

Motomachi-kōen

Old Public Hall of Hakodate Ward

Hakodate-yama

**HAKODATE**

**ACCOMMODATION**

| | |
|---|---|
| Auberge Kokian | 7 |
| Fitness Hotel 300 | 3 |
| Fukuisō | 1 |
| Hakodate Harbourview | 2 |
| Hakodate Kokusai | 4 |
| Hakodate Youth Guesthouse | 9 |
| Nagashima | 8 |
| Niceday Inn | 5 |
| Tabiji | 6 |

**RESTAURANTS**

| | |
|---|---|
| Aji-no-ichiban | B |
| Akachochin | C |
| BAY Hakodate | E |
| Beelongs | A |
| Hakodate Beer | D |
| Hishii | H |
| Lucky Pierrot | G |
| Nihombashi | F |

## HAKODATE AND AROUND

| | | |
|---|---|---|
| **Hakodate** | *Hakodate* | 函館 |
| Goryōkaku Fort | *Goryōkaku* | 五稜郭 |
| Hakodate City Museum of Northern Peoples | *Hoppōminzoku Shiryōkan* | 北方民族資料館 |
| Hakodate-yama | *Hakodate-yama* | 函館山 |
| Motomachi | *Motomachi* | 元町 |
| Seikan Tunnel | *Seikan Tonneru* | 青函トンネル |
| Trappistine Convent | *Torapisuchinu Shūdōin* | トラピスチヌ修道院 |
| | | |
| *ACCOMMODATION* | | |
| Auberge Kokian | *Oberuju Kokian* | オベルジュ古稀庵 |
| Fitness Hotel 330 Hakodate | *Fittonesu Hoteru 330 Hakodate* | フィットネスホテル330函館 |
| Fukuisō | *Fukuisō* | ふく井荘 |
| Hakodate Harbourview Hotel | *Hakodate Hābābyū Hoteru* | 函館ハーバービューホテル |
| Hakodate Kokusai Hotel | *Hakodate Kokusai Hoteru* | 函館国際ホテル |
| Hakodate Youth Guest House | *Hakodate Yūsu Gesuto Hausu* | 函館ユースゲストハウス |
| Nagashima | *Nagashima* | 長島 |
| Niceday Inn | *Naisudei In* | ナイスデイイン |
| Tabiji | *Tabiji* | 旅路 |
| | | |
| *EATING* | | |
| Akachōchin | *Akachōchin* | あかちょうちん |
| Aji-no-Ichiban | *Aji-no-Ichiban* | 味の一番 |
| Hishii | *Hishii* | ひしい |
| Nihombashi | *Nihombashi* | にほんばし |
| | | |
| *AROUND HAKODATE* | | |
| **Ōnuma** | *Ōnuma* | 大沼 |
| Chairo-tori | *Chairo-tori* | 茶色鳥 |
| Exander Ōnuma Youth Hostel | *Ekusandā Ōnuma Yūsu Hosuteru* | エクサンダー大沼ユースホステル |

of the first **ports** to open to foreign traders following the Japan-US amity treaty of 1854. Over the next few years, ten countries, including Britain, Russia and the USA, established consulates in Hakodate, and foreigners built fancy wooden homes, leaving the city with a legacy of European and American-style architecture. In 1868 the last of the Tokugawa shogun's forces was defeated in a siege of Hakodate's Goryōkaku fort, a victory celebrated each year in mid-May with a period costume parade through the town. A much larger parade is held during the Hakodate Port Festival, from August 1 to 5, when 20,000 people in cotton kimono and straw hats perform the "squid dance", an entertaining jig where hands are flapped and clapped in time to rythmic drumming.

Despite the fishy aroma that sometimes hangs in air, Hakodate has some compelling attractions. While you're here, be sure to check out the lively morning market of **Asa-ichi**, the turn-of-the-century settlers' homes in the **Motomachi** area, and the outstanding exhibition on **Ainu** culture at the main museum. Finally, no self-respecting traveller should leave before taking in the spectacular view from the top of **Hakodate-yama**, the mountain in the middle of the hammer-head tip of the peninsula. Within easy day-trip range of the city, is the **Ōnuma Quasi National Park**, a beautiful lakeland and mountain area, with good hiking trails.

## Arrival, information, orientation and city transport

Hakodate's **airport** (☎0138/57-8881) lies 8km north of the city; buses take around twenty minutes from here to reach the train station in the city centre, and cost around ¥300. **Trains** from Morioka and Aomori on Honshū, and Sapporo and New Chitose Airport on Hokkaidō terminate at Hakodate Station, on the eastern side of the harbour – the **bus** terminal is in front of here. If you're arriving by **ferry** from Honshū, you'll dock at Hakodate-kō Port, some 4km north of the train station. Buses #1 and #19 leave from the Hokkudai-mae stop, seven minutes' walk south of the port, to the city centre – or you can take a taxi for around ¥2000.

For a map of the city, call in at the **Hakodate Tourist Information Office** (daily: April–Oct 9am–7pm; Jan–March, Nov & Dec 9am–5pm; ☎0138/23-8366), next to Hakodate Station, where the assistants speak English and can also make accommodation bookings.

Squeezed into a narrow neck of land jutting into the Tsugaru Straits, Hakodate's sights are sprawled over a wide area. Immediately east of the station is the main **shopping** and **entertainment** district, while on the southern side of the harbour, rising up the slopes of Mount Hakodate-yama, is the **Motomachi** area of old residences and foreign consulates. Some 2km northeast of the station lies **Goryōkaku**, the site of the remains of the Tokugawa shogun's fort and another shopping and eating and drinking area.

Because Hakodate's sights are spread out, you'll need to use public transport to get around. This is no hardship as the city has a good **tram** system with two lines, both starting at the onsen resort of Yunokawa east of the city and running past Goryōkaku and the train station before diverging at the Jyūjigai stop in Motomachi. From here, Tram 5 heads west to Hakodate Dokku-mae, while Tram 2 continues further south to Yachigashira on the eastern side of Hakodate-yama. One-day (¥1000) and two-day passes (¥1700) can be bought from the tourist office for unlimited use of both the trams and city **buses** (but not Hakodate Bus Company buses). These passes, only worth buying if you plan to tour extensively around town, also cover the bus service up Hakodate-yama.

## Accommodation

There's a good range of **accommodation** in Hakodate, though the city gets crowded during the summer, when you'll need to book ahead. If you get stuck, head for the tourist office (see above), where staff can phone around to see what's available. The most interesting area to base yourself is **Motomachi**, at the foot of Hakodate-yama.

---

### THE SEIKAN TUNNEL

It took forty years to complete the mammoth civil engineering project that is the **Seikan Tunnel**. Joining Honshū with Hokkaidō, the tunnel is 53.9km long, and over half its length is underwater, making this the world's longest submarine transport link. Travelling through Seikan isn't recommended for the claustrophobic; even the fastest train takes an hour to complete the underground portion of the journey, with the tunnel sinking to 240m beneath sea level at its deepest point. If you're comfortable with being this far down however, you may want to go on a **tour** of the submarine facilities, which include a small exhibition area and a warren of passageways, one of which has its own cable car link with the shore. For an extra ¥820 on top of your train fare, you can get off at one of the mid-tunnel stations (145m below sea level), where you'll be shown around by a Japanese-speaking guide. The tours must be booked in advance at JR ticket counters and are held on the slower *kaisoku* (rapid), not *tokkyū* (limited express) trains.

Another option is to stay 20km north of the city in the tranquil Ōnuma Quasi-National Park, where there's a good youth hostel (see p.317).

**Auberge Kokian** 13-2 Suehiro-chō (☎0138/26-5753, fax 22-2710). This nineteenth-century Motomachi wooden house has been smartly renovated into a hotel with a restaurant and bar. Rates, at the low end of this scale, include breakfast and dinner. ⑦.

**Fitness Hotel 330 Hakodate**, 6-3 Wakamatsu-chō (☎0138/23-0330, fax 23-5377). Very decent rooms at this keenly priced business hotel, just across from the station. Guests can use the attached fitness club for an extra ¥700. ⑥.

**Fukuisō**, 30-16 Wakamatsu-chō (☎0138/23-5858, fax 26-8239). Homely minshuku, five minutes north of the station, with friendly management. The *tatami* rooms have air conditioning and TV. ④.

**Hakodate Harbourview Hotel**, 14-10 Wakamatsu-chō (☎0138/22-0111, fax 23-0154). Classy hotel next to the station, with smallish rooms but picturesque harbour views and a good range of restaurants. ⑦.

**Hakodate Kokusai Hotel**, 5-10 Ōtemachi (☎0138/23-5151, fax 23-0239). Hakodate's top hotel is in a grungy warehouse area between the station and Motomachi, and has spacious, comfortable rooms with harbour views, but lacks sparkle in its public areas. The ninth-floor restaurants are glamorous and pricey. ⑦.

**Hakodate Youth Guest House**, 17-6 Horai-chō (☎0138/26-7892). Delightful guesthouse with Western-style rooms and a top-floor lounge with a view of Hakodate-yama. Breakfast at ¥500 is served in the café, and free ice cream is offered every night at 9pm to tempt people back before the 11pm curfew. ②.

**Nagashima**, 18-5 Hourai-machi (☎0138/26-2101, fax 22-7298). Good-value, spotless minshuku near Hakodate-yama, offering mainly Western-style rooms, and a couple of nice *tatami* ones for the same price. For meals add ¥2300 per person. ④.

**Niceday Inn**, 9-11 Ōtemachi (☎0138/22-5919). Friendly hostel conveniently located between the station and Motomachi. All the rooms have two bunk beds and are very small, but if it's quiet you may get one to yourself. The owners speak English and there's free tea and coffee. ②.

**Tabiji**, 8-12 Ōtemachi (☎0138/26-7652). Simple minshuku in a wooden building on a side road between the station and Motomachi. The clean, Japanese-style rooms have TV but no air conditioning. Meals are available. ④.

## The City

Any tour of Hakodate should kick off at the atmospheric **Asa-ichi**, the morning market (Mon–Sat 5am–noon) immediately to the west of the station. Even if you arrive at the relatively late hour of 9am, there's still plenty see at the hundreds of tightly packed stalls in this waterside location. Old ladies in headscarves squat amid piles of vegetables and flowers at the back of the market, and huge, alien-like red crabs, squid and musk melons are the local specialities. Don't leave without stopping in one of the noodle stalls (see Eating and drinking, opposite).

A ten-minute walk west from the market will lead to **Hakodate-yama** and the Motomachi district – alternatively you can take a tram and get off at Jyūjigai. The 334-metre-high peak, crowned with television signal transmitters, is an excellent spot from which to soak up the town. On a clear day the view is spectacular, but best of all is the night-time panorama, when the twinkling lights of the port and the boats fishing for squid just off the coast create a magical scene – though be prepared for hordes of tourists hanging off the platform railings for a better view. The energetic can climb to the summit along a trail (May–Oct), but most people opt for the cable car (daily 10am–10pm, ¥640 one way, ¥1160 return), which is a seven-minute uphill walk from the Jyūjigai tram stop. The cheaper alternative is to take the bus (30min, ¥360) from Hakodate Station, which runs from April 25 to October 15 between 1.15pm and 9pm; the viewing platforms are above the summit cable car station, along with a couple of restaurants and gift shops.

Heading downhill, you'll find yourself in **Motomachi**, with its Western-style, late-nineteenth century architecture. The best thing to do here is simply wander about, stopping to explore some of the churches, which are free (few of the other buildings merit their entrance charges). The most striking is the white **Russian Orthodox Church**, seven minutes uphill from Jyūjigai tram stop, and built in 1919, complete with green copper-clad onion domes and spires. Inside, the icon-festooned carved wood altar piece is impressive and piped Russian choral music adds to the atmosphere. Nearby, the **Episcopal Church**, with its unusual modern architecture, is more interesting to observe from outside than in, while slightly downhill, the Gothic-style **Motomachi Roman Catholic Church** is worth stepping into for its decoration based on the stations of the cross.

Walking west for a couple of hundred metres across the hillside streets will bring you to the extraordinary **Old Public Hall of Hakodate Ward** (daily: April–Oct 9am–7pm; Jan–March, Nov & Dec 9am–5pm; ¥300), a sky-blue and lemon-painted confection with pillars, verandahs and fancy wrought-iron and plaster decoration. After a fire destroyed the original hall, this replacement was completed in 1910. In front of the hall is the small Motomachi Park, below which stands the rather twee **Old British Consulate**, which looked after the Empire's affairs in Hokkaidō from 1859 to 1934. The cream and blue building now houses a highly missable museum, a stuffy British tea room and a gift shop.

Far more interesting is the **Hakodate City Museum of Northern Peoples** (daily: April–Oct 9am–7pm, Jan–March, Nov & Dec 9am–5pm; ¥300), in an old bank down the Motoi-zaka slope, which leads away from the consulate. The museum's superb collection of artifacts relating to the **Ainu** and other races across the islands of Eastern Siberia and Alaska, has good written English explanations and is well worth the entrance fee. Some of the clothes on display are amazing – look out for the Chinese silk robe embroidered with dragons, an example of the trade that existed between China, the islanders of Sakhalin and the Ainu.

Hakodate's other attractions include the heavily hyped remains of **Goryōkaku**, a Western-style fort some 3km northeast of the station and five minutes' walk north of the Goryōkaku-kōen-mae tram stop. Built in the late-nineteenth century, the star-shaped fort was originally designed to protect Hokkaidō against attack from Russia. In the event however, it was used by Tokugawa's naval forces in a last-ditch battle to uphold the shogun against the emperor in the short-lived civil war that ushered in the Meiji restoration of 1869. What's left of the fort today – a leafy park, the moat and outer walls – looks best from the top of the rather ugly, sixty-metre-high viewing tower (daily 8am–7pm; ¥630) by the main entrance. It's best to visit here between late July to mid-August, when open-air plays about Hakodate's history are performed enthusiastically by five hundred amateur actors on Friday, Saturday and Sunday evenings.

Also rather disappointing is the **Trappistine Convent**, 10km southeast of Hakodate Station, established in 1868 by eight French nuns. You can't go inside; home-made cakes and biscuits are the real reason tour buses stop here. It takes at least one hour by public transport to reach the convent, either by an infrequent bus from Hakodate Station, or by tram to Yunokawa, then a bus.

On the way to the convent you'll pass the drab seaside area of Yunokawa, the oldest onsen resort in Hokkaidō and definitely looking it. A better (and cheaper) **onsen** option, closer to the town centre, is the huge public bath at **Yachigashira** (daily 6am— 9.30pm; ¥340), a couple of minutes' walk from tram terminus #2 on the eastern side of Hakodate-yama.

## Eating and drinking

**Seafood** is delivered fresh every day to the habour, and the best places to feast on it are the sushi bars scattered around the morning market near Hakodate Station. Look out for the **local speciality**, a bowl of ramen topped with a whole crab and other seafood. You'll find a limited range of **restaurants** on the main shopping street near the station – for good value, head for *The Don*, part of a chain serving bowls of rice topped with fish or meat. For a splurge, Motomachi's smart restaurants by the seafront can be fun.

Goryōkaku is the city's main **drinking** area. More central are the converted warehouses in Motomachi that serve the local *ji-biiru* (micro-brewery beer), Hakodate Beer; try *Beelongs* on the waterfront near the morning market and *Hakodate Beer*, just along from the *Kokusai Hotel*, towards Motomachi.

**Akachōchin**, 18-21 Wakamatsu-chō. The name means "red lantern" and there are plenty of these hanging inside this lively *robatayaki* (grilled food) restaurant, a couple of minutes' walk from the JR station. Expect to pay around ¥2500 per head.

**Aji-no-ichiban**. Noodle stall in the morning market serving up the local speciality for ¥1800, and plenty of cheaper dishes, plus delicious, freshly squeezed melon juice. Open daytime only.

**BAY Hakodate**, 11-5 Toyakawa-chō. Stylish buffet-style restaurant in one of the converted warehouses by the waterfront in Motomachi. The menu features a wide range of Western dishes, with lunch at ¥1500 and dinner at ¥2500 per head–both good value.

**El Paso**, 30-3 Goryōkaku-chō. Funky little Mexican café close to the fort, serving tacos, burritos, chilli and nachos. The lunch deals are all under ¥850. In the evening the place turns into a bar and has a wider food menu. Mon–Sat 11.30am—11.30pm.

**Hishii**, 9-4 Horai-chō. Elegant teashop, bar and antique clothes shop in this eighty-year-old wooden building, draped with ivy, near the Horai-chō tram stop. There's a *tatami* area on the second floor and the shop sells secondhand kimono from ¥5000. The café is open daily from 10am to 10pm, the bar from 8pm to midnight.

**Lucky Pierrot**. Just west of the Jyūjigai tram stop, towards the waterfront. Cheap fast food, Japanese-style, at this hamburger and curry restaurant. The shop sign says "Santa Claus has come to Hakodate" and there are plenty of the jolly red men decorating the front.

**Nihombashi**, 7-9 Motomachi. Good-value Japanese restaurant halfway along the pedestrianized street running across the top of Motomachi. Huge set meals and bowls of noodles are served in a relaxing atmosphere.

## Listings

**Airline offices** ANA, 14-10 Wakamatsu-chō (☎0138/22-1166); JAL, 7-16 Wakamatsu-chō (☎0138/27-5711).

**Banks** The banks close to the JR station only change US travellers' cheques. For other currencies go the central post office (see below; Mon–Fri only).

**Bookshops** A small selection of English-language paperbacks are available on the seventh floor of the Boni Moriya department store, opposite Hakodate Station.

**Car rental**, Eki Rent-a-car (☎0138/22-7864) is next to Hakodate Station.

**Hospitals** Hakodate City Hospital, 2-33 Yayoi-cho (☎0138/23-8651).

**Laundry** 24-hour JUN coin laundry, a block past the fire station, close by the city hall.

**Police** The main police station is on the western side of Goryōkaku-kōen. Emergency numbers are listed in Basics on p.70.

**Post office** The central post office, 1-6 Shinkawa-chō, is a ten-minute walk east of Hakodate Station, near the Shinkawa-chō tram stop. Opening hours are Mon–Fri 9am–7pm, Sat 9am–5pm, Sun 9am–12.30pm.

**Taxis** The main taxi rank is outside Hakodate Station.

**Travel agents** The main JTB office at 16-24 Yanagawa-chō (☎0138/56-1717) is a five-minute walk west of the Goryōkaku-kōen-mae tram stop.

## Ōnuma Quasi-National Park

The serene lakeland area of **Ōnuma Quasi National Park**, 20km north of Hakodate, can easily be visited in a day, but is worth considering as an overnight stop or even an alternative to staying in Hakodate itself. There are three **lakes** in the park – Ōnuma, Konuma, and Junsai-numa. The largest and most beautiful, **Ōnuma**, lying just east of the main tourist village outside Ōnuma-kōen Station, is carpeted with water lilies and contains over one hundred tiny islands.

The nicest way to take in the scenery is to walk around the islands, which are joined by bridges. The view towards the 1133-metre jagged peak of the dormant volcano of **Komaga-take** is rightly considered to be one of the most breathtaking in Japan. Unsurprisingly, Ōnuma is popular with the tour groups, but they are usually herded into the boats that depart every thirty minutes, leaving you to stroll in peace. **Cycling** is another good way of exploring – bikes can be rented for around ¥1500 a day from numerous shops around the station. Avid **hikers** can also tackle the **volcano**, which has two main routes, both taking around two and a half hours to complete – one route starts near the woodland shrine on the northern shore of Ōnuma Lake, while the other starts to the west on National Road 5.

Local **trains** from Hakodate to Ōnuma-kōen Station take around forty minutes, and you can do the journey in half the time on the less frequent and more expensive limited express trains. There are also five **buses** a day, taking around one hour. Apart from the **campsite** on the eastern shore of Ōnuma Lake, around 6km from the station, the cheapest **accommodation** is at the *Exander Ōnuma Youth Hostel* (☎0138/67-3419, fax 67-2655; [1]), ten minutes' walk south of Ōnuma-kōen Station. This is a large and friendly place with bunk bed dorms, serving good breakfasts and dinners and offering a wide range of activities such as canoeing or cross-country skiing, depending on the season. You can also pick up a discount coupon here to save ¥500 on bicycle rental. A good alternative is *Chairo-tori* (☎0138/67-2231; [5]), a homely minshuku opposite the station, with two meals included in the price. There are several touristy **restaurants** around the station, but the best place for lunch or dinner is *Wald* (daily except Thurs 10am–9pm), the log house on the way to the youth hostel; the menu here is in English and includes hearty sandwiches with chips, salad and beer.

# Shikotsu-Tōya National Park and around

Follow the coastal road or rail line around Uchiura-wan from Hakodate and you'll reach the eastern side of the **Shikotsu-Tōya National Park**, one of Hokkaidō's prettiest lakeland and mountain areas, but also its most developed, since it is within easy reach of Sapporo, some 80km north. It's difficult to say which of the park's two main caldera lakes – **Tōya-ko** to the east and **Shikotsu-ko** to the west – is the best to visit; both have gorgeous locations, are near active volcanoes and are surrounded by excellent hiking trails. Shikotsu-ko is certainly less touristy than Tōya-ko, but the latter is only 2km from the geological wonder Shōwa Shin-zan, a **volcano** that only started sprouting in the 1940s. Between the two lakes is **Noboribetsu Onsen**, the largest hot spring resort in Hokkaidō, worth visiting to soak up the other-worldly landscape of bubbling and steaming Jigokudani (Hell Valley). Between Norboribetsu and Shikotsu-ko, in the coastal town of Shiraoi, is **Poroto Kotan**, a recreated **Ainu village** that provides a rather nostalgic glimpse into the culture of Hokkaidō's original inhabitants. For a more accurate impression of how the Ainu live today press on to the real village of **Nibutani**, which has two fine museums and is the home of Japan's first Ainu MP, Kayano Shigeru.

## Tōya-ko and Shōwa Shin-zan

The beautiful caldera lake of **Tōya-ko** is punctuated dead centre by the ice-cream cone island of Ōshima, and on its southern shores is Tōya-ko Onsen. Hordes of visitors

Niseko △ ... Sapporo △
Chitose

Monbetsu-dake
(866 m) ... Chitose-gawa
*Yotei-san*
*(1893 m)* ... *Eniwa-dake* ... ▲
*(1320 m)* ... Poropinai ... Shikotsu Kohan
Morappu
*Shikotsu-ko*
Koke-no-dōmon
*Tarumae-zan*
*(1041 m)*
Tomakomai
*Tōya-ko*
Tōya-ko
Onsen ... *Orofure Pass* ... Porotokotan
... Shiraoi
Tōya ... ▲ ▲ *Shōwa Shin-zan*
*Usa-zan* *(402 m)*
*(732 m)* ... *Kuttara-ko*
Noboribetsu
Onsen
Date ... MUROBAN LINE

*Dōō Expressway*

N ... PACIFIC
OCEAN
Noboribetsu

Muroran ... **SHIKOTSU-TŌYA NATIONAL PARK**

0 ... 20 km

▽ *Aomori & Hachinohe* ... *Hachinohe, Nagoya, Sendai & Tokyo* ▽

regularly descend on this area, especially between May and October, when a spectacular nightly fireworks display illuminates the lake. Pretty as it is, the best reason for visiting Tōya-ko is to see the nearby dormant volcano Usu-zan, some 2km south, and its steaming "para-site volcano" **Shōwa Shin-zan**, which started to sprout out of the ground as recently as 1944.

On December 28, 1943, severe earthquakes began shaking the area around Usu-zan and continued to do so until September 1945. In the intervening period a new lava dome rose out of the ground, sometimes at the rate of 1.5m a day. By the time it had stopped growing, Shōwa Shin-zan, the "new mountain" named after the reigning emperor, stood 405m above sea level. The wartime authorities were desperate to hush up this extraordinary event for fear that the fledgling mountain would serve as a beacon for US bomber planes.

Fortunately, Shōwa Shin-zan's birth was carefully documented by local post master **Mimatsu Masao**, a 57-year-old amateur vulcanoligist who kept daily records of the mountain's growth. After the war, Mimatsu bought the land on which the mountain stood so it would be protected from the mining companies who were intent on digging up the rich mineral deposits beneath it. Despite tempting offers from the tourist indus-try (one rumoured to be ¥300 million), Mimatsu declared "I purchased the volcano to continue my research uninterrupted. I did not buy it to make money. Nor did I buy it for tourists to gawk at." His efforts were rewarded in 1958 when Shōwa Shin-zan was made a Special Natural Treasure by the government.

Nevertheless, Mimatsu never turned away gawking tourists – but nor did he charge them admission, a practice still upheld by Shōwa Shin-zan's current owner Mimatsu

| SHIKOTSU-TŌYA NATIONAL PARK AND AROUND | | |
|---|---|---|
| **Shikotsu-Tōya National Park** | *Shikotsu-Tōya Kokuritsu-kōen* | 支笏洞爺国立公園 |
| **Tōya-ko** | *Tōya-ko* | 洞爺湖 |
| Shōwa Shin-zan | *Shōwa Shin-zan* | 昭和新山 |
| Usu-zan | *Usu-zan* | 有珠山 |
| *ACCOMMODATION* | | |
| Ōno Pension | *Ōno Penshon* | 大野ペンション |
| Shōwa Shin-zan Youth Hostel | *Shōwa Shin-zan Yūsu Hosuteru* | 昭和新山ユースホステル |
| Tōya Sun Palace Hotel | *Tōya San Paresu Hoteru* | 洞爺サンパレスホテル |
| **Noboribetsu Onsen** | *Noboribetsu Onsen* | 登別温泉 |
| Jigokudani | *Jigokudani* | 地獄谷 |
| *ACCOMMODATION* | | |
| Akashiya-sō Youth Hostel | *Akashiya-sō Yūsu Hosteru* | あかしや荘ユースホステル |
| Dai-ichi Takamoto-kan | *Dai-ichi Takamoto-kan* | 第一瀧本館 |
| Ryokan Hanaya | *Ryokan Hanaya* | 旅館花屋 |
| Kanefuku Youth Hostel | *Kanefuku Yūsu Hosuteru* | 金福ユースホステル |
| Mahoroba | *Mahoroba* | まほろば |
| Muroran | *Muroran* | 室蘭 |
| Nibutani | *Nibutani* | 二風谷 |
| Poroto Kotan | *Poroto Kotan* | ポロトコタン |
| Shiraoi | *Shiraoi* | 白老 |
| Tomakomai | *Tomakomai* | 苫小牧 |
| **Shikotsu-ko** | *Shikotsu-ko* | 支笏湖 |
| Koke-no-dōmon | *Koke-no-dōmon* | コケの洞門 |
| Shikotsu Kohan | *Shikotsu Kohan* | 支笏湖畔 |
| Tarumae-zan | *Tarumae-zan* | 樽前山 |
| *ACCOMMODATION* | | |
| Marukoma Onsen | *Marukoma Onsen* | 丸駒温泉 |
| Shikotsu-ko Youth Hostel | *Shikotsu-ko Yūsu Hosuteru* | 支笏湖ユースホステル |
| Hotel Suimeikaku | *Hoteru Suimeikaku* | ホテル翠明閣 |

Saburō, Masao's son-in-law, who can often be found in the **Mimatsu Masao Memorial Hall** (daily 8am–5pm; ¥300). This small museum is tucked behind the ghastly row of giftshops at the base of the volcano, and contains an interesting collection of exhibits on the history of the fledgling volcano.

**Usu-zan**, Shōwa Shin-zan's neighbouring parent volcano is still frighteningly active; it last blew its top on August 7, 1977, showering Tōya-ko Onsen with volcanic rock and dust, and killing three people. The volcano still steams unpredictably, but it's safe enough for you to brave taking the cable car (daily 8.30am–5.30pm; ¥1450 return) up to a viewing platform 300m from the crater, for the stunning vistas over Shōwa Shin-zan, Tōya-ko and out to sea. The cable car station is at the end of the row of tourist shops by Shōwa Shin-zan. From April to October buses run every hour from the Donan Bus Terminal in Tōya-ko Onsen to Shōwa Shin-zan (¥330 one way, ¥600 return).

Back in Tōya-ko Onsen, you can learn a bit more about the 1977 eruption in the **Volcano Science Museum** (daily 9am–5pm; ¥600) above the bus station, although the lacklustre displays manage to make the eruption seem pretty dull. If you find yourself dropping off, pop into the "experience room", which rumbles along with the soundtrack of a movie showing the volcano in action. The best way to enjoy the positive side of volcanic activity – onsen water – is to pop into the huge *Tōya Sun Palace*, the hotel beside the lake, which has the pricey, but fun **Fantastic Large Hot Spring Bathhouse** (daily 10am–4pm; ¥2500), featuring two floors of over twenty different soaking pools, some with views across the lake, and a large swimming pool with artificial waves and a water slide.

Don't bother taking the kitsch yellow castle **ferry** *Espoir* (daily 8am–5pm, sailings every 30min; ¥1320) out to Ōshima, the largest of the islands in the centre of Tōya-ko, unless you have a burning desire to see Ezo deer grazing in the island's forests.

### Practicalities

**Trains** from Hakodate and Sapporo run to Tōya Station, on the coast, from where you can get a bus up the hill to Tōya-ko Onsen (¥320). There are daily **buses** to Tōya-ko Onsen from Sapporo and Hakodate, and from late April to October, five buses a day run to Noboribetsu Onsen from Tōya-ko Onsen (see opposite), along a scenic mountain route, via the Orufure Pass. Buses pull in at the Donan Bus Terminal, five minutes' walk from the shore of Tōya-ko; inside the terminal is a tourist office where you can pick up an English **map** of the area.

Tōya-ko Onsen has plenty of top-notch **hotels**, which usually include two meals in their rates and offer substantial discounts outside the busy summer season. The *Tōya Sun Palace* (☎0142/75-4126, fax 75-2875; ⑧) is a good upmarket option – you'll find cheaper places to stay outside of town, on the way to the volcanos. The *Shōwa Shinzan Youth Hostel* (☎0142/75-2283, fax 75-2872; ②), at the turn-off to Shōwa Shin-zan, a ten-minute bus ride (¥220) from Tōya-ko Onsen, has bunk-bed dorms and shared *tatami* rooms, and rents out bikes for ¥1000 a day. The *Ōno Pension* (☎0142/75-4128, fax 75-3880; ⑥), nearer to Tōya-ko Onsen on the lakeside road, is a good-value mid-range hotel, with two meals included in the price.

None of the **restaurants** at Tōya-ko Onsen or Shōwa Shin-zan make much of an effort to provide anything beyond the usual noodle and rice dishes; most people eat in their ryokan or hotel and you'd be wise to do the same. Of the small cluster of cafés at the turn-off from the lake to the volcanoes, *Ōdera* opposite the youth hostel, does good-value set meals, including sashimi, tempura and noodles, for ¥1500.

## Noboribetsu Onsen and around

Some 18km east of Tōya-ko and nestling amid lush green mountain slopes, ripped through by a bubbling wasteland of volcanic activity, lies **NOBORIBETSU ONSEN**. Although this small, purpose-built resort is Hokkaidō's top hot spring destination (and has huge, unsightly hotels to prove it), the dramatic landscape of **Jigokudani** – the source of Noboribetsu's fame – is less touristy than a similar area in Beppu in Kyūshū (see p.703), and is definitely worth seeing. Afterwards, don't miss out on a wallow in the luxurious baths of the **Dai-ichi Takimoto-kan**.

A ten-minute walk from the bus stop up Gokuraku, Noboribetsu's main street, will bring you to a roadside **shrine** guarded by two brightly painted statues of demons. This is the entrance to **Jigokudani** (Hell Valley) a steaming, lunar-like valley that is the result of an ancient volcanic eruption, and from where ten thousand tons of water are pumped out daily. It takes about thirty minutes to explore the area, wandering along wooden pathways through a landscape of rusty red rocks, streaked green and white by mineral deposits.

Close to the start of the valley walkway you'll notice a tiny wooden shrine where you can sip a cup of the onsen water, which tastes a bit like diluted vinegar. Twenty minutes' walk further on, a well-signposted pathway leads to **Oyu-numa**, a malevolent-looking hot-water lake which looks exactly what you'd expect to find in somewhere called "hell".

All of the hotels draw water from Jigokudani and many have built elaborate **baths** so that guests and visitors can enjoy the water's therapeutic benefits. The nicest baths open to the public are at the back of the **Dai-ichi Takamoto-kan** (daily 9am–3pm; ¥2000), with 29 different kinds of tubs, including several Jacuzzis, a *rotemburo* (outdoor pool), a cypress wood bath and a swimming pool with a water slide (you'll need to take a bathing costume with you to use this, or rent one on the premises). The main onsen bath hall, supported by Roman pillars, has a sweeping view across Jigokudani.

You're unlikely to be tempted by Noboribetsu's other main attraction, a deplorable **Bear Park** (daily 9am–4.30pm, longer hours April–Nov; entrance & cable car ¥2520) on the summit of Kuma-yama, the mountain that rises over the resort. Even if you find performing animals entertaining, the sight of scores of fully grown bears begging for snacks in spartan concrete bunkers is upsetting. The only pleasure to be had here is the panoramic view of the surrounding mountains you'll get from the cable car, which runs up to the park from the resort.

Returning from the onsen to Noboribetsu Station, the incongrous grey turrets of the red-brick Sea Fantasy Castle Nixe, loom into view. This is the main attraction of **Marine Park Nixe** (daily 9am–8pm; ¥2300), a kitsch medley of a Hans Christian Anderson-style amusement park, multi-storey aquarium and sea lion and dolphin shows.

## Practicalities

Noboribetsu Station is on the JR Muroran line and is served by **trains** from Hakodate and Sapporo. From the station, the onsen is a thirteen-minute bus ride away. There are also direct **buses** to Noboribetsu Onsen from Sapporo, Chitose Airport, and the nearby ports of Tomakomai to the north and Muroran to the south. If you're coming from or going to Tōya-ko Onsen from Noboribetsu Onsen between June and mid-October, consider taking the bus which goes via the beautifully scenic mountain-top Orofure Pass (¥1530).

The Donan and Chūō bus terminals stand opposite each other at the southern end of the resort's main shopping street, which runs uphill towards Jigokudani. Just up from the bus terminals is a **tourist information office** (daily 9am–6pm; ☎0143/84-3311); no English is spoken here, but you can pick up a decent English map and leaflet on the area.

For budget **accommodation**, head for the *Akashiya-sō Youth Hostel* (☎0143/84-2616; ①), roughly one minute's walk downhill from the bus station. This friendly hostel has standard bunk-bed and *tatami* dorms for four to eight people, an onsen bath, and a cosy lounge with TV, guitar and piano – dinner is also on offer. The more basic *Kanefuku Youth Hostel* (☎0143/84-2565, fax 84-2073; ①), is slightly cheaper, but less convenient-ly located, ten minutes' walk down the hill from the bus station, past the hospital. One of the nicest mid-range hotels is the modern *Ryokan Hanaya* (☎0143/84-2521, fax 84-2240; ⑤), opposite the hospital, five minutes' walk down the hill from the bus station. Run by English-speaking managers, the ryokan has comfortable Western- and Japanese-style rooms, as well as an ornamental garden, and a lovely *rotemburo*. Prices are slightly higher if you go for an en-suite bathroom and inclusive *kaiseki-ryōri* (Japanese haute cuisine) meals, which are mouth-watering. For something really swanky, try the *Dai-Ichi Takamoto-kan* (☎0143/84-2111, fax 84-2202; ⑧), or the over-the-top *Mahoroba* (☎0143/84-2211, fax 84-2218; ⑧) – the latter has the largest collection of residents-only baths in town.

As far as **eating** goes, there are plenty of ramen stalls and tourist restaurants along the main street – all good for a cheap lunch. Also worth trying is the *Takamoto Inn* opposite the Dai-ichi Takamoto-kan, which serves Japanese dishes and does a special set lunch for ¥800.

## Ainu Villages: Poroto Kotan and Nibutani

Some 30km north of Noboribetsu and outside of the national park area is **POROTO KOTAN** (daily: April–Oct 8am–5.30pm; Jan–March, Nov & Dec 8.30am–4.30pm; ¥650), a recreated Ainu village of thatched communal huts and a museum, beside a small lake, ten minutes' walk east of Shiraoi Station. Although it bears no relation to how Ainu live today, Poroto Kotan does provide the rare opportunity to see traditionally dressed Ainu men and women perform the ritual dance *Iyomante Rimse*. You can also listen to the haunting music of the *mukkur*, a mouth harp made of bamboo and thread that creates a strange, resonating sound. Lectures in Japanese on Ainu culture are given in the large straw huts, which have smoked fish hanging from their rafters. There's also a small museum of Ainu artifacts with good explanations in English, but it's somewhat overshadowed by the pathetic scene of caged bears outside. One of the Ainu's most important ceremonies involved the ritual slaughter and eating of bears; today these captured specimens react to their cramped jails by sleeping and no doubt dreaming of the forests where they should be. Limited express trains from Sapporo to Shiraoi take just over an hour.

Much better museums can be found in the real Ainu village of **NIBUTANI**, some 50km south of the port of the Tomakomai on road 237. Eighty percent of the five-hun-dred-strong population here are of Ainu blood. Just outside the village is the contro-versial Nibutani dam, which caused uproar in the community when it was built, since it flooded sacred Ainu sites and stopped the salmon runs along the river. A landmark legal verdict in 1997 declared the dam would stay, but also that it violated Ainu rights.

One of Nibutani's elder statesmen is Kayano Shigeru, an MP since 1994, and his per-sonal collection of Ainu artifacts is on display in the charming **Kayano Shigeru Ainu Memorial Museum** (daily April–Nov 9am–5pm; ¥300), a five-minute walk up the hill from the main road. Outside, you'll see a collection of traditional Ainu huts – inside, look out for the amazing perserved Emperor Fish, a prehistoric-looking giant salmon, and the evocative photographs of Ainu fishermen. During the winter, call in at the white house behind the museum and they will open it up for you.

The **Nibutani Ainu Culture Museum** (daily 9.30am–4.30; ¥300), on the opposite side of the main road through the village, is a strikingly modern concrete and glass facility, which also has some original Ainu huts outside. Inside the main building are carefully labelled and displayed sections on Ainu daily life and religion, plus videos in Japanese showing dances and explaining the language. Make sure you look through the pull-out display cases containing beautifully embroidered traditional costumes. To reach Nibutani by public transport you'll need to take a local train south from Tomakomai to Tomikawa Station from where buses run to the village – look out for the dam and get off when you see the cluster of Ainu gift shops.

## Shikotsu-ko

Even though it's the closest area of the Shikotsu-Tōya National Park to Sapporo and is also only 20km north of the port Tomakomai, where ferries dock from around Honshū, tourist development is remarkably low-key around the beautiful **lake of Shikotsu-ko**. At 360m deep, this is Japan's second deepest lake (after Tazawa-ko in Akita-ken) and its blue waters never freeze over.

Buses all stop at laid-back **SHIKOTSU KOHAN**, a village nestled in the woods beside the mouth of the Chitose-gawa on the east side of lake, and mercifully free of the multi-storey hotels and tourist tack seen at Tōya-ko. The **visitor centre** (daily 9.30am–4.30pm), just south of the bus terminal, has displays in Japanese on the area's nature and geology, and puts on a good slide show of the lake through the seasons – you can also pick up a free area map here. There are the usual boat rides on the lake, lasting thirty minutes (¥930), as well as a gentle, self-guided **nature walk**, lasting about forty minutes, over the bridge across the Chitose-gawa and along the lake shore to the camp-site at Morappu, 3km south. You'll get the best view of the lake by **hiking** to the peaks of any of the surrounding mountains and volcanoes. One of the easiest trails starts at the northern end of the village and leads up **Monbestu-dake**, a 866-metre peak which takes around one hour and twenty minutes to climb. The hike up **Eniwa-dake**, on the north side of the lake, above the Poropinai campsite, is more challenging and takes at least two and a half hours. After the climb, unwind in the lovely *rotemburo* at **Marukoma Onsen** (see Practicalities, below), beside the lake at the foot of the mountain.

Most people opt for the hike up **Tarumae-zan**, an active volcano (the last eruption was in 1955), south of the lake. The easiest way of reaching the start of the hike at the seventh station, three-quarters of the way up the volcano at the end of a dirt road, is to hitch a ride from Shikotsu-ko, although you may be lucky enough to catch one of the irregular buses (check at the bus terminal for times). The walk from the seventh station up to the summit (1024m), shouldn't take more than an hour, and at the top you'll be rewarded with great views, though the pungent aroma from the steaming crater discourages much lingering.

Following the northwest trail down from Tarumae-zan towards the lake will lead after a couple of hours to the impressive moss-covered gorge, **Koke-no-dōmon**. The sheer rock walls of this narrow passageway look as though they have been wallpapered with soft green velvet and even if you don't climb the volcano, it's worth hitching, walk-ing or cycling the 5km from Shikotsu-ko Kohan to view this natural wonder.

### Practicalities

The closest town to Shikotsu-ko is **Tomakomai**, a port with ferry connections to Honshū and a large train station. From here, three **buses** a day run to Shikotsu Kohan (¥640), leaving from outside the Sun Plaza department store opposite the south exit of Tomakomai Station. There are also daily buses from Chitose (the town, not the airport) and Sapporo to Shikotsu-kohan. If you're staying at the *Shikotsu-ko Youth Hostel*, you can make use of their free pick-up service from Chitose Station at 7pm and drop-off at Tomakomai at 8.30am, as long as you book at least a day ahead. **Getting around** the lake is best with your own transport, as there are no local buses. You can rent a bike from the youth hostel in Shikotsu Kohan for ¥1500 a day.

Most of the area's **ryokan and hotels** are within easy walking distance of the bus terminal at Shikotsu Kohan. *Hotel Suimeikaku* (☎0123/25-2131, fax 0123/25-2133; ⑥) beside the lake, is a good upmarket choice; rates here include two meals, with the cheaper rooms facing the mountain. The best budget place is the large *Shikotsu-ko Youth Hostel* (☎0123/25-2311, fax 25-2312; ①), which has reasonable bunk-bed and *tata-mi* rooms and a friendly atmosphere. In the winter, the hostel managers organize daily cross-country skiing tours (¥3000), while in the summer there's a canoeing school (¥2000 an hour). The hostel also serves decent food – a good thing, since there are few cheap options nearby. Of the three **campsites**, *Poropinai*, at the northern end of the lake, has the most attractive location, costs ¥300 per night, and is a good spot for swim-ming. Further around the lake is the plush ryokan *Marukoma Onsen* (☎0123/25-2341; ⑨), with wonderful *rotemburo* (open to non-residents between 10am and 3pm for ¥1000) and stunning views across Shikotsu-ko to Tarumae-zan.

# Central Hokkaidō

On the way to central Hokkidaidō or other points north, you're almost certain to find yourself passing through **Asahikawa**, Hokkaidō's second largest city and a major transport hub. Though there's little reason to linger here, Asahikawa is a good place to replenish supplies and change money. **Central Hokkaidō** is a sparsely populated area

| | | |
|---|---|---|
| **Asahikawa** | *Asahikawa* | 旭川 |
| Asahikawa Youth Hostel | *Asahikawa Yūsu Hosuteru* | 旭川ユースホステル |
| Asahikawa Washington Hotel | *Asahikawa Washinton Hoteru* | 旭川ワシントンホテル |
| Fitness Hotel 330 Asahikawa | *Fittonesu Hoteru 330 Asahikawa* | フィットネスホテル330旭川 |
| Station Hotel | *Sutéshou Hoteru* | ステーションホテル |
| | | |
| **Daisetsu-zan National Park** | *Daisetsu-zan Kokuritsu-kōen* | 大雪山国立公園 |
| Asahi-dake | *Asahi-dake* | 旭岳 |
| Asahidake Onsen | *Asahi-dake Onsen* | 旭岳温泉 |
| Kamikawa | *Kamikawa* | 上川 |
| Kuro-dake | *Kuro-dake* | 黒岳 |
| Sōunkyō gorge | *Sōunkyō* | 層雲峡 |
| Tenninkyō Onsen | *Tenninkyō Onsen* | 天人峡温泉 |
| | | |
| *ACCOMMODATION* | | |
| Daisetsuzan Shirakaba-sō Youth Hostel | *Daisetsuzan Shirakaba-sō Yūsu Hosuteru* | 大雪山白樺荘ユースホステル |
| Ezo Matsu-sō | *Ezo Matsu-sō* | えぞまつ荘 |
| Kitagawa | *Kitagawa* | 北川 |
| Lodge Nutapu-Kaushipe | *Rojji Nutapu Kaushipe* | ロッジヌタプカウシペ |
| Mount View Hotel | *Maunto Byū Hoteru* | マウントビューホテル |
| Sōunkyō Youth Hostel | *Sōunkyō Yūsu Hosuteru* | 層雲峡ユースホステル |
| | | |
| **Bibaushi** | *Bibaushi* | 美馬牛 |
| Bibaushi Liberty Youth Hostel | *Bibaushi Ribatii Yūsu Hosuteru* | 美馬牛リバテイーユースホステル |
| With You Farm Pension | *Fāmu Penshon Uizu Yū* | ファームペンションウイズユー |
| | | |
| **Furano** | *Furano* | 富良野 |
| Furano Prince Hotel | *Furano Purinsu Hoteru* | 富良野プリンスホテル |
| Furano White Youth Hostel | *Furano Howaito Yūsu Hosuteru* | 富良野ホワイトユースホステル |

dominated by the vast (2309sq km) and magnificent **Daisetsu-zan**, Japan's largest national **park**, which features Hokkaidō's highest mountain, **Asahi-dake** (2290m), and the spectacular **Sōunkyō gorge**. On the western fringes of the park lie the fertile farmlands which have given Hokkaidō the reputation for being a misplaced slice of Europe in the Orient. The fields around the picturesque village of **Bibaushi** are at their best in summer, when lavender, sunflowers and other blooms create a multi-coloured patchwork. Further south is **Furano**, one of Japan's top ski resorts and location of past World Cup competitions.

## Asahikawa

Straddling the confluence of the Ishikari, Biei, Chubetsu and Ushibetsu rivers, sprawling **ASAHIKAWA**, 136km northeast of Sapporo, is Hokkaidō's second-largest city. Although it has no compelling attractions, you may well find yourself passing through – and even having to stay – as this is an important railway junction, with lines heading from here north to Wakkanai and Abashiri. The city is also the main access point into the Daisetsu-zan National Park (see below), some 40km east, and a free bus runs daily from outside the train station to Asahidake Onsen.

Asahikawa Airport (☎0166/83-3716) lies 18km to the east of the city. **Trains** from Abashiri, Sapporo and Wakkanai arrive at the JR station, at the southern end of Heiwa-dōri, the city's main shopping street. There's a **tourist information booth** (daily except Tues 9.30am–5pm; ☎0166/22-6704) inside the station to the right as you exit through the ticket barrier – staff here don't speak English, but can provide a decent English-language map of the city. There are plenty of department stores and banks close to the JR station, and you should stock up on supplies and cash before venturing out into Hokkaidō's more remote regions.

Most **hotels** are within easy walking distance of the station. The cheapest central option is the *Station Hotel* (☎0166/23-9288, fax 23-6155; ④), on the sixth floor of the Asahi Building opposite the JR station, with simple, Western-style rooms, and singles for ¥3500. More upmarket is the *Asahikawa Washington* (☎0166/25-3311, fax 25-3319; ④), a good-value business hotel a couple of minutes' walk north of the station. The *Fitness Hotel 330 Asahikawa* (☎0166/26-0330, fax 26-9479; ⑤), opposite the Asahi Building, is even nicer, with a stylish café, a gym and swimming pool. You'll have to catch a bus to reach the city's **youth hostel** (buses #50, 444 or 550 from stand 11 outside the Chūō Bus Terminal, next to the Malsa department store; last bus 9.30pm). The *Asahikawa Youth Hostel* (☎0166/61-2751, fax 61-8886; ②) has Western-style dorms, serves hearty meals in a smart café, and rents out ski equipment for ¥2000 a day, which you can use at the small neighbouring ski slope.

There are plenty of places to **eat** around the Heiwa-dōri shopping street, including all the main fast-food outlets. One block west is the **Sanroku** entertainment district, where you'll find good-value *izakaya* and sushi bars.

# Daisetsu-zan National Park

**Daisetsu-zan National Park** may lack the picturesque lakes of Hokkaidō's other green spaces, but makes up for it with a spectacular range of gorges, hot springs and mountains – including **Asahi-dake**, the island's tallest peak – criss-crossed by hiking trails which could happily occupy you for days. There's generally a low-key approach to tourism in the park, especially at the charming village of **Asahidake Onsen**, though this may change over the next few years when a new cable car station is completed. Only **Sōunkyō Onsen,** on the northeast edge of the park, has been heavily developed. The highlight here is the famous **gorge**, a twenty-kilometre corridor of jagged cliffs, in places 150m high, where mother nature has run riot with her hammer and chisel. In July, the mountain slopes are covered with alpine flowers, while September and October see the landscape painted in vivid autumnal colours; these are the best months for hiking. During the winter, both Asahi-dake and **Kuro-dake** in Sōunkyō are popular skiing spots.

## Asahidake Onsen

Given that it's only 40km from Asahikawa, and is served by a free bus service, it's surprising that attractive **ASAHIDAKE ONSEN** has remained so uncommercialized. A handful of small hotels and pensions are dotted along the road which snakes up to the cable car station, from where hikers in the summer and skiers in the winter are whisked to within striking distance of the summit of Hokkaidō's highest mountain, **Asahi-dake**. There are plans to close the cable car in 1999 to build a new one, during which time Asahidake Onsen is likely to be even quieter, and patronized only by those who take their hiking and onsen pleasures very seriously.

Just before the cable car station is the **Visitors' Centre** (daily: June–Oct 9am–5pm; Jan–May, Nov & Dec 10am–4pm), which has some simple nature displays (all in

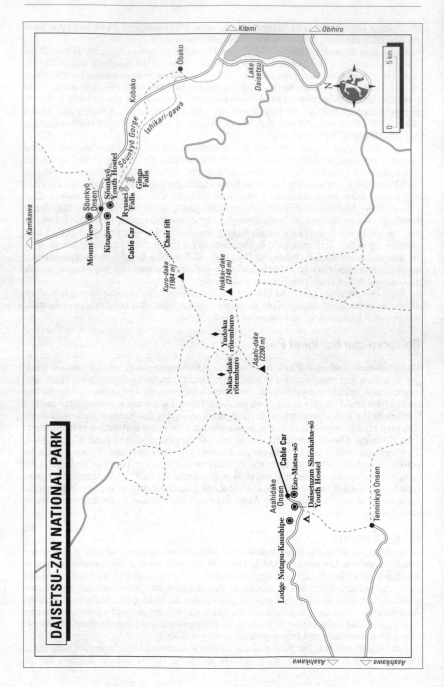

DAISETSU-ZAN NATIONAL PARK

Japanese), information on weather conditions on the mountain and a good hiking map in Japanese for ¥300. The **cable car** journey (daily, 6am–7pm; ¥1350 one way, ¥2700 return) is in two stages, and takes just under twenty minutes to reach the top station, where an ethereal landscape of steaming pools and rocky outcrops makes the trip worthwhile even if you're not planning to hike to the summit. Asahi-dake's peak is an arduous, one-hour-thirty-minute slog over slippery volcanic rock from the cable car station, but the view from the summit is fantastic.

Apart from the hike across to Sōunkyō (see below), there's a good two-hour walk, mainly downhill and through forests, from the campsite in Asahidake Onsen to **Tenninkyō Onsen**, where a gaggle of concrete tourist hotels stand at the mouth of a dramatic gorge. The soaring cliffs are draped in greenery and at the end of the gorge are two spectacular **waterfalls**. From the main car park at Tenninkyō Onsen you can catch the bus to Asahikawa or back to Asahidake Onsen. The youth hostel and the visitors' centre can advise on other hikes around the park, some of which pass by natural *rotemburo*.

From June to October there are three **buses** a day from Asahikawa Station to Asahidake Onsen, which stop at Tenninkyō Onsen en route. The one-hour-thirty-minute journey is free as long as you get off at either onsen, and free also for the return if you pick up a coupon from your hostel or hotel.

One of the best **places to stay** is the family-run *Daisetsuzan Shirakaba-sō Youth Hostel* (☎0166/97-2246, fax 97-2247; ①–②), a rustic building set back from the road, opposite the campsite bus stop, and next to a running stream. It's worth paying slightly extra to stay in the attached log house, with its convivial communal lounge. Evening meals include freshly caught river fish and the hostel staff can provide all you need to climb Asahi-dake, including a lunch of *onigiri* (rice balls) and a bell to warn off bears. There's a *rotemburo* in the woods behind the main building. Just beside the hostel, on the road, is the equally appealing *Lodge Nutapu-Kaushipe* (☎ & fax 0166/97-2150; ⑤), an attractive wooden cabin with comfortable, Japanese-style rooms; rates here include two meals. The lodge has a café, a winter-only sauna, and a two-level *rotemburo* overlooking the cascading river. The biggest hotel in the village, the *Ezo Matsu-sō* (☎0166/97-2321, fax 97-2324; ⑥), opposite the visitors' centre and designed to look like a Swiss chalet, caters mainly for large tour groups. Apart from the **café** at the *Lodge Nutapu-Kaushipe*, the best place for snacks and drinks are the **canteens** at the cable car stations.

## Sōunkyō Onsen

On the northeastern edge of Daisetsu-zan, some 60km east of Asahikawa, is **SŌUNKYŌ ONSEN**, the park's main resort, little more than a couple of streets lined with giftshops and tatty restaurants, surrounded by ugly hotel blocks poking out of the trees. Fortunately, this drab scene is amply compensated for by the main event here – the astonishing **Sōunkyō gorge**.

The best way to see the gorge, with its jagged rock walls carved out by the Ishikari-gawa, is to rent a **bike** from the shop by the bus station (¥1500) and follow the riverside route for 8km to Ōboke. Just east of the resort, leave the main road and pull into the car park next to the **Ginga and Ryusei waterfalls**. A twenty-minute climb up the opposite hill will lead to a viewpoint from where you'll get a fabulous view of the two cascades of white water tumbling down the cliffs. Continuing along the cycling and walking path, you may notice that the natural formations have been given poetic names, such as "Hime-iwa" (Princess rock). The narrowest section of the gorge is called **Kobako**, or "small box", because of the enclosed feeling imparted by the towering rock pillars shooting up from the river banks. The route crosses the new road and enters a tunnel before emerging at the decidedly touristy **Ōboke** ("big box"), where visitors line up to be photographed in front of the river that gushes through the narrow gap in the perpendicular cliffs.

While the Asahi-dake cable car is out of action, the classic Daisetsu-zan **hike** across the park's central mountain range is best started in Sōunkyō Onsen. Two minutes' walk south of the bus terminal you can catch a **cable car** (daily 6am–7pm; ¥800 one way, ¥1500 return), followed by a **chairlift** (¥280 one way, ¥500 return) up to within one hour's hike of the 1984-metre **Kuro-dake** (Black Mountain). From the summit, capped by a small shrine and giving marvellous views of the park, there's a choice of two trails to Asahi-dake – the southern route via Hokkai-dake (2149m) is the more scenic. By the time you reach Asahi-dake's summit you'll have spent around six hours walking, so returning on foot to Sōunkyō Onsen the same day is only possible if you set out at the crack of dawn. There are overnight huts on the mountain, but the more comfortable option is to continue down to Asahidake Onsen and rest there for the night. If you don't want to backtrack for your luggage, consider having it sent on by *Takkyūbin* (see Basics, p.54).

*PRACTICALITIES*

The closest **train** station to Sōunkyō Onsen is **Kamikawa**, some 22km north; buses take thirty minutes from here to reach the resort. Some of the **buses** passing through Kamikawa and Sōunkyō originate in Asahikawa and continue on to the central Hokkaidō town of Obihiro, to the south. There's a **tourist information office** (daily 8.30am–5.30pm) in the bus terminal building, where you can pick up a basic English map and pamphlet on the area.

Sōunkyō has no shortage of souless Western-style **hotels**, of which the *Mount View* (☎01658/5-3011; ⑦), in the valley just outside of the main village, is one of the least anonymous. Of the two youth hostels, the friendlier is the *Sōunkyō* (☎01658/5-3418, fax 5-3186; ①), ten minutes' walk up the path which runs behind the bus terminal, and near the *Prince Hotel*. The dorms here have bunk beds, meals are served in a rustic lounge area and there are lots of notes on hiking in the park – but all in Japanese. A good alternative is *Kitagawa* (☎01658/5-3515; ⑤), a reasonably priced minshuku and restaurant on the main drag up to the cable car station, with welcoming management, and nicely furnished *tatami* rooms.

Few of the tourist restaurants in the village are particularly appealing. About the best value place for a quick snack is the **café** above the cable car station, which serves Western-style dishes, such as cheese gratin, rice pilaf and spaghetti for under ¥1000.

# Bibaushi

Outside of Daisetsu-zan National Park, but overlooking its mountains from the east – including the active volcano Tokachi-dake – are the scenic farmlands surrounding the tranquil and picturesque village of **BIBAUSHI**. Known for its vast fields of lavender and expanses of sunflowers, the landscape here is faintly evocative of Provençale France, with bales of hay lying around and lone poplar trees etched against the backdrop of snow-capped peaks. The gently undulating countryside is ideal for gentle walks, bike riding and photography – some good examples of which you can check out in the **Post Card Gallery and Café** (daily 9am–6pm), next to *Bibaushi Liberty Youth Hostel*. It's also possible to use Bibaushi as a base for a hike up the 2077-metre active volcano of **Tokachi-dake**, some 20km southwest and within the Daisetsu-zan National Park.

Bibaushi is connected with Asahikawa by frequent **trains** and **buses** and can easily be visited as a day-trip, or en route to and from Sapporo. For **overnight stays**, there's the stylish *Bibaushi Liberty Youth Hostel* (☎0166/95-2141, fax 95-2142; ②), next to the train station, with bunk-bed dorms and excellent meals. Staff here can provide a cycling and hiking map of the area, mountain bikes for ¥2800 a day, and cross-country skiing and mountain treks. If you have your own transport, consider staying at *With You Farm Pension* (☎0166/95-2748, fax 95-2748; ⑤), ten minutes' drive from Bibaushi Station. This is in a lovely location overlooking the mountains and colourful fields and offers Western-style rooms as well as bunk-bed dorms, with rates that include two meals.

## Furano

The main reason to come to the sleepy farm town of **FURANO**, 120km northeast of Sapporo, is to **ski** at the renowned World Cup resort on the slopes of Mount Kitanomine. Famous for being the location of the old soap opera *Kita no Kuni Kara* (From the North Country), which followed the dramas of a Tokyo family adapting to life in Hokkaidō, Furano is also the focus of many a salaryman's dreams about escaping the rat race.

Furano's **ski** resort, overlooking Mount Furano and the smoking volcano Tokachi-dake (both within the southern border of Daisetsu-zan National Park), is run by the *Prince* hotel group. The slopes are challenging but not as varied or as long as those at Niseko (see p.309). Lift passes start at ¥1900 for a night ticket (5–9pm) and go up to ¥4500 for a one-day ticket.

Furano is best reached by direct **bus** from Sapporo, a service which takes around two and a half hours; ask to be dropped by the road leading up to *ski-jō*, rather than getting off in the centre of town, since you'll only have to backtrack. Check with tourist information in Sapporo (see p.301) about any special bus and lift-pass deals that are on offer. There is a **train** from the capital but it takes longer and costs more; if you're coming from Asahikawa, the train journey is only one hour and fifteen minutes. Buses run from the train station to the ski resort, and a taxi will cost less than ¥2000.

A good budget **place to stay** is *Furano White Youth Hostel* (☎0167/23-4807, fax 22-5284; ①), five minutes' walk from the ski lifts, with bunk-bed dorms, ski equipment for rent, and good-value package deals on accommodation and lift passes (for example, one night's stay and two day's skiing for ¥7500). The food is fantastic; the *nabe* stew feast especially is a great way to end a day on the slopes. The two *Prince* hotels are comfortable but pricey – the *Furano Prince* (☎0167/23-4111, fax 22-3430; ⑥), a giant, tent-shaped lodge rising out of the snow, is closer to the rest of the resort, while the *New Furano* (☎0167/22-1111, fax 22-1189; ⑦), a more modern, oval-shaped tower block, is tucked away on its own a few kilometres south, and has a heated swimming pool and several restaurants.

There's a decent range of **restaurants** on the mountain, though you're likely to eat in your hotel or pension at night. It's worth checking out the stylish *a dish* restaurant and bar (look for the English sign), a short walk uphill behind the youth hostel – as well as beer and cocktails, it also serves a wide range of coffees and teas. The owner, Tomita-san, speaks a little English and is a successful escapee from Tokyo.

# Wakkanai and Rishiri-Rebun-Sarobetsu National Park

The rather dreary port of **WAKKANAI**, 320km from Sapporo, is the gateway to the far northwestern tip of Hokkaidō and the idyllic Rishiri-Rebun-Sarobetsu National Park. The main reason for coming here is to press on to the islands of Rebun-tō and Rishiri-tō, and the quickest way of doing this is to hop on the overnight train from Sapporo, which will desposit you in Wakkanai in good time to board one of the early ferries. If you arrive during the day however, you'll find a few points of interest to keep you pleasantly occupied for a few hours.

One impressive spot is by the northern flank of the port, which is protected by the **North Breakwater Dome**, a 427-metre-long arched corridor supported by seventy concrete pillars. In July and August, a local **market** is set up here, along with a karaoke stage and barbecue pits at which you can sizzle your own fresh seafood and meat and guzzle beer – this is a fun place to hang out while waiting for a ferry. With more time to kill, head west of the JR station to the small cable car (¥180 one way, ¥240 return), which will whisk you up to **Wakkanai-kōen**, a grassy park from where, on a clear day, you can see right across to the Russian island of Sakhalin, some 60km northwest. Earlier this century Japan occupied Sakhalin and there's a monument in the park to nine female telephone operators who committed suicide in the post office on the island at the end of World War II, rather than be captured by the Russians. Sino-Japanese relations are now much improved and there is steady trade between Wakkanai and its northern neighbours.

There's not much point coming to cape **Sōya Misaki**, 27km east of Wakkanai, other than to say you've been to the northernmost point of Japan. A couple of monuments, "The Bell for World Peace" and the "Tower of Prayer", a memorial to the Korean Airlines plane shot down by Soviet Union just north of the cape, mark the flat and rather dull spot, served by infrequent buses from the Wakkanai.

Some 35km south of Wakkanai lies the **Sarobetsu Natural Flower Garden**, best visited between May and September, when its marshlands become a riot of colourful blooms. However, if you're heading over to Rebun, save your energy, as you'll see just as many flowers there, and in a far more dramatic setting. To reach the park, take a local train to Toyotomi Station, a forty-five minute journey from Wakkanai, and then catch a bus (¥400) for the last fifteen minutes.

## Practicalities

Direct **trains** from Sapporo and Asahikawa pull into Wakkanai Station, just south of the **ferry** terminal. Inside the station a **tourist information counter** (daily 10am–6pm), provides a Japanese map of the town, an English pamphlet and information on getting to the islands. Wakkanai's **airport** lies 10km east of the port; there are daily flights from here to and from Tokyo, Sapporo and both Rishiri-tō and Rebun-tō. From the airport, a bus into town will cost around ¥590 for the thirty-minute journey, and a taxi ¥3500.

If you're heading on to Rishiri-tō and Rebun-tō, make sure you're carrying enough Japanese currency, or change your money here, as there are no foreign exchange facilities on either of the islands. Tokugin Bank, two blocks west of the station, walking towards the hillside, has a **foreign exchange** desk on the second floor. From late-April to early-September a **ferry service** runs between Wakkanai and Korsakov on Sakhalin (¥40,000 one way, ¥57,000 return). The journey takes six hours and thirty minutes and departures are roughly every week.

There's no shortage of **accommodation** close to the station and around the port. The most convenient – though not the friendliest – budget option is *Wakkanai Moshiripa* (☎0162/24-0180; ②), a hostel just five minutes' walk north from the JR station and east of the ferry terminal; guests must check in before 8pm. More welcoming – but only open from April 21 to October 31 – is *Wakkanai Youth Hostel* (☎0162/23-7162, fax 23-7179; ①), a ten-minute walk south from JR Minami Wakkanai Station. The *Minshuku Nakayama* (☎0162/22-8868; ⑤) is a large, old-fashioned place opposite the port, where the rates include two meals, while the *Station Hotel* (☎0162/23-2111; ⑤), opposite the bus terminal, has nice *tatami* rooms and en-suite bathrooms. Most luxurious is the *ANA Hotel Wakkanai* (☎0162/23-8111, fax 23-8112; ⑦), directly in front of the ferry terminal.

There are plenty of tourist **restaurants** around the JR station, the most famous being *Takechan*, which specializes in fresh fish dishes, including sushi and *tako-shabu* (¥1500), an octopus stew that's worth trying for its novelty value.

## Rishiri-tō and Rebun-tō

The stunning and remote islands of **Rishiri-tō** and **Rebun-tō** should ideally be visited for two nights on each so you can do some real exploring. Both are quite different: Slender Rebun-tō is low-lying, and its gentle hills are sprinkled with alpine flowers;

Rishiri-tō is a Fuji-like volcano rising 1721m out of the sea. Because of their lovely scenery and mild weather, both islands are exceptionally popular with Japanese tourists in summer, when accommodation should be booked well in advance. At other times of the year, you're likely to have the islands to yourself.

## Rishiri-tō

Hiking up the volcano is the best reason to come to **RISHIRI-TŌ**, a circular island made up of the 1721-metre cone of **Rishiri-san**. The island is sometimes called Rishiri-Fuji because its shape resembles the famous southern volcano, but Westerners might find it looks more like a lone Swiss Alp. Even if the weather is unpromising, it's still worth making the ascent (which takes between ten and twelve hours) to break through the clouds on the upper slopes and be rewarded with panoramic views from the summit, which is crowned with a small shrine.

The most convenient route up the volcano starts some 3km south of the main port of **Oshidomari**, at the Rishiri Hokuroku campsite. Information and maps for the climb are available from the island's tourist information centre (see Practicalities, p.333) and daily climbing groups are organized by staff at the local youth hostel. Around fifteen minutes' climb from the peak of Mount Chokan, the eighth station up the volcano, there is a basic hut in which you can take shelter en route. Make sure you take plenty of water with you as there's none available on the mountain.

If you don't want to climb to the top of Rishiri-san, you can always embark on the less strenuous, three-hour hiking trail which starts at the pretty **Himenuma** pond, and continues across the slopes of two smaller mountains, Kopon-san and Pon-san, to the

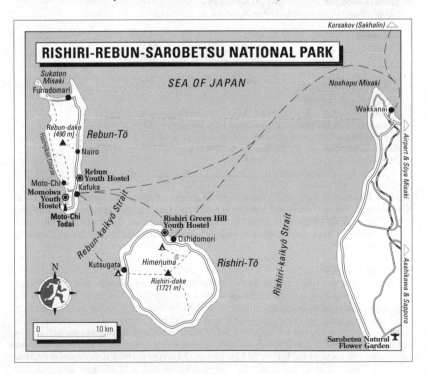

## RISHIRI-REBUN-SAROBETSU NATIONAL PARK

| | | |
|---|---|---|
| **Wakkanai** | *Wakkanai* | 稚内 |
| Sarobestu Natural Flower Garden | *Sarobetsu Gensei Kaen* | サロベツ原生花園 |
| Sōya Misaki | *Sōya Misaki* | 宗谷岬 |
| | | |
| *ACCOMMODATION* | | |
| ANA Hotel Wakkanai | *ANA Hoteru Wakkanai* | ＡＮＡホテル稚内 |
| Minshuku Nakayama | *Minshuku Nakayama* | 民宿中山 |
| Station Hotel | *Sutēshon Hoteru* | ステーションホテル |
| Wakkanai Moshiripa Youth Hostel | *Wakkanai Moshiripa Yūsu Hosuteru* | 稚内モシリパユースホステル |
| Wakkanai Youth Hostel | *Wakkanai Yūsu Hosuteru* | 稚内ユースホステル |
| | | |
| **Rishiri-tō** | *Rishiri-tō* | 利尻島 |
| Himenuma pond | *Himenuma* | 姫沼 |
| Kutsugata | *Kutsugata* | 沓形 |
| Oshidomari | *Oshidomari* | 鴛泊 |
| Rishiri-san | *Rishiri-san* | 利尻山 |
| | | |
| *ACCOMMODATION* | | |
| Kitaguni Grand Hotel | *Kitaguni Gurando Hoteru* | 北国グランドホテル |
| Pension Hera-san-no-ie | *Penshon Hera-san-no-ie* | ペンションへらさんの家 |
| Rishiri Green Hill Youth Hostel | *Rishiri Guriinhiru Yūsu Hosuteru* | 利尻グリーンヒルユースホステル |
| | | |
| **Rebun-tō** | *Rebun-tō* | 礼文島 |
| Funadomari | *Funadomari* | 船泊 |
| Kafuka | *Kafuka* | 香深 |
| Moto-chi | *Moto-chi* | 元地 |
| Sukoton Misaki | *Sukoton Misaki* | スコトン岬 |
| | | |
| *ACCOMMODATION* | | |
| Kaidō | *Kaidō* | 海憧 |
| Momoiwa-sō Youth Hostel | *Momoiwa-sō Yūsu Hosuteru* | 桃岩荘ユースホステル |
| Hotel Rebun | *Hoteru Rebun* | ホテル礼文 |
| Rebun Youth Hostel | *Rebun Yūsu Hosuteru* | 礼文ユースホステル |
| Seikan-sō | *Seikan-sō* | 星観荘 |

Rishiri Hokuroku campsite. To get to Himenuma from the ferry terminal at Oshidomari, follow the coastal road west until you reach a junction going up into the hills. The walk up to the pond is quite steep – you might be able to hitch a lift – and takes around an hour. At Himenuma, walk left around the lake to find the trail leading to the campsite.

### PRACTICALITIES

Daily **flights** from Wakkanai to Rishiri-tō take only fifteen minutes and cost around ¥14,120. The airport is a few kilometres west of Oshidomari. There are three **ferries** a day from Wakkanai to Oshidomari (1hr 40min; ¥1880 one way), rising to four between May and September and dropping to two in January and February. Daily ferry services also run between Kafuka on Rebun-tō and Oshidomari and Kutsugata on Rishiri-tō's west coast (40min; ¥730). If you book ahead, staff at the hostel and most minshuku on the island can meet you at the ferry terminal or the airport. The youth hostel reception group are well-known for their enthusiastic goodbyes to departing guests, when they sing and dance on the docks at Oshidomari.

The **tourist information counter** (daily 8am–5.40pm) inside the ferry terminal at Oshidomari, has a map of the island, plus English notes on the hikes to Rishiri-san and Himenuma pond. **Bicycles** – a good way to get around the island – can be rented from near the ferry terminal and from the youth hostel for around ¥1500 a day. Otherwise, **buses** run in both directions around the island, a circuit which takes one hour and forty five minutes and costs ¥2100. If you arrive by ferry at Kutsugata on the western side of Rishiri, you'll need to get a bus north to Oshidomari, which takes thirty minutes and costs ¥690.

The best **place to stay** is the *Rishiri Green Hill Youth Hostel* (☎01638/2-2507, fax 2-2383; ①), where the young staff throw their heart and soul into the nightly information and singing sessions. Accommodation is in *tatami* rooms, the food is good and the hostel organizes hiking up the mountain, starting at 4am. Near the ferry terminal is *Pension Hera-san-no-ie* (☎ & fax 01638/2-2361; ⑥), with nice *tatami* rooms and a couple of Western-style bedrooms, in a modern grey- and red-brick building next to the path leading up the rock which looms over the harbour. Rishiri-tō's most upmarket accommodation, the *Kitaguni Grand Hotel* (☎01638/2-1362, fax 2-2556; ⑨), is an unsightly red-brick tower that sticks out like a sore thumb amid the surrounding houses and is overpriced, even though rates include two meals. Pitching a tent at the Rishiri Hokuroku **campsite**, 3km south of the port, will cost you ¥340 – alternatively, you can kip in one of the wooden cabins, which sleep four people, for ¥2000 each a night. The campsite is on the main route up the volcano, so can get busy. For a quieter spot, head for the site in Kutsugata Misaki-kōen, the park on the promontory south of Kutsugata port.

The best place for **lunch** in Oshidomari is *Aji-no-ichi*, on the main road behind the ferry terminal, where the huge bowls of seafood-topped ramen (¥1000) are delicious. If you're climbing Rishiri-san, you can pick up supplies for a picnic at the grocery stores in town.

## Rebun-tō

Shaped like a crab's claw adrift in the Sea of Japan, **REBUN-TŌ** is most famous for its wildflower displays – the island's rolling green slopes are said to bloom with three hundred different types of alpine plants. At the southern tip of the island is the main port; small, attractive **Kafuka**, which rises uphill from the coast. In the north is the fishing village of **Funadomari**. The whole island is fabulous **hiking** territory (see box overleaf), and attracts hordes of visitors every summer – especially to its scenic western coast.

From May to September four **ferries** a day go from Wakkanai to Kafuka (1hr 55min; ¥2200), and at least a couple during the rest of the year. There are also two ferries a day to Oshidomari and Kutsugata on Rishiri-tō (40min; ¥730). The island has an **airport** in the north, near Funodomari village, with daily flights from Wakkanai. Infrequent buses run down the eastern coastal road from the airport to Kafuka; taxis are expensive, so it's better to hitch if you can't get a bus. Hostels and most minshuku will pick you up from the ferry terminal and the airport if you book in advance. As on Rishiri, the youth hostel staff loudly serenade departing guests at the port.

The island's **tourist information counter** (daily 8.30am–5.15pm) is in the ferry terminal at Kafuka, and has a good Japanese map of the island, marked with the main hiking routes. Staff here can also help with booking accommodation. **Getting around** the island is by bus, but fares are high, and given the scarcity of services, you'll probably find hitching a better way of exploring. If time is limited, consider taking one of the three **bus tours** (¥3100–3500) which cover all the scenic highlights and are timed to connect with the ferries. **Bike rental** is available from several shops near the ferry terminal at a rather pricey ¥3500 a day.

Most of Rebun's **accommodation** is in or around Kafuka. The luxurious *Hotel Rebun* (☎01638/6-1177, fax 6-2007; ⑨), in the modern block next to the ferry terminal, is

### REBUN-TŌ

The longest and most popular **hike** on Rebun-tō is the eight-hour **Hachi-jikan**, which runs for 32km along the west coast from Sukoton Misaki, the island's northernmost point, to Moto-chi in the south, passing through flower fields and forests. The cliffs at the end of this hike can be slippery and sometimes dangerous; if you don't enjoy struggling, try the easier **Yo-jikan** course, which consists of the first section of the Hachi-jikan course, thus lasting only four hours and missing the difficult coastal section from Uennai to Moto-chi. The island's youth hostels arrange walking groups for the two hikes and hold briefings the night before. If you want to hike on your own, aim to take the 6.50am bus from Kafuka to Sukoton, arriving at around 7.30am, so you can safely complete the walk during daylight. Stock up on food and drink before you start, as there are no refreshment stops along the way and it's not safe to drink river water on the island.

Another easy and enjoyable hike is the two-hour **Momoiwa** course, a return-trip starting just above Kafuka and running to the lighthouse, Moto-chi Todai, at the southern tip of the island. The well-marked cliff-top trail takes its name from the Momoiwa, or "peach-shaped rock" on the west coast, which it passes along the way. The views up the coast and over to Rishiri-tō are breathtaking, but be prepared for ferocious winds and some steep sections. If you don't feel like walking back the way you came, continue down to the road at the lighthouse, and return to Kafuka by bus.

Other hikes include the **Rebun Rindō Hanabatake** course, which runs across the centre of the island, through valleys blooming with flowers, and follows a dirt road. The course can be approached from either Kafuka or Kafukai, 8km to the north, and can also be used as a diversion from the dangerous part of the eight-hour hike. Finally, there's the **Rebun-dake Tozan** course, starting at either Nairo or Kitouse, both on the bus route north from Kafuka. The summit gives fine views of Rishiri-tō and the Hokkaidō mainland.

pricey, though two meals are included in the rates. Of the island's two hostels, *Rebun Youth Hostel* (☎01638/6-1608; ①), around fifteen minutes' walk north along the coastal road from the ferry terminal, is the more traditional, and has helpful staff and good food. At *Momoiwa-sō Youth Hostel* (☎01638/6-1421; ①), which gets packed to the gunnels at the height of the season, the atmosphere is akin to summer camp (no alcohol, lots of singing and dancing with the high-spirited staff). The hostel's location on the dramatically rocky western coast, fifteen minutes' drive from Kafuka and south of the small fishing village of Moto-chi, cannot be beat. It's also worth considering staying here if you plan to do the eight-hour hiking course, since the hostel is at the end of the walk and staff willl organize transport out to the start.

Tranquil **Funadomari**, the small fishing village at the northern end of the island, makes a good base for hikes out to the cape Sukoton Misaki. There's a comfortable minshuku, *Seikan-sō* (☎01638/7-2078; ④), where the rates include two meals, while *Kaidō* (☎01638/7-2717, fax 7-2183; ⑤), next to the beachside campsite, is larger, has nice *tatami* rooms (and some cheaper shared accommodation), and also includes two meals in its prices.

**Eating** is best arranged at your hotel or hostel – most can usually provide *bentō* picnic lunches for the hikes. Otherwise, there are grocery shops in both Kafuka and Funadomari where you can pick up supplies. Next to the *Momoiwa Youth Hostel* in Kafuka is a laid-back **café** which plays jazz and is a relaxing place to chill out.

## Northeastern Hokkaidō

Without your own transport you'll find it difficult to take the most direct coastal route from Wakkanai to the highlights of northeastern Hokkaidō. There are no through buses running along this sparsely populated coast and, by train, you'll have to return to

## NORTHEASTERN HOKKAIDŌ

| **Abashiri** | *Abashiri* | 網走 |
|---|---|---|
| Abashiri Prison Museum | *Hakubutsukan Abashiri Kangoku* | 博物館網走監獄 |
| Hokkaidō Museum of Northern Peoples | *Hokkaidō Hoppōminzoku Hakubutsukan* | 北海道北方民族博物館 |
| Okhotsk Ryūhyō Museum | *Ohōtsuku Ryūhyō-kan* | オホーツク流氷館 |

*ACCOMMODATION*

| Abashiri Central Hotel | *Abashiri Sentoraru Hoteru* | 網走セントラルホテル |
|---|---|---|
| Abashiri Ryūhyō-no-Oka Youth Hostel | *Abashiri Ryūhyō-no-Oka Yūsu Hosuteru* | 網走流氷の丘ユースホステル |
| Hotel Shimbashi | *Hoteru Shimbashi* | ホテルしんばし |

| **Shiretoko National Park** | *Shiretoko Kokuritsu-kōen* | 知床国立公園 |
|---|---|---|
| Kamuiwakka-no-taki | *Kamuiwakka-no-taki* | カムイワッカの滝 |
| Rausu | *Rausu* | ラウス |
| Rausu-dake | *Rausu-dake* | ラウス岳 |
| Shari | *Shari* | 斜里 |
| Shiretoko Go-ko | *Shiretoko Go-ko* | 知床五湖 |
| Shirctoko Shizen Centre | *Shiretoko Shizen Sentā* | 知床自然センター |
| Utoro | *Utoro* | ウトロ |

*ACCOMMODATION*

| Grand Hotel | *Gurando Hoteru* | グランドホテル |
|---|---|---|
| Rausu Youth Hostel | *Rausu Yūsu Hosuteru* | ラウスユースホステル |
| Shiretoko Iwaobetsu Youth Hostel | *Shiretoko Iwaobetsu Yūsu Hosuteru* | 知床岩尾別ユースホステル |
| Yūhi no-Ataru Ie | *Yūhi-no-Ataru Ie* | 夕陽のあたる家 |

| **Akan National Park** | *Akan Kokuritsu-kōen* | 阿寒国立公園 |
|---|---|---|
| Ainu Kotan | *Ainu Kotan* | アイヌコタン |
| Akan Kohan | *Akan Kohan* | 阿寒湖畔 |
| Kussharo-ko | *Kussharo-ko* | 屈斜路湖 |
| Mashū-ko | *Mashū-ko* | 摩周湖 |
| Me-Akan-dake | *Me-Akan-dake* | 雌阿寒岳 |
| Ō-Akan-dake | *Ō-Akan-dake* | 雄阿寒岳 |
| Teshikaga | *Teshikaga* | 弟子屈 |

*ACCOMMODATION*

| Akan Angel Youth Hostel | *Akan Enjeru Yūsu Hosuteru* | 阿寒エンジェルユースホステル |
|---|---|---|
| Ginrei | *Ginrei* | ぎんれい |
| Grand Hotel Akan | *Gurando Hoteru Akan* | グランドホテル阿寒 |
| Kiri | *Kiri* | 桐 |
| Kussharo-Genya Youth Guesthouse | *Kussharo-Genya Yūsu Gesutohausu* | 屈斜路原野ユースゲストハウス |
| Mashū-ko Youth Hostel | *Mashū-ko Yūsu Hosuteru* | 摩周湖ユースホステル |
| Nibushi-no-Sato | *Nibushi-no-Sato* | にぶしのさと |
| New Akan Hotel Shangrila | *Nyū Akan Hoteru Shangurira* | ニュー阿寒ホテルシャングリラ |
| Hotel Park Way | *Hoteru Pāku Uei* | ホテルパークウエイ |
| Pension Birao | *Penshon Birao* | ペンションビラオ |

*continued overleaf*

| NORTHEASTERN HOKKAIDO contd | | |
|---|---|---|
| Kushiro | *Kushiro* | 釧路 |
| Kushiro Shitsugen National Park | *Kushiro Shitsugen Kokusai-kōen* | 釧路湿原国際公園 |
| Obihiro | *Obihiro* | 帯広 |
| **Erimo Misaki** | *Erimo Misaki* | えりも岬 |
| Erimo Misaki Youth Hostel | *Erimo Misaki Yūsu Hosuteru* | えりも岬ユースホステル |
| Kaze-no-kan | *Kaze-no-kan* | 風の館 |
| Misakisō | *Misakisō* | 岬荘 |

Asahikawa before you can transfer to the line out to **Abashiri**. From this small port, 350km northeast of Sapporo and well known throughout Japan for its old maximum security prison, you can take winter boat tours through the drift ice floating down from Siberia into the Sea of Okhotsk. Jutting into this inhospitable expanse of water is the amazing **Shiretoko National Park**, one of the country's most remote and primevil peninsulas, featuring dramatic cliffs, ancient forests and a volcanically heated waterfall cascading down a mountain into natural bathing pools. Inland, south of the peninsula, the **Akan National Park** pales in comparison to Hakkaidō's other national parks, but is not without its own attractions, including three scenic lakes. A fittingly dramatic end to a tour of northeast Hokkaidō awaits at the rocky cape **Erimo Misaki**, the windiest place in Japan and home to a seal colony.

## Abashiri

The dead of winter is the best time to visit the compact fishing port of **ABASHIRI**, 350km from Sapporo, bordered by a couple of pretty lakes and overlooked by Mount Tento-zan, as this is when snow covers the less appealing, modern parts of the town, Siberian swans fly in to winter at Lake Tofutsu a few kilometres east of the harbour, and drift ice (called *ryūhyō* in Japanese) floats across the Sea of Okhotsk. By February the sea has frozen over in a remarkable sheet of blue-white ice which stretches as far as the eye can see. The ideal way to witness this astonishing phenomenon is to hop aboard the Aurora, an **ice-breaking sightseeing boat**, for a one-hour tour (Jan–April daily; ¥3000), which departs at least four times a day, depending on the weather. The boat cracks through the ice sheets, throwing up huge chunks, some over 1m thick, and during the journey you may well spot seals and eagles lounging on the floating white slabs.

An excellent vantage point from which to take in the full vista of the ice flows is the summit of Tento-zan, directly behind the train station, where you'll also find several enjoyable museums. For a taste of the extremes of winter in Abashiri, head for the modern and informative **Okhotsk Ryūhyō Museum** (daily: April–Oct 8am–6pm; Jan–March, Nov & Dec 9am–4.30pm; ¥500), where you can touch huge lumps of ice in a room where the temperature is kept at minus 15 C and coats are provided for warmth. A panoramic film of the drift ice is also screened regularly throughout the day. While you're up here, don't miss the **Hokkaidō Museum of Northern Peoples** (daily 9.30am–4.30pm; ¥200), a five-minute walk downhill from the ice museum, which has contemporary displays on the native peoples of northern Eurasia and America, prompting comparisons between the different cultures. A colour-coded chart at the start of the exhibition will help you identify which artifacts belong to the different races; look out for the Innuit cagools made of seal intestines.

Most Japanese associate Abashiri with its maximum security prison, featured in a popular series of jail drama films called *Abashiri Bangaichi*. The town's current prison no longer houses such high-grade criminals or political undesirables, and the original nineteenth-century penitentiary has been relocated to the foot of Tento-zan and transformed into the jolly **Abashiri Prison Museum** (daily: April–Oct 8am–6pm; Jan–March, Nov & Dec 9am–5pm; ¥1050). This large, open-air site features waxworks of various detainees (look out for the tatooed *yakuza* in the bathhouse and Shiratori Yoshie, a famous escapee, crawling across the rafters in the cell block), and is popular with Japanese tour groups. A regular **bus** runs a circular course from Abashiri Station up Tento-zan to the museums on the summit, stopping first at the prison museum on the way up.

## Practicalities

Apart from the flying, the fastest way to reach Abashiri is on the direct **train** from Sapporo, which takes five hours and twenty minutes. Cheaper and only a little slower are the seven daily **buses** from Sapporo. There's also an overnight bus and train from Sapporo if you want to save on a night's accommodation. Abashiri can also be reached by train from Asahikawa along the central Sekihoku line and by the plodding local train from the port of Kushiro (see p.342), 146km south, on the Senmō line. The nearest **airport** is Memanbetsu, 16km south of Abashiri, and twenty five minutes from the JR Station by bus (¥720).

Next to the JR station is the **tourist information office** (daily 9am–5pm; ☎0152/44-5809), where the friendly assistants can give you a Japanese map of the town, help with accommodation and supply discount tickets for the town's museums.

Of the several **hotels** near the JR station, the *Shimbashi* (☎0152/43-4307, fax 45-2091; ⑤), directly opposite, has decent *tatami* rooms, with singles for ¥6300. The town's top hotel, the *Abashiri Central Hotel* (☎0152/44-5151, fax 43-5177; ⑤), is well-located near the shopping district. To reach the nearest **youth hostel**, the *Abashiri Ryūhyō-no-Oka* (☎0152/43-8558; ②), you'll need to take a bus from the station to Meiji-iriguchi, an eight-minute journey, and then walk uphill for ten minutes. This modern hostel is in a great location overlooking the Sea of Okhotsk, and rents out bicycles for exploring the area.

Abashiri specializes in fresh **seafood** and you shouldn't leave town without trying some of succulent crabs. The best place to head for is *Sushiyasu*, a couple of blocks behind *Abashiri Central Hotel*, and easily spotted by its outside photograph menu and cheap prices. The *Shimbashi Hotel*'s restaurant serves good-value set meals, cheap noodle dishes and sushi, at tables and in screened-off *tatami* booths, while the stylish *Daihyogen* in the *Abashiri Central Hotel* does beautifully presented set meals of local delicacies for ¥2500 per person that are worth the splurge.

# Shiretoko National Park

Clearly visible from Abashiri is the Shiretoko peninsula, a seventy-kilometre-long finger of land thrusting out into the Sea of Okhotsk, 40km to the east. About half the peninsula is covered by the **Shiretoko National Park**. Shiretoko is an Ainu word, meaning "the end of the earth" and this volcanic corner of Hokkaidō, covered with virgin forest, certainly lives up to its name. Giant black rocks scattered along the coast look as though they were newly spewed from a volcano, roads are few, tourist facilities even fewer and wildlife is abundant – you're almost guaranteed to encounter wild deer, foxes, and even bears. In the winter, when freezing temperatures put off all but the hardiest of travellers, drift ice litters the shore. Most people visit between June and September, the best period for hiking up the mountainous volcanic spine of the peninsula and viewing the five small lakes at **Shiretoko Go-ko**. This is also a great time to soak in the natural *rotemburo*, including the hot waterfall of **Kamuiwakka-no-taki**.

Roads stop halfway up both sides of the peninsula, so the only way you'll get to see the rocky cape, with its unmanned lighthouse and waterfalls plunging over sheer cliffs into the sea, is to take a sightseeing boat from **UTORO**, the area's main onsen resort and fishing port. The boat tour lasts three hours and forty five minutes and runs between June and September daily, departing at midday (¥6000). Near Utoro's tiny harbour you'll notice several large rocks, one of which is nicknamed Godzilla, for reasons which become obvious when you see it.

Apart from being a useful stop-over, Utoro has few attractions, and you're best off pressing up the coast to the **Shiretoko Shizen Centre** (daily: April 20–Oct 20 8am–5.40pm; Oct 21–April 19 9am–4pm), which has displays on the national park and throughout the day shows a twenty-minute giant-screen film (¥500) with swooping aerial shots of the mountains and rugged coastline. Behind the centre, a few well-marked nature trails lead through forests and heathland covered with ferns, bamboo grass and wild flowers to cliffs, down which a waterfall cascades.

Some 9km further north, past the *Iwaobetsu Youth Hostel*, lies one of the peninsula's top attractions, **Shiretoko Go-ko**, where five jewel-like lakes are linked by wooden walkways and sinuous forest paths. If the weather is fine, some of the lakes reflect the mountains, and a lookout point west of the parking lot provides a sweeping view across the heathland to the sea. In summer, the first couple of lakes can be crowded with tourists, but the further you walk around the 2.4km circuit the more serene the landscape becomes. A bus from Utoro runs to the lakes four times a day – hitching is another option. You should allow at least an hour to see all five lakes.

Just before the turn-off to the lakes, a dirt road continues up the peninsula. Following this track for about twenty minutes by car, as it rises uphill, will bring you to **Kamuiwakka-no-taki**, a cascading warm-water river and series of waterfalls, creating three levels of natural *rotemburo*. To reach the bathing pools you'll have to climb up the river. Bring your bathing costume and some sandals to walk in since the rocks are very slippery; vendors make a hefty profit renting out straw sandals at ¥500 at the start of the climb. The climb becomes more treacherous the higher you go, but the reward is that the top-most pool is the warmest and has the loveliest waterfall. The water is mildly acidic, so be warned that if you have any cuts, it's going to sting. From June to mid-October three buses a day continue on from Shiretoko Go-ko to the falls; again, it's easy enough to hitch.

With more time, think about embarking on one of the challenging **hikes** up the volcanic backbone of the peninsula. The peak of **Rausu-dake**, at 1661m the tallest mountain in Shiretoko, can be reached in around four and a half hours from the *Iwaobetsu Youth Hostel*, passing a natural *rotemburo* on the way. It's a popular hike and the hostel staff can advise on weather conditions. From the top there are spectacular views along the whole peninsula and to the east you should be able to see Kunashiri-tō, one of the disputed Kuril islands, or "Northern Territories" as they are known in Japan (see box, opposite). It will take you a full day to continue across Rausu-dake to the quiet and unremarkable east-coast fishing village of Rausu.

**Iō-zan**, the active volcano that produces the hot water for the Kamuiwakka-no-taki waterfalls, is a more difficult climb. The trail begins beside the Shiretoko Ōhashi, the bridge just beyond the entrance to the falls. A hike to the 1562-metre summit and back takes at least eight hours and can be combined with a visit to the hot waterfall.

## Practicalities

The gateway to the Shiretoko National Park is the rather shabby town of **SHARI**, where there is a JR station on the Senmō line which links Abashiri with the port of Kushiro, some 100km south. Between May and October four buses a day (the last at 1.45pm) run up the western side of the peninsula to Shiretoko Go-ko, from Shari bus station opposite the JR station, all stopping at Utoro on the way. From June to mid-October a daily bus runs from Shari to Rausu, on the east coast, via the Shiretoko Pass in the middle of the peninsula. Rausu is also connected by bus with JR Nemuro-Shibetsu Station on the Nemuro line which runs out to the Nemuro peninsula some 40km east of Kushiro.

There's an **information office** in front of Utoro's bus station (daily 8am–7.30pm), where the assistants can help with accommodation, though they don't speak English.

## THE DISPUTED KURIL ISLANDS

In November 1997, Russian President Boris Yeltsin and Japanese Prime Minister Ryutaro Hashimoto set about putting an end to a half-century-long territorial dispute over the **Kuril Islands**, some of which can be seen clearly from the Shiretoko peninsula. Technically, Japan is still fighting World War II with the former Soviet Union; a peace accord has never been signed because of Russia's continued occupation of these volcanic islands strung across the Sea of Okhotsk between the Kamchatka Peninsula and northeastern Hokkaidō.

Known in Japan as the Northern Territories, or *Chishima* (the Thousand Islands) and in Russia as the Kurils, only five of the islands are permanently inhabited, with a third of the population of 23,000 being accounted for by Russian soldiers. Japan demands the return of the four southernmost islands of Kunashiri, Shikotan, Etorofu and the Habomai group, the closest of which is less than 20km off Hokkaidō's coast.

The islands themselves are fairly desolate; it is their rich mineral resources and the surrounding fishing grounds that make them so desirable. Also for Russia, the islands – blocking off the Sea of Okhotsk – have an important strategic military position. The meeting between Yeltsin and Hashimoto proved that relations between the two sides have warmed since the tense days of the Cold War. But although the leaders decided to settle the dispute by the year 2000, it is far from clear, given the delicate issues involved, how this will be achieved.

Of the four **youth hostels** in the area, the best and most convenient for the park is *Shiretoko Iwaobetsu* (☎01522/4-2311, fax 4-2312; ①), which nestles in a valley beside the Iwaobetsu-gawa. Large and well-managed, this hostel has welcoming staff and good food, though it gets busy in summer. In **Utoro**, there's the *Yuhi-no-Ataru Ie* (☎01522/4-2764, fax 4-2863; ②), a fifteen-minute hike up the second road off to the right after the bus station – take the pedestrian pathway and walk straight ahead until you see a building with a painting of a white-tailed eagle on it. The rooms are pretty good, but it's not as handy a base for hikes as *Iwaobetsu*. Next door is the *Shiretoko Yaei-jō*, a well-maintained **campsite** which costs ¥320 per person per night. At the other end of the scale, the opulent *Shiretoko Grand Hotel* (☎01522/4-2021, fax 4-2839; ⑦) has both Western- and Japanese-style rooms and a roof-top onsen bath and *rotemburo* with views across the harbour. On the opposite side of the peninsula in **Rausu** is the basic *Rausu Youth Hostel* (☎01538/7-2145; ①), one minute's walk from the Rausu Hon-chō bus stop. It's a good-value option, but the fishing village is a very quiet spot, inconvenient for public transport, and only worth visiting if you plan to hike across the central mountains.

Utoro has a reasonable selection of **restaurants**; try *Ichuya*, just north of the bus station, where large bowls of ramen noodles shouldn't cost you more than ¥700. Also worth searching out is *Shiakaze*, a small restaurant where a set lunch of grilled fish, soup, rice and pickles costs ¥800; you'll find it on the hill above the bus station, five minutes' walk east of the campsite.

## Akan National Park

Some 50km south of the Shiretoko pensinsula is yet another wilderness and lakeland area, the **Akan National Park**. In any other part of Japan this densely forested park, with its three **lakes** – Mashū-ko, Kussharo-ko and Akan-ko – and the **volcanic peaks** of Me-Akan and Ō-Akan, would rate as a major tourist attraction. In Hokkaidō though, where breathtaking scenery is par-for-the-course, Akan is a something of an also-ran, not nearly as beautiful as the Shikotsu-Tōya National Park in the south (see p.317), nor as dramatic as the Shiretoko National Park to the north (see p.337). Furthermore, patchy public transport makes this a difficult area to tour unless you have your own wheels, or don't mind hitching. However it does have some good onsens and in the resort of **Akan Kohan** you can see traditional Ainu dancing as well as the rare *marimo* weedballs.

## Akan Kohan

The compact onsen resort of **AKAN KOHAN**, on the southern shore of Akan-ko and bursting with ritzy hotels and giftshops, is the most commercialized part of the national park, but is worth considering as a base if you plan to hike up the nearby peaks of **Me-Akan-dake** (1499m) and **Ō-Akan-dake** (1371m). At the western end of town, a ten-minute walk from the bus station, is the **Ainu Kotan**, a depressingly fake Ainu "village" which is little more than a short road of gift shops selling identical carved wood figures. Two hundred Ainu are said to live here. Visitors can watch a performance of traditional dance and music in the thatched *chise* (house)at the top of the shopping parade, and there's a tiny **museum** (daily 10am–10pm; ¥300) in a hut beside the *chise*, where the most interesting exhibits are the traditional Ainu costumes.

Just beyond the Ainu Kotan is the **Akan Forest and Lake Culture Centre** (daily 10am–5pm; ¥500), a small exhibition area with an impressive slide show of owls and some excellent examples of wood carvings – much better than those you'll see in the giftshops. Look out also for a tank of *marimo*, the velvety green weedballs that are indigenous to Akan-ko. Much is made of the *marimo* in Akan Kohan; the lake is one of the few places in the world where this weed is found and you can buy bottled baby *marimo* in all the giftshops. It can take two hundred years for the weedballs to grow to the size of baseballs.

Dedicated botanists might want to take the boat trip across the lake to the small island of Churui-shima, where the **Marimo Exhibition Centre** (daily 7.30am–5.30pm; ¥400, or ¥1520 including the return boat trip) has an underwater viewing tank. If you're lucky, you'll see the *marimo* balls bobbing up to the surface of the lake to breathe. Back in Akan Kohan, there's yet more *marimo* on display in the **Visitors' Centre** (daily 9am–5pm) at the eastern end of town, but it's more interesting to head along the pleasant woodland trails which start behind the centre and lead to the **Bokke**, a small area of bubbling mud pools beside the lake.

Many of the hotels in Akan Kohan allow day visitors into their **onsen** baths, usually between 11am and 3pm. This will cost around ¥1500 at either the *New Akan Hotel Shangrila* or the *Grand Hotel Akan*, which has the most elaborate tubs, including rooftop baths for women and a landscaped *rotemburo* with a view across the lake, for men.

### PRACTICALITIES

There are daily **bus** connections to Akan Kohan from Asahikawa, travelling via Sōunkyō (see p.327), and from the port of Kushiro. Between July and September additional buses run between the lake and Utoro in the Shiretoko National Park and the central Hokkaidō town of Obihiro. The closest **train** station to the lake is in Teshikaga, but it's better to get off at Kawayu further north, where you can board the expensive tourist bus service that runs around the national park's main sights (2hr 30min; ¥3190), including lake Mashū-ko (see opposite), before stopping at Akan Kohan.

Help with accommodation bookings, plus English maps and leaflets on the area, including good hiking notes on the nearby mountains, are all available from the **Sightseeing Information Office** (daily 9am–6pm; ☎0154/67-2254), a five-minute walk towards the lake from Akan Kohan bus station. There's a rather run-down **youth hostel**, the *Akan Angel* (☎0154/67-2309, fax 67-2954; ①), five minutes' walk beyond the Ainu Kotan. The spartan feel is compensated for by friendly staff and the offer of meals and bike rental. In the woods opposite the hostel lies a decent **campsite** (¥300 per person). Of the several minshuku in the resort, *Kiri* (☎0154/67-2755; ⑤), opposite the *Grand Hotel Akan*, has English-speaking owners and is good value considering two meals are included in the price. At the other end of the scale, both the *Akan Grand Hotel* (☎0154/67-2531, fax 67-2754; ⑨) and the *New Akan Hotel Shangrila* (☎0154/67-2121, fax 67-3339; ⑧) have prime lake-side locations, opulent interiors, luxurious onsen baths and serve top-notch Japanese cuisine.

## Mashū-ko

Some 25km east of Akan-ko is the small and unexciting town of **Teshikaga**, which lies just outside the park boundaries and is where you'll find the JR station called Mashū. The reason for coming here is to see the **lake** and famed beauty spot of **Mashū-ko**, roughly 10km west and at the bottom of sheer cliffs that keep all tourists at bay and the waters pristine. There are three lookout points over the 212-metre-deep caldera lake, which on very rare occasions sparkles a brilliant blue. Unfortunately, it's likely that the view you'll get – if you get one at all – will be obscured by swirling mists and thick cloud. Given this mysterious atmosphere, it's not surprising that the Ainu called Mashū-ko "the Devil's Lake". The first lookout point tends to get crowded; a ten-minute walk further around the road will lead you to a quieter point from which to view the lake. If you want to see the lake in all its glory, your best bet is to pop into the giftshop at the first lookout point, where you can view a free video and slide show about Mashū-ko.

There are infrequent and costly **buses** from Teshikaga to Mashū-ko – it's much better to hitch here, especially if you're **staying** at the large and modern *Mashū-ko Youth Hostel* (☎01548/2-3098, fax 2-4875; ②), which is halfway to the lake. Meals are served next door in *The Great Bear* **restaurant** (the three-course dinner is especially good value). A reasonable alternative is in Teshigaka, about a five-minute taxi ride from the JR station, where the homely *Pension Birao* (☎ & fax 01548/2-2979; ⑥) offers neat, Western-style rooms, and two hearty meals of local cuisine served in the attached café and included in the rates.

## Kussharo-ko and around

To the west of Mashū-ko is the Akan National Park's largest lake, the picturesque **Kussharo-ko**, which at 80 square kilometres is the biggest **crater lake** in Japan. It's also famous for being the home of Kussie, Japan's answer to the Loch Ness Monster. Kussie's mythical status received a boost in 1997, when several people reported seeing a mysterious creature in the lake, though according to most locals, it was an oversized trout. Whether it has a monster or not, the lake is special because it is fed by onsen water, creating a warm temperature and several natural *rotemburo* around Kussharo-ko's edge, such as the piping hot pools at **Wakoto Hantō**, a mini-promontory on the lake's southern shore. You can hop into another lakeside *rotemburo* at **Kotan Onsen**, an easy cycle ride from the *Kussharo-Genya Guest House* (see below). This is also where you'll also find a small **Ainu museum** (daily 9am–4.30pm; ¥300) in a strikingly modern concrete building, worth going inside only if you've not checked out any of the other collections around Hokkaidō.

A strong whiff of sulphur from the nearby volcano Iō-zan drifts over the area's main village, **Kawayu Onsen**, 3km from the lake. Here you'll find several hotels and minshuku, as well as the bus terminal and the **Akan National Park Visitor Centre** (daily 9am–5pm, July & Aug closes at 7pm), where you can pick up leaflets and maps. Kawayu's train station is a ten-minute bus journey south of the village; if you arrive late (the last bus to the onsen is 5.30pm), you might **stay** at the *Hotel Park Way* (☎01548/3-2616; ⑤), which has decent *tatami* rooms and *rotemburo*. Beside the lake is *Nibushi-no-Sato* (☎01548/3-2294; ⑤), a minshuku run by a friendly, English-speaking manager, who'll come pick you up at Kawayu Onsen bus terminal if you phone ahead. Bike rental is available (¥1800 a day) and there's an indoor onsen bath with a lake view.

The park's best **youth hostel** is the *Kussharo-Genya Youth Guesthouse* (☎ & fax 01548/4-2609; ②), a distinctive, tent-like building made of wood, with a central atrium set amid potato fields, some thirty minutes' walk from the southern shore of Kussharo-ko. Accommodation is in Western-style rooms and superb Japanese meals are served. Mountain bikes can be rented (¥1000 a day) from here and the staff organize two-hour canoe tours from the lake up one of the local rivers (¥3500) and cross-country ski-tours in the winter.

## Eastern Hokkaidō: Kushiro and Erimo Misaki

The main southern gateway to the Akan National Park is the industrial town and port of **KUSHIRO**, which is also served by ferries from Tokyo. There's no reason to linger in this town, though nature-lovers will be interested in the nearby **Kushiro Shitsugen National Park**, a vast marshland and the winter habitat of around four hundred red-crested cranes (*tanchō*). Buses from just left of Kushiro Station take one hour to reach the main observation point within the park en route to Akan-ko (see p.339). If you have time to kill in Kushiro while waiting for a transport connection, you could do worse than head down to the colourful **Fisherman's Wharf**, a redeveloped waterside complex of shops and restaurants, which for some unfathomable reason is also called MOO. The ferry terminal is a fifteen-minute bus journey west of Kushiro Station.

By far the most fascinating place along Hokkaidō's eastern coast is the small fishing village of **ERIMO MISAKI**, 160km south of Kushiro and a popular stop with tour groups and bikers, who come to take in one of the windiest areas in Japan and gaze at the colony of three hundred Kuril Harbour seals living around the rocky cape. This is a dramatic place at any time of the year, but is particularly beautiful in summer, when the grassy hills which ripple down to the cape are dusted with wild flowers. Along the coast on the way to the cape you'll see people fishing for *kombu* seaweed, which is dried out in long strands on the pebbly black sand beaches.

The pride of this isolated community is reflected in the excellent **Kaze-no-kan** (May–Sept 8am–7pm; Jan–April & Oct–Dec 8.30am–5pm; ¥500), a "wind" **museum** just beyond the giftshops and car park at the cape, and set against a backdrop of surrounding hills. The exhibition halls are approached through a curved corridor resonating with swirly, tinkling music. Inside, a wind tunnel gives you the chance to experience what it is like to stand in a 25-metre-per-second gale (in case it's not so windy outside). Other highlights include film and slide shows on the area, with a slide screen that scrolls back to reveal a panoramic view of the cape. There's also a room dedicated to the seals with telescopes to view them – if you're lucky they'll be basking on the rocks below. Apart from visiting the museum, simply walking around the cape is extremely pleasant. It's also something of a ritual, if you stay overnight at Erimo Misaki, to visit the cape at dawn and watch the sun rise.

The closest train station to Erimo Misaki is at **Obihiro**, 115km northwest, from where you'll need to take two buses to reach the cape. The Tokachi bus departs outside Obihiro Station and takes an hour to reach **Hirō**, where you'll need to change to the less frequent (only four daily) JR bus running to the cape and around to **Samani**. From southern Hokkaidō, you can take a local train from Tomakomai which chugs for three hours along the coast to Samani, where you will pick up the JR bus to the cape.

If you decide to **stay**, you're best bet is the *Erimo Misaki Youth Hostel* (☎01466/3-1144; open April 26–Oct 31; ①), ten minutes' walk from the cape, next to the Erimo Gakomae bus stop. Both the bunk dorms and slightly pricier *tatami* rooms are comfortable and the dinner, including local salmon and seaweed and a complimentary beer, is well worth booking. But it's the nightly sing-a-long, when the staff rattle tamborines and dance around, which make this hostel such fun – not to mention the wild send-off you'll be given, with staff waving huge banners on the side of the road. A more sedate option is *Misakisō* (☎01466/3-1316, fax 3-1317; ④), a traditional ryokan just below the museum and overlooking the cape, where the rates include two meals. No English is spoken here, but the management is friendly and you're well placed to catch Erimo Misaki's sunrise.

# travel details

## Trains

The trains between the major cities listed below are the fastest, direct services. There are also frequent slower services, run by JR and several private companies, covering the same destinations. It is usually possible, especially on long-distance routes, to get there faster by changing between services.

**Abashiri** to: Asahikawa (6 daily; 3hr 44min); Kushiro (4 daily; 3hr); Sapporo (6 daily; 5hr 19min).

**Asahikawa** to: Abashiri (7 daily; 3hr 44min); Furano (10 daily; 1hr 8min); Sapporo (40 daily; 1hr 30min); Wakkanai (5 daily; 4hr 3min).

**Hakodate** to: Aomori (12 daily; 2hr); Morioka (4 daily; 4hr 20min); Ōnuma-kōen (12 daily; 20min), Sapporo (16 daily; 3hr 30min); Sendai (2 daily; 7hr); Tokyo (2 daily; 11hr 30min).

**Sapporo** to: Abashiri (7 daily; 5hr 19min); Asahikawa (40 daily; 1hr 30min), Hakodate (16 daily; 3hr 30min); Kushiro (8 daily; 3hr 30min); New Chitose airport (30 daily; 37min); Noboribetsu (20 daily; 1hr 13min); Osaka (daily; 22hr 15min); Otaru (30 daily; 30min); Tokyo (daily; 16hr); Tomakomai (25 daily; 50min).

**Wakkanai** to: Asahikawa (5 daily; 4hr, 3min); Sapporo (3 daily; 6hr).

## Buses

**Abashiri** to: Sapporo (6 daily; 6hr); Shari (5 daily; 1hr).

**Asahikawa** to: Asahidake Onsen (2 daily; 1hr 30min), Furano (daily; 1hr 30min); Sapporo (4 daily; 2hr 30min); Sōunkyō Onsen (8 daily; 1hr 45min); Tenninkyō Onsen (2 daily; 1hr); Wakkanai (daily; 4hr 45min).

**Hakodate** to: Ōnuma-kōen (5 daily; one hour); Tōya-ko (daily; 3hr 30min).

**New Chitose airport** to: Niseko (2 daily; 3hr); Sapporo (at least 20 daily; 70min); Shikotsu Kohan (3 daily; 45min).

**Sapporo** to: Abashiri (7 daily; 6hr); Furano (10 daily; 3hr); Kushiro (4 daily; 6 hours), Niseko (4 daily; 2hr 30min), Noboribestu (8 daily; 1hr 40min); Tōya-ko (daily; 3hr); Wakkanai (daily; 6hr 15min).

## Ferries

**Hakodate** to: Aomori (11 daily; 1hr 45min); Ōma (2 daily; 1hr 45min).

**Kushiro** to: Tokyo (daily; 31hr 35min).

**Otaru** to: Maizuru (weekly; 29hr); Niigata (2 weekly; 19hr); Tsuruga (weekly; 21hr).

**Muroran** to: Aomori (2 daily; 3hr); Naoetsu (3 weekly; 16hr 30min).

**Tomakomai** to: Nagoya (daily; 38hr 45min); Sendai (daily; 14hr 45min); Tokyo (4 weekly; 30hr).

**Wakkanai** to: Rebun-tō (2/4 daily; 2hr); Rishiri-tō (2/4 daily; 1hr 45min).

## Flights

**Asahikawa** to: Kansai International (2 daily; 2hr); Nagoya (daily; 1hr 50min); Tokyo (7 daily; 1hr 35min).

**Hakodate** to: Nagoya (3 daily; 1hr 20min); Kansai International (3 daily; 1hr 45min); Sapporo (5 daily; 45min); Sendai (3 weekly; 1hr); Tokyo (7 daily; 1hr 15min).

**Memanbetsu** to: Nagoya (daily; 2hr); Kansai International (daily; 2hr 10min); Sapporo (6 daily; 50min); Tokyo (6 daily; 1hr 40min).

**Sapporo (New Chitose)** to: Fukuoka (5 daily; 2hr 10min); Kansai International (10 daily; 2hr); Nagoya (12 daily; 1hr 30min); Tokyo (38 daily; 1hr 30min).

**Wakkanai** to: Rebun-tō (daily; 15min); Rishiri-tō (daily; 15min); Sapporo (daily; 50min); Tokyo (daily; 1hr 45min).

CHAPTER FIVE

# CENTRAL HONSHŪ

Located roughly midway along the Japanese archipelago, the seven prefectures of **CENTRAL HONSHŪ**, known as **Chūbu**, offer a wide choice of terrain and travel possibilities. Dominating the region are the magnificent **Japan Alps**, rising up in Nagano-ken and Gifu-ken, and providing spectacular mountain scenery, top onsen and ski resorts, old castle and temple towns, and villages in remote valleys caught in a time warp. Just as appealing is the rugged northern coast, **Hokuriku**, which covers Toyama-ken, Ishikawa-ken and Fukui-ken. Shaped by the savage waves of the Japan Sea, it feels very much set apart from the rest of the country. Expressways and train lines plough a direct route between Tokyo and Kansai through the hideously industrialized south-coast prefectures of Shizuoka-ken and Aichi-ken, yet even here, there are places worth stopping to see, including Japan's fourth main city, Nagoya.

Even on the shortest trip, make time for the majestic Japan Alps, now more accessible than ever, thanks to the new Hokuriku Shinkansen line that zips from Tokyo to the 1998 Winter Olympics city of Nagano in one hour and thirty minutes. Nagano's highlight is its venerable and atmospheric temple, **Zenkō-ji**, while southeast of the city, close to the summer resort of **Karuizawa**, don't miss the stunning lava landscape at **Onioshidashien**. Of the region's many skiing and onsen possibilities, perhaps the best is the charming village of **Nozawa Onsen**, northeast of Nagano, where you'll find excellent slopes and thirteen free hot spring baths. Northwest of the city, **Togakushi** offers ancient shrines surrounded by spiritual forests, and a wacky Ninja warrior museum.

The focus of the southern half of Nagano-ken is the charming castle-town of **Matsumoto**, easily reached from Shinjuku Station in Tokyo. The town is also the jumping-off point for the beautiful and tiny Alps resort of **Kamikōchi**, popular with mountaineers and hikers in summer, and for a handful of immaculately preserved post towns which line the old Nakasendō route from Kyoto to Tokyo. Between the best of these – **Tsumago** and **Magome** – is a lovely one-day hiking route.

Across the Alps, the small convivial city of **Takayama** is the centre of the Hida area famous for its skilled carpenters. Their craftsmanship is evident in many of the preserved houses and temples of the city, as well as in the unusual A-frame thatched

## ACCOMMODATION PRICE CODES

All accommodation in this book has been graded according to the following price codes, which refer to the cheapest double or twin room available for most of the year, and include taxes. Note that rates may increase during peak holiday periods, in particular around Christmas and New Year, the Golden Week (April 28–May 6) and Obon (the week around August 15), when accommodation is very difficult to get without an advance reservation. In the case of hostels providing dormitory accommodation, the code refers to the charge per bed. See p.36 for more details on accommodation.

| | | |
|---|---|---|
| ① under ¥3000 | ④ ¥7000–10,000 | ⑦ ¥20,000–30,000 |
| ② ¥3000–5000 | ⑤ ¥10,000–15,000 | ⑧ ¥30,000–40,000 |
| ③ ¥5000–7000 | ⑥ ¥15,000–20,000 | ⑨ over ¥40,000 |

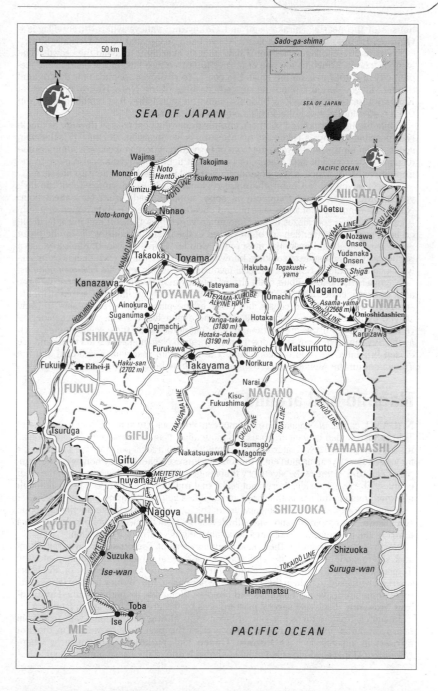

houses of the nearby Shirakawa-gō and **Gokayama** valleys where three villages – **Ogimachi, Suganuma** and **Ainokura** – have been designated World Heritage Sites.

Pretty as these villages are, you'll have to stay overnight to avoid the crowds. The same is true in **Kenroku-en**, one of Japan's top three gardens, in the historic and elegant city of **Kanazawa**, on the Japan Sea coast. To really escape, head for the tranquil fishing villages dotted around the rugged coastline of the **Noto Hantō**, northeast of Kanazawa, or the thriving Zen Buddhist community in **Eihei-ji**, a rambling temple in the forested foothills of Fukui-ken's mountains, to the south.

While the ugly, urbanized southern coast is generally best passed through as quickly as possible, **Nagoya**'s Tokugawa Art Museum is worth a visit, and the city is the main access point for the attractive castle-town of **Inuyama**, where you can see summer-time displays of the ancient skill of *ukai*, or cormorant fishing. Inuyama is also close to the impressive **Meiji Mura**, a vast outdoor museum of turn-of-the-century architecture.

Wherever you go in Chūbu, there are regional **foods** to be sampled, but the dish you'll come across most frequently is **soba**, noodles made from buckwheat flour. Nagano is renowned for its fresh fruit and chestnuts, while the Hida region of neighbouring Gifu-ken specializes in beef, mountain vegetables (*sansai*) and miso, fermented bean paste. *Ayu* river fish are often served in the inland regions, while on the Japan Sea coast, you should make the most of the wonderful fresh seafood. Kanazawa has a particularly refined style of cooking, known as *kaga ryōri* where each dish is exquisitely displayed, while in Nagoya, the local favourite is chicken with flat *kishimen* noodles.

Nagoya is home to Chūbu's main airport, but it's more likely that you'll approach the area by **train**, either from Tokyo or Kyoto. A couple of train lines cut across from the southern to the northern coasts, but many of the places in the mountains are only served by buses, which can be infrequent and expensive. It's well worth considering renting a car to tour this area, although note that some of the most scenic routes, such as the Skyline drive across the Alps from Gifu-ken to Nagano-ken are toll roads and are closed in winter because of deep snow. The mountain resort of Kamikōchi and the Tateyama-Kurobe Alpine route are similarly off limits between November and April.

# Nagano and around

**NAGANO**, capital of Nagano-ken, is a modern, compact city some 200km northwest of Tokyo. Surrounded by fruit orchards and mountains, Nagano came to world attention as the location of the 1998 Winter Olympics, but it's been a focal point for the Japanese for far longer. Every year, around eight million pilgrims come here to pay homage at the temple of **Zenkō-ji**, home of the legendary first image of Budda to arrive in Japan in the sixth century. The temple aside, there's not really that much to see in the city itself, although it's worth making full use of the shops and facilities before venturing into the Alps.

If you're travelling to the mountains from Tokyo, it's well worth considering a stop at **Karuizawa**, 90km from Nagano, where the lava flows from the nearby volcano Asama-yama have created a permanent record of a devastating eighteenth-century eruption.

Northwest of Nagano lies the scenic mountain area of **Togakushi**, a haven for hikers and skiers and home to the atmospheric shrine of Togakushi Okusha, and the Togakushi Minzoku-kan, a folklore museum with an entertaining section on the Ninja warriors who used to train in this area. To the northeast, the country town of **Obuse** features some attractive old buildings and temples, alongside its highlight, the **Hokusai-kan Museum**, displaying several masterpieces by the great *ukiyo-e* artist, **Hokusai**.

In winter, Nagano turns into one of Japan's top **skiing** destinations, with resorts in nearby Hakuba and Shiga Kōgen. This is also the best time to wallow in the **hot springs** in villages such as **Nozawa Onsen** and **Yudanaka Onsen**, near where *Nihonzaru* (Japanese long-tailed monkeys) also bathe in their own outdoor pool.

## Arrival, information and getting around

Nagano's sleek JR station, rebuilt for the Olympics, is the terminus for **trains** on the Hokuriku Shinkansen line from Tokyo and also the hub for local and express services around the prefecture and up to the Sea of Japan coastline. Most long-distance **buses** pull in at the bus terminal on Basu Tāminaru-dōri, on the west side of the JR station.

Another legacy of the Olympics is Nagano's excellent **tourist information centre** (daily 9am–6pm; ☎0262/26-5626), inside the station's main concourse. The helpful assistants speak English, can arrange accommodation and will provide you with a wide range of English maps and pamphlets for the city and prefecture. Information is also available from the International Exchange Lounge ANPIE (Mon–Fri 8.30am–5pm), outside the prefectural office around 1km west of the station. This facility also has a small library and is a good place to meet locals who speak English.

**Getting around** is best done on foot – walking the 2km up to Zenkō-ji (see p.349) is an especially good way of taking in the city. Alternatively, you can hop on a bus from the west side of the JR station, or take the local Nagano Dentetsu, a private railway with its terminus beneath the Midori department store – this is also the line for trains to Obuse (see p.353).

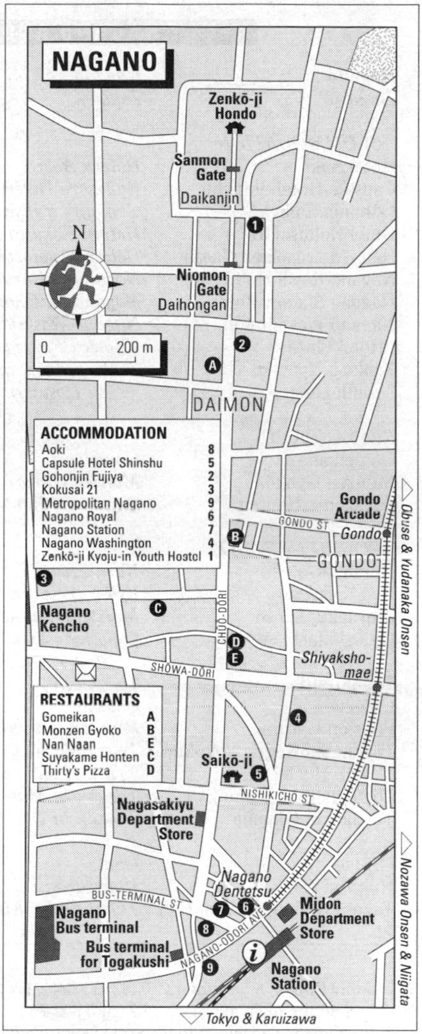


## Accommodation

The Olympics naturally caused a boom in **accommodation** and it's likely that, outside the busy summer and winter seasons and weekends, you'll be able to strike bargains at some places. The most atmospheric place to stay is near Zenkō-ji, where you can choose from several pricey ryokan and a youth hostel. Should you want to stay in temple lodgings (open only to genuine Zen Buddhist students), approach the tourist information centre in Nagano Station first.

**Hotel Aoki**, Suehiro-chō (☎0262/26-1271, fax 26-3445). One of the cheaper business hotels close to the west exit of the JR station. Singles are under ¥6000 and there's a café in the lobby. ⑤.

**Capsule Hotel Shinshu**, 860 Minami-Chitose (☎0262/23-4700, fax 23-4833). Men-only capsule hotel, five minutes' walk north of the JR station. The capsules are larger than usual and there's a sauna and large bath in the basement. ②.

## NAGANO AND AROUND

| | | |
|---|---|---|
| **Nagano** | *Nagano* | 長野 |
| Zenkō-ji | *Zenkō-ji* | 善光寺 |
| *ACCOMMODATION* | | |
| Hotel Aoki | *Hoteru Aoki* | ホテルアオキ |
| Capsule Hotel Shinshu | *Kapuseru Hoteru Shinshu* | カプセルホテル信州 |
| Gohonjin Fujiya | *Gohonjin Fujiya* | 御本陣藤屋 |
| Hotel Kokusai 21 | *Hoteru Kokusai 21* | ホテル国際２１ |
| Hotel Metropolitan Nagano | *Hoteru Metoroporitan Nagano* | ホテルメトロポリタン長野 |
| Nagano Royal Hotel | *Nagano Roiyaru Hoteru* | 長野ロイヤルホテル |
| Nagano Station Hotel | *Nagano Sutēshon Hoteru* | 長野ステーションホテル |
| Nagano Washington Hotel Plaza | *Nagano Washinton Hoteru Puraza* | 長野ワシントンホテルプラザ |
| Zenkō-ji Kyōju-in Youth Hostel | *Zenkō-ji Kyōju-in Yūsu Hosuteru* | 善光寺教授院ユースホステル |
| *RESTAURANTS* | | |
| Gomeikan | *Gomeikan* | 五明館 |
| Monzen Gyokō | *Monzen Gyokō* | 門前漁港 |
| Suyakame Honten | *Suyakame Honten* | すや亀本店 |
| *AROUND NAGANO* | | |
| **Karuizawa** | *Karuizawa* | 軽井沢 |
| Kyū-Karuizawa | *Kyū-Karuizawa* | 旧軽井沢 |
| Moritaku San-sō | *Moritaku San-sō* | もりたくさんそう |
| Onioshidashien | *Onioshidashien* | 鬼押出し園 |
| **Togakushi** | *Togakushi* | 戸隠 |
| Chūsha | *Chūsha* | 中社 |
| Pension Garnie | *Penshon Garuni* | ペンションガルニ |
| Togakushi Kōgen Yokokura Youth Hostel | *Togakushi Kōgen Yokokura Yūsu Hosuteru* | 戸隠高原横倉ユースホステル |
| Togakushi Minzoku-kan | *Togakushi Minzoku-kan* | 戸隠民族館 |
| Togakushi Okusha | *Togakushi Okusha* | 戸隠奥社 |
| **Obuse** | *Obuse* | 小布施 |
| Hokusai-kan | *Hokusai-kan* | 北斎館 |
| Takai Kōzan Memorial Hall | *Takai Kōzan Kinenkan* | 高井鴻山記念館 |

**Gohonjin Fujiya**, 80 Daimon (☎0262/32-1241, fax 32-1243). The stylish stone front of this venerable hotel on the main approach to Zenkō-ji is 75 years old, while the back is all Meiji-era elegance, with the most expensive *tatami* rooms facing onto manicured gardens. Meals are worth the indulgence, otherwise it's a grade cheaper. ⑥.

**Hotel Kokusai 21**, 576 Agatamachi (☎0262/34-1111, fax 34-2365). Nagano's top hotel, opposite the prefectural office on the west side of town, is spacious and well-appointed, but rather dull. It has a good selection of restaurants, serving large portions at lunch. ⑥.

**Hotel Metropolitan Nagano**, 1346 Minami-Ishido-chō (☎0262/91-7000, fax 91-7001). Good-value luxury hotel beside the west exit of the JR station, with high-standard Western-style rooms and a stylish lobby and restaurants. ⑥.

**Nagano Royal Hotel**, 1-28-3 Minami-Chitose (☎0262/28-2222, fax 28-0823). Service is polite and standards high at this slightly old-fashioned mid-range hotel opposite the JR station west exit. The rooms have tiled en-suite bathrooms, rather than the usual moulded plastic affairs. ⑥.

**Nagano Station Hotel**, 1359 Suehiro-chō (☎0262/26-1295, fax 26-1056). Stylish, good-value business hotel. The Western-style rooms are nicely decorated and singles start at ¥6000. ⑤.

**Nagano Washington Hotel Plaza**, 1177-3 Kami-Chitose (☎0262/28-5111, fax 28-4440). Reasonable value mid-range hotel. The rooms are plainly furnished and on the small side, but have bi-lingual TV with satellite channels. There are a couple of restaurants in the complex. ⑤.

**Zenkō-ji Kyoju-in Youth Hostel**, 479 Motoyoshi-machi (☎0262/32-2768). Ideal if you're planning an early-morning visit to Zenkō-ji, which is just one minute's walk away. The manager is very protective of this atmospheric old temple building and you'll have to leave your belongings in lockers in the entrance hall before being shown into the large *tatami* dorms. ①.

## Zenkō-ji

Believed to house the first image of Buddha to come to Japan, **Zenkō-ji**, Nagano's 1300-year-old temple, has long been a popular place of pilgrimage. It has traditionally welcomed believers of all Buddhist sects, has never barred women and is run alternately by an abbot of the Tendai sect and abbess of the Jōdo sect. Visitors can join the hundreds of daily petitioners searching for the "key to paradise" which lies beneath Zenkō-ji's main temple building (see below); find it and you'll have earned eternal salvation.

The traditional way to approach the temple is on foot. Head north along Chūō-dōri, west of the JR station, and you'll first pass **Saikō-ji**, a small temple tucked away in a quiet courtyard. Also known as Karukaya-san after the Buddhist saint who founded it in 1199, the main temple building contains two wooden statues of Jizō, the guardian of children, one carved by Karukaya, the other by his son Ishidō.

About three-quarters of the way up, the road begins to narrow around the area known as **Daimon**, where you'll find many gift shops, pilgrim stalls and ryokan. To the left is the **Daihongan**, the nunnery and residence of the high priestess of Zenkō-ji, who is also usually a member of the imperial family. In the courtyard, look out for the fountain with a statue of Mizuko Jizō, the patron saint of aborted and stillborn babies – little dolls and toys are left as offerings around the base.

Passing through the impressive 13.6-metre-tall Niō-mon (gate) and a short precinct lined with more souvenir stalls and lodgings, you'll see the **Roku-Jizō**, on the right, a row of six large metal statues symbolizing the guardians of the six worlds through which Buddhism believes the soul must pass: hell, starvation, beasts, carnage, human beings and heavenly beings. On the left is **Daikanjin**, the home of the high priest; the entrance is reached by crossing an attractive arched bridge and inside you'll find a pretty garden.

---

### ZENKŌ-JI

Zenkō-ji's most sacred object is the **Ikkō Sanzon Amida Nyorai**, a triad of Amida Buddha images sharing one halo. This golden statue is said to have been made by Buddha himself in the sixth century BC and is believed to have arrived in Japan some 1200 years later as a gift from Korea to the emperor. For a while, the image was kept in a specially built temple near Ōsaka, where it became became the focus of a clan feud. The temple was eventually destroyed and the statue dumped in a nearby canal, from where it was later rescued by **Honda Yoshimitsu**, a poor man who was passing by and apparently heard Buddha call. Honda brought the image back to his home in Nagano (then called Shinano). When news of its recovery reached Emperor Kōgyoku he ordered a temple to be built in its honour and called it Zenkō-ji after the Chinese reading of Honda's name. The emperor also ordered that the image should never be publically viewed again, so a copy was made and it is this that is displayed once every seven years in the grand Gokaichō festival, held from April 10 to May 20. The next festival is in 1999.

At the top of the precinct stands the **San-mon**, the huge, double-storey wooden gateway into the temple's central courtyard, the gathering place not only for pilgrims but also pigeons, who have their own elaborate metal coop on the left-hand side. On the same side is the **Kyōzo**, or sutra repository, an elegant wooden building that is only open occasionally. In the centre of the courtyard stands a large metal cauldron decorated with a lion whose mouth exhales the perfumed smoke of incense sticks. As a charm for health and good fortune, pilgrims waft the smoke around their bodies before moving on to the vast, imposing main hall, the Hondō, dating from 1707.

The **Hondō** houses the Amida triad (see box on previous page), and underneath is the dark tunnel where pilgrims grope around for the "key to paradise". Once you've entered the outer sanctuary of the hall, look straight ahead for the worn-out statue of Binzuru, a physician and fallen follower of Buddha; pilgrims rub the statue in the hope of curing their ailments. Just beyond is the awesome worshipper's hall, a vast space with golden ornaments dangling from the high ceiling, where pilgrims used to bed down on futons for the night. Now people traditionally come for the morning service, which starts around 5.30am; it's worth making the effort to attend this and witness Zenkō-ji at its most mystical, with the priests wailing, drums pounding and hundreds of pilgrims joined in fervent prayer. Afterwards. the Ojuzu Chodai ceremony takes place in the courtyard in front of the Hondō. Pilgrims kneel and wait for the high priest or priestess to rustle by in their colourful robes, shaded by a giant red paper umbrella, and bless them by tapping prayer beads on their heads.

If you're at all uncomfortable in the dark, don't enter the **Okaidan**, a pitch-black passage that runs beneath the Hondō's innermost sanctum, resting place of the revered original image of Buddha. However, if you fancy a feel of the "key of paradise," buy a ticket (¥300) from one of the machines to the right of Binzuru's statue, and follow the chattering crowds plunging into the darkness. Once you're in, keep your right hand on the wall and chances are you'll find the key (which feels more like a door knob) towards the end of the passage.

# Eating and drinking

You'll find most places to **eat** clustered on or around Chūō-dōri; in the evenings, try the lively Gondo arcade leading east from Chūō-dōri to Gondo Station. To sample *shōjin ryōri*, the expensive vegetarian cuisine prepared for the monks, head for the area around Zenkō-ji. Soba is available at most places around town. The many small **bars** around Gondo tend to be pricey, but if you're looking for a cool spot for a drink in summer, don't overlook the beer garden on top of Nagano Dentetsu Building, at the eastern end of the Gondo arcade.

## Restaurants and bars

**Giraffe**, Minami-Chitose. Beside the west exit of the JR station, this cheap chain café is a good spot for breakfast or a mid-day break, and turns into a bar in the evening.

**Gomeikan**, 515 Daimon-chō. Traditional tourist restaurant in an old white building halfway up Chūō-dōri. The lunch special is ¥1400, the *bentō* box of prepared tidbits is ¥2500, while full meals clock in at ¥5000 per person. Open 11am–2pm, 5–8pm, closed Wed.

**Kencho cafeteria**. On the tenth floor of the prefectural government building, this office canteen, open to the public, has two strong points in its favour: the cheap food and the view across the city. Check out the plastic food menu first, pay and take your chit to the kitchen counter to collect your meal.

**Liberty**. One of Nagano's most popular and relaxed *gaijin* bars, down the alley next to the Nagasakiya department store.

**Midori**. This department store, connected to the north end of the JR station, has a wide selection of restaurants on the fifth floor. *Keyaki* serves a good-value set meal of local specialities, including soba noodles, tofu and *konyaku* (root vegetable jelly) dipped in mustard and miso.

**Monzen Gyoko**, 5 Higashi-go-chō. Lively, modern *izakaya* by the Gondo arcade where a wide range of dishes and beers are served up by a largely *gaijin* staff. Around ¥3000 per person. Mon–Sat 11.30am–1.30pm & 5–11pm.

**Nan Naan**, 1271 Toigosho. Colourful Indian restaurant about halfway up Chūō-dōri, just after the crossing with Shōwa-dōri. The tasty lunch sets come in under ¥1000 and there's an English menu.

**Suyakame Honten**, 35-4022 Nishi-go-chō. A restaurant and shop that specializes in miso – they even serve miso ice-cream. Try the rice balls topped with three different types of miso sauce. Daily 11.30am–3pm.

**Thirty's Pizza**, Toigosho. Stylishly grungy pizza parlour and bar, with tables spilling out on to Chūō-dōri, which can get loud and boisterous at weekends. The pizza is the genuine article and the salads aren't bad either.

**Tokugyōbō**, 32-0264 Motoyoshi. A good place to sample *shōjin ryōri* close to Zenkō-ji. Prices from ¥5000 per person.

**Winds**, B1, 1-28-3 Minami-Chitose. Convivial bar, under the *Royal Hotel*, also serving a good range of snacks.

## Listings

**Airlines** ANA, Suehiro 1316, Minami Nagano (☎0262/25-0311); JAS, Minami-Ishido, Minami Nagano (☎0262/25-5888).

**Banks and exchange** Nagano's main bank, offering full foreign exchange facilities, is Hyaku Jū Ni (meaning "82") Ginkō, of which there are several branches around the city.

**Bookshops** Books Heiando (daily 10am–7.30pm), behind the Tōkyū department store, west of the station, has a small selection of English books and magazines on its second floor.

**Car rental** Eki Rent-a-car (☎0262/27-8500) is beside the Zenkō-ji exit of the JR station; Orix Rent-a-car, Kami-Chitose 1126-1, Tsuruga (0262/24-0543).

**Hospital** Nagano's main hospital is Nagano Sekijuji Byōin, 1512-1 Wakasato (☎0262/26- 4131).

**Police** The Prefectural Police Office is at 692-2 Habashita (☎0262/33-0110). Emergency numbers are listed in Basics on p.70.

**Post office** The Central Post Office is close to the Prefectural Office (Kencho) at 1085-4 Minami-Agata.

**Taxis** Try Utsunomiya Taxi (☎0262/32-8181); Nagano Kankō Jidōsha (☎0262/26-1234) or Nagano Taxi (☎0262/27-2222).

**Travel agency** The main JTB office is at 1-12-7 Minami-Chitose (☎0262/28-0489).

## Karuizawa and Onioshidashien

On the eastern edge of landlocked Nagano-ken, and lying on the slopes of Asama-yama (at 2568m Japan's highest triple-cratered active volcano), is the trendy summer resort of **KARUIZAWA**. From here you can visit nearby **Onioshidashien**, an incredible landscape of lava frozen in black clumps as it pursued a wide and destructive path down Asama-yama. The town itself is pleasant enough, though, with a low-key old district, **Kyū-Karuizawa**, where Crown Prince Akihito (now the emperor) met his future wife Michiko on the tennis courts in the 1950s. Things can get very hectic in summer, when a mass of clothing and gift shops open their doors to vacationing urbanites, but there are still traces of the natural tranquility that made Karuizawa so appealing to nineteenth-century visitors.

Karuizawa's sights are widely scattered, so the best plan of attack is to pick up the good English map and guidebook of the area from the **tourist information hut** (daily 9am–5pm; ☎0267/42-2491) at the station. The most enjoyable way of exploring is by **bicycle**; you can rent one from the many nearby outlets (¥500 for an hour). Otherwise, hop on a bus from in front of Karuizawa Station for Kyū-Karuizawa and the Old Mikasa Hotel (see overleaf).

Heading north from the station, past the row of shops brings you to a pedestrianized street dubbed "little Ginza", but more resembling Tokyo's teen-scene Takeshita-dōri (see p.134). At the end of this street, you'll emerge into forest; look out for the quaint wooden **Nihon Seikokai Chapel** with a bust of Archdeacon Shaw, who helped popularize the area as a retreat, standing in front. Services are held in the church every Sunday, and in the priest's old house, behind the church, you can see photographs of the man and his family. If you have time, it's a nice two-kilometre cycle ride or hike up to the secluded Old Mikasa Hotel, an elegant wooden building dating from 1905, which now houses a small missable museum. Follow the main road, Mikasa-dōri, due north from the chapel.

The fastest route to Karuizawa is by **train** on the Hokuriku Shinkansen between Tokyo and Nagano. Other services only go as far as Yokokawa Station from where you have to travel up to Karuizawa by bus from the valley below. There's no good-value **accommodation** to be had in fashionable Karuizawa – you're better off staying in nearby Nagano (see p.346). If you get stuck though, *try Moritaku San-sō* (☎0267/42-6721; [5]), a small ryokan a couple of blocks north of Karuizawa Station, where the room price includes two meals. By contrast, there are lots of reasonably priced places to **eat**, especially in Kyū-Karuizawa, where you can feast on the local speciality, soba noodles .

### Onioshidashien

Karuizawa'a main draw is the volcano Asama-yama which last erupted in 1973 and continues to steam ominously. No hiking is allowed within 4km of the crater, and the best place to get a glimpse of the volcano is on its north side at **Onioshidashien** (daily: May–Sept 7am–6pm; Jan–April & Oct–Dec 8am–5pm; ¥400), 21km from Karuizawa. Onioshidashien was the scene of a cataclysmic eruption on August 5, 1783, when ashes from the blow-out were said to have darkened the sky as far as Europe, and a seven-kilometre-wide lava flow swept away the nearby village of Kanbara. When the lava cooled, it solidified into an extraordinary landscape of black boulders and bizarre rock shapes which now sprout alpine plants. To get an idea of the scale of the place, head up to the observation floor in the gift shop and restaurant complex at the entrance. You can then explore the twisting paths that have been laid across the weird landscape. Most of the crowds head for the central temple, Kannon-dō, standing on a raised red platform amid the black rocks, but you can easily escape them by continuing past to the quieter area behind.

Regular **buses** run to Onioshidashien (¥950) from outside Naka-Karuizawa Station, one stop west of Karuizawa, in around thirty minutes. There are also direct buses from Karuizawa Station (45min; ¥1150). There's nothing to see in Naka-Karuizawa, but if you have time to kill while waiting for a train or bus, try the delicious noodles at *Chojuan*, an unpretentious restaurant left of the station.

## Togakushi

One of the best day-trips you can make from Nagano is to the refreshing alpine area of **Togakushi**, 20km northwest of the city, bounded on one side by the jagged ridge of Togakushi-yama and on the other by Mount Iizuna. As well as great scenery, there's a decent museum and a shrine to check out. The best way to approach the area is via the scenic **bus** route. Buses start from Nagano's Kawanakajima terminus one block west of *Hotel Metropolitan Nagano* and run along the vertiginous Bird-line Driveway, giving panoramic views of the city as they wind up the mountain around a series of hair-pin bends. Stay on the bus through the village of Chūsha (see below), about one hour from Nagano, and get off a couple of stops later when you reach the entrance to the Togakushi Okusha, the innermost of the three main sanctuaries of the Togakushi shrine.

Before heading off up to the shrine, it's worth crossing the road to the **Togakushi Minzoku-kan** (daily 9am–5pm; ¥500), a museum complex of traditional farm buildings, some of which have exhibits on the **Ninja warriors**, who were once trained in Togakushi (see box, opposite). Within the complex, the Togakure-ryu Ninpo Shiryōkan displays some amazing black and white photographs of the stealthy, black-garbed fighters in action, examples of their lethal weapons and even a model Ninja dangling from the rafters. The most fun is to be had next door in the Ninja House, a maze of hidden doors and staircases that is fiendishly difficult to find your way out of.

## NINJA: THE SHADOW WARRIORS

Long before their ancient martial art was nabbed by a bunch of cartoon turtles, the **Ninja** were Japan's most feared warriors, employed by lords as assassins and spies. They practiced **Ninjutsu**, "the art of stealth", which emphasized non-confrontational methods of combat. Dressed in black, Ninja moved like shadow warriors and used a variety of weapons, including *shuriken* (projectile metal stars) and *kusarikama* (a missile with a razor-sharp sickle on one end of a chain), examples of which are displayed in the Togakushi museum (see opposite).

According to legend, Ninjutsu was developed in the twelfth century when the warrior Togakure Daisuke retreated to the mountain forests of Iga, near Nara and met Kain Doshi, a monk on the run from political upheaval in China. Togakure studied Doshi's fighting ways and it was his descendants who devoloped them into the **Togakure-ryu school** of Ninjutsu. By the fifteenth century, there were some fifty family-based Ninjutsu schools across Japan, each jealously guarding their techniques.

Although the need for Ninja declined while Japan was under the peaceful rule of the Shogunate, the Tokugawa had their own force of Ninjutsu-trained warriors for protection. One ninja, Sawamura Yasusuke, even sneaked into the "black ship" of Commodore Perry in 1853 to spy on the foreign barbarians. Today, the Togakure-ryu school of Ninjutsu, emphasizing defence rather than offence, is taught by the 34th master, Hatsumi Masaaki, in Noda, Chiba-ken, just north of Tokyo.

The **Togakushi Okusha shrine** stands on the lower slopes of the jagged mountain, Togakushi-yama, which, according to ancient Shinto belief, was created when the god Amenotakjikarao tossed away the rock door of the cave where the Sun Goddess Amaterasu had been hiding (see p.781). The shrine is reached via a two-kilometre-long corridor of soaring cedar trees, and the truly adventurous can continue on along the route up the sharp ridge to the mountain summit – don't go unprepared, it's a strenuous route and you must write your name in the climbers' book at the start of the trail. Having looked round the inner shrine – a rustic collection of small wooden and stone buildings nestling under the rocks – the best option is to head back downhill along the pleasant and shaded woodland trails through the Togakushi Ōmine Recreational Forest to the attractive village of **CHŪSHA**, a good base for skiing in winter. Here you'll find the outer sanctuary of the shrine, the **Hōkōsha**, decorated with intricate wooden carvings, along with shops selling all manner of baskets and goods made of woven bamboo strips: the best one (where you can also see a basket-weaver at work) is downhill, opposite the Spar grocery store.

Chūsha has a couple of pleasant **accommodation** options, including the excellent-value *Togakushi Kōgen Yokokura Youth Hostel* (☎0262/54-2030, fax 54-2540; ①) which offers *tatami* dorms in a partly thatched, 150-year-old residence, five minutes' walk south of the shrine and near the ski resort. It's run by a friendly lady who speaks a little English and there's also a quaint log cabin café. On the road just north of Chūsha is *Pension Garnie* (☎0262/54-3130; ⑥), a convivial Western-style lodge with its own tennis court and two meals included in the rates. *Uzuraya*, in the thatched farmhouse opposite the Hōkōsha shrine, is Chūsha's top **restaurant** for freshly made soba; at weekends you'll have to stand in line for anything up to forty minutes for lunch.

## Obuse

Some 20km northeast of Nagano, the small town of **OBUSE** has several well-preserved Edo-era buildings, but its main attraction is the **Hokusai-kan** (daily: April–Oct 9am–5pm; Jan–March, Nov & Dec 9.30am–4.30pm; ¥500), a small museum displaying rare paintings and other works by the master of *ukiyo-e* woodblock prints, **Hokusai**

**Katsushika**. Pick up an English map of the town at Nagano's tourist information centre (see p.347) before setting off, so you can find your way straight from the station to the Hokusai-kan.

In 1842, the 83-year-old Hokusai was invited to live and work in Obuse by Takai Kōzan, the town's leading salt merchant and art lover. A special studio was built for the artist, and it was here that he completed four paintings for the ceilings of two large festival floats and a phoenix mural for the Ganshōin. The beautiful floats, decorated with dragons, seascapes and intricate carvings, are displayed in the museum along with some forty other works, including painted scrolls, delicate watercolours and woodblock prints. You can also watch a slide show on Hokusai's life, with English subtitles. The quiet **Ganshōin temple** (daily: April–Oct 9am–5pm; Jan–March, Nov & Dec 9.30am–4.30pm; ¥200), housing the phoenix mural, lies 1km east, towards the hills.

Opposite the Hokusai-kan is the **Takai Kōzan Memorial Hall** (daily: April–Oct 9am–5pm; Jan–March, Nov & Dec 9.30am–4.30pm; ¥200), the atmospheric former home of Hokusai's patron, who was also an accomplished artist and calligrapher. His drawings of ghosts and goblins are meant to be ironic comments on the turbulent early Meiji-era years and are quite intriguing, as is the giant mammoth sketch. In one of the rooms you can see long banners inscribed with *kanji* characters as well as the 2.5-metre-long brush used to paint them.

## Practicalities

Obuse is twenty minutes by **train** (¥650) from Nagano on the Nagano Dentetsu line. The museums are within easy walking distance of the station, but the best way of **getting around**, and also reaching Ganshōin temple, is to rent a bicycle from the station for around ¥340 per hour. If the weather is poor, take the shuttle bus that makes a circuit of the town's sights – all-day tickets cost ¥300.

Obuse is famous for its chestnut confectionery and one of the best places to sample these sweets and also **eat** lunch is *Senseki-tei*, which overlooks an exquisite ornamental garden – set menus here range from ¥500 to ¥2000. Nearby, is the *Obuse Guide Centre* (daily 9am–6pm), a smart modern café and Western-style **guesthouse** (☎0262/47-5050, fax 47-5700; ⑤) in a traditional, mustard-coloured building. You can pick up a map of the town here, if you don't already have one, and they rent out bicycles (¥400 for two hours).

# Ski resorts and onsen villages

Nagano-ken's spectacular mountains are home to several of Japan's best ski resorts and onsen villages. In the northeastern corner of the prefecture is the delightful **Nozawa Onsen**, self-proclaimed home of Japanese skiing and renowned hot spring village, with thirteen free bathhouses to dip into. West of Nagano is the skiing area known as **Hakuba**, a valley with seven different resorts to choose from, the most popular being Happo-one. **Shiga Kōgen**, 20km north of Nagano, is Japan's biggest skiing area, with 22 resorts sharing the same lift ticket. It lies within the Jōshinetsu Kōgen National Park, where you'll also find the village of **Yudanaka Onsen**, famous for its "snow monkeys" who splash about in their very own *rotemburo*.

## Nozawa Onsen

The most authentically Japanese skiing and hot-spring village around here is **NOZAWA ONSEN**, nestled at the base of Kenashi-yama (1650m), 50km northeast of Nagano. The ski resort, owned by the five thousand villagers, has a lively, yet traditional atmosphere, aided in no small part by the thirteen free bathhouses dotted along the narrow, twisting streets. Best of the lot is the **Ōyu bathhouse**, housed in a temple-

### NAGANO SKI & ONSEN RESORTS

| | | |
|---|---|---|
| **Nozawa Onsen** | *Nozawa Onsen* | 野沢温泉 |
| Marukaneya | *Marukaneya* | まるかねや |
| Museum of Skiing | *Sukii Hakubutsukan* | スキー博物館 |
| Nozawa St Anton Hotel | *Nozawa San Anton Hoteru* | 野沢サンアントンホテル |
| Pension Shune | *Penshon Shune* | ペンションシュネ |
| | | |
| **Hakuba** | *Hakuba* | 白馬 |
| Hakuba Valley Hotel | *Hakuba Bari Hoteru* | 白馬バリホテル |
| Happō-oné | *Happō-oné* | 八方尾根 |
| | | |
| **Shiga Kōgen** | *Shiga Kōgen* | 志賀高原 |
| Okushiga | *Okushiga* | 奥志賀 |
| Okushiga Kōgen Hotel | *Okushiga Kōgen Hoteru* | 奥志賀高原ホテル |
| Shiga Kōgen Prince Hotel | *Shiga Kōgen Purinsu Hoteru* | 志賀高原プリンスホテル |
| | | |
| **Yudanaka Onsen** | *Yudanaka Onsen* | 湯田中温泉 |
| Kameya Ryokan | *Kameya Ryokan* | 亀や旅館 |
| Kōrakukan | *Kōrakukan* | こうらく館 |
| Uotoshi Ryokan | *Uotoshi Ryokan* | うおとし旅館 |

like wooden building in the centre of the village; each side has two pools, one of which is so hot that it's almost impossible to get into.

Nozawa claims to be the "birthplace of Japanese skiing"; this was the place where, in 1930, Hannes Schneider, an Austrian who popularized the two pole technique, gave skiing demonstrations to an awestruck audience. One of the resort's runs is named after Schneider and photos of the man in action – impeccably dressed in suit and tie – can be seen in the **Japan Museum of Skiing** (daily except Thurs 9am–5pm; ¥300) in a white, church-like building at the bottom of the Hikage slope.

The resort, which hosted the biathlon events at the 1998 Olympics, has lots of English signs and varied terrain, from long easy runs for beginners to some challenging slopes for advanced skiers. A one-day lift pass costs ¥4600 and the season runs from mid-December to early May. If you can, time your visit to coincide with the spectacular **Doso-jin fire festival** held every January 15, when a burning portable shrine is paraded though the village.

JR trains runs to Togari-Nozawa-Onsen on the Iiyama line, around one hour by local train from Nagano; Nozawa Onsen is a twenty-minute bus or taxi ride from the station. It's also possible to catch direct buses from Nagano; check with the Nagano information officce for the timetable, or with the tourism section of the Nozawa village office (Mon–Fri 8.30am–5pm; ☎0269/85-3111), where there's an English speaker. Nozawa Onsen's **tourist information centre** (daily 8.30am–5.30pm), opposite the Ōyu bathhouse, has English brochures and maps.

**Accommodation** rates in Nozawa Onsen usually cover both breakfast and dinner. The prettiest place to stay is the Western-style *Pension Shune* (☎0269/85-2012; ⑥) on the mountainside – it's surrounded by snow in winter and flowers in summer, is run by a friendly couple who were once Olympic competitors, and has a great restaurant. For around the same price, you could also try the *Marukaneya* (☎0269/85-2203; ⑥), a recently refurbished inn closer to the village centre, with an English-speaking owner, offering *tatami* rooms and home-style cooking. In the heart of the village, near the restaurants and bars, is the upmarket, Western-style *Nozawa St Anton Hotel* (☎0269/85-3422; ⑦).

There are plenty of **restaurants** and cafés around the ski slopes; don't miss sampling *manjū*, deliciously plump dumplings with different fillings, best bought from the street vendors out of wooden steam boxes. To cool down after your onsen, slip into *Stay*, a convivial **bar** in the centre of town, named after the Jackson Brown song.

## Hakuba

There are more than a dozen ski areas around **Hakuba**, an impressive mountain range 60km northwest of Nagano, where many of top skiing events of the 1998 Olympics were held. The largest and most popular resort here is **HAPPŌ-ONE**, which has a wide range of runs covered by an extensive network of lifts (a one-day lift pass costs ¥4300). The village itself consists of an unruly gaggle of candy-coloured lodges, gift shops and cafés with silly English names, such as Coffee Cake Dude – but it makes a fine base for hiking and climbing in summer. A good English leaflet is available at the information centre in Nagano Station (see p.347) and covers some of the most popular hiking courses around here.

To get to Happō-One from Nagano, hop on a **bus** – the journey takes around an hour. By train the area is best reached from Matsumoto (see opposite) along the JR Ōito line. From Hakuba Station take a bus or taxi to Happō-One. A good place to **stay** is the friendly *Hakuba Valley Hotel* (☎0261/72-2448, fax 72-2137; ⑦), on the slopes of Nakiyama. This Japanese-style inn, popular with expats, is run by the English-speaking Hata-san. Rates include two meals, rooms are decorated with local pottery and there's a bar and pool table for après-ski socializing. To reach the hotel you need to take the chairlift up the slope from the Happō-One parking lot.

## Shiga Kōgen and Yudanka Onsen

The common complaint about Japanese ski resorts being too small certainly doesn't apply to mammoth **SHIGA KŌGEN**, a collection of 22 resorts strung out along the Shiga plateau within the Jōshinetsu Kōgen National Park, 20km northeast of Nagano. Between mid-December and late April, there's usually good snow here, and the huge variety of terrain makes the one-day ¥4900 lift pass, covering all 22 resorts, great value. You'll find it impossible to ski the whole area in a day, so the best plan of action is to head for northern end of the mountain range to the resorts at **Okushiga** and **Yakebitai-yama**, where the slalom events of the 1998 Olympics were held.

The closest **train station** to Shiga is Yudanaka (see below) – the ski resorts are a thirty-minute bus ride away from here. During the season, there are direct buses from Nagano to the resorts. The best **place to stay** in Okushiga is the comfortable, Western-style *Okushiga Kōgen Hotel* (☎0269/34-2034, fax 34-2827; ⑤–⑧); in Yakebitai you'll find the *Shiga Kōgen Prince Hotel* (☎0269/34-3111, fax 34-3132; ⑥–⑧), offering bland but reliably high-standard accommodation.

On the western fringe of the national park is the village of **YUDANAKA ONSEN** which has a small ski resort, Goringu Kōgen, but is more famous for the **snow monkeys** who bathe in a *rotemburo* at the nearby Jigokudani, or "Hell's Valley". Some two hundred Japanese long-tailed monkeys (*Nihon-zaru*) live in this area and they started to dip into the hot pools during the 1960s, when a local ryokan owner took pity on them and left food out in winter. The apes, dubbed snow monkeys by *Life* magazine, eventually had their own *rotemburo* built for them in a **Monkey Park** (daily 8am–5pm; ¥360). On winter mornings you can usually see them wallowing around the pool. Be warned though, that despite the amusing scene, the smell of droppings mingling with the sulphur in the water is less than pleasant. Winter is also the main mating season, so there's likely to be some simian hanky panky going on around the *rotemburo*.

Yudanaka is the terminus for the Nagano Dentetsu line from Nagano, forty minutes away by express train, and one hour by local train. From the station, it's a fifteen-minute bus journey to Kanbayashi Onsen. To reach the monkey pool, walk uphill from the bus stop until you find a sign for a trail leading through the woods for around 2km. On the way you'll pass the *Kōrakukan* (☎0269/33-4376, fax 33-3244; ⑥), a small ryokan offering basic Japanese-style accommodation, with rates which include two meals.

There are plenty more ryokan and minshuku in **Yudanaka Onsen**, one of the most convenient being the Japanese Inn Group member *Uotoshi Ryokan* (☎0269/33-1215, fax 33-0074; ④), seven minutes' walk from the station, across the Yomase-gawa. The owner is an expert in traditional archery (*kyūdō*) and is happy to demonstrate his skills if asked. Also worth checking out is the traditional *Kameya Ryokan* (☎0259/33-3585, fax 33-3587; ⑥), five minutes by bus from the station in nearby Shibu Onsen. This inn has lovely *tatami* rooms and its rates include two delicious meals.

# Matsumoto and around

Some 50km southwest of Nagano across the Hijiri Kōgen mountains is the prefecture's second largest city, **MATSUMOTO**, justly famous for its splendid **castle**, Matsumoto-jō, which has the oldest donjon (central keep) in Japan, dating from 1595. Also in the centre of this attractive town – gateway to the Japan Alps – is the **Nakamichi** area of traditional white-walled houses, many now renovated into ryokan and shops, while to the west is the **Japan Ukiyo-e Museum**, where beautiful traditional prints are displayed inside a surprisingly ugly modern building.

Matsumoto also has a reputation as a centre for classical music. It was the home of **Dr Suzuki Shini-ichi** (who died nine months short of his one-hundreth birthday in 1998), an internationally famous music teacher who encouraged children to learn to play instruments by using their natural gift for mimicry. His "Suzuki Method" is taught in the town's Suzuki Shin-ichi Talent Education Hall, around 1km east of Matsumoto Station. Every September Matsumoto also hosts the ten-day Saitō Kinen, a **classical music festival** in memory of another local talent, Saitō Hideo, celebrated conductor and mentor to many famous musicians, including Ozawa Seiji, director of the Boston Symphony Orchestra.

North of Matsumoto is the picturesque rural area of **Hotaka**, known for its *wasabi* (horseradish) farms and also a starting point for hikes up into the nearby Japan Alps. Serious mountaineers head straight from Matsumoto west to the beautiful lake and mountain resort of **Kamikōchi**, popularized by British missionary Walter Weston at the turn of the century. The mountains get so much snow that Kamikōchi is only open from late April to the end of October, when it can be very busy. A less crowded alternative is the nearby onsen and ski resort of **Norikura Kōgen**. The fabulous Skyline road runs through this area, across to Takayama in neighbouring Gifu-ken (see p.368); drive along it and you'll see why Nagano-ken is known as the "roof of Japan".

## Arrival, information, orientation and city transport

Matsumoto is connected to Nagano by **trains**, which take around an hour to get here, chugging across the mountains on the scenic Shinonoi line. From Nagoya, the limited express train takes two hours and thirty minutes. The fastest direct train from Tokyo is the Azusa limited express service from Shinjuku (2hr 45min). All long-distance **buses** stop in front of the train station. Matsumoto's small **airport** (☎0263/58-2517) is 8km southwest of the town centre; buses (¥540) are scheduled to meet the flights and take 25 minutes to reach the city centre.

You can pick up a town map from the excellent **tourist information office** (daily 9.30am–6pm; ☎0263/32-2814), outside Matsumoto Station, at the southern end of the building. This small bureau is staffed by friendly English speakers, who can make accommodation bookings and provide information on areas around Matsumoto, including the Japan Alps and Kamikōchi.

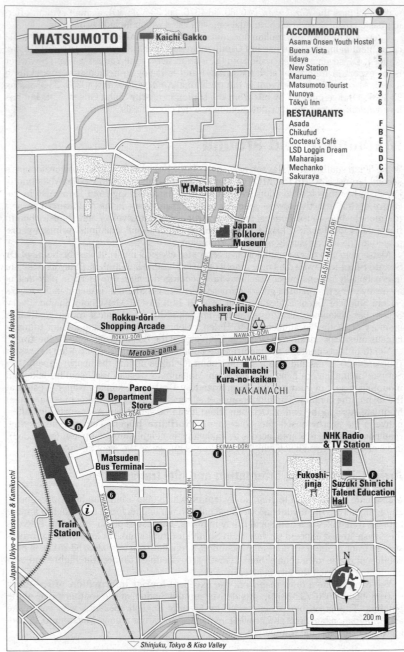

MATSUMOTO

Kaichi Gakko

**ACCOMMODATION**
Asama Onsen Youth Hostel 1
Buena Vista 8
Iidaya 5
New Station 4
Marumo 2
Matsumoto Tourist 7
Nunoya 3
Tōkyū Inn 6

**RESTAURANTS**
Asada F
Chikufud B
Cocteau's Café E
LSD Loggin Dream G
Maharajas D
Mechanko C
Sakuraya A

Matsumoto-jō

Japan Folklore Museum

HIGASHI-MACHI-DŌRI

DAIMYO-CHO-DŌRI

Yohashira-jinja

Rokku-dōri Shopping Arcade

ROKKU-DŌRI

NAWATE-DŌRI

Metoba-gama

NAKAMACHI

Nakamachi Kura-no-kaikan

NAKAMACHI

Parco Department Store

KOEN-DŌRI

EKIMAE-DŌRI

NHK Radio & TV Station

Matsuden Bus Terminal

HONMACHI-DŌRI

SHIRAKABA-DŌRI

Fukoshi-jinja

Suzuki Shin'ichi Talent Education Hall

Train Station

N

Hotaka & Hakuba

Japan Ukiyo-e Museum & Kamikochi

0    200 m

Shinjuku, Tokyo & Kiso Valley

## MATSUMOTO AND AROUND

| | | |
|---|---|---|
| **Matsumoto** | *Matsumoto* | 松本 |
| Japan Ukiyo-e Museum | *Nihon Ukiyo-e Bijutsukan* | 日本浮世絵美術館 |
| Matsumoto-jō | *Matsumoto-jō* | 松本城 |
| Nakamachi | *Nakamachi* | 中町 |

*ACCOMMODATION*
| | | |
|---|---|---|
| Asama Onsen Youth Hostel | *Asama Onsen Yūsu Hosuteru* | 浅間温泉ユースホステル |
| Hotel Buena Vista | *Hoteru Buena Bisuta* | ホテルブエナビスタ |
| Hotel Iidaya | *Hoteru Iidaya* | ホテル飯田屋 |
| Marumo | *Marumo* | まるも |
| Matsumoto Tourist Hotel | *Matsumoto Tsūristo Hoteru* | 松本ツーリストホテル |
| Hotel New Station | *Hoteru Nyu Sutēshon* | ホテルニューステーション |
| Nunoya | *Nunoya* | ぬのや |
| Tōkyū Inn | *Tōkyū In* | 東急イン |

*RESTAURANTS*
| | | |
|---|---|---|
| Asada | *Asada* | あさだ |
| Chikufudō | *Chikufudō* | ちくふどっ |
| Cocteau's Café | *Kokutōzu Kafue* | コクトウズカフェ |
| Mechanko | *Mechanko* | めちゃんこ |
| Sakuraya | *Sakuraya* | 桜家 |

| | | |
|---|---|---|
| **Hotaka** | *Hotaka* | 穂高 |
| Dai-ō Wasabi Farm | *Dai-ō Wasabi Nōjō* | だいおおわさび農場 |
| Rokuzan Art Museum | *Rokuzan Bijutsukan* | 碌山美術館 |

| | | |
|---|---|---|
| **Kamikōchi** | *Kamikōchi* | 上高地 |
| Gosenjaku Lodge | *Gosenjaku Rojji* | 五千尺ロッヂ |
| Kamikōchi Imperial Hotel | *Kamikōchi Teikoku Hoteru* | 上高地帝国ホテル |
| Nishiitoyasasō | *Nishiitoyasasō* | 西糸屋山荘 |
| Yari-ga-take | *Yari-ga-take* | 槍ヶ岳 |

| | | |
|---|---|---|
| **Norikura Kōgen** | *Norikura Kōgen* | 乗鞍高原 |
| Kyūka Mura | *Kyūka Mura* | 休暇村 |
| Lodge Suzurangoya | *Rojji Suzurangoya* | ロッジすずらんごや |
| Norikura Kōgen Youth Hostel | *Norikura Kōgen Yūsu Hosuteru* | 乗鞍高原ユースホステル |
| Pension Chimney | *Penshon Chimunii* | ペンションチムニー |

| | | |
|---|---|---|
| **Hirayu Onsen** | *Hirayu Onsen* | 平湯温泉 |

Most of Matsumoto's main sights are within easy walking distance of the train station. Heading due east from the station is Ekimae-dōri, crossed about 400m later by Honmachi-dōri which leads north over the Metoba river into the narrower Daimyō-chō-dōri up to the castle grounds. An alternative to walking is to rent a **bike** from the Nippon Rent-a-car office next to the tourist information booth (¥500 for two hours). **Local buses** from the Matsuden Bus Terminal, under the ESPA department store opposite Matsumoto Station, run north towards the onsen resort of Asama, where you'll find the local youth hostel – some buses pass near the castle along the way.

## Accommodation

The nicest area to **stay** is Nakamichi-dōri, where there are several good-value ryokan. The drab youth hostel is several kilometres from the city centre and has the usual curfew; if you want to enjoy a night on the town, check into one of the cheaper business hotels near the station.

**Asama Onsen Youth Hostel**, 1-7-15 Asama Onsen (☎0263/46-1335). Twenty minutes by bus from the JR station (take either the #6 or #7 from the bus terminal at the ESPA department store). Friendly management make up for the unappealing building and metal bunk beds. No meals are served. ②.

**Hotel Buena Vista**, 1-2-1 Honjo (☎0263/37-0111, fax 37-0666). Matsumoto's most opulent Western-style accommodation is five minutes' walk south of the station and has an excellent range of in-house restaurants and bars. ⑦.

**Hotel Iidaya**, 1-2-3 Chūō (☎0263/32-0027, fax 36-9223). Standard business hotel, just east of the station, with singles from ¥6500. ⑤.

**Marumo**, 3-3-10 Chūō (☎0263/32-0115). Appealing mix of old and modern Japan in this ryokan in a white-walled house and Meiji-era wooden building on the banks of the Metoba river. Has *tatami* rooms, a wooden bath, a small enclosed bamboo garden and a nice café. ⑤.

**Matsumoto Tourist Hotel**, 2-4-24 Fukashi (☎0263/33-9000, fax 36-6435). Small but decently decorated rooms in this business hotel five minutes' walk east of the station. The cheapest singles (¥5800) are in the older building. ⑤.

**Hotel New Station**, 1-1-11 Chūō (☎0263/35-3850, fax 35-3851). Good-value mid-range hotel, with quiet modern rooms, some with a Swiss-chalet feel to them. The attached *Izakaya Hakuba* is a smart place for a drink. ⑤.

**Nunoya**, 3-5-7 Nakamichi (☎ & fax 0263/32-0545). Delightful ryokan in a charming wooden building on Nakamichi-dōri, with high standard *tatami* rooms and separate bathroom and toilets. If you opt for meals, add about ¥3000 per person to the bill. ⑤.

**Tōkyū Inn**, 1-3-21 Fukashi (☎0263/36-0109, fax 36-0883). This mid-range chain hotel, a couple of minutes' walk south of the station, has good-sized rooms, but lacks atmosphere. ⑥.

## The City

Matsumoto's castle is its big attraction, but you'll find some nice surprises as you make your way to it. Check out the old houses along **Nakamachi-dōri**, which runs parallel to the southern bank of the Metoba river. Among the white-walled inns, antique shops and restaurants, look out for the Nakamachi Kura-no-Kaikan, a beautifully restored sake brewery with a soaring black-beam interior and traditional cross-hatching plasterwork outside. Cross over the river by any of several bridges and return to Daimyō-chō-dōri along the colourful market street Nawate-dōri. The castle grounds are just a couple of hundred metres north of here.

One of the great pleasures of approaching Matsumoto's castle is that it remains hidden from view until the very last moment. **Matsumoto-jō** (daily 8.30am–5pm; ¥520), also known as Karasu-jō (Crow Castle) because of its brooding black facade, makes its sudden dramatic appearance as you enter the outer grounds and approach the moat on which swans float by. The castle was started by the Ogasawara clan in 1504, but it was another lord, Ishikawa, who remodelled the fortress in 1593 and built the five-tier donjon that is now the oldest keep in Japan. You must take your shoes off before clambering up the dark, steep wooden stairs to the donjon's sixth storey (it has the traditional hidden floor of most Japanese castles) from which you can look out over the town and surrounding mountains. The entrance fee to the castle also includes access to the quirky **Japan Folklore Museum** (daily 8.30am–5pm), which is just before the moat. Inside, the displays include a good model of how Matsumoto looked in feudal times.

If you have time, head north of the castle for around 500m until you reach the attractive **Kaichi Gakkō** (Mon–Sat 8.30am–4.30pm; ¥310), the oldest Western-style school building in Japan, dating from 1876. It's just a dusty Victorian school inside, but the handsome, pale blue facade, decorated with temple-style plaster work, is worth a look.

Matsumoto's other main sight is the hideously modern, glass and concrete **Japan Ukiyo-e Museum** (Tues–Sun 10am–5pm; ¥900), some 3km west of the station, which houses 100,000 woodblock prints, including works by the great masters Hiroshige Utagawa and Hokusai Katsushika. Only a fraction of the museum's splendid collection is ever on display, and an English leaflet is available to help guide you around. The simplest way to reach the museum is to hop in a taxi, which will cost around ¥2000 from the town centre.

## Eating and drinking

Matsumoto is well served with places to **eat**, particularly around the train station. The local speciality is *shinshu* (the old name for Nagano) soba, best eaten cold in summer (ask for *zaru-soba*). A more expensive – and delicious – delicacy is *zazumushi*, eel steamed inside rice wrapped in bamboo leaves. There are several **bars** south of the station, one of the most popular being the *Gum Tree*, behind the *Hotel Buena Vista*, run by an Australian, and serving cans of Fosters and Castlemaine as well as Mexican snacks.

**Asada**, Fukashi. In a traditional white-walled building behind the NHK radio and TV station, this restaurant has the best reputation for soba in Matsumoto. Tues–Sun 11am–4pm.

**Chikufudō**. Local rice dishes and sweets made with chestnuts are served at this chain restaurant in one of the old whitewashed houses on Nakamachi-dōri. Set meals start at ¥900.

**Cocteau's Café**, Ekimae-dōri. Quietly trendy café and bar just after the crossing with Honmachi-dōri. The set lunch is good value at ¥750, while dinner costs ¥2800 and there's excellent French coffee.

**LSD Loggin Dream**, Honjo. American-style pizza parlour and bar facing the small park in front of the *Hotel Buena Vista*. There's an English menu and the place stays open until 2am.

**Maharajas**, 1 Chūō. Indian dishes are served with huge nan breads in this brightly decorated basement restaurant across from the station. Does a good-value set lunch for ¥700.

**Mechanko**, 1-7-2 Chūō. Large-scale sushi bar and *izakaya*, a couple of minutes' walk north of the station. For once, the food looks better than the photographs in the menu. The all-you-can-eat-and-drink set menus for ¥2300 are great value. Open daily 5pm–5am.

**Sakuraya**, 4-9-1 Ōtemachi (☎0263/33-2660). Elegant and traditional restaurant, with waitresses in kimonos, on the corner one block east of Daimyō-dōri. Eel dishes (*unagi*) are the speciality, and a set meal costs ¥2100.

## Hotaka

Thirty minutes by local train north of Matsumoto lies the quiet country town of **HOTAKA**, a base for hiking in the alps to the west and well known for its production of *wasabi*, the fiery green horseradish that, in a paste, accompanies sushi and sashimi. The best way to explore this tranquil area is to pick up a map from the **tourist information office** (May–Oct 9am–5pm; Jan–April, Nov & Dec 10am–3pm), to the right of the station exit, rent a bicycle from one of the many outlets around here (¥300 an hour, or ¥1500 for a day) and head east out of town through the paddy fields. Keep an eye open along the country roads for the charming *dosojin*, small stones on which guardian deity couples have been carved.

Some 2km east of Hotaka is the enjoyably touristy **Dai-ō Wasabi Farm** (9am–5pm; free). This is one of the largest such farms in Japan and the vast fields of *wasabi* growing in wide, waterlogged gravel trenches make an impressive sight. Within the landscaped grounds you can sample *wasabi* in all manner of foods, including ice-cream, which is surprisingly tasty.

Back in Hotaka, a ten-minute walk north of the station along a red-stone paved footpath will bring you to the serene **Rokuzan Art Museum** (Tues–Sun 9am–5pm; ¥500), an ivy-covered, church-like building and a couple of modern galleries. The museum houses the sculptures of Rokuzan Ogiwara, known in Japan as the "Rodin of the Orient". The artist, whose talent was cut short with his death at 32, was clearly influenced by the French master, but he also turned his hand to painting and sketches, some of which are also on display.

# Kamikōchi

Tucked away in the northern Alps at 1500m is the beautiful mountaineering and hiking resort of **KAMIKŌCHI**, nestling in the Azusa valley. Hardly more than a bus station and a handful of hotels scattered along the Azusa-gawa, Kamikōchi has some stunning alpine scenery, which can only be viewed between late April and the end of October before heavy snow blocks off the narrow roads and the resort shuts down for winter. As a result, during season the places buzzes with tourists and the prices at its few hotels and restaurants are as steep as the surrounding mountains.

Kamikōchi's history as a tourist destination dates back to the turn of the century, when British missionary **Walter Weston** (see box opposite) helped popularize the area as a base for climbing the craggy peaks known as the Northern Alps. The highest mountain here is the 3190-metre Hotaka-dake, followed by Yariga take (3180m). Both are extremely popular climbs; one trail up Yariga take has been dubbed the *Ginza Jūsō* (traverse), after Tokyo's busy shopping area, because it gets so crowded. However, the congestion on the mountain is nothing compared to that found at its base, where, at the height of the season, thousands of day-trippers tramp through the well-marked trails along the Azusa valley. The best way to appreciate Kamikōchi is to stay overnight so you can experience the valley minus the crowds in the evening and early morning. Alternatively, come here in June, when frequent showers put off fair-weather walkers.

## Hiking around Kamikōchi

With an early start, the scenic spots of the Azusa valley can all be covered in a day's **hike**. Pick up the English *Kamikōchi Pocket Guide* from the information office at the bus stop for a good map of all the main trails. On the way to the bus stop you'll pass the entrance to the valley, with its fantastic view across the Taishō-ike, a glass-like pond reflecting the snow-capped peaks: this is the best place to head first. The hour-long amble starts along the pebbly river bank and splits after the Tashiro bridge, one leg continuing beside the Azusa-gawa, the other following a nature-observation trail along wooden walkways, over chocolaty marshes. The Taishō-ike was formed when the Azusa-gawa was naturally dammed up after the eruption of the nearby volcano Yake-dake in 1915 and dead tree trunks still poke out of the water. Rowing boats can be rented from the hotel here for ¥800 for thirty minutes.

Returning the way you came, cross over the Tashiro bridge to the opposite bank of the river, where the path leads past some of Kamikōchi's hotels and the rock-embedded relief sculpture of Walter Weston. In the centre of the village the river is spanned by the much-photographed wooden suspension bridge Kappa-bashi. Cross this and continue north for a couple of minutes to the **visitors' centre** (daily 9am–5pm) where there are nature displays and evocative black and white photographs of Kamikōchi in times past.

The return trip north from the visitors' centre to the picturesque pond, Myōjin-ike, with its excellent lunch spot (see p.364), tiny shrine and mallard ducks, will take you around two hours if covered at a leisurely pace. The crowds begin to thin on this trail and really drop away on the "six-hour course" up the valley to the Tokusawa campground and the Shinmura suspension bridge, named after a famous climber, Shinmura Shoichi.

## Climbing around Kamikōchi

Beyond Tokusawa the serious hiking begins. The steep hike up the "Matterhorn of Japan" (so-called because of its craggy appearance), to the mountain huts at Ichinomata on the lower slopes of **Yariga-take** takes around five hours, and can be done in a long day from Kamikōchi. There are huts on the mountain for overnight stays; a futon and two meals costs around ¥8000 per person, but things can get very crowded during the season.

Reaching the summit of Yariga-take may well give you a taste for mountaineering. The popular route to follow is due south across the alpine ridge to **Hotaka-dake** (also known as Oku-Hotaka-dake), the third highest peak in Japan, a three-day loop that will bring you back to Kamikōchi. The route is well covered in the excellent *Hiking in Japan* by Paul Hunt (see Books, p.817).

An adventurous option for approaching Kamikōchi across the mountains from the west is to take the **cable car** (one way ¥1500, return ¥2800; ¥300 extra for large backpacks) up from Shin-Hotaka Onsen in **Gifu-ken**. This onsen resort, best reached by bus from Takayama (see p.368), has the longest cable car ride in the whole of Asia, which takes you halfway to the 2908-metre summit of Nishi-Hotaka-dake; from here Kamikōchi is a three-hour hike southeast.

Make sure you pack warm, waterproof clothing, as the weather can change rapidly in the mountains and even at the height of summer, temperatures on the peaks can be freezing, especially early in the morning.

## Practicalities

Private vehicles are banned in the village. If you're **driving**, park your car at the Sawando parking lot in the village of Nakanoyu, 8km outside Kamikōchi, for ¥500 a day. From here buses (¥1000) and taxis (¥4000) make regular runs to and from Kamikōchi, passing through narrow rock tunnels.

To get here from Matsumoto, take a twenty-minute **train** journey on the Matsumoto Dentetsu line to Shin-Shimashima Station (¥680), then transfer to a bus (¥2000), which takes one hour and fifteen minutes to reach Kamikōchi. From Takayama, hop on the bus to Hirayu Onsen (¥1530), where you'll have to transfer to the Kamikōchi bus (¥1550), which travels along the scenic Norikura Skyline Road. There's also a daily bus service between Norikura Kōgen (see overleaf) and Kamikōchi. Once you've arrived, make sure you reserve your seat on a bus *out* of Kamikōchi; the sheer number of visitors leaves many people at the mercy of the taxi drivers.

---

### WALTER WESTON

Born in Derbyshire, England, in 1861, British missionary **Walter Weston** was 29 years old when he first set foot in the mountains of Nagano-ken. Weston favoured Kamikōchi as a base from which to climb what he called "the grandest mountains in Japan" and he frequently visited the tiny village from his home in Kōbe. The phrase "Japan Alps" was actually coined by another Englishman, William Gowland, whose *Japan Guide* was published in 1888, but it was Weston's *Climbing and Exploring in the Japan Alps*, which appeared eight years later, that really put the peaks on the mountaineers' maps. Previously, these mountains, considered sacred, were only climbed by Shinto and Buddhist priests, but in fast-modernizing Japan, alpinism caught on as a sport and Weston became its acknowledged guru. Although he is honoured in Kamikōchi with a monument and a festival in his name on the first weekend in June, at the start of the climbing season, Weston is said to have wept at the prospect of mass tourism ruining his beloved mountains. His ghost can take comfort from the fact that the area's beauty survives largely intact, despite Kamikōchi's popularity.

There's an **information centre** (9.30am–5pm) at the bus terminal where you can pick up a good English map, showing the main hiking trails. The assistants don't speak English, so if you need more information or want to arrange accommodation, do this in Matsumoto (see p.357) before setting out.

The most convenient **campsite** is at Konashidaira (¥400 per person per night), just beyond the Kappa-bashi, near a visitors' centre. Otherwise the best budget option is in the large dorm at *Nishi-itoyasa-sō* (☎0263/95-2206, fax 95-2208; ④), which has both bunk beds and *tatami* areas. The rates here include two meals – a good deal for Kamikōchi. *Nishi-itoyasa-sō* also run a ryokan, where the rates are slightly pricer than those for the smallest rooms at the upmarket *Gosenjaku Lodge* (☎0263/95-2221; ⑦), next door. If you really want to push the boat out, book into the luxurious Western-style *Kamikōchi Imperial Hotel* (☎0263/95-2001, fax 95-2006); ⑧). Putting up at the excellent youth hostel in Norikura Kōgen (see opposite) and travelling into Kamikōchi for the day is also a viable option.

**Eating** options are a bit limited; most hotels serve up standard soba and curry rice at inflated prices. If you're visiting for the day or are planning a hike into the mountains, bring food with you. For lunch, *Kamonjigoya* beside Myōjin-ike, is worth stopping at for the *iwana* (river trout) lunch at ¥1500. The fish are roasted on sticks beside an *irori* (charcoal fire), making this an ideal refuge if the weather turns nasty.

## Norikura Kōgen Onsen

**NORIKURA KŌGEN**, an alpine village some 30km southwest of Matsumoto, isn't nearly as crowded as Kamikōchi and has some splendid mountain scenery, easy hiking trails and onsen baths. In winter, ski lifts whisk skiers up the lower slopes of **Norikura-dake**, while in summer the hike to the peak of the same mountain can be accomplished in an hour and thirty minutes from the parking lot where the Echo Line road leaves Nagano-ken and becomes the **Skyline Road** in Gifu-ken. This is the highest road in Japan, providing spectacular mountain-top views (the upper section is closed from November to June). The parking lot is an hour's drive from Norikura Kōgen; there is no public transport on this route.

The village is really no more than several widely spread out hotels and lodges. The closest thing to a centre is probably the modern onsen complex **Yukemuri-kan** (daily except Tues 10.30am–9pm; ¥700), which has both indoor wooden baths and *rotemburo* with mountain views. The nearby **Norikura Kōgen Visitors' Centre** (daily except Wed 9am–5pm; free) has unremarkable geology and nature displays in Japanese only; it's better to head on west towards the ski lifts. Continuing on foot up the mountain for around an hour, you'll reach the start of a short trail to **Sanbon-daki**, where three waterfalls converge in one pool.

An alternative route from the ski lifts is to hike south for twenty minutes to another beautiful waterfall, **Zengoro-no-taki**, reached along a clearly marked nature trail, with signs in English. In the morning, a rainbow often forms in the spray across this impressive fall. Twenty minutes' hike south of Zengoro, the small reflecting pond, **Ushidome**, provides a perfect view of the mountains. Continuing downhill from the pond, you can choose to walk towards another small lake, **Asami-ko**, or to the main picnic area, **Ichinose**, a picturesque spot at the confluence of two streams. A cycle and walking track leads directly north from Ichinose back to Yukemuri-kan, where the best plan of action is to soak in the *rotemburo*.

### Practicalities

Norikura Kōgen can be reached by infrequent **buses** from both Shin-Shimashima train station on the Matsumoto Dentetsu line (see previous page), and Takayama (see p.368), with a change of buses at Tatamidaira and Hirayu Onsen. From June to October there's also a daily bus between Norikura Kōgen and Kamikōchi. Some of these buses only run once a day, so it's best to check with local tourist offices on the current timetables in advance of your journey.

There's a **tourist information office** (daily 9.30am–4.30pm) opposite the Yukemurikan onsen complex; the staff don't speak English, but can provide a hiking map (in Japanese) of the area. Bicycles are handy for getting around and can be rented at the gift shop across from the visitors' centre for ¥500 a day.

As far as **accommodation** goes, the *Norikura Kōgen Youth Hostel* (☎0263/93-2748, fax 93-2162; ②), five minutes' walk north from the bus stop, and next to the ski lifts, is ideally placed for quick access to the slopes. The young, friendly staff can arrange ski rental (¥2000) and point out the most interesting hikes during the summer. Opposite the ski-lifts is *Pension Chimney* (☎0263/93-2902; ⑥), an appealing, European-style chalet with a steep, sloping roof and cosy rooms. Rates here include two meals and in the winter there's a heating charge. A similar deal is available at the large and friendly *Lodge Suzurangoya* (☎0263/93-2001, fax 93-2003; ⑥), near the tourist information office. The old rooms are the cheapest, but they're in good condition and in the same building. The "vacation village", *Kyūka Mura* (☎0263/93-2304, fax 93-2392; ⑥), near Ushidome pond, has fine *tatami* rooms and offers rates which include two meals – and an extra heating charge in the winter. For **eating**, you can get good, inexpensive Japanese food at *Kyūka Mura* café, where you pay first, are given a tag with a number and your meal is brought to you.

# The Kiso valley

For a taste of how Japan once looked, minus the concrete buildings and neon signs, head for the densely forested river valley of **Kiso**, southwest of Matsumoto, between the Central and Northern Alps. Shogun Tokugawa Ieyasu chose this valley as part of the route for the 550-kilometre Nakasendō, one of the five main highways linking his capital Edo (present-day Tokyo) with the rest of Japan. Eleven post towns (*juku*) lined the Kisoji (Kiso road) section of the Nakasendō, and three of them – **Narai, Tsumago** and **Magome** – have been preserved as virtual museums of the feudal past. This is also

## THE KISO VALLEY

| | | |
|---|---|---|
| **Narai** | *Narai* | 奈良井 |
| Iseya | *Iseya* | 伊勢屋 |
| Nakamura House | *Nakamura-tei* | 中村邸 |
| **Magome** | *Magome* | 馬籠 |
| Sakanoie | *Sakanoie* | 坂の家 |
| Tajimaya | *Tajimaya* | 但馬屋 |
| Tōson Kinenkan | *Tōson Kinenkan* | 藤村記念館 |
| **Tsumago** | *Tsumago* | 妻籠 |
| Daikichi | *Daikichi* | 大吉 |
| Kiso-Ryojoan Youth Hostel | *Kiso-Ryojoan Yūsu Hosuteru* | 木曽旅情庵ユースホステル |
| Matsushiro-ya | *Matsushiro-ya* | 松代屋 |
| Okuya Kyōdokan | *Okuya Kyōdokan* | 奥谷郷土館 |
| **Nagiso** | *Nagiso* | 南木曽 |
| **Kiso-Fukushima** | *Kiso-Fukushima* | 木曽福島 |
| **Nakatsugawa** | *Nakatsugawa* | 中津川 |

good **hiking** terrain; Tsugamo and Magome are linked by an easy three-hour hiking trail which follows the original route of the Nakasendō over the hills and through the forests.

## Narai

The thirty-fourth post town on the Nakasendō, attractive **NARAI**, 30km southwest of Matsumoto, was the most prosperous of the eleven *juku* along the Kisoji. The village's distinctive wooden buildings, with window shutters and *renji-gōshi* lattice work, have been beautifully preserved – Narai's only drawback are the cars that pass through the main street, making it hard to forget what century you're in.

The main road of restored houses and shops stretches for around 1km south from the train station at the north end of the village. Look out for the shop selling *kasira ningyō*, colourfully painted, traditional dolls and toys made of wood. About halfway down the road stands **Nakamura House** (daily 9am–4.30pm; ¥200), dating from the 1830s and once the home of a merchant who made his fortune in combs, one of the area's specialities. Side streets lead off to pretty temples and shrines in the foothills and on the other side, to the rocky banks of the Narai-gawa crossed by the Kiso-no-Ōhashi, an arched wooden bridge.

Narai is a forty-five-minute **train** journey from Matsumoto along the Chūō line. A lovely place to **stay** is *Iseya* (☎0264/34-3051; ⑥), a minshuku in a traditional house along the main street, with an ornamental garden – rates include two meals. Dotted along the main street are several **cafés** with soaring wooden-beamed ceilings and *irori*, central charcoal fires, serving soba noodles and other local dishes.

## Magome

The most southerly of the Kisoji's eleven *juku* is steeply-raked **MAGOME**, 55km south of Narai. Standing 800m up in the hills above the Kiso valley, Magome means "horse basket", because this was where travellers on the Nakasendō were forced to leave their nags before tackling the mountainous stretch of road ahead. Plaster and wooden buildings line either side of the stone-flagged path – many of the wooden roofs are still held down by stone. Despite appearances, most of the town's buildings date from the twentieth century, the village having suffered a history of fires, the most recent being in 1915, when 42 houses burnt to the ground.

Magome is famous for its native son, **Tōson Shimazaki** (1872–1943), an author whose historical novel, *Yoake Mae* (Before the Dawn), put the town on Japan's literary map. In the middle of the village, the **Tōson Kinenkan** (daily 8.30am–4.30pm; ¥500), celebrates the life of the author, and makes a pretty place to stroll around. The reverentially displayed fragments of Tōson's life are labelled in Japanese only.

To start the **hike** to Tsumago (see box) continue up the hill, past the *kōsatsu*, the old town notice board on which the Shogunate posted rules and regulations. The most notorious rule condemned to death anyone found illegally logging trees in the forests. The steepest part of the three-hour hike is over once you've reached the Magome-tōge (pass), where an old teahouse is beside the road and a stone monument engraved with a lyrical verse by the haiku master Shiki Masaoka (see p.641). From here, the route enters the forest and later passes two waterfalls, Ō-dake and Me-dake.

The closest **train station** to Magome is in the town of Nakatsugawa, just across the border in Aichi-ken, a fifty-five-minute journey northeast of Nagoya (see p.390) by limited express. **Buses** to Nakatsugawa also run from Nagoya. The bus journey up to Magome from outside Nakatsugawa Station (¥530) takes around thirty minutes.

Magome's **tourist information office** (daily 8.30am–5pm; ☎0264/59-2336), opposite the Tōson Kinenkan, has an English map of the area and the staff (who don't speak

English) can help with accommodation bookings at the village's numerous minshuku. Two good **places to stay** are *Sakanoie* (☎ 0264/59-2148; ⑥), which has a giant water-wheel outside, and *Tajimaya* (☎0264/59-2048; ⑥), further up the hill towards the information office – both places include two meals in their rates.

## Tsumago

Just thirty years ago the now thriving village of **TSUMAGO**, 80km south of Matsumoto, was virtually a ghost town, with most of its traditional Edo-era houses on the point of collapse. The concerted efforts of the locals helped restore the wooden houses that now line the long main street, earned the village protected status and helped spark the idea of cultural preservation across Japan. Electricity poles and TV antennae have been banished from sight so that the scene that greets you on the pedestrian-only street is probably very similar to that encountered by lords and their *samurai* passing through the village hundreds of years ago.

The highlight in Tsumago is the folk museum, **Okuya Kyōdokan** (daily 9am–4.45pm; ¥600), inside a rambling mansion that was once one of the villages' designated post inns where the *daimyō*'s retinue rested. Inside is a fine range of exhibits on the history of the Nakasendō and the village, including photographs showing just how dilapidated Tsumago once was. For an extra ¥100 you can also enter the Kyū-honjin on the opposite side of the street – this was where the *daimyō* used to stay. The front porch, when it's not thronged with day-trippers, is a fine place to sit and soak up Tsumago's quiet atmosphere. For a bird's-eye view of the village, head uphill to the former site of Tsumago castle, destroyed sometime in the late-sixteenth century. To get to the hill, follow the path just outside the village on the hiking route to Nagiso (see below).

The closest **train station** to Tsumago is at Nagiso, from where the village is an hour's walk south or a ten-minute bus ride. There's a **tourist information booth** beside Nagiso station, where you can pick up a map of the area, and another booth in the centre of Tsumago (daily except Wed 9am–5pm), where you can get help with accommodation and arrange to have your bag forwarded if you're planning to hike to Magome. Two good **places to stay** are the friendly minshuku *Daikichi* (☎0264/57-2595; ⑤), at the northern end of the village, where the rates include two meals of local specialities, and the more upmarket, 140-year-old *Matsushiro-ya* (☎0264/57-3022; ⑦), a ryokan in the centre of Tsumago with large *tatami* rooms and a shared bathroom.

---

### HIKING THE KISOJI

The traditional way of **hiking the Kisoji** is to go from Magome to Tsumago and experience how tough the initial climb up into the mountains is. Although the route is frequently signposted in English, it's a good idea to pick up a map from one of the tourist information offices before you start. If you don't fancy lugging around your bags, there's a baggage forwarding service in operation between March and November, charging ¥500 per piece, to and from the tourist information offices in both Tsumago and Magome. This service is offered daily from late July to the end of August and on the weekends and national holidays only at other times.

If you choose to walk in the easier direction downhill to Magome, start at Nagiso Station on the Chūō line, from which Tsumago is an hour's walk south through picturesque fields and small villages. If you're staying at the youth hostel near Kiso-Fukushima (see overleaf) and you want to walk the official route, it's still a good idea to alight at Nagiso and catch the bus to Magome, since this is cheaper than continuing on to Nakatsugawa and taking a bus from there. You'll need a whole day to explore both post towns and to complete the hike and you'll enjoy the experience all the more if you stay in either Tsumago or Magome overnight.

The area's only **youth hostel**, *Kiso-Ryōjōan* (☎0264/23-7716; ①), is nowhere near either Tsumago or Magome, but it's a gem worth making a detour for. Twenty-five minutes by bus from Kiso-Fukushima Station on the Chūō line between Narai and Nagiso, the hostel is in a large traditional building in the peaceful mountain village of **Ohara**. Excellent food, including *nabe* stews and *sukiyaki* (a succulent beef dish), is served by very friendly staff, and frequent bus connections to Kiso-Fukushima means you can use the hostel as a base from which to explore the valley's post towns.

There's no shortage of lunch-time **restaurants** and cafés in Tsumago. Most places serve *sansai soba* (buckwheat noodles topped with mountain vegetables) and *goheimochi* (balls of pounded rice on a skewer coated with a sweet nut sauce). A good place to sample these local specialities is *Enoki*, a bustling café a few doors north of the Okuya Kyōdokan museum.

# Takayama and around

On the Gifu-ken side of the Central Alps range, in an area known as Hida, lies the lovely town of **TAKAYAMA**, 110km northeast of Nagoya (see p.390). Once an enclave of skilled carpenters, employed by emperors to build palaces and temples in Kyoto and Nara, Takayama is now a sprawling, modern town, although most of its old merchant houses, small museums, tranquil temples and shrines are clustered into a compact area. Add on the area's specialized crafts and cuisine, not to mention warm-hearted locals, and you'll realize why it brings in the crowds. The best time to visit is out of sea-

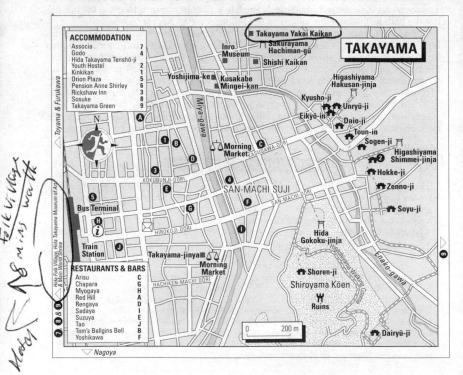

## TAKAYAMA AND FURUKAWA

| **Takayama** | *Takayama* | 高山 |
| Hida Folk Village | *Hida Minzoku-mura* | 飛騨民族村 |
| Hida Takayama Museum of Art | *Hida Takayama Bijutsukan* | 飛騨高山美術館 |
| Higashiyama Teramachi | *Higashiyama Teramachi* | 東山寺町 |
| Inrō Museum | *Inrō Bijutsukan* | 印籠美術館 |
| Kusakabe Mingei-kan | *Kusakabe Mingei-kan* | 日下部民芸館 |
| San-machi Suji | *San-machi Suji* | 三町筋 |
| Shishi Kaikan | *Shishi Kaikan* | 獅子会館 |
| Takayama-jinya | *Takayama-jinya* | 高山陣屋 |
| Takayama Yatai Kaikan | *Takayama Yatai Kaikan* | 高山屋台会館 |

*ACCOMMODATION*

| Hotel Associa | *Hoteru Asoshia* | ホテルアソシア |
| Godo | *Godo* | ごど |
| Hida Takayama Tenshō-ji Youth Hostel | *Hida Takayama Tenshō-ji Yūsu Hosuteru* | 飛騨高山天照寺ユースホステル |
| Kinkikan | *Kinkikan* | 金亀館 |
| Orion Plaza Hotel | *Orion Puraza Hoteru* | オリオンプラザホテル |
| Pension Anne Shirley | *Penshon An Shārī* | ペンションアンシャーリー |
| Rickshaw Inn | *Rikisha In* | 力車イン |
| Sosuke | *Sosuke* | 物助 |
| Takayama Green Hotel | *Takayama Guriin Hoteru* | 高山グリーンホテル |

*RESTAURANTS*

| Arisu | *Arisu* | アリス |
| Myōgaya | *Myōgaya* | みょうがや |
| Sadaya | *Sadaya* | さだや |
| Suzuya | *Suzuya* | 寿々や |
| Yoshikawa | *Yoshikawa* | よしかわ |

| **Furukawa** | *Furukawa* | 古川 |
| Furukawa Festival Hall | *Furukawa Matsuri Kaikan* | 古川まつり会館 |
| Hida Craftsman Culture Hall | *Hida-no-Sanshōkan* | 飛騨の山樵館 |
| Hida Furukawa Youth Hostel | *Hida Furukawa Yūsu Hosuteru* | 飛騨古川ユースホステル |
| Shirakabe-dozō | *Shirakabe-dozō* | 白壁土蔵 |

son or during the week, when it's quiet enough to appreciate the town's timeless atmosphere.

Takayama is famous throughout Japan for two of its **festivals** – the Sannō Matsuri (April 14–15) and the Yahata Matsuri (October 9–10). During these events eleven huge, elaborate floats, adorned with mechanical dolls (*karakuri*), are paraded around town, a spectacle which attracts hundreds of thousands of visitors.

You can also view these fabulous floats (*yatai*) at nearby **Furukawa**, a small town which, with its old houses, museums and temples is like a mini-Takayama, minus the crowds. Less accessible by public transport, but very popular with the tour bus brigade, are the picturesque villages in the **Shirakawa-gō** and **Gokayama valleys**, northwest of Takayama, where three villages of *gasshō-zukuri* A-frame thatched houses have been designated a UNESCO World Heritage Site.

## Arrival, information, getting around and accommodation

Takayama is connected by **train** to both Toyama (see p.378) in the north and Nagoya (see p.390) in the south. The bus terminus for services from Hirayu Onsen, where you'll need to transfer if you've taken the bus from Kamikōchi (see p.362), is next to Takayama Station, which is ten minutes' walk west of the San-machi Suji district, where many of the town's main sights are.

Staff at the **Hida tourist information office** (daily: April–Oct 8.30am–6.30pm; Jan–March, Nov & Dec 8.30am–5pm; ☎0577/32-5328), immediately in front of the JR station, are among the most clued-up you'll come across in this area – and there's always an English-speaker in the office. You can borrow a CD player to listen to recorded commentaries on local sights, history and tradition. The *Rickshaw Inn* (see Accommodation, below) also acts a tourist office – you can drop in to ask questions, pick up their restaurant map or just to read the daily English paper.

Takayama is best explored on foot or by **bicycle**. Bikes can be rented from the car park to the right of the station (¥300 per hour, ¥1300 per day) and, less expensively, from the youth hostel (see below) for ¥600 per day.

### Accommodation

If you're planning on **staying** in Takayama during either of the festivals, be sure to book well ahead. The best places are the town's ryokan and minshuku – a bit pricier than the business hotels near the train station, but a lot more atmospheric, and usually offering rates that include breakfast and dinner.

**Hotel Associa**, 1134 Echigo-chō (☎0577/36-0001, fax 36-0188). Elegant luxury hotel, eight minutes' drive southwest of Takayama Station, in the hills overlooking the town. It has several smart restaurants and bars and is next to *Kur Alp*, a modern onsen complex with baths, saunas, a swimming pool and a waterslide. A free-shuttle bus runs to and from the station. [7]–[8].

**Godo**, Kamisanno-machi (☎0577/33-0870). In the heart San-machi Suji, you pass through a low, paper-covered door to enter this quirkily-decorated ryokan. No English is spoken, so you might need to get some help making a booking from the information centre. [6].

**Hida Takayama Tenshō-ji Youth Hostel**, 83 Tenshō-ji-machi (☎0577/32-6345, fax 35-2986). If you don't mind the usual rules, this hostel, attached to one of the nicer temples in Teramachi, is a good (and tranquil) place to stay. For ¥1000 extra you can have a room to yourself, including a TV. Take a bus from the station to the Betsuin-mae stop and walk east for another couple of minutes. Bikes can be rented for ¥600 a day. [1].

**Kinkikăn**, 48 Asahimachi (☎0577/32-3131, fax 32-3130). Edo-period ryokan, a world away from modern Japan, where maids in kimono attend your needs in *tatami* rooms, decorated with local crafts. Most of the rooms overlook the beautiful 300-year-old garden. [8].

**Orion Plaza Hotel**, 6-15 Hana-satochiya (☎0577/34-5677, fax 34-5676). The large sign on the side of this business hotel beside the station offers rooms from ¥3600. For this you'll get a cramped, no-frills single room without bathroom – the cheapest hotel deal in Takayama. [4].

**Pension Anne Shirley**, 87 1297-1 Yamaguchi-chō (☎0577/32-6606, fax 36-0605). Delightful Western-style pension on the western edge of town, run by an English-speaking couple. There are also some *tatami* rooms, and evening meals (¥3000) include local delicacies such as *iwana* river trout. If you book in advance, the owner will pick you up at 5pm from the station. [5].

**Rickshaw Inn**, 54 Suehiro-chō (☎0577/32-2890, fax 320-2469). Friendly English-speaking owners run this excellent-value inn in the heart of town, with mainly *tatami* rooms – all furnished to a high standard. You can relax in the comfy lounge with a daily English newspaper and magazines and cook in a small kitchen. The cheapest single rooms are ¥4200. [5].

**Sosuke**, 1-64 Okamoto-machi (☎0577/32-0818). Good-value traditional minshuku, about ten minutes' walk west of the station, opposite the *Takayama Green Hotel*. If you have meals, add at least ¥3000 extra per person. [4].

**Takayama Green Hotel**, 2-180 Nishinoishiki-chō (☎0577/33-5500, fax 32-4434). The highlight of this vast upmarket hotel, eight minutes' walk west of the station, are its spacious onsen baths, which include landscaped *rotemburo* (open to the public 3–7pm; ¥1000). There's also a good range of restaurants, including one overlooking a Japanese-style garden. [8].

# The Town

Top of your sightseeing priorities should be the **Hida Folk Village**, an open-air museum of traditional houses gathered from all over the region into a park on the west side of Takayama. In the centre of town, across the Miya-gawa river, the **San-machi Suji** area of old merchants' houses is also a highlight, though it's often throbbing with visitors. To escape the crowds, you can head east to the **Higashiyama Teramachi** area of woodland temples and shrines.

## Hida Folk Village and around

The best place to start your explorations in Takayama is at the **Hida Folk Village** (daily 8.30am–5pm; ¥700), twenty minutes' walk west of Takayama Station, and in a lovely location overlooking the mountains. This outdoor museum of over twenty traditional buildings gathered from the Hida area is a fascinating place to wander around, especially if you're not planning on visiting the *gasshō-zukuri* thatched houses of the Shirakawa-gō and Gokayama districts (see p.375).

The main entrance is roughly 600m uphill, past the first car park and old houses and opposite a row of gift shops. The ticket office has a good English map of the museum and a rather lyrical English-language taped commentary, which you can listen to while wandering the grounds. The route winds in a clockwise direction around a central pond and you're free to explore inside the houses, many of which have displays of farm implements and folk crafts relating to their former owners. At the end of the route, next to the ticket gate, are four old houses where you might catch real artists at work on traditional crafts such as lacquering and wood carving. The old houses at the bottom of the hill comprise the Hida Folk Museum, but are little different from those in the main village. If you don't fancy walking or cycling to the museum, take a bus from the terminal beside Takayama Station to the village every thirty minutes during the day. One way is ¥250, while the *Hida-no-Sato Setto-ken* discount return ticket (¥1000) includes entrance to the village.

Roughly 1km west of Hida Folk Village is the enormous **Main World Shrine**, headquarters of the religious sect, Sukyo Mahikari. You'll be able to see its golden roof, topped with a huge red snooker ball, quite clearly from the village. It's worth getting closer to check out the shrine's stupendous architecture – including an unbelievably accurate copy of Mexico's Quetzalcoatl Fountain and two vaguely Islamic-looking towers. The interior, operatically kitsch, is built like a stage set for a cast of thousands. On leaving you'll probably welcome the offer of a sip of sake to jolt you back to reality.

On the road up to the Hida Folk Village look out for the elegant and modern **Hida Takayama Museum of Art** (daily 9am–5pm; ¥1300). Although admission is pricey, it's worth forking out to see one the best collections of works of art made from glass and Art Nouveau interiors you'll find in Japan. Near the entrance is a beautiful glass fountain by René Lalique which once stood in the Paris Lido; further on, the collection includes exquisite sixteenth-century goblets, Tiffany glass lamps and rooms decorated with the interior designs of Charles Rennie Mackintosh. The museum also has a pleasant café (see p.373).

## San-machi Suji

Before you cross over the Miya-gawa to the area of old merchants' houses, make your way to the town's feudal-era government complex, **Takayama-jinya** (April–Oct 8.45am–5pm; Jan–Mar, Nov & Dec 8.45am–4.30pm; ¥420), at the end of Hachikenmachi-dōri, five minutes' walk southeast of the station. This small-scale palace, originally built in 1615 and the only building of its kind left in Japan, was the seat of power for the Hida area's governor, appointed by the shogun. Most of the buildings seen today, including a torture chamber and a rice storehouse, date from reconstruction in 1816 and the best way to explore them is to go on one of the free guided tours in English which take around forty-five minutes.

Every day country women come into town from the surrounding mountains to sell vegetables, fruit and flowers at one of Takayama's two **morning markets** (*asa ichi*) in front of the *jinya*. The more attractive market is strung out along the east bank of the Miyagawa, between the bridges Kaji-bashi and Yayoi-bashi, and takes place from 7am until around noon. You can buy local handicrafts here, and grab a cheap coffee or local beer.

Cross the Naka-bashi from Takayama-jinya and you'll find the **San-machi Suji** area of dark wooden merchant houses dating from the mid-nineteenth century and at its most evocative at dusk when the crowds have thinned. During the day, along the quarter's three narrow streets you'll have to negotiate your way through rickshaws and tourists pottering in and out of craft shops, cafés and sake breweries, marked out by the giant balls of cedar leaves hanging in front of their entrances.

You can easily overdose on San-machi Suji's plethora of small and frequently uninteresting museums, many of which are a waste of time and money. The best plan is to head to the north end of the district to the handsome **Kusakabe Mingei-kan** (daily 8.30am–5pm; ¥500), the home of the Kusakabe family, dating from 1879, and an outstanding example of the carpentry skills Takayama is renowned for. In the shaded courtyard between the main home and the storehouses, now stocked with folkcrafts, you'll be offered a refreshing cup of tea and a rice cracker. The **Yoshijima-ke** (daily 9am–5pm; ¥300) next door is a very similar house and you'd be better off walking east for a minute to the delightful **Inro Museum** (daily April–Nov 9am–5pm; ¥500). *Inro* are the antique ornamental boxes of tiered compartments held together on a cord with a *netsuke* (toggle fastener). The highly detailed decoration on the boxes and the *netsuke* is a valued Japanese art and this museum has some exquisite examples among its collection of three hundred pieces.

### Festival floats, temples and shrines

From the Inro Museum hang a right and walk east to the precincts of the Sakurayama Hachiman-gū shrine where you'll find the **Takayama Yatai Kaikan** (daily 9am–4.30pm; ¥820), a large exhibition hall for four of the multi-tiered and elaborately decorated *yatai* (floats) used in the town's spring and autumn parades. At least once a year all eleven floats and the golden *mikoshi* (portable shrine) are displayed inside the huge glass case that you wind your way around at different levels so you can see all of the *yatai* decoration including the *karakuri*, mechanical dolls operated by up to eight puppeteers. Many of the floats date from the seventeenth century and they are usually stored in the tall storehouses (*yatai-gura*) which you'll notice around Takayama. The entrance charge also includes the **Sakurayama-Nikkō-kan**, a hall displaying a dazzling one-tenth scale replica of 28 buildings from Nikkō's Tōshōgū shrine (see p.170), where a computer controls the lighting to reproduce sunrise and sunset.

If you have time, check out the enjoyable demonstration of automated *karakuri* puppets in the **Shishi Kaikan** (daily 8am–5pm; ¥600), on the south side of the shrine. A video of a *shishi* (mythical lion) dance, common to festivals in the Takayama area, is screened at regular intervals during the day and you can also see displays of many lion masks and musical instruments used in these dances.

Following the narrow Enako-gawa southeast towards the hills from the Sakurayama Hachiman-gū, will bring you to the tranquil area of **Higashiyama Teramachi**, where thirteen temples and five shrines are dotted among the soaring pine trees. None of the holy places are particularly significant, but they are linked by a pleasant walk that goes over the river to Shiroyama-kōen, a wooded park standing on the remains of Lord Kanamori's castle, destroyed over three hundred years ago; you can still trace the donjon's foundations on the top of the hill, but the view across Takayama is now largely obscured by trees. The route is signposted and you can pick up a map from the tourist information office. The youth hostel (see p.370) is in Tensō-ji, one of the temples in the middle of the route, around which are clustered the most interesting of the other temples and shrines.

# Eating and drinking

The best thing to sample at Takayama's numerous **restaurants** is the area's speciality, *sansai ryōri*, dishes which use local mountain vegetables, ferns and wild plants. Try *sansai soba*, buckwheat noodles topped with the greens, or *hoba miso*, vegetables mixed with miso paste and roasted on a magnolia leaf. A delicious snack you'll see sold around town is *mitarashi-dango* – pounded rice balls dipped in soy sauce and roasted on skewers.

For breakfast or a snack a good place to head for is the *Sunahara Pan* bakery on a backstreet, two minutes' walk northwest of the *Rickshaw Inn*. Many of the San-machi Suji tourist restaurants are only open at lunch when they can get very busy. It's best to head closer to the station for dinner.

The Asahimachi area between the station and the Miya-gawa is the best place to track down convivial **bars**. You shouldn't leave town without sampling some of the local **sake**; the breweries in San-machi Suji hold free tastings of new sake in January and February. The town has also embraced the *ji-biiru* (regional beer) boom and several places around the shopping street Kokubunji-dōri now stock the Hida Takayama, Konkon and Ginga Biiru labels.

## Restaurants and bars

**Arisu**, Yashugawa-dōri. *Arisu* feels a bit like a prim 1920s café, with its waitresses in pinnies serving faithfully executed *Yōshoku*, Japanese takes on Western dishes such as steak and omlettes. The lunchtime set menus for around ¥1000 are good value.

**Chapara**. Small and friendly bar between Kokubunji-dōri and Hirokoji-dōri, which also serves Mexican food from around ¥600 per dish. Closed Sun.

**The Mackintosh Tearoom**. Attached to the Hida Takayama Museum of Art (see p.371) and modelled after the famous tearooms in Glasgow, designed by Charles Mackintosh. Pasta and pizza cost around ¥1000. The specially blended tea is a pricey ¥500 a cup, but the view across the mountains is lovely and you can eat outside. Open daily 9am–5.30pm

**Myogaya**. Excellent vegetarian food on offer at this relaxed natural food restaurant and shop, a block east of Takayama Station. The brown rice and organic veggie set menu is good value at ¥1000 and the cook will avoid using salt and fat if you tell her. Closed Sun.

**Red Hill**. This small bar at the northern end of the Asahimachi entertainment district is a little difficult to locate, but you'll get a warm welcome on arrival. Serves a wide range of bottled beer from around the world and food with a Middle Eastern slant, including pitta and houmous.

**Rengaya**. Modern *izakaya* on the west side of the Kaji-bashi, serving some of the local micro-brews on tap. A good place to go with a crowd of people and share a range of nibbly dishes.

**Sadaya**, 11-3 Kamisanno-machi. Excellent set lunches of *sansai ryōri* (¥1300 per person) served in the *tatami* rooms of one of the San-machi Suji's old merchants' houses. Open daily 11am–3pm.

**Suzuya**, 24 Hanakawa. Just off Kokubunji-dōri, this beamed family restaurant is a great place to sample *sansai ryōri*, and especially the nutty miso paste cooked on a leaf over a charcoal brazier. Has an English menu with pictures and friendly waitresses to assist you. Can either sit at tables or on *tatami*. Best for lunch or an early dinner since it closes promptly at 8pm.

**Tao**. This trendy hangout has a good bar and serves pasta and pizzas in a vaguely Southeast Asian setting. On the second floor of a parking lot arcade – look for the outcrop of potted plants on the balcony.

**Tom's Bellgins Bell** (☎0577/33-6507). A few blocks northwest of the Kaji-bashi look for the Swiss flag outside this pleasant restaurant, run by a Swiss resident of Takayama, who cooks a mean rosti and fondue. Best to phone before setting off since it has erratic opening hours.

**Yoshikawa**, 83 Kamisanno-machi. This small artsy café with a photo menu is a good place to sample traditional Japanese sweets, with green tea or coffee. Open daily 9am–6pm.

# Furukawa

With an area of old storehouses by a canal, some charming temples and several good museums, **FURUKAWA** is like a compact version of Takayama, 15km north, and all the more delightful because of that. This little riverside town, surrounded by mountains, is generally free of the crowds and giftshops; the only time it's busy is during the Furukawa Matsuri (April 19 & 20), which celebrates the coming of spring with a grand parade of wonderfully decorated floats. The highlight is the midnight procession, *Okoshi Daiko*, where hundreds of men, clad only in baggy white underpants and belly bands, compete to place small drums, tied to long logs, on top of a portable stage bearing the huge main drum, which all the while is being solemnly thumped. The men also balance atop tall poles and spin around on their stomachs.

It shouldn't take you more than three hours to cover the town's main sights, which are all within easy walking distance of Furukawa Station. West of the station is the **Shirakabe-dozo** district, where a row of white earthern storehouses have been preserved beside a narrow, gently flowing canal, packed with carp. Follow the canal for five minutes to your left until you reach the main road leading to the river. Beside the bridge you'll see **Honko-ji**, an attractive temple decorated with the intricate carving and carpentry for which the town is famous. If you arrive around lunchtime you're likely to find a service in full swing.

From the temple walk back towards the centre of town along Ichino-machi-dōri, where the two-hundred-year-old candle shop Mishimaya stands; demonstrations by a candlemaker take place in the front of the shop. Further along, look up for the cedar leaf balls hanging outside the sake breweries. On the corner of the street, in front of the town's central square, you'll see a shop where paper lanterns are made.

It's worth buying the ¥900 joint ticket to visit both **museums** in the square. The **Hida Craftsman Culture Hall** (daily 9am—5pm) has displays highlighting local carpenters' art and skills. Here you can see how buildings are made from jointed wooden beams so that no nails are necessary. In the **Furukawa Festival Hall** (daily 9am–5pm), apart from being able to get up close to two of the nine *yatai* used in the *matsuri* parade, you can watch a three-dimensional film of the festival, see a computer-controlled performance by one of the puppets on the floats and check out local craftsmen at work. Look out for the convincing crushed beer cans and bowls of peanuts carved from wood in the display cabinets. The drums used in the festival are in an open hall on the square and on the second Sunday in October all the *yatai* are displayed in the square, too.

If you've time to spare, head for the **Hida Forestry Museum** (9am–5pm; ¥300), a couple of minutes' walk east of the station, which has displays of more local crafts and industries, including sculptures woven from straw. There's also a slide show of local beauty spots. The best time to visit is at the weekends, when there are demonstrations of rice straw sculpture and traditional weaving.

## Practicalities

Furukawa is an easy day-trip from Takayama, with frequent trains and buses taking at most thirty minutes to reach the town. The local train is the cheapest option at ¥230. The station name is Hida-Furukawa and the **Kita-Hida tourist information** booth (daily 9am–5.30pm), where you can pick up a map of the town, is just outside. Staff here are helpful, but don't speak English; it's best to make detailed enquiries at Takayama first.

About the only reason for **staying** overnight is if you're planning on hiking up into the surrounding mountains, The best base to do this from is the *Hida Furukawa Youth Hostel* (☎0577/75-2979; ②), set amid rice-fields, a fifteen-minute bus ride from Hida-Furukawa Station. This is a modern hostel in a homely wooden cabin, where the food is good and you can arrange bike rental. You need to take a bus to Shinrin-kōen from the stand opposite the JR station – check with the tourist information booth as to the times.

The main **eating** options in Furukawa are clustered within a minute's walk of the station. The best deal is at *Shinanoya* (daily 11.30am–1pm 5.30pm–midnight), a cosy bar with counter seats, serving a ¥800 buffet lunch where the freshly cooked dishes just keep coming. Next door is *Matsuya* (daily except Thurs, 11am–11pm), serving set meals of *san-sai ryōri* dishes from ¥2000. You can also try out the tender local beef; *Maida*, on the right-hand corner of the junction with the road from the station, has set meals starting at ¥2500.

## Shirakawa-gō and Gokayama

No longer quite as remote as they once were, the quaint World Heritage Site **villages** of the **Shirakawa-gō** and **Gokayama** areas, northwest of Takayama, number among the many fabled bolt holes of the Taira clan after their defeat at the battle of Dannoura (see History, p.771). Until earlier this century these villages, with their distinctive, thatched A-frame houses, were almost entirely cut off from fast-modernizing Japan. The damming of the Shō-kawa in the 1960s, together with the drift of population away from the countryside, threatened the survival of this rare form of architecture called *gasshō-zukuri* (see box below). In 1971 local residents began a preservation movement which has been so successful that the three tiny communities of Ogimachi in Gifu-ken and Suganuma and Ainokura in neighbouring Toyama-ken are in danger of being swamped by the million visitors who now tramp through each year in search of the lost Japan of the popular imagination.

The glut of tourists is unlikely to abate at these villages, designated a World Heritage Site by UNESCO in 1995, but it's still worth braving the crowds to see the remarkable thatched buildings, which remain in idyllic valleys surrounded by forests and mountains. The most popular village is the largest, **Ogimachi**, which has several small museums and the Gasshō-zukuri Folklore Park, a showcase for 25 of the rare buildings. If you want to experience a more authentic atmosphere, head for the smaller villages of Suganuma and Ainokura and stay overnight in a minshuku in a *gasshō-zukuri* house.

---

### PRAYING HANDS HOUSES

*Gasshō-zukuri* – the style of architecture of which there are less than two hundred examples left in the Hida region – means "praying hands", because the sixty-degree slope of the thatched roofs is said to recall two hands joined in prayer. Although the locals were once fervent Buddhists, it is likely that the roofs were built like this for more practical reasons; the sharp angle protects the buildings from the effects of the heavy snowfall in this area.

The houses are large because land and resources were scarce in this remote and mountainous area. Many generations of the same family had to live together and the upper storeys of the home were used for industries such as making gunpowder and cultivating silkworms. The thatched roofs – often with a surface area of around six hundred square metres – are made of *susuki* grass, native to the northern part of the Hida region (wooden shingles were used in the south) and have to be replaced every thirty to forty years.

Since it can cost ¥20 million to rethatch an entire roof, many of the houses fell into disrepair until the government stepped in with grants in 1976, enabling the locals to keep up their housebuilding traditions. The local preservation society decides which buildings are most in need of repair each year and helps organize the *yui*, a two-hundred-strong team who co-operate to rethatch one side of a roof in two days flat.

## SHIRAKAWA-GŌ AND GOKAYAMA

| | | |
|---|---|---|
| **Shirakawa-gō** | *Shirakawa-gō* | 白川郷 |
| **Ogimachi** | *Ogimachi* | 荻町 |
| Doburoku Matsuri Exhibition Hall | *Doburoku Matsuri-no-Yakata* | どぶろく祭りの館 |
| Gasshō-zukuri Folklore Park | *Gasshō-zukuri Minka-en* | 合掌造り民家園 |
| Museum of Daily Life | *Seikatsu Shiryōkan* | 生活資料館 |
| Myōzen-ji Temple Museum | *Myōzen-ji Hakubutsukan* | 明善寺博物館 |

*ACCOMMODATION*

| | | |
|---|---|---|
| Etchū Gokayama Youth Hostel | *Etchū Gokayama Yūsu Hosuteru* | 越中五箇山ユースホステル |
| Furusato | *Furusato* | ふるさと |
| Yosobe-e | *Yosobe-e* | よそべえ |

| | | |
|---|---|---|
| **Gokayama** | *Gokayama* | 五箇山 |
| **Suganuma** | *Suganuma* | 菅沼 |
| **Ainokura** | *Ainokura* | 相倉 |
| Murakami-ke | *Murakami-ke* | 村上家 |

## Ogimachi

In the shadow of the sacred mountain Hakusan, **OGIMACHI** village, some 30km northwest of Takayama, is where you'll find the largest collection of *gasshō-zukuri* houses within the Shirakawa-gō area of the Shō-kawa valley. Many of the thatched houses were moved here when threatened by the damming of the Shō-kawa, and this makes for rather a contrived scene, not helped by the major road that cuts through its centre, bringing a daily overdose of tourists. It's not all about hype; the village is populated by families living in most of the homes, farming rice and other crops in the surrounding rice-fields.

A good way to start your explorations is by hiking up to the lookout spot (*tenbodai*), about ten minutes' walk north of the main Gasshō-Shuraku bus stop, from where you can get a good view of the village's layout and a great photo of the thatched houses. The **Wada-ke** (daily 9am–5pm; ¥300), with a lily pond in front, is the first of several "museum" houses you'll pass on your way back to the village centre. Inside, lacquerware and other household items used by the Wada family who lived here for over two hundred years are displayed. Five minutes' walk further south stands the five-storey **Myōzen-ji Temple Museum** (daily 8.30am–5pm; ¥300). This huge building was once the living quarters for the priests and monks at the attached temple and in its upper floors you can see where over 1000 kilograms of silk cocoons were cultivated a year. The gaps in the floor boards allowed the smoke from the *irori* fire to permeate the whole building, preserving the wood and thatch. The thatched temple is connected by a narrow passageway to the main house and outside you'll also notice a thatched bell-tower.

Continuing south of the temple will bring you to the village's main shrine, **Shirakawa Hachiman-jinja**, next to which stands the **Doburoku Matsuri Exhibition Hall** (daily May–Nov 9am–4pm; ¥300) devoted to the annual festival, (Oct 14–19), which involves the making of *doburoku*, a rough milky sake. The exhibition itself is small, but you can watch a good video in Japanese about life in the village and try a drop of the thick and potent alcohol on the way out. At the far southern end of Ogimachi you'll find the ramshackle **Museum of Daily Life** (daily 8.30am–4.30pm; ¥300), where you can weave your way through all kinds of intriguing junk, including

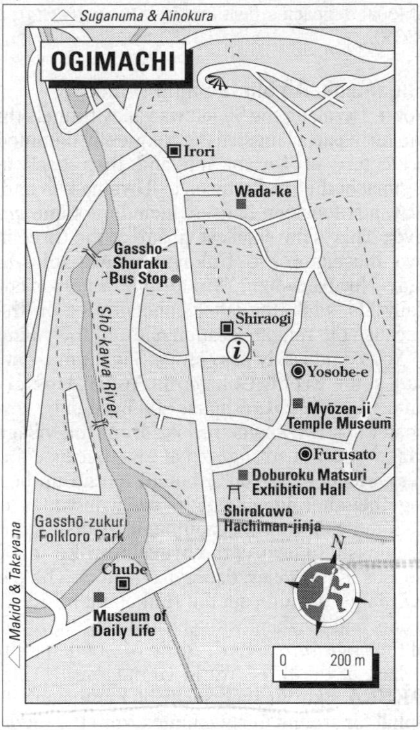


bearskins and beautifully carved wooden headrests.

Reached by a footbridge across on the west side of the Shō-kawa is the **Gasshō-zukuri Folklore Park** (daily except Thurs: April, May, July & Sept–Nov 8.40am–5pm; Jan–March, June & Dec 9am–4pm; Aug daily 8am–6pm,; ¥700), an open-air museum of some 25 buildings gathered together from around the region. This is a lifeless place to wander around compared to the real village on the opposite river bank, but it is quiet and you can see demonstrations of handicrafts, such as weaving and carving, in some of the buildings, as well as rest and have a free cup of tea in the Nakano Chojiro family house near the entrance. Just outside the park is the **Minka-en**, the village hall where you can don a pinny and learn how to make soba noodles. The two-hour sessions cost ¥1800 and must be booked in advance (☎05769/6-1231).

*PRACTICALITIES*

If you're coming to Ogimachi from Takayama by public transport, first take an infrequent **bus** to Makido (50min; ¥1930), where you'll need to change for another journey of around an hour (¥1430). There are direct buses from Nagoya (see p.390) which also take around two hours and cost ¥4760 and Takaoka (see p.378), to the north, which has the most frequent service (four daily) and costs ¥2350. Between July and mid-November there is also one bus a day from Nagoya to Kanazawa (see p.380) on the Japan Sea coast, which stops in Ogimachi. This is a good area to **rent a car**; try Eki Rent-a-car at Takayama Station (☎0577/33-3522).

The **tourist information office** (Daily except Wed 8.30am–6pm), next to the car park opposite the Gasshō-Shuraku bus stop, is staffed by helpful assistants, who don't speak English, but can provide you with a good English booklet about the village and help arrange accommodation. The only way of seeing Ogimachi minus the crowds is to **stay** overnight. There are several nice minshuku in the thatched-roof homes to choose from, all of which include breakfast and dinner in their rates. *Yosobe-e* (☎05769/6-1172; [6]) is a small place, one minute's walk northeast of the tourist office, with an *irori* fire. *Furusato* (☎05769/6-1033; [5]), just south of Myōzen-ji, is larger, has a stuffed bear in the hall and other more endearing touches throughout its *tatami* rooms. The closest youth hostel is near Suganuma (see overleaf).

For **eating**, try *Irori* on the main road at the north end of the village, opposite the petrol station, where you can sit around a raised hearth and have good-value set lunches (¥1000), which include fish, noodles or tofu. Next to the Museum of Daily Life, *Chube* is a large restaurant overlooking the river, where you can feast on the mountain vegetable cuisine, *sansai ryōri*, from ¥1300 per person. *Shiraogi*, opposite the tourist information office, is a bit more expensive, but has an English menu and offers a set menu of local delicacies (ask for the *Shiraogi-setto*), including trout and miso bean paste, for ¥2600.

## Suganuma, Ainokura and around

Route 156 along the Shō-kawa valley tunnels through the mountains keeping course for the main part alongside the frequently dammed river as it meanders north into the next prefecture of Toyama-ken and then back again into Gifu-ken. Some 10km from Ogimachi the road returns to Toyama-ken and passes the quaint hamlet of **SUGANU-MA**, just fourteen houses, including some *gasshō-zukuri*, beside a sharp bend in the river. This is the smallest village of the three in the World Heritage Site, but it still has two museums, the **Gokayama Minzoku-kan** and the **Ensho-no-Yakata** (daily May–Nov 9am–4pm; ¥210 for one, ¥300 for both). The former has more artifacts from daily life, while the latter concentrates on the production of gunpowder, made here because the remote location allowed the ruling Kaga clan to keep it secret.

You could easily pass on by Suganuma, but you'll need to come here if you want to stay at the **Ecchū Gokayama Youth Hostel** (☎0763/67-3331; ①), which is in a magnificent *gasshō-zukuri* house still lived in by several generations of the same family. The hostel is a two-kilometre hike from the village, across the river and up a steep road. Make sure you arrange to eat here because there's nothing else around. The family are very friendly and you're bound to end up beside the large sunken *irori* fire chatting together after dinner which usually includes local delicacies.

Some 4km from Suganuma, it's worth stopping off briefly in the modern village of Kaminashi to inspect the **Murakami-ke** (daily; 8.30am–5pm; ¥300), one of the oldest houses in the valley, dating from 1578. The owner gives guided tours around the *tatami* rooms, pointing out the sunken pit beside the entrance where gunpowder was once made, and finishing with spirited singing of folk tunes accompanied by a performance of the *bin-zasara*, a rattle made of wooden strips.

Last of the three World Heritage Site villages and possibly the loveliest, is **AIN-OKURA**, 4km further north of Kaminashi. To reach the village, you'll need to hike uphill for around thirty minutes from the modern village of Shimonashi; you could also try hitching a lift, not a problem since Ainokura attracts so many visitors. This is its main problem. Despite the idyllic hillside location and lack of motorized transport in the village itself, Ainokura can feel like hell on earth as you battle past yet another group of camera-toting day-trippers. Catch it on a quiet day, or after the crowds have gone home, and you'll think quite the opposite.

Look out for the English map on a sign in the parking lot at the entrance to the village which shows various trails up into the surrounding hills. There's nothing available in English from the gift shop in the white building in the centre of the village which is also the minshuku information centre; if you want to stay overnight in one of the thatched houses, this is the place to head first. There's also the **Ainokura Minzoku-kan** (daily 8.30am–5pm; ¥200) a tiny museum of daily life, including examples of the handmade paper and toys local to the area.

The infrequent buses that run between Ogimachi and Takaoka (see opposite) also pass by Ainokura and Suganuma. The JR Jōhana line runs from Takaoka to Jōhana, where you can also pick up a bus to the Gokayama area.

# Takaoka, Toyama and around

Head northeast from the Gokayama valley and you'll reach the modern coastal cities of **Takaoka** and, further west, the prefectural capital of **Toyama**. Neither city is worth stopping over in and you'd do well to press on south along the Japan Sea coast to Kanazawa and the more scenic Noto Hantō peninsula (see p.387).

**TAKAOKA, TOYAMA AND AROUND**

| | | |
|---|---|---|
| **Takaoka** | *Takaoka* | 高岡 |
| **Toyama** | *Toyama* | 富山 |
| Dai-ichi Inn Toyama | *Dai-ichi In Toyama* | 第一イン富山 |
| Toyama Youth Hostel | *Toyama Yūsu Hosuteru* | 富山ユースホステル |
| **Tateyama-Kurobe Alpine Route** | *Tateyama-Kurobe Arupen Rūto* | 立山黒部アルペンルート |
| Murodō | *Murodō* | 室堂 |
| Shinano-Ōmachi | *Shinano-Ōmachi* | 信濃大町 |

The only thing **TAKAOKA** is famous for is its Daibutsu, a large statue of Buddha, cast in 1933, about ten minutes' walk north of the station, and only worth seeing if you have time to kill while waiting for a train. This might be the case if you're using the JR Jōhana line which starts in Takaoka and goes part of the way towards Gokayama (see p.375). You can pick up a map of town from the tourist information booth (daily 10am–6pm), beside the ticket gate at the station where the friendly assistant speaks a little English and can make accommodation bookings if you're stuck for somewhere to stay.

Some 17km further west, straddling the mouth of the Jinzū-gawa is the workaday prefectural capital **TOYAMA**, a good starting point for excursions along the Alpine Route (see below) to Nagano ken. The city's castle, 1km south of the station is a replica of the original and houses the missable Museum of Local History (Tues–Sun 9am–4.30pm; ¥210); if you have time to spare the best place to head is the **Toyama Municipal Folkcraft Village** (Tues–Sun 9am–4.30pm; ¥620), where eight museums highlighting local arts, crafts and industries are gathered together at the foot of Kureha hills. Beside the museums you'll also find the atmospheric temple **Chokei-ji**, with its Gohyaku Rakan, terraces of over 500 mini stone statues of Buddha's disciples. To reach the village take a bus from stop 14 in front of the Hokuriku Bank Building opposite Toyama Station to Anyobo and then walk for five minutes.

The **tourist information booth** (daily 8am–8pm; ☎0764/32-9751), beside the central exit at Toyama Station, has a good selection of leaflets on local attractions and English-speaking staff who will help book accommodation. You should also be able to get here a copy of *What's Happening*, a monthly English newsletter (with parts in Chinese, Portugese and Russian), put out by the Toyama International Centre (☎0764/44-2500). Toyama's banks, main post office and shops are all within easy walking distance of the station.

The *Toyama Youth Hostel* (☎0764/37-9010; ①) is several kilometres north of the city, beside a pine-fringed beach which would be lovely if not for all the rubbish on the shore. The hostel itself is a pleasant place and serves meals. If you want more convenient accommodation for the city centre, there are plenty of business hotels around Toyama Station; a good option is the *Dai-ichi Inn Toyama* (☎0764/42-6611, fax 42-8153; ⑤), at the east end of the station, with singles from around ¥7000.

## Tateyama-Kurobe Alpine Route

If you're in no hurry and don't mind shelling out over ¥10,000 – or the constant changes of transport – a leisurely and scenic way to travel from the Japan Sea coast across the alps to Nagano-ken or visa versa is to follow the **Tateyama-Kurob Alpine Route**. The 90km route, using buses, trains, funicular and cable cars, is c open from the end of April to the beginning of November depending on the snow is at its busiest between August and October when it's best to make advance reservations.

Starting from Toyama take the Toyama Chiho Tetsudō line to the village of **Tateyama** (45min; ¥1100), at the base of Mount Tateyama one of the three most sacred mountains in Japan after Mount Fuji and Mount Hakusan. Change to the Tateyama Cable Railway for a seven-minute journey (¥620) up to the small resort of Bijo-daira (beautiful lady plateau). One of the best parts of the journey follows, taking the Tateyama Kōgen bus (55min; ¥1630) up the twisting alpine road, which early in the season is still piled high either side with snow, to the terminal at **Murodō**. Only five minutes north of the bus terminal is the Mikuriga-ike, an alpine lake in a fifteen-metre-deep volcanic crater and, twenty minutes' walk further on, Jigokudani (Hell Valley), an area of boiling hot springs. There are also several longer hikes you can do around Murodō, which is the best place to end your journey along the alpine route, if you're concerned about the cost, and return to Toyama.

The next section of the journey – a ten-minute bus ride along a tunnel cut through Mount Tateyama to Daikanbō – is the most expensive at ¥2060. The view from Daikanbō across the mountains is spectactular and you'll be able to admire it some more as you take first the Tateyama Ropeway cable car (¥1240) down to the Kurobe Cable Railway (¥840) for a five-minute journey to the edge of the Kurobe-ko lake formed by the enormous **Kurobe dam**. You'll now have to walk 800 metres to the catch the trolley bus (¥1240) for a sixteen-minute journey through tunnels under Harinoki-dake to the village Ogisawa, across in Nagano-ken. Here you'll transfer to a bus (40min; ¥1300) down to the station at Shinano-Ōmachi, where you can catch both local and express trains to Matsumoto.

# Kanazawa and around

Like several other historic cities on the Japan Sea coast, **KANAZAWA**, the modern, refined capital of Ishikawa-ken, south of Toyama-ken, has become something of a backwater. Only 150 years ago, this old castle town was the fourth largest city in Japan, with a sophisticated population whose riches rested on the area's abundant production of rice and long periods of peace. Today, despite being a sprawling city with artistic pretentions, its main attraction is the lovely **Kenroku-en**, one of Japan's top three gardens, within which you'll find the elegant Seison-kaku villa. The city also has many museums, a compact area of *samurai* houses and the fascinating "ninja" temple **Myōryū-ji**. There's also a conscious effort made to make *gaijin* welcome, demonstrated by Kanazawa's many international centres.

Kanazawa's history stretches back over seven hundred years to when the region was known as Kaga, a name which is still applied to the city's exquisite crafts, such as silk dyeing and lacquerware, and its delicately prepared cuisine. The city's heyday was a golden century from 1488 when the ruling Togashi family was overthrown by a collective of farmers and Buddhist monks, and Kanazawa became Japan's only independent Buddhist state. Even though autonomy ended in 1583, when the *daimyō* Maeda Toshiie was installed as ruler by the warlord Oda Nobunaga who unified Japan, Kanazawa (which means "golden marsh") continued to thrive as the nation's richest province, churning out five million bushels of rice a year.

You'll still see plenty of rice growing on the way out to the **Noto Hantō**, a rural peninsula north of Kanazawa, and a great place to kick back in a charming fishing village and enjoy a slower pace of life. Also possible as a long day-trip south of Kanazawa, in the hills of Fukui-ken, is **Eihei-ji**, one of the Japan's most atmospheric temples, surrounded by forests and still an active monastery. You can also stay in the temple overnight and experience part of the monks' daily routine.

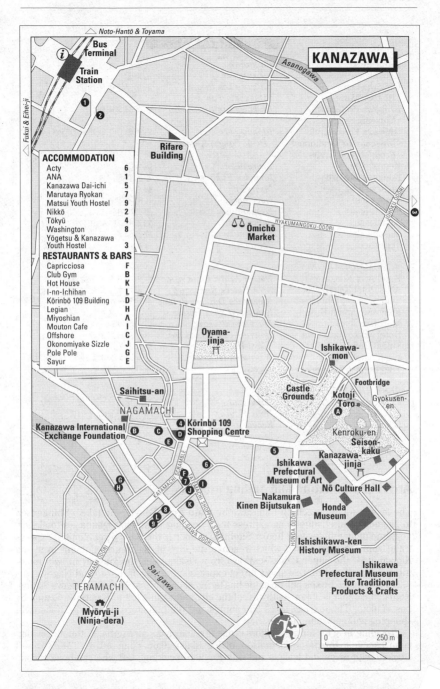

△ *Noto-Hantō & Toyama*

Bus Terminal

Train Station

*Asanogawa*

# KANAZAWA

◁ *Fukui & Eihei-ji*

Rifare Building

**ACCOMMODATION**

| | |
|---|---|
| Acty | 6 |
| ANA | 1 |
| Kanazawa Dai-ichi | 5 |
| Marutaya Ryokan | 7 |
| Matsui Youth Hostel | 9 |
| Nikkō | 2 |
| Tōkyū | 4 |
| Washington | 8 |
| Yōgetsu & Kanazawa Youth Hostel | 3 |

**RESTAURANTS & BARS**

| | |
|---|---|
| Capricciosa | F |
| Club Gym | B |
| Hot House | K |
| I-no-Ichiban | L |
| Kōrinbō 109 Building | D |
| Legian | H |
| Miyoshian | A |
| Mouton Cafe | I |
| Offshore | C |
| Okonomiyake Sizzle | J |
| Pole Pole | G |
| Sayur | E |

Ōmichō Market

*HYAKUMANGOKU-ŌDŌRI*

*ŌHINTI-ŌDŌRI*

Oyama-jinja

Ishikawa-mon

Saihitsu-an

**NAGAMACHI**

Castle Grounds

Kotoji Tōrō

Footbridge

Gyokusen-en

Kanazawa International Exchange Foundation

Kōrinbō 109 Shopping Centre

*KATAMACHI SCRAMBLE*

Kenroku-en

Seison-kaku

Kanazawa-jinja

Ishikawa Prefectural Museum of Art

*KATAMACHI SHOPPING STREET*

Nakamura Kinen Bijutsukan

Nō Culture Hall

*SAIGAWA-ŌDŌRI*

Honda Museum

*HONDA-ŌDŌRI*

Ishishikawa-ken History Museum

*MINAMI-ŌDŌRI*

Ishikawa Prefectural Museum for Traditional Products & Crafts

*Sai-gawa*

**TERAMACHI**

Myōryū-ji (Ninja-dera)

N

0    250 m

| | | |
|---|---|---|
| **KANAZAWA** | | |
| **Kanazawa** | *Kanazawa* | 金沢 |
| Gyokusen-en | *Gyokusen-en* | 玉泉園 |
| Ishikawa-ken History Museum | *Ishikawa-ken Rekishi Hakubutsukan* | 石川県歴史博物館 |
| Ishikawa Prefectural Museum of Art | *Ishikawa-ken Bijutsukan* | 石川県美術館 |
| Ishikawa Prefectural Museum for Traditional Products and Crafts | *Ishikawa-kenritsu Dentō-Sangyō Kōgeikan* | 石川県立伝統産業工芸館 |
| Kenroku-en | *Kenroku-en* | 兼六園 |
| Komatsu Airport | *Komatsu Kūkō* | 小松空港 |
| Myōryū-ji | *Myōryū-ji* | 妙立寺 |
| Nagamachi | *Nagamachi* | 長町 |
| Oyama-jinja | *Oyama-jinja* | 尾山神社 |
| Saihitsu-an | *Saihitsu-an* | 彩筆庵 |
| Seison-kaku | *Seison-kaku* | 成巽閣 |
| Teramachi | *Teramachi* | 寺町 |
| | | |
| *ACCOMMODATION* | | |
| Hotel Acty Kanazawa | *Hoteru Akutei Kanazawa* | ホテルアクティ金沢 |
| ANA Hotel Kanazawa | *ANA Hoteru Kanazawa* | ＡＮＡホテル金沢 |
| Kanazawa Dai-ichi Hotel | *Kanazawa Dai-ichi Hoteru* | 金沢第一ホテル |
| Kanazawa Youth Hostel | *Kanazawa Yūsu Hosuteru* | 金沢ユースホステル |
| Marutaya Ryokan | *Marutaya Ryokan* | 村田屋旅館 |
| Hotel Nikkō Kanazawa | *Hoteru Nikkō Kanazawa* | ホテル日光金沢 |
| Tōkyū Hotel | *Tōkyū Hoteru* | 東急ホテル |
| Washington Hotel | *Washinton Hoteru* | ワシントンホテル |
| Yōgetsu | *Yōgetsu* | 陽月 |
| | | |
| *RESTAURANTS* | | |
| Capricciosa | *Kapurichōza* | カプリチョーザ |
| Hot House | *Hotto Hausu* | ホットハウス |
| Legian | *Rejian* | レジアン |
| Miyoshian | *Miyoshian* | みよしあん |
| Sayur | *Sayuru* | サユル |

## Arrival, information and getting around

The fastest way of reaching Kanazawa by **train** from Tokyo is to take a Shinkansen to Nagaoka and change to an express train heading west, via Toyama – a total journey time of just under four hours. Slightly cheaper is the daily direct limited express train from Ueno in Tokyo which reaches the city in six hours. Coming from the Kansai area, the Super Raichō express from Ōsaka does the journey in two hours, thirty minutes and there's also a direct express service from Kyoto and Nagoya.

Long-distance **buses** pull up at the bus terminal on the east side of Kanazawa Station. Komatsu Airport is 30km southwest of the city and connected to Kanazawa Station by bus (¥1050). The journey takes 55 minutes and the bus stops first in the Katamachi shopping and entertainment district.

Providing help for foreign visitors is one of Kanazawa's strengths. Within the station is an excellent **tourist information office** (daily 10am–6pm; ☎0762/32-6200), well stocked with maps and leaflets and with English-speaking staff who can book accommodation. You may also be able to arrange for a guide to show you around town for free. Another good place to pop in is the **Ishikawa Foundation For International Exchange** (Mon–Fri 9am–6pm, Sat 9am–5pm; ☎0762/62-5931) on the third and fourth floors of the Rifare Building, five minutes' walk southeast of the station. This has a library with foreign newspapers and magazines and two wide-screen TVs, one showing CNN, the other BBC World, and it's also a good place to meet up with Japanese who want to practice their English. Finally, the **Kanazawa International Exchange Foundation**, or KIEF (☎0762/20-2522), is on the second floor of Nagamachi Kenshukan Hall, on the western side of the Nagamachi *samurai* house district. KIEF can arrange homestays as well as volunteer guides.

**Getting around** is easy enough; although Kanazawa is a sprawling city, its main sights are clustered within walking distance of Kōrinbō and Katamachi, the neighbouring downtown areas, ten minutes by bus from the terminal outside the east exit of Kanazawa Station. Kenroku-en is five minutes' walk east of Kōrinbō, and the Nagamachi district of *samurai* houses lies immediately to the west. **Buses** leave frequently from stops 7, 8 and 9 for both Kōrinbō and Katamachi and cost ¥200.

## Accommodation

There are plenty of **hotels** – luxury and mid-range – near the train station, but the most convenient place to be based is in the central **Kōrinbō** district, within easy walking distance of Kenroku-en and other sights. On the east side of the city, **Higashiyama** is also a pleasant and atmospheric area to stay.

**Hotel Acty**, 1-2-44 Katamachi (☎0762/33-3900, fax 33-3005). Good-value rooms at this well-located modern business hotel, above the *Sapporo Lions* beer hall. ⑤.

**ANA Hotel Kanazawa**, 16-3 Shōwa-machi (☎0762/24-6111, fax 24-6100). Luxury hotel, next to Kanazawa Station, with a grand atrium lobby and comfortable rooms. Its Japanese restaurant overlooks a miniature version of Kenroku-en. ⑦.

**Kanazawa Dai-ichi Hotel**, 1-2-25 Hirosaka (☎0762/22-2011, fax 62-0363). Decent business hotel, one minute's walk away from the entrance to Kenroku-en. Twin rooms are at the bottom of this scale and a single room, including breakfast, is ¥6000. ⑤.

**Kanazawa Youth Hostel**, 37 Suehiro-machi (☎0762/52-3414, fax 52-8590). Up in the wooded hills on the east side of the city, the larger and more modern of Kanazawa's two hostels has some very nice *tatami* rooms, does good-value meals, has a kitchen where you can cook for yourself and rents out bikes. However, the twenty-minute steep hike up the hill is a disadvantage. ①.

**Marutaya Ryokan**, 1-5-2 Katamachi (☎0762/63-0455, fax 63-0456). This small ryokan in the heart of the Katamachi entertaiment district has some original touches and is run by friendly people used to dealing with foreign guests. The *tatami* rooms are on the small side, but are well maintained. Singles are ¥4500 and you can get a Western-style breakfast for ¥450. ④.

**Matsui Youth Hostel**, 1-9-3 Katamachi (☎0762/21-0275). Small, friendly hostel in the heart of Katamachi, with *tatami* dorms and private rooms for just a little extra. No meals, but free tea and coffee. The 10pm curfew puts a dampener on a night out in the surrounding bars. ①-②.

**Hotel Nikkō Kanazawa**, 2-15-1 Honmachi (☎0762/34-1111, fax 34-8802). Thirty-storey upmarket hotel opposite Kanazawa Station, with a sophisticated modern European design feel to its sleek lobby, restaurants and rooms. ⑦.

**Tōkyū Hotel**, 2-1-1 Kōrinbō (☎0762/31-2411, fax 63-0154). Upmarket hotel with old fashioned decoration in an ideal downtown location, a short walk from Kenroku-en. The rooms are more spacious than those at business hotels. ⑥.

**Washington Hotel**, 1-10-18 Katamachi (☎0762/24-0111, fax 24-2800). Mid-range business hotel chain. As well as the usual amenities the rooms have TVs with bi-lingual reception. Singles start at around ¥7000 and there's also a Japanese and Chinese restaurant in the hotel. ⑥.

**Yōgetsu**, 22 Higashiyama (☎0762/52-0497). Cosy minshuku in a wooden-beamed house dating from the last century, once the home of a *geisha*. The *tatami* rooms are small but the management is friendly and you can stay for ¥4500 per person without meals. ④.

## Kenroku-en and around

You and thousands of others will be heading straight to Kanazawa's star attraction, **Kenroku-en** (daily: March 1–Oct 15 7am–6pm; Oct 16–Feb 28 8am–4.30pm; ¥300, free third Sun of month), and it is best to bear this in mind before setting off for the gardens, five minutes' walk north of Kōrinbō. Early morning or late afternoon are the best times for catching the garden at its most tranquil, although you're bound to have your thoughts interrupted at least once by a megaphone-toting guide and party of tourists.

Of the official top three gardens in Japan (Kairaku-en in Mito and Kōraku-en in Okayama are the other two) **Kenroku-en** – developed over two centuries from the 1670s – is generally regarded as the best. Originally the outer grounds of Kanazawa castle, thus the private garden of the ruling Maeda clan, Kenroku-en was opened to the public in 1871. Its name, which means "combined six garden" refers to the six horticultural graces that the garden embraces: spaciousness, seclusion, artificiality, antiquity, water and panoramic views. Crowds notwithstanding, it's a lovely place to stroll around, all the more remarkable because an ingenious pumping system keeps the hillside pools full of water and the fountains working.

The main gate to Kenroku-en is on the slope leading up to its western edge and there's another a little further north beside the Renchimon, the original gate to the garden, next to the row of gift shops. From either entrance you'll first see the three-hundred-year-old Hisago-ike (Gourd Pond), so called because it's supposed to have the shape of the vegetable. Into the pond drops the Midori-taki (Green Waterfall), an unusual feature for a Japanese garden and built in 1774, at the same time as the nearby Yugaotei, a teahouse where you can still take tea for ¥500.

Walking in a clockwise direction up the hill you'll pass Japan's first fountain, constructed in 1861, and operated by the natural pressure of water flowing down from the mountains outside Kanazawa. At the top of the hill is the **Kasumi-ga-ike** (Misty Lake), the largest of Kenroku-en's four ponds and the heart of the garden. The pedestrian jam here is in front of the two-legged Kotoji Tōrō, the most famous stone lantern among Kenroku-en's eighteen, and an obligatory photo opportunity for all the tourist groups.

Looking in the opposite direction from the pond, take in the sweeping prospect across towards Kanazawa's old *geisha* district Higashiyama and, weather permitting, the Japan Sea coast. Throughout the park are many marvellous pine trees, pruned carefully throughout the centuries to achieve a certain shape; look out for the "married pines" at the southern end of the Kasumi-ga-ike, whose trunks are lovingly entwined.

One minute's walk east of the pond is the entrance to the delightful **Seison-kaku** (daily except Wed 8.30am–4.30pm; ¥500), an elegant two-storey shingle-roofed mansion built in 1863 by the *daimyō* Maeda Nariyasu as a retirement home for his mother. A good English leaflet lists the main architectural and decorative features to look out for, including paintings of fish, shellfish and turtles on the wainscots of the *shōji* sliding screens in the formal guest rooms downstairs. The view from the Tsukushi-no-rōka (Horsetail corridor) across the mansion's own raked-gravel garden is particularly enchanting, while upstairs, the decorative style is more adventurous, using a range of striking colours and materials including, unusually for a Japanese house, glass windows, imported from the Netherlands. These were installed so that the occupants could look out in winter at the falling snow.

If you return to the northernmost exit to the gardens you'll be immediately opposite the footbridge leading to the **Ishikawa-mon**, an impressive eighteenth-century gate and turret, about all that remains of Kanazawa castle. Walk across the now empty castle grounds and you'll emerge on the western side beside the back of the intriguing **Oyama-jinja**, a large shrine dedicated to first Maeda lord, Toshiie. It's fronted by the Shinmon, a square arched gate with multi-coloured stained glass in its upper tower, designed in 1875 with the help of Dutch engineers and once used as a lighthouse to guide ships towards the coast.

Heading in the opposite direction from Kenroku-en's north exit, along its eastern flank, will bring you to the small traditional garden, **Gyokusen-en** (daily April–Nov 9am–4pm; ¥500), an ideal escape from the crowds. Built on two levels of a steep slope, the garden has many lovely features, including mossy stone paths leading past two ponds and a mini waterfall. For ¥500 extra you can enjoy green tea and a sweet in the main villa's tearoom.

## City museums

There are several museums immediately to the southwest of Kenroku-en, one of the best being the informative **Ishikawa Prefectural Museum for Traditional Products and Crafts** (April–Nov daily 9am–5pm, closed every 3rd Thurs Jan–March & Dec daily except Thurs; ¥250), in a concrete building beside the Seison-kaku, next to the garden's east exit. Across two floors are displayed prime contemporary examples of Kanazawa's rich artistic heritage, including lacquerware, dyed silk, pottery, musical instruments and fireworks. None of the articles are for sale but all have a price tag, so if you take a fancy to one of the gold leaf and lacquer Buddhist family altars, for example, you'll know that it costs ¥4.5 million.

Heading downhill from the gardens, past the **Nō Culture Hall**, where Nō plays are often performed (check with one of the tourist offices for programme details, p.382), look for the Ishikawa-ken History Museum (daily 9am–5pm; ¥250) housed in the striking red-brick army barracks buildings, dating from 1910. Among the displays to look out for here is a detailed miniature reconstruction of a *samurai* parade, a grainy black and white film of Kanazawa from earlier this century and a reconstruction of a silk spinning factory.

If you're pressed for time, pass by the small **Honda Museum** (daily except Thurs 9am–5pm; ¥500), with its family collection of robes, armour and knicknacks, and the **Nakamura Kinen Bijutsukan** (daily except Tues 9am–4.30pm; ¥300), specializing in tea ceremony objets d'art, in favour of the larger **Ishikawa Prefectural Museum of Art** (daily 9.30am–5pm; ¥350), where beautiful examples of calligraphy, kimono, pottery, lacquerware and other relics of the Maeda clan are displayed along with a more eclectic collection of contemporary local art. There are usually special exhibitions held here which cost extra.

## Nagamachi and Teramachi

Kanazawa escaped bombing during World War II and so has been able to preserve some of its traditional inner-city areas. Directly behind Kōrinbō, the **Nagamachi** quarter has a few twisting cobbled streets of *samurai* houses, protected by thick yellow and grey earthen walls, topped with ceramic tiles. It's an evocative area to wander around, although the graffiti scratched into the walls is somewhat distracting. Inside one of the old wooden houses is the *kaga-yūzen* (silk dyeing) workshop **Saihitsu-an** (daily except Thurs 9–11.45am & 1–4.30pm; ¥500), where a short lecture and demonstration in Japanese is given on this painstaking, highly detailed process of dyeing silk for kimono, and then you can wander around the house and see some of the artists at work behind a glass screen.

A ten-minute walk south of Nagamachi flows the Sai-gawa, on the other side of which is **Teramachi** (temple town), an area of narrow streets and several temples. Religious buildings were often grouped together at the entrance to a city in an attempt to deter enemies, a defensive role that is clearly apparent at the unique **Myōryū-ji**, also known as Ninja-dera (daily: March–Nov 9am–4.30pm; Jan, Feb & Dec 9am–5.30pm; ¥700), five minutes' walk south of the river. The temple, completed in 1643 and belonging to the Nichiren sect of Buddhism, is associated with the *ninja* assassins (see p.353) because of its many secret passages, trick doors and concealed chambers, including a lookout tower that once commanded a sweeping view of the surrounding mountains and coast. To see around the temple you must reserve a place on one of several daily tours (call ☎0762/41-2877), conducted in Japanese but pretty self explanatory.

# Eating, drinking and entertainment

Kanazawa has a great range of **restaurants**. The local cuisine, *kaga ryori*, is expensive and best sampled for lunch or at the major hotels where special set menus are often available. Also worth trying is seafood and sushi; the best place to head is north of Kōrinbō to the teeming alleys of Ōmichō Ichiba, the daily market around which you'll find many small sushi bars and *shokudō* (cafeterias) serving rice bowl dishes (*donburi*).

The neon-lit drag running south towards the Sai-gawa from Kōrinbō is known locally as the Katamachi Scramble. The warren of streets around here are chock-full of **bars**. Katamachi also has several cinemas; pick up a copy of *Cosmos* from one of the international exchange offices (see p.383) for performance times. This free English-language newsletter also has details of Nō plays (enthusiastically nurtured by Kanazawa's arty citizens) and classical music performances.

## Restaurants

**Capricciosa**, Tatemachi. Italian chain restaurant which serves huge portions of pasta. Close by the Katamachi Scramble, opposite the cafés *Doutor* and *Mr Donut*.

**Hot House**, 3-11 Tatemachi. Lunch is best value at this small Indian restaurant just south of the main shopping street, at ¥900 for the set menu. For dinner, expect to pay ¥3000 per person. Open daily 11am–3pm, 5–10pm.

**Kōrinbō**, 109 Bldg. The fourth floor of this shopping mall is the place to head if you can't decide what to eat. There's a wide selection of restaurants, all serving set meals and many with window displays of plastic food you can point at.

**Legian**. Scruffy Indonesian café on the east side of Katamachi overlooking the Sai-gawa. Sometimes has satay sticks being cooked on a cart outside. Serves a good-value lunch from noon to 3pm daily.

**Miyoshian**, 1-11 Kenroku-machi (☎0762/21-0127). Specializes in *kaga ryōri*. Best to try the ¥2000 *bentō* boxed lunch at this atmospheric 100-year-old restaurant within Kenroku-en. Dinners require reservations and are much more expensive.

**Mouton Café 1999**. Tatemachi. Faux-French café-bar on the main shopping street with outdoor tables covered with yellow table cloths and excellent-value set meals. Lunch sets start at ¥600, dinners at ¥2000. A carafe of wine is ¥900.

**Okonomiyaki Sizzle**, Tatemachi. Fun D-I-Y Japanese pancake restaurant. A photo menu helps you choose which set of ingredients to sizzle up on the hot-plate at your table. Reckon on ¥1000 per person.

**Sayur**, 2-6-8 Katamachi. Easily missed basement veggie restaurant and bar, shortly after the Chinese on the corner of Kigura-machi-dōri. Serves a wide range of imported microbrew beers and tasty organic food. The cover charge of ¥600 is dropped if you eat. The set dinner menus at ¥1500 are excellent value and there's an English menu. Open Mon–Sat 7pm–11pm, closed 2nd and 3rd Sat of month.

## Bars and clubs

**Club GYM**, 2-10-14 Katamachi. Techno dance club and bar in basement of a silver tube building towards end of Kigura-machi-dōri. Free Mon–Thurs, ¥2500 with two drinks Fri & Sat. Open Mon–Thurs 8pm–1am, Fri & Sat 9pm–5am, but doesn't get going till midnight.

**I-no-Ichiban**, 1-9-20 Katamachi. The entrance to this hip, modern *izakaya*, on the ground floor of the Sekano Bldg, is hidden behind a mini bamboo grove. Sit at the bar beside the open kitchen so you can watch the chefs at work. Mon–Sat 6pm–3am, Sun 6pm–midnight.

**Offshore**. Stylish Australian beach bar, with roof-top seating in summer, behind the cinemas, east of Kōrinbō. Beers start at ¥500, other drinks ¥700. Daily 6pm–2am.

**Pole Pole**, 2-31-30 Katamachi. Directly behind the Indonesian restaurant *Legian*, on the road running parallel to the Sai-gawa. Cramped and raucous reggae bar serving forty different cocktails and a range of beers, as well as abundant supplies of monkey nuts, the shells of which litter the floor. Daily 8pm–5am.

## Listings

**Airlines** For ticket reservations call ANA (☎0762/31-3111); JAS (☎0762/24-7111) or JAL (☎0120–25-5971).

**Airport information** ☎0761/21-9803.

**Banks and exchange** There are several banks along the main road leading southeast from Kanazawa Station as well as around Kōrinbō.

**Bike rental** Bicycles can be rented (daily 9am–5pm) from outside the west exit of Kanazawa Station. Two hours for ¥300, or ¥1000 a day; the *Kanazawa Youth Hostel* (see p.383) is cheaper, but you'll have to push the bike up a steep hill on the way back to the hostel.

**Bookshops** The best selection of English-language books and magazines can be found in the Rifare Building underneath the Ishikawa Foundation for International Exchange, five minutes' walk south east of Kanazawa Station.

**Car rental** Both Toyota Rent-a-lease Ishikawa (☎0762/61-4100) and Nippon Rent-a-car (☎0762/63-0919) are close by Kanazawa Station.

**Hospital** The main hospital is Kanazawa University Hospital, 13-1 Takaramachi (☎0762/62-8151), around 1km southeast of Kenroku-en.

**Police** The Prefectural Police Office is at 2-1-1 Hirosaka (☎0762/62-1161). Emergency numbers are listed in Basics on p.70.

**Post office** The Central Post Office is a long way from any of Kanazawa's main tourist spots. The most convenient branch is the one at Kōrinbō.

**Taxis** Try Ishikawa Kōtsū (☎0762/31-4131) or Daiwa Taxi (☎0762/21-5166).

## Noto Hantō

Jutting out like a gnarled finger into the Japan Sea is the **Noto Hantō**, a rural escape best explored by car or bicycle. One story is that the name Noto is derived from an Ainu word, *nopo*, meaning "set apart" but regardless of whether this is true, the peninsula's quieter way of life, tied to agriculture and fishery, is certainly worlds away from modern Japan. The rugged and windswept west coast has the bulk of what constitutes the Noto Hantō's low-key attractions, while the calmer, indented east coast harbours several sleepy fishing ports, where the silence is broken only by the lapping of waves and the phut phut of boat engines.

Going up the west coast of the peninsula from Kanazawa you're best off driving past the wide, sandy Chiri-hama beach, cluttered with day-trippers and their litter, to secluded **Keta-taisha**, Noto's most important shrine. The complex, set in a wooded grove near the sea, dates from the 1650s, although the shrine is believed to have been founded in the eighth century. A few kilometres further up the coast, **Myōjō-ji** is a seventeeth-century temple with an impressive five-storey pagoda, but you have to pay ¥300 to enter, so press on the **Noto-kongō**, a sixteen-kilometre stretch of coast where the pounding Japan Sea has created fascinating rock formations and cliffs.

Around the mid-point of the west coast is the small town of **MONZEN**, where the most famous attraction is the temple **Sōji-ji** (daily 8am–5pm; ¥300), a training centre for Zen monks. Most of what you can see are twentieth-century reconstructions of much older buildings, but you can take part in the meditation sessions, if you get to the temple early enough.

The peninsula's main tourist centre is **WAJIMA**, an appealing fishing port 16km further up the coast, with a colourful morning market. Every day between 8am and 11.30pm, except for the tenth and twenty-fifth of each month, around two hundred vendors set up stalls along the town's main street selling fish, vegetables and other local products. While at the market you'll be intrigued to see an Italian palazzo in the middle of the street. Inside this grand facade is the **Inachu Cosmopolitan** (daily 8am–5pm; ¥600) a bizarre museum where reproductions of famous art pieces, such as the Venus de Milo, sit side by side with original European and Japanese antiques, including a huge pair of jet-black ornamental jars that once belonged to Tokugawa Iemetsu, the third Tokugawa shogun.

Wajima is renowned for its black lacquerware and you'll find many shops around town selling it; one of the best to head for is the **Wajima Lacquerware Centre**, beside the Shin-bashi bridge across the Kawarada-gawa on the west side of town. The centre has a display hall on the second floor (daily 9am–5.30pm; ¥200) where you can see craftsmen at work and view many prime examples of their art, some dating from the sixteenth century. If lacquerware isn't your bag, head across to the **Kiriko-kaikan** (daily 8am–5pm; ¥460) to see the giant colourful paper lanterns paraded around town in Wajima's lively summer and autumn festivals. The museum also shows videos of the festivals.

The Sosogi coastline between Wajima and the cape Rokkō-zaki is wonderfully scenic and is a great place for hiking past more strange rock formations. Near the village of Sosogi you'll pass the **Senmaida**, where over a thousand rice paddies cling to the sea-facing slopes in diminishing terraces. Heading inland towards Iwakura-yama, a steep 357m mountain, are two traditional thatched-roof houses that once belonged to the wealthy Tokikuni family, supposed descendants of the vanquished Taira clan (see Contexts, p.771). The family split in two in the sixteenth century, one part staying in the **Kami Tokikuni-ke** (daily: April–Nov 8.30am–6pm; Jan–March & Dec 8.30am–5pm; ¥420) the other building the smaller **Shimo Tokikuni-ke** (daily: April–Nov 8am–5pm; Jan–March & Dec 9am–5pm; ¥420), with its attractive attached garden.

On the Noto Hantō's gentler east coast the nicest place to head for is crinkly **Tsukumo-wan**, meaning "99 indentation bay". View the bay's inlets, islands and shoals of fish by hopping on the glass-bottomed boats (daily 8am–5pm; ¥800) that depart from the dock a minute's walk from Tsukumo-wan-Ogi Station on the Noto line. Heading down the coast around Nanao-wan look out for the *Boramachi-yagura*, pyramid-shaped wooden platforms on top of which fishermen once perched waiting for the fish to swim into their nets.

### Practicalities

The main access point for the Noto Hantō is Kanazawa, from where you can catch direct **trains** across the lower half of the peninsula to the uninteresting east coast town of Nanao. More convenient are the **buses** which cruise up the peninsula's central highway from Kanazawa to Wajima, with some going on to Sosogi. There are also direct bus services between Kanazawa and Suzu near the tip of the east coast.

Nanao, which can also be reached from Toyama, with a change of trains at Tsubata, is where JR is replaced by the Noto railway, although some JR trains do continue one further stop to the modern resort of Wakura Onsen. The Noto railway is the best option for sightseeing on the east coast, especially since its carriages have large windows to take in the pleasant views. The line runs as far as Takojima on the southern side of the peninsula's tip, with a branch cutting across country from Anamizu to Wajima.

Local **buses** also connect up most places of interest around the peninsula, but they're infrequent and you might want to try hitching instead. The quiet and mainly flat coastal roads make the Noto Hantō an ideal place in which to cycle or hire a car. If you're pushed for time, there are also several daily **tour buses** from Kanazawa which take in all the sights, with an unrelenting Japanese commentary, for around ¥5000.

It's best to pick up **tourist information** at the desk in Kanazawa station (see p.382) before setting out. In Wajima Station, there's also a tourist information booth (daily 10am–6pm; 0768/22-1503), where the assistants speak some English and can provide you with maps of the town and the peninsula and book accommodation. There are lockers at the station and you can rent bicycles from the nearby Okina Rent-a-cycle, ¥800 for eight hours.

#### *ACCOMMODATION*

Wajima has the widest choice of accommodation and is about the best place to be based for making day-trips around the peninsula. There are plenty of minshuku and ryokan in other villages around the coast as well as campsites and four youth hostels; the nicest is the one Tsukumo-wan.

**Fukasan** (☎0768/22-9933). Spotless minshuku beside the coast at Wajima, around ten minutes' walk north of the station. Some rooms have sea views and it's a grade cheaper if you opt for no meals. [5].

**Heguri** (☎0768/22-1018). Delightful minshuku on the west side of Wajima, across the Kawarada-gawa, five minutes' walk from the morning market. Run by friendly people who speak a little English, in a century-old wooden house. Some rooms overlook a traditional garden. [5].

**Noto Isaribi Youth Hostel** (☎ & fax 0768/74-0150). New hostel facing onto Tsukumo-wan, in the sleepy village of Ogi, twenty minutes' walk from Tsukumo-wan-Ogi station. Has good-quality *tatami* dorm rooms and is run by a friendly man who rustles up local seafood feasts. If you're lucky, he might give you a lift across the bay in his fishing boat to the station. [2].

**Wajima Chōraku-ji Youth Hostel** (☎0768/22-0663). Down-at-heel hostel next to a small temple on the west side of Wajima, a minute's walk from the Shin-bashi bridge. The only things in its favour are the friendly monks who run the place and that it's cheap. [1].

## Fukui and Eihei-ji

Some 75km south of Kanazawa is **FUKUI**, the modern capital of Fukui-ken, rebuilt after World War II and a severe earthquake in 1948 left the old city in a heap of rubble. There's little reason to linger here when **Eihei-ji**, the serene "temple of eternal peace" and headquarters of the Soto sect of Zen Buddhism, awaits on a mountain side surrounded by forests, 19km northeast of Fukui.

The main approach to Eihei-ji is lined with the usual tacky souvenir shops, but at the top of the hill the temple complex of over seventy buildings blends seamlessly with the trees. Eihei-ji is one of the few ancient temples in Japan where a community is visibly functioning, breathing life into what would otherwise be an attractive but sterile place. Touring around the main seven buildings of the complex, all connected by covered wooden walkways, you'll pass many shaven-headed monks busily going about their daily chores and religious duties.

Eihei-ji is closed on several dates throughout the year for special services, so it's wise to check first with Fukui tourist information (see below) or with the temple (☎0776/63-3631; fax 63-3640) before setting off. The best way to experience the temple is as a *sanrosha*, or religious trainee, and to stay the night. Enquiries should be made at least two weeks (preferably a month) in advance to see if the dates you would like to stay are available – if they are, you'll be sent an application form.

Overnight visits begin around 3pm with a bath to cleanse your body in preparation for the instruction. At 5pm a meal of simple vegetarian food is served, after which you'll take part in your first *zazen* **meditation** session, lasting around thirty minutes. Next comes a video about life in the temple and then bedtime at 9pm. This might seem rather early, but you'll be up at 3.10am for a second *zazen* session before the morning service at 5pm, followed by a tour of the temple complex. At 8.30am, after a breakfast of rice gruel and pickles, you're free to leave.

One night at Eihei-ji costs ¥8000, while for ¥1000 extra you can take part in the three night/four day programme, which follows more closely the rigorous daily routine of the monks. If this sounds all too much, there's a nearby **youth hostel**, *Eihei-ji Monzen Yamaguchi-sō* (☎0776/63-3123; ①), where the food is slightly more luxurious, even if the accommodation is quite basic, in large *tatami* rooms.

### Practicalities

Fukui can be reached by **train** from Kanazawa on the JR Hokuriku line. Alternatively, from Maibara, on the Tōkaidō Shinkansen line, direct express trains take just over an hour to reach Fukui. There are direct buses (¥1030) from Komatsu airport to Fukui bus terminal, a couple of blocks from the JR station. Buses also run to Fukui from the port of Tsuruga, which is connected by ferry to Otaru in Hokkaidō.

You can get information on the city and the prefecture from **Fukui City Sightseeing Information** (daily 8.30am–5pm; ☎0776/20-5348), next to the Fukui Station's central exit ticket barrier. No English is spoken, but the assistants can supply an English city and prefecture maps and leaflets and help arrange accommodation. You can change money at the Hokurika Bank opposite the central exit of the JR station and there are plenty of fast-food restaurants in the area should you need a quick bite to eat.

Trains to Eihei-ji (¥710) start from the Keifuku Denki Testudō Station, accessible from the east exit to the JR Fukui Station or via an underground tunnel that runs from outside the central exit. The journey takes 35 minutes and you'll have to change trains at Higashi-Furuichi. The temple is five minutes' walk uphill from the Eihei-ji Station.

# Nagoya and around

Japan's fourth largest city is **NAGOYA**, the concrete capital of Aichi-ken and major transport hub on central Honshū's industrial southern coast. Completely rebuilt after a wartime drubbing, it's an overwhelmingly modern city of high-rise buildings, multi-lane highways and flyovers, more suited to business than sightseeing. This is where

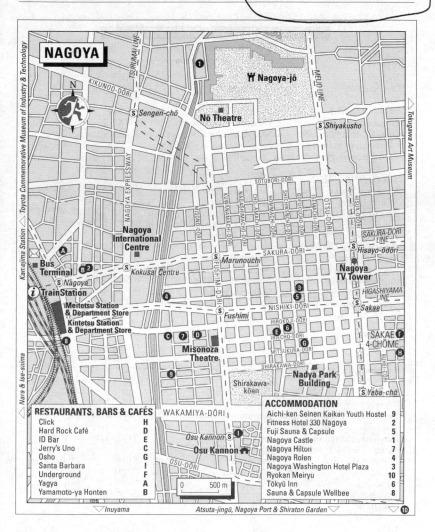

**NAGOYA**

N

♦ Nagoya-jō

❶

S *Sengen-chō*

Nō Theatre

S *Shiyakusho*

KIKUNOO-DORI

TSURUMAI LINE

MEIJO LINE

Toyota Commemorative Museum of Industry & Technology ◁

NAGOYA EXPRESSWAY

Kanejima Station ◁

Tokugawa Art Museum ▷

SOTOBORI-DORI

Nagoya
International
Centre

Bus
Terminal ❷

Nagoya
Train Station

Meitetsu Station
& Department Store

Kintetsu Station
& Department Store

S *Kokusai Centre*

S *Nagoya*

MISONO-DORI

FUSHIMI-DORI

SAKURA-DORI

S *Marunouchi*

SAKURA-DORI LINE

S *Hisayo-ōdōri*

Nagoya
TV Tower

HIGASHIYAMA LINE

S *Sakae*

❸
❺

S *Fushimi*

NISHIKI-DORI

HIROKOJI-DORI

IRECHO-DORI

MITSUKURA-DORI

SHIRAKAWA-DORI

SAKAE
4-CHŌME

❻

❼

Misonoza
Theatre

Shirakawa-
kōen

Nadya Park
Building

S *Yaba-chō*

❾

OTSU-DORI

HISAO-DORI

OSU-DORI

❶ A B C ❼ D E F G H

Nara & Ise-saima ◁

**RESTAURANTS, BARS & CAFÉS**

| Click | H |
| Hard Rock Café | D |
| ID Bar | E |
| Jerry's Uno | C |
| Osho | G |
| Santa Barbara | I |
| Underground | F |
| Yagya | A |
| Yamamoto-ya Honten | B |

WAKAMIYA-DORI

Osu Kannon ❶

Osu Kannon ♦

OSU-DORI

0        500 m

**ACCOMMODATION**

| Aichi-ken Seinen Kaikan Youth Hostel | 9 |
| Fitness Hotel 330 Nagoya | 2 |
| Fuji Sauna & Capsule | 5 |
| Nagoya Castle | 1 |
| Nagoya Hilton | 7 |
| Nagoya Rolen | 4 |
| Nagoya Washington Hotel Plaza | 3 |
| Ryokan Meiryu | 10 |
| Tōkyū Inn | 6 |
| Sauna & Capsule Wellbee | 8 |

▽ Inuyama      ▽ Atsuta-jingū, Nagoya Port & Shiraton Garden ▽      ▽ ❿

Japan's top past-time, *pachinko* (see p.810), was born; the mind-numbing pinball game's mix of flashing lights and noise are a reflection of the city.

Despite the bustle and grime, Nagoya is still more laid-back than Tokyo or Ōsaka and it has a few decent attractions, the most interesting of which is the grand **Tokugawa Art Museum**, housing belongings of the powerful family who once ruled Japan, and the **Toyota Commemorative Museum of Industry and Technology**, an appropriate tribute to Nagoya's industrial heritage. The city's most hyped attractions – the castle **Nagoya-jō** and the sacred shrine **Atsuta-jingū** – are hardly outstanding examples of their kind, but they're worth checking out if you have the time.

West of Nagoya, the Kiso-gawa forms the border between Aichi-ken and Gifu-ken, and the ancient night spectacle of *ukai*, cormorant fishing (see box, p.397) is still prac-

## NAGOYA AND AROUND

| | | |
|---|---|---|
| **Nagoya** | *Nagoya* | 名古屋 |
| Atsuta-jinja | *Atsuta-jinja* | 熱田神社 |
| Nagoya-jō | *Nagoya-jō* | 名古屋城 |
| Ōsu Kannon | *Ōsu Kannon* | 大須観音 |
| Sakae | *Sakae* | 栄 |
| Shirotori Garden | *Shirotori-teien* | 白鳥庭園 |
| Tokugawa Art Museum | *Tokugawa Bijutsukan* | 徳川美術館 |
| Toyota Commemorative Museum of Industry and Technology | *Sangyō Gijutsu Kinenkan* | 産業技術記念館 |

*ACCOMMODATION*

| | | |
|---|---|---|
| Aichi-ken Seinen Kaikan Youth Hostel | *Aichi-ken Seinen Kaikan Yūsu Hosuteru* | 愛知県青年会館ユースホステル |
| Fitness Hotel 330 Nagoya | *Fittonesu Hoteru 330 Nagoya* | フィットネスホテル３３０名古屋 |
| Fuji Sauna & Capsule | *Sauna to Kapuseru Fuji* | サウナ＆カプセル富士 |
| Ryokan Meiryū | *Ryokan Meiryū* | 旅館名龍 |
| Hotel Nagoya Castle | *Hoteru Nagoya-jō* | ホテル名古屋城 |
| Nagoya Hilton | *Nagoya Hiruton* | 名古屋ヒルトン |
| Nagoya Rolen Hotel | *Nagoya Rōren Hoteru* | 名古屋ローレンホテル |
| Nagoya Washington Hotel Plaza | *Nagoya Washinton Hoteru Puraza* | 名古屋ワシントンホテルプラザ |
| Sauna & Capsule Wellbee | *Sauna to Kapuseru Uerubii* | サウナ＆カプセルウェルビー |
| Tōkyū Inn | *Tōkyū In* | 東急イン |

*RESTAURANTS*

| | | |
|---|---|---|
| Oshō | *Oshō* | おしょう |
| Yagya | *Yagya* | やぎゃ |
| Yamamoto-ya Honten | *Yamamoto-ya Honten* | やまもとや本店 |

| | | |
|---|---|---|
| **Inuyama** | *Inuyama* | 犬山 |
| Cormorant fishing | *ukai* | 鵜飼 |
| Inuyama Artifacts Museum | *Inuyama-shi Bunka Shiryōkan* | 犬山市文化史料館 |
| Inuyama International Youth Hostel | *Inuyama Kokusai Yūsu Hosuteru* | 犬山国際ユースホステル |
| Inuyama-jō | *Inuyama-jō* | 犬山城 |
| Meiji Mura | *Meiji Mura* | 明治村 |
| Ōgata-jinja | *Ōgata-jinja* | 大縣神社 |
| Tagata-jinja | *Tagata-jinja* | 田県神社 |
| Uraku-en | *Uraku-en* | 有楽苑 |

| | | |
|---|---|---|
| **Gifu** | *Gifu* | 岐阜 |
| Ryokan Banshōkan | *Ryokan Banshōkan* | 旅館萬松館 |
| Gifu-jō | *Gifu-jō* | 岐阜城 |
| Gifu Youth Hostel | *Gifu Yūsu Hosuteru* | 岐阜ユースホステル |
| Hotel 330 Grande | *Hoteru 330 Gurande* | ホテル３３０グランデ |

ticed in **Inuyama**. This small castle town, where you'll find the classical Jo-an teahouse in a beautiful traditional garden, is also the jumping-off point for the vast outdoor architectural museum, **Meiji Mura**. Across the river in Gifu-ken, the capital **Gifu** serves up a similar combination of castle, parks and *ukai*, and is well-known for its production of lanterns and umbrellas made of paper.

## Arrival, information, orientation and city transport

The lines of three railway companies converge on Nagoya and their stations are all close to each other on the west side of the city. The main station belongs to JR and is where you'll alight from Tokaidō Shinkansen services coming from Tokyo, Ōsaka or Kyoto. Direct JR services also run to Nagoya from Takayama (see p.368) to the north and Ise and Toba (see pp.500 & 503), south in Mie-ken.

Immediately south of the JR station, beneath the Meitetsu department store, is the Meitetsu line terminus for trains to and from Inuyama and Gifu (see pp.397 & 399), while next door is the Kintetsu department store, with its Kintetsu line for services to Nara and the Shima Hantō region (see p.498). Most long-distance buses pull in at the terminal at the north end of the JR station.

Some 10km south of the train stations is the Nagoya-ko port area, where ferries arrive from Hokkaidō and Okinawa. The quickest way to reach the city from the port area is to hop on the Meijo line of Nagoya's subway system (see below). **Nagoya airport**, 12km north of the city, serves some 27 local and some 30 international destinations, but it's nowhere near as high-tech as Narita or Kansai; expect delays during peak holiday periods. Buses run from the airport both to the JR station and the neighbouring Meitetsu Bus Centre on the third floor of the Melsa Building.

The first stop for information should be the **Nagoya Station Tourist Information Centre** (daily 9am–7pm; ☎052/541-4301) on the central concourse of the JR station. The English-speaking assistants can provide you with maps and guides to the city and help with accommodation bookings. Another useful place to drop by is the International Centre (Mon–Sat 9am–8.30pm, Sun 9am–5pm; ☎052/581-0100), on the third floor of the **Nagoya International Centre Building**, some seven minutes' walk east of the JR station, along Sakura-dōri. Among the many services on offer here are an excellent library, English-language television, a bulletin board and the opportunity to meet English-speaking locals and arrange home visits. You can also pick up free copies of the glossy English-language monthly magazines *Nagoya Avenues* and *Eyes*, and weekly newspaper *Chūbu Weekly*, all of which carry entertainment listings and features on local attractions.

### Orientation and city transport

In front of Nagoya's three railway stations a giant swirling airvent heads up **Sakura-dōri**, the main highway cutting directly east towards the Nagoya TV Tower in the heart of the city. Immediately south of here is the main shopping and entertainment district of **Sakae**, where you'll find most hotels, department stores and restaurants. Around 1km north lie the **castle grounds**, while a similar distance south is the temple **Ōsu Kannon**. Some 3km south of the Ōsu Kannon is the main shrine **Atsuta-jingū**. Keep heading south and you'll hit the **Nagoya-ko port area**.

The easiest way to get around is on the **subway**, which has four colour-coded lines: Higashiyama (yellow), Meijo (purple), Sakura-dōri (red) and Tsurumai (blue). Both the Sakura-dōri and Higashiyama lines connect with the train stations. The extensive **bus** system can also be handy, but it's not as *gaijin*-friendly as the subways, which have everything labelled in English. Single journeys by subway or bus around the city centre cost ¥200; if you plan to travel a lot, think about buying one of the day tickets: ¥740 for subways only; ¥600 for buses only; ¥850 for subways and buses.

## Accommodation

The cheapest hotel **accommodation** is around the railway stations, but the nicest area to stay in is Sakae. Apart from the central *Aichi-ken Seinen Kaikan Youth Hostel*, there's also the cheaper *Nagoya Youth Hostel* (☎052/781-9845, fax 781-7023; ①), out on a limb at Higashiyama-kōen, some 5km southeast of the city centre – no good if you want to enjoy Nagoya at night. For men only, there are also a handful of capsule hotels worth considering as cheap overnight digs.

**Aichi-ken Seinen Kaikan Youth Hostel**, 1-18-8 Sakae, Naka-ku (☎052/221-6001, fax 204-3508). Great location and very good value since it's more like a hotel, with big rooms and a huge top-floor communal bath. The downside is the 11pm curfew. ②.

**Fitness Hotel 330 Nagoya**, 3-25-6 Meieki, Nakamura-ku (☎052/562-0330, fax 562-0331). Pleasantly decorated business hotel, a couple of blocks east of JR Nagoya Station. Has single rooms for under ¥8000 and an Aussie café in the lobby. ⑤.

**Fuji Sauna & Capsule**, 3-22-31 Sakae (☎052/962-5711). Nagoya's largest and cheapest capsule hotel is a snazzy affair, one block north of Maruzen bookstore, with its own restaurant, sauna and huge bath. ②.

**Ryokan Meiryu**, 2-4-21 Kamimaezu, Naka-ku (☎052/331-8686, fax 321-6119). To find this friendly ryokan, take exit three at Kamimaezu subway station and walk a couple of minutes east towards the YMCA. All rooms are *tatami* with air-conditioning and TVs; bathrooms are communal and there's a little café for breakfast and dinner. ④.

**Hotel Nagoya Castle**, 3-19 Hinokuchi-chō, Nishi-ku (☎052/521-2121, fax 531-3313). The best thing about this upmarket hotel is its views across to the neighbouring castle. Rooms are spacious but old-fashioned. There's also a free shuttle bus from the JR station. ⑦.

**Nagoya Hilton**, 1-3-3 Sakae, Naka-ku (☎052/212-1111, fax 212-1225). Classy luxury hotel, with fine rooms and an excellent range of facilities. The location is good, and it's worth checking on the special package deals throughout the year. ⑧.

**Nagoya Rolen Hotel**, 1-8-40 Sakae, Naka-ku (☎052/211-4581, fax 211-4588). Functional, no-frills business hotel in a good location. The rooms are plain, but clean. The cheapest share communal bathrooms. Singles from ¥4100. ④.

**Nagoya Washington Hotel Plaza**, 3-12-33 Naka-ku (☎052/962-7111, fax 962-7122). Chain business hotel, with the usual functional but cramped rooms, especially the limited number of singles at ¥6121. ⑤.

**Sauna & Capsule Wellbee** (☎052/586-2641). Capsule hotel, a couple of minutes' walk south of the railway stations in the Lejac Building. You get your capsule from noon to noon the next day. Also a branch in Sakae opposite the Nadia Park Building. ②.

**Tōkyū Inn**, 3-1-8 Sakae, Naka-ku (☎052/251-0109, fax 251-0299). This mid-range chain hotel is in an excellent location and has comfortable rooms. If you want something fancier try its luxury big brother *Nagoya Tōkyū Hotel*, 1km further east along Nishiki-dōri. ⑥.

## Central Nagoya

After the bombings of World War II, all that remained of **Nagoya-jō** (daily 9am–4.30pm; ¥500), some 2km northeast of the railway stations, were three turrets, three gates and sequestered screen paintings from the destroyed Honmaru palace. A handsome, ¥600-million concrete replica of the original castle, built by Tokugawa Ieyasu in 1612, was completed in 1959, and the central donjon was topped by huge 18-carat-gold-plated *shachi*, mythical dolphins which have become a symbol of the city.

More interesting is the **Tokugawa Art Museum** (Tues–Sun 10am–5pm; ¥1200), 2km further east, along Dekimachi-dōri, which houses a vast array of heirlooms from the Owari branch of the Tokugawa family, who once ruled Nagoya. The collection, displayed in large modern galleries with English explanations, includes items inherited by the first Tokugawa shogun, Ieyasu, reconstructions of the formal chambers of the *daimyō*'s residence and a Nō stage, around which are ranged beautiful traditional costumes. The museum's star attraction is a twelfth-century painted scroll of *The Tale of Genji* (see Contexts, p.792). The original is too precious to be continually exhibited, so most of the time you'll only be able to see reproduced panels and video programmes about the scroll.

A handful of other central Nagoya sights are worth checking out. Made up of two main pavilions – one housing textile machinery, the other cars – **The Toyota Commemorative Museum of Industry and Technology** (Tues–Sun 9.30am–5pm;

¥500), in an old red-brick Toyota factory, is nowhere near as dull as it sounds. This local firm, now famous worldwide for its cars, began as a textile producer, and rows of early twentieth-century looms make an incredible racket in the first pavilion. In contrast, a computer-controlled air-jet loom at the end of the display purrs like a kitten. In the automobile pavilion, it's the car-making robots, some of which look like giant, menacing aliens, that grab the attention. The museum is around 1km north of JR Nagoya Station and only two minutes' walk east of Sako Station on the Meitetsu Nagoya line.

In the heart of Sakae, the stimulating **Design Museum** (daily except Tues 11am–8pm; ¥500), on the fourth floor of the Nadya Park Design Centre Building, charts commerical design of modern products, such as telephones and radios, and has high-tech displays and computer simulations. Rather more traditional is the **Ōsu Kannon**, a vermilion-painted temple bustling with a steady stream of petitioners, 1km south of Sakae and beside the Ōsu Kannon stop on the Tsurumai subway line. Immediately to the east, check out the bargain hunters' district of **Ōsu**, where old-style arcades are lined with shops selling discount electronic goods, cheap clothes and used kimono.

## Atsuta-jingū and around

Some 5km south of central Nagoya, amid extensive wooded grounds, lies the venerable shrine of **Atsuta-jingū**, home of the *kusanagi-no-tsurugi* or "grass-cutting sword". This, along with the sacred jewels in Tokyo's Imperial Palace and the sacred mirror at Ise-jingū (see p.501), forms part of the imperial regalia, and remains hidden – if it exists at all – deep within the shrine, which had to be rebuilt after the war.

Within the shrine grounds there's a small **museum** (daily 9am–4.30pm, except last Wed and Thurs of the month; ¥300), where you can see many other swords offered to the Shinto gods at Atsuta-jingū, including a ferocious two-metre-long blade in the entrance hall. Also within the grounds look out for the giant camphor tree, said to have been planted by the Buddhist saint Kōbō Daishi (see p.784), 1300 years ago. It takes around twenty minutes by subway from Nagoya Station to reach Jingū-Nishi station on the Meijo line, the closest stop to Atsuta-jingū.

While you're out at the shrine, it's worth strolling west from the subway station towards the Hori-kawa, on the other side of which is the charming **Shirotori Garden** (Tues–Sun 9am–4.30pm; ¥200). This classical stroll-garden, arranged around ponds and streams, has an elegant traditional teahouse which is supposed to resemble a swan landing on the water.

# Eating, drinking and nightlife

Unlike Tokyo, Kyoto and Ōsaka, Nagoya doesn't have a gourmet reputation to uphold, which makes dining out here a relaxing experience of simple pleasures and hearty food. Sakae is the main district to head for, the grid of streets around 3-chōme being packed with lively **restaurants** and bars. There are also underground arcades filled with restaurants beneath the train stations. The town's signature dish is **kishimen**, flat, floury noodles served in a variety of ways; one of the tastiest is in a kind of salad called *komasu*.

The main **drinking** area is around Sakae Ō-chōme on the far eastern side of the central park. Here you'll find many multi-storey buildings, decked out in neon, where numerous *nomiya*, clubs, and more dubious establishments, are piled on top of each other.

Traditional performing arts are well supported in Nagoya, with a newish Nō theatre opposite the castle and the grand Kabuki theatre Misono-za in the downtown area of Fushimi; for details of shows contact the International Centre or check out the listings in the free city magazines (see p.393).

## Restaurants and cafés

**Café de Crie**. At several locations around the city including Sakae and near the *Hilton*. A chain café offering cheap and tasty breakfasts and snacks.

**Hard Rock Café**. Hirokoji-dōri, Sakae, next to the *Hilton* hotel. You know the score before you enter. The same American-style burgers, fries and rock'n'roll nick nacks found at other outlets around the world.

**Nagoya Hilton**, 1-3-3 Sakae. Head to this hotel for a fantastic range of good-value lunches in all six of its restaurants, ranging from a curry and salad buffet (¥1600) to Japanese specialities such as *sukiyaki* and tempura (¥1900–¥3000 per person).

**Jerry's Uno**. Laid-back Mexican café-cum-American-diner next to the cinema on the corner a block west of the *Hilton*. Serves spicy buritos, cheesy tacos and crispy tacos, as well as an impressive range of beers from around the world.

**Matsuzakaya**. On the seventh floor of the department store, next to JR Nagoya Station, is a wide range of restaurants where you can sample the noodle dish, *kishimen*.

**Ōsho**. Cheap and cheerful Chinese café, one block south of the Maruzen book shop on one of Sakae's main shopping streets. Has an English menu and pictures of the excellent-value set meals which rarely cost over ¥1000. Daily 11am–11.30pm.

**Yagya**, 3-13-21 Meieki. Ultra modern Southeast Asian and Japanese restaurant with a vaguely Balinese feel to its interior. Look for the huge Aztec ruin facade, 2min walk northeast of JR Nagoya Station. A good deal if you come with a crowd and share dishes. There's also a branch in Sakae. Daily 5pm–midnight.

**Yamamoto-ya Honten**, B1, Horiuchi Bldg, Meieki. Chief outlet of noodle café chain, on Sakura-dōri a few minutes' walk from the JR station. The specialities are *miso nikomi* (thick udon noodles in a bean paste) and locally-reared *tori kochin* (chicken). Around ¥1500 per head. Daily 11am–7.30pm.

## Bars & clubs

**Click**, 3F, Toe Bldg, 4-11-6 Sakae. Small bar and club where the music ranges from blue grass and jazz to hip hop. Entrance on Fri & Sat is ¥1500 including two drinks, while women get in free from 8–10pm.

**ID Bar**, 3-1-15 Sakae. Psychadelic flowers decorate this multi-level bar and club with a funky vibe. ¥1000 to enter gets you two tokens that can be used for food or drinks, all priced at ¥500. Open Tues–Sun 6pm–midnight.

**Santa Barbara Restaurant and Bar Grill**, beside exit 3 of the Ōsu Kannon subway station. Most people come to drink, play pool and just hang out at this California-style restaurant. With special events every night, good music and a outdoor wooden deck you'll find most of Nagoya's *gaijin* community here.

**Underground**, 4-3 Sakae. On third and fourth floors of a corner building. Look for the London Underground symbol on the door to this long-running club, also known as *Lush*. Dark, crowded at weekends, but a good place to dance. Entrance is ¥1500 on Fri & Sat, including two drinks. Daily 9pm–5am.

# Listings

**Airlines** ANA, Sumitomo Shoji Bldg, 1-1-6 Higashi-Sakura (international ☎0120–029333, domestic ☎0120–029222); JAL, Sakae Sun City Bldg, 4-1-8 Sakae (international ☎0120–255931, domestic ☎0120–255971); JAS, 2F, Tōkyū Bldg, 1-17-18 Marunouchi (international ☎0120–711283, domestic 0120–511283).

**Airport information**, ☎0568/29-0765

**Banks and exchange** There are several major bank branches around the stations, along Sakura-dōri and Nishiki-dōri in Sakae.

**Bookshops** The best places for English-language books are Maruzen, 3-2-7 Sakae (daily except Wed 10am–7pm) and Kinokuniya, within the Loft department store in the Nadya Park Building in Sakae (daily except Tues 11am–8pm).

**Car rental** Eki Rent-a-car (☎052/581-0882); Japan Rent-a-car (☎052/221-7631).

**Consulates** Australia, 8F, Ikko Fushima Bldg, 1-20-10 Nishiki, Naka-ku (☎052/211-0603); Canada 6F, Nakato Marunouchi Bldg, 3-17-6 Marunouchi (☎052/972-0450); USA, 6F, Nishiki SIS Bldg, 3-10-33 Nishiki, Naka-ku (☎052/203-4011).

**Hospital** Nagoya's main hospital is Nagoya University Hospital, 65 Tsuruma, Shōwa-ku, but it's best to first call the International Centre (☎052/581-0100) and they'll tell you the most appropriate place to go.

**Police** The Prefectural Police Office is at 2-1-1 Sannomaru (☎052/951-1611). Emergency numbers are listed in Basics on p.70.

**Post office** The Central Post Office is at 1-1-1 Meieki, a minute's walk north of the JR station. Open Mon–Fri 9am–7pm, Sat 9am–5pm, Sun 9am–12.30pm.

**Travel agency** The main JTB office is near Nagoya JR station (☎052/582-9481), and there's also a useful branch in the *Hilton* hotel (☎052/221-8768).

# Inuyama

Easily visited in a day-trip from Nagoya is the castle town of **INUYAMA**, 25km north of the city, beside the Kiso-gawa. The town feels like an affluent suburb of Nagoya, but on summer evenings, displays of *ukai*, or cormorant fishing (see box below), to which the castle's floodlit exterior provides a dramatic backdrop, will transport you back centuries.

During the day it won't take you long to explore the town's small, original castle, **Inuyama-jō**; you're more likely to be tempted to linger in **Uraku-en**, the delightful garden. Otherwise Inuyama's best attraction is the nearby open-air architectural museum **Meiji Mura**, which brings together a fascinating range of Meiji-era buildings in a huge landscaped park.

## Inuyama-jō and around

Although the castle is slightly closer to Inuyama-Yuen Station, if you approach it from the west side of Inuyama Station – which takes around ten minutes on foot – you'll pass

---

### UKAI

Inuyama on the Kiso-gawa, and Gifu on the Nagara-gawa 20km west (see p.399), are two of the main locations for **ukai**, or night-time **fishing with cormorants**, a skill developed back in the seventh century. The slender-necked birds are used to catch *ayu*, a sweet freshwater fish, in season between May and September. The fishermen, dressed in traditional straw skirts and pointed hats, handle up to twelve cormorants on long leashes, attached at the birds' throats with a ring to prevent them from swallowing the fish. The birds dive into the water, hunting the *ayu* which are attracted to the light of the fire blazing in the metal braziers hanging from the bows of the narrow fishing boats. The birds are specially bred and trained for the job and get well fed afterwards.

The fast-moving show usually only lasts around twenty minutes, but an *ukai* jaunt is not just about fishing. Around two hours before the start of the fishing, the audience boards long, canopied boats, decorated with paper lanterns, which sail up river and then moor to allow a pre-show picnic. Unless you pay extra you'll have to bring your own food and drink, but sometimes a boat will drift by selling beer, snacks and fireworks – another essential *ukai* component. Although you can watch the show for free from the river bank, you won't experience the thrill of racing alongside the fishing boats, the birds splashing furiously in the reflected light of the fire.

The *ukai* season in Inuyama runs from June 1 to September 30, with boats sailing from the dock beside the Inuyama-bashi bridge, five minutes' walk north of Inuyama Yuen Station. In June, July and August the boats depart at 6pm and the fishing show begins at 7.50pm, while in September the start time is 5.30pm, with the *ukai* kicking off at 7.20pm. In June and September the cost is ¥2500, rising to ¥2800 during the peak months of July and August, when it's best to reserve a place at your hotel or the booking office (☎0568/61-0057). *Ukai* is not performed on nights of the full moon or during and after heavy rain, when the rivers become too muddy.

through an area of old wooden houses culminating in the small **Inuyama Artifacts Museum** (daily 9am–5pm; ¥100). Here you can see two of the thirteen towering, ornately decorated floats (*yatai*), paraded around Inuyama during the town's major festival on the first weekend of April, and a video of the *matsuri*. If you visit the museum on Friday or Saturday, you can also see a craftsman demonstrating the art of making *karakuri*, the mechanical wooden puppets that perform on the *yatai*.

The museum is just in front of **Haritsuna-jinja**, the plain shrine at which the colourful festival takes place. One minute's walk up the hill behind the shrine will bring you to the entrance of the only privately owned castle in Japan, **Inuyama-jō** (daily 9am–5pm; ¥400). This toy-like fortress was built in 1537, making it the oldest in Japan (despite parts of it having been extensively renovated), and has belonged to the Naruse family since 1618. Inside, the donjon is nothing special, but there's a pretty view of the river and surrounding country from the top, where you can appreciate the defensive role that this white castle played.

East of Inuyama-jō, within the grounds of the luxury *Meitetsu Inuyama Hotel* beside the river, is the beautiful garden **Uraku-en** (daily: Mar–Nov 9am–5pm; Jan, Feb & Dec 9am–4pm; ¥1000). The mossy lawns and stone pathways act as a fancy frame for the subdued **Jo-an**, a traditional teahouse and national treasure. Originally built in Kyoto by Oda Uraku, the younger brother of the warlord Oda Nobunaga, the yellow-walled teahouse has floor space for just over three *tatami* mats and can only be viewed from the outside. If you want tea (¥500) you'll have to go to one of the garden's larger modern teahouses.

## Meiji Mura and around

Some 7km southeast of Inuyama lie the extensive grounds of **Meiji Mura** (March–Oct 9.30am–5pm; Jan, Feb, Nov & Dec 9.30am–4pm; ¥1500), one of the best of several open-air architecutural museums dotted around Japan. The park's one million square metres contain 67 structures, including lamps that once stood on a bridge to the Imperial Palace in Tokyo, churches, banks, a Kabuki theatre, a lighthouse and a telephone exchange from Sapporo. The common factor is that all date from around the Meiji era (1868–1912), when Western influences were flooding into Japan, resulting in some unique hybrid architecture, such as the front of Frank Lloyd Wright's original Imperial Hotel. This highlight, at the north end of the park, is a survivor of the Great Kantō Earthquake, which hit Tokyo the day after the hotel opened in 1923.

The sheer size of Meiji Mura means that tour groups are easily swallowed up and you may be tempted to hop on the electric bus (¥600) that beetles from one end of the park to the other, or the old Kyoto tram (¥300) and steam locomotive (¥500) that only go part of the way. Give yourself half a day and you can cover most of the park on foot. There are several places to snack or eat **lunch** within the park. Coffee and cake inside the *Imperial Hotel* is rather pricey at ¥800; hold out instead for lunch at the reasonable, modern restaurant, opposite the elegant reception hall of the Marquis Saigō Tsugumichi (younger brother of Kagoshima's famous general Saigō Takamori, at the southern end of the park, run by Inuyama's prestiguous *Meitetsu Inuyama Hotel*.

**Buses** leave at regular intervals from the east side of Inuyama Station for the twenty-minute journey to Meiji Mura (¥820 return), or you can go directly from Nagoya's Meitetsu bus station (¥1190 return), which takes one hour.

If you're in the mood for a **country walk**, head 3km west towards Gakuden Station on the Meitetsu Komaki line between Inuyama and Nagoya, until you reach the **Ōgata-jinja**, one of a pair of fertility shrines dedicated to the Shinto deities, Izanagi and Isanami. Ōgata-jinja is the female's shrine and as such is packed with cleft rocks and the like resembling female genetalia, while **Tagata-jinja**, further southwest, the male shrine, is where you'll find all shapes and sizes of carved penises. Both shrines have festivals, one week apart in early March, which involve the parading of a giant vagina and penis around town and lots of sake drinking. Ōgata-jinja stands around 1.5km east of Gakuden Station and Tagata-jinja is beside Tagata-jinja-mae Station, one stop further south on the Meitetsu Komaki line.

## Practicalities

Inuyama is roughly thirty minutes from both Nagoya and Gifu (see below) by the Meitetsu railway and is best visited as a day-trip from either city. At the **tourist information booth** (daily 9am–5pm; ☎0568/61-6000) beside the central exit of Inuyama Station, the assistants speak a little English and will provide you with English maps and leaflets. If you need more detailed assistance head for the Inuyama International Sightseeing Centre "FRUEDE" (daily 9am–7pm), five minutes' walk east of the station.

**Places to stay** include the *Inuyama International Youth Hostel* (☎0568/61-1111, fax 61-2770; ③), which has no dorms and is really a modern hotel. Japanese-style rooms cost ¥2800 per person, Western-style ones start at ¥3600, the restaurant is fine and the laundry free. With such good facilities, you'll need to book well in advance. To reach the hostel, walk for fifteen minutes from Inuyama-Yuen Station following the Kiso-gawa upstream until you reach the first major turning off to the right, where there's a park and a sign pointing up a steep flight of steps to the hostel. Alternatively, take the monorail from Inuyama-Yuen Station to the Monkey Park (¥150) and walk north for ten minutes past the park, across the main road, and up the hill on your left.

## Gifu

On the other side of the Kiso-gawa from Inuyama is Gifu-ken, with its capital, **GIFU**, 20km further west. The city pretty much repeats the formula of *ukai* on a meandering river overlooked by a hilltop castle, but is otherwise a bigger and more modern place, rebuilt after the double whammy of an earthquake in 1891 and blanket bombings during World War II. The city is also renowned for its production of **paper umbrellas** and lanterns and it's possible to visit a couple of workshops, although you might not always be able to see the craftspeople at work.

The Meitetsu Shin-Gifu Station is 200m north of Gifu's JR Station, on the main road leading to the Nagara-gawa, around 2km further north. This is where the **ukai** displays (see box p.397) run each year from May 11 to October 15. You'll have to bring your own picnic for the boat, and the cormorant fishing lasts only thirty minutes and, at ¥3300, it's more expensive than in Inuyama, which may persuade you to view the whole thing for free from the riverside. If the water is low, you'll be able to walk out across the rocky river bed for a better view of the proceedings. If you do want to go on the boats, book first at the boat office (☎0582/62-0140; English spoken) beside the Nagara-bashi. To reach this bridge it's best to take bus 11 (¥200) from either of the stations.

The small white castle of **Gifu-jō** (daily 9am–5pm; ¥200), perched atop Kinka-zan, is the city's main daytime attraction and is in Gifu-kōen, the park around the densely-forested hillock looming over the Nagara-gawa. The castle itself is an unremarkable re-creation, but the reason for going up to it on the cable car (daily 9am–5pm; ¥600 one way; ¥1050 return) is for the panoramic view of the river winding its way past the hump-backed outcrops on Gifu's surrounding plains. The park is reached on the same bus that goes out to the Nagara-bashi. While you're out here, pop into **Shōhō-ji**, a temple opposite the park, housing an imposing 13.7m-tall sculpture of Buddha made of lacquered bamboo.

Around 1km south of Gifu-kōen at 1-18 Koguma-chō, is Ozeki Shōten, a company which produces traditional **paper lanterns** which sell for around ¥20,000 with a stand. The workshops here are closed to the public, but in the shop (Mon–Sat 9am–5pm) you'll find a display outlining the process. To see craftsmen at work, head for the paper umbrella company, Sakaida Honten, 27 Kanō-Naka Hiroe (Mon–Sat 7am–noon, 2–5pm). If you ask nicely, the assistants will show you a range of the colourful umbrellas, which start at ¥3000 and rise to ¥100,000 for the giant red parasols often seen outside the most traditional of ryokan. The shop is less than ten minutes on foot south of the JR station, but tricky to locate; get the assistants at Gifu tourist information to draw you a map.

## Practicalities

Gifu has two **train stations** – JR and Meitetsu – within five minutes' walk of each other at the south end of the city's commercial district. The main **tourist information office** (daily 9am—7pm; ☎0582/62 4415) is inside JR Gifu station, beside the ticket barrier at the Nagara-guchi exit. The helpful assistants speak a little English, can provide English maps and pamphlets on the city and the prefecture, and point you towards accommodation.

There's a good range of both Western and Japanese style **hotels** and ryokan in the city. As usual, several business hotels are clustered close by the train stations. One of the better ones is the comfortable *Hotel 330 Grande* (☎0582/67-0330, fax 64-1330; [5]), with singles from ¥8000. The *Gifu Youth Hostel* (☎0582/63-6631; [1]) is a cheap and clean place run by a chatty manager who speaks a little English and writes about local nature. Its location on top of hilly Kashimori-kōen on the east side of town means you'll save a lot of sweat by taking a taxi there from the station (around ¥2000) rather than lugging your bags 2km up the hill. Many tourist ryokan line the Nagara-gawa, where the *ukai* displays take place, but if you can afford it, head for *Ryokan Banshōkan* (☎0582/62-0039; [7]), a traditional wooden building, with raked gravel gardens, beside the entrance to Gifu-kōen.

As far as **eating** goes, you'll find a handful of fast-food joints underneath the JR station, including *Mos Burger* and the pastry shop *Vie de France*. Around the main road heading north from the station, along which trams run, are many other dining options, including the *Gurume-kan*, a corner building with different restaurants on each level.

## travel details

### Trains

The trains between the major cities listed below are the fastest, direct services. There are also frequent slower services, run by JR and several private companies, covering the same destinations. It is usually possible, especially on long-distance routes, to get there faster by changing between services.

**Kanazawa** to: Echigo-Yuzawa (10 daily; 2hr 30min); Fukui (60 daily; 50min); Kyoto (24 daily; 2hr 20min); Niigata (5 daily; 3hr 40min); Ōsaka (24 daily; 2hr 45min); Tokyo (Ueno Station; daily; 6hr 5min); Toyama (20 daily; 40min).

**Matsumoto** to: Hakuba (12 daily; 55min); Hotaka (34 daily; 15min); Nagano (34 daily; 45min); Nagoya (13 daily; 2hr); Ōsaka (1 daily; 4hr); Tokyo (Shinjuku Station;18 daily; 2hr 30min).

**Nagano** to: Matsumoto (13 daily; 50min); Nagoya (13 daily; 2hr 50min); Niigata (2 daily; 3hr); Ōsaka (1 daily; 4hr 50min); Tokyo (23 daily; 1hr 30min).

**Nagoya** to: Fukui (8 daily; 2hr 5min); Fukuoka (Hakata Station; 24 daily; 3hr 25min); Gifu (every 30 min; 30min); Hiroshima (at least 30 daily; 2hr 20min); Inuyama (every 30 min; 35min); Kanazawa (8 daily; 2hr 55min); Kii-Katsuura (4 daily; 3hr 20min); Kyoto (every 10 min; 45min); Matsumoto (13 daily; 2hr); Nagano (13 daily; 2hr 50min); Okayama (every 30 min; 2hr); Ōsaka (every 10 min; 1hr); Takayama (9 daily; 2hr 35min); Toba (8 daily; 1hr 30min); Tokyo (every 10 min; 1hr 50min); Toyama (11 daily; 3hr 40min).

**Toyama** to Kanazawa (20 daily; 40min); Nagoya (4 daily; 3hr 40min); Niigata (5 daily; 3hr); Ōsaka (14 daily; 3hr 15min); Takayama (4 daily; 1hr 30min); Tateyama (21 daily; 1hr); Tokyo (Ueno Station 1 daily; 5hr 40min).

### Buses

The buses listed below are mainly long-distance services – often travelling overnight – between the major cities, and local services where there is no alternative means of transport. For shorter journeys, however, trains are almost invariably quicker and often no more expensive.

**Kanazawa** to: Fukuoka (1 daily; 12hr 45min); Nagoya (10 daily; 3hr 50min); Niigata (2 daily; 4hr 40min); Kyoto (5 daily; 3hr 50min); Sendai (1 daily; 8hr 30min); Tokyo (Ikebukuro Station 4 daily; 7hr 30min); Wajima (4 daily; 2hr).

**Matsumoto** to: Nagano (16 daily; 1hr 20min); Ōsaka (1 daily; 6hr 50min); Tokyo (Shinjuku Station; 12 daily; 3hr 10min).

**Nagano** to: Matsumoto (16 daily; 1hr 20min); Nozawa Onsen (5 daily; 1hr 15min); Togakushi (5 daily; 1hr 30min); Tokyo (1 daily; 6hr 30min).

**Nagoya** to: Kanazawa (1 daily; 8hr 20min); Kyoto (24 daily; 2hr 15min); Magome (1 daily; 2hr); Ogimachi (1 daily; 4hr); Ōsaka (6 daily; 3hr); Tokyo (14 daily; 6hr).

**Ferries**

**Nagoya** to: Naha (1 daily; 21hr) Sendai (1 daily; 21hr); Tomakomai (1 daily; 38hr 45min).

**Tsuruga** to: Otaru (weekly; 21hr).

**Flights**

**Komatsu** to: Fukuoka (2 daily; 1hr 15min); Hiroshima (3 daily; 1hr 20min); Izumo (6 weekly; 1hr 5min); Kagoshima (5 weekly; 1hr 40min); Naha (1 daily; 2hr 15min); Okayama (2 daily; 55min); Sapporo (1 daily; 1hr 35min); Sendai (1 daily; 1hr 5min); Tokyo (8 daily; 1hr).

**Matsumoto** to: Ōsaka (2 daily; 1hr); Sapporo (1 daily; 1hr, 30min); Fukuoka (1 daily; 1hr 30min).

**Nagoya** to: Akita (2 daily; 1hr 10min); Aomori (2 daily; 1hr 20min); Asahikawa (1 daily; 1hr 40min); Fukuoka (13 daily; 1hr 15min); Hakodate (2 daily; 1hr 25min); Kagoshima (5 daily; 1hr 20min); Kōchi (2 daily; 55min); Kumamoto (2 daily; 1hr 15min); Matsuyama (2 daily; 1hr); Memanbetsu (1 daily; 1hr 50min); Miyazaki (5 daily; 1hr 15imin); Nagasaki (4 daily; 1hr 20min); Narita (1 daily; 1hr); Niigata (2 daily; 55min); Oita (3 daily; 1hr 10min); Okinawa (6 daily; 2hr 10min); Sapporo (10 daily; 1hr 35min); Sendai (6 daily; 1hr 5min); Takamatsu (2 daily; 1hr 5min); Tokushima (1 daily; 1hr) Toyama (2 daily; 55min);

**Toyama** to: Fukuoka (1 daily; 1hr 30min); Hakodate (1 daily; 1hr 45min); Kansai International (1 daily; 1hr 15min); Nagoya (2 daily; 55min); Sapporo (1 daily; 1hr 25min); Tokyo (6 daily; 1hr 5min).

CHAPTER SIX

# KANSAI

In a country so devoid of flat land, the great rice-growing plains of **KANSAI**, the district around Ōsaka and Kyoto, are imbued with an almost mystical significance. This was where the first proto-nation took root, in the historic region known as Yamato, and where a distinct Japanese civilization evolved from the strong cultural influences of China and Korea. Kansai people are tremendously proud of their pivotal role in Japanese history and tend to look down on Tokyo, which they regard as an uncivilized upstart. Today, its superb legacy of temples, palaces, shrines, gardens, sculpture and crafts makes Kansai one of Japan's top tourist destinations.

The opening of the spectacular Kansai International airport in 1994 created a new gateway into Japan which is already providing stiff competition for Tokyo. At the same time it has given a significant tourism impetus to **Ōsaka**, the country's second-largest metropolis. A much-maligned city, Ōsaka is not short of impressive attractions and easily makes up for its superficial shortcomings with an excess of commercial spirit – the source of its long-established wealth – and an unqualified love of eating, drinking and general bonhomie. Even on the briefest stay in Kansai you won't be disappointed if you spend time visiting the city's fabulous **aquarium**, the handsomely restored castle **Ōsaka-jō** and the laudable **Liberty Ōsaka**, an uncompromising civil rights museum.

From Ōsaka, you could also take a trip out to **Takarazuka**, home of Japan's show-stopping all-female musical drama troupe and the imaginative **Tezuka Osamu Manga Museum**, celebrating a Japanese master of comic-book art.

Though **Kyoto** is nowhere near as big as Ōsaka, it's still a major city which keeps many of its charms hidden from view. You could spend a lifetime exploring Kyoto's bewildering array of ancient Buddhist **temples** and gorgeously decorated **imperial palaces** wrapped round with exquisite **gardens**. Until Emperor Meiji decamped for the bright lights of Tokyo in 1868, Kyoto was Japan's imperial capital and to this day represents the last word in cultural refinement. Its elaborate cuisine, traditional theatre, even its everyday crafts reflect this incomparable lineage. To avoid cultural overload, it's best to take Kyoto in small chunks, and to spend at least one day in the surrounding districts. **Hiei-zan**, in particular, offers not only majestic temples but also an escape from the city streets, while in **Uji**'s Byōdō-in you'll find one of the country's supreme architectural masterpieces.

## ACCOMMODATION PRICE CODES

All accommodation in this book has been graded according to the following price codes, which refer to the cheapest double or twin room available for most of the year, and include taxes. Note that rates may increase during peak holiday periods, in particular around Christmas and New Year, the Golden Week (April 28–May 6) and Obon (the week around August 15), when accommodation is very difficult to get without an advance reservation. In the case of hostels providing dormitory accommodation, the code refers to the charge per bed. See p.36 for more details on accommodation.

| | | |
|---|---|---|
| ① under ¥3000 | ④ ¥7000–10,000 | ⑦ ¥20,000–30,000 |
| ② ¥3000–5000 | ⑤ ¥10,000–15,000 | ⑧ ¥30,000–40,000 |
| ③ ¥5000–7000 | ⑥ ¥15,000–20,000 | ⑨ over ¥40,000 |

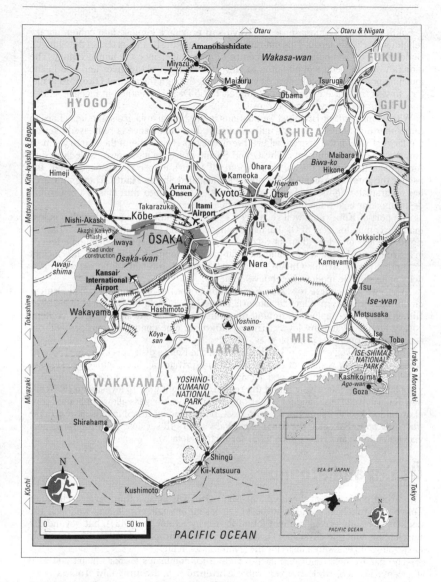

Before Kyoto even existed, the monks of **Nara** were busily erecting their great monuments to Buddha under the patronage of an earlier group of princes and nobles. This relaxed, appealing town holds the distinction of being Japan's first permanent capital, founded in the early eighth century. A surprising number of buildings survive, notably the great **Tōdai-ji** with its colossal bronze Buddha, but Nara's real glory lies in its wealth of statues. Nowhere is this more evident than the nearby temple complex of **Hōryū-ji**, a treasure-trove of early Japanese art.

South of Nara, the monasteries of **Kōya-san** provide a glimpse into contemporary religious practice in Japan. This mountain-top retreat – the headquarters of the Shingon Buddhist sect – has been an active centre of pilgrimage since the ninth century. The monks welcome people of all faiths to stay in their quiet old temples and join in the morning prayer service. Afterwards you can walk through the ancient **Okunoin** cemetery to visit the grave of Shingon's founder, Kōbō Daishi, wreathed in incense smoke under the towering cryptomeria trees.

With so many major Buddhist foundations in the Kansai area, it's sometimes hard to remember that Shinto is Japan's native religion. But the balance is redressed over on the far east side of the district, where **Ise-jingū** represents one of the country's most important Shinto monuments. The Grand Shrine of Ise, as it's known, is dedicated to Amaterasu, the Sun Goddess, from whom all Japan's emperors are descended. **Ise** itself is the gateway to an attractive neck of land called **Shima Hantō**. Though the area has no dramatic sights, the lovely island-speckled bay of **Ago-wan** makes a rewarding destination for boat rides through its unspoilt scenery.

The port of **Kōbe**, now well recovered from 1995's devastating earthquake, is less than thirty minutes west of Ōsaka, in a dramatic location on the edge of Ōsaka Bay. Its sights are less of a draw than its relaxed cosmopolitan atmosphere, best experienced in a stroll around Kōbe's shops and harbour-side developments. Close by is the ancient hot spring resort, **Arima Onsen**, which has managed to retain a little old-world rusticity alongside the modern hotel developments.

Wherever you choose to stay in Kansai, don't miss the opportunity to visit **Himeji**, on the area's western edge, to explore **Himeji-jō**, Japan's most impressive castle. Himeji also has a couple of intriguing museums in buildings designed by top contemporary architects and the lovely **Himeji Kōko-en**, nine connected gardens laid out according to traditional principles.

The most convenient way of **getting around** the Kansai district is by train. The area is criss-crossed by a skein of competing JR and private rail lines, while the Tōkaidō Shinkansen provides a high-speed service between Ōsaka, Kyoto, Kōbe and Himeji. If you plan to travel intensively round the region, you might want to investigate JR-West's new Kansai Area Pass. Valid for either one or four days, the pass allows unlimited travel on all local services operated by JR-West, but excluding the Shinkansen. For those travelling on to Fukuoka, the Sanyō Area Pass covers JR services from Kansai airport via Ōsaka, Kōbe and Himeji (see p.521 for further details).

# Ōsaka and around

The urban equivalent of the Elephant Man, **ŌSAKA**, Japan's third largest city after Tokyo and Yokohama, yearns to be loved despite its ugliness. It may well lack the pockets of beauty and refinement found in nearby Kyoto (see p.424), but beyond the unrelenting concrete cityscape, Ōsaka is a vibrant metropolis, inhabited by famously easy-going citizens with a taste for the good things in life.

The handsomely renovated castle, **Ōsaka-jo**, dominates Ōsaka's heart just as it did centuries ago, while the venerable **Shitennō-ji** and **Sumiyoshi Taisha** hark back to the city's past importance as a religious centre. In contrast, bizarre modern buildings, such as the spaceship-like **Ōsaka Dome** sports stadium and the fantastic **aquarium** at the Tempozan Harbour Village, thrust forth from the urban sprawl like shiny gems.

But what is really special about Ōsaka is its people, who speak one of Japan's more earthy dialects **Ōsaka-ben**, and are as friendly as Kyoto folk can be frosty. Ōsakans may greet each other saying "Mō kari makka?" (Are you making any money?), but they also know how to enjoy themselves once work has stopped. Whereas Tokyo has shut down its

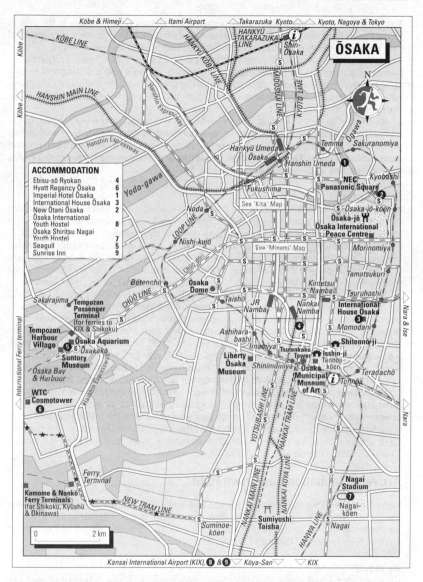

once thriving Harajuku band scene, Ōsakans still thrash out rock tunes by the castle every Sunday, while across town in Tennōji-Kōen, you'll find entertaining al fresco karaoke song and dance shows. Downtown Shinsaibashi is an eternal fancy dress parade of matronly shoppers and boozy bon viveurs, where bequiffed lads cast their nets for mini-skirted girls on the Ebisu-bashi (fishing bridge). In a city which cultivated high **arts**, such as Bunraku puppetry, the locals also have a gift for low-life comedy; Takeshi "Beat" Kitano, the internationally famous film director, started his career as a comedian in Ōsaka, while "Knock"

Yokoyama, another retired funny man, was recently elected mayor. Ōsaka is also one of Japan's great **food** cities, but Ōsakans are not precious about their cuisine, a typical local dish being *takoyaki*, the battered octopus balls, usually sold as a street snack.

Ōsaka also feels a more welcoming place for foreigners. It has Japan's largest community of Koreans and a growing *gaijin* population. There's also a willingness to face up to uncomfortable social issues, exemplified by the city's admirable civil rights museum **Liberty Ōsaka**, which among other things focuses on Japan's untouchables, the Burakumin.

If you want to escape Ōsaka's urban landscape and preoccupations for a day, take a trip out to **Takarazuka**, home of the eponymous musical drama troupe. As well as taking in one of the all-female troupe's glitzy shows, you can check out the imaginative art work at the **Tezuka Osamu Manga Museum**, a showcase for local artist Tezuka, widely regarded as the god of *manga* (comic books).

## Some history

Ōsaka's history stretches back to the fifth century when it was known as **Naniwa** and its port served as a gateway to the more advanced cultures of Korea and China. For a short period, from the middle of the seventh century, the thriving city served as Japan's capital, but in the turbulent centuries that followed it lost its status, changed its name to Ōsaka and developed as a temple town. It was on the site of the temple Ishiyama Hongan-ji that the warlord **Toyotomi Hideyoshi** decided to build his castle in 1583 (see box, p.414) and it became a key bastion in his campaign to unite the country.

With Toyotomi's death in 1598, another period of political instability loomed in Ōsaka for his supporters, as rival **Tokugawa Ieyasu** shifted the capital to Edo. The shogun's troops besieged the castle in 1614 and destroyed it, along with the Toyotomi clan's hopes for power, a year later. With Japan firmly under their control the Tokugawa shoguns were happy to allow the castle to be rebuilt and for Ōsaka to continue developing as an economic and commercial centre, which it did with spectacular success. The wealth of what became known as the "kitchen of Japan" led to patronage of the arts, such as a Kabuki and Bunraku, and an appreciation of fine food, still retained today.

In the twentieth century, Ōsaka has dragged itself up from rubble of World War II bombings to become one of the wealthiest cities in the world, its gross domestic product exceeding that of Australia. Although its hopes of hosting the 2008 Olympic Games are probably misplaced (Nagano having held the 1997 Winter Olympics), the development programme being pushed through will result in many new facilities, including a Universal Studio theme park on Ōsaka Bay.

# Arrival, information and orientation

Served by two airports, numerous ferries and buses, not to mention a slew of railway companies, you can arrive in Ōsaka from almost any point in Japan and, via Kansai International airport, from many places overseas, too. There's also a twice-monthly ferry service between Ōsaka and Shanghai in China.

## By plane

All international and many domestic flights now arrive at **Kansai International airport (KIX)**, on a man-made island in Ōsaka Bay, some 35km south of the city centre. International arrivals are on the first floor of the sleek modern building, topped with a wave-like roof, where you'll also find the small **Kansai Tourist Information Centre** (daily 9am–9pm; ☎0724/56-6025), a separate desk where you can make hotel reservations and several **bureau de change** booths. Domestic arrivals are on the second floor.

The fastest way into the city is by **train**. Services depart from the station connected to the second floor of the passenger terminal building. The regular **Nankai Express**

## ŌSAKA

| Ōsaka | Ōsaka | 大阪 |
|-------|-------|------|

### ARRIVAL

| Hankyū Umeda Station | Hankyū Umeda-eki | 阪急梅田駅 |
|---|---|---|
| Hanshin Umeda Station | Hanshin Umeda-eki | 阪神梅田駅 |
| JR Namba Station | JR Namba-eki | ＪＲ難波駅 |
| JR Ōsaka Station | JR Ōsaka-eki | ＪＲ大阪駅 |
| Kamome Terminal | Kamome-futō | かもめ埠頭 |
| Kansai International airport | Kansai Kokusai-Kūkō | 関西国際空港 |
| Namba Nankai Station | Namba Nankai-eki | 難波南海駅 |
| Nankō Terminal | Nankō-futō | 南港埠頭 |
| Ōsaka International airport (Itami) | Ōsaka Kokusai-Kūkō | 大阪国際空港（イタミ） |
| Shin-Ōsaka Station | Shin-Ōsaka-eki | 新大阪駅 |
| Tempozan Terminal | Tempozan-futō | 天保山埠頭 |

### ACCOMMODATION

| Hotel California | Hoteru Kariforunia | ホテルカリフォルニア |
|---|---|---|
| Capsule Hotel Asahiplaza Shinsaibashi | Kapuseru Hoteru Asahi Puraza Shinsaibashi | カプセルホテル朝日プラザ心斎橋 |
| Capsule Inn Namba | Kapuseru In Namba | カプセルＩＮＮ難波 |
| Ebisu-sō Ryokan | Ebisu-sō Ryokan | えびす荘旅館 |
| Hotel Hokke Club Ōsaka | Hotel Hokke Kurabu Ōsaka | ホテル法華倶楽部大阪 |
| Hyatt Regency Ōsaka | Haiatto Rejenshii Ōsaka | ハイアットレジェンシー |
| Imperial Hotel Ōsaka | Teikoku Hoteru Ōsaka | 帝国ホテル大阪 |
| Hotel International House Ōsaka | Hoteru Kokuritsu Hausu Ōsaka | ホテル国立ハウス大阪 |
| Namba Oriental Hotel | Namba Orientaru Hoteru | 難波オリエンタルホテル |
| New Ōtani Ōsaka | Nyū Ōtani Ōsaka | ニューオオタニ大阪 |
| Hotel Nikkō Ōsaka | Hoteru Nikkō Ōsaka | ホテル日光大阪 |
| Ōsaka International Youth Hostel | Ōsaka Kokusai Yūsu Hosuteru | 大阪国際ユースホステル |
| Ōsaka Shiritsu Nagai Youth Hostel | Ōsaka Shiritsu Nagai Yūsu Hosuteru | 大阪市立長居ユースホステル |
| Ritz Carlton Ōsaka | Za Rittsu Kāruton Ōsaka | ザリッツカールトン大阪 |
| Hotel Seagull | Hoteru Shiigaru | ホテルシーガル |
| Sunrise Inn | Sanraizu In | サンライズイン |

### THE CITY

| Dōtomburi | Dōtomburi | 道頓堀 |
|---|---|---|
| Liberty Ōsaka | Ribati Ōsaka | リバティ大阪 |
| Museum of Oriental Ceramics | Tōyo Tōji Bijutsukan | 東洋陶磁美術館 |
| Namba | Namba | 難波 |
| National Bunraku Theatre | Kokuritsu Bunraku Gekijō | 国立文楽劇場 |
| Ōsaka-jō | Ōsaka-jō | 大阪城 |
| Ōsaka Aquarium | Kaiyūkan | 海遊館 |
| Ōsaka Nō Hall | Ōsaka Nōgaku-kaikan | 大阪能楽会館 |
| Ōsaka Shōchiku-za | Ōsaka Shōchiku-za | 大阪松竹座 |
| Shinsaibashi | Shinsaibashi | 心斎橋 |
| Shin-Sekai | Shin-Sekai | 新世界 |
| Shitennō-ji | Shitennō-ji | 四天王寺 |
| Sumiyoshi Taisha | Sumiyoshi Taisha | 住吉大社 |
| Tempozan Harbour Village | Tempozan Hābā Birejji | 天保山ハーバービレッジ |
| Tennōji-kōen | Tennōji-kōen | 天王寺公園 |
| Umeda | Umeda | 梅田 |

*continued oveleaf*

| ŌSAKA contd | | |
| --- | --- | --- |
| **RESTAURANTS** | | |
| Aisaitei | *Aisaitei* | 愛菜亭 |
| Fun Fun Plaza | *Fan Fan Puraza* | ファンファンプラザ |
| Gochisō Biru | *Gochisō Biru* | ごちそうビル |
| Herbis Plaza | *Hābisu Puraza* | ハービスプラザ |
| Kagetsu | *Kagetsu* | かげつ |
| Kani Dōraku | *Kani Dōraku* | かに道楽 |
| Kisoji | *Kisoji* | きそじ |
| Kuidaore | *Kuidaore* | くいだおれ |
| Madonna | *Madonna* | マドンナ |
| Nawasushi | *Nawasushi* | 縄寿司 |
| Ninniku-ya | *Ninniku-ya* | にんにく屋 |

or *kaisoku* (¥870), takes just over forty minutes to reach Nankai Namba Station, although it's hard to resist the chic **Rapi:t** (pronounced Rapid), designed like a train from a sci-fi comic, which costs ¥1370 and does the journey in around thirty minutes. From Nankai Namba Station, you can take a subway or taxi to other parts of the city.

**JR** also runs trains directly to several stations in and around Ōsaka from KIX, and if you have a rail pass voucher you can exchange it at KIX Station. For pass holders, the services to JR Namba Station (1hr; ¥1010) are a good alternative to the Nankai Express. The **Haruka** limited express is a convenient, but pricey option, stopping at Tennōji Station (30min; ¥2230), handy for the Nagai Youth Hostel; Shin-Ōsaka Station (45min; ¥2930), where you can catch the Shinkansen; and then on to Kyoto (1hr 15min; ¥3390). If you're in no hurry, the regular JR express trains to Tennōji Station (45min; ¥1010) and Ōsaka Station (70min; ¥1140), in the Umeda area of the city, are worth considering.

To avoid the hassle of dragging your luggage on and off trains, there are also **limousine buses** and taxis for various locations around Ōsaka, including several hotels, departing from international arrivals. All central city locations take around one hour to reach, depending on the traffic, and cost ¥1300. There's also a direct bus to Itami airport (see below; 1hr 20min; ¥1700), and there are services to Kyoto, Kōbe and Nara. **Taxis** to central Ōsaka are expensive and no faster than the buses.

As KIX is an island airport, you also have the option of hopping on a **boat** into the city. Ferries to Ōsaka's Tempozan Harbour Village (7 daily; ¥1650) take around forty minutes. From the dock it's a seven-minute walk south to Ōsakakō Station on the Chūō subway line. Additionally, jet foils frequently zip across to Kōbe's Port Island in thirty minutes (¥2650), and there's a regular ferry service to Tokushima on Shikoku (1hr 20min; ¥2000).

**Itami airport**, 10km north of the city centre, is also known as Ōsaka International Airport even though it no longer handles overseas flights. From the airport there are regular buses into the city (25–50min depending on destination; ¥340–680) and also to Shin-Ōsaka Station (25min; ¥480), where you can connect to the Shinkansen. There are also direct limousine buses to KIX (1hr 20min; ¥1700) and on to Kyoto and Kōbe. A taxi to Umeda in central Ōsaka costs around ¥5000.

## By train

Shinkansen, taking around three hours from Tokyo or Fukuoka in Kyūshū (the two termini of the line), pull into **Shin-Ōsaka Station**, north of the city centre. You can transfer here both to other JR services around the area, or to the subway lines.

JR services, along the Tōkaidō line connecting Nagoya, Kyoto and Kōbe with Ōsaka, arrive at the central **Ōsaka Station**, in Umeda, where you'll also find the termini for the Hankyū and Hanshin lines, both of which provide cheaper connections with Kyoto and Kōbe than JR if you're not using a rail pass. Services from Nara (see p.479) on the Kintetsu line arrive at **Kintetsu Namba Station**, in the heart of the Minami district. Those from Ise (see p.500) arrive at Uehonmachi, also on the Kintetsu network.

## By bus

Ōsaka's main long-distance **bus stations** are beside JR Ōsaka Station in Umeda; the Namba Kaisoku Bus Terminal and Ōsaka City Air Terminal in Namba; Kintetsu Uehonmachi, south of the castle; and Abenobashi near Tennōji, 1km further south of the castle. All are beside or near subway and train stations for connections around the city.

## By boat

Ōsaka is still a major port of call for many of the **ferries** plying routes around Japan, and sailing into Ōsaka Bay is a memorable way of approaching the city. From the port, there are good transport links to hotels via the subway and train network.

---

### MOVING ON FROM ŌSAKA

At Kansai International **airport**, the international departure lounge is on the fourth floor, and you must pay a ¥2650 departure tax here before leaving. Domestic departures are on the second floor. It's worth noting that Kyoto, Nankai Namba and JR Namba stations all have **CAT** (city air terminal) facilities, as does the jet foil terminal on Kōbe's Port Island, where you can go through check-in procedures for Japanese and some other airlines.

If you plan to depart Ōsaka by **bus**, check first with one of the tourist information centres (see below) on timetables and which station to go to.

Among other places, there are **ferry** services from Ōsaka to Beppu, Miyazaki and Shin-Moji on Kyūshū (see p.656) and to Kōchi, Matsuyama and Tokushima on Shikoku (see p.614). In addition, there's a slow boat to Shanghai, China which leaves twice a month from Ōsaka Nankō International Ferry Terminal, close by Cosmosquare Station, where the Techno Port line meets the New Tram line. It's always best to check current timetables and fares with the tourist information office.

---

## Information

The Ōsaka Tourist Association beats both Tokyo and Kyoto hands down. There are **tourist information** offices all over the city, as well as at KIX (see p.406), so that no matter where you arrive, you're sure to be within walking distance of one. All are open daily from 8am to 8pm, have English-speaking staff and can help you book accommodation. Make sure you also pick up a free copy of the **Ōsaka City Map**, which includes a handy subway and local train map, too.

There's an office in Shin-Ōsaka Station (☎06/305-3311), handy if you've arrived by Shinkansen, while the main office is in Umeda's JR Ōsaka Station (☎06/345-2189) tucked away beside the Midōsuji East Gate opposite the Hankyū department store. You should apply at either of these if you're interested in participating in the home visit programme (see Listings, p.422). You'll also find tourist information counters beneath the OCAT train terminal at JR Namba Station (☎06/643-2125) and in Tennōji Station (☎06/774-3077).

If you're going to be in Ōsaka for a while, it's well worth visiting the International House Ōsaka, 8-2-6 Uehonmachi (☎06/772-5931), which has a well-stocked library and cultural exchange facilities.

At all the information counters and in most top hotels you'll find the free quarterly booklet *Meet Ōsaka*, which carries basic **listings** of events. A better outline of what's happening appears in the monthly *Kansai Time Out*, one of Japan's best English-language magazines, which carries detailed information and listings for the whole Kansai area as well interesting features. (Check out their Web site at *www.kto.co.jp*). *The Japan Times, Daily Yomiuri* and *Asahi Evening News* newspapers also carry special weekly sections on what's on in the Ōsaka area.

## Orientation

Like all big Japanese cities, Ōsaka is divided into wards (ku), but you'll often hear locals talking of Kita (north) and Minami (south), the split being along Chūō-dōri. **Kita** covers the areas of Umeda, where all the main railway companies have stations, and Shin-Ōsaka, north of the Yodo-gawa river and location of the Shinkansen station. On the east side of this area is Ōsaka-jō, the castle. The shopping and entertainment districts of Shinsaibashi, Dōtombuni and Namba are all part of **Minami**.

Slightly further south is **Tennōji**, where you'll find Tennōji-kōen and the temple Shitennō-ji, and further south again, the ancient shrine Sumiyoshi Taisha. West of these districts lies the patchwork of landfill islands edging Ōsaka Bay; the Ōsaka Aquarium is at **Tempozan Harbour Village**, while the Kansai area's tallest building, the WTC Cosmotower, is further south at **Nankō**.

## City transport

Ōsaka's extensive **subway and train system** operates exactly like Tokyo's (see p.87). It even has an overground circular line, called the JR Loop line, with trains running both clockwise and anticlockwise, just like the Yamanote line in Tokyo. The Loop line is handy, especially if you're using a rail pass, but most of the time you'll find the subway more convenient and quicker for getting around the city. You can transfer between the seven subway lines and the New Tram line on the same ticket, but if you switch to any of the railway lines at a connecting station, you'll need to buy either another ticket or a special transfer ticket when you start your journey. Most journeys across central Ōsaka cost around ¥200.

Because Ōsaka's attractions are widely scattered, investing in a **one-day pass** (¥850) is worth considering if you're up for a hectic round of the sights. The pass, like a thin telephone card, is valid on all the subways and will be date stamped when you pass it through the gate machines the first time. On the twentieth of each month (or twenty-first if the twentieth falls on a Sunday) you can buy the "No-My-Car-Day" pass, which is the same as the one-day pass, but only costs ¥600 (a consciousness-raising scheme to encourage people to use public transport instead of their cars).

There are plenty of **buses**, but you'll find the subways and trains with their English signs and maps much easier to use. If you do need to go short distances quickly, flag down a **taxi**; a city-centre journey shouldn't cost more then ¥2000.

## Accommodation

Being a commercial city, Ōsaka's **accommodation** ranges from scores of business hotels near the main train stations to some of the swankiest luxury hotels you'll come across in Japan. If you're in search of more traditional ryokan, you'll be better off staying in Kyoto (see p.424). The most convenient locations in Ōsaka are **Umeda** and the shopping and nightlife districts of **Shinsaibashi** and **Namba**. However, local transport is so efficient that it's no great problem to be based elsewhere, such as around Ōsaka Bay or even south of the city closer to Kansai International airport. The following reviews give the nearest subway or train station.

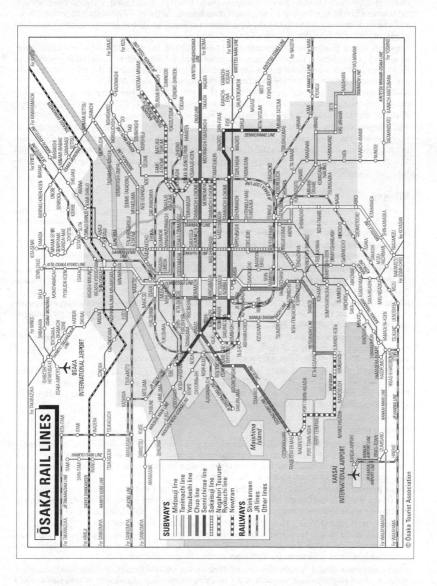

ŌSAKA RAIL LINES

SUBWAYS
Midosuji line
Tanimachi line
Yotsubashi line
Chuo line
Sennichimae line
Sakaisuji line
Nagahori Tsurumi-
Ryokuchi line
Newtram

RAILWAYS
Shinkansen
JR lines
Other lines

© Osaka Tourist Association

## Kita

**Hotel Hokke Club Ōsaka**, 12-19 Togano-cho (☎06/313-3171, fax 313-4637). One of the city's oldest business hotels, and looking its age, but it does have a choice of Western-style or *tatami* rooms and a large public bath in which to soak. Singles start at ¥6000 and the in-house restaurant also does a reasonable buffet breakfast. Umeda/Ōsaka stations. ⑤.

**Imperial Hotel Ōsaka**, 1-8-50 Temmabashi (☎06/881-1111, fax 881-1200). This new hotel, overlooking the Ō-kawa river, is just as luxurious as its famous Tokyo parent and reproduces many of Frank Lloyd Wright's original touches. Perfumed air, a golf driving range and a select range of elegant restaurants are all part of the experience. Sakuranomiya Station. ⑦–⑧.

**New Ōtani Ōsaka**, 1-4-1 Shiromi (☎06/941-1111, fax 941-9769). Deservedly one of the city's top hotels, with many of the comfortable rooms overlooking the castle and the sweep of the rivers. Excellent service and a wide range of restaurants and other facilities. Ōsaka-jō-kōen Station. ⑧.

**Ritz Carlton Ōsaka**, 2-5-25 Umeda (☎06/343-7000, fax 343-7001). New luxury hotel with the intimate feel of a European country house, sprinkled liberally with antiques and Japanese *objets d'art*. Rooms have fantastic views across the cityscape, there's a great range of restaurants, and the pool and gym are free to guests. It's always worth enquiring if they're running any special price packages. Ōsaka/Umeda stations. ⑧.

## Minami

**Hotel California**, 1-9-30 Nishi-Shinsaibashi (☎06/243-0333, fax 243-0148). Not quite what The Eagles had in mind: step into a world of kitsch in the mirrored, gilt lobby and bar, brimming with foliage. Decoration in the good-value rooms is more restrained. Shinsaibashi Station. ⑤.

**Capsule Hotel Asahiplaza Shinsaibashi**, 2-12-22 Nishi-Shinsaibashi (☎06/213-1991). Reasonably smart capsule hotel, for men only, with a large bath, sauna and restaurant. Shinsaibashi Station. ②.

**Capsule Inn Namba**, 1-7-16 Namba (☎06/633-2666). There are capsules, single rooms and small doubles on offer at this basic hotel close by all the Namba stations. Also has capsules for women. Namba Station. Capsules ①. Rooms ④.

**Ebisu-sō Ryokan**, 1-7-33 Nipponbashi-nishi (☎06/643-4861). The *tatami* rooms in this ryokan are a little shabby, but the welcome is friendly and the location, close to Namba, is handy for sampling the city's nightlife. Singles for ¥5500. Ebisuchō Station. ⑤.

**Namba Oriental Hotel**, 2-8-17 Sennichi-mae (☎06/647-8111, fax 632-9979). Good-value mid-range hotel in a fine location. Some of the spacious rooms have small balconies overlooking a courtyard with an Italianate fountain. Singles from ¥8500. Namba/Nipponbashi stations. ⑤.

**Hotel Nikkō, Ōsaka**, 1-3-3 Nishi-Shinsaibashi (☎06/244-1111, fax 245-2432). Spacious comfortable rooms, some decorated by the Japanese designer Hanae Mori, at this top-class hotel close to Ōsaka's best nightlife. Attentive service and a good range of restaurants, including a coffee shop which does a huge buffet breakfast. Shinsaibashi Station. ⑦.

## Other areas

**Hotel International House Ōsaka**, 8-2-6 Uehonmachi (☎06/773-8181, fax 773-0777). Used mainly by those attending meetings at the International House, the large rooms here are very good value, but there is a midnight curfew. Most of the rooms are singles at ¥6600 and there's a restaurant and café in the building. Uehonmachi Station. ⑤.

**Hyatt Regency Ōsaka**, 1-13-11 Nankō-Kita (☎06/612-1234, fax 614-7800). Good luxury choice near the Ōsaka World Trade Centre offering well-appointed rooms with a minimalist design theme, elegant public areas and restaurants, and indoor and outdoor pools. Nakafutō Station. ⑦–⑧.

**Ōsaka International Youth Hostel**, 4-1-56 Hagoromo, Takaishi-shi (☎0722/63-1271, fax 63-1271). The Ōsaka area's newest hostel is midway between KIX and the city centre, ten minutes' walk from Hagoromo Station on the Nankai Main line. Has both *tatami* dorm rooms and Western-style twin rooms with en-suite bathrooms for ¥4300 per person. Hagoromo Station. ②.

**Ōsaka Shiritsu Nagai Youth Hostel**, 1-1 Nagai-kōen (☎06/699-5631, fax 699-5644). Excellent modern hostel running along one side of the Nagai sports stadium. Bunk dorms have six beds and there are spacious private rooms for only a little extra. Staff are friendly and speak some English. The meals are reasonable, but for ¥50 you can use the kitchen for self catering. The main drawback is the 11pm curfew. Tsurugaoka/Nagai stations. ①.

Autumn in Nikkō National Park

Ainu carving, Nibutani, Hokkaidō

Jizō statue and offerings, Nikkō

Rice planting, Northern Honshū

Nagano, Central Honshū

The Inland Sea from Shōdo-shima, Western Honshū

Niseko ski resort, Hokkaidō

Traditional house, Ogimachi, Central Honshū  Jigokudani, Yudanaka, Central Honshū

Adachi Museum of Art gardens, Western Honshū

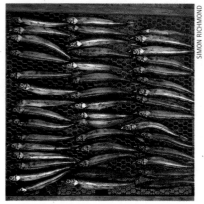

Drying fish, Central Honshū

Detail of Zen garden, Ryōan-ji, Kyoto

Lava beach, Osore-zan, Northern Honshū

## Umeda and around

Around 1km west of the castle, sandwiched between the Dojima and Tosabori rivers, lies a thin island, Nakanoshima, the eastern tip of which is a small park with a Parision feel to it. Here, in a squat brick building, you'll find the **Museum of Oriental Ceramics** (Tues–Sun 9.30am–5pm; ¥500), housing an exemplary collection of mainly ancient Chinese and Korean pottery. Only around a tenth of the museum's collection of 1300 pieces are displayed in a hushed, reverential atmosphere, a world away from the bustling city outside.

Just outside the museum stands the handsome **Central Public Hall**, a Neoclassical beauty dating from 1918, which looks its best floodlit at night. Heading north across the Oe-bashi bridge and along the broad avenue Midōsuji-dōri, brings you to the heart of the **Umeda** area, the meeting point of the JR, Hankyū and Hanshin railway lines. Tucked into a side street just before the stations is the **Ohatsu-Tenjin**, an atmospheric shrine where local shopkeepers pray for good business and which has a flea market on the first Friday of each month.

Even if you don't plan to take a train, the baroque entrance hall of the **Hankyū Umeda Station** is worth a look. Immediately west of the station, a tunnel leads under the railway sidings to the Umeda Sky Building, one of the city's more striking skyscrapers, where you can take a glass elevator up to the **Floating Garden Observatory** (daily 10am–10pm; ¥1000), 170m above the ground. Although there are some other attractions in the tower, this is a rather expensive way to get a bird's-eye view of Ōsaka

MINAMI

0    500 m

▽ *Tennōji & Kansai International Airport (KIX)*    ▽ *KIX*    ▽ ⑥

and if you've been up the castle already, it's not worth doing. In contrast, the basement of the same complex is styled as a turn-of-the-century street and offers a somewhat surreal shopping and dining experience (see p.418).

## Around Tennōji & Sumiyoshi Taisha

The first state Buddhist temple in Japan, **Shitennō-ji**, some 2km southeast of Namba, has retained its classical layout, but contains none of the buildings originally erected in 593. The oldest feature of this windswept, concrete complex, with turtle ponds and a five-storey pagoda at its centre, is the late thirteenth-century *torii* at the main entrance gate, five minutes' walk south of Shitennō-ji-mae subway station and fifteen minutes' north of the Tennōji overground station. The **treasure house** (Tues–Sun: April–Sept 8.30am–4.30pm; Jan–March & Oct–Dec 8.30am–4pm; ¥200), in the modern white building behind the central courtyard, contains gorgeous orange costumes and enormous mandalas, carved with fantastic birds and dragons, used for the ceremonial *bugaku* dances held at the temple on April 22, August 8 and October 22.

Festival days apart, spacious Shitennō-ji swallows up visitors with ease, but the more compact precincts of nearby **Isshin-ji**, five minutes' walk west, are always bustling with crowds of petitioners. This atmospheric temple is adorned with striking modern sculptures of the gods of thunder and wind (Raijin and Fūjin) and bare-breasted dancing girls on the steel gate doors. You can leave the temple through its adjacent graveyard and walk south towards the **Ōsaka Municipal Museum of Art** (Tues–Sun 9.30am–5pm; ¥300) which contains fine examples of ancient and modern oriental art in its permanent collection and which usually has special exhibitions.

Behind the gallery is **Keitakuen**, a pretty traditional Japanese garden arranged around a central pond. The garden, left to the city by Baron Sumitomo, whose family owned the mammoth trading company of the same name, is now part of **Tennōji-kōen** (Tues–Sun 9.30am–5pm; ¥150), which also includes the modern Great Conservatory, a giant glasshouse brimming with plants and flowers from around the world. The best reason for visiting the park, though, is for the Sunday **karaoke** fests on the pedestrian street which cuts through to Tennōji Zoo. These song and dance performances have been a regular fixture since the 1980s, when homeless people got together to entertain the crowds who visited the park at the weekends. Would-be *enka* (folk song) chanteurs can belt out a tune for ¥100.

On the western side of the zoo, soak up the low-rent atmosphere of **Shin-Sekai** (New World), a raffish district of narrow shopping arcades, cheap bars and restaurants and *pachinko* parlours. At its centre stands the appealingly retro **Tsutenkaku Tower** (daily 10am–6.30pm; ¥600), a postwar city landmark but, at 103m, long since lorded over by Umeda's skyscrapers to the north and the 256m WTC Cosmotower by Ōsaka Bay.

From Ebisuchō Station, immediately north of Shin-Sekai, it's a fifteen-minute subway or tram ride south to **Sumiyoshi Taisha**, Ōsaka's grandest shrine, home of the Shinto gods of the sea. Built in 211, after the grateful Empress Jingō returned from an expedition to subjugate Korea, its buildings, with logs jutting out at angles from the thatched roofs, exemplify *sumiyòshi zukuri* one of Japan's oldest styles of shrine architecture. Unlike similar complexes at Ise (see p.500) and Izumo Taisha (see p.590), Sumiyoshi Taisha is painted bright red, a sharp contrast with its wooded surrounding. The approach to the complex takes you over the elegant humpbacked Sori-hashi bridge, donated to the shrine by Yodogimi, Toyotomi Hideyoshi's lover.

## Liberty Ōsaka and Ōsaka Bay

The factory and flyover wasteland, some 2km west of Tennōji, is the unlikely location for the city's most stimulating museum, **Liberty Ōsaka** (Tues–Sun 10am–5pm; ¥250). Its longer name is the Ōsaka Human Rights Museum and it contains remarkable exhibits which tackle Japan's most taboo subjects. There's an excellent English-language leaflet and a portable tape recording to guide you around the displays which include the untouchable caste, the Burakumin, Japan's ethnic minorities and the disabled, the sexist treatment of women, and the effects of pollution, most tragically seen in the exhibition about Minamata disease (see p.696). The museum is an eight-minute walk south of Ashiharabashi Station on the JR Loop line.

To reach the **Ōsaka Bay** area, take the JR Loop line to Bentenchō Station; on the way you'll pass the UFO-like **Ōsaka Dome**, home of the Kintetsu Buffaloes pro-baseball team. From Bentenchō Station take the Chūō line subway to Ōsakako Station (the Chūō line subway will bring you all the way from other parts of the city), and walk north towards the huge ferris wheel beside Tempozan Harbour Village. Inside an exotic butterfly-shaped building, decorated with a giant fish-tank mosaic, is the fabulous **Ōsaka Aquarium** (daily 10am–7pm; ¥2000), which provides an eye-popping tour around the "Ring of Fire", the seismic and volcanic belt encircling the Pacific Ocean.

The aquarium is constructed so that you wind your way down around fourteen elongated tanks, each representing a different acquatic environment, from Antartica to the Aleutian Islands. The beauty of the design means you can, for example, watch seals basking on the rocks at the top of the tank and see them swimming, torpedo-like, through the lower depths later. The huge central tank represents the Pacific Ocean and is home to a couple of whale sharks and several manta rays, among many other fish. The giant spider crabs, looking like alien invaders from *The War of the Worlds*, provide a fitting climax to far and away Japan's best aquarium.

While at Tempozan, check out what's showing at the **Suntory Museum** (daily 10am–7.30pm; ¥950), housed in a striking glass and concrete inverted cone, designed by star local architect Andō Tadao. The museum specializes in twentieth-century graphic art and has a collection of over 10,000 posters. There's also an IMAX movie theatre (daily 11am–7pm; ¥1000) showing films on a twenty-metre-high screen.

# Eating

Ōsaka has a reputation as a foodies' paradise, but it can be a daunting task finding the best places to eat in a city crammed with so many restaurants. The trick is to stick to particular areas and to hunt around until something takes your fancy. Both **Umeda** and **Dōtomburi** offer rich pickings, while **Tsuruhashi**, on the JR Loop line to the east, is the main place to head for Korean food. The magazine *Kansai Time Out* reviews the latest additions to the restaurant scene and it's always a good idea to ask the locals what their favourite places are.

Of the several dishes that Ōsaka specializes in you shouldn't leave town without going to an **okonomiyaki restaurant**, preferably one where you can fry the thick pancakes yourself. Ōsaka's own style of **sushi** is *oshizushi*, layers of vinegared rice, seaweed and fish cut into bite-size chunks, and the city also has a favourite way of cooking chunky **udon noodles**; simmering them in a veggie, seafood or meat broth.

## Restaurants and cafés

The best choice of **restaurants and cafés** is around the Kita areas of Umeda and Sonezaki, and the Minami areas of Shinsaibashi, Dōtomburi and Namba. Strolling around the narrow streets dotted with stand-up noodle and *takoyaki* bars, and restaurants dolled up with flickering neon signs and crazy displays – especially along Dōtomburi-dōri – is an appetizing experience in itself. The major **hotels** and **department stores** are also worth checking out, especially at lunchtime when many restaurants offer special deals. Reviews give the nearest subway or train station and there are phone numbers for restaurants where you'll need to book.

### KITA

**Café Isn't It?**, 3-2-15 Sonezaki. Adopting the "same price for everything" concept of *Bar Isn't It?* (see p.420), the pizzas, pasta, meat dishes, sandwiches and good salads at this stylish café-bar all cost ¥500. Place your orders at the bar and go early evening if you want to avoid the crowds. Sun–Thurs 5pm–midnight, Sat & Sun 5pm–5am. Higashi-Umeda Station.

**Court Lodge**, Konishi Bldg, 1-4-7 Sonezaki-Shinchi (☎06/342-5253). Tiny Sri-Lankan restaurant serving mild curries, flavoured with coconut milk, and excellent set menus; lunches start at ¥800. Daily 11am–9pm. Nishi-Umeda Station.

**Fun Fun Plaza**, B1 Umeda Sky Bldg. This evocative recreation of a 1920s shopping street, beneath one of Ōsaka's high-tech towers, has some fifteen different restaurants to choose from all serving traditional dishes, including noodles, tempura and *okonomiyaki*. Most places open daily 11am–2pm & 5–9pm. Ōsaka/Nishi-Umeda stations.

**Herbis Plaza**, 2-5-25 Umeda. Excellent range of restaurants serving all kinds of cuisine in imaginative settings, on the B2 level of this new shopping development west of Ōsaka Station. Try *Takara-no-Kura*, a hip *izakaya* serving *mukokuseki* dishes. Ōsaka/Nishi-Umeda stations.

**Kagetsu**, B1 Furukawa Ōsaka Bldg, 2-1-29, Dōjimahama. There's a warm welcome at this excellent, cheap noodle restaurant, behind the *Dōjima Hotel*, which uses organic ingredients and serves up large portions. Try their *zarusoba* (cold buckwheat noodles). Nishi-Umeda Station.

**Kisoji**. This cubby-hole *izakaya* on the second floor of the warren of small cafés and restaurants behind Hankyū Umeda Station, serves a good-value ¥500 buffet lunch that has local office workers lining up out the door. Ōsaka/Umeda stations.

**Madonna**, B2 Hilton Plaza, 1-8-16 Umeda. Small *okonomiyaki* restaurant, where you cook at your own table or sit at the kitchen counter and watch the chefs. Also serves *yakisoba* (fried noodles). Most dishes under ¥1500. Daily 11am–11pm. Ōsaka/Nishi-Umeda stations.

**Nawasushi**, 2-14-1 Sonezaki. Among the many sushi restaurants in this area, east of the Hanshin department store, this one stands out for serving three rather than two pieces of sushi per dish for around ¥400. Daily noon–12.30am. Higashi-Umeda Station.

## MINAMI

**Aisaitei**, 2-8-11 Higashi-Shinsaibashi. Interesting spin on *takoyaki* at this second-floor restaurant, with a kitsch line in Seventies decor: the octopus balls are served as part of a *nabe* stew. Reasonable salads and there's a three dish and drink deal for ¥1000. Shinsaibashi Station.

**Capricciosa**, 2-8-110 Nambanaka. Well-established chain Italian restaurant that has prospered by serving up huge helpings of pasta, in a casual atmosphere popular with youngsters. Daily 11am–11pm. Namba Station.

**Cirque de Haagen Dazs**, 2-4-9 Shinsaibashi-suji. Playfully decadent but inexpensive ice-cream bar and café, beside Ebisu-bashi, with decor that's Alice in Wonderland meets Clockwork Orange. Enjoy your cookies-and-cream cone while scantily clad mannequins ride a merry-go-round downstairs, or sit upstairs in an absurdly silly lounge that would do Salvador Dali proud. Namba Station.

**Hard Rock Café**, 2-8-110 Nambanaka. The large burgers, beer and rock'n'roll outlet beside the retired Ōsaka Stadium, has a lively all-American atmosphere. Daily 11am–11pm, Fri and Sat until 3am. Namba Station.

**Il Gemello**, 2F Daiki Bldg, 2-4-8 Nishi-Shinsaibashi (☎06/211-9542). Traditional and friendly Italian restaurant, where the chefs are all trained in Rome. English is spoken and a meal costs around ¥2000 per person. Mon–Fri 5.30pm–midnight, Sat & Sun 11.30am–2.30pm & 5.30–midnight. Namba Station.

**Kanadian**, B1 Miyoshi Manshuon, 2-1-64 Teramachi. Long-running, inexpensive Asian food restaurant, now without its pet goat. The curries, samosa and chai are all made from organic products and, on Saturday there is often live music for which there's an extra charge. Tani-machi 9-chōme Station.

**Kani Doraku**, 1-6-2 Dōtomburi. There are now outlets of this seafood restaurant – always easily spotted by the giant red crab above the door wiggling its claws – all over Japan, but this is one of the originals. Fresh crab served in a vast range of dishes. Daily 11am–11pm. Namba Station.

**Kuidaore**, 1-8-25 Dōtomburi. One of Ōsaka's oldest restaurant department stores, easily indentified by the giant drumming clown outside. Set meals, covering a wide range of cuisines, start at around ¥1000 and there are good plastic food displays. Head to the fourth floor for *nabe* and *shabu-shabu* stews. Namba Station.

**Namaste**, No. 2 Rose Bldg, 3-7-28 Minami-Semba. To the east of the Shinsaibashi shopping arcade, on the cross street before the Maruzen bookshop. Not the cheapest Indian restaurant in Ōsaka, but a good one, serving lots of vegetable dishes and with set lunches from ¥750. Mon–Sat 11.30am–3pm & 5.30–11pm. Shinsaibashi Station.

**Ninniku-ya**, 6F Daimondo Bldg, Shinsaibashi (☎06/212 5770), plus two further branches in Umeda. There's a South Sea Islands feel at this garlic-with-everything restaurant. The portions are large so it pays to go with friends and share a few dishes, and there's an English menu. Namba Station.

## OTHER AREAS

**Bofinger**, Fureai Minato-kan, 1-10-12 Nankō-Kita (☎06/612-3381).This outlet of the famous Parisian brasserie/café, in a modern waterfront complex, is a fine place for a slap-up lunch (¥1450–1900). While here, you could also check out the wine museum in the basement of the building. Cosmosquare Station.

**Gochi-so Biru**. Restaurant building with eleven floors next to the Kintetsu department store opposite Tennōji Station, offering a good range of reasonably priced cuisines. Head to the basement for excellent-value set Japanese meals. The bakery *Hokuo* on the ground floor is a good place to pick up a breakfast snack. Tennōji Station.

**Sun Tempo**, 1-5-10 Kaigan-dōri. Rustic-style Italian restaurant behind the Suntory Museum, with views across Ōsaka Bay, which serves imaginative pizzas and pasta and has a decent salad bar. A much better option than the large but lacklustre food court at the nearby Tempozan Harbour Village complex. Daily 11am–10pm. Ōsakakō Station.

**WTC Cosmotower**, 1-14-16 Nankō-Kita. Ōsaka's tallest building has several good-value restaurants worth checking out, including *Ōtanko*, a sushi restaurant on the 47th floor, and the *World Buffet Restaurant* on the 48th. Cosmosquare Station.

# Nightlife and entertainment

The apex of Ōsaka's frenetic nightlife, where neon coruscates off the Dōtomburi canal, is **Ebisu-bashi**, a dazzling area to wander around, if only to check out the wild youth fashion – skirts for men are a current hot item. If you've seen the movie *Black Rain*, you'll recognize the jet black glass and steel *Kirin Plaza* beside the bridge, but there are much better bars around the area. Don't miss out on strolling through **Amerika-mura**, immediately west, a street crowded with trendy shops and bars. In contrast, the **Hozen-ji Yokochō** area, around the paper-lantern-festooned temple Hozen-ji, is old-time Ōsaka, a narrow alley of tiny watering holes. Check the listings magazine *Kansai Time Out* for the latest info on clubs, bars and one-off dance events.

## Bars and clubs

**Balabushka**, 4F Nippo Mittera Kaikan, 2-9-5 Nishi-Shinsaibashi. Unusually spacious bar, in Amerika-mura, with a pool table and darts, and a Happy Hour Sun–Thurs 6–8pm. Daily 6pm–midnight, Fri & Sat until 2am. Shinsaibashi Station.

**Bar Isn't It?**, 4F Yoshimoto Bldg, 2-5-5 Shinsaibashi-suji. The original outlet of what has now become a Japan-wide phenomenon – the one-price (¥500) only bar, big on space and loud atmosphere. Hosts occasional dance parties and live music gigs, when there's an entry charge of ¥1000. Namba Station.

**Canopy**, IM Excellence Bldg, 1-11-20 Sonezaki-Shinchi. A healthy mix of *gaijin* and Japanese rub shoulders in the least likely looking "American delicatessen" in Ōsaka. Cool down on the outdoor terrace and enjoy the 5–8.30pm Happy Hour when beers are ¥400. Mon–Sat 5pm–6am, Sun 5pm–midnight. Higashi-Umeda Station.

**Club Karma**, Kasai Bldg, 1-5-18 Sonezaki-Shinchi. Stark, yet roomy bar and club which hosts a range of trendy dance events and happenings, with the added bonus of a good food menu and a Happy Hour until 9pm. The all-night techno raves are usually held on Friday and Saturday when there's a cover charge of ¥2500. Nishi-Umeda Station.

**The Cellar**, B1 Dai-3 Hirata Bldg, 2-17-13 Nishi-Shinsaibashi. Reasonably priced drinks and a daily Happy Hour 6–9pm at this quiet basement cocktail bar with a conservative 1950s feel. Live music on Wednesday, Friday and Saturday. Mon–Thurs 6pm–2am, Fri & Sat 6pm–4am, Sun 6pm–midnight. Shinsaibashi Station.

**Murphy's**, 6F Lead Plaza Bldg, Higashi-Shinsaibashi. Even though Ōsaka now has a branch of Sapporo's *The Dubliners'*, this is the city's original Irish bar with a cracking atmosphere to go with the draught Guinness and Kilkenny beer. Also serves food and has live music on Wednesday & Friday. Daily 5pm–1am, Fri & Sat till 3am. Nagahoribashi Station.

**Pig & Whistle**, B1 Ohatsutenjin Bldg, 2-5 Sonezaki (Higashi-Umeda subway station) & 2F "is" Bldg, 2-chōme Shinsaibashi-suji (Shinsaibashi subway station). The place to head if you're feeling nostalgic about the old boozer. Both branches of this British-style pub have Guinness on tap, fish and chip suppers, and darts.

**Rockets**, 6025 Namba-pia, 2-8-13 Nambanaka. Grunge chic club, nestling under the railway tracks running south from Namba station. DJs spin everying from drum & bass to reggae and punk depending on the night of the week. It's best to check local media since it's not open every night. 11pm–5am. Entrance ¥2500 including one drink. Namba Station.

**Tin's Hall**, 10-3 Minami-Kawahori, Tennōji. Lively bar, on the north side of the station, which serves a good range of food, including smoked salmon bagels and salads for ¥700, and has a Mon–Thurs Happy Hour 6–9pm. Mon–Thurs 6pm–2am, Fri & Sat 6pm–5am. Tennōji Station.

## Traditional performing arts

Ōsaka is where **Bunraku** puppetry flourished during the seventeenth century and performances are still held at the **National Bunraku Theatre** (☎06/212-1122), Namba, in January, April, June, August and November at 11am and 4pm. Tickets (¥5700 and ¥4500) sell out quickly, but you can try at the theatre box office, a three-minute walk from exit 7 of Nipponbashi Station.

The place to catch **Kabuki** plays is the handsomely restored **Ōsaka Shōchiku-za** (☎06/214-2211), five minutes' walk north of Namba Station, beside the Dōtomburi canal. Tickets start at ¥6000. If you're interested in sampling the more difficult **Nō** plays, the **Ōsaka Nō Hall** (☎06/373-1726) near Nakazakichō Station on the Tanimachi line, or a short walk east of Hankyū Umeda Station, often holds free performances, usually beginning around 9.30am. Details of all traditional arts performances appear in the free quarterly booklet *Meet Ōsaka*, available at all the tourist offices, and in the magazine *Kansai Time Out*.

# Listings

**Airlines** ANA (domestic ☎06/534-8800; international ☎06/372-1212); JAL (domestic ☎06/223-2255, international ☎06/223-2345); JAS (☎06/241-5511); Japan Asia Airways (☎06/223-2258); Aeroflot (☎06/271-8471); Air Canada (☎0120–891890); Air China (☎06/946-1702); Air France (641-1211); Air India (☎06/246-1781); Air New Zealand (☎0120–300747); Air Pacific (☎06/311-2004); Alitalia (☎06/341-3951); American Airlines (☎0120–000860); Ansett Australia (☎06/346-2556); British Airways (☎0120–122881); Canadian Airlines International (☎06/346-5591); Cathay Pacific (☎06/245-6731); China Eastern Airlines (☎06/448-5161); China Southern Airlines (☎06/448-6655); Continental Micronesia (☎0120–242414); Delta Air Lines (☎0120–333742); Finnair (☎06/347-0888); Garuda Indonesia Airways (☎06/445-6985); Iberia (☎06/347-7201); KLM (☎06/345-6691); Korean Air (☎06/264-3311); Lufthansa (☎06/341-4966); Malaysia Airlines (☎06/635-3070); Northwest Airlines (☎06/228-0747); Philippine Airlines (☎06/444-2541); Qantas Airways (☎0120–207020); Sabena World Airlines (☎06/341-8081); Scandinavian Airlines (☎06/348-0211); Swissair (☎06/345-7851); Thai Airways International (☎06/202-5161); United Airlines (☎0120–114466); Vietnam Airlines (☎06/533-5781).

**Airport information** Kansai International (KIX) ☎0724/55-2500; Itami ☎06/856-6781.

**American Express** The office at Ōsaka Yotsuhashi Dai-ichi Seimei Bldg, 1-4-24 Shinmachi, Nishi-ku (☎06/578-5035) has recently closed. See Tokyo Listings for Japan's main office.

**Banks and exchange** There are plenty of banks around the Umeda, Shinsaibashi and Namba areas of central Ōsaka. Major department stores also have foreign exchange desks as does the Central Post Office, beside JR Ōsaka Station.

**Bookshops** Kinokuniya, behind the main entrance to Hankyū Umeda Station, is open daily 10am–9pm, except the third Wednesday of the month. Peynet (daily 10am–8pm), below the *Ōsaka Hilton Hotel,* is smaller, but has a good selection of English-language books and magazines at cheaper prices than Kinokuniya.

**Car rental** There are several major car rental firms at both Shin-Ōsaka and Ōsaka stations (all open daily 8am–8pm). Eki Rent-a-car (Shin-Ōsaka ☎06/303-0181, Ōsaka ☎06/341-3388, Tennoji ☎06/773-0341) and Nippon Rent-a-car (Shin-Ōsaka ☎06/394-4919, Hankyū Umeda Station ☎06/371-9354).

**Consulates** Australia, 29F, Twin 21 MID Tower, 2-1-61 Shiromi, Chūō-ku (☎06/941-9271); Belgium, 8F Takahashi Bldg, 5-9-3 Nishitemma, Kita-ku (☎06/361-9432); Canada, 12F Daisan Shoho Bldg, 2-2-3 Nishi-Shinsaibashi, Chūō-ku (☎06/212-4910); China, 3-9-2 Utsubohommachi, Nishi-ku (☎06/445-9481); France, 20F Ōbayashi Bldg, 4-33 Kita-hamahigashi, Chūō-ku (☎06/946-6181); Germany, 36F Umeda Sky Bldg Tower East, 1-1-81 Oyodonaka, Kita-ku (☎06/440-5070); India, 10F Semba IS Bldg, 1-9-26 Kyutaromachi, Chūō-ku (☎06/261-7299); Indonesia, 6F Daiwa Bank Bldg, 4-4-21 Minami-Semba, Chūō-ku (☎06/252-9823); Italy, 31F Twin 21 MID Tower, 2-1-61 Shiromi, Chūō-ku (☎06/949-2970); Netherlands, 6F Twin 21 MID Tower, 2-1-61 Shiromi, Chūō-ku (☎06/944-7272); New Zealand, 28F Twin 21 MID Tower, 2-1-61 Shiromi, Chūō-ku (☎06/942-9016); Philippines, 101/103 Advan Bldg, 2-3-7 Uchiawajimachi, Chūō-ku (☎06/910-7881); Russia, 1-2-2 Nishimidorigaoka, Toyonaka-shi (☎06/848-3452); Singapore, 14F Ōsaka Kokusai Bldg, 2-3-13 Azuchimachi, Chūō-ku (☎06/261-5131);

South Korea, 2-3-4 Nishi-Shinsaibashi, Chūō-ku (☎06/213-1401); Thailand, 4F Konoike East Bldg, 3-6-9 Kita-Kyuhojimachi, Chūō-ku (☎06/243-5563); UK, 19F Seiko Ōsaka Bldg, 3-5-1 Bakuromachi, Chūō-ku (☎06/281-1616); USA, 2-11-5 Nishitemma, Kita-ku (☎06/315-5900).

**Home visits** Ōsaka runs a programme which allows you to meet local people in their homes for a few hours so you can learn a bit more about Japanese life. If you want to participate you need to take your passport to either of the tourist information desks at Ōsaka or Shin-Ōsaka stations (see p.409) and allow a couple of days for visiting arrangements to be made.

**Hospitals and medical advice** Yodogawa Christian Hospital, 2-9-26 Awaji, Higashi-Yodogawa-ku (☎06/322-2250) or the more central Sumitomo Hospital, 5-2-2 Nakanoshima, Kita-ku (☎06/443-1261). For medical advice and the closest hospital call the International Medical Information Centre (Mon–Wed, Fri & Sat 9am–5pm; ☎06/213-2393). Outside these times contact one of the tourist information counters (see p.409).

**Immigration** Osaka's immigration bureau is a three-minute walk from exit 3 of Temmabashi Station on the Keihan line at 2-1-17 Tanimachi, Chūō-ku (☎06/06-941 0771).

**Internet access** To surf the net at the Internet Square "Ring Ring" (Tues–Sun 10am–8pm), on the ground floor of the National Tower, Twin 21, 2-1-61 Shiromi, costs ¥1000 per hour. You'll need to become a member first, but registration is free. The nearest station is Ōsaka-jō-kōen on the JR Loop line. Also try Bean's B:t Café, 6-2-29 Uehonmachi, Tennōji-ku (daily 8.30am–9pm; ☎06/766-3566; *www.interfarm.co.jp*), which offers special rates for foreigners. Closest subway stations are Tanimachi 9-chōme and Uehonmachi on the Kintetsu line.

**Lost property** The lost and found department for Ōsaka's buses and subways is at 1-17 Motomachi (☎06/633-9151).

**Police** The main Ōsaka Police Station, 3-1-16 otemae, chūō-ku, is open Mon–Fri 9.15am–5.30pm (☎06/941-1386; after hours 943-1234 ext 3023). Numbers for the emergency services are listed in Basics on p.70.

**Post office** The Central Post Office is immediately west of JR Ōsaka Station.

**Shopping** Den-Den Town, the electronic goods area of Ōsaka 5min walk east of Namba, has over 300 discount outlets, those with tax-free signs selling export models. The shops here are closed on Wednesday. Nearby, beside Nipponbashi Station, is the Kuromon-Ichiba, a large food market open Mon–Sat 10am–5pm and worth a browse. North of Namba, Amerika-mura and Europe-mura are the main areas to shop for trendy clothes and knick-knacks, while Umeda has several classy department stores and shopping plazas, good for souvenir hunting.

**Sports** Ōsaka's fifteen-day sumo tournament is held mid-March at Ōsaka Furitsu Taiikukan, 10min walk from exit 5 of Namba Station. Seats for the bouts, which begin at 10am and run through to 6pm, sell out quickly, and you'll need to arrive early to snag one of the standing-room tickets (¥1500) which go on sale each day at 9am. The Kintetsu Buffaloes play at the huge Ōsaka Dome during the professional baseball season, but the highlights of the city's sporting summer is the All-Japan High School Baseball Championship, held at Kōshien Stadium, 5min walk from Kōshien Station on the Hanshin line. For ticket availability, check first with tourist information.

**Taxis** Ōsaka Taxi Companies Association (☎06/768-1281).

**Travel agencies** For international tickets try one of the following English-speaking discount agents: Academy Travel (☎06/303-3538); A'cross Travellers Bureau (☎06/345-0191); Maptour (☎06/361-7171); No 1 Travel (☎06/363-4489); STA (☎06/262-7066); Travel Kingdom (☎06/309-2199). For domestic travel JTB's foreign tourist division is on 7F Sakai-suji-honmachi Centre Bldg, 2-1-6 Honmachi, Chūō-ku (☎06/271-6195).

# Takarazuka

When the Hankyū railway tycoon Kobayashi Ichizo laid a line out to the tiny spa town of **TAKARAZUKA**, 20km northwest of Ōsaka, in 1911, he had an entertainment vision that extended way beyond soothing onsen dips. By 1924 he'd built the first Takurazuka Grand Theatre, home to the all-female musical drama troupe **Takarazuka** (see box, opposite). Some 2.5 million people – mainly women – flock to the town each year to see the reviews and musicals at the plush **Takarazuka Grand Theatre**, ten minutes' walk southeast of the train stations, through the Sonio shopping centre and along an avenue of cherry trees. Shows start at 11am, 1pm and 3pm, with no performances on Wednesday, and tickets cost from ¥3500. Reservations should be made up to a month

| Takarazuka | Takarazuka | 宝塚 |
| Daihonzan Nakayama-dera | Daihonzan Nakayama-dera | 大本山中山寺 |
| Kiyoshikōjin Seichō-ji | Kiyoshikōjin Seichō-ji | 清荒神清澄寺 |
| Takarazuka Grand Theatre | Takarazuka Gurando Gekijō | 宝塚グランド劇場 |
| Tezuka Osamu Manga Museum | Tezuka Osamu Kinenkan | 手塚治虫記念館 |

### ACCOMMODATION AND RESTAURANTS

| Otafuku | Otafuku | おたふく |
| Petit House | Puchi Hausu | プチハウス |
| Takarazuka Washington Hotel | Takarazuka Washinton Hoteru | 宝塚ワシントンホテル |
| Hotel Wakamizu | Hoteru Wakamizu | ホテル若水 |

before performances (10am–5pm; ☎0797/86-7777; no English spoken, but tourist offices can often make calls on your behalf). Your show ticket also gets you into the bland fun-fair and zoo **Takarazuka Family Land** (daily except Wed 9.30am–5.30pm; ¥1400), opposite the theatre, although you'll have to pay extra to go on any of the tame rides.

A much more entertaining place for both children and adults is the **Tezuka Osamu Manga Museum** (daily except Wed 9.30am–5.30pm; ¥500), just beyond the Grand Theatre, which celebrates the comic-book genius Tezuka Osamu, creator of Astro Boy and Kimba the White Lion, an inspiration for Disney's *The Lion King*. Considered Japan's "god of manga", Tezuka (1928–1989), who was raised in Takarazuka, was much more than a Walt Disney figure who penned cuddly characters. He helped pioneer story book comics – the mainstay of today's mammoth *manga* industry – and tackled difficult, adult material, such as anti-semitism in his epic masterpiece *Adorufu ni Tsugu* (Tell Adolf). This colourful museum charts his career, displays art from his books, comics and animated films, screens cartoons and gives you the chance to become an animator in the basement workshop.

## THE WONDERFUL WORLD OF TAKARAZUKA

There's a long tradition of men performing female roles in Japanese theatre, acting out a male fantasy of how women are supposed to behave. It's not so strange, then, that actresses playing idealized men have struck such a cord with contemporary female audiences. Along with the glitter, this has been the successful formula of the 700-strong all-female **Takarazuka Review Company**, founded in 1914.

The company's founder, Kobayashi Ichizo, was mightily impressed by performances of Western operas he'd seen in Tokyo. He sensed that Japanese audiences were ripe for lively Western musical dramas, but he also wanted to preserve something of Japan's traditional theatre, too. So as well as performing dance reviews and musicals, Takarazuka also act out classical Japanese plays and have developed shows from Western novels, including *Gone With The Wind* and *War and Peace*.

Thousands of young girls apply annually to join the troupe at the age of 16, and devote themselves to a punishing routine of classes that will enable them to embody the "modesty, fairness and grace" (the company's motto) expected of a Takarazuka member. They must also forsake boyfriends, but in return are guaranteed the slavish adoration of an almost exclusively female audience. The male impersonators or *otoko-yaku* attract the most attention from the fans, who buy so many cut flowers for their idols that the town's shops and restaurants receive free daily deliveries of unwanted bouquets.

There are a couple of atmospheric **temples** in the hills around Takarazuka that merit a look as part of a day-trip to the spa town. The liveliest, especially on the festival days held on the 27th and 28th of each month, is **Kiyoshikōjin Seicho-ji**, a rambling complex dedicated to a fire deity, high above Hankyū Kiyoshikōjin Station, one stop from Takarazuka. The long slope leading up to the temple from the station is lined with stalls selling souvenirs and traditional sweets, and each autumn the woods surrounding Kōjin-san, as it's nicknamed, burst into a range of rustic colours. The ideal time to visit the nearby **Daihonzan Nakayama-dera** temple, three minutes' walk from Hankyū Nakayama Station, is the end of February when six hundred *ume* (plum) trees blossom with pink and white buds. Although there's been a temple on this spot for 1400 years, the present buildings date from 1610, and people come here to worship the eleven-faced goddess of mercy, Jūichimen Kannon Bosatsu, a statue believed to have been carved from a nutmeg tree in the tenth century.

### Practicalities

The fastest **train** on the Hankyū Takarazuka line from Ōsaka's Umeda Station takes 36 minutes to reach Takarazuka Station (¥270). There are also direct trains on the JR Fukuchiyama line, taking much the same time from JR Ōsaka Station to JR Takarazuka Station, next to the Hankyū terminus and department store. The town's **tourist information** office (daily 9.30am–5.45pm; ☎0797/81-5344) is on the ground floor of the Hankyū department store and is always staffed by English speakers. You can pick up a map of the town here, but everything is so close that you don't really need one.

Given that performances take place during the day, there's no need to stay over in Takarazuka, especially since **accommodation** is generally expensive and difficult to book depending on the popularity of the shows. However, the town is much quieter than Ōsaka and several of the hotels along the Muko-gawa have their own onsen. One of the nicest is *Hotel Wakamizu* (☎0797/86-0151, fax 86-2846; ⑦), a top-class establishment with *tatami* and Western rooms and beautifully designed onsen baths, directly across the river from Hankyū Takarazuka Station. The *Takarazuka Washington Hotel* (☎0797/87-1771, fax 86-2287; ⑤–⑥), beside the station, is part of the national business hotel chain; singles from ¥6800. The cheapest accommodation is the women-only dorm at *Petit House* (☎0797/84-8753; ②), a small hotel opposite the *manga* museum, where you can mull over Takarazuka performances with die-hard fans.

There a several **places to eat** in the Sorio 1 shopping mall that you'll pass through on the way to the Takarazuka Grand Theatre, including a *Mr Donuts*. The theatre complex also has a range of restaurants, but they tend to serve rather delicate portions. The best bet is *Otafuku*, a smart *okonomiyaki* restaurant, on the opposite bank of the Muko-gawa from the theatre, which has set lunches from ¥850. If you really want to make a day of it, go for the lunch and bath package at *Hotel Wakamizu*, starting at ¥3500 per person.

# Kyoto

The capital of Japan for more than one thousand years, **KYOTO** is endowed with an almost overwhelming legacy of ancient Buddhist temples, majestic palaces and gardens of every size and description, not to mention some of the country's most important works of art, its richest culture and its most refined cuisine. For many people the very name Kyoto conjures up the classic image of Japan: streets of traditional wooden houses, the click-clack of *geta* on the paving stones, *geisha* in a flourish of brightly coloured silks, and the inevitable weeping cherry. While you can still find all these things, and much more, first impressions of Kyoto are invariably disappointing. For the most part it's a sprawling, overcrowded city with a population of 1.5 million and a thriving industrial sector. The die-straight streets certainly simplify navigation, but they also give the city an oppressive uniformity which you won't find among the tortuous lanes of Tokyo. And, perhaps not surprisingly, Kyoto is a notoriously exclusive place, where it's difficult for outsiders to peek through the centuries-thick layer of cultural refinement into the city's secretive soul.

However, there's plenty for the short-term visitor to enjoy in Kyoto. In fact, the array of top-class sights is quite mind-boggling: more than 1600 Buddhist temples, hundreds of Shinto shrines, two hundred classified gardens, a clutch of imperial villas and several first-rate museums. With so much choice, the biggest problem is where to start, but it's perfectly possible to get a good feel for Kyoto even in a couple of days. Top priority should go to the eastern, Higashiyama district, where you can walk from the famous **Kiyomizu-dera** to **Ginkaku-ji**, the Silver Pavilion, taking in a whole raft of interesting temples, gardens and museums on the way. The following day, head for the northeastern hills to contemplate the superb Zen gardens of **Daitoku-ji** and **Ryōan-ji**, and then gorge on the wildly extravagant Golden Pavilion, **Kinkaku-ji**. With more time, you can visit some of the central sights, of which the highlight is **Nijō-jō**, a lavishly decorated seventeenth-century palace, while nearby **Nijō-jinya** is an intriguing place riddled with secret passages and hidey-holes. Try also to visit at least one of the imperial villas, such as **Shūgaku-in Rikyū** or **Katsura Rikyū**, or the sensuous moss gardens of **Saihō-ji**, all located in the outer districts. It's also well worth making time to wander off the beaten track into Kyoto's old merchant quarters. The best of these, surprisingly, are to be found in the central district north of **Shijō-dōri** and across the river in **Gion**. Here you'll find the traditional **crafts shops** and beautiful old **ryokan** for which the city is justly famous.

Kyoto's **festivals** tend to be more stately than rumbustious. The most famous feature grand costume parades, esoteric ritual and elegant *geisha* dances and take place in spring and autumn. These two seasons are undoubtedly the **best time to visit** Kyoto, though also the busiest; after a chill winter, the cherry trees put on their finery in early April, while the hot, oppressive summer months (June through August) are followed in October by a delightful period of clear, dry weather when the maples erupt into fiery reds.

## Some history

Kyoto became the **imperial capital** in the late eighth century when Emperor Kammu relocated the court from Nara (see p.480). His first choice was Nagaoka, southwest of today's Kyoto, but a few inauspicious events led the emperor to move again in 794 AD. This time he settled on what was to be known as **Heian-kyō**, "capital of peace and tranquillity", which he modelled on the Chinese Tang-dynasty capital Chang'an (today's Xi'an). The new city was built on a rectangular grid of streets, symmetrical about a north–south axis, with the imperial palace to the north and the main entrance in the south. By the late ninth century the city was already overflowing onto the eastern hills and soon had an estimated population of 500,000. For the aristocrats at least, it was a life of exquisite refinement, characterized by boating parties and poetry-writing competitions, while Japanese arts were evolving their own identity independent of earlier Chinese influences.

From then on the city had a rather roller-coaster ride. In the late twelfth century a fire practically destroyed the whole place, but two centuries later the **Ashikaga shoguns** were busily building some of the city's finest monuments, among them the Golden and Silver Pavilions (Kinkaku-ji and Ginkaku-ji). Many of the great Zen temples were established at this time and the arts reached new levels of sophistication. Once again, however, almost everything was lost during the **Ōnin Wars** (1467–78), which were waged largely within the city over an Ashikaga succession dispute.

Kyoto's knight in shining armour, however, was **Toyotomi Hideyoshi** who came to power in 1582 and sponsored a vast rebuilding programme. The **Momoyama period**,

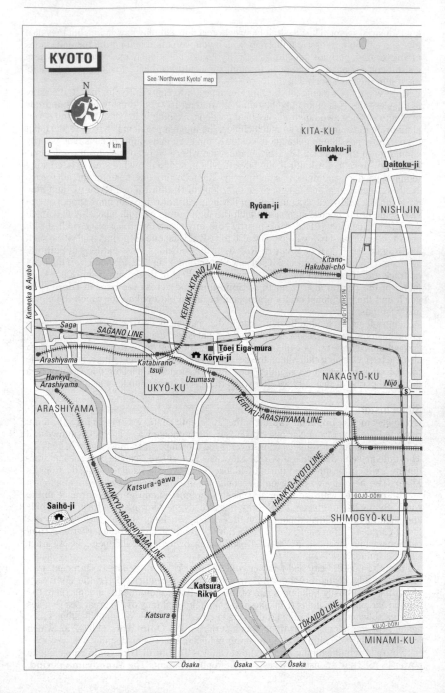

# KYOTO

N

0       1 km

See 'Northwest Kyoto' map

KITA-KU

Kinkaku-ji

Daitoku-ji

NISHIJIN

Ryōan-ji

Kitano-
Hakubai-chō

*Kameoka & Ayabe*

KEIFUKU-KITANO LINE

*Saga*

SAGANO LINE

Tōei Eiga-mura

*Arashiyama*

Katabirano-
tsuji

Kōryū-ji

*Hankyū-
Arashiyama*

*Uzumasa*

NAKAGYŌ-KU

*Nijō*

S

UKYŌ-KU

ARASHIYAMA

KEIFUKU-ARASHIYAMA LINE

HANKYŪ-ARASHIYAMA LINE

*Katsura-gawa*

HANKYŪ-KYOTO LINE

GOJŌ-DŌRI

Saihō-ji

SHIMOGYŌ-KU

Katsura
Rikyū

*Katsura*

TŌKAIDŌ LINE

KUJŌ-DŌRI

MINAMI-KU

▽ *Ōsaka*      *Ōsaka* ▽    ▽ *Ōsaka*

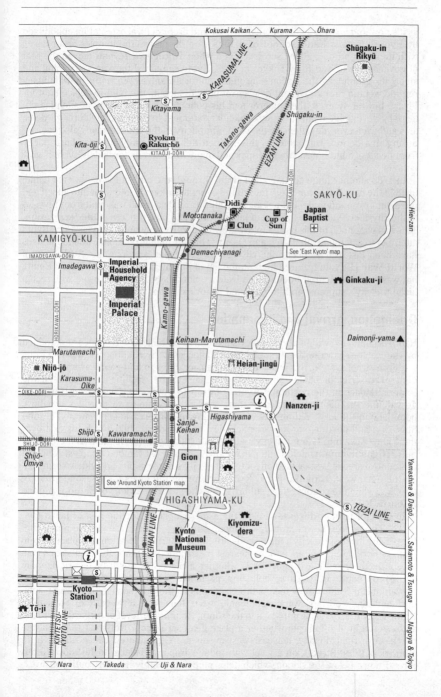

Kokusai Kaikan △   Kurama △△ ▷ Ōhara

Shūgaku-in
Rikyū

*KARASUMA LINE*

Kitayama

Kita-ōji

Takano-gawa

Shūgaku-in

Ryokan
Rakuchō
KITAŌJI-DŌRI

*EIZAN LINE*

SHIRAKAWA-DŌRI

SAKYŌ-KU

△ Hiei-zan

Didi

KAMIGYŌ-KU

Mototanaka

Club

Cup of
Sun

Japan
Baptist

IMADEGAWA-DŌRI

See 'Central Kyoto' map

Demachiyanagi

See 'East Kyoto' map

Imadegawa

Imperial
Household
Agency

Ginkaku-ji

HORIKAWA-DŌRI

Kamo-gawa

HIGASHIŌJI-DŌRI

Imperial
Palace

Daimonji-yama ▲

Keihan-Marutamachi

Marutamachi

Heian-jingū

Nijō-jō

Karasuma-
Oike

OIKE-DŌRI

Nanzen-ji

KARASUMA-DŌRI

KAWARAMACHI-DŌRI

Shijō

Kawaramachi

Sanjō-
Keihan

Higashiyama

Yamashina & Daigō ▷

Shijō-
Ōmiya

SHIJŌ-DŌRI

Gion

*TŌZAI LINE*

Sakamoto & Tsuruga ▷

See 'Around Kyoto Station' map

HIGASHIYAMA-KU

KEIHAN LINE

Kyoto
National
Museum

Kiyomizu-
dera

Nara & Tokyo ▷

Kyoto
Station

Tō-ji

KINTETSU-
KYOTO LINE

▽ Nara   ▽ Takeda   ▽ Uji & Nara

as it's now known, was a golden era of artistic and architectural ostentation epitomized by Kyoto's famous **Kanō school of artists** who decorated the temples and palaces with their sumptuous, gilded screens. Even when **Tokugawa Ieyasu** moved the seat of government to Edo (now Tokyo) in 1603, Kyoto remained the imperial capital and stood its ground as the nation's foremost cultural centre. While the new military regime went in for extravagant displays of power, such as the **Nijō-jō** palace built for Ieyasu but rarely used, the emperor and his cohorts cocked a snook at such lack of taste by developing a talent for superb understatement in their architecture, gardens, arts and even everyday utensils; the rustic simplicity of the tea ceremony also evolved during this period. Undoubtedly, this sudden delight in simplicity was born partly from necessity, but it nevertheless spawned many of the crafts for which Kyoto is now famous.

In 1788 another huge conflagration swept through the city, but worse was to come; in 1868 the new **Emperor Meiji** moved the court to Tokyo. Kyoto went into shock and the economy foundered – but not for long. In the 1890s a canal was built from Biwa-ko to the city, and Kyoto, like the rest of Japan, embarked on a process of **modernization**. This has continued to this day – amidst growing controversy in recent years – as Kyoto attempts to catch up with Tokyo and Ōsaka. Though many traditional wooden houses have been lost to developers, the city narrowly escaped a worse fate. At the end of **World War II** Kyoto featured high on the list of potential targets for the Atom Bomb, but was famously spared by American Defence Secretary, Henry Stimson, who recognized the city's supreme architectural and historical importance.

## Orientation, arrival and information

Kyoto is contained within a wide valley surrounded by hills on three sides and drained by the Katsura-gawa to the west and the smaller, easterly Kamo-gawa. Thanks to its grid-iron street system, this is one of Japan's easier cities to find your way around. The **central district** of banks, shops and the main tourist facilities lies between the Imperial Palace in the north and **Kyoto Station** to the south. Nijō-jō and Horikawa-dōri define the district's western extent, while the Kamo-gawa provides a natural boundary to the east. Within this core, the **downtown** area is concentrated around Shijō-dōri and north along Kawaramachi-dōri to Oike-dōri. Shijō-dōri leads east over the Kamo-gawa into **Gion**, the city's major entertainment district, and to the eastern hills, **Higashiyama**, which shelter many of Kyoto's most famous temples. Much of this central area is best tackled on foot, but the city's other sights are widely scattered. To the northwest, **Kinkaku-ji** and **Ryōan-ji** provide the focus for a second group of temples, while the southwestern suburbs hide the superb gardens of **Saihō-ji** and the **Katsura Rikyū**.

In general Kyoto **addresses** follow the same pattern as for the rest of Japan (see p.21). There are, however, a few added subtleties which are worth mastering. Unusually, most of the city's main roads are named and the location of a place is generally described by reference to the nearest major junction. Since the land slopes gently south, the most usual indicator is whether a place lies north of (*agaru*, literally above) or south of (*sagaru*, below) a particular east–west road. For example, Kawaramachi Sanjō simply means the place is near the intersection of Kawaramachi-dōri and Sanjō-dōri; Kawaramachi Sanjō-agaru tells you it's north of Sanjō-dōri; Kawaramachi Sanjō-sagaru that it's to the south. At a higher level of sophistication, the address might also indicate whether a place lies east (*higashi*) or west (*nishi*) of the north-south road. Finally, ten east–west avenues are numbered consecutively from Ichijō-dōri (First Street), on a level with today's Imperial Palace, to Jūjō-dōri (Tenth Street) down below the station, which helps pinpoint roughly how far south you are.

## Arrival

Most visitors arrive at Kyoto's splendid new **train station**. The city is linked by Shinkansen to Tokyo and Nagoya to the north and Ōsaka, Hiroshima and Fukuoka to the south. If you're coming direct from **Kansai International airport** (see p.406) the quickest and easiest option is a JR Haruka Limited Express train which whisks you direct to Kyoto in just over an hour (¥3490); JR rail passes are valid on this service. Trains on the private Keihan or Hankyū railways are cheaper (roughly ¥2000) but can take around two hours – from the airport take a JR train to either Kyōbashi or Ōsaka stations respectively and then change to the private line. Alternatively, **airport limousine** buses do the journey in under two hours, traffic permitting, terminating on the south (Hachijō-guchi) side of Kyoto Station (1–2 hourly 5am–9pm; ¥2300). Limousine buses also run direct from Ōsaka's **Itami airport** to Kyoto Station (every 30min 6am–7.30pm; 55min; ¥1280), from where local buses and two subway lines fan out to all destinations around the city.

**Long-distance buses** from Tokyo and other cities terminate outside Kyoto Station. Keihan buses arrive at the southern terminal in front of Avanti department store, while other companies use a stand at the front (north side) of the station.

---

### MOVING ON

If you're heading from Kyoto direct **to Kansai International airport**, it's a good idea to reserve your transport in advance. Limousine buses depart from outside the Avanti department store on the south side of Kyoto Station (hourly 5am–9pm; 1hr 45min; ¥2300; ☎075/682-4400); tickets are available from the ground floor of the nearby *Keihan Hotel*. Reservations are essential on JR's Haruka Limited Express trains, for which you can buy tickets either at an ordinary JR ticket office or in **Kyoto City Air Terminal** (9.30am–5.30pm), in the first basement of Kyoto Station. Ticket holders on international flights with JAL and JAA can also check in here (6am–5pm), as long as you're travelling by Haruka train; you need to check in at least three hours before your flight departs. Finally, remember that there's a ¥2650 **departure tax** at Kansai airport.

Long-distance **buses** depart from terminals either side of Kyoto Station. JR Highway Buses and other services to Tokyo, Nagoya, and Kanazawa depart from a stand on the north side of the station, while Keihan Bus uses a terminal on the south side, outside the *Keihan Hotel*. Keihan services cover Nagasaki, Kumamoto, Fukuoka, Tokyo and Kanazawa.

---

## Information

Conveniently, the station area also contains Kyoto's main **information** services. The most useful is the **Kyoto Tourist Information Centre** (TIC; Mon–Fri 9am–5pm, Sat 9am–noon; closed Sun & hols; ☎075/371-5649), located on the east side of the Kyoto Tower building, opposite the station's front, Karasuma exit. The staff are often besieged, so take a number from the dispenser and while you're waiting browse through the information on hand, including details of festivals and other local events. The staff can help arrange volunteer Goodwill Guides (see p.23) – worth considering for visiting those sights where guided tours are in Japanese only – and home visits, as long as you give a couple of days' notice. There's also a Welcome Inn Reservation counter where you can make bookings with member hotels and ryokan anywhere in Japan, though note that it's best to have your Kyoto accommodation sorted out well in advance (see p.432 for more on accommodation).

If the TIC's closed, the next best bet is the **Kyoto City Information Office** (daily 8.30am–7pm) on the station's second floor, near the entrance to Isetan department store. There's usually an English speaker on hand who can also help with accommodation,

---

To visit some of Kyoto's most famous palaces and gardens it's necessary to apply in advance. In most cases this is a simple procedure and well worth the effort.

Tours of the **Imperial Palace**, **Sentō Gosho**, **Katsura Rikyū** and **Shūgaku-in Rikyū** are all handled by the **Imperial Household Agency** (Mon–Fri 8.45am–noon & 1–4pm, closed hols & Dec 28–Jan 4; ☎075/211-1215). Their office is located on the west side of the Imperial Park, near Imadegawa subway station. It's best to book your tour at least two days in advance, though you can often visit the Imperial Palace itself on the same day. All tours are free and conducted in Japanese, with the exception of the Imperial Palace where there may be an English guide. Note that anyone under twenty years old (still a minor in Japanese law) has to be accompanied by an adult when visiting the Sentō Gosho, Katsura Rikyū or Shūgaku-in Rikyū. Finally, take your passport with you to the office and also for the tour itself, in case it's requested.

Other sights which require reservations are **Nijō-jinya**, the interior of **Nishi-Hongan-ji** and **Saihō-ji**. See the individual accounts for details.

---

maps and city-wide information. Failing that, head for the **JR Railway information office** (daily 5.30am–11pm) on the ground floor, which also has English-speaking staff and can make hotel reservations (¥525 commission) for that night only.

Closer to the city centre, near Nanzen-ji, **Kyoto International Community House** (Tues–Sun 9am–9pm; ☎075/752-3010, fax 752-3510) is aimed primarily at foreign students or longer-term residents, but will happily assist tourists where possible. They have a message board, foreign-language papers and magazines, and CNN or BBC World news playing in the first-floor lobby. There's also a fax machine, word-processor and printer available for a small charge.

For most purposes the combined Kyoto–Nara **maps**, available free from the TIC, are perfectly adequate. If you feel in need of something more detailed, look out for the *Kyoto Information Map* (¥300), a book of large-scale maps in English and Japanese, which you should find in major bookstores (see p.466).

The monthly freesheet, *Kyoto Visitor's Guide*, is the best source of information regarding **what's on** in Kyoto. It includes details of festivals and cultural events, as well as area spotlights and selective listings of restaurants, bars and shops; you can usually pick it up in the TIC, major hotels and other tourist haunts. The monthly magazine, *Kansai Time Out* (¥300), has good coverage of the Kyoto arts scene, from cinema, theatre and live music to museums and galleries. Keep an eye out in bars, shops and the information centres for the free, weekly *Kansai Flea Market* which contains classified adverts for accommodation, employment, courses and so on.

## City transport and tours

Kyoto has two **subway** lines, offering the quickest way to scoot around the city. The Karasuma line runs from southerly Takeda, via Kyoto Station and Kita-ōji, to Kokusai Kaikan in the north, while the new Tōzai line starts at Nijō in the west and cuts east through Sanjō-Keihan and Higashiyama to Daigō in the southeast suburbs; the junction between the two lines is Karasuma-Oike Station. Trains run from 5.30am to 11.30pm and fares range from ¥200 to ¥320. Tickets are available from station vending machines. As well as single tickets, you can also buy stored-fare cards (*Torafica Kyō Kādo*) for ¥1000 or ¥3000, which you can then use to buy subway tickets and also use on City Bus services.

Several private **railways** also operate within the city. Trains on the Hankyū-Kyoto line for Ōsaka (Umeda) run beneath the city centre from Kawaramachi Station west along Shijō-dōri; a branch line heads northwest from Katsura Station in west Kyoto to

Arashiyama (see p.475). Arashiyama is also served by the Keifuku Electric Railway from Shijō-Ōmiya Station, with another branch line (the Kitano line) looping north. In northeast Kyoto, Demachiyanagi is the terminus for the Eizan line, which covers Shūgaku-in Rikyū and Yase-yūen, one of the routes up Hiei-zan (see p.473). Keihan mainline services start from a separate station in Demachiyanagi and then head south via Sanjō-Keihan to Ōsaka (Yodayabashi). Finally, trains on the Kintetsu-Kyoto line depart from the south side of Kyoto Station, from where they link into the main Kintetsu network, with services to Nara, Kōya-san and Ise.

Kyoto has an excellent **bus system** which is relatively easy to use. The buses are colour-coded, the majority show their route numbers on the front and the most important stops are announced in English, either on the electronic display or over the loudspeakers. Within the city there's a flat fare of ¥220 which you pay on exit. In most cases you enter via the back door, where you may need to take a numbered ticket if the bus is going into the suburbs, though the flat fare still applies within the central zone. The only problem is that most services stop running around 11pm, or even earlier on less popular routes.

Before leaping on board, get hold of the English-language route map from the information offices (see p.429) or the bus terminals. This shows the central zone boundary and routes operated by both **Kyoto City Bus** (light green with a darker stripe) and the far less comprehensive **Kyoto Bus** (cream with a red stripe). You'll need to use Kyoto Bus services for Ōhara and Arashiyama, but otherwise you can stick to City Bus for the central districts. The **main bus terminal** is outside Kyoto Station's Karasuma exit. Nearly all City Bus stands are coded: "A" before the stand number indicates buses headed for east Kyoto and "B" for the western districts. Of several loop lines around the city, the most useful is #206, with stops near the National Museum, Gion, Heian-jingū, Daitoku-ji and Nijō-jō; buses running clockwise leave from stand B-4, anticlockwise from A-2. The other major terminals are at **Sanjō-Keihan**, in east Kyoto, and **Kita-ōji** in the north. Some loop line buses terminate at Kita-ōji, so check with the driver if you're going that way; the stands at Kita-ōji are colour-coded red for eastbound buses and blue for westbound.

The bus companies offer a range of **discount tickets**. The simplest, *kaisūken*, are booklets of ¥220 tickets available at a small reduction at the bus terminals or from the driver in denominations of ¥1000, ¥3000 and ¥5000, valid on all buses. Next up are the one-day passes (*shi-basu ichi-nichi jyōshaken*; ¥700) which allow unlimited travel on City Bus services within the central zone; if you want to visit anywhere further out, you just pay for the bit outside the zone. These passes are available at information centres, hotels and bus terminals, but not on the bus itself. To validate the pass, put it through the machine beside the driver when you get off the first bus – after that just show it as you exit. Finally, there are combined subway and bus passes, either one-day (*shi-basu chikatetsu ichi-nichi jyōshaken*; ¥1200) or two-day (*shi-basu chikatetsu futsuka jyōshaken*; ¥2000), covering unlimited travel on the subways, City Bus and Kyoto Bus within a wider area marked on the bus maps in white. They're sold at hotels, the TIC, bus terminals, subway information windows or travel agents. You can buy them in advance, though you have to specify a date.

Though traffic in central Kyoto often gridlocks during rush hour, **taxis** (see Listings, p.469) can be useful for hopping short distances. The minimum fare is ¥580 for 2km. Renting a **bike** is a viable option for exploring central Kyoto, though not much use along the eastern hills, where you're better off walking. See Listings p.468 for outlets.

### City tours

Kyoto is best appreciated at a leisurely pace, but if you're really short of time, JTB's Sunrise Tours (☎075/341-1413) offers English-speaking guides on their **city tours**; prices start at ¥5200 for a half-day tour of selected sights. Alternatively, Keihan Bus and City Bus run a more varied programme at slightly cheaper prices, but all in Japanese. Tickets for all these tours are available through travel agents or at the bus terminals. If you fancy a more

## KYOTO: ACCOMMODATION

### CENTRAL KYOTO

| | | |
|---|---|---|
| Hotel Gimmond | *Hoteru Ginmondo* | ホテルギンモンド |
| Hiiragiya | *Hiiragiya* | 柊屋 |
| Hiiragiya Bekkan | *Hiiragiya Bekkan* | 柊屋別館 |
| Ryokan Hinomoto | *Ryokan Hinomoto* | 旅館ひのもと |
| Kinmata | *Kinmata* | 近又 |
| Marukō Inn | *Marukō In* | マルコーイン |
| Hotel Oaks | *Hoteru Ōkusu* | ホテルオークス |
| Palace-Side Hotel | *Paresu Saido Hoteru* | パレスサイドホテル |
| Sanjō Karasuma Hotel | *Sanjō Karasuma Hoteru* | 三条烏丸ホテル |
| Sun Hotel | *San Hoteru* | サンホテル |
| Yoshikawa Ryokan | *Yoshikawa Ryokan* | 吉川旅館 |

### AROUND THE STATION

| | | |
|---|---|---|
| Hotel Granvia | *Hoteru Guranvia* | ホテルグランヴィア |
| Heianbō | *Heianbō* | 平安坊 |
| Ryokan Hiraiwa | *Ryokan Hiraiwa* | 旅館平岩 |
| Kyoto 2 Tower Hotel | *Kyōto Dai-Ni Tawā Hoteru* | 京都弟2タワーホテル |
| Matsuba-ya Ryokan | *Matsuba-ya Ryokan* | 松葉家旅館 |
| New Hankyū Hotel | *Shin-Hankyū Hoteru* | 新阪急ホテル |
| Pension Station Kyoto | *Penshon Sutēshon Kyōto* | ペンションステーション京都 |
| Riverside Takase | *Ribāsaido Takase* | リバーサイド高瀬 |
| Ryokan Yuhara | *Ryokan Yuhara* | 旅館ゆはら |

### EAST KYOTO

| | | |
|---|---|---|
| Higashiyama Youth Hostel | *Higashiyama Yūsu Hosuteru* | 東山ユースホステル |
| Kiyomizu Sansō | *Kiyomizu Sansō* | 清水山荘 |
| Miyako Hotel | *Miyako Hoteru* | 都ホテル |
| Ryokan Seiki | *Ryokan Seiki* | 旅館晴輝 |
| Shinnyo-sansō | *Shinnyo-sansō* | 真如山荘 |
| Three Sisters' Inn | *Ryokan Surii Shisutāsu* | 旅館スリーシスターズ |
| Travellers' Inn | *Toraberāzu In* | トラベラーズイン |

### NORTH KYOTO

| | | |
|---|---|---|
| Aoi-sō Inn | *Aoi-sō In* | あおい荘イン |
| Kitayama Youth Hostel | *Kitayama Yūsu Hosuteru* | 北山ユースホステル |
| Myōken-ji | *Myōken-ji* | 妙顕寺 |
| Myōren-ji | *Myōren-ji* | 妙蓮寺 |
| Ryokan Rakuchō | *Ryokan Rakuchō* | 旅館洛頂 |
| Tani House | *Tani Hausu* | 谷ハウス |
| Utano Youth Hostel | *Utano Yūsu Hosuteru* | 宇多野ユースホステル |

personal tour, the English-speaking Johnny Hillwalker (otherwise known as Hirōka Hajime) takes small groups on a slow amble through southern Kyoto from Higashi-Hongan-ji to Kiyomizu-dera (March–late Nov; ¥1000–¥2000 per person; ☎075/622-6803).

## Accommodation

Kyoto's **accommodation** options range from basic guesthouses, youth hostels and temple lodgings (*shukubō*) to luxurious international hotels and top-class ryokan. One night in a full-blown Kyoto **ryokan**, where meals are served in your room, maybe overlooking a miniature garden, and where you're treated to the most meticulous service in the world, is an experience not to be missed. Some are hideously expensive, and may refuse to accept foreigners or anyone without a prior recommendation, but we've listed one or two of the more accessible traditional ones below. Needless to say, it's essential to make **reservations** at these places as far in advance as possible, but all accommodation in Kyoto gets pretty busy during the autumn and spring peaks, at holiday weekends and around the major festivals (see p.463). Note that during these times, room rates may rise considerably.

Central Kyoto is obviously a popular choice, with its easy access to the main shopping and nightlife districts as well as good transport links to sights around the city. That said, most downtown hotels are either big, luxury places or offer poor value for money, with a few notable exceptions. Because city transport is so good, however, you can stay in the cheaper outer districts and still enjoy everything the city has to offer. Many places in **eastern Kyoto** are within walking distance of Gion and the city centre, while also being in quieter, more attractive surroundings. It's also worth considering one or two nights in **northern** Kyoto to explore the region around Kinkaku-ji and west to Arashiyama. Even the **station area** has a lot going for it, especially the group of inexpensive ryokan to the northeast.

## Central Kyoto

*All the following hotels are marked on the map on p.438.*

**Hotel Gimmond**, Takakura Oike, Nakagyō-ku (☎075/221-4111, fax 221-8250). Elegant, mid-market hotel with an English touch to its newly revamped lobby. The rooms are nicely done, all en suite, and there's an in-house restaurant. ⑤.

**Hiiragiya**, Fuyachō Anekoji-agaru, Nakagyō-ku (☎075/221-1136, fax 221-1139). One of Kyoto's most famous traditional ryokan which has hardly changed since *samurai* were staying here in the mid-nineteenth century. You need to book up well in advance, but it's worth it for this quintessential Kyoto experience. ⑨.

**Hiiragiya Bekkan**, Gokomachi Nijō-sagaru, Nakagyō-ku (☎075/231-0151, fax 231-0153). The annexe of Hiiragiya (see above) offers slightly less grand accommodation. Though you can stay without meals, their *kaiseki* cuisine is superb. Located five minutes' walk northwest of Kyoto Shiyakusho-mae subway station. ⑧.

**Ryokan Hinomoto**, 375 Kotake-chō, Kawaramachi Matsubara-agaru, Shimogyō-ku (☎075/351-4563, fax 351-3932). One of the few inexpensive places to stay in the central area, a few minutes' walk south of Shijō-dōri. The recently refurbished rooms are nicely done in Japanese style, though none have private bathrooms. City Bus #17 and #205 stop at the nearby Kawaramachi Matsubara junction. ④.

**Kinmata**, 407 Gokomachi Shijō-agaru, Nakagyō-ku (☎075/221-1039, fax 231-7632). Leave the hustle and bustle of Shijō-dōri behind in this beautiful old inn, established in 1801. It offers the full ryokan experience, with *kaiseki ryōri* served in your room, a cedar-wood bath, meticulous service and a tiny classical garden – the modern breakfast room is a tad incongruous. Prices are a little less than the competition and, while you really should try one evening meal, they do offer breakfast-only rates. English spoken. ⑧–⑨.

**Marukō Inn**, Nishinotōin Shijō minami-iru, Shimogyō-ku (☎075/361-0505, fax 361-7340). A modest hotel offering decent rooms on the fringes of central Kyoto. Four minutes' walk from Shijō subway station. ⑤.

**Hotel Oaks**, Nishinotōin Shijō, Shimogyō-ku (☎075/371-0941, fax 371-4222). This comfortable, mid-range business hotel offers excellent value for its location, five minutes' walk west of Shijō subway station along Shijō-dōri. All rooms come with small bathroom, phone, TV and mini-bar as standard. ⑤.

**Palace-Side Hotel**, Shimodachiuri Karasuma, Kamigyō-ku (☎075/431-8171, fax 414-2018). Large, slightly bland hotel overlooking the Imperial Palace from the west, with good views from the more expensive, higher rooms. Three minutes north of Marutamachi subway station. ⑤.

**Sanjō Karasuma Hotel**, 80 Mikura-chō, Sanjō Karasuma nishi-iru, Nakagyō-ku (☎075/256-3331, fax 256-2351). This large, modern hotel offers well-priced, comfortable rooms, all with satellite TV, extra-wide beds and en-suite bathrooms. There's also a communal bath with garden views, a bar, restaurant and coffee lounge. ⑤.

**Sun Hotel**, Kawaramachi Sanjō-sagaru, Nakagyō-ku (☎075/241-3351, fax 241-0616). Nothing special, but the best of several lower-end hotels bang in the centre of town. Inevitably boxy but more than adequate. English spoken. ⑤.

**Yoshikawa Ryokan**, Tominokoji Oike-sagaru, Nakagyō-ku (☎075/221-5544, fax 221-6805). Intimate, traditional inn that's also renowned for its *tempura kaiseki* cuisine. Cypress-wood bath, immaculate garden and all the understated luxury you could want. ⑨.

## Around the station

*All the following hotels are marked on the map on p.441.*

**Hotel Granvia**, 657 Higashi-Shiokoji-chō, Karasuma Shiokoji-sagaru, Shimogyō-ku (☎075/344-8888, fax 344-4400). Sleek new hotel incorporated into the Kyoto Station building, with rooms on the upper floors. Facilities include a range of restaurants and bars, indoor swimming pool, boutiques and business suites. ⑥–⑦.

**Heianbō**, 725 Heian-chō, JR Kyoto-eki-mae, Shimogyō-ku (☎075/351-0650). This little wooden inn, just behind Kyoto Tower, is a real surprise among all the highrises. Rooms are nicely refurbished in Japanese style, some with bathrooms. ⑤.

**Ryokan Hiraiwa**, 314 Hayao-chō, Ninomiyachō Kaminokuchi-agaru, Shimogyō-ku (☎075/351-6748, fax 351-6969). Efficient, popular place in an attractive area of backstreets east of the Takase Canal. The *tatami* rooms are slightly spartan, and none are en suite, but they're all clean and tidy. It's a fifteen-minute walk northeast of the station, or two minutes from the Kawaramachi-shōmen stop on City Bus #17 or #205. ④.

**Kyoto 2 Tower Hotel**, Higashinotōin Shichijō-sagaru, Shimogyō-ku (☎075/361-3261, fax 351-6281). Immediately outside the station, this is the nicest of the three *Kyoto Tower* hotels, with fairly cheerful rooms and English-speaking staff. ⑤.

**Matsuba-ya Ryokan**, Kamijuzumachi Higashinotōin nishi-iru, Shimogyō-ku (☎075/351-3727, fax 351-3505). Homely ryokan in an atmospheric Meiji-era building. All rooms are Japanese style, none en suite; the more expensive rooms overlook a tiny garden. Well-placed only eight minutes' walk from Kyoto Station, east of Higashi-Hongan-ji. ④–⑤.

**New Hankyū Hotel**, JR Kyoto-eki-mae, Shiokoji-dōri, Shimogyō-ku (☎075/343-5300, fax 343-5324). An efficient, upmarket hotel that's a cut above the neighbouring *Kyoto Tower* hotels. ⑥.

**Pension Station Kyoto**, Shinmachi Shichijō-sagaru, Shimogyō-ku (☎075/882-6200, fax 862-0820). Cheerful, relaxed place with a choice of Western and Japanese rooms – those without bath are better value. In an interesting old neighbourhood west of Higashi-Hongan-ji. ④–⑤.

**Riverside Takase**, Kiyamachi Kaminokuchi-agaru, Shimogyō-ku (☎075/351-7925, fax 351-7620). Though basic, these *tatami* rooms are among the cheapest available in the city centre. On the Takase Canal near Ryokan Hiraiwa. ③.

**Ryokan Yuhara**, Kiyamachi Shōmen-agaru, Shimogyō-ku (☎ & fax 075/371-9583). Slightly more elegant ryokan on the Takase Canal with comfortable *tatami* rooms and English-speaking owners. ④.

## East Kyoto

*All the following hotels are marked on the map on p.444.*

**Higashiyama Youth Hostel**, 112 Sanjō-dōri Shirakawa-bashi, Higashiyama-ku (☎075/761-8135, 761-8138). Kyoto's smartest hostel is conveniently located three minutes' walk east from Higashiyama subway station. Against that, it's run like a boarding school, there's a 10.30pm curfew and at the time of writing they were insisting that everyone paid for breakfast and dinner. The food's not bad, but you definitely want to eat out at night in Kyoto. ②.

**Kiyomizu Sansō**, 3-341 Kyomizu, Higashiyama-ku (☎075/561-6109). There are only four rooms in this hundred-year-old, family inn hidden down an alley off the Sannen-zaka pedestrian street. Meals are optional, but excellent value. Reservations essential. ④–⑤.

**Miyako Hotel**, Sanjō Keage, Higashiyama-ku (☎075/771-7111, fax 751-2490). Huge, efficient, top-class hotel complete with landscaped gardens, bird sanctuary and range of restaurants. There's a choice of elegant Japanese-style rooms, some in the garden annexe, or Western-style accommodation, where higher rates get you balconies with views over Kyoto. Free shuttle buses operate between the hotel, Sanjō-dōri and Kyoto Station. ⑦–⑨.

**Ryokan Seiki**, 188-1 Kadowaki-chō, Yamatoōji Gojō-agaru higashi-iru, Higashiyama-ku (☎075/551-4911, fax 551-9251). Pleasant, modern ryokan within walking distance of Gion. Rooms are small but adequate, all with shared washing facilities. Take City Bus #206 heading anticlockwise to the Gojō-zaka stop, then walk back down Gojō-dōri till you find their sign on the right. ④.

**Shinnyō-sansō**, 82 Shinnyō-chō, Jōdo-ji, Sakyō-ku (☎075/751-8073, fax 771-1304). A modern *shukubō* in the grounds of Shinnyō-dō temple, in a quiet corner of northeast Kyoto, offering *tatami* rooms with bath and toilet separate. You can order mini-*kaiseki* dinners (¥3150), or other meals as required. The nearest bus stop, Kinrin-shako-mae, is six minutes' walk east on Shirakawa-dōri. Note that there's an 11pm curfew.④–⑤.

**Three Sisters' Inn**, Kurodani-mae, Okazaki, Sakyō-ku (☎075/761-6336, fax 6338). The Yamada sisters run this homely ryokan and a nearby annexe set in a small garden. All rooms are beautifully appointed, some with en-suite bathrooms and they're located in an interesting residential area behind Heian-jingū. Meals are optional. English spoken. ⑤.

**Travellers' Inn**, 91 Enshoji-chō, Okazaki, Sakyō-ku (☎075/771-0225, fax 771-0226). Tidy, no frills Japanese- and Western-style rooms at an excellent price for the location, within walking distance of Heian-jingū and the surrounding sights. From the station, take City Bus #5. ⑤.

## North Kyoto

*All the following hotels are marked on the map on p.452.*

**Aoi-sō Inn**, Karasuma Shimei, Kita-ku (☎075/431-0788). Popular *gaijin* guesthouse, offering functional private rooms with shared toilets and showers. Weekly and monthly rates also available. Two minutes' walk west from Kuramaguchi subway station. ②.

**Kitayama Youth Hostel**, Takagamine, Kita-ku (☎075/492-5345). This small, older hostel on the northwest fringes of Kyoto makes a good base for Kinkaku-ji and surrounding sights. You'll get a warm welcome and lots of local information from the jovial, English-speaking manager and, though there's a 9.30pm curfew, it's all pretty relaxed. From Kyoto Station, take a City Bus (#6) to the Genkō-an-mae stop (30–40min), then walk west until you find the signed right-hand turn. ①.

**Myōken-ji**, Teranouchi Shinmachi nishi-iru, Kamigyō-ku (☎075/414-0808). Lovely, traditional *shukubō* with a delightful garden at the back of the temple complex. At busy times you'll be asked to share the *tatami* rooms. Three minutes' walk west of Horikawa Teranouchi bus stop, northwest of the Imperial Palace. From the station, take City Bus #9. 10pm curfew. ④–⑤.

**Myōren-ji**, Teranouchi Ōmiya higashi-iru, Kamigyō-ku (☎075/451-3527). Welcoming, relaxed *shukubō* with refurbished *tatami* rooms behind a thirteenth-century temple with a celebrated rock garden. There's no bath – you'll be given tickets to the local public bath – and no meals, but guests can attend the 6.30am service. Myōren-ji lies two minutes west from the Horikawa Teranouchi bus stop, in the opposite direction to Myōken-ji (see above); look for an unusual bell tower in the front courtyard. English spoken. 11pm curfew. ④.

**Ryokan Rakuchō**, 67 Higashi-Hangi-chō, Shimogamo, Sakyō-ku (☎075/721-2174, fax 791-7202). Friendly, well-kept inn with *tatami* rooms and shared washing facilities. It's ten minutes' walk east from Kita-ōji subway and bus station and also on the #206 City Bus loop line (Furitsu-daigaku-mae stop); turn north off Kitaōji-dōri in front of the sub-post office. English spoken. ④.

**Tani House**, 8 Daitokuji-chō Murasakino, Kita-ku (☎075/492-5489, fax 493-6419). Reservations are essential at this welcoming, cluttered house among quiet lanes to the east of Daitoku-ji. There's a choice of shared *tatami*-mat dorms, or basic private rooms, plus use of a shared kitchen and cheap bikes for rent (¥500 per day). They also run an annexe in central Kyoto, though it's often filled with long-term guests. To find Tani House, walk west from the Kenkun-jinja-mae stop (City Bus #206) and turn north beside the walls of Daitoku-ji. English spoken. ①–②.

**Utano Youth Hostel**, 29 Nakayama-chō, Uzumasa, Ukyō-ku (☎075/462-2288, fax 462-2289). A big, bustling hostel with a good atmosphere and helpful, English-speaking staff, set in its own grounds on Kyoto's western outskirts. The buffet breakfast is excellent value, and you can work it off by biking (¥800 per day) to nearby Ryōan-ji and Kinkaku-ji, or west to Arashiyama. There's a 10.30pm curfew. Three City Bus lines (#10, #26 and #59) stop near the hostel, just within the ¥700-bus pass zone. ①.

# The City

For decades Kyoto-lovers have been lamenting the loss of old wooden neighbourhoods to concrete modernity, the diminishing number of traditional craftsmen and the demise of their ancient city's unique culture. While the onslaught has been relentless

## KYOTO: THE CITY

| Kyoto | *Kyōto* | 京都 |
|---|---|---|

**CENTRAL KYOTO AND AROUND THE STATION**

| Higashi-Hongan-ji | *Higashi-Hongan-ji* | 東本願寺 |
|---|---|---|
| Imperial Palace | *Kyōto Gosho* | 京都御所 |
| Kyoto Station | *Kyōto-eki* | 京都駅 |
| Museum of Kyoto | *Kyōto Hakubutsukan* | 京都博物館 |
| Nijō-jō | *Nijō-jō* | 二条城 |
| Nijō-jinya | *Nijō-jinya* | 二条陣屋 |
| Nishi-Hongan-ji | *Nishi-Hongan-ji* | 西本願寺 |
| Pontochō | *Pontochō* | 先斗町 |
| Tō-ji | *Tō-ji* | 東寺 |

**EAST KYOTO**

| Chion-in | *Chion-in* | 知恩院 |
|---|---|---|
| Eikan-dō | *Eikan-dō* | 永観堂 |
| Fureaikan | *Fureaikan* | ふれあい館 |
| Kiyomizu-dera | *Kiyomizu-dera* | 清水寺 |
| Kōdai-ji | *Kōdai-ji* | 高台寺 |
| Kyoto National Museum | *Kyōto Kokuritsu Hakubutsukan* | 京都国立博物館 |
| Ginkaku-ji | *Ginkaku-ji* | 銀閣寺 |
| Gion | *Gion* | 祇園 |
| Gion Kōbu Kaburenjō | *Gion Kōbu Kaburenjō* | 祇園甲部歌舞練場 |
| Heian-jingū | *Heian-jingū* | 平安神宮 |
| Kawai Kanjirō's House | *Kawai Kanjirō Kinenkan* | 河合寛次郎記念館 |
| Murin-an | *Murin-an* | 無隣庵 |
| Nanzen-ji | *Nanzen-ji* | 南禅寺 |
| Sanjūsangen-dō | *Sanjūsangen-dō* | 三十三間堂 |
| Shinbashi | *Shinbashi* | 新橋 |
| Shōrin-in | *Shōrin-in* | 勝林院 |
| Shūgaku-in Rikyū | *Shūgaku-in Rikyū* | 修学院離宮 |
| Yasaka-jinja | *Yasaka-jinja* | 八坂神社 |
| Yasui Konpira-gū | *Yasui Konpira-gū* | 安井金比羅宮 |

**WEST KYOTO**

| Daisen-in | *Daisen-in* | 大仙院 |
|---|---|---|
| Daitoku-ji | *Daitoku-ji* | 大徳寺 |
| Katsura Rikyū | *Katsura Rikyū* | 桂離宮 |
| Kinkaku-ji | *Kinkaku-ji* | 金閣寺 |
| Kita-ōji Station | *Kita-ōji-eki* | 北大路駅 |
| Kōryū-ji | *Kōryū-ji* | 広隆寺 |
| Ryōan-ji | *Ryōan-ji* | 竜安寺 |
| Ryōgen-in | *Ryōgen-in* | 龍源院 |
| Saihō-ji | *Saihō-ji* | 西芳寺 |
| Tōei Uzumasa Eiga-mura | *Tōei Uzumasa Eiga-mura* | 東映太秦映画村 |

– witness the controversial new station and the more insidious redevelopment of countless private plots – Kyoto's "world of shadows" still exists, lurking behind the secretive screens of traditional inns or exclusive restaurants, and within the lantern-lit façades of Gion and Pontochō. The spirit of old Kyoto is not all so elusive, however, and the key to enjoying this massive city is to leave the tourist haunts behind occasionally and delve into the quiet backstreets, among age-old craftshops and distinctive *machiya* houses (see box, p.446), or to seek out the peaceful garden of some forgotten temple.

The account below starts in central Kyoto and then heads south to the station before crossing east over the Kamo-gawa to work anticlockwise around the outer districts. Much of the city centre and the eastern hills can be covered on foot, but you'll need to hop on a few trains and buses to explore the more scattered sights to the north and west.

## Central Kyoto

Before the Emperor moved to Tokyo in 1868, Kyoto's **Imperial Palace** symbolized the nation's physical and spiritual centre. Today's palace is by no means a high priority among Kyoto's wealth of sights, but it's a good idea to come here early in your stay to make arrangements for visiting the city's more rewarding imperial villas and gardens (see box, p.430). If you're not pushed for time, then the **Sentō Gosho** garden, also in the Imperial Park, is worth seeing, but otherwise it's better to concentrate on **Nijō-jō**'s magnificent screen paintings and the intriguing **Nijō-jinya**.

### THE IMPERIAL PARK

Dun-coloured earth walls enclose the **Imperial Park**, inside which wide expanses of gravel and clipped lawns have replaced most of the former palaces and subsidiary buildings. In the park's northwest corner, the **Imperial Household Agency** office handles applications to visit the former royal palaces (see box, p.430); the nearest subway station is Imadegawa, or take a bus to Karasuma Imadegawa. As long as you arrive at least twenty minutes before, it's usually possible to sign up for the next tour of the nearby **Imperial Palace** (Mon–Fri & occasionally Sat 10am & 2pm, closed hols & Dec 25–Jan 5; free). The tour lasts around one hour and is often in English, though it's still worth investing in the English-language guide book (¥200) for its interior views. Though it originally stood about 2km further west, the palace was relocated to the present site in the late twelfth century. Nearly all the buildings, however, date from the mid-nineteenth century and the overwhelming impression is of sterile spaces of pure white gravel set off against regal halls built in austere Heian style (794–1185). The most important building is the ceremonial **Shishin-den**, flanked by two cherry and citrus trees, where the Meiji, Taishō and Shōwa emperors were all enthroned. Further on, you can peer inside the Seiryō-den which was once the emperor's private residence, while beyond there's a tantalizing glimpse of a pond-filled stroll-garden (see p.439) designed by the landscape gardener Kobori Enshū (1579–1647).

You can enjoy Enshū's work to the full in the **Sentō Gosho** which occupies the southeast quadrant of the Imperial Park. Again, you have to join a guided tour (Mon–Fri 11am & 1.30pm, closed hols & Dec 25–Jan 5; free), and this time it's all in Japanese. Originally built as a retirement home for former emperors, the palace last burnt down in 1854 and now only the peaceful garden remains. Apart from several graceful pavilions, its main features are a zig-zag bridge – stunning when its wisteria-trellis is in full bloom – and a cobbled "seashore" which lends the garden an extra grandeur.

### NIJŌ-JŌ AND NIJŌ-JINYA

One kilometre southwest of the Imperial Park, the swaggering opulence of **Nijō-jō** (daily 8.45am–5pm; last entry 4pm; ¥600) provides a complete contrast to imperial understatement. Built as the Kyoto residence of Shogun Tokugawa Ieyasu (1603–1616), the castle's double moats, massive walls and watchtowers demonstrate the supreme confidence of his new, Tokyo-based military government. Inside, the finest artists of the day filled the palace with sumptuous gilded screens and carvings, the epitome of Momoyama style (see Contexts, p.794). The increasingly impoverished Emperor was left in no doubt as to where power now lay. The castle took 23 years to

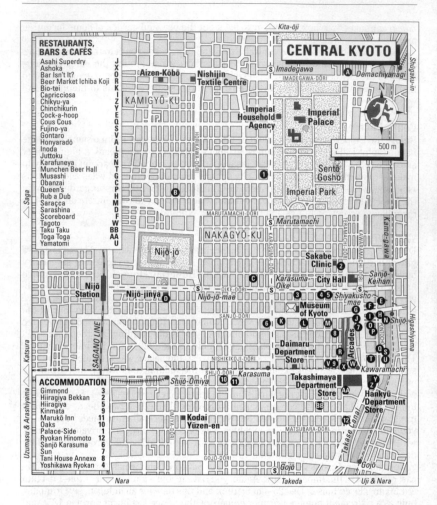

**CENTRAL KYOTO**

**RESTAURANTS, BARS & CAFÉS**

| | |
|---|---|
| Asahi Superdry | J |
| Ashoka | X |
| Bar Isn't It? | O |
| Beer Market Ichiba Koji | R |
| Bio-tei | K |
| Capricciosa | I |
| Chikyu-ya | Z |
| Chinchikurin | Y |
| Cock-a-hoop | E |
| Cous Cous | Q |
| Fujino-ya | S |
| Gontaro | V |
| Honyaradō | A |
| Inoda | L |
| Juttoku | B |
| Karafuneya | N |
| Munchen Beer Hall | T |
| Musashi | G |
| Obanzai | C |
| Queen's | P |
| Rub a Dub | H |
| Saraçca | M |
| Sarashina | D |
| Scoreboard | F |
| Tagoto | W |
| Taku Taku | BB |
| Toga Toga | AA |
| Yamatomi | U |

**ACCOMMODATION**

| | |
|---|---|
| Gimmond | 3 |
| Hiiragiya Bekkan | 2 |
| Hiiragiya | 5 |
| Kinmata | 9 |
| Marukō Inn | 11 |
| Oaks | 10 |
| Palace-Side | 1 |
| Ryokan Hinomoto | 12 |
| Sanjō Karasuma | 6 |
| Sun | 7 |
| Tani House Annexe | 8 |
| Yoshikawa Ryokan | 4 |

complete, paid for by local *daimyō*, but Nijō-jō was never used in defence and rarely visited by a shogun after the mid-1600s. More than two hundred years later, however, it was here that the young Emperor Meiji had the satisfaction of receiving the resignation of the last Tokugawa shogun in 1867.

The entrance to Nijō-jō lies via the main East Gate on Hirokawa-dōri, near the Nijō-jō-mae subway station and bus stop. Inside, follow the crowds through Kara-mon gate and under the magnificent, sweeping roofs of the **Ninomaru Palace**. Its five buildings face onto a lake-garden created by Kobori Enshū and run in a staggered line connected by covered corridors. Each room is lavishly decorated with **screen paintings** by the brilliant Kanō school of artists, notably Kanō Tanyū and Naonobu, while some of the intricately carved transoms are attributed to Hidari Jingoro. In keeping with the rigid stratification of feudal society, each room's function was reflected in the degree of decoration and in the motifs themselves. *Daimyō* seeking an audience with the shogun cooled their heels among scenes of imposing leopards and tigers – animals the artists had never seen – before being ushered into the Second Grand Chamber (in the third building). Here they would prostrate themselves before the shogun on his raised dais, surrounded by bold, shimmering screens of pines and peacocks beneath an equally ornate ceiling. The fourth building, reserved for the trusted Inner Lords, eschews such grandeur for more delicate herons and cherry blossoms, while the fifth is positively subdued. This last was the shogun's living quarters which only his female attendants were allowed to enter; it's decorated with monochrome screens of craggy, Chinese landscapes and sleeping sparrows.

Ieyasu built Nijō-jō in the grounds of the original, Heian-era Imperial Palace. Today only a tiny fragment of the earlier palace remains – a pond-garden, **Shinsen-en** – trapped between two roads immediately south of the castle walls. Through the garden, continue walking south down Ōmiya-dōri to find the mysterious **Nijō-jinya** behind a fence on the right-hand side. Since this is a private house, **tours** (four daily; 1hr; ¥1000; ☎075/841-0972) are by appointment only and must be booked by phone, in Japanese, at least a day before; they also ask that non-Japanese-speakers bring an interpreter. All this effort is rewarded with a glimpse into a treacherous world – the seemingly ordinary house is riddled with trap doors, false walls and ceilings, squeaking "nightingale" floors, escape hatches, disguised staircases and confusing dead ends to trap intruders. It was built in the early seventeenth century as an inn for feudal lords who came to pay homage to the emperor. As these were days of intrigue and high skulduggery, the owner spent thirty years incorporating this splendid array of security devices. It's the stuff of countless *samurai* epics, but Ian Fleming, researching locations for *You Only Live Twice* (see Books, p.819) found it excessive: "I wouldn't dare write this for Bond," he said. "There must be some show of plausibility".

## DOWNTOWN KYOTO

Kyoto's **downtown** district is contained within the grid of streets bounded by Oike-dōri and Shijō-dōri to the north and south, Karasuma-dōri to the west and the Kamo-gawa in the east. While there's little in the way of specific sights, the backstreets still hide a number of traditional, wooden buildings, including some of Kyoto's finest ryokan (see Accommodation, p.432). You'll also come across fine old craft shops (see p.467) among the boutiques and department stores, while the colourful, somewhat touristy arcades of **Teramachi** and neighbouring **Shinkyōgoku** are worth a browse. The alleys east of Shinkyōgoku are home to a scattering of forgotten temples which were banished to this area in the late sixteenth century. Beyond this lies **Pontochō**. Though best at night, when lantern-light fills the narrow lanes, this former *geisha* district is also attractive by day, particularly along the willow-lined Takase Canal. In July and August Pontochō restaurants open terraces over the cooling Kamo-gawa – their mellow lamps are a memorable feature of Kyoto's sweltering summer nights.

Walking west, **Nishiki-koji** street market provides a feast for the eyes and nose. Since the early seventeenth century this narrow, covered alley has been one of Kyoto's main fish and vegetable markets, supplemented nowdays by the city's famous *tsuke-mono* – great vats of brightly coloured pickled vegetables. Where the stalls end, turn north on Takakura-dōri to find the downtown district's only conventional sight, the new **Museum of Kyoto** (daily 10am–6/7.30pm; closed 3rd Wed of each month; ¥500), in a trendy area of galleries and cafés. The museum incorporates a Meiji-era bank building and a replica Edo-period shopping street with craft shops and some reasonable restaurants. Upstairs, the main display halls deal with local history, culture and modern crafts. Despite the charming historical dioramas, the exhibitions are rather disappointing – ask for one of the museum's volunteer guides if you want to fathom what's going on. However, the small section on Kyoto's film industry is enlivened by screenings of classic movies (in Japanese only) at 1.30pm and 5pm on weekdays.

## Around the station

Historically, the principal entrance to Kyoto lay through its great southern gate, so it's only fitting that this district, south of the city centre, should be home to the monumental **Kyoto Station**. Uncompromisingly modern, the shiny new station and its associated developments have already begun to revitalize the area, which also contains a few of the city's more venerable temples. In their day, **Nishi-Hongan-ji** and **Higashi-Hongan-ji** were probably equally awe-inspiring as today's architecture, with their massive wooden halls full of shimmering gold. Across the tracks, **Tō-ji** boasts Japan's tallest wooden pagoda and some of the city's oldest-surviving buildings.

### *NISHI-HONGAN-JI*

One of Japan's most popular and wealthy Buddhist sects is the Jōdo Shinshū (True Pure Land) which was founded by the Kyoto-born priest Shonin Shinran (1173–1262). His simple creed, which at the time was regarded as heresy, asserts that merely chanting the *nembutsu*, "Praise to Amida Buddha", can lead to salvation. Not surprisingly, the sect grew rapidly despite opposition from the established hierarchy, until eventually Toyotomi Hideyoshi granted them a plot of land in southern Kyoto in 1591. By 1602, however, Shogun Tokugawa Ieyasu was sufficiently alarmed at the sect's power to sponsor a splinter group just a few hundred metres to the east – even today the two groups continue to differ over doctrinal affairs.

The more interesting of the two temples is the original **Nishi-Hongan-ji** (daily 6am–5/6pm; free) which faces onto Horikawa-dōri about ten minutes' walk north of Kyoto Station. The gravel courtyard contains two huge halls, the oldest of which is the Founder's Hall (1636) on the left, dedicated to Shinran, while the Amida Hall dates from 1760. Both are decked with gold, including some screens by Kanō artists in the Amida Hall, but the temple's real highlights are the even more ornate buildings behind. If you've developed a taste for Momoyama-era extravagance after Nijō-jō (see p.437), then it's worth applying for their next guided **tour** (2–4 days each month; 1.30pm & 2.30pm; free; ☎075/371-5181) – ask in the green-roofed building, left of the Founder's Hall. To be on the safe side, however, it's best to reserve at least two weeks before by writing to the Nishi-Hongan-ji Reception Office, Hanayachō-sagaru, Horikawa-dōri, Shimogyō-ku, Kyoto 600, giving your name, address, phone number, number of people and dates you'll be in Kyoto; remember to enclose a stamped-addressed envelope, or an international reply coupon if sending from abroad.

The tour starts with an introductory talk – you'll be lent an English-language pamphlet – after which you can explore at your own pace. The halls date from the mid-seventeenth century and were relocated here from various palaces around the city by order of Tokugawa Ieyasu. Kanō-school artists covered the walls and screens with what are regarded as some of the finest Momoyama-period paintings, of classical landscapes, birds and flowers, all lavishly sprinkled with gold. The temple's dry garden is noted for its exotic cycad palms and is similarly elaborate, in stark contrast to the two austere Nō stages. Dated 1581, the northern stage is held to be the oldest in Japan.

### *HIGASHI-HONGAN-JI*

Shōmen-dōri leads east from Nishi-Hongan-ji, past shops selling Buddhist accessories, to the back wall of **Higashi-Hongan-ji** (daily 6am–4.30/5pm; free). Though similar in style to its rival, Higashi-Hongan-ji had to be completely rebuilt after a fire in 1864. Only the two main halls are open to the public, of which the northerly Founder's Hall counts among Japan's largest wooden buildings. When the new halls were built, ordinary ropes proved too weak to lift the massive roof beams so female devotees from around the country sent in enough hair to plait 53 ropes; an example of these black coils is preserved in the open corridor connecting the halls. Two blocks further east, the temple's shady **Kikoku-tei** garden (daily 9am–4/4.30pm; free) provides a welcome respite from the surrounding city blocks.

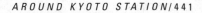

△ Nagoya & Tokyo

# AROUND KYOTO STATION

N

## ACCOMMODATION

| | |
|---|---|
| Granvia | 9 |
| Heianbō | 6 |
| Kyoto 2 Tower | 8 |
| Matsuba-ya Ryokan | 4 |
| New Hankyū | 7 |
| Pension Station Kyoto | 5 |
| Riverside Takase | 1 |
| Ryokan Hiraiwa | 2 |
| Ryokan Yuhara | 3 |

## RESTAURANTS, CAFÉS & BARS

| | |
|---|---|
| Chikara | A |
| Izusen | B |
| Suishin | C |

500 m

△ Sanjō-Keihan
Gojō
△ Kita-ōji
S Gojō
GOJŌ-DŌRI
△ Saga
△ Osaka

Kamo-gawa
Takase Canal
Gojō
Shichijō
KAWARAMACHI-DŌRI
Kikoku-tei
Higashi-Hongan-ji
KARASUMA-DŌRI
SHICHIJŌ-DŌRI
SHIMOGYŌ-KU
Nishi-Hongan-ji
HORIKAWA DŌRI
ŌMIYA-DŌRI

Tōfukuji
△ Uji & Nara
S Tōji
△ Takeda
KUJŌ-DŌRI
Kyoto Tower
Kyoto Station
Tōji
△ Nara
To-ji

## KYOTO STATION AND KYOTO TOWER

There's been tremendous controversy about the new **Kyoto Station**, designed by Tokyo architect Hara Hiroshi, the steel-grey bulk of which dominates the southern aspect of this low-rise city. In fact, the hugely ugly 1960s **Kyoto Tower** is far more objectionable, so save your money on the tower's observatory (daily 9am–9pm; ¥770) and head for the station's twelfth-floor Sky Garden instead. The views may be less dramatic, but it's free and the building's extraordinary central atrium, with its grand stairways and suspended walkway, is well worth exploring. Apart from the station itself, there's a department store, restaurants and underground shopping malls, plus a hotel, theatre and an unusually good Joypolis amusement hall (daily 10am–11pm; from ¥1500 for 3 attractions). Already the station is providing a new focus to southern Kyoto and it's likely that this area will see more development.

## TŌ-JI

There's little reason to venture into the bleak districts south of Kyoto Station, with the noteworthy exception of **Tō-ji** (daily 9am–4.30pm). This historic temple, founded by Emperor Kammu in 794, contains some of Japan's finest Esoteric Buddhist sculpture. If possible, it's best to visit during the monthly flea market (21st of each month), when Tō-ji throngs with pilgrims, hustlers and bargain-hunters.

The main entrance to eighth-century Heian-kyō lay through the great south gate, Rashō-mon, which stood at the junction of Kujō-dōri and Senbon-dōri. After the problems in Nara (see p.481), Emperor Kammu permitted only two Buddhist temples within the city walls: Tō-ji and Sai-ji, the East and West temples, stood either side of Rashō-mon and were charged with the young capital's spiritual well-being. While Sai-ji eventually faded in the thirteenth century, Tō-ji prospered under **Kōbō Daishi**, the founder of Shingon Buddhism (see p.784), who was granted the stewardship in 823. Over the centuries, the temple gathered a treasure trove of calligraphy, paintings and Buddhist statuary, the oldest of which were supposedly brought from China by the Daishi himself.

The back gate of Tō-ji lies about ten minutes' walk southwest of Kyoto Station. Its most distinctive feature is a **five-storey pagoda** – Japan's tallest – which was erected in 826 and last rebuilt in the mid-seventeenth century. It now stands in an enclosure alongside Tō-ji's greatest treasures, the Kō-dō and more southerly Kon-dō (¥500, or ¥800 including the Hōmotsu-kan). These solid, confident buildings both date from the early seventeenth century, but it's the images inside that are the focus.

The red-lacquered **Kō-dō** (Lecture Hall) is the temple's most important building. Inside the cool, slightly musty hall, 21 gilded and polychrome statues are arranged in a mandala representing the eternal realm. Five Buddhas hold centre stage, flanked by two splendid groups of statues, all of which date from the early Heian period. To the right (east) five bodhisattvas sit on their lotus thrones and to the left stand the Godai Myō-ō (Five Fearful Kings), whose ferocious demeanour is meant to scare off evil. The mandala's corners are protected by the no-less fierce Shi-Tennō (Four Heavenly Kings), with between them the glorious Taishaku-Ten, astride a lumpy, white elephant, and the four-headed, four-armed Bon-Ten perched precariously on a quartet of geese.

By contrast, the plain wooden **Kon-dō** (Main Hall) contains just three images within its dark, high-roofed sanctuary. Here, Yakushi Nyorai, the Buddha of physical and spiritual healing, is accompanied by his two assistants, Nikkō and Gakkō, all carved around four centuries ago. Take a close look at the twelve sacred generals gathered around Yakushi's throne – one of these small but lusty characters shades his eyes to search out evil while another eagerly tests the edge of his sword.

Kōbō Daishi is said to have lived in the **Miei-dō**, the Founder's Hall, located in the temple's northwest corner. The present building, erected in 1380, houses a thirteenth-century statue of the saint which can be seen on the 21st of each month. On this day, which marks the entry of the Daishi into nirvana, hundreds of pilgrims queue up to pay their respects. Beyond the Miei-dō, the modern **Hōmotsu-kan** contains Tō-ji's remaining treasures, including priceless mandala, portraits of Kōbō Daishi and a six-metre-tall Senjū Kannon (1000-arm Buddhist Goddess of Mercy) carved in 877. The museum opens twice a year (March 20–May 25 & Sept 20–Nov 25 daily 9am–4.30pm; ¥500), with a different exhibition on each occasion.

## East Kyoto

If you only have time for one day in Kyoto, then it would be wise to concentrate on the wealth of temples and museums lining the eastern hills. Not only does this district include many of Kyoto's more rewarding sights, but it's also fairly compact and contains areas of attractive lanes and traditional houses against the wooded slopes behind. With a comfortable pair of shoes and an early start, you'll be able to sample some of the best Kyoto has to offer.

Beginning in the south, the massed statues of **Sanjūsangen-dō** are a tremendous sight, but if you're pushed for time, head straight for **Kiyomizu-dera**, with its distinctive wooden terrace, and then follow the cobbled lanes of **Sannen-zaka** north. **Gion**, the famous entertainment district traditionally associated with *geisha* and teahouses, retains a surprising number of wooden façades and photogenic corners, though its seductive charms are best savoured after dark. Further north, **Heian-jingū** rings the changes as both a major shrine and a relatively recent addition to the cityscape, while the nearby **Fureaikan** provides a comprehensive introduction to Kyoto's myriad traditional crafts. It's worth seeking out the quiet gardens of **Murin-an** and **Konchi-in**, before taking the philosopher's path north to **Ginkaku-ji** – the Silver Pavilion may be unexpectedly low-key, but it makes a startling combination with the garden's mass of sculpted white sand. Garden-lovers should also arrange to visit **Shūgaku-in Rikyū** on the northeast edge of Kyoto for its inspired use of borrowed scenery on a grand scale – you'll need an extra half day for this.

### *SANJŪSANGEN-DŌ TO KIYOMIZU-DERA*

Don't be put off by the turn-stile entrance to **Sanjūsangen-dō** (daily: April–mid-Nov 8am–5pm; mid-Nov–March 9am–4pm; ¥500), on the southeastern edge of Kyoto – the ranks of 1001 gilded statues inside the hall are a truly awe-inspiring sight. At first the impassive, haloed figures appear as identical images of Kannon, the Buddhist Goddess of Mercy, portrayed with eleven heads and one thousand arms. But they all have subtle differences in their faces, clothes, jewellery or the symbols held in their tiny, outstretched hands. Rather than a thousand arms, the statues have been given only forty apiece (excluding the two hands in prayer), but each of these can save 25 worlds. In addition, every figure represents 33 incarnations, giving a total of 33,033 Kannon to help save mankind. It's perhaps not surprising to learn that they were commissioned by the devout former-Emperor Go-Shirakawa in 1164, during the bloody Genpei Wars (see p.771).

The statues were carved by some seventy craftsmen under the direction of the renowned sculptor, **Tankei** (c.1173–1256). He completed the central, seated Kannon at the age of 82 and is also attributed with several of the superb images along the front row. Of these, 28 are disciples of Kannon, while Fūjin and Raijin, the muscular gods of Wind and Thunder, bring up the two ends. Unfortunately, many of the original statues were lost in a fire in 1249, but 156 Kannon and the head of the main image were saved, and by 1266 a replica hall had been completed with the Kannon back up to full strength. In the early seventeenth century, the west veranda of the 118-metre-long hall became a popular place for *samurai* to practice their **archery**. This developed into a competition, **Tōshiya**, in which archers had to fire arrows from a squatting position along the length of the building without hitting a pillar. Nowadays, the event is commemorated with an archery display outside the hall on January 15.

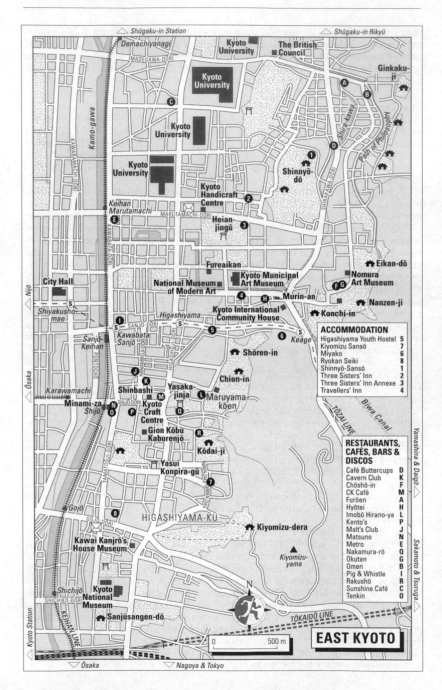

△ Shūgaku-in Station      △ Shūgaku-in Rikyū

Demachiyanagi

Kyoto University
The British Council

MADEGAWA-DORI

Kyoto University

Ginkaku-ji

**A**

**B**

**C**

Kyoto University

Shira-kawa

**D**

Path of Philosophy

Kamo-gawa

Kyoto University

**1**

Shinnyō-dō

Kyoto Handicraft Centre

Keihan Marutamachi

**2**

MARUTAMACHI-DORI

**E**

Heian-jingū

**3**

SHIRAKAWA-DORI

Fureaikan

Eikan-dō

City Hall

National Museum of Modern Art

Kyoto Municipal Art Museum

Nomura Art Museum

**F G**

Shiyakusho-mae

**S**

**4**

Murin-an

**H**

Nanzen-ji

Kyoto International Community House

Konchi-in

**I**

SANJŌ-DORI

Higashiyama

**S**

**S**

**ACCOMMODATION**

Sanjō-Keihan

Kawabata Sanjō

**5**

Keage

**6**

**S**

Higashiyama Youth Hostel    5
Kiyomizu Sansō            7
Miyako                   6
Ryokan Seiki             8
Shinnyō-Sansō            1
Three Sisters' Inn        2
Three Sisters' Inn Annexe 3
Travellers' Inn           4

Shōren-in

**J**

**K**

Chion-in

Shinbashi

Yasaka-jinja

**M**

**L**

Maruyama-kōen

Minami-za

Shijō

**N**

**O**

Kyoto Craft Centre

TŌZAI LINE

Biwa Canal

Karawamachi

**P**

Gion Kōbu Kaburenjō

**R**

Kōdai-ji

**RESTAURANTS, CAFÉS, BARS & DISCOS**

Yasui Konpira-gū

**7**

Café Buttercups      D
Cavern Club          K
Chōshō-in            F
CK Café              M
Furōen               A
Hyōtei               H
Imobō Hirano-ya      L
Kento's              P
Malt's Club          J
Matsuno              N
Metro                E
Nakamura-rō          Q
Okutan               G
Omen                 B
Pig & Whistle        I
Rakushō              R
Sunshine Café        C
Tenkin               O

Gojō

**8**

HIGASHIYAMA-KU

Kiyomizu-dera

Kawai Kanjrō's House Museum

Kiyomizu-yama

Shichijō

Kyoto National Museum

**N**

Sanjūsangen-dō

△ Kyoto Station

△ Ōsaka

TŌKAIDŌ LINE

0      500 m

**EAST KYOTO**

▽ Ōsaka      ▽ Nagoya & Tokyo

Yamashina & Daigo

Sakamoto & Tsuruga

Sanjūsangen-dō lies south of Shichijō-dōri (on bus routes #100, #206 and #208), immediately across from the **Kyoto National Museum** (Tues–Sun: April–Nov 9am–8pm; Jan–Mar & Dec 9am–4.30pm; ¥420, plus extra for special exhibitions). Rotating exhibitions of the museum's permanent collection, covering Kyoto culture from pre-history up to 1868, are held in its "new" wing while the original hall, built in 1895, is reserved for special exhibitions two or three times a year. Many of the items on display are National Treasures and the museum is a manageable size, if rather old-fashioned in style.

Heading north along Higashiōji-dōri, anyone interested in Japanese folk crafts should make a brief detour to **Kawai Kanjirō's House** (Tues–Sun 10am–5pm; closed Aug 10–20 & Dec 4–Jan 7; ¥900). Though it's a trifle expensive, this is the tastefully rustic home of the innovative potter Kawai Kanjirō (1890–1966), who helped revive *mingei* (folk crafts) in the 1930s. The house is as he left it, beautifully furnished with ceramics and sculptures from his long career, including the kilns where many of these pieces were made. To find the house, turn west off the main road shortly before the Gojō-dōri fly-over.

Just north of the fly-over a right fork brings you to Chawan-zaka, a road lined with shops selling local pottery. This is also a quieter, back entrance to **Kiyomizu-dera** (daily 6am–6pm; ¥300). If you'd rather use the traditional approach, continue to Kiyomizu-zaka, where you'll find a colourful, crowded parade of souvenir shops and craft galleries. The closest bus stops are Kiyomizu-michi or Gojō-zaka on Higashi-ōji-dōri (served by #202, #207 or #206).

Kiyomizu-dera, with its trade-mark wooden platform overhanging the valley, is one of Kyoto's defining sights. There's been a temple here since 778 when a visionary priest came across its fount of clear water (*kiyo-mizu*). Nearly all the buildings you see today, however, date from 1633. Passing the newly painted three-storey pagoda, the monumental **Hon-dō** (Main Hall) is strangely peaceful inside, though there's little to see – its principal image, an eleven-headed Kannon, only goes on show every 33 years (next scheduled for 2000). Instead, most people head straight for the terrace in front, originally a stage for sacred dances, for the famous view over the wooded gorge and Kyoto beyond.

On the hill behind the Hon-dō a jumble of shrine buildings competes for the attention of students and young couples. **Jishū-jinja** is dedicated to several Shinto gods, of whom the most popular is Okuninushi-no-mikoto, an ancient deity in charge of love and good marriages; his messenger is a rabbit. To test your current relationship, try walking in a straight line between the two "love stones", set 18m apart, with your eyes closed and intoning your partner's name. Finally, head down beside the wooden terrace to the **Otowa waterfall**, a sip of which is reputed to cure any illness, and then follow the short path up the opposite hillside from where you get the best views of Kiyomizu-dera.

## NORTH TO GION

Leaving Kiyomizu-dera via Kiyomizu-zaka, head north down a set of stone steps along an inviting, cobbled lane. Known as **Sannen-zaka** (Three-Year Slope) and **Ninen-zaka** (Two-Year Slope), these lanes preserve some of the last vestiges of the old Kyoto townscape (see box overleaf). A few paving stones were laid in the ninth century, while the two-storey wooden townhouses date from the late 1800s. Many still cater to passing pilgrims and souvenir-hunters in time-honoured fashion, peddling Kiyomizu pottery, bamboo-ware, pickles and refreshments. Just at the bottom of the steps, look out for Hyōtan-ya which has been selling gourd flasks (*hyōtan*) for at least two hundred years. Be careful walking along these two lanes, though: according to popular belief, a fall here brings two or three years' bad luck.

At the north end of Ninen-zaka, make a dog-leg round to the left to find the entrance to the peaceful gardens of **Kōdai-ji** (daily 9am–4/4.30pm; ¥600). This temple was granted to Kita-no-Mandokoro, the wife of Toyotomi Hideyoshi, when she became a nun

## BEDROOMS OF EELS

Kyoto's **traditional townhouses**, *machiya*, were built to a unique architectural style known colloquially as "bedrooms of eels" (*unagi no nedoko*). As might be imagined, they consist of a succession of rooms along a single corridor stretching back up to one hundred metres – the reason for this was because taxes were levied according to street frontage. *Machiya* were usually built by **merchants**, with a shop space at the front, followed by living quarters and with a warehouse at the rear. They generally have at least one courtyard-garden to allow in light and air.

*Machiya* were also built almost entirely of wood, which means that few today are more than a century old. While some of the best are now protected by law, *machiya* are still being destroyed at an alarming rate. But walk along **Sannen-zaka** (see previous page) or through **Shinbashi** (see opposite), two of the city's historical **preservation areas**, and you'll find some almost complete rows of these beautiful old houses, each dark façade shows subtle variations on the same overall design. Note the distinctive gutter-guards made of curved bamboo and the narrow-slatted ground-floor windows, which keep out both the summer heat and prying eyes.

after his death in 1598. Kōdai-ji owes its finery, however, to the generosity of Hideyoshi's successor, Tokugawa Ieyasu, who donated buildings from his own castles and financed paintings by Kanō artists, before he wiped out the Toyotomi dynasty at Ōsaka in 1615 (see box, p.414). Nowdays, the temple buildings blend beautifully into their attractive, hillside garden, its two ponds graced by a moon-viewing pavilion and the aptly named "Reclining Dragon Corridor". Between the two, the ceilings of the pretty Kaisan-dō are made from recycled panels from Ieyasu's ship and from the carriage of Kita-no-Mandokoro. But the temple's most important building lies at the top of the scaly-backed corridor – you have to walk round by path – where statues of Hideyoshi and his widow are enshrined. The exquisite gold-inlay lacquerwork is among the finest of its kind in Japan.

Continuing north, a phoenix-tipped tower is a bizarre 1920s replica of a float from the *Gion Matsuri* (see opposite). A right turn in front of it brings you to an attractive public park called **Maruyama-kōen**, beyond which lie a pair of markedly different temples. The first, **Chion-in**, is a big, busy complex, where everything is built on a monumental scale. Chion-in was founded in 1175 by the priest Hōnen, and is the headquarters of his popular Jōdo (Pure Land) sect of Buddhism. On entering via the huge San-mon gate, look up to the right, and you'll see the colossal Daishō-rō bell, the biggest in Japan, hanging in its belfry; at New Year it takes seventeen priests to ring the 67-ton monster. Behind the cavernous main hall – all dark wood and sumptuous gold – red arrows lead to the entrance to the Ōhōjō and Kohōjō halls and a garden representing Amida's paradise (daily 9am–4/4.30pm; ¥400). The halls' main features are their rooms filled with Momoyama-period screens, but, since you can only peer in, they've placed replicas in a room behind the ticket desk – the most famous features a cat with uncannily life-like eyes.

Next-door, **Shōrin-in** (daily 9am–5pm; ¥500), on the other hand, is a quiet little place surrounded by gardens and ancient camphor trees. The temple started life in the ninth century as lodgings for Tendai-sect priests from Enryaku-ji (see p.469) and later served as a residence for members of the imperial family. After seeing the collection of painted screens, there's not a lot to do here but enjoy the paths winding through the hillside garden.

Back in Maruyama-kōen, take any path downhill to come in at the back of **Yasaka-jinja**. The main entrance to this bustling shrine faces west onto Higashiōji-dōri where, instead of the usual *torii*, there's a brightly coloured Buddhist-style gate – a legacy of the days before 1868 when Buddhism and Shinto often cohabited. Yasaka-jinja lies on the eastern edge of **Gion** and each July hosts one of Kyoto's biggest spectacles, the **Gion Matsuri**. This festival dates back to the ninth century, since when the ritual purification to ward off plague in the humid summer months has developed into a grand procession of richly decorated floats.

From Yasaka-jinja, Shijō-dōri runs west through the heart of Gion and across the Kamo-gawa into Kyoto's main downtown district (see p.439). One of the most distinctive buildings along here, on the corner overlooking the river, is the **Minami-za**. This famous Kabuki theatre was established in the early seventeenth century, though last rebuilt in 1929; each December it's the venue for a major Kabuki festival featuring Japan's most celebrated actors. Kabuki has been an integral part of Gion life since the late sixteenth century when a female troupe started performing religious dances on the river banks. Eventually this evolved into an equally popular, all-male theatre and, patronized by an increasingly wealthy merchant class, Kabuki joined *geisha* and the teahouses in Kyoto's vibrant **pleasure quarters**. Of these, Gion was perhaps the most famous, and you can still get a flavour of this "floating world" if you walk south along Hanamikoji-dōri where many of the lovely wooden buildings still function as exclusive teahouses with *geisha* holding court. It's best after dark when red lanterns hang outside each secretive doorway, allowing the occasional glimpse down a stone-flagged entrance-way; early evening is also a good time to spot *geisha*, or trainee *maiko*, arriving for an appointment.

During April's *Miyako Odori* local *geisha* give performances of traditional dance at the **Gion Kōbu Kaburenjō**, a theatre near the south end of Hanamikoji-dōri. This is also the venue for a touristy display of traditional arts known as **Gion Corner** (March–Nov daily 7.40pm & 8.40pm; ¥2800; ☎075/752-0225). Though it's far better to spend a little extra for the real thing, this is an opportunity to see brief extracts of court dance, Bunraku puppet theatre and the slap-stick *kyōgen*. (See p.463 for further details of events in Kyoto.)

On the southern fringes of Gion "love hotels" have replaced the brothels of earlier times. This area is also home to a little-visited shrine, **Yasui Konpira-gū**, and a couple of unusual museums (Tues–Sun 10am–4pm; ¥500); to get there turn left at the end of Hanamikoji-dōri and then second right. Founded in 1659, the shrine itself is relatively new, but over the years it's amassed an interesting collection of *ema*, the wooden boards on which people write their prayers. Ask the priest if you can also see the Glass Gallery which features some lovely Art-Deco pieces and a huge, under-floor work, layered like a sea-shell, by American Dale Chihuly.

Gion north of Shijō-dōri consists mainly of highrise blocks packed with clubs, bars and restaurants. But walk up Kiritoshi, one block west of Hanamikoji-dōri, and you eventually emerge into another area of teahouses. **Shinbashi**, as the district's known, only comprises two short streets, but the row of slatted façades reflected in the willow-lined Shirakawa Canal makes a delightful scene, day or night.

## HEIAN-JINGŪ AND AROUND

In the late nineteenth century, after Emperor Meiji had moved his imperial court to Tokyo, Kyoto authorities felt the need to reaffirm their city's illustrious past. The result is **Heian-jingū** (daily 8.30am–4.30pm; free), an impressive though rather garish shrine which was modelled on a scaled-down version of the original, eighth-century emperor's Hall of State. Completed in 1895 to commemorate the 1100th anniversary of the founding of the city, it is dedicated to emperors Kammu and Komei (1846–67), Kyoto's first and last imperial residents. The present buildings are a 1979 rebuild, but this is still one of Kyoto's most famous landmarks. The shrine lies about ten minutes' walk north of Higashiyama subway station, or take one of the many bus routes along Higashiōji-dōri.

The shrine's bright orange and white halls have an unmistakably Chinese air. Two wings embrace a huge, gravelled courtyard at the north end of which sits the main worship hall flanked by a couple of pretty two-storied towers representing the protective "Blue Dragon" and "White Tiger". More interesting are the gardens behind (same hours; ¥600) which were also designed in Heian style. They're divided into four sections, starting in the southwest corner and ending beside a large pond in the east. The south garden features a collection of plants mentioned in Heian literature, while the middle (third) garden is famous for a row of stepping stones made from the columns of two six-teenth-century bridges. Lastly, the more spacious, east garden boasts the shrine's most attractive buildings – the graceful Taihei-kaku pavilion and its covered bridge.

Heian-jingū faces south towards a large vermilion *torii* across a park dotted with museums and other municipal buildings. The most rewarding of these is the **Fureaikan**, or Kyoto Museum of Traditional Crafts (Tues–Sun 10am–6pm; free), in the basement of the modern Miyako Messe building. Well-designed and informative, the museum provides an excellent introduction to the whole range of Kyoto crafts, from roof tiles and metalwork to textiles, confectionery and ornamental hair pins. Allow plenty of time to take it all in.

The **National Museum of Modern Art** (Tues–Sun 9.30am–5pm; April–Oct also Fri 9.30am–8pm; ¥420; extra for special exhibitions) and the brick-built **Kyoto Municipal Art Museum** (Tues–Sun 9am–5pm; varying prices) stand on opposite sides of the big *torii*. The modern art museum focuses on local twentieth-century artists, while the Municipal Museum hosts temporary exhibitions from its vast collection of post-1868 fine arts.

At the same time as Heian-jingū was being built, Marshal Yamagata Aritomo, a lead-ing member of the Meiji government, was creating a delightful haven for himself beside the Biwa Canal. From the *torii*, walk east along the canal to find his villa, **Murin-an** (daily 9am–4.30pm; ¥350), where the road bends to the right. Even today, as you look east from the garden to the Higashiyama hills beyond, it's hard to believe you're in the middle of a busy city. Designed by Yamagata himself, the unusually naturalistic garden incorporates a meandering stream, pond and lawns in a surprisingly small space. There are also three buildings; take a look upstairs in the two-storied brick house, where par-quet floors and wood-panelling blend beautifully with Kanō-school painted screens. In 1903, this room was the venue for the "Murin-an Conference" when Yamagata and three other ministers thrashed out government policy during the run-up to the Russo-Japanese War (1904–5).

Continuing east, cross over the canal again in front of **Kyoto International Community House**, an excellent resource centre for Kyoto's foreign residents (see p.430), and head uphill towards **Nanzen-ji**. This large, active temple belongs to the Rinzai sect of Zen Buddhism and is one of the most important in Kyoto. Before enter-ing the main compound, however, it's worth exploring its quiet sub-temple, **Konchi-in** (daily 8.30am–4.30/5pm; ¥400), on the right in front of the first gate. An arched gate leads straight into one of Kyoto's most beautiful dry gardens – one of the rare works by the ubiquitous Kobori Enshū with documents to prove it. Its centrepiece is a large rec-tangle of raked gravel with two groups of rocks set against a bank of clipped shrubs. The right-hand, vertical rock group represents a crane, in balance with the horizontal "tortoise" topped by a twisted pine, on the left; both these animals symbolize longevity.

After Konchi-in, the looming bulk of **San-mon**, the main gate to Nanzen-ji, seems excessively monumental. It was erected in 1628 to commemorate the soldiers killed during the siege of Ōsaka Castle (see p.414). However, Nanzen-ji's prize possessions are in the **Hōjō** (daily 8.30am–4.30/5pm; ¥400), up to the right behind the San-mon. These include the "Leaping Tiger" garden, also attributed to Enshū though working in a much more confined space, and a series of screens painted by Kanō Tanyū depicting tigers in a bamboo grove. Before leaving the area, note that Nanzen-ji is also famous for its *shōjin-ryōri*, Buddhist vegetarian cuisine, which can be sampled in a number of sub-temples (see Eating, p.456).

## NORTH TO GINKAKU-JI

The final sight along this stretch of Kyoto's eastern hills is the famous Ginkaku-ji. Though you can get there by bus (see below), by far the best approach is to walk along the canal-side **Path of Philosophy** which starts just north of Nanzen-ji (see opposite). The name of the two-kilometre-long path refers to a respected philosopher, Nishida Kitarō (1870–1945), who took his daily constitutional along the wooded hillside. To reach the path from Nanzen-ji, follow the road curving northeast past the small, extremely esoteric **Nomura Art Museum** (Tues–Sun 10am–4.30pm; closed mid-June–early Sept & Dec–mid-March; ¥600), which holds rotating exhibitions of tea-ceremony utensils and related paraphernalia. A little further on, you might want to pop into **Eikan-dō**, also known as Zenrin-ji (daily 9am–4/5pm; ¥500), for its unusual Amida statue. Eikan-dō was founded in the ninth century by a disciple of Kōbō Daishi (see p.784), but later became the headquarters of a sub-sect of Jōdoshū (Pure Land Buddhism). In 1082 the then head priest, Eikan, was circling the altar and chanting the *nembutsu*, "Praise to Amida Buddha", when the Amida statue stepped down and started walking in front of him. When Eikan stopped in his tracks, Amida turned to encourage him. Soon after, the priest commissioned the statue you see today of Amida looking over his left shoulder.

On exiting Eikan-dō, the first right turn leads to the philosopher's path. Every so often stone bridges link the tempting residential lanes on either side, while the occasional souvenir shop or bijou teahouse provides an additional distraction. Without too many halts, however, you should emerge beside the Ginkaku-ji bridge about thirty minutes later. If you're coming by bus, on the other hand, routes #5, #203 and #204 stop nearby at Ginkaku-ji-michi.

The Temple of the Silver Pavilion, **Ginkaku-ji** (daily: mid-March–Nov 8.30am–5pm; Jan–mid-March & Dec 9am–4.30pm; ¥500), numbers among Kyoto's most celebrated sights. Though modelled on its ostentatious forebear, the golden Kinkaku (see p.451), this simple building sits quietly in the wings. Here, it's the garden that takes centre stage, dominated by a truncated cone of white sand whose severity offsets the soft greens of the surrounding stroll-garden. Ginkaku originally formed part of a much larger villa built in the fifteenth century for Shogun **Ashikaga Yoshimasa** (1436–90), the grandson of Kinkaku's Ashikaga Yoshimitsu. Interrupted by the Ōnin Wars (1467–77) and plagued by lack of funds, the work continued for thirty years until Yoshimasa's death in 1490. During those years, however, it became the focal point of Japanese cultural life. Yoshimasa may have been a weak and incompetent ruler, but under his patronage the arts reached new heights of aesthetic refinement. In this mountainside retreat, significantly turned away from the city, he indulged his love of the tea ceremony, poetry and moon-viewing parties while Kyoto burned. After 1490, the villa became a Rinzai Zen temple (Jishō-ji) and eventually fires razed all except two buildings, one of which was the famous pavilion.

It's worth savouring the approach to Ginkaku-ji. Despite the crowds, there's a wonderful sense of anticipation as you're funnelled between tall, thick hedges down an apparently dead-end lane. Turning the corner, a high wall now blocks the view except for one teasing glimpse through a small, low window. Inside, you're directed first to the **dry garden**, comprising a raised, rippled "Sea of Silver Sand" – designed to reflect moonlight – and a large "moon-facing" cone. The jury's out on whether these enhance the garden or intrude, but it's almost certain that they weren't in the original design, and were probably added in the early seventeenth century. Behind the cone to the west, the small, dark two-storied building with the phoenix top-knot is **Ginkaku**. Some scholars argue that Yoshimasa never intended to cover it with silver, while others say he ran out of money; whatever, it must be a glorious, ethereal sight under the reflected light of a full moon.

The villa's other extant building, the Tōgū-dō, lies east of the main hall. Though not generally open to the public, it contains a small, *tatami* room with a central sunken hearth and decorative *tokonoma* (alcove) which is considered to be the forerunner of the tea-ceremony house. The more classical pond-garden in front of the Tōgū-dō is attributed to the gifted Sōami (died 1525) and is full of literary allusions.

## SHŪGAKU-IN RIKYŪ

In the far northeast of Kyoto, the foothills of Hiei-zan (see p.469) provide a superb setting for one of Japan's finest examples of garden design using borrowed scenery. Entry to **Shūgaku-in Rikyū**, an imperial villa, is by appointment only (see box, p.430) and requires you to join a guided tour (Mon–Fri & occasionally Sat five tours daily; closed hols & Dec 25–Jan 5; free). To get there, hop on City Bus #5 to the Shūgaku-in Rikyū-michi stop on Shirakawa-dōri, from where the villa's a signed ten-minute walk to the east. Alternatively, take a train on the private Eizan line from Demachiyanagi Station (in northeast Kyoto) to Shūgaku-in Station (10min), located a couple of minutes west of Shirakawa-dōri.

Emperor Go-mizuno'o (1611–1629) built Shūgaku-in Rikyū in the late 1650s as a pleasure garden rather than a residence. Just 15 years old when he ascended the throne, the artistic and highly cultured Go-mizuno'o fiercely resented the new Shogunate's constant meddling in imperial affairs – not least being forced to marry the shogun's daughter. After Go-mizuno'o abdicated, however, the shogun encouraged him to establish an imperial villa. He eventually settled on the site of a ruined temple, Shūgaku-in, and set about designing a series of gardens which survived more than a century of neglect before the government rescued them in the 1820s. Though some of the original pavilions have been lost, Go-mizuno'o's overall design remains – a delightfully naturalistic garden which blends seamlessly into the wooded hills.

In fact, Shūgaku-in Rikyū is made up of three separate gardens, each in their own enclosure among the terraced rice-fields. Of these, the top lake-garden is the star attraction, though the middle villa's **Kyaku-den** guest house is also of interest. Look out for a complicated, fragile set of shelves – the "shelves of mist" – hanging in one alcove, and some painted wooden panels. One set shows festival floats from the Gion Matsuri (see p.463), while another is embellished with three scaly carp – it's said that the nets were added later to keep the fish from slipping out at night to the nearby pond.

From here you start climbing towards the upper villa, passing between tall, clipped hedges before suddenly emerging at the garden's highest point. An airy pavilion, **Rin-un-Tei**, occupies the little promontory, with views over the lake, the forested, rolling hills in the middle distance and the mountains beyond. Walking down through the garden, the grand vistas continue with every twist and turn of the path, passing the intricate Chitose bridge, intimate tea ceremony pavilions and rustic boat houses which decorate the garden.

## West Kyoto

Compared to east Kyoto, sights in the city's **western districts** are more dispersed and therefore require a little more effort to get to. Nevertheless, it's well worth devoting at least one day to this area, particularly the northwest fringes where the city meets the encircling hills. Here you'll find the outrageously extravagant **Kinkaku-ji**, the Golden Pavilion, rubbing shoulders with **Ryōan-ji**'s supreme example of an austere, enigmatic Zen garden. If puzzling over Zen riddles is your thing, then don't miss the dry gardens of **Daitoku-ji**, where **Daisen-in** attracts all the attention though several other subtemples allow quieter contemplation.

Moving south, **Kōryū-ji** houses one of Japan's most perfect images, a serene statue of the Future Buddha, carved fourteen centuries ago. Nearby **Tōei Uzumasa Eigamura**, on the other hand, celebrates the celluloid world. This "movie village", styled "Japan's Hollywood", turns working film sets and studios into a theme park, complete with battling *samurai*, winsome *geisha* and sci-fi monsters. The city's southwestern suburbs contain two outstanding gardens. **Katsura Rikyū**, one of Japan's first stroll-gardens, belongs to the languid world of moon-viewing parties and tea ceremonies, while the dappled mosses of **Saihō-ji** herald from an older tradition of Buddhist paradise gardens.

## DAITOKU-JI

Lying halfway between the Kamo-gawa and the Kitayama hills, **Daitoku-ji** is one of Kyoto's largest Zen foundations, with over twenty sub-temples in its large, walled compound. Of these only four are open to the public, but within them you'll find a representative sampler of the dry gardens (*kare-sansui*), for which Japanese Zen Buddhism is renowned. The temple lies roughly 1500m west of Kita-ōji subway station (on the Karasuma line), or can be reached by City Bus (routes #101, #205 and #206) – get off at Daitoku-ji-mae.

Entering from the south, head past the huge San-mon gate to **Daisen-in** (daily 9am–5pm; ¥400) in the north of the compound. This sub-temple contains two gardens, of which the most famous lies to the right as you enter the main hall. In fact, you'd be forgiven for overlooking it – the miniaturized, allegorical landscape is squeezed into a narrow strip, then cut in two by a corridor with a bell-shaped window. Replicating a Chinese landscape painting, the garden uses only carefully selected rocks, pebbles and a few scaled-down plants to conjure up jagged mountains, from which a stream tumbles down to the plain, then broadens into a gently flowing river. Just in front of the bell-window, a boat-shaped rock "floats" seawards – enhancing the garden's allusion to the passage of life.

Follow the "river" south and it opens into the second, larger garden. Here an expanse of raked, white gravel represents the "Sea of Nothingness", into which two cones of purity are sinking; the idea is that a soul must be pure, or empty, to face its destiny. A statue of Kogaku Shukō, the temple's founder, sits in the room behind. He's also credited with the river-and-mountain garden, which dates from the early sixteenth century, possibly in collaboration with the great Sōami, while it's likely that the south garden was added later.

It pays to visit Daisen-in early in the day before the crowds arrive. However, Daitoku-ji's other sub-temples remain surprisingly quiet. Of these, probably the most interesting is **Ryōgen-in** (daily 9am–4.30pm; ¥350), lying just south of the San-mon gate. The temple was also founded in the early sixteenth century and claims Japan's smallest Zen rock garden. As you enter, the first garden is another narrow rectangle of gravel containing three rocks. This represents "A-un", the essential dichotomy and harmony of the universe – heaven and earth, male and female, inhale and exhale – which lies at the heart of Zen. Once you've got that sorted out, move on to the minuscule Tōtekiko garden, on your right. The meaning's a bit less obtuse here: waves of sand round a rock symbolize a Zen saying that the harder a stone is thrown, the bigger the ripples. The hall's south side looks out on a bigger garden, Isshi-dan, where vertical rocks represent the mythical Mount Horai which lies at the centre of the Buddhist universe, flanked by its Crane and Turtle islands (symbols of longevity). Finally, Ryōgin-tei, the north garden, is not only the oldest in Daitoku-ji but is also attributed to Sōami. Again its subject is the essential truth at the core of the universe, rising from a sea of moss.

## KINKAKU-JI AND RYŌAN-JI

West of Daitoku-ji, the wooded hills of Kitayama harbour two highly individual gardens. The first of these is a lake-garden belonging to **Kinkaku-ji** (daily 9am–5pm; ¥400), the famous Temple of the Golden Pavilion, and provides the setting for the gilded extravaganza after which the temple is named. The pavilion originally formed part of a larger retirement villa built by the former Shogun Ashikaga Yoshimitsu (1358–1408) on the site of an earlier aristocratic residence; on his death it was converted into a Zen temple.

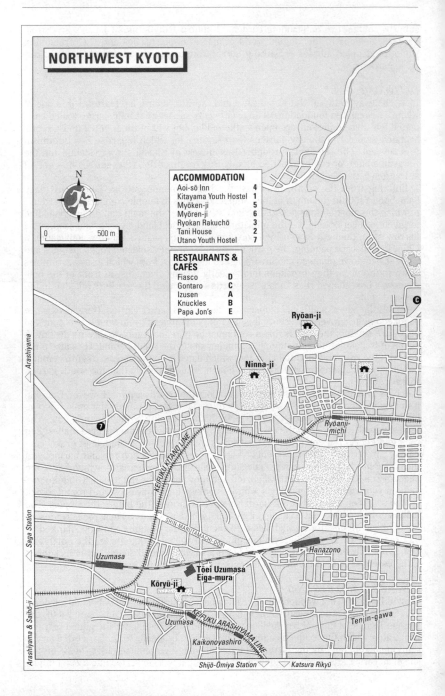

## NORTHWEST KYOTO

N

0          500 m

### ACCOMMODATION
| | |
|---|---|
| Aoi-sō Inn | 4 |
| Kitayama Youth Hostel | 1 |
| Myōken-ji | 5 |
| Myōren-ji | 6 |
| Ryokan Rakuchō | 3 |
| Tani House | 2 |
| Utano Youth Hostel | 7 |

### RESTAURANTS & CAFÉS
| | |
|---|---|
| Fiasco | D |
| Gontaro | C |
| Izusen | A |
| Knuckles | B |
| Papa Jon's | E |

Ryōan-ji

Ninna-ji

Ryōanji-michi

Arashiyama

KEIFUKU KITANO LINE

SHIN-MARUTAMACHI-DORI

Saga Station

Uzumasa

Hanazono

Tōei Uzumasa
Eiga-mura

Kōryū-ji

Uzumasa

KEIFUKU ARASHIYAMA LINE

Tenjin-gawa

Arashiyama & Saihō-ji

Kaikonoyashiro

Shijō-Ōmiya Station ▽        ▽ Katsura Rikyū

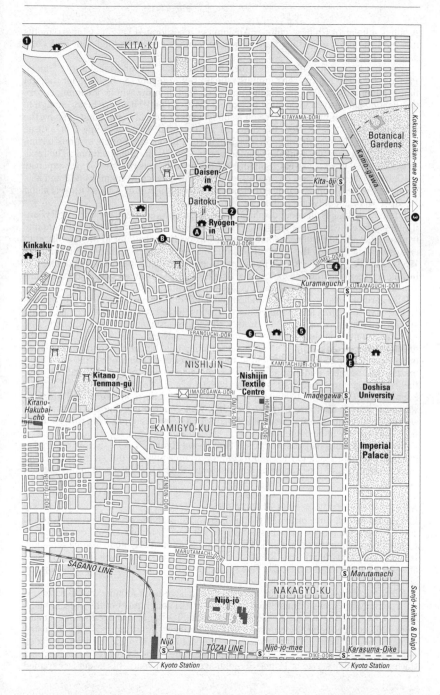

KITA-KU

KITAYAMA-DŌRI

Botanical
Gardens

Kokusai Kaikan-mae Station

Daisen-
in

Daitoku-
ji

Kita-ōji S

Ryōgen-
in

KITAŌJI-DŌRI

Kinkaku-
ji

SHIMEI-DŌRI

Kuramaguchi

KURAMAGUCHI-DŌRI

S

TERANOUCHI-DŌRI

NISHIJIN

Nishijin
Textile
Centre

KAMITACHIURI-DŌRI

Doshisa
University

Kitano
Tenman-gū

IMADEGAWA-DŌRI

Imadegawa S

Kitano-
Hakubai-
chō

KAMIGYŌ-KU

Imperial
Palace

KARASUMA-DŌRI

SAGANO LINE

MARUTAMACHI-DŌRI

Marutamachi S

NAKAGYŌ-KU

Nijō-jō

Nijō
S

TŌZAI LINE

Nijō-jō-mae

Karasuma-Oike S

DIKE-DŌRI

Kyoto Station

Kyoto Station

Sanjō-Keihan & Daigō

Kamo-gawa

A noted scholar of Chinese culture, Yoshimitsu incorporated various Chinese motifs into both the pavilion and the garden, whose focus is a lake studded with rocks and pine-covered islets.

Beautiful though it is, the garden merely serves as a foil for Kinkaku, the Golden Pavilion. Even the crowds can't diminish the impact of seeing the building for the first time – a hint of gold glimpsed though the trees, and then the whole, gleaming apparition floating above the aptly named Kyōko-chi (Mirror Pond). If you're lucky enough to see it against the autumn leaves, or on a sunny winter's day after a dusting of snow, the effect is doubly striking. Note the different architectural styles of the pavilion's three floors and the phoenix standing on the shingle roof. It's an appropriate symbol: having survived all these years, Kinkaku was torched in 1950 by an unhappy monk. The replica was finished in just five years, and in 1987 the building was regilded at vast expense.

Kinkaku-ji lies on several bus routes, of which the most convenient are #12 and #59. To get to the next stop, Ryōan-ji, either hop back on a #59 bus, or walk southwest along Kitsuji-dōri for about twenty minutes.

While Kinkaku-ji is all about displays of wealth and power, the dry garden of **Ryōan-ji** (daily: March–Nov 8am–5pm; Jan, Feb & Dec 8.30am–4.30pm; ¥400) hides infinite truths within its riddle of rocks and sand. It was probably laid out in the late fifteenth century (some say it's the work of Sōami), but went largely undiscovered until the 1930s. Now it's probably Japan's most famous garden, which means you're unlikely to be able to appreciate the Zen experience thanks to intrusive tape-recorded explanations and almost constant crowds, though very early morning tends to be better.

The garden consists of a long, walled rectangle of off-white gravel in which fifteen stones of various sizes are arranged in five groups, some rising up from the raked sand and others almost completely lost. In fact, the stones are placed so that wherever you stand one of them is always hidden from view. The only colour is provided by electric-green patches of moss around some stones, making this the simplest and most abstract of all Japan's Zen gardens. It's thought that the layout is a *kōan*, or riddle, set by Zen masters to test their students, and there's endless debate about its "meaning". Popular theories range from tigers crossing a river to islands floating in a sea of infinity. Fortunately, it's possible to enjoy the garden's perfect harmony and inbuilt tension without worrying too much over the meaning. Walk round the veranda of the main hall and you'll find a stone water basin inscribed with a helpful thought from the Zen tradition: "I learn only to be contented".

Leaving the main hall, it's worth strolling round Ryōan-ji's refreshingly quiet lake-garden. This dates back to the twelfth century, when a noble of the Fujiwara clan built his villa here, before the estate was donated to the Rinzai Buddhist sect in the fifteenth century.

## KŌRYŪ-JI AND TŌEI UZUMASA EIGA-MURA

**Uzumasa** district, due south of Ryōan-ji, is home to both the art treasures of Kōryū-ji and the Tōei film studios. The easiest way to get here is to take a train on the private Keifuku Arashiyama line from Shijō-Ōmiya Station in central Kyoto to Uzumasa Station. If you're coming straight from Ryōan-ji, it's probably quickest to back-track into Kyoto and pick up the train or a bus; City Bus #11 and Kyoto Bus #71, #72 and #73 all stop outside Kōryū-ji.

**Kōryū-ji** (daily 9am–4.30/5pm; ¥600) is said to have been founded in the early seventh century by Nara's Prince Shōtoku (see p.480). Though most of the present buildings are much more recent, the Kōdō (Lecture Hall) – the first inside the gate – dates from 1165 and is one of the oldest in Kyoto. The three Buddhas inside are imposing enough, but Kōryū-ji's main attraction are the statues kept in the modern Reihōden (treasure house) at the back of the compound. The "newest" of these images is a thirteenth-century statue of Prince Shōtoku aged sixteen years, his sweet face framed by bun-shaped pigtails, while the oldest dominates the room with its sheer beauty. This is the exquisite **Miroku Bosatsu**, the Future Buddha rendered as a bodhisattva pondering how to save mankind. It is believed to have been gilded originally and was probably a gift to Shōtoku from the Korean court in the early seventh century; its soft, delicate features are certainly unlike contemporary Japanese images. The small, slim figure sits, elbow on knee, leaning forward slightly and head tilted in a pose of utter concentration.

Having come out this way, you might want to walk behind the temple to visit **Tōei Uzumasa Eiga-mura** (daily: April–Nov 9am–5pm; Dec–March 9.30am–4pm; closed Dec 21–1 Jan; ¥2200 plus extra for some attractions), where Tōei, one of Japan's major film companies, opens its sets to the public. Their new entertainment complex, Padios, is more like a theme park with its roller-coaster rides, games arcades and huge souvenir malls, but the studios behind hold more general appeal. One of the indoor studios is usually in action, nowadays mostly making TV dramas, while the outdoor sets – an Edo-period street, thatched farms, Meiji-era Western-style buildings and so on – are enlivened by roaming *geisha*, battling *samurai* and a superbly cheesy "special effects" zone. On the way out, don't miss the Movie Museum where film buffs can take a nostalgic romp through the archives.

## KATSURA RIKYŪ

Few people trek out to the southwest corner of Kyoto, but the journey is rewarded with two magnificent gardens. Before setting off, however, note that in both cases admission is by appointment only. The more accessible garden belongs to **Katsura Rikyū** (Mon–Fri & occasionally Sat four tours daily; closed hols & Dec 25–Jan 5; free), a former imperial palace, and applications should be made through the Imperial Household Agency (see p.430). Located on the west bank of the Katsura-gawa, it's fifteen minutes' walk from the Katsura Station, on the private Hankyū line from central Kyoto. Alternatively, City Bus #33 will drop you at Katsura Rikyū-mae, the first stop after crossing the river, from where it's a five-minute walk north to the gate. Note that this bus stop lies just outside the bus-pass zones so, if you want to save a few yen, get off before the river and walk over.

Katsura palace was built in the early seventeenth century as a residence for the imperial Prince Toshihito, and then expanded by his son, Toshitada, in the 1650s. Toshihito was a highly cultured man, who filled his villa and garden with references to *The Tale of Genji* and other literary classics, while also creating what is considered Japan's first **stroll-garden**. As the name suggests, these gardens were to be enjoyed on foot – rather than from a boat or from a fixed viewpoint – and were designed to look "natural". In fact they were planned in minute detail so that scenes unfold in a particular order as the viewer progresses round the garden. Focused on a large, indented lake, the Katsura garden is famed for its variety of footpaths and stone pavings, and for its stone lanterns, all of which helped create the desired mood. Several tea pavilions occupy prime spots around the lake, the most attractive of which is **Shokin-tei**, but perhaps the most interesting aspect about the Katsura garden is the designer's sheer ingenuity. Unlike Shūgaku-in Rikyū (see p.450), there's no help here from the site itself and very little opportunity to use borrowed scenery to expand the view. Instead, Toshihito managed to wrestle a splendidly harmonious, seemingly spacious garden out of an unexciting bit of floodplain.

Unfortunately, the **palace** buildings themselves are not open to the public, though even from outside they're beautiful structures. The low-slung, wood and shingle pavilions were all built in the seventeenth century in an innovative architectural style. Two sections are raised up on platforms to allow cooling air to circulate in summer, while individual rooms are variously oriented to avoid the fierce summer sun, catch the winter rays or face the full autumn moon.

*SAIHŌ-JI*

Three kilometres northwest of Katsura Rikyū, you'll find the voluptuous moss gardens of **Saihō-ji** (daily; ¥3000; ☎075/391-3631), also known as Koku-dera (the "Moss Temple"), on a narrow, tree-filled valley. Not surprisingly, many people are put off by the exorbitant entry fee (termed a "donation"), but if you've got time to spare after the major sights, this temple is well worth visiting, not least because it's one of the few you really can enjoy in peace.

To visit Saihō-ji you have to make an **application**. Japanese speakers can try phoning a few days before to see if there's space – or ask someone to phone on your behalf. But the more assured method is to write to Saihō-ji, 56 Kamigatani, Matsuo, Nishikyō-ku, Kyoto-shi, Kyoto-ken, giving your name, address, age, occupation and proposed date of visit. It's best to allow at least one or two weeks' notice – longer if sending from abroad – and remember to enclose a stamped-addressed postcard or international reply-coupon. Within Japan you can buy special reply-paid "double postcards" (*ofuku hakagi*) at post offices for this type of application.

Saihō-ji lies at the terminus of the #73 Kyoto Bus route, which takes a circuitous route from Kyoto Station via Arashiyama (see p.475). Unless you're visiting Arashiyama at the same time, it's quicker to take a City Bus (#28 or #29) to Matsuo Taisha-mae, just west of the river, and change to the #73. At the end of the line, walk up the road for a minute or so to find the temple gate on your right. All visitors are required to attend a short Zen service during which you'll chant a sutra, trace the sutra's characters in *sumi-e* ink and finally write your name, address and "wish" before placing the paper in front of the altar. After that you're free to explore the garden at your leisure.

Like Kōryū-ji (see p.454), the temple apparently started life in the seventh century as another of Prince Shōtoku's villas. Soon after, Jōdo Buddhists adopted the site for one of their "paradise gardens", after which the gifted Zen monk, **Musō Kokushi** was invited to take over the temple in 1338 and restore the gardens. The present layout dates mostly from his time, though the lake-side pavilion – the inspiration for Kinkaku-ji (see p.451) – and nearly all Saihō-ji's other buildings burnt down in the Ōnin Wars (1467–77). In fact, given the temple's history of fire, flooding and periods of neglect, it seems unlikely that today's garden bears much resemblance to Musō's original. Saihō-ji was in complete ruins by the eighteenth century and some sources even attribute the famous mosses to accident, arguing that they spread naturally as the garden reverted to damp, shady woodland.

Whatever their origin, the swathes of soft, dappled moss – some 120 varieties in all – are a magical sight, especially after the rains of May and June when the greens take on an extra intensity. The garden is divided into two levels with the serene, strangely melancholic lake area followed by an upper slope where a powerful, rocky cascade tumbles down the hillside. This "dry waterfall" is held to be one of the first examples of *kare-sansui*, dry gardening; though it's a world away from Zen's enigmatic rocks and gravel, the design was also conceived as an aid to meditation.

# Eating

With such an august history, it's not surprising that Kyoto is home to Japan's most refined cuisine, **Kyō-ryōri** (Kyoto cooking), which is known for its subtle flavours and use of only the freshest ingredients. The ultimate Kyoto dining experience is **kaiseki**, originally designed to accompany the tea ceremony, and a feast for both the eyes and taste buds. Everything about the meal is an expression of cultured refinement, from the artful arrangement of seasonal delicacies, each on its carefully chosen lacquer or earthenware dish, to the picture-perfect garden outside the window. Of course, such meals aren't cheap (generally ¥10,000 per head), but at lunchtime many *kaiseki* restaurants offer a usually excellent-value mini-*kaiseki* or *bentō* – a boxed sampler of their specialities.

Kyoto's other gastronomic highlight is **fucha-ryōri**, a Zen version of the exquisite Buddhist vegetarian cuisine, *shōjin-ryōri*, and still mostly found in restaurants near the

## KYOTO: RESTAURANTS

*CENTRAL KYOTO*

| | | |
|---|---|---|
| Bio-tei | *Bio-tei* | びお亭 |
| Capricciosa | *Kapurichōza* | カプリチョーザ |
| Chikyū-ya | *Chikyū-ya* | 地球屋 |
| Chinchikurin | *Chinchikurin* | 珍竹林 |
| Fujino-ya | *Fujino-ya* | 藤の家 |
| Gontaro | *Gontaro* | 権太呂 |
| Honyaradō | *Honyaradō* | ほんやら洞 |
| Musashi | *Musashi* | むさし |
| Obanzai | *Obanzai* | おばんざい |
| Saraçça | *Sarasa* | サラサ |
| Sarashina | *Sarashina* | 更科 |
| Tagoto | *Tagoto* | 田ごと |
| Yamatomi | *Yamatomi* | 山とみ |

*AROUND THE STATION*

| | | |
|---|---|---|
| Chikara | *Chikara* | 泉仙 |
| Izusen | *Izusen* | ちから |
| Suishin | *Suishin* | すいしん |

*EAST KYOTO*

| | | |
|---|---|---|
| Chōshō-in | *Chōshō-in* | 聴松院 |
| Furōen | *Furōen* | ふろうえん |
| Hyōtei | *Hyōtei* | 瓢亭 |
| Imobō Hirano-ya Honten | *Imobō Hirano-ya Honten* | いもぼう平野家本店 |
| Matsuno | *Matsuno* | 松乃 |
| Nakamura-rō | *Nakamura-rō* | 中村楼 |
| Okutan | *Okutan* | 奥丹 |
| Omen | *Omen* | おめん |
| Tenkin | *Tenkin* | 天金 |

*NORTHWEST KYOTO*

| | | |
|---|---|---|
| Gontaro | *Gontaro* | 泉仙 |
| Izusen | *Izusen* | 権太呂 |

great Zen temples of Daitoku-ji and Nanzen-ji. *Fucha-ryōri* includes a good deal of *yuba* (dried soybean curd) and *fu* (wheat gluten), dressed up in the most appetizing ways, while restaurants around Nanzen-ji also specialize in *yudōfu*, which is tofu simmered in a kelp-flavoured stock. Though generally cheaper than *kaiseki*, the best of these restaurants are also found in lovely old houses overlooking a classic garden.

It's well worth treating yourself to at least one traditional Kyoto restaurant, but after that there are plenty of more modest establishments to choose from. Some of these have been serving their simple homecooking for a century or more and are as much a part of Kyoto life as the high-class places. There's also a fair sprinkling of Indian, Italian and other international cuisines nowdays, as well as a growing number of vegetarian and health food restaurants.

## Central Kyoto

*All the following restaurants are marked on the map on p.438.*
The best place to look for somewhere to eat in Kyoto is the central shopping district focused around **Shijō-dōri and Kawaramachi-dōri**, including the backstreets north of Shijō. Among the plethora of fast-food chains, there are a number of decent foreign

restaurants and also several old Kyoto establishments hiding down alleys and among the more expensive names of **Pontochō**. Below, we've also recommended one or two places on the fringes of this central district where they're handy for nearby sights.

**Ashoka**, 3F, Kikusui Bldg, Teramachi Shijō-agaru. Once you've tried a few of the Japanese restaurants below, give your taste buds a work-out at Kyoto's most popular Indian restaurant. It's a smart place, but their lunchtime sets offer reasonable value (¥700–¥1500). Daily 11.30am–2.30pm & 5–8.30/9pm.

**Bio-tei**, 2F, Higashinotōin Sanjō. Laid-back health food restaurant with an appetizing range of vegetarian daily specials, plus some meat dishes. Count on spending around ¥1500 for a good feast. Tues–Sat 11.30am–2pm & 5–8.30pm, closed Thurs eve and Sat lunch.

**Capricciosa**, 2F, Vox Bldg, 44 Daikoku-chō, Kawaramachi Sanjō. Ever-popular member of the cheerful Tokyo chain, selling huge portions of pizza and pasta. Daily 11.30am–10.30pm.

**Chikyu-ya**, Kawaramachi Shijō-sagaru. There's a faintly hippy air to this bustling, student *izakaya*, with its shared wooden tables and rug-covered ceiling. Prices are cheap and the food's not bad – standard *izakaya* fare of small dishes ranging from tofu to tuna salad or french fries, some listed on their English menu. Daily 5pm–midnight.

**Chinchikurin**, Kiyamachi Shijō-sagaru. Inexpensive country-style restaurant specializing in *kamameshi*, kettle-steamed rice with a whole range of toppings. In winter, *nabe* stews or *zōsui* rice gruel make a good choice. Daily except Wed 11.30am–3pm & 5–9.30pm.

**Cous Cous**, Kiyamachi Shijō-agaru. Bright, cheerful "African" restaurant serving ostrich, alligator and kangaroo as well as cous cous and other less exotic fare. Wash it all down with Tusker beer, cane spirit or coffee-bean liqueur. Moderately expensive. Daily 5pm–1am.

**Fujino-ya**, Pontochō Shijō-agaru. One of the more affordable Pontochō restaurants with a river view. The simple menu (in English) offers either tempura or *kushi-katsu* (deep-fried pork skewers), with standard sets from around ¥1500. Daily except Wed 5–10pm.

**Gontaro**, Fuyachō Shijō-agaru. Home-made noodles are the order of the day at this welcoming little restaurant just north of busy Shijō-dōri. Despite the elegant entrance, prices are reasonable, starting at under ¥1000 for standard dishes and rising to around ¥4000 for the house speciality, *Gontaro nabe*. Daily except Wed 11.30am–10.30pm.

**Honyaradō**, Teramachi Imadegawa nishi-iru. Cluttered, relaxed café/restaurant just northeast of the Imperial Palace. Great for a Western breakfast, long coffee break or a satisfying meal. The food's wholesome – don't miss their home-made bread – and excellent value, with set meals around ¥500–¥800 for lunch or dinner. English menu. Daily 9.30am–9.30pm.

**Musashi**, Kawaramachi Sanjō-agaru. Excellent *kaitenzushi* (conveyor-belt sushi) joint right on the junction, where the cheapest plate (two pieces) is only ¥100. Also does a brisk trade in take-away *bentō*. Daily 11am–10pm.

**Obanzai**, Koromonotana Oike-agaru. It's well worth searching out this nicely designed, cafeteria-style restaurant to the east of Nijō-jō for their excellent-value vegetarian buffets (¥840–¥1050 for lunch, ¥2100 at night). Very popular. Mon, Tues & Thurs–Sun 11am–2pm, 2.30–4pm & 5–9pm, Wed 11am–2pm.

**Saracça**, Wood Inn, Tominokoji Sanjō-sagaru. This friendly haven in the midst of central Kyoto is difficult to define – a restaurant, café, bar and record shop all in one. There's a definite arty touch to its high ceilings, wooden tables, *ikebana* and scattered fabrics, while the menu is similarly eclectic – tofu with tuna and spicy miso, sandwiches, preservative-free wine and home-made cheesecake. English menu. Daily except Wed noon–10pm, Sat till midnight.

**Sarashina**, Ōmiya Aneyakoji-agaru. If you're feeling peckish out near Nijō-jō, join the locals for a hearty bowl of soba or udon. Prices are very reasonable and there's an English menu. Mon–Sat 10.30am–7.30pm.

**Tagoto**, Shijō Teramachi higashi-iru. This welcoming little restaurant is a good place to sample *Kyōryōri* without breaking the bank. Try their beautiful *kōetsu-mizusashi-bentō* (¥3000) or, at lunchtime only, choose between a smaller *bentō* (¥1500) and a mini-*kaiseki* (¥3000). Reservations are required for an evening *kaiseki* meal (from ¥6000). Tagoto's just off Shijō-dōri up a tiny alley near the *Central Hotel*. Daily 11am–9pm.

**Volks**, 2F, Kikusui Bldg, Teramachi Shijō-agaru. This well-known steak and burger chain is recommended mainly for its salad bar, though some of its weekday lunch sets are also good value. It's below the *Ashoka* at the south end of Teramachi-dōri. Daily 11am–10pm.

**Yamatomi**, Pontochō Shijō-agaru. Another unpretentious, Pontochō restaurant a few doors down from *Fujino-ya*. There's plenty of good, wholesome fare on offer (English menu available), such as sashimi, *oden* and *okonomiyaki*. In summer you can eat on their riverside terrace. Daily except Tues noon–midnight.

## Around the station
*All the following restaurants are marked on the map on p.441.*
Unlike most Japanese cities, the area around **Kyoto Station** is not particularly well endowed with restaurants. Apart from those places recommended below, your best bet is the eleventh-floor "Eat Paradise" in the station's Isetan department store or the Porta underground shopping mall. Next to Isetan, there's a self-service, fast-food area on the tenth floor of The Cube; it's cheap and easy, but rather grim.

**Chikara**, Horikawa Shichijō. Cheap and cheerful soba joint south of Nishi-Hongan-ji. Also serves udon and simple *donburi* (rice) dishes, with sets from under ¥1000. Daily except Thurs 11am–8pm.

**Izusen**, 2F, Kintetsu department store, Karasuma Shichijō-sagaru. Not the most brilliant surroundings, but *Izusen*'s Zen vegetarian cuisine is, nonetheless, beautifully presented. Sets start at ¥1800; there's an English menu and also a window display to choose from. Daily except Thurs 11am–8pm.

**Suishin**, SK Bldg, Kyoto-eki-mae. The ground floor of this big restaurant is a clean, modern sushi bar (daily 11.30–3pm & 5–11.30pm), offering better value at lunchtime, while in the evening head for the huge, popular *izakaya* in the basement (daily 5–11pm).

## East Kyoto
*All the following restaurants are marked on the map on p.444, except for Didi which appears on p.427.*
If you want to treat yourself to traditional Kyoto cuisine, then head for the city's **eastern districts**. We've recommended one or two of the more affordable restaurants below, which still offer a glimpse into the world of kimono-clad waitresses, elegant *tatami* rooms, carp ponds and tinkling bamboo water spouts. Northeast Kyoto, on the other hand, is home to a number of lively student cafeterias which make a welcome break on the temple trail.

**Café Buttercups**, 103 Shimobanba, Jōdo-ji. Arty *gaijin* hangout serving a well-priced menu of scrumptious daily specials including sandwiches, fried rice and tacos, accompanied by fruitshakes and free coffee refills. English spoken; newspapers, books and video rental available. Daily except Tues 10am–10pm.

**Chōshō-in**, Fukuchi-chō, Nanzen-ji. A sub-temple of Nanzen-ji which offers Zen *yudōfu* cuisine in its attractive gardens, with the option of an outside terrace in fine weather. If you don't want the full "Matsu" meal (around ¥3000), there are individual dishes such as *fu no dengaku*, three wheat-gluten cakes with different toppings. English menu. Daily except Tues 11am–4pm; last order 3pm.

**Didi**, Higashiōji Imadegawa-agaru. Follow your nose to this cheerful ethnic restaurant, using all natural ingredients to create delicious curries, wholewheat pancakes and blueberry muffins. It's a great place for breakfast, and lunch sets are a snip at ¥750. Daily except Wed 9.30am–10pm.

**Furōen**, Ishibashi-chō, Jōdo-ji. Earthen walls, bamboo fixtures, rustic tables and Elvis make odd bedfellows, but this little place is less touristy than most around Ginkaku-ji. The food's equally eclectic, and prices aren't bad, with a choice of *teishoku* at under ¥1500. Daily except Tues 11.30am–2pm & 5.30–10pm.

**Hyōtei**, Nanzen-ji (☎075/771-4116). Hidden behind Murin-an garden, this thatch-roofed, garden-restaurant started serving *kaiseki* cuisine more than a hundred years ago. Their specials are *asagayu*, a summer breakfast, and *uzuragayu* (rice gruel with quail eggs) in winter. Prices are lower in the new annexe, but even here expect to pay ¥4000 for the cheapest meal. Reservations essential; English spoken. April–Nov 8am–7.30pm; Jan–March & Dec 11am–7.30pm.

**Imobō Hirano-ya**, Maruyama-kōen-uchi. Delightful, 300-year-old restaurant located inside the north entrance to Maruyama park. Their specialities are *imobō* incorporating an unusual type of potato (*ebi-imo*), and finding ingenious ways to make preserved fish taste superb. Try an *imobō teishoku* for about ¥2500. Daily 10.30am–8pm.

**Matsuno**, Shijō-dōri. If you like eel (*unagi*), this is the place for you. The Matsuno family have been broiling eels for at least a century and devising all sorts of delicious ways to present them. Sets start at around ¥2000. English menu. Daily except Thurs 11.30am–9pm.

**Nakamura-rō**, 509 Gion-machi minami-gawa. This wonderful old restaurant has been serving exquisite Kyoto cuisine for the last four hundred years. It's surprisingly relaxed and informal, with *tatami* rooms overlooking a lush garden, but even a lunchtime *bentō* will set you back ¥3600, or ¥5000 for a mini-*kaiseki* meal – worth every yen, of course. Daily 11.30am–7.30pm; closed last Thurs of the month.

**Okutan**, 86-30 Fukuchi-chō, Nanzen-ji. If Chōshō-in (see previous page) is full, try this small restaurant half-hidden in a bamboo grove on the east side of the same garden. Daily except Thurs 10.30–6pm.

**Omen**, Shishigadani-dōri. This informal noodle restaurant makes a useful pit-stop at the north end of the Philosopher's Path. Lunchtime sets (around ¥2000), plus daily specials. English menu. Daily except Thurs 11am–11pm.

**Sunshine Café**, 4 Ushinomiya-chō, Yoshida. A veritable jungle of pot plants fills this popular organic café near Kyoto University, serving tasty, innovative meals in generous portions. There's a daily lunch for ¥800, a longer evening menu (around ¥800 for a main dish) plus sandwiches, salads, herb teas and organic beer. Daily 10am–11pm.

**Tenkin**, Shijō Yamatoōji nishi-iru. A spick-and-span sushi restaurant a few doors east of the Minami-za. Prices aren't bad for the location (around ¥2000 for a reasonable selection). There's a plastic window display to choose from, and English-speaking staff. Daily except Wed 11.30am–9pm.

## Northwest Kyoto

*All the following restaurants are marked on the map on p.453.*

This **northwestern district** covers a huge area with no particular centre to aim for. Instead, the restaurants below are chosen for their proximity to several major sights. These include a reliable place just north of the Imperial Palace, near Doshisha University, and a couple of restaurants near Daitoku-ji and Kinkaku-ji.

**Fiasco**, 2F, Kamidachiuri Karasuma higashi-iru. Bright, sunny Italian restaurant known for its fresh pasta, California cuisine and adventurous pizzas – go wild with Masala chicken and shrimp, or Chicken Quesadilla. Count on at least ¥2000 per head. No smoking. Daily except Wed 11.30am–10pm.

**Gontaro**, Kinkaku-no-michi. Useful branch of the Shijō soba shop just a few minutes' walk west of Kinkaku-ji. Nothing fancy, but you'll still find the same welcome and well-priced noodle dishes. Daily 11am–10pm.

**Izusen**, Daitoku-ji (☎075/491-6665). One of the nicest places to sample vegetarian *shōjin-ryōri* at an affordable price, though still around ¥3000 for the simplest meal. It's located in the garden of Daiji-in, a sub-temple of Daitoku-ji, with tables outside in fine weather. Reservations are recommended in spring and autumn. They also have a cheaper branch near the station (see p.459). Daily except Thurs 11am–5pm.

**Knuckles**, 1-9 Murasakino Nishinochō. A "New York deli" just west of Daitoku-ji's Zen gardens. As you'd expect, there are bagels and rye-bread sandwiches, plus a few Mexican dishes. The lunch deal includes soup and tea or coffee for ¥850. English menu available. Tues–Sun 11am–10pm.

# Drinking and nightlife

Kyoto isn't all about high culture. After you've finished tramping the streets, there are plenty of **coffee houses** and cosy **bars** where you can kick back and quench your thirst. And, if the aching feet can stand it, Kyoto's late-night scene offers a fair range of **clubs**, **discos** and **live music** venues. It may not compete with the likes of Ōsaka and Tokyo, but you should be able to find somewhere to party till the wee hours. The prime entertainment districts are **Pontochō** and **Gion**, both of which are stuffed to the gunnels with bars, clubs and much else besides. But be warned; even fairly innocuous-looking establishments can be astronomically expensive, so check first to make sure you know exactly what you're letting yourself in for. And don't be surprised if you get a frosty reception, or are even turned away. It may be because you're a foreigner or because you need a formal introduction – which is invariably the case with the exclusive *geisha* houses.

## Coffee shops and teahouses

Caffeine addicts need never go short in Japan, and Kyoto is no exception. If all you want is a quick break, then look out for the *Colorado* and *Pronto* chains – they're cheap, reasonably smart and the coffee's drinkable. For something more classy you might want to try the places listed below, while *Rakushō* offers traditional green tea in delightful surroundings.

**Inoda**, Sakaimachi Sanjō-sagaru. It's hard to ignore the delicious aroma of roasting coffee outside this traditional coffee shop, established over one hundred years ago. Behind the old façade a 1920s Western-style tea room overlooks a small garden. They have a range of coffees (from ¥450), plus sandwiches, cakes and other snacks. *Inoda* now has a small chain in Kyoto – not as atmospheric as the original, but the coffee tastes as good. Daily 7am–6pm.

**Karafuneya**, Pontochō Sanjō-sagaru. Member of the *Karafuneya* chain that's recommended for its riverside location at the north end of Pontochō. It's also open till late and has an open-air terrace in summer. Mon–Fri noon–midnight, Sat & Sun noon–5am.

**Papa Jon's**, Kamidachiuri Karasuma higashi-iru. Downstairs from *Fiasco* (see opposite), this airy little coffee shop serves luscious home-made cheesecake, as well as herbal teas and all kinds of coffee – from espresso, latte and frothy cappuccino to liqueur coffees with attitude. No smoking. Daily except Tues 11am–10pm.

**Rakushō**, Washiyo-chō Kōdai-ji-mae. On the hike through eastern Kyoto, stop off at this charming old tea shop for a cup of green tea and *warabi mochi* (green-tea rice cake). They also serve coffee, ice cream, cakes and other light snacks. Don't miss their tiny pond filled with enormous carp. Open 9am–6pm; closed one day each week.

## Bars, clubs and live music

From dingy dives to swanky hostess **bars**, Kyoto is well-endowed with places to while away the evening. The epicentre of this activity is Gion and Pontochō, the two traditional pleasure quarters either side of the Kamo-gawa in downtown Kyoto. Even if you're not keen on propping up bars, make sure you take an evening stroll up Pontochō-dōri and along Gion's Hanamikoji-dōri. In summer, look out for roof-top **beer gardens** on top of the big hotels – the *Miyako Hotel* is a popular venue.

The contemporary music scene is also alive and well in Kyoto. Whether you're into jazz, rock, folk or drum'n'bass, or simply want a good bop, the city has enough **clubs**, discos and **live music** venues' to satisfy most tastes. To find out who or what's on, pick up a copy of the *Kyoto Visitors' Guide* or *Kansai Time Out* (¥300).

### CENTRAL KYOTO AND PONTOCHŌ

**Asahi Superdry**, Kawaramachi Sanjō-sagaru. This big, casual beer restaurant on the main Kawaramachi-dōri drag is a fine place to start the evening. Daily noon–10pm.

**Bar Isn't It?**, B1, 67-3 Daikoku-chō, Kawaramachi Sanjō-sagaru. Loud, lively beer-hall-cum-disco with a predominantly *gaijin* crowd. Drinks and snacks are all ¥500. There's a DJ on Fri and Sat, and live music most Sun (¥1000 entry, including one drink). Daily 6pm–2/3am.

**Cock-a-hoop**, 7F, Empire Bldg, Kiyamachi Sanjō-agaru. Relaxed, inexpensive bar with river views and salsa on the turntable (daily except Wed 6pm–2am). In the same building, there's the cool *Teddy's* bar, and *Live Spot Rag* with local and international bands most nights (from ¥1600).

**Beer Market Ichiba Koji**, B1, With You Bldg, Teramachi Shijō-agaru. The decor's fun and they serve a well-priced pint in this high-tech micro-brewery doubling as a restaurant. Find it in the Teramachi shopping arcades. Daily 11.30am–2pm & 5–11pm, Sat & Sun 11.30am–11pm.

**Munchen Beer Hall**, Shijō Kawaramachi-agaru higashi-iru. No-nonsense beer restaurant in an interesting area of back alleys between Kawaramachi and Pontochō. Daily noon–10/11pm.

**Queen's**, Kiyamachi Rokkaku-sagaru. This large, attractive bar opens onto the west bank of the Takase Canal. All drinks are ¥500 – order at the bar – and they also do a range of snacks, mostly ¥500, plus a few set meals. Daily 6pm–2am.

**Rub a Dub**, B1, Kiyamachi Sanjō-sagaru. Sup a pina colada in this reggae beach bar decked out with fairy-lights, palm trees and plastic fruit. Somehow they occasionally squeeze in a live musician (cover charge). It's at the north end of canal-side Kiyamachi-dōri – look for a small sign-board on the pavement. Daily 6pm–3/4am.

**Score Board**, B1, Hitosujime higashi-iru, Kawaramachi Sanjō-agaru. Watch the big match live at this "sports bar" in the northwest corner of Pontochō. Not the cheapest drinks, but there's a small discount during Happy Hour (7–9pm). Daily 7pm–2/3am.

**Taku Taku**, Tominokoji Bukkoji-sagaru. This *kura* (traditional storehouse) makes a great live venue. The music's pretty varied but tends towards rock and blues, with someone on stage most nights (7–9pm), including the occasional international artist. *Taku Taku* lurks in the blocks southwest of Takashimaya department store. Cover charge ¥1600, including one drink.

**Toga Toga**, B1, Teramachi Shijō-sagaru. Loud, hard and fairly pricey live house just south of Shijō-dōri with bands two or three times a week (from ¥1500).

## GION

**Cavern Club**, B1, Shinsei Bldg, Hanamikoji Sueyoshichō-agaru. Branch of Tokyo's long-running tribute to The Beatles, located on Hanamikoji-dōri. The cover bands sound pretty authentic – shut your eyes and you could almost be there. ¥1300 cover charge. Daily 6.30pm–1am.

**CK Café**, 4F Gion-kaikan, 323 Kitagawa, Higashiōji Shijō-agaru. The hottest nightspot in Kyoto, with a large dance floor and live bands to suit every taste. Find it on Higashiōji-dōri near Yasaka-jinja. ¥2500 cover charge, including two drinks. Fri, Sat and any day before a national holiday 8pm–midnight.

**Kento's**, 2F, Hitosujime nishi-iru, Hanamikoji Shijō-sagaru. Just south of Shijō-dōri behind an old Gion façade, it's all greased quiffs, polka dots and naff suits. The golden fifties are still rocking and rolling in Kento's live house. Cover charge ¥1300. Daily 6.30pm–2pm, Sun till midnight.

**Malt's Club**, Nexus Bldg, Hanamikoji Shinbashi nishi-iru. If you're exploring Shinbashi, a lovely corner of old Gion, pop into this extraordinary "concept" bar. The food's a bit expensive but the drinks aren't so bad and worth it for the decor – choose between jazz lounge, casual Japanese or Mongolian yurt. Daily 5pm–midnight.

## OTHER AREAS

**Club**, Mototanaka-eki-mae. Mellow, second-floor bar with a great record/CD collection, including Okinawa folk. They also put on the occasional jazz concert (around ¥600). It's located on the east side of Higashiōji-dōri, beside the Eizan line tracks across from Mototanaka Station. Daily except Tues 6pm–2am.

**Cup of Sun**, Kitashirakawa Sennouchi-chō. Tiny bar which hosts local acoustic, folk and bluegrass bands on Fri and Sat (¥200–¥1000). It's out near the Foreign Languages Institute in northeast Kyoto, on City Bus route #204. Mon–Sun 11am–11pm.

**Juttoku**, 815 Higashiya-chō, Ōmiya Marutamachi-agaru. A bit out of the way, north of Nijō-jō, but this is another wonderful old *kura* hosting mostly rock and blues bands. Cover charge ¥800–3000. Daily 5.30pm–midnight.

**Metro**, exit 2, Keihan Marutamachi Station. Small, loud and very popular live house in the guts of the railway station. Various local and foreign bands, from drum'n'bass to reggae, rock and latin, alternating with wild, DJ theme nights. Entrance ¥500–¥2000, including one drink. Daily from around 9pm.

**Pig & Whistle**, 2F, 115 Ōhashi-chō, Sanjō-ōhashi higashi-iru. If you're craving fish 'n chips or a jar of Sam Smith's, then hurry along to this fair imitation of a British pub just east of Sanjō-Keihan Station. Daily 5pm–midnight/1am.

# Dance, theatre and cinema

Kyoto is famous for its performances of traditional **geisha dances**. *Geisha* and the trainee *"maiko"* from each of the city's former pleasure quarters have been putting on these *Odori* since the late nineteenth century, though the music and choreography are much older. By turns demure and coquettish, they glide round the stage in the most gorgeous kimono, straight out of an Edo-period woodblock print of Japan's seductive "floating world". If you're in Kyoto at the time, it's well worth going along. Performances take place several times a day, so it's usually possible to get hold of tickets; you can buy them from the theatre box offices, ticket agencies, travel agents (see p.469) and major hotels.

京都 kyoto station

湖西線 kosai line
ko sai sen

志賀 shiga station

(琵琶湖)
bi wa ko
biwa-Lake.

三井海上

## MAJOR KYOTO FESTIVALS AND ANNUAL EVENTS

Thanks to its central role in Japanese history, Kyoto is home to a number of important **festivals**, of which the major celebrations are listed below. The **cherry-blossom** season hits Kyoto in early April – famous viewing spots include the Imperial Park, Heian-jingū and Arashiyama – while early November brings dramatic **autumn colours**. Many **temples** hold special **openings** in October and November to air their inner rooms during the fine, dry weather. This is a marvellous opportunity to see paintings, statues and other treasures not normally on public display; details are available in the free *Kyoto Visitor's Guide*. Note that Kyoto gets pretty busy during major festivals and national holidays (especially the late-April/early-May "Golden Week" period).

**Feb 2–4 Setsubon**. The annual bean-throwing festival is celebrated at shrines throughout the city. "Ogres" scatter beans and pray for good harvests at Yasaka-jinja, while Heian-jingū hosts performances of traditional *kyōgen* theatre (see p.796) on Feb 3.

**April 1–30 Miyako Odori**. Performances of traditional *geisha* dances held in Gion (see p.447).

**May 15 Aoi Matsuri**. The Hollyhock Festival dates back to when this plant was believed to ward off earthquakes and thunder. Now it's an occasion for a gorgeous parade of people dressed in Heian-period costume (794–1185). They accompany the imperial messenger and an ox cart decked in hollyhock leaves from the Imperial Palace to the Shimo-gamo and Kami-gamo shrines, in north Kyoto.

**May 1–24 Kamo-gawa Odori**. Performances of traditional dances by *geisha* in Pontochō (see p.439).

**June 1 & 2 Takigi Nō**. Nō plays performed by torchlight at Heian-jingū.

**July 17 Gion Matsuri**. One of Kyoto's great festivals, the *Gion Matsuri* also dates back to Heian times when ceremonies were held to drive away epidemics of the plague – a curse of the hot, humid summer months. The festivities focus on Yasaka-jinja and culminate on July 17 with a grand parade of tall, pointy *yama-boko* floats, richly decorated with local Nishijin silk.

**Aug 16 Daimonji Gozan Okuribi**. Five huge bonfires etch *kanji* characters on the hills around Kyoto; the most famous is the character for *dai* (big) on Daimonji-yama, northeast of the city. The practice originated from lighting fires after Obon (see p.59) to guide the ancestral spirits back "home".

**Oct 22 Jidai Matsuri**. A comparative newcomer, this "Festival of the Ages" was introduced in 1895 to mark the city's 1100th anniversary. More than 2000 people, wearing costumes representing all the intervening historical periods, parade from the Imperial Palace to Heian-jingū.

**Oct 22 Kurama-no-Himatsuri**. After the Jidai parade, hop on a train north to see Kurama's more boisterous Fire Festival. In 940 Yuki-jinja, the local shrine, was moved here from central Kyoto, a journey which was accomplished by torchlight over three nights. To commemorate the event, the villagers light bonfires outside their houses and local lads carry giant, flaming torches (weighing up to 50kg) up to the shrine. Events climax around 9pm, after which there's heavy-duty drinking, drumming and chanting till dawn. It's primitive, exciting and extremely crowded. To get to Kurama, take the Eizan line from Kyoto's Demachiyanagi Station (30min); it's best to arrive early and leave around 10pm unless you want to see it through.

**Dec 1–25 Kabuki Kaomise**. Grand Kabuki festival (see overleaf).

**Dec 31 Okera Mairi**. The best place to see in the New Year is at Gion's Yasaka-jinja. Apart from the normal festivities (see p.57), locals come here to light a flame from the sacred fire with which to rekindle their hearths back home. As well as general good luck, this supposedly prevents illness in the coming year.

The year kicks off with the **Miyako Odori** (April 1–30) performed by *geisha* from the Gion teahouses. These dances, on a seasonal theme, take place in the local theatre, Gion Kōbu Kaburenjō (see p.447; ☎075/541-3391; tickets from ¥1900). The ladies of Pontochō stage their **Kamo-gawa Odori** twice a year (May 1–24 & Oct 15–Nov 7) in Pontochō Kaburenjō, at the north end of Pontochō-dōri (☎075/221-2025; tickets from ¥2000). In fact, autumn brings a whole flurry of activity: the **Onshukai** dances are held between October 1 and 10 at the Gion Kaikan theatre, near Yasaka-jinja (☎075/561-0224; from ¥4000), followed by **Kotobukikai** (Oct 8–12) in northwest Kyoto's Kitano Kami-shichiken Kaburenjō (☎075/461-0148; ¥6000); finally, the **Gion Odori** wraps things up in early November (Nov 1–10; from ¥3300), again in the Gion Kaikan.

If your visit doesn't coincide with any of these, you can see a rather disappointing sampler of traditional arts from March to November at **Gion Corner** (see p.447; ☎075/561-1119). As well as a dance by *maiko*, there are short extracts from court dances, a puppet play (Bunraku) and *kyōgen* theatre, and demonstrations of the tea ceremony and flower arranging (*ikebana*).

Colourful and dramatic, **Kabuki** theatre is said to have originated in Kyoto. Unfortunately, performances these days are fairly sporadic, but in December there's a major Kabuki-fest at Gion's eye-catching Minami-za theatre (see p.447; ☎075/561-1155). During this *kaomise*, or "face-showing" (Dec 1–25), big-name actors give snippets from their most successful roles. **Nō** theatre is a far more stately affair – and often incomprehensible even to Japanese, though it can also be incredibly powerful. Kyoto's main venue is the Kanze Kaikan (☎075/771-6114), south of Heian-jingū, with performances of Nō or *kyōgen* most weekends (tickets from ¥2500; occasional free performances). Both the Kongo Nō-gakudō (☎075/221-3049; around ¥6000), near west Kyoto's Karasuma Shijō junction, and Kawamura Nō Kaikan (☎075/451-4513; from ¥4000) put on plays every month or so. The latter is a lovely old theatre run by the Kawamura family – a long line of famous Nō actors – located on Karasuma-dōri near Doshisha University.

For those with more contemporary tastes, **Kyoto Connection** deserves a special mention for its contribution to the local arts scene. On the last Saturday of every month (except Aug & Dec; 8.30–11.30pm; ¥500) up-and-coming musicians, dancers, poets, comedians, video artists and actors of all nationalities gather in northwest Kyoto. The "programme" varies from month to month, but there's usually something interesting happening. If you want to contribute, or simply watch, phone Ken Rodgers (☎075/712-7129) for further information and directions.

Alternatively, you can catch the latest Hollywood **movies** at the local cinema. These are mostly grouped along Kawaramachi-dōri north of Shijō and in the backstreets immediately to the west. For art-house movies, try Asahi Kaikan, on Kawaramachi-dōri south of the *Royal Hotel*, which often screens them in their original language, and Minami Kaikan, near the junction of Ōmiya and Kujō, southeast of Kyoto Station. The Japan Foundation, 8F Yasuda Kasai Bldg, Karasuma Nishikinokoji-agaru (☎075/211-1312), hosts free showings of Japanese classics for foreigners only; films are subtitled in English and are usually on Wednesday at 2pm. Finally, the British Council occasionally puts on home-grown English-language films (see Listings, p.468).

Details of these and other events in Kyoto are available at the Tourist Information Centre (see p.429), and also in the two monthly publications, the *Kyoto Visitor's Guide* and *Kansai Time Out*.

## Crafts and shopping

Over the centuries the finest craftsmen in Japan were drawn to Kyoto's Imperial Court as the city's workshops spawned an array of exquisite crafts. Gold-dusted **lacquerware**, shimmering **brocades** and folding paper **fans** were all favourites of the royal household. In the sixteenth century the popularity of the formal tea ceremony, with its appreciation of rustic understatement, created a fashion for rough-cast **pottery** and simple **bamboo utensils**. The nouveau-riche merchants, on the other hand, favoured a more flamboyant style, epitomized by the gorgeous **silks** and ornate **hair ornaments** worn in the pleasure quarters. Even everyday items, such as **boxwood combs**, brooms and buckets, show a certain pizazz in Kyoto.

To learn more about local crafts, take a look round the Fureaikan museum (see p.448), or join a **demonstration class** and have a go yourself. Without too much effort you can still find **shops** in Kyoto producing crafts in the traditional way, using skills passed down the generations. These offer superb, if often pricey, souvenirs of the city. And there's no shortage of conventional shops, department stores and even one or two flea markets where you can pick up less august mementos.

## Textiles

Kyoto has long been famous for its high-quality **weaving**. The centre of the city's textile industry is the **Nishijin** district, located northwest of the Imperial Palace. Even today you'll still hear the clatter of looms in dozens of family-run workshops as you walk through the area. Some of these families have been here since the early 1500s when their ancestors, returning to Kyoto after the ravages of the Ōnin Wars (1467–77), settled in an abandoned military camp called Nishi-jin. They revived the production of *aya*, a unique style of elaborately patterned weave, which eventually became synonymous with Nishijin. During the Edo period (1603–1868) these sumptuous **silk brocades** were much in demand – it's estimated that the area boasted more than 5000 looms at its peak – but business collapsed after the Meiji Restoration as Western fashions took over. To counteract the decline, several Nishijin craftsmen travelled to France to study modern techniques, and came back with the revolutionary Jacquard mechanical loom. Nowdays, the vast majority of Nishijin fabrics are produced on computerized looms, but the more complex designs are still woven on the Jacquard or the even more labour-intensive hand loom.

You can see samples of these gorgeous fabrics and demonstrations of traditional Nishijin weaving at the **Nishijin Textile Centre** (daily 9am–5pm; free), just south of the Horikawa Imadegawa junction. Take a close look at the incredibly painstaking *tsuzurebata* technique, aptly known as fingernail weaving; it can take a whole day to complete one centimetre. The centre also puts on several kimono shows each day (¥600; tickets available at the ground-floor information desk), featuring this season's fashions.

In Nishijin weaving, silk threads are dyed before being woven into their intricate patterns. Originally, only the aristocracy could afford these fabrics, and when merchants began to patronize the same tailors in the late seventeenth century, the shogun promptly forbade such extravagance. However, an enterprising Kyoto craftsman, Yūzensai Miyazaki, soon came up with a method for hand-dyeing fabrics to create the same elaborate effect. **Yūzen dyeing** is still an incredibly complex process, involving successive applications of glutinous-rice paste and dye to produce detailed, multicoloured designs. Afterwards, the pattern is often augmented with powdered gold or silver leaf, or embroidered with gold threads. Some of these wonderful fabrics are on display in the **Kodai Yūzen-en** gallery (daily 9am–5pm; ¥500), located on Takatsuji-dōri, southwest of the Hirokawa Shijō junction. Ask to see their introductory video in English first and then, if you're inspired, you can try it yourself on a handkerchief or table centre-piece (from ¥1050).

When luxury fabrics went out of fashion in the Meiji era, many weavers turned to other areas of textile production. One of these was the Utsuki family, who saw the potential in making good-quality indigo-dyed cloth which was traditionally worn by farmers. They still produce handwoven clothes, *noren* curtains, bags and so forth in their lovely old workshop, **Aizen-kōbō** (Mon–Sat 9am–5.30pm; free), two blocks west of the Nishijin Textile Centre, on Nakasuji-dōri. The English-speaking owner will explain the laborious techniques involved in hand-dyeing the cloth with natural indigo and then sun-drying it to give a glorious, rich shade of blue.

## Craft classes and cultural activities

In addition to Yūzen dyeing (see previous page), you can try several other crafts at various venues around the city. The Kyoto Handicraft Centre (see Shopping, opposite) offers **demonstration classes** for beginners in woodblock printing, *cloisonné* (enamel-work) and doll-making (¥1500 for 1hr; book at the ground-floor information desk 1–4pm). Classes in *ikebana*, origami and calligraphy, among other things, are available through Kyoto International Community House (see p.430). They also do longer courses on the tea ceremony, the *koto* (a type of zither) and Nō theatre (¥5000 per term; ¥1000 for a demonstration class). At Tō-ji temple, south of Kyoto Station (see p.442), you can also try painting on lacquerware (daily 9.30am–3pm; ¥1000–¥1500).

Kyoto's most famous **tea-ceremony** school, Urasenke, is open to visitors one afternoon a week (¥1000). After an English-language introduction to the ceremony's form and history, you'll take part in the ritual itself. Phone the centre on ☎075/451-8516 for the latest schedule and to make a reservation. Alternatively, the *Miyako Hotel* offers the tea ceremony every day (10am–7pm; ¥1150); no reservation required.

Recently it's become popular to dress up as a *maiko* (trainee *geisha*) and, if you can afford it, wander round the streets of Kyoto for an hour or two – much to the horror of the genuine *maiko*. Some hotels and guesthouses now offer the opportunity to their guests, or you can don a kimono, wig and make-up at the Nishijin Textile Centre (see previous page) for around ¥10,000 and have your photo taken.

## Shopping

Kyoto's main shopping district is focused around the junction of **Shijō-dōri** and **Kawaramachi-dōri**, and spreads north of Shijō along the Teramachi and Shinkyōgoku arcades. Here you'll find the big-name **department stores**, notably Takashimaya, Hankyū and Daimaru, as well as all manner of souvenir shops, smart boutiques and even a few traditional craft shops, especially on Sanjō-dōri just west of the river. The **station area** has improved enormously with the opening of the huge Isetan department store and a revamped underground shopping mall, Porta, under the northern bus terminal.

**East Kyoto** is best known for its wealth of shops around Kiyomizu-dera selling the local pottery, while nearby Sannen-zaka is a lovely parade of traditional craft shops. Further north, Gion's Shinmonzen-dōri specializes in antiques. The prices are predictably high, but it's a good area to browse. Below we suggest some of the more interesting shops to aim for, but anyone in Kyoto for more than a few days should invest in a copy of Diane Durston's labour of love, *Old Kyoto* (see Books, p.817).

### BOOKS AND MUSIC

Kyoto's largest range of foreign-language **books** is to be found on the eighth floor of the Maruzen store on Kawaramachi-dōri north of the Shijō junction. Imported magazines and newspapers are kept on the ground floor. Alternatively, you'll find a more limited selection of foreign-language titles in the Kinokuniya bookstore; it's in the Zest underground mall beneath the Kawaramachi Oike crossroads.

For the city's biggest choice of **records and CDs**, try the Virgin Megastore, on Kawaramachi-dōri just up from Maruzen, or Tower Records in the backstreets to the west. Joe's Garage, at 82-3 Nishimachi, Kitashirakawa (11am–11pm) is also worth seeking out if you're into nostalgia; this tiny outlet specializes in records, posters and pop memorabilia of the 1960s and 1970s – with a soft spot for Zappa. It's on Imadegawa, the road leading east to Ginkaku-ji, about halfway between Higashiōji and Shirakawa-dōri.

## CRAFTS AND SOUVENIRS

**Asahi Tōan**, 1-287-1 Kiyomizu. The best and most famous of several pottery shops on the road up to Kiyomizu-dera. They sell a wide variety of locally produced *Kiyomizu-yaki*.

**Jūsan-ya**, Shijō Teramachi higashi-iru. This little shop on Shijō-dōri is crammed with beautiful combs and hair ornaments in plain boxwood or covered in lacquer. All the items are hand-crafted using traditional techniques.

**Kungyoku-dō**, Horikawa-dōri, Nishi-Hongan-ji-mae. Though you wouldn't guess it from its modern, grey-stone frontage, this shop has been selling incense since 1594. Originally their customers were Buddhist temples and court nobles indulging in incense parties (players had to guess the ingredients from the perfume). The shop lies opposite the west gate of Nishi-Hongan-ji. Closed 1st and 3rd Sun of the month.

**Kyoto Handicraft Centre**, Marutamachi-dōri. Five floors packed with souvenirs from all over Japan at a range of prices. The smaller Amita Plaza, next door, is also worth a look for its selection of foodstuffs. Both shops offer tax-free prices for goods over ¥10,000 (see p.63 for more on this). Find them near the northwest corner of Heian-jingū.

**Kyoto Craft Centre**, Shijō-dōri. This large modern shop showcases the best of Kyoto's contemporary designers working with traditional crafts. Great for unusual, stylish souvenirs. It's located in Gion, towards the east end of Shijō-dōri. Closed Wed.

**Kyoto Tojiki Kaikan**, Gojō-zaka. West of Kiyomizu-dera, this shop stocks a good selection of *Kiyomizu-yaki* and other local ceramics. It's also worth popping in the next-door gallery to see what's on display.

**Naitō**, Sanjō-ōhashi. You might not be in the market for a broom, but this old shop just west of the Sanjō bridge is a treasure trove of beautifully made hemp brushes of every size and description. The traditional shop selling rice crackers and confectionery next door is also a delight.

**Tachichiki**, Shijō Tominokoji. An elegant shop on Shijō-dōri with fine ceramics and china on three floors and modern crafts in the basement. Closed occasionally on Wed.

**Tanakaya**, Shijō Yanaginobanba. Dolls of all shapes and sizes fill this shop on Shijō-dōri. There's also a gallery upstairs with changing exhibitions of antique dolls. Closed Wed.

**Tsujikura**, Kawaramachi Shijō-agaru. Traditional paper and modern plastic umbrellas spill out of Tsujikura onto the pavement of Kawaramachi-dōri. They also stock jaunty paper lanterns in a variety of styles. Closed Wed.

**Yamato Mingei-ten**, Kawaramachi Takoyakushi-agaru. The best place in Kyoto to buy folk crafts. The main shop has two floors stuffed full of tempting items from all over Japan, while the annexe round the corner displays furniture and more modern designs. Find them on Kawaramachi-dōri near Maruzen bookstore. Closed Tues.

## FOOD AND MARKETS

Kyoto is as famous for its beautiful **foodstuffs** as it is for crafts, all made with the same attention to detail and love of refinement. You can see this in even the most modest restaurant, but also in the **confectionery** shops whose window displays look more like art galleries. In the centre of Kyoto, take a look in Masune (closed Thurs), on the southeast corner of the Sanjō Kawaramachi junction, or Kagiya Yoshifusa (closed Mon) on Gion's Shijō-dōri, for a sample of the best. This latter shop has a tea-room upstairs where you can enjoy one of their dainty sweetmeats (*wagashi*) over a cup of green tea.

The other local delicacy is **pickled vegetables** (*tsukemono*). You'll be eating them at every meal, but if you want to buy some pickles – they're often sold vacuum-packed – head for **Murakami-jū** (closed occasionally on Wed). This traditional shop, southeast of Hankyū department store, is famous throughout Japan for the quality of it's old-style pickles. Otherwise, take a walk down **Nishiki-koji** market street (see p.439), where pickles predominate among a whole range of foodstuffs.

If you're in Kyoto on the 21st or 25th of the month, don't miss the two big **flea markets** held respectively at Tō-ji temple (see p.442) and Kitano Tenman-gū, a shrine in northwest Kyoto with its entrance on Imadegawa-dōri. Both kick off at 7am and it's worth getting there early if you're looking for bargains. There's a fantastic carnival atmosphere at these markets, where stalls sell everything from pots and socks to lacquerware and long-johns.

## Listings

**Airlines** ANA, Teramachi Oike higashi-iru, Nakagyō-ku (☎0120–029333 international; 0120–511283 domestic); JAL, 2F, Recruit Meiji Seimei Blg, Karasuma Oike, Nakagyō-ku (☎0120–255931 international; 0120–255971 domestic); JAS, Karasuma Dai-ichi Seimei Blg, Karasuma Bukkoji-agaru, Shimogyō-ku (☎0120–711283 international; 0120–511283 domestic); Korean Airlines, 6F Toho Seimei Blg, Ainomachi Oike higashi-iru, Nakagyō-ku (☎0088–212001).

**Airport information** Kansai International ☎0724/55-2500; Itami ☎06/856-6781.

**Banks and exchange** Kyoto's main banking district is around the Karasuma Shijō junction, extending east towards the river and north to Oike-dōri, where Sumitomo, Sanwa and Tokyo Mitsubishi banks all have foreign-exchange facilities. However, note that most banks in Kyoto don't open their exchange desks until 10.30/11am. Down near the station, the Central Post Office (see opposite) also handles foreign exchange (Mon–Fri 9.30am–6pm). ATM machines in the All Card Plaza (in the Teramachi arcade, just north of Shijō-dōri) and the underground Zest Mall (under the Kawaramachi Oike junction, near Kyoto City Hall) accept a range of credit cards, including some cards registered on foreign accounts. Otherwise, you can get cash advances over the counter without a PIN number at the following: for Visa go to Sumitomo Bank's main branch on Karasuma just south of Sanjō-dōri, or a handy sub-branch in Hankyū department store; for MasterCard head for Nanto Bank, on the Karasuma Oike junction; and Sanwa Bank, at Shijō Karasuma, for American Express.

**Bike rental** Renta-cycle Yasumoto (daily 9am–5pm; ☎075/751-0595), on the river bank just north of Sanjō-Keihan Station, charges ¥1000 per day and asks for a deposit of ¥10,000 or an ID of some sort. Nearby, the fishing shop Nagaharaya Mohachi (daily 8am–9pm; ☎075/761-3062) has the same rates but doesn't require a deposit. Ordinary town bikes at Taki Renta Bike (☎075/341-7586), near *Hiraiwa Ryokan*, cost ¥1000 for 24hr, or ¥1300 for three-speed machines. If you're staying at either *Utano Youth Hostel* or *Tani House* (see p.435), their bikes are a more reasonable ¥500–¥800 per day.

**British Council** The Council's library, at 77 Kitashirakawa Nishimachi (Mon–Fri 10am–6pm; ☎075/791-7151), stocks English-language newspapers and magazines. They also have occasional screenings of British films (¥500; free to members) and a varied lecture programme. Membership costs ¥2000 per year.

**Car rental** Nippon Rent-a-car (☎075/671-0919), Nissan Rent-a-car (☎075/351-4123) and Eki Rent-a-car (☎075/371-3020) all have offices near Kyoto Station.

**Hospitals and clinics** The main Kyoto hospital with English-speaking doctors is the Japan Baptist Hospital (☎075/781-5191), 47 Yamanomoto-chō, Kitashirakawa, Sakyō-ku. Otherwise, Sakabe Clinic (closed Thurs pm, Sat pm & Sun; ☎075/231-1624), 435 Yamamoto-chō, Gokomachi Nijō-sagaru, is run by the English-speaking Dr Sakabe. They have a general clinic (6.30–8.30pm), or take appointments between 9am and 12.30pm. Consultations cost around ¥4000 for the first visit and ¥2000 thereafter. For more information about medical facilities with English-speaking staff in Kyoto or throughout the region, call the AMDA International Medical Information Centre (☎06/636-2333).

**Immigration** To renew your tourist or student visa, apply to the Immigration Bureau, 4F, 34-12 Higashi Marutamachi, Kawabata higashi-iru, near Keihan Marutamachi Station.

**Internet access** At the time of writing, the best place to log on is NTT Multimedia World, Kawaramachi-dōri (10.30am–8pm; free for 30min). Alternatively, it costs ¥250 for 30min at *Café Buttercups* (see Eating, p.459) and at the Kyoto Prefectural Tourist office, on the 9th floor of Isetan department store in Kyoto Station, or ¥500 at Netsurf, 8F, Kawabata Bldg, Shijō Takakura nishi-iru (daily except Wed noon–8pm).

**Language courses** Some of the most prominent language schools are the Kyoto Japanese Language School, Ichijō-dōri Muromachi-nishi, Kamigyō-ku (☎075/414-0449); Kyoto Kokusai Gaikokugo Centre, 21 Kamihate-chō, Kitashirakawa, Sakyō-ku (☎075/722-5066); Kyoto YMCA Japanese Language School, Sanjō Yanaginobanba (☎075/255-3287); and Kyoto International Academy, Sanjō Hanamikoji (☎075/752-2837). The Kyoto International Community House, 2-1 Torii-chō Awataguchi, Sakyō-ku (☎075/752-3010), also runs basic courses in survival Japanese (¥5000 per term), while Berlitz, 9F, Ishizumi Bldg, Shijō Tominokoji nishi-iru, Shimogyō-ku (☎075/255-2311), is recommended for its intensive courses.

**Post office** The Central Post Office, 843-12 Higashi Shiokoji-chō, Shimogyō-ku, Kyoto-shi, is located in front of Kyoto Station. They accept poste restante mail and there's a 24hr window for stamps and express mail.

**Taxis** If you phone in advance, MK Taxi (☎075/721-2237) can provide English-speaking drivers. Otherwise, Kyōren (☎075/672-5111) offers decent rates.

**Ticket agencies** Tickets to theatre, films, concerts and sports events are available at Pia (☎075/252-7190) on the 7th floor of Takashimaya department store. There are also similar agencies in the Daimaru and Hankyū stores.

**Travel agents** For international tickets, A'cross Travellers Bureau, 2F Royal Plaza Bldg, Rokkaku-sagaru Higashinotōin (☎075/255-3559), and No 1 Travel, 3F Shinkyōgoku Shijō-agaru (☎075/251-6970), have English-speaking staff. Or, try T.I.S (☎075/352-5339) in the first basement of Kyoto Station. The main domestic agents are Japan Travel Bureau (JTB; ☎075/341-6331) and Kinki Nippon Tourist (☎075/255-0489), with branches all over the city.

# Around Kyoto

There's so much to see in Kyoto itself that most people forget the surrounding area. However, you should try to make at least one day-trip out of the city. First priority should probably go to **Hiei-zan**, the mountain overlooking northeast Kyoto, where age-old cedars shelter the venerable temples of **Enryaku-ji**. Below Hiei-zan, **Ōhara** contains a scattering of beguiling temples in an attractive valley, while out on the west side of Kyoto, the more urbanized **Arashiyama** is also famous for its gardens and temples. Arashiyama has less high-brow attractions as well: take a toy-town train through the Hozu-gawa gorge and then ride the rapids back down. It's back on the temple trail south of Kyoto, where **Uji** is home to the magnificent **Byōdō-in**, whose graceful Phoenix Hall is a masterpiece of Japanese architecture.

## Hiei-zan

Protecting Kyoto's northeastern flank, the sacred mountain of **Hiei-zan** is the home of Tendai Buddhism, its headquarters comprising an atmospheric collection of buildings, **Enryaku-ji**. There's not much else up on the mountain, so it's a good area to take at a leisurely pace, following ancient paths among the cedar forests to the less-frequented halls. Though there are several ways of getting to Enryaku-ji (see Practicalities, p.473), the easiest route is by bus from Kyoto, wriggling up the mountain side and then following a ridge road north. On a clear day you'll be rewarded with huge views west over **Biwa-ko**, Japan's largest lake and the second oldest fresh-water lake in the world after Lake Baikal in Siberia.

### Enryaku-ji

The top of Hiei-zan consists of a narrow ridge, at the south end of which stand the central halls of **Enryaku-ji** (daily 8.30/9am–4/4.30pm; ¥500, including all temple buildings). From this core area, known as the **Tō-tō** (Eastern Pagoda), the ridge slopes gently northwest down to the **Sai-tō** (Western Pagoda). A third compound, Yokawa, lies further north again, but this was a later addition and contains little of immediate interest. Most buses from Kyoto terminate at the Tō-tō carpark beside a souvenir shop; walk behind it to find the temple's main entrance.

Enryaku-ji was founded in 788 AD by a young Buddhist monk called **Saichō** (767–822), later sanctified as Dengyō Daishi. Saichō built himself a small hut on the mountain and a temple to house an image of Yakushi Nyorai (the Buddha of Healing), which he carved from a fallen tree. He then went to China for a year to study Buddhism. On returning to Hiei-zan in 805 AD, he founded the Japanese **Tendai sect** (see Contexts, p.784). Based on the Lotus Sutra, Tendai doctrine holds that anyone can

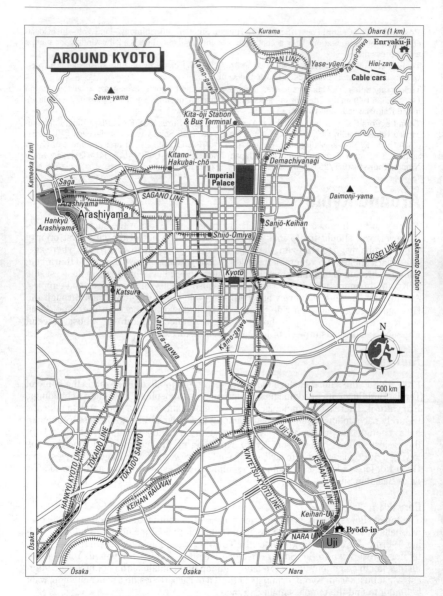

achieve enlightenment through studying the sacred texts and following extremely rigorous practices. Its followers went on to establish a whole host of splinter groups: Hōnen (who founded the Jōdo sect), Shinran (Jōdo Shinshū), Eisai (Rinzai Zen) and Nichiren all started out as Tendai priests.

In the early days, Enryaku-ji received generous imperial funding and court officials were sent up the mountain for a twelve-year education programme. As the sect expanded so it become both enormously rich and politically powerful, until there were 3000 buildings on the mountain. It owned vast areas of land and even maintained an army of several hundred well-trained **warrior monks** – many of whom were not really monks at all. They spent a good deal of time fighting other Buddhist sects, notably their great rivals at Nara's Kōfuku-ji (see p.483), but in the end, the warlord **Oda Nobunaga** (see p.772) put a stop to it all in 1571. He led 30,000 troops up Hiei-zan and proceeded to lay waste to the complex, including the monks and their families. Nobunaga died eleven years later and his successor, Toyotomi Hideyoshi, was more kindly disposed to the Tendai sect, encouraging the monks to rebuild.

## TŌ-TŌ

Enryaku-ji's most important buildings are concentrated in the southerly **Tō-tō** compound. Immediately inside the entrance you'll find a modern treasure hall, the **Kokuhō-den**, for which there's a separate entrance fee of ¥450. Its most interesting exhibits are a fine array of statues, including a delicate, thirteenth-century Amida

| AROUND KYOTO | | |
|---|---|---|
| **Arashiyama** | *Arashiyama* | 嵐山 |
| Daikaku-ji | *Daikaku-ji* | 大覚寺 |
| Giō-ji | *Giō-ji* | 祇王寺 |
| Ōkōchi Sansō | *Ōkōchi Sansō* | 大河内山荘 |
| Seiryō-ji | *Seiryō-ji* | 清涼寺 |
| Tenryū-ji | *Tenryū-ji* | 天竜寺 |
| *ACCOMMODATION AND RESTAURANTS* | | |
| Hōsen-ji Zen Centre | *Hōsen-ji Zen Sentā* | 宝泉寺禅センター |
| Nishiki | *Nishiki* | 錦 |
| Sagano | *Sagano* | 嵯峨野 |
| Minshuku Tsujimura | *Minshuku Tsujimura* | 民宿つじむら |
| **Hiei-zan** | *Hiei-zan* | 比叡山 |
| Eizan Cable | *Eizan Kēburu* | 叡山ケーブル |
| Enryaku-ji | *Enryaku-ji* | 延暦寺 |
| Jōdo-in | *Jōdo-in* | 浄土院 |
| Konpon Chū-dō | *Konpon Chū-dō* | 根本中堂 |
| Ninai-dō | *Ninai-dō* | にない堂 |
| Sai-tō | *Sai-tō* | 西塔 |
| Sakamoto Cable | *Sakamoto Kēburu* | 坂本ケーブル |
| Shaka-dō | *Shaka-dō* | 釈迦堂 |
| Tō-tō | *Tō-tō* | 東塔 |
| Yase-yūen Station | *Yase-yūen-eki* | 八瀬遊園駅 |
| **Ōhara** | *Ōhara* | 大原 |
| Hōsen-in | *Hōsen-in* | 宝泉院 |
| Jakkō-in | *Jakkō-in* | 寂光院 |
| Jikkō-in | *Jikkō-in* | 実光院 |
| Sanzen-in | *Sanzen-in* | 三千院 |
| Seryō | *Seryō* | 芹生 |
| Shōrin-in | *Shōrin-in* | 勝林院 |
| **Uji** | *Uji* | 宇治 |
| Byōdō-in | *Byōdō-in* | 平等院 |
| Magozaemon | *Magozaemon* | 孫左エ門 |

## MARATHON MONKS

Followers of the Buddhist **Tendai sect** believe that the route to enlightenment lies through chanting, esoteric ritual and extreme physical endurance. The most rigorous of these practices is the "thousand-day ascetic mountain pilgrimage", in which **marathon monks**, as they're popularly known, are required to walk 40,000km through the mountains and streets of Kyoto in a thousand days – the equivalent of nearly a thousand marathons. The thousand days are split into hundred-day periods over seven years, but during that period the monk has to go out every day, in all weathers, regardless of his physical condition. He must adhere to a strict vegetarian diet and, at one point during the seven years, go on a week-long fast with no food, water or sleep, just for good measure. Not surprisingly, many monks don't make it – in the old days they were expected to commit ritual suicide if they had to give up. Those that do finish (nowadays, about one person every five years), are rewarded with enlightenment and become "living Buddhas". Apparently, the advice of modern marathon monks is much sought after by national baseball coaches and others involved in endurance training.

Buddha and a lovely Senjū Kannon (thousand-armed Kannon) of the ninth century. You can also see a scroll apparently recording Saichō's trip to China in 804AD. Up the hill from the museum, the first building on your left is the **Daikō-dō**, the Great Lecture Hall, where monks attend lectures on the sutras and discuss doctrinal subtleties. Keeping an eye on them are life-size statues of Nichiren, Eisai, Hōnen, Shinran and other great names from the past – a sort of Tendai Hall of Fame.

Continuing uphill, you can take your turn at the huge bell, whose thundering peal reverberates around the mountain, and then go down the steps to the temple's most sacred hall, the **Konpon Chū-dō**. This powerful, faded building allegedly marks the spot where Saichō built his first hut; his statue of Yakushi Nyorai is kept inside, though hidden from view. Despite the crowds, the atmosphere in the dark, cavernous hall is absolutely compelling. Unusually, the altars are in a sunken area below the worship floor, where they seem to float in a swirling haze of incense smoke lit by low-burning lamps. It's said that the three big lanterns in front of the main altar have been burning ever since Saichō himself lit them 1200 years ago. Some sources hold that the lanterns did go out after Nobunaga's attack, and that a monk was sent up to Yamadera, north of Tokyo (see p.235), to bring back a light from their sacred flame, which had itself originally come from Enryaku-ji. Monks tending the flames nowdays wear a mask in case they sneeze.

From Konpon Chū-dō, walk ahead to the paved road and then follow it generally west, passing the bell again on your right. The next little hillock sports the pretty **Kaidan-in**, the Ordination Hall, and beyond it stand the recently reconstructed **Amida-dō** and its two-storey pagoda. Behind this bright-red hall, a path leads off through the woods to the Sai-tō compound.

### SAI-TŌ

It takes around thirty minutes to walk from the Amida-dō to the centre of the **Sai-tō** compound, with a few stops on route. First of these is the **Jōdo-in** which you'll come to after about ten minutes at the bottom of a lantern-lined staircase. Inside the temple's courtyard and round to the right of the main hall, Saichō's mausoleum, a red-lacquered, sun-burnt building, stands in a carefully tended gravel enclosure.

Continuing northwest, the path eventually leads to two identical square halls standing on a raised area. These are commonly known as **Ninai-dō**, which roughly translates as "shoulder-carrying hall". The name refers to the legendary strength of Benkei (see p.247), who's said to have hoisted the two buildings onto his shoulders like a yoke. Their official names are Jōgyō-dō, the Hall of Perpetual Practice on the left, and the Hokke-dō, or Lotus

Hall. They're used for different types of meditation practice: in the former monks walk round the altar for days reciting the Buddha's name, in the *nembutsu*, in the latter they alternate between walking and sitting meditation while studying the Lotus Sutra.

Walk between the pair of buildings and down more steps to reach the **Shaka-dō**, another imposing hall, which marks the centre of the Sai-tō area. Though smaller and not so atmospheric as Konpon Chū-dō, this building is much older. It was originally erected in the thirteenth century on the shores of Biwa-ko, but was moved here in 1595 to replace the earlier hall destroyed by Nobunaga's armies. It enshrines an image of Shaka Nyorai (Sakyamuni, the Historical Buddha), which is also attributed to Saichō, but again you can't see it. Otherwise the Shaka-dō is similar to the Tō-tō, with its sunken centre and three lanterns. It's a lovely, quiet place to rest before you start heading back.

### Practicalities

The quickest and simplest way of getting to Enryaku-ji is to take a **direct bus** (1hr; ¥800) from either Kyoto Station or Sanjō-Keihan Station in east Kyoto. The timetable varies according to the season, so check in Kyoto for the latest schedule, and note that in winter the road is sometimes closed by snow. Enryaku-ji lies about 800m above sea level and can get pretty chilly in winter. Even in summer, you'll find it noticeably cooler than Kyoto.

The alternative is one of two **cable cars** up the mountain. The most convenient of these is the eastern **Sakamoto Cable** (every 30min; 11min; ¥840, or ¥1570 return), which has the added benefit of views over Biwa-ko. To reach the cable car, take a JR Kosei line train from Kyoto Station to Hiei-zan Sakamoto Station (every 15min; 20min; ¥320), then a bus (¥210). From the top station it's a 700m-walk north to the central Tō-tō area along a quiet road. The main disadvantage of the western, **Eizan Cable** (every 30min; 20min; ¥840 one way, or ¥1640 return) is that it dumps you about 1500m away from the Tō-tō at the Sanchō Station, from where you can catch a shuttle bus (see below), or walk along a footpath from behind the ski-lift. However, it's slightly cheaper, especially if you've got a bus pass covering Kyoto's outer districts (see p.431). Eizan Cable leaves from near Yase-yūen Station; to get there, either take a Kyoto Bus headed for Ōhara, or a train on the private Eizan line from Kyoto's Demachiyanagi Station (every 12min; 13min; ¥250).

Once you've arrived on the mountain, the best way to get around is on foot. If you're in a hurry, however, **shuttle buses** run during most of the year from Sanchō via the central Tō-tō car park to Sai-tō and Yokawa (March 20–Dec 1; every 30min). The whole journey only takes about twenty minutes and costs ¥740. If you plan to use this bus a lot, buy a one-day pass (*Hiei-zannai ichi-nichi jyōshaken*; ¥900) from the bus driver or at the Tō-tō bus terminal. The pass allows unlimited travel and also entitles you to a ¥100 discount on the entrance to Enryaku-ji.

## Ōhara

Though only a short bus ride from Kyoto, the collection of temples that makes up **ŌHARA** is almost in a different world. They are all sub-temples of Enryaku-ji (see p.469), but the atmosphere here is quite different; instead of stately cedar forests, these little temples are surrounded by maples and flower-filled gardens, fed by tumbling streams. The sights are divided into two sections: the easterly **Sanzen-in** and the melancholy **Jakkō-in** across the rice-fields.

### The temples

From the Ōhara bus terminal, cross over the main road and follow the lane leading east, uphill beside a small river and between stalls selling "beefsteak-leaf" tea (*shiso-cha*), mountain vegetables and other local produce. At the top of the steps, roughly ten minutes from the bus terminal, a fortress-like wall on the left contains Ōhara's most important temple, **Sanzen-in** (daily 8.30am–4/4.30pm; ¥550). It's said to have been founded by Saichō, the founder of Tendai Buddhism but it's main point of interest is the twelfth-century **Hon-dō**, a small but splendid building standing on its own in a mossy garden. Inside is an astonishingly well-preserved tenth-century Amida Buddha flanked by smaller statues of Kannon (on the right as you face them) and Seishi which were added later.

The hillside behind Sanzen-in is covered with hydrangeas, at their best in June, but at other times of year walk back past the entrance and north along the lane a short distance to **Jikkō-in** (daily 9am–5pm; ¥500, including green tea). This monastery's prime attraction is a quiet garden, landscaped in the late Edo period, fringed by a row of tufted pines. It also houses a collection of antique musical instruments.

Continuing north, the lane takes a sharp left in front of **Shōrin-in** (daily 9am–5pm; ¥200) where, if you're lucky you might hear monks chanting, though it's generally deserted. The large hall, reconstructed in the 1770s and containing another image of Amida, is used for studying *shōmyō*, Buddhist incantations practised by followers of Tendai. *Shōmyō* were first introduced from China in the eighth century and have had a profound influence on music in Japan; some temples have CDs for sale if you're interested in hearing more.

The last temple in this section, **Hōsen-in** (daily 9am–5pm; ¥500, including green tea) lies at the end of the lane, on the left. Like Jikkō-in, it's the garden that you've really come to see, this one much more enclosed and almost swamped by a magnificent, aged pine and a lovely maple. The attendants will give you a brief history of the temple while you sip tea.

The last of Ōhara's temples lies on the other side of the main road. Walk back past the bus terminal and across the valley floor, following the main river southwest for a while before turning northwest up a tributary – signposts are erratic. After about fifteen minute's walk, look out on the right for some old stone steps leading to **Jakkō-in** (daily 9am–5pm; ¥500). The oldest temple in the area, Jakkō-in was founded in 594 AD, by Prince Shōtoku (see p.480) in honour of his father, Emperor Yōmei. It's an attractive spot, with its pond-garden and gurgling waterfall, but if you detect a note of sadness in the air, it's not surprising. Jakkō-in is most famous as the nunnery where **Empress Kenreimon-in**, the only surviving member of the Taira clan after the battle of Dannoura (see p.771), lived out her life. At the end of the naval battle, in 1185, as her clan's armies were slaughtered by the Minamoto, she watched her son and her mother drown. Kenreimon-in tried to follow them but she was plucked out of the sea by a Minamoto sailor and eventually made her way to Jakkō-in to mourn until her death in 1213.

The temple has been rebuilt on occasion but otherwise remains much as it was in those days. In the main hall, Kenreimon-in's statue sits in prayer, to the left as you're facing the altar, her legendary beauty apparent even beneath the white cowl. The woman to the right is the Empress's loyal lady-in-waiting, Awa no Naiji.

### Practicalities

To reach Ōhara from central Kyoto, take a cream-and-red **Kyoto Bus** either from Kyoto Station (#17 & #18), Sanjō-Keihan Station (#16) or Kita-ōji Station (#15). The journey takes between thirty and fifty minutes and costs a maximum of ¥600, or you can use the Kyoto-wide subway and bus pass (see p.431). The route takes you past Yaseyūen, the starting point of the Eizan cable car up Hiei-zan (see p.473), making it possible to visit both places in one rather hectic day.

There are numerous small **restaurants** in Ōhara, but one of the nicest places to eat is *Seryō* (daily 11am–5pm), which you'll find at the top of the steps up to Sanzen-in, on the left. They serve a beautifully presented *bentō* of seasonal vegetables (¥3000) as well as more expensive meals; in good weather you can eat outside on a riverside terrace. If you want to enjoy Ōhara once the crowds have gone, they also run a fine **ryokan** with a choice of *tatami* or Western-style rooms (☎075/744-2301; ⑦, including two meals).

# Arashiyama

At its western edge, the modern city of Kyoto ends in a pleasant, leafy suburb beside the Hozu-gawa. **ARASHIYAMA** was originally a place for imperial relaxation, but the palaces were later converted into Buddhist temples and monasteries. The most famous of these is **Tenryū-ji**, noted for its garden, while the smaller, quieter temples have a more intimate appeal. In contrast with Tenryū-ji's somewhat introspective garden, that of **Ōkōchi Sansō** – the home of a 1920s movie actor – is by turns secretive and dramatic, with its winding paths and sudden views over Kyoto. For a break from temples and gardens, take the little Torokko train tootling up the Hozu valley to **Kameoka**, from where boats ferry you back down the fairly gentle **Hozu rapids**.

A good way to explore the area is to rent a bike and spend a day pottering around the lanes and through magnificent bamboo forests. Or, if you're pushed for time, you can combine Arashiyama with the sights of western Kyoto (see p.450). Note that central Arashiyama can get unbearably crowded, particularly on spring and autumn weekends. Just head north along the hillside, however, and you'll soon begin to leave the crowds behind.

## Temples and gardens

Arashiyama is centred on the long **Togetsu-kyō** bridge which spans the Hozu-gawa (known as the Katsura-gawa east of the bridge). This is a famous spot for viewing spring cherry blossoms or maples in autumn, and is also the scene of night-time fishing expeditions using cormorants. An ancient, ingenious method of catching fish (see box on p.397), **cormorant fishing** (*ukai*) still takes place at Arashiyama in summer; boats depart for an hour-long fishing trip (July & Aug 7pm & 8pm, Sept 1–15 7.30pm; ¥1700) from the river's north bank just upstream from the bridge.

The town's most interesting sights, as well as the majority of its shops, restaurants and transport facilities, lie north of the Hozu-gawa. First of these is the Zen temple of **Tenryū-ji** (daily 8.30am–5/5.30pm; ¥600, or ¥500 for the garden only) which started life as the country retreat of Emperor Kameyama (1260–1274), grandfather of the more famous **Emperor Go-Daigo** (1318–1339). Go-daigo overthrew the Kamakura Shogunate (see p.771) and wrested power back to Kyoto in 1333 with the help of a defector from the enemy camp, **Ashikaga Takauji**. The ambitious Takauji soon grew exasperated at Go-Daigo's incompetence and staged a counter coup. He placed a puppet emperor on the throne and had himself declared shogun, thus also gaining the Arashiyama palace, while Go-Daigo fled south to set up a rival court in Yoshino, south of Nara. After Go-Daigo died in 1339, however, a series of bad omens convinced Takauji to convert the palace into a temple to appease Go-Daigo's restless soul.

The temple buildings are nearly all twentieth-century reproductions, but the **garden** behind dates back to at least the thirteenth century. It's best viewed from inside the temple, from where you get the full impact of the pond and its artfully placed rock groupings against the tree-covered hillside. The present layout of the garden is the work of **Musō Kokushi**, the fourteenth-century Zen monk also responsible for Saihō-ji (see p.456), who incorporated Zen and Chinese motifs into the existing garden. There's still an argument, however, over who created the garden's most admired feature, the dry, Dragon Gate waterfall on the far side of the pond. Apparently inspired by Chinese Sung-dynasty landscape paintings, the waterfall's height and bold vertical composition are extremely unusual in Japanese garden design.

When you've had your fill, follow the paths through the garden to its back (north) entrance where you'll emerge into some of the bamboo groves for which Arashiyama is renowned. Heading northwest along the hillside, look out on the left for the entrance to **Ōkōchi Sansō** (daily 9am–5pm; ¥900 including green tea), just before you reach the train tracks. This was once the home of Ōkōchi Denjirō, a silent-movie idol of the 1920s, who chose a spectacular location for his traditional Japanese villa. The route takes you winding all over the hillside, past tea ceremony pavilions, a moss garden, a dry garden and convenient stone benches, up to a ridge with views over Kyoto on one side and the Hozu gorge on the other. Finally, you drop down to a small museum devoted to the actor.

From here continue north past Torokko Arashiyama Station, where you can join the train for Kameoka (see below), and keep following the attractive lanes along the hillside. After passing two minor temples, Jōjakkō-ji and Nison-in, a left turn leads up to **Giō-ji** (daily 9am–5pm; ¥300). Giō-ji, a pretty little Buddhist nunnery, with a mossy, maple-shaded garden and more bamboo groves, is named after one of its former inhabitants. Princess Giō was concubine to the notoriously ruthless Taira Kiyomori (1118–1181), who was head of the Taira clan and effective ruler of Japan for a number of years. On falling from favour, Giō came to Arashiyama to drown her sorrows, bringing along her mother, sister and a friend. Their statues are on display in a small pavilion – from the left, Giō's mother, Giō, her sister and her friend – alongside a Buddha image and Kiyomori half-hidden from view.

While the lanes carry on along the hills, the last two sights in Arashiyama – both of moderate interest – are off to the west. It's only worth popping into **Seiryō-ji** (daily 9am–4pm; ¥300), 1km from Giō-ji, on the eighth day of the month when the statue of Shaka Nyorai (the Historical Buddha) is on show. The image was carved in China in 985 AD as a copy of a much older, Indian statue which in turn was said to have been modelled on the Buddha while he was alive. The rest of the time you'll have to be content with his internal organs – when the statue was opened in 1953, they found several little silk bags in the shape of a heart, kidneys and liver, which are now on display in the temple museum. One kilometre northeast from here, the more impressive **Daikaku-ji** (daily 9am–4.30pm; ¥500) was founded in 876 when Emperor Saga ordered that his country villa be converted to a Shingon-sect temple. The main Shin-den hall was moved here from Kyoto's Imperial Palace in the late sixteenth century and still contains some fine screens painted by renowned artists of the Kanō school. Behind this building, the Shoshin-den is also noted for its panels of a hawk and an endearing group of rabbits. Afterwards you can wander along the banks of Ōsawa-ike, Emperor Saga's boating lake.

## Along the Hozu-gawa

Northwest of Arashiyama the **Hozu-gawa** flows through a fairly narrow, twisting gorge just over 15km long. It's a popular, though fairly costly, half-day excursion to take the old-fashioned Torokko train upriver to **Kameoka** and come back down by boat. You can board the train at Torokko Arashiyama Station, just north of Ōkōchi Sansō (see previous page), or at the Torokko Saga terminus one stop further east. Wherever you get on it's the same price (¥600 one way) for the 25-minute journey which takes you through tunnels and criss-crosses the river. It's a good idea to reserve seats in advance during the main holiday periods, especially when the cherries and autumn colours are at their peak, though at other times you should be able to buy tickets on the day. Reservations can be made through JTB and other major travel agents, at JR's Green Windows or by phone direct to Torokko (☎075/861-7444). Trains leave hourly between 9.25am and 5.25pm.

At the Torokko Kameoka terminus buses wait to take you to the landing stage (15min; ¥280), from where fairly chunky, wooden **punts** set off down the Hozu-gawa on the *Hozu-gawa Kudari* (at least four daily; ¥3900). The **rapids** aren't the most fearsome in the world, but it's a fun trip and the gorge is that much more impressive from water level. Back in Arashiyama, the boats land on the river's north bank just short of the Togetsu bridge. Regular **sightseeing boats** depart from this same landing stage for a very over-priced thirty-minute jaunt to the mouth of the gorge (¥1100 per person), or you can rent your own three-person rowboat for ¥1400 per hour.

## Practicalities

Three train lines and several bus routes connect Arashiyama with central Kyoto. Unless you've got a bus or JR rail pass, the quickest and nicest way to get here is to take a **train** on the private Keifuku Electric Railway from Kyoto's Shijō-Ōmiya Station (every 10min; 20min; ¥230). This brings you into the main Arashiyama Station in the centre of town. Keifuku offers a one-day pass (¥650) covering unlimited travel on this Arashiyama line and also the Keifuku Kitano line which connects with Kitano-Hakubai-chō Station in northwest Kyoto. Alternatively, the JR Sagano line runs from Kyoto Station to Saga Station (every 20min; 20min; ¥230), which is handy for the Torokko trains, but it's roughly fifteen minutes' walk to central Arashiyama from here; make sure you get on a local JR train and not the express which shoots straight through. Finally, there's the less convenient Hankyū Electric Railway; from central Kyoto you have to change at Katsura Station, and you end up in the Hankyū Arashiyama Station on the south side of the river.

**Buses** are slightly more expensive and take longer, especially when the traffic's bad. However, Arashiyama is on the main Kyoto bus network and falls within the limits for the combined bus and subway pass (see p.431). City Bus routes #11, #28 and #93, and Kyoto Bus routes #61, #71, #72 and #73 all pass through central Arashiyama.

If you plan to do more than just the central sights, it's worth considering **bike rental**. There are rental outlets at each of the train stations (¥800–¥1000 per day).

### ACCOMMODATION

If you want **to stay** out here, the nicest option is *Minshuku Tsujimura* (☎075/861/3207, fax 862-0820; ⑤). It's a small, tidy place, with *tatami* rooms and shared washing facilities, located a few minutes west of JR Saga Station – walk along the north side of the tracks to find it just across a small river.

Kameoka's **Hosen-ji Zen Centre**, 52 Nakajō, Yamamoto Shino chō, Kameoka (☎ & fax 0771/22-3649; Web site *www.jin.zen.or.jp/~kyotozen*; ②), offers accommodation and the chance to study Zen. They'll accept anyone who is interested in experiencing temple life, as long as you're prepared to join in with everything from chanting sutras at 5.30am and *zazen* meditation, to cleaning and helping in the garden. Rates are per person in dormitory accommodation and include three meals. The Centre is located fifteen minutes' walk from JR Umahori Station on the Sagano line. Reservations are essential.

### RESTAURANTS

Arashiyama is famous for its Buddhist vegetarian cuisine, *shōjin-ryōri*, and particularly for *yudōfu* (simmered tofu) which is closely associated with the Zen tradition. Of several **restaurants** serving *shōjin ryōri*, Tenryū-ji's *Shigetsu* (daily 11am–2pm; ☎075/881-1235) offers the best surroundings, though you're a bit on public display. There's a choice of three meals (from ¥3150) and reservations are recommended; note that if you're eating in the restaurant, the temple's ¥600 entry fee will be waived. A good alternative is *Sagano* (daily 11am–7pm; ☎075/871-6946) which is a cheerful little place buried in a bamboo grove south of Tenryū-ji. Their *yudōfu* set meal, with lots of sauces and non-meat side dishes, costs ¥3500. But the town's most famous restaurant is undoubtedly *Nishiki* (daily except Tues 11am–7.30pm; ☎075/871-8888) which is located on the low island in the middle of the Hozu-gawa. They specialize in Kyoto cuisine, whose subtle flavours and exquisite presentation follow a seasonal theme; course menus start at ¥3800. Though not too busy on weekdays, it's a good idea to reserve at weekends. Arashiyama also has plenty of cheaper places to eat, mostly clustered around the main station.

# Uji

Thirty minutes' train ride south of Kyoto, **UJI** doesn't look particularly promising as you cross its broad, fast-flowing river among the electricity pylons and industrial suburbs. However, the town has a long, illustrious past and boasts one of Japan's most fabulous buildings, the **Byōdō-in** – for a preview, look at the reverse side of a ¥10 coin. Somehow this eleventh-century hall, with its glorious statue of Amida Buddha, survived war, fire and years of neglect and preserves a stunning display of Heian-period art at its most majestic. Unfortunately, there's not a lot else to do in Uji, except sample their famous green tea; since the fourteenth century this area's tea leaves have been rated among the best in the country. Most people visit Uji on a half-day excursion from Kyoto, but it's only a little bit further from Nara (see opposite).

## Byōdō-in

Arriving at JR Uji station, cross over the main road and turn left along the next, parallel, road for a quieter route down to the Uji-gawa. Just before the bridge – a modern successor to the seventh-century original – turn right on to a narrow shopping street and follow the river southeast through a fragrant haze of roasting tea. Then, where the lane forks left onto the embankment, continue straight ahead and you'll find the entrance to the **Byōdō-in** (daily: March–Nov 8.30am–5.30pm; Jan, Feb & Dec 9-4.30; ¥500), roughly ten minutes' walk from the station.

After the imperial capital moved to Kyoto in 794 AD, Uji became a popular location for aristocratic country retreats. One such villa was taken over in the late tenth century by the emperor's chief advisor, **Fujiwara Michinaga**, when the Fujiwara clan was at its peak (see History, p.770). His son, Yorimichi, continued developing the gardens and pavilions until they were the envy of the court. Those pavilions have long gone, but you can still catch a flavour of this golden age through the great literary masterpiece, *The Tale of Genji* (see Books, p.818), written in the early eleventh century. The book's final chapters are set in Uji which the authoress, Murasaki Shikibu, would have known intimately – a distant relative of Fujiwara Michinaga, she served as lady-in-waiting to his daughter, Empress Akiko. In 1052, some years after *The Genji* was completed, Yorimichi decided to convert the villa into a temple dedicated to Amida, the Buddha of the Western Paradise. By the following year the great Amida Hall, popularly known as the **Phoenix Hall** (*Hōō-dō*) was completed. Miraculously, it's the only building from the original temple to have survived.

The best place to view the Phoenix Hall is from the far side of the pond in which it sits on a small island. The hall itself is surprisingly small, but the architect has added two completely ornamental wings which extend in a broad U, like a pair of open arms. The whole ensemble is in perfect balance, while the little turrets, upward-sweeping roofs and airy, open spaces create a graceful, almost gossamer-light structure which appears to float on the reflecting water. A third corridor extends west behind the main hall, giving the building its distinctive, bird-like ground plan from which its name is said to derive. However, the phoenix is also an ancient Chinese image of rebirth, which is what this building, and its now much-diminished garden, represents. According to Buddhist teachings, Amida promised to save all souls who faithfully beseech his name and to lead them to the Pure Land, the Western Paradise. The splendour of the hall and the images inside are all reminders of that promise of ultimate salvation.

The gilded statue of **Amida** dominates the hall. It was created by a sculptor-priest called Jōchō, using a new method of slotting together carved blocks of wood, and is in remarkably fine condition. Interestingly, at this time Chinese influence in Japan was waning and artists were establishing a fresh, purely Japanese stylistic form. Already, the statue's gentle expression and softer, more human body set it apart from earlier Buddhist images. Again the impression is one of Amida floating on his lotus throne – a clever, stylistic trick in which a narrow pedestal supports four layers of gilded petals in strict alignment rather than the normal staggered arrangement. A golden, flaming halo, decorated with twelve, barely visible Bodhisattvas, swoops up behind the statue to a richly decorated canopy inlaid with mother-of-pearl.

At one time the hall must have been a riot of colour, but now only a few traces of the **wall paintings** remain, most of which are reproductions. If you look very carefully, you can just make out faded images of Amida and a host of heavenly beings descending on billowing clouds to receive the faithful. Meanwhile the white, upper walls are decorated with a unique collection of 52 carved bodhisattvas, which were also painted at one time. Each delicate, wooden figure rides a wisp of clouds, and they're all busy either dancing, playing an instrument, praying or carrying religious symbols.

The original wall paintings, as well as the temple bell and two phoenixes, are now preserved in a modern **treasure hall** (*Hōmotsu-kan*; ¥300) on a hill behind the Phoenix Hall. Unfortunately, the treasures only go on view in spring and autumn, but if you get the chance, it's worth seeing the artwork close up. These are now the oldest examples of the emerging Yamato-e style of painting (see p.792) still in existence.

On the opposite, north side of the temple compound, the twelfth-century **Kannon-dō** houses a gently smiling statue of the eleven-headed Kannon, while behind it you'll find a fenced-off triangle of grass. This **"fan-shaped lawn"** is revered as the place where Minamoto Yorimasa, a valiant warrior of the Genpei Wars (see p.771), committed ritual suicide in 1180, at the age of 76. After a bitter struggle, his small army was completely overrun when the rival Taira army swept across the river. Yorimasa retreated inside the temple gates and, while his son held off the attackers, penned a quick poem on his war fan before disembowling himself. His words: "How sad that the old fossil tree should die without a single blooming."

### Practicalities

Uji lies on the JR Nara line between Kyoto and Nara, with **trains** roughly every fifteen minutes from Kyoto (15–30min) and every twenty minutes from Nara (30–50min). There's a **tourist information office** (daily 9am–5pm; ☎0774/23-3334) further along the river bank from the Byōdō-in, next door to a traditional **teahouse**, the *Taiho-an*, where you can try Uji's famous green tea (Feb 1–Dec 20 daily 10am–4pm; ¥500). On summer evenings the river here is used for demonstrations of **cormorant fishing** (see p.397); it's best experienced from one of the boats (mid June–early Sept 7–8.30pm; ¥1800).

In fine weather it's a nice idea to buy a *bentō* and eat it on the little island in the Uji-gawa. You'll find plenty of snack shops and **restaurants** as you walk down from the station, but *Magozaemon*, opposite the entrance to the Byōdō-in, has especially good and inexpensive handmade noodle dishes – try their green-tea udon, either hot or cold.

# Nara and around

Before Kyoto became the capital of Japan in 794 AD, this honour was held by **NARA**, a town some 35km further south in an area which is regarded as the birthplace of Japanese civilization. During this period, particularly the seventh and eighth centuries, Buddhism became firmly established within Japan under the patronage of court nobles who sponsored magnificent temples and works of art, many of which have survived to this day. Fortunately, history subsequently left Nara largely to its own devices and it's now a relaxed, attractive place set against a backdrop of wooded hills. Its greatest draw is undoubtedly the monumental bronze Buddha of **Tōdai-ji**, while **Kōfuku-ji** and several of the smaller temples boast outstanding collections of Buddhist statuary. However, even these are outclassed by the images housed in **Hōryū-ji**, a temple to the southwest of Nara, which also claims the world's oldest wooden building. The nearby temples of **Yakushi-ji** and **Tōshōdai-ji** contain yet more early masterpieces of Japanese art and architecture.

Nara has the added attraction of packing all these sights into a fairly compact space. The central area is easily explored on foot, and can just about be covered in a long day,

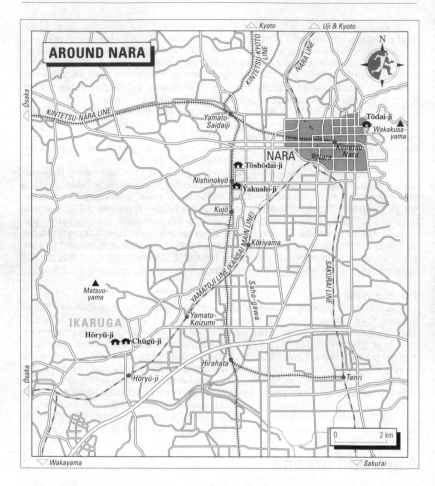

with the more distant temples fitting into a second day's outing. Many people visit Nara on a day-trip from Kyoto, but it more than deserves an overnight stop, not least to enjoy it once the crowds have gone. If at all possible, try to avoid Nara on Sundays and national holidays.

## Some history

During the fifth and sixth centuries a sophisticated culture evolved in the plains east of Ōsaka, an area known as **Yamato**. Close contact between Japan, Korea and China saw the introduction of Chinese script, technology and the Buddhist religion, as well as Chinese ideas on law and administration. Under these influences, the regent **Prince Shōtoku** (574–622) established a strictly hierarchical system of government. However, he's probably best remembered as a devout Buddhist who founded numerous temples, amongst them the great **Hōryū-ji**. Though Shōtoku's successors continued the process of centralization, they were hampered by the practice of relocating the court after each emperor died. In 710 AD, therefore, it was decided to establish a permanent capital modelled on China's imperial city, Chang'an (today's Xi'an). The name chosen for this new city was **Heijō**, "Citadel of Peace", today known as **Nara**.

In fact Heijō lasted little more than seventy years, but it was a glorious period, which saw Japanese culture beginning to take shape. A frenzy of building and artistic creativity culminated in the unveiling of the great bronze Buddha in **Tōdai-ji** temple by **Emperor Shōmu** in 752 AD. But beneath the surface, things were starting to unravel. As the temples became increasingly powerful, so the monks began to dabble in politics until one Dōkyō seduced a former empress and tried to seize the throne in 769. In an attempt to escape such shenanigans, Emperor Kammu decided to move the court out of Nara in 784 and eventually founded Kyoto.

## Arrival, information and city transport

Nara has two, competing **train stations**: JR Nara Station, on the west side of the town centre, and the private Kintetsu-Nara Station right in the thick of things. Arriving **from Kyoto**, the quickest option is a Limited Express train on the private Kintetsu-Kyoto line (every 30min; 33min; ¥1110); the ordinary express takes a little longer and you have to change at Yamato-Saidaiji (1–2 hourly; 45min; ¥610). JR also has a choice of express trains (8 daily; 45min; ¥740) and regular trains (every 30min; 1hr 20min; ¥740) from Kyoto. Travelling **from Ōsaka**, trains on the private Kintetsu-Nara line (from Ōsaka's Kintetsu-Namba Station) arrive at the Kintetsu-Nara Station (every 15min; 35–50min; ¥540–1040). Alternatively, take a JR line train from Ōsaka Station (every 20min; 40min; ¥780), or from JR Namba Station (every 20min; 30–40min; ¥740) to JR Nara Station. If you're coming here **from Kansai International airport**, you can go into central Ōsaka to pick up a train, or hop on a limousine bus (hourly; 1hr 35min; ¥1800) which stops at both Nara's train stations.

Nara is also well provided with **information offices**. The most useful of these is the Nara City Tourist Information Centre (daily 9am–9pm; ☎0742/22-3900) located on Sanjō-dōri. They have English-speaking staff, plentiful **maps** and information, and can also help arrange volunteer "Goodwill Guides" (see p.23). There's also an office in the JR Station (daily 9am–5pm; ☎0742/22-9821), again with English-speaking staff who can, in this case, make hotel bookings, and another in the Kintetsu Station (daily 9am–5pm; ☎0742/24-4858). Finally, there's a small booth on the hill above the Sarusawa pond (daily 9am–5pm; ☎0742/26-1991), on the eastern edge of central Nara. The Nara City office carries some information about **what's on**, as does the region-wide magazine, *Kansai Time Out* (see p.410).

### City transport

The centre of Nara is small enough to be covered on foot, though you'll need to use local **buses** for some of the more far-flung sights. The main terminuses are outside the JR and Kintetsu-Nara train stations. Nearly all the timetables and route maps are in Japanese, but the one-sheet "Nara Sightseeing Map" available at the tourist offices has a summary of the most useful routes. The standard fare is ¥180 within the city centre, which you usually pay as you get on, though buses going out of central Nara employ a ticket system – take a numbered ticket as you board and pay the appropriate fare on exit. If you're heading for the sights around Nara, there are a range of bus passes, of which the most helpful is the *Nara Nishinokyō Ikaruga Furii-ken* (¥1600). This covers unlimited travel for one day in central Nara and the western districts, including Hōryū-ji, Yakushi-ji and Tōshōdai-ji. You can buy the pass in the Nara Kōtsu bus office (daily 8.30am–6pm) across Ōmiya-dōri from the Kintetsu train station.

Nara Kōtsu (☎0742/22-5263) runs a number of **bus tours** where you'll be given a cassette recorder with taped information in English. Again, the tours covering the surrounding sights are most useful: a full day-trip round the Nishinokyō and Ikaruga areas, for example, costs ¥6560. JTB's Sunrise Tours (☎075/341-1413) also offers half-day excursions to Nara from Kyoto and Ōsaka. They're accompanied by an English-speaking guide, but only cover Tōdai-ji and Kasuga Taisha.

Another option for central Nara is **bike rental**. You'll find Eki Rent-a-cycle (daily 9am–5pm; ¥1000 per day) outside the JR Station and Sunflower Rent-a-cycle (daily 9am–5pm; ¥1000–¥1200 per day, or ¥2000 for two days) southeast of the Kintetsu Station.

## Accommodation

To make the most of Nara it's best to stay at least one night, which gives you some unusual **accommodation** options, ranging from a former *geisha* house to the grand old *Nara Hotel*. There's plenty of choice within the city centre but you'll need to book ahead at weekends and during the spring and autumn peaks. Note that the smarter places tend to put their rates up at these times.

**Hotel Fujita**, 47-1 Sanjō-chō (☎0742/23-8111, fax 22-0255). A reasonably smart, surprisingly affordable business hotel right on Sanjō-dōri. The rooms are nothing exciting, but they're all comfortable and en suite. ⑤.

**Ryokan Hakuhō**, 4-1 Kamisanjō-chō (☎0742/26-7891, fax 26-7893). This friendly little guest house on Sanjō-dōri offers a choice of *tatami* rooms with or without bath. Slightly aged, but reasonable value for the location. ④–⑤.

**Kotton 100%**, 1122-21 Bodai-chō, Takabatake (☎0742/22-1717). The rooms are small and rather worn, but this place is located on the edge of Nara-kōen, just east of Sarusawa-ike. ⑤.

**Ryokan Matsumae**, 28-1 Higashi-Terabyashi-chō (☎0742/22-3686, fax 26-3927). Welcoming ryokan in an interesting area south of Sarusawa-ike. The spruce, Japanese-style rooms come with or without private bathrooms. ④–⑤.

**Nara Hotel**, Nara Deer Park (☎0742/26-3300, fax 23-5252). Nara's top hotel occupies a stylish, Meiji-era building, set in its own gardens within Nara-kōen. Ask for a room in the old wing for the full works – high ceilings, fireplaces, period furniture and the original baths. ⑦.

**Nara Youth Hostel**, 1716 Horen-chō (☎0742/22-1334, fax 22-1335). Large, modern hostel with dormitory rooms and good facilities, though a little soulless. Check in is from 4.30pm and there's a 10pm curfew. The hostel's in northwest Nara, ten minutes' bus ride (bus #108, #109, #111, #115 or #130) from either the JR or Kintetsu stations; get off at the Shieikujō stop in front of the hostel. ①.

**Nara-ken Seishōnen Kaikan Youth Hostel**, 72-7 Ikenoue Handa, Hiraki-chō (☎ & fax 0742/22-5540). You're assured of a friendly welcome at the Nara Prefecture hostel, located in a residential area just behind the main *Nara Youth Hostel* (see above). They also offer very reasonable bike rental (¥300 per day). Again there are several buses from the stations (#12, #13, #131, #140) which will drop you at the Ikuei Gakuen-mae stop, five minutes' walk from the hostel. Room ②. Dorm ①.

**Ryokan Seikan-sō**, 29 Higashi-Kitsuji-chō (☎ & fax 0742/22-2670). Though it's a little out of the centre and the rooms are a bit frayed, this old ryokan has a lovely atmosphere and a colourful past – half of it was once a *geisha* house. It's in the Nara-machi area, about ten minutes' walk south of Sanjō-dōri. ④.

**Hotel Sunroute**, Bodai-chō, Takabatake (☎0742/22-5151, fax 27-3759). A standard business hotel in a prime location overlooking Sarusawa-ike. The rooms are all Western-style with en-suite bathrooms and of a fairly decent size, though not brilliant value. ⑥.

## The City

More a large town than a city, Nara is an enjoyable place to explore. There are plentiful English-language signs, the grid street-system makes for easy navigation, and the main sights are all gathered on the city's eastern edge in the green expanse of **Nara-kōen**. The route outlined below starts with the most important temples, **Kōfuku-ji** and **Tōdai-ji**, before ambling south along the eastern hills. Here you'll find a sprinkling of second-tier sights, including Nara's holiest shrine, **Kasuga Taisha**, and splendid displays of Buddhist statuary in two historic temples, **Sangatsu-dō** and **Shin-Yakushi-ji**.

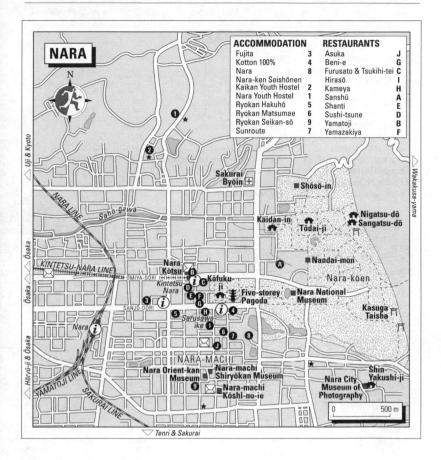

With an extra hour or two to spare, it's worth wandering the streets of southerly **Nara-machi**, a traditional merchants' quarter where some attractive, old shophouses have been converted into museums and craft shops.

## Nara-kōen

The most pleasant route into **Nara-kōen** is along Sanjō-dōri, which cuts across the central district and brings you out near Sarasuwa-ike with the **Five-Storey Pagoda** rising from the trees to your left. The pagoda belongs to **Kōfuku-ji** which in the eighth century was one of Nara's great temples. It was founded in 669 AD by a member of the Fujiwara clan, and moved to its present location when Nara became the new capital in 710. For a while it prospered greatly, but when the Fujiwara star began to fade in the twelfth century, Kōfuku-ji lost its powerful patrons and now only a handful of buildings remain from that period. But the prime draw here is the fine collection of Buddhist statues contained in the Tōkon-dō (daily 9am–5pm; ¥300) and the Kokuhōkan (same hours; ¥500).

The **Tōkon-dō**, a fifteenth-century hall to the north of the Five-Storey Pagoda, is dominated by a large image of Yakushi Nyorai, the Buddha of Healing. He's flanked by three bodhisattvas, the Four Heavenly Kings and the Twelve Heavenly Generals, all beady-eyed guardians of the faith, some of which date from the eighth century. Perhaps the most interesting statue, though, is the seated figure of Yuima Koji to the left of Yakushi Nyorai; depicting an ordinary mortal rather than a celestial being, it's a beautifully realistic portrait.

Meanwhile, the modern **Kokuhōkan** is a veritable treasure trove of early Buddhist statues. The most famous image is the standing figure of **Ashura**, one of Buddha's eight protectors, instantly recognizable from his three, red-tinted heads and six spindly arms. Look out, too, for his companion Karura (Garuda) with his beaked head. Though they're not all on display at the same time, these eight protectors are considered to be the finest dry-lacquer images of the Nara period. Surprisingly, the large, **bronze Buddha head**, with its fine, crisp features, comes from an even earlier period. Apart from a crumpled left ear, the head is in remarkably good condition considering that the original, complete statue was stolen by Kōfuku-ji's warrior priests from another temple sometime during the Heian period (794–1185). Then, after a fire destroyed its body, the head was buried beneath the replacement Buddha, only to be rediscovered in 1937 during renovation work.

From Kōfuku-ji you can stroll generally northeast through the park, towards Tōdai-ji. The large, grassy area is kept trim by more than a thousand semi-wild **deer**. They were originally regarded as divine messengers of one of Kasuga-jinja's Shinto gods, and anyone who killed a deer was liable to be dispatched shortly after. During World War II the numbers dwindled to just seventy beasts, but now they're back with a vengeance – which makes picnicking impossible and presents something of a hazard to young children.

In the midst of the park you'll come across a grey, Western-style building, erected in 1894, which houses the main exhibits of the **Nara National Museum** (Tues–Sun 9am–4.30pm; ¥400, extra for special exhibitions). As you'd imagine, the museum's strong point is its superb collection of statues, of which only a small part is on display at any one time. They're arranged chronologically, so you can trace the development of the various styles, and there's plenty of English-language information available, though the presentation is pretty unexciting. Each autumn (late Oct–early Nov) the museum is closed for two weeks while an exhibition of the **Shōsō-in treasures** takes place in the newer annexe next door. This priceless collection was donated to Tōdai-ji in 756 by Empress Kōmyō, on the death of her husband Emperor Shōmu, and then added to in 950. It contains unique examples of Buddhist art and ritual objects, musical instruments, household utensils, glassware and games, not only from eighth-century Japan but also from China, Korea, India and Persia. The exhibition takes a different theme each year, so what you see is very much the luck of the draw.

## Tōdai-ji

For many people Nara is synonymous with **Tōdai-ji**. This great temple was founded in 745 by **Emperor Shōmu**, ostensibly to ward off the terrible epidemics that regularly swept the nation, but also as a means of cementing imperial power. In doing so he nearly bankrupted his young nation, but the political message came across loud and clear and soon an extensive network of sub-temples spread throughout the provinces, where they played an important role in local administration. It took more than fifteen years to complete Tōdai-ji, which isn't surprising when you learn that the main hall is still the world's largest wooden building. Even so, the present structure (last rebuilt in 1709) is only two-third's the size of the original.

The main entrance to Tōdai-ji lies through the suitably impressive **Nandai-mon**, or Great Southern Gate. Rebuilt in the thirteenth century, it shelters two wonderfully expressive guardian gods (*Niō*), each over 7m tall. Beyond, you begin to see the horned, sweeping roof of the **Daibutsu-den**, the Great Buddha Hall (daily: March–Oct 7.30am–5/5.30pm; Jan, Feb, Nov & Dec 8am–4.30pm; ¥400), which houses Japan's largest bronze statue. A fifteen-metre-tall, blackened figure on a lotus throne, the great Buddha (*Daibutsu*) seems to strain at the very walls of the building. It depicts Rushana (later known as Dainichi Nyorai), the Cosmic Buddha who presides over all levels of the Buddhist universe, and was a phenomenal achievement for the time. Not surprisingly, several attempts at casting the Buddha failed, but in 752 the then retired Emperor Shōmu, his wife Empress Kōmyō and the reigning Empress Kōgen gathered to dedicate the gilded statue by symbolically "opening" its eyes. To achieve this an Indian priest stood on a special platform and "painted" the eyes with a huge brush, from which coloured strings trailed down to the assembled dignitaries, enabling them to participate in the ceremony. Not only were there hundreds of local monks, but also ambassadors from China, India and further afield, bearing an amazing array of gifts, many of which have been preserved in the Shōsō-in treasury – as has the original paint brush.

The Buddha has had a rough time of it since then. As early as the ninth century an earthquake toppled his head, then it and his right hand melted in a fire in 1180, only to be repeated in 1567. As a result only tiny fragments of the original statue remain, but it's hard not be impressed at least by the technological triumph. As you walk round the hall, don't be surprised to see people trying to squeeze through a hole in one of the rear supporting pillars; success apparently reserves you a corner of paradise.

Walk west from the Daibutsu-den compound and you'll find the more modest **Kaidan-in** (daily 7.30/8am–4.30/5pm; ¥400), which was established in 754 as Japan's first, and foremost, ordination hall. It was founded by a Chinese high priest, Ganjin, who Emperor Shōmu hoped would instil some discipline into the rapidly expanding Buddhist priesthood. He had to be patient, however; poor Ganjin's ship eventually arrived on the sixth attempt, by which time the priest was 67 years old and completely blind. His ordination hall was rebuilt in the Edo period, but the statues inside include eighth-century representations of the Four Heavenly Kings (*Shi-Tennō*). These small, beautifully crafted clay figures, each standing on a different demonic beast, protect a diminutive Buddha inside a wooden pagoda.

If you've got time to spare, circle round behind the Daibutsu-den to take a peak at the **Shōsō-in** (Mon–Fri 10am–3pm; free). Though it looks like a modern log-cabin on stilts, this storehouse was erected in the eighth century to hold the massed treasures of Tōdai-ji. Whatever the secret, it preserved them in immaculate condition – as witnessed at the National Museum's annual exhibition (see previous page). Nowdays, however, they're kept in a specially designed concrete repository.

## Along the eastern hills

Two of Tōdai-ji's sub-temples were built on the slopes of Wakakusa-yama, which forms Nara's eastern boundary. Northerly **Nigatsu-dō** offers good views over the city from its wooden terrace, but the next-door **Sangatsu-dō** (daily 8am–4.30/5pm; ¥400) is notable as Nara's oldest building, completed in 729. It also contains another rare collection of eighth-century, dry-lacquer statues. The main image is a dimly lit, gilded figure of Kannon, bearing a silver Amida in its crown, while all around stand gods, guardians, bodhisattvas and other protectors of the faith.

From Sangatsu-dō it's a pleasant stroll south along the Wakakusa hillside, past a handy string of restaurants, and up the lantern-lined approach to **Kasuga Taisha**. Kasuga Grand Shrine was founded in 768 as the tutelary shrine of the Fujiwara family and, for a while, held an important place in Shinto worship; indeed, the emperor still sends a messenger to participate in shrine rituals. As with many shrines, however, there's not a great deal to see unless you happen to coincide with a special service or festival (see p.488). The four sanctuaries, gleaming after their fifty-ninth reconstruction, are just visible in the inner compound, while the thousand beautifully crafted bronze **lanterns** hanging round the outer eaves are easier to admire. Donated over the years by supplicants, they bear intricate designs of deer, wisteria blooms, leaves or geometric patterns. The best time to see them is in early February (Feb 2 & 3) and mid-August (Aug 14 & 15), when these and the nearly two thousand stone lanterns are lit at dusk.

Continuing south through the woods from Kasuga Taisha, cross over the main road into an attractive residential area. Five minutes further on you'll come to the venerable **Shin-Yakushi-ji** (daily 9am–5pm; ¥500). This quiet temple stands in a courtyard full of bush clover, much as it has done for the last 1250 years. It was founded by Empress Kōmyō to pray for Emperor Shōmu's recovery from an eye infection; apparently she had some success since he lived for another decade. Though the hall may not look terribly imposing, it's the original and inside you'll find more Buddhist statues of a similar age. The central image is a plump-faced, slightly cross-eyed Yakushi Nyorai (the Buddha of Healing) carved from one block of cypress wood. He's surrounded by clay statues of the Twelve Heavenly Generals, of which only one has had to be replaced. It's worth the walk just to see their wonderful expressions and innovative hair-dos.

Another good reason for visiting this area is the **Nara City Museum of Photography** (Tues–Sun 9.30am–5pm; ¥500), which lies a few metres west of Shin-Yakushi-ji in a sleek, modern building that's almost totally buried. Its core collection consists of some 80,000 photos by the late Irie Taikichi who spent most of his life capturing Nara and its temples. In addition, there's a fascinating group of 2000 photos of Nara during the Taishō period (1912–1925) taken by Kudo Risaburo. The exhibitions change every three months, but the collection can always be viewed on video in the museum's Hi-Vision gallery.

### Nara-machi

The southern district of central Nara is known as **Nara-machi**. There are no great temples here, but instead an attractive area of traditional shops and lattice-front houses off the main tourist path. The best approach is to start by the southwest corner of willow-fringed Sarusawa-ike, a good spot for views of the Five-Storey Pagoda, and then head south. At the end of the road is an enticing little shop, **Kikuoka-kōge** (closed Mon), selling linen goods and, next door, **Nara-machi Monogatori-kan** (daily 10am–5pm; free) which shows changing exhibitions of local crafts. Turn right (west) in front of these two and you'll find **Nara-machi Shiryōkan** (Tues–Sun 10am–4pm; free), on the next corner. This small museum, marked by strings of red-cloth monkeys hanging outside, occupies the former warehouse of a mosquito-net manufacturer. It's a wonderful jumble of household utensils, shop signboards, Buddhist statues, pots and so forth from the local area.

Turn left (south) beside the Shiryōkan for a collection of oriental art. Exhibits in the **Nara Orient-kan** (Tues–Sun 10am–5pm; ¥300) illustrate the influence of Persian art on Japanese aesthetics during the Nara period. But rather more interesting is the building itself, an old merchant's house consisting of two traditional storehouses (*kura*) linked by a long corridor. Follow this road round to the left and turn south again, past a sub-post office. Just before the next corner the lovingly restored latticed façade of **Nara-machi Kōshi-no-ie** (Tues–Sun 9am–5pm; free) announces one of the area's best-preserved traditional townhouses. Inside, you can see the line of *tatami* rooms off a high-ceilinged corridor, inner courtyard garden and beautiful wooden furniture favoured by successful Edo-period merchants.

You're now near the southern limits of Nara-machi. To return to central Nara, take the next road parallel to the west which will eventually lead to the arcades and Sanjō-dōri. On the way, look out for **Ashibi-no-gō**, an old-style shop selling pickles and tea, where you can also have light meals, and **Esaki** on the corner – unmissable thanks to its jaunty lanterns and shopful of traditional umbrellas.

## Eating

You're rather spoilt for choice when it comes to eating in Nara. The central Higashimuki arcade is the best place to look, or along Sanjō-dōri, where you'll find a range of hamburger joints, coffee shops and a clutch of decent **restaurants** serving classy local cuisine. Like Kyoto, Nara has its own brand of *kaiseki*, the elaborate meals that originally accompanied the tea ceremony, but **local specialities** also include some rather less appetizing dishes. *Cha-ga-yu* evolved from the poor people's breakfast into a fairly expensive delicacy, but there's no escaping the fact that it's basically a thin rice gruel, boiled up with soy beans, sweet potatoes and green tea leaves. It's best as part of a *teishoku*, when the accompaniments add a bit of flavour. *Tororo* is pretty similar: it's thickened grated yam mixed with soy sauce, seaweed and barley, then poured over a bowl of rice – full of protein and rather sticky. Less of an acquired taste is sushi wrapped in persimmon leaves and *Nara-zuke*, vegetables pickled in sake.

**Asuka**, 1 Shonami-chō. A sleek tempura restaurant in the attractive Nara-machi district. At lunchtime you can feast on their beautifully presented *bentō* (¥1600), or menus from around ¥2000. Daily except Wed 11.30am–2.30pm & 5–9.30pm.

**Beni-e**, Higashimuki-dōri. In central Nara, look for this small tempura restaurant on the main arcade tucked down an alley beside Regal Shoes. Sets start at ¥1600 at lunch or around ¥2000 in the evening. Daily except Wed 11.30am–2pm & 5–8.30/9pm.

**Furusato**, 10 Higashimuki-dōri. This unpretentious restaurant serving a range of Japanese foods is hidden behind a traditional sweet shop near the north end of the arcade. There's an English menu, or see what catches your eye in their window display. Tues–Sun 11.30am–8.30pm.

**Hirasō**, 30-1 Imanikadō-chō. Hirasō specializes in persimmon-wrapped sushi, though you'll also find all sorts of other tasty delicacies on the menu. Sushi sets start at ¥790, with more varied meals from around ¥2400, including *cha-ga-yu*. Tues–Sun 11am–9pm.

**Kameya**, 6 Hashimoto-chō. Popular, nicely decorated *okonomiyaki* joint. Prices start at ¥600 and there's an English menu available. Daily except Tues 11am–2pm & 5–9.30pm.

**Sanshū**, Isui-en. *Tororo* won't be everyone's cup of tea, but this is an attractive place to find out, located in an old wooden house overlooking the secluded, Meiji-era Isui-en garden. There are just two meals on the menu: plain *mugi tororo* (¥1200) or *unagi tororo* laced with eels (¥2500). Daily except Tues 11.30am–1.30pm.

**Shanti**, 5 Konishi-chō. If you're craving something hot and spicy, head straight for this cheerful Indian restaurant in the backstreets north of Sanjō-dōri. The thali set is highly recommended for ¥1000. 11.30am–10pm. Closed one Tues each month.

**Sushi-tsune**, Konishi-dōri. Tastefully decorated sushi bar in a traditional building opposite Vivre department store. They do a good-value lunchtime *teishoku* for around ¥1000, as well as *chirashi* (a

---

## FESTIVALS AND ANNUAL EVENTS

Several of Nara's **festivals** have been celebrated for well over a thousand years. Many of these are dignified court dances, though some of the fire rituals are more lively affairs. In spring and autumn the New Public Hall (☎0742/27-2630) in Nara-kōen stages a series of **Nō dramas**, while the biggest cultural event of the year is undoubtedly the autumn exhibition of **Shōsō-in treasures** at the National Museum (see p.485).

**Jan 15 Yama-yaki** (Grass-burning festival). On a winter evening at 6pm, priests from Kōfuku-ji set fire to the grass on Wakakusa-yama – watched by a few hundred firemen. The festival commemorates the settlement of a boundary dispute between Nara's warrior monks.

**March 1–14 O-Taimatsu and O-Mizutori** (Torch lighting and water drawing). A 1200-year-old ceremony which commemorates a priest's dream about Kannon drawing water from a holy well. The climax is on the night of March 13. At around 6.30pm priests on the second-floor veranda light huge torches and scatter sparks over the assembled crowds to protect them from evil spirits. At 2am the priests collect water from the well, after which they whirl more lighted flares round in a frenzied dance.

**May 11 & 12 Takigi Nō.** Outdoor performances of Nō dramas by firelight. At Kōfuku-ji.

**Mid–late Oct Shika-no-Tsunokiri** (Antler cutting). You might want to give Sundays a miss during October. This is the season when the deer in Nara-kōen are wrestled to the ground and have their antlers sawn off by Shinto priests. It all takes place in the Roku-en deer pen, near Kasuga Taisha.

**Dec 17 On-matsuri.** At around midday a grand costume parade sets off from the Prefectural offices to Kasuga Wakamiya-jinja, stopping on the way for various ceremonies. It ends with outdoor performances of Nō and various courtly dances.

box of rice topped with sashimi and vegetables), or individual pieces (from ¥350). Daily except Tues 11am–9.30pm.

**Tsukihi-tei**, 2F, Higashimuki-dōri (☎0742/23-5470). One of the best places to sample Nara *kaiseki* at an affordable price. A full *kaiseki* course starts at ¥6300, with mini-*kaiseki* from ¥4200; reservations are required for your own *tatami* dining room. They also do cheaper *teishoku*. Daily 11am–10pm.

**Yamatoji**, 4F & 5F, 6 Nakasuji-chō. Located above the Nara Kōtsu bus office, these two restaurants offer reasonable-value meals. The fourth floor is an *izakaya*-style place where you can get *cha-ga-yu* for breakfast (¥860) and cheap *teishoku*. Upstairs is smarter, with tempura, *shabu-shabu* and so on (sets from ¥2000). 4F daily 6.30am–8.30am, 11.30am–3pm & 5–10pm. 5F daily 11am–2pm & 5–10pm.

**Yamazakiya**, Higashimuki-dōri. Pleasantly relaxed restaurant behind a pickle shop in the arcade. They offer *kaiseki* cuisine from ¥4000 for a sampler and *cha-ga-yu* (¥2200 for a *teishoku*), or try the excellent-value *Nara bentō* (¥1500). Tues–Sun 11.30am–9pm.

## Listings

**Banks and exchange** You'll find several banks, with foreign exchange desks, including Dai-ichi Bank, Asahi Bank and Nara Bank, on Sanjō-dōri.

**Buses** Long-distance buses for Tokyo (Shinjuku) and Yokohama stop outside both the Kintetsu and JR Nara train stations. Buses for Fukuoka, however, skip the JR station.

**Car rental** Eki Rent-a-car (☎0742/26-3929) is next door to JR Nara Station, while Toyota Rentals (☎0742/26-2229) and Nippon Rent-a-car (☎0742/24-5701) have branches near the Kintetsu Station.

**Hospital** Nara's main hospital is the Sakurai Byōin, 2 Imako-chō (☎0742/26-0277), with a 24hr emergency department. It's located on the main road, Tegai-dōri, northwest of Tōdai-ji.

**Internet access** The NTT Multimedia Gallery, on Sanjō-dōri, offers free Internet connection, plus fax and phone services. Daily 9am–4pm.

**Post offices** Nara's Central Post Office is on Ōmiya-dōri, a fair walk west of centre. It has 24hr mail services, but for other purposes the sub-post offices in the centre of town are more convenient (see map on p.483).

**Shopping** Among a range of local crafts, Nara is particularly renowned for its high-quality *sumi-e* ink, calligraphy brushes (*fude*), tea whisks (*chasen*) and bleached hemp cloth (*sarashi*). You'll find all these on sale along the main shopping streets, or try the Nara Prefectural Commerce, Industry and Tourist Hall, on Ōmiya-dōri to the east of Kintetsu-Nara Station, which stocks the full range of Nara crafts.

**Taxis** The main taxi companies are Kintetsu Taxi (☎0742/22-5501), Hattori Taxi (☎0742/22-5521) and Kai-Nara (☎0742/22-7171).

## Around Nara

Even before Nara was founded, the surrounding plains were sprinkled with burial mounds, palaces and temples. A few of these still survive, of which the most remarkable is **Hōryū-ji**, about 10km southwest of Nara in *Ikaruga* district. In 1993 this temple complex was recognized by UNESCO as a World Heritage Site for its unique collection of Buddhist statues (some of which are now housed in Tokyo's National Museum; see p.118) and its architecture. The temple was founded when Buddhism was gaining a foothold in Japan and its statues and buildings are a fascinating record of the transition from monumental Chinese to a more intimate Japanese artistic style. A supreme example of this is the delicate Miroku Bosatsu statue housed in the **Chūgū-ji** nunnery. Closer to Nara, the two temples of Nishinokyō district, **Yakushi-ji** and **Tōshōdai-ji**, continue the story of the transition from Chinese to Japanese art and architecture.

   The route described below starts at Hōryū-ji and then works back towards Nara. All these temples are served by the same **buses** (routes #52, #97 & #98) from Nara's JR and Kintetsu stations. If you're just doing the journeys outlined here, it's cheaper to buy single tickets. For anything more complicated, however, it would be worth investigating the discount bus passes offered by Nara Kōtsu (see p.481). Note that it's a good idea to take a **flashlight** when visiting Hōryū-ji as the statues can be difficult to see on grey days.

## Hōryū-ji and Chūgū-ji

As you walk round the historic temple of **Hōryū-ji** (daily: April–Oct 8am–5pm; Jan–March, Nov & Dec 8am–4pm; ¥1000), completed in 607 AD, it's worth bearing in mind that Buddhism only really got going in Japan some fifty years earlier. The confident scale of Hōryū-ji and its superb array of Buddhist statues amply illustrate how quickly this imported faith took hold. One of its strongest proponents was Prince Shōtoku (574-622), the then Regent, who founded Hōryū-ji in accordance with the dying wish of his father, Emperor Yōmei. Though the complex burnt down in 670, it was soon rebuilt, making this Japan's oldest-surviving Buddhist temple.

The simplest way of getting to Hōryū-ji from Nara is by **bus** (every 30min; 50min; ¥720); get off at the Hōryū-ji-mae stop. However, JR's Ōsaka-bound trains stop at Hōryū-ji Station (every 10min; 15min; ¥210), from where it's a good twenty-minute walk to the temple on a fairly busy road, or you can wait for a #72 bus (1–2 hourly; 10min; ¥170).

The main approach to Hōryū-ji is from the south, which takes you past the helpful **information centre** (daily 8.30am–6pm; ☎0745/74-6800), where you can pick up English-language maps and look at their displays about the temple. At the end of the wide, tree-lined avenue, Nandai-mon (the Great South Gate) marks the outer enclosure. Inside lies a second, walled compound known as the **Sai-in Garan**, or Western Precinct.

Within the Sai-in Garan's cloister-gallery, the **Five-Storey Pagoda** inevitably catches the eye first. This is Japan's oldest five-tier pagoda, and for a change you can see the statues inside. In this case they're all early-eighth-century clay images, of which the most appealing is that in the north alcove, portraying Buddha entering nirvana watched by a nicely realistic little crowd. But it's actually the right-hand building, the **Kon-dō** (Golden Hall) which is Hōryū-ji's star attraction, the world's oldest wooden structure, dating from the late seventh century. It's not very large, but when you look closely it's a very striking building, with its multi-layered roofs, sweeping eaves and elaborate, second-floor balustrade – the dragons propping up the roof were added later.

Entering the Kon-dō's south door, you're greeted by a bronze image of Shaka Nyorai (the Historical Buddha) flanked by two bodhisattvas still bearing a few touches of original gold leaf; this **Shaka triad** was cast in 623 AD in memory of Prince Shōtoku, who died the previous year. To its right stands **Yakushi Nyorai**, the Buddha of Healing to which Hōryū-ji was dedicated in 607, and to the left a twelfth-century **Amida Buddha** commemorating the Prince's mother. Four Heavenly Kings (*Shi-Tennō*), carved of camphor wood in the late seventh century, protect the corners of the platform. Though they're perched symbolically on chunky demons, these images are stolid and rather half-hearted compared to the far more aggressive figures introduced in the eighth century – for example, the *Shi-Tennō* of Nara's Kaidan-in (see p.486). On the walls behind, it's possible to make out murals depicting the Buddhist paradise, similar to those of the Byōdō-in near Kyoto (see p.478); sadly, the original frescoes were damaged by a fire in 1949 and these are now replicas.

Exiting the Sai-in compound, walk east past two long, narrow halls, once monks' quarters, and a small shrine dedicated to Prince Shōtoku's horse. By the time you read this the new Kudara Kannon hall may be open off to left; until then the Kannon statue is displayed in the **Daihōzō-den** alongside Hōryū-ji's other priceless temple treasures. This museum consists of two halls. The first building features statues of Prince Shōtoku aged two and seven, as well as a portrait of him as a young man, and the bronze **Yume-chigae Kannon**. A delicate creature with a soft, secretive smile, this "Dream-Changing" Kannon, is credited with turning bad dreams into good. In the next room the temporarily residing wooden **Kudara Kannon** is also thought to be from the sev-

<table>
<tr><td colspan="3">AROUND NARA</td></tr>
</table>

| Chūgū-ji | *Chūgū-ji* | 中宮寺 |
|----------|------------|-------|
| Hōryū-ji | *Hōryū-ji* | 法隆寺 |
| Tōshōdai-ji | *Tōshōdai-ji* | 唐招提寺 |
| Yakushi-ji | *Yakushi-ji* | 薬師寺 |

enth century. Nothing is known about where this unusually tall, willowy figure came from or who carved it, but it's long been recognized as one of Japan's finest Buddhist works of art.

The second of the Daihōzō-den buildings contains more images of Prince Shōtoku and a small, very faded panel from the Kon-dō murals. But its most important treasures are two unique Buddhist altars. The first you come to, in the second room, is known as the **Tamamushi Altar** after the *tamamushi* beetle, whose iridescent wings once decorated the bronze filigree-work round its base – there's an example just in front. Paintings on the sides depict scenes from Buddha's life, of which the most famous shows him neatly folding his shirt, hanging it on a tree and then throwing himself off a cliff to feed a starving tigress and her cubs. In the next room, the **Lady Tachibana Altar** once belonged to Prince Shōtoku's consort. It's larger and less beautifully ornamented, but contains bronze statues of Amida – wearing a loveable grimace – and two attendant bodhisattvas balanced on long-stemmed lotus blossoms.

From the treasure house a lane leads east between old clay walls to the **Tō-in Garan** (same ticket). This eastern precinct was added in 739 when the monk Gyōshin Sōzu dedicated a temple to Shōtoku on the site of the Prince's former palace. Its centrepiece is the octagonal **Yume-dono** (Hall of Dreams) with its magnificent statue, the **Kuze Kannon**. Until recently this gilded wooden figure, said to be the same height as Prince Shōtoku or even modelled on him in the early seventh century, was a *hibutsu*, a hidden image, which no one had seen for centuries. Somewhat surprisingly it was an American art historian, Ernest Fenellosa, who was given permission to unwrap the bundle of white cloth in the 1880s. He revealed a dazzling statue in an almost perfect state of repair, carrying a sacred jewel and wearing an elaborate crown, with the famous enigmatic smile playing around its youthful lips. Unfortunately, the Kannon is still kept hidden for most of the year, except for brief spells in spring and autumn (April 11–May 5 & Oct 22–Nov 3). Also inside the Yume-dono, you'll find a Nara-period dry-lacquer statue of Gyōshin Sōzu, holding a rod, on the east side, and on the west, a clay statue of a thin, worried-looking monk. This is Dōsen Risshi who supervised repairs to the hall during the Heian era (794–1185).

## CHŪGŪ-JI

A gate in the northeast corner of the Tō-in Garan leads directly into **Chūgū-ji** (daily 9am–4/4.30pm; ¥400). This intimate, surprisingly quiet nunnery was originally the residence of Prince Shōtoku's mother, which he converted into a temple on her death in 621. The main reason for coming here, however, sits inside a modern hall facing south over a pond. If you've already visited Kyoto's Kōryū-ji (see p.454), you'll recognize the central image of a pensive, boy-like **Miroku Bosatsu** (the Future Buddha) absorbed in his task of trying to save mankind from suffering. In this case the statue is of camphor wood, burnished black with age, and is believed to have been carved by an immigrant Korean craftsman in the early seventh century. The pose is the same – his right arm rests on his knee, one leg is crossed and one hand raised to the chin in a classic gesture of deep concentration – but here the figure dressed in cascading robes has an even softer, more natural quality and its gently smiling face a mystical realism.

Beside the altar, a few fragments of silk embroidery are replicated remnants of a pair of tapestries known as the **Tenjukoku Mandala**. The mandala was commissioned by Lady Tachibana in 623 to commemorate Prince Shōtoku's death by depicting him in Buddha's Paradise. A thirteenth-century nun rescued what she could and patched the pieces together into the square that survives today. It's still possible to make out some celestial figures as well as symbolic tortoises and phoenixes.

Chūgū-ji marks the eastern extent of the Hōryū-ji complex. From here it's about an eight-minute walk south down to the main road and the Chūgū-ji-mae bus stop. Buses heading south will take you back to JR Hōryū-ji Station, while those going north pass Yakushi-ji en route to Nara; in either case, you'll want a #52, #97 or #98 bus.

## Yakushi-ji and Tōshōdai-ji

Six kilometres northwest of Hōryū-ji, the *Nishinokyō* area is home to two great temples which are again famed for their age and wealth of statuary. The older of the pair is southerly **Yakushi-ji** (daily 8.30am–5pm; ¥500). Emperor Tenmu first ordered its construction sometime around 680 AD when his wife was seriously ill. Although she recovered, Tenmu died eight years later, leaving the empress to dedicate Yakushi-ji in 697. Over the centuries, fires have destroyed all but one of the original buildings, though the statues themselves have fared better.

Arriving by **bus** from Hōryū-ji (35min; ¥560) or Nara (20min; ¥240) – buses #52, #97 or #98 – get off at the Yakushi-ji Higashi-guchi stop, from where it's roughly ten minutes' walk to the temple's north gate. Alternatively, Kintetsu-line **trains** run from Nara to Nishinokyō Station with a change at Saidai-ji; the north gate is a three-minute walk east of the station.

Since Yakushi-ji faces south, you are, in effect, entering by the back door. The first building, in the compound's northeast corner, is a modern **treasure hall**. It's only open twice a year (Jan 1–15 & Oct 8–Nov 10; ¥500), when a rare, Nara-period painting of Kissho-ten, the Buddhist goddess of peace, happiness and beauty, is the prime attraction. She is portrayed as a voluptuous figure with cherry-red, butterfly lips, and dressed in an intricately patterned fabric whose colours are still remarkably clear.

Continuing south through the outer compound you come to a long, low wooden hall on your left, the **Tōin-dō**. This hall, rebuilt around 1285, houses a bronze image of **Shō-Kannon**, an incarnation of the Goddess of Mercy, which dates from the early Nara period. The graceful, erect statue framed against a golden aureole shows distinctly Indian influences in its diaphanous robes, double necklace and strands of hair falling over its shoulders.

The only building of note in Yakushi-ji's inner compound is the three-storied **East Pagoda** which Ernest Fenellosa famously described as "frozen music". Apart from its obvious beauty, he was referring to the rhythmical progression of smaller double roofs which punctuate the pagoda's upward flow. It's the sole surviving remnant of the original temple and stands out like a sore thumb against the spanking red lacquer of the new West Pagoda and the **Kon-dō** (Golden Hall), both of which were rebuilt in the last 25 years. But inside the Kon-dō the temple's original seventh-century, bronze **Yakushi triad** sits unperturbed. Past fires have removed most of the gold and given the statues a rich, black sheen, but otherwise they are in remarkably fine condition. A rather pudgy, seated Yakushi Nyorai, Buddha of Healing, is flanked by two only slightly less ample bodhisattvas of the sun and moon. Their poses are symmetrical, resting gracefully on one leg, though there are subtle differences in their ornate jewellery, headresses and the drape of their garments; Nikkō, the sun, stands on the right (east), with Gakkō the moon to the left. As you leave by the back of the hall, take a look at Yakushi's **pedestal** which is decorated with so-far unexplained figures with Polynesian features, and a grape-vine motif of Middle-Eastern origin.

## TŌSHŌDAI-JI

Retracing your steps, head north from Yakushi-ji's north gate for five minutes and you'll find the front entrance to **Tōshōdai-ji** (daily 8.30am–4.30/5pm; ¥500). Here the weathered, wooden halls in their shady compound are superb examples of late eighth-century architecture. The temple was founded in 759 by the eminent Chinese monk Ganjin – he of Nara's Kaidan-in (see p.486) – when he was granted permission to move from the city to somewhere more peaceful.

The first building inside the south gate is the **Kon-dō**, or Golden Hall, whose majestic roof and uncompromising solidity are typical of Tang Chinese architecture. Craftsmen who accompanied Ganjin from the mainland are also responsible for the three dry-lacquer statues which fill the hall. Pole position goes to a seated Rushana Buddha, a slightly later cousin of Tōdai-ji's Daibutsu (see p.486), surrounded by a halo of a thousand mini-Buddhas. Yakushi Nyorai stands on one side and a phenomenally busy Senjū Kannon, this time with the full complement of a thousand arms, on the other. The Four Heavenly Kings who are supposed to protect this trio do their best to look menacing, but they're way outclassed on the height stakes.

The **Kō-dō**, Lecture Hall, behind also dates from the late eighth century, though this low-slung hall with its gabled roof is more Japanese in styling. In spring and autumn Tōshōdai-ji's treasures go on display in the concrete **Shin-Hōzō** (March 21–May 19 & Sept 15–Nov 3; ¥100) on the compound's east side. Again, these are mostly statues, of which the most celebrated is a headless Buddha known as the "Venus of the Orient". Just once a year – on June 6, the anniversary of Ganjin's death – the doors of the **Mieidō** are opened to reveal a lacquered image which was carved just before he died in 763 at the grand age of 76. He's buried next door, in the far northeast corner of the compound, in a simple grave within a clay-walled enclosure.

When you've finished, walk back to the main gate and then east for about five minutes to the main road where you can pick up a bus back to Nara – the same #52, 97 or 98 (20min; ¥240).

# Kōya-san

Ever since the Buddhist monk Kōbō Daishi founded a temple here in the early ninth century, **KŌYA-SAN**, some 50km south of Ōsaka, has been one of Japan's holiest mountains. On top is an elongated, cedar-filled valley perched 800m above sea level, where more than one hundred monasteries cluster round the head temple of the Shingon sect, **Kongōbu-ji**. This isolated community is then protected by two concentric mountain chains of eight peaks each, which are said to resemble an eight-petalled lotus blossom.

Whatever your religious persuasion, there's a highly charged, slightly surreal atmosphere about this group of temples suspended among the clouds. The journey alone, a dramatic ride by train and cable car, more than repays the effort, but Kōya-san is also a good place to step out of Japan's hectic city life for a day or two. One of its great delights is to stay in a *shukubō*, or **temple lodgings**, and attend a dawn prayer service. Afterwards, head for the **Garan**, the mountain's spiritual centre, or wander among the thousands of ancient tombs and memorials which populate the **Okunoin cemetery**, where Kōbō Daishi's mausoleum is honoured with a blaze of lanterns.

Of course, Kōya-san is not undiscovered. Some 6000 people live in the valley and each year thousands of pilgrims visit the monasteries. Even here, loudspeakers, ugly concrete buildings and commercialization intrude, and one or two women travelling alone have complained of some mildly unmonkish behaviour. Be aware also that, while the mountain can be pleasantly cool in summer, winter temperatures often fall below freezing.

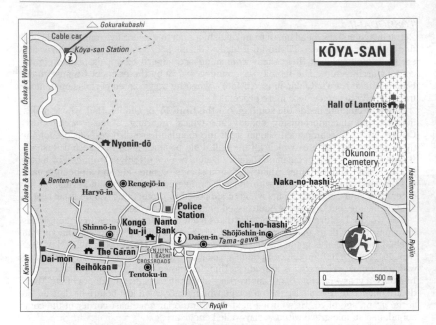

The biggest **festival** in Kōya-san takes place on the twenty-first day of the third lunar month (usually mid-April), when all the monks gather for a service at the Mie-dō. Everyone's out in force again for Kōbō Daishi's birthday (June 15), while during Obon, several thousand lanterns light the route through Okunoin cemetery as part of Japan's festival for the dead (Aug 13).

## Some history

The first monastery on Kōya-san was founded in the early ninth century by the monk **Kūkai** (774–835), known after his death as **Kōbō Daishi**. As a young monk Kūkai travelled to China to study Esoteric Buddhism for two years. On his return in 806 he established a temple in Hakata (now Fukuoka), before moving to Takao-san near Kyoto, where his ardent prayers for the peace and prosperity of the nation won him powerful supporters. Kūkai was soon granted permission to found the **Shingon** sect which, in a break from contemporary belief, held that enlightenment could be achieved in one lifetime (see p.784 for more on Shingon Buddhism). But city life was too disruptive for serious meditation, so Kūkai set off round Japan to find a suitable mountain retreat.

According to legend, when Kūkai left China he prayed for guidance on where to establish his monastery. At the same time he flung his three-pronged *vajra* (the ritual implement of Shingon monks) clear across the ocean. Later, as he drew near **Kōya-san**, he met a giant, red-faced hunter who gave him a two-headed dog. The dog led Kūkai to the top of the mountain where, of course, he found his *vajra* hanging in a pine tree. In any event, the historical records show that Kūkai first came to Kōya-san in 816 and returned in 819 to consecrate the first temple. For a while after 823 he presided over Kyoto's Tō-ji temple (see p.442), but eventually returned to Kōya-san, where he died in 835, aged 62. Even without his religious work it seems that Kūkai was a remarkable man; he's credited with inventing the *hiragana* syllabary and founding Japan's first public school, as well as being a gifted scholar, calligrapher, and spiritual healer.

After his death, Kūkai's disciple **Shinzen** continued developing the monasteries, then collectively known as **Kongōbu-ji**, until at its height there were more than 1500 monasteries and several thousand monks on the mountain top. The sect then had its ups and downs, of which the most serious was during the anti-Buddhist movement following the 1868 Meiji Restoration. In recent years, however, the temples have been extensively repaired and Kōya-san is once again a major centre of pilgrimage.

## Arrival, information and accommodation

Access to Kōya-san's mountain-top hideaway is via a cable car (5min; ¥380) which departs at least every thirty minutes from Gokurakubashi Station. To get to this lower station there are direct express and super-express trains on the private Nankai line **from Ōsaka**'s Namba Station (every 20–30min; 1hr 15min–1hr 40min; ¥850–¥1600); note that reservations are required on the super-express. **From Nara and Kyoto** you can either travel via Ōsaka or use the JR network as far as Hashimoto and then change onto the Nankai line.

At the top cable-car station you'll find **buses** waiting for the ten-minute ride into town (every 20–30min). Nearly all buses stop at the central Senjuin-bashi crossroads, where the routes then divide, with the majority of services running east to Okunoin and fewer heading past Kongōbu-ji to the western, Dai-mon gate; take a ticket as you board the bus and pay the driver on exit. Once you're in the centre it's more pleasant to explore on foot, but if you plan on doing a lot of bus journeys, you can buy a one-day pass (*ichi-nichi furii kippu*; ¥800) at the station terminus.

There's a small **information office** inside the cable-car station (daily 8.30am–5/5.30pm), or try the central office (daily 8.30am–5pm; ☎0736/56-2616) beside the Senjuin-bashi junction. Both offices can provide maps and help fix accommodation, while the main office also offers **bikes** for rent (¥1200 per day). **Taxis** wait outside the station, or call Kōya-san Taxi on ☎0736/56-2628.

### Accommodation

Around fifty monasteries on Kōya-san offer **accommodation** in *shukubō* (temple lodgings) run by the monks. The rooms are all Japanese-style with communal washing facilities, and in some cases look out over beautiful gardens or are decorated with painted screens or antique hanging scrolls. These are primarily places of worship, so don't expect hotel-style service, and you'll be asked to keep to fairly strict meal and bath times. However, guests are usually welcome to attend the early-morning prayers (around 6am or 6.30am) and all the *shukubō* offer excellent **vegetarian meals**, *shōjin-ryōri*.

While the local information offices (see above) can help book *shukubō*, it's a good idea to make reservations in advance. Either approach the temples recommended below direct, or contact the Kōya-san Tourist Association at 600 Kōya-san, Kōya-chō, Itō-gun, Wakayama-ken (☎0736/56-2616, fax 56-2889). Prices generally start at around ¥9000 per person per night, including two meals.

**Daien-in**, ☎0736/56-2009, fax 56-2971. Small, highly recommended *shukubō* near the centre of Kōya-san. No English spoken, but it's a friendly place. [6].

**Haryō-in**, ☎0736/56-2702, fax 56-2936. One of the cheapest places to stay on the mountain. They even offer rooms without meals, though it would be a shame to miss out. The temple's located about ten minutes' walk from the centre of town on the road to the cable-car station, or take a bus to the Isshin-guchi stop. [5].

**Rengejō-in**, ☎0736/56-2233, fax 56-4743. Foreigners are assured a warm welcome at this lovely old temple, founded in 1190, opposite *Haryō-in*. They'll even conduct the prayer ceremony in English if there's enough demand, and again rooms are available without meals. [5]–[6].

**Shinnō-in**, ☎0736/56-2227, fax 56-3936. One of Kūkai's leading disciples founded this attractive temple in a secluded spot just behind the Garan. No English spoken. [6].

**KŌYA-SAN**

| | | |
|---|---|---|
| **Kōya-san** | *Kōya-san* | 高野山 |
| Danjō Garan | *Danjō Garan* | 壇上伽藍 |
| Gokurakubashi Station | *Gokurakubashi-eki* | 極楽橋駅 |
| Hashimoto | *Hashimoto* | 橋本 |
| Kongōbu-ji | *Kongōbu-ji* | 金剛峯寺 |
| Okunoin | *Okunoin* | 奥ノ院 |
| Reihōkan | *Reihōkan* | 霊宝館 |
| *ACCOMMODATION* | | |
| Daien-in | *Daien-in* | 大円院 |
| Haryō-in | *Haryō-in* | 巴陵院 |
| Rengejō-in | *Rengejō-in* | 蓮華定院 |
| Shinnō-in | *Shinnō-in* | 親王院 |
| Shōjōshin-in | *Shōjōshin-in* | 清浄心院 |
| Tentoku-in | *Tentoku-in* | 天徳院 |

**Shōjōshin-in**, ☎0736/56-2006, fax 56-4770. One of the larger temples, located on the edge of town near Okunoin's west entrance, *Shōjōshin-in* started life as a grass hut erected by Kūkai himself. It boasts a lovely garden, a warm atmosphere and there's usually someone who speaks English. [6].

**Tentoku-in**, ☎0736/56-2714, fax 56-4725. On a lane south of Kongōbu-ji, *Tentoku-in* is best-known for its sixteenth-century garden. More expensive rooms come with glorious garden views. [6].

## The Town

The road into Kōya-san from the cable-car station winds through cool, dark cryptomeria forests for about 2km before passing a small temple called **Nyonin-dō**. This "Women's Hall" marks one of the original seven entrances to the sacred precincts, beyond which women weren't allowed to proceed; the practice continued until 1906 despite an imperial edict issued in 1872. In the meantime, female pilgrims worshipped in special temples built beside each gate, of which Nyonin-dō is the last. Beyond the hall, you begin to see the first monasteries and, 1km further on, reach the main **Senjuin-bashi crossroads**. This junction lies at the secular centre of Kōya-san. Nearby you'll find the information office, post office, police station and restaurants alongside shops peddling souvenirs and pilgrims' accessories. The main sights are located either side of this crossroads: head west for Kōya-san's principal temple, **Kongōbu-ji**, and its religious centre, the **Garan**, or east for the mossy graves of **Okunoin cemetery**.

### Kongōbu-ji and the Garan

Though it originally applied to the whole mountain community, the name **Kongōbu-ji**, Temple of the Diamond Mountain (daily: April–Oct 8am–5pm; Jan–March, Nov & Dec 8.30am–4.30pm; ¥350), now refers specifically to the sect's chief monastery and administrative offices located three minutes' walk west of the central crossroads. In fact, this temple was a late addition to the complex, being founded in 1592 by the then ruler Toyotomi Hideyoshi in honour of his mother. It only later became Shingon's headquarters.

Rebuilt in 1861 in the original style, the graceful building is famous largely for its late-sixteenth-century **screen paintings** by Kyoto's Kanō school of artists. The best of these are the cranes and pine trees by Kanō Tanyū decorating the Great Hall, and Kanō Tansai's *Willows in Four Seasons* two rooms further along. This Willow Room is also the spot where Hideyoshi's nephew **Toyotomi Hidetsugu** killed himself in 1595.

Hidetsugu was the adopted heir of the childless Hideyoshi, but things got complicated when Hideyoshi fathered a lusty son, Hideyori, in 1593. To forestall any arguments over the succession, Hideyoshi ordered his now inconvenient nephew to commit suicide and then had Hidetsugu's wife and family murdered just to be on the safe side.

Beside the temple's front entrance, the **Rokuji-no-kane** (Six O'clock Bell), cast in 1547, sits on a castle-like foundation; a monk comes out to ring it every even hour (6am–10pm). Opposite the bell a gravelled path leads into the **Danjō Garan**, Kōya-san's sacred precinct. This large sandy compound, filled with cryptomeria trees, lanterns and wooden halls wreathed in incense, is where Kōbō Daishi founded his original monastery. Only one of those early buildings still stands and many are much newer, such as the **eastern stupa** which marks the entrance to the Garan from this side. It's followed by three older halls, of which the most interesting is the middle **Daie-dō**, housing an impressive statue of Amida Buddha attended by two bodhisattvas. The Daie-dō was rebuilt in 1638, while the hall in front of it, the **Fudō-dō**, is the oldest building in the Garan, dating from 1198.

The Garan's most important building, however, is the monumental **Konpon Daitō** (¥100), the Fundamental Great Stupa covered in strident, orange lacquer – it was last rebuilt in the 1930s. Inside, Dainichi Nyorai and four other blue-coiffed Buddhas symbolize the ideal universe. They're surrounded by a gaudy forest of pillars painted with bodhisattvas while the eight patriarchs who helped propagate Shingon decorate the walls. South of the stupa, the more restrained **Kon-dō** (¥100), also rebuilt in the 1930s, marks the spot where Kūkai gave his first lectures. He reputedly lived where the **Mie-dō** now stands, just to the west. There's nothing much to see inside, but this attractive building, dating from 1843, is regarded as one of the mountain's most holy places. Note the two sacred pines in front which are said to be offspring of the tree in which Kūkai's *vajra* landed.

Continuing west past the little **Juntei-dō** and **Kujakū-dō** – peer in to see a mini Kannon and a statue of the peacock divinity Kujakū – you finally reach the nicely weathered **western stupa**. Circling round to the south, the pretty hexagonal building was once a scripture repository, and the long, low wooden hall is where priests still hold monthly debates and monks sweat over their exams. Behind the exam hall, there's a reminder that Kōya-san was a sacred mountain long before Kūkai arrived; the ornate, vermilion Shinto shrine **Miyō-jinja** is dedicated to Kōya-san's guardian deities – Kūkai's red-faced hunter and his mother.

The main road in front of the Garan eventually leads to the **Dai-mon**, or Great Gate, that was Kōya-san's main entrance until the cable car was built in the 1930s. The huge, rust-red gate sits on the mountain's western edge but the views are blocked by trees and it's not really worth the five-minute walk. Instead, follow the main road back towards town to see the temples' greatest treasures in the **Reihōkan** (daily 8.30am–4.30pm; ¥500). Though the old buildings don't really do the exhibits justice, and there's very little in English, this collection includes a number of priceless works of art. The displays are changed five times a year, but look out for a triptych of Amida welcoming souls to the Western Paradise, painted in 965, and a Heian-era silk painting of Buddha entering nirvana. Among the statues there's the original Kujakū Myō-ō, the peacock deity, and an apoplectic Fudō Myō-ō. In Shingon Buddhism this god is regarded as an incarnation of Dainichi Nyorai and he's usually accompanied by eight youthful servants – those in the museum are attributed to the gifted twelfth-century sculptor, Unkei. The rest of the collection is made up of mandala, scrolls and documents, including some by Kūkai, and also a number of ritual implements (*vajra*) he's said to have brought back from China.

## Okunoin

About 1km east of Kōya-san's central crossroads, the buildings give way once more to stately cedar trees. Turn left here over a broad, white bridge, **Ichi-no-hashi**, to follow the path into a mysterious, mossy forest. This is **Okunoin**, Kōya-san's vast **cemetery**.

Stretching away to either side, the forest floor is scattered with more than 200,000 stone stupas of all shapes and sizes, some jumbled and decaying like fallen logs, others scraped clear of lichen so that you can make out vague inscriptions. Here and there you'll also find Jizō statues, their red bibs bright against the muted greens, and the occasional war memorial. The most obvious is a white-winged structure beside Ichi-no-hashi, commemorating students who died in the Pacific War, but along the path keep an eye open for campaign maps of Papua New Guinea and Borneo. A great number of historical characters are also buried here, among them the great general Oda Nobunaga, and the monks Dōgen, Shinran, Nichiren and Hōnen, all founders of Buddhist sects.

It's best to walk through Okunoin in the early morning or around dusk when lamps light up the path; at these times the only other people you're likely to meet are the occasional, white-garbed pilgrims with their tinkling bells. It takes roughly twenty minutes to reach the cemetery's spiritual centre beyond the little **Tama-gawa** river. Before entering the sacred precinct, people offer paper or bamboo strips bearing names of deceased relatives to one of the seven bronze statues – five Jizō, Fudō and Miroku, the Future Buddha – and then douse the statue with water as a service to the dead. Above the bridge, a line of wooden stakes in the river represent memorials to those who died by drowning and to miscarried foetuses.

Across the bridge you begin the approach the **mausoleum of Kōbō Daishi**. First comes the **Hall of Lanterns** where thousands of oil lamps donated by the faithful are kept constantly alight. Two of them are said to have been burning since the eleventh century, one donated by the former Emperor Shirakawa and another by an anonymous poor woman. After this blaze of light and colour, the **tomb** itself is mercifully restrained. Indeed, it's only just visible within a gated enclosure behind the hall, sheltered by lofty cryptomeria trees.

According to Shingon tradition, the Great Master, Daishi, did not die in 835 but rather entered "eternal meditation". He's now waiting the coming of Miroku, the Future Buddha, when he will help lead the faithful to salvation – which is one reason why so many Japanese wish to have their ashes buried on Kōya-san. Next to the Daishi's tomb you'll see the octagonal ossuary where ashes are collected. Many of these are destined for the **modern cemetery** which lies south of the Tama-gawa bridge on a short cut back to the main road. It's the custom now for big companies to maintain plots on Kōya-san for past employees – the space rocket is probably the most famous memorial, but look out, too, for familiar names such as Yakult and UCC's coffee cup. And note also the "letter boxes" on some monuments for company employees to leave their *meishi* (business cards), just to say they called or perhaps to petition a former colleague for a bit of spiritual assistance.

You emerge on to the main road beside a clutch of restaurants and a buspark. If you don't want to walk back, take any bus heading west from the Okunoin-mae stop across the road.

# Shima Hantō

East of Ōsaka and Nara, on the far side of the Kii Peninsula, a small knuckle of land sticks out into the ocean. Known as the **Shima Hantō**, this peninsula has been designated a **national park**, partly for its natural beauty but also because it contains Japan's spiritual heartland, **Ise-jingū**. Since the fourth century the Grand Shrine of Ise, on the edge of **Ise** town, has been venerated as the terrestrial home of the Sun Goddess Amaterasu, from whom all Japanese emperors are descended. Unfortunately, there's not a great deal to see, but if you're passing through Ise it's worth making a brief excursion, joining the reverent throng of Japanese tourists who try to make a pilgrimage

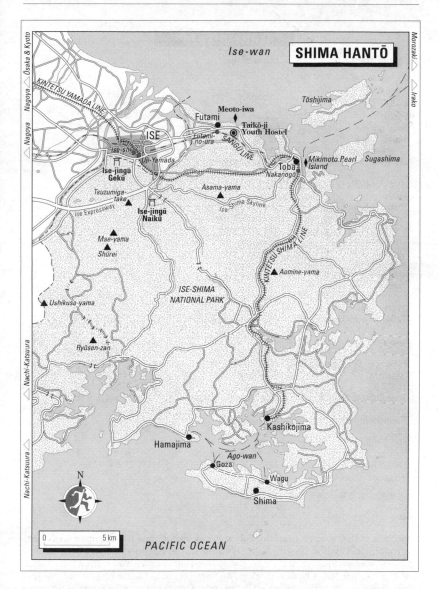

here at least once in their lifetimes. Beyond Ise it's **pearl** country. The world-famous Mikimoto company started up in **Toba** when an enterprising restaurant owner discovered the art of cultivating pearls. Now there's a whole island dedicated to his memory, including a surprisingly interesting museum. Most of today's pearls are raised further east in **Ago-wan**, where hundreds of rafts are tethered in a beautiful, island-speckled bay.

| | SHIMA HANTŌ | |
|---|---|---|
| **Shima Hantō** | *Shima Hantō* | 志摩半島 |
| **Ise** | *Ise* | 伊勢 |
| Akafuku Honten | *Akafuku Honten* | 赤福本店 |
| Ise-shi Station | *Ise-shi eki* | 伊勢市駅 |
| Gekū | *Gekū* | 外宮 |
| Ise-jingū | *Ise-jingū* | 伊勢神宮 |
| Naikū | *Naikū* | 内宮 |
| Oharai-machi | *Oharai-machi* | おはらい町 |
| Uji-Yamada Station | *Uji-Yamada eki* | 宇治山田駅 |
| *ACCOMMODATION AND RESTAURANTS* | | |
| Daiki | *Daiki* | 大喜 |
| Hoshide-kan | *Hoshide-kan* | 星出館 |
| Ise City Hotel | *Ise Shitii Hoteru* | 伊勢シティーホテル |
| Kawasaki-kan | *Kawasaki-kan* | 河崎館 |
| Okadaiya | *Okadaiya* | 岡田屋 |
| Okuno | *Okuno* | おく乃 |
| Yamada-kan | *Yamada-kan* | 山田館 |
| **Futami** | *Futami* | 二見 |
| Futami-no-ura Station | *Futami-no-ura eki* | 二見浦駅 |
| Meoto-iwa | *Meoto-iwa* | 夫婦岩 |
| Taikō-ji Youth Hostel | *Taikō-ji Yūsu Hosuteru* | 太江寺ユースホステル |
| **Toba** | *Toba* | 鳥羽 |
| Awami | *Awami* | 阿波海 |
| Mikimoto Pearl Island | *Mikimoto Shinju-shima* | 御木本真珠島 |
| Sazanami | *Sazanami* | さざなみ |
| Tenbinya | *Tenbinya* | 天びん屋 |
| Toba International Hotel | *Toba Kokusai Hoteru* | 鳥羽国際ホテル |
| **Kashikojima** | *Kashikojima* | 賢島 |
| Goza | *Goza* | 御座 |
| Hamajima | *Hamajima* | 浜島 |
| Ryokan Ishiyama-sō | *Ryokan Ishiyama-sō* | 旅館石山荘 |
| Shima Kankō Hotel | *Shima Kankō Hoteru* | 志摩観光ホテル |
| Wagu | *Wagu* | 和具 |

# Ise

The town of **ISE** wears its sanctity lightly. Many visitors find it a disappointingly ordinary place, and even at **Ise-jingū**, Japan's most sacred Shinto shrine, it's hard for non-Japanese visitors to appreciate its deeper spiritual significance. Apart from their historical significance, there is, nevertheless, an unquestionable sense of awe and mystery about these simple buildings buried in the cedar forest. After you've seen the two sanctuaries, however, there's really nothing else to detain you in Ise.

Ise-jingū is naturally a top choice for the first shrine visit of the New Year (*hatsumode*) on January 1. This is followed by more than 1500 annual **ceremonies** in honour of Ise's gods. The most important of these revolve around the agricultural cycle, culminating in offerings of sacred rice (Oct 15–17). In spring (April 5–6) and during the autumn equinox (around Sept 22) ancient Shinto dances and a moon-viewing party take place at the inner shrine.

## The Town

Central Ise is bounded to the north by the JR and Kintetsu line train tracks and by the Seta-gawa river to the east. The southwestern quarter, however, is taken up by a large expanse of woodland in the midst of which lies the first of **Ise-jingū**'s two sanctuaries, the **Gekū**. While this Outer Shrine is within easy walking distance of both train stations, to reach the **Naikū** (Inner Shrine), some 6km to the southeast, you'll need to take a bus (see Practicalities, overleaf). The two shrines follow roughly the same layout, so if you're pushed for time, head straight for the more interesting Naikū.

The Grand Shrine of Ise was established sometime in the fourth century to house a **mirror** representing the Sun Goddess, **Amaterasu**. According to legend, this was the very mirror which Amaterasu gave her grandson Ninigi-no-Mikoto when she sent him to rule Japan (see Contexts, p.781). At first it had been stored in the imperial palace, along with the sacred sword and beads (these are now held respectively in Nagoya's Atsuta-jingū and Tokyo's Imperial Palace), but the goddess gave instructions to move her mirror to somewhere more remote. Eventually they settled on a wooded spot beside Ise's Isuzu-gawa which has been the mirror's home ever since and the country's most sacred centre. The Outer Shrine was added in the fifth century to honour the god of food and industry. Not that the shrines look old; according to custom they are rebuilt every twenty years in order to re-purify the ground. Each is an exact replica of its predecessor, following a unique style of architecture that has been passed down the centuries and is free of any Chinese or Korean influences. Only plain *hinoki* (Japanese cypress) and grass thatch are used, plus a few gold embellishments, but the most distinctive features are the two cross-pieces (*chigi*) standing up at each end of the roof and the chunky, horizontal bars (*katsuogi*) lined up between them. When the buildings are dismantled the old timbers are passed on to other shrines around the country to be recycled.

### GEKŪ

The entrance to the **Gekū** (sunrise to sunset; free) lies over a small humped bridge and along a gravel path leading into the woods. After passing under two unpainted *torii* you reach a sacred dance platform and, nearby, the shrine office – ask for a copy of their excellent English-language leaflet. Just beyond, a high wooden fence contains the shrine itself, a thickly thatched, gleaming structure in a sea of white gravel. It's dedicated to the goddess **Toyouke-no-Ōmikami**, who was sent by Amaterasu to look after the all-important rice harvests. Another of her duties is to provide Amaterasu with sacred food, so twice a day priests make offerings to Toyouke in a small hall at the back of the compound. Presumably she then passes this on to the Sun Goddess.

As you leave, take a look at the empty plot next door. This is reserved for the new shrine which will be built in 2013, when the Naikū will also be reconstructed. It takes about a year to complete the buildings and refurbish them with hundreds of sacred objects all of which are handmade according to age-old techniques. The dedication of the new shrine takes place at night when the secret treasures symbolizing the goddess are carried from one building to the other. This solemn ceremony is believed to renew the blessings brought by the gods on the Japanese people.

Having paid their respects to Toyouke by bowing deeply twice, clapping and bowing deeply a third time, most people hurry off to visit the inner shrine. Buses heading east leave from a stand on the main road opposite the Gekū's main entrance; hop on either a #55 or #51 for the Naikū stop (every 10min; 15min; ¥410).

*NAIKŪ*

Ise-jingū's inner shrine, dedicated to Amaterasu Ōmikami, the ancestress of the imperial family, is a much grander affair. The **Naikū** (sunrise to sunset; free) stands on the edge of a large expanse of sacred woodland across a beautiful arched bridge, **Uji-bashi**, which spans the Isuzu-gawa. On the far side, turn right and walk through a small, formal garden to reach the purification fountain just in front of the first sacred *torii*. A little further on, the path goes down to the river. Traditionally, pilgrims would purify themselves here as well, but most people nowadays just go to see the fat, multi-coloured carp that laze in the shallows.

The path turns away from the river towards an assembly of buildings which include the shrine office – where they also stock the English-language leaflets – and a purple-curtained music hall. Here worshippers dedicate performances of **sacred dance** or Nō theatre to the gods for services rendered or in the hope of securing divine intervention. Next come various halls where **sacred foods** are stored and prepared; to ensure their purity, rice, sake, salt, fruit and vegetables are all produced on plots of shrine land. Finally, the path loops round to approach the **inner sanctum** from the south. As in the Gekū, the main building is contained within four increasingly sacred enclosures, though in this case it's further away and even more difficult to see the details. Nevertheless, the architecture's pure, strong lines hold the same mystical power. Only members of the imperial family and head priests can enter the inner sanctuary where Amaterasu's **sacred mirror** is enshrined. It's wrapped in layers of cloth and, according to the records, no one's laid eyes on it for at least a thousand years.

Rather than retracing your steps, follow the paths round to the west of the main sanctuary. This route takes you past an attractive rice storehouse and treasury, to the auxiliary shrine of Aramatsurinomiya, where you can get a better look at the architecture.

If you've got time to spare after exploring the Naikū, turn right immediately over the Uji-bashi and take a stroll down the main street of **Oharai-machi**. This pedestrian-only area replicates a Meiji-era merchants' quarter; it's all rather touristy, but the buildings are well done and there are some decent places to eat (see Practicalities, below). If you just want a snack, head for **Akafuku Honten** about halfway along on the right beside a little bridge – look for the lovely red wood-burning steamers in front. They serve the local speciality *akafuku mochi*, steamed rice cakes covered with red-bean paste (¥230 for three pieces including tea); in summer try them cold with ice. To return to central Ise from the Naikū area take a bus (#51 or 55 again) from stop #1 (every 30min; 15–20min; ¥410).

## Practicalities

There are regular **trains** to Ise from Nagoya, Kyoto and Ōsaka. In all cases the private Kintetsu network offers the quickest and most convenient service, particularly if you're travelling from Kyoto or Ōsaka. Note that there are two stations in central Ise. The more easterly, Uji-Yamada Station is Kintetsu's main station. However, some Kintetsu trains also stop at Ise-shi Station, which is shared with JR. **From Nagoya** the fastest option is an express on the Kintetsu-Ise line to Uji-Yamada Station (hourly; 1hr 20min). If you've got a JR Rail Pass, you can use JR's limited express trains direct from Nagoya to Ise-shi (hourly; 1hr 35min), but note that you have to pay a small supplement (¥440) for travelling on a section of Kintetsu track. Kintetsu also runs direct trains **from Ōsaka**'s Uehonmachi Station (every 15min; 1hr 45min) and **from Kyoto** (hourly; 2hr).

Each train station has its own **bus** terminal, with regular departures for the two shrines; buses #51 and #55 run via the Gekū to Naikū, after which the #51 route circles back round to the stations.

Ise's main **tourist information** office (Mon–Fri 8.30am–5pm, Sat & Sun 9am–3/4pm; ☎0596/28-3705) is located opposite the entrance to the Gekū. You can pick up maps and brochures at the ground-floor window, but if you need English-language help try the office upstairs (Mon–Fri only). Alternatively, there's a useful office with English-speaking staff in the Uji-Yamada Station (daily 9am–5.30pm; ☎0596/23-9655), where staff can also help arrange accommodation throughout the Shima Hantō area.

Ise's main **shopping area** lies south of Ise-shi Station. For **foreign exchange**, try the Daisan Bank opposite the JR Station, or walk down the pleasant, lantern-lined street leading from the station to the Gekū where'll you'll find Daiwa Bank. **Car rental** is available through Kinki Nippon Rent-a-car (☎0596/28-0295), at Uji-Yamada Station, and Eki Rent-a-car (☎0596/25-5019) at Ise-shi Station.

### ACCOMMODATION

Surprisingly, Ise doesn't have a great choice of **accommodation**. One of the most interesting places is *Yamada-kan* (☎0596/28-2532, fax 28-4440; ⑦ including two meals), in a distinctive seventy-year-old building on the lantern-lined road in front of Ise-shi Station. This traditional ryokan offers Japanese-style rooms with shared bathroom facilities. On the main road north of Uji-Yamada Station, the *Ise City Hotel* (☎0596/28-2111, fax 28-1058; ⑤), is a reasonable business hotel with English-speaking staff and comfortable en-suite rooms; they also have a slightly more expensive annexe. Continue up this road to find *Hoshide-kan* (☎0596/28-2377, fax 27-2830; ④), on the right before the next main junction. This delightful, higgledy-piggledy old ryokan offers *tatami* rooms, all with shared bathrooms, and serves excellent vegetarian meals in the restaurant next door. Behind the *Hoshide-kan* there's a small, interesting area of old streets, known as Kawasaki, along the Seta-gawa river.

### RESTAURANTS

Ise's **speciality foods** include lobster (*Ise-ebi*) and the rather less exciting *Ise udon* which consists of thick, handmade noodles served in a thin soy sauce – in summer they'll ask if you want it cold. By far the nicest **restaurant** in town is the *Daiki* (daily 11am–9pm; ☎0596/28-0281), despite its rather unpromising location on the north side of the Uji-Yamada Station forecourt. The restaurant made its name catering to the emperor, but it's a nicely relaxed place and eating here doesn't have to blow the budget. Set meals start at under ¥2000, though if you want to splurge, they also do *Ise-ebi* at ¥6000. In the Naikū area, *Okadaiya* (daily except Fri 10.30am–5pm) and *Okuno* (daily 1am–5pm) both serve *Ise udon* (¥400) and well-priced set meals – find them on the main street of Oharai-machi before the Akafuku shop. Finally, if you're wandering the Kawasaki area, look out for the jazz coffee house *Kawasaki-kan* (daily 8am–7pm) in a nicely restored traditional warehouse. They serve a variety of freshly roasted coffees, as well as cakes and light snacks.

# Toba and Ago-wan

East of Ise the ragged Shima Peninsula juts out into the Pacific Ocean. Most of this mountainous area belongs to the Ise-Shima National Park, whose largest settlement is the port of **Toba**, home to the famous **Mikimoto Pearl Island**. After learning everything you ever wanted to know about cultured pearls, you can head on east to **Kashikojima** on the shores of **Ago-wan**. This huge, sheltered bay is scattered with wooded islands, between which float banks of oyster rafts – it's magical at sunset.

Travelling from Ise, there's a choice of routes into the area. If the weather's clear the best option is via the **Ise-Shima Skyline** which runs between Ise and Toba over the summit of Asama-yama. From the top you get excellent views over Ise-wan and, on an exceptional day, all the way to Mount Fuji. **Buses** depart three times a day (Mon–Sat 11am, 1pm & 3pm; 40min; ¥1120) from outside Ise's Naikū shrine (see opposite), with hourly departures on Sundays and national holidays (11am–3pm).

Alternatively both Kintetsu and JR **trains** continue east of Ise. Of these the JR services are less frequent and don't go beyond Toba. However, their lines are routed closer to the coast where they pass through **Futami** which is famous for its "wedded rocks", **Meoto-iwa**. Joined by a hefty sacred rope, this pair of "male" and "female" rocks lies just offshore about fifteen minutes' walk northeast of Futami-no-ura Station. They're revered as representations of Izanagi and Izanami, the two gods who created Japan (see p.781), and it's the done thing to see the sun rise between them – the best season is from May to August when the sun's in the right place. Perhaps more interesting, however, is Futami's excellent **youth hostel**, located ten minutes' walk inland from the rocks; ask at the train station for a map. As the name suggests, the *Taikō-ji Youth Hostel*, 1659E, Futami-chō (☎0596/43-2283; ③) is located in a temple. It's on a quiet knoll among trees, nothing luxurious but a lovely relaxed place to recharge the batteries.

## Toba

Although it's on an attractive bay, the town of **TOBA** is not somewhere to linger. The seafront is a strip of car parks, ferry terminals and shopping arcades, behind which run the main road and train tracks. Really the only point in stopping here, unless you need accommodation or are catching a ferry, is to pay homage to the birth-place of cultured pearls.

In 1893 **Mikimoto Kokichi** (1858–1954), the son of a Toba noodle-maker, produced the world's first cultivated pearl using tools developed by a dentist friend. Just six years later he opened his first shop in Tokyo's fashionable Ginza shopping district, from where the Mikimoto empire spread worldwide. His life's work is commemorated – and minutely detailed – on **Mikimoto Pearl Island** (daily 8.30am–5/5.30pm, Dec 9am–4.30pm; ¥1500), lying just offshore five minutes' walk south of Toba's train and bus stations. Even if you're not a pearl fan, the museum is extremely well put together, with masses of information in English describing the whole process from seeding the oyster to grading and stringing the pearls. There's also a section devoted to Mikimoto's extraordinary pearl artworks, including a spinning globe, a model of the Yume-dono pavilion (see p.491) with a revolving top, and a modest little crown containing 872 pearls and 188 diamonds. The unsung heroines of all this are the **women divers** (*ama*) who stoically come out every hour or so in all weathers to demonstrate their skills. Though *ama* are no longer employed in the pearl industry, some 2000 local women still earn their living this way, collecting abalone, sea urchins and seaweed from the rocky coast. On average they'll spend three to four hours a day in the water, going down to a depth of 10–15m, and some are still diving at the age of sixty. The argument for using women is that they can apparently hold their breath longer then men and are blessed with an extra layer of insulating fat.

### PRACTICALITIES

Toba's JR and Kintetsu **stations** and the bus terminal are all located next door to each other in the centre of town. There's an **information booth** (daily 9am–5pm; ☎0599/25-2844) beside the taxi stand at the bottom of the Kintetsu Station steps. The staff don't speak English, but can help with accommodation.

If you're leaving the Shima Hantō area, one of the nicest ways to travel is by **ferry** across the bay to a couple of ports south of Nagoya. Ise-wan Ferry (☎0599/25-2880) operates regular services to both Irako (50min; ¥1050) and Morozaki (1hr 10min; ¥1150), from where buses connect with the rail network. The boats leave from Ise-wan Ferry Terminal, two minutes' walk south along the seafront from Mikimoto Pearl Island; if you're travelling by Kintetsu line train, get off at Nakanogō Station. Alternatively, Meitetsu (☎0559/25-2023) runs frequent high-speed passenger ferries to Irako (30min; ¥1530) from a wharf immediately opposite Toba Station – walk through the Pearl Building and keep going to find their ticket desk in the Bay Centre.

Toba is not well-endowed with **accommodation** options, so you'd be better off staying in Ise (see p.500) or travelling on to Kashikojima (see below). If you're stuck, one of the most reasonable places to stay is *Awami*, 300-7 Kohama (☎0599/25-2423, fax 25-2701; ⑤). This small, friendly ryokan is actually located in the Kohama district, an attractive fishing port ten minutes' walk north of Toba Station; follow the train tracks but keep going straight ahead when they veer left. The rooms are simple but clean, meals are available and the owners speak a little English. Otherwise, the choice is a resort hotel, such as the *Toba International Hotel*, 1-23-1 Toba (free dial ☎0120–108593, fax 0599/21-0054; ⑦), in a fine position on the headland overlooking Toba Bay. It takes about fifteen minutes on foot from the station.

**Eating** in Toba is less of a problem. Seafood restaurants abound, with oyster as the predictable speciality. Though it looks a bit grim, the Pearl Building, opposite Toba Station, offers a pretty good choice on its *Ichibangai* restaurant floor. Here *Tenbinya* is recommended for its well-priced seafood *teishoku*, but you'll also find noodle shops and pizza parlours. If you're after something smarter, try *Tenbinya*'s main shop (closed Mon) in the streets just inland from Mikimoto Pearl Island, where you can eat well for under ¥2000. Nearby, *Sazanami* is another popular seafood restaurant with slightly higher prices.

## Ago-wan

The Shima Hantō ends in a chaos of islands known as **Ago-wan**. This large, sheltered bay is a classic ria coastline, formed by the sea rising along river valleys to create myriad islands and deep inlets. For centuries, divers have been collecting natural pearls from its warm, shallow waters, but things really took off when Mikimoto started producing his cultured pearls in Ago-wan earlier this century. Nowdays, hundreds of rafts moored between the islands trace strangely attractive patterns on the water while, in the nets beneath, thousands of oysters busily work their magic.

The main reason to visit Ago-wan is to take a **boat trip** round the bay. Boats depart from the tiny port of **KASHIKOJIMA** at the end of the Kintetsu train line. The station lies just one minute north of the harbour, where you'll find a choice of sightseeing boats and ferries. For ¥1500 you can cruise in a very mock-Spanish galleon (every 30min according to demand; 50min), and there are also small boats (*uransen*) which take you further in among the islands (50–60min; ¥1400). But perhaps the best option is one of the passenger **ferries** (*teikisen*). There are two ferry routes: across to **Goza**, on the long arm forming the bay's southern edge, and back via **Hamajima** to the west of Kashikojima (at least 6 daily; 1hr 15min; ¥1800 for the round trip); the second goes via Monsaki island in the middle of the bay to **Wagu**, a village east of Goza (at least hourly; 25min; ¥600 one way). You can get tickets and information about the ferries and Spanish cruise boats from an office beside the harbour – on the right as you walk down from the station – or buy *Yūransen* tickets from a small booth opposite.

For local maps and general **information**, try the Kintetsu office (daily 8am–8pm; ☎0559/43-1211) in the station building, or Kashikojima Ryokan Annaijo (daily except Thurs 10am–5pm; ☎0599/43-3061). Both offices can help with **accommodation**, though note that the station office only handles Kintetsu hotels, while the latter handles all the rest. Kintetsu mainly owns big, resort establishments, such as their flagship *Shima Kankō Hotel* (☎0599/43-1211, fax 43-3538; ⑥) in a magnificent position overlooking the bay; there's a free shuttle bus for the two-minute ride from the station. At the other end of the scale, the wonderfully atmospheric *Ryokan Ishiyama-sō* (☎0599/52-1527, fax 52-1240; ④–⑤ including Western breakfast) is a great place to spend the night. The rooms are nothing fancy but the main thing here is its location on an island, Yokoyama-jima, two minutes by boat from Kashikojima pier – the English-speaking owner will collect you. After dining on a feast of fresh seafood you can watch the sun go down over Ago-wan.

# Kōbe and around

An historic port and distinct city in its own right, **KŌBE**, the capital of Hyōgo-ken, now seems more like the fashionable western suburb of sprawling Ōsaka, 33km east around Ōsaka Bay. You don't visit Kōbe for the sights, which are of limited interest, but more for its human scale, dramatic location on a sliver of land between the sea and Rokkō-san, its cosmopolitan atmosphere and great range of food.

Although Kōbe has almost totally recovered from the 1995 **earthquake** (see below) it has far from forgotten this horrific event; one of the city's most interesting new "attractions" is the **Kōbe Phoenix Plaza** which documents the quake and its aftermath. The nearby **Kōbe City Museum**, covering the port's earlier illustrious history, is also worth a look, as is the space-age **Fashion Museum** on the man-made Rokkō Island, east of the city harbour.

Heading into hills, you can relax at **Arima Onsen**, one of Japan's oldest spa resorts. West of the city is the **Akashi Kaikyō Ōhashi**, the longest suspension bridge in the world (see p.598), linking Kansai directly with Shikoku via Awaji-shima. Continue some 55km further west along the coast and you'll arrive at **Himeji**, home of Japan's best original castle Himeji-jō, a UNESCO World Heritage Site since 1993.

### Some history

Kōbe's history is dominated by two important events; the opening of Japan's ports to foreign trade in 1868 and the Great Hanshin Earthquake of 1995. Although it had been a port as long ago as the eighth century, Kōbe's fortunes really took off when **foreign traders** set up shop in the city in the latter part of the nineteenth century, bringing their new ways and styles of living with them. Japan got its first taste of beef and soccer in 1871 in Kōbe, the first cinema film was shown here in 1896, and the first golf course was laid down close to the city in 1903, designed by Arthur Gloom, a Brit.

This trend-setting nature and booming trade made Kōbe a very popular place and, despite suffering heavy bombing during World War II, by the 1960s the city was bursting in its narrow stretch of land between the mountains and the sea. A solution was found by levelling the hills and dumping the rubble in the sea to create Port Island and Rokko Island in the bay. All this came to a sudden halt, though, at 5.46am, January 17, 1995, when a devastating **earthquake** struck the city and surrounding area. As dawn broke, Kōbe resembled a war zone with buildings and highways toppled, whole neighbourhoods in flames, some 5500 people dead and tens of thousands homeless. Although the authorities were criticized for not responding promptly to the disaster, Kōbe has quickly got back to business and the city bears little physical sign of its tragedy today.

## Arrival, information and getting around

Shinkansen **trains** stop at Shin-Kōbe station at the foot of Rokkō-san, around 1km north of Sannomiya Station in downtown Kōbe. As well as JR trains, those on the Hankyū and Hanshin lines also stop at Sannomiya Station, and are the cheaper way of connecting with Ōsaka and Kyoto to the east if you're not using a JR pass.

The fastest way of getting directly to Kōbe from Kansai International airport (KIX) is by **jet foil boat**. The thirty-minute journey across Ōsaka Bay to the Kōbe City Air Terminal (KCAT) on Port Island, costs ¥2200. From KCAT, take a bus to Sannomiya Station. **Ferries** from Shikoku, Kyūshū and Awaji-shima arrive at Naka Pier next to the Port Tower, ten minutes' walk south of Motomachi Station, and at Rokkō Island Ferry Terminal, east of the city. From here you can take the Rokkō Liner monorail to JR Suiyoshi or Hanshin Uozaki stations.

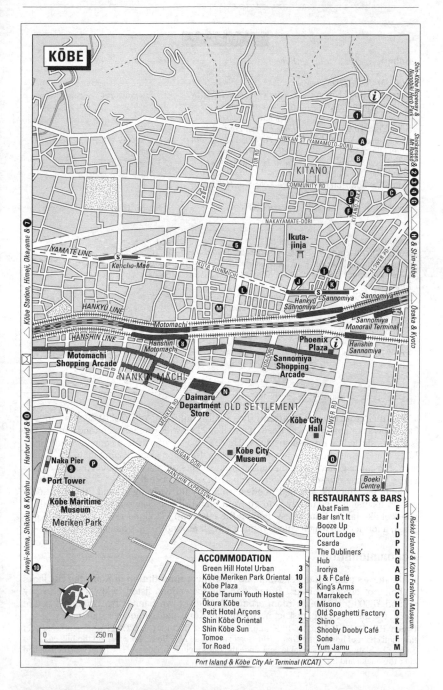

**KŌBE**

KITANO

JINKAN ST (YAMAMOTO-DORI)

COMMUNITY RD

NAKAYAMATE-DORI

Ikuta-jinja

YAMATE LINE

Kencho-Mae

IKUTA SUJINMICHI

HANKYŪ LINE

Motomachi

Hankyū Sannomiya

Sannomiya

Sannomiya Monorail Terminal

HANSHIN LINE

Hanshin Motomachi

Phoenix Plaza

Hanshin Sannomiya

Motomachi Shopping Arcade

NANKIN-MACHI

Sannomiya Shopping Arcade

Daimaru Department Store

OLD SETTLEMENT

Kōbe City Hall

Kōbe City Museum

Naka Pier

Port Tower

Kōbe Maritime Museum

Meriken Park

Boeki Centre

TOR RD

KITANO-ZAKA

FLOWER RD

NUNOBIKI RD

FLOWER RD

MERIKEN RD

KAIGAN-DORI

HANSHIN EXPRESSWAY 3

Shin-Kōbe Ropeway & Nunobiki Herb Park

Shinkansen & Mt Rokkō ❷ ❸ ❹ Ⓖ

Ⓗ & Shin-kōbe

Ōsaka & Kyoto

Rokkō Island & Kōbe Fashion Museum

Kōbe Station, Himeji, Okayama & ❼

Awaji-shima, Shikoku & Kyūshū

Harbor Land & ⓪

Port Island & Kōbe City Air Terminal (KCAT)

0    250 m

N

**RESTAURANTS & BARS**

| | |
|---|---|
| Abat Faim | E |
| Bar Isn't It | J |
| Booze Up | I |
| Court Lodge | D |
| Csarda | P |
| The Dubliners' Hub | N |
| Iroriya | G |
| J & F Café | A |
| King's Arms | B |
| Marrakech | Q |
| Misono | C |
| Old Spaghetti Factory | H |
| Shino | O |
| Shooby Dooby Café | K |
| Sone | L |
| Yum Jamu | F |
| | M |

**ACCOMMODATION**

| | |
|---|---|
| Green Hill Hotel Urban | 3 |
| Kōbe Meriken Park Oriental | 10 |
| Kōbe Plaza | 8 |
| Kōbe Tarumi Youth Hostel | 7 |
| Ōkura Kōbe | 9 |
| Petit Hotel Arçons | 1 |
| Shin Kōbe Oriental | 2 |
| Shin Kōbe Sun | 4 |
| Tomoe | 6 |
| Tor Road | 5 |

## KŌBE

| Kōbe | *Kōbe* | 神戸 |
|------|--------|-----|

### ACCOMMODATION

| English | Japanese (romaji) | Japanese |
|---------|-------------------|----------|
| Green Hill Hotel Urban | *Guriin Hiru Hoteru Āban* | グリーンヒルホテルアーバン |
| Kōbe Meriken Park Oriental Hotel | *Kōbe Merikenpāku Orientaru Hoteru* | 神戸メリケンパークオリエンタルホテル |
| Kōbe Plaza Hotel | *Kōbe Puraza Hoteru* | 神戸プラザホテル |
| Kōbe Tarumi Youth Hostel | *Kōbe Tarumi Yūsu Hosuteru* | 神戸垂水ユースホステル |
| Hotel Ōkura Kōbe | *Hoteru Ōkura Kōbe* | ホテルオークラ神戸 |
| Petit Hotel Arçons | *Puchi Hoteru Aruson* | プチホテルアルソン |
| Shin-Kōbe Oriental Hotel | *Shin-Kōbe Orientaru Hoteru* | 新神戸オリエンタルホテル |
| Shin-Kōbe Sun Hotel | *Shin-Kōbe San Hoteru* | 新神戸サンホテル |
| Tomoe | *Tomoe* | ともえ |
| Hotel Tor Road | *Hoteru Toa Rōdo* | ホテルトアロード |

### THE CITY

| English | Japanese (romaji) | Japanese |
|---------|-------------------|----------|
| Kitano | *Kitano* | 北野 |
| Kōbe City Museum | *Kōbe Shiritsu Hakubutsukan* | 神戸市立博物館 |
| Kōbe Fashion Museum | *Kōbe Fasshon Hakubutsukan* | 神戸ファッション博物館 |
| Kōbe Maritime Museum | *Kōbe Kaiyō Hakubutsukan* | 神戸海洋博物館 |
| Motomachi | *Motomachi* | 元町 |
| Nankin-machi | *Nankin-machi* | 南京町 |
| Phoenix Plaza | *Fenikkusu Puraza* | フェニックスプラザ |
| Sannomiya Station | *Sannomiya-eki* | 三ノ宮駅 |
| Shin-Kōbe Station | *Shin-Kōbe-eki* | 新神戸駅 |

### RESTAURANTS

| English | Japanese (romaji) | Japanese |
|---------|-------------------|----------|
| Misono | *Misono* | みその |
| Shino | *Shino* | 志乃 |

The main **tourist information** office (daily 9am–7pm; ☎078/322-0222) is south of Sannomiya Station on Flower Road. It's well stocked with English maps and leaflets and is always staffed by English speakers. There's also an information counter inside Shin-Kōbe Station and one at the top of Kitana-zaka, the main slope leading up to the Kitano area. For more general information on what's happening around Kōbe, pick up a copy of the magazine *Kansai Time Out* (see p.410), which has full listings of local events.

Being less than 3km wide, Kōbe is a great city for **walking** around. About the only reason for using the subway is to go from Shin-Kōbe to Sannomiya Station (¥160). If you feel like taking things easy, hop on the **city loop** (¥250 per ride, or ¥650 for a day pass), a tourist bus which runs a regular circuit around Kōbe's main sights.

## Accommodation

While there's plenty of top-end and mid-range **accommodation** in Kōbe, the city lacks a choice of cheaper places. Other than the exceptions listed below, expect to pay around ¥8000 for a single room around the downtown Sannomiya Station. If you're stuck, try the love hotel district between Shin-Kōbe and Sannomiya stations.

**Green Hill Hotel Urban**, 2-5-16 Kanno,Chūō-ku(☎078/222-1221, fax 242-1194). The cheapest of this mini-chain of hotels (the *Green Hill Hotel* and *Green Hill Hotel Annex* are up the hill, closer to Shin-Kōbe Station) is a reasonable deal since the rates include breakfast. The hotel was refurbished after the quake and includes a café. ⑨.

**Kōbe Meriken Park Oriental Hotel**, 5-6 Hatoba-chō (☎078/325-8111, fax 332-3900). The most striking feature of this reasonably priced upmarket hotel, jutting out into Kōbe Harbour, is its hump-backed design. The rooms have balconies and lovely views and there's a good range of in-house restaurants. Single rooms are just over ¥10,000. [7]

**Kōbe Plaza Hotel**, 1-13-12 Motomachi-dōri (☎078/332-1141, fax 331-2630). Slightly old-fashioned decor at this otherwise good-value mid-range hotel in a convenient location opposite Motomachi Station, near Chinatown. [5].

**Kōbe Tarumi Youth Hostel**, 5-58 Kaigan-dōri, Tarumi-ku (☎078/707-2133). This hostel, eight train stops west of Sannomiya Station, is worth considering because there's no curfew in the dorm, the trains are frequent and there are kitchen facilities to make your own meals. Also has single rooms for ¥5000. To reach the hostel from Tarumi Station, walk west along the main road running parallel to the shore for around ten minutes. The main road and construction along the beach does make it a noisy choice, however. [1].

**Hotel Ōkura Kōbe**, 2-1 Hatoba-chō (☎078/333-0111, fax 333-6673). Elegant luxury hotel, with smartly designed rooms, beside the Port Tower. Facilities include indoor and outdoor swimming pools and several restaurants and bars. It's worth stopping by to check out the beautiful paintings by Hirayama Ikuo in the main lobby. [7].

**Petit Hotel Arçons**, 3-7-1 Kitano-chō. There's nothing French at all about this small hotel in a white building with an outdoor deck in the heart of Kitano. Large, simply furnished rooms and a café. [5].

**Shin-Kōbe Oriental Hotel**, 1-7-14 Kitano-chō (☎078/291-1121, fax 291-1154). Soaring skyscraper upmarket hotel next to Shin-Kōbe Station. Fanstastic views from the smallish rooms, and a good range of restaurants both in the hotel and the connected shopping plaza. [7].

**Shin-Kōbe Sun Hotel**, 2-1-9 Nunobiki-chō (☎078/272-1080, fax 272-1088). Reasonably priced, if undistinguished business hotel towards the Shin-Kōbe end of the Flower Road. Singles are ¥7000. [5].

**Tomoe**, 5-4-19 Koto-no-ochō (☎078/221-1227). The cheapest business hotel you'll find near to Sannomiya Station; it's just a couple of blocks north on a side street. *Tatami* and Western-style rooms, with the ¥5700 single rooms sharing a communal bathroom. [5].

**Hotel Tor Road**, 3-1-19 Nakayamate-dōri (☎078/391-6691, fax 391-6570). Mid-range hotel with spacious rooms and a little more character than similar establishments. The British theme extends as far as draping a Union Jack outside and calling the café, *Muffin*. [6].

## The City

Kōbe's sights are split into three main areas. South of the band of rail lines passing through Sannomiya Station, Kōbe's focal point, is the city's commercial centre covering the **old settlement** area and, to the west, **Nankin-machi**, Kōbe's Chinatown. Immediately south of here are the **harbour** developments of Meriken Park, Kōbe Harbor Land, Port Island and Rokkō Island. North of Sannomiya Station lies Shin-Kōbe Station and **Kitano** where the *ijinkan*, or foreigners' houses dating from the turn of the century (most reconstructed after the 1995 quake) are clustered on the slopes of Maya-san. For the best view of the whole city and the Inland Sea, take the cable car up Rokkō-san.

### South of Sannomiya

Heading south along Flower Road from Sannomiya Station brings you to **Phoenix Plaza** (daily 10am–7pm; free), next to the main tourist office, where you can find out more about the Great Hanshin Earthquake and the area's rise from the rubble. It mainly functions as a base to promote social recovery, but there are also displays on the ground floor showing the impact of the tremor, including video footage of the disaster, all of which will give you a much better impression of how Kōbe suffered than the few cracks that remain in the pavements outside.

Around a century ago this area was Kōbe's principal foreign settlement, although there's little evidence of it today. To get a better idea of what it once looked like head for the **Kōbe City Museum** (Tues–Sun 10am–5pm; ¥200), ten minutes' walk south of either Sannomiya or Motomachi stations, which contains a finely detailed scale model of turn-of-the-century Kōbe and many woodblock prints from the same era. The highlight of the museum, however, is its collection of *Namban* (southern barbarian) art. These paintings, prints and screens – some of extraordinary detail and beauty – by Japanese artists of the late sixteenth and seventeenth century, show how they were influenced by the art of the first Europeans, or "southern barbarians", to come to Japan. Most of the pieces are so precious that they're only displayed for short periods each year.

Immediately west of the museum is **Nankin-machi**, Kōbe's Chinatown, the entrance to which is marked by the ornate Choan-mon gate opposite the Daimaru department store. The area is packed with Chinese restaurants and is a coulouful spot to browse for Asian trinkets, CDs and old vinyl records.

## Kōbe Harbour and Kitano

Kōbe's **harbour** lies directly south of Nankin-machi. Here you'll find the city's most striking architectural feature – the filigree roof of **Kōbe Maritime Museum** (Tues–Sun 10am–5pm; ¥500 or ¥700 including entrance to the Port Tower), a swooping white framework symbolizing waves and sails, contrasting with the tapered red casing of the adjacent **Port Tower**, best viewed at dusk from the wharf of the Harbor Land development. The museum itself contains detailed models of a wide range of ships, intriguing audio-visual displays and has good English explanations, but ultimately fails to have the impact of its exterior. If you want a bird's-eye view of the city, go up to the top of Kōbe City Hall, back on Flower Road, rather than pay ¥500 to enter the Port Tower.

The surrounding **Meriken Park** is a pleasant place to chill out and take in harbour views, as is the newer **Harbor Land** development, directly across the bay, where spruced up brick wharf buildings have been joined by modern shopping malls and a huge ferris wheel. East of Meriken Park is **Port Island**, but there's no reason to head out here on the monorail, unless you plan to attend a conference or exhibition in the area.

Kōbe's other area of reclaimed land, **Rokkō Island**, is something of a *gaijin* ghetto of multi-national offices and expat apartments, but it does have the high-tech **Kōbe Fashion Museum** (Mon, Tues, Thurs & Sat 11am–6pm, Fri 11am–8pm; ¥500). Housed inside what looks like a docked Starship Enterprise, this museum is a must for clothes junkies, and has a slide-show scored by The Orb and an extensive library of fashion mags and books. The only disappointment is that it's surprisingly light on Japanese fashion. To reach the museum, take the Rokkō line monorail from JR Suiyoshi or Hanshin Uozaki stations to Island Centre Station, from where it's a a couple of minutes' walk from the southeast exit.

Of primary interest to the hordes of Japanese visitors to Kōbe, but less so to others, are the *ijinkan*, or Western-style brick and clapboard houses of **Kitano**, 1km north of Sannomiya Station. The area's steep, narrow streets, lined with fashionable cafés, restaurants and shops, are pleasant to explore and throw up odd surprises, such as a mosque and a Jain temple. However, virtually all the *ijinkan* had to be reconstructed after the 1995 earthquake and most are just not that interesting inside for Westerners.

From the top of Kitano it's a short walk across to the **Shin-Kōbe Ropeway** (Mar 20–July 19 & Sept 1–Nov 30 Mon–Fri 9.30am–5.30pm, Sat 9.30am–9pm, Sun 9.30am–8pm; July 20–Aug 31 daily 9.30am–9pm; Dec 1–Mar 19 daily 9.30am–5pm; ¥550 one way, ¥1000 return), a cable car which provides sweeping views of the bay on the way up to the restful **Nunobiki Herb Park** (opens 30min later and closes 30min earlier than cable car hours; ¥200), a flower garden with a field of lavender and glass houses stocked with more exotic blooms. Hiking up the hill along the course starting behind Shin-Kōbe Station takes around thirty minutes.

# Eating, drinking and nightlife

Kōbe is a gourmet's paradise, its long history of international exchange blessing it with a diverse range of excellent **restaurants**. The most cosmopolitan dining area is around **Kitano-zaka**, where you can eat everything from Sri Lankan curries to the local delicacy Kōbe Beef – expensive slices of meat heavily marbled with fat. Another exciting place to head of an evening is the **Harbor Land** development, where you can take your pick from a multitude of cafés and restaurants in the bayside Mosaic mall. Fans of Chinese cuisine shouldn't miss out on **Nankin-machi** (Chinatown), where long queues form outside the most popular restaurants; if you can't wait, there are plenty of street stalls selling takeaway dumplings, noodles and other dishes.

While Kōbe doesn't have as strong a club scene as neighbouring Ōsaka, it does have a good range of **bars**, most clustered around Sannomiya and Motomachi – all within easy walking distance of each other. There are also several **cinemas** around Sannomiya, and at the Mosaic mall there's a four-screen multiplex.

## Restaurants and cafés

**Abat Faim**, 1-23-16 Kitano-chō. Tasty pasta and other Italian dishes in a stylish, contemporary restaurant with an open kitchen. Lunch specials for ¥770 are a great deal and there's an English menu. Tues–Sun 11.30am–10pm.

**Court Lodge**, 1-23-16 Kitano-chō. Next door to *Abat Faim*, this Sri Lankan restaurant serves rich coconut-milk-flavoured curries, best eaten with *godamba* bread. The set lunches are the best deal at around ¥1000. Daily 11am–10pm.

**Iroriya**, 3 Kitano-chō (☎078/231-6777). Large, traditional restaurant, where the waitresses wear kimono, specializing in dishes using the famous Kōbe beef, such as *shabu-shabu* and *sukiyaki* stews. Expect to pay at least ¥4000 per person. Daily noon–10pm.

**J&F Café**, 2-14-28 Yamamoto-dōri. On the main Kitano drag, this bright and airy café in a whitewashed wooden shack is above a shop and has English magazines to leaf through. Sandwiches for ¥700, and set lunches including a drink for ¥1000. Daily 11am–7pm.

**King's Arms**, 4-2-15 Isobe-dōri. On Flower Road just past the City Hall, this Olde England pub and steak restaurant, complete with darts, wooden beams and a portrait of Churchill, is a Kōbe institution. Lunch is the best time to sample the beef, with prices starting from ¥1300. Fish and chips, duck and daily specials are also on the menu. Expect to pay at least ¥3000 for dinner. Mon–Sat 11am–10pm, Sun 11.30am–9.30pm.

**Marrakech**, 1-20-15 Nakayamate-dōri. This long-running Morrocan restaurant, in a basement a couple of blocks east of Kitano-zaka, is not cheap, but it's authentic and serves true North African food, including *tajine* stews and couscous. Tues–Sun 5pm–11pm, Sat & Sun noon–2pm.

**Misono**, 3-3-19 Ikuta-chō. Photos of customers decorate the walls of this convivial *izakaya*, on the way up to Shin-Kōbe station to the east of Flower Road, specializing in *okonomiyaki* pancakes and serving a wide range of other Japanese dishes at inexpensive prices. Also good for a beer and late-night dining. Mon–Sat 11am–2pm & 6pm–1am.

**Old Spaghetti Factory**, 1-5-5 Higashi-Kawasaki-chō. Large, funky Italian restaurant, serving sixteen different spaghetti dishes in a converted turn-of-the-century brick warehouse in Harbor Land. A tram dominates the dining area and there's an English menu. Around ¥1500 per person, less for lunch. Mon–Sat 11am–2pm & 5–10.30pm, Sun 11am–10.30pm.

**Shino**, 6F, 1-20-2 Kitanagasa-dōri. Ladies in kimono greet you at this delightful and cosy Japanese restaurant, high above the traffic along Ikuta Shinmichi. Dishes such as grilled fish, tempura and sashimi are beautifully presented and the green tea *mochi* rice cake melts in the mouth. Set lunches are fantastic value from ¥1650; dinner starts at ¥3000. Mon–Sat 11.30am–2pm & 5–10pm.

**Shooby Dooby Café**, 3-12-3 Kitanagasa-dōri. Trendy diner, attracting Kōbe's stylish youth, with colourful leather banquette seats and a counter bar. Serves Western snack dishes, including sandwiches and pizza. The ¥1000 set lunch includes a beer and salad. Daily 11.30am–10.30pm.

**Yum Jamu**, 3F Hirose Bldg, 3-2-17 Kitanagasa-dōri. Eclectic oriental restaurant and good veggie choice using organic and additive-free produce. Has an English menu. Around ¥1000 per person. Daily noon–2pm & 5–10pm.

## Bars and clubs

**Bar Isn't It**, 6F Algo Bldg, 1-1-8 Shimoyamate-dōri. Lively atmosphere, but the notices warning patrons not to bring in weapons or hassle women set the tone at this chain bar, which is well past its best days. Daily 6pm–5am.

**Booze Up**, 2-15-3 Nakayamate-dōri. Laid-back bar, tucked away in the backstreets north of Ikuta Shinmichi, with a great collection of classic soul LPs. Opposite is the *Hurdy Gurdy Company* a funky *izakaya* specializing in *mukokuseki*.

**Csarda**, Meriken Park guchi. Micro-brewery, pronounced "Charuda", serving up at least seven types of beer, brewed by a Czech brewmeister on the the premises. Less interesting Western-style snack foods also available.

**The Dubliners'**, 47 Akashi-chō. Branch of the nationwide Irish pub chain owned by Sapporo Beer, in a basement opposite the Daimaru department store. Has quickly established itself as Kōbe's main *gaijin* hangout, due to its relaxed atmosphere and good food, including fish and chips. Daily 11.30am–11.30pm.

**Hub**, 2F OPA Bldg, 1 Kitano-chō. It's worth dropping by this British-style pub close to Shin-Kōbe Station, for the Happy Hour which runs from 5 till 7pm when all drinks are a bargain ¥180. Otherwise, Bass beer on tap is ¥800 a pint. Daily 5pm–midnight.

**Sone**, Kitano-zaka. This famous jazz club, just north of Nakayamate-dōri and run by the Sone family, is the best in the Kansai area. Attracts many top international artists as well as local talent. The first live set starts around 7pm and there's a ¥500 cover charge.

## Listings

**Airlines** JAL (☎078/331-2811), JAS (☎078/391-7611).

**Banks and exchange** Tokyo Bank and Hyōgo Bank are a 5min walk south of Sannomiya Station, just off Flower Road.

**Bookshops** The excellent secondhand bookstore Wantage Books, 1-13 Ikuta-chō (Mon–Fri 10am–5.30pm), is just south of Shin-Kōbe Station. Above are the offices of the monthly magazine *Kansai Time Out*. For new books head to Maruzen (daily 11am–8pm), on the Motomachi Ichibangai shopping arcade.

**Car rental** Nippon Rent-a-Car (☎078/252-0522), Mazda Rent-a-Car (☎078/251-6421) and Oki Rent-a-Car (☎078/232-1268) all have branches near Sannomiya Station.

**Hospital and medical advice** Kōbe Adventist Hospital, 8-4-1 Arinodai, Kita-ku (☎078/981-0161) has many English-speaking staff, but is a 30min drive north of the city. Kōbe University Hospital, 7-5-2 Kusunoki-chō (☎078/341-7451), is ten minutes' walk north of Kōbe Station. You could also try CHIC (Community House and Information Centre) for medical advice in English (Mon–Fri 9.30am–4.30pm; 078/857-6540).

**Internet access** Netsurf Kōbe, 1-13-19 Motomachi-dōri, close by Motomachi Station (daily 11am–9pm; ¥500 for 30min; ☎078/331-5173).

**Police** Kōbe Police Station, 5-4-1 Shinoyamate-dōri, chūō-ku (☎078/341-7441). Emergency numbers are listed in Basics on p.70.

**Post office** Kōbe Central Post Office is a two-minute walk northeast of Kōbe Station. There's also a convenient branch in Sannomiya Station.

**Shopping** Kōbe has several large department stores, including Daimaru, south of Motomachi Station and Kōbe Hankyū, part of the Harbor Land development beside Kōbe Station. The shopping arcades shadowing the railway tracks between Motomachi and Sannomiya stations are a favourite cruising ground of Kōbe's youth, while the arcades around Nankin-machi have several cut-price electrical outlets.

**Taxis** Try ABC Musen (☎078/241-8484) or Kōbe Sogō Taxi (☎078/431-0081).

**Travel agency** The main JTB office is at Sannomiya Station (☎078/231-4118).

# Arima Onsen

It may be one of Japan's oldest hot spring resorts, but **ARIMA ONSEN**, on the northern slopes of Rokkō-san, northeast of the city, has become blighted by ugly overpriced tourist hotels and gift shops galore. Fortunately there's still an area of small wooden ryokan, twisting narrow streets and several rustic temples and shrines dotted up the hillside. If you've not been to an onsen resort, Arima is worth dropping by to see what one is like, and it's also possible to hike to the top of the mountain in around an hour.

The small **public bath** (daily 8am–9pm, closed first and third Tues of every month; ¥5200) is five minutes' walk uphill from the train station, close by the bus station and **tourist information office** (daily 9am–7pm; ☎078/904-0708). It's nothing special and is usually full of pensioners who come to take the sludgy brown waters for their health. Slightly more attractive, but more expensive, are the baths at **Kan I Hoken Hoyo Centre** (daily 10.30am–3.30pm; ¥1000), a hotel, ten minutes' walk further up the hill past a cluster of shrines.

To reach the resort by **train** from Kōbe, take the subway to Tanigami, transfer to the Kōbe Dentetsu line to Arima Guchi, where you may have to change again to reach the terminus at Arima Onsen. The journey takes around thirty minutes and costs ¥970. There are also direct **buses** from Sannomiya and Shin-Kōbe station to Arima which take around forty minutes and cost ¥680. If you're coming from Ōsaka, take a local JR train to Sanda, where you can change to the Kōbe Dentetsu line.

The tourist office has a hand-drawn English map of the town and can help arrange **accommodation** should you wish to stay over. One of the more traditional small ryokan is *Kami-ō-bō* (☎078/904-0531, fax 904-0515; ⑥), just up the main street from the public bath, where the rates include two meals. For lunch, *Goshobo*, opposite the tourist office in the rustic lodge has set menus of local dishes from around ¥2000 per person.

## Himeji

By far the most impressive of Japan's twelve surviving feudal-era fortresses is the one in **HIMEJI**, 55km west of Kōbe, the memorable backdrop to the Bond adventure *You Only Live Twice* as well as countless *samurai* dramas. The splendid gabled donjons of **Himeji-jō** – also known as Shirasagi-jō, or "white egret castle" because the complex is supposed to resemble the shape of the bird in flight – miraculously survived the World War II bombings that laid waste to much of the rest of the city. Himeji is best visited as a day-trip: after you've explored the castle, it's also worth taking in the beautiful **Himeji Kōko-en**, nine linked traditional-style gardens, and a couple of intriguing **museums** around the fortress walls.

### Himeji-jō

Around 1km directly north of Himeji Station lies the main gateway to **Himeji-jō** (daily: Jan–May 9am–4pm; June–Dec 9am–5pm; ¥500). The present complex of moats, thick defensive walls, keeps and connecting corridors dates from the early seventeenth century, although there has been a fortress in the town since around 1346. By the time Tokugawa Ieyasu's son-in-law, Ikeda Terumasa, took control of the area in 1600, the country was at peace and so when he set about rebuilding Himeji-jō, adding the central five-storey donjon and three smaller donjons, the aim was to create something visually impressive. Even so, the castle incorporates many cunning defensive features, only really appreciated if you go on one of the **free guided tours in English** which take around ninety minutes; guides are usually waiting at the main castle gate, but to be sure of meeting one make an advance reservation on ☎0792/85-1146.

If you don't have a guide, finding your way around the castle is no problem because a route is clearly marked and there are English explanations on plaques at many points of interest. The main gateway is the Hishi-no-mon, to the west of which are the open grounds of the Nishi-no-maru (western citadel), where the *daimyō* and his family lived, the central donjon only being used in times of war. All that remains of the original

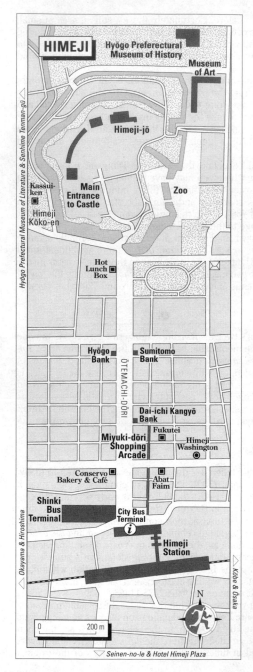

HIMEJI

Hyōgo Preferectural Museum of History

Museum of Art

Himeji-jō

*Hyōgo Prefectural Museum of Literature & Senhime Tenman-gū*

Kassui-ken

Himeji Kōko-en

Main Entrance to Castle

Zoo

Hot Lunch Box

Hyōgo Bank

Sumitomo Bank

ŌTEMACHI-DŌRI

Dai-ichi Kangyō Bank

Fukutei

Miyuki-dōri Shopping Arcade

Himeji Washington

Conservo Bakery & Café

Abat-Faim

Shinki Bus Terminal

City Bus Terminal

*Okayama & Hiroshima*

Himeji Station

*Kōbe & Ōsaka*

N

0     200 m

▽ *Seinen-no-le & Hotel Himeji Plaza*

palace are the outer corridor and "cosmetic tower" where Princess Sen (see box, p.516) adjusted her kimono and powdered her nose during the mid-seventeenth century. It was Sen's dowry that enabled the castle to be built in its present form.

A zigzag path through more gates and past turrets and walls from which defending soldiers could fire arrows, shoot muskets and drop stones and boiling liquids, leads up to the **Honmaru** (inner citadel), dominated by the magnificent central donjon **Daitenshū**. There are six levels within the dark and chilly keep, supported by a framework of huge wooden pillars, one of which is made from a 780-year-old cypress tree; touch it and it's said you'll have long life. On the top level, where the lord and his family would commit suicide if the castle was captured (which it never was), you can now look out across the city and as far as the Inland Sea on clear days.

Beside the **Harakiri-maru**, a small courtyard on the east side of the Daitenshū where *samurai* are believed to have committed ritual suicide (*Seppuku*), is an alternative route to the donjon from the moat grounds. Before leaving, pass by **Okiku-ido**, a well on south of the donjon, the scene of the castle's most famous ghost story *Banshu Sara-Yashiki*. The soul of the servant girl Okiku, tortured to death after she was falsely accused of stealing a valuable dish, is said to wail in this well into which her body was dumped.

## Other sights

Himeji's other sights are conveniently located around Himeji-jō's moats. On the west side of the castle is the splendid **Himeji Kōko-en** (daily: Jan–May & Sept–Dec

## ARIMA ONSEN AND HIMEJI

| | | |
|---|---|---|
| **Arima Onsen** | *Arima Onsen* | 有馬温泉 |
| Goshobo | *Goshobo* | ごしょぼ |
| Kami-ō-bō | *Kami-ō-bō* | かみおおぼう |
| Kan I Hoken Hoyō Centre | *Kan-ichi Hoken Hoyō Sentā* | かんいちほけん保養センター |
| | | |
| **Himeji** | *Himeji* | 姫路 |
| Himeji-jō | *Himeji-jō* | 姫路城 |
| Himeji Kōko-en | *Himeji Kōko-en* | 姫路好古園 |
| Hyōgo Prefectural Museum of History | *Hyōgo-ken Rekishi Hakubutsukan* | 兵庫県歴史博物館 |
| Hyōgo Prefectural Museum of Literature | *Hyōgo-ken Bungaku Hakubutsukan* | 兵庫県文学博物館 |

*ACCOMMODATION AND RESTAURANTS*

| | | |
|---|---|---|
| Fukutei | *Fukutei* | ふく亭 |
| Hotel Himeji Plaza | *Hoteru Himeji Puraza* | ホテル姫路プラザ |
| Himeji Washington Hotel | *Himeji Washinton Hoteru* | 姫路ワシントンホテル |
| Seinen-no-Ie | *Seinen-no-Ie* | 青年の家 |

9am–4.30pm; June–Aug 9am–5.30pm; ¥300 or ¥640 combined ticket with the castle), nine connected Edo-era style gardens built in 1992, on the former sight of the Nishi Oyashiki, the *daimyō*'s west residence for his *samurai*. The gardens are separated by mud walls topped with roof tiles, like those which would have stood around each *samurai* villa, and include mini forests, carp-filled pools, rockeries and elegant teahouses.

Ignore the depressing zoo on the east side of Himeji jō and follow the moat grounds north past the red-brick building that once housed an armoury and is now the **Museum of Art** (Tues–Sun 9am–5pm; ¥200), mainly displaying changing exhibitions of Western art. Ahead, in a striking building designed by the founding father of modern Japanese architecture, Tange Kenzō, is the informative **Hyōgo Prefectural Museum of History** (Tues–Sun 10am–5pm; ¥200), which includes detailed scale models of the twelve donjons across Japan which survive in their original form, plus Tokyo's Edo Castle, the largest of the keeps, which was largely destroyed by fire in 1657 and finally destroyed during World War II. There's also the opportunity to try on a twelve-layered court kimono and *samurai* armour (11am, 2pm & 3.30pm).

Tange's contemporary rival, Andō Tadao, has made his mark on Himeji at the **Museum of Literature** (Tues–Sun 10am–4.30pm; ¥200), some 600m directly west of the History Museum across the moat and just beyond the entrance to Princess Sen's shrine, **Senhime Tenman-gū**. The exhibits inside the museum are all in Japanese and their authors are unknown in the West, but the imaginative displays and an excellent English-language leaflet make the entrance fee worth considering. If nothing else, come here to admire Ando's ultra modern design – a disjointed arrangement of squares, circles and walkways made from rough concrete – which also respects traditional principles, such as the *shakkei* (borrowed scenery) of the castle behind the museum and the use of water.

## Practicalities

Himeji is a stop on the **Shinkansen** line between Ōsaka and Okayama, and is also served by slower and cheaper limited express **trains**, which take around fifty minutes from Kōbe to the east or Okayama to the west. Long-distance **buses**, from Tokyo, Ōsaka and Kōbe, also stop beside the train station which is around 1km south of the castle at the end of Ōtemae-dōri, the main shopping street.

### SENHIME THE SURVIVOR

As pawns in political power games go, Senhime, eldest daughter of the second shogun Tokugawa Hidetada, was dealt some rough calls during her life, but had the strength of character to outlive all her warrior relations. She was cynically married off by her grandfather Tokugawa Ieyasu at the age of six to Toyotomi Hideyori, son of the future shogun's arch enemy Hideyoshi. When Hideyori came to power after his father's death, Ieyasu laid seige to Ōsaka castle despite Senhime being trapped inside. The lord of Tsuwano (see p.579), Sakazaki, risked his life to rescue her from the burning fortress on the understanding that he would later marry her. Ieyasu had other ideas, and a year after the suicide of her first husband, Senhime was married to Honda Heihachirō Tadatoki, son of the *daimyō* of Himeji. For ten years, the princess lived a peaceful life in Himeji-jō where special apartments were built for the couple. After Honda's death in 1626, Senhime took the veil in preference to marrying yet again, and passed the next forty years in Tokyo until her death in 1666.

Himeji's major sights are within easy walking distance of the station. Stash your bags in one of the station's coin lockers, and pick up a map of the town from the **Himeji Tourist Information Centre** (daily 9am–5pm; ☎0792/85-3792), staffed by English speakers between 10am and 3pm. If you decide to stop over, the assistants can also make **accommodation** bookings, although there's little reason for staying overnight in Himeji beyond walking around the floodlit castle.

Only if you're running low on cash, consider the run-down *Seinen-no-Ie* (☎0792/93-2716; ①), which has very cheap dorms, with cooking facilities, but is also very basic. To reach the hostel, take bus #37 to the Chūō-kōen-guchi bus stop, and walk 600m west across the river and past a Japanese garden. Immediately south of Himeji Station is the *Hotel Himeji Plaza* (☎0792/81-9000, fax 84-3549; ⑤), one of the cheaper mid-range business hotels, with singles from ¥5900 and a sauna and communal bath. The singles are slightly more expensive, but the rooms more modern at the *Himeji Washington Hotel* (☎0792/25-0111, fax 25-0133; ⑤), part of the national chain of business hotels, three blocks east of the north side of the station.

The Miyuki-dōri covered shopping arcade, to the north from the station, is a good place to stop off for a **snack** or to pick up a *bentō* to enjoy within the castle grounds. The *Conservo* bakery and café on Ōtemae-dōri does reasonably priced sandwiches, salads and cakes, while closer to the castle, the *Hot Lunch Box*, serves heated takeaway *bentō*. For something classier, try the *Kassui-ken* **teahouse** within Himeji Kōko-en, where the lunch of *anago* (grilled conger eel) is a local speciality and is worth the expense if only for the beautiful views you'll have of castle and gardens. A block behind the *Washington Hotel*, is the traditional Japanese **restaurant** *Fukutei*, which does good-value set lunches including sashimi and tempura, while almost opposite the hotel is a branch of the excellent Kōbe-based Italian restaurant *Abat Faim*. Pasta lunch specials here are under ¥1000 and it's open until 9pm if you fancy dinner after seeing the castle.

## travel details

### Trains

The trains between the major cities listed below are the fastest, direct services. There are also frequent slower services, run by JR and several private companies, covering the same destinations. It is usually possible, especially on long-distance routes, to get there faster by changing between services.

**Himeji** to: Fukuoka (Hakata Station; 20 daily; 3hr); Hiroshima (at least 20 daily; 1hr 22min); Kōbe (at least every 30min; 20min); Kyoto (at least

30 daily; 1hr); Nagoya (at least 30 daily; 1hr 55min); Okayama (at least every 30min; 25min); Ōsaka (at least every 30 min; 35min); Tokyo (14 daily; 3hr 45min).

**Ise** to: Futaminoura (1–3 hourly; 8min); Kashikojima (1–3 hourly; 50min–1hr); Kyoto (hourly; 2hr); Nagoya (every 20–30min; 1hr 20min–1hr 35min); Nara (every 15–20min; 2–3hr); Ōsaka (every 15min; 1hr 45min); Toba (every 20–30min; 15–20min).

**Kashikojima** to: Ise (1–3 hourly; 50min–1hr); Kyoto (hourly; 2hr 45min); Nagoya (1–2 hourly; 2hr 15min); Ōsaka (1–2 hourly; 2hr 20min).

**Kōbe (Shin-Kōbe)** to: Fukuoka (Hakata Station; at least 20 daily; 3hr 5min); Himeji (every 30min; 20min); Hiroshima (at least every 30min; 1hr 15min); Kyoto (35 daily; 35min); Nagoya (35 daily; 1hr 25min); Okayama (at least every 30min; 35min); Ōsaka (every 15min; 15min); Tokyo (33 daily; 3hr 30min).

**Kōya-san** (Gokurakabashi) to: Hashimoto (every 20–30min; 45min); Nara (every 15–20min; 3hr); Ōsaka (every 20–30min; 1hr 15min–1hr 40min).

**Kyoto** to: Fukuoka (Hakata Station; 1–2 hourly; 2hr 50min–3hr 20min); Himeji (1–3 hourly; 50min); Hiroshima (1–2 hourly; 2hr 15min–1hr 40min); Ise (hourly; 2hr); Kanazawa (1–2 hourly; 2hr–2hr 40min); Kansai International (every 30min; 1hr 15min); Kashikojima (hourly; 2hr 45min); Kobe (1–3 hourly; 35min); Nagoya (at least every 15min; 40min–1hr); Nara (every 15–20min; 33min–1hr 20min); Ōsaka (at least every 15min; 17min); Toba (hourly; 2hr 20min); Tokyo (at least every 15min; 2hr 10min–4hr); Toyama (hourly; 2hr 40min–3hr); Uji (every 15–20min; 15–25min).

**Nara** to: Ise (every 15–20min; 2–3hr); Kōya-san (every 15–20min; 3hr); Kyoto (every 15–20min; 33min–1hr 20min); Ōsaka (at least every 15min; 30–40min).

**Ōsaka (Hankyū Umeda)** to: Takarazuka (at least every 30min; 36min).

**Ōsaka (Kintetsu-Namba)** to: Nara (at least every 15min; 30–40min).

**Ōsaka (Namba)** to: Kansai International (every 30min; 35min); Kōya-san (every 20–30min; 1hr 15min–1hr 40min).

**Ōsaka (Ōsaka Station)** to: Akita (1 daily; 10hr); Aomori (1 daily; 12hr 35min); Kanazawa (24 daily; 2hr 30min); Matsumoto (1 daily; 4hr); Nagano (1 daily; 4hr 50min); Takarazuka (every 30 min; 40min); Toyama (14 daily; 3hr 5min).

**Ōsaka (Shin-Ōsaka)** to: Fukuoka (Hakata Station; at least every 30min; 2hr 17min); Himeji (every 20min; 35min); Hiroshima (at least every 15min; 1hr 15min); Kansai International (30 daily; 45min); Kōbe (every 15min; 15min); Kyoto (at least every 15min; 17min); Nagoya (at least every 15min; 1hr 7min); Okayama (at least every 15min; 1hr 5min); Tokyo (at least every 15min; 2hr 30min).

**Ōsaka (Uehonmachi)** to: Ise (every 15min; 1hr 45min); Kashikojima (1–2 hourly; 2hr 20min); Toba (every 20–30min; 2hr).

**Toba** to: Kashikojima (every 30min; 30–40min); Kyoto (hourly; 2hr 20min); Nagoya (every 20–30min; 1hr 45min); Ōsaka (every 20–30min; 2hr).

## Buses

The buses listed below are mainly long-distance services – often travelling overnight – between the major cities, and local services where there is no alternative means of transport. For shorter journeys, however, trains are almost invariably quicker and often no more expensive.

**Himeji** to: Tokyo (Shibuya; 1 daily; 9hr).

**Ise** to: Toba (at least 3 daily; 40min).

**Kyoto** to: Fukuoka (1 daily; 9hr 25min); Kanazawa (5 daily; 4hr); Kansai International (hourly; 1hr 45min); Kumamoto (1 daily; 10hr 45min); Nagasaki (1 daily; 11hr); Nagoya (13 daily; 2hr 30min); Ōsaka (Itami; every 30min; 55min); Tokyo (3 daily; 8hr); Yokohama (1 daily; 7hr 30min).

**Nara** to: Fukuoka (1 daily; 10hr); Tokyo (1 daily; 8hr); Yokohama (1 daily; 9hr).

**Ōsaka** to: Beppu (1 daily; 9hr); Fukuoka (1 daily 9hr); Niigata (1 daily; 9hr); Hagi (1 daily; 12hr); Kagoshima (1 daily; 12hr); Kansai International (at least every 15min; 1hr); Kumamoto (1 daily; 9hr); Miyazaki (1 daily; 12hr); Nagano (1 daily; 8hr); Nagasaki (1 daily; 10hr); Ōsaka (Itami; every 20–30min; 50min); Tokyo (3 daily; 8hr 50min).

## Ferries

**Kōbe** to: Imabari (1 daily; 7hr 20min); Kansai International (frequent; 30min); Kita-Kyūshū (1 daily; 12hr 20min); Nishi-Ōita (2 daily; 11hr 50min).

**Ōsaka** to: Ashizuri (6 weekly; 10hr 20min); Beppu (1 daily; 13hr 20min); Kannoura (1 daily; 5hr); Kōchi (1 daily; 9hr 10min); Matsuyama (1 daily; 9hr 20min); Miyazaki (1 daily; 12hr 50min); Shibushi (1 daily; 14hr 40min); Shinmoji (2 daily; 12hr).

**Toba** to: Irako (frequent; 30–50min); Morozaki (4 daily; 1hr 10min).

**Flights**

**Ōsaka (Itami)** to: Akita (1 daily; 1hr 20min); Aomori (2 daily; 1hr 30min); Fukuoka (5 daily; 1hr); Kagoshima (9 daily; 1hr 10min); Kumamoto (6 daily; 1h 5min); Miyazaki (8 daily; 1hr 5min); Nagasaki (6–7 daily;1hr 10min ); Niigata (3 daily; 1hr 5min); Ōita (5 daily; 1hr); Okinawa (Naha; 3 daily; 2hr); Sapporo (Chitose; 3 daily; 2hr); Sendai (6 daily; 1hr 10min); Tokyo (9 daily; 1hr); Yamagata (2 daily; 1hr 20min).

**Ōsaka (Kansai International)** to: Akita (1 daily; 1hr 30min); Aomori (1 daily; 1 hr 35min); Fukuoka (6–7 daily; 1hr); Ishigaki (1 daily; 2hr 40min); Kagoshima (2–3 daily; 1hr 10min); Kōchi (8 daily; 40min); Kumamoto (2 daily; 1hr 5min); Matsuyama (4 daily; 50min); Miyako (1 daily; 2hr); Miyazaki (2 daily; 1hr 5min); Nagasaki (2–3 daily; 1hr 10min); Niigata (3 daily; 1hr 10min); Ōita (2–3 daily; 1hr); Okinawa (Naha; 3 daily; 2hr); Sapporo (10 daily; 2hr ); Sendai (1–2 daily; 1hr 40min); Shōnai (Tsuruoka; 1 daily; 1hr 20min); Tokyo (Haneda; 9 daily; 1hr); Yamagata (1 daily; 1hr 15min).

# CHAPTER SEVEN

# WESTERN HONSHŪ

lso known as Chūgoku meaning "middle country", **Western Honshū** used to be at the centre of the Japanese nation, lying between the country's earliest settlements in Kyūshū and the imperial city of Kyoto. The region is split geographically into two distinct areas, with the southern **San-yō coast** being blighted by heavy industry but bordering the enchanting Inland Sea, while the rugged and sparsely populated northern **San-in coast** boasts some delightful small towns and a generally pristine landscape. The southern coast is easy to travel around, with Shinkansen lines, good local railway services and highways, while the northern coast takes more planning to tour by public transport, but easily repays the effort.

Though Chūgoku is rich in history, with burial mounds on both coasts dating from the first century, it's a more contemporary event that brings most visitors to the region. Lying midway along the San-yō coast, **Hiroshima**, site of the world's first atom-bomb and the region's largest city, is the one place you'll want to stop off en route to or from Kyūshū. If you only have a few days, you should also aim to take in the old towns of **Kurashiki** and **Matsue**, as well as the island **Miya-jima**. In a couple of weeks, you could make a circuit of both coasts taking in most of the region's highlights.

## THE INLAND SEA

*"They rise gracefully from this protected, stormless sea, as if they had just emerged, their beaches, piers, harbors all intact... Wherever one turns there is a wide and restful view, one island behind the other, each soft shape melting into the next until the last dim outline is lost in the distance."*

Donald Richie, *The Inland Sea*, 1971.

It's difficult to improve on American author Richie's sublime description of the Inland Sea (*Seto Naikai*) and, despite his fears that it would all be ruined in Japan's rush to the twenty-first century, this priceless panorama has changed remarkably little. Boxed in by the islands of Honshū, Kyūshū and Shikoku, and dotted with more than 3000 other islands, this sea is one of Japan's scenic gems, often likened to the Aegean in its beauty. But as Richie rightly says, given the choice, you'd always want to swim to one of these inviting Japanese islands rather than a rugged Greek rock.

Several islands are now connected by bridges and fast ferries to the mainland, reducing their isolation and much of their charm, but on many others you'll be struck by the more leisurely pace of life and by the relative lack of modern-day blight. The most popular islands to head for are Awaji-shima (p.621), Ikuchi-jima and Ōmi-shima (p.543), Miya-jima (p.556) and Shōdo-shima (p.609), although a host of others are served by ferries and have accommodation and tourist facilities.

If you don't have time to linger, consider taking one boat trip across the sea or heading to a vantage point such as Washū-zan (p.536) or Yashima (p.608) to look out over the islands. JNTO publishes a fact sheet, detailing several sightseeing cruises, which are expensive for what they offer; you're better off putting together your own itinerary using individual ferry services. If you take a ferry between Kyūshū and Kōbe, Ōsaka and Tokyo, you'll pass through the Inland Sea, anyway, although check it will be daylight.

At the eastern end of the San-yō coast, **Okayama** has one of Japan's top gardens, **Kōrakuen**, and makes a good base for visiting the beautifully preserved Edo-era town of **Kurashiki**. One of the best things about travelling around Okayama-ken is a stay in its International Villas, unique to the prefecture and dotted around some of its more remote parts. Heading west along the coast, one of the treasures of Hiroshima-ken is the timeless fishing village of **Tomo-no-Ura** with its gorgeous views across the Inland Sea. The raffishly appealing port of **Onomichi**, slightly further west, is also the jumping-off point for the laid-back island, **Ikuchi-jima**, home to Japan's wackiest temple complex and a lovely art museum.

The one island of the Inland Sea you won't want to miss is verdant *Miya-jima*, just west of Hiroshima, site of the ancient shrine **Itsukushima-jinja** with its water-bound red *torii*. On the southern coast of neighbouring Yamaguchi-ken, the only prefecture to span Chūgoku, pause to admire the elegant bridge Kintai-kyō at **Iwakuni** and the spectacular view across the narrow Kanmon Straits to Kyūshū from Hino-yama in **Shimonoseki**, the port at the tip of Honshū. Inland, the highlights of the prefecture's small capital, **Yamaguchi**, are an impressive pagoda and classic Zen rock and moss garden.

Turning east along the frequently deserted San-in coast, **Hagi**, an old castle town and hot-bed of pre-Meiji era revolt, boasts a lovely cluster of old *samurai* houses and atmos-

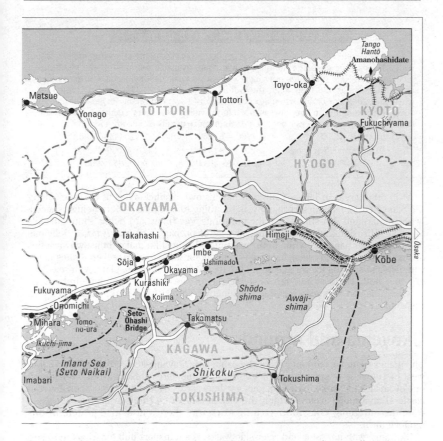

pheric temples. Perhaps even more beautiful is **Tsuwano**, another small castle town nestling in a tranquil valley, further east in Shimane-ken. This prefecture is the heartland of Japan's eight million Shinto deities, who gather each year in October at the venerable shrine Izumo Taisha, near the appealing waterbound capital of **Matsue**. Roughly mid-point along the San-in coast, Matsue has the region's only original castle tower as well as some old *samurai* houses and interesting museums. The sand spit **Amanohashidate**, at the far eastern reaches of the region, marks the end of the San-in coast, and provides some of Japan's most scenic views.

A regular JR Rail Pass is the most convenient way of getting around the region, but if you plan to stick only to the San-yō coast consider the cheaper **JR West San-yō Area Pass**, which covers all Shinkansen and local rail routes between Ōsaka and Fukuoka (see Basics, p.31). If you need quicker access to the region there are several **airports**, including two near Hiroshima, Okayama, Ube close to Shimonoseki, and Yonago near the San-in city of Matsue. If time isn't an issue, then don't miss out on a leisurely **ferry** ride across the Inland Sea (see box, p.519). **Renting a car** is a good idea, especially if you're planning to tour the quieter San-in coast, as the fast **Chūgoku Expressway** threads its way through the region's central mountainous spine, from where you can branch off to sights on either coast.

---

### ACCOMMODATION PRICE CODES

All accommodation in this book has been graded according to the following price codes, which refer to the cheapest double or twin room available for most of the year, and include taxes. Note that rates may increase during peak holiday periods, in particular around Christmas and New Year, the Golden Week (April 28–May 6) and Obon (the week around August 15), when accommodation is very difficult to get without an advance reservation. In the case of hostels providing dormitory accommodation, the code refers to the charge per bed. See p.36 for more details on accommodation.

| | | |
|---|---|---|
| ① under ¥3000 | ④ ¥7000–10,000 | ⑦ ¥20,000–30,000 |
| ② ¥3000–5000 | ⑤ ¥10,000–15,000 | ⑧ ¥30,000–40,000 |
| ③ ¥5000–7000 | ⑥ ¥15,000–20,000 | ⑨ over ¥40,000 |

---

As in other areas of Japan, Chūgoku has it's own distinct styles of **cuisine**. Along the San-yō coast, fish, unsurprisingly, is the thing to eat, with oysters being especially popular around Hiroshima, and the notorious *fugu* (blowfish) being Shimonoseki's top dish. Hiroshima also has a special way of preparing *okonomiyaki*, a delicious Japanese batter pancake, while both Iwakuni and Kurashiki make their own varieties of sushi. On the San-in coast, Matsue is renown for it *kyōdo ryōri*, seven dishes made with fish and seafood from Lake Shinji-ko. It's worth a look at the plates you're eating off, too: both Hagi, at the far western end of the San-in coast, and Imbe, east of Okayama, are famous for their distinctive pottery, Hagi-yaki and Bizen-yaki respectively.

# Okayama and around

The main reason for stopping off in the capital of Okayama-ken, **OKAYAMA**, 730km west of Tokyo, is to stretch your legs in its famous garden, **Kōrakuen**, considered one of Japan's top three. The spacious gardens are overlooked by the reconstructed castle **Okayama-jō** around which the city developed in the Edo period, but aside from the intriguing **Okayama Orient Museum**, there's little else of note in this modern town.

Okayama, with its trams and river-side walks, is a transport hub for trips out to surrounding attractions. The top draw is **Kurashiki**, just fifteen minutes west of the city, with its well-preserved enclave of picturesque old merchant houses and canals. From Kurashiki you can head inland to **Takahashi** to discover Japan's highest castle **Bitchū-Matsuyama**, looking down from its mountain-top over a town of old temples. For a spectacular view of both the Inland Sea and the Seto-Ōhashi bridge, aim for **Washū-zan** on the southern tip of the prefecture. To discover fragments of the area's ancient history, consider pedalling along the **Kibi bicycle route**, west of the city, past fifth-century burial mounds and rustic temples and shrines. And even more off-the-beaten-track sights will be within your reach if you opt to stay at one of the prefecture's **International Villas**, self-catering accommodation in scenic locations specially reserved for foreign visitors.

## Arrival and information

Shinkansen and regular **trains** stop at Okayama Station, just over 1km west of Kōrakuen. This is where you'll need to change from the Shinkansen to the JR Seto Ōhashi line if you're heading across to Shikoku (see p.598). Long-distance **buses** arrive either at the Eki-mae Bus Station on the east side of Okayama Station or the Tenmaya

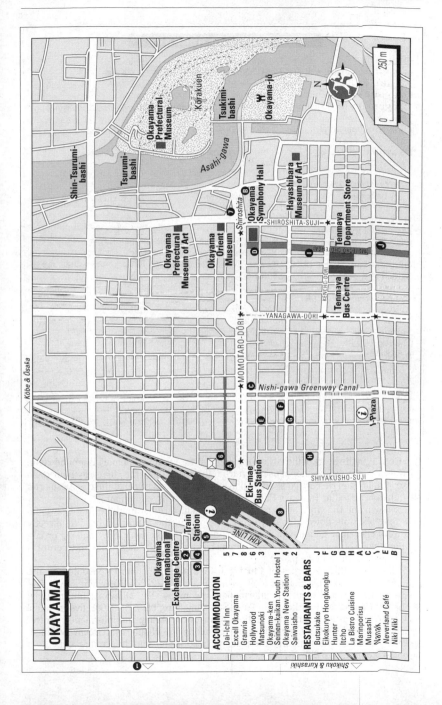

# OKAYAMA

△ Kōbe & Ōsaka

Shikoku & Kurashiki ▽

Shin-Tsurumi-bashi

Tsurumi-bashi

Tsurumi-bashi

Kōrakuen

Okayama Prefectural Museum

Tsukimi-bashi

Okayama-jō

Asahi-gawa

Okayama Prefectural Museum of Art

Okayama Orient Museum

Shiroshita

Okayama Symphony Hall

Hayashibara Museum of Art

SHIROSHITA-SUJI

Tenmaya Department Store

KENCHO-DORI

Tenmaya Bus Centre

YANAGAWA-DŌRI

MOMOTARO-DŌRI

Nishi-gawa Greenway Canal

I-Plaza

Eki-mae Bus Station

SHIYAKUSHO-SUJI

KIHI LINE

Train Station

Okayama International Exchange Centre

0    250 m

N

**ACCOMMODATION**

| Dai-Ichi Inn | 5 |
| Excell Okayama | 7 |
| Granvia | 8 |
| Hollywood | 6 |
| Matsunoki | 3 |
| Okayama-ken Seinen-kaikan Youth Hostel | 1 |
| Okayama New Station | 4 |
| Saiwaisho | 2 |

**RESTAURANTS & BARS**

| Butsukake | J |
| Eikokuryo Hongkongku | F |
| Hunter | G |
| Itcho | D |
| La Bistro Cuisine | H |
| Marinporisu | A |
| Musashi | C |
| Nayak | I |
| Neverland Café | E |
| Niki Niki | B |

## OKAYAMA AND AROUND

| | | |
|---|---|---|
| **Okayama** | *Okayama* | 岡山 |
| Hayashibara Museum of Art | *Hayashibara Bijutsukan* | 林原美術館 |
| Kōraku-en | *Kōraku-en* | 後楽園 |
| Okayama-jō | *Okayama-jō* | 岡山城 |
| Okayama Orient Museum | *Okayama-shiritsu Oriento Bijutsukan* | 岡山市立オリエント美術館 |
| Okayama Prefectural Museum of Art | *Okayama-kenritsu Bijutsukan* | 岡山県立美術館 |
| Okayama Prefectural Museum | *Okayama-kenritsu Hakubutsukan* | 岡山県立博物館 |

*ACCOMMODATION*

| | | |
|---|---|---|
| Excel Okayama | *Ekuseru Okayama* | エクセル岡山 |
| Hotel Granvia | *Hoteru Guranvia* | ホテルグランヴィア |
| Hollywood | *Hariuddo* | ハリウッド |
| Matsunoki Ryokan | *Matsunoki Ryokan* | まつのき旅館 |
| Okayama-ken Seinen-Kaikan Youth Hostel | *Okayama-ken Seinen-Kaikan Yūsu Hosuteru* | 岡山県青年会館ユースホステル |
| Okayama New Station Hotel | *Okayama Nyū Sutēshon Hoteru* | 岡山ニューステーションホテル |
| Saiwai-sō | *Saiwai-sō* | 幸荘 |

*INTERNATIONAL VILLAS*

| | | |
|---|---|---|
| Kokusai Kōryū Vira | *Kokusai Kōryū Vira* | 国際交流ヴィラ |
| Koshihata | *Koshihata* | 越畑 |
| Shiraishi-jima | *Shiraishi-jima* | 白石島 |
| Takebe | *Takebe* | 建部 |
| Ushimado | *Ushimado* | 牛窓 |

*RESTAURANTS*

| | | |
|---|---|---|
| Butsukake-tei | *Butsukake-tei* | ぶっかけ亭 |
| Itchō Sushi | *Itchō Sushi* | いっちょう寿司 |
| Musashi | *Musashi* | むさし |
| Marinporisu | *Marinporisu* | マリンポリス |

Bus Centre, in the heart of the city's shopping district. Okayama **airport** is around 20km northwest of the train station; buses run from the airport into the city every hour or so (¥680; 40min). **Ferries** arrive at Shin-Okayama Port, 10km south of the city; buses run from the port into the Tenmaya Bus Centre every hour or so (30min).

Kōrakuen and the city's other main sights are clustered around the Asahi-gawa, fifteen minutes' walk down Momotarō-dōri (see p.526), the main road heading directly east from Okayama station, which **trams** run along. If you don't fancy walking or taking the tram, a bicycle is a good way to travel around; the cheapest daily **bike rental** is from the youth hostel (see p.526).

Of the city's three sources of **tourist information**, the most convenient is the counter inside Okayama Station (daily 9am–6pm; ☎086/222-2912), where you'll find English speakers and plenty of information and maps. The Okayama International Exchange Centre, 2-2-1 Hokanchō (Tues–Sun 9am–5pm; 086/256-2000), five minutes' walk from the eastern exit of the station, has a good library and information centre. Finally, I-Plaza, the city's international centre along the Nishi-gawa Greenway Canal, 500m southeast of the station, is the place to head if you want to arrange a visit to a Japanese home (see p.23).

## Accommodation

There are plenty of inexpensive business hotels around Okayama Station, with the marginally cheaper ones and the youth hostel being on the west side. If you want to stay in a ryokan or minshuku, head for nearby Kurashiki (see p.529).

**Excel Okayama**, 5-1 Ishiseki-chō (☎086/224-0505, fax 224-2625). This good-value, mid-range hotel is smartly decorated and conveniently located near Kōrakuen and Okayama's shopping arcades. ⑤.

**Hotel Granvia**, 1-5 Ekimoto-machi (☎086/234-7000, fax 234-7099). The city's top Western-style hotel, conveniently located next to the station, with tastefully furnished, spacious bedrooms and elegant public areas. Also has several restaurants, bars and a swimming pool. ⑦.

**Hollywood**, 1-2-4 Ekimae-chō (☎086/226-2188). This men-only capsule hotel and sauna, in the shopping arcade opposite Okayama Station, may have a tacky name, but inside it's spacious and clean. Capsules are available from 5pm–10am, and there's another branch at 10-4 Chūō-chō if this is full. ②.

**Matsunoki**, 19-1 Ekimoto-machi (☎086/253-4111, fax 253-4110). Five minutes' walk from the west side of the station, this hotel has both Western-style and *tatami* rooms. The cheapest rates are for

### OKAYAMA'S INTERNATIONAL VILLAS

Okayama-ken set up the first of its **International Villas** in Fukiya in 1988 in order to provide foreign visitors with affordable, authentic accommodation. The villas range from restored farmhouses to specially commissioned modern buildings, and are all in interesting locations. The six properties can be booked up to six months in advance with the Okayama International Villa Group, Okayama International Centre, 2-2-1 Hokanchō, Okayama 700 (☎086/256-2535, fax 256-2576; *www.harenet.or.jp/villa*). All the villas cost ¥3000 per person per night for non-members, ¥2500 for members, and ¥500 extra for single occupancy; a two-year membership costs ¥500. You may have to share your villa with other visitors, but all the properties have separate bedrooms, fully equipped kitchens and basic cooking ingredients, though in practice, the cookers are fiddly to use and supplies are often missing: the more traditional Japanese properties tend to be in better condition than the modern ones. Each villa has booklets of information in English about where to get food locally and what to do in the area. There should also be a caretaker around to let you in and answer any questions. Few of the villas are easy to reach by public transport, so your own car would be very useful.

Two of the nicest villas are at **Fukiya** (see p.535) and **Hattoji** (see p.537). One of the smallest, sleeping a maximum of eight people, is at **Koshihata** in a nineteenth-century, thatched farmhouse in the remote Chūgoku mountains, north of Okayama. The nearest train station is Tsuyama (on the Tsuyama line from Okayama, Kishin line from Himeji and Imbi line from Tottori), from where two buses a day make the seventy-minute journey to the villa. **Shiraishi-jima**, a modern villa with one *tatami* and four Western-style rooms, is highly popular because of its idyllic location on a small island in the Inland Sea. The villa has sea views and a sun deck, as well as access to the island's several hiking trails, small temples and rocky coastline. To reach Shiraishi-jima, take a ferry from Kasaoka, forty-five minutes west of Okayama by train. Despite its modern design, **Takebe** International Villa is showing its age, with damaged furniture and an interior that is too minimalist. Its pluses are an adjacent onsen overlooking the gushing Asahigawa, and an easily accessible location, one hour north of Okayama by direct train or bus to Fukuwatari Station. Sadly, the spacious, modern villa at **Ushimado**, spectacularly perched on a hill overlooking the Inland Sea, is also fraying at the edges. However, it still makes a good base for exploring the seaside town, the neighbouring olive groves or the small island of Maejima, a five-minute boat ride from Ushimado harbour. The easiest way to reach Ushimado, some 20km east of Okayama, is by direct bus from Okayama Station. The nearest JR station is Oku from where you can take a twenty-five-minute bus ride to Ushimado.

rooms without en-suite bathrooms, with singles starting at ¥5000. Japanese-style breakfast (¥700) is served in a communal dining hall. ⑤.

**Okayama-ken Seinen-Kaikan Youth Hostel**, 1-7-6 Tsukura-chō (☎086/252-0651). In a residential area, ten minutes by bus from the JR station, this hostel is a little run-down, but has friendly management and a relaxed atmosphere. Accommodation is in shared *tatami* rooms, there's a dining room and you can rent bikes for ¥300 a day. ②.

**Okayama New Station Hotel**, 18-19 Ekimoto-machi (☎086/253-6655). Simple Western-style rooms at this business hotel on the west side of the station. If it's full, try the nearby *Dai-ichi Inn*, run by the same management, which charges the same rates (¥5500) for a single. ④.

**Saiwai-sō**, 24-8 Ekimoto-machi (☎086/254-0020, fax 254-9438). Only *tatami* rooms at this small, good-value business hotel. The cheaper rooms are without en-suite bathroom. ④.

## The City

Although you can hop on a tram and travel the length of **Momotarō-dōri** to Shiroshita (¥140), the closest stop to Kōrakuen, the walk is easy enough and takes you across the tree-lined **Nishi-gawa Greenway Canal**, a pleasant spot for a stroll. At the main crossroad, Shiroshita-suji, turn north and you'll soon arrive at the atmospheric **Okayama Orient Museum** (Tues–Sun 9am–5pm; ¥300), an unusual and well-presented collection of Near-Eastern antiquities, ranging from Mesopotamian pottery to Syrian mosaics and Roman sculptures. A block further north, you'll see an angular modern building which is home to the **Okayama Prefectural Museum of Art** (Tues–Sun 9am–5pm; ¥300), a collection of more recent and local art. As well as dreamy ink paintings by the fifthteenth-century artist and priest Sesshū Tōyō, there are examples of the local pottery style Bizen-yaki (see p.536), and regularly changing special exhibitions for which you'll have to pay an additional fee.

Just north of the museum, turn east and head across the Tsurumi-bashi (bridge) to the northern end of the comma-shaped island on which you'll find Okayama's star attraction, **Kōrakuen** (daily: April–Sept 7.30am–6pm; Jan–March & Oct–Dec 8am–5pm; ¥350). Founded in 1686 by lord Ikeda Tsunamasa, this landscaped garden is notable for its wide, lush green lawns, highly unusual in Japanese garden design. Other than this, all the traditional elements, including tea houses, artificial lakes, islands and hills, and borrowed scenery (in this case, the black keep of Okayama-jō), are present. The strange bleeting sound you'll hear on entering the garden comes from a flock of caged red-crested cranes. Fortunately Kōrakuen is large enough to soak up the crowds that deluge other famous gardens, such as Kenrokuen in Kanazawa (see p.384) and Ritsurin-kōen in Takamatsu (see p.606), both of which are more interesting.

Outside the main gate to Kōrakuen is the lacklustre **Okayama Prefectural Museum** (Tues–Sun: April–Sept 9am–6pm; Jan–March & Oct–Dec 9.30am–5pm; ¥200), where the historical exhibits are presented with little ceremony and no English captions. Better to head for the smartly renovated castle, **Okayama-jō** (daily 9am–5pm; ¥300), reached by walking round the island and crossing the Tsukimi-bashi (Moon-viewing bridge). Its nickname *U-jō* (Crow Castle) refers to the black wooden cladding of the donjon, from the top of which you get an excellent view of the surrounding area. Founded in 1573 by lord Ukita Hideie, the adopted son of the great warlord Toyotomi Hideyoshi, the castle fell foul to both the Meiji restoration and World War II bombings, with the only original bit of the building now being the *Tsukimi Yagura* (Moon-viewing turret), at the western corner of the compound. You can pick up a good English-language leaflet from the ticket desk at the entrance to the donjon, and inside there's the chance to dress up in regal kimono as a lord or lady.

A final pit-stop on the way back to the station is the small **Hayashibara Museum of Art**, 2-7-15 Marunouchi (daily 9am–5pm; ¥300), which displays selections from the oriental art collection of local businessman Hayashibara Ichiro. There are some beautiful

---

**COMBINED TICKETS**

You can save a little money if you buy combined tickets to enter Kōrakuen and other attractions in Okayama. The gardens and the Okayama Prefectural Museum ticket is ¥440; the gardens and castle ticket ¥520; and the gardens, castle and Hayashibara Art Museum ticket is the best value at ¥670.

---

items in the collection, including delicate ink scroll paintings and exquisite Nō theatre robes from the sixteenth century, but they're not always on display, so take a moment to leaf through the catalogue while sipping a free cup of green tea in the lounge.

# Eating, drinking and entertainment

Okayama has the widest range of **eating and drinking** options between Kōbe and Hiroshima. The main districts to head for are immediately east of Okayama Station, where you'll find all the usual fast-food outlets and many other restaurants, and along Ōmotechō-shotengai, the covered shopping street closer to the river. Local dishes include *somen*, handmade noodles dried in the sun and often served cold in summer, and *Okayama barazushi* (festival sushi), a mound of vinegared rice covered with seafood and regional vegetables.

There's not a huge variety of **nightlife**, but there are several jolly *izakaya* catering mainly for a younger crowd. The mauve cylindrical building at the start of the Ōmotechō-shotengai is the **Okayama Symphony Hall**; check with tourist information as to what concerts are on. Towards the southern end of the arcade are several **cinemas** showing mainstream films, while more arty films get an airing at Cinema Claire near the Okayama Prefectural Museum of Art; for schedules pick up a copy of *Okayama Insider*, a free monthly English newsletter available from the tourist information centres.

## Restaurants

**Applause**, *Hotel Granvia*, 1-5 Ekimoto-machi. The main lounge bar on the nineteenth floor of this upmarket hotel often does good value buffet lunches. The cityscape view, especially at night, is unbeatable, and there are several other restaurants in the hotel, including *Prix d'Or* for French food and *Bisai* for *teppan-yaki* (beef and seafood cooked at your table). *Applause* daily 11am–midnight; *Prix D'Or* daily 11.30am–2.30pm & 5–10pm; *Bisai* daily 11.30am–2.30pm & 5–10pm.

**Butsukake**, 2-6-59 Ōmotechō-shotengai. Inside a shopping arcade, this homely restaurant specializes in udon noodles, served in cheap set menus (around ¥800 per head) with tempura on rice. Look upwards to the second floor for the grand piano playing by itself. Daily except Tues 11am–7.30pm.

**Itcho Sushi**, Ōmotechō-shotengai. Traditional sushi restaurant at the Momotarō-dōri end of the arcade, with good-value set meals including soba and the usual trimmings. Daily except Tues 9.30am–8pm.

**La Bistro Cuisine**, 6-8 Nishiki-chō. This compact bistro a couple of minutes' walk east of the station, serves dainty portions of French-style food, and can get very busy at lunchtimes. Daily 11.30am–2pm & 5.30–9.30pm.

**Marinporisu**, Ekimae-shotengai. Brightly lit revolving sushi restaurant in the arcade immediately opposite the east exit of Okayama Station. As well as fingers of vinegared rice and fish, you can take your pick from plates of melon, jelly and potato chips. Daily 11am–9pm.

**Musashi**, Momotarō-dōri. Near where the main road crosses the Nishi-gawa Greenway Canal, this traditional restaurant is the best place in which to try Okayama cuisine. The set lunches from ¥1200 are the best value, while dinner starts at ¥3000 per head.

**Nanak**, Ōmotechō-shotengai (call ☎086/224-7900 to check times). This fine Indian restaurant in the middle of the shopping arcade is part of a chain with branches throughout Western Honshū and Kyūshū. As usual, the lunchtime set meals are the best value.

## KIBI PLAIN BICYCLE ROUTE

The fifteen-kilometre-long **Kibi Plain bicycle route**, accessed either from Okayama or Kurashiki (see opposite), is an enjoyable way to see an area of countryside studded with ancient burial grounds, shrines and temples. Running from Bizen-Ichinomiya Station in the east to Sōja Station in the west, the route takes about four hours to cycle, or a full day to walk. Bikes can be hired at either station (¥200 per hour, or ¥1000 for the day) and dropped off at the other end.

In the fourth century this area was known as Kibi-no-kuni and was the centre of early Japanese civilization. Lords were buried in giant key-hole-shaped mounds known as *kofun*, one of which can be visited along the cycle route. Starting from **Bizen-Ichinomiya** Station, three stops from Okayama on the JR Kibi line, cross the tracks and follow the cycle path to Kibitsuhiko-jinja, an ordinary shrine beside a pond notable only for its huge stone lantern, one of the largest in Japan. Around 300m further south-west is the much more impressive **Kibitsu-jinja**, dating from 1425 and dedicated to Kibitsu-no-mikoto, the valiant prince who served as the inspiration for the legend of **Momotarō**, Japan's famous fairytale of a child who pops out of the centre of a giant peach after being rescued from a river by a childless farmer's wife. This shrine nestles at the foot of Mount Naka and has a magnificently roofed outer sanctum, with twin gables.

Several kilometres further west, is the **Tsukuriyama-kofun**, a burial mound constructed in the fifth century in the characteristic shape of a keyhole (only really appreciated from the air). Measuring 350m in length and 30m at its highest point, this wooded mound in the midst of rice-fields is the fourth largest *kofun* in Japan. Around a kilometre east of here is a cluster of sights, including the foundation stones of Bitchū Kokubun-niji, an eighth-century convent, another burial mound and the five-storied pagoda of **Bitchū Kokubun-ji**, a temple, dating from the seventeenth century.

It's another couple of kilometres to the train station at **Sōja**, from where you can either return to Okayama or to Kurashiki. Before leaving check out **Iyama Hōfuku-ji**, a pretty Zen Buddhist temple, 1km north of Sōja Station along a footpath that follows the railway line. The celebrated artist and landscape gardener Sesshū Tōyō (1420–1506) trained here as a priest.

| | | |
|---|---|---|
| **Kibi Plain Bicycle Route** | *Kibi-ji Saikuringu Rūto* | 吉備路サイクリングルート |
| Bitchū Kokubun-ji | *Bitchū Kokubun-ji* | 備中国分寺 |
| Bizen Ichinomiya Station | *Bizen Ichinomiya-eki* | 備前いちのみや駅 |
| Kibitsu-jinja | *Kibitsu-jinja* | 吉備津神社 |
| Sōja | *Sōja* | 総社 |
| Tsukuriyama-kofun | *Tsukuriyama-kofun* | 造山古墳 |

**Niki Niki**, 1-2-4 Marunouchi. Stylish *mukokuseki* restaurant, with a Mediterranean feel, opposite Okayama civic hall, on the way to Kōrakuen. Lunch specials start at ¥700. Daily 11.30am–3.30pm & 5pm–midnight.

## Bars and izakaya

**Eikokuryo Hongkongku**, 6-18 Maya-chō. Funky *izakaya*, serving food as well as cocktails and beers, a block west of the Nishi-gawa canal. There are wild cartoons on the walls and tables behind prison bars. Daily 9am–5pm.

**Hunter**, 2F, YA Bldg, 3-22 Nishikimachi. Spacious American-style bar, where you can play pool for free if you buy a drink (around ¥800). The food is also worth checking out, with lunchtime specials of hamburgers and sandwiches under ¥1000. Daily until 3am.

**Neverland Café**, Honmachi. The low tables make you feel like one of Peter Pan's Lost Boys at this cheerfully designed *izakaya*. Half-price drinks before 7pm and a varied and reasonably priced food menu, including fish and chips in newspaper. Daily 5pm–2am.

# Listings

**Airlines** ANA (☎0120–029222); JAC and JAS (☎0120–511283); JTA (☎0120–255971); KAL (☎086/221-3311).

**Banks and exchange** There are several banks along Momotarō-dōri and you can also change money at the Central Post Office (see below).

**Bookshops** Beneath the Symphony Hall Maruzen, (daily 10am–8pm; closed 2nd Tues of month), has the best selection of English books and magazines, or try Kinokuniya, a block west of Tenmaya Bus Station (daily 10am–7.30pm daily).

**Car rental** Nippon Rent-a-car (☎086/235-0919); and Toyota Rent-a-car (☎086/2421-9898).

**Hospital** The Okayama University Medical Research Hospital, 2-5-1 Shikata-chō (☎086/223-7151).

**Police station** Okayama Prefectural Police HQ, 2-4-6 Uchisange, Ok City (☎086/234-0110).

**Post office** Central Post Office, 2-1-1 Nakasange (Mon–Fri 9am–7pm, Sat 9am–5pm, Sun 9am–12.30pm).

**Shopping** A good one-stop emporium for local arts and crafts, including Bizen-yaki pottery, masks and weaving is the Okayama Tourist Product Centre (daily 10am–8pm) on the ground floor of the Symphony Hall.

# Kurashiki

At first sight, **KURASHIKI**, 26km west of Okayama, looks like just another bland iden-tikit Japanese town with a recreation of Copenhagen's Tivoli Park tacked onto one side. But ten minutes' walk south of the station the modern buildings and shops are replaced by a delightful enclave of black and white, walled merchants' homes (*machiya*) and store-houses (*kura*) dating from the town's Edo-era heyday, when it was an important centre for trade in rice and rush reeds. The compact **Bikan** historical area, cut through by a nar-row, weeping-willow-fringed canal, in which swans drift and carp swim, is overly endowed with museums and galleries, the best of which is the excellent **Ōhara Museum of Art**, containing four separate halls for Western art, contemporary Japanese art and local crafts. Hugely popular with tourists, Kurashiki can get very busy during the day; to best appreciate its charm, stay overnight and take an early morning or evening stroll through the Bikan district, or visit on Monday when most of the museums and galleries are shut.

## Arrival and information

Local **trains** arrive at Kurashiki Station, fifteen minutes west of Okayama on the Sanyō line. Shinkansen don't stop at Kurashiki, so you'll need to change to a local train at Okayama. Regular **buses** from Okayama and Kojima (see p.536) stop in front of Kurashiki Station.

At the **tourist information** office (daily 9am–5pm; ☎086/426-8681) inside Kurashiki Station, you can pick up a map of the town's sights and the English-speaking staff can make accommodation bookings. There's also another helpful tourist information office in the Bikan district (daily 9am–5pm; ☎086/422-0542), beside the canal, with a rest area where you can grab a drink from a bank of vending machines.

## Accommodation

Kurashiki is an excellent place to stay if you want to experience a traditional ryokan or minshuku, the best being in the Bikan district. The town is also well served with upmar-ket Western-style hotels. In contrast, the cheaper business hotels tend to be shabby and overpriced and are best avoided in favour of those in Okayama. Rates at most hotels rise by a couple of thousand yen at weekends and during holidays.

**Hotel 330 Grande Kurashiki**, 2-2-26 Chūō (☎086/421-0330, fax 421-0335). Stylish modern hotel, with tastefully decorated rooms that are surprisingly well-priced for what they offer. Also has a restaurant next to the lobby. ⑨.

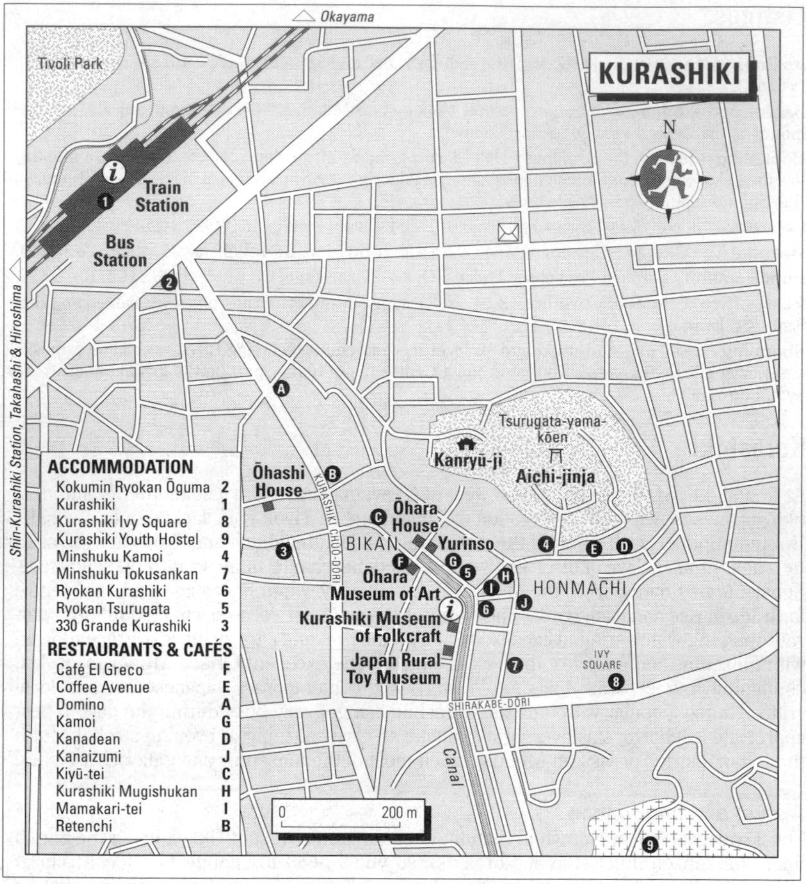
Okayama
Tivoli Park
KURASHIKI
N
Train Station
Bus Station
Shin-Kurashiki Station, Takahashi & Hiroshima
Tsurugata-yama-kōen
Kanryū-ji
Aichi-jinja
Ōhashi House
KURASHIKI CHŪŌ-DŌRI
Ōhara House
BIKAN
Yurinso
HONMACHI
Ōhara Museum of Art
Kurashiki Museum of Folkcraft
Japan Rural Toy Museum
IVY SQUARE
SHIRAKABE-DŌRI
Canal
0
200 m
ACCOMMODATION
Kokumin Ryokan Ōguma 2
Kurashiki 1
Kurashiki Ivy Square 8
Kurashiki Youth Hostel 9
Minshuku Kamoi 4
Minshuku Tokusankan 7
Ryokan Kurashiki 6
Ryokan Tsurugata 5
330 Grande Kurashiki 3
RESTAURANTS & CAFÉS
Café El Greco F
Coffee Avenue E
Domino A
Kamoi G
Kanadean D
Kanaizumi J
Kiyū-tei C
Kurashiki Mugishukan H
Mamakari-tei I
Retenchi B

**Minshuku Kamoi**, 1-24 Honmachi (☎086/422-4898, fax 427-7615). On the slope leading up to Tsurugata-yama park, this modern minshuku, built in traditional style, has some rooms overlooking the Bikan district and good rates considering meals are included. There are antiques in the entrance hall and a pretty garden. The owners also run the *Kamoi* sushi restaurant (see p.533). ⑤.

**Kokumin Ryokan Ōguma**, 3-1-2 Achi (☎086/422-0250, fax 422-0497). There's a friendly welcome at this small ryokan, with simple *tatami* rooms, in the narrow arcade on the west side of Kurashiki Chūō-dōri. If you opt for meals, add around ¥2000 per person extra to the rates. ⑤.

**Hotel Kurashiki**, 1-1-1 Achi (☎086/426-6111, fax 426-6163). Although it's above Kurashiki Station, this reasonably priced upmarket hotel owned by JR, has a hushed atmosphere and attractive rooms, some with views over the neighbouring Tivoli Park. ⑤.

**Ryokan Kurashiki**, 4-1 Honmachi (☎086/422-0730, fax 422-0990). Classic ryokan housed in three converted rice and sugar storehouses in the midst of the Bikan district. Each individual suite of rooms is filled with antiques, and women in blue kimono minister to your needs. Expensive, but the genuine article. ⑨.

**Kurashiki Ivy Square Hotel**, 7-2 Honmachi (☎086/422-0011, fax 424-0515). Part of a renovated factory complex at the southern corner of the Bikan district, this is a good mid-range hotel with pleasantly decorated rooms and a couple of restaurants. Rates are cheaper for rooms without en-suite baths. ⑥.

**Kurashiki Youth Hostel**, 1537-1 Mukoyama (☎086/422-7355, fax 422-7364). Homely hostel, atop a hill overlooking the Bikan district at the southern end of Kurashiki. Has dorms with bunk beds (¥2900 per person), the food is excellent and there's a comfortable lounge area with a bilingual TV and a daily English newspaper. You can also use their kitchen to cook your own meals.

**Minshuku Tokusankan**, 6-12 Honmachi (☎086/425-3056, fax 425-3053). This reasonably priced minshuku, with simply furnished *tatami* rooms, is tucked one street east of the southern end of the Bikan canal above a gift shop of the same name. Rates include two meals. ⑤.

**Ryokan Tsurugata**, 1-3-15 Chūō (☎086/424-1635). Slightly cheaper than *Ryokan Kurashiki*, this ryokan is in a 250-year-old canal-side merchant's house and has atmospheric *tatami* rooms overlooking a traditional-style rock garden. Guests are served top-class *kaiseki ryōri* meals, which are also available to non-residents. ⑧.

## The Town

It's around a 1km walk from Kurashiki Station along Kurashiki Chūō-dōri to the Bikan district of seventeenth-century granaries and merchant houses, but before heading there, peel off west after the fourth set of traffic lights to check out the recently restored **Ōhashi House** (Tues–Sun 9am–5pm; ¥500). A poor *samurai* family, the Ōhashi turned to trade and prospered through salt production and land holdings. When they built their home in 1796, it was designed like those of the high-ranking *samurai* class, indicating how wealth was beginning to break down previously rigid social barriers. After passing through a gatehouse and small courtyard, you're free to wander through the spacious, unfurnished *tatami* rooms.

| **KURASHIKI** | | |
|---|---|---|
| **Kurashiki** | *Kurashiki* | 倉敷 |
| Bikan | *Bikan* | びかん |
| Japan Rural Toy Museum | *Nihon Kyōdo Gangukan* | 日本郷土玩具館 |
| Kurashiki Museum of Folkcraft | *Kurashiki Mingeikan* | 倉敷民芸館 |
| Kurashiki Tivoli Park | *Kurashiki Chibori-kōen* | 倉敷チボリ公園 |
| Ōhara Museum of Art | *Ōhara Bijutsukan* | 大原美術館 |
| Ōhara House | *Ōhara-tei* | 大橋邸 |
| | | |
| *ACCOMMODATION* | | |
| Hotel 330 Grande Kurashiki | *Hoteru 330 Gurande Kurashiki* | ホテル３３０グランデ倉敷 |
| Minshuku Kamoi | *Minshuku Kamoi* | 民宿カモ井 |
| Kokumin Ryokan Ōguma | *Kokumin Ryokan Ōguma* | 国民旅館大熊 |
| Hotel Kurashiki | *Hoteru Kurashiki* | ホテル倉敷 |
| Ryokan Kurashiki | *Ryokan Kurashiki* | 旅館くらしき |
| Kurashiki Ivy Square Hotel | *Kurashiki Aibii Sukuea Hoteru* | 倉敷アイビースクエアホテル |
| Kurashiki Youth Hostel | *Kurashiki Yūsu Hosuteru* | 倉敷ユースホステル |
| Minshuku Tokusankan | *Minshuku Tokusankan* | 民宿特産館 |
| Ryokan Tsurugata | *Ryokan Tsurugata* | 旅館鶴形 |
| | | |
| *RESTAURANTS AND BARS* | | |
| Café El Greco | *Kafe Eru Gureko* | カフェエルグレコ |
| Kamoi | *Kamoi* | カモ井 |
| Kanadean | *Kanadean* | カナデアン |
| Kanaizumi | *Kanaizumi* | かないずみ |
| Kiyū-tei | *Kiyū-tei* | 亀遊亭 |
| Kurashiki Mugishukan | *Kurashiki Mugishukan* | 倉敷麦酒館 |
| Mamakari-tei | *Mamakari-tei* | ままかり亭 |
| Retenchi | *Retenchi* | 煉天地 |

Returning to the main road, the start of the **Bikan** district is marked by the inevitable cluster of shops and dawdling tourists. Either side of the willow-lined canal are beautifully preserved houses and warehouses, including the **Ōhara House**, with its typical wooden lattice windows, and the adjacent **Yurinsō**, the Ōhara family guesthouse with distinctive green roof tiles. Opposite, across a stone bridge decorated with carved dragons, is the **Ōhara Museum of Art** (see below), the best of Kurashiki's many galleries and museums. The next most engaging is the **Kurashiki Museum of Folkcraft** (Tues–Sun: March–Nov 9am–5pm; Dec–Feb 9am–4pm; ¥700) in a handsomely restored granary around the canal bend, next to a stylish Meiji-era wooden building which houses the tourist information centre. The museum displays a wide range of crafts, including Bizen-yaki pottery, baskets and traditional clothes, and has a small shop attached, selling souvenirs a cut above those found in most of Kurashiki's other gift shops.

A few doors down from the folkcraft museum, another excellent shop attached to the **Japan Rural Toy Museum** (daily 8am–5pm; ¥500) sells colourful, new versions of the traditional playthings on display in the museum. Among this vast collection of dolls, spinning tops, animals, and such like – most faded and tatty with age and use – the best displays are of huge kites and masks in the hall across the garden at the back of the shop.

Rather than spending more yen at Kurashiki's other lacklustre museums, retrace your steps north over the canal and amble past the seventeenth-century merchant houses in the district of **Honmachi**, where you'll find some artsy craft shops, or stroll up the hillside to **Tsurugata-yama Park** which includes the grounds of the simple shrine Aichi-jinja and temple Honei-ji. If you have time, you could also potter around **Ivy Square**, east of the canal, the ivy-covered late-nineteenth-century Kurashiki Spinning Mill redeveloped into a shopping, museum and hotel complex. There's another good craft shop here, as well as an **atelier** where you can try your hand at pottery (¥1800).

Grafted on to the town as if from another planet is **Kurashiki Tivoli Park** (Mon–Fri 10am–8pm; Sat, Sun and holidays 9am–10pm; ¥2000), a mini-Danish theme park in storybook colours, immediately north of Kurashiki Station. Modelled on the famous Copenhagen funfair, the park, with its street entertainers, giant ferris wheel, Hansiatic palaces and shopping plazas, landscaped gardens and artificial lakes, is amusingly kitsch, and has some reasonably priced restaurants and cafés. However, the rides are all tame and cost extra on top of the already expensive entrance fee. Hang around, though, to watch the Hans Christian Anderson-inspired automatons spring to life on the hour from inside the musical clock between the station and the park.

## ŌHARA MUSEUM OF ART

Apart from the Bikan district's historical townscape, Kurashiki's top draw is the impressive **Ōhara Museum of Art** (Tues–Sun 9am–5pm; ¥1000), easily spotted by its creamy Neoclassical facade. This is the entrance to the original gallery established by local textile tycoon Ōhara Magosaburō in 1930 to house his collection of Western art, including works by Cézanne, El Greco, Matisse, Monet, Picasso and Rodin, which were hand-picked by his friend the painter Kōjima Torajirō in Europe in the 1920s. The first gallery to exhibit Western art in Japan, the museum was a raging success and has expanded ever since, with Magosaburō's heirs adding Western and Japanese contemporary art to the collection, as well as ancient Chinese artworks and an excellent range of top-class Japanese folkcrafts.

The entrance to the **Main Gallery** is flanked by bronze sculptures of St John the Baptist and the Burghers of Calais by Rodin, both of which were nearly melted down to make armaments during World War II. Starting with Ōhara's nineteenth-century purchases, the paintings are displayed in roughly chronological order, with works by Kandinsky, Pollock, Rothco and Andy Warhol included in the twentieth-century and contemporary art sections. Despite the impressive range of artists displayed, however, there are few truly memorable works in this collection.

In contrast, the **Craft Art Gallery**, housed in an attractive quadrangle of converted wooden-beamed storehouses, leaves a much stronger impression. The ceramics rooms display beautiful and unusual works by four potters who were prime movers in the resurgence of interest in Japanese folk arts (*mingei*) earlier this century: Hamada Shōji (1894–1978), Kawai Kanjirō (1890–1966), Kenkichi Tomimoto (1886–1963) and Bernard Leach (1887–1979), the British potter who worked with Hamada both in Japan, at Mashiko (see p.178), and in Britain, at St Ives. A room filled with the strikingly colourful and sometimes abstract woodblock prints of Munakata Shikō (1903–1975) follows, with the last section devoted to Serizawa Keisuke, a textile dyer and painter whose exquisite work features on kimono, curtains and fans, and who designed both the craft galleries and the adjoining **Asiatic Art Gallery**. This smaller collection, on two levels, provides another change of pace with its cool displays of ancient East-Asian art, including seventh-century Tang Dynasty ceramics and sculptures, and serene Buddhas.

The ground floor of the **Annexe**, in a separate building behind the main gallery, displays unmemorable pastiches of modern Western-style art by Japanese artists, while downstairs you'll find bizarre contemporary works, made from Day-Glo perspex and the like.

## Eating, drinking and entertainment

There's a bewildering choice of **restaurants** in Kurashiki, with the Bikan district being the place to head for excellent-value set-lunch deals. In the evenings many places are closed, so you might have to head towards the station area, which is also where you should go if you want fast food. The town's signature dish is *mamakari sushi*, a vinegared sardine-like fish on top of sushi rice.

Bars and evening entertainment are not Kurashiki's strong point, although the Bikan district does have its own **microbrewery**, which is worth a try. Otherwise, the liveliest spot at night is Tivoli Park (see opposite), which certainly is more charming once the fairy lights spark into action.

### *RESTAURANTS AND CAFÉS*

**Café El Greco**. Classic Bikan café, in an ivy-clad building facing the canal next to the Ohara Museum of Art. It's a favourite pit-stop with visitors, even though it has a limited menu of drinks and cake. Seating is at shared tables and a coffee will set you back ¥400. Tues–Sun 10am–5pm.

**Domino**, Kurashiki Chūō-dōri. Small café in a pink and grey wooden building midway between the station and the Bikan district. It serves cheap Western/Japanese dishes, such as hamburger, rice pilaf and spaghetti. Tues–Sun 10am–9pm.

**Kamoi**, 1-3-17 Chūō. Good-value *sushi-ya* in a old granary facing the canal. Choose from the plastic food display in the restaurant window. Tues–Sun 9am–6pm.

**Kanadean**, Honmachi. The curries at this funky Indian-style restaurant, run by a Japanese couple, are on the weak side, but the set lunches including rice, nan bread, salad, samosa or yoghurt are good value for ¥1000. Tues–Sun noon–9pm.

**Kanaizumi**, Honmachi. Koto music tinkles in the background at this traditional restaurant, specializing in freshly made noodles, and serving excellent-value set-meals throughout the day, all illustrated in a photo menu. A good place to sample *mamakari sushi* at only ¥750 for a set meal. Daily 11.30am–8pm.

**Kiyū-tei**, Chūō. Rustic steak restaurant at the head of the canal running through the Bikan district. The lunches start at ¥880 for a beef steak, cake and coffee. There's also a salad bar. The fixed three-course dinner menu for ¥2800 is also worth considering. Daily 11.30am–3pm & 5–8.30pm.

**Mamakari-tei**, 3-12 Honmachi. Fine place to try the local speciality *mamakari sushi*. A set lunch including the sushi, along with baked fish, tofu and soup is ¥2500. Look for the giant *ikebana* flower display outside the restaurant. Daily 11am–2pm & 5–10pm.

**Retenchi**, Kurashiki Chūō-dōri. Dimly lit Italian restaurant, with an intimate atmosphere, next to a pop-art junk shop. Pasta and pizza are on the menu, and a meal comes to around ¥1500 per person. Daily 11am–3pm & 5–10pm.

**Terrace de Ryokan Kurashiki**, 4-1 Honmachi. Elegant café at the back of the *Ryokan Kurashiki*, opening out onto a beautiful traditional garden which is particularly enchanting at dusk. Indulge in tea and biscuits for ¥840. Daily 9am–8pm.

## BARS

**Coffee Avenue**, Honmachi. At 7pm this cool coffee shop in the middle of a street of old merchant houses transforms into the *Your Jazz Life* bar. There's a cover charge of ¥500, for the live jazz played nightly on a grand piano and other instruments.

**Kurashiki Mugishukan**, 1019 Honmachi. Microbrewery with attached restaurant and bar in an old storehouse. Try the combination taster of three types of Kurashiki Beer – Weizen, Kölsch and Alt – for ¥580 before deciding which one to go for. Snacks are available and a ¥950 set lunch is served daily 11.30am–2.30pm. Daily 11am–11pm.

**Ivy Square**, 7-2 Honmachi. In July and August you can chill out at the beer garden in the inner courtyard of this red-brick, ivy-adorned complex. July & Aug daily 6–9.30pm.

# Takahashi

Some 40km northwest of Okayama, in the foothills of the mountain range which divides Western Honshū, is **TAKAHASHI**, a small and charming time-warped castle town. Few visitors venture here despite the town's preserving several fine old buildings and temples in the Furusato Mura (hometown village) area, a name evoking images of a long lost Japan. Except for the steep hike up to the castle – Japan's highest – all of Takahashi's sights are in easy walking distance of Bitchū-Takahashi Station and can be covered in half a day. Finding your way around is simple since there are plenty of direction signs in English.

The row of temples, ranged attractively at staggered levels along the hillside and heading north towards Furusato Mura, lies on the eastern side of the railway tracks. The single most impressive is **Raikyū-ji** (daily 9am–5pm; ¥300), ten minutes' walk from the train station, with its serenely beautiful raked-gravel garden. The exact date the temple was built is lost in the mists of time, but it is known that in 1604, Kobori Enshū, governor of the province and expert gardener, lived in the temple. The Zen garden is maintained today exactly as he designed it, with its islands of stones, plants and trimmed hedges carefully placed to resemble a crane and a tortoise and the distant borrowed scenery of Mount Atago.

Rest by Raikyū-ji's garden before tackling the short but strenuous hour-long hike up to the castle, **Bitchū Matsuyama-jō**, following a shaded track through the hillside forest. Takahashi's fortunes prospered from the mid-thirteenth century when warlord Akiba Saburoshigenobu built the original fortress, on top of the nearby Mount Gagyū. You'll fully appreciate the scale of this engineering feat after having climbed up to the castle. Even if you take a taxi from the station (¥1200), there's still a steep fifteen-minute walk ahead of you from the car park. The reward is that the castle's remote location keeps the crowds away. Don't bother paying to go into the **donjon** (daily 9am–4pm; ¥300), restored this century, since there are few relics inside and little view from its narrow windows. The view on the walk back downhill makes the effort of hiking up worthwhile.

On returing to the town, if you have time, explore the **Furusato Mura** area of old merchant houses and buildings, sandwiched beween the rail tracks and the Takahashi-gawa, and cut through by a stream crossed by stone bridges topped with miniature shrines. Of the several buildings turned into museums, the most interesting is the wooden Meiji-era Takahashi Elementary School, now the **local history museum** (daily 9am—5pm; ¥300). Inside is a jumble of possessions, running from *mikoshi* (portable shrines) to a morse code machine. At the back of the ground floor are some evocative black-and-white photos of the town, while on the second floor you should look

| TAKAHASHI, KOJIMA AND IMBE | | |
|---|---|---|
| **Takahashi** | *Takahashi* | 高梁 |
| Bitchū Matsuyama-jō | *Bitchū Matsuyama-jō* | 備中松山城 |
| Bitchū-Takahashi Station | *Bitchū-Takahashi-eki* | 備中高梁駅 |
| Raikyū-ji | *Raikyū-ji* | 頼久寺 |
| *ACCOMMODATION* | | |
| Fukiya | *Fukiya* | 吹屋 |
| Takahashi-shi Cycling Terminal | *Takahashi-shi Saikuringu Tāminaru* | 高梁サイクリングターミナル |
| Takahashi Kokusai Hotel | *Takahashi Kokusai Hoteru* | 高梁国際ホテル |
| Takahashi Youth Hostel | *Takahashi Yūsu Hosuteru* | 高梁ユースホステル |
| **Kojima** | *Kojima* | 児島 |
| Bridge Museum | *Seto-Ōhashi Kinenkan* | 瀬戸大橋記念館 |
| Seto-Ōhashi | *Seto-Ōhashi* | 瀬戸大橋 |
| Washū-zan | *Washū-zan* | 鷲羽山 |
| Washū-zan Youth Hostel | *Washū-zan Yūsu Hosuteru* | 鷲羽山ユースホステル |
| **Imbe** | *Imbe* | 伊部 |
| Hattōji | *Hattōji* | 八塔寺 |
| Shizutani School | *Shizutani Gakkō* | 閑谷学校 |

out for the dancing doll models made from old cigarette packets – a nod to Japan Tobacco which has a factory in Takahashi.

## Practicalities

Takahashi's railway station, **Bitchū-Takahashi**, is on the JR Hakubi line, just under an hour from Okayama or forty-five minutes from Kurashiki. You can pick up a Japanese map of the town from the **information office** (daily 7.15am–6.40am; ☎0866/22-6789) at the bus terminal, next to the station. The staff here only speak Japanese, but are welcoming and can point you towards accommodation, if you decide to stay overnight.

The *Takahashi Youth Hostel* (☎0866/22-3149; ①), a small place run by a chatty old lady, is next to the temple Kofuku-ji on the way to Raikyū-ji, and overlooks the temple's gardens. Budget accommodation is also available some way out of town at the *Takahashi-shi Cycling Terminal* (☎0866/22-0135, fax 22-0935; ③), which has both Japanese and Western-style rooms, the cheapest being on a shared basis. Bicycles can be rented here for ¥500 for four hours. To reach the *Cycling Terminal* you need to take a twenty-minute bus journey from the bus terminal to Wonderland Iri-guchi and walk for a further twenty minutes. For upmarket accommodation, try the *Takahashi Kokusai Hotel* (☎0866/21-0080, fax 21-0075; ⑦), two minutes' walk north of the station. Alternatively, you could explore Takahashi from one of the prefecture's International Villas (see p.525) in the charming hamlet of **Fukiya**, an old copper-mining centre with streets of nineteenth-century merchants' houses made of wood, plaster and tiles. The villa is a modern building mixing Western and Japanese styles, about an hour by bus from Bitchū-Takahashi (3 daily).

**Dining** options in Takahashi are centred around the station, where there are several restaurants with plastic food displays. Near the *Takahashi Kokusai Hotel* is *Jyūjyū-tei*, an inexpensive *okonomiyaki* restaurant, while across the road is *Sushi Hana-kan*, a take-out sushi shop, ideal for a picnic lunch at the castle.

## Kojima and Seto-Ōhashi

Twenty-five kilometres south of Okayama, **KOJIMA**, with its sprawling shopping centres and newly laid roads, has boomed since the opening in 1988 of the nearby 12.3km-long **Seto-Ōhashi**, a series of six bridges and four viaducts hopping from island to island, across the Inland Sea to Shikoku. One of the most memorable ways to view this engineering wonder is to take an hour-long **boat tour** (daily: Mar–Nov 9am–4pm; Jan, Feb & Dec 10am–2pm; ¥1550) from the sightseeing pier immediately to the east of Kojima Station. The boats depart on the hour, except at noon.

If you'd prefer to view the Seto-Ōhashi and islands from dry land, head 4km south of Kojima to **Washū-zan**, a 134-metre-high hill jutting out into the Inland Sea. Regular buses run to the lookout point, from outside both Kojima and Kurashiki (see p.529) stations. Stay on the bus past Washū-zan Highland, a tacky amusement park, and get off at the car park by the official lookout spot. From here you can climb to Washū-zan's summit and take in what has to be one of Japan's most glorious panoramas.

Back in Kojima, the **Bridge Museum** (Tues–Sun 9am–5pm; ¥210), a ten-minute walk west of the train station, is a wacky attraction, well worth a look if you have the time. You can actually walk over the arched museum building, inspired by a *taiko-bashi* (drum bridge), and enjoy a small park containing eleven amusing mini-bridges and a chequerboard square decorated with bizarre silver statues (supposedly symbolizing the seasons) and a model of Stevenson's Rocket. Inside the museum, which displays scale models of bridges from around the world, the eye is drawn immediately to the roof, painted with a lively mural of Edo-era travelling performers, craftsmen, merchants and priests. Nowhere near as unique is **Nozaki House** (Tues–Sun 9am–4.30pm; ¥500), the handsomely kept mansion of salt tycoon Nozaki Buzaemon. Five minutes' walk northwest of the Bridge Museum, the house dates from the 1830s and includes three picturesque storehouses, identical to those found in Kurashiki.

At the **tourist office** (daily 9am–6pm; ☎086/472-1289) in Kojima Station, the friendly assistant speaks English and can provide you with an English map and booklet on the area. The best **place to stay** in the area is at the *Washū-zan Youth Hostel* (☎ & fax 086/479-9280; ①), which has bunk-bed dorms and good food as well as impressive views of the Seto-Ōhashi and the Inland Sea from its location at the tip of a promontory. It takes twenty minutes to reach the hostel on one of the frequent buses leaving for Washū-zan from platform two outside Kojima Station.

## Imbe and around

Only dedicated lovers of ceramics will want to linger in drab **IMBE**, 30km east of Okayama and home of Bizen-yaki, Japan's oldest method of making pottery, developed here over 1000 years ago. The ceramics' distinctive earthy colour and texture is achieved without the use of glazes, by firing in wood-fuelled kilns, whose brick chimneys you'll see dotted around Imbe Station. Beside the station is a **tourist information** counter (daily except Tues 9am–5pm; ☎0869/64-1100), where you can pick up an English leaflet about Bizen-yaki and get directions to the local pottery museums, the best being the **Bizen Pottery Traditional and Contemporary Art Museum** (Tues–Sun 9.30am–5pm; ¥500), in the grey concrete block immediately north of the station. This museum displays both old and new examples of the ceramics, providing an overview of the pottery's style and development.

There are plenty of kilns with attached shops which you can mooch around in Imbe, and at some there are studios where you can sculpt your own blob of clay, for around ¥3000. This is then fired and shipped to your home (for overseas deliveries you'll need to pay extra). The most convenient place to try your hand at making pottery is the **Bizen-**

yaki **Traditional Pottery Centre** (☎0869/64-1001) on the third floor of Imbe Station, where workshops are held each weekend and on holidays from April to November.

If you have a car, it's worth exploring the area around Imbe and in particular heading northeast to visit the **Shizutani School** (daily 9am–4pm; ¥300), 3km south of the Yoshinaga Station on the JR Sanyō line. Secluded in a leafy vale, this elegant walled compound of buildings was established by feudal lord Ikeda Mitsumasa in 1666 as a school open to all, regardless of social postion. The gateways and large lecture hall are roofed with warm brown and grey Bizen-yaki tiles, contrasting sharply with the green lawns and gently rounded stone walls.

Returning to Yoshinaga Station, you can catch occasional buses north to the picturesque village of **Hattoji**, setting for the anti-war movie *Black Rain*, by Imamura Shohei, and home to the oldest and perhaps loveliest of Okayama's International Villas (see p.525). The restored thatched-roof village farmhouse, on the slopes of Mount Hattoji, has an open hearth and a *goemonburo* – a traditional stone and metal bath – and all the rooms have *tatami* and *fusuma* (sliding screens).

# Fukuyama and around

Some 65km west from Okayama along the industrialized San-yō coast is the old castle town of **Fukuyama**, now the key industrial city of Hiroshima-ken's Bingo district. The main reason to visit Fukuyama, apart from a few quirky museums, is as a jumping-off point for the nearby characterful seaside towns of **Tomo-no-Ura** and **Onomichi**, from where you can also explore the islands of the Inland Sea.

## The Town

One of Japan's less interesting castles, **Fukuyama-jō**, immediately north of the train station, can be safely ignored in favour of the more memorable **Hiroshima Prefectural Museum of History**, just west of the station (Tues–Sun 9am–5pm; ¥290). Designed around the excavation of the ruins of Kusado Sengen, a medieval town buried in the nearby riverbed of the Ashida-gawa, the museum has some imaginatively displayed artefacts, and haunting background music, as well as a reconstructed village street from Kusado Sengen, lit to recreate twilight in May. Next door is the **Fukuyama Museum of Art** (Tues–Sun 9am–5pm; ¥300), with a permanent collection of mainly Japanese art, focussing on contemporary works by local artists. The most striking pieces of sculpture are in the surrounding gardens. The gallery also hosts visiting exhibitions for which there is an extra charge.

Fifteen minutes' walk north of Fukuyama Station is the odd **Fukuyama Automobile and Clock Museum** (daily 9am–6pm; ¥900, or ¥700 with a discount coupon from the tourist information desk) combining vintage vehicles, including a motorbike taxi, with clocks and music machines. To liven things up there are also waxwork models of celebrities such as Elvis Presley and James Dean. If you don't fancy walking there, take a bus to Kitayoshizu-Jūtaku from platform 3 outside the east exit of Fukuyama Station.

Keeping up the quirky museum theme are the **Japan Footwear Museum** and the **Japan Folk Toy and Doll Museum** (daily 9am–5pm; ¥1000 joint ticket), five minutes' walk east of Matsunaga Station, two stops west of Fukuyama. It's only natural that the town of Matsunaga, which has produced *geta* (traditional wooden sandals) for over a century, hosts Japan's only museum dedicated to shoes. It's a large and surprisingly intriguing collection – from straw sandals to a pair of lunar boots used on one of the Apollo missions – that would make Imelda Marcos drool with envy. The toy museum next door is less unique, but just as extensive, with over 50,000 colourful exhibits. Most

## FUKUYAMA, TOMO-NO-URA AND ONOMICH

| | | |
|---|---|---|
| **Fukuyama** | *Fukuyama* | 福山 |
| Fukuyama Automobile and Clock Museum | *Fukuyama Jidōsha Tokei Hakubutsukan* | 福山自動車時計博物館 |
| Hiroshima Prefectural Museum of History | *Hiroshima-kenritsu Rekishi Hakubutsukan* | 広島県立歴史博物館 |
| Japan Folk Toy and Doll Museum | *Nihon Kyōdo Gangu Hakubutsukan* | 日本郷土玩具博物館 |
| Japan Footware Museum | *Nihon Hakimono Hakubutsukan* | 日本はきもの博物館 |
| | | |
| *ACCOMMODATION* | | |
| Fukuyama Kokusai Hotel | *Fukuyama Kokusai Hoteru* | 福山国際ホテル |
| Fukuyama Oriental Hotel | *Fukuyama Orientaru Hoteru* | 福山オリエンタルホテル |
| Marunouchi Hotel | *Marunouchi Hoteru* | まるのうちホテル |
| New Castle Hotel | *Nyū Kyassuru Hoteru* | ニューキャッスルホテル |
| | | |
| **Tomo-no-Ura** | *Tomo-no-Ura* | 鞆の浦 |
| Fukuzen-ji | *Fukuzen-ji* | 福善寺 |
| Hosen-ji | *Hosen-ji* | 法宣寺 |
| Io-ji | *Io-ji* | 医王寺 |
| Nunakuma-jinja | *Nunakuma-jinja* | 沼名前神社 |
| Sensui-jima | *Sensui-jima* | 仙酔島 |
| Tomo-no-Ura Museum of History | *Tomo-no-Ura Rekishi Minzoku Shiryōkan* | 鞆の浦歴史民族資料館 |
| Uonosato | *Uonosato* | うおの里 |
| | | |
| *ACCOMMODATION* | | |
| Keishōkan | *Keishōkan* | 景勝館 |
| Kokuminshukusha Sensui-jima | *Kokuminshukusha Sensui-jima* | 国民宿舎仙酔島 |
| Hotel Ōfūtei | *Hoteru Ōfūtei* | ホテル鴎風亭 |
| Tomo Seaside Hotel | *Tomo Shiisaido Hoteru* | 鞆シーサイドホテル |
| | | |
| **Onomichi** | *Onomichi* | 尾道 |
| Fukuzen-ji | *Fukuzen-ji* | 福善寺 |
| Jōdo-ji | *Jōdo-ji* | 浄土寺 |
| Saikoku-ji | *Saikoku-ji* | 西国寺 |
| Senkō-ji | *Senkō-ji* | 千光寺 |
| Senkō-ji-kōen | *Senkō-ji-kōen* | 千光寺公園 |
| | | |
| *ACCOMMODATION* | | |
| Alpha-1 | *Arufa-1* | アルファ1 |
| Dai-Ichi Hotel | *Dai-Ichi Hoteru* | 第一ホテル |
| Kaizan-sō | *Kaizan-sō* | 海山荘 |
| Uonobu | *Uonobu* | 魚信 |

of the toys are linked to festivals and religious beliefs and there's also a fascinating display of Kachina dolls made by the Hopi people in Arizona.

## Practicalities

Fukuyama Station is on both the Shinkansen and JR Sanyō **train** lines. The **bus** terminus, from where services run to Tomo-no-Ura (see opposite), is beside the station's south exit. Inside the station, beside the north exit, is the **tourist information desk** (daily 8.30am–5pm; ☎0849/22-2869), where the helpful assistants speak English and can provide you with English maps and leaflets on Fukuyama and Tomo-no-Ura.

If for some reason you need **to stay** overnight, the best selection of business hotels is north of the station. The *Marunouchi Hotel* (☎0849/23-2277, fax 23-6557; ④) has the cheapest rates, while the *Fukuyama Oriental Hotel* (☎0849/27-0888, fax 27-0991; ⑤) and the *Fukuyama Kokusai Hotel* (☎0849/24-7000; ⑤) both offer smart, spacious rooms with TVs, fridges and en-suite bathrooms. Top-of-the-range is the characterless *New Castle Hotel* (☎0849/22-2121, fax 23-6813; ⑥), one minute south of the station.

There are plenty of **restaurants** near the south side of the JR station, including the usual fast-food outlets. *Amochan*, in the row of cheap noodle bars and cafeterias directly under the railway tracks to the right of the station's south exit, does good-value tempura and *sashimi* set meals for ¥800. Italian food with a Japanese flavour is served at *Studebaker*, on the third floor of the building on the west side of the bus station. The set lunches offer the best value at around ¥750, while an evening meal here shouldn't set you back more than ¥2000. Worth checking out for lunch and/or beer is *Prost Beer Restaurant*, behind the Tenmaya department store on the Motomachi arcade, five minutes' walk south of Fukuyama Station. It serves a wide range of bottled beers, including several brews from Belgium and the UK.

## Tomo-no-Ura

There are few more pleasant ways to spend half a day or more in Japan than exploring the enchanting fishing port of **TOMO-NO-URA**, at the tip of the Numakuma Peninsula, 14km south of Fukuyama. The town has one of the most beautiful locations on the Inland Sea, and its narrow, twisting streets and surrounding hills, liberally sprinkled with picturesque temples and shrines, are easily explored on foot or by bicycle. Boats unload their catch daily beside the horseshoe-shaped **harbour**, which has hardly changed since the town's Edo-era heyday, when trading vessels waited here for the tides to change direction or rested en route to mainland Asia. Now, you're just as likely to see locals dreaming the day away on the sea walls, rod in hand, waiting for the fish to bite, or selling catches of prawns, squirming crabs, and other seafood on the streets.

The best way to get your bearings is by climbing up to the ruins of the castle **Taigashima-jō** on the headland immediately above the ferry landing and pausing to take in the view from the temple Empuku-ji, where you'll also find a small monument to the celebrated haiku poet Bashō. To the West, you can see the gentle sweep of the harbour and the temple-studded slopes of Taisiden hill, while to the east is tiny Benten-jima, an outsized rock crowned with a temple to the Buddhist deity, and the larger island Sensui-jima, the best place to stay the night (see overleaf).

Heading west into the town from the bus terminal, you'll soon hit the steps leading up to the **Tomo-no-Ura Museum of History** (Tues–Sun: April–Sept 9am–5pm; Jan–March & Oct–Dec 9am–4.30pm; ¥150), which has a few mildly diverting exhibits including a miniature model of the sea-bream-netting show held every day in May, when the local fishermen use age-old methods to herd the fish into their nets. Even if you don't go into the museum, the view from its hill-top location in the middle of the town, across a patchwork of grey and blue tiled roofs dropping away to the harbour is one of Tomo-no-Ura's most pleasant.

Returning to the foot of the hill, follow the narrow road west past the ships' chandlers shop and then turn left into the street lined with wood and plaster warehouses dating from the eighteenth and nineteenth centuries, some of which have been converted into gift and coffee shops. At the end of the street is the confusingly named **Shichikyō-ochi Ruins**, a perfectly intact old sake brewery that briefly sheltered a band of anti-shogun rebels in the turbulent times prior to the Meiji Restoration. The water-washed steps of the harbour, topped off by a handsome stone lantern, are directly ahead.

Much of the locally caught fish ends up being processed at **Uonosato** (Tues–Sun 9am–5pm; free), a surprisingly engaging snackfood factory in a commanding hillside postion on the far western side of the harbour. There's more of a craft shop than a factory atmosphere inside and you can try your hand at making prawn paste *sembei* (crackers) and other snacks after watching demonstrations by the friendly, blue-clothed workers. Outside the workshops, seafood dries in the sunlight on large wooden racks and there are craft shops on the surrounding terraces, all of which provide marvellous views across the harbour.

Returning towards the town, keep an eye open for the sign pointing up Taishiden hill to the pretty temple **Io-ji**. If you're cycling it's best to leave your bike on the main road before hiking up to the temple, one of many founded by the revered Buddhist priest Kōbō Daishi (see p.784). You can hike down the hill eastwards past several more temples, include **Hosen-ji**, where only a truncated stump remains of the previously 14.3m-wide Tengai pine tree. As the street turns the corner just beyond Hosen-ji, glance down to see the mini-stone bridge **Sasayaki**, where a couple of ill-fated lovers are said to have once whispered sweet nothings before drowning.

Continuing north for a couple of minutes you'll arrive at the hillside approach to **Nunakuma-jinja**, a large shrine which, although ancient, has been recently rebuilt in concrete. More impressive is the traditional wooden Nō stage within the shrine grounds that used to be taken around battlefields so the warlord Toyotomi Hideyoshi could be entertained. A couple of minutes' walk further north is **Ankoku-ji**, founded around 1270, and containing two wooden statues of Buddha designated as national treasures. Neither they nor the temple's tatty sand and rock garden are worth going out of your way for.

Either wind your way back to the ferry landing along the narrow streets or follow the seafront to the west, then hike up the hill immediately to the north to take in one more view from the Taichoro reception hall of the temple **Fukuzen-ji** (daily 10am–5pm). It costs ¥200 to enter the airy *tatami* space with paper screens which open to a reveal a striking panorama of the Inland Sea, a view which has changed little since 1711, when a visiting Korean envoy hailed it "the most beautiful scenery in Japan."

### Practicalities

**Buses** leave platform 11 at Fukuyama bus terminus roughly every fifteen minutes, and take around thirty minutes to reach Tomo-no-Ura. They stop at the ferry landing building, inside which is an **information desk** (daily 9am–5.45pm), where you can pick up an English map of the town. **Bikes** can be hired from the adjoining parking lot for ¥100 for two hours, plus a ¥500 deposit.

The main **accommodation** in Tomo-no-Ura is limited to expensive ryokan-type hotels in charmless modern buildings. Both the *Keishōkan* (☎0849/82-2121, fax 82-2510; ⑧) and the *Tomo Seaside Hotel* (☎0849/83-5111, fax 82-3122; ⑦) have traditional *tatami* rooms with sea views, but are geared towards the tastes of old-fashioned tour parties. The most upmarket choice is the *Hotel Ōfūtei* (☎0849/82-2480; ⑨), whose highlight is its collection of huge roof-top baths; thankfully the strikingly ugly building is safely out of view at the north end of the town. However, a much better option is to take the ferry that regularly shuttles across to **Sensui-jima**, (a five-minute hop for ¥240 return), and stay in the smartly refurbished *Kokuminshukusha Sensui-jima* (☎0849/70-5050, fax 70-5035; ④), which has superior-quality *tatami* rooms and a relaxing set of public baths, including an outdoor roof-top pool. Breakfast and dinner are ¥2800 per person extra and, admirably for a Japanese hotel, there are no TVs in rooms; instead there are pens and paper and a note encouraging guests to write a letter or even a poem. At a small visitor's centre beside the hotel, you can pick up a map showing four trails around the island, including one across its hilly centre and another passing secluded beaches.

Being a fishing port, Tomo-no-Ura has a decent range of seafood **restaurants**, the best being *Chitose* (daily except Tues 11.30am–3pm & 6–8.30pm), a friendly joint just behind the car park on the town's eastern waterfront. A delicious set-meal of many dishes including Tomo's trademark catch of *tai* (sea bream) costs ¥1680. In the same row of shops, pop into the charming *Tomo-no-Tsu*, a café serving *matcha* tea and *dango* rice balls in winter and ice-shaving desserts in the summer. Also worth checking out is *Shyomachi-jaya* (Tues–Sun 9am–5pm), which serves tempura set-meals for ¥1400, in an atmospheric wooden building near the chandlers shop on the east side of the harbour.

## Onomichi

The appealingly raffish port of **ONOMICHI**, overlooked by the houses and temples that tumble down the steep face of the wooded hill, Senkōji-san, is only 20km west of Fukuyama. Many Japanese come here to linger along the town's vertiginous byways, imagining scenes from their favourite movies by local director Ōbayashi Nobuhiko. Onomichi is also a gateway to some of the islands of the Inland Sea, including Ikuchi-jima and Ōmi-shima (see p.543), and to Shikoku via ferries and, soon by road, along the Nishi-Seto Expressway, a sixty-kilometre highway to Imabari which, when it opens in 2000, will cross ten bridges and nine islands (see p.651).

There's a pleasant **walk** from Onomichi Station past most of the town's twenty-five temples; to complete the full course takes the better part of a day, by which time you'll be sick of temples, so skip those at the start by hopping on the regular bus from platform 2 outside Onomichi Station and heading east for five minutes to the Nagaeguchi stop (¥130). From here, you can catch the **ropeway** (daily 9am–5.15pm; ¥280 one way, ¥440 return) up to the park **Senkō-ji-kōen**, which blooms with cherry blossom and azaleas each spring. The views from its hill-top observatory across the town and narrow sea channel to the nearest island Mukai-shima are impressive.

The most colourful temple on the hill is the scarlet-painted **Senkō-ji**, packed with *jizo* statues and doing a lively trade in devotional trinkets, particularly heart-shaped placards to scribble a wish and leave dangling in the temple for good luck. Heading back downhill from here, you can follow the "literary path", so-called because famous writers' words are inscribed on stone monuments along the way. The most celebrated of the local writers is Hayashi Fumiko, a female poet who lived in Onomichi from 1917 and whose bronze statue – something of a landmark – can be found crouching pensively beside a wicker suitcase and brolly at the entrance to the shopping arcade a minute east of the station.

The "literary path" continues past the pagoda at the temple **Tennei-ji**, just behind the ropeway base station, from where you can head east back up the hill towards **Fukuzen-ji**. This temple, dating from 1573, has a vast spreading pine tree in its grounds, said to be shaped like an eagle, and its main gate is decorated with some beautiful wood carvings of cranes and dragons. On the steps up to the temple, look out for **Tile-ko-michi** (Little Tile Street), a narrow alley which has been plastered over the last 25 years with ceramic slabs inscribed by visitors.

Continuing east along the flagstoned streets, head north up the hill when you hit the next main crossroads, and you'll arrive at **Saikoku-ji**, one of the largest temple complexes in western Japan and easily spotted by the giant straw sandals which hang either side of the imposing entrance gate; pray here and it's said you'll find the strength to continue your journey.

The last temple worth visiting is **Jōdo-ji** at the eastern end of the route. Pigeons flock around its squat two-storey pagoda, and an elegant Zen garden, with a tea ceremony room transported from Kyoto's Fushimi castle, is hidden behind the main hall of worship. To see the garden you'll have to pay the grumpy attendant ¥500; he'll perk up once the money's handed over and take you on a personally guided tour with a non-stop commentary in Japanese.

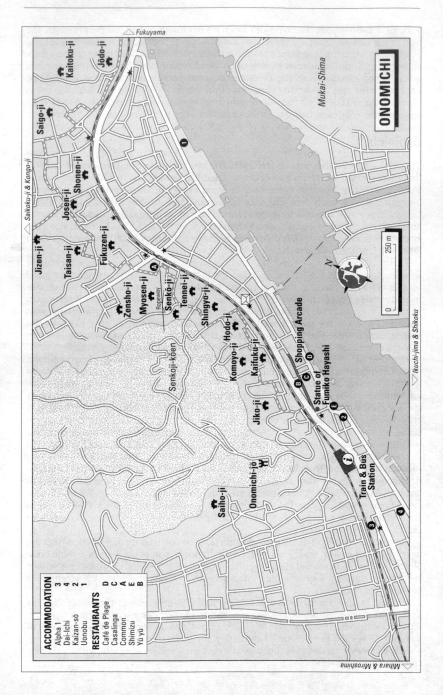

ONOMICHI

△ Fukuyama

Mukai-Shima

Kaitoku-ji
Jōdo-ji

Saigo-ji

△ Saikoku-ji & Kongo-ji

Shonen-ji
Josen-ji

Jizen-ji
Taisan-ji
Fukuzen-ji

Zensho-ji
Myosen-ji
Ropeway
Senko-ji
Tennei-ji
Shingyo-ji

Hodo-ji
Komoyo-ji
Kaifuku-ji

Senkoji-kōen

Jiko-ji

Shopping Arcade

Statue of
Fumiko Hayashi

Onomichi-jō

Saiho-ji

Train & Bus
Station

Ikuchi-jima & Shikoku ▽

△ Mihara & Miroshima

N

0          250 m

Don't get too hung up in Onomichi's temples to miss pottering around the evocative waterfront and **shopping arcade** near the train station. Here you'll find remnants of old Asia rare in squeaky-clean modern Japan, including a small crescent of shacks by the sea that have miraculously survived the combined forces of earthquakes, typhoons and general redevelopment. In and around the arcades are several antique and junk emporiums that are also worth a browse.

### Practicalities

**Trains** on the JR Sanyō line stop at Onomichi Station, a minute's walk from the waterfront. The closest Shinkansen station, Shin-Onomichi is 3km north of the town; from here a regular bus takes fifteen minutes to reach Onomichi Station (¥210). **Buses** leave from outside Onomichi Station for Ikuchi-jima (see below) and Hiroshima Airport (see p.549), thirty minutes west. **Ferries** to Setoda on Ikuchi-jima and Imabari and Matsuyama on Shikoku leave from the jetty immediately in front of Onomichi Station. Tourist **information** is available at the office just to the left as you come out of Onomichi Station (Mon–Fri 9am–5.30pm). The assistants don't speak English, but you can pick up an English map here marking out the walking route around the temples.

The cheapest **accommodation** options are business hotels, of which there are several immediately west of the station. The *Alpha-1* (☎0848/25-5600; [5]) has good standard singles from ¥4600, while the rooms at the *Dai-Ichi Hotel*, just round the corner (☎0848/23-4567, fax 23-2112; [5]), have sea views. There are also a couple of excellent ryokan, where the rates include two meals: *Kaizan-sō* (☎0848/22-8338, fax 22-2221; [7]), a couple of minutes' walk east from the station towards the harbour, is beautifully decorated and has one room where the ceiling looks like a giant bird's nest. The owner speaks Japanese only, but is very friendly. You could also try *Uonobu* (☎0848/3-4175, fax 37-3849; [8]), a larger, equally elegant establishment with a seaside location and a tea ceremony room.

Onomichi fancies itself as something of a gourmet destination and the tourist office produces a map in Japanese detailing an impressive range of **eating** options. Being a port, fresh seafood is the thing to go for, especially at the sushi restaurants clustered along the harbour front east of the station. One of the best places to try is *Shimizu*, a cramped three-table joint in a tumbledown shack on Onomichi's waterfront. Real food is displayed in the window and they do noodles, too. If you go for the whole grilled *tai* (sea bream), when you've finished eating the cook will stick the fish head and bones in a bowl of soup for afters. There are plenty of Western-style restaurants, too, such as *Casalinga*, a funky Italian joint between the shopping arcade and the waterfront, with red-checked tablecloths and graffiti on the walls; lunch here costs around ¥1000, with dinner not much more. Just round the corner on the waterfront, you can get a cheap lunch of salad and a drink at the trendy *Café de Plage*. In the arcade itself, you'll find *Yūyū*, a café-bar and gift shop with a 1920s feel, while at the base of the ropeway, *Common* specializes in freshly made Belgian waffles, costing ¥400–670, with a drink.

## Ikuchi-jima and Ōmi-shima

Among the Geiyo archipelago of islands clogging the Inland Sea between Onomichi and the northwest coast of Shikoku, **IKUCHI-JIMA** and **ŌMI-SHIMA** are both worth a visit. Of the two, Ikuchi-jima is the place to stay and has the best attractions, including **Kōsan-ji**, a dazzling Disneyland-esque temple complex, and the exquisite **Hirayama Ikuo Museum of Art**.

Whilst part of the fun of visiting these islands is the **ferry** ride there, you can also get to Ikuchi-jima by **bus** from Onomichi since the island is connected to the mainland by a series of bridges that will eventually carry the Nishi-Seto Expressway (see p.651). The bridge linking Ikuchi-jima to Ōmi-shima is due to be completed in 1999; if it's not yet open, the island is only a short ferry hop from Ikuchi-jima and is best explored, like its neighbour, by bicycle.

# Ikuchi-jima

Sun-kissed **IKUCHI-JIMA** is covered with citrus groves and attracts plenty of tourists each summer to its palm-fringed beaches, in particular the sweeping man-made Sunset Beach on the west coast. The potato-shaped island can comfortably be toured by bicycle in a day, as can the islet Kōne-shima linked by bridge to Ikuchi-jima's main settlement, the quaint **Setoda** on the island's northwest coast. Around the island, you should look out for the fourteen bizarre contemporary outdoor sculptures, including a giant saxaphone and a stack of yellow buckets, which form part of Ikuchi-jima's "Biennale" modern art project.

## Kōsan-ji

A gift-shop-lined street leads directly from Setoda's ferry landing to the unmistakably gaudy entrance to Ikuchi-jima's wackiest attraction – the technicolour temple complex of **Kōsan-ji** (daily 9am–4pm; ¥1000). Built by Kanemoto Kozo, an arms manufacturer turned priest, Ikuchi-jima's top tourist attraction includes not only replicas of famous temple buildings from Nikkō, Kyoto and Nara, but also a Grand Guignol grotto, aviaries of exotic birds and a contrastingly sober art museum.

Once inside the gate, modelled on one from an imperial palace in Kyoto, the buildings you see are no less overwhelming, with the central focus being a faithful reproduction of the Yōmei-mon (Sunshine Gate) from Tōshō-gū in Nikkō. To the right of the main temple building is the entrance to the **Senbutsudo** (cave of a thousand Buddhas) and the Valley of Hell. An underground passage leads past miniature tableaux of the horrors of eternal damnation (the cramped bird cages outside provide a more graphic real-life depiction), followed by the raptures of a heavenly host of Buddhas. You'll then wind your way up from this mock grotto to emerge beneath the beatific gaze of a 15-metre-tall statue of the Buddhist goddess of mercy, Kannon.

Kōsan-ji's five-storied pagoda, modelled on the one at Murō-ji in Nara, is the last resting place of Kanemoto's beloved mother, whose holiday home, **Chōseikaku**, is right by the exit (¥300). The home is a fascinating combination of Western and traditional styles, with two of the rooms having beautiful painted panels on their ceilings and a Buddha-like model of Mrs Kanemoto resting in one of the alcoves. From the mother's retreat, a tunnel leads under the road to Kōsan-ji's **art gallery**, a contrastingly plain building housing sober displays of mainly religious paintings and statues, many rated as important cultural assets.

## Hirayama Ikuo Museum of Art and around

Topping Kōsan-ji's treasures takes some doing, but the **Hirayama Ikuo Museum of Art**, next door to the temple's art gallery (daily: April–Sept 9am–5.30pm; Jan–March & Oct–Dec 9am–4.30pm; ¥600), has eclipsed it with a superior calibre of art. Hirayama Ikuo, one of Japan's greatest living artists, was born in Setoda in 1930, and was a junior high school student in Hiroshima when the bomb dromped. Despite travelling the world and becoming famous for his series of paintings on the Silk Road, he continually returns to the Inland Sea for inspiration.

Hirayama uses a traditional painting technique for his giant canvases, giving the finished paintings a distinctively dreamy quality. Because the special paint (*iwaenogu*) needed for this method is much less flexible and dries faster than oil paint, each picture has its own series of preparatory sketches. These full-sized blueprints for the final painting are known as *oshitazu*, and this museum contains many such sketches of Hirayama's most celebrated works, as well as original paintings and watercolours.

After the Hirayama museum, you can take in the view that inspired one of the artist's most beautiful paintings, by hiking to the summit of the hill behind Setoda. A small park here overlooks the attractive three-storey pagoda of **Kōjō-ji**, breaking out of the pine trees below, with the coloured tiled roofs of the village and the islands of the Inland Sea beyond. If you have some time to kill while waiting for a ferry or bus, you could drop by the **Folk Museum** (daily except Tues 10am–4.30pm; free) in the old building beside the ferry terminal. Inside, you'll find a mildly diverting collection of antique boats and everyday household objects.

## Practicalities

There are plenty of **ferries** to Ikuchi-jima from either Onomichi (p.541) or Mihara, slightly further along the coast, which is on both the Shinkansen and Sanyō rail lines

---

### A DISNEYLAND OF TEMPLES

**Kōsan-ji** is the creation of steel tube manufacturer Kanemoto Kozo, who made much of his fortune from the arms trade. A devoted son, Kanemoto used some of his funds to build his mother a holiday retreat in their home town of Setoda. When she died, the bereft Kanemoto decided to build a temple in her honour, so bought a priesthood from Nishi-Hongan-ji temple in Kyoto and took over the name of a minor-league temple, Kōsan-ji, in Niigata. He resigned from his company, grew his hair, changed his name to Kōsanji Kozo, and began drawing up plans for the new Kōsan-ji, a collection of the most splendid examples of Japanese temple buildings.

Although many of the re-creations are smaller than the originals, Kanemoto cut no corners when it came to detail, even going as far as to add his own embellishments, most famously to the already over-the-top replica of the Yōmei-mon from Nikkō's Tōshō-gū. It was this gate, completed in the mid-1950s that earned Kōsan-ji its nickname Nishi-Nikkō, the Nikkō of the west. Behind Kanemoto's seemingly barmy project lay sound business sense. Despite its costly upkeep, Kōsan-ji has attracted millions of paying visitors since its opening in 1936 and continues to do so. And since it's recognized as an official temple, Kōsan-ji's considerable income is tax-free.

and offers the cheapest ferry fare of ¥670 one way. The **bus** from Onomichi (¥1080) leaves from platform one in front of Onomichi Station and terminates at the southern end of Setoda; you might have to change buses at the terminus on Ino-shima along the way. For a map of Ikuchi-jima and a well-illustrated brochure on the island's attractions, partly in English, drop by the **tourist information** booth (daily 10am–3pm; ☎08452/7-0051), next to Setoda's ferry terminal. **Bikes** can also be rented from here from ¥100 an hour, or ¥700 for the day; if the information booth is closed, go to the office on the second floor of the ferry terminal.

The island has two youth hostels, both of which provide cheap **accommodation** and bike rental: the distinctive *Setoda Youth Hostel* (☎08452/7-0224; [1]) is easily spotted, on the hill five minutes' walk south of the ferry terminal, by the rainbow painted on one side. Inside, the hostel is just as colourful, decorated with many dolls, including the Seven Dwarfs skulking under the stairs. The *tatami* rooms have fans and TVs and are generally in better condition than those at *Ikuchi-jima Seaside Youth Hostel* (☎08452/7-3137; [1]), beside Sunset Beach, a couple of kilometres south of Setoda. Both hostels serve meals. Setoda also has several ryokan where the rates include two meals: *Sazanami* (☎ & fax 08452/7-3373; [5]), a couple of blocks from the waterfront along the main approach to the Kōsan-ji, is one of the cheapest, while the nicest is *Suminoe* (☎08452/7-2155, fax 7-2156; [7]), a very traditional establishment next to the ferry terminal, with an elegant courtyard garden and spacious *tatami* rooms.

Most of Setoda's **eating** options are along the street leading up to the temple. Opposite Kōsan-ji, *Mansaku* and *Ikoi* are two smart fish restaurants serving pricey set lunches of local cuisine. For something cheaper try the more down-to-earth *Keima* or *Juregoyun*, both close to the ferry terminal and serving a mish-mash of dishes. If you're cycling around the island, pack a picnic from Setoda's shops, or stop off at *Mien*, a small *okonomiyaki* joint run by an elderly lady on the coastal road, near the Kōmyōbo temple.

## Ōmi-shima

While Ikuchi-jima's top attraction is a temple, the big draw of neighbouring **Ōmi-shima** is one of the oldest shrines in the country, **Ōyamatsumi-jinja**, dating back to the end of the Kamakura era (1192–1333). Dedicated to Ōyamazumi, the elder brother of the Shinto deity Amaterasu, the shrine is around a fifteen-minute walk from the small, undistinguished port of **Miyaura**, on the west side of the island. Between the twelfth and sixteenth centuries, it used to be a place of worship for pirates who used the island as a base before being brought to heel by the warlord Toyotomi Hideyoshi.

To the right of the main shrine grounds you'll find three modern buildings comprising Ōyamasumi-jinja's **museum** (daily 8.30am–5pm; ¥1000 including entrance to the Kaiji Musuem). The Shiyōden hall and connected Kokuhō-kan are reputed to contain the largest collection of armour in Japan, but unless you're a *samurai* freak, you'll find the dry displays very dull. More intriguing is the **Kaiji Museum**, next door, (same hours and entrance fee as above), which houses the Hayama-maru, the boat built for Emperor Hirohito so he could undertake marine biology research. Beside the boat are some meticulously catalogued displays of fish, birds and rocks, some of the sealife looking like pickled aliens.

After visiting the shrine, there's not a huge amount to do on Ōmi-shima, other than explore the coast by bike (the best way of getting around the island), which will take half a day, or linger on some of its less than fine beaches. The interior is hilly, but there is a decent 5km cycle track mainly downhill from **Inokuchi**, the ferry port closest to Ikuchi-jima, across the island to Miyaura.

Miyaura is connected by ferry to Matsuyama and Imabari on Shikoku and there are also regular sailings from Mihara on Honshū to Inokuchi. There's also a ferry from

Tarumi, beside Sunset Beach on Ikuchi-jima, to Inokuchi taking fifteen minutes and costing ¥410 each way with a bike.

# Hiroshima and around

Because of the events of August 6, 1945, western Honshū's largest city needs little introduction. **HIROSHIMA** has become a by-word for the devastating, horrific effects of the atom bomb and for this reason alone millions visit the city every year to pay their respects at the Peace Park and museum. But more than either of these formal monuments, the reconstructed city – bigger, brighter and more vibrant than ever – is eloquent testimony to the power of life over destruction. Where once there was nothing but ashes for as far as the eye could see, now stands a modern city that still retains an old-world feel with its trundling trams and sunny disposition.

Poised on the coast at the western end of the Inland Sea, Hiroshima is also the jumping-off point for several islands, most notably verdant **Miya-jima**, home of the beautiful shrine **Itsukushima-jinja**. The view out to the red *torii* gate standing in the shallows in front of the shrine is rightly one of Japan's most celebrated, and although the island is often swamped by day-trippers, it's a delightful place to spend the night.

| HIROSHIMA | | |
|---|---|---|
| **Hiroshima** | *Hiroshima* | 広島 |
| A-bomb Dome | *Genbaku Dōmu* | 原爆ドーム |
| Hiroshima-jō | *Hiroshima-jō* | 広島城 |
| Peace Memorial Museum | *Heiwa Kinenkan* | 平和記念館 |
| Peace Memorial Park | *Heiwa Kinen-kōen* | 平和記念公園 |
| Hiroshima City Museum of Contemporary Art | *Hiroshima-shi Gendai Bijutsukan* | 広島市現代美術館 |
| Hiroshima Prefectural Museum of Art | *Hiroshima Kenritsu Bijutsukan* | 広島県立美術館 |
| Shukkei-en | *Shukkei-en* | 縮景園 |
| | | |
| *ACCOMMODATION* | | |
| ANA Hotel | *Zennikū Hoteru* | 全日空ホテル |
| Aster Plaza International Youth House | *Asutēru Puraza Kokusai Yūsu Hausu* | アステールプラザ国際ユースハウス |
| Hiroshima Kokusai Hotel | *Hiroshima Kokusai Hoteru* | 広島国際ホテル |
| Hiroshima Youth Hostel | *Hiroshima Yūsu Hosuteru* | 広島ユースホステル |
| Minshuku Ikedaya | *Minshuku Ikedaya* | 民宿池田屋 |
| Mikawa Ryokan | *Mikawa Ryokan* | 三河旅館 |
| Rihga Royal Hotel | *Riiga Roiyaru Hoteru* | リーガロイヤルホテル |
| Hotel Sunroute | *Hoteru Sanrūto* | ホテルサンルート |
| World Friendship Centre | *Sekai Yūkō Sentā* | 世界友好センター |
| | | |
| *RESTAURANTS* | | |
| Geishu | *Geishu* | げいしゅ |
| Kissui | *Kissui* | 吉水 |
| Kuimonoya | *Kuimonoya* | くいものや |
| Namche Bazar | *Namuchi Bazāru* | ナムチバザール |
| Okonomi-mura | *Okonomi-mura* | お好み村 |
| Pacela | *Pasēra* | パセーラ |
| Tokugawa | *Tokugawa* | 徳川 |
| Suishin | *Suishin* | 酔心 |

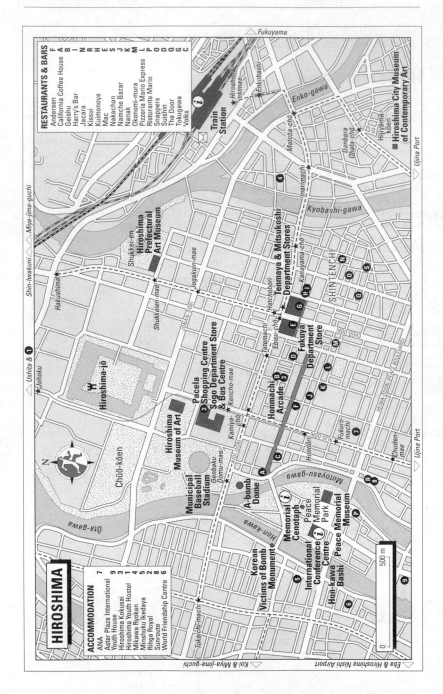

## Some history

Hiroshima's story began long before the bomb was dropped. During the twelfth century the delta of the Ōta-gawa on which Hiroshima now stands was known as Gokamura (five villages) and was ruled by **Taira no Kiyomori**, a scion of the Taira clan who commissioned the shrine Ikutsushima-jinja on Miya-jima and for a while was the power behind the Emperor in Kyoto. All this ended when the Taira were vanquished by the Minamoto clan (or Genji) at the Battle of Dannoura in 1185.

However, Gokamura continued to grow and became crucial in the campaign of the warlord **Mōri Motonari** to take control of Chūgoku, during the latter half of the fifteenth century. When Motonari's grandson Terumoto built his castle, the city was renamed Hiroshima (wide island). By the Meiji era the city had become an important base for the imperial army, a role that placed it firmly on the path to its terrible destiny.

As a garrison town, Hiroshima was an obvious target during World War II, but until August 6, 1945 it had been been spared Allied bombing. It's speculated that this was an intentional strategy by the US military so that the effects of the atom bomb when exploded could be fully understood. Even so, when the B29 bomber Enola Gay set off on its mission, Hiroshima was one of three possible targets (the others being Nagasaki and Kokura), whose fate was sealed by reconnaissance planes above the city reporting clear skies.

When "Little Boy", as the bomb was nicknamed, exploded 580m above the city at 8.15am it unleashed the equivalent of the destructive power of 15,000 tonnes of TNT. Beneath, some 350,000 people looked up and saw the sun fall to earth. In less than a second a kilometre-wide radioactive fireball consumed the city. The heat was so intense that all that remained of some victims were their shadows seared onto the rubble. Immediately some 70,000 buildings and 80,000 people were destroyed. But this was only the start. By the end of the year, 60,000 more had died from burns, wounds and radiation sickness. The final death toll is still unknown, the figure offered by the Hiroshima Peace Memorial Museum being "140,000 (plus or minus 10,000)".

Many survivors despaired of anything growing again for decades in the city's poisoned earth, but their hopes were raised on seeing fresh buds and blossom on the trees less than a year after the blast. The reborn Hiroshima, with its population of more than a million, is now a self-proclaimed "city of international peace and culture", and one of the most memorable and moving days to visit the city is August 6, when a **memorial service** is held in the Peace Park and 10,000 lanterns for the souls of the dead are set adrift on the Ōta-gawa delta.

For all Hiroshima's symbolic importance, though, it's important to remember that the city is far from top of the league table of war-time suffering. In the Battle of Okinawa, 265,000 people were killed in a few weeks, more than in Hiroshima and Nagasaki combined. In a single night of bombing in 1945, close on 200,000 died in Tokyo, while the Japanese themselves are said to have brutally massacred a similar number of soldiers and civilians in Nanking, China.

# Arrival and information

Hiroshima Station, on the east side of the city, is where local **trains** and Shinkansen arrive. Long-distance **buses** also arrive beside Hiroshima Station, although some also terminate at Hiroshima Bus Centre on the third floor of Sogō department store in the city centre. **Ferries** from Beppu in Kyūshū, Imabari and Matsuyama in Shikoku and various other locations around the Inland Sea, arrive at Hiroshima Port, some 4km south of Hiroshima Station and connected to the city by regular trams (¥130).

There are two airports serving the city, the closest being **Hiroshima Nishi Airport**, on the bay around 4km from the city centre. Apart from flights to Kansai International, Hiroshima Nishi handles services to smaller regional airports, such as Niigata and

Tottori; buses from the airport to the city centre leave every forty minutes or so, take thirty minutes and cost ¥230; a taxi will set you back around ¥2500. Flights from Tokyo Haneda airport and several other cities arrive at **Hiroshima Airport**, some 40km east of the city; regular buses run from here to Hiroshima Station and the central bus centre, in around fifty minutes (¥1250) or you can take a bus to nearby Shiraichi Station and transfer to a local train to the city.

There are two small **tourist information** booths in Hiroshima Station, one in the concourse at the south (*minami*) entrance, and another at the north (*kita*) Shinkansen entrance. Both are open daily 9am–5.30pm and can provide maps, leaflets in a wide range of languages and assist with hotel bookings. Hiroshima's main tourist information centre is the Hiroshima City Tourist Association (daily: April–Sept 9.30am–6pm; Jan–March & Oct–Dec 8.30am–5pm; ☎082/247-6738) in the Hiroshima Rest House beside the Motoyasu bridge to the Peace Park. The association has the best range of tourist literature, including information on other areas of Hiroshima-ken, and a small souvenir shop.

If you want to arrange a **home visit**, you'll need to apply in person at the International Conference Centre (daily: May–Nov 9am–7pm; Jan–April & Dec 10am–6pm; ☎082/247-8715) at the southwest end of the Peace Park, at least a day in advance. The centre also provides information on local events and has an excellent library and reading area with many international magazines and newspapers. Look out for free copies of the entertaining monthly listings magazine *The Outsider* at the centre, tourist offices and *Andersen*'s bakery (see p.554).

## Orientation and city transport

Hiroshima's main attraction, the Peace Park and museum, are around 2km west of Hiroshima Station, at the tip of a finger of land bounded by two of the six main channels of the Ōta-gawa that flow through the city. The city's central shopping and entertainment district, defined by the covered Hondōri arcade, is immediately east of the park, while the reconstructed castle Hiroshima-jō is directly north. Closer to Hiroshima Station is the pretty traditional garden Shukkei-en and 1km south is the hilly park Hijiyama-kōen and Hiroshima City Museum of Contemporary Art.

The city is well served by **public transport**, with nine **tramlines**, an extensive network of **city buses** and the zippy new Astram **monorail** line which transforms into a subway in the city centre, terminating beneath the Hondōri arcade. In practice, however, traffic can make catching a bus or a tram a frustratingly slow business; to get around the central sights quickly you're often better off **walking**.

Within the city centre the minimum tram and city bus fares are ¥130, with the numbered trams being easier to use if you don't read Japanese. From the station, trams #1 and #5 head south to Hiroshima Port past Hijiyama-kōen, while #2 and #6 head west to the Peace Park and beyond. Tram #9 shuttles back and forth from Hatchobori past the Shukkei-en garden. If you need to transfer from one tram to another to get to your destination, ask for a *norikai-kippu* from the driver (¥180); drop this in the fare box when you leave the second tram. If you need to transfer again, a second *norikai-kippu* costs ¥50.

With fares so cheap, neither of the one-day tram tickets are worth buying. A better option is the **pre-paid travel card** which can be used on the buses, trams and monorail/subway – the ¥1000 card gets you ¥1100 worth of travel. These cards can only be bought at the tram terminus at Hiroshima Station, the bus centre and the main JTB office on Rijo-dōri.

One off-beat way of seeing Hiroshima is to take a **taxi tour** with Stephen Outlaw-Spurell, possibly Japan's only *gaijin* taxi-driver. The American has become something of a local celebrity and offers a range of fully guided tours of the city at ¥5200 per hour, worth considering if there's a group of you to split the cost. Bookings are made through the taxi firm Tsubame Kōtsū on ☎082/222-8180, fax 082/228-5200.

## Accommodation

Hiroshima has plenty of inexpensive **accommodation**, and the only time of year you might have a problem finding somewhere to stay is August 6 when the annual peace ceremony is held. Although there are many business hotels in the charmless area around Hiroshima Station (charging around ¥7000 for a single room, ¥11,000 for a twin), it's better to stay closer to Peace Park, west of which are more business hotels, minshuku and, if all else fails, love hotels. Hiroshima's main **youth hostel** is a couple of kilometres to the north of the city centre, though if you're planning on visiting near-by Miya-jima (p.556) you might find it more convenient to stay at the *Miyajima-guchi Youth Hostel* and travel into Hiroshima for the day. This island also has some luxury ryokan..

**ANA Hotel**, 7-20 Nakamachi, Naka-ku (☎082/241-1111, fax 241-9123). Reasonably priced luxury hotel with spacious rooms only a couple of minutes' walk east of the Peace Park. The comfy lobby overlooks an ornamental garden and there's a swimming pool as well as several restaurants. Has a few singles for ¥9000. ⑥.

**Aster Plaza International Youth House**, 4-17 Kakomachi, Naka-ku (☎082/247-8700, fax 246-5808). Accommodation at this municipal culture centre a block south of the Peace Park is meant for students, but is also available at the same rates to foreign tourists. The large, comfortable Western and *tatami* rooms both have en-suite bathrooms and good views. Single rooms are ¥3620 and there's a midnight curfew. ③.

**Hiroshima Kokusai Hotel**, 3-13 Tatemachi, Naka-ku (☎082/248-2323, fax 248-2622). Good-value mid-range hotel, a minute's walk from the Hondōri shopping arcade. Some of the rooms are a bit flowery in their design, but it also has a few economy singles for just over ¥8000, a fourteenth-floor revolving restaurant and a recommended Japanese restaurant, *Geshui*. ⑤.

**Hiroshima Youth Hostel**, 1-13-6 Ushita-shinmachi, Higashi-ku (☎082/221-5343, fax 221-5377). This large institutional hostel, with bunk-bed dorms, is Hiroshima's cheapest option. There are extra charges, though, for bedsheets (¥140), heating in winter and air-conditioning in summer (¥170), and for use of the outdoor swimming pool. The main drawbacks are its distance from the sights and the 10pm curfew. If you arrive by train, the information counter in Hiroshima Station can give details of where to catch the bus to the hostel; if you arrive at the Bus Centre, take any bus from platform 11 and get off at Ushita-shinmachi-ichōme (¥210). From here, the hostel is an eight-minute uphill walk. ①.

**Minshuku Ikedaya**, 6-36 Dobashi-chō, Naka-ku (☎082/231-3329, fax 231-7875). Excellent-value, spacious *tatami* rooms at this Japanese Inn Group minshuku, five minutes' walk west of the Peace Park, run by friendly English-speaking staff. Singles start at ¥4000 for rooms without en-suite baths, while slightly higher rates are charged for the rooms in the newer *Bekkan* building. ④.

**Mikawa Ryokan**, 9-6 Kyobashi-chō, Minami-ku (☎082/261-2719). Small minshuku, a member of the Japanese Inn Group, five minutes' walk from Hiroshima Station towards the city centre. Cheap rates, from ¥3150 for a single, but the *tatami* rooms, sharing a common bathroom, are gloomy. ③.

**Rihga Royal Hotel**, 6-78 Motomachi, Naka-ku (☎082/502-1121, fax 228-5415). Hiroshima's grand-est hotel soars 33 floors and is supposedly designed in the image of its neighbour, the reconstruct-ed castle. Has spacious rooms, several restaurants, a pool and fitness centre. Also check out the stunning painting of Itsukushima-jinja, by Hirayama Ikuo, in the plush lobby. ⑦.

**Hotel Sunroute**, 3-3-1 Ōtemachi, Naka-ku (☎082/249-3600, fax 249-3677). One of the more upmar-ket in this nationwide chain of business hotels. Features a couple of good restaurants (the Italian *Viale* and the Japanese *Kissui*), a non-smoking floor and rooms specially equipped for disabled guests. Five minutes' walk east of the Peace Park, on Heiwa-dōri. ⑥.

**World Friendship Centre (WFC)**, 8-10 Higashi-Kannonmachi, Nishi-ku (☎082/503-3191, fax 503-3179). The first night's stay at this small, homely B&B with *tatami* rooms costs ¥3200 per person, dropping to ¥3000 for additional nights. Run by a friendly American couple on behalf of the WFC, which aims to bring different nationalities together to promote peace. About a ten-minute walk south of the Peace Park, the WFC can also arrange meetings with A-bomb survivors and guided tours around the park for non-guests. ②.

# The Peace Memorial Park and Museum

The most appropriate place to start exploring Hiroshima is beside the twisted shell of the Industrial Promotion Hall, built in 1914 and now better known as the **A-bomb Dome**. Almost at the hypocentre of the blast, the hall was one of the few structures for the surrounding 3km that remained standing. It's been maintained ever since in its distressed state as a historical witness of Hiroshima's suffering and packs a powerful punch as you emerge from the modern-day hustle and bustle of the Hondōri arcade.

On the opposite bank of the Motoyasu-gawa is the verdant **Peace Memorial Park**, dotted throughout with dozens of statues and monuments to the A-bomb victims. One of the most touching is the **Children's Peace Monument**, a statue of a young girl standing atop an elongated dome and holding aloft a giant origami crane – the symbol of health and longevity. The monument's base is eternally festooned in multicoloured garlands of origami cranes, folded by school children from all over Japan and many other countries, a tradition that started with radiation victim Sasaki Sadako who fell sick with leukaemia in 1955. The twelve-year-old Sasaki started to fold cranes on her sickbed in the hope that if she reached a 1000 she'd be cured; she died before reaching her goal, but her classmates continued after her death and went on to build this monument.

The main monument – a smooth concrete and granite arch aligned with the A-bomb Dome and the Peace Memorial Museum – is the **Memorial Cenotaph**, designed by architect Kenzō Tange in the style of protective objects found in ancient Japanese burial mounds. Underneath the arch lies a stone coffin holding the names of all the direct and indirect A-bomb victims and beside it burns the **Flame of Peace**, which will be put out once the last nuclear weapon on earth has been destroyed. It is before this monument that a memorial service is held every August 6 when white doves are released.

One final monument to take note of before proceeding to the museum is the **Monument in Memory of the Korean Victims of the Bomb**, on the western bank of the Hon-kawa, outside the Peace Park, beside the Hon-kawa-bashi. Some 2000 of the 20,000 forced labourers from Korea, a Japanese colony at the time of the war, died anonymously in the A-bomb blast, but it took decades before this monolith mounted on the back of a turtle was erected in their memory.

The **Peace Memorial Museum** (daily: May–Nov 9am–6pm; Jan–April & Dec 9am–5pm; ¥50) deserves to be seen by every visitor to Hiroshima. Expanded into two sections for the fiftieth anniversary of the bombing, it presents a balanced picture of why the atrocity took place as well as its harrowing effects. The newer displays in the **east building** revolve around two models of the city before and after the explosion, and explain the lead-up to the bombing, including Japan's militarism. A watch in one case is forever frozen at 8.15am. To one side of the ground floor is a **video theatre** where you can see two short documentary films in English; in one a doctor's voice breaks as he recalls his realization that vast numbers of childhood leukaemia cases were caused by radiation.

On the third floor, after displays on the nuclear age post-Hiroshima, is a connecting corridor to the old museum in the **west building**. There are counters here where you can rent a taped commentary (¥150) in one of sixteen different languages – worth doing, although the appalling injuries shown in photographs and recreated by models need no translation. This is strong stuff, which shirks none of the horror of the bomb's aftermath. At the end, you'll walk along a corridor overlooking the Peace Park and the resurrected city, providing a chance for contemplation on the bomb that wiped it all out half a century ago.

## THE HIBAKUSHA

*"I saw, or rather felt, an enormous bluish white flash of light, as when a photographer lights a dish of magnesium. Off to my right, the sky split open over the city of Hiroshima."*

Ogura Toyofumi, *Letters From the End of the World* (Kodansha).

There are more than 300,000 *hibakusha* (war survivors) in Japan who, like Ogura, lived through the A-bomb, and some 95,000 still live in Hiroshima today. Ogura's poignant account – a series of letters penned to his dead wife in the immediate aftermath of the war – stands alongside many others, including the video-taped testamonies of survivors that can be viewed at the Peace Museum.

Through the museum it's also possible to meet with a *hibakusha*. To do this you need to make a request in writing to the Heiwa Bunka Centre (fax 082/242-7452), stating the dates you'd prefer and whether you'll need an interpreter. The World Friendship Centre (see Accommodation, p.551) also arranges meetings and occasionally hosts discussions with experts and visiting scholars.

## North of the Peace Park

At the northern end of the Peace Park, east of the T-shaped bridge Aioi-bashi, that was the A-bomber's target is the **Municipal Baseball Stadium**, home ground of the Toyo Carp, Hiroshima's professional team. Locals are avid supporters of the team and it's well worth trying to catch a game. Tickets start from ¥1500 and can be bought on the gate; for information and advance bookings call ☎082/223-2141.

Five minutes' walk north of the stadium is the pricey **Hiroshima Museum of Art** (daily 9am–5pm; ¥1000), which specializes in late nineteenth- and twentieth- century French art, including minor works by Monet, Renoir, Matisse, Van Gogh and Picasso. The airy museum with an elegant central dome also has a less enthralling section of modern, Western-style, Japanese paintings. If you have limited time, skip this and head for some of Hiroshima's better art museums (see below).

If you've seen other castles in Japan, there's little reason either to proceed to **Hiroshima-jō** (daily: April–Sept 9am–5.30pm; Jan–March & Oct–Dec 9am–4.30pm; ¥300), whose main entrance is directly behind the museum, next to three reconstructed turrets, containing temporary exhibitions and fronting the Ninomaru compound beside the castle moat. The original castle was built in 1589 by Mōri Terumoto, one of Toyotomi's Hideyoshi council of "five great elders", but just eleven years later he was forced to retreat to Hagi (see p.573) following defeat in the battle of Sekigahara. Eventually the shogun passed control of Hiroshima to the Asano clan who held sway until the Meiji restoration. Inside the smartly rebuilt five-floor donjon are various historical displays, the most entertaining of which is the combined model and video show with a guard giving a comical English commentary.

## Shukkei-en and the Hiroshima Prefectural Museum of Art

Ten minutes' walk east of Hiroshima-jō (or catch tram #9 from the Hatchobori stop, getting off at Shukkei-en-mae), is a much better post-bomb reconstruction, **Shukkei-en** (daily: April–Sept 9am–6pm; Jan–March & Oct–Dec 9am–5pm; ¥250), a beautiful strollgarden with a central pond and several teahouses. Built originally by Asano Nagaakira after he'd been made *daimyō* of Hiroshima in 1620, the gardens aim to present in miniature the Xihu lake from Hangzhou, China, and its name aptly means "shrunk scenery garden".

Adjacent to the garden is **Hiroshima Prefectural Museum of Art** (Tues–Sun 10am–6pm; ¥500) an impressive modern facility worth visiting to see two paintings alone: the fiery, awe-inspiring "Holocaust at Hiroshima" by Hirayama Ikuo (see p.545) who was in the city when the bomb dropped, and the floppy watches of Salvador Dali's surreal masterpiece "Dreams of Venus." Check out what's showing in the temporary exhibition area, too, for which you'll pay an extra fee. A *combined ticket* for the museum and garden costs ¥600; you'll need to buy this in the museum and enter the garden from there.

## Hiroshima City Museum of Contemporary Art

Around 1km south of Hiroshima Station, on the crest of Hiji-yama is the challenging **Hiroshima City Museum of Contemporary Art** (daily 10am–5pm, except July 20–Aug 31 10am–7pm; ¥300) with its ultra-modern collection of art inspired in part by the atomic bombing. Whether or not the often weird, sometimes wonderful, sculptures and paintings in this museum are to your taste, it's a collection that the city has clearly lavished money on. The surrounding leafy park, **Hijiyama-kōen**, is dotted with more modern sculptures, including some by Henry Moore, and provides splendid views across the city. To reach the museum take trams #1, #3 or #5 to Hijiyama-shita and hike up the hill. On Saturday, Sunday and holidays, there's a free shuttle bus from the bus centre to the museum.

## Eating

Hiroshima's excellent selection of **restaurants** are the best you'll find in this part of Japan. There's also the usual **fast-food** chains, including a branch of the American sandwich bar *Subway*, just south of the east end of the Hondōri arcade, the epicentre of Hiroshima's entertainment district. The *Pacela* complex connecting the *Rihga Royal Hotel* and Sogo department store also has four floors of restaurants and a food court in the basement with many fast-food operations and cafés, including *Mister Donut* and *Café du Monde*.

Hiroshima's specialities are fresh seafood from the Inland Sea, in particular oysters which are cultivated on thousands of rafts in Hiroshima Bay and *okonomiyaki*. The local tradition is to make these delicious batter pancakes with the diner's choice of separate layers of cabbage, beansprouts, meat, fish and noodles, unlike in Ōsaka, where all the ingredients are mixed up. Don't leave Hiroshima without sampling one. Where the reviews below list a telephone number, it's a good idea to book.

**Andersen**, 7-1 Hondōri. With its ground floor deli, bakery and café and second floor Swedish-style restaurants – including the classy *Midnight Sun* which serves free champagne at its weekend brunch buffets – this is a true gourmet's paradise. Ideal for breakfast, lunch or an early dinner. Daily except Wed 10am–8pm.

**Geishu**, 2F, *Hiroshima Kokusai Hotel*, 3-13 Tate-machi. Pricey, but one of the best places to enjoy beautifully presented local seafood dishes. On the top floor of the same hotel you'll find the revolving restaurant *Le Train Blue*, worth dropping by for a romantic evening cocktail. *Geishu* Mon–Sat 11am–11pm, Sun and hols 11am–10pm: *Le Train Blue* Mon–Sat 11.30am–midnight, Sun & hols 11.30am–11pm.

**Kissui**, 15F, *Hotel Sunroute*, 3-3-1 Ōte-machi (☎082/249-3600). Elegant *shabu shabu* (beef) restaurant overlooking the Peace Park, where the waitresses wear pale green kimono. Dinner is very pricey, but the ¥1800 lunch is a much more affordable option. Daily 11.30am–2pm & 5–9.30pm (last orders 8.30pm).

**Kuimonoya**, 2F, Apple 2 Bldg, 3-15 Ebisu-machi. A photo menu helps simplify the ordering at this trendy Southeast Asian restaurant with a casual atmosphere. Daily 11.30am–2pm & 5.30–midnight (2pm on Saturday).

**Namche Bazar**, 2F, K Bldg, 2-22 Fukuro-machi (☎082/246-1355). Oriental trinkets decorate this compact *mukokuseki* (no nationality) restaurant which serves dishes like Spanish omelette alongside Thai salads and Japanese-style beef stew. There's an English menu and they cater for vegetarians. Daily 5pm–midnight.

**Nanak**, 2-2 Fukuro-machi. Popular Indian chain restaurant with reasonably restrained decor, and waiters wearing orange turbans. Curries to suit all tastes and a decent lunch special for ¥880. Daily 11am–10pm.

**Okonomi-mura**, 5-13 Shin-tenchi. Behind the Parco department store, in the heart of the lively entertainment district, this building has 28 small *okonomiyaki* stalls crammed into three floors. You're unlikely to go wrong at any of them, but *Itsukushima*, the first stall you see on emerging from the elevator on the fourth floor is reputed to be one of the best in town. Daily 11am–9pm.

**Pizzeria Mario Expresso**, 7-9 Fukuro-machi. The more casual of the two *Mario* operations, this lively pizzeria has pavement tables and overlooks a small park. A nice spot to chill out over a coffee and dessert if you don't fancy a full meal. Daily 11am–11pm.

**Ristorante Mario**, 4-11 Nakaji-machō (☎082/248-4956). Authentic and deservedly popular Italian restaurant in the ivy-clad mock-Tuscan villa beside the Peace Bridge. As usual, the set lunches for ¥1200 and ¥1800 offer the best deal, but it's not too expensive for dinner and they have half bottles of wine. Daily 11.30am–2.30pm & 5–11.30pm (last orders 10.30pm).

**Tokugawa**, 5F, Tohgeki Bldg, Ebisu-machi. Cook up your own *okonomiyaki* for around ¥1000 at this restaurant whose entrance is halfway down the covered arcade running behind Tenmaya department store. Has an English menu and a bright, family-orientated atmosphere. Daily 10am–10.30pm.

**Suishin**, 6-7 Tatemachi (☎082/247-4411). Long-established fish restaurant which serves dishes in the local style, in particular *kamameshi* (rice casseroles). Daily except Wed 11.30am–10pm.

**Volks**, Hondōri. At the west end of the main shopping arcade this inexpensive chain steak restaurant is also a good choice for vegetarians because of its all-you-can-eat salad bar. Daily 10.30am–10.30pm.

## Drinking and entertainment

Come sundown, the thousands of **bars** crammed into the Nagarekawa and Shin-tenchi areas of the city, at the east end of the Hondōri arcade, fling open their doors. In summer, several beer gardens sprout on city rooftops, including one at the *ANA Hotel*. The best source of **information** on the latest in-places is the monthly magazine *The Outsider*, which also has listings for **concerts** and **cinema**; Salon Cinema (☎082/241-1781), near the city hall, has by far the most adventurous programme of European and American art-house films and revivals.

**California Coffee House**, west end of Hondōri. Outdoor tables make this a convivial spot near the river to hang out on sultry nights. Serves beers as well as coffee and snacks, but keeps erratic hours.

**The Door**, 3F, Maritai Bldg, 6-7 Yagenbori. Mellow, arty bar whose friendly owner is married to a Canadian; no cover charge. Has occasional live accoustic sets. Mon–Sat 7pm–5am.

**Harry's Bar**, B1, Apple 2 Bldg, 3-15 Ebisu-machi. Not quite up to its Venice namesake, but does have a more spacious and stylish ambience than many other bars. Cocktails cost around ¥1000, snacks are available and there's sometimes live music. Daily 6pm to at least midnight.

**Jacara**, 5F, Shatore No.3 Bldg, 13-13 Ginzan-chō, Naka-ku. The best of Hiroshima's late-night dance bars, *Jacara* has a friendly vibe and the DJs play a wide range of crowd-pleasing sounds, from Abba to Jamiroquai via the Gypsy Kings. The entry charge of ¥1000 includes one drink. Mon–Thurs 1pm–1am, Fri & Sat 7pm–3am, closed Sun.

**Mac**, Chūō-dōri. It's rumoured that this building on the corner of the arcade will be torn down, but the owner of the laid-back bar on the fourth floor insists he'll still be there. You can choose from his vast CD collection as you sip beers from ¥500. Daily 8pm–late.

**Nakachan**. This shack at the south end of Yagenbori, near the police box (*kōban*), has bags of atmosphere, especially late at night, with pavement tables where you can sip beers and tuck into dishes such as grilled fish. You'll find things more easy-going if you take a Japanese speaker. Daily 6am–4pm.

**Public**, Jizō-dōri. Set apart from the central district, a couple of blocks south of the crossing with Heiwa-dōri, this friendly bar has an open-air section, an English menu and most drinks under ¥1000. Look out for the blue awning. Mon–Fri 11.30am–1am, Sat & Sun noon–2am.

**Snappers**, 4F Miya Bldg, 1-7 Yagenbori. A well-known *gaijin* hangout, this tiny bar is often packed, and turns into a disco should the crowd feel in the mood to dance. Happy Hour is Mon–Sat 8–9pm, and bands occasionally play. Daily 8pm–1am.

## Listings

**Airlines** ANA, 2-1 Ōtemachi (domestic flights ☎082/246-0211; international flights ☎243-2231); JAL, 1-1-17 Kamiya-chō (☎082/242-6375); JAS, Kamiya-chō (☎082/245-1111).

**Banks and exchange** There are several banks clustered around the Hondōri arcade as it crosses Rijo-dōri, including Hiroshima Bank, Sumitomo Bank and Tokyo Mitsubishi Bank. Sumitomo Bank has an ATM (8am–10pm daily) from which you can make cash withdrawals with international cash cards, including Visa and Mastercard. Foreign exchange is also available at the central post office (see below) and Higashi post office next to Hiroshima Station.

**Bookshops** There's a small selection of English-language books and magazines at Kinokuniya on the sixth floor of Sogō department store and Maruzen in the Hondōri arcade, opposite *Andersen*. The Book Nook, in the editorial offices of *The Outsider* magazine, 201 Nakano Bldg., 1-5-17 Kamiya-chō, Naka-ku, near the *Hiroshima Kokusai Hotel,* also has an excellent selection of secondhand books (Mon–Fri 10am–9pm, Sat 10am–6pm, Sun &hols 1–6pm).

**Car rental** Eki Rent-a-car is at Hiroshima Station (☎082/263-5933). You can also try local branches of Hertz (☎082/262-4455) and Budget (☎082/222-0543).

**Hospital** Hiroshima Municipal Hospital is at 7-33 Moto-machi (☎082/221-2291).

**Police** The central police station is at 9-48 Moto-machi (☎082/224-0110). Emergency numbers are listed in Basics on p.70.

**Post office** The main central post office on Rijo-dōri near the Shiyakusho-mae tram stop is open Mon–Fri 9am–7pm, Sat 9am–5pm and Sun 9am–12.30pm. Other convenient branches are the Higashi post office beside the south exit of Hiroshima Station (also open Sat until noon) and the Miru Paruku post office next to Sogō department store.

**Shopping** Most of the city's main department stores open 10am–7pm, with Mitsukoshi being closed on Monday, Sogō on Tuesday, Fukuya on Wednesday and Tenmaya on Thursday.

**Sports** The Big Wave sports centre, with a swimming pool in summer and two ice-rinks during the winter is beside the Ushita stop on the Astram line. There's also a pool and other fitness facilities at the Hiroshima Prefectural Sports Centre behind the Municipal Baseball Stadium.

**Travel agent** The main JTB office is at Kamiyachō Biru, 2-2-2 Kamiyachō (☎082/542-5001).

## Miya-jima

The most famous attraction on **MIYA-JIMA**, officially known as Itsuku-shima, is the venerable shrine of **Itsukushima-jinja**, whose vermilion gate rising grandly out of the sea is considered one of Japan's most beautiful views. In the right light, when the tide is high and the many day-trippers have left, you may be tempted to agree that it is, in fact, *the* best.

The shrine and temples clustered around Miya-jima's only village at the northern tip of this long, mountainous island can comfortably be seen in a half-day trip from Hiroshima. If you have more time, there's plenty of other attractions, including beaches to laze on, and hikes over **Misen-san**, whose summit provides panoramic views across the Inland Sea. Consider splashing out on a night's accommodation at one of the island's classy ryokan, so that you can enjoy the after-hours atmosphere with only tame deer and a few other guests for company.

### Getting there and information

From Hiroshima you can get to Miya-jima either directly by ferry or by a combination of tram and ferry or train and ferry. High-speed **ferries** (¥1440) from Hiroshima's port, connected by tram to Hiroshima Station and the city centre, take twenty minutes.

Alternatively, **tram #3** runs out to Nishi-Hiroshima where you might have to change to tram #2, which will take you to the ferry terminal at Miyajima-guchi, a fifty-five-minute journey in total. A one-way costs ¥250, and the ten-minute ferry fare is ¥170. If you plan to return to Hiroshima the same day and travel a bit around the city, you'll save money buying a ¥840 one-day ticket. The **train** plus ferry route is only worth considering if you have a rail pass or special excursion ticket which will cover the cost of both the thirty-minute journey from Hiroshima to Miyajima-guchi Station and the crossing on the JR-run ferry.

There's a **tourist information** booth (daily 8.30am–7pm; ☎0829/44-2011) inside the island's ferry terminal, where you can pick up a basic map and book accommodation. The assistants speak a little English. Also in the terminal, you can **rent bikes** from the JR ticket counter from ¥320 for two hours; the only reason you'd want to do this is to pedal to the northern beaches since all the main sights are within easy walking distance of the ferry.

## Accommodation

The only budget accommodation options around Miya-jima are the **campsight** at the northern end of the island (☎0829/44-2903; ¥300 per person per night) and the **youth hostel** on the mainland at Miyajima-guchi. The best deal on the island is the *Kokuminshukusha*, but if you can afford it, you should splash out on one of the island's more upmarket

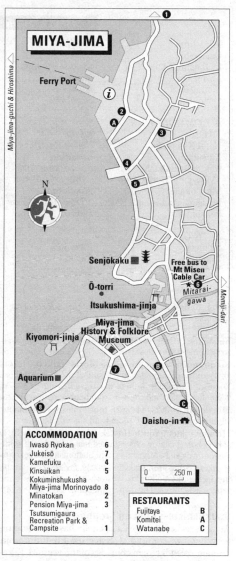

**ACCOMMODATION**

| Iwasō Ryokan | 6 |
| Jukeisō | 7 |
| Kamefuku | 4 |
| Kinsuikan | 5 |
| Kokuminshukusha Miya-jima Morinoyado | 8 |
| Minatokan | 2 |
| Pension Miya-jima | 3 |
| Tsutsumigaura Recreation Park & Campsite | 1 |

0      250 m

**RESTAURANTS**

| Fujitaya | B |
| Komitei | A |
| Watanabe | C |

ryokan or the excellent Western-style pension. Also try and visit mid-week since at weekends and during peak holiday seasons, rates at many of the hotels rise.

**Jukei-sō** (☎0829/44-0300, fax 44-0388). This ryokan has an excellent hillside location south of Itsukushima-jinja and overlooking the shrine. There's a choice of Western and *tatami* rooms and of Japanese and French restaurants. It's possible to stay here without taking meals, which start at ¥8000 per person. ⑨.

**MIYA-JIMA**

| | | |
|---|---|---|
| **Miya-jima** | *Miya-jima* | 宮島 |
| Daisho-in | *Daisho-in* | 大聖院 |
| Itsukushima-jinja | *Itsukushima-jinja* | 厳島神社 |
| Misen-san | *Misen-san* | みせん山 |
| Momiji-dani | *Momiji-dani* | もみじ谷 |
| Senjōkaku | *Senjōkaku* | 千畳閣 |
| *ACCOMMODATION* | | |
| Jukeisō | *Jukeisō* | じゅ景荘 |
| Hotel Kamefuku | *Hoteru Kamefuku* | ホテルかめ福 |
| Kinsuikan | *Kinsuikan* | きんすい館 |
| Kokuminshukusha Miya-jima Morinoyado | *Kokuminshukusha Miya-jima Morinoyado* | 国民宿舎みやじま杜の宿 |
| Minatokan | *Minatokan* | みなと館 |
| Miyajima-guchi Youth Hostel | *Miyajima-guchi Yūsu Hosuteru* | 宮島口ユースホステル |
| Pension Miya-jima | *Penshon Miyajima* | ペンション宮島 |
| *EATING* | | |
| Fujitaya | *Fujitaya* | ふじたや |
| Komitei | *Komitei* | こみ亭 |
| Watanabe | *Watanabe* | わたなべ |

**Hotel Kamefuku** (☎0829/44-2111, fax 44-2554). Large modern waterfront hotel, with spacious Japanese and Western-style rooms. Rooms have nice touches including fresh flowers, and there are luxurious public baths and several restaurants. ⑧.

**Kinsuikan** (☎0829/44-2131, fax 44-2137). Luxurious ryokan on the waterfront a minute's walk from the ferry. Some of the *tatami* rooms also have sunken *irori* charcoal fires, ideal for chilly winter nights. ⑧–⑨.

**Kokuminshukusha Miya-jima Morinoyado** (☎0829/44-0430, fax 44-2248). Book ahead for Miya-jima's only accommodation bargain, at the quiet southern end of the island, beyond the aquarium. Rooms are available without meals from around ¥5000 per person, a choice of meal plans start at ¥2000 for dinner, and there's a good public bath which non-residents can use for ¥300. ⑤.

**Minatokan** (☎0829/44-0362). Small minshuku a minute's walk south of the ferry terminal, with slightly cramped *tatami* rooms and shared bathrooms. No meals are served. ⑤.

**Miyajima-guchi Youth Hostel**, 1-4-14 Miyajima-guchi, Ono-machi (☎ & fax 0829/56-1444). Down-at-heel hostel run by a friendly old man who speaks some English. Meals are available and it's conveniently close to Miyajima-guchi Station and the ferry to the island.

**Pension Miya-jima** (☎0829/44-0039, fax 44-2773). Set back in the village a couple of minutes from the ferry, this delightful Western-style pension is undergoing renovations that may add some Japanese features. The owner Kikugawa-san speaks a little English and is an excellent chef. ⑦.

## Itsukushima-jinja and around

Ancient records tell that a sea deity has been worshipped on Miya-jima since the sixth century, but it wasn't until 1168 that **Itsukushima-jinja** (daily 6.30am–6pm; ¥300) took on its present splendid form courtesy of the warlord Taira-no-Kiyomori. When the sea is lapping beneath its low-slung halls and red-colonnaded, lantern-fringed corridors, you can see why it's called the "floating shrine". More than likely, though, the tide will be out and the muddy seabed revealed. Still, the classical beauty of the architectural ensemble, modelled after the *shinden*-style villas of the Heian period, endures, although the shrine is at its most enchanting come dusk when the lights of the surrounding stone lanterns flicker on.

From the ferry landing the shrine is around a ten-minute walk south either along the seafront, where the island's many tame deer amble, or through the parallel shopping arcade crammed with gift shops and cafés. There is only one way to walk through the shrine, from its most northern entrance to its southern exit beside the Nishi-matsubara sand spit. Most of the attached halls are closed, but in the centre, 200 metres ahead of the projecting stage for Nō plays, you'll see the famed sixteen-metre-tall **Ō-torii**, dating from 1875. This is the seventeenth incarnation since the original gate was erected by Taira-no-Kiyomori, its position in the sea indicating that the entire island is a Shinto holy place.

The shrine is the obvious place to head, which is why it's often better to hang back from the crowds and explore some of the other surrounding attractions first. From the ferry landing, head up the hill to the south towards the red-painted five-storey pagoda that you'll see poking through the trees. Beside this is the "hall of a thousand *tatami*" **Senjōkaku** (daily 9am–5pm; ¥350), part of Hokoku-jinja, a shrine started by Toyotomi Hideyoshi, but left unfinished when the warlord died. Votive plaques decorate the inside of the large, airy hall, which was originally a library for Buddhist sutras.

Better still is the island's main temple **Daisho-in**, on the hillside around ten minutes' walk south of Itsukushima-jinja. This attractive temple complex with ornate wooden pavilions, arched bridges across lily-pad-dotted ponds and stone lanterns, belongs to the Shingon sect of Buddhism associated with the revered Kōbō Daishi, who blessed the island with a visit in the ninth century. Look out for the "universally illuminating cave" towards the back of the complex, hung with hundreds of lanterns and packed with mini-Buddhas laden down with lucky talismans.

## Misen-san and around

If you're feeling energetic, the 530m **Misen-san**, Miya-jima's sacred mountain, can be climbed in a couple of hours. Otherwise a two-stage **ropeway** (daily: April–Sept 8am–6pm; Jan–March & Oct–Dec 9am–5pm; ¥900 one way, ¥1500 return) provides a thrilling and somewhat scary 1.7km cable-car ride up to within easy walking distance of the summit. The ropeway base-station is beside **Momiji-dani** (Maple Valley), a leafy hillside park around a twenty-minute hike from the ferry terminal; a free mini-bus runs up to the station from opposite the *Iwaso Ryokan*.

---

### MIYA-JIMA FESTIVALS

As well as the regular festivals, such as New Year, there are special **festivals** held most months on Miya-jima at both the shrine Itsukushima-jinja and the main temple Daisho-in. From time to time, *bugaku* (traditional court dancing) is also performed on the shrine's Nō stage; check with the main tourist information offices in Hiroshima (see pp.549–50) for details.

February 11: **Kaki Matsuri**. Free oysters, an island speciality, are served to sightseers.

March 20: **Kiyamori Matsuri**. Held in memory of Taira no Kiyomori, this festival includes a colourful costume parade recreating the warlord's visit to his shrine.

April 15 & November 15: **Spring and Autumn festivals** at Daisho-in including fire-walking displays by the resident monks.

April 16–18: **Jin-Nō**. Sacred Nō plays, first performed for the *daimyō* Mōri Motonari in 1568, are re-enacted on the shrine's stage as part of the spring peach blossom festival.

June 16: **Kangensai**. Itsukushima-jinja's main annual festival includes an atmospheric night-boat parade, accompanied by traditional music.

August 14: **Hanabi Matsuri**. The largest fireworks display in western Japan explodes in front of Itsukushima-jinja.

December 31: **Chinkasai**. Huge pine torches, blazing in front of Itsukushima-jinja, are fought over by groups of young men.

Around the Shishiwa station on top of the mountain, you'll see a colony of wild monkeys as well as more deer. Cute as they may look, it's important to keep your distance from the monkeys, who can occasionally turn vicious. There's an excellent look-out spot across the Inland Sea near the station, but the actual summit is a good twenty minutes further on. The path initially drops down but then starts to climb past various small temples built in honour of Kōbō Daishi. Opposite the Misen Hondō, the main hall of worship on the mountain, is the **Keizu-no-Reikadō**, in which a sacred fire said to be originally lit by the Daishi has burned for over 1600 years. Legend has it that if you drink tea made from the boiling water in the suitably blackened iron pot which hangs over the fire, all your ills will be cured.

Five more minutes' climb will take you past giant mysterious boulders to the rest-house at the summit; if you haven't packed refreshments you can buy them here, but at accordingly high prices. The main route down passes more small temples and provides stunning views over Itsukushima-jinja, especially as you near Daisho-in.

If you have enough time, the beachside walks along a pine-tree-lined sand spit south of the shrine are pleasant, and there's a rather dated **aquarium** (daily 8.30am–5pm; ¥1050) nearby, which has sea-lion and sea-otter feeding shows. Opposite the aquarium is the marginally diverting **Miya-jima History and Folklore Museum** (daily 8.30am–4.30pm; ¥100), with a mish-mash of exhibits, including traditional boats, farm equipment and furniture, in an attractive nineteenth-century merchant's home.

Several kilometres north of the ferry landing is the **Tsutumigaura Recreation Park**, with a long stretch of sandy beach and shallow waters ideal for paddling in. The nearby **campsite** is a popular spot for families in the summer (see Accommodation).

### Eating and drinking

Because most people dine at their hotels, other than at lunch **eating** options on the island are limited. Besides oysters another local speciality is *anago*, a long eel-like fish, cooked and served sliced on top of rice (*anagoburi*). The most famous place to sample this dish is the refined *Fujitaya*, a small, busy restaurant a couple of minutes' walk uphill from the shrine, towards Daisho-in. A large serving of *anagoburi*, accompanied by soup and pickles costs ¥2300. Less expensive is the café attached to the *Watanabe* ryokan, beside the main gate to Daisho-in, which has an *anago* set lunch for ¥1600 as well as many other dishes.

The arcade of tourist shops leading to the shrine has several restaurants, all with plastic food displays. *Komitei*, closer to the ferry terminal, serves *okonomiyaki*, as well as having an English menu and a pretty ornamental garden at the back. You can have your *okonomiyaki* Hiroshima-style (layered and cooked for you) or Kansai-style (cook it yourself).

# Iwakuni

Heading south along the San-yō coast from Miya-jima, you'll soon cross the border into western Honshū's last prefecture Yamaguchi-ken. The first place to pause briefly is the pleasant old castle town of **IWAKUNI**, some 40km west of Hiroshima and home to an American military base. Two kilometres west of the present town centre, **Kintai-kyō** is one of the country's top three bridges, an elegant five-arched structure, spanning the rocky Nishiki-gawa like a tossed pebble skipping across the water. It was *daimyō* Kikkawa Hiroyoshi who ordered the construction of the bridge in 1673 to solve the problem of crossing the Nishiki-gawa every time it flooded. The most advanced civil engineering techniques of the time were used and even though the 210-metre-long bridge was built without a single nail, bound together with clamps and wires, the

| IWAKUNI | | |
|---|---|---|
| **Iwakuni** | *Iwakuni* | 岩国 |
| Iwakuni Kokusai Kankō Hotel | *Iwakuni Kokusai Kankō Hoteru* | 岩国国際観光ホテル |
| Iwakuni Youth Hostel | *Iwakuni Yūsu Hosuteru* | 岩国ユースホステル |
| Kikkō-kōen | *Kikkō-kōen* | 吉香公園 |
| Kintai-kyō | *Kintai-kyō* | 錦帯橋 |
| Shiratame Ryokan | *Shiratame Ryokan* | しらため旅館 |

original stood in place until Typhoon Kezia swept it away in 1950. What you see today – and can walk across for ¥210 – is the 1953 reconstruction, no less impressive for that. For once, the hordes of tourists add something to the bridge's attraction, as they parade across the steep arches like figures in a *ukiyo-e* print.

Out of regular office hours, you're supposed to drop the bridge toll in the box beside the ticket office, or you can avoid it all together by crossing the river on the nearby modern concrete span, the Kinjō-kyō, a good vantage point for a photo. It's also worth checking out the bridge at night, since it's glamorously floodlit until 10pm. The ticket office also sells a combination ticket (¥820) for the bridge, the return cable-car ride up Shiro-yama and entry to the castle, which, if you intend to do all three, will give you a small saving.

Adjoining the bridge on the west bank of the Nishiki-gawa is a landscaped park, **Kikko-kōen**, once the estate of the ruling Kikkawa clan. With it grass lawns and cooling fountains, the park preserves some of the layout and buildings of the former estate, despite also having some modern features. Immediately ahead from the bridge, on the left, is the **Nagaya-mon**, the wooden gate to the home of the Kagawa family, *samurai* to the Kikkawa *daimyō*. There are several other *samurai* houses you can wander around and, at the far west side of the park, the Kikkawa family **graveyard**, a compact series of white-walled enclosures, with moss-covered gravestones. In addition, there's a mildly interesting collection of old maps and plans from feudal times, as well as craftwork from Iwakuni's past, on display at the **Choko-kan** (daily 9am–5pm; ¥500), at the north end of the park.

Just outside the park, opposite the cable-car station, is a small **white snake research centre** (daily 9am–5pm; entry free, ¥100 donation for an English pamphlet) worth a visit for those interested in the area's zoological oddity. The albino-like snakes are unique to Iwakuni and are thought to have evolved here because of the slightly warmer temperatures in winter. A guide will show you the observation tanks where four of the snakes live; the oldest, He-chan, is twelve, while the youngster, Mari-chan, is a mere six-year-old.

Just next to the cable-car station, the **Iwakuni Historical Art Museum** (daily 9am–5pm; ¥500) displays the unexceptional art collection of local resident Nishimura Shigenori.

The **cable car** (¥520 return) saves a forty-minute hike up Shiro-yama, but if you fancy the work-out, the route begins beside the youth hostel in the south-west corner of Kikko-kōen. An impressive view of the meandering river, town and Inland Sea from the summit makes the effort worthwhile. Unless you're interested in displays of armour, swords and a miniature wooden model of the Kintai-kyō, the **castle** (daily 9am–8pm; ¥260) is not worth entering. Set back from the 1960 reconstruction is the original base of the fortress built by Kikkawa Hiroie in 1608, and torn down by the *daimyō*, just seven years later, in obeyance of the Tokugawa government's edict that each province should only have one castle (Hagi's took precedence). If you have time, follow the nature trail along the mountain ridge for just over 1km to the lonely **Gokanjin** shrine, keeping an eye out for the many giant spiders in their webs along the way.

If you are in Iwakuni overnight between June 1 and August 31, don't miss the **cormorant fishing** (*ukai*), which takes place on the Nishiki-gawa beside the bridge between 6.30pm and 9pm. This colourful and exciting method of fishing with birds (see box, p.397) can be viewed from boats for ¥3500, or for free from the pebbly riverbank.

### Practicalities

The Kintai-kyō is roughly midway between Ikawunki's Shinkansen and local train stations. **Shinkansen** stop at Shin-Iwakuni Station, twenty minutes by bus west of the bridge, while **trains** on the JR Sanyō line stop at Iwakuni Station, a twenty-minute bus journey east of the centre. **Buses** from both stations are operated by both the Shiden bus company and JR, and fares on both routes cost ¥240. Rail pass holders can use the JR buses free of charge, but the Shiden service is more frequent.

There's a **tourist information** booth (Tues–Sun 9am–5pm; ☎0827/21-6050) in Iwakuni Station which can provide maps and pamphlets and where the assistants might speak some English. Another information booth, by the bridge, has the same leaflets, but is only open daily during the peak holiday seasons, and at weekends during the rest of the year (8.30am–5pm).

All of Iwankuni's sights can be comfortably seen in a couple of hours. If you decide **to stay** the night, the cheapest option is *Iwakuni Youth Hostel* (☎0827/43-1092, fax 43-0123; ②) in the southwest corner of the park, ten minutes' walk from the bus stop by the bridge. It's an old, large building, with shared Japanese-style rooms with TVs. Its peaceful location and considerate managers make this a good place to stay. The best ryokan is the pretty *Shiratame Ryokan* (☎0827/41-0074, fax 41-1174; ⑧), which has rooms overlooking the bridge; even if you can't afford to stay, try to go for lunch. The *Iwakuni Kokusai Kankō Hotel* (☎0827/43-1111, fax 41-2483; ⑧), has branches on both sides of the river, with the east bank main hotel being decorated in kitsch 1970s style.

There are several **eating** options on the east side of the bridge: try the local fish dishes, such as *Iwakuni-zushi*, a block of vinegared rice topped with bits of cooked fish and vegetables, at *Yoshida*, which lies just beyond some interesting antique shops leading up to the Kintai-kyō. The best place to eat within Kikko-kōen is *Kinjō-en*, next to the Nagaya-mon (daily 11am—5pm), which has an ornamental garden to sit out in on warm days. Their set lunch for ¥1200 includes a choice of udon or soba noodles, *oden* (boiled vegetables and fish cakes) and *Iwakuni-zushi*. Otherwise, pack a picnic and enjoy it in the park.

# Yamaguchi and around

Yamaguchi-ken is perhaps Chūgoku's most appealing prefecture, but the coastal route further west from Iwakuni is undeniably blighted by heavy industry. Better to head inland to the hills where an old-world atmosphere hangs over the sleepy prefectural capital, **YAMAGUCHI**, cut through by the narrow scenic river, Ichinosaka-gawa. It's a modern city, but one can see why it's also known as the "Kyoto of western Japan." The local highlights are the beguiling temple garden of **Jōei-ji**, designed by the fifteenth-century artist and priest Sesshū, the handsome five-storey pagoda at **Rurikō-ji**, and the recently reconstructed **St Francis Xavier Memorial Cathedral** an ultra-contemporary church commemorating the first Christian missionary to Japan.

Many of the temples spread around Yamaguchi, not to mention its artistic sensibilities, date from the late fifteenth century, when war raged around Kyoto, and the city became an alternative capital for fleeing noblemen and their retinues. The tolerant ruling family of **Ouchi Hiroyo**, who settled in the area in 1360, allowed the missionary Francis Xavier to stay in Yamaguchi in 1549. By the Edo period the **Mōri** clan had gained power over the whole of western Japan and several of the Mōri lords are buried

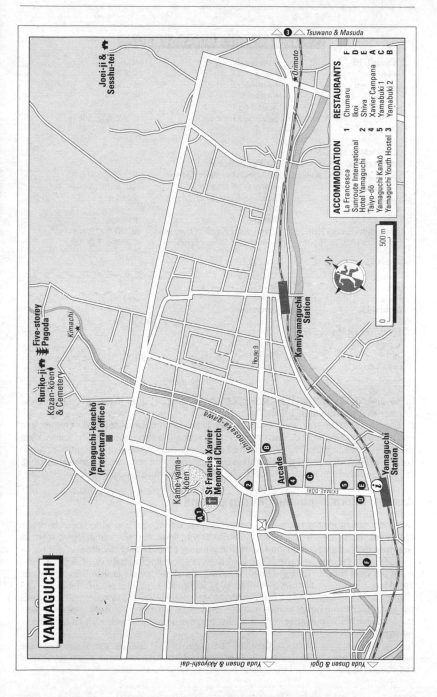

YAMAGUCHI

Joei-ji & Sesshu-tei

Five-storey Pagoda
Ruriko-ji
Kōzan-kōen & Cemetery
Kimachi

Yamaguchi-kenchō (Prefectural office)

Kame-yama-kōen

St Francis Xavier Memorial Church

Ichinosaka-gawa

Route 9

Arcade

EKIMAE-DORI

Yamaguchi Station

Kamiyamaguchi Station

Orimoto

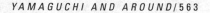
Tsuwano & Masuda

| ACCOMMODATION | | RESTAURANTS | |
|---|---|---|---|
| La Francesca | F | Chumaru | 1 |
| Sunroute International Hotel Yamaguchi | D | Ikoi | 2 |
| Taiyo-dō | E | Shiva | 4 |
| Yamaguchi Kankō | A | Xavier Campana | 5 |
| Yamaguchi Youth Hostel | C | Yamabuki 1 | 3 |
| | B | Yamabuki 2 | |

0          500 m

N

Yuda Onsen & Akiyoshi-dai
Yuda Onsen & Ogōri

in Kōzan-kōen, including Mōri Takachika, who was a key figure in the overthrow of the Tokugawa government in 1867.

The closest of the surrounding attractions is the hot-spring resort **Yuda Onsen**, just one train-stop to the west of Yamaguchi, and practically a suburb of the city. Some 20km northwest are the intriguing caverns and rocky plateau of **Akiyoshi-dai** quasi-national park. The **SL Yamaguchi-gō**, a highly popular steam train service, also passes through the city on its way to the delightful castle town of **Tsuwano** (see p.579).

## Arrival, information and getting around

To reach Yamaguchi by **train**, take the branch JR Yamaguchi line which runs between **Ogōri** on the southern coast (also a Shinkansen stop) and the north coast town of **Masuda** in Shimane-ken. From Ogōri, the journey takes twenty minutes.

The line is famous because it's one of the very few left in Japan on which a **steam train** service, the SL Yamaguchi-gō, operates most weekends and holidays between late March and November. A gleaming 1937 locomotive, pulling restored antique carriages, takes two hours to run from Ogōri to the castle town of Tsuwano, where it waits for just under three hours before making the return journey. Seat bookings are essential for this highly popular service. For the current schedule check with JR and tourist information offices.

Regular **bus** services run to the city from Hagi (p.573) and Tsuwano, and there are also connecting buses for flights into **Yamaguchi Ube Airport**, some 40km south near the coastal city of Ube. All buses stop in front of Yamaguchi Station.

The **tourist information** centre (daily 9am–5pm; ☎0839/33-0090) is on the second floor of Yamaguchi Station. An English map and leaflets are available, but the assistants do not speak English. There's also an information counter at Ogōri Station beside the exit from the Shinkansen tracks, where you can get English-language leaflets on most attractions in Yamaguchi-ken.

Yamaguchi might be the smallest of Japan's prefectural capitals, but its main sights are too widely spread out to walk between them. There are plenty of local buses, but the easiest way to get around is to rent a **bicycle** at the station ticket office (¥320 for two hours; ¥840 for the day). The city's commercial heart is where Ekimae-dōri, the main street heading northwest towards the hills from the station, crosses the shopping arcade of Komeya-chō. The central **post office** is on the west side of the arcade, and there are **banks** and a JTB **travel agent** to the east. All the main sights are north of here.

## Accommodation

An overnight stay in Yamaguchi will allow you to enjoy the city's relaxed atmosphere or take a hot spring bath in nearby Yuda Onsen. The cheapest option, *Yamaguchi Youth Hostel*, is several kilometres east of the city, although easily reached by JR buses from Yamaguchi Station or city buses from Miyako Station, two stops along the line from Yamaguchi.

**La Francesca**, 7-1 Kame-yama (☎0839/34-1888, fax 34-1777). This romantic Tuscan-style villa hotel, nestling at the base of the hilltop Xavier Cathedral, has Western-style suites with twin beds, as well as a lovely garden and a top-class Italian restaurant. [8].

**Kokuminshukusha Koteru**, 4-3-15 Yuda Onsen (☎0839/22-3240, fax 28-6177). Good-value Japanese-style accommodation in Yuda Onsen, around ten minutes' walk northwest of the station. Singles are ¥5000, with two meals costing ¥2000 extra per person. [5].

**Matsudaya Hotel**, 3-6-7 Yuda Onsen (☎0839/22-0125, fax 25-6111). A historic three-hundred-year-old ryokan, cocooned by high walls, on the main road running through the onsen resort. Has a modern high-rise extension, but the elegant *tatami* rooms and a lovely traditional garden make it worth the expense. There's also a small display area of hanging scrolls, lacquerware and pottery. [9].

**Sunroute International Hotel Yamaguchi**, 1-1 Nakagawara-chō (☎0839/23-3610, fax 23-2379). Standard business hotel, part of a nationwide chain, in a convenient location, fifteen minutes' walk from the station. The cheapest singles are ¥6000. [5].

**Taiyo-dō**, Komeya-chō (☎0839/22-0897, fax 22-1152). The entrance to this surprisingly large ryokan, with a small central garden, is on the east side of Komeya-chō arcade. All the rooms are *tatami*, and have shared bathrooms. It's good value when you consider that rates, starting at ¥6000 for a single, include two meals. [5].

**Yamaguchi Kankō Hotel** (☎0839/22-0356, fax 25-5668). This convenient budget hotel option is five minutes' walk from the station on Ekimae-dōri. By the entrance are plastic herons and a bamboo garden. Inside, the atmosphere is no less cheesy, but the *tatami* rooms are clean and there are singles for ¥4750. [4].

**Yamaguchi Youth Hostel**, 801 Miyano-kami (☎0839/28-0057). Well away from the city, this hostel is in a peacefully rural location near fields which bloom with pastel-coloured Cosmos flowers each autumn. The ivy-clad building has *tatami* dorms, good food, English-speaking owners, a quirky art collection and some scratchy LPs to play in the common room. If you take the JR bus, the nearest stop is on the hill above the hostel; follow the signs down into the valley. The city bus stop is closer, at around five minutes' walk through a village.

## The City

The first place to pause on your bike tour from the station is the modern **St Francis Xavier Memorial Church**, whose twin towers are easily spotted atop Kame-yama-kōen on the northwest side of the city. It was named after the pioneering Spanish missionary Xavier, who, having already had success in Goa and Malacca, landed in Japan on August

15, 1549, and in the following year was granted leave to preach in Yamaguchi. When he left, the city had a community of more than five hundred Christians, many of whom later died for their beliefs under the less tolerant Tokugawa government.

In 1991, the original church, built in 1951 to commemorate the four hundreth anniversary of Xavier's visit, burned down. It has recently been completely replaced by a striking contemporary structure incorporating a pyramid-like main building, and twin square towers topped by metalic sculptures, one hung with nine bells.

A more traditionally Japanese place of worship is the charming temple and park of **Rurikō-ji** and **Kōzan-kōen**, in the foothills around 1km north of Kame-yama-kōen. The temple dates from the high point of the Ouchi clan's reign and epitomizes the Kyoto style of the Muromachi era (1333–1573). Its highlight is a beautifully preserved **five-storey pagoda** made from Japanese cypress and picturesquely sited beside an ornamental pond. Beside the temple is a small exhibition hall (daily 8.30am–5pm; ¥300), containing a diverting collection of model pagodas, photographs of the other 53 pagodas scattered around Japan, and strange masks.

Next to Rurikō-ji, the park **Kōzan-kōen**, with its peaceful and atmospheric graveyard, is the last resting place of the *daimyō* Mōri Takachika and his offspring. Takachika was one of the prime movers in planning the overthrow of the Tokugawa government at the end of the Edo era and there are a couple of old wooden houses preserved in the park where he secretly met with fellow plotters. The closest bus stop to Rurikō-ji is Kimachi.

Some 2km east of the park, along the major road Route 9, is the enchanting **Sesshū-tei** garden at the temple **Jōei-ji** (daily 8am–5pm; ¥300). The priest and master painter Sesshū, born in Okayama-ken in 1420, settled in Yamaguchi at the end of the fifteenth century. After travelling to China to study the arts, he was asked by the *daimyō* Ouchi Masahiro to create a traditional garden for the grounds of his mother's summer house. Sesshū's Zen-inspired rock and moss design remains intact behind the temple and if you're fortunate enough to avoid the arrival of a tour group, you'll be able to sit in quiet contemplation of the garden's simple beauty, looking for the volcano-shaped rock that symbolizes Mount Fuji. The surrounding forest, and the lily-pad pond add brilliant splashes of colour particularly in autumn, when the maple trees flame red and gold. Orimoto, the closest bus stop to Jōei-ji, is around ten minutes' walk south of the temple.

On the way back to the city centre, follow the meandering path of the **Ichinosaka-gawa**, a pretty stream crossed by pedestrian bridges. The cherry trees along the river banks turn candy-floss pink each spring while in early summer fireflies (*genji botaru*) buzz around the azaleas and reeds.

One train station before Yamaguchi or a short bus ride south of the city centre is **Yuda Onsen**, easily spotted by the cluster of large and not particularly attractive hotels. A cute legend about a white fox curing an injured leg in the natural springwater explains both how the onsen developed and the town's mascot, immortalized by an eight-metre-high cartoon-like fox statue beside the station. **Onsen no Mori** (daily 10am–midnight; ¥1000), a modern spa complex about ten minutes' walk north from Yuda Onsen Station, has several different jaccuzzi baths, a sauna and a *rotemburo* (an outdoor pool) and you're given towels to use when you enter.

## Eating

There's a limited range of **restaurants** in Yamaguchi, with most of the options being clustered along Eki-mae-dōri and the Komeya-chō arcade. The local dish is the fresh-water fish *ayu*, and many shops also sell *uiro*, a glutinous sweet made from pounded rice, a supposed favourite of the ruling Ouchi clan six hundred years ago.

**Chumaru**. Head two blocks south of Yamaguchi Station and hang north to find this cosy café specializing in cheap pasta and curry dishes. The wooden interior and local art adds some character to the place. Open daily 11am–8.30pm.

**Ikoi**, Eki-mae-dōri. *Shokudō* serving a decent range of Japanese staple dishes, including fish. The plastic food display outside will help you choose from the menu. Daily 10am–10pm.

**La Francesca**, 7-1 Kame-yama. Top-class Italian restaurant attached to the hotel which does excellent-value pasta lunches for either ¥1200 or ¥2200. Daily 11am–10pm, sometimes closes at lunchtime on Sat & Sun.

**Shiva**, Eki-mae-dōri. Small Indian restaurant opposite Yamaguchi Station, serving a good set lunch for ¥800. Also open in the evenings, 5–9pm.

**Xavier Campana**, 5-2 Kame-yama. Mouthwatering bakery and restaurant, serving a wide range of breads, cakes, salads and a mixture of European cuisines including German-style dishes, fondu and pasta. The bakery is open daily 9am–8pm; the restaurant for breakfast from 8am–10.30pm and for lunch and dinner from 11.30am–9pm.

**Yamabuki**. There are a couple of outlets of this inexpensive and authentic noodle operation, one east off Eki-mae-dōri, the block before the arcade, the other north of the arcade near the crossing with Route 204. The shops are identified by their traditional wooden exteriors, and bowls of tempura, udon or soba cost as little as ¥470. Daily 11.30am–5.30pm.

# Akiyoshi-dai

Midway between Yamaguchi and the northern coast city of Hagi (see p.573), in the heart of the prefecture, are the vast caverns and rock-strewn tablelands of **AKIYOSHI-DAI**. This bleak Scottish-highland-like landscape has been designated a quasi-national park, but is not so impressive to go out of your way for.

The park's main attraction is **Akiyoshi-dō** (daily 8.30am–4.30pm; ¥1240), the largest limestone cave in Japan, stretching around 10km underground, although only about a tenth is open to the public. The main entrance is a five-minute walk from Akiyoshi-dō bus station along a pedestrianized street of gift shops, a sure sign that the cave gets its full complement of tour groups. Look out for the cheeky *He-no-Kappa* statues, a bug-eyed water sprite clutching his penis.

A raised walkway through a copse of lofty, moss-covered pine trees provides an atmospheric introduction to the gaping cavern mouth. However, inside, the booming loudspeakers of competing tour group leaders, combined with unimaginative lighting, detracts from the huge cave's potential impact. It took more than 300,000 years of steady erosion and dripping to create some of the rock walls and formations, which have since been given names like the "Big Mushroom" and the "Straw-wrapped Persimmon", in an effort to spark interest.

From the bowels of the earth an elevator whisks you up to the alternative cave entrance **Yano-ana**, a short walk from the Akiyoshi-dai, Japan's largest karst plateau. A look-out point commands an impressive view of rolling hills spread out in all directions and there are a range of hikes you can follow across the 130 square kilometres of the plateau. If you return to the cave in the elevator, you'll be charged ¥100, but you can just as easily either walk down the hill or catch a bus back to the station.

## Practicalities

**Buses** run to Akiyoshi-dō from Hagi, Ogōri, Shimonoseki and Yamaguchi. The fastest connection is from Ogōri Station, a Shinkansen stop, which takes 45 minutes. If you have a JR Rail Pass, it's best to take the JR bus service from Yamaguchi.

**Tourist information** is available from the counter inside the bus centre (daily 8.30am–5pm; ☎08376/2-1620), where you can pick up an English-language pamphlet on the area.

The only reason **to stay** overnight is if you arrive late in the day and want to see the cave early the next morning before the tour buses arrive. The *Akiyoshi-dai Youth Hostel* (☎08376/2-0341, fax 2-1546; ①) on the hill leading up to the plateau, is a twenty-minute steep hike from the bus centre. If you have heavy luggage, you can take a taxi there for ¥570. It's an institutional place, geared to large groups, but the food is fine. In a more scenic location overlooking the plateau is the down-at-heel *Kokuminshukusha Wakatakesan-sō* (☎08376/2-0126, fax 2-0127; ⑨). Rates include two meals (or you can have a room only for ¥4200 per person).

**Eating** options are thin on the ground, and practically non-existent at night. The pedestrian arcade, however, has one pleasant surprise, a snazzy Italian café, *La Gurota* (Mon–Fri 10am–6pm, Sat & Sun 10am–9pm), serving freshly baked pizza, focaccia and other light nibbles, as well as good expresso and cappuccino. For a ¥1000 lunch you could almost believe yourself in Rome.

# Shimonoseki and around

Most travellers pass through the port of **SHIMONOSEKI** at the southern tip of Honshū, 65km west of Yamaguchi, as quickly as possible en route to Kyūshū, or to Pusan in South Korea on the daily ferry. However, this unpretentious city is not without its attractions. The narrow **Kanmon Channel**, which separates Honshū from Kyūshū, is best viewed from Hino-yama, the mountain park that rises above the port. The channel was the scene of the battle of Dannoura, the decisive clash between the Taira and Minamoto clans in 1185, and the colourful shrine **Akama-jingū** is dedicated to the defeated Taira. If you have enough time, you should consider a short trip to the neighbouring town of **Chōfu**, with its authentic enclave of *samurai* houses and streets, sleepy temples and lovely garden.

## Arrival, information and city transport

If you're travelling by **Shinkansen**, you'll need to change **trains** at Shin-Shimonoseki Station, and go two stops on the Sanyō line to Shimonoseki Station. Long-distance **buses** arrive at the bus station in front of Shimonoseki Station. The fastest way of connecting with Kyūshū is by train or road across Kanmon suspension bridge; traditionalists can still make the short **ferry** hop (¥150) from Karato Pier, around 1.5km east of Shimonoseki Station, to Moji on Kyūshū's northwest tip. If you arrive by ferry from South Korea, you'll come in at the Shimonoseki Port International Terminal, five minutes' walk from Shimonoseki Station.

Maps and local sightseeing literature in English are available from the **tourist information** booth in Shin-Shimonoseki Station (daily 9am–5pm; ☎0832/56-3422) by the Shinkansen exit, where the main tourist office, where the assistants speak English and can help arrange accommodation, is on the concourse of Shimonoseki Station (daily 9am–7pm; ☎0832/32-8383).

Shimonoseki's main sights are several kilometres east along the waterfront from the station so it's best to use the local **buses** to get around. The buses departing from platforms 1 and 2 outside Shimonoseki Station are the most convenient, passing Akama-jingū and Hino-yama on their way to Chōfu.

## Accommodation

It doesn't take long to see the port's sights, but if you do want to stay overnight there's the usual cluster of business **hotels** around Shimonoseki Station and the international ferry terminal. More spectacular views can be had from the youth hostel and the *kokuminshukusha* on the slopes of Hino-yama, around 2km east of the station, near the Kanmon Bridge.

**Kokuminshukusha Kaikan-sō**, 3-58 Mimosusogawa-chō (☎0832/23-0108). This low-rise concrete block, with a fantastic prospect across the Kanmon Channel, has spacious, excellent-value *tatami* rooms; the rates include two meals. A single with meals is ¥3500. ⑨.

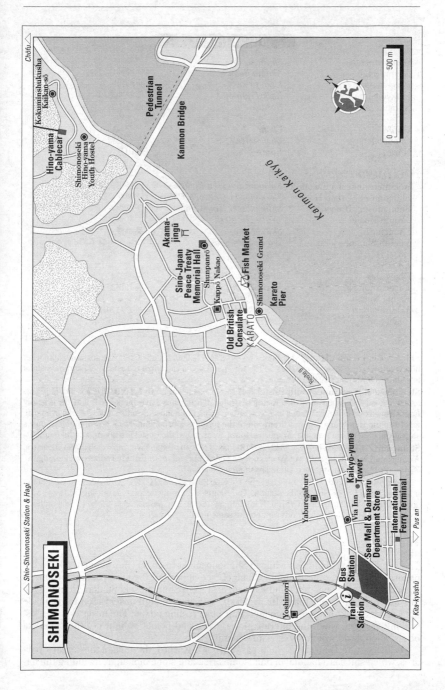

SHIMONOSEKI

△ Shin-Shimonoseki Station & Hagi

△ Chōfu

Kokuminshukusha
Kaikan-sō

Hino-yama Cablecar

Shimonoseki
Hino-yama
Youth Hostel

Pedestrian
Tunnel

Kanmon Bridge

Akama-
jingū

Sino-Japan
Peace Treaty
Memorial Hall

Shunpanrō

Kappō Nakao

Old British
Consulate

Shimonoseki Grand

Fish Market

Karato
Pier

KARATO

Kanmon Kaikyō

Route 9

Kaikyō-yume
Tower

Yaburegabure

Via Inn

Sea Mall & Daimaru
Department Store

International
Ferry Terminal

Bus
Station

Yoshimori

*i*

Train
Station

△ Kita-kyūshū

▽ Pus an

N

0          500 m

| SHIMONOSEKI | | |
|---|---|---|
| **Shimonoseki** | *Shimonoseki* | 下関 |
| Akama-jingū | *Akama-jingū* | 赤間神宮 |
| Hino-yama | *Hino-yama* | 火の山 |
| Kaikyō-yume | *Kaikyō-yume* | 海峡ゆめ |
| Karato | *Karato* | 唐戸 |
| | | |
| **Chōfu** | *Chōfu* | 長府 |
| Chōfu-teien | *Chōfu-teien* | 長府庭園 |
| Kōzan-ji | *Kōzan-ji* | 功山寺 |
| | | |
| *ACCOMMODATION* | | |
| Kokuminshukusha Kaikan-sō | *Kokuminshukusha Kaikan-sō* | 国民宿舎海関荘 |
| Shimonoseki Grand Hotel | *Shimonoseki Gurando Hoteru* | 下関グランドホテル |
| Shimonoseki Hino-yama Youth Hostel | *Shimonoseki Hino-yama Yūsu Hosuteru* | 下関火の山ユースホステル |
| Shunpanrō | *Shunpanrō* | 春帆楼 |
| Via Inn Shimonoseki | *Via In Shimonoseki* | ヴィアイン下関 |
| | | |
| *EATING* | | |
| Chayashō | *Chayashō* | ちゃやしょう |
| Furue Shōji | *Furue Shōji* | 古江小路 |
| Kappō Nakao | *Kappō Nakao* | 割烹なかお |
| Yaburekabure | *Yaburekabure* | やぶれかぶれ |
| Yoshimori | *Yoshimori* | よしもり |

**Shimonoseki Grand Hotel**, 31-2 Nabe-chō (☎0832/31-5000, fax 35-0039). Comfortable, upmarket hotel with Western-style rooms, beside Karato Pier. Also has a couple of restaurants and bars and a few singles for under ¥10,000. ⑥.

**Shimonoseki Hino-yama Youth Hostel**, 3-47 Mimosusogawa-chō (☎ & fax 0832/22-3753). Fine hostel with good views across to the Kanmon Bridge. The dorms have bunk-beds, and the friendly English-speaking manager is not a bad cook either. From Shimonoseki Station, take the bus from platform 1 to the Hino-yama ropeway, from where the hostel is a two-minute walk downhill. More buses stop at the base of Hino-yama at Mimosuso-gawa, from where the hostel is a ten-minute hike uphill.

**Shunpanrō**, 4-2 Amida-dera (☎0832/23-7181, fax 32-7980). Expensive, top-notch hotel, near the Akama-jingū, with large suites of Western-style bedrooms and *tatami* sitting-rooms overlooking the Kanmon Channel. The meals include lavish *fugu* dishes. ⑨.

**Via Inn Shimonoseki**, 4-2-33 Takezaki-chō (☎0832/22-6111, fax 24-3261). One of the newest of the many business hotels close to the station. The rooms are plainly decorated, but the beds are wide and comfortable. Singles from ¥5700. If it's full, try the nearby *Shimonoseki Station Hotel* or *Hotel 38 Shimonoseki*, both of which offer much the same deal.

## The City

The one thing you should do while in Shimonoseki is head up Hino-yama to take in the panoramic view over the Kanmon Channel (see opposite). If you're pushed for time, a similar view can be had ten minutes' walk east from Shimonoseki Station, from the top of **Kaikyō-yume** (daily 10am–10pm; ¥600), a 153-metre-high observation tower made of glass, that looks like a giant golf tee with a ball resting on top. The tower is at its most striking at night, when the interior glows green and points of light dot the spherical observation deck, which also has a restaurant.

On the way to Hino-yama you'll pass through **Karato**, the turn-of-the-century port area, which still has a handful of handsome brick and stone buildings, including the former British Consulate. On the waterfront is the **Karato Fish Market**, a lively place to drop by if you're up early in the morning.

Ten minutes' stroll further east is **Akama-jingū**, the shrine dedicated to Antoku, an eight-year-old emperor who drowned along with the Taira clan when they were routed in the naval battle of Dannoura. The clash took place in the straits overlooked by the striking vermilion, gold and pale green shrine, originally built as a Buddhist temple to appease the souls of the dead Taira warriors, and known at the time as Amida-ji. When Shinto and Buddhism were separated in the Meiji period, the temple became a shrine and was renamed Akama-jingū.

The Chinese-style arched gate, Suite-mon, dates from 1958 when the shrine was rebuilt after being damaged in the war, and the courtyard beyond is the scene of the colourful Sentei Matsuri festival. Held on April 23–25, this festival is based around the legend that the surviving Taira women, who after their clan's defeat were forced to turn to prostitution, came to the shrine each year to purify themselves. In a small graveyard to the right of the courtyard are fourteen ancient graves for notable Taira warriors and a small statue of the blind and deaf priest, Houichi Miminashi, the "earless Houichi" in one of the Irish writer Lafcadio Hearn's most famous ghost stories (see p.587).

If you've got time, nip up the hillside road before the shrine to check out the **Sino-Japan Peace Treaty Memorial Hall** (free), in an ornate, gabled building next to the *Shunpanrō* hotel. Built in 1936, the hall includes a re-creation of the room in the hotel where a peace treaty was signed between China and Japan on April 17, 1895, after nearly a month of negotiations. Around 1km further east, just beside the Kanmon Bridge, is a kilometre-long pedestrian tunnel through which you can walk under the straits to Moji, on Kyūshū.

Uphill from the bridge is **Hino-yama**, with a number of trails leading up to the 268m summit. If you don't fancy walking, there's a **ropeway** (daily: April 9am–6pm; May–Oct 9am–6.40pm; Nov–March 9am–5pm; ¥200 one way), that will take you close to the top. The view from the roof of the cable-car station takes in the whole of the Kanmon Straits and the islands to the west of Shimonoseki, and is particularly memorable towards sunset. Over a thousand ships a day sail through this narrow waterway, making it one of Asia's busiest maritime crossroads.

### Chōfu

Heading east along Route 9 from Hino-yama for around 3km, ignore the lacklustre aquarium and amusement park in favour of the elegant garden **Chōfu-teien** (April–May & Sept–Oct 9am–8pm; rest of the year 9am–5pm; ¥200), which makes a civilized introduction to **CHŌFU**, an old castle town of the Mōri family. The garden dates

---

#### THE KAMPU FERRY TO SOUTH KOREA

Every day at 6pm the Kampu Ferry service to Pusan, South Korea, leaves from the **Shimonoseki Port International Terminal**, five minutes' walk from Shimonoseki Station. The ticket booking office is on the second floor of the terminal building (daily 8.30am–4.30pm; ☎0832/24-3000), and the cheapest one-way ticket is ¥8500 (¥6800 if you're a student), for the *tatami* resting areas. If you want a bed, the cheapest fare is ¥12,000. Although there's a ten percent discount on a return ticket, it's still cheaper to buy another one-way ticket in Pusan.

The ferry is one of the cheapest routes out of and back to Japan, and is often used by people working illegally who need to renew their tourist visas. For this reason, the immigration officials at Shimonoseki have a reputation for being tough on new arrivals, so be prepared for a less than warm reception. It's also important to note that if you need a visa for South Korea, you must arrange it before arriving in Shimonoseki; the nearest consulate is in Hiroshima.

---

## FUGU

Shimonoseki revels in its role as Japan's centre for **fugu**, the potentially deadly blowfish or globefish, which provides inspiration for many local sculptures and souvenirs of spiky, balloon-shaped fish. About half the entire national catch (3000 tonnes a year) passes through Haedomari, the main market for *fugu*, at the tip of the island Hiko-shima, some 3km west of Shimonoseki Station.

Chomping on the translucent slivers of the fish which are practically tasteless, you may wonder what all the fuss is about. Only the *fugu*'s ovaries, liver and a few other internal organs contain dangerous amounts of tetrodotoxin, a poison more lethal than cyanide, and *fugu* chefs spend up to seven years in training before they can obtain a government licence to prepare the fish. Even so a small number of people do die, the most famous fatality being Kabuki actor Bandō Mitsugorō – a living national treasure – who dropped dead after a globefish banquet in Kyoto in January 1975.

---

from the Taishō era and has several teahouses dotted around an ornamental pond and babbling river.

After the garden, branch off from the main road at the next turning and head inland towards a compact enclave of old **samurai houses**, shielded by wooden gates and crumbling earthen walls, topped with glazed tiles, with the roads bordered by narrow water channels. Further up the hill in a leafy glade approached by a broad flight of stone steps is **Kōzan-ji**, the Mōri family temple dating from the fourteenth century. Next to the temple, you'll see the small **Chōfu Museum** (Tues–Sun 9am–5pm; ¥200) displaying some beautiful scrolls decorated with calligraphy and some intriguing old maps, as well as a statue of General Nogi Maresuke, a key military figure in both the Sino-Japanese War of 1894–95 and the Russo-Japanese War of 1904–05.

One of the joys of Chōfu is a relative lack of tourist development, making it easy to slip back several centuries while wandering round the *samurai* district. The one shop you should search out is Chayashō, a marvellous antique emporium selling kimono, pottery and other colourful knick-knacks, with a special display area in the *kura* (storehouse) at the back; it also serves coffee and tea in an atmospheric lounge (see below). Look for the large red paper umbrella by the entrance to the century-old house, downhill from Kōzan-ji.

Buses to Chōfu (25min; ¥350) run from platforms 1 and 2 at Shimonoseki Station, every 40 minutes or so. For the *samurai* district get off at **Jōka-machi** bus stop and head uphill.

## Eating

Shimonoseki is packed with **restaurants** specializing in *fugu* (see box above), but the daily ferry connection with Pusan means that Korean cuisine is almost as popular in the port. There are several restaurants around the Green Mall near the station that specialize in Korean barbecue dishes, called *yakiniku*, while for *fugu* head for the parade running parallel to Route 9. Another good area for fish restaurants is Karato.

The area around the station has plenty of **fast-food** options too, with branches of *KFC*, *Lotteria* and *Mister Donuts* in the Sea Mall. The seventh floor of Daimaru department store, connected to the mall, also has a variety of restaurants, all with inexpensive set menus and plastic food displays.

### Restaurants and cafés

**Chayashō**, Chōfu. Delightful café within an antique shop, where ladies in kimono serve tea and coffee with cakes for ¥500. The delicious chocolate cake comes on indigo china plates and is decorated with a gold maple leaf.

**Furue Shōji**, Chōfu (☎0832/45-5233). Elegant *kaiseki ryōri* restaurant in an old *samurai* house. The light but visually splendid lunch for ¥2500 is worth trying (11.30am–2.30pm). Dinner is at least twice the price.

**Kappō Nakao**, Karato. (☎0832/31-4129). Excellent fish restaurant where a team of motherly waitresses serve hearty set lunches for around ¥1200. The *fugu* course is ¥5000 at dinner. Mon–Sat 11am–2pm & 6–10pm.

**Yaburekabure** (☎0832/34-3711). Live *fugu* swim in the tank in the window of this restaurant, on the shopping parade east of the station. The speciality is a meal which includes seven different *fugu* dishes for ¥5000.

**Yoshimori** 2-1-13 Takezaki-chō. One of Shimonoseki's best *yakiniku* restaurants about ten minutes' walk north of the station along the Green Mall shopping street. You order plates of raw meat and vegetables to sizzle on a table-top cooker. Also try *pivinpa*, a traditional mix of rice and vegetables in a stone bowl. Around ¥2000 per person. Open daily except Thurs 11am–midnight.

# Hagi and around

Heading east from Shimonoseki along the **San-in** coast you'll immediately notice how much more rugged and sparsely populated the landscape becomes. Here the savage Sea of Japan has eroded the rocks into jagged shapes and, if you take the train, you'll see some marvellously bleak shorelines. The next town of any consequence is **HAGI**, some 70km northeast of Shimonoseki, which dates back to 1604 when warlord Mōri Terumoto built his castle at the tip of an island between the Hashimoto and Matsumoto rivers.

Hagi's castle is long ruined, but the atmospheric graveyards of the Mōri *daimyō* and the layouts of the *samurai* and merchants' quarters, **Horiuchi** and **Jōkamachi**, and the temple district of **Teramachi** still remains, with several significant buildings intact. These attractive plaster-walled streets are the town's main attraction, together with its renowned pottery, **Hagi-yaki**, considered Japan's next best style of ceramics after Kyoto's Raku-yaki. You can hardly move around Hagi without coming across a shop selling the pastel-glazed wares. The town is also famous for the role that some of its citizens played in the Meiji Restoration, such as Yoshida Shōin (see box, p.578), enshrined at **Shōin-jinja**, who was executed by the Tokugawa Shogunate, for his radical beliefs.

Sharing the relaxed, friendly atmosphere of other Yamaguchi-ken towns, Hagi is certainly worth visiting. If you rent a bike (see p.575), you can easily take in the most important sights in a day and still have time to lay back on **Kikugahama**, a fine stretch of beach beside the castle ruins.

## Arrival, information and getting around

There are three **train** stations around Hagi, of which **Hagi Station**, is the least useful. The main train station, close to the modern side of town, is **Higashi-Hagi**, where the infrequent limited-express (*tokkyū*) services, which pass through Shimonoseki from Kokura in Kyūshū, stop. If you're staying near the remains of Hagi-jō, then **Tamae Station**, two stops west of Higashi-Hagi, is more convenient.

Long-distance **buses** all stop in the centre of town at the bus centre, near the Tamachi shopping arcade. **Iwami Airport** (☎0856/24-0010) is an hour east along the coast, and is served only by flights from Tokyo and Ōsaka. A connecting bus (¥1560) runs to the town's bus station, a short walk east of Jōkamachi.

There are **tourist information** booths at Higashi Hagi and Hagi stations (daily 9am–5.30pm), both to the left as you leave the station buildings. Both provide English maps and pamphlets, including the useful, pocket-sized *Hagi Sightseeing Guide*. However, neither is staffed by English-speakers, so if you have more detailed enquiries contact the tourism section (desk 14) at Hagi City Office (Mon–Fri 8.30am–5.15pm; ☎0838/25-3131), where there's a helpful, English-speaking assistant.

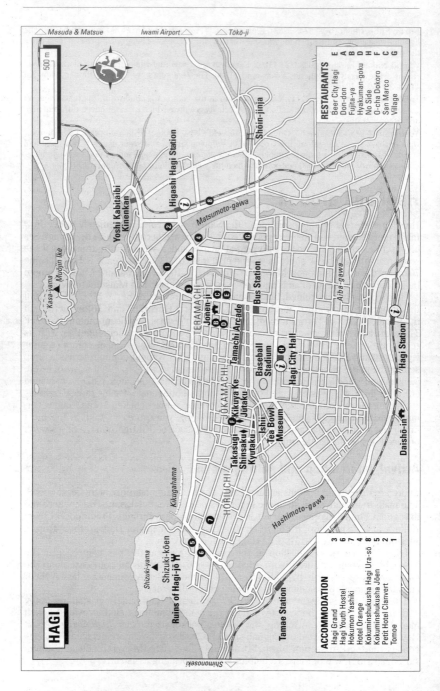

△ Masuda & Matsue    Iwami Airport △    △ Tōkō-ji

**HAGI**

500 m
0

N

Shoin-jinja

Yoshi Kabitaibi Kinenkan

Higashi Hagi Station

Matsumoto-gawa

❷

ℹ

❽

Muqjin Ike

Kasa-yama

❶

Ⓐ

❹

Ⓖ

TERAMACHI

❸

Ⓑ Ⓒ Ⓔ

Jonen-ji

Ⓑ

Ⓓ

Tamachi Arcade

Bus Station

Aiba-gawa

ℹ Hagi Station

ŌKAMACHI

Kikuya Ke Jutaku

Baseball Stadium

Hagi City Hall

ℹ ⑪

Kikugahama

HORIUCHI

Takasugi Shinsaku Kyutaku

Ishii Tea Bowl Museum

Hashimoto-gawa

Daishō-in

❼

Shizuki-yama

Shizuki-kōen
Ruins of Hagi-jō ⛩

❺

❻

Tamae Station

△ Shimonoseki

**RESTAURANTS**

| Beer City Hagi | E |
| Don-don | A |
| Fujita-ya | B |
| Hyakuman-goku | D |
| No Side | H |
| O-cha Dokoro | F |
| San Marco | C |
| Village | G |

**ACCOMMODATION**

| Hagi Grand | 3 |
| Hagi Youth Hostel | 6 |
| Hokumon Yashiki | 7 |
| Hotel Orange | 4 |
| Kokuminshukusha Hagi Ura-sō | 8 |
| Kokuminshukusha Jōen | 5 |
| Petit Hotel Clanvert | 2 |
| Tomoe | 1 |

Hagi's sights are spread over a wide area. From Higashi-Hagi Station, the *samurai* district of Jōkamachi and the remains of Hagi-jō in Shizuki-kōen are a good thirty minutes' walk west, while other major temples and shrines are similar distances to the east and south. The best way of getting around, therefore, is by **bicycle** and there are plenty of bike rental shops at Higashi-Hagi Station, with rates starting from ¥150 per hour. The cheapest day rentals are available from the outfit directly opposite the station entrance, beside the river, and the youth hostel; both charge ¥500 per day

## Accommodation

Hagi has a good range of **accommodation** spread evenly between Higashi-Hagi Station and Shizuki-kōen. The two main ryokan – *Hokumon Yashiki* and *Tomoe* – are top-notch places to indulge in traditional Japanese hospitality and cuisine at hefty prices. At the opposite end of the scale, there are a couple of *kokuminshukusha* and a fairly decent youth hostel.

**Hagi Grand Hotel**, 25 Furuhagi-chō (☎0838/25-1211, fax 25-4422). Large Western-style hotel with rather dated decor, but spacious, well-furnished rooms. Close to the modern heart of town. ⑥.

**Hagi Youth Hostel**, 109-22 Horiuchi (☎0838/22-0733). Beside Shizuki-kōen, this hostel has bunk-bed dorms around a central open courtyard. It's not a modern place, but the manager is very helpful and can advise on the area's attractions. Bike rental is also available. From Tamae Station, walk fifteen minutes' north across the Hashimoto-gawa. ①.

**Hokumon Yashiki**, 210 Horiuchi (☎0838/22-7521, fax 25-8144). Hagi's most luxurious ryokan, in a picturesque area close to the castle ruins, is set back from the main road in a private compound. It combines traditional Japanese rooms, gardens and cuisine with a Western-style lobby backed by an English garden. ⑨.

**Kokuminshukusha Hagi Ura-sō**, Higashi Hagi Kaisaku (☎0838/22-2511, fax 26-0143). Five minutes' walk south of Higashi-Hagi Station, facing the Matsumoto-gawa, is one of Hagi's two people's lodges. It's nothing fancy, but the manager is friendly, the Japanese-style rooms clean and the rates include two meals. Singles are ¥4725. ⑤.

**Kokuminshukusha Jōen**, Horiuchi (☎0838/22-3939, fax 26-0471). Beside Shizuki-kōen, this people's lodge is more glamorous than its partner on the other side of town. Still, the decor is old fashioned and there are squat toilets in the otherwise spacious and well-kept *tatami* rooms. Rates include two meals. Singles are ¥5775. ⑥.

**Hotel Orange**, 370-48 Hijiwara (☎0838/25-5880, fax 25-7690). This business hotel, three minutes' walk from Higashi-Hagi Station across the Matsumoto-gawa, doesn't look much from outside, but the rooms are all well turned out with conveniences such as air-conditioning, TV and compact en-suite bathrooms. ④.

**Petit Hotel Clanvert**, 370-9 Hijiwara (☎0838/25-8711). Good-value, modern hotel, three minutes' walk from Higashi-Hagi Station, with comfy Western-style rooms, all with twin beds, a kids' play area and a smart café. You'll pay ¥3600 extra for breakfast and dinner. ⑤.

**Tomoe**, Hijiwara (☎0838/22-0150, fax 22-0152). The warm orange walls of this modern ryokan offset the Zen minimalism of the rest of the decor. Rooms overlook the surrounding raked-gravel gardens, rather than the less-than-scenic stretch of the Matsumoto-gawa. ⑨.

## The Town

Much of Hagi's charm lies in its suitability for meandering strolls and bike rides. The tourist map suggests several cycling routes varying from two to six hours, but if you set off early, the main sights can be seen in a day. There are frequent direction signs in English around the town, and at each of the sights you'll usually find an English explanation, too.

If time is limited, head first to the scenic **Jōkamachi** district where the narrow streets are often over-run by tour groups. If you're starting from Higashi-Hagi Station, you'd be wise to check out the temples and shrines in the hills to the south or the coastal routes first, leaving Jōkamachi as the final stop, to be enjoyed once most of the day-trippers have gone home.

## Jōkamachi and around

From Higashi-Hagi Station, the most direct route to the Jōkamachi district is along the main road heading west across the river, which will take you through Hagi's central shopping area and the **Teramachi** district (so-called because it contains some twenty temples or "tera"). Bordering Teramachi is the surprisingly clean and picturesque **Kikugahama** beach, "officially" open for swimming only from mid-July to mid-August, after which you'll have to watch out for jellyfish.

At the end of the beach, across a narrow channel, rises Shizuki-san, a 143m hill surrounded by **Shizuki-kōen** (daily 8am–5.30pm; ¥210). The park is home to an atmospheric shrine, the rustic Hananoe teahouse (tea costs ¥500) and the moat and sloping stone walls of **Hagi-jō**, all that remains of the castle destroyed in 1874 when Mōri Takachika shifted court to Yamaguchi (see p.562). It takes twenty minutes to hike to the top of Shizuki-san, or you can relax beside the quiet cove with modern sculptures on the west side of the park.

Immediately south of the park are several large pottery factories with showrooms, and a long wood and plaster tenement building where soldiers of the Mōri clan once lived. Entry to the house is covered by the same ticket as for Shizuki-kōen. From here, return east through the **Horiuchi** quarter, where high-ranking *samurai* once lived. In

| HAGI AND AROUND | | |
|---|---|---|
| **Hagi** | *Hagi* | 萩 |
| Daishō-in | *Daishō-in* | 大照院 |
| Higashi-Hagi Station | *Higashi-Hagi-eki* | 萩市萩駅 |
| Horiuchi | *Horiuchi* | 堀内 |
| Ishii Tea Bowl Museum | *Ishii Chawan Bijutsukan* | 石井茶碗美術館 |
| Jōkamachi | *Jōkamachi* | 城下町 |
| Kasa-yama | *Kasa-yama* | 笠山 |
| Kikugahama | *Kikugahama* | 菊ヶ浜 |
| Kikuya-ke Jūtaku | *Kikuya-ke Jūtaku* | 菊屋家住宅 |
| Shizuki-kōen | *Shizuki-kōen* | 指月公園 |
| Shōin-jinja | *Shōin-jinja* | 松陰神社 |
| Takasugi Shinsaku Kyūtaku | *Takasugi Shinsaku Kyūtaku* | 高杉晋作旧宅 |
| Tamae Station | *Tamae-eki* | 玉江駅 |
| Tōkō-ji | *Tōkō-ji* | 東光寺 |
| Yoshikataibi Kinenkan | *Yoshikataibi Kinenkan* | 吉賀大眉記念館 |
| | | |
| *ACCOMMODATION* | | |
| Hagi Grand Hotel | *Hagi Gurando Hoteru* | 萩グランドホテル |
| Hagi Youth Hostel | *Hagi Yūsu Hosuteru* | 萩ユースホステル |
| Hokumon Yashiki | *Hokumon Yashiki* | 北門屋敷 |
| Kokuminshukusha | *Kokuminshukusha* | 国民宿舎萩浦荘 |
|   Hagi Ura-sō |   *Hagi Ura-sō* | |
| Kokuminshukusha Jōen | *Kokuminshukusha Jōen* | 国民宿舎城苑 |
| Hotel Orange | *Hoteru Orenji* | ホテルオレンジ |
| Petit Hotel Clanvert | *Puchi Hoteru Kuranbēru* | プチホテルクランベール |
| Tomoe | *Tomoe* | 常茂恵 |
| | | |
| *RESTAURANTS* | | |
| Don-don | *Don-don* | どんどん |
| Fujita-ya | *Fujita-ya* | ふじた屋 |
| Hyakuman-goku | *Hyakuman-goku* | 百萬石 |
| O-cha Dokoro | *O-cha Dokoro* | お茶処 |
| San Marco | *San Marco* | サンマルコ |

summer you'll notice *natsu mikan* (summer orange) trees heavily laden with fruit behind the high stone and mud walls; these were planted in 1876 as a way for the redundant *samurai* to earn some money.

The neighbouring quarter, **Jōkamachi**, contains the old homes of lower-ranking *samurai* and rich merchants, and is the most picturesque part of Hagi, with narrow lanes lined by whitewashed buildings decorated with distinctive black and white lattice plasterwork. Several of the houses are open to the public, the most interesting being the **Kikuya-ke Jūtaku** (daily 8.30am–5pm; ¥500), built in 1604 for a wealthy merchant family. The house has a particularly lovely garden which you can see from the main *tatami* guest room, as well as displays of many household items. Just south of the Kikuya residence is the **Takasugi Shinsaku Kyūtaku** (daily 9am–5pm; ¥100), home of Takasugi Shinsaku, a leading figure in the fight to restore the emperor to power. Like his mentor Yoshida Shōin (see box, overleaf), Takasugi died tragically young at 29 from tuberculosis, a year before the Meiji Restoration in 1868.

If you have time to kill or are particularly interested in the tea ceremony, drop by the tiny **Ishii Tea Bowl Museum** (daily except Tues 9am–11.30pm & 1–5pm; ¥500), at the southern end of Jōkamachi, which contains the bizarre collections of Ishii Kigensai, a merchant who died in 1982. In addition to a few prime examples of Hagi-yaki tea bowls, the museum's second floor contains a jumble of knick-knacks including toys, lamps and old cameras.

## South of Higashi-Hagi Station

Five minutes south-east of Higashi-Hagi Station, on the mountain side of the Mastumoto-gawa, is **Shōin-jinja**, Hagi's largest shrine, dedicated to the nineteenth-century scholar and revolutionary figure Yoshida Shōin (see box, overleaf). Within the shrine grounds is **Shōka Sonjuku** the small academy where Yoshida lived and taught in the final years of his life. There's also a small **museum** (daily: March–Nov 9am–5pm; Jan, Feb & Dec 9.30am–4.30pm; ¥100) containing some not particularly interesting displays on Yoshida.

Following the riverside cycle path uphill from the shrine leads to one of the family temples of the Mōri clan, **Tōkō-ji** (daily 8.30am–5pm; ¥100), worth visiting for its atmospheric graveyard packed with neat rows of more than 500 moss-covered stone lanterns. The temple, founded in 1691, has a Chinese flavour to its many handsome buildings and gates. Look out for the giant, wooden carp gong hanging in the courtyard as you walk behind the main hall towards the graveyard. Here you'll find the tombs of five Mōri lords, all odd-numbered generations, save the first lord buried with the even-numbered generations in nearby Daishō-in (see below), guarded by an army of lanterns. On August 15, during the Obon festival, the lanterns are lit to send off the souls of the dead.

Cycling up the hill behind the temple will bring you to **Tanjōchi**, the birthplace of Yoshida Shōin, marked by a bronze statue of the *samurai* revolutionary and one of his followers. Take in the view of the town before heading back downhill, past the small thatched home of **Itō Hirobumi**, another Yoshida disciple later to become prime minister and draft the Meiji constitution. Cross over to the west bank of the Matsumoto-gawa and follow the river south to the start of the **Aiba-gawa**, a narrow canal teeming with carp.

The final sight to check out on a tour of this side of Hagi is the temple **Daishō-in** (daily 8am–5pm; ¥200), around ten-minutes' bike ride from the Aiba-gawa, west of Hagi Station on the south bank of the Hashimoto-gawa. The temple was built after the death of Mōri Hidenari, the first lord of Hagi branch of the Mōri clan. A rickety gate leads to another lantern-filled graveyard, where you'll find the tombs of all the even-numbered Mōri lords, as well as Hidenari's and those of eight *samurai* who committed *seppuku* (ritual suicide) on his death. The serenity of the spot can be ruined, though, by the squealing of pigs from the farm next door.

## YOSHIDA SHŌIN

Born into a Hagi *samurai* family in 1830, the charismatic **Yoshida Shōin** believed that the only way self-isolated, military-ruled Japan could face up to the industrialized world – knocking at the country's door in the insistent form of Commodore Perry (see p.774) – was to ditch the Tokugawa government, re-instate the emperor and rapidly emulate the ways of the West. To this end, he tried to leave Japan in 1854 on one of Perry's ships, together with a fellow *samurai*, but was handed over to the authorities who imprisoned him in Edo (Tokyo) before banishing him back to Hagi.

Once at home, Yoshida didn't let up in his revolutionary campaign to "revere the emperor, expel the barbarians". From 1857 he was kept under house arrest in the Shōka Sonjuku (now within the shrine grounds of Shōin-jinja), where he taught many young disciples, including the future Meiji-era prime minister Itō Hirobumi. Eventually Yoshida became too big a thorn in the shogunate's side and he was executed in 1860, aged 29, for plotting to assassinate an official.

Five years later, *samurai* and peasants joined forces in Hagi to bring down the local Togukawa government. This, together with similar revolts in western Japan (see p.775), led to Yoshida's aim being achieved in 1867– the restoration of the emperor to power.

### North to Kasa-yama

Along the coastal route Highway 191, directly north of Higashi-Hagi Station, is **Yoshikataibi Kinenkan** (daily 9am–5pm; ¥500), one of Hagi's most respected pottery kilns, with an attached museum displaying an outstanding collection of Hagi-yaki. If you call in advance (☎0838/26-5180), you can make your own pottery for ¥2000, which will be fired and sent to you (for an extra fee) after a couple of months. Unlike some other kilns, this one will post pottery abroad.

A fifteen-minute bike ride further north along the indented coast will take you past several fishing villages, where drying squid hang on lines like wet underwear, out along a narrow peninsula to the **Myōjin-ike**, a salt-water pond teeming with fish, at the foot of a mini-volcano, **Kasa-yama**. Set back from the pond, beside a small shrine, is an interesting natural phenomenon: the **Kazeana**, a shaded glade cooled by cold air rushing from cracks in the lava. Naturally, there's a café in this amenable spot which is a good place to cool down after hiking the 112m up Kasa-yama. At the summit there are panoramic views along the coast and you can inspect the 30m crater, one of the smallest in the world.

## Eating and drinking

You'll find many of Hagi's **restaurants** around the central Tamachi shopping arcade and the main cross street, Route 262. There's not a huge choice, but you won't go wrong if you opt for a cheap noodle bar or fish restaurant. The local speciality is whitebait, and in spring you'll see fishermen on the Matsumoto-gawa sifting the water for the fish with giant nets hung from their narrow boats.

At night the town reveals its true colours as a fishing village, where everyone goes to bed early. This is not a town to party in, but if you're in search of a **drink**, one of the best bets is *No Side*, a spacious, relaxed bar next to the City Hall, where you stand the best chance of running into the few *gaijin* who live in the area. The jazz café-bar *Village* (see opposite) is also worth a try and you might be lucky enough to catch a live performance.

### Restaurants and cafés

**Beer City Hagi**, 19-4 Tōdachō. Surprisingly stylish and modern *izakaya* serving a good range of beers, cheap set lunches and the usual selection of nibbly dishes in the evening. Daily 11.20am–2pm & 5pm–11pm.

**Don-don**, 177 Hijiwara 3-ku. Bustling, inexpensive noodle joint near the Hagi-bashi across the Matsumoto-gawa. A bowl of udon noodles plus a salad costs ¥700. Daily 9am–8pm.

**Fujita-ya.** Very small but popular noodle shop on a street north of the Tamachi arcade and one block west of the temple Jonen-ji. Specializes in *sairo soba*, handmade buckwheat noodles served in five-tiered cypress wood boxes.

**Hyakuman-goku**, Shimogoken-machi. North of the Tamachi arcade, this fish restaurant inside an old storehouse does excellent-value set menus for around ¥1500. Sit at the counter bar and you can watch the sushi chefs at work.

**O-cha Dokoro**, Jōkamachi. A pleasant place to rest and sample various types of Japanese tea (¥500). Sit either on *tatami* or at a low table, admire the mini-garden, and try the pounded rice and bean paste cake, served by waitresses in kimono.

**San Marco**, on the second floor of the building next to *Beer City Hagi* (see opposite). This bright Italian restaurant has a photo-menu and does passable pizza as well as pasta, pilaff rice and gratin dishes. A meal is around ¥1300. Daily 11am–9pm.

**Village**, 291-1 Hijiwara. Laid-back café/bar on the second floor of a white building on the way to the Matsumoto-bashi. Serves cheap meals of spaghetti or pilaff as well as yummy yoghurt drinks. Top jazz artists drop by and play when they're in town. Daily except Tues 10am–11pm.

# Tsuwano

Some 80km east of Hagi, in the neighbouring prefecture of Shimane-ken, is the older and even more picturesque castle town of **TSUWANO**. Nestling in the shadow of the 908m-high extinct volcano, **Aono-yama**, around which mists swirl moodily each autumn, this is yet another small town that touts itself as a "little Kyoto" and, for once, there really is an air of courtly affluence along the tourist-jammed streets.

    **Tonomachi**, the well-preserved central area of *samurai* houses, with their distinctive cross-hatched black and white plaster walls, is famous for its narrow canals teeming with carp and and flowerbeds bursting with purple and white irises each June. Overlooking the town from the west are the ruins of the **castle** built in 1295 by the lord

| TSUWANO | | |
|---|---|---|
| **Tsuwano** | *Tsuwano* | 津和野 |
| Kakuozan Yōmei-ji | *Kakuozan Yōmei-ji* | 覚皇山永明寺 |
| Katsushika Hokusai Museum | *Katsushika Hokusai Bijutsukan* | 葛飾北斎美術館 |
| Maria Seidō | *Maria Seidō* | マリア聖堂 |
| Musée de Morijuku | *Morijuku Bijutsukan* | 杜塾美術館 |
| Taikodani Inari-jinja | *Taikodani Inari-jinja* | 太鼓谷稲荷神社 |
| Tonomachi | *Tonomachi* | 殿町 |
| | | |
| *ACCOMMODATION* | | |
| Hoshi Ryokan | *Hoshi Ryokan* | 星旅館 |
| Meigetsu | *Meigetsu* | 明月 |
| Mimuraya | *Mimuraya* | みむらや |
| Tsuwano Lodge | *Tsuwano Rojji* | 津和野ロッジ |
| Tsuwano Youth Hostel | *Tsuwano Yūsu Hosuteru* | 津和野ユースホステル |
| Wakasaginoyado | *Wakasaginoyado* | 若さぎの宿 |
| | | |
| *EATING* | | |
| Furusato | *Furusato* | ふる里 |
| Iwami-ji | *Iwami-ji* | 石見路 |
| Saranoki Shōintei | *Saranoki Shōintei* | 沙羅のき松韻亭 |
| Yu-uki | *Yu-uki* | 遊亀 |

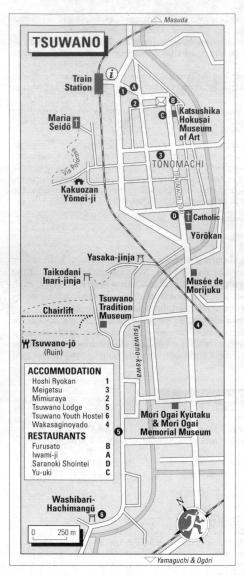

**TSUWANO**

△ Masuda

Train Station (i)

Maria Seidō

Via Ponovia

Katsushika Hokusai Museum of Art

TONOMACHI

TONOMACHI-DŌRI

Kakuozan Yōmei-ji

Catholic

Yōrōkan

Yasaka-jinja

Taikodani Inari-jinja

Musée de Morijuku

Tsuwano Tradition Museum

Chairlift

Tsuwano-kawa

Tsuwano-jō (Ruin)

**ACCOMMODATION**
Hoshi Ryokan          1
Meigetsu              3
Mimiuraya             2
Tsuwano Lodge         5
Tsuwano Youth Hostel  6
Wakasaginoyado        4
**RESTAURANTS**
Furusato              B
Iwami-ji              A
Saranoki Shointei     D
Yu-uki                C

Mori Ogai Kyūtaku & Mori Ogai Memorial Museum

Washibari-Hachimangū

0    250 m

▽ Yamaguchi & Ogōri

Yoshimi Yoriyuki as protection against potential Mongol invaders. The Yoshimi clan followed their allies the Mōri to Hagi after they both fought on the losing side in the Battle of Sekigahara in 1600. Sakazaki Maomori was installed in Tsuwano by the Tokugawa clan, but even though he later proved his loyalty by rescuing the Princess Senhime (see p.516) from the siege of Ōsaka castle, he was refused her hand in marriage. The castle was dismantled at the start of the Meiji era, then an earthquake in June 1997 made what was left of it unsafe to visit.

At the foot of the hill on which the castle stood is the bright red shrine complex of **Taikodani Inari-jinja**, approached through a zig-zag tunnel of a thousand vermilion *torii*. Closer to Tsuwano Station is the serene Zen Buddhist temple **Kakuozan-Yōmei-ji** and the tranquil **Maria Seidō**, a chapel in a mountain glade, dedicated to the martyrdom of Japanese Christians. Also worth a look are the small **Katsushika Hokusai Museum**, with its collection of works by the master print maker and artist Hokusai, and the **Musée de Morijuku**, displaying twentieth-century art in an old farm building with some unusual features.

## Arrival, information and getting around

By **train**, Tsuwano is reached on the cross-country JR Yamaguchi line. From Ogōri, where the Shinkansen stops, the fastest journey is just over an hour, while from **Masuda** (near Iwami Airport, see p.573), on the San-in coast, express trains take thirty minutes, only ten minutes faster than the local service. Tsuwano is also the terminus for the **SL Yamaguchi-gō** steam train service (see p.564); the fare for this popular service from Ogōri to Tsuwano is ¥1650 and reservations are essential.

There are also daily direct **bus** services to Tsuwano from Hagi (1hr 20min), Hiroshima (2hr 30min), Iwakuni (2hr) and Yamaguchi (1hr). The buses all stop in front of Tsuwano Station, at the northern end of town, seven minutes' walk from Tonomachi, the heart of the old *samurai* district.

To the left of the station is the **tourist information** centre (daily 9am–5pm; ☎08567/2-1771), where the friendly assistants speak no English, but are used to helping foreign visitors. It's worth picking up the excellent English guidebook to the town (¥200), updated every April by the local tourism association.

Tsuwano's sights are somewhat spread out so, if you intend to explore beyond Tomomachi, rent a **bicycle** from one of the many operations around the station, all charging ¥500 for two hours, ¥800 for the day. Alternatively, infrequent buses run to the southern end of town from where you can walk back towards the station seeing most of the sights in a couple of hours.

## Accommodation

There's little more than a day's leisurely sightseeing and walks around Tsuwano, but an overnight stay is recommended if you want to sample a traditional ryokan or minshuku, of which the town has several. Rates mostly start at a reasonable ¥6000 per person including two meals, and the tourist office by the Tsuwano Station can help you find a place if the ones below are full.

**Hoshi Ryokan**, Eki-mae (☎08567/2-0136) This is the most convenient ryokan for the station, just a minute's walk away. All the rooms are *tatami* and the rates include two meals. ⑤.

**Meigetsu**, Uochō (☎08567/2-0685, fax 2-0637). Tsuwano's most charming ryokan, with paper umbrellas by the front door, polished wood fittings, spacious *tatami* rooms and a small traditional garden. The rates include two meals, which feature seasonal mountain vegetables and carp. ⑦.

**Mimuraya**, Shinchō (☎08567/2-1171, fax 2-3053). Small minshuku five minutes' walk south of Tsuwano Station, above a fishmonger's, so you know the fish served in the meals will be fresh. All *tatami* rooms, and the rates include two meals. ⑤.

**Tsuwano Lodge**, Washibara (☎08567/2-1683, fax 2-2880). A good fifteen minute walk south of Tonomachi, on the west bank of the Tsuwano-kawa, this friendly hotel has a small *rotemburo* (open-air bath). ⑤.

**Tsuwano Youth Hostel**, Washibara (☎08567/2-0373). Run-down hostel near the the fourteenth-century shrine Washibari-Hachiman-gū, several kilometres south of the station. Although it may seem cheap, it's not so much of a bargain once you factor in the breakfast and dinner you'll be missing at Tsuwano's minshuku and ryokan, not to mention the inconvenience of being so far away from most of the sights. Infrequent buses run from the station to within easy walking distance of the hostel. ①.

**Wakasaginoyado**, Mori (☎ & fax 08567/2-1146). Around ten minutes' walk south of Tonomachi, this homely minshuku has an English-speaking owner, good *tatami* rooms with TVs and air-conditioning and the rates include two meals. ⑤.

## The Town

If you're in town on Sunday, head for the early-morning market beside Tsuwano Station, otherwise you should aim straight for the old streets of **Tonomachi**, around seven minutes' walk southeast. At the north end of the main pedestrian thoroughfare, Tonomachi-dōri, pause at the small **Katsushika Hokusai Museum of Art** (daily 9.30am–5pm; ¥450) to view its refined collection of woodblock prints, illustrations and paintings by the famous nineteenth-century artist Hokusai Katsushika.

Tonomachi's streets are bordered by narrow canals, home to carp which outnumber the town's 9000 residents by more than ten to one, and which were originally bred as emergency food supplies in the event of famine. The town's prosperity born of peace and enlightened rule by local *daimyō* is evident from the handsome buildings. Look out for sake breweries and shops selling traditional sweets, including *genji-maki*, a soft sponge filled with sweet red-bean paste.

Easily spotted behind the white, tile-capped walls is the grey spire of the **Catholic Church**, built in 1931, which combines stained-glass windows and an organ with *tatami* flooring. Further along, near the banks of the Tsuwano-kawa, is the **Yōrōkan**, the former school for young *samurai*, now containing an uninspiring folk art museum (daily 8.30am–5pm; ¥200).

Make a short detour across the Tsuwano-kawa, around which the fireflies buzz each June, to the fancifully named **Musée de Morijuku** (9am–5pm; ¥300), a restored farmhouse fronted by raked-gravel gardens and smartly converted into a modern gallery for local contemporary artists. The museum also has a small collection of etchings by the Spanish artist Goya. Upstairs, get the attendant to show you the pinhole camera in the *shōji* screen, capturing an image of the garden outside.

Back across the river, just west of the train tracks is the shrine **Yasaka-jinja** where each July 20–27, the ancient Sagi-Mai (heron dance) is perfomed by men dressed as the white birds, complete with flapping wings and long-necked hats. Nearby, a path, covered by a tunnel of over thousand red *torii*, leads uphill towards the **Taikodani Inari-jinja**, one of the five largest Inari shrines in Japan. The bright red and gold shrine bustles with tourists who say prayers to the local Shinto deities outside the splendid main hall.

The views of Tsuwano from the shrine's hillside location are good, but not as good as those from the top of the hill where the castle **Tsuwano-jō** used to stand. If you fancy an energetic hike, follow the pathway leading up to the old castle grounds (around a thirty-minute walk), or you could take the **chair lift** (daily 9am–5pm; ¥450 return). However, due to a recent earthquake, the castle ruins themsleves are out of bounds.

Immediately below the bottom of the chair lift, the **Tsuwano Tradition Museum** (daily 8.30am–5pm; ¥310), is worth a look for its collection of photographs of the town throughout the seasons, videos of local festivals and culture, and the bizarre masks and costumes worn in the heron dance. Continuing downhill, you'll find yourself at the southern end of Tsuwano. If you cross over the river and head south along the main road, you'll pass several more inconsequential museums, before reaching the **Mōri Ogai Kyūtaku**, on the right, the preserved wood and mustard-plaster home of a famed Meiji era novelist. Personal effects of the writer, including his death mask, are displayed next door in the modern **Mōri Ogai Memorial Museum** (daily 9am–5pm; ¥500).

## Maria Seidō to Kakuozan Yōmei-ji

If you have an hour or so to spare, there's a very pleasant woodland hike in the hills immediately west of Tsuwano Station. Head south and cross the train tracks at the first opportunity, then double back and continue to the car park from where a footpath leads up to the cosy chapel **Maria Seidō**, nestling in a leafy glade. In 1865, the Tokugawa Shogunate transported some 150 Christians from Nagasaki to Tsuwano; 36 were eventually put to death for their beliefs before the new Meiji government bowed to international pressure, lifting the ban on the religion in 1874. This chapel was built in 1951 to commemorate the martyrs and the quaint wooden building is the scene of the **Otometoge festival** on May 3, when pilgrims from across Japan celebrate an outdoor Mass.

From the chapel a series of wooden signs count down the stations of the Cross along the **Via Dolorosa footpath**, winding up the hillside. The path emerges from the forest onto a wider dirt track leading downhill to the charming temple of **Kakuozan Yōmei-ji** (daily 8.30am–5pm; ¥300). Stone steps lead up to the elegant collection of wooden, thatched buildings, used by generations of Tsuwano lords since 1420. Inside, look out for the lovely screen paintings decorating some of the *tatami* rooms and take a moment to sit and admire the verdant traditional garden. From the temple it's around a fifteen-minute walk back to Tsuwano Station.

# Eating

Being a tourist town, Tsuwano is not short of **restaurants**, with several *shokudō* and noodle shops close to the station and around the scenic Tonomachi area of town. Finding an evening meal can be more tricky since most visitors who stop over eat in their ryokan or minshuku. *Uzume-meishi*, the traditional local dish of rice in a broth with shredded green mountain vegetables, pieces of tofu and mushrooms, is worth trying, as is the carp.

**Furusato**, Gion-chō. A short walk south of the station, opposite the post office, this small restaurant in a traditional plaster house, specializes in *uzume-meishi* (see above), served as part of a set meal with slices of white root-vegetable jelly coated in lemon sauce and pickles, for ¥1200. Daily 11am–3pm.

**Iwami-ji**, Eki-dōri. One of the better restaurants close to the station, this small place does good set meals including tempura and sashimi for around ¥1500. Also a good option for dinner. Daily except Thurs 11.30am–9pm.

**Saranoki Shointei**, Yamanechō. From the large *tatami* room you can gaze out on a lovely traditional garden while eating either the ¥2000 or ¥3000 set meal of *kaiseki ryōri* haute cuisine. Daily 11am–6pm.

**Yu-uki**, Honmachi. At the northern end of Tonomachi, this famous and busy restaurant has lots of traditonal touches, including a stream running through the dining room filled with carp, some of whom end up on the plate as sashimi or in the miso soup. The best deal is the ¥2000 *Tsuwano teishoku*, a set meal of local dishes. Daily except Thurs 10am–7pm.

# Matsue and around

Stradling the strip of land between the lagoons of Nakaumi-ko and Shinji-ko is **MATSUE**, the appealing prefectural capital of Shimane-ken, 180km east of Tsuwano, and one of the highlights of the San-in coast. Although the city's main sights – one of Japan's few original castles, **Matsue-jō**, an area of *samurai* residences, the museum and onetime home of nineteenth-century expat writer **Lafcadio Hearn** (see box, p.588) – are so closely grouped together that they can all easily be seen in half a day, there are good reasons for lingering in Matsue. The lakes, rivers and castle moat lend this modern city a soothing, faintly Venetian atmosphere. It's still possible to catch glimpses of the old Japan that so enchanted Hearn a century ago, such as fishermen casting their nets in **Shinji-ko**, or prodding the lake bed with poles, searching out shellfish.

A timelessness also pervades Matsue's elegant eighteenth-century **Meimei-an** teahouse and garden, its beauty exceeded only by the stunning landscapes on view at the **Adachi Museum of Art**, 20km east of the city. Also out of town, the shrines and first-century burial tumuli at **Fudoki-no-Oka** are testimony to the ancient history of the area, while **Izumo Taisha**, 35km west, is one of Japan's most important shrines, holiday home of the Shinto pantheon of deities, and the reason that Matsue was dubbed "chief city of the province of the gods," by Hearn.

## Arrival, information and getting around

JR **trains** arrive at **Matsue Station**, south of the Ōhashi-gawa, while **Matsue Onsen Station**, just north of where the river flows into Lake Shinji, is the terminus for Ichibata trains from the grand shrine Izumo Taisha (see p.590). The most convenient Shinkansen stop is Okayama, from where the fastest local train takes two hours twenty minutes to reach Matsue. There are also sleeper train services from Tokyo via **Yonago**, the main San-in coast railway junction, some 25km east of Matsue. Most long-distance **buses** arrive beside Matsue Station, the rest at Matsue Onsen Station. There are overnight services to Tokyo and Fukuoka and daily services to Ōsaka and

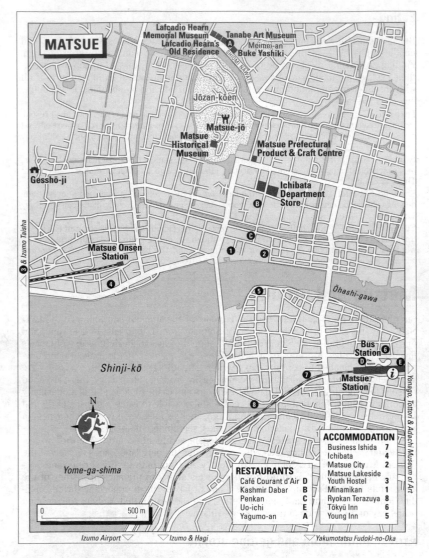

**MATSUE**

Lafcadio Hearn
Memorial Museum
Lafcadio Hearn's
Old Residence

Tanabe Art Museum
Meimei-an
Buke Yashiki

Jōzan-kōen

Matsue-jō

Matsue
Historical
Museum

Matsue Prefectural
Product & Craft Centre

Gesshō-ji

Ichibata
Department
Store

3 & Izumo Taisha

Matsue Onsen
Station

Ōhashi-gawa

Shinji-kō

Bus
Station

Matsue
Station

N

Yome-ga-shima

Yonago, Tottori & Adachi Museum of Art

0          500 m

**RESTAURANTS**

| | |
|---|---|
| Café Courant d'Air | D |
| Kashmir Dabar | B |
| Penkan | C |
| Uo-ichi | E |
| Yagumo-an | A |

**ACCOMMODATION**

| | |
|---|---|
| Business Ishida | 7 |
| Ichibata | 4 |
| Matsue City | 2 |
| Matsue Lakeside Youth Hostel | 3 |
| Minamikan | 1 |
| Ryokan Terazuya | 8 |
| Tōkyū Inn | 6 |
| Young Inn | 5 |

Izumo Airport          Izumo & Hagi          Yakumotatsu Fudoki-no-Oka

Hiroshima. For **flights** the closest airport is **Izumo airport**, 35km west, although **Yonago airport** to the east is also an option. There are direct buses from Izumo to Matsue Station (¥920), while from Yonago it's best to take the frequent buses to Yonago Station and then catch a train to Matsue.

The **tourist information** office (daily 9.30am–6pm; ☎0852/21-4034), next to *Mister Donuts* on the north side of Matsue Station, has plenty of leaflets and maps and is staffed by an English-speaking assistant (daily except Tues 10am–4pm), who can help with accommodation bookings.

The best way to **get around** is to walk or cycle. **Bikes** can be rented from the Nippon Rent-a-car office next to Matsue Onsen Station (daily 8am–6pm; ¥500 for two hours, ¥1100 for the day). Regular **buses** connect Matsue Onsen with Matsue Station, from where you can catch buses to other parts of the city and surrounding area. From outside both stations you can also pick up the **Lakeside bus** service, a motorized red trolley bus that makes a leisurely circuit of Matsue's sights (¥200 a trip). The day-pass for ¥500 is hardly worth it, since it's far quicker to walk parts of the route. However, if you're planning to visit Izumo Taisha (see p.590) the same day, you will save money if you buy the one-day L&R ticket (¥1000), which covers the Lakeside bus and Ichibata trains.

If you visit Matsue between March and November, an ideal way to appreciate the city's watery charms is to take an hour-long **boat** trip around the castle moat and canals. Departures are between 9am and 5pm (June–Aug 9am–6pm) from the Karakoro Hiroba beside Matsue's shopping district, west of the castle. The fare is ¥1200 and the open-top boats don't run if it's raining.

## Accommodation

**Accommodation** options in Matsue are split across two main areas. There's the usual cluster of business hotels around Matsue Station, while on the lake south of Matsue Onsen Station are the upmarket, expensive hotels catering to the hot-spring crowd.

**Business Ishida**, 205-11 Tera-machi (☎0852/21-5931). All the rooms in this plain hotel, five minutes west of the north side of Matsue Station, are Japanese-style with shared bathrooms. It doesn't look much, but it's clean and they're used to *gaijin*. Singles are ¥4000. [4].

**Hotel Ichibata**, 30 Chidori-chō (☎0825/22-0188, fax 22-0230). The more modern section of this upmarket lakeside hotel in Matsue Onsen is in the newer east building. The cheapest Western-style rooms, half the price of the *tatami* rooms, don't have lake views, but you can always admire the scenery from the top-floor onsen. [5].

**Matsue City Hotel**, Suetsugu-Honmachi (☎0852/25-4100, fax 25-5100). There's a Spanish flavour to the decoration at this convenient and comfortable business hotel, with a quirky display of eighteenth-century antique clocks on one floor. Most rooms are singles starting from ¥5250. [5].

**Matsue Lakeside Youth Hostel**, 1546 Koshoshi-chō (☎ & fax 0852/36-8620). Although its countryside location, beyond walking distance from Matsue's sights, is a disadvantage, this spacious hostel has fine bunk-bed dorms, friendly staff and serves good meals. The view across Shinji ko is also good. Take the Ichibata line one stop from Matsue Onsen Station to Furue, and follow the signs for around ten minutes to the hillside hostel. [1].

**Minamikan**, 14 Suetsugu-Honmachi (☎0852/21-5131, fax 26-0351). Matsue's top ryokan is in a modern complex, but has a distinctly tradtional feel, from the courteous service to the neatly clipped pines in the gravel garden. Huge suites of *tatami* rooms and the best local cuisine push up the prices. [8].

**Ryokan Terazuya**, 60-3 Tenzin-machi (☎0852/21-3480, fax 21-3422). Excellent-value ryokan, in a quiet location above a sushi restaurant, about ten minutes' walk west of Matsue Station. Run by a friendly English-speaking couple, its well-kept Japanese-style rooms have air-conditioning and TV. For two meals add ¥3000 per person. [4].

**Tokyu Inn**, 590 Asahi-machi (☎0852/27-0109, fax 25-1327). Very conveniently located opposite Matsue Station, this national chain hotel has smart, but dated Western-style rooms. [5].

**Young Inn**, 5 Uo-machi (☎ & fax 0852/22-4500). There's a Seventies retro feel to this business hotel and bar. The rooms are cheap because they're cramped and share communal shower rooms (no

### TICKETS FOR MATSUE'S SIGHTS

If you plan to visit Matsue-jō, the Lafcadio Hearn Museum and the Buké-yashiki *samurai* residence it's best to buy the **Universal Pass** (¥800) at the first of the sights you visit. This ticket, which is valid for three days, will save you money on the separate entrance fees, and get you discounts at other attractions around the city.

## MATSUE AND AROUND

| | | |
|---|---|---|
| **Matsue** | *Matsue* | 松江 |
| Buke Yashiki | *Buke Yashiki* | 武家屋敷 |
| Lafcadio Hearn Memorial Museum | *Koizumi Yakumo Kinenkan* | 小泉八雲記念館 |
| Lafcadio Hearn's Old Residence | *Koizumi Yakumo Kyūkyo* | 小泉八雲旧居 |
| Matsue Historical Museum | *Matsue Kyōdokan* | 松江郷土館 |
| Matsue-jō | *Matsue-jō* | 松江城 |
| Matsue Onsen Station | *Matsue Onsen-eki* | 松江温泉駅 |
| Meimei-an | *Meimei-an* | 明々庵 |
| Tanabe Art Museum | *Tanabe Bijutsukan* | 田部美術館 |
| | | |
| *ACCOMMODATION* | | |
| Business Ishida | *Bijinesu Ishida* | ビジネス石田 |
| Hotel Ichibata | *Hoteru Ichibata* | ホテル一畑 |
| Matsue City Hotel | *Matsue Shitii Hoteru* | 松江シティーホテル |
| Matsue Lakeside Youth Hostel | *Matsue Reikusaido Yūsu Hosuteru* | 松江レイクサイドユースホステル |
| Minamikan | *Minamikan* | 皆美館 |
| Ryokan Terazuya | *Ryokan Terazuya* | 旅館寺津屋 |
| Tōkyu Inn | *Tōkyū In* | 東急イン |
| Young Inn | *Yangu In* | ヤングイン |
| | | |
| *EATING* | | |
| Kashmir Dabar | *Kashimiiru Dabā* | カシミールダバー |
| Penkan | *Penkan* | ペンカン |
| Uo-ichi | *Uo-ichi* | 魚一 |
| Yakumo-an | *Yakumo-an* | 八雲庵 |
| | | |
| *AROUND MATSUE* | | |
| **Yakumotatsu Fudoki-no-Oka** | *Yakumotatsu Fudoki-no-Oka* | 八雲立つ風土記の丘 |
| Izumo Kanbe-no-sato | *Izumo Kanbe-no-sato* | 出雲かんべの里 |
| Kamosu-jinja | *Kamosu-jinja* | 神魂神社 |
| | | |
| **Adachi Museum of Art** | *Adachi Bijutsukan* | あだち美術館 |
| | | |
| **Izumo Taisha** | *Izumo Taisha* | 出雲大社 |
| Arakiya | *Arakiya* | 荒木屋 |
| Ebisuya Youth Hostel | *Ebisuya Yūsu Hosuteru* | えびすやユースホステル |
| Hino-misaki | *Hino-misaki* | 日御碕 |
| Takenoya | *Takenoya* | 竹の屋 |

baths), but they're clean, and the hotel is conveniently sited just south of the main sights. Singles are ¥3465. ③.

## Matsue-jō and around

The brooding, five-storey donjon of **Matsue-jō** (daily: April–Sept 8.30am–6pm; Jan–March & Oct–Dec 8.30am–5pm; ¥500), standing on top of the hill Oshiro-yama, is still the focal point of the city, as it was when the *daimyō* Horio Yoshiharu first built his castle in 1611. Compared to Himeji-jō's donjon (see p.513), this one looks as if it's been squashed, but it is, in fact, the largest of the twelve remaining original castle towers scattered around Japan and its sinister aspect is enhanced by the black-painted wood decorating the walls. It was extensively renovated in the 1950s and the surrounding grounds defined by the inner moat have been turned into a pleasant park, **Jōzan-kōen**.

If you're taking a bus from Matsue Station to the castle, get off at Kencho-mae, and you'll see the castle grounds dead ahead. You'll have to change into slippers before entering the donjon, but if you have large feet it will be safer to climb the slippy wooden stairs to the fifth-floor *Tengu* (long-nosed goblin) room in your socks. This is where the lords would have commanded their armies if there had been any battles (which there weren't), and the room now has displays of armour, weapons and other artefacts, including the original *shachi* (mythical dolphins) that topped the roof. The views across the city towards the lake and sea are still splendid.

Within Jōzan Kōen you'll also find the **Matsue Historical Museum** (daily 8.30am–5pm; ¥200), in an elegant whitewashed wooden building, whose combination of pillars, verandahs and ornate gabled roof are typical of the hybrid style of the Meiji era. The two-storey mansion was built in 1903 to accommodate the emperor on the off-chance that he might visit the city, which he never did. It now contains an interesting collection of colourful local arts and crafts, including plenty of tea-ceremony utensils.

Leave the park by the bridge in the northwest corner, follow the moat as it turns east and you'll come to **Shiomi Nawate**, a parade of *samurai* residences, some converted into museums, that remain protected by high walls capped with grey tiles. On the corner is the **Lafcadio Hearn Memorial Museum** (daily 8.30am–5pm; ¥250), which provides an excellent introduction to the life and works of the revered writer (see box overleaf) and is curated by Hearn's great-grandson, Bon Koizumi. There are lots of English explanations and you can also see Hearn's favourite writing desk and chair, specially designed so that he could work closer to his one good eye. Next door is **Lafcadio Hearn's Old Residence** (daily 9am–4.30pm; ¥200), the small, old *samurai* house where the writer lived from May to November 1891 and in which he began work on two of his most famous books, *Glimpses of Unfamiliar Japan* and the ghost story collection *Kwaidan*. Sit in the calm of the *tatami* rooms, read the English leaflet containing extracts from Hearn's essay *In a Japanese Garden*, which is about the house, and see how little has changed.

The next high wall shields the contemporary building of the **Tanabe Art Museum** (Tues–Sun 9am–5pm; ¥500), established by the late prefectural governor Tanabe Chōemon XXIII, who was also a respected artist with a particular interest in the aesthetics of the tea ceremony. The museum contains the Tanabe family's refined collection, centring around pottery tea bowls and tea utensils. There's a pleasant, airy café where you can take tea (¥350) overlooking the museum's garden.

Further along Shiomi Nawate is the largest *samurai* house remaining in Matsue, the **Buké-yashiki** (daily 8.30am–5pm; ¥250), built in 1730 as the home of the Shiomi family, high-ranking retainers to the ruling Matsudaira clan. The attractive complex of buildings has been well preserved and you can wander round the exterior looking into *tatami* and wood rooms which give some sense of what eighteenth-century *samurai* life was like.

The dusty grounds of the Buké-yashiki are a contrast to the precise Zen beauty of the raked gravel and artfully positioned stones around the **Meimei-an** teahouse (grounds daily 9am–5pm; ¥200), a short walk up the hill directly behind Shiomi Nawate. Originally designed by the *daimyō* Matsudaira Fumai to exact tea-ceremony principles, the tiny cottage has creamy beige plaster walls which hardly look capable of holding up the heavily thatched roof. Meimei-an was restored and moved to this spot – an existing *samurai* mansion with a good prospect of the castle – in 1966 to celebrate its 150th anniversary. You cannot enter the teahouse itself, but it's still worth taking time to admire it from the verandah of the adjoining mansion.

## LAFCADIO HEARN

*"There is some charm unutterable in the morning air, cool with the coolness of Japanese spring and wind-waves from the snowy cone of Fuji..."*
Lafcadio Hearn, *My First Day in the Orient.*

From the moment he set foot in the country, the journalist **Lafcadio Hearn** was clearly enchanted by Japan. Of all expat writers, Hearn is by far the most respected by the Japanese, and has been adopted as a mascot of Matsue, where he lived on and off between August 1890 and November 1891. Books such as *Glimpses of Unfamiliar Japan* and *Kwaidan* are considered classics, but if Hearn had chosen to chronicle his own remarkable life he'd have surely had a best-seller on his hands.

The son of a passionate but doomed liaison between an Anglo-Irish army surgeon and a Greek girl, and named after the Greek island of Lefkada on which he was born on June 27, 1850, Hearn was destined to be an outsider. Growing up in Dublin, a contemporary of Bram Stoker and Oscar Wilde, it was also on the cards that he would become a writer. A schoolyard accident in 1866 left Hearn permanently blind in his left eye, something he remained ashamed of for the rest of his life, as shown by the many photographs where the writer carefully presents his right profile.

In 1869, the young and penniless Hearn decided to chance his fortune in the United States eventually becoming a reporter for the *Cincinnati Inquirer*, where he built a reputation as a brilliant but difficult writer. However, in 1875 Hearn was sacked and had to leave the city because he broke a social taboo, not to mention the law, by marrying a black girl. The marriage didn't last, but Hearn ended up in more tolerant New Orleans, where he threw himself into writing about Creole culture.

After a couple of years living on the West Indian island of Martinique and penning his first novel, *Chita*, Hearn was commissioned by *Harper's Monthly* to write about Japan. He arrived in Yokohama at 6am on April 4, 1890, and by the end of the day had decided to stay, get a teaching job and write a book. The teaching post brought Hearn to Matsue where he met and married Koizumi Setsu, the impoverished daughter of a *samurai* family.

Hearn would happily have stayed in Matsue, but the freezing winter weather made him ill and he was forced to move south to Kumamoto, in Kyūshū, closer to Setsu's relatives. The couple had four children and in 1896 he adopted the name Koizumi Yakumo (eight clouds) and Japanese nationality. By the beginning of the new century, Hearn's novels and articles had become a great success, he had started teaching at the prestigious Waseda University in Tokyo, and was invited to give a series of lectures at London University and in the United States. However, he was never to return to the West, since on September 30, 1904, at the age of 54, Hearn suffered a series of heart attacks and died. His grave at Zoshigaya cemetry near Ikebukuro in Tokyo is marked by a stone that proclaims him a "man of faith, similar to the undefiled flower blooming like eight rising clouds who dwells in the mansion of right enlightment."

Hearn's books stand as paeans to the beauty and mystery of old Japan, something he believed worth recording because it seemed to be fast disappearing in the non-stop modernization of the early Meiji years.

The best place to head at the end of the day, especially if the weather is good, is the eastern shore of **Shinji-ko**. This is where a mass of photographers gather, lenses poised, to capture the golden sunset behind Yōme-ga-shima, a tiny pine-studded island in the lake.

## Eating and drinking

Matsue doesn't have a wide range of **restaurants**, but those it does have are of a high quality and reasonably priced; a good place to head for is the Suetsugu Honmachi area

### KYŌDO RYŌRI IN MATSUE

Epicurians flock to Matsue for its *Kyōdo ryōri*, seven types of dishes using fish and seafood from Shinji-ko, best sampled in winter when all the fish are available and tasting their freshest. The seven dishes are *Amasagi*, smelt either cooked as tempura or marinated in *teriyaki* sauce; *Koi*, carp baked in a rich, sweet sauce; *Moroge-ebi*, steamed prawns; *Shijimi*, small shellfish usually served in miso soup; *Shirauo*, whitebait eaten raw as sashimi or cooked as tempura; *Suzuki*, bass wrapped in paper and steam-baked over hot coals; and *Unagi*, grilled freshwater eel. To sample the full seven courses make an advance reservation with one of the top ryokan, such as *Minami-kan* (☎0852/21-5131) and have at least ¥10,000 in your wallet.

beside the canal just south of the castle. If you're on a budget, pack a picnic to enjoy in the castle grounds or at Meimei-an. For **fast-food** fans there's a *Mister Donuts* by Matsue Station, and a *McDonald's* on the main road, Kunibiki-dōri, to the east of the town centre. There are few cheap **drinking** options. *Filament*, about five minutes' walk from Matsue Station, is generally recommended as a *gaijin*-friendly bar, but is also expensive. If your Japanese is up to it, take pot luck in the Isemiya district near Matsue Station or Tohonchō between the canal and the Ōhashi-gawa, two areas teeming with small bars and *izakaya*.

**Café Courant d'Air**, 494-13 Asahi-machi. This sophisticated café, with subdued lighting, classical music and classy decor, is close by Matsue Station. Specializes in thick slices of creamy sponge cake and fancy coffees. Mon–Sat 11am–11pm.

**Kashmir Dabar**, 79 Tonomachi. Authentic Indian restaurant, run by a friendly Indian chef and his Japanese wife, not far from the castle. The decor is tasteful, the portions healthy and videos of Indian songs play in the background. Lunch curries start from ¥800 and dinner set menus from ¥2500. Also has occasional live music performances. Daily except Wed 11am–3pm, 6–10pm.

**Penkan**, Suetsugi Honmachi. Small, highly recommended Thai restaurant, with a picture menu of the spicy dishes available. Set lunch is ¥900, while dinner starts from ¥2500. On the second floor above the Fukujiya chemist by the canal. Daily except Thurs 11am–2pm & 5–10pm.

**Uo-ichi**, Matsue Station. At the end of the New Orleans shopping arcade running east under the train tracks, this is a good place to try some of the *Kyōdo ryōri* fish dishes. The set course costs ¥3500, but there are cheaper meals, starting around ¥1000 that include sashimi and tempura. Also a possible beer and snack option in the evening. Daily 11am–9pm.

**Yagumo-an**, Shiomi Nawate. Highly popular, picturesque restaurant in a former *samurai* residence, with central garden, teahouse and carp-filled pond, specializing in soba and udon noodles, including *warago soba*. Most dishes under ¥1000. Daily 9am–4.30pm.

## Yakumotatsu Fudoki-no-Oka

The area around Matsue, once known as Izumo, is one of the longest settled in Japan and was written about in *Izumo-no-Kuni Fudoki* (The Topography of Izumo), a text dating from the seventh century. Keyhole-shaped burial tumuli (*kofun*) from this period can be seen breaking out of the rice-field-dotted countryside at **Yakumotatsu Fudoki-no-Oka**, a museum and park thirty minutes by bus south of Matsue Station.

The dry **museum** (Tues–Sun 9am–4.30pm; ¥300), mainly of interest to archeology and history buffs, has a small display of finds from excavations of nearby burial tumuli, including impressive pottery horses, and some first- and second-century bronze daggers and bells. From the roof you can overlook some of the tumuli, while close by you can go inside and look around a re-created thatched hut, half-buried in the ground.

Within the park, which has several pleasant forest and nature walks, is also the **Izumo Kanbe-no-sato**, a couple of buildings promoting local culture, including the **Kogei-kan** (Tues–Sun 9am–5pm), an "Industrial Arts Hall" where you can watch woodworkers, basket makers, weavers, potters and a specialist in *temari*, the art of making colourful thread-decorated balls. With an advance reservation, arranged via the Matsue tourist information office (see pp.583–4), you can also take lessons in the crafts.

Before leaving, check out the nearby fourteenth-century shrine **Kamosu-jinja**, dedicated to the Shinto mother deity Izanami. The impressive raised wooden structure, in a glade of soaring pines reached via stone steps lined by cherry trees, is one of the few remaining examples of *Taisha-zukuri* or "Grand shrine style" left in Japan.

## Adachi Museum of Art

While in Matsue don't miss taking a trip to the stunning **Adachi Museum of Art** (Apr–Sept 9am–5.30pm; Jan–March & Oct–Dec 9am–5pm; ¥1100 for *gaijin*), some 20km east of the city near the village of Yasugi. The large collection of contemporary Japanese artworks dating from 1870 to the present day, including masterpieces by Yokoyama Taikan and Uemura Shoen, take second place to the exquisite surrounding gardens, covering 43,000 square metres.

The founder of the museum, Adachi Zenko, was an enthusiastic gardener and his passion for the art form shows through in the beautiful landscapes which envelope the galleries and steal your attention at every turn. The museum is designed so that, as you move around, the views of the Dry Landscape Garden, the White Gravel and Pine Garden, the Moss Garden and the Pond Garden, seem like pictures, changing with the seasons. A couple of the gardens have traditional tea houses where you can take tea from ¥850; the two coffee shops in the museum are cheaper and provide just as nice views.

Give yourself plenty of time here because once you've dragged yourself away from the gardens, the art itself is not bad either. The museum has the largest collection of paintings by Yokoyama Taikan, whose delicate ink drawings and deep colour screens set the standard for modern Japanese art. The curators can't resist pandering to the Japanese love of the cute by including a section of kitsch art from children's books, but recover credibility in the tasteful ceramics hall, which includes works by Kitaoji Rosanjin, a local potter known as the "poet of fire" for his daring work with glazes.

Direct buses from Matsue's JR station take around fifty minutes to reach the museum (get off at Saginoyu Onsen), or you can take a train to Arashima, which is only thirteen minutes away from the museum by bus.

## Izumo Taisha and around

The grand, graceful shrine of Izumo Oyashiro, second only in importance to that at Ise (see p.500) is better known as **IZUMO TAISHA**, after the town it is sited in, 33km west of Matsue. Although most of the current buildings date from the nineteenth century, the original shrine was built, if you believe the legend, by Amaterasu, the Sun Goddess, and is still visited each October by all eight million Shinto deities for their annual get-together. Since the shrine is dedicated to Okuninushi-no-kami, the god of good relationships, many couples visit in the hope that they will live happily ever after. It's also a popular stop for tour groups, but the shrine precincts are large enough to absorb the crowds and most pass through pretty quickly anyway.

A giant concrete *torii* stands at the southern end of Shinmon-dōri, the main approach to the shrine, along which you'll also find Izumo Taisha Station, the terminus for the Ichibata train from Matsue Onsen. More in keeping with the shrine's natural grace is the wooden *torii* that marks the entrance to the forested grounds at the foot of Yakumo-yama. To the left, you'll pass an old steam locomotive, quietly rusting away, while closer to the central compound, to the right of the Seki-no-Baba, an avenue of gnarled pine trees leaning at odd angles, is a large, modern statue of the deity Okuninushi.

Straight ahead, beyond the bronze *torii* is the shrine's central compound, the **Oracle Hall**, in front of which hangs a giant *shimenawa*, the traditional twist of straw rope. Inside the hall, Shinto ceremonies take place all day, with accompanying drumming and flute playing. To the right is a modern building containing the **treasure hall** (daily 8.30am–4.30pm; ¥150) on the second floor of which you'll find a small collection of swords, statues, armour, painted screens and a map of the shrine, dating from 1248, painted on silk and in remarkably good condition. There's also an illustration of the shrine as it was supposed to have been in the Middle Ages, when it was 48 metres tall and the highest wooden structure in Japan, topping Nara's Tōdai-ji, home of the great statue of Buddha (see p.485).

The current inner shrine, or **Honden**, last rebuilt in 1744 and directly behind the Oracle Hall, is still the country's tallest at 24 metres in height, with projecting rafters that shoot out from the roof. Unless you've paid to take part in a Shinto ceremony, you'll have to stand outside the **Eight-legged East Gate** entrance, decorated with beautiful unpainted wooden carvings and peer through to the inner coutyard. Even pilgrims are not allowed anywhere near the central Holy of Holies hall, buried deep within the Honden and the province only of the head priest.

The branches of the trees surrounding the shrine, on which visitors tie *omikuji* (fortune telling) papers for good luck, are so heavily laden they look as if they have been coated with snow. In the woods behind the Honden is the **Shōkōkan** (¥50), the former treasure house, now displaying many jolly statues of Daikoku (one of the guises of Okuninushi), and his *bon viveur* son Ebisu, who usually has a fish tucked under his arm.

Leaving the shrine by the west exit (the closest to the Bus Centre and main car park), you'll see a large modern hall, where more daily ceremonies take place and which is also used for the sacred *kagura* dances performed on festival days. In front of the hall hangs another *shimenawa* into which people fling coins, hoping they will stick and bring them luck.

Apart from the shrine, there are only a couple of other sights worth seeing in the town of Izumo Taisha. Near the cement *Ōtorii* is the **Kikyo-kan** (Tues–Sun 9am–5pm; ¥500), a modern hall with colourful exhibits on the town's festival, including costumes, banners and video films. Also look out for **Iwaidakoten**, where traditional Izumo kites have been made for over seventy years (the large ones cost ¥40,000); it's on the same street as the soba shop *Arakiya* (see opposite), close to Shinmon-dōri.

If you have time, head 10km northwest to the scenic cape of **Hino-misaki**, where you'll find a quieter shrine complex, **Hinomisaki-jinja**, built in 1644 under the shogun Tokugawa Ieyasu, and a 44-metre-tall white stone lighthouse dating from 1903. Climb the steep spiral staircase to the top of the lighthouse (April–Sept 8.30am–4pm; Jan–March & Oct–Dec 9am–4.30pm; ¥150) for a splendid view out to the nearby islands. Around the cape are several bathing beaches, too. Hino-misaki is a twenty-minute bus ride (¥490) from Izumo Taisha Bus Centre.

## IZUMO-TAISHA FESTIVALS

Apart from the usual Shinto festival days (see Basics, p.57), the important festivals at Izumo Taisha are:

May 14–16: **Imperial Grand Festival**. The welcome mat is rolled out for an envoy from the imperial family.

Oct 11–17: **Kamiari-sae**. Celebration for the annual gathering of the Shinto gods.

## Practicalities

From Matsue, the easiest way to reach Izumo Taisha is by **train** on the Ichibata line from Matsue Onsen Station, on the west side of town. You'll have to change at Kawato for the final leg to Izumo Taisha. The journey takes an hour and costs ¥790, but if you're travelling round both Matsue and Izumo Taisha in the same day, you should buy the ¥1000 L&R Free Kippu (see p.585). JR trains stop at Izumo-shi Station, from where you'll have to transfer to the Ichibata line, changing again at Kawato. The Izumo Taisha-mae terminus is five minutes' walk south of the shrine. There's also a direct Ichibata **bus** from Izumo-shi Station, which is slower and more expensive than the train; both the train and bus leave from the Ichibata department store beside the JR station. Buses stop at the Izumo Taisha bus centre, a minute's walk west of the shrine, where you can also catch buses to Hino-misaki.

The **tourist information** office (daily 9am–5.30pm; ☎0853/53-2298) is on Shinmon-dōri between the station and the shrine grounds. No English is spoken, but a few English leaflets are available. It's only worth renting a bicycle at the station (¥500 for three hours, ¥800 for the day), if you plan to cycle out to Hino-misaki, which takes around thirty minutes.

With Matsue so close, there's no pressing reason to stay overnight in Izumo Taisha, and especially not at the *Ebisuya Youth Hostel* (☎0853/53-2157; ①), which has plain bunk-bed dorms and a sterile, unwelcoming atmosphere. A ryokan is a better option, especially since you'll be served dinner, almost impossible to come by otherwise, as all the tourist restaurants shut around 5pm. The *Hi-no-Izukan* (☎0853/53-3311, fax 53-2014; ⑦) and the slightly more expensive, but better kept *Takenoya* (☎0853/53-3131, fax 53-3134; ⑦) are both attractive, friendly places on the main Shinmon-dōri approach to the shrine.

Around the bus centre near the shrine are many **restaurants** catering to the bland tastes of mass tourism; don't expect any culinary surprises. The local speciality is **wari-go soba**, cold buckwheat noodles seasoned with seaweed flakes, served in three-layer dishes, over which you pour *dashi* stock. The best place to sample this dish is at *Arakiya*, a hospitable outfit, about five minutes' walk south of the main throng of tourist canteens. You'll pay ¥780 for *warigo soba*, or you can try one layer of noodles for just ¥250. Both are served with a cup of hot soba-water soup which you can flavour with *dashi*.

# Tottori

The main rail and road routes east of Matsue continue along the coast, crossing into the neighbouring prefecture Tottori-ken and through **Yonago**, an uninteresting industrial city with a nearby airport. Trains from Okayama on the JR Hakubi line terminate at Yonago. Stick to the coast until you reach the prefectural capital of **TOTTORI**,

| **TOTTORI** | | |
| --- | --- | --- |
| **Tottori** | *Tottori* | 鳥取 |
| Dunes | *Sakyū* | 砂丘 |
| | | |
| *ACCOMMODATION* | | |
| Hotel New Ōtani Tottori | *Hoteru Nyū Ōtani Tottori* | ホテルニューオータニ鳥取 |
| Sakyū Centre Hotel | *Sakyū Sentā Hoteru* | 砂丘センターホテル |
| Tottori Green Hotel Morris | *Tottori Guriin Hoteru Mōrisu* | 鳥取グリーンホテルモーリス |
| Washington Hotel | *Washinton Hoteru* | ワシントンホテル |

famous in Japan for the 16km-long **sand dunes** at nearby Hamasaka. Although they've been designated a national monument, there's nothing especially unique about the dunes and they're not worth going out of your way to see. However, it is an atmospheric place, where tourists get swallowed up by the enormity of the sand hills and there are also camels imported for would-be Lawrence of Arabia's to pose on.

The dunes are a twenty-minute bus journey north of Tottori Station. Buses leave from platform 3 at the bus centre next to the station and pass through the city centre on the way to either Sakyū Kaikan, beside the dunes, or the Sakyū Centre, overlooking them from a hill. The centre is nothing more than a souvenir and food stop for the tour buses that pile in daily. There is a chair lift (daily 8am–5pm; ¥200) which runs between the centre and the edge of the dunes, but you can just as easily walk between the two.

### Practicalities

Tottori Station, on the San-in line, is the terminal of the JR Tsuyama line from Okayama. The **bus terminal** next to the station is where long-distance buses from Tokyo, Himeji, Hiroshima, Kyoto and Ōsaka stop. Tottori **airport** (☎0857/28-1402), 10km northwest of the city, has daily flights to Tokyo and Hiroshima. A bus to the city from the airport takes twenty minutes and costs ¥450.

The **tourist information booth** (daily 9am–7pm; ☎0857/22-3318) is inside Tottori Station, to the right of the north exit. The assistants don't speak English, but there are English leaflets and maps for the city and prefecture. If you need a **hotel** there are several options close to the station's north side. *Tottori Green Hotel Morris* (☎0857/22-2331, fax 26-5574; [5]) is a good-value business hotel behind the Daimaru department store across from the station. It has neat rooms, serves Western-style breakfast for ¥480 and has single rooms from ¥5250. Nearby is the ever reliable *Washington Hotel* (☎0857/27-8111, fax 27-8125; [6]), while the upmarket *Hotel New Ōtani Tottori* (☎0857/23-1111, fax 23-0979; [6]) is next to Daimaru. If you want to stay out by the dunes, the *Sakyū Centre Hotel* (☎0857/22-2111, fax 24-8811; [6]) is old-fashioned, but has good-value Japanese-style rooms, overlooking the coast, with two meals included in the rates and, in summer, an outdoor pool.

Although there are a handful of **restaurants** at the dunes, you'll be better served by the choice near Tottori Station. There are several restaurants in the shopping arcades that run under the train tracks, all with plastic food displays. Directly across from the station is *Mister Donuts*, and on the fourth floor of the Daimaru department store is *Marguerite* (11am–6.30pm), a Japanese restaurant with a good range of set meals and special daily dishes.

## Amanohashidate and around

At the far eastern end of the San-in coast, some 90km from Tottori, the stubby peninsula Tango-hantō leans protectively over Wakasa Bay, shielding the sandspit **AMANOHASHIDATE**, the "Bridge to Heaven". As one of the trio of top scenic views in Japan (the other two being Matsushima and Miya-jima), Amanohashidate has a lot to live up to. The "bridge" is actually a 3.6km ribbon of white sand and pine trees slinking its way from **Monjū** to **Fuchū** across the bay, and the recommended way to view it is from the hillside on either side with your head stuck between your legs.

Once you're standing upright, you'll find that Amanohashidate and the surrounding attractions of the Tango-hantō are to northern Kyoto-ken what Hakone is to Tokyo – a pleasureland of scenic delights, old temples and shrines and, rarest of all for Japan, good beaches. Expensive and limited public transport keeps the crowds down, particularly out of season, but this also means that your own transport will help you get the most out of this cut-off corner of the Japan Sea coast.

## AMANOHASHIDATE AND AROUND

| | | |
|---|---|---|
| **Amanohashidate** | *Amanohashidate* | 天橋立 |
| Chion-ji | *Chion-ji* | 智恩寺 |
| Fuchū | *Fuchū* | 府中 |
| Hashidate Jaya | *Hashidate Jaya* | 橋立茶や |
| Ine | *Ine* | 伊根 |
| Monjū | *Monjū* | 文殊 |
| Nariai-ji | *Nariai-ji* | 成相寺 |
| Tango-hantō | *Tango-hantō* | 丹後半島 |
| Toyooka | *Toyooka* | 豊岡 |
| | | |
| *ACCOMMODATION* | | |
| Amanohashidate Youth Hostel | *Amanohashidate Yūsu Hosuteru* | 天橋立ユースホステル |
| Amanohashidate Kankōkaikan Youth Hostel | *Amanohashidate Kankōkaikan Yūsu Hosuteru* | 天橋立観光会館ユースホステル |
| Genmyōan | *Genmyōan* | 玄妙庵 |
| Maruyasu | *Maruyasu* | まるやす |
| Monjūsō Shōrotei | *Monjūsō Shōrotei* | 文殊荘松露亭 |
| Young Inn | *Yangu In* | ヤングイン |

On Mount Nariai above Fuchū, the splendidly atmospheric **Nariai-ji** is one of the thirty-three temples on the Saigoku Kannon pilgrimage route, while closer to the summit there is a fantastic view of the bay and coast as far as away as the Noto-hantō, some 500km northeast. East along the Tango-hantō is the picturesque fishing hamlet of **Ine**, while across the bay in Monjū, another attractive wooden temple, **Chion-ji**, stands on the brink of the sandbar, which is a lovely area for a quiet stroll or cycle ride, or lazing on the beach.

## Arrival, information and getting around

**Trains** to Amanohashidate Station in Monjū run along the scenic Kita-kinki Tango Tetsudō line. If you're approaching the Tango-hantō from the west you'll need to change from the JR line at **Toyo-oka**. The standard fare from here for the one-hour, twenty-minute journey to Amanohashidate is ¥1160, but for ¥930 extra you can save yourself thirty minutes by taking the more comfortable limited express trains, whose carriages have large picture windows and TV screens showing the view from the front of the train. There are a few direct JR trains from Kyoto and Ōsaka, which take around two hours and thirty minutes, but you'll have to pay for the Kita-kinki Tango Tetsudō portion of the journey if you're using a JR rail pass. **Buses** from both Kyoto and Ōsaka take around two hours and forty minutes.

Inside Amanohashidate Station, at the **tourist information desk** (daily 10am–6pm; ☎0772/22-8030), the helpful assistants don't speak much English, but can provide a couple of English-language pamphlets on the area and help with accommodation bookings.

**Buses** across the bay to Fuchū, where you'll find the two youth hostels, and around the Tango-hantō leave from outside the station until 7pm, and take twenty minutes. Alternatively you can take the regular **ferry** (12min; ¥520), from the jetty beside Chion-ji, five minutes' walk from the station, to the Fuchū side jetty at Ichinomiya. If you fancy some excercise, **bicycles** can be rented from the shops close to the station for ¥500 for two hours, or you could stroll the 4km across the sandbar.

## Accommodation

Monjū is the main tourist hub of Amanohashidate and has the widest range of **accommodation**, including several inexpensive minshuku near the station and a couple of top-class ryokan. Both the youth hostels are across the bay in Fuchū.

**Amanohashidate Youth Hostel**, Fuchū (☎0772/27-0121, fax 27-0939). The more modern of the town's two hostels has bunk-bed dorms, a comfy lounge and a helpful English-speaking manager. Bike rental is also cheap at ¥500 a day. The secluded location is a ten-minute hike uphill to the right from the ferry and bus stop at Ichinomiya, behind the shrine, Kono-jinja. [1].

**Amanohashidate Kankōkaikan Youth Hostel**, Fuchū (☎0772/27-0046). Old waterfront hostel with *tatami* rooms, all with TVs, some overlooking the sandbar. The management is friendly. [1].

**Genmyoan** (☎0772/22-2171, fax 25-1641). On the hillside above Monjū, with good views of the sand bar, this ryokan has the feel of an English cottage with its dark wooden beams and white plaster walls. The rooms are traditional *tatami* and there's also an outdoor pool in the summer. [9].

**Maruyasu**, Eki-dōri, Monjū (☎0772/22-2310, fax 22-8200). Cosy minshuku, a minute's walk to the right of the station. *Tatami* rooms, with shared bath and the rates include two meals. [5].

**Monjūsō Shōrotei** (☎0772/22-2151, fax 22-2153). Exquisite ryokan, behind the temple Chion-ji, surrounded by private gardens at the tip of a mini-peninsula overlooking the sandbar. Rates can climb as high as ¥60,000 per person, depending on the room and your choice of meals. [9].

**Young Inn**, Eki-dōri (☎0772/22-0650, fax 22-7735). No-frills Western-style hotel, beside the lake, a minute's walk left from the station exit. The cheaper rooms, at the bottom end of the scale, share a bathroom. [5].

## Monjū and Amanohashidate

Five minutes' walk north of Amanohashidate Station, at the end of a shopping street leading towards the sandspit, is the attractive temple **Chion-ji**, dedicated to the Buddhist saint Chie-no-Monnjū. Beside the main hall (*Monnjū-do*), which houses a revered image of the saint, stands the Tahoto, a squat wooden pagoda dating from 1500 and designated an Important Cultural Property. In the temple precincts, near the ferry jetty, you'll also see the Chie-no-wa Torō, a granite ring monument symbolizing wisdom which has been adopted as an emblem of the town.

To reach the pine-forested sandbar, **Amanohashidate**, cross the red bridge Kaisenkyō, which swings around to allow boats through the narrow channel to the open sea. The sandy crescent-shaped beaches on the east side of the spit are at their busiest from July to August. The pine-shaded lane is a lovely spot for a quiet stroll or you can hop in one of the pedicabs (¥3000 for thirty minutes).

The best place from which to view the sand spit in its entirety is from Kasamatsu-kōen above Fuchū (see below), but if you're pushed for time there's also a look-out point in the hills behind Monjū. A five-minute walk over the rail tracks and up the hill behind Amanohashidate Station brings you to the **chair-lift** (daily 8.30am–5pm; ¥850 return) which takes six minutes to reach the touristy Amanohashidate View Park, a mini-amusement park where loudspeakers pump out a 1950s musical soundtrack.

## Fuchū and around

The walking trail across Amanohashidate and the ferry brings you close to the precincts of **Kono-jinja**, the oldest shrine in the area and guarded by a pair of stone dogs dating from the Kamakura era. A short walk up the hill to the left, past a row of souvenir stalls, is the station for both the funicular railway and chair-lift (¥320 one way) up the lower slopes of Mount Nariai to Kasamatsu-kōen, the principal look-out point over Amanohashidate, where tourists gather for official group photos. Signs demonstrate how best to stand, with your head between your legs, so the sand spit seems to float in mid-air.

From the park you can either catch a bus or walk for twenty minutes further up the mountain to the gate to **Nariai-ji** (daily 8am–5pm; ¥400), a charmingly rustic temple surrounded by lofty pines, founded in 704 and dedicated to Kannon, the Buddhist goddess of mercy. This is one of the thirty-three temples on the Saigoku Kannon pilgrim route, so attracts a steady stream of visitors, many of who are clutching elaborate hanging scrolls which are specially inscribed at each temple. Legend has it that if you pray at the temple and make a vow to Kannon, your prayer will be granted.

As you climb the stone steps leading up to the main temple building you'll pass a 33-metre-tall pagoda, currently being rebuilt for the first time since it burned down five hundred years ago, and a small wooden bell tower. An interesting legend is attached to the bell, which has never been rung since it was first cast in 1609. A mother who had been too poor to contribute money to the temple, accidentally dropped her baby into the vat of molten copper being cast as the bell. When the bell was first stuck it is said that the people could hear the baby calling out for its mother, so it was decided never to ring the bell again.

If you have time, it really is worth making the effort to continue on to the **Nihon Ichi Tenbodai**, a panoramic look-out spot around 1km further up the mountain from Nariai-ji. The sublime view across Amanohashidate and Wakasa Bay, as far away as the Noto-hanō (p.387) and the sacred mountain Hakusan on the Hokuriku coast, is straight out of a woodblock print.

If you have time, back down in Fuchū you can catch a bus 16km up the coast to the charming fishing hamlet of **Ine**, sheltering in a hook-like inlet towards the eastern end of the Tango-hantō. The best way to see the traditional wooden houses built over the water, with space beneath for the boats to be stored, is to take a yellow sightseeing boat from Ine harbour (March–Jan daily 9am–4.30pm; ¥660) on a thirty-minute tour of the inlet. If you have your own transport, you'll find it easier to proceed around the rest of the rugged penninsula, with its dramatic cliffside roads, sweeping coastal views and quiet beaches.

## Eating and drinking

You'll find more **restaurants** and **cafés** in Monjū than Fuchū, although there are few star options. One of the nicest places is *Hashidate Jaya* (daily except Thurs 9am–5pm), nestling amid the pines at the Monjū end of the sand spit, which serves good-value meals and snacks, including *asari-don*, small shellfish and spring onions on a bowl of rice. The *Young Inn* (see previous page) has an attached French restaurant with views of the bay, and does a four-course lunch deal for ¥1500. Over in Fuchū, try *St John's Bear* (daily except Wed 8.30am–5pm) at the water's edge down from the chair-lift station, a Western-style café/bar which also serves pizza.

## travel details

**Trains**

The trains between the major cities listed below are the fastest, direct services. There are also frequent slower services, run by JR and several private companies, covering the same destinations. It is usually possible, especially on long-distance routes, to get there faster by changing between services.

**Amanohashidate** to: Kyoto (2 daily; 2hr 30min); Ōsaka (2 daily; 2hr 30min), Toyo-oko (8 daily; 1hr, 20min).

**Hagi** to: Matsue (1 daily; 3hr 45min); Shimonoseki (1 daily; 2hr).

**Hiroshima** to: Fukuoka (Hakata station; every 15 min; 1hr 10min); Kyoto (every 15 min; 1hr 50min); Matsue, via Okayama (1 hourly; 4hr); Okayama (every 15 min; 40min); Shin-Ōsaka (every 15 min; 1hr 30min), Tokyo (at least 25 daily; 4hr 50min).

**Matsue** to: Izumo Taisha (10 daily; 1hr); Kokura (daily; 5hr 35min); Okayama (14 daily; 2hr 20min); Tokyo (daily; 13hr).

**Okayama** to: Hiroshima (every 15min; 40min), Matsue (14 daily; 2hr 20min), Shin-Ōsaka (every 30min; 45min), Takamatsu (34 daily; 1hr), Tokyo (25 daily; 3hr 53min).
**Yamaguchi** to: Tsuwano (16 daily; 50min–1hr 15min).

## Buses

The buses listed below are mainly long-distance services – often travelling overnight – between the major cities, and local services where there is no alternative means of transport. For shorter journeys, however, trains are almost invariably quicker and often no more expensive.
**Amanohashidate** to: Kyoto (daily; 2hr 40min); Ōsaka (daily 2hr 40min).
**Hagi** to: Ōsaka (daily; 9hr); Tokyo (daily; 14hr).
**Hiroshima** to: Hagi (4 daily; 3hr 45min); Izumo (8 daily; 3hr 30min); Kyoto (daily; 7hr); Matsue (12 daily; 4hr); Nagasaki (2 daily; 7hr); Ōsaka (daily; 7hr 30min); Tokyo (daily; 12hr).
**Kurashiki** to: Ōsaka (2 daily; 5hr); Tokyo (daily; 11hr).
**Ogōri** to: Akiyoshi-dai (4 daily; 40min); Hagi (6 daily; 1hr 26min)
**Okayama** to: Chiba (daily; 10hr 55min); Fukuoka (daily; 9hr); Kōbe (2 daily; 2hr 50min); Kōchi (8 daily; 2hr 30min); Matsue (4 daily; 3hr 10min); Matsuyama (6 daily; 2hr 40min); Ōsaka (2 daily; 4hr); Tokyo (2 daily; 10hr 20min); Yonago (6 daily; 2hr 10min).
**Tottori** to: Himeji (8 daily; 2hr 30min); Hiroshima (3 daily; 4hr 50min); Kyoto (3 daily; 4hr); Ōsaka (13 daily; 3hr 35min); Tokyo (daily; 10hr 30min).
**Yamaguchi** to: Akiyoshi-dai (13 daily; 55min); Hagi (15 daily; 1hr 23min).

## Ferries

**Hiroshima** to: Miyajima (every 20min; 10min); Matsuyama (daily; ferry 3hr; hydrofoil 1hr).

**Okayama** to: Shōdo-shima (1 hourly; 1hr 10min).
**Onomichi** to: Ikuchi-jima (9 daily; 30min); Imabari (daily; 1hr 30min).

## Flights

**Hiroshima** to: Aomori (4 weekly; 1hr 35min); Hakodate (3 weekly; 1hr 40min); Kagoshima (2 daily; 50min); Miyazaki (1 daily; 50min); Okinawa (10 weekly; 1hr 40min); Sapporo (2 daily; 2hr); Sendai (2 daily; 1hr 35min); Tokyo Haneda (10 daily; 1hr 15min).
**Hiroshima Nishi** to: Izumo (2 daily; 35min); Kansai International (1 daily; 1hr); Komatsu (2 daily; 1hr 10min); Matsuyama (2 daily; 20min); Niigata (3 daily; 1hr 45min); Oita (2 daily; 30min); Tottori (3 daily; 45min).
**Iwami (Hagi)** to: Tokyo (2 daily; 1hr 40min); Ōsaka (daily; 1hr).
**Izumo** to: Tokyo (4 daily; 1hr 20min); Fukuoka (daily; 1hr 15min); Hiroshima Nishi (2 daily; 40min); Komatsu (daily; 1hr 5min); Nagoya (daily; 1hr 10min); Ōsaka (5 daily; 1hr 5min); Sapporo (daily; 1hr 55min).
**Okayama** to: Kagoshima (3 daily; 1hr 15min); Komatsu (2 daily; 1hr 5min); Okinawa (daily; 2hr); Sapporo (daily; 2hr); Sendai (daily; 1hr 30min); Tokyo (4 daily; 1hr 15min).
**Tottori** to: Hiroshima Nishi (3 daily; 55min); Ōsaka Nishi (daily; 50min); Tokyo Haneda (3 daily; 1hr, 10min).
**Yonago** to: Fukuoka (daily; 1hr 25min); Nagoya (daily; 1hr 5min); Ōsaka Itami (3 daily; 1hr); Tokyo Haneda (4 daily; 1hr 15min).
**Yamaguchi Ube** to: Tokyo (5 daily; 1hr 30min); Okinawa (daily; 1hr 40min); Sapporo (4 weekly; 2hr 10min).

CHAPTER EIGHT

# SHIKOKU

Despite its beautiful scenery, laid-back atmosphere, friendly people and several notable sights, **SHIKOKU**, the fourth main island of the Japanese archipelago, is usually at the bottom of most visitors' itineraries – if it appears at all. This is a shame since this quiet island, which nestles in the crook between Honshū and Kyūshū, offers elements of traditional Japan that are often hard to find elsewhere. An ancient Buddhist pilgrimage, original castles and distinctive arts and crafts are some of Shikoku's attractions – but the real appeal for travellers lies in the island's rural, less frantically modern pace of life and its little-visited villages. You'll need a week or so to absorb the tranquil pleasures of Shikoku's four prefectures and their small coastal capitals. If you only have a day, head straight for either of the island's justly famous draws: Matsuyama's splendid Dōgo hot springs and the landscape gardens of Ritsurin-kōen in Takamatsu.

According to legend, Shikoku was the second island (after Awaji-shima) born to Izanagi and Izanami, the gods who are considered to be Japan's parents. Its ancient name was Iyo-no-futana and it was divided into four main areas: Awa (now Tokushima-ken), Iyo (Ehime-ken), Sanuki (Kagawa-ken) and Tosa (Kōchi-ken). These epiphets are still used today when referring to the different prefectures' cuisines and traditional arts. Apart from being the scene of a decisive battle between the Taira and Minamoto clans in the twelfth century (see History, p.771), Shikoku has had a relatively peaceful history, due in part to its isolation from the rest of Japan. This seclusion is fast disappearing as links to mainland Japan spring up. Since the opening of the Seto Ōhashi, the main **bridge** from Honshū, in 1989, trains and cars regularly zip across the series of six bridges leapfrogging the islands of the Inland Sea to Shikoku. The new Akashi Kaikyō Ōhashi – the longest single-span suspension bridge in the world – connects Shikoku to Honshū via Awaji-shima, the island to the west of Tokushima. Finally, the ultimate road link with Honshū – ten bridges joining nine islands between Onomichi in Hiroshima-ken and Imabari on Shikoku's northern coast – is set for completion in 2000.

Most of Shikoku's population of around four million is to be found in its four main cities; Takamatsu, Tokushima, Kōchi and Matsuyama. The island is split by a vast mountain range that runs from Tsurugi-san in the east, to Ishizuchi-san, the island's

## ACCOMMODATION PRICE CODES

All accommodation in this book has been graded according to the following price codes, which refer to the cheapest double or twin room available for most of the year, and include taxes. Note that rates may increase during peak holiday periods, in particular around Christmas and New Year, the Golden Week (April 28–May 6) and Obon (the week around August 15), when accommodation is very difficult to get without an advance reservation. In the case of hostels providing dormitory accommodation, the code refers to the charge per bed. See p.36 for more details on accommodation.

| | | |
|---|---|---|
| ① under ¥3000 | ④ ¥7000–10,000 | ⑦ ¥20,000–30,000 |
| ② ¥3000–5000 | ⑤ ¥10,000–15,000 | ⑧ ¥30,000–40,000 |
| ③ ¥5000–7000 | ⑥ ¥15,000–20,000 | ⑨ over ¥40,000 |

## THE SHIKOKU PILGRIMAGE

Wherever you are in Shikoku, you'll seldom be far from Japan's longest and most famous **pilgrimage** – the pilgrim trail of the Buddhist saint **Kōbō Daishi**, founder of Shingon Buddhism. It takes two months to walk the one thousand kilometres between the 88 temples on the route, and plenty of pilgrims, known as *henro*, still complete the journey on foot, though more travel the route by car or on bus tours. It's even possible to do the tour by helicopter. The number of temples represents the 88 evils which, according to Shingon Buddhism, bedevil human life.

*Henro* are easy to spot, since they usually dress in traditional short white cotton coats, coloured shoulder bands and broad-rimmed straw hats, and generally clutch rosaries, brass bells and long wooden staffs – for support on the steep ascents to most of the temples. The characters on their robes and staffs translate as "Daishi and I go together". Most pilgrims are well past retirement age, as few young Japanese have the inclination or the vacation time needed for such a pilgrimage.

Kōbō Daishi (known during his lifetime as Kūkai), was born in 774, 30km from Takamatsu. This pious man, who walked all over the island as an itinerant priest and spent two years in China studying esoteric Buddhism before apparently gaining enlightenment at Muroto Misaki in Kōchi-ken, founded the **Shingon** (True Word) sect of Buddhism. Shingon was influenced by Central Asian tantric Buddhist traditions and this is reflected in the Shikoku temples, with their often exotic decor and atmosphere.

Kūkai died on April 22, 835, the exact day he predicted he would. For his achievements, he was posthumously awarded the title **Daishi** (Great Saint) by the imperial court. Soon after his death, his disciples began a tour around the temples of Shikoku associated with the Daishi – thus establishing the pilgrimage as it is known today.

The present-day headquarters of the Shingon sect is **Kōya-san**, in Wakayama-ken (see p.493) and this is the traditional start of the once-in-a-lifetime pilgrimage. The first temple visited on Shikoku is **Ryōzen-ji**, near Naruto in Tokushima-ken. Pilgrims then follow a circular route that winds its way clockwise around the island, stopping at all the temples on the way to the eighty-eighth temple, **Ōkubo-ji**, in Kagawa-ken. Around half the temples allow pilgrims to stay for around ¥4000 per person including meals. You'll see many pilgrims dropping coins by the thousands of Buddhas along the way, and they fork out again at the temples, where an official stamp costs around ¥300.

tallest peak, in the west. The northern coast, facing the Inland Sea, is heavily developed, in contrast to the rugged, more rural south, where the unimpeded *kuroshio* (black current) of the Pacific Ocean has carved a dramatic coastline of sheer cliffs and outsized boulders. The climate throughout the island is generally mild, although the coasts can be lashed by typhoons and the mountains see snow in the winter.

Shikoku's best all-round destination is Matsuyama, but you're more than likely to begin your journey around the island in **Kagawa-ken** on the northern coast, after crossing the Seto Ōhashi. Highlights in this area include the delightful gardens of **Ritsurin-kōen** in the capital Takamatsu, the **Yashima** plateau, to the east, site of the historic clan battle, and, in the west of the prefecture, the shrine at **Kotohira**. Eastern Shikoku and the central mountain areas of Ōboke and Iya are part of **Tokushima-ken**, famous for its capital city Tokushima's annual **Awa Odori** dance festival, the whirlpools at **Naruto** and the turtles who come to lay their eggs at **Hiwasa** each summer. Shikoku's southern coast, fanning out between the capes at Ashizuri and Muroto, is covered by **Kōchi-ken**, where fighting sumo dogs and long-tailed roosters are the local attractions, along with an original castle in the capital Kōchi. **Matsuyama**, the capital of the eastern prefecture of **Ehime-ken**, has an even better castle – one of the best in Japan – along with the renowned onsen at Dōgo, where emperors and commoners have come to bathe for centuries. Just outside Matsuyama, the small towns of Uwajima and

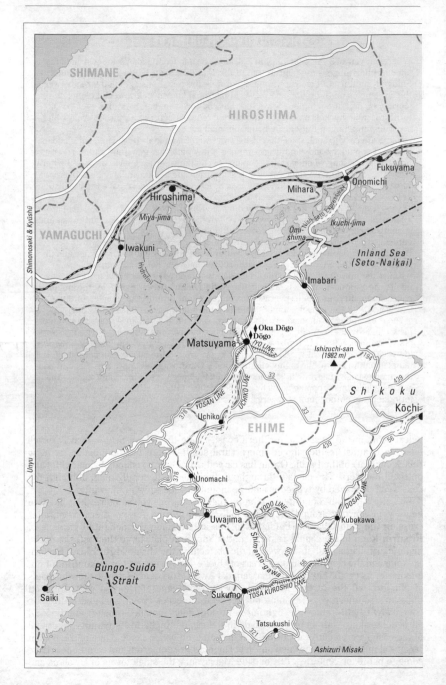

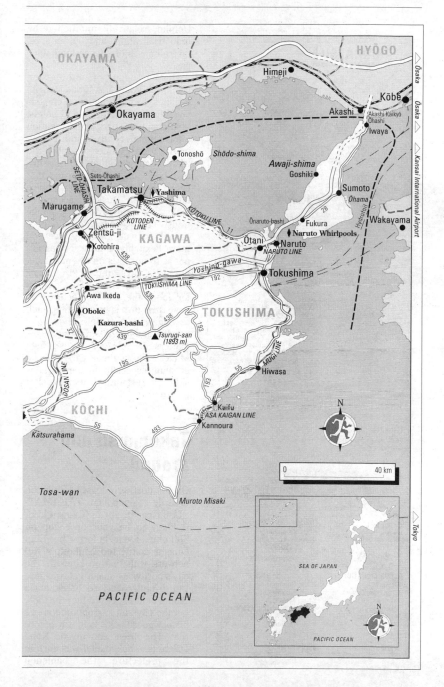

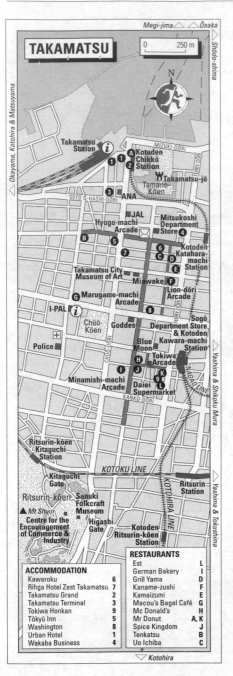

Uchiko, relatively untouched by industrialization and commerce, give glimpses of a Japan long since past.

Despite being off the beaten track, Shikoku has good tourist facilities. In the prefectural capitals you'll find a decent range of hotels, restaurants and bars, not to mention international centres and tourist information offices, while the island's famous 88 temple **pilgrimage** (see box, p.599), means that even in the countryside you're unlikely to be stuck for accommodation. **Getting around** by public transport is easy enough, though a rented car will obviously give you more flexibility. Train services are not as frequent as on the mainland, but the island's compact size means you can easily cross it in a day. As for **food**, the four prefectures all have their own special dishes, such as Kagawa-ken's tasty *sanuki udon* noodles and Kōchi-ken's *tosa ryōri* – platters of delectable fresh fish. Make sure you eat early in the evening, especially in the countryside, as restaurants usually shut before 9pm.

# Takamatsu and around

On the northern coast of Shikoku, breezily cosmopolitan **TAKAMATSU**, the capital city of **Kagawa-ken**, is likely to be your first stop on Shikoku. Even before the Seto Ōhashi connected Shikoku's rail network with that on Honshū, the city's port was a major gateway into the island. Warlord Chikamasa Ikoma built his castle here in 1588, but the city and surrounding area's history goes back a long way before that. The priest and mystic Kōbō Daishi (see box, p.599) was born in the prefecture, the banished

Emperor Sutoku was murdered here in 1164, and 21 years later, the Taira and Minamoto clans clashed at nearby **Yashima**. In air raids during World War II, Chikamasa's castle was virtually destroyed, along with most of the city.

Today, Takamatsu is a sprawling, yet fairly attractive modern city of 350,000 inhabitants, peppered with covered shopping arcades and designer stores. The current focus of development is the central port area as the city aims to take full advantage of its position looking out at the Inland Sea. A new JR train station is under construction and new port facilities, a convention centre, hotels and a seaside promenade are planned. But the city's star attraction is **Ritsurin-kōen**, one of Japan's most spacious and beautifully designed gardens. The gardens are easily accessible in a day-trip from Honshū, but it's well worth staying overnight so you can also take in **Shikoku Mura**, the open-air museum of traditional houses at Yashima, or **Kotohira-gū** (see p.612), the ancient shrine less than one hour by train west of the city. And if you're on your way to Kotohira, consider visiting **Zentsū-ji**, the atmospheric temple at the birth place of Kōbō Daishi, some 30km west of Takamatsu.

## Arrival, information and getting around

Takamatsu's JR **train** station is at the northern, seaside end of the city's central artery, Chūō-dōri, and is ten minutes' walk from the heart of the city. Several direct trains arrive daily from Kōchi, Matsuyama, Okayama and Tokushima. **Buses** pull in nearby, at the north end of Chūō-dōri. The **high-speed boat** from Ōsaka (twice daily; ¥5990) docks at the Prefectural Pier, five minutes' walk east of the train station, as do **ferries** from the island of Shōdo-shima. Ferries from Kōbe arrive at the main port complex, fifteen minutes to the east by bus (¥250). Takamatsu **airport** (☎0878/35-8110) lies 16km south of the town centre, 35 minutes away by bus (¥700) or taxi (¥4000).

The **tourist information office** (daily 9am–5pm; ☎0878/51-2009), on the western side of the train station, usually has someone who can speak English and provides useful free maps and booklets on the area. Alternatively, pay a visit to the **Kagawa International Exchange Centre**, better known as I-PAL, at 1-11-63 Banchō (Tues–Sun 9am–6pm). This is an excellent facility with a library of English books, magazines and newspapers from around the world, free use of Internet terminals and a TV lounge where you can catch up on the CNN news. It's also a good place to meet Japanese who speak English and foreigners who live in town, and you can pick up the free *Kagawa Journal*, which has details of what's on in town. From the JR station, I-PAL is a twenty-minute walk down Chūō-dōri to the crossing with Central Park – turn right and I-PAL is just on the left.

### Getting around

If you're up for some exercise, walking or cycling around Takamatsu is a fine idea, and bicycles can be rented at the JR station (see Listings, p.607). Otherwise, you'll find trains and buses perfectly user-friendly, and good for getting to sights outside the city. As well as local JR train services, Takamatsu has the **Kotoden** network, which uses old-fashioned trains and which is useful for getting to Yashima or Kotohira. Kawara-machi Station, where the Kotoden's three main lines intersect, is beside the Sogō department store at the end of the Tokiwa arcade, while Chikkō Station is opposite the JR station. Buses for Ritsurin-kōen and Yashima also run from the stops outside the *Takamatsu Grand Hotel*, at the top of Chūō-dōri.

## Accommodation

If you're on a tight budget and want to stay in the centre of Takamatsu, your choice is pretty much limited to one of the many business **hotels** clustered just south of the JR

## TAKAMATSU AND AROUND

| | | |
|---|---|---|
| **Takamatsu** | *Takamatsu* | 高松 |
| Kotoden line | *Kotoden-sen* | 琴電線 |
| Ritsurin-kōen | *Ritsurin-kōen* | 栗林公園 |
| Takamatsu Museum of Art | *Takamatsu Bijutsukan* | 高松美術館 |
| Tamamo-kōen | *Tamamo-kōen* | 玉藻公園 |

*ACCOMMODATION*

| | | |
|---|---|---|
| Kawaroku | *Kawaroku* | 川六 |
| Rihga Hotel Zest Takamatsu | *Riiga Hoteru Zesuto Takamatsu* | リーガホテルゼスト高松 |
| Takamatsu Grand Hotel | *Takamatsu Gurando Hoteru* | 高松グランドホテル |
| Takamatsu Terminal Hotel | *Takamatsu Tāminaru Hoteru* | 高松ターミナルホテル |
| Takamatsu Tōkyū Inn | *Takamatsu Tōkyū In* | 高松東急イン |
| Takamatsu Washington Hotel | *Takamatsu Washinton Hoteru* | 高松ワシントンイン |
| Tokiwa Honkan | *Tokiwa Honkan* | 常盤本館 |
| Urban Hotel | *Āban Hoteru* | アーバンホテル |
| Wakaba Business Hotel | *Wakuba Bijinesu Hoteru* | わくばビジネスホテル |

*EATING*

| | | |
|---|---|---|
| Grill Yama | *Guriru Yama* | グリル山 |
| Kaname-zushi | *Kaname-Zushi* | 要寿司 |
| Kamaizumi | *Kamaizumi* | かま泉 |
| Kikugestu-tei | *Kikugeshi-tei* | 菊月底 |
| Tenkatsu | *Tenkatsu* | 天勝 |
| Uo Ichiba | *Uo Ichiba* | 魚市場 |

| | | |
|---|---|---|
| **Shōdo-shima** | *Shōdo-shima* | 小豆島 |
| Choshi-kei | *Choshi-kei* | 銚子渓 |
| Eigamura | *Eigamura* | 映画村 |
| Kanka-kei | *Kanka-kei* | 寒霞渓 |
| Kusakabe | *Kusakabe* | 草壁 |
| Oriibu-kōen | *Oriibu-kōen* | オリーブ公園 |
| Sakate | *Sakate* | 坂手 |
| Tanoura | *Tanoura* | 田の浦 |
| Tonoshō | *Tonoshō* | 土庄 |

*ACCOMMODATION*

| | | |
|---|---|---|
| Maruse | *Maruse* | まるせ |
| Shōdo-shima Olive Youth Hostel | *Shōdo-shima Oriibu Yūsu Hosuteru* | 小豆島オーリブユースホステル |
| Uchinomi-chō Cycling Terminal | *Saikuringu Tāminaru Uchinomi-chō* | サイクリングターミナル内海町 |

| | | |
|---|---|---|
| **Yashima** | *Yashima* | 屋島 |
| Shikoku Mura | *Shikoku Mura* | 四国村 |
| Takamatsu Yashima Sansō Youth Hostel | *Takamatsu Yashima Sansō Yūsu Hosuteru* | 高松屋島山荘ユースホステル |

*EATING*

| | | |
|---|---|---|
| Ikkaku | *Ikkaku* | 一鶴 |
| Waraya | *Waraya* | わら家 |

| | | |
|---|---|---|
| **Marugame** | *Marugame* | 丸亀 |
| **Zentsū-ji** | *Zentsū-ji* | 善通時 |

station — the better ones are listed below and have single rooms from around ¥6000. More upmarket hotels can be found on and around Chūō-dōri. There is no youth hostel in Takamatsu and the nearest one at Yashima (see p.609) is very basic.

**Kawaroku**, Hyaken-machi (☎0878/21-5666, fax 21-7301). The city's top ryokan has excellent *tatami* rooms, and decent Western-style accommodation, but is disappointingly modern (the original was bombed during World War II), though an attempt has been made to add some old-style ambience with raked gravel gardens on the lobby roof, overlooked by some of the guest rooms. ⑦.

**Rihga Hotel Zest Takamatsu**, 9-1 Furujin-machi (☎0878/22-3555, fax 22-7516). The upmarket *Rhiga* is pleasantly designed, has comfortable, good-value rooms and three restaurants, as well as being conveniently located near the entertainment district on Chūō-dōri. ⑨.

**Takamatsu Grand Hotel**, 10-5-1 Kotobuki-chō (☎0878/51-5757, fax 21-9422). Good-value upmarket hotel, close to the JR station and castle park, and with excellent views of the port and nearby islands from the top-floor *Yashima* restaurant. ⑨–⑥.

**Takamatsu Terminal Hotel**, 10-17 Nishinomaru-chō (☎0878/22-3731, fax 22-0749). Western- and Japanese-style rooms are available at this clean and reasonably priced business hotel. Some rooms have a sofa that can be turned into a bed if you want to share a room between three and bring the cost down. ⑨.

**Takamatsu Tōkyū Inn**, 9-9 Hyogo-machi (☎0878/21-0109, fax 21-0291). Nothing fancy, but you'll find good-value rooms at this chain hotel close to the shopping and entertainment districts. ⑥.

**Takamatsu Washington Hotel**, 1-2-3 Kawara-machi (☎0878/22-7111, fax 22-7110). Upmarket business hotel, with high-standard rooms and lots of restaurants. ⑥.

**Tokiwa Honkan**, 1-8-2 Tokiwa-chō (☎0878/61-5577, fax 61-5584). The Chinese-style green tiled roof of this traditional ryokan sticks out from the mass of shops in the heart of Takamatsu. The *tatami* rooms are spacious, but a little gloomy. Meals, included in the price, are served in your room – a pity since the ryokan's highlights are the ornate dining hall, dripping in gold leaf and lacquer decoration, and the inner courtyard garden it overlooks. ⑦.

**Urban Hotel**, 2-23 Nishnomaru-chō (☎0878/21-1011, fax 21-1012). Basic business hotel at two locations close to the train station, with Western- and Japanese-style rooms. They're well furnished, with small en-suite bathrooms and coin-operated TVs. ⑨.

**Wakaba Business Hotel**, 2-20 Uchi-machi (☎0878/23-7177, fax 23-7182). Modern business hotel close to the Mitsukoshi department store. The small but smart rooms are a cut above others in this range. ⑨.

# The City

Takamatsu's highlight, Ritsurin-kōen, is 2km south down Chūō-dōri from the JR station, but on the way are several sights worth a stop. Just beside the Kotoden Chikkō Station, opposite the JR station, is the entrance to **Tamamo-kōen** (daily 9am–5pm; ¥150), a park which contains the ruins of the castle **Takamatsu-jō**. Four hundred years ago this was one of the three major Japanese fortresses protected by sea, with three rings of moats surrounding the central keep. There's little left of the original buildings today – just a couple of turrets and parts of the moat, and the grounds are only a ninth of their original size. Still, it's a pleasant enough park, with winding pathways and a fantastic display of blossom on the cherry trees in spring. If you climb the raised mound of the keep, you'll get a great view out across the Inland Sea.

South of the park, heading down Chūō-dōri, are the main commercial, entertainment and shopping districts of Takamatsu, threaded through with covered shopping arcades – one of which is said to be the longest (at 2.7km) in Japan. Just off Chūō-dōri on Bijutsukan-dōri is the modern **Takamatsu City Museum of Art** (Tues–Sun 9am–5pm; ¥200). The small permanent collection includes Sanuki lacquerware and Western and Japanese contemporary art. There's also a library of art books and videos – some in English – and the spacious entrance hall is sometimes used for dance and music performances. A fifteen-minute walk further down Chūō-dōri will bring you to the main entrance to the gardens of Ritsurin-kōen.

### Ritsurin-kōen

At the foot of Mount Shuin lies Takamatsu's biggest draw, **Ritsurin-kōen** (daily 7am–5pm; ¥350), at 750,000 square metres, the largest garden in Japan. Three feudal lords had a hand in constructing these gardens over a period of one hundred years, starting in the early seventeenth century. In the following century Ritsurin became the private gardens of the powerful Matsudaira family and was opened to the public in 1875. The gardens were designed to present magnificent vistas throughout the seasons, from an arched red bridge amid a snowy landscape in winter, to ponds full of purple and white irises in early summer.

You're most likely to enter the park from the East Gate, a twenty-minute walk from the port. Alternatively you can take the bus from platform 2 outside the *Takamatsu Grand Hotel* (¥220) to the East Gate. JR trains stop at least once an hour at Ritsurin-kōen Kita-guchi, one minute's walk from the North Gate – a quieter entrance to the park. At the East Gate, there is an **information booth** where you can pick up a free English map of the gardens and buy tickets, at a modest discount, combining entrance with tea in the Kikugetsu-tei Pavilion (see opposite). Ignore the shabby zoo to the left of the East Gate, and head instead for the **Sanuki Folkcraft Museum** (daily 8.45am–4.30pm, Wed until 4pm; free), worth checking out for its good examples of local basketwork, ceramics and furniture and especially its huge, brightly painted banners and kites. By contrast, the rather pompously named Centre for the Encouragment of Commerce and Industry – housed in an impressive two-storey traditional building – is little more than a glorified gift shop.

From the East Gate you can either follow a route through the Nantei (South Garden) to the left or Hokutei (North Garden) to the right, though your priority will probably be to head in the opposite direction to the many tour groups that descend daily on the park. The more stylized **Nantei** garden has paths around three lakes, dotted with islands sprouting carefully pruned pine trees. The highlight here is the delightful *Kikugetsu-tei,* or "Scooping the Moon" **teahouse**, overlooking the South Lake. Dating from around 1640 and named after a Tang-dynasty Chinese poem, the teahouse exudes tranquility, with its empty *tatami* rooms with screens pulled back to reveal perfect garden views. The Nantei also has the less elaborate, more secluded *Higurashi-tei* teahouse set in a shady forest.

The **Hokutei** has a more natural appearance, and is based around two ponds – the Fuyosho-ike, dotted with lotus flowers, and the Gunochi-ike, where feudal lords once hunted ducks and which now blooms with irises in June. Keep an eye out for the Tsuru Kame no Matsu, just to the left of the main park building, a black pine tree shaped like a crane spreading its wings and considered to be the most beautiful of the 29,190 trees in the gardens. Behind this is a line of pines called the "Byōbu-matsu", after the folding-screen painting (*byōbu*) they are supposed to resemble.

## Eating, drinking and nightlife

Takamatsu has a wide range of **restaurants** and **cafés**, many conveniently concentrated around the central arcade district, just off Chūō-dōri. Like Shikoku's other seaside cities, this is a great place to sample fish and **seafood** – in some restaurants served, still wriggling, on your plate. The other local speciality is **sanuki udon**, thick white noodles usually served with a separate flask of stock and condiments. For snacks and fast food, there's a *Willie Winkie* bakery at the station (as there is at all major JR stations in Shikoku) which serves up freshly baked pastries, cakes and sandwiches. There are also a couple of branches of *Mr Donuts* and *McDonald's* around town.

*Est,* 2-3-4 Tokiwa-chō, is a laid-back **bar** which also serves food – the English-speaking owner here, Toshi, spins soul classics from his impressive record collection and cooks up decent versions of Italian dishes. Worth checking out later in the evening is *Goddes* at 1-1 Kameichō. Set in a back room of Big hairdressers, this cosy place has no cover charge, prices all its drinks at ¥500, has walls you can scribble on and live music at the weekends.

Takamatsu's **nightlife** centres around the dense, neon-lit grid of streets radiating from the Marugame-machi arcade, filled mainly with small, pricey bars. There aren't many clubs; one that's worth checking out is the *Blue Moon*, 2-8-44 Kawaramachi, on the sixth floor, which occasionally has live bands. Entry is ¥2500 including one drink – pick up a flier from *Est* for the DJ schedule. There are several **cinemas** around the Tokiwa arcade that show English-language films; you'll find details of what's showing and of other events in town in *Kagawa Journal*, available from I-PAL (see p.603).

### Restaurants and cafés

**German Bakery**, Tokiwa Arcade. In the square behind the police box at the end of the Tokiwa arcade, this pleasant, European-style café attracts office workers and students with its cakes and lunch-time set menus. Around ¥800 for lunch. Daily 9am–7.30pm.

**Grill Yama**, Lion arcade. Plenty of red meat on offer at this restaurant which specializes in steak dishes. There's an open kitchen and set menus including rice, salad and a glass of wine start at ¥2000.

**Kaname-zushi**, Lion arcade. Smart sushi shop on a corner halfway down the arcade. Does good-value evening set meals of sushi, tempura, sashimi and fried fish for ¥1500.

**Kamaizumi**, Ferry-dōri. One of Takamatsu's best *sanuki udon* restaurants, where you can see the noodles being made in the shop window each afternoon. There's a picture menu and the set meals are good value at around ¥1500. Look for the huge red paper lantern hanging outside the entrance.

**Kikugetsu-tei**, Ritsurin-kōen. The best way to fully appreciate Ritsurin-kōen's beautiful "Scooping the Moon" teahouse is to sip *sencha* (green tea) for ¥510 or *matcha* (powdered green tea) for ¥710. You can buy a ticket at either of the garden's gates, which will get you into the grounds and entitle you to a cup of tea at a small discount.

**Macou's Bagel Café**. Close to I-PAL, this is one of the hippest places to hang out in Takamatsu. Authentic bagels are freshly made on the premises, and served up with an imaginative range of fillings, either to eat in or take away. Also does a properly frothy cappuccino. Ideal for breakfast, lunch or a late cuppa, since it's open daily 7.30am–midnight.

**Spice Kingdom**, corner of Minamishin-machi and Tokiwa arcades. This second-floor Indian chain restaurant, decorated in dusky pink drapes, does the full range of classic dishes, has a picture menu and a copy of the English-language *Daily Yomiuri* to leaf through. The set lunches are good value at ¥850 (dinner is around ¥2000) and the curries are available in different grades of spiciness.

**Tenkatsu**, Nishizumi Hiroba, Hyogo-machi (☎0878/21-5380). Reputable fish restaurant in the square at the far west end of the Hyogo-machi arcade. The interior is dominated by a central sunken tank around which you can sit either at the jet black counter bar or in *tatami* booths. Kimono-clad waitresses will bring you your pick of the fish served raw or cooked in *nabe* stews. Expect to fork out at least ¥3000 per head, but the experience is worth it.

**Uo Ichiba**, Hyaken-machi. Colourfully decorated, lively restaurant on several floors, just off the Marugame-machi arcade, with a circular wooden tank of fish ready for the picking. Lunchtime set menus start as low as ¥900, but dinner is considerably more expensive.

## Listings

**Airlines** Both ANA (☎0878/25-0135) and JAL (☎0878/22-2323) have offices at the north end of Chūō-dōri, five minutes from the JR station. JAS is at 1-1-5 Banchō (☎0878/26-1111).

**Banks and exchange** The main branch of Hyakujyushi Bank is at 5-1 Kameichō; Kagawa Bank is at 6-1 Kameichō; and Mitsui Shintaku Bank is at 9-4 Konya-machi. Fuji Bank, 7-10 Marugame-machi, changes US dollars only.

**Bike rental** From the rent-a-cycle shop beside the *Willie Winkie* bakery outside the JR Takamatsu station.

**Bookshops** Miawake, 4-8 Marugame-chō (daily 9am–8pm), has a good selection of English-language books and magazines on the fifth floor.

**Car rental** Eki Rent-a-car Shikoku, 1-10 Hamanchō (☎0878/21-1341); X Rent-a-lease Kagawa, 4-1 Uchi-machi (☎0878/23-3741); Toyota Rent-a-lease Kagawa, 2-2-5 Kotobuki-chō (☎0878/51-0100).

**Hospitals and clinics** Kagawa Kenritsu Chūō Byōin (Prefectural Central Hospital) is at 5-4-16 Banchō (☎0878/35-2222).

**Laundry** Flower Coin Laundry, 1-11-15 Hananomiya-chō is open daily 8am–10pm.

**Police** The main police station is at 4-1-10 Banchō (☎0878/33-2111). Emergency numbers are listed in Basics on p.70.

**Post office** The main post office is at the north end of the Marugame arcade, opposite the Mitsukoshi department store. Opening hours are Mon–Fri 9am–7pm, Sat 9am–5pm, Sun 9am–12.30pm.

**Shopping** Sanuki lacquerware and papier-mâché dolls are the main local crafts. Apart from the gift shop in Ritsurin-kōen, shops in the arcades and the Mitsukoshi and Sogō department stores are the best places for souvenirs.

**Taxis** Try Okawa Taxi (☎0878/51-3358) or Tosan (☎0878/21-0777).

**Travel agencies** The main JTB office (☎0878/51-4981) is on Chūō-dōri close to Chūō-kōen. The assistants speak some English.

# Yashima

Twenty minutes by train to the east of Takamatsu lies **YASHIMA**, a 293-metre-high plateau formed from volcanic lava, and best reached by cable car. The name literally means "rooftop island" (which thousands of years ago it once was) and it was here that, in 1185, the Taira and Minamoto clans famously battled to determine who ruled Japan (see "History", p.771). A small detachment of Minamoto forces surprised the Taira by attacking from the land side of the peninsula – the Taira had expected the attack to come from the sea. Within a month the Taira were defeated at the battle of Dannoura and forced to flee to the mountainous hinterland of Shikoku.

JR trains run at least every hour to Yashima station, from where it's a ten-minute walk north to the base of the plateau. More convenient is the Kotoden line as the Kotoden Yashima station is only a couple of minutes' walk to the plateau, and to the outdoor Shikoku Mura museum. A bus also runs from outside the *Takamatsu Grand Hotel* directly to the top of the plateau three times a day (35min; ¥740).

Yashima's rather antiquated **cable car** takes five minutes (daily 8am–5.40pm, every 20min; ¥700 one way, ¥1300 return) to reach the park on the top of the plateau. You can also hike up a steep winding path starting to the west of the cable-car station. Once at the top, apart from the stunning views (weather permitting) of the Inland Sea, you might be a little disappointed. On the southern ridge of the plateau are some rather dingy tourist hotels, souvenir shops, and the tacky Yashima Sanjo Aquarium, where dolphins and sea lions are kept in appallingly small pools. More appealing is **Yashima-ji**, a temple supposedly constructed in 754, and which is number 84 on the Shikoku pilgrimage. Look out for the sexual granite carvings of racoons next to the temple. Yashima-ji's Treasure House (daily 9am–5pm; ¥500) is worth popping into for its collection of screens, pottery and a mixed bag of relics from the battle between the Heike and Genji. There's also a traditional garden worth inspecting behind the Treasure House, with the distinctly unbloody "Pond of Blood", believed to be the spot where the Genji soldiers cleansed their swords.

By far the best reason for visiting Yashima is **Shikoku Mura** (daily: April–Oct 8.30am–5pm, Jan–March, Nov & Dec 8.30am–4.30pm; ¥800), which lies at the base of the plateau, five minutes' walk to the east of the cable-car station. Twenty-one traditional houses and buildings were relocated here from across the island, and a cleverly landscaped park links the buildings. The park starts with a replica of the Iya Valley's Kazura-bashi, a bridge made of vines and bamboo which crosses a pond to a traditional thatched-roof Kabuki theatre from Shōdo-shima. Plays are occasionally performed here – check with the tourist information office in Takamatsu (see p.603). Look out also for the circular Sato Shime Goya (Sugar press hut) with a conical roof – a unique feature for Japanese architecture. There's also a guardhouse of the Marugame clan, and a fisherman's hut, complete with a couple of boats. Each of the houses has an English explanation of its history.

### Practicalities

Being so close to Takamatsu, there's little reason to search for **accommodation** at Yashima. If you're desperate though, head for the *Takamatsu Yashima Sansō Youth Hostel*, 77-4 Yashima Naka-machi (☎0878/41-2318; ①), next to the entrance to Shikoku Mura. This is a run-down place, with grubby futons in the small *tatami* dorm rooms, and no meals. Fortunately there are several good **restaurants** nearby. *Ikkaku*, a minute's walk east of the Kotoden Yashima station, is an ultra-modern beer hall, specializing in spicy chicken, served on silver platters with leaves of raw cabbage, at around ¥1000 a head. Wash it down with a beer (¥850 for a large glass), brewed on the premises. *Waraya* is a justly famous *sanuki udon* restaurant at the foot of the plateau next to Shikoku Mura. The main building has a thatched roof and a water wheel and gets so busy that there's an overflow section in a temporary wooden building in the car park. You sit at shared tables and slurp the noodles (¥380) from large wooden bowls.

## Shōdo-shima

The third largest island in the Inland Sea, **Shōdo-Sshima** is also one of the most interesting to visit, with splendid natural scenery and some worthwhile sights. The moutainous, forested island styles itself as a Mediterranean retreat, and has whitewashed windmills and mock Grecian ruins strategically placed in its terraced olive groves. But native culture also gets a look in since Shōdo-shima – which translates as "island of small beans" – promotes its own version of Shikoku's 88 temple pilgrimage and its connection with the classic Japanese book and movie *Nijūshi-no-Hitomi* (Twenty-four Eyes), the anti-war tale of a teacher and her twelve young charges set on Shōdo-shima between the 1920s and 1950s, written by local author Tsuboi Sakae.

Outside of July and August, and especially mid-week, Shōdo-shima makes a delightfully peaceful escape, and you may find yourself tempted to linger. However, the main sights can be covered in a day. If you're short of time, it's best to start exploring at the main port of **Tonoshō** and then head up into the mountains on the bus bound for the 612-metre-high spot of Kanka-kei. Along the way the bus stops for thirty minutes at **Choshi-kei** monkey park (daily 8am–5pm; ¥370), where apes from Africa, Southeast Asia and South America are kept in cages while the local wild monkeys roam free. It's rather unsettling to be surrounded by so many monkeys, especially as the apes often fight viciously among themselves over the food. The bus makes a five-minute stop at a lookout point before arriving at the park at **Kanka-kei**, which has breathtaking vistas across the Inland Sea. Another way of getting here is by **cable car** (daily 8am–5pm; ¥700 one way, ¥1250 return) from Kountei a fifteen-minute bus ride from Kusakabe port on the south of the island. From the cable car you can look down into the three million-year-old granite gorge, where the rocks sprout trees that explode in a palate of brown, gold and red every October. To hike up the gorge takes fifty minutes from Kountei, and to continue up to the summit of Hoshigajō, at 817m the island's highest point, will take another hour. The youth hostel (see Practicalities, overleaf) can provide a basic hiking map in Japanese.

The best way to appreciate the indented **coast** of Shōdo-shima is to rent a bicycle or motor scooter; the seventy-kilometre circuit of the island will take you a day to cover. Along the main Highway 436 heading east from Tonoshō, lies **Olive-kōen**, a pleasant but touristy park of olive groves and fake Grecian ruins, where among other things you can buy green olive chocolate. Just as touristy, but more interesting, is the **Eigamura** film set (daily 9am–5pm; ¥630), located at the tip of a crooked isthmus sticking out into Uchinomi Bay on the south of the island. The film set was left over from the 1980s remake of *Nijūshi-no-Hitomi*, and you can wander around a re-created village, do some souvenir shopping and watch the movie. Just before Eigamura is the rustic fishing village of **Tanoura**, where the original schoolhouse that served as an inspiration for the book is also open to visitors (daily 9am–5pm; ¥200).

The east and north coasts of the island are less attractive, scattered as they are with stone quarries. At Omi and Iwagatani, however, you can see **Zannen Ishi**, "rocks which are sorry to be left behind". These huge chiselled blocks were originally ordered by Toyotomi Hideyoshi (the warlord who unified Japan) in the sixteenth century as construction materials for Ōsaka castle. Every block is stamped with the seal of the general in charge of its shipment.

### Practicalities

The best way to get to Shōdo-shima is from Takamatsu via one of the many **ferries** (1hr; ¥510 one way) and **high-speed boats** (30min; ¥1020 one way) which depart daily for several ports on the island. If you're coming from Honshū, there are also ferries from Himeji, Hinase, Kōbe, Ōsaka, Okayama and Uno. The main port of Tonoshō, on the west coast, is served by the most services. If you intend to stay at the youth hostel, take a ferry from Takamatsu to Kusabe, and if you're heading for the *Uchinomi-chō Cycling Terminal*, take the boat to Sakate.

Inside Tonoshō's ferry terminal is a **tourist information desk** (daily 8.30am–5.15pm; ☎0879/62-6256) with an assistant who speaks a little English and can provide you with an English map and bus timetables. If you're coming from Takamatsu, you can pick up information on the island from the tourist information centre there (see p.603).

**Buses** for main points around the island depart from next to the Tonoshō Port building, two minutes' walk from the ferry terminal. At the bus company office you can buy a one-day ticket for ¥1980, or a two-day ticket for ¥2550 – a good deal if you intend to make your way around the island's main sights by bus, since individual fares are expensive. The best deal for **motor scooters** is from Ryōbi Rent-a-bike (¥2990 a day including fuel; ☎0879/62-6578), near Tonoshō ferry terminal, while **bicycles** are available at either the youth hostel or the Cycling Terminal at Sakate (4hr; ¥500; mountain bike: 4hr; ¥1000).

Tonoshō has plenty of business and tourist **hotels** charging around ¥8000 per person, including two meals (a safe bet, as restaurants are thin on the ground). A slightly cheaper option is the *Maruse* (☎0879/62-2385; ④), a small, clean minshuku next to the Tonoshō post office. The real flavour of Shōdo-shima, however, is best appreciated at the smaller seaside villages along the southern coast. The friendly *Shōdo-shima Olive Youth Hostel* (☎0879/82-6161, fax 82-6060; ②), a ten-minute walk west of Kusabe port, has high-standard dorms and private *tatami* rooms for ¥4000 per person, and serves good meals. A fine alternative is the *Uchinomi-chō Cycling Terminal* (☎ & fax 0879/82-1099; ①), beside Sakate port, which has the cheapest dorm rooms on the island and is run by Yokoyama-san, president of Shōdo-shima's International Friendship Club (☎ & fax 0879/82-0469) and author of an informative free English booklet on the island. For **lunch**, try *Santarō*, next to Kusabe port, where you can enjoy a sea breeze while tucking into delicious freshly made udon noodles.

## West of Takamatsu: Marugame and Zentsū-ji

Heading west from Takamatsu, you'll first pass the lush green slopes of **Goshiikidai**, five forested peaks each believed to have a subtly different colour (which they do seem to, at sunset). Enjoy this burst of unspoilt countryside while you can; the rest of the coastline is heavily developed, a consequence of the proximity of the Seto Ōhashi.

Some 30km from Takamatsu, the port of **MARUGAME** has a few points of minor interest. The castle **Marugame-jō**, 1km south of the station, dates from 1597, and is one of only twelve left in Japan with an original wooden donjon, and the **Nakatsu Banshō-en** (daily 9.30am–5pm; ¥1000) is a pretty, Edo-period garden beside the sea. From the port you can reach the **Shiwaku Islands**, once the hideout of pirates who terrorized the Inland Sea.

At Tadotsu the railway line splits into the Yosan line, which continues around the coast to Matsuyama, and the Dosan line, which runs south to Kotohira and Kōchi. Taking the inland route and alighting one train stop before Kotohira will get you to atmospheric **Zentsū-ji**, the seventy-fifth temple on the pilgrim circuit, and featuring a picturesque five-storey pagoda, treasure hall (daily 9am–5pm; ¥500) and wooded grounds. Kōbō Daishi was born here, so the temple is one of the three most sacred places associated with the Buddhist saint (the others are Kōya-san, in Wakayama-ken, and Tō-ji in Kyoto). A map outside the JR station will direct you up the main road to the temple, a twenty-minute walk away. A visit here is well worth combining with Kotohira as a day-trip from Takamatsu.

# Kotohira

Some 30km southwest of Takamatsu, **KOTOHIRA**, with its ancient shrine Kotohira-gū – popularly known as Kompira-san – should be high on your list of places to see in Shikoku. After the Grand Shrines of Ise (see p.500), and Izumo Taisha (see p.590), Kotohira is one of the major places of pilgrimage of the Shinto religion, attracting around four million visitors a year. The town itself is pleasantly located, straddling the Kanakura-gawa at the foot of the mountain Zozu-san, so called because it is said to resemble an elephant's head (*zozu*). Kotohira can easily be visited on a day-trip from Takamatsu, one hour away by train, or en route to Kōchi or the mountainous interior.

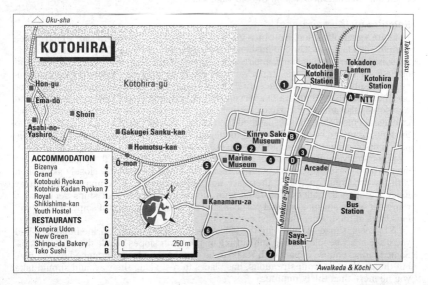

| KOTOHIRA | | |
|---|---|---|
| Kotohira | *Kotohira* | 琴平 |
| Kanamaru-za | *Kanamaru-za* | 金丸座 |
| Kinryō Sake Museum | *Kinryō-no-Sato* | 金陵の郷 |
| Kotohira-gū | *Kotohira-gū* | 琴平宮 |
| Saya-bashi | *Saya-bashi* | 鞘橋 |
| | | |
| *ACCOMMODATION* | | |
| Bizenya | *Bizenya* | 備前屋 |
| Kotobuki Ryokan | *Kotobuki Ryokan* | ことぶき旅館 |
| Kotohira Grand Hotel | *Kotohira Gurando Hoteru* | 琴平グランドホテル |
| Kotohira Royal Hotel | *Kotohira Roiyaru Hoteru* | 琴平ロイヤルホテル |
| Kotohira Youth Hostel | *Kotohira Yūsu Hosuteru* | 琴平ユースホステル |
| Shikishima-kan | *Shikishima-kan* | 敷島館 |
| | | |
| *EATING* | | |
| Konpira udon | *Konpira Udon* | こんぴらうどん |
| New Green | *Nyū Guriin* | ニューグリーン |
| Shinpu-da | *Shinpu-da* | しんぷだ |
| Tako Sushi | *Tako Sushi* | たこ寿司 |

## The Town

Kotohira is compact and easily negotiated by foot. The main sights lie across the river from the train and bus stations; this is where you'll find the approach to the shrine and the main shopping street, as well as most hotels and restaurants. If you haven't got long, head straight for the shrine, which will take you at least a couple of hours to explore fully. With more time on your hands, you could check out the Kanamaru-za, a traditional Kabuki theatre, and the old sake factory.

### Kotohira-gū (Kompira-san)

Kotohira's main attraction, **Kotohira-gū**, is usually known as "Kompira-san" which comes from the nickname for Omono-nushi-no-Mikoto, the spiritual guardian of seafarers. This is appropriate enough, since Kompira was originally Kumbhira, the Hindu crocodile god of the River Ganges, and was imported as a deity from India well before the ninth century when Kōbō Daishi chose the shrine as the spot for one of his Buddhist temples. For one thousand years Kompira-san served as both a Buddhist and Shinto holy place and was so popular among the Japanese that those who could not afford to make the pilgrimage themselves either dispatched their pet dogs, with pouches of coins as a gift to the gods, or tossed barrels of rice and money into the sea, in the hope that they would be picked up by sailors, who would take the offering to Kompira-san on their behalf.

When the Meiji Restoration began, Shinto took precedence, and the Buddhas were ousted from the shrine, along with Kompira, who was seen as too closely associated with the rival religion. While there are no representations of Kompira at the shrine today, an open-air gallery decorated with pictures and models of ships serves as a reminder of the shrine's original purpose, and the Chinese-flavour of some of the buildings hints at the former Buddhist connection.

A big deal is made of climbing the 785 steps to reach the main shrine buildings, and you'll see many people huffing and puffing on the lower slopes beside the tourist shops. Some tourists choose to part with ¥5000 to be carried up in rather cramped palanquins, but the climb is far from strenuous, has places to rest along the way, and should take you no more than thirty minutes.

The shrine grounds begin at the Ō-mon, a stone gateway just inside of which you'll pass the Gonin Byakushō – five red painted stalls, shaded by large white umbrellas. The souvenir sellers here stand in for the five farmers who were once allowed to hawk their wares in the shrine precincts. Further along to the right of the main walkway, lined with stone lanterns, are the Hōmotsu-kan (Treasure House) and the Gakugei Sankō-kan (both daily 9am–4pm; ¥200), two small museums which can be passed over in favour of the **Shoin** (daily 9am–4pm; ¥200), a study and reception hall built in 1659. You can walk around the verandahs and peer through the grills at the delicate screen paintings by the celebrated artist Okyo Maruyama (1733–1795) – look out too for the screens he painted with playing tigers, which have been designated an Important Cultural Property.

Just before climbing up to the next stage of the shrine you'll notice a giant gold ship's propeller, a gift from a local shipbuilders. At the top of the steps is the grand **Asahi-no-Yashiro** (Sunshine Shrine), dedicated to the Sun Goddess Amaterasu, decorated with intricate wood carvings of flora and fauna and topped with a green copper roof. A couple of paths lead from here to the thatched-roof **Hon-gū**, the main shrine, built in 1879 and centre of Kompira-san's daily activities. Priests and their acolytes in traditional robes rustle by along a raised wooden corridor linking the shrine buildings. Visitors bow deeply, clap their hands, toss their coins and sigh with relief on reaching here, but the hardy, and truly faithful, trudge on up a further 583 steps to the **Oku-sha**. This inner shrine, located almost at the top of Zozu-san, sports a rather cartoonish stone carving of the long-nosed demon Tengu on the side of a cliff.

Returning to the main shrine area, head for the wooden platforms for magnificent views of the surrounding countryside – on a clear day you can see as far as the Inland Sea. To the left of the main shrine is the open-air **Ema-dō** gallery, which displays votive plaques, paintings and models of ships. These are from sailors who hope to be granted good favour on the seas. The commendations extend to one from Japan's first cosmonaut, a TV journalist who was a paying passenger on a Russian Soyuz launch in 1990.

## Other sights

Kotohira's other sights include the **Takadōrō Lantern**, an intriguing wooden tower next to the Kotoden station, which was built in 1856 and served as a warning beacon in times of trouble. Also worth a look is the **Kinryō Sake Museum** (daily 9am–5pm; ¥310), located at the start of the shrine approach. There has been a sake brewery on this spot since 1616, and the buildings arranged around a large courtyard have been kept pretty much as they have always been. Inside, the exhibition runs step by step through the sake-making process, using life-size displays. Ask for the leaflet with an English explanation. You can also sample three types of sake, at ¥100 per shot.

Closer to the shrine steps, a road to the left leads past the lacklustre Marine Museum (daily 9am–5pm; ¥400) up the hill to the **Kanamaru-za** (Mon & Wed–Sun 9am–4pm; ¥500). This performance hall, built in 1835, is said to be the oldest surviving Kabuki theatre in Japan and was fully restored when it was moved to this location from the center of Kotohira in 1975. Plays are only peformed here in April, but the theatre itself merits a visit, especially for its wooden-beamed and lantern-lit auditorium.

Just before the turning up the hill to the Kanamaru-za, a twisting path leads down to the river, and if you head south along the banks, you'll soon come to the **Saya-bashi**, an attractive arched wooden bridge with a copper-covered roof. The bridge is only used during the grand Otaisai festival, in which sacred *mikoshi* are paraded through the town, held every October.

# Practicalities

Arriving from Takamatsu by JR **train**, you'll pull into Kotohira Station, a ten-minute walk northeast of the town centre. Inside the station look for the travel agency (daily

9am–5pm) next to the ticket window, from where you can pick up a **map** of the town – no English is spoken here. To the left as you exit the station there's a cloakroom where left luggage costs ¥200 per bag (daily 6.30am–9pm). If you've travelled by Kotoden train from Takamatsu, you'll arrive at the smaller station closer to the town centre on the banks of the Kanekura-gawa. **Buses** from Takamatsu terminate at the bus station at the eastern end of the covered shopping arcade leading to the main approach to the shrine. Drivers should take Route 32 west from Takamatsu to reach Kotohira in around one hour.

## Accommodation

**Accommodation** in Kotohira is in high demand, and prices rise by as much as fifty percent at weekends and public holidays. The town is famed for its top-notch ryokan, several of which line the main approach to Kotohira-gū. Although the ryokan are pricey, it's worth remembering that their rates also cover two meals and personal service. Those on a tight budget should consider staying at the youth hostel in Awa Ikeda (see p.623), 20km to the south; Kotohira's youth hostel (the only cheap place to stay) is depressingly shabby.

**Bizenya** (☎0877/75-4131, fax 75-4133). The friendly manager speaks a little English at this large ryokan at the start of the main approach to the shrine steps. There's a traditional garden and a large communal bath. ⑦.

**Kotobuki Ryokan** (☎ & fax 0877/73-3872). The best deal in Kotohira. A charming, small ryokan, run by a friendly young couple, that oozes with tradition. Conveniently located, right by the river and the shopping arcade. Very good value considering the rates include two meals. ⑤.

**Kotohira Grand Hotel** (☎0877/75-3218, fax 73-5669). On the slopes of Zozu-san, this large hotel has both Japanese and Western-style rooms and is convenient for the shrine and the Kabuki theatre. It's comfortable enough, but slightly old-fashioned. ⑧.

**Kotohira Royal Hotel** (☎0877/75-1000, fax 75-0600). The town's most modern hotel is set back from the river on the approach to the shrine. Designed to accommodate busloads of pilgrims, it's a touch impersonal, though the large rooms offer good value in this price range. ⑦.

**Kotohira Youth Hostel** (☎0877/73-3836). This run-down, old-style hostel, with drafty, echoing rooms and bunk beds, is the only budget accommodation in Kotohira. The building is on a side road just a little lower down the hill from the Kabuki theatre, a 15min walk from the train stations. ①.

**Shikishima-kan** (☎0877/75-5111, fax 73-2617). The wonderfully ornate carved wooden exterior of this traditional ryokan is, unfortunately, not matched inside; the rooms are gloomy and have seen better days. ⑦.

## Eating and drinking

The best advice for **lunch** in Kotohira is to pack a picnic and enjoy it with the view from Kompira-san. You can stock up on supplies at *Shinpu-da*, a bakery on the route from the JR station to the shrine, serving rolls, sandwiches and cakes. The ryokan-lined approach to the shrine also has several tourist restaurants, many with stout ladies outside shouting the praises of the food inside. Try *Konpira Udon*, where the speciality is *shōyu udon*, thick noodles topped with dried fish flakes and bits of tempura batter – you add your own soy sauce – for ¥500 a bowl. Closer to the shopping arcade, on the corner beside the bridge, is the *New Green*, a quirkily decorated café which serves both Japanese and Western food and does good-value set menus for ¥700 – it's open until 9pm, so is also good for dinner. For a more traditional setting, try *Tako Sushi*, easily spotted on the main shopping street by the large red octopus (*tako*) above the door. Apart from sushi (a set plate costs ¥800), the restaurant also does the usual noodle dishes.

# Tokushima and around

Built on the delta of the Yoshino-gawa – Shikoku's longest river – and bisected by the Shinmachi-gawa, **TOKUSHIMA**, the capital of Tokushima-ken, is known across Japan

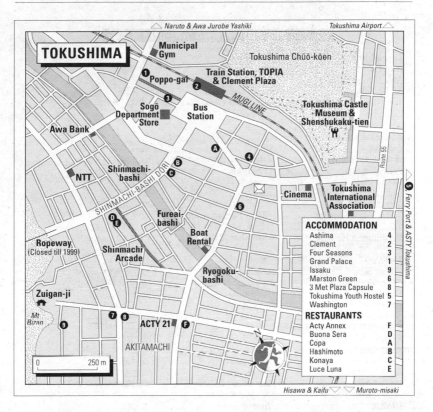

△ Naruto & Awa Jurobe Yashiki　　Tokushima Airport △

**TOKUSHIMA**

Municipal Gym

Tokushima Chūō-kōen

① Poppo-gai　　Train Station, TOPIA & Clement Plaza ②

MUGI LINE

③

Sogō Department Store

Bus Station

Tokushima Castle Museum & Shenshukaku-tien

Awa Bank

Ⓐ

④

Route 55

Shinmachi-bashi

Ⓑ

NTT

Ⓒ

SHINMACHI-BASHI DORI

⑤ Ferry Port & ASTY Tokushima

Cinema

Tokushima International Association

Fureai-bashi

Ⓓ Ⓔ

Boat Rental

⑥

Ropeway (Closed till 1999)

Shinmachi Arcade

Ryogoku-bashi

**ACCOMMODATION**
| | |
|---|---|
| Ashima | 4 |
| Clement | 2 |
| Four Seasons | 3 |
| Grand Palace | 1 |
| Issaku | 9 |
| Marston Green | 6 |
| 3 Met Plaza Capsule | 8 |
| Tokushima Youth Hostel | 5 |
| Washington | 7 |

**RESTAURANTS**
| | |
|---|---|
| Acty Annex | F |
| Buona Sera | D |
| Copa | A |
| Hashimoto | B |
| Konaya | C |
| Luce Luna | E |

Zuigan-ji

Mt Bizan

⑨

⑦ ⑧

ACTY 21 Ⓕ

AKITAMACHI

N

0 ⸻ 250 m

Hisawa & Kaifu ▽ ▽ Muroto-misaki

for its summer **dance festival** (the Awa Odori), which is attended every year by over one million people. The city has other attractions besides the festival: the high-tech **ASTY** crafts and exhibition centre; the historic **Awa Jūrōbē Yashiki**, where Bunraku puppet performances are held; and Akitamachi, the lively entertainment district. The opening in 1998 of the Akashi Kaikyō Ōhashi – providing a new road route from Honshū to Shikoku, via Awaji-shima (p.621) – is bringing more visitors and development to Tokushima, but for the time being it remains a laid-back, friendly place.

Tokushima also makes a good jumping-off point from which to explore the rest of the prefecture. North of the city are the whirlpools of **Naruto** and several **craft villages**, while the island of **Awaji-shima** has some attractive beaches and is worth considering as an alternative route to Shikoku from Kōbe. Heading south, there's the pretty coastal village of **Hiwasa**, where turtles lay their eggs on the beach each summer and, across the border in Kōchi-ken, the jagged cape at **Muroto**. Inland to the west are mountains, which cover eighty percent of the prefecture, the spectacular **Iya Valley**, the gorge at **Ōboke** and the **Kazura-bashi**, an ancient bridge made of vines and bamboo.

Tokushima (meaning "virtuous island"), was named by Hachisuka Iemasa, a supporter of the warlord Toyotomi Hideyoshi. Hachisuka built his castle here in the 1586, and his clan ruled the area until the fall of the Tokugawa Shogunate in 1867. The following year the prefecture of Tokushima-ken was established.

## Arrival, information and accommodation

**Trains** from Takamatsu via the Kotoku line, and from Kōchi via the Dosan and Tokushima lines, pull in at Tokushima Station, next to the Clement Plaza shopping centre, at the head of Shinmachibashi-dōri, the main thoroughfare. Tokushima's **airport** (☎0886/23-5111) lies 8km north of the city centre. Buses from here to the city's bus terminal, in front of

Clement Plaza, take 25 minutes and cost ¥430. The city's sights are all within easy walking distance of the train and bus stations. **Ferries** from several locations on Honshū and the **hydrofoil** from Kansai International Airport dock at the port, 3km east of centre, and fifteen minutes by bus. **Buses** for around the city and further afield arrive and depart from the bus terminal outside Clement Plaza; there's an information office to help you find the right platform.

For **information** on the city and prefecture, head for the Tokushima Prefecture International Exchange Association (TOPIA), on the sixth floor of Clement Plaza (daily 10am–6pm; ☎0886/56-3303). Staff here are helpful and speak English and there's a small library of English books and magazines and information on other parts of Japan. Offering a similar service, but in a less convenient location, is the Tokushima International Association (Mon–Fri 9am–6pm; ☎0886/22-6066), one block beyond the city hall to the east of the JR station.

## Accommodation

Tokushima has a decent range of **accommodation**, most of it of a high standard and conveniently located around the JR station. More cheap business hotels can be found across the river, the Shinmachi-gawa, about five minutes' walk from the station. The only time of year you'll have to **book** well in advance is during the Awa Odori in August. If you're having problems finding somewhere to stay, pop into TOPIA (see above), who can make enquiries for you. The closest youth hostel is a thirty-minute bus journey south of the city, and has a delightful beachside location.

**Ashima**, 2-26 Ichiban-chō (☎0886/53-6151). Small business hotel, close to the station, with rooms that are a cut above others in this range. The management is friendly and there's a coffee shop next to the lobby. ④.

**Hotel Clement**, 1-16 Terashima Honchō Nishi (☎0886/56-3111, fax 56-3132). Right beside the JR station, this glitzy hotel has spacious and tastefully furnished rooms. There is a roof-top swimming pool, an 18th-floor bar with a view of Mount Bizan, and Chinese, French and Japanese restaurants on the premises. ⑤.

**Four Seasons**, 1-54 Terashima Honchō Nishi (☎0886/22-2203, fax 56-6083). Small, stylish business hotel, a minute's walk west of the station, where the young English-speaking chef rustles up a special curry-rice dish in the attached café. ④.

**Grand Palace**, 1-60 Terashima Honchō Nishi (☎0886/26-1111). Upmarket hotel going for the sleek black look in a big way. The lobby is all gleaming surfaces and odd angles and the rooms are large with decent-sized en-suite bathrooms. ④.

**Isaku**, 1 Igachō (☎0886/22-1392, fax 23-8764). Just to left of Zuigan-ji temple, this is one of the most traditional ryokans in Tokushima. Japanese only is spoken, but the *tatami* rooms are very nice, and there's an ornamental garden. Rates include two meals. ⑦.

**Marston Green**, 1-12 Honmachi (☎0886/54-1777, fax 52-8104). The green theme is carried through the building in its unimpressive decor. There's a small restaurant and a swimming pool and sauna in the basement, which cost an extra ¥500. ④.

**Hotel Sunroute Tokushima**, 1-12 Tomidahama (☎0886/26-0311, fax 54-7765). Business hotel, part of a nationwide chain, beside the Shinmachi-gawa and handy for Tokushima's Akitamachi entertainment district. The rooms are pretty standard. ④.

**3 Met Plaza Capsule**, 1-8 ōmichi (☎0886/22-1177). Men-only 24hr sauna and capsule hotel, next to the Akitamachi entertainment district. Not as seedy as some capsule hotels can be. Overnight stays are available from 4pm–10am. ②.

**Tokushima Youth Hostel**, 7-1 Hama, Ohara-machi (☎0886/63-1505, fax 63-2407). Next to a cresent-shaped stretch of beach fringed by pine trees, this hostel has a peaceful location and friendly, English-speaking management. Meals are available, and bikes can be rented for ¥800 a day. Take the bus bound for Omiko, the last one leaving from outside Tokushima Station at 6.05pm. You'll then have to catch the bus to Omiko-guchi and walk the remaining 3km to the beach. ①.

**Tōkyū Inn**, 1-24 Motomachi (☎0886/26-0109, fax 26-0686). Not much to look at from the outside, with slightly old-fashioned, but good-value rooms, in a convenient location close to the JR station. ⑤.

**Washington Hotel**, 1-61-1 Ōmichi (☎0886/53-7111, fax 54-3111). Another of the upmarket identik-it business hotels that can be relied on for efficient service and standards. The rooms are nothing special, but the lobby coffee shop is a light, popular spot, which gives free coffee refills. ⑨.

## The City

Five minutes' walk to the east of the JR station is the attractive **Tokushima Chūō-kōen**, a park on the site of the fortress of *daimyō* Hachisuka Iemasa, built in 1586. His clan lived in the castle for the next 280 years and created the town that is now Tokushima. The building was destroyed in 1896 and all that remains of the castle today are a few stone walls, part of the moat and the Shenshuku-tien, a beautiful formal garden, which has been designated a national scenic spot. Beside the garden is the small **Tokushima Castle Museum** (Tues–Sun 9:30am–5pm; ¥300), with informative, modern displays explaining the history of the Hachisuka clan and a large model which gives a good idea of what the castle and its surrounding compound once looked like.

Walking directly south out of the JR station along the main road brings you to Tokushima's river, the Shinmachi-gawa. There are several bridges and prettily designed promenades, with places to sit and some clever pieces of modern sculpture – look out for the street mosaics of Awa Odori dancers reflected in the metallic bollards on the bridge Shinmachi-bashi. Boats can be rented from ¥500 for thirty minutes at a booth beside the Ryogoku-bashi.

Five minutes' walk south of the river is the base of the 280-metre-high **Mount Bizan**. On a clear day, it's worth hiking up to the mountain top; a route starts from the temple to the left of the cable-car station at the end of Shinmachibashi-dōri. At the summit there's a park with a pagoda monument to the soldiers who served in Burma during the war and the mariginally interesting Moraesu-kan **museum** (daily except Tues

---

### THE DANCING FOOLS

Every year, in mid-August, many Japanese return to their family homes for **O-bon** (Festival of the Dead), which is as much a celebration as remembrance of the deceased. Towns all over the country hold *bon* dances, but none can compare to Tokushima's **Awa Odori** – the "great dance of Awa" – a four-day festival, which runs every year from August 12 to 15. Over 1.3 million spectators and 80,000 participants, dressed in colourful *yukata* (summer kimono) and half-moon-shaped staw hats, parade throughout the city, waving their hands and shuffling their feet to an insistent two-beat rhythm, played on *taiko* drums, flutes and *shamisen* (traditional stringed instruments). With plenty of street parties and side shows, this is as close as Japan gets to Rio's Mardis Gras.

The history of the Awa Odori goes back to 1587, when the first *daimyō* of Tokushima, Hachisuka Iemasa, is said to have initiated the celebration on the completion of his castle. The people enjoyed themselves so much that the party was held again the following year, and so on for the centuries that followed. The festival only became known as the Awa Odori after World War II, and it now also attracts participants from abroad. Some feel the festival has become too big and organized – for example, there are now viewing stands for which you must purchase tickets. But there's still plenty of fun to be had – mostly from mingling with the dancers, who famously chant, "The dancing fool and the watching fool are equally foolish. So why not dance?".

If you plan to attend the festival, book your accommodation well in advance or arrange to stay in one of the nearby towns and travel in for the dances which start at 6pm and finish at 10.30pm (street parties continue well into the night). If you fancy taking part as a dancer, contact the Tokushima International Association (see p.617), which organizes a dance group on one of the festival nights.

9am–5pm; ¥200), dedicated to Wenceslāo de Morães, a Portuguese naval officer and former consul-general in Kōbe who wrote many books on Japan.

A better use of time would be to walk east around the base of Bi-zan from the cable-car station to the delightful Buddhist temple, **Zuigan-ji**. The street approaching the temple has an ornamental stream running down one side and you can see a picturesque red pagoda poking out of the mountainside woods. Built in the Momoyama-style, Zuigan-ji dates from 1614 and has an elegant traditional garden with carp-filled pools, a waterfall and rock paths across mossy lawns.

If you're not in town at the right time for the Awa Odori, the next best thing is to make your way to the **ASTY Tokushima**, a state-of-the-art conference and exhibition hall, some 2km southeast of Tokushima Station (the name stands for Attractive Space in Tokushima Yamashiro). Head for the second floor of the complex, where you'll find the **Experience Tokushima Area** (daily 9am–5pm, closed third Tues of the month; ¥900), an impressive exhibition with high-tech devices, including simulated bus, bike and windsurf rides. The highlight is a 360-degree cinema in which you are surrounded by the story of three childhood friends who are reunited as adults at the Awa Odori, travelling from some of the prefecture's most scenic locations in the process. Outside the cinema, assistants will help you practice the festival dance routines and play the instruments. Look out for the *ningyō jōruri* section, where puppets are displayed, and shows are performed daily by robots and at the weekends by human puppeteers. Also worth checking out is the "arts village" (*Kōgei mura*) – a large shopping area where you can watch, and participate in, the making of local crafts, including *washi* paper, indigo dying and lacquer work. There are regular buses from the bus terminal to ASTY which take ten minutes. The centre has several restaurants.

If you're interested in Bunraku puppetry, known locally as *ningyō jōruri*, head for the historic premises of the Jūrobei family, **Awa Jūrōbē Yashiki** (daily 8.30am–5pm; ¥350), 4km to the north of Tokushima Station. This former *samurai* residence, with an enclosed garden and display room of beautifully made antique puppets, was once the home of the tragic figure Jūrōbē, immortalized in *Keisei Awa no Naruto*, the epic eighteenth-century play by Chikamatsu. You can see part of the play performed here, usually the classic scene where the Jūrōbē's wife Oyumi turns away their daughter Otsuru as a stranger. Live performances are held in the wooden outdoor theatre on Saturdays and Sundays at 3pm, and between April and November at 10.30am on Sunday (call ☎0886/65-2202 first to check). A video of the play is also shown inside a large *tatami* hall. To reach the building, take a fifteen-minute bus journey from platform seven at the bus terminal.

## Eating, drinking and nightlife

Fot the best choice of **restaurants**, make your way to the Clement Plaza, next to Tokushima Station; there are several places on the fifth floor serving Japanese, Chinese and Western food, as well as an outlet of *Spice Kingdom* (daily 11am–9.30pm), with good Indian curries and other dishes. The major hotels in town do inexpensive buffet lunches – *Café Clements*, on the ground floor of *Hotel Clement*, is a good bet.

For Japanese food, *Hashimoto*, a cheap soba shop, and *Konaya*, which specializes in *okonomiyaki*, can both be found along Shinmachibashi-dori, while for Italian food, you could try *Buona Sera*, on the second floor at 1 Higashi-shinmachi (☎0886/55-8472), where a meal is around ¥3000 per head. Save some space for the delicious home-made *gelato* served at the *Luce Luna* ice-cream bar (daily 11.30am–9.30pm) on the ground floor of the same building. Also worth trying is *Copa* (daily from 7.30am) a narrow café/bar close to the train station on Terashimahonchō, serving giant bagels and salads. There's a good selection of English magazines to browse through and in the evening an upstairs bar opens up, with occasional live music performances.

During the summer months, several hotels, including the *Marston Green*, have rooftop **beer gardens**. **Akitamachi**, Tokushima's lively entertainment area, bulges with bars and restaurants; a popular hangout is *Club Marrs* on the fifth floor of the Kirinsiguramu Biru, a **nightclub** which charges foreigners a bargain ¥500 entrance, including one drink, and where you'll bump into most of Tokushima's expat community. *Bar Drug Store*, on the fourth floor of the ASTY Annex, is a dark and rowdy place which plays loud music, and has the virtue of being more spacious than most other bars.

## Listings

**Airlines** ANA, 2-11 Yaoya-chō (☎0886/24-2565); JAS, 2-28 Shinmachi-bashi (☎0886/23-5111).

**Banks and exchange** The main branch of Awa Bank, beside the Kasuga-bashi, offers the full range of foreign exchange services. Dai-ichi Kangyō Bank is just off from Shinmachi-dōri, while Sanwa bank can only exchange US dollars.

**Bookshops** There's a very limited selection of English-language books at the Koyama bookstore, opposite the JR station.

**Car rental** Eki Rent-a-car (☎0886/22-1014) is in front of Tokushima Station, while Kōkō Rent-a-car (☎0886/99-6671) is at the airport; both offer similar rates.

**Hospitals and clinics** Tokushima Prefectural Central Hospital (Kenritsu Chūō Byōin), 1-10-3 Kuramoto-chō (☎0886/31-7151).

**Laundry** A short walk from the station is the Aozara coin laundry at 3-3 Nakajo-sanjima, open daily from 8am–10pm.

**Police** The main police station is close to Kachidoki-bashi (☎0886/22-3101). Emergency numbers are listed in Basics on p.70.

**Post office** The central post office is a 3min walk south of the JR station at 1-2 Yaoya-chō. Opening hours are Mon–Fri 9am–7pm, Sat 9am–5pm & Sun 9am–12.30pm.

**Shopping** Clement Plaza, beside the JR station, and Sogō department store are the best places to hunt out souvenirs and food supplies, but the main shopping arcade is the covered Higashi Shinmachi, just off Shinmachi-dōri.

**Taxis** Try the Taxi Association on ☎0886/31-8203 or Tomida Taxi on ☎0886/22-5158

**Travel agents** The main JTB office is at 1-29 Ryogoku Honmachi (☎0886/23-3181).

## Around Tokushima: craft villages and Naruto

Tokushima makes a good base for visiting local **craft factories** that specialize in indigo-dying, papermaking and pottery. **ŌTANI**, around 10km north of of the city on the JR Naruto line, is the home of Ōtani-yaki, the name given to the distinctive local pottery, which has a heavy, earthen texture and is traditionally crafted into enormous standing vessels. There are several workshops where you can try your hand at creating your own cups or plates, but you need to make an appointment first – two workshops to try are Yano Toen (☎0886/89-0023) and Harumoto Togyo Kaikan (☎0886/89-0048). Making a simple pottery cup will cost you around ¥3000.

You can learn about natural indigo dyeing at the **Aizomi-chō Historical Museum** (daily 9am–5pm; ¥300), 10km east of Tokushima near the Yoshino-gawa. In Tokushima this craft dates back at least four hundred years and until the late eighteenth century was the source of much of the area's wealth. As well as visiting the museum, with informative mini-dioramas showing the whole colouring process and examples of blue patterned cloth, you can wander around the old buildings that make up the complex and have a go at dyeing yourself – a handkerchief costs ¥500, a T-shirt ¥2800. The museum is about twenty minutes by bus from Tokushima Station (get off at Higashi Nakatomi).

Some 30km west of Tokushima is the **Hall of Awa Japanese Handmade Paper** (Tues–Sun 9am–5pm; ¥300), which holds exhibitions, sells a wide range of multicoloured papers and has a huge working space where you might catch a glimpse of master papermaker Fujimori Minoru at work. You can also make your own *washi* postcards. To get there, take the JR Tokushima line and get off at Awa Yamakawa Station, from where the hall is a fifteen-minute walk south.

**NARUTO**, around 13km north of Tokushima, marks the start on Shikoku of the 88 temple pilgrimage (see p.599), but the town is more famous for the **whirlpools** which form as the tides change and water is forced through the narrow straits between Shikoku and Awaji-shima. This is one of Tokushima's most heavily hyped attractions, but it's not an event you can bank on catching. The whirlpools are at their most dramatic on days of the full and new moon, but to avoid a wasted journey, check first on the tidal schedule with tourist information in Tokushima (see p.617). For the closest view of the whirlpools, hop on one of the **boats** that cruise daily around the whirlpools and under the Naruto-Ōhashi bridge. The trip lasts thirty minutes and costs between ¥1500 and ¥2000, depending on the boat. Again, check first with tourist information in Tokushima, as the cruises can be cancelled because of bad weather and mechanical trouble. The cheaper alternative is a bird's-eye view from Naruto-kōen, the park on Oge island, just to the north of Naruto town.

There are several trains a day from Tokushima to Naruto, taking forty minutes, and buses run regularly to the park from Naruto Station.

## Awaji-shima

Lying less than 1km off the northeastern tip of Tokushima-ken is **AWAJI-SHIMA**, the largest island in the Inland Sea after Shikoku. Best known for its largely unspoilt beaches, the island provides an escape for Kansai residents from the urban sprawl of Honshū, and is especially appealing in spring and summer, when flowers and fruit crops scent the air and colour the landscape.

Awaji-shima was at the epicentre of the Great Hanshin Earthquake of 1995 and took the brunt of the tremor's force. Luckily, the island is not nearly as populated as Kōbe, so although the damage was extensive, the loss of life was not. The most notable casualty was the new bridge, the Akashi Kaikyō Ōhashi, which grew longer by a metre as Awaji-shima moved away from Honshū. With the bridge and fast boat connections to Kansai International Airport, Awaji-shima is quickly shedding its sleepy demeanour and get-away-from-it-all atmosphere – if this is what you're after, you'd be better off visiting one of the smaller islands of the Inland Sea, such as Shōdo-shima (see p.609). The biggest changes are afoot at **Iwaya**, the landing point for the Akashi Kaikyō Ōhashi. Construction of a mountain-side park is underway behind the small fishing village and seaside spa; the focal point will be a huge arch, a present to Japan from France. This will completely dwarf Iwaya's current claim to fame: a splodge of rock next to the ferry port called **Esima-jima**, which is believed to be Japan's first island created by the ancient gods, and is so small that it's hardly worth visiting.

Of Awaji-shima's **beaches**, Ōhama, on the east of the island, is a long sandy stretch that attracts crowds during summer, and Goshiki, on the west, is pebbly but more tranquil, better for swimming and renowned for its golden sunsets.

### Practicalities

Direct **buses** from several places in central Ōsaka and Kōbe run to Awaji-shima across the Akashi Kaikyō Ōhashi, with many continuing on to Tokushima. From Tokushima, several buses a day leave from outside the bus terminal and go directly to Awaji-shima, stopping in Naruto on the way. **Ferries** run roughly every twenty minutes during the day from Akashi, on the main JR line from Kōbe, to Iwaya, and cost ¥400 one way. Buses running the length of the island (a trip of around two hours) depart from outside the ferry terminal.

There's a fairly good range of **accommodation** around the island, particulary in the tourist resorts, such as Ohama. The youth hostel (☎0799/52-0460; open March–Aug;

②), 4.5km from Fukura on the southern coast, is isolated, basic, and very institutional, but does have a splendid view across to the bridge joining the island to Shikoku. Meals are available, but if you want something tasty, pack your own food. A pricier, but good-value year-round option is *Qkamura Minami-Awaji* (☎0799/52-0291, fax 52-3651; ⑥), a national vacation village on the opposite side of Fukura Bay from the youth hostel. Accommodation is in *tatami* rooms and the rates include two meals.

## South to Hiwasa

Heading south by rail or road from Tokushima you'll be following the rugged coastline, passing by a string of small fishing villages – the best one to stop at is picturesque **HIWASA**, 55km from the city, for its intriguing temple, quaint harbour and beach. You'll see **Yakuō-ji**, the twenty-third temple on the Shikoku pilgrimage, on the hillside as you pull into the train station; the temple's base is surrounded by hotels and giftshops catering to the hordes of pilgrims who regularly pass through. Climb the steps to the main temple area, where the buildings date from 815, and you'll notice a striking statue of a goddess carrying a basket of fish and flanked by lotus blooms. Off to the right is a more recently built single-storey pagoda. There's a good view of Hiwasa's harbour from the platform, but the highlight here is to descend into the pagoda's darkened basement, where for ¥100 you can fumble your way around a pitch-black circular corridor to a central gallery containing Brügel-like painted depictions of all the tortures of hell. In a second gallery is long scroll showing the steady decay of a beautiful, but dead, young woman.

About 1km south of the harbour, the reconstructed castle **Hiwasa-jō** (daily 9am–5pm; free) is only worth visiting for its impressive view of the town. The better option is to head directly to Ōhama beach, north of the harbour, where **turtles** lay their eggs between May and August. During this time, the beach is roped off and spectators must watch the action from a distance. For a closer look at the turtles, make your way to **Hiwasa Chelonian Museum** (daily 8.30am–5pm; ¥500), beside the beach. The displays are mainly in Japanese, but are very visual, with step-by-step photos of turtles laying eggs and you'll see the turtles themselves swimming in indoor and outdoor pools.

Hiwasa is 55 minutes from Tokushima by limited express **train** or one hour and 45 minutes by the more frequent local trains, and makes a good day-trip or a stop en route to or from Muroto Misaki (see below). There's a very run-down **youth hostel** on the road to the beach (☎08847/7-0755; ①), but you're better off staying at one of the hotels near the beach – try the *White Lighthouse* (☎08847/7-1170; ⑦), where the rates include two meals in a restaurant with a good view of the beach.

## On to Kannoura and Muroto Misaki

Some 26km south of Hiwasa is **Kaifu**, a popular surfing spot, where the JR train line ends and is replaced with the private Asa Kaigan railway. You won't always have to change trains, but you will have to pay ¥260 extra to travel the remaining two stops to **KANNOURA** at the end of the line. Kannoura is a sleepy village with a pleasant stretch of gravely sand, framed with rocky outcrops. It has a surprisingly stylish **place to stay**, the *White Beach Hotel* (☎08872/9-3344 fax 9-3032; ⑦), with a decent **restaurant** serving good-value set lunches. If you want to continue south from Kannoura, you'll have to take the bus – several continue around the cape to Kōchi.

You can reach the cape, **MUROTO MISAKI**, an important stop on the pilgrimage route, by bus from either Kannoura (1hr; ¥1480) or Kōchi (2hr 30min; ¥2770). The route from Kannoura will take you past rocky, black sand beaches and two huge rock outcrops between which a ceremonial rope has been strung, creating a natural shrine. Virtually at the cape, you can't fail to notice the towering white **statue of Kōbō Daishi**, commemorating the spot where the priest gained enlightenment when he had a vision of the

Buddhist deity Kokūzō in a nearby cavern. Pilgrims pay their respects here before heading up to a glade of lush vegetation high above the sharp cliffs and boulders at the cape where **Hotsumisaki-ji** stands. This appealingly shabby Buddhist temple, known locally as Higashi-dera (East temple), is the twenty-fourth on the pilgrimage circuit.

There's little more to Muroto Misaki other than a few weather-beaten shops and small hotels, and a series of pathways along the shore and up the mountainside to the temple. If you decide to **stay**, your best option is to head for *Hotsumisaki-ji Youth Hostel* (☎08872/3-0024 fax 2-0055; ③), just behind the temple, which has spacious *tatami* rooms and offers good-value **meals**. Be prepared for a long steep climb up the mountainside. Pop into the **information centre** (daily 8.30am–5pm; ☎08872/2-0574) close to the bus stop, if you get stuck for somewhere to stay – the kindly assistant might even offer you a ride up to the hostel.

## Inland to Ōboke Gorge

Highway 192 shadows the JR Tokushima line for around 70km inland from Tokushima to the railway junction at **AWA IKEDA**, also easily reached from Kotohira (see p.611). If you want to explore the mountainous heart of Shikoku, this is where you'll need to change trains. There's little of interest in the town itself, aside from a fine **youth hostel** (☎ & fax 0883/72-5277; ③), part of a brand new temple with a spectacular location on the side of the mountain overlooking the town and the Yoshino-gawa river. The priest Kondo-san will pick you up at the station if you call. Accommodation is in high-standard *tatami* rooms, there's a cosy lounge with TV and Kondo-san's wife cooks excellent meals.

From Awa Ikeda the road and railway enter the spectacular **Ōboke Gorge**, one of Japan's top three "hidden regions". The vertiginous mountains here and in the adjacent Iya Valley can be thickly coated in snow during the winter, while less than one hour south, the palms of Kōchi sway in the sunshine. This remoteness from the rest of the island made the gorge an ideal bolthole for the Taira clan after their defeat at Yashima in 1185. Here the warriors traded their swords for farm implements and built distinctive thatched-roof cottages on the mountain sides. Hardly any of these remain, but what has survived is the impressive **Kazura-bashi**, a bridge made out of *shirakuchi* (mountain vines) and bamboo, so that it could easily be cut down to block an enemy.

The Taira would have a tougher time chopping down the Kazura-bashi today since it is strengthened with carefully concealed steel cables. The 45-metre-long bridge is rebuilt every three years, and though it is not that high, the swaying motion as you cross induces enough of a thrill to justify the rather expensive admission price of ¥420. Otherwise, you can get a perfectly good view for free from the secure footing of the adjacent concrete bridge.

Unless you have a car, Kazura-bashi is far from easy to reach. There are very infrequent buses to the bridge from Awa Ikeda and Ōboke (check with the information office beside Awa Ikeda station for details). Alternatively, if you're staying at the *Jōfuku-ji Youth Hostel* (see overleaf), you can borrow a bicycle, but be prepared to pedal up some seriously steep roads. Following the road up from Ōboke you'll eventually reach a toll tunnel (¥30 walkers and cyclists, ¥260 cars) which takes you into the west side of the Iya valley. On the route down to the bridge you'll pass the Hikyo-no-Yu, a new onsen complex.

A model of the bridge graces the station platform at Ōboke, where you can alight the train to take a thirty-minute boat trip (¥1000) down the spectacular river gorge. To learn more about this area's geology, pop into the **Lapis Ōboke Stone Museum** (daily 9am–5pm; ¥500), in the modern building with the distinctive rippling roof across the river from the station. The exhibition over two floors begins with a clever piece of technology that transposes a video of a Japanese Indiana Jones character on to a model of the gorge and includes all manner of stones, including a meteorite from Mars and many glittering gems.

## Practicalities

Several limited express **trains** to and from Kōchi stop at Ōboke. The slower local trains will give you time to take in the scenery and get off at Toyanaga Station, from where *Jōfuku-ji* **youth hostel** (☎0887/74-0301, fax 74-0302; ②), the ideal base for exploring the area, is roughly a twenty-minute uphill walk. Set in the grounds of a beautiful hillside temple, the hostel is surrounded by little stone statues (*jizō*) considered guardians of children and travellers. Tsurui-san is the beaming Buddhist priest who runs the hostel and he has devised a series of cycling and walking routes in the mountains and valleys. You can also join the priest in **zazen meditation** at the temple daily at 7am. Accommodation is either in bunk beds or huge *tatami* rooms. Bike rental is ¥1000 per day and the hostel is only open Friday through Sunday between December and April – there's no food, so bring your own supplies. For something more luxurious, head for the *Kazura-bashi Hotel* (☎0883/87-2171, fax 87-2175; ⑨), a ryokan on the main road, about twenty minutes' walk from the bridge, with open-air baths and a restaurant with barbecue pits at each table.

Several tourist **restaurants** around the Kazura-bashi serve *yakisakana* – fish roasted on sticks over hot coals; set meals start at around ¥1000. If you have a sweet tooth, try the café in Ōboke's stone museum, which does freshly made waffles and a drink for ¥700.

# Kōchi and around

Sun-kissed **KŌCHI** lies dead centre of the arch-shaped southern prefecture of Shikoku. Texts from 712 refer to the area as "Takeyoriwake", meaning "brave and manly country" – a reputation enforced by the city being the birthplace of some of Japan's most impressive historical figures. Tosa was the next name of the area and is still used by people today, particularly when referring to the local cuisine. It wasn't until 1603, when ruling *daimyō* Yamaguchi Katsutoyo named his castle Kōchiyama (now Kōchi-jō), that the city adopted its present name.

The **castle** is still the highlight of any visit to Kōchi. To see anything else of interest requires a short journey out of the city centre. The most immediately rewarding trip is to **Godai-san-kōen**, a mountain-top park overlooking the city, and the nearby **Chikurin-ji**, the thirty-first temple on the pilgrimage circuit. South of the city lies Katsurahama, with its celebrated beach and Tosa fighting dogs, though in fact the most interesting attraction here is the **Sakamoto Ryōma Memorial Museum**, dedicated to a local hero of the Meiji Restoration.

Kōchi-ken, one of Japan's poorest prefectures, is predominantly rural, and the people here are refreshingly down-to-earth, something you'll discover if you time your visit to coincide with a three-hundred-year-old institution, the weekly **Sunday market** on Kōchi's Otesuji-dōri when farmers from all over the prefecture bring their produce to town. Even so, the capital is no hick town. On the contrary, Kōchi has a distinctly cosmopolitan feel, with its wide, palm-lined avenues, network of rivers and shopping arcades, and gently trundling trams.

## Arrival, information, orientation and city transport

All **trains** and most **buses** arrive at Kōchi Station, at the head of Harimaya-bashi-dōri, north of the city centre. Buses coming from Muroto Misaki to the east arrive at the bus station next to the Seibu department store at Harimaya-bashi. Kōchi's **airport** (☎0888/82-6171) is by the coast, a forty-minute drive east of the city; a bus (¥700) runs to opposite Kōchi Station, while a taxi into the city will cost around ¥4000. **Ferries** from Tokyo (via Katsura in Wakayama-ken) and Ōsaka arrive at the port, which is a ten-minute tram ride south of Harimaya-bashi in the city centre.

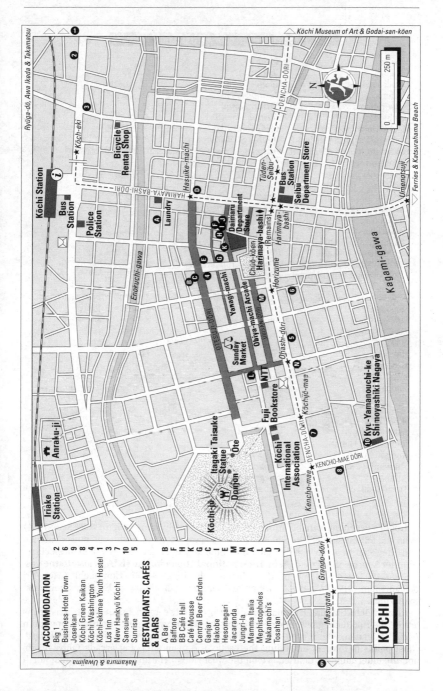

KŌCHI

**ACCOMMODATION**

| | |
|---|---|
| Big 1 | 2 |
| Business Hotel Town | 6 |
| Joseikan | 9 |
| Kōchi Green Kaikan | 8 |
| Kōchi Washington | 4 |
| Kōchi-ekimae Youth Hostel | 1 |
| Los Inn | 3 |
| New Hankyū Kōchi | 7 |
| Sansuien | 10 |
| Sunrise | 5 |

**RESTAURANTS, CAFÉS & BARS**

| | |
|---|---|
| A Bar | B |
| Baffone | F |
| BB Café Hall | H |
| Café Mousse | K |
| Central Beer Garden | G |
| Ganjar | C |
| Hakobe | I |
| Hesomagari | E |
| Jacaranda | M |
| Jungri-la | N |
| Mamma Italia | A |
| Mephistopholes | L |
| Nakamachi's | D |
| Tosahan | J |

Ryūga-dō, Awa Ikeda & Takamatsu

Kōchi Museum of Art & Godai-san-kōen

Kōchi Station

Kōch-eki

Bicycle Rental Shop

Bus Station

Police Station

HARIMAYA-BASHI-DŌRI

Enokuchi-gawa

Hasuike-machi

DENCHA-DŌRI

Tūden-Seibu

Bus Station

Seibu Department Store

Umenotsuji

Ferries & Katsurahama Beach

Laundry

Daimaru Department Store

Harimaya-bashi

Chūō-kōen

Harimaya-bashi (Remains)

Kagami-gawa

Horizume

Yanagi-machi

Ōtesuji-dōri

Ōbiya-machi Arcade

Sunday Market

NTT

Ōhashi-dōri

Kōchijō-mae

Kōchi-mae

Fuji Bookstore

Kyu-Yamanouchi-ke Shimoyashiki Nagaya

Kōchi International Association

Kencho-mae

DENCHA-DŌRI

KENCHO-MAE DŌRI

Itagaki Taisuke Statue

Ōte

Kōchi-jō Donjon

Iriake Station

Anraku-ji

Nakamura & Uwajima

Masugata

Grando-dōri

N

250 m

0

## KŌCHI AND AROUND

| Kōchi | *Kōchi* | 高知 |
|---|---|---|
| Chikurin-ji | *Chikurin-ji* | 竹林寺 |
| Godai-san-kōen | *Godai-san-kōen* | 五台山公園 |
| Haramaya-bashi | *Haramaya-bashi* | はらまや橋 |
| Katsurahama | *Katsurahama* | 桂浜 |
| Kōchi-jō | *Kōchi-jō* | 高知城 |
| Kōchi Museum of Art | *Kōchi Bijutsukan* | 高知美術館 |
| Makino Botanical Garden | *Makino Shokubutsu-en* | 牧野植物園 |
| Sakamoto Ryōma Memorial Museum | *Sakamoto Ryōma Kinenkan* | 坂本竜馬記念館 |

*ACCOMMODATION*

| Big 1 | *Biggu 1* | ビッグ1 |
|---|---|---|
| Business Hotel Town | *Bijinesu Hoteru Taun* | ビジネスホテルタウン |
| Jōseikan | *Jōseikan* | 城西館 |
| Katsurahama Kokuminshukusha | *Katsurahama Kokuminshukusha* | 桂浜国民宿舎 |
| Kōchi Green Kaikan | *Kōchi Guriin Kaikan* | 高知グリーン会館 |
| Kōchi Washington Hotel | *Kōchi Washinton Hoteru* | 高知ワシントンホテル |
| Kōchi-ekimae Youth Hostel | *Kōchi-ekimae Yūsu Hosuteru* | 高知駅前ユースホステル |
| Los Inn | *Rosu In* | ロスイン |
| New Hankyū Hotel Kōchi | *Shin-Hankyū Hoteru Kōchi* | 新阪急ホテル高知 |
| Sansuien Hotel | *Sansuien Hoteru* | 三翠園ホテル |
| Sunrise Hotel | *Sanraizu Hoteru* | サンライズホテル |

*EATING*

| Hakobe | *Hakobe* | はこべ |
|---|---|---|
| Hesomagari | *Hesomagari* | へそまがり |
| Jacaranda | *Jakaranda* | ジャカランダ |
| Jungri-la | *Jangurira* | ジャングリラ |
| Tosahan | *Tosahan* | 土佐藩 |

*WESTERN KŌCHI-KEN*

| Ashizuri Misaki | *Ashizuri Misaki* | 足摺岬 |
|---|---|---|
| John Mung House | *Jon Mung Hausu* | ジョン万ハウス |
| Kongōfuku-ji | *Kongōfuku-ji* | 金剛福寺 |
| Shimanto-gawa | *Shimanto-gawa* | 四万十川 |
| Sukumo | *Sukumo* | 宿毛 |
| Tatsukushi | *Tatsukushi* | 竜串 |

Kōchi's excellent **tourist information centre** (daily 9am–9.40pm; ☎0888/82-1634) is on the left outside Kōchi Station. There is always someone who can speak English and they can provide useful maps and booklets both for the city and prefecture. Another source of help is **Kōchi International Association (KIA)** close to the castle, on the second floor of the Marunouchi Biru, 4-1-37 Honmachi (Mon–Fri 8.30am–5pm; ☎0888/75-0022), which also has a small library of English books and magazines.

From Kōchi Station, Harimaya-bashi-dōri, the city's main north–south axis, runs across the Enokuchi-gawa, before reaching the **Harimaya-bashi**, two tram stops south of the JR station, where it intersects with Dencha-dōri, the main east–west boulevard. Most points of interest, including the castle, the main shopping arcade Obiya-machi and the entertainment district, are on the west side of Harimaya-bashi-dōri. Just north of the arcade is Otesuji-dōri, which leads to the castle. Kōchi's port, Mount Godai-san, and the beach at Katsurahama are south of the city.

While central Kōchi is easily negotiated on foot, the distances between the major sights makes catching a **tram** or **bus** a sensible option. The tram terminus is just to the left as you exit Kōchi Station. The system consists of two lines, one running north to south from the station to the port, crossing the east–west tracks at Harimaya-bashi. To travel within the city area costs a flat ¥180, paid to the driver on leaving the tram; you'll need to ask for a transfer ticket (*norikai-ken*) when you switch lines at Harimaya-bashi. Buses for Godai-san and Katsurahama leave from both Kōchi Station and the Seibu department store at Harimaya-bashi. If you're travelling on to Matsuyama, the most direct route is via JR express bus from Kōchi Station.

## Accommodation

Kōchi has a good range of **accommodation**, ranging from a well-run youth hostel to top-class ryokan – as usual, there's also a cluster of hotels close to the train station. More convenient for the shopping and entertainment districts are the hotels between Dencha-dōri and the city's principal river, Kagami-gawa. If you want to stay by the beach, head for the good *kokuminshukusha* (national lodging house) at Katsurahama.

**Big 1**, 3-9-45 Kitahonmachi (☎0888/83-9603) Large, men-only sauna and capsule hotel, with a swimming pool and relaxation area where you can watch wide-screen movies (some in English). Capsules are available from 4pm. ②.

**Business Hotel Town**, 1-5-26 Honmachi (☎0888/25-0055, fax 25-0048). One in a chain of five no-frills business hotels around the city. The rooms are nothing special, but they're clean and have en-suite bathrooms. ④.

**Jōseikan**, 2-5-34 Kamimachi (☎0888/75-0111, fax 24-0557). The most elegant and expensive ryokan in Kōchi is close to the castle. The spacious *tatami* rooms offer what you would expect for a place where the emperor stays when he visits town. Rates include two meals. ⑨.

**Katsurahama Kokuminshukusha**, Katsurahama (☎0888/41-2201, fax 41-2249). 13km south of central Kōchi, and decorated on the outside with turquoise tiles, this modern hotel has spectacular views across the beach from its cliff-top location. The high-standard rooms are very good value and the rates include two meals. ⑥.

**Kōchi Green Kaikan**, 5-6-11 Honmachi (☎0888/25-2701, fax 25-2703). Good-value mid-range hotel, close to the castle and with friendly management. Rooms are a decent size and have all the usual amenities. ⑤.

**Kōchi Washington Hotel**, 1-8-25 Otesuji-dōri (☎0888/23-6111, fax 25-2737). The central location, handy for the Sunday market which is on the same street, and close by the entertainment district, makes this national chain hotel a Kōchi landmark. The rooms are standard, though, and overpriced for their size. ⑥.

**Kōchi-ekimae Youth Hostel**, 3-10-10 Kitahonmachi (☎0888/83-5086, fax 83-0925). Small, friendly hostel, run by English-speaking Toyata-san and his wife. Apart from the dorms, there are private rooms (¥4300) with attached bath and TV. A drawback is the 11pm curfew. A 10min walk east of the JR station – look for the sign opposite the filling station. ①.

**Los Inn**, 2-4-8 Kitahonmachi (☎0888/84-1110, fax 84-1095) Hotel close to the station with a rather eccentric, kitsch feel to its decor, a mixture of reproduction antiques, heavy leather sofas and 1970s-style chandeliers. The manager speaks English and the rooms are quite comfortable. ⑤.

**New Hankyū Kōchi**, 4-2-50 Honmachi (☎0888/73-1111, fax 73-1145). Kōchi's top Western-style hotel has well-appointed rooms, a good selection of restaurants, a fitness centre and a swimming pool. ⑦.

**Sansuien Hotel**, 1-3-35 Honmachi (☎0888/22-0131, fax 22-0145). Ryokan housed in a large, ugly building. However, its interior is refined and the attached traditional gardens and buildings beside the Kagami-gawa add some atmosphere. ⑧.

**Sunrise Hotel**, 2-31-2 Honmachi (☎0888/22-1281, fax 22-1282). The staff are helpful and speak a little English at this chain business hotel. There's a men-only communal bath and sauna on the ninth floor, with a view of the city skyline, and a café on the ground floor. ⑤.

## The City

Kōchi's best-known fable concerns a romantic monk who courted a lady beside the **Harimaya-bashi**. Today all that remains of this bridge, ten minutes' walk south from the station, are the red-painted railings, but the spot has become so popular with visitors that the river buried beneath the road is being disinterred and given a pair of promenades. Look out for the telephone box on the left as you emerge from Kōchi Station; it is crowned with a small statue of the monk and his kimono-dressed paramour. Once you've checked out the bridge, proceed on to the city's main attraction, Kōchi **castle**, best followed up with a visit to the **Museum of Art** to the east. Kōchi's other main sights – **Godai-san-kōen**, the temple **Chikurin-ji** and the beach at **Katsurahama** – are all short journeys from the city centre by bus.

### Kōchi-jō and two museums

To the west of Harimaya-bashi, at the end of the Obiya-machi shopping arcade, is the hilltop castle of **Kōchi-jō** (daily 9am–4.30pm; ¥350 to enter the donjon). Construction was begun in 1601 by the feudal lord Yamaguchi Katsutoyo and finished in 1611, when the outer walls went up, but what you see today dates mainly from 1748, when reconstruction of the donjon turrets and gates was completed, following a major fire 21 years earlier.

The main approach is through the Ōte-mon, an impressive gateway flanked by high stone walls at the end of Otesuji-dōri. On the walk up to the donjon you'll pass a statue of Itagaki Taisuke, the founder of the People's Rights Movement, which promoted democracy in Japan during the early years of the Meiji era. For his efforts, Itagaki suffered an assassination attempt, during which he cried out "Itagaki may die, but liberty never!". The politician survived the knife attack, living to the ripe old age of 82, and his defiant phrase was adopted across Japan as the patriotic *cri de coeur* for democracy.

In the anti-feudal fervour that heralded the start of the Meiji era, almost all the castle's buildings were demolished, leaving the steeply sloping walls surrounding empty courtyards. The exception was the three-storey donjon, within the inner citadel (*honmaru*), reached through the Tsume-mon gate. To left of the entrance there's an exhibition of old *samurai* armour and a scroll from 1859 showing the English alphabet, written by John Mung (see p.632). In the main building look out for a beautifully painted palanquin, before you ascend to take in the superb view from the uppermost storey. To the right is the corridor leading to the *daimyō's* main chambers. By the time the donjon was rebuilt, the threat of war had evaporated, so these rooms did not need to be heavily fortified, hence the sliding screens and wooden balconies.

From the castle, it's only a five-minute walk south along Kenchomae-dōri to Kōchi's other main building of historic interest. The **Kyu-Yamanouchi-ke Shimoyashiki Nagaya**, on the banks of the Kagami-gawa, and next to the *Sansuien Ryokan*. Once the barracks of foot-soldiers during the late Tokugawa period, the narrow two-storey wooden building is now a National Treasure and houses a small museum (daily 7am–5pm; free) with some mildly interesting models of boats and displays showing the original use of the rooms.

In stark contrast is the stylish modern building housing Kōchi's **Museum of Art** (Tues–Sun 9am–5pm; ¥300). Set in landscaped grounds some 3km east of the city centre, the two-storey facility houses an impressive permanent collection of modern Japanese and Western art, including a gallery of lithographs and paintings by Marc Chagall, and a theatre with a specially designed stage for Nō plays. Films and other performances are occasionally held here, too. The museum is a fifteen-minute tram journey east of Harimaya-bashi (ask to get off at Kenritsu Bijutsukan-dōri).

### Gōdai-san-kōen and Chikurin-ji

Perched on the wooded mountain top overlooking Kōchi's harbour is **Godai-san-kōen**, an attractive park 2km south of the city centre. Alongside this are the equally pleasant grounds of the temple Chikurin-ji and the Makino Botanical Gardens. Several buses run to the park from Kōchi Station, a journey of around twenty minutes. The bus first stops at the Godai-san Tembo Service Centre, the main park building housing a café and souvenir shop, before turning around further along opposite the temple to return to town. It's a good idea to get off at the service centre and admire the panoramic view of Kōchi and its port from the platform above the café. From here you can walk towards the temple's five-storey pagoda, visible through the trees.

**Chikurin-ji** was founded in 724, making it one of oldest temples in the prefecture and its atmospheric main building, decorated with intricate carvings of animals, dates from the Muromachi period. The pagoda, built in the 1970s, is said to contain a bone of Buddha from Bodh Gaya in India, but there's no way of verifying this since the tower is closed to the public. The Treasure House (daily 9am–5pm; ¥400), to the right of the temple's main entrance gate, is worth seeing for its tranquil traditional gardens overlooked by an Edo-era villa and the small collection of Tantric statues and Buddhas.

Opposite the temple lies the large **Makino Botanical Garden** (daily 9am–5pm; ¥350), which has lovely views out to the coast and is dedicated to celebrated local botanist Dr Makino Tomitaro, who died aged 95 in 1957. It includes a large greenhouse and a fossil gallery, easily spotted since it has a giant model of a Tyrannosaurus Rex outside.

## Katsurahama

**Katsurahama**, some 13km south from the centre of Kōchi, is famous for two things: its beach and the Tosa fighting dogs, who compete in mock sumo tournaments. Neither attraction is what it's cracked up to be. The cresent-shaped beach, though capped off at one end with a picturesque cliff-top shrine, is rather pebbly and swimming is not allowed, while the dogs in the **Tosa Tōken Centre** (daily 9am–4pm; ☎0888/41-5184) are such lethargic, over-fed lumps that it's hard to believe they walk for 10km every day, let alone take part in sometimes bloodily vicious fights. Animal-lovers should give these bouts a wide berth, and the small museum, which includes several *Onagadori* roosters cooped up in cramped boxes designed to display their long tail feathers, and a Tosa dog lounging in a small cage. The rest of the centre is a giant gift shop selling tacky souvenirs, including cuddly toy sumo dogs.

Far more interesting is the **Sakamoto Ryōma Memorial Museum** (daily 9am–5pm; ¥350), the architecturally stunning building on the headland above the beach. Dedicated to local hero Sakamoto (see box), the building uses bold colours and a radical free-standing design for the main exhibition halls. Inside, as well as state-of-the-art displays using computers, you can see the blood-spotted screen from the room in which Sakamoto was assassinated in Kyoto. Next to the beach is a large statue of

### SAKAMOTO RYŌMA

You'd have to be blind to miss the scowling features of **Sakamoto Ryōma** on posters and other memorabilia around Kōchi. The city is immensely proud of this romantic figure who died young, but whose political ideas helped lay the groundwork for the Meiji Restoration of 1868. Born in 1835 to a half-*samurai*, half-farmer family, Sakamoto directly challenged the rigid class structure of the Shogunate years by leaving Kōchi to start a trading company in Nagasaki (*samurai* never normally dirtied their hands in business). In his travels around Japan, he gathered support for his pro-Imperial views, eventually forcing the shogun, Tokugawa Yoshinobu, to agree to give supreme power back to the Emperor. But, one month later, on November 15, 1867, Salamoto was assassinated in Kyoto. Although he was just 33 at the time, his writings included an enlightened plan for a new political system for Japan, aspects of which were later embraced by the Meiji government.

Sakamoto and a small aquarium (daily 8.30am–5pm; ¥950), which has dolphin and sea-lion shows.

To get to Katsurahama from Kōchi by public transport, you'll need to take a **bus** (¥530) from beside Kōchi Station – the journey to the beach takes 35 minutes.

# Eating, drinking and entertainment

The streets around Obiya-machi arcade are the best places for **eating and drinking** in Kōchi. The top floor of the Seibu department store, next to the Harimaya-bashi has a range of restaurants with picture menus and plastic-food window displays. There are plenty of **cafés** in Kōchi, none of them particularly cheap, but often strong on atmosphere. If you are looking for a cheap pick-me-up, *Mr Donut* is your best bet: it does bottomless cups of coffee at two outlets on Dencha-dōri.

For a relatively small city, Kōchi has an awful lot of *pachinko* parlours and amusement arcades. If these forms of entertainment don't thrill, you can always head for one of the several **cinemas** along the Obiya-machi arcade, which sometimes show English-language films. You could also check with the tourist information centre (see p.626) to see whether there are any **cultural perfomances** happening out at the Museum of Art.

## Restaurants and cafés

**Baffone**, 1-2-10 Yanagimachi. At the Harimaya-bashi end of Kōchi's famous drinking street, you can watch the drunken revellers pass by from this Continental-style café's outdoor tables. The daily menu, prepared by Matthew, the English-speaking chef, is a mixture of French and Italian styles. Around ¥2500 per head.

**Café Mousse**, Obiya-machi arcade. This popular, inexpensive café has a window packed with colourful plastic-food displays and serves up standard Japanese and Western grub to mainly high school students and office workers.

**Hakobe**, Obiya-machi arcade. *The* place to go for *okonomiyaki* and *yakisoba*. The ingredients are served in stainless steel pots and you cook up the dish yourself at the hotplate on your table. Difficult to spend over ¥1000. Closed Wed.

**Hesomagari**, Otesuji-dōri. Cheap, lively Chinese noodle shop, which serves milk ramen – which tastes much better than it sounds. Good spot for a late-night snack since it's open until 2am. Closed Wed.

**Jacaranda**, Obisan-dōri. Small, second-floor restaurant serving set menus of Southeast Asian cuisine. Attention to detail means you pay a little more (around ¥1500) but it's certainly worth it. Only open for lunch from 11.30am–3pm, closed Sun.

**Jungri-la**, Densha-dōri. Above the corner *pachinko* parlour, this pub/restaurant has palms and vines which sprout up and around the large dining space, built around a fake waterfall. The standard *izakaya* food is a lot less adventurous, but they do have Guinness on tap for ¥650.

**Mamma Italia**, Nijudai-machi. Opposite the *Kōchi Palace Hotel*, this stylish Italian is run by an English-speaking chef, who learnt his craft in Rome. The speciality is pizza baked in a wood-fired oven. Around ¥2500 a head. Closed Wed.

**Mephistopholes**. Opposite the west end of Obisan-dōri. The decor at this popular café is best described as that of an eclectic English country cottage. A wide range of coffees and set-meal menus from as little as ¥500. Daily 7am–9.30pm.

**Tosahan**, Obiya-machi Arcade. The place to go to savour *Tosa ryōri*, the local speciality fish cuisine. The decor is all dark wood beams and red lanterns and the set lunches at around ¥1000 are good value. For dinner expect to pay at least ¥4000 per head.

## Bars and clubs

As the largest city on Shikoku's southern coast, Kōchi attracts many people looking for a night on the town, so it's not short of a **bar** or ten and has a lively atmosphere, especially on weekends. The city's famous drinking street is **Yanagi-machi**, which runs parallel to the Obiya-machi arcade. During the summer Kōchi's outdoor and roof-top beer gardens are the ideal places to relax with a cold brew on a sultry night.

**A Bar**. Look for the white corrugated-iron building on a street behind Otesuji-dōri – the door is decorated with a giant orange A. This is a spacious, laid-back place with comfy sofas and the owner plays in a blues band. All drinks ¥600. Closed Sun.

**BB Café Hall**. A basement nightspot just off the Obiya-machi arcade, which attracts a trendy young crowd and triples up as a café, bar and live music venue. The cover charge for the live music ranges from ¥500 to ¥2500, depending on who is playing.

**Central Suntory Beer Garden**. Only open from May to September, this open-air beer garden is on the corner of Yanagi-machi, close to the *Washington Hotel*.

**Ganjar**. Seventh-floor bar on Otesuji-dōri, decorated with exposed ducts and pipes, has a giant video screen and a DJ who'll let you to choose records from his collection.

**Nakamachi's**. Funky hangout for the foreign teaching community on the second floor of a building just off Harimaya-bashi-dōri, on the east side of Otesuji-dōri. Spacious interior with scatter cushions around low tables on one side and a long bar on the other. Also serves food.

## Listings

**Airlines** ANA, 1-5-1 Harimaya-chō (☎0888/82-0747); JAS, Dentetsu Taminaru Biru, 1-5-15 Harimaya-chō (☎0888/83-9611).

**Banks and exchange** Shikoku Bank is on the corner at Harimaya-bashi; there's a branch of Kōchi bank further west, along Dencha-dōri.

**Bike rental** Bikes can be rented from Kagiyama Rental Cycle, 4-11 Aioi-chō (☎0888/82-1585) for ¥600 for 2 hours and ¥1200 for a day.

**Bookshops** Fuji Bookstore, on the corner of Kōchijōmae-dōri (Mon–Sat 9am–9pm, Sun & hols 10am–7pm), has a few English books on the second floor.

**Car rental** Try Eki Rent-a-car (☎0888/82-3022); Toyota Rent-a-car (☎0888/23-0100) Nissan (☎0888/83-4485); or Budget (free dial ☎0120–23-0543).

**Hospitals and clinics** The Red Cross Hospital (☎0888/22-1202) is behind Kōchi Station.

**Internet access** NTT, opposite the castle at the end of Obiya-machi arcade, has a section with free Internet access. Opening hours are Mon–Fri 9am–5pm.

**Laundry** There's a self-service laundry (daily 7am–10pm) on Nijudai-machi, one block after the Enokuchi-gawa on the right as you walk towards Harimaya-bashi.

**Police** The main police station is opposite Kōchi Station. Emergency numbers are listed in Basics on p.70.

**Post office** The main post office is just to the west of Kōchi Station. Opening hours are Mon–Fri 9am–7pm, Sat 9am–5pm, Sun 9am–12.30pm.

**Sports** There's an outdoor swimming pool at the Sogō Taikokan (City Gym) next to the baseball stadium across the Yanagihara-bashi south of the Kagami-gawa.

**Taxis** Call Kenko Hire (☎0888/82-6166) or Mikuni Hire (☎0888/82-3660).

**Travel agents** The main branch of JTB is at Harimaya-bashi, but you're not guaranteed to be served by English-speaking staff.

## Western Kōchi-ken

The western side of Kōchi-ken has some of Shikoku's best scenery, especially along the rugged coast, which is washed by the savage current from the Pacific Ocean. The rocky cape at **Ashizuri Misaki**, 180km southwest of Kōchi, with its twisting coastal roads, temple and lush foliage, is well worth the journey. Continue around the coast and you'll reach **Tatsukushi**, where outlandish rock formations stretch out towards the coral reefs under the ocean, and **Sukumo**, a recommended spot for scuba diving and jumping-off point for the undeveloped islands of Okino-shima and Uguru-shima.

Inland, the **Shimanto-gawa**, said to be the last free-flowing river in Japan, is the place to head if you want to enjoy boating, canoeing and fishing. A good base for these activities is the *Shimantogawa Youth Hostel* (☎0880/54-1352; ②), run by a friendly couple and about as far off the beaten track as you could wish for in Shikoku; you'll need a car to get there. The nearest train station is Ekawasaki on JR's plodding Yodo line, which runs from Kubokawa on the bay side of Kōchi-ken, to Uwajima (see p.634) along a beautifully scenic route. From March to November, open-air carriages are hitched to the train on most weekends and holidays.

Also on the Tosa-wan side of Kōchi's coast are several of the fishing villages which used to be bases for Japan's whaling industry. These days, instead of slaughtering the rare creatures, the fisherman conduct **whale-watching tours** for around ¥4500 per person. For details contact the Ōgata Town Leisure Fishingboats Owners Association (☎0880/43-1058) or Saga Town Fishermen's Association (☎0880/55-3131).

## Ashizuri Misaki

The tourist trail has beat a steady path to the small, scenic village of **ASHIZURI MIS-AKI**, standing on the most southerly point of Shikoku, but don't let this put you off checking it out. Pilgrims have long been coming here to pay their respects at **Kongōfuku-ji**, the thirty-eighth temple on the sacred circuit (see p.599). This picturesque temple, dedicated to the Buddhist deity Kannon, who symbolizes infinite compassion, has a two-storey pagoda and nestles amid a palm grove in the centre of the village. Ashizuri's white-painted lighthouse stands atop the eighty-metre-high cliffs, while at shore level there's a natural rock arch, crowned by a small shrine. All these sights are within easy walking distance of each other, along cliff-top pathways that each February burst forth with crimson camellia blossoms.

On the way to the lighthouse you'll pass the statue of Nakahama Manjirō, better known as **John Mung** (see box), the local lad who travelled the world and pioneered relations between Japan and the USA in the early years of the Meiji Restoration. Opposite Kongōfuku-ji is a small museum, **John Mung House** (daily 8am–5pm; ¥200), dedicated to the man, which includes some of Mung's personal items and miniature tableaux describing his life and the whaling industry he was once part of.

Reaching the cape by public transport can be costly (around ¥4000) and time consuming. There are direct **buses** from Kōchi to Ashizuri Misaki which take around four

---

### JOHN MUNG

In the normal course of life, Nakahama Manjirō, born in 1827 into a poor family living in Tosa Shimizu, near Ashizuri Misaki, would have lived and died a fisherman. His lucky break came when he was marooned on Tori-jima, a uninhabited volcanic island some 580km south of Tokyo, along with five shipmates. After nearly five months, they were saved by a landing party from a passing US whaling ship, who had come to the island in search of fresh water.

The ship's captain, John Whitfield, took a shine to the fourteen-year-old Nakahama and renamed him **John Mung**. When the ship docked at Honolulu, Mung decided to remain with the Americans and served with Whitfield's crew for four years, before returning with the captain to his home in Bedford, Massachussetts. The bright lad mastered English, mathematics, surveying and navigation, and undertook journeys to Africa, Australia and around Southeast Asia. After making some money in the California Gold Rush of 1849, Mung returned to Japan in 1851. He was sought out by the feudal lord of Tosa, who realized it was only a matter of time before Japan would open up to the West and so was eager to have the likes of Mung on his side.

Two years later, Mung was summoned to Tokyo to assist with the drawing up of international trade treaties. In 1860 he returned to the US as part of a national delegation and in 1869 paid visits to London and other places in Europe. Before his death in 1898 he taught at the Kaisei School for Western Learning in Tokyo (later to become part of the prestigious Tokyo University), sharing the knowledge he'd accumulated during a period when Japan was still living in self-imposed isolation from the rest of the world.

hours forty minutes. **Trains** only go as far as Nakamura, where you'll have to catch one of the local buses from directly outside the station. The bus journey takes around an hour and becomes progressively more spectacular the closer to the cape you get, the driver skilfully whipping the bus around the narrow, cliff-hugging road. In your own car, you can opt for the less hair-raising, but equally scenic Skyline road down the middle of the peninsula to the cape. The bus stop is next to Kongōfuku-ji.

Buses run regularly to the nearby town of Tosa Shimizu (¥820) where you'll usually have to change to continue north up the coast. There are two **youth hostels** at Ashizuri Misaki: *Kongōfuku-ji* (☎08808/8-0038, fax 8-0688; [1]), next to the temple, is the slightly more attractive, though it's often busy with groups of pilgrims; and *Ashizuri* (☎08808/8-0324; [1]), which is next to the small shrine, and offers accommodation in *tatami* rooms. Both hostels serve breakfast and evening meals. There are several ryokans in town, including *Hotel Kaijokan* (☎08808/8-0503, fax 8-0211; [6]) where the rates cover breakfast only, and *Ashizurien* (☎08808/8-0206, fax 8-0033; [8]), which includes dinner in its rate.

## Tatsukushi and Sukumo

Heading north for 24km around the coast from Ashizuri Misaki will bring you to the small town of **TATSUKUSHI**, which gets its name (meaning "dragon's skewers") from the remarkable rock pillars that protrude, like dinosaur bones, from the sea. The various formations have been given names like "dragon's skeleton" and "big bamboo tree" to jolly things up, but there's really no need; the honeycombed rocks, split by swirling indentations where the sea water has sluiced in, are fascinating enough in their own right.

The Minokoshi coastline around Tatsukushi was designated a national underwater park in 1970 and is the first of its kind in Japan. It's possible to take glass-bottomed boats (¥850) from the jetty near the bus station to view the coral reefs and then explore the weird rock formation along the coast, created over tens of thousand of years. Don't expect much from the reefs – they're hardly up to tropical standards, but the oddly-shaped cliffs on what is dubbed the "hidden coast" make it worth the trip.

Tatsukushi is one hour's bus ride from Tosa Shimizu. You can leave your bags at the bus station (¥100) while exploring the area. Next to the bus station, in the Chinese-style red and green building is the **Coral Museum** (daily 8am–5.30pm; ¥300), which has a large collection of *sango*, the pink coral found in the area. Mini-dioramas show how the coral used to be raised to the surface and there are some showpiece models made from the stuff, including a detailed castle and a life-size tiger. The café next to the shop on the ground floor is also about the best bet for something to **eat**. Five minutes' walk around the coast, past a sandy beach and an unremarkable aquarium, is the **Ashizuri Sea-floor Museum** (April–Aug 8am–5.30pm; Jan–March & Sept–Dec 9am–4.30pm; ¥800). You walk out to the red, white and blue cross-shaped pod, stranded in the ocean, along a gantry from the rocks and then descend a spiral staircase to the sea bed to watch the fish swirling around the observation room's windows. Emperor Hirohito, a keen marine biologist, visited here many times, but unless you're mad on fish you could give it a miss.

Buses continue up the coast for 50km to **SUKUMO** (¥1500), a small and quiet fishing port where it is possible to take a trip out to the nearby islands, **Okino-shima** and **Uguru-shima**. On these islands you can camp, follow hiking trails, fish and go scuba diving. Ferries also make a three-hour crossing from Sukumo to Saeki in Kyushu. The Tosa Kuroshio railway also links Sukumo with Nakamura, bypassing the cape.

A very pleasant **place to stay**, although it is far from convenient to reach by public transport, is the *Sukumo Youth Hostel* (☎0880/64-0233, fax 64-0162; [1]). Run by an enthusiastic young couple, the hostel is 9km out of town, next to a river where fireflies appear in June, and has an *irori* – a central charcoal fire. There is a school bus which runs from Sukumo to Matsudagawa, a fifteen-minute walk from the hostel. If you miss this, you can call the wardens, who speak a little English and may be able to pick you up.

# Uwajima and around

From Sukumo, Route 55 continues through countryside before emerging on the coast. The gently turning cliffside road, passing though small fishing communities, provides spectacular views of the deep-blue sea, carpeted with nets held up by a criss-cross network of buoys. The next major stop is the port of **UWAJIMA**, 60km north of Sukumo, famous for its sumo-style bull fights, when the otherwise quiet and compact town comes alive (see box, p.637). The main sights – which include an original castle and a fertility shrine – can be seen easily in half a day. An overnight stop will allow you more time to explore the tranquil backstreets lined with old wooden houses and temples.

You can easily walk between Uwajima's main sights, but they are a little scattered, so renting a bike (available from the youth hostel or the information centre at ¥100 per hour) is a good idea if your time is limited. The castle is a fifteen-minute walk south of the JR station, while the Taga-jinja sex shrine, across the Suka-gawa river, is a ten-minute walk to the north. The municipal bull fighting ring is a twenty-minute walk up the hill to the east. Route 55 cuts through the centre of Uwajima, running past the castle and the JR station and parallel to the main covered shopping arcade Uwajima Gintengai.

## The City

Uwajima's most notorious attraction, the fertility shrine **Taga-jinja**, is set back from the Suka-gawa river, a short walk north of the JR station. The shrine has an attached **sex museum** (daily 8am–5pm; ¥800) and is set in a small compound, which is packed with various statues, some of which assume the shape of penises if looked at from a certain angle – there's no mistaking the shape of the carved log beside the main shrine building, though. To the right you'll see a smaller shrine, clogged with dolls, strings of paper cranes, women's clothes and other articles – all fertility offerings. The museum is spread over three floors of a modern building. Inside, it's wall-to-wall erotica, with display cases packed with all manner of sexual objects, literature and art. There's nothing in the way of an explanation – or even logical order – to what's on show, and it soon becomes more entertaining to watch the reactions of the Japanese tour groups guffawing their way round the museum.

Taga-jinja is to the left as you cross the bridge over the Suka-gawa, while the larger shrine to the right is **Warei-jinja**, the starting point of the Warei Taisai, one of Shikoku's major festivals. Held on July 23 and 24, the festival involves huge models of devil bulls (*ushi-oni*) being paraded in the streets, along with ornate portable shrines, the aim being to dispel evil. The bulls, like giant pantomime horses, eventually do battle in the river.

Walking back into the town, keep an eye out for the rather forlorn-looking **Uwajima-jō** (daily 9am–4pm; ¥200), at the top of the hillside park that rises west of Route 55. The compact, three-storey donjon may be original and certainly gives a fine view of the surrounding city and port, but there's little reason to pay the entrance charge, unless you want to look at the photos of other Japanese castles displayed inside.

There are two routes up to the donjon, either from the north through the gate of the Kōri *samurai* family (transferred to the castle ground in 1952), tucked back from the main road behind the post office, or from the Noboritachi-mon gate on the south side of the castle hill. On the way up, it's worth popping into the **Shiroyama Museum**

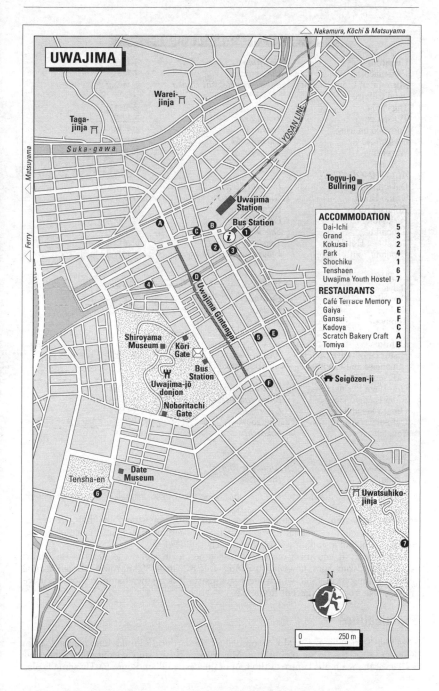

UWAJIMA

△ Nakamura, Kōchi & Matsuyama

Warei-jinja

Taga-jinja

Suka-gawa

△ Matsuyama

△ Ferry

YOSAN LINE

Togyu-jo
Bullring

Uwajima
Station

Bus Station

A

B

C

1

i

2

3

D

Uwajima Gintengai

4

Shiroyama
Museum

Kōri
Gate

5

E

Bus
Station

Uwajima-jō
donjon

Noboritachi
Gate

F

Seigōzen-ji

Date
Museum

Tensha-en

6

Uwatsuhiko-
jinja

7

ACCOMMODATION
Dai-Ichi          5
Grand             3
Kokusai           2
Park              4
Shochiku          1
Tenshaen          6
Uwajima Youth Hostel 7

RESTAURANTS
Café Terrace Memory  D
Gaiya                E
Gansui               F
Kadoya               C
Scratch Bakery Craft A
Tomiya               B

N

0        250 m

(daily 9.30am–4pm; free), housed in a half-timbered one-storey building, to see an eclectic collection of local antiques and artifacts, ranging from giant masks of a long-nosed goblin and a smiling woman to an early radio set.

Don't worry if you miss out Uwajima's other main sight, the **Tensha-en** (daily: April–July 8.30am–5pm; Jan–March & Aug–Dec 8.30am–4.30pm; ¥300), a small, formal garden, dating from 1866, which feels lacklustre. It is further hampered by intrusive traffic noise from the adjacent Route 55.

## Practicalities

Uwajima Station is the **train** terminus for both the JR Yodo line running from Kubokawa and the JR Yosan line from Matsuyama. Buses stop in front of the station as well as at the main bus centre at the foot of the castle hill on Route 55. Uwajima is also

(☎089/933-9230), south of the city centre, close to the Tachibana-bashi across the river Ishite-gawa. Theatre, dance and orchestral perfomances are held at the Matsuyama City Hall (☎089/921-8222) and the Prefectural Cultural Centre (Kenmin Bunka Kaikan) (☎089/923-5111). Check the monthly *What's Going On?* booklet for details.

## Restaurants and cafés

**à table,** 2-5-6 Chifune-machi (☎089/947-8001). It may have odd decoration (tinsel, wooden beams, saucy postcards), but the excellent French country cooking is done by a real French chef. The set lunches for ¥850 are a taster of the delights on offer at dinner, which averages ¥3000 without drinks.

**Atom Boy,** Minato-machi. Popular conveyor-belt sushi shop opposite the Shi-eki tram stop. Dishes are priced either ¥150 or ¥200 each. Takeaway packs are also available.

**Café do Namo,** Dōgo. Artsy café, easily spotted halfway along the covered shopping arcade: it's in the stone igloo-like building with the wooden interior. The set lunches for ¥700 are good value.

**Cappuccio,** 3 Sanban-chō. Next to the Sunshine Cinema, on the second floor, overlooking the Ōkaidō. The pizzas here get the best reviews and a standard range of Italian dishes is also on offer, at around ¥1000 a plate.

**Castle Grill,** *ANA Hotel* (☎089/933-5511). The most romantic restaurant in Matsuyama serves European dishes, and has a lovely view of Katsuyama Hill and the Bansui-sō villa, especially when the buildings are spotlit at night.

**Charlie,** Minato-machi. This sparklingly clean operation on a side road off from the Gintengai arcade is one of the cheapest ramen shops in town, with bowls of noodles costing as little as ¥250. Lunchtime sets with rice and salad are ¥490.

**Dan Raku,** Niban-chō. A modern *izakaya*, which specializes in *mukokuseki*, the no-nationality mish-mash of cuisines. The menu is in Japanese, but you can easily point at the array of food on the counter, which will be freshly cooked for you. Expect to pay around ¥3000 a head.

**Goose,** 3 Chifune-machi. Angels are painted on the walls of this cheap coffee shop, popular with teenagers, that does home-made cakes, waffles and crepes, also served from a takeaway hatch on the street. Coffee is ¥150. Closed Wed.

**Goshiki,** 3-5-4 Sanban-chō (☎089/933-3838). Matsuyama's most famous place to sample *sōmen*, the five-coloured noodles. In front of the restaurant is a shop where you can buy the noodles, packed as souvenir sets from around ¥300. Lunchtime set menus start at ¥1100; noodles on their own are cheaper.

**Kaiseki Club Kawasemi,** 2-5-18 Niban-chō (☎089/933-9697). Avant-garde *kaiseki* (Japanese haute-cuisine) restaurant. The portions are small, but your tastebuds will be subtly challenged. Look for the world "club" in English on the sign and go up to the second floor. Best visited for lunch (around ¥1500), dinner is a much more expensive affair.

**Komadon,** Ōkaidō. On the floor above Italian restaurant *Santo Santo*, this arty café does things in style. Choose from a wide range of teas, coffees and delicious home-made cakes, then ponder which of the many designs of china cup you would like. An egg-timer is provided so you know exactly when the tea is brewed. At least ¥1000 a head, but worth splashing out for.

**Murasaki,** Niban-chō. Look for the large red lantern hanging outside of this appealingly ram-shackle *izakaya* near the Ōkaidō. There's a picture menu and it's popular with a young, lively Japanese crowd.

**Nikitatsu-an,** Dōgo Shitamachi (☎089/924-6617). Imaginative modern Japanese cooking comple-ments the local beer. Seating is on *tatami* in a contemporary setting. The set meals (lunch starts at ¥1000) include a range of tasty morsels, beautifully presented on a wicker plate, and accompanied by special rice and soup. There's also an outdoor deck for quaffing beer on balmy nights.

## Bars and clubs

**Dejavu,** Ciel Biru, 2-3-5 Sanban-chō. This narrow basement bar east of the Ōkaidō, with a seating area at the back dominated by a table decorated with a poster for *Clockwork Orange*, plays rock music and is popular with the local *gaijin*. Open until 4am.

**Dōgo Bakushukan,** opposite Dōgo Onsen Honkan. An *izakaya* owned by the same independent brewery that runs Nikitatsu-an (see above). The two beers to try are the *Botchan* lager or the dark-er *Madonna* ale, slightly sweet and very refreshing after an onsen dip.

**Ex**, 3 Niban-chō. Matsuyama's main dance club is in the same block as *Kentos*, (a national chain club where house bands play cover-versions of classic rock songs). Men pay ¥2000 entrance, includng one drink, women ¥1500. Open to 4pm on Friday and Saturday.

**Moonglow**, Chifune-machi. Sophisticated piano-bar with a genial English-speaking host and live jazz every night from 9.15pm. ¥300 cover charge.

**Piccadilly Circus**, 3 Sanban-chō. Calls itself a British antique bar and charges aristocratic prices. There's a Triumph motorbike propped up in one corner and the kind of dusty fittings last seen in an eccentric Aunt's living room.

## Listings

**Airlines** ANA, 5 Minato-machi (☎089/948-3131); JAL, 4 Chifune-machi (☎089/943-6111); JAS, 5-2-2 Minato-machi (☎089/948-3281).

**Banks and exchange** Ehime Ginkō and Iyo Ginkō have several branches in downtown Matsuyama. There's also a Ehime Ginkō branch by the Dōgo tram terminus.

**Bookshops** Kinokuniya, 5 Chifune-machi, has an extensive range of English books and magazines on the fourth floor. Open daily 10am–5.30pm.

**Car rental** Budget Rent-a-car (☎089/973-0543) is at the airport.

**Hospital and clinics** The central prefectural hospital, Ehime Kenritsu Chūō Byōin (☎089/947-1111), is in Kasuga-machi, south of the Shi-eki Station.

**Internet access** Free surfing of the Net and coffee is available at NTT's main office, 4 Ichiban-chō, opposite EPIC.

**Laundry** Okaya Coin Laundry, 43 Minami-Mochida, is open daily from 6am to 10.30pm.

**Police** The main police station is at 2 Minami Horibata (☎089/941-0111). Emergency numbers are listed in Basics on p.70.

**Post office** Matsuyama's main post office is at 3 Sanban-chō. Opening hours are Mon–Fri 9am–7pm, Sat 9am–5pm, Sun 9am–12.30pm. There's also a branch in Dōgo (Mon–Fri 9am–5pm), to the west of the shopping arcade.

**Sports** There's an open-air public swimming pool in the park beside EPIC (closest tram stop is Shiyakusho-mae). Open only July and August it costs ¥200.

**Shopping** Local products to look out for include *iyo-gasuri*, an indigo dyed cloth; *hime temari*, colourful thread-covered balls that bring good luck; and *Tobe-yaki*, distinctive blue-patterned pottery. Check out the Ōkaidō and Gintengai arcades for souvenir shops. Also try the Mistukoshi and Sogō department stores. There's a branch of Muji, the trendy, no-brand goods shop, in the Laforet building next to Mitsukoshi. Hamashō, a large shop specializing in basket weaving, is close by Ishite-ji, on the way from Dōgo.

**Taxi** Daiei Taxi can be called for free on ☎0120–015151.

**Travel agents** For cheap international flights try HIS, Yasui Biru 3-2, Hanazono-machi (☎089/931 6121). For domestic travel arrangements JTB's main office, where English is spoken, is at 4 Sanban-chō (☎089/931-2281).

## Ishizuchi-san

Some 45km south of Matsuyama rises **ISHIZUCHI-SAN**, at 1982m Shikoku's tallest mountain and a sacred place of pilgrimage. Legend has it that it was first climbed in 682 by En no Ozuno, a *yamabushi*, or mountain ascetic, while Kōbō Daishi undertook the hike in 797. Ishizuchi's temple, **Ōhō-ji**, in the valley below the mountain, is the sixtieth on the pilgrimage route.

At one time, the mountain was climbed only by male pilgrims – women were strictly forbidden from setting foot on it. This tradition is still upheld for the annual official opening ceremony on July 1, when *yamabushi*, dressed in white robes and blowing on conch shells, hike up to the shrine at the summit. It is possible to scale the mountain from April, once the winter snow has melted, but the climbing season officially runs from July until the end of August and there are more frequent bus connections to the trails during this time, enabling you to get up and down the mountain in a day as long as you set off early from Matsuyama.

The Ishizuchi Quasi National Park, in which the mountain stands, was established in 1955 and has several hiking trails, plus limited skiing in the winter. The relatively warm climate means there are trees on the slopes of the mountain, almost to the summit. There's also a **cable car** (¥900 one way, ¥1700 return) which cuts out much of the foot slogging, taking you within three hours' hike of the top. The "official" route partly involves negotiating sheer cliffs, using *kusari*, thick metal chains hammered into the rock, but if this doesn't appeal there's an easier walking path. Most people stop at the mountain-top shrine (beside which, during the climbing season, is a refreshments hut) but the official summit is the even higher peak of Tengu-dake, approached along a razor-edge ridge, about ten minutes away.

Buses run to Tsuchigoya (you might have to change buses at Mimido), from where the summit is a two-hour hike. The one-way fare for the journey is ¥3140. Alternatively, plenty of trains from Matsuyama go to Iyo Saijō, on the Yosan line, from where it's a 55-minute bus ride (¥950) to the cable car at Nishi-no-Kawa. From Jōyu, the cable car terminus, the summit is a four-kilometre hike. Standard Japanese **meals**, such as noodles and curry rice, are available at various mountain huts and in the tourist restaurants at Tsuchigoya, but you'd do better to pack a picnic and enjoy it at the summit.

## Imabari

The only reason you're likely to find yourself in **IMABARI**, perched on Shikoku's northwest coast 45km from Matsuyama, is at the start or end of the ferry journey to or from Honshū or the nearby islands of Ōmi-shima and Ikuchi-jima (see p.543). The town itself is nothing special, but it does have a rare example of a castle in an open field; **Imabari-jō**, built in 1602 by local warlord Todo Takatora. The present buildings date from 1980, but are surrounded by the original moat. Inside the castle grounds is an attractive shrine with lots of red-painted *torii*, while the keep contains a rather musty museum (daily 9am–4.30pm; ¥300), displaying armour and painted screens, plus a natural history section with local rocks, embalmed fish and stuffed birds.

Imabari's future is set to liven up as the **Kurushima bridges**, a few kilometres north of the port, near completion. This mammoth civil engineering project involves ten bridges, spanning nine islands, and will eventually provide the route for the Nishiseto Expressway, a sixty-kilometre-long road joining Onomichi in Hiroshima-ken with Imabari. The expressway is expected to open in 1999. In the meantime, the bridges can be viewed from a promontory near Itoyama. There are regular buses from Imabari to Itoyama, but you'll need to take a taxi to get to the viewing point.

**Maps** and booklets on the area are available at the helpful tourist information centre (daily 9am–5pm; no English spoken) inside the JR station, a five-minute bus ride from the port. If you need to stay in Imabari, your best budget choice of **accommodation** is the *Komechō Ryokan* (☎0898/32-0554, fax 33-0843; ③), conveniently located close by the ferry piers and bus terminal. The ryokan, which has large *tatami* rooms, is part of the Japanese Inn Group. The manager speaks some English and meals are available.

## travel details

### Trains

The trains between the major cities listed below are the fastest, direct services. There are also frequent slower services, run by JR and several private companies, covering the same destinations. It is usually possible, especially on long-distance routes, to get there faster by changing between services.

**Kōchi** to: Awa Ikeda (9 daily; 2hr 20min); Kotohira (6 daily; 1hr 30min); Nakamura (8 daily; 1hr 50min); Okayama (4 daily; 2hr 25min); Takamatsu (7 daily; 2hr 15min); Tokushima (daily; 2hr 34min).

**Matsuyama** to: Okayama (8 daily; 2hr 45min); Takamatsu (9 daily; 2hr 23min); Uwajima (14 daily; 1hr 30min).

**Takamatsu** to: Matsuyama (9 daily; 2hr 23min); Kōchi (7 daily; 2hr 15min); Kotohira (20 daily; 1hr); Okayama (34 daily; 1hr); Tokushima (13 daily; 1hr 15min).

**Tokushima** to: Awa Ikeda (20 daily; 1hr 53min); Kaifu (7 daily; 2hr 20min) Kōchi (daily; 2hr 34min); Naruto (14 daily; 40min); Takamatsu (13 daily; 1hr 15min).

**Uwajima** to: Matsuyama (16 daily; 1hr 30min); Kubokawa (7 daily; 2hr 15min).

## Buses

The buses listed below are mainly long-distance services – often travelling overnight – between the major cities, and local services where there is no alternative means of transport. For shorter journeys, however, trains are almost invariably quicker and often no more expensive.

**Kōchi** to: Okayama (8 daily; 2hr 30min); Ōsaka (daily; 5hr 35min); Tokyo (1 daily; 11hr 40min).

**Matsuyama** to: Kōchi (13 daily; 3hr); Ōsaka (1 daily; 7hr); Tokyo (2 daily; 12hr 40min).

**Takamatsu** to: Kōchi (3 daily; 2hr); Kotohira (12 daily; 1hr); Nagoya (1 daily; 7hr 30min); Matsuyama (12 daily; 2hr 30min); Tokyo (1 daily; 11hr); Yokohama (1 daily; 10hr 30min).

**Tokushima** to: Awaji-shima/Fukura (4 daily; 1hr 6min); Awaji-shima/Tsuna (14 daily; 1hr 45min); Ōsaka (4 daily; 3hr 10min); Takamatsu (12 daily; 2hr); Tokyo (1 daily; 10hr 40min).

## Ferries

**Ashizuri** to: Kōbe (1 daily; 10hr 10min).

**Kōchi** to: Ōsaka (1 daily; 9hr 10min); Tokyo via Katsūra in Wakayama-ken (3 weekly; 21hr 20min).

**Imabari** to: Hiroshima (1 daily; 1hr 50min); Kōbe (1 daily; 7hr 20min); Mihara (1 daily; 1hr); Onomichi (1 daily; 1hr 30min); Ōsaka (1 daily; 11hr 30min).

**Matsuyama** to: Aga (1 daily; 1hr 50min); Beppu (1 daily; 3hr 40min); Hiroshima (1 daily; ferry 3 hr, hydrofoil 1hr); Iwakuni (1 daily; 1hr 25min); Kōbe (daily; 8hr 10min); Kokura (1 daily; 6hr 55min); Oita (1 daily; 3hr 15min); Onomichi (1 daily; 1hr 25min); Ōsaka (1 daily; 9hr 20min); Yanai (1 daily; 2hr 25min).

**Sukumo** to: Saeki (1 daily; 3hr).

**Takamatsu** to: Kōbe (by hydrofoil 2hr, by ferry 4hr, 10min); Ōsaka (2hr, 10min); Shōdo-shima (by hydrofoil 30min, by ferry 1hr); Uno (1hr)

**Tokushima** to: Awaji-shima/Fukura (4 daily; 55min); Kansai International Airport (7 daily; 1hr 20min); Kōbe (9 daily; 1hr 50min); Kitakyūshū (3 weekly; 17hr); Ōsaka (6 daily; 1hr 45min); Tokyo (3 weekly; 18hr); Wakayama (9 daily; by hydrofoil 1hr, by ferry 2hr).

**Uwajima** to: Beppu (1 daily; 3hr).

## Flights

**Kōchi** to: Fukuoka (2 daily; 50min); Nagoya (2 daily; 55min); Miyazaki (1 daily; 45min); Ōsaka (8 daily; 40min); Tokyo (6 daily; 1hr 15min).

**Matsuyama** to: Fukuoka (4 daily; 40min); Miyazaki (1 daily; 55min); Nagoya (2 daily; 1hr); Naha (daily; 1hr 55min); Ōsaka (4 daily; 50min); Sapporo (1 daily; 2hr); Seoul (3 weekly; 1hr 30min); Tokyo (8 daily; 1hr 20min).

**Takamatsu** to: Fukuoka (2 daily; 1hr); Kansai International (1 daily; 40min); Naha (1 daily; 2hr, 5min); Ōsaka (1 daily; 45min); Sapporo (1 daily; 1hr 50min); Sendai (1 daily; 1hr 20min); Seoul (daily; 1hr 55min); Tokyo (8 daily; 1hr 10min).

**Tokushima** to: Fukuoka (1 daily; 1hr 40min); Ōsaka (6 daily; 30min); Tokyo (7 daily; 1hr 10min).

CHAPTER NINE

# KYŪSHŪ

Lying off the south end of Honshū, Japan's third largest island, **KYŪSHŪ** is surrounded by a spray of smaller islands which trail off in a long arc across the East China Sea. It's a relaxed, uncomplicated place, with its own distinctive character and enough variety to make Kyūshū a feasible holiday destination on its own. Though it has no absolutely compelling sights, there's something for everyone here, from dynamic cities, to ancient folk dances, grumbling volcanoes and steaming hot spring baths. It's perfectly possible to scoot round Kyūshū's main cities in a week, but you'll need more like two to do it justice, allowing time for the splendid mountainous interior and a few of the more far-flung islands.

This area has long had close links with the Asian mainland, and Kyūshū's chief city, **Fukuoka**, is again becoming an important regional hub. An energetic city on the island's heavily developed north coast, most people pass Fukuoka by, but it's a shame to miss out on its superb modern architecture and vibrant nightlife. If you've only got a couple of days on Kyūshū, however, **Nagasaki** represents the best all-round destination. Though its prime draw is the A-Bomb museum and related sights, the city also has a picturesque harbour setting, a laid-back cosmopolitan air and a spattering of temples and historical museums. From here it's a short hop east to **Kumamoto**, famous for its castle and landscaped garden, and the empty, rolling uplands of central Kyūshū beyond. Dominated by the spluttering, smouldering cone of **Aso-san**, this is great hiking country, while hot-spring enthusiasts will also be in their element – from **Kurokawa Onsen**'s delightful *rotemburo* to the bawdy pleasures of **Beppu** on the east coast. The mountain village of **Takachiho** requires a fair detour, but it's worth it for the thrilling train ride along the Gokase gorge and for the local traditional dance performances depicting the antics of Japan's ancient gods.

The island's southern districts contain more on the same theme – volcanoes, onsen and magnificent scenery – and, if you're pushed for time, there's no need to linger. However, there are some real highlights, including one of the world's most active volcanoes, **Sakurajima**, which looms over the city of **Kagoshima**. Nearby, **Chiran** was a World War II airbase for kamikaze pilots who are the subject of a somewhat perturbing museum, after which **Yakushima** provides the perfect tonic. This lush, lumpy island,

### ACCOMMODATION PRICE CODES

All accommodation in this book has been graded according to the following price codes, which refer to the cheapest double or twin room available for most of the year, and include taxes. Note that rates may increase during peak holiday periods, in particular around Christmas and New Year, the Golden Week (April 28–May 6) and Obon (the week around August 15), when accommodation is very difficult to get without an advance reservation. In the case of hostels providing dormitory accommodation, the code refers to the charge per bed. See p.36 for more details on accommodation.

| | | |
|---|---|---|
| ① under ¥3000 | ④ ¥7000–10,000 | ⑦ ¥20,000–30,000 |
| ② ¥3000–5000 | ⑤ ¥10,000–15,000 | ⑧ ¥30,000–40,000 |
| ③ ¥5000–7000 | ⑥ ¥15,000–20,000 | ⑨ over ¥40,000 |

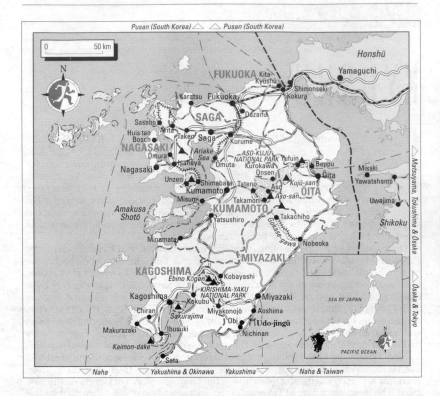

Pusan (South Korea) △ △ Pusan (South Korea)

Honshū

Yamaguchi

FUKUOKA Kita-Kyūshū

Karatsu Fukuoka Shimonoseki Kokura

Sasebo SAGA Dazaifu

Huis-ten Bosch Arita Takeo Saga Kurume

NAGASAKI Ariake Sea ASO-KUJŪ NATIONAL PARK Yufuin

Ōmura Isahaya Ōmuta Kurokawa Onsen Beppu Misaki

Nagasaki Kumamoto Unzen Shimabara Tateno Aso Kujū-san Ōita Yawatahama

Misumi Takamori Aso-san ŌITA Uwajima

Amakusa Shotō KUMAMOTO Yatsushiro Takachiho Shikoku

Minamata Gokase-gawa Nobeoka

MIYAZAKI

KAGOSHIMA Ebino Kōgen Kobayashi

Kagoshima KIRISHIMA-YAKU NATIONAL PARK Kokubu Miyazaki

Chiran Sakurajima Miyakonojō Aoshima

Makurazaki Ibusuki Obi Udo-jingū

Kaimon-dake Nichinan

Sata

▽ Naha ▽ Yakushima & Okinawa Yakushima ▽ ▽ Naha & Taiwan

*(map margin labels: Matsuyama, Tokushima & Ōsaka; Ōsaka & Tokyo)*
*(inset: SEA OF JAPAN; PACIFIC OCEAN)*

roughly 100km south of Kyūshū, has recently been designated a World Heritage Site, in honour of its towering, thousand-year-old cedar trees.

Kyūshū is connected to the main island of Honshū by road and rail. **Trains** on the Tōkaidō Shinkansen terminate in Fukuoka's Hakata Station and are covered by JR West's Sanyō Area Pass (see p.521). From Hakata, JR Kyūshū trains fan out to all the major cities, and the company offers its own five- and seven-day **rail passes** (¥15,000 & ¥20,000) for travelling round the island. These allow unlimited travel on all local, limited express and express trains, but not the Shinkansen or JR buses, and note that you have to buy the exchange voucher before arriving in Japan; see p.28–32 for more on JR passes and discount tickets.

In the central uplands and southern Kyūshū, however, you'll be more reliant on **local buses**, particularly in the south, and a limited number of private train lines. For exploring these more remote areas, **car rental** is an excellent option – as elsewhere in Japan, there are car rental outlets in almost every town and in all the main tourist areas.

### Some history

The ancient chronicles state that **Emperor Jimmu**, considered to be Japan's first emperor, set out from southern Kyūshū to found the Japanese nation in 660 BC. Though these records are open to dispute, there's evidence of human habitation on Kyūshū from before the tenth century BC, and by the beginning of the Yayoi period (300 BC–300 AD) the small kingdom of **Na** was trading with China and Korea. Local merchants brought rice-farming and bronze-making techniques back to Japan while, in the twelfth century, monks introduced Zen Buddhism to northern Kyūshū. Less welcome visitors arrived in 1274 and 1281 during the **Mongol invasions** under Kublai Khan. The first ended in a narrow escape when the Mongols withdraw, and the shogun ordered a protective wall to be built around Hakata Bay. By 1281 the Japanese were far better prepared, but their real saviour was a typhoon, subsequently dubbed *kami-kaze*, or "wind of the gods", which whipped up out of nowhere and scattered the Mongol fleet on the eve of their massed assault.

Three hundred years later, in 1543, the first **Europeans** to reach Japan pitched up on the island of Tanegashima, off southern Kyūshū. Finding an eager market for their guns among the local *daimyō*, the Portuguese sailors returned a few years later, bringing with them **missionaries**, among them the Jesuit priest **Francis Xavier**. Within fifty years the Catholic Church, now also represented by Spanish Franciscans and Dominicans, was claiming some 600,000 Christian converts. The centre of activity was **Nagasaki**, where Chinese, Dutch and British merchants swelled the throng. In the early 1600s, however, the government grew increasingly wary of the Europeans in general and Christians in particular. By fits and starts successive shoguns stamped down on the religion and restricted the movement of all foreigners, until eventually only two small communities of Dutch and Chinese merchants were left in Nagasaki.

This period of isolation lasted until the mid 1850s, when suddenly **Western learning** was again all the rage. For a brief period Nagasaki and Kagoshima in particular were at the forefront of the modernizing revolution which swept Japan after the **Meiji Restoration**. Indeed, it was the armies of the Satsuma and Choshu clans, both from Kyūshū, which helped restore the emperor to the throne, and many members of the new government hailed from the island. In 1877, however, Kagoshima's **Saigō Takamori** led a revolt against the Meiji government in what became known as the **Satsuma Rebellion**. Saigō's army was routed, but he's still something of a local hero in Kyūshū, where they pride themselves in being different from the rest of Japan – perhaps not surprising, when Kyūshū is closer to Korea than it is to Tokyo.

# NORTH KYŪSHŪ

Kyūshū's five northern prefectures (Fukuoka, Saga, Nagasaki, Kumamoto and Ōita) contain the bulk of the island's population, industry and economic power. Though coal-mining and shipbuilding, the region's traditional money-earners, have been in slow decline for many years, there's been a massive boom in electronics industries – so much so that Kyūshū now produces ten percent of the world's semiconductors and has been dubbed "silicon island". Nowhere is this renewed optimism more visible than in **Fukuoka**, with its high-tech research centres reflected in futuristic urban renewal projects, but the upturn is also visible in other cities such as Kita-Kyūshū and Kumamoto.

But north Kyūshū isn't just about industry. Its ragged western shores, from Fukuoka round to **Nagasaki**'s misshapen headland and down through the Amakusa Islands, display magnificent stretches of coastal scenery. From here the route strikes east via **Unzen-dake**, one of Kyūshū's several active volcanoes, to the castle-town of **Kumamoto**. This is the main jumping-off point for exploring **Aso-san**'s vast caldera, which dominates the island's wild, relatively empty central highlands. Most people then continue on to **Beppu**, on Kyūshū's east coast, where bathing is taken to such an extreme that's it's earned the accolade of Japan's hot-spring capital. Further south, on the edge of the central highlands, the isolated village of **Takachiho** is accessible from either Aso or Beppu. It's a bit of a trek, but the effort is amply rewarded with a dramatic journey and the opportunity to see lively folk-dances recalling the ancient gods and goddesses.

# Kita-Kyūshū

A narrow strip of water little more than 1km wide separates Kyūshū from the southern tip of Honshū. Three tunnels and a soaring suspension bridge funnel road and rail traffic south from Shimonoseki (see p.568) into the sprawling, industrial conurbation of **KITA-KYŪSHŪ**. Most people travel straight through to Fukuoka (see opposite), but if you're arriving by ferry or changing trains for Beppu and other east-coast towns, you may need to make an overnight stop here. Kita-Kyūshū was created in 1963 out of five towns, of which **Kokura** is the largest. Here you'll find the city's main train station, administrative offices, the majority of its hotels and ferries to Matsuyama (Shikoku). Neighbouring **Yahata**, however, offers the area's cheapest accommodation, while over on the east coast, **Shin-Moji** now serves as the area's main ferry terminal.

Despite its surroundings, central **Kokura** is not an unattractive place. It has a small but lively downtown area south of Kokura JR Station, while the northern, port-side districts are catching up fast. It also boasts the area's only notable sight, a reconstructed castle with a moderately interesting museum, twenty minutes' walk west of the station. Built in the mid-sixteenth century, **Kokura-jō** (daily: April–Oct 9am–6pm; Jan–March, Nov & Dec till 5pm; ¥350) was home to the Ogasawara clan for two hundred years until they were forced to abandon it in 1866. It then lay in ruins until 1959 when the keep was rebuilt in the original style, including its distinctive, overhanging fifth floor. While it's now all concrete inside, it's worth venturing in to see a scale model of seventeenth-century Kokura peopled by 1500 paper figures, full of life and energy despite their diminutive size; use the knee-high telescopes to take a closer look.

## Practicalities

Kita-Kyūshū's main **train station** is the new Kokura Station, a stop on the Shinkansen between Tokyo and Fukuoka where you can pick up trains to Beppu and Miyazaki. **Ferries** from Matsuyama (Shikoku) pull in at the Sunatsu pier, a five-minute walk north of Kokura Station. Boats from Kobe, Ōsaka and Tokushima (also on Shikoku) use Shin-Moji-kō over on the east coast; from the port take a taxi (around ¥2000) to JR Moji Station, then a train (6min; ¥200) to Kokura. There's a **tourist information** booth (daily 9am–8pm; ☎093/541-4189) beside the station's north-exit ticket barrier, where you can make hotel reservations and get basic information in English. For anything more complicated, try Kita-Kyūshū International Association's desk (Mon–Fri

| KITA-KYŪSHŪ | | |
|---|---|---|
| **Kita-Kyūshū** | *Kita-Kyūshū* | 北九州 |
| **Kokura** | *Kokura* | 小倉 |
| Chisan Hotel | *Chisan Hoteru* | チサンホテル |
| Kurofune | *Kurofune* | 黒舟 |
| Rihga Royal Hotel | *Riiga Roiyaru Hoteru* | リーガロイヤルホテル |
| Yutaka Business Hotel | *Yutaka Bijinesu Hoteru* | ユタカビジネスホテル |
| **Shin-Moji-kō** | *Shin-Moji-kō* | 新門司港 |
| **Yahata** | *Yahata* | 八幡 |
| Ginga-no-chanpon | *Ginga-no-chanpon* | 銀河のチャンポン |
| Kisaragi | *Kisaragi* | きさらぎ |
| Kita-Kyūshū Youth Hostel | *Kita-Kyūshū Yūsu Hosuteru* | 北九州ユースホステル |
| Hotel Townhouse Matsuya | *Hoteru Taunhausu Matsuya* | ホテルタウンハウスまつや |

9am–5.30pm; ☎093/551-0555) on the ground floor of the distinctive, modern Conference Centre, next to Sunatsu pier. At weekends, only their main office in Yahata is open (Tues–Sun 9am–5.30pm; ☎093/662-0055); it's in a black-glass building about ten minutes' walk south of Yahata Station.

You'll find a clutch of middle- and top-end **hotels** immediately north of Kokura Station, including the rather incongruous *Rihga Royal Hotel* (☎093/531-1121, fax 521-2068; ⑦), behind the Laforet department store – its deluxe, top-floor tower rooms are the work of Japanese designer Hanae Mori. In the next block east, the new *Chisan Hotel* (☎093/531-4000, fax 531-5120; ⑤) is a more straightforward business hotel offering well-appointed, comfortable rooms at reasonable rates. The *Yutaka Business Hotel* (☎093/511-0101, fax 511-0120; ④) is decidedly functional but this represents about the best budget accommodation in central Kokura; it's located two blocks west of the Laforet store, overlooking the station car parks. Otherwise, hop down the line to Yahata where *Hotel Townhouse Matsuya* (☎093/661-7891, fax 671-5648; ④), a small, friendly member of the Japanese Inn Group, offers modest Western and *tatami* rooms, all with bath and TV, right beside the station. *Kita-Kyūshū Youth Hostel* (☎093/681-8142; ①) lies 25 minutes' walk from Yahata Station on the opposite hillside. Head south past Kita-Kyūshū International Centre, over the expressway and then up to the Sarakura-yama cable-car station – the hostel is the low, white building hidden among trees to the right.

The warren of streets south of Kokura Station is a good area to trawl for **restaurants**. One of the most atmospheric places is *Kurofune* (daily 5–11pm), a giant *izakaya* where you can wash down the local speciality, *karashi mentaiko* (salted cods' roe marinated in salt and red pepper), with a jar or two of beer. To find it, walk south from the station down the main road, Mikage-dōri, till you spot its large, black triangular sign on the corner opposite Quest bookstore. On the way you'll pass *Kashi* (daily 11.30am–10pm), a cheerful Indian restaurant a few blocks north on Mikage-dōri, which offers good-value set lunches every day except Sunday. Outside Yahata Station, *Gingano-chanpon* (Mon–Sat 11am–7.30pm) is a great place to eat, identifiable by its bright yellow frontage and matching flags. Locals come here to slurp steaming bowls of *chanpon*, thick noodles laced with deep-fried chicken chunks, or sizzling hot-plates of *yakisoba* for ¥700–900. Out on the ring road (walk past Kita-Kyūshū International Centre and turn right), you'll find two reasonable restaurants, *Kisaragi* (daily 10am–10pm), on the left next to a golf-driving range, which serves well-priced Japanese sets from ¥700, and, a bit further along, *Skylark* (daily 9am–10pm) offering everything from sandwiches to *tonkatsu*.

# Fukuoka

A big, semi-industrial city at the southern end of the Shinkansen, **FUKUOKA** was, until recently, simply a place to negotiate as quickly as possible en route to Kyūshū's more picturesque regions. However, over the last few years it has established itself as western Japan's major cultural centre and an important international gateway. Though not a huge place (just under 1.3 million people), the city combines tremendous vitality with a determination to make the rest of Japan sit up and take notice – already it claims the country's biggest hotel, longest bar, largest cinema complex and most advanced baseball stadium. For the visitor this translates into a thoroughly modern city with all the energy and atmosphere of a Tokyo or Ōsaka, contained within manageable proportions.

Though Fukuoka offers few historical sights, it does have one or two excellent museums plus more than enough outstanding modern architecture to justify at least a day in transit. The highlights are **Canal City**, a sparkling new, self-contained cinema, hotel and shopping complex built around a semi-circular strip of water, and **Hawks Town**, which forms part of a major seafront redevelopment. The city is also renowned

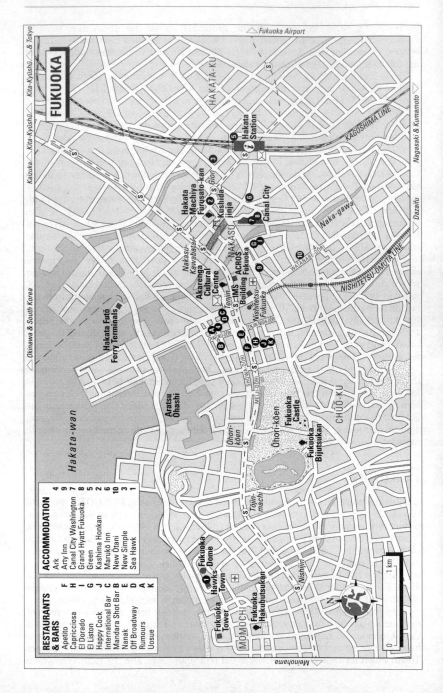

△ Fukuoka Airport

**FUKUOKA**

HAKATA-KU

Hakata Station

KAGOSHIMA LINE

Hakata Machiya Furusato-kan

Kushida-jinja

Canal City

Naka-gawa

Nakasu-Kawabata

Akarenga Cultural Centre

ACROS Building Fukuoka

NAKASU

Nishitetsu-Fukuoka

IMS Building

NISHITETSU-ŌMUTA LINE

WATANABE-DŌRI

Hakata Futō Ferry Terminals

Hakata-wan

Aratsu Ōhashi

TENJIN NISHI-DŌRI

SHŌWA-DŌRI

MEIJI-DŌRI

Ōhori-kōen

Ōhori-kōen

Fukuoka Castle

Fukuoka Bijutsukan

CHŪŌ-KU

Tōjin-machi

**RESTAURANTS & BARS**

| | |
|---|---|
| Apetito | F |
| Capricciosa | H |
| El Dorado | I |
| El Liston | G |
| Happy Cock | J |
| International Bar | C |
| Mandara Shot Bar | B |
| Nanak | E |
| Off Broadway | D |
| Rumours | A |
| Uosue | K |

**ACCOMMODATION**

| | |
|---|---|
| Ark | 4 |
| Arty Inn | 9 |
| Canal City Washington | 7 |
| Grand Hyatt Fukuoka | 8 |
| Green | 5 |
| Kashima Honkan | 2 |
| Marukō Inn | 6 |
| New Otani | 10 |
| New Simple | 3 |
| Sea Hawk | 1 |

Fukuoka Dome

Hawks Town

Fukuoka Tower

Fukuoka Hakubutsukan

MOMOCHI

N

0    1 km

△ Meinohama

△ Okinawa & South Korea

◁ Kaizuka △ Kita-Kyūshū △ Kita-Kyūshū △ & Tokyo

▷ Nagasaki & Kumamoto

▷ Dazaifu

Nishijin

for its festivals and folk crafts, which are presented at **Hakata Machiya Folk Museum**. As with any self-respecting Japanese city of this size, Fukuoka maintains a lively entertainment district, in this case crammed onto the tiny island of **Nakasu**, though it's safer on the wallet to head for the less glitzy bars and restaurants of **Tenjin**, the city's main downtown area.

## Arrival, information and city transport

Central Fukuoka is split in two by the Naka-gawa. To the east of this river, **Hakata** district centres on Fukuoka's main **train station**, confusingly known as Hakata Station – a historical legacy of when the two neighbouring towns of Fukuoka and Hakata were combined. Hakata Station is the terminus of the Tōkaidō Shinkansen and the focal point of Kyūshū's local JR services. West of the Naka-gawa, in **Tenjin**, the city's commercial heart, stands Nishitetsu-Fukuoka Station, where trains from Dazaifu terminate (see p.667). These central districts are linked by subway to **Fukuoka airport**, handily located only two stops down the line from Hakata (5min; ¥220). From the **ferry** terminal, however, you have to take a Nishitetsu city bus for the ten-minute ride to either Tenjin or Hakata Station (¥200). **Long-distance buses** call at the Tenjin Fukuoka Bus Centre (above the Nishitetsu Station), before terminating at the Fukuoka Kōtsu Centre outside Hakata Station.

Fukuoka has a good sprinkling of **information** offices. There are desks at the airport, but the main tourist information centre (daily 9am–7pm; ☎092/431-3003) is located in Hakata Station's central concourse, where English-speaking staff are reasonably helpful and can provide city maps, hotel lists and the *Fukuoka City Visitor's Guide*. If you're in Tenjin, or need more serious English-language assistance, Fukuoka International Association (daily 10am–8pm; ☎092/733-2220) offers a broad range of information, from tourist brochures to local events and English-speaking doctors; you'll find them in the Rainbow Plaza, on the eighth floor of Tenjin's IMS Building. Finally, the Prefectural Information Centre (Tues–Sun 10am–7pm; ☎092/725-9100) is in east Tenjin, on the second floor of the ACROS Fukuoka building.

All these places dish out free city **maps**, but it's also worth asking in the subway for the useful English booklet, *Guide to Main Subway Station Vicinities*, which contains five detailed area maps. *Rainbow* is a free monthly **newsletter** aimed at residents but with some interesting articles and listings of what's on, while *Metro* gives snippets of local news together with details of clubs and restaurant reviews. You can pick both up at Rainbow Plaza.

The easiest way of **getting around** Fukuoka is on its fast and efficient **subway** system. There's plenty of English-language information and, though there are only two lines, most places of interest fall within walking distance of a station. The main Kūkō line runs from the airport through central Fukuoka, via Hakata Station and Tenjin, to Meinohama in the west, while the shorter Hakozaki line splits off at Nakasu-kawabata (one stop east of Tenjin) for the northeast suburb of Kaizuka. Trains run from 5.30am to around 11pm, every three to eight minutes depending on the time of day, and the minimum fare is ¥180; buy your tickets at the station vending machines. If you anticipate doing a lot of journeys, it might be worth buying a one-day subway card (¥850), which also gets you small discounts at several museums and the Fukuoka Tower. For those places not within striking distance of the subway, such as the Hawks Town area, you'll need to use Nishitetsu **city buses**, most of which funnel through the Hakata Station–Tenjin corridor. Take a numbered ticket from the machine as you enter and pay the driver on exit; the screen at the front of the bus shows how much you have to pay – the minimum fare is ¥170. A day-pass (¥600) is available for the central zone, but you probably won't cover enough ground in a day to make it worthwhile.

| FUKUOKA | | |
|---|---|---|
| Fukuoka | *Fukuoka* | 福岡 |
| Fukuoka Bijutsukan | *Fukuokai Bijutsukan* | 福岡市美術館 |
| Fukuoka Hakubutsukan | *Fukuoka Hakubutsukan* | 福岡市博物館 |
| Fukuoka Tower | *Fukuoka Tawā* | 福岡タワー |
| Hakata | *Hakata* | 博多 |
| Hakata Machiya Furusato-kan | *Hakata Machiya Furusato-kan* | 博多町家ふるさと館 |
| Hawks Town | *Hōkusu Taun* | ホークスタウン |
| Kushida-jinja | *Kushida-jinja* | 櫛田神社 |
| Nakasu | *Nakasu* | 中洲 |
| Ōhori-kōen | *Ōhori-kōen* | 大濠公園 |
| Tenjin | *Tenjin* | 天神 |
| **ACCOMMODATION** | | |
| Ark Hotel | *Āku Hoteru* | アークホテル |
| Arty Inn | *Aruti In* | アルティイン |
| Canal City Fukuoka Washington Hotel | *Kyanaru Shiti Fukuoka Washinton Hoteru* | キャナルシティ福岡ワシントンホテル |
| Grand Hyatt Fukuoka | *Gurando Haiatto Fukuoka* | グランドハイアット福岡 |
| Green Hotel | *Guriin Hoteru* | グリーンホテル |
| Kashima Honkan | *Kashima Honkan* | 鹿島本館 |
| Marukō Inn | *Marukō In* | マルコーイン |
| Hotel New Ōtani | *Hoteru Nyū Ōtani* | ホテルニューオオタニ |
| Hotel New Simple | *Hoteru Nyū Shinpuru* | ホテルニューシンプル |
| Sea Hawk | *Shii Hōku* | シーホーク |
| **RESTAURANTS** | | |
| Ume-no-hana | *Ume-no-hana* | 梅の花 |
| Uosue | *Uosue* | 魚末 |

## Accommodation

Fukuoka has several modern, world-class **hotels** which aren't a bad deal compared to what you'd pay for similar accommodation in Tokyo. For those on more modest budgets, there's a good choice of business hotels and some truly bargain-basement rooms, mostly located around Hakata Station. You can make hotel **reservations** in the station at a desk (Mon–Sat noon–2.30pm & 3.30–8pm, Sun & hols 11am–12.30pm & 3.30–7pm) next to the tourist information centre – note that there's a small commission charge – and at the airport.

**Ark Hotel**, 3-7-22 Tenjin (☎092/781-2552, fax 781-2606). Spruce, marble-lobbied business hotel in the thick of the Tenjin restaurant and bar district, five-minutes' walk from the subway. Though not outstanding, the rooms are well equipped and reasonably priced for such a central location. ⑤.

**Arty Inn**, 5-1-2 Watanabe-dōri (☎092/724-3511, fax 714-3200). The name alone is endearing, but this business hotel is also good value. The rooms are simple but well decorated, with unusually large beds and bathrooms. ⑤.

**Canal City Fukuoka Washington Hotel**, 1-2-20 Sumiyoshi (☎092/282-8800, fax 282-0757). This slightly upmarket member of the *Washington* chain is a good option if you want to stay in Canal City but can't afford the *Hyatt* (see below). Rooms are relatively spacious and come with TV, fridge and phone, and good-size bathrooms. ⑥.

**Grand Hyatt Fukuoka**, 1-2-82 Sumiyoshi (☎092/282-1234, fax 282-2817). Fukuoka's top hotel occupies a large chunk of Canal City, between Hakata Station and the Nakasu nightlife district. The understated entrance opens into an oval-shaped lobby and a plunging atrium looking out over fountains. The big, beautifully designed rooms incorporate Japanese touches, such as *shōji* screens and contemporary artwork, and have huge bathrooms. ⑦–⑧.

**Green Hotel 1 & 2**, 3-11 Hakataeki-chūōgai (☎092/451-4111, fax 451-4508). The two *Green* hotels offer some of the cheapest accommodation around Hakata Station. The mostly single rooms are basic boxes, but come with TV and tiny bathroom. They also have a few doubles with very small beds, plus slightly more expensive and larger twins. ④.

**Kashima Honkan**, 3-11 Reisen-machi (☎092/291-0746, fax 271-7995). This homely, eighty-year-old ryokan is located on a pleasant backstreet, just round the corner from Gion subway station. The 23 *tatami* rooms are traditional and elegant, with antique screens and wall-hangings. Rooms are available with or without meals. English spoken. ⑤.

**Marukō Inn**, 3-30-25 Hakataeki-mae (☎092/461-0505, fax 475-2680). A short walk west of Hakata Station, this good-value, mid-range business hotel offers rooms that are comfortable, cheery and well kept, all with TV, mini-bar and bathroom. ⑤.

**Hotel New Ōtani**, 1-1-2 Watanabe-dōri (☎092/714-1111, fax 715-5658). Predictably efficient hotel offering all the usual facilities, including restaurants, shopping arcade, non-smoking rooms, CNN and BBC TV. The bedrooms are slowly being revamped in brighter tones, but they're all a good size and well appointed. The only drawback is its location, about fifteen minutes' walk south of Tenjin subway station. ⑥–⑦.

**Hotel New Simple**, 1-23-11 Hakataeki-mae (☎092/411-4311, fax 411-4312). Basic but welcoming hotel near Gion subway station, behind the smarter *President Hotel*. It has the cheapest, hardest beds you'll find in Fukuoka, mostly in single rooms with communal washing facilities. They also have two dorms with bare, wooden cubicles, though they are sometimes reluctant to use them. English spoken. Dorms ①; rooms ③.

**Sea Hawk**, 2-2-3 Jigyohama (☎092/844-8111, fax 844-7887). Japan's biggest hotel, out near Momochi Seaside Park, vies with the *Grand Hyatt* for pole position. Most of its 1052 rooms overlook Hakata Bay, with sea-view Jacuzzis at the luxury end. They're stylish but no means as spacious or luxurious as the *Hyatt*'s. The hotel has any number of bars and restaurants, while baseball enthusiasts can walk to the next-door Fukuoka Dome. ⑥–⑦.

# The City

Even today the old cultural and economic divide between the original castle town, Fukuoka, and the former merchants' quarter of Hakata can be traced, albeit faintly, in the city's streets. Much of **Hakata** consists of dull office blocks, but the district is also home to the city's oldest **shrine** and its most rumbustious festival. Here too, you'll still find the occasional wooden building, narrow lane or aged wall, and can discover some of the unique, Hakata culture in its well-presented **folk museum**. Not surprisingly, many **craft industries** originated in this area, most famously Hakata dolls and *ori* silks, while *geisha* still work the traditional **entertainment district** of Nakasu. Nevertheless, Hakata has also managed to throw up a startling exception, and one of Fukuoka's most famous landmarks, in **Canal City**. West of the Naka-gawa, **Tenjin** has upmarket boutiques, department stores and "fashion buildings", but there's little in the way of sights until you go further west to the ruins of Fukuoka castle in **Ōhori-kōen**. As well as an attractive lake, this park also contains an **art museum** with an important collection of twentieth-century works. North and west again, you reach the high-tech **Fukuoka City Museum** of local history and, beyond, the coastal **Momochi** area dominated by the **Fukuoka Tower** and the **Hawks Town** development.

## Hakata and Tenjin

**Kami-Kawabata-dōri**, now a covered arcade, was once the city's main shopping street, and its small stores, selling a mix of clothes, daily provisions, crafts and household shrines, now have a pleasantly old-world feel. Exit 5 of Hakata's Nakasu-Kawabata subway station brings you out straight onto the street. At weekends, look out for a towering festival float filling one of the shops, where you can sample *Kawabata zenzai*, a hot, sweet red-bean soup topped with rice cakes, washed down with green tea (Sat, Sun & hols 11am–5pm; ¥400).

At the far end of the arcade, a left turn under a *torii* brings you to the back entrance of Hakata's principal shrine, **Kushida-jinja**, founded in 757 AD. However, since its halls are reconstructed every 25 years, the prime attraction is another of the twelve gaudy, top-heavy floats displayed during Hakata's annual **Gion Yamakasa festival** (July 1–15). The climax of these lively celebrations is a five-kilometre, dawn race finishing at Kushida-jinja, in which seven teams manhandle one-ton floats through the streets while spectators dowse them with water. Like Kyoto's Gion festival (see p.463), this harks back to the Kamakura period (1185–1333) when Buddhist priests sprinkled sacred water to drive away summer epidemics. There's a small **museum** (daily 10–5pm; ¥200) of shrine treasures in the grounds, not of great interest, though it stocks English-language leaflets about Kushida-jinja and the festival. As you leave by the main, east gate, look out for a couple of hefty, stone anchors, supposedly left behind by the Mongol fleet (see p.655), lying beneath a thousand-year-old gingko tree.

A short walk east of Kushida-jinja you can't miss the traditional whitewashed walls and grey roofs of **Hakata Machiya Furusato-kan** (daily 10am–6pm; ¥200) which records the history of Hakata over the last two hundred years. Made up of three buildings, the museum is well designed, with plenty of scale models, reconstructed interiors and good coverage of Hakata's many festivities, including a twenty-minute video of the Gion Yamakasa festival (regular shows 10am–5pm). The middle block comprises a late-nineteenth-century weaver's workshop, with a soaring roof space, where craftsmen demonstrate traditional *Hakata-ori* silk weaving on aged looms.

Immediately west of Kushida-jinja, **Nakasu** entertainment district is built on a sandbank in the middle of the Naka-gawa. At its most atmospheric at night, the district can still be an interesting wander during daylight. The island is a mere 1500m long by 250m wide, but its size is deceptive – somehow more than 2500 restaurants, bars and food-stalls manage to squeeze themselves on. Its southernmost point lies just off the weird and wonderful, multicoloured blocks of **Canal City**, Fukuoka's vision of the future. Apart from two large hotels, a major theatre, a thirteen-screen cinema with seating for nearly 2600, and an amusement hall, the complex also houses a shopping arcade and multimedia store, plus a host of bars and restaurants. The liveliest part, however, is the interior court, where the pink, purple and blue buildings wrap round the "canal", which erupts occasionally into five-storey-high jets of water.

From Nakasu, a pedestrian bridge leads west across the Naka-gawa to Tenjin. Immediately over the river, the European-style, wooden building is the **former Prefectural Hall** (Tues–Sun 9am–5pm; ¥220). Built for a trade fair in 1910, the hall's interior plaster cornices, marble fireplaces and wooden panelling will probably be of greater interest to Japanese visitors. The next block west, however, is dominated by a bizarre building with a name to match. **ACROS Fukuoka**, meaning "Asian Crossroads Over the Sea", was completed in 1995 as a cultural centre. Its terraced south side forms a "step garden" (daily 9am–5.30pm; free), giving it the vague air of an Inca ruin, while inside lurk a symphony hall, information centre (see p.659), shops and restaurants. The **Akarenga Cultural Centre** (Tues–Sun 9am–9pm; free), one block north of ACROS Fukuoka, was erected in 1909 for a life insurance company and designed by Tatsuno Kingo, one of Japan's first modern architects, who went in for busy, white-stone detailing, domes and turrets. The interior offices, now given over to exhibition space and a coffee shop, are more sedate and have some attractive touches, particularly the cashiers' windows and iron grille-work.

## The western sights

In 1601 the Kuroda lords built their castle on a low hill sitting among coastal marshes to the west of the Naka-gawa. Today, just a few old stone walls and ruined watchtowers remain, but the castle grounds have been landscaped to form **Ōhori-kōen**, a large public park. It's most easily accessible from the subway; exit 3 of Ōhori-kōen Station brings you up beside a large lake spanned by a pleasing necklace of islets and bridges. The park's foremost attraction is the city's art museum, **Fukuoka Bijutsukan** (Tues–Sun 9.30am–5.30pm; ¥200), situated in its southeast corner about ten minutes' walk from the subway. Its three ground-floor galleries contain a hotchpotch of early Japanese and Asian art, including the Kuroda family treasures and several eye-catching statues of Buddhism's twelve guardian generals (*Jūni Jinsho*), each crowned with his associated zodiacal beast. Upstairs you leap a few centuries to the likes of Warhol, Miro and Lichtenstein in a great retrospective of twentieth-century Western art, displayed alongside contemporary Japanese works.

The district northwest of here, known as **Momochi**, has only recently been reclaimed from the sea and handed over to ambitious city planners. By far their most striking project is the 234-metre, pencil-thin **Fukuoka Tower** which has become one of the city's most famous icons. The closest subway station is Nishijin, about fifteen minutes' walk to the south, or city bus number #305 from Tenjin stops right outside. Primarily a communications tower, the first section is an empty shell coated with 8000 sheets of mirror glass, while the top third bristles with radio transmitters. In between, at 123m, the architects slipped in an observation deck (daily 9.30am–9pm, March–Sept till 10/11pm; ¥800) to capitalize on the spectacular views of Fukuoka and Hakata Bay. On the ground-floor there's a moderately interesting **Doll Museum** (daily 9.30am–6pm, July & Aug till 7pm; ¥300), displaying just some of the 30,000 dolls amassed by a local collector.

Five minutes' walk south from the tower, the excellent local history museum, **Fukuoka Hakubutsukan** (Tues–Sun 9.30am–5.30pm; ¥200) occupies an imposing, late 1980s structure of mirrored glass and grey stone. The museum's most famous exhibit is the two-centimetre-square **Kin-in gold seal**, ornamented with a dumpy, coiled snake. According to its inscription, the seal was presented by China's Han emperor to the King of Na (see p.654) in 57 AD – it was only rediscovered in 1784 on an island in Hakata Bay. The main exhibition hall, containing the seal, is divided into seven chronological periods from the kingdom of Na to the 1950s, with a final section devoted to folk culture. An English-language guidebook provides selective details, or you can borrow headphones for a fuller commentary. The museum is well laid-out and enlivened by videos, maps and models, including one of the Yamakasa Festival (see opposite).

Before heading back to central Fukuoka, it's worth walking over to the neighbouring reclamation area, roughly 800m east through an area of high-tech research centres, to visit **Hawks Town** and the *Sea Hawk* hotel. Owned by the Daiei retail group and designed by Caesar Perri, this is one of Fukuoka's top hotels. It also passes muster as a tourist attraction, partly for its extraordinary boat-shaped floor plan and luxurious interior design, but mainly for the jungle-filled, hot-house atrium on the seaward side. Parrots squawk unhappily from cramped cages, but that apart it works well: a waterfall slides down one wall, model giant stag beetles and crabs hide among the palms, while tropical sunshades, exotic birdcalls and the sound of rustling leaves add extra "authenticity". The humidity is boosted regularly with a fine spray and, so they say, alpha waves transmitted to ensure "stable bio-rhythms and a tranquil spirit" – which makes ¥700 for a coffee at the atrium's *Luggnagg Café* an absolute steal.

Daiei, which also owns the Hawks baseball team, gave them an equally luxurious home-ground next to the hotel. Opened in 1993, **Fukuoka Dome** easily outclasses Tokyo's older rival (see p.107): it's not only larger but is the first stadium in Japan to sport a retractable roof. The Dome also boasts the world's longest bar, *The Big Life*, an 188-metre counter overlooking the pitch, though it's marred by a rather tacky row of themed service outlets and game machines (daily 11am–midnight; cover charge ¥500; during matches, ¥1000 after 4pm).

To return to central Fukuoka from the Dome you can walk south for fifteen minutes to Tōjin-machi subway station. Alternatively, for a scenic ride along the seafront expressway and over the Aratsu-Ōhashi suspension bridge, pick up a Nishitetsu bus either from the *Sea Hawk* or the Fukuoka Dome-mae bus stop on the main road; bus #305 goes via Tenjin to Hakata Station.

## Eating, drinking and entertainment

Fukuoka's most notorious **speciality food** is *fugu*, the poisonous blow-fish eaten only in winter (Nov–March); though you'll find *fugu* throughout Japan, the best is said to come from this region. Cheaper food is on offer at the city's mobile street-kitchens, **yatai**, the plastic sheets cocooning a steamy, pungent world where you squeeze in at the counter for hearty bowls of ramen, or, less traditionally, *oden* and tempura, accompanied by flasks of sake. A typical stall charges roughly ¥500 for ramen, though some are going more upmarket. *Yatai* can be found around the intersection of Tenjin Nishidōri and Shōwa-dōri, and along the southwest bank of Nakasu island. Tenjin is also a good bet for more traditional **restaurants**, particularly the blocks west and north of Tenjin Station. Sun Plaza, under the west side of Hakata Station, has a host of mostly downmarket eating houses, while the station itself is a cheap place to try out *karashi mentaiko*, the spicy fish eggs for which north Kyūshū is famed; you'll find both *mentaiko onigiri* (rice balls) and *bentō* at the station stalls.

Fukuoka's famous **Nakasu** nightlife district occupies an island in the Naka-gawa, seemingly just staying afloat under the weight of clubs, restaurants, bars and soft-porn cinemas. It's a great area to wander round, but most places are extortionately expensive and only take customers by recommendation, if they accept foreigners at all. A happier hunting ground lies around Tenjin's main crossroads, particularly **Oyafuko-dōri** and streets immediately to the east which are packed with bars and clubs. Roughly translated, Oyafuko-dōri means street of disobedient children, originally referring to a local school but nowadays more applicable to groups of college kids in various stages of inebriation who gather here at weekends under the blind eye of the *kōban* on the corner.

As for more formal **entertainment**, Fukuoka is large enough to be on the circuit for pop stars, musicals and major theatre productions. The main venues are Canal City's new Fukuoka City Theatre, ACROS Symphony Hall, or Fukuoka Dome for the real biggies. To find out what's on, consult the *Rainbow* or *Metro* newsletters (see p.659) or ask at any of the information centres; tickets are available through PIA (☎092/708-9999). Movie fans should check the current week's showings at Japan's biggest **cinema**, AMC Canal City 13, on Canal City's fourth floor; cut-price seats (¥1000) are available on weekdays up to 7pm (ring ☎092/272-2222 for 24hr recorded information). Finally, **blues** aficionados should check out the *Blue Note* club, at 2-7-6 Tenjin (☎092/715-6666).

### Restaurants

**Apetito**, 29-5 Daimyō. Hugely popular bakery-cum-restaurant on Tenjin's Meiji-dōri, especially for the excellent-value lunchtime deals. Western food from sandwiches and salads to more substantial fish and meat dishes, all for well under ¥2000. But star attraction is the bread bar – help yourself for an extra ¥200. Daily 8am–11pm.

**Capricciosa**, 2-6-5 Daimyō (☎092/716-7701). The well-known Tokyo chain of Italian restaurants has hit Kyūshū, offering the same value for money, mammoth portions and queues at peak times. Daily 11.30am–10.30pm.

**Food Live**, *Grand Hyatt Fukuoka*, 1-2-82 Sumiyoshi. This basement-floor food court is your best option for somewhere to eat in Canal City, both for atmosphere and value for money. Choose between the appetizing aromas of five open-plan, stylish eating spaces; a moderate meal should cost around ¥2000 per person.

**Nanak**, 2F, 3-2-1 Maizuru. One of whose reliable Indian chain whose lunchtime sets are excellent value. They also do reasonable evening menus, but outside these special deals count on at least ¥2000 per head. Daily 11am–3pm & 5–10pm.

**Sizzler**, B2, ACROS Fukuoka, 1-1-1 Tenjin. This large, bright, steak restaurant does a great salad-bar lunch, kids' menus and a decent evening buffet. As well as big, juicy steaks, they serve hamburgers and other variations on the theme. Daily 10am–10pm.

**Ume-no-hana**, 4F, Canal City. If you can't get to the Dazaifu outlet of this popular tofu restaurant (see p.670), this is the next best thing. Try the silky-smooth *yudōfu*, cooked in famously pure water from Ureshino onsen. The restaurant is non-smoking. Daily 10am–4pm & 5–11pm.

**Uosue**, 2-1-30 Daimyō. A small, traditional restaurant famous for having the freshest fish in town. Menus change daily and there aren't any displayed prices, but count on at least ¥2500 for a satisfying evening meal. Even on weekdays it pays to get here before 6pm. Daily 11am–late.

## Bars

**El Liston & El Dorado**, *Il Palazzo Hotel*, 3-13-1 Haruyoshi. Two of several high-tech bars in the basement of the whimsical *Il Palazzo Hotel*. *El Liston* is the more elegant, with warm coral tones, soft lighting and comfy chairs, while the main bar, *El Dorado*, by Italian designer, Aldo Rossi, is dominated by a magnificent, gilded icon of the hotel's distinctive facade. Not surprisingly, prices aren't cheap: there's a ¥500 cover charge and the lowliest beer is ¥600. Opening times vary.

**Happy Cock**, 9F, 2-1-51 Daimyō. It's elbow-room only at weekends in this large, laid-back bar opposite *Capricciosa* (see Restaurants). Drinks are all ¥500 – buy your own beer from vending machines – and they do a range of foods, such as nachos, pizzas and Thai soup, with an all-you-can-eat-and-drink deal in the early evening (6–9pm; ¥2500). Tues–Thurs 6pm–2am, Fri & Sat 6pm–4am.

**International Bar**, 4F, 3 Tenjin. This ordinary little bar is a good place to network with local *gaijin*. No cover charge and inexpensive snacks. Look out for the English sign on the main street opposite Matsuya Ladies store, north of the main Tenjin crossroads. *Bolero*, in the basement of the same building, is a similarly relaxed, inexpensive place. Mon–Sat 7pm–1am.

**Mandara Shot Bar**, 3F Maria House, 1-8-26 Maizuru. It's worth paying the ¥500 cover charge to see inside this wonderful bar, fashioned on the theme of Kali, India's black goddess. Greeted by a statue of the Dance of Death, you lounge on floor cushions in a hushed cavern partitioned by thin muslin screens and lit by flickering candles. Drinks start at ¥500, and there's an eclectic food menu. Daily 7pm–3am, Fri & Sat till 5am.

**Off Broadway**, 2F, 3-2-13 Tenjin. They play everything from jazz to hip-hop in this dark, lively bar with regular reggae and latin nights. Though there's no cover charge, you're expected to buy at least one drink, with prices starting at ¥400 for a beer; midweek, beer pitchers are half price until 10pm. They claim to serve the "best hamburgers in Kyūshū", besides large portions of fries, buffalo wings and daily set meals. One street west of Oyafuki-dōri. Daily 7.30pm–2am, Fri & Sat till 4am.

**Rumours**, 1F, PI Stage Bldg, 3-8-1 Tenjin. A popular *gaijin* hangout, west of the *Ark Hotel*, with plenty of seating and music at conversation-levels. Live bands two or three times a month. Mon–Sat 7.30pm–3pm.

# Listings

**Airlines** Air China (☎092/282-5611); Air Lanka (☎092/451-2855); Air New Zealand (☎092/724-3211); ANA (☎0120–029222); Asiana Airlines (☎092/471-7788); Cathay Pacific (☎092/441-1806); China Airlines (☎092/471-7788); China Eastern Airlines (☎092/472-8383); Eva Air (☎092/412-3553); Garuda (☎092-475-3400); JAL (☎0120–255971); Korean Air (☎092/441-3311); Northwest Airlines (☎092/262-2771); Philippine Airlines (☎092/415-3232); Qantas (☎092/761-1821); Singapore Airlines (☎092/481-7007); Thai International (☎092/734-6409).

**Airport information** ☎092/621-6059. Note that Fukuoka airport has three terminals: numbers 1 and 2 for domestic flights and 3 for international.

**Banks and exchange** There's a whole cluster of banks with foreign exchange desks outside the front, west entrance of Hakata Station, including Tokyo Mitsubishi Bank and Dai-ichi Kangyō Bank. In Tenjin, head for Meiji-dōri, near the junction with Watanabe-dōri, where you'll also find Fuji Bank and Sanwa Bank.

**Buses** Long-distance buses depart from outside Hakata JR Station, with a stop at Tenjin. There are connections to cities on Kyūshū, as well as express buses to Kyoto, Ōsaka and Tokyo.

**Consulates** Australia, 7F, Tsuruta-keyaki Bldg., 1-1-5 Akasaka (☎092/734-5055); Canada, 9F, FT Bldg., 4-8-28 Watanabe-dōri (☎092/752-6055); China, 1-3-3 Jigyohama (☎092/713-1121); South Korea, 1-3-3 Jigyohama (☎092/771-0461); USA, 2-5-26 Ōhori (☎092/751-9331).

**Car rental** Eki Rent-a-car (☎092/431-8775), Nissan Rent-a-car (☎092/471-1634), Nippon Rent-a-car (☎092/414-7535) and Toyota Rent-a-car (☎092/441-0100) all have offices in or near Hakata Station.

**Ferries** The RKK Line (☎092/291-3362) operates weekly ferries from Hakata Futō, northwest of Hakata Station, to Naha on Okinawa (25hr; ¥12,970). There's also a choice of services to Pusan in South Korea, from Hakata Futō's International Terminal. Beetle 2 is a daily hydrofoil service (2hr 55min; ¥12,400; ☎092/281-2315), with a free shuttle bus to the port from Hakata Station, while the Camellia Line (☎092/262-2323) operates conventional ferries on Monday, Wednesday and Friday (15hr 40min; from ¥9000).

**Festivals** Hakata celebrates a whole host of festivals, of which the biggest are the summer-time *Gion Yamakasa* (July 1–15) and the *Hakata Dontaku*, now held during Golden Week (May 3 & 4). In feudal times, Hakata townspeople were permitted across the river once a year to convey New Year greetings to their lord. Today's festival centres on a parade along Meiji-dōri to the old castle.

**Hospitals** The largest general hospital with English-speaking staff is National Kyūshū Medical Centre, 1-8-1 Jigyohama (☎092/852-0700), near Hawks Town. In a more central location, there's the Saiseki Fukuoka General Hospital, 1-3-46 Tenjin (☎092/771-8151), south of the ACROS building.

**Immigration** For visa renewals, contact Fukuoka Regional Immigration Bureau, 1–22 Okihama-chō, Hakata-ku (☎092/281-7431).

**Police** ☎092/641-4141. Emergency numbers are listed in Basics on p.70.

**Post offices** Fukuoka Central Post Office, just north of Tenjin subway station at 4-3-1 Tenjin, offers a poste restante service. There's also another big branch beside the west exit of Hakata Station.

**Shopping** Fukuoka's main department stores are Iwataya and Daimaru in Tenjin, and Izutsuya built over Hakata Station. All of these sell a selection of local crafts, the most famous of which are *Hakata ningyō*, hand-painted, unglazed clay dolls fashioned as *samurai*, Kabuki actors, or demure, kimono-clad women. *Hakata ori* is a rather more transportable, slightly rough silk fabric traditionally used for *obi* (sashes worn with kimono), but now made into ties, wallets and bags. *Chanpon* are totally impractical – a long-stemmed, glass toy with a bowl at the end which makes a clicking sound when you blow into it. Apart from the big stores, try Hakata Machiya Furusato-kan (p.662), the Kawabata-dōri arcade (p.661) or Hakata Station's Ming arcade for local souvenirs.

**Sumo** Japan's last *basho* of the season, the Kyūshū Grand Sumo Tournament, takes place in Fukuoka's Kokusai Centre (☎092/272-1111) during November. Phone the centre for tickets and information.

**Taxis** For a taxi, call the station's central booking desk (☎092/431-3003), or Nishitetsu Taxi (☎093/651-5661).

**Travel agents** For domestic travel, JTB (☎092/752-0700) has English-speaking staff; their main office is in the Yamato Seimei Bldg, on Meiji-dōri west of the ACROS building. International tickets are available at A'cross Travellers Bureau, 2F, Dayton Bldg, 2-4-5 Tenjin (☎092/761-9309) and H.I.S No 1 Travel, 1F, Tenjin Yōmei Bldg, 1-2-1 Maizuru (☎092/761-0957).

# South to Nagasaki

The plains south of Fukuoka are pretty much built-up all the way to the ancient, temple town of **Dazaifu**, once the seat of government for all southern Japan, but now a pleasant backwater best known for its collection of temples and shrines set against a backdrop of wooded slopes. For centuries, Dazaifu's monks, priests and officials sought solace in the healing waters of nearby **Futsukaichi Onsen**. Both towns are easily accessible by train and can either be combined as a day-trip from Fukuoka or treated as a stop-over en route to Nagasaki. Travelling on from Futsukaichi, the Nagasaki line peels off south on a picturesque run beside the Ariake Sea, while the Sasebo line continues via **Takeo**, another recommended dip for hot-spring enthusiasts, and through the pottery town of **Arita** towards Kyūshū's west coast. Arita's 150 kilns punch out the world-renowned *Arita-yaki*, but it's not a particularly attractive town and, unless you're

| SOUTH TO NAGASAKI | | |
|---|---|---|
| **Dazaifu** | *Dazaifu* | 太宰府 |
| Dazaifu Youth Hostel | *Dazaifu Yūsu Hosuteru* | 太宰府ユースホステル |
| Kanzeon-ji | *Kanzeon-ji* | 観世音寺 |
| Kōmyōzen-ji | *Kōmyōzen-ji* | 光明禅寺 |
| Rankan | *Rankan* | 蘭館 |
| Tenman-gū | *Tenman-gū* | 天満宮 |
| Ume-no-hana | *Ume-no-hana* | 梅の花 |
| | | |
| **Futsukaichi Onsen** | *Futsukaichi Onsen* | 二日市温泉 |
| Daimaru Bessō | *Daimaru Bessō* | 大丸別荘 |
| Maizuru-sō | *Maizuru-sō* | 舞鶴荘 |
| | | |
| **Takeo** | *Takeo* | 武雄 |
| Ryokan Kagetsu | *Ryokan Kagetsu* | 旅館花月 |
| Sagi-no-yu | *Sagi-no-yu* | 鷺乃湯 |
| Takeo Onsen Youth Hostel | *Takeo Onsen Yūsu Hosuteru* | 武雄温泉ユースホステル |
| | | |
| **Arita** | *Arita* | 有田 |
| Kakiemon | *Kakiemon* | 柿衛門 |
| | | |
| **Huis ten Bosch** | *Hausu ten Bosu* | ハウステンボス |

a real enthusiast or happen to be here during the annual pottery fair (April 29–May 5), there's little reason to stop. At the coast, the line splits again: the southern branch passing the improbable yet intriguing **Huis ten Bosch**, a replica Dutch town which doubles as a holiday resort, and then skirting round the shores of Ōmura Bay before dropping down into Nagasaki.

# Dazaifu and around

A mere 15km from Fukuoka, **DAZAIFU** only just squeaks free of the urban sprawl, but enough to possess a definite country air. The town is very much on Kyūshū's tourist map, especially in late February and March when cherry blossoms signal both the start of spring and the onset of the exam season. Anxious students descend on **Tenman-gū**, Japan's foremost shrine dedicated to the god of learning, but the nearby **temples** and other historical relics remain surprisingly peaceful. Everything is within easy walking distance of the station, making it possible to cover the main sights in a day. A popular stop en route to or from Dazaifu is **Futsukaichi Onsen**, around 3km further south, where you can take a dip in its healing waters.

Dazaifu rose to prominence in the late seventh century, when the emperor established a regional seat of government and **military headquarters** (known as the *Dazaifu*) here, responsible for defence, trade, and diplomatic ties particularly with China and Korea. For more than five hundred years successive governor generals ruled Kyūshū from Dazaifu, protected by a series of ditches, embankments and hill-top fortresses, until political circumstances changed in the twelfth century and the town gradually fell into decline.

## The Town

Dazaifu Station sits on the town's main crossroads, facing north, with the tourist information right outside. From here it's a short walk east along Kazami-dōri to Dazaifu's main

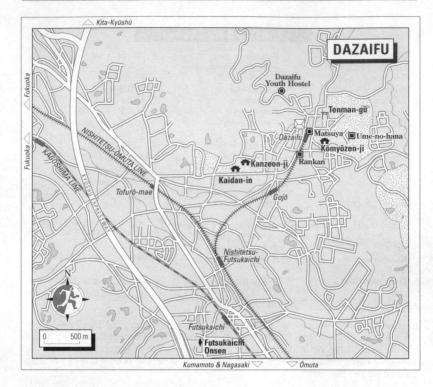

sight, **Tenman-gū** (daily 8.30am–5pm; free), a tenth-century shrine dedicated to Tenjin, the guardian deity of scholars (see box). The shrine information office (daily 8.30am–5pm), on the right as you enter the grounds, rents out radio-headsets (¥300) providing English-language information about Tenman-gū, though the quality of reception is not brilliant.

The approach to Tenman-gū lies over an allegorical stone bridge, **Taiko-bashi**; its first, steep arch represents the past, the present is flat, while the final, gentler hump indicates difficulties yet to come. While negotiating the bridge, take a close look at the second of the two little shrines on the right, which was constructed in 1458 – its intricate, Chinese-style roof shelters some particularly fine carving. Beyond, a two-storey gate leads into a courtyard dominated by the main **worship hall**, built in 1591 but now resplendent in bright red and gold lacquer under a freshly manicured thatch. A twisted **plum tree** stands immediately to the right (east) of the hall. Known as the "flying plum tree", it's said to be over 1000 years old and, according to legend, originally grew in Michizane's Kyoto garden. On the eve of his departure he wrote a farewell poem to the tree, but that night it upped roots and "flew" ahead of him to Dazaifu. Behind the worship hall, a modern building houses a small **museum** (daily 9am–4.30pm; ¥200) detailing the life of Michizane through a series of tableaux.

To escape the crowds at Tenman-gū just walk south from the shrine entrance for about 100m to the nearby temple of **Kōmyōzen-ji** (daily 8am–5pm; free), founded in the mid-thirteenth century. This small, serene temple is an appealing collection of simple, wooden buildings whose *tatami* rooms contain Buddha figures or works of art. There's usually no one around, but you're free to walk around – take off your shoes and follow the polished wooden corridors round to the rear, where there's a contemplative garden made up of a gravel sea swirling round moss-covered headlands and jutting rocks, caught against a wooded hillside. Dazaifu's three other major sights lie about twenty minutes' walk west of the station; to avoid the main road, follow signs to the right after the post office. This route brings you in at the back of **Kanzeon-ji** – watch out for the footpath off to the left just before a set of old foundation stones lying in the grass. Founded in 746 AD by Emperor Tenji in honour of his mother, Empress Samei, at one time Kanzeon-ji was the largest temple in all Kyūshū and even rated a mention in the great, eleventh-century novel, *The Tale of Genji* (see Books, p.669). Only the bronze **bell**, the oldest in Japan, remains from the original temple, while the present buildings – unadorned and nicely faded – date from the seventeenth century.

Kanzeon-ji's main hall holds a graceful standing Buddha, but you'll find its most magnificent statues in the modern **treasure house** (daily 9am–4.30pm; ¥400) next door. The immediate impression is the sheer power of the thirteen, huge wooden figures, of which even the newest is at least 750 years old. The oldest is Tobatsu-Bishamonten, standing second in line, which was sculpted from a single block of camphor wood in the eighth century. An informative English brochure provides further details, starting with the Jizō figure facing you as you come up the stairs and working clockwise.

From the Treasure Hall, walk west in front of Kanzeon-ji towards the two-tiered roof of **Kaidan-in**, built in the late eighth century for the ordination of Buddhist priests. This is one of just three such ordination halls in Japan – the other two being in Tochigi and Nara – and again the statuary is of interest, in this case an eleven-headed Kannon from the Heian period, dressed in fading gold.

## Practicalities

The easiest way of **getting to Dazaifu** from Fukuoka is a private Nishitetsu train from Tenjin's Nishitetsu-Fukuoka Station direct to Dazaifu (40min; ¥360). Alternatively, Japan Rail pass holders can save a few yen by travelling via Futsukaichi (see opposite); from JR Futsukaichi Station it's a ten-minute walk north to Nishitetsu-Futsukaichi Station, where you can join a Nishitetsu train for the last five minutes to Dazaifu (¥130).

The town's **tourist information office** (daily 8.30am–5pm; ☎092/925-1880) is located right outside Dazaifu Station, where you can pick up local maps and brochures in English. Though no one speaks English, they do offer **bike rental** (¥200 per hour), which is worth considering for the western sights.

The only **place to stay** in town is the *Dazaifu Youth Hostel* (☎092/922-8740, fax 920-1963; ①) in a grand position up on a hill ten minutes' walk north of the station. It's a relaxed, welcoming hostel with four *tatami* rooms, laundry and cooking

### THE STORY OF TENJIN

Tenjin is the divine name of **Sugawara-no-Michizane**, a brilliant scholar of the Heian period, who died in Dazaifu in 903 AD. By all accounts, Michizane was a precocious youngster – composing *waka* poems at 5 years old and Chinese poetry by the age of 11 – and went on to become a popular governor of Shikoku before rising to the second highest position at court as Minister of the Right. Not surprisingly, he found no favour with his powerful superior, Fujiwara Tokihira, who persuaded the emperor to banish Michizane. So, in 901 Michizane, accompanied by his son, daughter and a retainer, travelled south to take up a "post" as deputy governor of Dazaifu. He was kept under armed guard until he died in despair – though still loyal to the emperor – two years later. Soon after, a succession of national disasters were attributed to Michizane's restless spirit, so in 919 Tenman-gū was built to pray for his repose. This was the first of an estimated 12,000 shrines dedicated to Tenjin in Japan.

facilities, though no evening meals. The English-speaking manager is a mine of local information.

There's more choice when it comes to **restaurants**. By far the best is *Ume-no-hana* (daily 11am–3pm & 5–9pm), east of Kōmyōzen-ji, which is worth tracking down for its melt-in-the-mouth tofu creations served in *tatami* rooms overlooking a pretty garden. Prices rise steeply in the evening, but their set lunches and *bentō* are reasonable at just over ¥2000; try to arrive before noon or be prepared for a wait. Youth Hostel members can get a small discount at *Rankan* (daily 8.30am–10pm), on the main road south of the station, which serves good coffee and a basic selection of meals. Otherwise, there are a number of places along Kazami-dōri, including a couple of cheap noodle restaurants behind the tourist office. *Matsuya*, second on the right walking east from the station, is a good place to sample the local delicacy, *Umegae-mochi*, a steamed rice-cake stuffed with sweet, red-bean paste.

### Futsukaichi Onsen

People have been coming to **FUTSUKAICHI ONSEN** since at least the eighth century to soothe muscle pain, skin complaints and digestive troubles in its healing waters. Despite being the closest hot spring to Fukuoka, the resort is still surprisingly undeveloped. There are three **public baths** (daily 9am–9pm), all grouped together in the centre of Futsukaichi, about ten minutes' walk south of JR Futsukaichi Station. The first, and easiest to spot by its English sign, is Baden House (¥450) – it's also the newest and biggest, with a *rotemburo* and sauna as well as a whole variety of other pools. Next door, Hakata-yu (¥100) is a tiny old bath-house favoured by Futsukaichi's senior citizenry, while over the road Gozen-yu (¥200) is the perfect compromise, with three large pools in an attractive, old-style building.

There are frequent **trains** from Fukuoka's JR Hakata Station direct to Futsukaichi Station (20min; ¥270). Coming from Dazaifu, take a train to Nishitetsu-Futsukaichi Station, then a local bus (6min; ¥150). The local **information office** (daily 9am–6pm; ☎092/922-2421), inside the JR station, provides useful town maps, in Japanese only, as well as Dazaifu maps if you're heading that way. As usual, you can leave bags in the station lockers, but if you're doing a return trip the two main bath-houses will take care of luggage while you soak.

If you fancy combining your bath with gourmet dining, or even an overnight stay, *Daimaru Bessō* (☎092/924-3939, fax 924-4126; [8]) is an atmospheric old **ryokan** on the south side of town, set round a traditional garden of pine trees and carp-ponds. The beautifully appointed *tatami* rooms come with two meals included, and the excellent restaurant also serves good-value set lunches (from ¥1500), and includes the use of their huge, hot spring bath. For more affordable accommodation, try *Maizuru-sō* (☎092/922-2727, fax 922-6750; [5]), a new business hotel on the road in from the station, with just eleven cheerful rooms and a small, black-stone onsen bath.

## Takeo

Roughly one hour from Futsukaichi by train on the JR Sasebo line, **TAKEO** is another **onsen resort** which makes a relaxed stop-over on the way to Nagasaki. Squeezed in a narrow valley between low hills, the town is more developed than Futsukaichi, though its **public baths** draw fewer day-trippers. According to legend, it's also a lot older, dating back to the late third century AD when Empress Jingu rested here on her way home from invading Korea. Out walking one day, the tip of her staff slipped between two stones, causing a spring of crystal-clear water to gush forth. Later, in the sixteenth century, Toyotomi Hideyoshi used Takeo as a watering hole for his troops on their way to another Korean invasion (see p.772).

The town centre lies ten minutes' walk northwest of the station, where the onsen buildings are clustered behind a dumpy, Chinese-style gate. First on the left through the gate is Moto-yu (daily 6.30am–9pm; ¥260), the most traditional of the public baths, where locals lying out on the hot stones swap gossip. If you prefer outdoor bathing, the nearby *Ryokan Kagetsu* (see below) has a beautiful *rotemburo* (¥700), while the recently refurbished *Sagi-no-yu* boasts a smaller *rotemburo* and sauna (daily 9am–4.30pm; ¥600). The waters are renowned, amongst other things, for their power to heal burns and cure physical exhaustion.

You'll find Takeo **information centre** (daily 9am–5.30pm, Sat & Sun 9am–5pm; ☎0954/22-2542) upstairs in the JR train station, directly opposite the ticket barriers. Among several **ryokan** gathered round the onsen, the *Kagetsu* (☎0954/22-3108, fax 22-2120; [6]) offers elegant, *tatami* rooms with or without meals, while *Sagi-no-yu* (☎0954/23-2111, fax 23-9205; [5]) charges lower rates for a simple *tatami* room including breakfast. *Takeo Onsen Youth Hostel* (☎ & fax 0954/22-2490; closed late May/early June; [1]) provides the cheapest option with its bunk beds, though it's a seven-minute bus ride south of town on a pine-covered hilltop. Buses for the hostel – direction Hōyō Centre, also known as Kanpo – stop on the road outside the station (¥220), but note that the last bus up leaves just after 5pm. If you arrive later, the English-speaking hostel manager will collect you, but after 7pm the choice is a taxi (¥800) or a steep, forty-minute hike.

## Huis ten Bosch

Where the train from Takeo turns south beside Ōmura Bay there's a surprise in store as the horizon fills with an unmistakably European-style building, announcing your arrival at **HUIS TEN BOSCH**. Opened in 1992 at a cost of ¥250 billion, this **resort town** is a meticulously engineered replica of a Dutch port caught somewhere between the seventeenth and twenty-first centuries. As such it might not seem a natural destination for most Western visitors, but the overall concept – part theme park, part serious experiment in urban living – and its top-quality design lift it above the ordinary.

Huis ten Bosch (meaning "house in the forest" in Dutch) owes its existence to the drive and vision of **Kamichika Yoshikuni**, a local entrepreneur who was so impressed with Dutch land reclamation and environmental management that he persuaded his financiers it could work in Japan as a commercial venture. After three years planning, the complex took only another three to build on an abandoned block of reclaimed land. Twenty million baked clay bricks were imported from Holland and Dutch technicians came to advise, but Huis ten Bosch is predominantly a Japanese venture. It employs thousands of local people and has boosted the economy not only of Nagasaki, but all Kyūshū through increased tourism, especially from Southeast Asia.

While Huis ten Bosch may seem quaintly olde worlde, it's equipped with the latest technology developed specially to manage its sophisticated heating systems, wave control, desalination, water recycling and security. All the pipes, cables and wires are hidden underground and, as far as possible, it's designed to be environmentally benign. Though no one's putting a date on it, the long-term goal is to launch Huis ten Bosch as a fully functioning city.

### The Town

**Huis ten Bosch** (daily 9am–9pm; Jan, Feb, Nov & Dec 9am–7/8pm; last admission two hours before closing) is divided into an exclusive residential district, Wassenaar, and the public areas where you'll find a bewildering choice of museums and attractions, plus dozens of souvenir shops and numerous restaurants. Fortunately, there are plenty of signposts in English, while the 105-metre-high Utrecht tower (Domtoren) provides a prominent landmark, and a bird's-eye view from its observatory.

It's just a couple of minutes' walk from Huis ten Bosch Station to the entrance gate where there's a choice of three **tickets**, known as "passports". The One Day Free

Passport (¥5800), allows entry to all the museums and attractions; the Two Day Special Passport (¥6800; only available to foreign tourists staying in the resort) covers one-time admission to all facilities in Huis ten Bosch and Holland Village, an older prototype mostly of interest to children; and the ordinary Passport (¥4200) covers admission only. Though there's a fair amount to explore for "free" inside, especially in summer when they stage more outdoor events, it's worth visiting at least a couple of the attractions.

The best way to get around Huis ten Bosch is on foot, wandering along the canals and past quaint, brick-faced houses on streets refreshingly free of advertising hoardings, loudspeakers and the electrical spaghetti you find elsewhere in Japan. In the far southwest corner, **Paleis Huis ten Bosch** is a perfect replica of the Dutch royal palace – at least on the outside. It's used for art exhibitions but, unless there's something special on, there's not a lot to see, beyond a vast love-it or hate-it mural designed on computer by Dutch artist Rob Scholte. The palace's formal gardens follow an original eighteenth-century design, never realized at the time, by Frenchman Daniel Marot for the Hague. Among other museums, the **Porcelain Museum** is notable for its impressive reproduction of the Charlottenburg's porcelain room as well as some actual genuine pieces of local Imari-ware.

Most of Huis ten Bosch's **attractions** are a touch on the cutesy side. However, three stand out for their high-quality special effects and outrageous ambition. The **Great Voyage Theatre** shows a short film about the first Dutch ships to reach Japan, during which the whole seating area pitches and rolls – sit in the middle if you get seasick. In **Mysterious Escher** you enter a topsy-turvy world to watch a sickly-sweet but well-executed 3D film based on Escher's famous graphics. Last but not least, **Horizon Adventure** stages a real-life flood with 800 tons of water cascading into the theatre.

### Practicalities

The easiest way of getting to the resort is JR's special **Huis ten Bosch Express** from Fukuoka, or the Seaside Liner from Nagasaki. For those in a hurry, high-speed **boats** zip across Ōmura Bay direct to Huis ten Bosch from Nagasaki airport (9 daily; 45min; ¥1420).

You'll find **information** counters at the entrance gate and in the main square, as well as a bank, post office, medical centre and even an Internet café. Huis ten Bosch can easily be explored in a day. Should you decide to stay, however, the cheapest **accommodation** is the nearby *Hotel Tulip* (☎0956/58-7777, fax 58-7788; [5]), which runs a shuttle bus to the resort entrance. The four hotels on site are top quality and expensive, but if you want to push the boat out, the *Hotel Den Haag* (☎0956/27-0011, fax 27-0912; [8]) is the most attractive option. **Eating** inside Huis ten Bosch won't break the bank. There's a huge choice of restaurants and cafés, serving everything from sandwiches and tacos to sushi and fresh seafood. Note that you're not allowed to take your own food into the resort.

# Nagasaki

> *"As the passage into the harbour widened we had our first glimpse of Nagasaki town in the haze of the morning, nestled in a most beautiful inlet at the foot of wooded hills."*

Although few visitors these days arrive by boat and the woods are diminished, many would agree with British landscape painter Sir Alfred East, who came here in 1889, that **NAGASAKI** is one of Japan's more picturesque cities, gathered in the tucks and crevices of steep hills rising from a long, narrow harbour supposedly shaped like a crane in flight. It's not a particularly ancient city, nor does it possess any absolutely compelling sights. Instead, Nagasaki's appeal lies in its easy-going attitude and an

| NAGASAKI | | |
|---|---|---|
| Nagasaki | *Nagasaki* | 長崎 |
| Atomic Bomb Museum | *Nagasaki Genbaku-shiryōkan* | 長崎原爆資料館 |
| Dejima | *Dejima* | 出島 |
| Dutch Slopes | *Oranda-zaka* | オランダ坂 |
| Glover Garden | *Gurabā-en* | グラバー園 |
| Inasa-yama | *Inasa-yama* | 稲左山 |
| Kōshi-byō | *Kōshi-byō* | 孔子廟 |
| 26 Martyrs' Memorial | *Nihon Nijū-roku seijin junkyōchi* | 日本26聖人殉教地 |
| Megane-bashi | *Megane-bashi* | 眼鏡橋 |
| Peace Park | *Heiwa-kōen* | 平和公園 |
| Shōfuku-ji | *Shōfuku-ji* | 聖福寺 |
| Sōfuku-ji | *Sōfuku-ji* | 崇福寺 |
| Suwa-jinja | *Suwa-jinja* | 諏訪神社 |

*ACCOMMODATION*

| | | |
|---|---|---|
| Capsule Inn | *Kapuseru In* | カプセルイン |
| Capsule Inn Nagasaki | *Kapuseru In Nagasaki* | カプセルイン長崎 |
| Dai-ichi Hotel | *Dai-ichi Hoteru* | 第一ホテル |
| Fumi | *Fumi* | 富美 |
| Holiday Inn | *Horidei In* | ＩＫホテル |
| IK Hotel | *IK Hoteru* | 長崎ユースホステル |
| Miyuki-sō | *Miyuki-sō* | ホテルニュー長崎 |
| Nagasaki Grand Hotel | *Nagasaki Gurando Hoteru* | ホリデイイン |
| Nagasaki Youth Hostel | *Nagasaki Yūsu Hosuteru* | 長崎グランドホテル |
| Hotel New Nagasaki | *Hoteru Nyū Nagasaki* | 三幸荘 |
| Park Side Hotel | *Pāku Saido Hoteru* | ワシントンホテル |
| Minshuku Tanpopo | *Minshuku Tanpopo* | パークサイドホテル |
| Washington Hotel | *Washinton Hoteru* | 民宿たんぽぽ |

*RESTAURANTS*

| | | |
|---|---|---|
| Hamakatsu | *Hamakatsu* | 浜勝 |
| Kagetsu | *Kagetsu* | 花月 |
| Kouzanrou | *Kouzanrou* | 江山楼 |
| Robin Hood no Mori | *Robin Fuddo no Mori* | ロビンフッドの森 |
| Shirokiya | *Shirokiya* | 白木屋 |

unusually cosmopolitan culture, resulting from over two centuries of contact with foreigners when the rest of Japan was closed to the world, and cemented by its isolation from Tokyo.

Nagasaki would probably have remained just a pleasant, attractive city with a bustling harbour if a chance break in the clouds on August 9, 1945 hadn't seared it into the world's consciousness as the target of Japan's second **atomic bomb**. It's the A-Bomb hypocentre and nearby museum, as harrowing as that in Hiroshima (see p.552), that brings most people to Nagasaki, yet the city has much else to offer. Successive communities of Chinese, Dutch, Portuguese and British have left their mark here to varying degrees, including colourful **Chinese temples**, Catholic **churches** and an array of European-style houses gathered in **Glover Garden**, as well as imported cuisines and festivals. Despite efforts to stamp out another European import, the Catholic faith, Nagasaki remains Japan's centre of **Christianity**, claiming one sixth of the country's believers. It's possible to cover the two main areas – the hypocentre and around Glover Garden – in a day, but Nagasaki deserves at least one extra night's stopover to explore its backstreets, soak up some atmosphere and sample a few of the city's culinary treats.

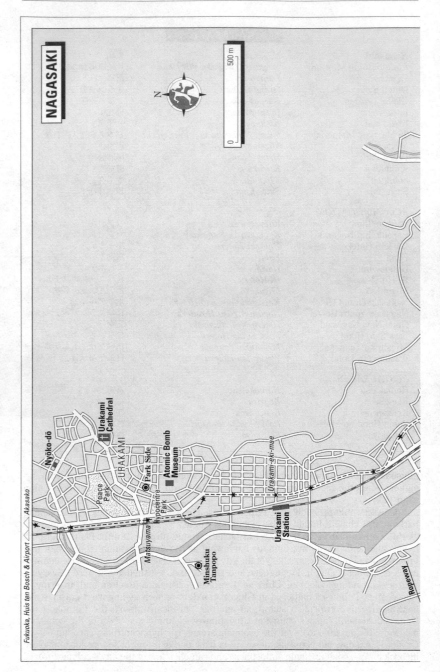

NAGASAKI

N

500 m

0

*Fukuoka, Huis ten Bosch & Airport* △ △ *Akasako*

Nyoko-dō

Urakami
Cathedral

URAKAMI

Peace
Park

Park Side

Atomic Bomb
Museum

Hypocentre
Park

*Matsuyama*

*Urakami-eki-mae*

Urakami
Station

Minshuku
Tanpopo

*Ropeway*

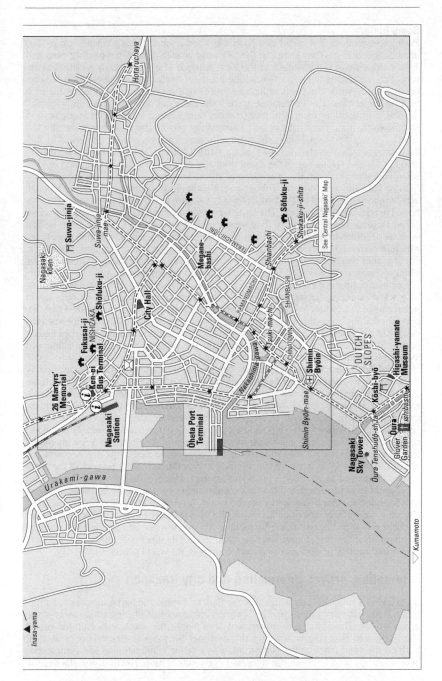

Inasa-yama

Urakami-gawa

26 Martyrs' Memorial

Nagasaki Station

Ken-ei Bus Terminal

Fukusai-ji

NISHIZAKA

Shōfuku-ji

Nagasaki-kōen

Suwa-jinja

Suwa-jinja-mae

City Hall

Megane-bashi

TERAMACHI-DŌRI

Sōfuku-ji

Shokaku-ji-shita

Shianbashi

See Central Nagasaki Map

HAMANOMACHI

Tsuki-machi

SHIANBASHI

CHINA-TOWN

Nakashima-gawa

Ōhata Port Terminal

Shimin Byōin

Shimin Byōin-mae

DUTCH SLOPES

Higashi-yamate Museum

Kōshi-byō

Ōura

Ishibashi

Nagasaki Sky Tower

Ōura Tenshudō-shita

Glover Garden

Kumamoto

Hotaruchaya

## Some history

Portuguese traders first sailed into Nagasaki, then a small fishing village of just 1500 inhabitants, in 1570. They returned the following year to establish a **trading post** and **Jesuit mission** at the invitation of the local *daimyō*, who was already a Catholic convert. The merchants built up a flourishing business exchanging Chinese silks for copper and silver, while the Jesuit fathers financed their missionary activities by taking a turn on the profits. The Portuguese were soon the most powerful force in Nagasaki, despite competition from Chinese traders and, later, Spanish Franciscan and Dominican fathers. For a brief period, Christianity was all the rage, but in the late sixteenth century Toyotomi Hideyoshi, fearing the missionaries would be followed by military intervention, started to move against the Church. Though the **persecutions** came in fits and starts, one of the more dramatic events occurred in Nagasaki in 1597 when Hideyoshi ordered the crucifixion of 26 Franciscans.

After 1616 the new shogun, Tokugawa Hidetada, gradually took control of all dealings with foreigners and by the late 1630s only Chinese and Portuguese merchants continued to trade out of Nagasaki. The latter were initially confined to a tiny island enclave called **Dejima**, but in 1639 even they were expelled following a Christian-led rebellion in nearby Shimabara (see p.689). Their place on Dejima was filled by Dutch merchants who had endeared themselves to the shogun by sending a warship against the rebels. For the next two hundred years this tiny Dutch group together with a slightly larger Chinese community provided Japan's only link with the outside world.

Eventually, the restrictions began to ease, especially after the early seventeenth century when technical books were allowed into Nagasaki, making the city once again Japan's main conduit for **Western learning**. Nevertheless, it wasn't until 1858 that five ports, including Nagasaki, opened for general trade. America, Britain and other nations established diplomatic missions as Nagasaki's foreign community mushroomed and its economy boomed. New inventions flooded in: the printing press, brick-making and modern shipbuilding techniques all made their Japanese debut in Nagasaki.

In the early twentieth century the city's industrial development was spearheaded by the giant **Mitsubishi dockyards**. Nagasaki became an important naval base with huge munitions factories, an obvious target for America's second **atomic bomb** in 1945. Even so, it was only poor visibility at Kokura, near Fukuoka, that forced the bomber, critically short of fuel, south to Nagasaki. The weather was bad there too, but as "Bock's Car" flew down the Urakami-gawa at 11am on August 9 a crack in the cloud revealed a sports stadium just north of the factories and shipyards. A few moments later "Fat Boy" exploded. It's estimated that 73,000 people died in the first seconds, rising to 140,000 by 1950, while 75,000 were injured and nearly forty percent of the city's houses destroyed in the blast and its raging fires. Horrific though these figures are, they would have been higher if the valley walls hadn't contained the blast and a spur of hills shielded southern Nagasaki from the worst. An American naval officer visiting the city a few weeks later described his awe at the "deadness, the absolute essence of death in the sense of finality without resurrection. It's everywhere and nothing has escaped its touch". But the city, at least, did rise again to take its place with Hiroshima as a centre for anti-nuclear protest and an ardent campaign for world peace.

## Orientation, arrival, information and city transport

Nagasaki is a long, thin city which fills the flatland beside the harbour, spreads its tentacles along tributary valleys, and is slowly creeping up the hillsides, eating away at the green woods. The city's main **downtown** area lies in the south, concentrated round Hamanomachi shopping centre and the compact Shianbashi entertainment district, both on the south bank of the Nakashima-gawa, while administrative and commercial offices occupy land between the river and Nagasaki Station. North of the station, the city slims down to a narrow corridor along the **Urakami valley**, with Inasa-yama rising to the west.

Nagasaki **airport** occupies an artificial island in Ōmura Bay, 40km from town and connected by limousine bus (¥1150) to Nagasaki Station in just under one hour. The **train station** sits at the south end of the highway running into Nagasaki, roughly 1km north of the city's main downtown area. Most long-distance **buses** either stop outside the station or pull into Ken-ei bus terminal on the opposite side of the road. **Ferries** from Kumamoto dock at the Ōhato Port Terminal, fifteen minutes' walk south of Nagasaki Station.

The best source of **information** is Nagasaki Prefectural Tourist Federation (Mon–Sat 9am–5.30pm; ☎0958/26-9407), located on the second floor above Ken-ei bus station. The English-speaking staff can help with hotel reservations and there's plentiful information about the local sights and transport to them. When the office is closed, city maps and a few English pamphlets are available at Nagasaki City Tourist Information (daily: March–Oct 8am–7pm; Jan, Feb, Nov & Dec 8am–5.30pm; ☎0958/23-3631), immediately outside the station on the left, though staff here don't speak English.

## City transport

Given its elongated shape, Nagasaki's sights are all fairly spread out. However, it's one of the easier cities for getting around thanks mainly to its cheap and easy **tram system**. There are four lines, numbered 1 to 5 (#2 is missing), each identified and colour coded on the front. The two north–south lines (#1 and #3) are the most handy, running from either side of the downtown area to meet at the station and then continuing north to the A-Bomb sights. To reach the Glover Garden area, however, you'll need Line 5 for Ishibashi; you can transfer on to this line at Tsuki-machi – ask for a transfer ticket (*norikae-ken*). Trams run from approximately 6.30am to 11pm, though check the timetables at each stop for precise times, and there's a flat fare of ¥100 which you feed into the driver's box on exit. Alternatively, you can buy a one-day pass (¥500) at the information centres and hotels, but not on the trams themselves. While you're clanking along, take a look around: some of these trolley-cars are museum pieces – the oldest dates from 1911 – which were snapped up when other Japanese cities were merrily ripping up their tram lines.

**City buses** are more complicated, but the only time you're likely to need them is getting to the Inasa-yama ropeway (see p.684). In this case you need a Nagasaki Bus (#3 or #4) from a stop on the road outside Nagasaki Station. The normal system operates: take a numbered ticket on entry and pay the driver as you get off according to the fare-display board.

# Accommodation

Nagasaki offers a broad range of **accommodation** widely dispersed around the city. Cheaper places cluster round the station, but otherwise the main choice is whether to stay near the station or in the southern, downtown district. There are also a couple of reasonable places near the hypocentre, in the north of the city, if that's your main area of interest.

## Around Nagasaki Station

**Capsule Inn**, 6F, Nagasaki Kenko Centre, 6-6 Daikoku-machi (☎0958/28-1126). Capsules for both sexes are available in this well-run hotel right opposite the station, sandwiched between two *pachinko* parlours. ①.

**Capsule Inn Nagasaki**. A smaller, men-only capsule hotel behind the *Dai-ichi*. It's good and clean, with a large Japanese bath. Apply to the *Dai-ichi*. ①.

**Dai-ichi Hotel**, 2-1 Daikoku-machi (☎0958/21-1711, fax 23-8475). Friendly and efficient business hotel with some English-speaking staff and a wide range of rooms, up to a six-berth family room. The standard rooms aren't enormous but are comfortable enough, and all en suite. ⑤.

**Fumi**, 4-9 Daikoku-machi (☎0958/22-4962, fax 22-6110). After the capsules, this minshuku is the cheapest place near the station, located behind the Ken-ei bus terminal. Its *tatami* rooms and shared bathrooms have seen better days, but the welcome is warm and there's lots of local information available. Charges are on a room-only basis. ④.

**IK Hotel**, 7-17 Ebisu-machi (☎0958/27-1221, fax 27-1241). Newish, mid-range business hotel, five minutes' walk from the station. The rooms are decked out in smart pinks and peaches, but the beds are a touch on the small size. ⑤.

**Nagasaki Youth Hostel**, 1-1-16 Tateyama (☎0958/23-5032, fax 23-4321). A good location and great breakfast buffet (all-included) make this hostel popular among budget travellers. Despite the raft of regulations, it's a fairly relaxed place, with laundry facilities and a small kitchen (¥100), but no evening meals on offer. All accommodation is in bunk-bed dorms. ①.

**Hotel New Nagasaki**, 14-5 Daikoku-machi (☎0958/26-8000, fax 23-2000). Nagasaki's best hotel, conveniently placed outside the station, with all the trimmings: grand marble lobby, shopping arcade, restaurants and fitness centre (¥2000). The rooms are mostly Western-style, some boasting harbour views, with not a lot of character but generous on the floor space. ⑦.

## Downtown

**Holiday Inn**, 6-24 Doza-machi (☎0958/28-1234, fax 28-0178). For mid-range accommodation in central Nagasaki, you can't beat this elegant, well-priced hotel. The lobby sets the tone with its low-level lighting, Japanese screens and antique silk embroideries, mixed with European dark-wood furniture and deep sofas. The standard rooms don't quite go that far, but they're more than adequate in pinky browns with a choice of three different bed sizes. ⑥.

**Miyuki-sō**, 6-46 Kajiya-machi (☎0958/21-3487, fax 21-7831). It's worth tracking down this good-value budget hotel, in a five-storey red-brick building with a blue sign, on the far east side of town. Its basic *tatami* and Western rooms have recently been refurbished, offering pay-TV and phone, while the more expensive have their own bathroom and toilet. The owner speaks a little English. ④.

**Nagasaki Grand Hotel**, 5-3 Manzai-machi (☎0958/23-1234, fax 22-1793). This big, older hotel offers reasonable rates in a good location midway between the station, downtown and Glover Garden area. The cheaper rooms are pretty standard, all equipped with TV, bathroom and mini-bar. ⑤–⑥.

**Washington Hotel**, 9-1 Shinchi-machi (☎0958/28-1211, fax 25-8023). This new member of the *Washington* chain is more expensive than usual, but offers a good selection of rooms including singles from ¥6500 plus tax. ⑥.

## North Nagasaki

**Park Side Hotel**, 14-1 Heiwa-machi (☎0958/45-31919, fax 46-5550). This smart, spacious hotel benefits from a peaceful, out of town location. All its rooms are Western style, of a generous size with bigger than average bathrooms, while modern art works jolly up the cool, cream walls. ⑥

**Minshuku Tanpopo**, 21-7 Hoei-chō (☎0958/61-6230, fax 64-0032). A member of the Japanese Inn Group, this small, tidy minshuku is about ten minutes' walk from the Peace Park. Overnight rates aren't bad for its *tatami* rooms, all without bath, and well-priced meals are also on offer. *Tanpopo* is ten minutes on foot from the Matsuyama tram stop and fifteen from JR Urakami Station; if you phone from Urakami Station, the owners will collect you. ④.

## The City

Nagasaki's principal sights are widely spread, starting in the north with the **Peace Park** and the gruelling but informative **Atomic Bomb Museum**. From there it's a tram ride down to Nagasaki Station and a gentle stroll along the slopes of Nishizaka from the **26 Martyrs' Memorial** round to Nagasaki's most imposing shrine, **Suwa-jinja**. The focus of interest in the central district is a row of quiet temples, notably **Sōfuku-ji**, founded by the city's Chinese community, while **Chinatown** itself consists of a colourful, compact grid of streets. Slightly further west, the former Dutch enclave of **Dejima** is commemorated with a museum and scale model of the old settlement.

Down in the far south, several European houses have been preserved on the former hilltop concession, now known as **Glover Garden**, overlooking Nagasaki's magnificent harbour and a colourful **Confucian shrine**. To round it all off, take a twilight ropeway ride up to the top of **Inasa-yama** before hitting the bars and clubs of **Shianbashi**. There's more than enough here to fill two days; if you've only got one to spare, it's probably best to skip the sights along Nishizaka and head straight for Sōfuku-ji or Glover Garden.

## North Nagasaki: A-Bomb Hypocentre

As you walk around **Urakami** these days it's hard to link these quiet, reasonably prosperous residential suburbs with the scenes of utter devastation left by the atomic explosion in August 1945. If you've already visited Hiroshima (see p.547), which was destroyed by uranium bomb three days earlier, Nagasaki's memorials might seem a little less striking. However, the new museum is notable for its balanced approach.

Urakami's main sights can be covered on a circular route from Matsuyama tram stop, roughly ten minutes north of Nagasaki Station. A long flight of steps leads up into the **Peace Park**, which is as popular among anti-nuclear lobbyists trolling for signatures as it is for young kids skate-boarding among the donated plaques and memorials, watched over by sculptor Kitamura Seibō's muscular **Peace Statue**. The figure, right hand pointing skyward at the threat of nuclear destruction, left extended to hold back the forces of evil, was unveiled in 1955. As Ishiguro Kazuo remarked in *A Pale View of the Hills* (see Books, p.819), from a distance the figure resembles a "policeman conducting traffic", but when some elderly figure pauses on the way past, head bowed, it's not easy to be so cynical.

Signs behind the Peace Statue point the way to Nyōko-dō (Tues–Sun 9am–5pm; free), the former home of **Dr Nagai Takashi**, who wrote the *Bells of Nagasaki* amongst a dozen other books about the atomic bomb's aftermath. Though his house, now a public library with a few personal mementoes, isn't particularly worth the detour, his lifestory is remarkable. A radiologist working in Nagasaki, Dr Nagai had already developed leukaemia before he received further exposure from the bomb. He continued to help other survivors until he himself became bed-ridden, and lived for another four years, cared for by his two young children in a tiny shack, courageously recording his experiences with radiation victims right up to his death, aged 43, in 1951.

From the Peace Park you can see the twin, red-brick towers of **Urakami Cathedral** dominating a small rise 400m to the east. The present building is a postwar replica of the original, completed in 1925, which was destroyed when the atomic bomb exploded only 500m away. The blast left scorch marks on the statues now preserved beside the front porch, and tore off huge chunks of masonry, including a section of the tower which still rests on the bank under the north wall. All that remained of the congregation were a few melted rosaries.

Nowadays, a pleasant shopping street leads southwest from the cathedral back towards Matsuyama. Before reaching the main road, turn left into the **Hypocentre Park**, where an austere black pillar marks the exact spot where the bomb exploded 500m above the ground. Overlooking the park to the east, behind an incongruous row of Love Hotels peering over the willows, you'll find the **Atomic Bomb Museum** (daily 8.30am–5.30pm; ¥200). You enter via a symbolic, spiralling descent, then views of pre-war Nagasaki lead abruptly into a darkened room full of twisted iron girders, blackened masonry and videos constantly scrolling through horrific photos of the dead and dying. It's strong stuff, occasionally too much for some, but the most moving exhibits are always those single fragments of an individual life – a charred lunch-box, twisted pair of glasses or the chilling shadow of a man etched on wooden planks.

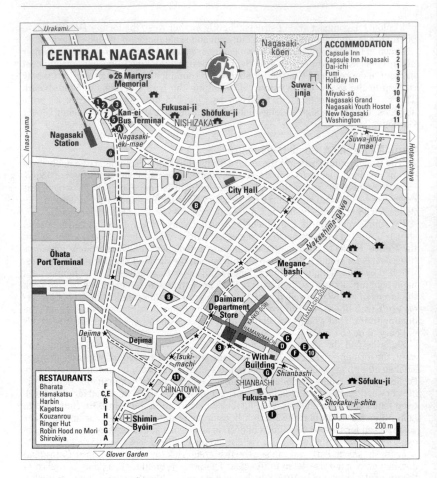

The purpose of the museum isn't only to shock, and the displays are packed with information, much of it in English, tracing the history of atomic weapons, the effects of the bomb and the heroic efforts of ill-equipped rescue teams who had little idea what they were facing. There's a fascinating video library of interviews with survivors, including some of the foreigners present in Nagasaki at the time; figures vary but probably more than 12,000 foreigners were killed in the blast, mostly Korean forced-labour working in the Mitsubishi shipyards, as well as Dutch, Australian and British prisoners of war. The museum then broadens out to examine the whole issue of nuclear weapons and ends with a depressing film about the arms race and test-ban treaties.

## Along Nishizaka

East of Nagasaki Station, a quiet lane hugs **Nishizaka** hillside, starting in the north at a bizarre, mosaic-clad church dedicated to Japan's first Christian martyrs. In 1597 six foreign missionaries and twenty Japanese converts were the unlucky victims of the shogunate's growing unease at the power of the Church. They were marched from Kyoto and Ōsaka to Nagasaki where they were crucified on February 2 as a warning to others. The group were canonized in 1862 and a century later the **26 Martyrs' Memorial** was erected on the site, together with a small **museum** (daily 9am–5pm; ¥250) telling the history – mostly in Japanese – of the martyrs and of Christianity in Japan. A surprising amount survives, including tissue-thin prayer books hidden in bamboo and statues of the Virgin Mary disguised as the goddess Kannon. One document records the bounties offered to informers: 500 silver pieces per priest, down to 100 for a lowly catechist.

Heading south along Nishizaka, a giant statue of Kannon marks **Fukusai-ji** (daily 8am–5pm; ¥200), founded in 1628 by a Chinese Zen priest. The original temple was destroyed in 1945 and replaced with a tasteless, turtle-shaped building topped by the eighteen-metre-tall, aluminium-alloy goddess and a circle of supplicating infants. Inside, a 25-metre-long Foucault's pendulum represents a perpetual prayer for peace, oscillating over the remains of 16,500 Japanese war-dead buried underneath. Nearby **Shōfuku-ji**, on the other hand, survived the bomb and consists of an attractive collection of aged, wooden buildings surrounded by rustling bamboo stands and shady trees. Another early-seventeenth-century Zen temple, rebuilt in 1715, its main attributes are some detailed carving on the gates and unusual decorative features such as the red balustrade around the worship hall.

From Shōfku-ji it's a ten-minute walk east along the hillside, along the edge of Nagasaki-kōen, to the side entrance of Nagasaki's major shrine, **Suwa-jinja**, which was founded in 1625 when the Shogunate was promoting Shintoism in opposition to the Christian Church. Ask at the office, beside a bronze horse by Kitamura Seibō, for their comprehensive English brochure. Suwa-jinja's main hall, rebuilt in 1869, is fresh and simple, but for most foreigners its greatest attraction is the English-language fortune papers on sale beside the collecting box (¥200). The grounds are scattered with unusual subsidiary shrines, notably two *koma-inu* (guardian lions) known as the "**stop lions**", where people vowing to give up unwanted habits fasten paper strings round the front legs, like plaster casts; you'll find them in a small garden to the left as you face the main hall.

Each autumn, Suwa-jinja hosts the famous **Kunchi Matsuri** (October 7–9). This festival is believed to have originated in 1633 when two courtesans performing a Nō dance attracted huge crowds during celebrations to mark the ninth day of the ninth lunar month. Gradually, European and Chinese elements were incorporated – this was one of the few occasions when Dutch merchants were allowed to leave Dejima – and the jollities now consist of dragon dances and heavy floats, some fashioned as Chinese and Dutch ships, being spun round outside the shrine.

## Central Nagasaki: down the Nakashima-gawa

Below Suwa-jinja the **Nakashima-gawa** flows west through central Nagasaki under a succession of stone bridges linked by a pleasant riverside walk. The most noteworthy of these is the double-arched **Megane-bashi**, aptly named "spectacles bridge", which is Japan's oldest stone bridge, dating from 1634. Across Megane-bashi, Teramachi-dōri (Temple-town Street) parallels the river along the valley's eastern slopes.

Turn right here, past a row of traditional shops, and then follow signs pointing left to **Sōfuku-ji** (daily 8am–5pm; ¥300). This is Nagasaki's most important Chinese Zen temple, founded in 1629 by Fujian immigrants, and it contains rare examples of Ming-period Chinese architecture. The entrance lies under a stocky, vermilion gate followed by a wooden inner gate, **Dai-ippon-mon**, decorated with polychrome, jigsaw-puzzle eaves. Both this gate and the **Buddha hall**, first building on the left inside the temple's stone-flagged courtyard, were actually shipped over from China and then pieced back together in Nagasaki in 1646 and 1696 respectively. Sakyamuni, the historical Buddha, occupies the hall's altar, flanked by eighteen individually expressed, gilded statues of Buddhist saints. A smaller, more faded hall lies at the back of the compound, its interior gloom broken only by the gorgeous robes and spangly headdress of a Chinese goddess, the protectress of sailors, and her two assistants. Finally, don't miss the vast cauldron, against the courtyard's south wall, in which monks supposedly boiled up porridge for five thousand people per day during a famine in 1681.

In the seventeenth century, Nagasaki's Chinese community comprised over fifteen percent of the population. Like the Europeans, they were restricted to a designated area which lay just inland from Dejima, near today's **Chinatown**. Four elaborate gates, recently built by Chinese craftsmen, signpost this colourful grid of six blocks packed with restaurants, while a bare-earth park over on the south side houses an older wooden gate and a Chinese pavilion where old men sit and gossip over the chess pieces.

There's more to see a few metres further south where traces of **Dejima**, the Portuguese and then Dutch enclave, can still be found along a curve of the old sea wall. Created in 1636 and enlarged after 1641, this fan-shaped, artificial island extended a mere 100 by 300m. For over two hundred years Dejima provided Japan's only access to the Western world and, similarly, the lone point of contact for European academics studying in Japan until 1854, when the enclave was officially disbanded. The island was swallowed up in later land reclamations, but you can get an idea of the place from a scale model, in a small garden beside the river, belonging to the next-door **Nagasaki Museum of History and Folklore** (Tues–Sun 9am–5pm; free). The museum itself contains a few bits and pieces related to the island, while nearby several old European buildings are being restored and there's a full-size replica of Dejima's original wooden gate.

## South Nagasaki

When Japan's period of isolation effectively ended in the mid-1850s, the newcomers were allowed to live in Nagasaki itself, although still only within a proscribed area until 1899. Trading companies and customs offices sprouted along the seafront south of Dejima, while houses soon clothed the steep slopes above. A small river split the area into two districts known as the south and east bluffs: Minami-yamate and Higashi-yamate. Today a fair number of the old buildings still survive, most notably in the southern **Glover Garden** and in pockets along Higashi-yamate's **Dutch slopes**, where you'll also find an exotic little piece of China in Nagasaki's **Confucian shrine**.

### GLOVER GARDEN

From the Ōura Tenshudō-shita tram stop (Line 5), a parade of souvenir shops leads to Japan's oldest existing church, **Ōura Catholic Church** (daily: April–Nov 8am–6pm; Jan–March & Dec 8.30am–5pm; ¥250). A pretty little white structure, with nothing much to see inside, it was built by French missionaries in 1864 to serve Nagasaki's growing foreign community. A few months later Father Petitjean was astonished to find outside his door a few brave members of Nagasaki's "hidden Christians" who had secretly kept the faith for more than two centuries (see p.787).

The path continues on up to **Glover Garden** (daily: Mar 1–July 19 & Nov 8am–6pm; July 20–Oct 31 8am–9.30pm; Jan, Feb & Dec 8.30am–5pm; ¥600), which is named after the bluff's most famous resident, Thomas Glover. Despite the crowds and piped music, the garden's seven late-nineteenth-century, European-style buildings are surprisingly interesting, mostly for the life-stories of their pioneering inhabitants. The houses are designed in full colonial style with wide verandahs and louvred shutters, while their high-ceilinged, spacious rooms contain odds and ends of furniture and evocative family photos. The best approach is to start at the top – there are escalators up the hill – and work down, visiting at least the four houses recommended below.

A modest bungalow, **Walker House** was built in 1877 for the British-born Captain of a Japanese passenger ship after he helped provide transport for government troops in the Satsuma Rebellion (see p.710). On retiring from the sea in 1898 he joined Thomas Glover in setting up Japan's first soft drinks company which produced a popular line in

"Banzai Lemonade" and "Banzai Cider". **Ringer House** is a more comfortable, stone-built bungalow erected in 1865. Frederick Ringer began life as a tea inspector in Canton, then moved to Nagasaki in 1864 where he ran a tea export business, flour-mill, gas and electricity company, as well as founding an English-language paper, the *Nagasaki Press*. The **Alt House**, also built in 1865, is more imposing with its deep verandahs, carriage porch and fountain, while the servants made do in the red-brick kitchen block behind. William Alt, another tea merchant, only lived here for three years before heading on to Ōsaka and then Yokohama.

By far the bluff's most colourful and illustrious resident, however, was the Scotsman **Thomas Glover**, who arrived from Shanghai in 1859, aged just 22 years, and became involved in various enterprises, including arms dealing. In the mid-1860s, rebels seeking to overthrow the shogun approached Glover for his assistance. Not only did he supply them with weapons, but also furthered their revolutionary cause by smuggling some of them abroad to study, including Ho Hirofumi who eventually served as prime minister in the new Meiji government. For this, and his subsequent work in modernizing Japanese industry, Glover was awarded the Second Class Order of the Rising Sun, a rare honour, shortly before his death in Tokyo aged 73.

Thomas built the bungalow now known as **Glover House** in 1863, where he lived with his wife Tsuru, a former *geisha*, and his son from an earlier liaison, Tomisaburo. After his father's death, Tomisaburo was a valued member of both the Japanese and foreign business communities, but as Japan slid towards war in the mid-1930s his companies were closed and Tomisaburo came under suspicion as a potential spy. Forced to move out of Glover House, with its bird's-eye view of the harbour, and kept under virtual house arrest, he committed suicide two weeks after the atomic bomb flashed above Nagasaki.

The exit from Glover Garden takes you through the **Museum of Traditional Performing Arts** (same ticket), which displays the beautifully fashioned floats and other paraphernalia used during the Kunchi festivities (see p.681). There's also a short film giving a glimpse of the action, including lithe dragon dances and ships spinning furiously.

---

### MADAME BUTTERFLY

Puccini's opera, written in the early twentieth century, tells the story of an American lieutenant stationed in Nagasaki who marries a Japanese woman known as **Madame Butterfly**. Whereas she has given up her religion and earned the wrath of her family to enter the marriage, Lt. Pinkerton treats the marriage far less seriously, and is soon posted back to the States. Unknown to Pinkerton, Butterfly has given birth to their son and is waiting faithfully for his return when he arrives back in Nagasaki three years later. Butterfly pretties up her house and prepares to present her child to the proud father. Pinkerton, meanwhile, has remarried in America and brings his new wife to meet the unsuspecting Butterfly. When he offers to adopt the child, poor Butterfly agrees and tells him to come back later, then embraces her son and falls on her father's sword.

The opera was adapted from a play by David Belasco, though some attribute it to a book by Frenchman Pierre Loti who wrote *Madame Chrysanthème* after spending a month in Nagasaki in 1885 with a young Japanese woman called Kane. Whatever its origin, the opera was not well received at its debut and Puccini was forced to rewrite Pinkerton and his American wife in a more sympathetic light. Efforts to trace the real Pinkerton have led to a William B Franklin, but it was common practice in the late nineteenth century for Western males stationed in Japan to "marry" a *geisha* in order to secure their companion's faithfulness and reduce the spread of venereal disease. In return, they provided accommodation plus some remuneration. As soon as the posting ended, however, the agreement was considered null and void.

*THE DUTCH SLOPES*

From Ōura Church, take the footpath heading east through a little graveyard and along the valley side until you pick up signs to the **Dutch Slopes**. Though it's only five minutes, few visitors bother to venture into this area where several more Western-style period houses have been preserved on the terraced hillsides reached by roads still paved with their original flagstones. The first group of wooden houses you see on the left consists of two neat rows: the lower three house a **photography museum** (Tues–Sun 9am–5pm; ¥200) displaying early photos of Nagasaki, while the **Higashi-yamate Museum** (same hours; free), in the middle of the upper row, exhibits materials about the district and efforts to rescue the old buildings.

Walking along the Dutch slopes you can't miss the bright yellow roofs of **Kōshi-byō** (daily 8.30am–5pm; ¥515), nestling at the foot of the hill within its stout, red-brick wall. Interestingly, the land beneath this **Confucian shrine**, completed in 1893, belongs to China and is administered by the embassy in Tokyo. Its present pristine state is due to an extensive 1980s rebuild using materials imported from China, right from the glazed roof tiles to the glittering white marble flagstones and statues of Confucius's 72 disciples filling the courtyard. After the restrained tones of Japan's religious architecture, Kōshi-byō's exuberant use of colour comes as a bit of a surprise, as does the gorgeously bedecked statue of Confucius flashing an endearing pair of snow-white, buck-teeth in the old, incense-stained sanctuary. Behind, the shrine museum is packed with priceless treasures, including hefty silver ingots, gold seals and rich brocades.

## Inasa-yama

Nagasaki is not short of good viewpoints, but none can compare with the spectacular night-time panorama from **Inasa-yama**, a 330-metre-high knobble to the west of the city. A **ropeway** (daily: April–Nov 9am–10pm; Jan–March & Dec 10am–8pm; closed for maintenance early Dec; ¥600 one way), whisks you up there in just five minutes; cars run every twenty minutes and you can pick up discount vouchers at most hotels. To reach the ropeway, take Nagasaki Bus #3 or #4 from outside the train station and get off across the river at Ropeway-mae bus stop, from where the entrance is up the steps in the grounds of a shrine.

# Eating, drinking and entertainment

Nagasaki's international heritage extends to its most famous **speciality food**, *shippoku*, which combines European, Chinese and Japanese tastes in lots of small dishes eaten Chinese-style at a round table. It's not a cheap meal, starting at around ¥4000 per head, and for the best *shippoku* you need to reserve the day before, although most of the big hotels also offer a less formal version. Nagasaki's other home-grown dishes include the cheap and cheerful *chanpon*, in which morsels of seafood, meat and vegetables are served with a dollop of thick noodles in piping-hot soup. *Sara udon* uses similar ingredients but blends them into a thicker sauce on a pile of crispy strands.

You can sample *chanpon* and *sara udon* at most of the **restaurants** listed opposite, or try the little street immediately across from Nagasaki Station, where yellow flags announce a couple of good-value eating houses. Though you'll find a few such places around the station, there's a far better choice of restaurants in the southern districts, specifically around Teramachi-dōri and across the tram tracks into Shianbashi and Chinatown.

Nagasaki's entertainment district, **Shianbashi**, is sandwiched between Hamanomachi shopping district and Chinatown, in the south of the city. Ironically, *shian* translates something like "peaceful contemplation", which is the last thing you'll find in this tangle of lanes, packed with bars, clubs, *pachinko* parlours, *izakaya* and "soaplands", where nothing really gets going until 10pm and ends at dawn. The choice, as ever, is bewildering, and prices can be astronomical, but a safe place to start is the With Nagasaki Building, on the east edge of the district on Kankō-dōri. It's a one-stop night-out, starting in the basement with Asahi Brewery's mellow *Ancient Time* beer restaurant, and working upward through a host of bars and nightclubs.

## Restaurants

**Bharata**, Street Yasaka Bldg, 2-10 Aburaya-machi. It's worth tracking down this little, homely Indian for its excellent-value sets. There's a limited range of curries, including vegetarian, tandoori dishes and thali. Not haute cuisine, but the food is spicy and plentiful. Tues–Sun 11.30am–3pm & 5–10pm.

**Hamakatsu**, 1-14 Kajiya-machi. Popular restaurant on Teramachi-dōri specializing in *tonkatsu* (pork cutlets). Though it looks smart, with its gold signboard and iron lantern, prices are extremely reasonable and you can eat all you want of the extras – soup, rice and salad. Daily 11.30am–10pm.

**Hamakatsu**, 6-50 Kajiya-machi (☎0958/26-8321). This smarter *Hamakatsu* offers *shippoku* meals at reasonable prices. You can try a mini-*shippoku* at around ¥3000 or the real thing from ¥4000 up to ¥15,000 per person; note that you must order in advance and they require at least two people per group. Daily 11.30am–10pm.

**Harbin**, 2-27 Kozen-machi (☎0958/22-7443). On the main road west of City Hall, this Nagasaki institution has been serving French and Russian cuisine since 1959. It's nicely decked out with dark wooden furniture and an impressive array of vodkas. There's plenty of choice, from *borsch* to Azerbaijan-style *pot au feu*, and good lunchtime sets for ¥1500. Tues–Sun 11.30am–2.30pm & 6–10.30pm.

**Kagetsu**, 2-1 Maruyama-machi (☎0958/22-0191). Even more famous than *Harbin*, *Kagetsu* started life as a brothel, but in the early twentieth century began cooking top-notch Nagasaki cuisine. On the corner of an attractive square and surrounded by a traditional garden, this is the best place for *shippoku*. Prices start at ¥4550 for a lunchtime *bentō* or ¥8000 for the regular set; expect to pay at least double that in the evening. Booking is essential and you need two people or more. Daily noon–3pm & 5–10pm.

**Kouzanrou**, 12-2 Shinchi-machi. Chinatown is packed with tempting restaurants, but this Fukien establishment is recommended for its reasonably priced *chanpon* and *sara udon* as well as more mainstream Chinese dishes. Daily 11.30am–9.30pm.

**Ringer Hut**. Towards the south end of Teramachi-dōri, this basic, reliable café-style restaurant belongs to another Kyūshū chain. The extensive menu includes *chanpon* sets from ¥600. Daily 11am–4am.

**Robin Hood no Mori**, 4F, 5-8 Motoshikkui-machi. Look for their small Robin Hood logo just as you walk south into Shianbashi, and make sure you're hungry enough to appreciate their eat-and-drink-all-you-want deals (from ¥2100). Men pay slightly more than women, there's a two-hour time period and everyone in the group must choose the same type of menu. *Shabu-shabu*, barbecue-beef and seafood are the main options, though there's also a salad bar. It's a bit of a scrum at peak times, when you'll have to queue. Daily 5–10.30pm, Fri & Sat till midnight.

**Shirokiya**, 9-28 Daikoku-machi. Big, bright *izakaya* opposite the station with something for everyone on its picture-menu – sushi, *sukiyaki*, *yakitori*, salads and so on. Service can be slow, but the beers are cheap and you can count on ¥2000 or less per person for a good feast. Upstairs is a more formal restaurant under the same management. Daily 5pm–5am.

# Listings

**Airlines** ANA (☎0120–029222); China Eastern Airlines (☎0958/28-1510); JAL (☎0120–255971); JAS (☎0120–511283); Korean Air (☎0958/24-3311).

**Airport information** ☎0957/52-5555.

**Banks and exchange** The 18th Bank, next to the *New Nagasaki Hotel*, is the closest foreign exchange service to the train station. Otherwise, there are branches of major banks around the central Hamanomachi shopping district.

**Bookshops** Nagasaki's biggest bookshop, Kobundo, is located in Hamanomachi arcade. Foreign titles are up on the second floor. Look out for *Crossroads* (¥600), an excellent journal about Nagasaki history and culture published annually by two American academics.

**Car rental** Eki Rent-a-car (☎0958/26-0480); Nippon Rent-a-car (☎0958/21-0919); Nissan Rent-a-car (☎0958/25-1988); Toyota Rent-a-car (☎0958/47-0100).

**Ferries** Yasuda company (☎0958/20-5055) operates daily "Sea Bird" high-speed ferries from Nagasaki's Ōhato Port Terminal, fifteen minutes' walk south of the train station, to Kumamoto (1hr 45min; ¥4500).

**Festivals** New Year is celebrated in Chinatown with a Lantern Festival, dragon dances and acrobatic displays (Jan 1–3). Dragon-boat races, here called *Peiron*, were introduced by the Chinese in 1655 and are still held in Nagasaki harbour every summer (June–July). The last evening of *Obon* (Aug 15) is celebrated with a "spirit-boat" procession, when recently bereaved families lead lantern-lit floats down to the harbour. But the biggest bash of the year occurs at the *Kunchi Matsuri* held in early October at Suwa-jinja (see p.681).

**Hospitals** Nagasaki Hospital, 6-41 Sakuragi-chō (☎0958/23-2261), is located on the city's southeastern suburbs. Closer to the centre, Shimin Byōin, 6-39 Shinchi-machi (☎0958/22-3251) is an emergency hospital on the western edge of Chinatown.

**Police** 6-13 Okeya-machi (☎0958/22-0110). Emergency numbers are listed in Basics on p.70.

**Post office** Nagasaki Central Post Office is 300m east of the station at 1-1 Ebisu-machi and has a poste restante service.

**Shopping** The main department stores, Daimaru and Hamaya, are in the Hamanomachi shopping arcades. The most popular local souvenir is *kasutera*, a honey-sponge cake introduced from Spain by Portuguese cooks in the sixteenth century. The best-known *kasutera* bakeries are Fukusa-ya and Bunmei-dō, both of which have outlets all over the city. If you want to buy it at source, however, try Fukusa-ya's original shop in a picturesque building on the edge of Shianbashi – look for its distinctive bat logo (daily 8.30am–8pm).

**Taxis** Lucky Cab ☎0958/22-4123.

**Travel agencies** For domestic travel, the main JTB office is at 1-95 Onoue-machi (☎0958/24-5194), near Nagasaki Station. International tickets can be bought at H.I.S, 5F, Yamato-seimei Bldg, 3-4 Manzai-machi (☎0958/20-6839), in the streets west of the City Hall.

# Shimabara Hantō

East of Nagasaki, the **Shimabara Hantō** bulges out into the Ariake Sea, tethered to mainland Kyūshū by a neck of land just 5km wide. The peninsula owes its existence to the past volcanic fury of **Unzen-dake** which still grumbles away, pumping out sulphurous steam, and occasionally spewing lava down its eastern flanks. Buddhist monks first came to the mountain in the eighth century, followed more than a millennium later by Europeans from nearby Nagasaki attracted by the cool, upland summers and mild winters. Even today, **Unzen**, a small onsen resort surrounded by pine trees and billowing clouds of steam, draws holidaymakers to its hot springs, malodorous "hells" and scenic hiking trails. One of the most popular outings is to the lava dome of **Fugen-dake**, which roared back into life in 1990 after two centuries of inactivity, and now smoulders menacingly above **Shimabara**. The old castle town was protected from the worst of the eruption by an older lava block, but still suffered considerable damage to its southern suburbs, which are slowly being rebuilt. Previously, Shimabara was famous largely for its association with a Christian-led rebellion in the seventeenth century when 37,000 peasants and their families were massacred. Both towns can be covered on a long day's journey between Nagasaki and Kumamoto, but if time allows Unzen makes a relaxing overnight stop.

## Unzen

You can feel the air temperature dropping as the road from Obama leaves sea level and climbs up towards the **Unzen plateau** (727m). The name means "fairyland among the clouds", perhaps inspired by the pure, mountain air and colourful flourishes of vegetation – azaleas in spring and autumn leaves – against which the **onsen** and their *alter*

| **SHIMABARA HANTŌ** | | |
|---|---|---|
| **Unzen** | *Unzen* | 雲仙 |
| Kaseya | *Kaseya* | かせや |
| Kokuminshukusha Seiun-sō | *Kokuminshukusha Seiun-sō* | 国民宿舎青雲荘 |
| Unzen Kankō Hotel | *Unzen Kankō Hoteru* | 雲仙観光ホテル |
| | | |
| **Shimabara** | *Shimabara* | 島原 |
| Hotel Hakusan | *Hoteru Hakusan* | 姫松屋 |
| Himematsu-ya | *Himematsu-ya* | ホテル白山 |
| New Queen Hotel | *Nyū Kuiin Hoteru* | ニュークイーンホテル |
| Ōsaka-ya | *Ōsaka-ya* | 大阪屋 |
| Shimabara-jō | *Shimabara-jō* | 島原城 |
| Shimabara Youth Hostel | *Shimabara Yūsu Hosuteru* | 島原ユースホステル |
| Sumiyoshikan | *Sumiyoshikan* | 住吉館 |
| Sushi-katsu | *Sushi-katsu* | すし勝 |
| Toraya | *Toraya* | とらや |

*egos*, the spitting, scalding **jigoku** ("hells"), compete for attention. Unzen town consists largely of resort hotels and souvenir shops strung out along the main road, but fortunately there's plenty of space around and a variety of **walking trails** lead off into the surrounding national park. The best hikes explore the peaks of Unzen-dake, though at the time of writing the highest paths are still off-limits following the 1990 eruption. However you can take a **ropeway** part way up **Fugen-dake**, affording splendid views of the Ariake Sea and, if you're lucky, across to Aso-san's steaming cauldron.

Without your own transport, the best way of **getting to Unzen** is by bus. Frequent direct services depart from either Nagasaki's Ken-ei bus terminal or outside the station (¥1750), or JR pass holders can take the train to Isahaya and pick up the bus there. Isahaya's bus station is right in front of the JR station, under the building with the National Panasonic hoarding on top. From here, both Ken-ei and Shimatetsu buses run up to Unzen (¥1200).

## The Town

UNZEN is pretty much a one-street town. The main road enters from the southwest, does a dog-leg east and then north, before exiting east towards Shimabara. Unzen's commercial centre lies in the north, concentrated round the bus stations, while its geographical centre consists of a steaming, barren area known as **jigoku**. These *jigoku* and an assortment of **onsen baths**, renowned for their silky smooth water, constitute Unzen's foremost attractions. The first commercial onsen bath was opened in 1653, while two hundred years later Europeans arriving from Nagasaki, Hong Kong, Shanghai and east Russia prompted the development of a full-blown resort, complete with mock-Tudor hotels and one of Japan's first golf courses, laid out in 1913.

The nicest of Unzen's **public baths** is the newly renovated **Kojigoku** (daily 9am–9pm; ¥400) which occupies two octagonal wooden buildings opposite the *Seiun-sō* hotel, roughly ten minutes' walk south of town. More in the centre of things, **Shin-yu** (daily 10am–11pm; ¥100) is a small but traditional bathhouse just south of the *jigoku*. Lastly, there's the more glitzy **Unzen Spa House** (daily 10am–6pm; ¥1500; ¥800 after 4pm), offering sauna, Jacuzzi and all sorts of baths, including a *rotemburo*, in a half-timbered building on the main road into town.

A Shingon Buddhist priest is credited with "founding" Unzen when he built a temple here in 701 AD. The area developed into a popular retreat where monks could contemplate the 84,000 tortures awaiting wrongdoers in the afterlife as they gazed at

Unzen's bubbling mudpools. The volcanic vents are less active nowdays but still emit evil, sulphurous streams and waft steam over a landscape of bilious-coloured clay. Only the hardiest of acid-tolerant plants can survive, and local hoteliers have added to the satanic scene by laying a mess of rusting, hissing pipes to feed water to their onsen baths.

Nevertheless, the *jigoku* provide an interesting hour's diversion, particularly the more active eastern area. The paths are well signposted, with lots of maps and information along the way, and there's also a descriptive English-language brochure, *A Round in Unzen Hell*, available at the Visitors' Centre (see Practicalities, below). The highest and most active *jigoku*, **Daikyōkan Jigoku**, takes its name from the "scream" produced as it emits hydrogen sulphide steam at 120°C. The noise is likened to the cries of souls descending to hell, but could well be the howls of 33 Christian martyrs, commemorated on a nearby monument, who were scalded to death here around 1630 by the Shimabara lords (see box opposite). Another unhappy end is remembered at **Oito Jigoku** which, according to legend, broke out the day a local adulteress, Oito, was executed for murdering her husband. The tiny, bursting bubbles of **Suzume Jigoku**, on the other hand, supposedly resemble the twittering of sparrows. Over in the western section, the main point of interest is the temple founded nearly 1300 years ago. **Mammyō-ji** has recently been restored, and inside the gilded Shaka Buddha with his startling blue hair-do is an intriguing sight.

## Fugen-dake

While Unzen-dake is the name of the whole volcanic mass, **Fugen-dake** (1488m) refers to a newer cone on its east side that now forms the highest of the Unzen peaks. Fugen-dake erupted suddenly in November 1990 and reached a crescendo in June 1991 when the dome collapsed, sending an avalanche of mud and rocks through Shimabara town. Forty three people were killed and nearly 3000 homes destroyed. Since then Fugen-dake continues to smoke gently, but the eruption officially ended in May 1995.

A **ropeway** (daily 8.30am–5pm; ¥600 one way) takes visitors up to an observation platform to the west of Fugen-dake. Cars run every twenty minutes, though not in bad weather or if the volcano is misbehaving; last ride down is at 5.30pm. From the top station, you can walk to the nearest summit, Myōken-dake (1333m), in just ten minutes and then continue to Kunimi-dake (1347m). Buses to the ropeway depart from Unzen's Ken-ei bus terminal (25min; ¥700 return), with two up in the morning and two or three in the afternoon. The last bus down to Unzen leaves at 4.30pm, after which you'll have to walk; the path, which takes an hour, starts to the west of the information centre in the ropeway car park and ends beside the Ikenohara golf course, on the main road 1km east of Unzen town.

## Practicalities

Unzen has two **bus terminals**: Ken-ei buses, by far the most frequent, pull in at the north end of town, while Shimatetsu buses stop a little further back down the main road. For general **information** about accommodation and transport, try Unzen Information Centre (daily 9am–5pm; ☎0957/73-3434) located on the main road in from the south. Where the main road turns north, the Visitors' Centre (daily except Thurs 9am–5pm) has information about the national park, including a few walking maps and nature trails. Neither office has English-speaking staff.

Most **accommodation** in Unzen consists of expensive resort hotels, but there are a couple of reasonable choices, which it's advisable to reserve even out of season. The best option is *Kokuminshukusha Seiun-sō* (☎0957/73-3273, fax 73-2698; ③–⑤). It's a rambling place offering basic *tatami* rooms, a big onsen bath and excellent-value meals – or the option of room only – in a nicely wooded position ten minutes' walk south of town (phone to be collected from the bus station). *Kaseya* (☎0957/73-3321, fax 73-3322;

[5]), an attractive old ryokan on the main road near the bus stations, has clean bright *tatami* rooms and optional meals. Set in gardens at the south end of town, the *Unzen Kankō Hotel* (☎0957/73-3263, fax 73-3419; [5]) is one of the original European-style hotels, built in 1935. The cheaper rooms are all Western style; small, but comfortable, and equipped with large, old-fashioned bathtubs.

When it comes to **eating**, you're best off taking meals in your hotel. However, the *Unzen Kankō Hotel* has a good restaurant which is open to non-residents, and there are a few uninspiring but inexpensive cafés along the main road.

## Shimabara

The port town of **SHIMABARA** has had a chequered history. Following the ructions of the **Shimabara Rebellion** (see box), it was decimated when Unzen-dake erupted in 1792, sending rock and hot ash tumbling into Shimabara Bay. An estimated 15,000 people died in the disaster, mostly from huge tidal waves that swept the Ariake Sea. The volcano then lay dormant until Fugen-dake burst into life again in 1990 (see opposite) and cut a swathe through the town's southern reaches. They're still busily restoring the roads and rice terraces, while photos of the eruption appear all over Shimabara. Though the brooding mountain makes a dramatic backdrop, the only reason to stop here is to visit its castle, **Shimabara-jō**, which hosts an interesting museum about Japan's early Christians and the local rebellion.

Completed in 1625, the castle took seven years to build – it was partly the taxes and hard-labour demanded for its construction that provoked the Shimabara Rebellion. Entry to the grounds is free, while the reconstructed turrets contain three **museums** (daily: April–Oct 8am–6pm; Jan–March, Nov & Dec 9am–5pm; ¥510) of which priority should go to the main keep's local history exhibits, including some interesting relics of clandestine Christian worship. The modern building in the northwest corner displays a short video in English about Fugen-dake's most recent eruption, while fans of Nagasaki's Peace Statue (see p.679) will be interested in the Kitamura Seibō Memorial Museum located in the southeast turret. Kitamura, a local sculptor who died in 1987, specialized in powerful bronzes, the best of them gripped by a restless, pent-up energy.

### Practicalities

Shimabara straggles along the coast for more than 2km from its southerly **Shin-kō ferry terminal** to the main centre, **Ōte**, just below the castle. **Buses** from Unzen call at the Shin-kō terminal before proceeding into town, where they either terminate at the Shimatetsu bus terminal or stop a little further on in Ōte. **Trains** running south from Isahaya on the private Shimabara line stop at the main Shimabara Station, a couple of

> **THE SHIMABARA REBELLION**
>
> In 1637, exorbitant taxes and the oppressive cruelty of two local *daimyō* sparked off a large-scale **peasant revolt** in the Shimabara area, though the underlying motive was anger at **Christian persecutions** taking place at the time. Many of the rebels were Christian, including their leader, a 16-year-old boy known as Amakusa Shirō, who was supposedly able to perform miracles. His motley army of 37,000, including women and children, eventually sought refuge in abandoned Hara castle, roughly 30km south of Shimabara town. For three months they held off far-superior government forces, but even Shirō couldn't save them when Hara was stormed in April 1638 and, so it's said, all 37,000 were massacred. Rightly or wrongly, Portuguese missionaries were implicated in the rebellion and soon after all foreigners were banished from Japan as the country closed its doors.

minutes' walk east of Ōte, and then continue three more stops to Shin-kō Station (also known as Gai-kō Station) near the ferry port.

Shimabara's **information office** (daily 8.30am–5pm; ☎0957/63-1111) is inside the Shin-kō terminal building. For **onward transport** to Kumamoto, there's a choice of two ferry crossings: either to Kumamoto Shin-kō or Misumi (last sailings 6.35pm and 4.40pm respectively), both of which take one hour and cost ¥580 for foot passengers. There are buses from Kumamoto Shin-kō into the city (35min; ¥470), while from Misumi it's a longer, fifty-minute train ride, though free to JR pass holders.

If you need **accommodation**, one of the nicest central places is *Sumiyoshikan* (☎0957/63-0032, fax 63-1659; [5]), a small, bright business hotel five minutes' walk southwest from Shimabara Station. Near the ferry terminal, there's the cheap and basic *Toraya* (☎0957/63-3332; [4]), offering either Western or *tatami* rooms, or *Shimabara Youth Hostel* (☎0957/62-4451; [1]), roughly three minutes' walk west across the train tracks. For something smarter, try either the *New Queen Hotel* (☎0957/64-5511, fax 63-0051; [4]–[5]) or the slightly cheaper *Hotel Hakusan* (0957/63-5400, fax 62-3334; [4]), both on the main road north.

Shimabara's **speciality food**, *guzoni*, consists of clam broth packed with rice-cakes, fish, pork, lotus root, tofu and egg. You can try it at *Himematsu-ya* (daily 10am–8pm), an attractive **restaurant** opposite the entrance to Shimabara-jō, or there's a choice of well-priced sets and mainstream Japanese dishes. *Sushi-katsu* (daily 10am–8pm) is a fine, old sushi bar on Ōte's central square, where you should be able to eat for under ¥2000. For a late-night bite, *Ōsaka-ya* (daily 6pm–3am), south of this square, serves a cracking, mixed-cheese *okonomiyaki*.

# Kumamoto

Situated halfway down the west coast, within striking distance of Aso to the east and Unzen to the west, **KUMAMOTO** makes a good base for exploring central Kyūshū. The city itself is reasonably attractive and boasts a couple of worthwhile sights, namely the fearsome, fairy-tale **castle** dominating the town centre, and one of Japan's most highly rated gardens, **Suizenji-kōen**, in the western suburbs. Wars and development have left little else of particular note, though you've got to admire a city which invented the endearingly offbeat "Kobori-style" swimming which "involves the art of swimming in a standing posture attired in armour and helmet".

Kumamoto owes its existence to the Katō clan who were given the fiefdom in the late sixteenth century in return for supporting Tokugawa Ieyasu during his rise to power. **Kato Kiyomasa**, first of the feudal lords, not only built a magnificent fortress but is also remembered for his public works, such as flood control and land reclamation. However, political intrigue resulted in the Kato being ousted in 1632, in favour of the **Hosokawa** clan who had previously held Kokura. Thirteen generations of Hosokawa lords ruled Kumamoto for more than two centuries, during which time the city thrived as Kyūshū's major government stronghold, until feudal holdings were abolished in 1871. Six years later, the final drama of the Meiji Restoration was played out here when Saigō Takamori's rebel army was defeated by government troops, but not before destroying much of Kumamoto's ultimately impregnable castle.

## Orientation, arrival, information and city transport

Central Kumamoto occupies the north bank of the **Shira-kawa**, between the river and the castle. This is where you'll find the main shopping mall, Shimo-tōri, as well as major hotels, banks and, Kumamoto Kōtsū Centre, the city's central bus terminal. The main station, however, lies 2km to the south, creating a secondary hub, with its own hotels and bus services.

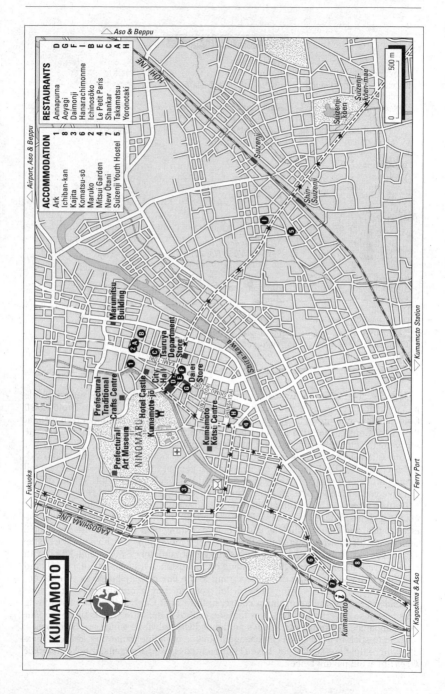

△ *Aso & Beppu*

△ *Airport, Aso & Beppu*

◁ *Fukuoka*

▽ *Kagoshima & Aso*

▷ *Ferry Port*

▽ *Kumamoto Station*

# KUMAMOTO

N

| ACCOMMODATION | |
|---|---|
| Ark | 1 |
| Ichiban-kan | 8 |
| Kajita | 3 |
| Komatsu-sō | 6 |
| Maruko | 2 |
| Mitsui Garden | 4 |
| New Ōtani | 7 |
| Suizenji Youth Hostel | 5 |

| RESTAURANTS | |
|---|---|
| Annapurna | D |
| Aoyagi | G |
| Daimonji | F |
| Hanarachimonme | I |
| Ichinosōko | B |
| Le Petit Paris | E |
| Shankar | C |
| Takamatsu | A |
| Yoronotaki | H |

HOHI LINE

KAGOSHIMA LINE

Marumitsu-
Building

Prefectural
Traditional
Crafts Centre

Prefectural
Art Museum

NINOMARU Hotel Castle

Kumamoto-jō

Tsuruya
Department
Store

City
Hall

Daiei
Store

KAMI-TŌRI

SHIMO-TŌRI

SHINSHIGAI

Kumamoto
Kōtsu Centre

SHIRAKAWA

Suizenji

Shin-
(Suizenji)

Suizenji-
kōen

Suizenji-
kōen-mae

0        500 m

## KUMAMOTO

| | | |
|---|---|---|
| **Kumamoto** | *Kumamoto* | 熊本 |
| Kumamoto-jō | *Kumamoto-jō* | 熊本城 |
| Kumamoto Kōtsū Centre | *Kumamoto Kōtsū Sentā* | 熊本交通センター |
| Kumamoto Shin-kō | *Kumamoto Shin-kō* | 熊本新港 |
| Prefectural Art Museum | *Kumamoto-kenritsu Bijutsukan* | 熊本県立美術館 |
| Suizenji-kōen | *Suizenji-kōen* | 水前寺公園 |
| Prefectural Traditional Crafts Centre | *Kumamoto-ken Dentō Kōgei-kan* | 熊本県伝統工芸館 |

*ACCOMMODATION*

| | | |
|---|---|---|
| Ark Hotel | *Āku Hoteru* | アークホテル |
| Hotel Ichiban-kan | *Hoteru Ichiban-kan* | ホテル一番館 |
| Kajita | *Kajita* | 梶田 |
| Komatsu-sō | *Komatsu-sō* | 小松荘 |
| Hotel New Otani | *Hoteru Nyū Ōtani* | ホテルニューオオタニ |
| Maruko Hotel | *Maruko Hoteru* | 丸小ホテル |
| Mitsui Garden Hotel | *Mitsui Gāden Hoteru* | 三井ガーデンホテル |
| Suizenji Youth Hostel | *Suizenji Yūsu Hosuteru* | 水前寺ユースホステル |

*RESTAURANTS*

| | | |
|---|---|---|
| Annapurna | *Annapuruna* | アンナプルナ |
| Aoyagi | *Aoyagi* | 青柳 |
| Daimonji | *Daimonji* | 大文字 |
| Hanarachimonme | *Hanarachimonme* | 花らちもんめ |
| Ichinosōko | *Ichinosōko* | 壱之倉庫 |
| Takamatsu | *Takamatsu* | 高松 |
| Yōrōnotaki | *Yōrōnotaki* | 養老の滝 |

Arriving at Kumamoto **airport**, roughly 15km northwest, limousine buses shuttle into town in roughly one hour (¥670), stopping at Shimo-tōri and the Kumamoto Kōtsū Centre before ending up at the train station. Most **long-distance buses** terminate at the Kōtsū Centre, though a few continue to Kumamoto Station, while buses from the **ferry** port, Kumamoto Shin-kō, stop at the station first.

Kumamoto's helpful **tourist information** service (daily 9am–5.30pm; ☎096/352-3743) occupies a desk inside the train station's central exit, and there's also a small branch office in the airport (daily 8am–8.30pm). English-language staff at both offices can give you a number of useful maps and guides, and help with hotel reservations.

Getting around central Kumamoto is made fairly easy by a **tram** system which covers most sights. There are just two lines (#2 and #3), both of which run from the eastern suburbs and through the city centre before splitting near the Kōtsū Centre. Line 2 then heads off south to Kumamoto Station, while Line 3 loops north round the castle. Trams run every five to ten minutes between approximately 6.30am and 11pm, with fares ranging from ¥130 to ¥190 depending on the distance travelled; take a numbered ticket on entry and pay the driver according to the fare-display board as you get off. Alternatively, if you're moving about a lot, you can buy a one-day pass (*ichi-nichi jyōshaken*; ¥500) at the information centre, in the Kōtsū Centre or on the tram itself. This pass also covers Shiei **buses** within the central zone; however, as there are four bus companies in Kumamoto and it's not immediately obvious which are Shiei buses, it's best to stick to trams. You can change from one tram line to another at Karashima-chō, where the lines split; if you haven't got a day pass, ask for a transfer ticket (*norikae kippu*) to avoid paying twice.

## Accommodation

You'll find the majority of **hotels** concentrated in Kumamoto's central district, where there are a couple of reasonable ryokan plus a wider selection in the business category and above. Most cheaper places are located around Kumamoto Station, with the main youth hostel lying out west near Suizenji-kōen.

**Ark Hotel**, 5-16 Jōtō-machi (☎096/351-2222, fax 326-0909). Nicely designed mid-range hotel beside the castle. The rooms are a reasonable size and decked out with batik-style bed covers and contemporary prints. You pay slightly more for a castle view, though the NHK radio mast intrudes. ⑤–⑥.

**Hotel Ichiban-kan**, 1-3-9 Nihongi (☎096/359-6600, fax 359-6949). Five minutes' walk east of the station, this bottom-end business hotel is a friendly place with English-speaking staff and very green decor. Rooms are basic but clean and bright, in Western or Japanese style. The cheapest come without bath. ④.

**Kajita**, 1-2-7 Shin-machi (☎ & fax 096/353-1546). Tucked away on the castle's west side, this homely minshuku is one of the few budget places within walking distance of central Kumamoto. The *tatami* rooms are simple yet smart, with TV but no en-suite facilities. Prices are good and the owners helpful. ④.

**Komatsu-sō**, 1-8-23 Kasuga (☎096/355-2634). Welcoming if rather run-down little minshuku offering good rates for the location, on a lane just five minutes from the train station. Prices include bread and coffee for breakfast, or you can use the small communal kitchen. ③.

**Hotel New Ōtani**, 1-13-1 Kasuga (☎096/326-1111, fax 326-0800). The smartest hotel near Kumamoto Station, where you'll find the usual efficient service, plus a choice of formal restaurants and a coffee shop, sauna and shopping area. Rooms are well equipped and ample, with generous-size beds. ⑥.

**Maruko Hotel**, 11-10 Kamitōri-chō (☎096/353-1241, fax 353-1217). Modern, well-decorated hotel in an interesting area to the north of the centre. Rooms are mostly Japanese style and all en suite, and there's also a Japanese bath with views on the sixth floor. English spoken. ⑤.

**Mitsui Garden Hotel**, 1-20 Koyaima-machi (☎096/352-1131, fax 322-5847). Despite the grand marble lobby, prices at this mid-range business hotel on the south edge of the centre aren't too bad. The rooms are comfortable and come with bathroom, TV and mini-bar. ⑤.

**Suizenji Youth Hostel**, 1-2-20 Hakuzan (☎096/371-9193). It's wise to book ahead for this small, spotless hostel out near Suizenji-kōen. All accommodation is in *tatami* rooms and there are no meals or cooking facilities on offer. It's located five minutes' walk west of Shin-Suizenji Station on the JR Hōhi line, and two minutes from the Misotenjin-mae tram stop; from the tram, walk back (west) to the last crossroads, turn left and follow the road round and you'll find the hostel before the next main road. ①.

## The City

Most of Kumamoto's sights are conveniently located in and around the castle. The outer citadel has been turned into a public park, **Ninomaru**, dominated by the remaining turrets of **Kumamoto-jō** to the east and containing various public facilities, of which the **Prefectural Art Museum** is the most rewarding. Beneath the castle walls, the well-arranged and informative **Traditional Crafts Centre** is worth a visit. Out in the western districts, the landscaped garden of **Suizenji-kōen** with its manicured mini-Fuji, vies with the castle as Kumamoto's most popular sight.

### The central sights

Completed in 1607 after only seven years' labour, **Kumamoto-jō** is Japan's third largest castle (after Ōsaka and Nagoya) and one of its most formidable. It was designed by lord **Kato Kiyomasa**, a brilliant military architect, who combined superb fortifications with exquisitely graceful flourishes – as Alan Booth observed in *The Roads to Sata* (see Books, p.816), the main keep seems like "a fragile bird poised for flight". At its peak, Kumamoto-jō had an outer perimeter of 13km and over 5km of inner wall built in what's called *musha-gaeshi* style, meaning that no invading warrior – or mouse in the more popular version – could scale their smooth, gently concave surfaces. In case of prolonged attack, 120 wells were sunk, while camphor and gingko trees provided firewood and edible nuts. These defences were severely tested during the 1877 **Satsuma Rebellion** (see p.710), when Saigō Takamori's army besieged Kumamoto-jō for fifty days. Government reinforcements eventually relieved the garrison and trounced the rebels soon after. Though the castle held, most of its buildings were burnt to the ground and were left in ruins until 1960, when the main keep was magnificently restored around a concrete shell.

The best approach to the castle is from its south side which brings you up into the grassy expanse of **Ninomaru**. Before entering the inner citadel, you might want to visit the **Prefectural Art Museum** (Tues–Sun 9.30am–5pm; ¥250, plus extra for special exhibitions), over to the west, which takes in a broad sweep from ancient ornamented tombs to an impressive collection of contemporary Japanese and Western art. Otherwise, pass through the castle's main, west gate into the **Honmaru** (daily 8.30am–5.30pm; Jan–March, Nov & Dec till 4.30pm; ¥200 entry plus ¥300 for the keep). Inside to the left, **Uto Yagura** was the only turret to survive the 1877 battle, while straight on, a high-sided defile leads to the imposing central keep. It now hosts an excellent historical **museum** about the castle and the Hosokawa lords.

Continuing down the castle's eastern slope, you reach **Akazu-no-mon**. Traditionally this northeastern gate was never opened – the northeast being the direction from which evil was thought to emanate – but castle waste was pushed through a nearby sluice to be collected by local farmers for fertilizer. One enterprising gatekeeper made such a profit selling the refuse that he was later deified by grateful benefactors in his hometown.

Opposite the Akazu gate, the **Prefectural Traditional Crafts Centre** (Tues–Sun 9am–5pm) hosts free exhibitions promoting local artists and an excellent display of Kumamoto crafts on the second floor (¥190). The most famous traditional craft is *Higo zogan*, a painstaking technique of inlaying gold and silver in a metal base. Developed in the seventeenth century for ornamenting sword hilts, it's now used for jewellery, decorative boxes and the like. Look out among the toys for a little red-faced fellow with a black hat, known as *Obake-no-kinta* who is supposedly a ghost – try pulling the string.

## Suizenji-kōen

It pays to visit **Suizenji-kōen** (daily: April–Oct 7.30am–6pm; Jan–March, Nov & Dec 8am–5.30pm; ¥400) early, before crowds arrive. In any case, the garden's at its best with an early-morning mist over the crystal clear, spring-fed lake, its surface broken by jumping minnows or the darting beak of a vigilant heron. Plump, multicoloured carp laze under willow-pattern bridges, while staff sweep the gravel paths or snip back an errant pine tuft. Considered to be one of Japan's most beautiful stroll-gardens, Suizenji-kōen was created over eighty years, starting in 1632, by three successive Hosokawa lords. The temple from which the garden took its name is long gone, but the immaculate, undulating landscape, dotted with artfully placed shrubs and trees, has survived. The design supposedly mimics scenes on the road between Tokyo and Kyoto, known as the "53 stations of the Tōkaidō", of which the only ones most people will recognize are Fuji and Lake Biwa.

Considering Suizenji's prestige, it's surprising to find the garden cluttered with souvenir stalls, and it's also quite small, taking only thirty minutes to walk round. On the way, you'll pass the Izumi shrine, dedicated to the Hosokawa lords, and a four-hundred-year-old teahouse overlooking the lake. If it's not too early, you can drink a cup of green tea on the benches outside (9am–5.30pm; ¥500) or in the tea ceremony room (¥600), while admiring one of the best views of the garden; the price includes a *mangetsu mochizuki*, a white, moon-shaped cake made using pure spring water.

# Eating, drinking and nightlife

Central Kumamoto splits into two distinct areas either side of the tram tracks. South of the tracks, **Shimo-tōri** arcade and its offshoots, Sannenzaka-dōri, Ginza-dōri and Shinshigai-Sunroad, are the classic entertainment district, packed with neon-lit **bars**, **clubs** and a mix of **restaurants** from fast food to expense-account dining. North of the tracks, on the other hand, there's a younger, less hectic feel among the small boutiques and ethnic cafés around **Kami-tōri**.

Local **speciality foods** include horse-meat sashimi (*basashi*) eaten with lots of garlic, and *karashi renkon* which consists of lotus-root slices stuffed with a mustard and bean paste, dipped in batter and deep fried. In addition to the restaurants listed below, most big hotels, notably the *Castle* and *New Ōtani*, have well-rated dining-rooms, while Kumamoto Station has a good variety of outlets on its second floor. You'll find the usual chains either at the station or in the central arcades, including *Capricciosa*, *Nanak* and *Ringer Hut*.

## Restaurants

**Annapurna**, 2F, 3-12 Tetorihon-chō. This cheerful, vegetarian restaurant serves excellent-value lunchtime *bentō* from ¥700, with prices only slightly higher in the evenings. All ingredients are organically grown and there's dandelion ice cream for afters. Mon–Sat 11am–3pm & 5–9pm.

**Aoyagi**, 1-2-10 Shimotōri-chō. Large, elegant restaurant behind the Daiei store, with a choice of counter, *tatami* room or tables. Despite appearances, prices aren't astronomical; lunch sets start at just over ¥1000, though you could spend a lot more. Beautifully presented house specialities include *basashi* (from ¥2000). Daily 11.30am–10pm.

**Daimonji**. Tiny *okonomiyaki* place on the second floor above *Angelus Bakery* at the north end of Shimo-tōri. There are plastic examples to choose from, with a big bowl for around ¥600 to cook yourself. Cheap, cheerful and filling. Daily 11am–10pm.

**Hanarachimonme**. A good bet if you're staying at the nearby Suizen-ji Youth Hostel. It's a bit run-down but friendly and very cheap, serving up huge helpings of curry-rice, chicken cutlets and fried noodles, or occasionally *basashi*. The garrulous host speaks a modicum of English and can regale you with songs in any language. Daily 5–11pm.

**Ichinosōko**, 2-8 Kachikōji. A tiny door leads into this spacious, wood-beamed beer restaurant which started life as a silk-weaving workshop. The food is a typical mix of Western and Japanese, both snacks and full meals, where you should be able to eat well for around ¥2000. Daily 5–11pm.

**Le Petit Paris**, 3-12 Tetorihon-chō (☎096/359-5252). Pink table clothes and classical music set the tone at this little French restaurant above a pharmacy. There's a choice of four different menus, with midday prices starting at around ¥1300. Daily except Tues 11.30am–2.30pm & 6–9.30pm.

**Shankar**, 7-11 Kamitōri-chō. This atmospheric Indian restaurant above a pharmacy on Kami-tōri is worth tracking down for its excellent-value set meals (from ¥600), including salad, *chai* and yoghurt. Daily 10.30am–10/11pm.

**Takamatsu**, 11-10 Kamitōri-chō. You can hear the buzz outside this popular basement restaurant which serves an East–West menu (in English) plus daily specials. Portions are on the small side, but the authentic pasta dishes are recommended. With careful ordering, expect to pay around ¥2000 per head. Daily 5–11pm.

**Yoronotaki**, Shinshigai-Sunroad. Popular *izakaya* which attracts a young crowd with its cheap beers and lively atmosphere. There's a big choice of well-priced dishes on its picture menu. Daily 11.30am–11.30pm.

# Listings

**Airlines** ANA (☎0120–029222); JAL (☎0120–255971); JAS (☎0120–511283); Korean Air (☎096/323-3311).

**Airport information** ☎096/232-2810.

**Banks and foreign exchange** You'll find foreign exchange desks in Higo Bank and Fuji Bank, beside the Tsuruya department store, and Daiwa Bank near the Kumamoto-jō-mae tram stop. Higo Bank also has a branch just north of Kumamoto Station.

## MINAMATA'S POISONED SEA

In the mid-1950s, fisherfolk living around Minamata, a town in south Kumamoto Prefecture, began suffering from a mysterious disease. The illness attacked the nervous system, causing convulsions, loss of speech and hearing, often severe mental disability and an agonizing death. The first case of what came to be known as **Minamata disease** was officially diagnosed in 1956, but it took another three years to identify the cause as organic mercury poisoning and it was nearly another decade before Chisso, a local chemical company, stopped pumping their mercury-laden waste into the sea.

The victims aided by a local teacher, **Ishimure Michiko**, battled for years against the local authorities, the company and the national government to win recognition of their suffering and adequate compensation. Eventually, a number of families took the company to court in 1969, by which time a nationwide support movement had evolved. Four years later, Chisso was finally judged liable – too late for many, of course.

To date nearly 2000 people have died of Minamata disease, while around 13,000 have been certified as afflicted and eligible for compensation. Though we will never know the true extent of the tragedy, some estimates put the total number of people affected as high as 100,000.

The government recently declared the bay mercury free, but it will be many years before Minamata's nightmare is over.

**Bookshops** The best is Kinokuniya, under the Sunroute Hotel on the corner of the Shimo-tōri and Ginza-dōri arcades.

**Car rental** Nippon Rent-a-car (☎096/324-0335), Eki Rent-a-car (☎096/352-4313), and Mazda Rent-a-car (☎096/366-4141) all have branches near Kumamoto Station.

**Ferries** Kyūshū Shōsen (☎096/354-6131) operates hourly ferries from Kumamoto Shin-kō to Shimabara (1hr; ¥580). To get to the port, take a bus from Kumamoto Station (35min; ¥470).

**Festivals** Kumamoto's main event is the Fujisaki Hachiman-gū autumn festival (Sept 11–15). On the final day there are two processions, morning and afternoon, when some 20,000 people parade through the streets in historical garb.

**Hospital** The Kumamoto National Hospital (*Kokuritsu Kumamoto Byōin*; ☎096/353-6501) is conveniently located immediately south of Ninomaru park.

**Internet cafés** The *Internet Café* (daily 10am–11pm; ¥500 per 30min) is on the second floor of the Marumitsu Building above a *pachinko* parlour. The *Internet Gallery* (7-7 Kamitōri-chō; daily except Tues 10am–7pm; same rates), near *Shankar* restaurant (see previous page), is more convenient but less wacky on the decor.

**Travel agents** JTB (☎096/322-4111) is a good bet for domestic travel, while HIS (☎096/351-0561) handles international tickets.

# Aso and the central highlands

Central Kyūshū is dominated by sparsely populated, grassy highlands, in places rising to substantial peaks, which offer some of the island's most magnificent scenery and best walking country. These mountains are relics of ancient volcanic upheavals and explosions of such incredible force they collapsed one gigantic volcano to create the world's largest crater. Today the floor of the **Aso caldera** is a patchwork of fields like so many *tatami* mats, and the surrounding uplands a popular summer playground, but at its centre, **Aso-san** provides a potent reminder that the volcano is still very much alive. Most people come here to peer inside its steaming crater, eruptions permitting, and then scale some of the neighbouring peaks or walk over the lush green meadows at its base.

All this subterranean activity naturally means a wealth of hot springs to wallow in, mostly within the caldera itself, although there are a few gems hidden deep in the highlands. One such is the picturesque village of **Kurokawa Onsen**, squeezed in a narrow gorge on the Senomoto plateau, which makes an indulgent overnight stop on the road to Beppu. The village lies a few kilometres off the **Yamanami Highway**, the main tourist route between Aso and Beppu, providing a spectacular mountain ride through the Aso–Kuju National Park. Heading in the opposite direction, another dramatic road climbs over the crater wall and heads southeast to **Takachiho**. Perched above an attractive gorge of angular basalt columns, this is where Amaterasu, the mythical Sun Goddess, hid according to legends governing the birth of the Japanese nation. A riverside cave and its neighbouring shrine make an easy excursion, but a more compelling reason to stop here is to catch a nightly performance of the story told through traditional folk dances.

The Aso region is one place where having your own **transport** is a definite advantage; it's perfectly feasible to get around by public transport, but everything just takes a lot longer. From Kumamoto the recommended route is the JR Hōhi line across the caldera floor, which is a great journey in its own right, to spend a night or two in Aso Town. It's also possible to visit Aso-san on a day-trip from Kumamoto, or break the journey here for a couple of hours on route to Beppu. If you're heading that way, the Yamanami Highway offers the most scenic option, though the train continues via Ōita

| ASO AND THE CENTRAL HIGHLANDS | | |
| --- | --- | --- |
| **Aso** | *Aso* | 阿蘇 |
| Aso-no-Fumoto | *Minshuku Aso-no-Fumoto* | 民宿阿蘇のふもと |
| Aso-san | *Aso-san* | 阿蘇山 |
| Aso Volcano Museum | *Aso Kazan Hakubutsukan* | 阿蘇火山博物館 |
| Aso Youth Hostel | *Aso Yūsu Hosuteru* | 阿蘇ユースホステル |
| Kokuminshukusha Aso | *Kokuminshukusha Aso* | 国民宿舎阿蘇 |
| Kokuminshukusha Nakamura | *Kokuminshukusha Nakamura* | 国民宿舎なかむら |
| Naka-dake | *Naka-dake* | 中岳 |
| Pinochio | *Pinokio* | ピノキオ |
| **Kurokawa Onsen** | *Kurokawa Onsen* | 黒川温泉 |
| Kyūho-kan | *Kyūho-kan* | 九峯館 |
| Okyaku-ya | *Okyaku-ya* | 御客屋 |
| Senomoto-kōgen | *Senomoto-kōgen* | 瀬の本高原 |
| Shinmei-kan | *Shinmei-kan* | 新明館 |
| Yamabiko Ryokan | *Yamabiko Ryokan* | やまびこ旅館 |
| **Takachiho** | *Takachiho* | 高千穂 |
| Amano Iwato-jinja | *Amano Iwato-jinja* | 天岩戸神社 |
| Asagi | *Asagi* | あさぎ |
| Hatsu-e | *Hatsu-e* | 初栄 |
| Kamino-ya | *Kamino-ya* | かみの家 |
| Kenchan | *Kenchan* | けんちゃん |
| Nobeoka | *Nobeoka* | 延岡 |
| Takachiho-jinja | *Takachiho-jinja* | 高千穂神社 |
| Takachiho gorge | *Takachiho-kyō* | 高千穂峡 |
| Takamori | *Takamori* | 高森 |
| Tateno | *Tateno* | 立野 |
| Yamato-ya | *Yamato-ya* | 大和屋 |

to Beppu and is a good alternative for JR pass holders on a strict budget. You'll have to overnight in Aso, however, if you're combining the crater with Takachiho.

## The Aso Caldera

The train from Kumamoto changes direction twice as it zigzags up the formidable wall of the **Aso Caldera**. This ancient crater, 18km from east to west, 24km north to south and over 120km in circumference, was formed about 100,000 years ago when a vast volcano collapsed. As the rock cooled, a lake formed, but the eruptions continued, pushing up five smaller cones, today known collectively as **Aso-san**, in the crater's centre. Eventually the lake drained and the area became inhabited; local people attribute their fortune to the god Takawatsu-no-mikoto, grandson of Emperor Jimmu, who kicked a gap in the western wall – the same gap the train uses – to give them rice-land. Now some 70,000 people live within the crater, working the rich volcanic soils, while cattle and horses graze the higher meadows in summer.

   **Aso Town** is a grandiose name for a scattered group of villages located in the northern caldera, including a tourist area around Aso Station where you'll find an information desk (see Practicalities, opposite), accommodation and buses heading up the mountain or north to Beppu.

### Aso-san

The five peaks of **Aso-san** line up across the caldera with the two highest, Taka-dake (1592m) and the distinctively craggy Neko-dake (1433m) lying at the chain's eastern

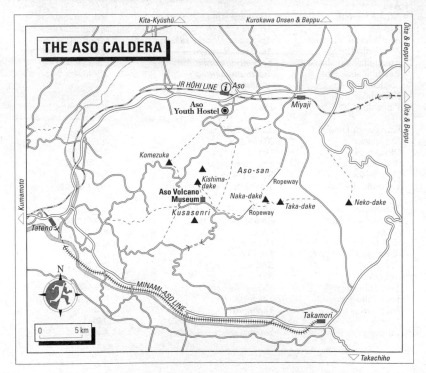

end. Of the five, only Naka-dake (1323m), really just a gash on the side of Taka-dake, is still active – particularly so over the last two decades. Its most recent eruptions occured in the early 1990s, since when it's calmed down considerably, but it's wise to treat the mountain with respect. Notices are posted in Aso Station when the mountain's closed, but if you plan to do any long-distance walks around the crater it would be wise to check at the station's information desk. Note that anyone suffering from asthma or other respiratory problems is advised not to approach the crater rim because of strong sulphur emissions.

Seven daily buses shuttle visitors from the Sankō terminal outside Aso Station on a dramatic thirty-minute journey up the mountain (¥700; last bus up 3.20pm). There's a five-minute photo break at the pass, from where you look down on the perfect cone of **Komezuka**, the "hill of rice". Its dimpled top is said to have been created when Takawatsu-no-mikoto scooped up a handful of rice to feed his starving people. Turning the other way, you get your first glimpse of Naka-dake's gaping mouth across the grassy bowl of **Kusasenri** speckled with shallow crater lakes.

Before continuing to Naka-dake, you might want to get off at the next bus stop for a quick tour of the informative **Aso Volcano Museum** (daily 9am–5pm; ¥820). Satellite photos reveal Japan's major fault lines in awesome clarity and there are films of recent eruptions around the world, but the museum's most fascinating display takes you inside Naka-dake crater courtesy of two cameras inserted in the mountain wall. Afterwards, you can hop on the next passing bus, or walk 3km across the plateau to the base of Naka-dake. Alternatively, there's a popular detour up **Kishima-dake** (1321m), an easy thirty-minute climb from behind the museum, and then descend via a ski slope to join the road about halfway along.

Buses terminate at the foot of **Naka-dake** in a scruffy area of souvenir shops and restaurants, while a toll road continues to the top for cars. You can walk up in twenty minutes, or there's a **ropeway** (daily 9am–5pm; ¥410) running every eight minutes or so from the bus terminus. However you arrive, the crater's evil-coloured rocks and glimpses of a seething grey lake through turbulent, sulphurous clouds of steam, is a sobering sight. Most activity takes place in a hundred-metre-deep cauldron at the northern end and this area is strictly off limits. Near the ropeway, however, you can approach the unfenced crater lip and then walk south beside barren, dormant craters – mercifully out of earshot of the loudspeakers.

Rather than backtracking, there's a great **hiking trail** round the crater's southern rim to the summit of Naka-dake, with a possible side trip to Taka-dake, and then down to Aso-san Higashi-guchi. It takes between four and five hours, depending whether you include Taka-dake, and the path's a little tricky to find at the beginning. After that it's not too difficult as long as you've got good boots, plenty of water and keep well away from the edge. With any luck, you'll coincide with the cable car down the eastern, Sansuikyō ropeway (every 25min; ¥610) and there'll also be a bus waiting at the bottom to whisk you back to Aso Station in under half an hour (April–Nov 3 daily; ¥390); otherwise try hitching or set off on the ninety-minute downhill trot to Miyaji Station, one stop east of Aso Station.

## Practicalities

Aso **train station** is the centre of local life. **Buses** congregate at the Sankō terminal, on the left as you exit the station, while inside there's a well-organized **tourist information centre** (daily except Wed 9am–7pm; ☎0967/34-0250), with English-speaking staff and a wealth of information on local transport and accommodation.

You'll find a couple of **places to stay** right outside Aso Station with little to choose between them. The yellow *Kokuminshukusha Aso* (☎0967/34-0111, fax 34-0112; ④) lies immediately opposite, while the slightly more expensive *Kokuminshukusha Nakamura* (☎0967/34-0317, fax 34-1882; ④) occupies a white concrete building to the right; both offer basic *tatami* rooms either with or without meals. Five minutes' walk west, the welcoming *Aso-no-Fumoto* (☎0967/34-0624; ④) offers eight nicely decorated *tatami* rooms in an attractive setting among old farms. The owners, who speak a little English, will collect you from the station; otherwise, walk west along the main highway, Route 57, for a couple of minutes until you see their blue signboards pointing right. Dormitory beds are available at *Aso Youth Hostel* (☎0967/34-0804; ①) which lies twenty minutes' walk uphill from the station on the road to Aso-san; buses heading up the mountain stop outside the hostel (¥130), or a taxi should cost around ¥500. The manager speaks good English and is a real enthusiast for the mountains, with a detailed knowledge of hiking routes and bus timetables.

Most people eat where they're staying, but there are a handful of **restaurants** around the station, of which *East Coffee Plaza* (daily 9am–10.30pm) is recommended for its range of well-priced Japanese and Western meals, including substantial breakfast sets. They're on the main highway, two minutes' walk straight ahead from Aso Station. Alternatively, continue south on the Aso-san road where you'll find *Pinochio* after about five minutes' walk on the left, opposite the post office; the decor is a bit grim but they dish up cheap, hearty fare such as noodles and curry-rice from ¥500 up.

Finally, if you fancy a soak at the end of the day, *Yume-no-yu* (daily 10am–11pm; ¥400) is a decent **onsen** in the centre of town, with a large *rotemburo* and sauna. It's between *Nakamura* ryokan and *East* restaurant.

## North on the Yamanami Highway

From Aso the **Yamanami Highway** heads north over the Kujū mountains to Beppu. The road breaches the caldera wall at Ichinomiya, from where the classic profile of Aso-san's five peaks supposedly conjures up a sleeping Buddha with head to the east and Naka-dake's steaming vent at his navel. North of this, the only signs of life on the rolling grasslands are herds of cattle and notices for *Patio Ranch* or *El Rio Grande*, though if you want to break the journey, **Kurokawa Onsen** offers a choice of *rotemburo* along a picturesque valley. The highway then climbs again through the Kujū range, which for some reason receives far less attention than Aso-san or Ebino Kōgen, although it contains Kyūshū's highest peaks (up to 1787m) and offers good hiking. This may be because Kujū-san is no longer active, but even here wisps of steam mark vents high on the north slopes while more spa towns lie strung along the valley and then break out again at Yufuin before the road makes its final descent into Beppu.

Though the Yamanami Highway is best avoided during peak holiday periods, for the most part it's fairly traffic free. Every day, four sightseeing **buses** ply the route between Kumamoto and Beppu, stopping at Aso, Senomoto, Yufuin and a few other places en route. You can join or leave the bus at any stop, either buying your ticket in advance at the local station or taking a numbered ticket on entry and paying the driver when you get off, as with any normal bus. The cheapest fare between Aso and Beppu, for example, costs ¥2950, but note that prices and journey length vary according to whether lunch is included.

### Kurokawa Onsen

The twenty-odd ryokan that make up **KUROKAWA ONSEN** lie higgledy-piggledy at the bottom of a steep-sided, tree-filled valley scoured into the **Senomoto plateau** some 6km west of the Yamanami Highway. The village is completely devoted to hotspring bathing and most of its buildings are at least traditional in design, if not genuinely old, while *yukata*-clad figures wandering the lanes add to its slightly quaint atmosphere. The village is particularly famous for its *rotemburo*: there are 23 in total, in all shapes and sizes of rocky pools shrouded in dense vegetation. Out of season, when all the crowds have gone, it's well worth the effort of getting here, and if you don't mind paying a little extra on accommodation, Kurokawa makes an excellent overnight stop.

Though it helps if you have your own **transport**, it's possible to reach Kurokawa Onsen on the daily bus from Aso Town, leaving the Sankō bus station mid-morning and taking roughly an hour – check locally for current times. The return bus leaves Kurokawa less than two hours later, allowing for just one leisurely dip, unless you stay the night. If you're heading for Beppu, however, you can take a taxi (approximately ¥1000) back up to the Senomoto Kōgen junction to connect with the last, mid-afternoon Yamanami Highway bus; the bus shelter lies just north of the crossroads and make sure you arrive at least ten minutes early since these buses occasionally run ahead of schedule.

Arriving in Kurokawa, you'll find the **tourist information** office (daily 9am–6pm; ☎0967/44-0076) beside a car park on the north side of the river, next to the bus stop and taxi rank. While there's nothing in English, they have good maps showing the location of all the **public rotemburo** (daily 8.30am–9pm) with photos and a key indicating whether they're mixed or segregated. All the baths are attached to ryokan and you can either buy tickets at reception (¥500) or get a day pass (¥1200) at the tourist office allowing entry to any three. If you only have time for one and don't mind mixed bathing, try the central **Shinmei-kan** for its cave-bath and choice of open-air pools, or **Yamabiko Ryokan** for its unusually large *rotemburo*.

*Yamabiko Ryokan* (☎0967/44-0311, fax 44-0313; ⑦) is also a pleasant **place to stay** in the mid-price range. For something a touch cheaper, both *Okyaku-ya* (☎0967/44-0454, fax 44-0551; ⑦) and the slightly more rustic *Kyūho-kan* (☎0967/44-0651, fax 44-0563; ⑦) are atmospheric ryokan right in the centre of things. All these rates include two meals.

## Takachiho

The small town of **TAKACHIHO** lies on the border between Kumamoto and Miyazaki prefectures, where the Gokase-gawa has sliced a narrow channel through layers of ancient lava. In winter, when night temperatures fall below freezing, local villagers perform time-honoured **Yokagura dances** in the old farmhouses, bringing back to life the gods and goddesses who once inhabited these mountains. The main reason for visiting Takachiho is to see a few excerpts from this dance-cycle, but combine that with **Takachiho gorge**, a pretty spot whose strange rock formations are woven into local myths, plus a dramatic journey from whichever direction you arrive, and Takachiho becomes somewhere to include on any Kyūshū tour.

According to legend, the **Sun Goddess Amaterasu**, took umbrage at the offensive behaviour of her brother, the Storm God Susano-ō, after he destroyed her rice-fields and desecrated her sacred palace. So she hid in a cave and plunged the world into darkness. The other gods tried to entice her out with prayers and chants, but nothing worked until, finally, a goddess broke into a provocative dance. The general merriment was too much for Amaterasu who peeped out to see the fun, at which point they grabbed her and hauled her back into the world. Locals also claim that this Takachiho – not the mountain of Ebino Kōgen (see p.728) – is where Amaterasu's grandson, Ninigi-no-mikoto, descended to earth with his mirror, sword and jewel to become Japan's first emperor.

**To get here** from Aso Town and points west, you need to take a private Minami-Aso line train from Tateno round the caldera's south side as far as Takamori (¥470), from where buses continue to Takachiho (¥1440). Coming from the east coast, or vice versa, the private TR Takachiho line links Takachiho with Nobeoka's JR station (¥1440); its one-car train tracks the Gokase valley, criss-crossing high above the river before pausing over the gorge as it draws in to Takachiho.

## The Town

Takachiho sits on the north bank of the Gokase-gawa, with its main street, National Highway 218, running southwest from the town's central crossroads. Both the gorge and Takachiho-jinja, where nightly *Yokagura* dances are held, are within easy walking distance down this road, on the southwest edge of town, while its other main sight, a mildly interesting riverside cave, lies a short bus ride to the east. It's possible to cover both areas in a day, see a *Yokagura* performance in the evening and travel on the next morning.

The main road southwest to the gorge first passes **Takachiho-jinja**, roughly 600m from the town's central crossing. It's a simple, wooden building, engulfed in ancient cryptomeria trees and mainly of interest for a carving on its east wall of the guardian deity despatching a demon. The new, wooden **Kagura-den** next door is where the nightly **Yokagura** (8pm; ¥500) dances are held. Though this is a much-shortened version of the complete cycle, it still gives a good flavour. In one hour you see three dances relating the story of Amaterasu and her cave, followed by an explicit rendition of the birth of the Japanese nation in which the two "gods" leave the stage to cavort with members of the audience – to the great delight of all concerned. The performers are drawn from a pool of around 500 local residents, aged from 5 to 80 years, who also dance in the annual **Yokagura festival** which takes place between mid-November and mid-February. A combination of harvest thanksgiving and spring festival, 24 troupes perform all 33 dances in sequence, lasting through the night and into the next day. The locations vary, so check in the tourist office (see Practicalities, below) for the current schedule.

Rather than continuing on the main road for the last kilometre to **Takachiho gorge**, a steep footpath you can take that cuts down from behind the shrine to emerge beneath a soaring road bridge. Cross the old, stone bridge and you can follow another path running 600m along the gorge's most scenic stretch. At it's narrowest point, where you re-cross the river, it's just 3m wide and plunges 100m between cliffs of basalt columns which in one place fan out like a giant cockle shell. To see what it looks like from below, you can hire rowboats at the southern end (¥1500 for 40min; 3 people per boat); though it's a little expensive, the gorge is more impressive viewed from the emerald-green river. By the boat station another road heads back into town, but it's more pleasant to retrace your tracks along the river. On the way, you might want to stop off at the restaurant-cum-souvenir shop beside the stone bridge for a sup of the local speciality, *kappo saké*, in which sake is heated in a pipe of fresh green bamboo (¥950).

Suitably revived, next stop is the central bus terminal to board a bus for an attractive ride east along the Iwata-gawa to **Amano Iwato-jinja**, some 8km from Takachiho (hourly; 20min; ¥340). The shrine buildings are closed to the public, but it's an attractive setting among more venerable cedars, and from behind the shrine it's just possible to make out Amaterasu's cave on the river's far bank. Unfortunately, you can't reach it but, when her fellow-gods were deciding their strategy, they fortunately convened in the more accessible **Amano Yasugawara**, on the same side as the shrine. It's about a fifteen-minute walk east, down some steps and beside the river, to find the cave with its diminutive shrine beneath a sacred rope.

## Practicalities

From Takachiho **train station**, on the north side of town, it takes roughly ten minutes to walk to the central crossroads, while the **bus station** lies a couple of hundred metres southeast. The **tourist information** office (daily 8.30am–5pm; ☎0982/72-4680) resides in a small white hut outside the station, where you can pick up maps and a brief English-language brochure plus hotel information, but can't make reservations. **Bus tours** leave four times daily from the bus station, with a choice of a full three-hour tour (¥1660) or a shorter trip missing out Amano Iwato-jinja (¥1150); though all commen-

Traditional wooden houses, Kyoto

Buddhist nun collecting alms

The great bronze Buddha of Tōdai-ji, Nara

Downtown Ōsaka

Five-Storey Pagoda, Kōfuku-ji, Nara

Uji-bashi, the Grand Shrine of Ise, Shima Hantō

SARAH CHAPLIN

Salarymen on an office outing to Nara

SIMON RICHMOND

SIMON RICHMOND

Himeji-jō, Kansai

Painted screen, Himeji, Kansai

Orchards protected from volcanic ash, Sakurajima, Kyūshū

Hot sand bath, Ibusuki, Kyūshū

White sand beach, Miyako-jima, Okinawa

Ashizuri Misaki, Shikoku

tary is in Japanese, these are an efficient way of seeing the sights. Local **shops** are full of dried mushrooms, sweet potatoes and other mountain produce, alongside *kagura* dolls and locally crafted camphor-wood masks which make an unusual souvenir.

Takachiho has a good choice of **places to stay**. On the main road just below the NTT radio mast, *Yamato-ya* (☎0982/72-2243, fax 72-6868; dorm ①; room ④) serves as both a youth hostel and an affordable ryokan, though the latter's rates may well increase after a planned refurbishment. All the rooms are Japanese style and, while you don't have to eat in, it's well-worth opting for at least the evening meal. If you phone from the station, *Yamato-ya's* English-speaking owner will come to collect you; alternatively, take a taxi (around ¥600), or it's only a fifteen-minute walk. *Kamino-ya* (☎0982/72-2111, fax 72-5040; ④), a couple of minutes' walk south of the central junction, is another friendly ryokan with a nice, rustic atmosphere, where the screens and corridors are decorated with original ink paintings by an artist friend. Again, their meals are good value, though you can opt for room only, and they'll also collect you from the train station.

There are plenty of decent **restaurants** in town. On the main crossing, you can't miss the farmhouse-style frontage of *Asagi* (daily 8am–10pm), a souvenir shop which also serves simple snacks, such as udon and soba, and a tasty, hot-ginger drink called *syōga-yu*. In the backstreets just northeast of here, *Hatsu-e* (Mon–Sat 10am–10pm) provides a warm welcome on cold evenings with its table-top braziers for cooking *yakiniku*; sets start at ¥1000. Finally, *Kenchan* (Mon–Sat 5pm–midnight) is a cosy *yukitori* opposite *Kamino-ya*; a good meal, excluding drinks, will set you back about ¥2000 per person.

# Beppu

The best approach to **BEPPU**, on Kyūshū's northeast coast, is on the Yamanami Highway which drops down into town from the western hills. It's an extraordinary sight: spirals of steam rise from chimneys and billow out of the ground itself in dramatic confirmation that this is one of the world's most geothermally active regions. Over 100 million litres a day of near-boiling water gush out of more than 3000 springs, to be harnessed for local swimming pools, heating and medicinal purposes or to fill the dozens of public and private baths that make this one of Japan's most popular **onsen** resorts. Unashamedly dedicated to pleasure, from the refined to the bawdy, this town of only 130,000 people receives over twelve million visitors a year. Most of these are domestic tourists; many foreigners who come here find Beppu all too tacky, but its sheer vulgarity can also be huge fun – the trick is just to jump in and enjoy yourself.

When not soaking in a tub or buried in hot sand, there isn't a lot else to do in Beppu. The most popular attractions are the nine **jigoku**, or "hells", which spew out steaming, sulphurous mud or form simmering lakes in lurid hues. Despite the hype, only two or three are of any real interest, and you'll be better off instead heading for **Tsurumi-dake** and the hills ringing Beppu to the west. If you're leaving Kyūshū from here, be sure to take the daytime ferry for Kōbe and Ōsaka, a glorious voyage right through the island-spattered Inland Sea.

## Orientation, arrival, information and city transport

Beppu is a medium-size, low-rise city wrapped round an attractive, east-facing bay with mountains to both south and west. The main highway, Route 10, hugs the coast while the railway loops through the city centre, sandwiching **downtown** Beppu between the tracks and the sea. **Ekimae-dōri** splits this central district in two, running from the station concourse east past banks, post office and department stores to end where it meets

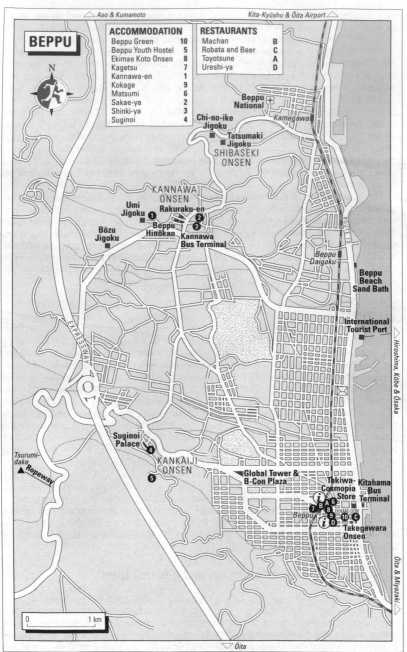

Aso & Kumamoto

Kita-Kyūshu & Ōita Airport

# BEPPU

N

| ACCOMMODATION | | RESTAURANTS | |
|---|---|---|---|
| Beppu Green | 10 | Machan | B |
| Beppu Youth Hostel | 5 | Robata and Beer | C |
| Ekimae Koto Onsen | 8 | Toyotsune | A |
| Kagetsu | 7 | Ureshi-ya | D |
| Kannawa-en | 1 | | |
| Kokage | 9 | | |
| Matsumi | 6 | | |
| Sakae-ya | 2 | | |
| Shinki-ya | 3 | | |
| Suginoi | 4 | | |

Beppu
National

Chi-no-ike
Jigoku

Kamegawa

Tatsumaki
Jigoku

SHIBASEKI
ONSEN

KANNAWA
ONSEN

Umi
Jigoku   Rakuraku-en

Bōzu
Jigoku   Beppu
Hinōkan

Kannawa
Bus Terminal

Beppu
Daigaku

Beppu
Beach
Sand Bath

International
Tourist Port

ROUTE 10

EXPRESSWAY

Tsurumi-
dake   Ropeway

Suginoi
Palace

KANKAIJI
ONSEN

Global Tower &
B-Con Plaza

Tokiwa-
Cosmopia
Store

Kitahama
Bus
Terminal

EKIMAE-DORI

Beppu

Takegawara
Onsen

Hiroshima, Kōbe & Osaka

Ōita & Miyazaki

0          1 km

Ōita

Route 10 at the **Kitahama** junction. Though Beppu's onsen are scattered far and wide, most *jigoku* are clustered in the northerly **Kannawa** district.

Beppu is served by **Ōita airport** located on the north side of the bay, from where frequent airport buses run south to Ōita city, stopping at Kitahama on the way (1hr; ¥1800). **Ferries** from Ōsaka, Kōbe and Hiroshima dock a couple of kilometres north of the centre at the grandly named International Tourist Port; take a local Kamenoi bus (#10 or #16) from outside the terminal to either Kitahama or the station. Long-distance **buses** mostly stop at Kitahama, but the Yamanami Highway Bus continues up Ekimae-dōri to terminate at Beppu Station.

The town's main **information desk** (daily 9am–5pm; ☎0977/24-2838) lies just inside the central east exit of Beppu Station. They supply English-language maps and brochures, information on local bus routes and will also assist with hotel reservations. If you need English-language assistance, Beppu's Foreign Tourist Information Service (Mon–Sat 10am–4pm; ☎0977/23-1119), run by volunteer staff, should be able to help. Their office is clearly signed, a couple of minutes' walk south of the station's east exit.

**Local buses** are the best way of getting around Beppu. Fortunately, they're not too complicated and there's a fair amount of information in English for the major routes. In general, Kamenoi buses, in blue and white livery with route numbers indicated on the front, cover most places within the city limits. Nearly all their routes start at Beppu Station's east exit and pass along Ekimae-dōri, though a few use the station's west side. If you're going to be doing more than a couple of long journeys – say, from the station out to Kannawa's *jigoku* and back – it's worth investing in a "My Beppu Free" one-day "mini pass" (¥900). This includes all buses within the city centre after 9.30am, which covers the *jigoku*, Suginoi Palace and the sand baths, though you can also use them to go further afield by paying the difference at the end. The passes are available at the station information desk or the Kamenoi bus stations in both Kitahama and Kannawa.

## Accommodation

The most convenient place to look for **accommodation** is around Beppu Station, where you'll find a clutch of business hotels and a couple of good-value ryokan. Though less central, the Kannawa area offers some interesting alternatives buried among its old streets, while the youth hostel rubs shoulders with Beppu's top hotel in Kankaiji district on the town's western outskirts.

### Around the station

**Beppu Green Hotel**, 1-3-11 Kitahama (☎0977/25-2244, fax 25-2236). Well-priced, bottom-end business hotel halfway along Ekimae-dōri with a few small semi-doubles and much larger twin rooms, all en suite with phone and TV. ③–④.

**Ekimae Koto Onsen**, Ekimae-dōri (☎0977/21-0541). This old, half-timbered onsen building doubles as a cheap, clean lodging house offering dormitory beds (men only) and four spartan *tatami* rooms with no windows and no bath. Dorm ①; room ③.

**Kagetsu**, 7-22 Tanoyu-chō (☎0977/24-2355, fax 23-7237). You'll find a warm welcome from the English-speaking owners of this minshuku on the west side of Beppu Station. The rooms, both Japanese and Western style, are a bit worn, but they all have their own onsen bath, TV and air-con. Make sure you book ahead. ③–④.

**Kokage**, 8-9 Ekimae-chō (☎0977/23-1753, fax 23-3895). Another popular place in a great location on a little alley two minutes' walk east of the station. Though slightly more upmarket than the *Kagetsu*, it's still excellent value with a choice of *tatami* or Western rooms, with or without bath, plus an onsen downstairs. ④.

**Matsumi**, 6-28 Ekimae-honchō (☎0977/24-1122, fax 24-1121). This smart, new business hotel is surprisingly reasonable for a central location. The rooms are mostly Western style and not huge, but all nicely decorated in beige or peach, with good views from the upper floors. ④–⑤.

## BEPPU

| | | |
|---|---|---|
| **Beppu** | *Beppu* | 別府 |
| Beppu Beach Sand Bath | *Beppu Kaihin Suna-yu* | 別府海浜砂湯 |
| Beppu Hinōkan | *Beppu Hinōkan* | 別府秘宝館 |
| Bōzu Jigoku | *Bōzu Jigoku* | 坊主地獄 |
| Chi-no-ike Jigoku | *Chi-no-ike Jigoku* | 血の池地獄 |
| International Tourist Port | *Kokusai Kankō Kō* | 国際観光港 |
| Kankai-ji | *Kankai-ji* | 観海寺 |
| Kannawa | *Kannawa* | 鉄輪 |
| Kitahama | *Kitahama* | 北浜 |
| Rakuraku-en | *Rakuraku-en* | 楽々園 |
| Takegawara Onsen | *Takegawara Onsen* | 竹瓦温泉 |
| Tsurumi-dake | *Tsurumi-dake* | 鶴見岳 |
| Umi Jigoku | *Umi Jigoku* | 海地獄 |

| *ACCOMMODATION* | | |
|---|---|---|
| Beppu Green Hotel | *Beppu Guriin Hoteru* | 別府グリーンホテル |
| Beppu Youth Hostel | *Beppu Yūsu Hosuteru* | 別府ユースホステル |
| Ekimae Kōto Onsen | *Ekimae Kōto Onsen* | 駅前高等温泉 |
| Kagetsu | *Kagetsu* | 花月 |
| Kannawa-en | *Kannawa-en* | 神和苑 |
| Kokage | *Kokage* | こかげ |
| Matsumi | *Matsumi* | 松美 |
| Sakae-ya | *Sakae-ya* | サカエ家 |
| Shinki-ya | *Shinki-ya* | しんきや |
| Suginoi Hotel | *Suginoi Hotel* | 杉乃井ホテル |

| *RESTAURANTS* | | |
|---|---|---|
| Machan | *Machan* | まちゃん |
| Toyotsune | *Toyotsune* | とよ常 |
| Ureshi-ya | *Ureshi-ya* | うれしや |

## Kannawa and Kankaiji

**Beppu Youth Hostel**, 2 Kankaiji (☎0977/23-4116, fax 22-0086). Large, friendly hostel with English-speaking staff and dormitory accommodation in either bunk beds or *tatami* rooms. Panoramic views of Beppu make up for its inconvenient location, 25 minutes by bus from the station; take Kamenoi bus #10 or #14 from the station's east exit as far as the Kankaiji-bashi stop, near the *Suginoi Hotel*. The hostel is signed left over the bridge and up a steep, lantern-lined road, two minutes from the bus stop. ①.

**Kannawa-en**, Kannawa (☎0977/66-2111). This beautiful old ryokan boasts nineteen lovely *tatami* rooms, some in individual buildings, set in a classic, hillside garden. Rates include breakfast and an evening meal. ⑧.

**Sakae-ya**, Kannawa (☎0977/66-6234, fax 66-6235). Another attractive, wooden building hidden in the eastern, less touristy part of Kannawa. They offer twelve rooms at either minshuku rates or in the more upmarket ryokan, with an option on meals, though this would definitely be missing out. ④–⑥.

**Shinki-ya**, Kannawa (☎ & fax 0977/66-0962). Near the *Sakae-ya*, this simple, homely minshuku is worth seeking out for its well-priced *tatami* rooms. There's a shared onsen bath and meals can be provided or there's also a small kitchen area. You'll find it three minutes downhill from the Kamenoi bus terminal, past the "Young Centre" theatre and then right up an alley behind a coin-laundry. ③–④.

**Suginoi Hotel**, 1 Kankaiji (☎0977/24-1141, fax 21-0010). Beppu's top hotel is a one-stop holiday, complete with vast bathing complexes, an ice-rink and baseball- and golf-simulators, as well as shopping malls, restaurants and nearly 600 rooms. There's a complicated scale of room charges depending on the day of the week, season, if meals are included and whether you're in the main building or newer "Hana" block. The rooms are bland but comfortable, and the best have stunning views over Beppu bay. ⑥–⑧.

## The Town

There are eight distinct hot spring "towns", dotted about Beppu, each characterized by the varying proportions of iron, sulphur and other minerals in the water. Most activity, however, is concentrated in **Kannawa**. Not only is this northern district home to seven of the nine *jigoku* ("hells"), but it's also a spa in its own right with a beautiful, garden *rotemburo*, as well as an outrageously tacky museum of erotica. Dedicated bathers might want to try one of Beppu's **sand baths** or take a dip in the vast, jungle-filled atriums of the **Suginoi Palace**. Alternatively, you can ride the ropeway to the top of **Tsurumi-dake** for superb views over Beppu bay and inland to the Kujū mountains.

### Kannawa and the jigoku

Noxious pools of bubbling mud, super-heated lakes, geysers and other geothermal outpourings are generally known in Japan as **jigoku**, after the word for Buddhism's hell. Beppu's *jigoku* (daily 8am–5pm) are located in three clusters: six in central Kannawa, one on Kannawa's western edge and two in Shibaseki Onsen, 3km further north. Though each *jigoku* has its own "personality" and you could cover them all in two to three hours, only those recommended below are really worth it – any more and you'll tire of the tacky commercialism, loudspeakers and tour groups. You can buy individual **tickets** (¥400) as you go round, or get a day pass (¥2000) covering all except Bōzu Jigoku. Frequent buses ply between Beppu Station and Kannawa (30min; ¥330).

Starting from Kannawa's Kamenoi bus terminal, signs point west to a line of six *jigoku* in quick succession. At the far end, **Umi Jigoku** is the most attractive, set in a bowl of hills among well-tended gardens. It's main feature is a sea-blue pool – 120m deep and, at 90°C, hot enough to cook eggs – set off by a bright-red humped bridge and *torii* swathed in clouds of roaring steam. From here it's about 750m on up the main road to **Bōzu Jigoku** which takes its name from the resemblance between mud bubbles and the bald pate of a Buddhist monk, a *bōzu*. Again it's surrounded by greenery, but the speciality here is mud – boiling, smelly, steaming, hiccuping pools of mud

The remaining Kannawa *jigoku* are generally best avoided, being either full of gaudy statues or unfortunate elephants, crocodiles and monkeys in their own personal hell. However, it's definitely worth walking through the beautiful, classic garden of **Kannawa-en** (daily 7am–10pm; ¥100), belonging to a ryokan of the same name (see Accommodation, opposite). Built on a hillside to the east of Umi Jigoku, the garden is a haven of peace and good taste. It encloses a small lake, hidden rocky pools reached by winding paths and a picturesque, milky-white *rotemburo* which is open to the public (same times; ¥800).

On the way back down to Kannawa bus station, connoisseurs of the bizarre might like to join the giggling young couples at **Beppu Hinōkan** (daily 9am–11pm; ¥1000), a sex museum. Buxom statuary graces the entrance while inside there's a collection of erotic *ukiyo-e*, sacred phalluses from Shinto shrines and then a downhill slide into pornographic tableaux, notably a gleeful Snow White and her seven dwarfs, which grind into action at the push of a button. Finally, if you fancy trying another of Kannawa's baths, **Rakuraku-en** (daily 8am–midnight; ¥200) in a ryokan behind the bus station would be a good, inexpensive choice. It offers a mixed and women-only *rotemburo*, sand bath, sauna and ordinary indoor pool.

Beppu's last two *jigoku* are in **Shibaseki Onsen**, five minutes' bus ride north of Kannawa (#16 or #2 from Kannawa bus terminal). **Chi-no-ike Jigoku**, "Blood Pond", is the better of the two, a huge bubbling pool whose vermilion fringes result from a high iron-oxide content. Fifty metres down the road, **Tatsumaki Jigoku** consists of an unimpressive geyser which spouts 20m into the air roughly every half hour; it used to reach 60m until they put a stone block over it for safety.

## The sand baths

Beppu is one of only two places in Japan where it's possible to take a genuine sand bath, or *suna-yu*. Ibusuki (see p.718) may be more famous and have the better scenery, but Beppu's two sand baths are less touristy and far more relaxed. **Takegawara Onsen** is a grand, old Meiji-era edifice in the backstreets south of Ekimae-dōri. Its ordinary bath (daily 6.30am–10.30pm; ¥60) is nicely traditional, but first of all try the sand bath (8am–9pm; ¥610). After rinsing in hot water, you lie face up – take a towel to cover your front – on a bed of coarse, black sand while an attendant gently piles a heavy, warm cocoon (around 42°C) up to your neck. Then just relax as the heat soaks in for the recommended ten minutes, followed by another rinse before soaking in the hot tub.

On a fine day, the seaside location of **Beppu Beach Sand Bath** (daily: April–Oct 8.30am–6pm; Jan–March, Nov & Dec 9am–5pm; ¥610) sounds preferable, but it's slightly marred by a busy main road behind and a concrete breakwater dominating the view – the end result, however, is still an overall sense of well being. You'll need a swimsuit, but they provide *yukata* to wear in the "bath". Shoninga-hama lies on Kamenoi bus route #20 or #26 from central Beppu (20min; ¥230), near Beppu Daigaku Station.

### Kankaiji and Tsurumi-dake

**Kankaiji** onsen spews out its hot water high up on a hill overlooking western Beppu, where it feeds the multifarious baths of the *Suginoi Hotel's* **Suginoi Palace** (daily 9am–11pm; ¥2000, or ¥1000 after 5pm; free to hotel guests). This is Beppu's foremost bathing extravaganza. Two huge hothouses contain pools of every shape, size and temperature surrounded by jungle vegetation: the "Dream Bath" features a Shinto *torii* with waterfalls and slides, while the "Flower Bath" is dominated by a statue of Kannon, the Buddhist goddess of mercy, revolving slowly atop a fish tank; the baths are segregated and alternate each day.

On the way up to Kankaiji, you pass by the futuristic **Global Tower** (daily 9am–7pm, May–Nov till 9.30pm; ¥300) which serves as both viewing platform and a landmark for **B-Con Plaza**, Beppu's lavish convention centre and concert hall. The hundred-metre-high open observation deck provides giddying views, but if you've got time you'll get a better, all round panorama from the western hills. A ropeway (daily 9am–4.30/5pm; ¥1400) carries you to the top of **Tsurumi-dake** (1375m) in five minutes, from where you can see Shikoku on a clear day. Kamenoi buses #31 to #37 depart Beppu Station every half hour for the forty-minute ride to the ropeway (¥490; ¥180 extra on the minipass), passing below *Suginoi Hotel* on route.

## Eating and drinking

Beppu's **speciality foods** include *fugu* (blowfish) and *karei* (flounder), both winter dishes, and the piping-hot *dango-jiru*. This cheap, filling soup comes with thick, white noodles, assorted vegetables and chunks of either chicken or pork. When it comes to finding a **restaurant**, you're best off in the downtown area. There are dozens of *izakaya* and Japanese restaurants in the streets south of Ekimae-dōri, while the Tokiwa–Cosmopia store on Ekimae-dōri also has a decent choice of outlets on its fourth floor "Gourmet Plaza" (10am–7.30pm).

**Machan**, Beppu Station. This rustic little place in the station's north shopping arcade is one of the best places to try *dango-jiru*. They also serve hearty meals of *chanpon*, *donburi* and tempura at reasonable prices. Daily 9am–7pm.

**Robata and Beer**, 1-15-7 Kitahama. Popular *robatayaki* at the east end of Ekimae-dōri with English-speaking staff and an English menu listing a good range of fish, vegetable and tofu dishes, as well as *yakitori* skewers and daily specials. Service is a bit slow and prices are not the cheapest, but you should be able to eat for under ¥2000, and it's open till late. Daily 5pm–midnight.

**Toyotsune**, Ekimae-chō. Traditional restaurant opposite Beppu Station specializing in *fugu*, either as sashimi (¥2500 per person) or a full, two-hour long meal (¥7000). Other, more reasonable fare includes tempura and sashimi sets, and they offer a good range of local *shōchū*. Daily except Wed 11am–2pm & 5–10pm.

**Ureshi-ya**, 7-12 Ekimae-chō. Tables fill up early at this small, friendly restaurant where you can choose from a tempting array of ready-prepared dishes, such as vegetable tempura, pumpkin, sashimi and fried fish. They also do standard rice and noodle dishes for under ¥800. Open from 5pm.

## Listings

**Airport information** ☎0975/37-2800.

**Banks and exchange** You can change money at banks along Ekimae-dōri, including Iyo Bank, Beppu Sinyo Bank and Fukuoka City Bank.

**Buses** Long-distance buses between Ōita and Nagoya, Nagasaki and Fukuoka stop at the Kitahama junction in passing.

**Car rental** Eki Rent-a-car (☎0977/24-4428), Nippon Rent-a-car (☎0977/22-6181) and Toyota Rent-a-car (☎0977/22-7171) all have offices in Beppu.

**Ferries** Kansai Kisen (☎0977/22-1311) operates two ferries daily from Beppu's International Tourist Port to Ōsaka via Kōbe, with one service daily to Matsuyama (Shikoku). Hirobetsu Kisen (☎0977/21-2364) has a daily sailing to Hiroshima, while Uwajima Onyu Ferry (☎0977/21-2364) services connect Beppu with Misaki, Yawatahama and Uwajima, all on Shikoku.

**Hospital** Beppu National Hospital (☎0977/67-1111) is in north Beppu's Kamegawa district, inland from Kamegawa Station.

**Police** The main police station is opposite the post office on Route 10 (☎0977/21-2131).

**Post office** Beppu Central Post Office (4-23 Motigahama-chō), opposite the International Tourist Port, offers post restante. There's also a more convenient sub-office on Ekimae-dōri.

**Shopping** The Beppu region is famed for its bamboo handicrafts, which you'll find in the station arcades and main department stores on Ekimae-dōri. Another popular souvenir is *yu-no-hana*, natural bath salts to create that instant, hot-spring feel back home. These are on sale all over Kannawa district.

# SOUTH KYŪSHŪ

Southern Kyūshū consists of two huge, empty prefectures which offer few historical or cultural sights, but buckets of scenery – mostly of the volcanic variety – and further stops on the onsen trail. The most interesting area is westerly **Kagoshima**, whose main city sits in the shadow of a grumbling, ash-spewing volcano, **Sakurajima**. Most people come simply to view this troublesome beast, but Kagoshima also has one or two worthwhile museums celebrating its role in the Meiji Restoration, and provides a gateway to the Satsuma Peninsula. Here, the small town of **Ibusuki** is devoted to hot-spring bathing, including a seaside sand bath, while nearby **Chiran** houses another of Japan's disturbingly ambiguous war museums. In this case it commemorates the kamikaze suicide bombers, many of them mere teenagers, who rallied to the imperial cause at the end of World War II. From either Kagoshima or Ibusuki, ferries ply south to **Yakushima**. A paradise for botanists and hikers, this mountainous island is covered in ancient, misty forests where only in the last few decades five-thousand-year-old cedar trees have been discovered. Back on the Kyūshū mainland, there's very different walking country around **Ebino Kōgen**, a high, open plateau ringed by volcanic peaks, before the mountains fade out towards **Miyazaki**. The only large town on southern

Kyūshū's southeast coast, Miyazaki is a useful base but has little to detain you. Its artificial, indoor beach, **Seagaia**, is an extraordinary concept, though the real coast probably holds more of immediate interest, notably **Aoshima**'s sub-tropical gardens and the celebrated cave-shrine of **Udo-jingū**.

# Kagoshima

With a population of nearly 500,000, **KAGOSHIMA** curls round the west shore of Kagoshima Bay, a mere 4km from one of the world's most active volcanoes. **Sakurajima**'s smouldering cone constitutes the city's most obvious and compelling attraction, but Kagoshima contains a few sights of its own which justify a day's exploration. Foremost of these are its classical garden, **Iso-teien**, which uses Sakurajima in the ultimate example of "borrowed scenery", and several excellent **museums** of local history and culture. The best are devoted to Kagoshima's mid-nineteenth-century heyday when Saigō Takamori, amongst other local heroes, played a major role in Japan's modernization.

### Some history

Originally known as **Satsuma**, the Kagoshima region was ruled by the powerful **Shimazu** clan for nearly seven centuries until the Meiji reforms put an end to such fiefdoms in 1871. The area has a long tradition of overseas contact and it was here that Japan's first Christian missionary, the Portuguese Jesuit **Francis Xavier**, arrived in 1549. Welcomed by the Shimazu lords – who were primarily interested in trade and acquiring new technologies – he spent ten months working in Kagoshima, where he found the poorer classes particularly receptive to Christian teachings. After just a few months Xavier declared "it seems to me that we shall never find among heathens another race to equal the Japanese".

Soon after, Japan was closed to foreigners and remained so for the next two hundred years. As central control crumbled in the mid-nineteenth century, however, the farsighted **Shimazu Nariakira** began introducing Western technology, such as spinning machines, the printing press and weapons manufacture. Not that all relations were cordial. In 1862 an Englishman was decapitated in Yokohama by a Shimazu retainer for crossing the road in front of the *daimyō*'s procession. When the Shimazu refused to punish the loyal *samurai* or pay compensation, seven **British warships** bombarded Kagoshima Bay in 1863. Fortunately there was little loss of life and the Shimazu were so impressed by this show of force that three years later they dispatched nineteen "**young pioneers**" to study in London. Many of these young men went on to assist the new Meiji government in its mission to modernize Japan, but Kagoshima's most famous son by far is **Saigō Takamori**.

Born in 1827, Saigō made his name as one of the leading figures in the **Meiji Restoration**. Though aware of the need for Japan to modernize, he grew increasingly alarmed at the loss of traditional values and eventually left the government to set up a military academy in Kagoshima. He soon became a focus for opposition forces – mainly disaffected *samurai* but also peasants protesting at punitive taxes. Things came to a head in January 1877 when Saigō led an army of 40,000 against the government stronghold in Kumamoto, in what came to be known as the **Satsuma Rebellion**. After besieging the castle for nearly two months, the rebels were forced to withdraw before the 60,000-strong Imperial Army. They retreated to Kagoshima where they were gradually pinned down on Shiroyama. On September 24, the imperial forces closed in and Saigō, severely wounded, asked one of his comrades to kill him. His courage, idealism and heroic death earned Saigō enormous popular support – so much so that he was officially pardoned by imperial decree in 1891.

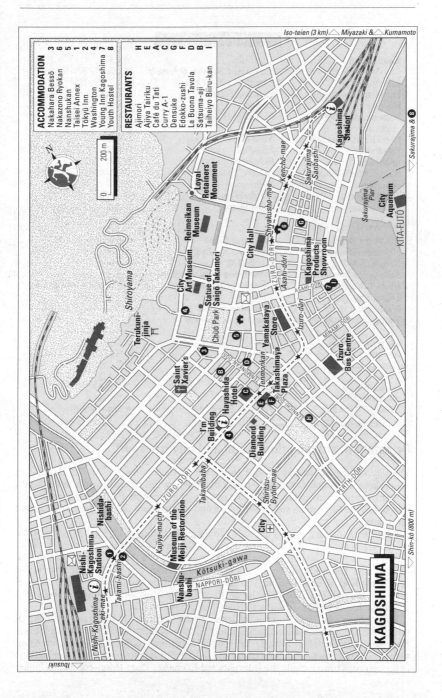

Iso-teien (3 km) △ Miyazaki & △ Kumamoto

**ACCOMMODATION**
Nakahara Bessō          3
Nakazono Ryokan         6
Nanshukan               5
Taisei Annex            1
Tōkyū Inn               2
Washington              4
Young Inn Kagoshima     7
Youth Hostel            8

**RESTAURANTS**
Ajimori                 H
Aiiya Tairiku           E
Café du Tati            A
Curry A-1               C
Densuke                 G
Edokko-zushi            F
La Buona Tavola         D
Satsuma-aji             B
Taiheiyo Biiru-kan      I

200 m

0

Shiroyama

Loyal Retainers' Monument

Reimeikan Museum

City Hall

Kagoshima Station

Sakurajima Sanbashi

Kenchō-mae

Shiyakusho-mae

Sakurajima Pier

City Aquarium

KITA-FUTŌ

Sakurajima & 8

City Art Museum

Statue of Saigō Takamori

Terukuni-jinja

Chūō Park

IZURO-DŌRI

Asahi-dōri

Izuro-dōri

Kagoshima Products' Showroom

ASAHI-DŌRI

MINAMI-DŌRI

Saint Xavier's

Hayashida Hotel

I'm Building

Tenmonkan Yamakataya Store

Takashimaya Plaza

Izuro Bus Centre

TENMONKAN-DŌRI

Diamond Building

PERTH-DŌRI

IZURO-DŌRI

Kajiya-machi

Takamibaba

Museum of the Meiji Restoration

Nishida-bashi

Shiritsu-Byōin-mae

City

Nishi-Kagoshima Station

Kōtsuki-gawa

Nanshu-bashi

NAPPORI-DŌRI

Shin-kō (800 m)

Nishi-Kagoshima-eki-mae

Takami-bashi

Ibusuki

**KAGOSHIMA**

| | **KAGOSHIMA** | |
|---|---|---|
| Kagoshima | *Kagoshima* | 鹿児島 |
| City Art Museum | *Kagoshima Shiritsu Bijutsukan* | 鹿児島市立美術館 |
| City Aquarium | *Kagoshima Suizokukan* | かごしま水族館 |
| Furusato Onsen | *Furusato Onsen* | 古里温泉 |
| Iso-teien | *Iso-teien* | 磯庭園 |
| Museum of the Meiji Restoration | *Ishinfurusatokan* | 維新ふるさと館 |
| Nishi-Kagoshima Station | *Nishi-Kagoshima eki* | 西鹿児島駅 |
| Kita-Futō | *Kita-Futō* | 北埠頭 |
| Reimeikan | *Reimeikan* | 黎明館 |
| Saint Xavier's Church | *Zabieru Kyōkai* | ザビエル教会 |
| Sakurajima | *Sakurajima* | 桜島 |
| Terukuni-jinja | *Terukuni-jinja* | 照国神社 |
| Tenmonkan | *Tenmonkan* | 天文館 |
| | | |
| *ACCOMMODATION* | | |
| Nakahara Bessō | *Nakahara Bessō* | 中原別荘 |
| Nakazano Ryokan | *Nakazano Ryokan* | 中薗旅館 |
| Nanshūkan | *Nanshūkan* | 南洲館 |
| Sakurajima Youth Hostel | *Sakurajima Yūsu Hosuteru* | 桜島ユースホステル |
| Hotel Taisei Annex | *Hoteru Taisei Anekkusu* | ホテルタイセイアネックス |
| Tōkyū Inn | *Tōkyū In* | 東急イン |
| Washington Hotel | *Washinton Hoteru* | ワシントンホテル |
| Young Inn Kagoshima | *Yangu In Kagoshima* | ヤングインかごしま |
| | | |
| *RESTAURANTS* | | |
| Ajimori | *Ajimori* | あぢもり |
| Ajiya Tairiku | *Ajiya Tairiku* | 味屋大陸 |
| Densuke | *Densuke* | でんすけ |
| Edokko-zushi | *Edokko-zushi* | 江戸ッ子寿司 |
| Satsuma-aji | *Satsuma-aji* | さつま路 |
| Taiheiyō Biiru-kan | *Taiheiyō Biiru-kan* | 太平洋ビール館 |

## Orientation, arrival, information and city transport

The city of Kagoshima lies on the west side of Kagoshima (or Kinkō) Bay facing Sakurajima. The main downtown area is bounded by the **Kōtsuki-gawa** to the south and **Shiroyama** rising to the west. Most of the sights are located in a fairly compact district below the Shiroyama ridge, with a second group about 3km to the north around **Iso-teien**.

Kagoshima **airport**, served by flights to Seoul and Hong Kong as well as domestic routes, is located some 30km away at the top of the bay. Limousine buses depart roughly every ten or twenty minutes for the hour's ride into town (¥1200), stopping at central Kagoshima's **Tenmonkan** crossroads before terminating just south of the river at the new **Nishi-Kagoshima Station**. Though this is the main station, some trains also call at the old **Kagoshima Station** to the north of the city. Most **long-distance buses** stop at Tenmonkan before proceeding to Nishi-Kagoshima Station.

Kagoshima's two main **tourist offices** are located outside the train stations. Of these, the Kagoshima Station branch (daily 8.30am–5pm; ☎0992/22-2500) is a lot quieter and more helpful, though the Nishi-Kagoshima office (daily 8.30am–6pm; ☎0992/53-2500) can provide city maps and assist with accommodation. Other options in the centre of town include the International Exchange Plaza (Mon–Sat 9am–5.30pm;

☎0992/25-3279) and the Update Visitors Centre (Mon–Fri 10am–4.30pm; ☎0992/24-8011) which you'll find on the eleventh floor and ground floor of the I'm Building on Izuro-dōri. Finally, there's the Prefectural Information Office (Mon–Fri 8.30am–5.15pm; ☎0992/23-5771) on the third floor above Kagoshima Products shop on Asahi-dōri. All of these offices have English-speaking staff.

Moving around central Kagoshima is simplified by a highly efficient **tram system** which has been in operation since 1912 – some of the original cars are still working. There are only two lines, both of which start outside Kagoshima Station and run down the main street, past the City Hall (Shiyakusho-mae) and Tenmonkan before splitting at Takamibaba, just past the *Washington Hotel*. Trams on Line 2 then continue southwest to Nishi-Kagoshima Station, while Line 1 turns southeast. There's a flat fare of ¥160, which you pay on exit, and trams run roughly every eight minutes from 6.30am to 10.30pm.

The **local bus system** is a lot more complicated, with five different companies in operation. The **City View** tourist bus does a circuit of the main sights from Nishi-Kagoshima Station (stand #4) via the Museum of the Meiji Restoration, Reimeikan and Shiroyama observatory to Iso-teien, before returning through the city centre. These retro-style buses are easily recognizable, they run every half hour and there's a flat fee of ¥180. Alternatively, you can buy a one-day pass (¥600) which also covers the trams; it's available at the tourist information centres, or from bus and tram drivers.

Local **ferries** to Sakurajima depart from a pier near Kagoshima Station. The new Kita-Futō (North Pier) next door is used by services to Yakushima, Ibusuki and Okinawa. However, "A Line" ferries to Okinawa operate out of the more southerly Shin-kō.

## Accommodation

Kagoshima is well provided with mid-range business hotels, offering comfortable if unexciting **accommodation**, but has little in the way of good-value budget places. If you need to keep costs down, your best option is the youth hostel on Sakurajima.

**Nakahara Bessō**, 15-19 Higashi-Sengoku-chō (☎0992/25-2800, fax 26-3688). Nicely decorated onsen hotel in the city centre overlooking Chūō Park, where the Japanese-style rooms are better value. Though they do offer room-only rates, the meals are highly recommended. ⑥–⑦.

**Nakazano Ryokan**, 1-18 Yasui-chō (☎0992/26-5125, fax 26-5126). The best budget option in central Kagoshima, this welcoming ryokan offers homely *tatami* rooms with shared facilities. It's tucked behind a temple opposite Kagoshima City Hall, about five minutes' walk from Kagoshima Station and handy for the Sakurajima pier. ④.

**Nanshukan**, 19-17 Higashi-Sengoku-chō (☎0992/26-8188, fax 26-9383). Well-priced business hotel with fair-sized rooms – all en suite – in a good location near Chūō Park. ④.

**Sakurajima Youth Hostel**, Hakama-goshi Sakurajima-chō (☎0992/93-2150). Kagoshima's cheapest accommodation is this big, relaxed hostel on Sakurajima (see p.715), signed about ten minutes' walk uphill from the ferry terminal. It also boasts an onsen bath. ①.

**Hotel Taisei Annex**, 4-32 Chūō-chō (☎0992/57-1111, fax 57-1113). Reasonable business hotel near Nishi-Kagoshima Station. The rooms are nothing special, but they're clean, comfortable and all en suite. ④–⑤.

**Tōkyū Inn**, 5-1 Chūō-chō (☎0992/56-0109, fax 53-3692). Smartish business hotel three minutes' walk from Nishi-Kagoshima Station. The rooms are all Western style and come with TV, phone and bath as standard. There's also a coffee shop and restaurant. ⑤.

**Washington Hotel**, 12-1 Yamanokuchi-chō (☎0992/25-6111, fax 24-2303). This well-appointed business hotel is conveniently located on Izuro-dōri, slightly south of the centre. Rooms are a good size, with satellite TV and telephone; ask for one on the back with views of Sakurajima. ⑤.

**Young Inn Kagoshima**, 16-23 Izumi-chō (☎0992/23-1116). Small, basic guesthouse with a few Japanese and Western rooms. It's buried in the backstreets east of the centre, towards the ferry terminals. ④.

## The City

Kagoshima's handful of central sights are gathered round the informative **Reimeikan** museum at the foot of Shiroyama. Next, you can either walk or take a tram south to the banks of the Kōtsuki-gawa, where there's a gimmicky but entertaining **Museum of the Meiji Restoration**. A few kilometres north of town, the **Iso-teien** area is of interest not only for its traditional garden, but also for a museum celebrating the modernizing zeal of the enterprising Shimazu lords. All these sights are served by the City View bus (see previous page), but you'll need to catch a ferry over to **Sakurajima** itself. A circuit of the volcano includes lava fields and observatories, but it's also worth stopping off at **Furusato** village to soak in a superb, sacred hot spring.

### The central sights

The best place to start exploring Kagoshima is in **Chūō-kōen**, west of the Tenmonkan arcades. A bronze statue of the close-cropped, portly Saigō Takamori (see p.710 above) stares seaward across the park's north corner. Unlike the more relaxed portrait in Tokyo's Ueno-kōen (see p.117), this shows Saigō as the uncompromising military leader. Behind him, carp-filled moats and some bullet-pocked walls are all that remain of **Tsurumaru-jo** following the 1877 Satsuma Rebellion. The castle site is now occupied by a collection of public buildings, kicking off with the **City Art Museum** (Tues–Sun 9.30am–6pm; ¥200). This spacious, modern building houses a good collection of Impressionist and twentieth-century Western art, besides well-rated local artists Kuroda Seiki and Fujishima Takeji.

Walking north, an arched wooden bridge leads up to the **Reimeikan** (Tues–Sun 9am–5pm, closed 25th of every month; ¥260) which provides an excellent introduction to local history and culture. Dioramas, life-size models and video presentations take you from Stone-age villages to post-1945 recovery on the ground floor, while upstairs is devoted largely to folk culture and festivals. Apart from a delightful mock-up of the Tenmonkan arcade in the 1930s, the most interesting displays cover the southern islands' distinct traditions, showing the strong influence of Okinawan and Melanesian culture.

Follow the castle walls round to the northwest and you'll find the **Loyal Retainers' Monument** dedicated to Kagoshima labourers who died in Gifu-ken, central Honshū, in 1755. On the shogun's orders the Satsuma clan sent a thousand men to tame the wild Kiso-gawa. It took two attempts and fifteen months to complete the embankments, in appalling conditions which cost the lives of 84 men from disease, accident and suicide. One of these was the chief retainer, Hirata Yukie, who killed himself in order to atone for the project's huge financial and human cost. Beside the otherwise uninteresting monument, a path leads up through impressive stands of mature, sub-tropical trees to the top of **Shiroyama**. The twenty-minute climb is worth it for superb views over Kagoshima and the smouldering cone of Sakurajima.

Heading back downhill, the right fork brings you down a gentler route to **Terukuni-jinja**. This shrine is dedicated to Shimazu Nariakira (see p.710), whose statue – with its determined face and oversize shoes – stands immediately to the north. Straight ahead from the shrine you're back in Chūō-kōen. Take the road heading down to the Kōtsuki-gawa from the park's south corner and after a couple of minutes you'll reach **Saint Xavier's Church**. The small gothic building was erected in 1949 to commemorate the four-hundredth anniversary of Francis Xavier's landing. Across the road a memorial park occupies the site of a stone church, built in 1891 by a French Jesuit, which was destroyed in 1945 bombing raids.

From here it's about 600m further south to where the stone **Nishida-bashi**, built in 1846, spans the Kōtsuki-gawa. Turn left before the bridge for a pleasant, riverside stroll down to the splendid **Museum of the Meiji Restoration** (daily 9am–5pm;

¥300). No expense has been spared to recreate the "golden age" of Kagoshima, when Saigō and other local luminaries were instrumental in returning power to the emperor and then spearheading the Meiji reforms. The highlight is a 25-minute *son et lumière* in which robots re-enact scenes from the restoration. It's best to sit near the doors, facing the white screen, from where you get the best view of Saigō and his disconcertingly realistic eyes. All the dialogue is in Japanese, so it's a good idea to visit the rest of the museum first, by which time you should be able to identify the main characters. The show takes place roughly once an hour in the basement theatre (9.15am–4.30pm).

The final sight in central Kagoshima is the **City Aquarium** (daily 9am–5pm;¥1500) recently opened on a manmade island in the harbour. Thanks to the warm Kuroshio current sweeping across from the East China Sea, the waters around Kagoshima's southern islands are rich in temperate and sub-tropical aquatic life. A broad range is on show in this well-designed installation, from Sakurajima's unique tube worm, to colourful sea anemones, sharks and dolphins in a huge glass-sided tank.

## Iso-teien

When their base at Tsurumaru-jo was destroyed during the Satsuma Rebellion, the Shimazu lords set up residence in their lovely garden-villa now known as **Iso-teien** (daily 8.30am–5/5.30pm; ¥800, or ¥1400 including entry to the residence). Though the villa itself is a beautiful building, the main points of interest are the garden, with its views of Sakurajima, unfortunately now interrupted by the main road and train tracks, and the neighbouring history museum. The easiest way to reach Iso-teien is to take the City View Bus or a local Hayashida Bus from Nishi-Kagoshima Station or Tenmonkan (every 15min; 7min; ¥180); check the destination when you get on, as a few buses skip Iso-teien.

The entrance to Iso-teien lies through a raft of souvenir shops and restaurants, selling everything from Satsuma glass to *imo* (sweet potato) ice cream. Inside, it's worth joining a tour of the **villa** (an English leaflet is provided) as much for the fine interior decoration, including ornamental nail heads, painted screens and carved transoms, as the views of the volcano. Apart from this stunning backdrop, the **garden** is also noted for its collection of stone lanterns and an Okinawa-style Bōgaku-rō pavilion, presented by the King of the Ryūkyū Islands. The cliffs behind are etched with an eleven-metre tall *kanji* saying "thousand-fathom crag"; it takes about thirty minutes to walk up beside the stream for even more dramatic panoramas of the bay.

Beside Iso-teien, an old, stone machine factory, known as the **Shōko Shūseikan** (same times and ticket as Iso-teien), serves as a local history museum. Inside, you'll find a moderately interesting array of Shimazu family heirlooms, from early cannon balls and carding machines to tea-ceremony utensils. An annexe hosts changing exhibitions, behind which are a series of workshops where they still make Satsuma glass and ceramics.

## Sakurajima

Just 4km from Kagoshima, the volcanic cone of **Sakurajima** grumbles away, pouring a column of dense black ash into the air. This is one of the world's most active volcanoes. Major eruptions have been recorded from the early eighth century to as recently as 1947, though the most violent in living memory was that of 1914. After a period of increased activity in the early 1990s, the volcano is now fairly quiet and makes an enjoyable half-day excursion from Kagoshima. A single road (40km) circles Sakurajima at sea level, with stops along the way at lava fields, onsen baths and a couple of observatories.

**Ferries** from Kagoshima (15min; ¥150) dock at a small pier on Sakurajima's west coast. The service operates 24 hours a day, with hourly sailings between 10pm and

5am, and at least every fifteen minutes during peak hours (7am–8pm); buy a ticket from the machines before boarding. At the other end, a handy **sightseeing bus**, the "JR Red Liner", departs twice daily for a circuit of the volcano from beneath Sakurajima ferry terminal (9.30am and 1.30pm; ¥1,700, free to JR pass holders). Tickets are available in the terminal or from JR stations and travel agents.

Before setting off round the volcano, it's a good idea to pop along to the **Sakurajima Visitors' Centre** (Tues–Sun 9am–5pm; ☎0992/93-2443), located less than ten minutes' walk south of the ferry terminal. With the aid of an English-language guide tape you can bone up on volcanoes, and gauge Sakurajima's present mood from a seismograph. There's also interesting material about how the islanders cope with their restless home, whose fertile soils produce the world's largest radish – up to 40kg in weight and over 1m in diameter – and its smallest mandarin, measuring a mere 3cm across.

You'll see some of these prolific crops as you tour **the island**, particularly on the more gentle, northern slopes. This is Sakurajima's most attractive side, where the road wriggles through the pine trees, past coves filled with fishing hamlets. As you turn down the east coast, however, Sakurajima's brooding presence becomes more apparent as you start to see the first grey lava fields. Look out on the right, too, for the **buried torii** of Kurokami-jinja. Originally 3m tall, now just the top cross-bars protrude from a bed of ash and pumice left by the 1914 eruption. During this particularly violent explosion enough lava spilled down the southeast slopes to fill a 400-metre-wide channel that previously separated Sakurajima from the mainland.

Just beyond this narrow neck of land, you can explore the still-barren 1914 lava fields at the **Arimura Observatory**. A little further on the settlements start again, at **Furusato Onsen**, but here it's all resort hotels capitalizing on the abundant supplies of hot water. The best of these, the *Furusato Kankō Hotel* (☎0992/21-3111, fax 21-2345; ⑧), features a large, cliff-side *rotemburo* (closed Mon am & Thurs; ¥720) shaded by a sacred camphor tree. Since it doubles as a shrine, you'll be given a white *yukata* to wear when bathing.

The final port of call on Sakurajima takes you up a tortuous road on the volcano's west flank to the **Yunohira Observatory** (373m). This is the closest you can get to the deeply creviced summit, which in fact comprises three cones, from the highest, northerly Kita-dake (1117m) to Minami-dake (1040m), the most active, in the south. Weather permitting, you'll also be treated to sweeping views of Kagoshima.

## Eating, drinking and nightlife

Kagoshima's most popular **speciality food** is *Satsuma-age*, a deep-fried, slightly sweet patty of minced fish and sake, eaten with ginger and soy sauce. The prettiest dish, however, is *kibinago sashimi*, in which slices of a silvery, sardine-like fish are arranged in an eye-catching flower head. *Keihan chicken* mixes shredded meat with carrot, egg, mushroom and spring onions over a bowl of rice in a hot, tasty broth, while *saké-zushi* consists of sushi with a drop of sake. For snacks, there's *Satsumo-imo* ice cream (made with sweet potato) and *Jambo mochi* – rice cakes smothered in sweet sauce on bamboo skewers. Kagoshima is also Japan's biggest producer of *shōchū*, a potent liquor traditionally brewed from grain but also sweet potato.

The city's prime **restaurant** area focuses around the Tenmonkan and Sennichi arcades, to either side of Izuro-dōri, though you'll also find places around Nishi-Kagoshima Station and in Iso-teien. As for **nightlife**, head east of Izuro-dōri to the Sennichi-gai area, where the Diamond Building alone provides a good night out. You can start off with a few jars in the ground-floor *Cotton Club* (daily 6pm–2/3am) before heading down to the basement where you'll find *Kento's* (daily 7pm–1/2am; ¥1700 cover charge) playing Sixties rock, and mellow jazz in *Rusty's* bar (daily 7pm–late; ¥500 cover charge).

## Restaurants

**Ajimori**, 13-21 Sennichi-chō. Nicely informal *tonkatsu* (fried pork cutlets) restaurant on Sennichi-dōri, east of the arcade with a good choice of set meals (¥700–2800). There's a more formal *shabu-shabu* restaurant upstairs. Daily 11.30am–2.30pm & 5.30–9pm.

**Ajiya Tairiku**, 1-17 Sennichi-chō. Well-designed, basement beer restaurant on a broadly Asian theme, backed by a Seventies Western sound track. The menu's equally eclectic, including *oden*, *yakitori*, pizza, Korean *kimchi* and salads. Expect to pay around ¥2000 per head. Daily 5.30–11.30pm.

**Café du Tati**, Shiroyama-chō. Look out for this small, jolly café in an interesting area of backstreets west of Chūō-kōen, offering a short menu of sandwiches, crêpes and cakes. (Daily noon–9/10pm). Upstairs, there's a tree growing through the middle of the nicely relaxed *Treetop Terrace* bar.

**Curry A-1**, 12-22 Higashi-Sengoku-chō. Cheap and cheerful, Japanese-style curry house on Izuro-dōri under the *Hayashida Hotel*, with a branch nearer Kagoshima Station. Their lunch menus (¥700) are particularly good value. Daily 11am–8pm.

**Densuke**, 5-16 Yasui-chō. Join the locals at the counter of this welcoming, traditional *izakaya* for sashimi, *yakitori* and copious glasses of *shōchū*. It's just round the corner from *Nakazano Ryokan*. Mon–Sat 5pm–midnight.

**Edokko-zushi**, 2-16 Sennichi-chō. Sparkling sushi bar on the corner opposite *Ajiya Tairiku* (see above), which is best at lunchtime for its reasonably priced sets (around ¥1000). They also do sashimi and tempura dishes. Daily 10.30am–midnight.

**La Buona Tavola**, 16-19 Higashi-Sengoku-chō (☎0992/24-4741). This sunny trattoria, also know as *Budonoki*, uses imported ingredients for its authentic taste. Good-value evening menus start at ¥2000, while the set lunch is a mere ¥1000. They do a great *antipasto* and excellent cappuccino. Daily except Tues 11am–3pm & 5.30–10pm.

**Satsuma-aji**, 6-29 Higashi-Sengoku-chō. Though fairly pricey, this elegantly rustic restaurant is one of the nicest places to try Kagoshima's local speciality dishes, such as *Satsuma-age*, *kibinago sashimi* and *sake-zushi*. There's a picture-menu and lunch deals from ¥2000. Daily 11.30am–10pm.

**Taiheiyo Biiru-kan**, Izumi-chō. It's a bit out of centre, but this old stone storehouse near the harbour makes a great venue for a microbrewery and beer restaurant. The speciality is barbecues cooked at the table (¥1500 per head). Mon–Sat 5–10pm.

## Listings

**Airlines** Air Nippon (☎0992/25-4134); ANA (☎0120–029222); Dragon Air (☎0992/27-2911); Korean Air (☎0992/27-3311); Japan Air Commuter (☎0995/58-2673); JAL (domestic ☎0120–255971; international ☎0120–255931); JAS (☎0992/24-6111).

**Airport information** ☎0995/58-2113.

**Banks and exchange** You'll find foreign exchange banks, such as Sumitomo, Fuji and Dai-ichi Kangyō, along Izuro-dōri near Yamakataya department store and around the junction with Asahi-dōri.

**Buses** Airport buses leave from Nishi-Kagoshima Station, stand #8 (every 10–20min; 1hr; ¥1200), with a stop in front of Tenmonkan's *Hayashida Hotel*. Most long-distance buses either depart from Nishi-Kagoshima Station or the city-centre, Izuro bus terminus, but also stop at Tenmonkan. Buses to Chiran and Ibusuki use the Yamakataya bus centre, under the department store.

**Car rental** Eki Rent-a-car(☎0992/58-1412), Nippon (☎0992/58-3336) and Nissan Rent-a-car (☎0992/50-2123) all have offices near Nishi-Kagoshima Station.

**Ferries** A Line ferries (☎0992/26-4141) sail to Okinawa from Kagoshima Shin-kō, the city's southern harbour, while RKK Line (☎0992/26-1652) uses Kita-Futō. This "North Pier" is also the departure point for Orita Kisen (☎0992/26-0731) ferries to Yakushima, and for Toppy jetfoils (Kagoshima Shōsen; ☎0992/55-7888) to both Yakushima and Ibusuki.

**Hospitals and medical care** The most central hospital with English-speaking staff is the Kagoshima City Hospital, 20-17 Kajiya-chō (☎0992/24-2101), near the Shiritsu Byōin-mae tram stop (line #1). Otherwise, contact the International Exchange Plaza (see p.712) for lists of English-speaking doctors.

**Post office** Kagoshima Central Post Office, 1-2 Chūō-chō, next to Nishi-Kagoshima Station, operates a poste restante service. There's also a handy sub-office on Asahi-dōri near Chūō-kōen.

**Shopping** Local crafts include *Satsuma-yaki* (cracked-glaze, or earthy black ceramics), Ōshima hand-woven silks and various concoctions made from sweet potato. You'll find all these in the

Kagoshima Products Showroom, at the east end of Asahi-dōri, in the sprawling Yamakataya store and Nishi-Kagoshima Station's shopping malls. For sweet-potato products check out Satsuma Imono-yakata, near the west end of Tenmonkan arcade.

**Taxis** Kagoshima City Taxi (☎0992/26-5966).

# Ibusuki and around

South of Kagoshima, the great claw of the Satsuma Peninsula extends into the East China Sea, to culminate in a perfect, cone-shaped mountain and a clutch of onsen resorts. The most famous of these is **Ibusuki**, whose trademark is a piping-hot, open-air sand bath on Surigahama beach. The town also has a certain sub-tropical appeal, with average annual temperatures of 19°C, but its prime attraction is as a base for the surrounding region. Dominating the landscape, **Kaimon-dake**'s volcanic cone makes a good hike and a perfect backdrop for the flower gardens of nearby **Nagasaki-bana**, the peninsula's most southerly point. Heading north, the road skirts a large crater lake, **Ikeda-ko**, then climbs to join the Ibusuki Skyline – a dramatic ridge road – before dropping down to **Chiran**. The centre of this small town contains a strip of beautifully preserved *samurai* houses, each with a diminutive traditional garden, but it's perhaps best known as the air-base from which kamikaze suicide pilots took off during the closing days of World War II.

The easiest and quickest way **to reach Ibusuki** is by JR train or Toppy jetfoil from Kagoshima – both offer good views across Kagoshima Bay to Sakurajima and the Sata Peninsula. Jetfoils also operate between Yakushima (see p.723) and Ibusuki; see Practicalities, opposite for more about these ferries.

## Ibusuki

Claiming to be Japan's third-largest hot-spring resort by volume of water, the small town of **IBUSUKI** is a strange mix of luxury hotels and expensive restaurants next to seedy bars and nightclubs. Its saving grace is an attractive setting on a sweeping bay and a **sand bath** where you get buried up to the neck in hot sand – a more enjoyable experience than it sounds. Once you've rinsed off the grains and strolled the promenade, however, you're best heading off to Chiran and other places in the neighbourhood (see p.721, below).

Ibusuki lies spread out along a bay between the Iwasaki promontory to the south and Uomi-dake hill and Chirin island in the north. The main north–south avenue, Hibiscus Road, is shadowed a few hundred metres inland by a road passing in front of the JR station. Chūō-dōri, Ibusuki's prime shopping street, leads from the station to meet the sea at the bay's mid-point. Ten minutes' walk south of here, there's a second clutch of shops and restaurants gathered around the famous sand bath.

This southern stretch of beach is known as **Surigahama**. Like much of Japan's coast it's protected by concrete break-waters, but a few stretches of black, volcanic sand remain, from which wisps of scalding steam mark the presence of hot springs. It's the done thing in Ibusuki to take a **sand bath** (*suna-yu*), which is best at low tide when everyone is buried on the beach itself, leaving a row of heads under snazzy sunshades; at high tide a raised bed beside the sea wall is used. You can buy tickets and change into a *yukata* in the modern **Saraku** bath house immediately behind the beach (daily 8.30am–noon & 1–9pm; ¥900, including *yukata* rental). You then troop down to the beach and lie down – take a small towel to wrap round your head. At over 50°C, the sand temperature is much hotter than Beppu's rival bath (see p.708) and most people find it difficult to last the recommended ten minutes. Once you've rinsed off the sand, however, it's a wonderfully invigorating feeling.

Ibusuki also has several indoor onsen baths which are open to the public. The best of these is the charming, traditional **Moto-yu** (daily 6am–10pm, closed 5th and 25th of each month; ¥200). It's located five minutes' walk from Saraku; head north on Hibiscus Road and take the first left turn to find the bath house on the next corner.

## Practicalities

Ibusuki's bright-yellow and orange **train station** lies on the west side of town. You'll find the tourist **information desk** (daily 9am–7.30pm; ☎0993/22-4114) inside, while

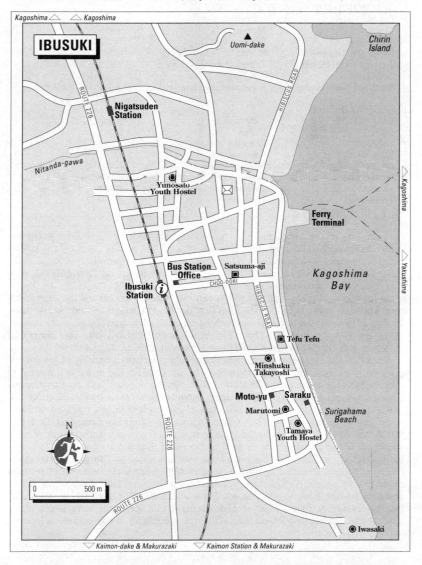

Kagoshima △  △ Kagoshima

**IBUSUKI**

▲ *Uomi-dake*

*Chirin Island*

HIBISCUS ROAD

**Nigatsuden Station**

*Nitanda-gawa*

ROUTE 226

**Yunosato Youth Hostel**

✉

△ *Kagoshima*

**Ferry Terminal**

**Bus Station Office**

Satsuma-aji

*Kagoshima Bay*

**Ibusuki Station** *i*

CHŪO-DŌRI

HIBISCUS ROAD

△ *Yakushima*

▣ **Tefu Tefu**

**Minshuku Takayoshi**

**Moto-yu** ▣ **Saraku**

**Marutomi** ◉

*Surigahama Beach*

**Tamaya Youth Hostel**

N

ROUTE 226

0    500 m

ROUTE 226

◉ *Iwasaki*

▽ *Kaimon-dake & Makurazaki*    ▽ *Kaimon Station & Makurazaki*

## IBUSUKI AND AROUND

| | | |
|---|---|---|
| **Ibusuki** | *Ibusuki* | 指宿 |
| Ibusuki Station | *Ibusuki eki* | 指宿駅 |
| Ibusuki Port | *Ibusuki minato* | 指宿港 |
| Moto-yu | *Moto-yu* | 元湯 |
| Saraku | *Saraku* | 砂楽 |
| *ACCOMMODATION AND RESTAURANTS* | | |
| Iwasaki Hotel | *Iwasaki Hoteru* | いわさきホテル |
| Marutomi | *Marutomi* | まるとみ |
| Satsuma-aji | *Satsuma-aji* | さつま味 |
| Minshuku Takayoshi | *Minshuku Takayoshi* | 民宿たかよし |
| Tamaya Youth Hostel | *Tamaya Yūsu Hosuteru* | 圭屋ユースホステル |
| Tefu Tefu | *Tefu Tefu* | てふてふ |
| Yunosato Youth Hostel | *Yunosato Yūsu Hosuteru* | 湯の里ユースホステル |
| *AROUND IBUSUKI* | | |
| Buké-yashiki | *Buké-yashiki* | 武家屋敷 |
| Chiran | *Chiran* | 知覧 |
| Chōju-an | *Chōju-an* | 長寿庵 |
| Kaimon-dake | *Kaimon-dake* | 開聞岳 |
| Nagasaki-bana | *Nagasaki-bana* | 長崎鼻 |
| Special Attack Peace Hall | *Tokkō Heiwa Kaikan* | 特攻平和会館 |
| Taki-an | *Taki-an* | 高城庵 |
| Tōsen-kyō | *Tōsen-kyō* | 唐船峡 |

the main **bus terminal** occupies the station forecourt, with the Kagoshima Kōtsū bus office on the opposite corner. The most useful local bus service connects the station with Ibusuki port (4–5 daily; 5min; ¥130), from where Toppy **jetfoils** (☎0992/55-7888) sail to Kagoshima (daily; 40min; ¥2100) and Yakushima (daily; 1hr 15min; ¥6000); note that reservations are required on these boats.

As Ibusuki is so spread out, it's worth **renting bikes** to get around the central district. The main outlet is Eki Rent-a-car (¥1310 per day) outside the station, while those staying at *Yunosato Youth Hostel* (see below) can take advantage of their more reasonable rates (¥600 per day). Apart from Eki Rent-a-car (☎0993/23-3879), other **car rental** outlets include Toyota (☎0993/22-4009) and Hibiscus (☎0993/22-5909).

Among all the expensive resort **hotels**, Ibusuki does have a number of reasonable places to stay, including no less than three youth hostels. The nicest and newest of these is *Yunosato Youth Hostel* (☎0993/22-5680; ①), ten minutes' walk north of the station beside a small park. Slightly cheaper, *Tamaya Youth Hostel* (☎0993/22-3553; ①), is fifteen minutes from the station but more in the thick of things, on Hibiscus Road just south of the sand bath. Going more upmarket, *Minshuku Takayoshi* (☎ & fax 0993/22-5982; ④–⑤), offers cheerful *tatami* rooms and an onsen bath; it's ten minutes southeast of the station and west of Hibiscus Road, just before you reach the sand bath; meals are optional. You'll need to book well in advance for *Marutomi* (☎0993/22-5579, fax 22-3993; ⑤ including meals), an attractive old ryokan famous for its seafood dinners – it's also in the backstreets inland from the sand bath. Finally, one of the smartest options around is the *Iwasaki Hotel* (☎0993/22-2131, fax 24-3215; ⑤) on the headland south of Ibusuki. Set in lush gardens, this sprawling hotel boasts three onsen baths (including a spectacular, cliff-edge *rotemburo*), a golf course, swimming pool and numerous restaurants; it's on several bus routes from the station, or a taxi will cost around ¥700.

In general, you're probably best **eating** in your hotel, since the choice of restaurants in Ibusuki is pretty limited, especially in the winter season. For a bit of atmosphere try *Satsuma-aji* (daily 11.30am–3pm & 5–10pm), about halfway along Chūō-dōri, which offers a good choice of local specialities such as *Satsuma-age* and *kibinago* (see p.716) and excellent seafood; you'll get a decent meal for around ¥2500 and there's a helpful English menu. Another possibility is the modern *Tefu Tefu* (Tues–Sun noon–midnight) on the seafront south of Chūō-dōri. It's primarily a coffee shop and bar, but they'll also rustle up hamburgers, pizza, curry-rice and other light meals.

## Around Ibusuki

The Ibusuki region is dominated by a beautifully proportioned extinct volcano, **Kaimon-dake**, and a crater lake whose giant eels have fostered tales of a mythical monster named "Isshie". Sub-tropical gardens and nurseries also thrive in the mild climate, particularly near the tip of the peninsula, **Nagasaki-bana**. The rest of the area is peppered with missable tourist developments, though **Tōsen-kyō**, a narrow canyon full of outdoor noodle restaurants, makes a fun snack stop. One sight you shouldn't miss, however, is **Chiran** with its museum commemorating the notorious kamikaze pilots and a less controversial street of old, *samurai* houses.

If you're travelling on public transport, the most convenient way of exploring the region is the **sightseeing bus** shuttling between Ibusuki and Chiran, which calls at some fifteen sights en route. Even if you're just going to Chiran and back, it's worth buying the "My Plan" bus pass (one day ¥2000, or ¥2500 for two days' unlimited travel). The passes are available from the driver or the Kagoshima Kōtsū office opposite Ibusuki Station, and buses depart roughly every hour (8.30am–2.30pm) from a stand outside; note that the last bus back from Chiran leaves at 4.20pm. You can also reach Chiran by bus direct from Kagoshima (1hr 20min; ¥900) – buses depart from the Yamakataya bus centre (see p.717).

### The southern sights

The Satsuma Peninsula comes to a halt 13km southwest of Ibusuki at **Nagasaki-bana**. This is a popular tourist spot, but it's still worth walking past the souvenir stalls and out along the rocky promontory to get a classic view of Kaimon-dake and, on clear days, the distant peaks of Yakushima. Next to the bus stop and car park, the oddly named **Parking Garden** (daily 8.20am–5pm, July–Sept to 6pm; ¥1800) is a moderately interesting sub-tropical garden where parrots, monkeys and flamingos roam free.

Though a rather pint-size version at 922m, the triangular peak of **Kaimon-dake** is known locally as "Satsuma Fuji". The volcano last erupted some 15,000 years ago and now much of it is a nature park (daily 6am–6pm; ¥350) inhabited by wild Tokara ponies. The classic route up Kaimon-dake is from Kaimon Station, the start of a five-kilometre-long path which spirals round the cone. It takes about two hours and the effort is rewarded with views south to the Satsunan Islands and north beyond Sakurajima to Kirishima. Kaimon Station is a stop on the JR line between Ibusuki and Makurazaki (6 daily; 1hr).

From Kaimon-dake the route turns inland towards **Tōsen-kyō** where three noodle restaurants shelter in the bottom of a narrow, tree-filled gorge. They specialize in *sōmen*, thin wheat-noodles, which you fish out from a spinning bowl of ice-cold spring water in the centre of the table. It's gimmicky but quite fun, especially in summer when the gorge makes a welcome refuge from the heat, and pretty cheap – one helping of *sōmen* costs ¥500, and set meals start from ¥1200. In winter they also do hot stews, while at any time of year fresh rainbow trout, raised in the nearby fish farms, makes a tasty side dish. Of the three restaurants, southernmost *Chōju-an* (daily 10am–5pm, or 7pm in summer) is recommended for its natural setting beside a waterfall. All the restaurants have plastic-food displays and you pay first at the cashier's window.

The Tōsen-kyō river is fed by a spring from the crater lake, **Ikeda-ko**, lying just over the ridge. Apart from being Kyūshū's largest lake, it's famous for its giant eels which grow up to 2m long and a hefty 5kg in weight. But there's no real reason to stop here, other than to admire Kaimon-dake rising above the crater's southern rim. Turning north, the **Ibusuki Skyline** climbs over Sansu-yama, flanked by immaculate tea-fields, and follows a ridge of hills north towards Chiran.

## Chiran

A small town lying in a broad valley, **CHIRAN** owes its fortune to the Shimazu lords of Kagoshima (see p.710). In the eighteenth century, the Shimazu's chief retainers, the Sata family, were permitted to build a semi-fortified village and a number of their lovely **samurai houses** survive today. After exploring the *samurai* quarter, next stop is a former airfield on the outskirts of town where the kamikaze suicide bombers were based. The site has now been turned into a **museum**, documenting the history of the kamikaze and commemorating the hundreds of young pilots who died.

Central Chiran consists of one main road oriented roughly east–west. The **samurai houses**, *buké-yashiki* (daily 9am–5pm; ¥310), are grouped along an attractive lane running parallel to the south of this road, behind ancient stone walls topped by neatly clipped hedges. Arriving by bus, you should get off at the Buké-yashiki-iriguchi stop near the east end of the *samurai* street; it's the last stop on the sightseeing bus from Ibusuki.

Since many of the houses are still occupied, you can't see inside, but the main interest lies in their small but intricate **gardens**, some said to be the work of designers brought from Kyoto. Seven gardens, indicated by signs in English, are open to the public. Though each is different in its composition, they mostly use rock groupings and shrubs to represent a classic scene of mountains, valleys and waterfalls taken from Chinese landscape painting. In the best of them, such as the gardens of Hirayama Soyo and Hirayama Ryoichi, the design also incorporates the hills behind as "borrowed scenery". Look out, too, for defensive features such as solid, screened entry gates and latrines beside the front gate – apparently, this was so that the occupant could eavesdrop on passers by.

If you've got time to spare, the **Anglo-Satsuma Museum** (daily except Wed 9.30am–4.30/5pm; ¥390) is moderately interesting for its coverage of the "war" between Britain and the Shimazu clan in 1863. Most exhibits are in Japanese, but newspaper reports from London indicate how seriously the incident was taken at the time. The museum is on the main road near the Buké-yashiki bus stops – look for the red double-decker bus. Alternatively, take a pit-stop in *Taki-an* **restaurant** (daily 10am–5pm), in a thatch-roofed building on the *samurai* street; their speciality is homemade soba and udon.

The last stop in Chiran is a five-minute ride southwest from the Buké-yashiki-iriguchi bus stop, where the **Special Attack Peace Hall** (daily 9am–5pm; ¥500, or ¥600 including Museum Chiran) marks the site of a military airfield established in 1942. At first it was a training camp, but from mid-1944 Chiran became the base for the "Special Attack Forces" whose mission was to crash their bomb-laden planes into American ships – they're better-known in the West as the **kamikaze**, in reference to a "divine wind" which saved Japan from Mongol invasions in the late-thirteenth century (see p.655). Hundreds of young men, some mere teenagers, rallied to the call, eager to die for the emperor in true *samurai* style. Their opportunity came during the battle of Okinawa (see p.745), when an estimated 1035 pilots died, including a number from Taiwan and other bases. Before leaving they were given a last cigarette, a drink of sake and a blessing, after which they donned their "rising sun" headband and set off on the lonely, one-way mission with enough fuel to last for two hours. It seems that many never reached their target: the toll was 56 American ships sunk, 107 crippled and 300 seriously damaged.

The "peace hall", which was only established in 1975, is essentially a memorial to the pilots' undoubted courage and makes little mention of the wider context or moral argument. This aside, the photos, farewell letters and often childish mascots are tragic mementos of young lives wasted. Several pilots' letters reveal that, though they knew the war was lost, they were still willing to make the ultimate sacrifice – you'll see many older Japanese people walking round in tears and it's hard not to be moved, despite the chilling overtones.

While waiting for the next bus, you might like to visit the more cheerful **Museum Chiran** (daily except Wed 9am–5pm; ¥300) beside the peace hall. Concentrating on local history and culture, the exhibits are beautifully displayed, with the most interesting showing the strong influence of Okinawan culture on Kagoshima's festivals and crafts.

# Yakushima

Kagoshima Prefecture includes an arc of islands trailing south over nearly 500km of ocean to Okinawa. Among the most northerly of these, long, low **Tanegashima** has the dubious distinction of being both where the first firearms were introduced to Japan – by ship-wrecked Portuguese in 1543 – and the home of Tanegashima Space Centre, Japan's Cape Canaveral. A little further south, some 120km off Kyūshū, a great lump of rock

## YAKUSHIMA

| | | |
|---|---|---|
| **Yakushima** | *Yakushima* | 屋久島 |
| Anbō | *Anbō* | 安房 |
| Hirauchi Kaichū onsen | *Hirauchi Kaichū onsen* | 平内海中温泉 |
| Jōmon-sugi | *Jōmon-sugi* | 縄文杉 |
| Kurio | *Kurio* | 栗生 |
| Miyanoura | *Miyanoura* | 宮之浦 |
| Mountain hut | *Koya* | 小屋 |
| Nagata | *Nagata* | 永田 |
| Ōko-no-taki | *Ōko-no-taki* | 大川の滝 |
| Onoaida | *Onoaida* | 尾之間 |
| Yakushima Environmental and Cultural Centre | *Yakushima Kankyō Bunka Mura Sentā* | 屋久島環境文化村センター |
| Yaku-sugi Land | *Yakusugi-rando* | ヤクスギランド |

ACCOMMODATION
| | | |
|---|---|---|
| Chinryū-an | *Chinryū-an* | 枕流庵 |
| Kamome-sō | *Kamome-sō* | かもめ荘 |
| Seaside Hotel Yakushima | *Shiisaido Hoteru Yakushima* | シーサイドホテル屋久島 |
| Minshuku Shiho | *Minshuku Shiho* | 民宿志保 |
| Shisuikan | *Shisuikan* | 紫水館 |
| Minshuku Takesugi | *Minshuku Takesugi* | 民宿岳杉 |
| Minshuku Yaedake | *Minshuku Yaedake* | 民宿八重岳 |
| Yakushima Iwasaki Hotel | *Yakushima Iwasaki Hoteru* | 屋久島いわさきホテル |
| Yakushima Youth Hostel | *Yakushima Yūsu Hosuteru* | 屋久島ユースホステル |

RESTAURANTS
| | | |
|---|---|---|
| Kabochaya | *Kabochaya* | かぼちゃ家 |
| Wakatake | *Wakatake* | 若竹 |
| Rengaya | *Rengaya* | れんが屋 |

clothed in dripping, sub-tropical rainforest rises from the ocean. This is **Yakushima**, blessed with an average annual rainfall of at least 2m on the coast and a staggering 6m in its mountainous interior. Not surprisingly, the locals are a little touchy about their weather, and it doesn't sound an obvious holiday destination, but all this rain feeds tumbling streams and a lush, primeval forest famous for its magnificent **Yaku-sugi**. These are cedar trees at least 1000 years old – younger trees are known as *Ko-sugi*, or "small cedars" – and are honoured with individual names. The oldest is the **Jōmon-sugi**, a 5000-year-old monster growing high in the mountains, where its mossy, tattered trunk looks more like rock face than living tissue. Logging companies worked Yakushima's forests until the early 1970s, but most of the area is now protected within the Kirishima-Yaku National Park, and in 1993 was placed on UNESCO's World Heritage list.

Yakushima's fairly sizeable population is concentrated in **Miyanoura**, its main town, **Anbō** and other small settlements scattered round the coast. An increasingly popular tourist destination, the island now boasts a number of swish hotels in addition to more basic accommodation. Most people, however, come to hike and camp among the peaks, where the older cedars are found. For the less adventurous, **Yaku-sugi Land** contains a few more accessible trees and can be reached by public bus. Otherwise, there's a good **local museum**, a seaside **onsen** and several beaches. There are no dry months here, but the **best time to visit** is May or during the autumn months of October and

November. June sees by far the highest rainfall, followed by a steamy July and August, while winter brings snow to the peaks, though the sea-level temperature stays around 15°C.

## The island

The first impressions of **MIYANOURA** aren't very favourable. It's a fairly scruffy little port, backed by smoking chimneys, but it's home to the informative **Yakushima Environmental and Cultural Centre** (Tues–Sun 9am–5pm; ¥500), in a dramatic new building five minutes' walk up from the ferry terminal. The exhibits are arranged in a spiral, proceeding from the ocean up through village life and the cedar forests to the mountain tops. Allow time to see the Omnimax film (hourly; 25min) which takes you on a fabulous helicopter ride swooping over the island – not recommended for anyone prone to motion sickness.

From Miyanoura, the main road leads east past the airport to **ANBŌ**, a much more attractive place to stay. From here you can turn inland for a fantastic, forty-minute ride up into the mountains. In places almost washed away or blocked by fallen trees, the single-track road corkscrews up into a lost world wreathed in drifting cloud banks. Every so often there are glimpses of plunging, tree-filled valleys, the lush greens accentuated by cascading, ice-white torrents. Keep an eye open, too, for wild deer (*shika*) and red-faced macaque monkeys (*zaru*) which often feed beside the road at dusk.

Twelve kilometres later, 1000m above sea level, a wooden resthouse marks the entrance to **Yaku-sugi Land** (daily 9am–5pm, Jan, Feb & Dec till 4.30pm; closed one day each month; ¥300). This forest reserve contains four walking courses varying in length from thirty minutes to two hours. The three shortest and most popular walks wind along an attractive river valley which is home to two 1000-year-old cedar trees, their gnarled roots clinging to the rock. Since the route consists mostly of wooden pathways with hand rails, a pair of flat, non-slip shoes will do, but hiking boots are a must on the longer trail. If you've got the time and energy, this course is by far the most interesting, taking you deeper into the forest, past another four Yaku-sugi, of which the oldest is the 2600-year-old **Jamon-sugi**. Alternatively, continue up the paved road from the resthouse for about 6km to the **Kigen-sugi**, a grand lady of 3000 years.

All these are mere saplings compared to the great **Jōmon-sugi** which is estimated to be at least 5000 years old. Growing 1300m up and five-hours' hike from the nearest road, the tree was only discovered in 1968. This event sparked moves to protect the forests and also created the tourist industry which now accounts for over half the island's economy. The Jōmon-sugi stands on the north face of **Miyanoura-dake** (1935m), the highest of Yakushima's seven peaks. There are two main routes up to the tree: the Kusugawa Hiking Path from east of Miyanoura, and the eastern, Arakawa trail starting at the Arakawa Dam. In both cases you can get a fair way up by road if you've got your own transport.

These are just two of the many **hiking** trails snaking through Yakushima's mountains. If you're going to be walking, try to get hold of Shōbunsha's 1:50,000 "Area map" #66 (¥714), and note that even in summer you'll need warm clothes at higher altitudes. The paths are so steep in places that 1km per hour is good going, and trails often get washed away, so check locally for the latest information. It's also a good idea to leave your itinerary with someone; special forms (*tozan todoke*) are available in the ferry building, airport and at information offices. There are plenty of places to camp and very basic mountain huts along the trails.

One of the hiking paths climbs up from **ONOAIDA** on the south coast, which also has some good accommodation options. Around here you'll see orchards of tropical fruits, such as mango, papaya and lychee, alongside the more traditional orange groves, while bright sprays of bougainvillea and bird-of-paradise flowers decorate the villages. A few kilometres west of Onoaida, **Hirauchi Kaichu onsen** (free) makes the perfect place to kick back with the locals in a hot rockpool overlooking the sea. You just have to get the timing right – the pool is only uncovered for an hour or so either side of low tide.

## Practicalities

Miyanoura is the largest centre for supermarkets and other facilities. The main **post office** is located in the town centre, just west of the river, but there's no **money exchange** on Yakushima, so stock up with cash in Kagoshima. Both Anbō and Onoaida have sub-post offices and supermarkets.

### Arrival and getting away

Kagoshima serves as the main **access** point for Yakushima, though you can also reach the island from Miyazaki and Ibusuki. There are at least four **flights** daily from Kagoshima airport (40min; around ¥10,000 one way) operated by an associate of JAS (☎0120–511283). Yakushima airport (☎09974/2-1200) lies on the island's northeast coast roughly midway between the two main towns, Miyanoura and Anbō, and is served by local buses and taxis.

By the time you've included transport to and from the airports, however, the Toppy **jetfoil** is almost as speedy. There are four sailings daily from Kagoshima's Kita-Futō terminal (2hr–2hr 30min; ¥7000, or ¥12600 return), one of which comes via Ibusuki, and a daily service from Miyazaki. Note that some of these jetfoils also stop at Tanegashima en route and that while most dock at Miyanoura, one or two use Anbō port, so check beforehand. Reservations are required and can be made through a travel agent or with the ferry company (Kagoshima Shōsen; ☎0992/55-7888), or you can buy advance tickets at the terminals. When making your plans, it's also worth bearing in mind that jetfoils stop running in bad weather.

Finally, daily **ferries**, operated by Orita Kisen (☎0992/26-0731), depart from Kagoshima's Kita-Futō (3hr 50min; from ¥3900). If you're not in a hurry, these ships are a great way to travel – there's even a sauna and coin-laundry on board – and reservations aren't necessary except for private rooms. You might want to bring your own food, however, since there's not a great choice, and there's very little seating, just *tatami* mats or carpets.

For jetfoil information and reservations on Yakushima call the Toppy office in Miyanoura (☎09974/2-0034) or Anbō (☎09974/6-3399). Orita Ferry's local office is on ☎09974/2-0008.

### Information

Both Yakushima's main towns have **information offices**. In Miyanoura there's a useful desk in the ferry terminal building (daily 9am–noon & 2–5pm; ☎09974/2-1019) where you can pick up bus timetables, hotel lists and maps – look out for the colour "Landsat Map", which gives names in Japanese and English. For English-language assistance walk up the road to the smart new Yakushima Island Environmental and Cultural Centre (Tues–Sun 9am–5pm; ☎09974/2-2900). Though not an official tourist office, the staff will usually help call hotels and so on, if you're stuck. Anbō's tiny office (daily 9am–5.30pm; ☎ 09974/6-2333) is located in the centre of town on the main road just north of the river.

### Getting around

Yakushima's road system consists of one quiet highway circumnavigating the island, plus a few spurs running up into the mountains. **Buses** depart from the Miyanoura ferry terminal for Nagata in the west (30min; ¥900), or on the more useful route east via the airport and Anbō to terminate in Kurio or a little further on at Ōko-no-taki (1hr 30min; ¥2000). There's roughly one bus per hour between Miyanoura and Kurio, with the last service in each direction leaving around 5pm. For most of the year (March–Nov) buses also operate twice daily from Miyanoura via Anbō to Yaku-sugi Land (1hr 15min; ¥1300). The timetable varies according to the season so check locally, and note that there's an extra charge for large rucksacks and luggage over 10kg; for example, you'll pay an additional ¥390 from Miyanoura to Yaku-sugi Land.

It's well worth renting your own transport. A day's **car rental** ranges from ¥6000 to ¥10,000 for the smallest car depending on the season. Local companies are generally cheaper, such as Terada Rent-a-car (☎09974/2-0460) and Matsubanda Rent-a-car (☎09974/3-5241), while Hertz (☎09974/6-3782) and Nippon Rent-a-car (☎09974/6-3322) also have offices here. Make sure you keep the tank topped up. There are no petrol stations on west Yakushima between Onoaida and Nagata and those on the rest of the island close at 6pm. On Sunday, only one station – in Miyanoura – stays open on a rotating basis. **Motorbikes** are available at Miyanoura's Nakashima Motors (☎09974/2-1772), just east of the river, and at You Shop (April–Oct; ☎09974/6-2705) on the main road in Anbō. You Shop also has pedal-bikes for rent, while in Miyanoura you'll find them at the Yakushima Kankō Centre, on the main road opposite the ferry terminal. The three main **taxi** companies on the island are Kagoshima Kōtsū Taxi (☎09974/6-2321), Anbō Taxi (09974/6-2311) and Matsubanda Kōtsū Taxi (☎09974/2-0027).

## Accommodation

Yakushima has a fair range of **accommodation**, but you still need to plan well ahead during holiday periods. In **Miyanoura**, you can't get more convenient than the *Seaside Hotel Yakushima* (☎09974/2-0175, fax 2-0502; ⑦), built on the promontory overlooking the ferry port. It's a comfortable place with Western and *tatami* rooms, and several restaurants. For something cheaper, try the modern *Minshuku Takesugi* (☎ & fax 09974/2-0668; ④–⑥), easily identified by its "Lodging House" sign on the main road overlooking the harbour, or *Minshuku Yaedake* (☎ & fax 09974/2-2552; ④–⑤), a couple of minutes further east where the road starts to descend to the river.

If you'd rather stay in **Anbō**, book early for the welcoming *Shisuikan* (☎09974/6-2018; ⑤–⑥) in a traditional, white building 100m west of the main road, two streets north of the river; the owner speaks English and lays on excellent meals. On the same street the *Kamome-sō* (☎09974/6-2544, fax 6-3104; ⑤–⑥) is less attractive but offers a couple of en-suite rooms, while *Minshuku Shiho* (☎09974/6-3288; ④–⑤) is the best option near the port. A white bungalow shaded by palm trees, it's the first building you come to on the road up from the pier, and provides spick-and-span, no-frills *tatami* rooms.

Continuing round the island, **Onoaida** is home to the island's plushest hotel, the *Yakushima Iwasaki Hotel* (☎09974/7-3888, fax 7-3788; ⑦), complete with its own Yaku-sugi in the atrium. Guests are met at the airport or ferry terminal, but the hotel's also on the public bus route, west of central Onoaida. At the other end of the scale, the nearby *Chinryu-an* (☎ & fax 09974/7-3900; dorm ②; room ④) offers dormitory bunks or private *tatami* rooms in a cedar-wood chalet buried among trees. The cheerful, English-speaking owner is a fount of local information and also provides hearty meals, though you can use the kitchen for a small fee. To get here, take the bus to the Iwasaki Hoteru-iriguchi stop and walk west for a few minutes, keeping your eyes peeled for a sign on the right.

Last but not least, there's the equally friendly *Yakushima Youth Hostel* (☎09974/7-3751, fax 7-2477; ①) in **Hirauchi**, about 5km west of Onoaida. The hostel, run by an enthusiastic couple from Tokyo, only has six rooms, so make sure you book ahead. It's five minutes' walk east from the Hachimansho gakkō, signed down a quiet lane.

**Eating and drinking**

All the places above offer room rates without meals, but in general you're best off **eating** in your accommodation, especially in the evenings. **Miyanoura** has a few restaurants along the main road, of which *Kabochaya* (Tues–Sun 11am–3pm) makes a good, inexpensive lunch stop. The English-speaking chef rustles up a pretty fair curry-rice, but his real speciality is *Yakushima* ramen made with smoked fish. The restaurant is on the main road, halfway between the two minshuku (see above), near the Nisseki gas station.

**Anbō** has a lively little *izakaya* called *Wakatake* (Mon–Sat 11.30am–1.30pm & 6–10pm) beside the river immediately south of the *Kamome-sō* ryokan. Fresh seafood is the order of the day, served as sashimi or as part of their *omakase* course-menu (from ¥3000); get here early to be sure of a seat. The pleasantly rustic *Rengaya* (daily 10am–2pm & 6–10pm), on the road down to the harbour, is another popular spot. It offers a varied menu, including *yakiniku* (barbecued meat), *tonkatsu* (pork cutlets) and steaks, with set meals from around ¥1400.

# Kirishima National Park

No less than 23 volcanic mountains, ten crater lakes and numerous hot springs provide the substance of **Kirishima National Park**. Its main base is the plateau-village of **Ebino Kōgen**, a cluster of shops, hotels and campsites, from where it's a short scramble up the park's highest peak, Karakuni-dake (1700m). The easternmost peak, Takachiho-no-mine (1574m), however, holds greater significance. According to legend, this is where Ninigi-no-mikoto, grandson of the Sun Goddess Amaterasu (see p.781) and founder of the Japanese imperial line, descended to earth. The traditional approach to Takachiho is from the park's southern gateway, **Kirishima Jingū**, stopping first at a shrine shrouded in cryptomeria trees. The peaks are linked by a skein of **hiking** trails – it's worth scaling at least one of them for superb views over a foreground of jagged craters filled with spherical, cobalt-blue lakes to Sakurajima puffing angrily on the southern horizon.

The Kirishima range lies at the north end of Kagoshima Bay, with sporadic **transport** links to both Kagoshima and Miyazaki. Coming **from Kagoshima**, the quickest option is a bus from Nishi-Kagoshima Station to Ebino Kōgen (1hr 45min–3hr; ¥1800). Operated by Hayashida Bus company, these services run three times daily, but note that only the first bus is direct; the others involve a change at the *Hayashida Onsen Hotel* just below the park. If you're using a JR pass, take a train from Kagoshima to Kirishima Jingū Station, then a bus to Hayashida Onsen to connect with the Ebino Kōgen buses. Miyakō Bus runs daily services **from Miyazaki**'s Miyakō City bus terminal to Ebino Kōgen (2hr 15min–3hr; ¥2310) via Kobayashi in the north. Again, JR pass holders can save a few yen by taking a train from Miyazaki to Kobayashi Station (3 daily; 1hr 30min) before joining the bus.

## Ebino Kōgen

Whichever route you take to **EBINO KŌGEN** the views are stunning. At 1200m above sea level, temperatures on the plateau rarely exceed 20°C in summer and dip well below freezing when winter gives the peaks a dusting of snow and hoar frost. This is the best time to appreciate the local **onsen** – Kirishima is Japan's highest hot spring resort – while spring and autumn provide perfect hiking weather.

The centre of Ebino Kōgen consists of a coach park, beside which you'll find the bus centre **information desk** (daily 8am–5pm; ☎0984/35-1111) and, opposite, a small **Visitors' Centre** (daily 8.30am–5pm). Both these places provide local sketch-maps,

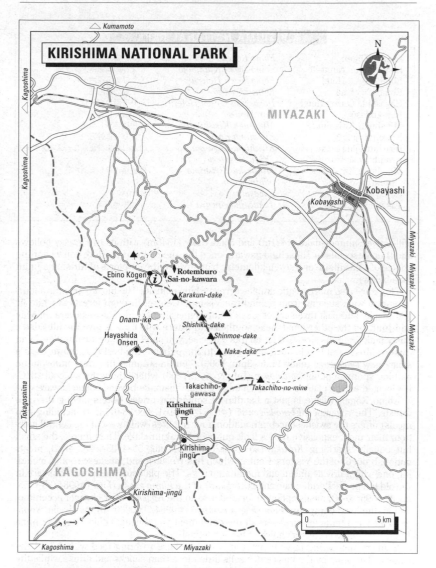

## KIRISHIMA NATIONAL PARK

△ *Kumamoto*

*Kagoshima* ◁

*Kagoshima* ◁

MIYAZAKI

*Kagoshima* ◁

Kobayashi

*Kobayashi*

*Miyazaki* ▷   *Miyazaki* ▷

*Miyazaki* ▷

▲ **Rotemburo**
**Sai-no-kawara**

Ebino Kōgen ⓘ

*Karakuni-dake*

*Tokagoshima* ◁

*Onami-ike*

*Shishiko-dake* ▲

Hayashida
Onsen

▲ *Shinmoe-dake*

▲ *Naka-dake*

▲ *Takachiho-no-mine*

Takachiho-
gawasa

**Kirishima-
jingū**
⛩

Kirishima-
jingū

KAGOSHIMA

*Kirishima-jingū*

N

0        5 km

▽ *Kagoshima*                ▽ *Miyazaki*

though you'll need something more detailed for the longer **hikes**. If it's a clear day, try tackling **Karakuni-dake** at the very least. The quickest trail starts 1km northeast of the village beside a steaming, sulphurous scar known as Sai-no-kawara, and then climbs steeply along a heavily eroded ridge. It's not a difficult climb, taking under two hours, though you'll want good footwear on the loose stones. From here you can circle south to Ōnami-ike, a crater lake, but the classic walk is east along Kirishima's magnificent volcanic peaks. It takes four hours to hike from Karakuni-dake to Takachiho-gawara; remember to carry plenty of water. The path leads over Shishiko-dake (1428m), the

| | KIRISHIMA NATIONAL PARK | |
|---|---|---|
| Ebino Kōgen | *Ebino Kōgen* | えびの高原 |
| Ebino-kōgen campsite | *Ebino-kōgen Kyanpu-jō* | えびの高原キャンプ場 |
| Ebino-kōgen Hotel | *Ebino-kōgen Hoteru* | えびの高原ホテル |
| Ebino-kōgen-sō | *Ebino-kōgen-sō* | えびの高原荘 |
| Hayashida Onsen Hotel | *Hayashida Onsen Hoteru* | 林田温泉ホテル |
| Karakuni-sō | *Karakuni-sō* | からくに荘 |
| Minshuku Kirishima-ji | *Minshuku Kirishima-ji* | 民宿きりしま路 |
| Kirishima-jingū | *Kirishima-jingū* | きりしま神宮 |
| Kirishima-jingū-mae | *Kirishima-jingū-mae* | きりしま神宮前ユースホステル |
| Youth Hostel | *Yūsu Hosuteru* | |
| Minshuku Kirishima | *Minshuku Kirishima* | 民宿きりしま清水荘 |
| Shimizu-sō | *Shimizu-sō* | |
| Kobayashi | *Kobayashi* | 小林 |
| Takachiho-gawara | *Takachiho-gawara* | 高千穂河原 |

still-active Shinmoe-dake (1421m) and Naka-dake (1345m) with its two grassy hollows and then descends to Takachiho-gawara, once the site of a shrine. Here you've got the choice of a **campsite** or a seven-kilometre trot down to the comforts of Kirishima Jingū (see below).

There are also more gentle ambles across Ebino plateau. The most popular is a four-kilometre walk starting from behind the Visitors' Centre, through forests of white fir and maple, and past three crater lakes before emerging beside Sai-no-kawara. In May and June, on the other hand, head southeast to where wild azaleas give the hillsides a dusty-pink tinge. As a reward for all this exercise, you can't do better than wallow in an **onsen**. Most local hotels open their baths to the public – the best is *Ebino-kōgen-sō*'s smart new *rotemburo* (daily 11am–3pm; ¥500) – but in summer the most atmospheric bathing spot is a public *rotemburo* (July & Aug; ¥200) where the water's a cool 28°C. It's located on the plateau's northern edge a short distance beyond Sai-no-kawara.

Ebino Kōgen village is just a handful of somewhat pricey **hotels** among the pine forests. The revamped *Ebino-kōgen-sō* (☎0984/33-0161, fax 33-0114; ⑦ including two meals) offers the swishest accommodation, four minutes' walk west of the central junction; their most expensive rooms look out over Karakuni-dake. Then there's the small but equally sparkling *Karakuni-sō* (☎0120–888847, fax 0984/33-4928; ⑤–⑦, meals optional) north of the Visitors' Centre, which has Western and Japanese rooms, including one with a private onsen and mountain views. The plateau's cheapest rooms are in the old but perfectly adequate annex (*bekkan*) of the *Ebino-kōgen Hotel* (☎0984/33-1155, fax 33-5395; ⑤–⑥, meals optional) located next to the *Kōgen-sō*. For cheaper accommodation, the local **campsite**, *Ebino-kōgen camp-jō* (☎0984/33-0800; ①), has basic, wooden cabins and tents for hire, plus all the equipment you'll need. Otherwise, Kirishima Jingū (see below) offers a choice of homely minshuku.

If you're not **eating** in your hotel, it would be wise to bring food with you to the plateau. The shop by the bus centre sells little more than snacks and drinks, while the restaurant opposite closes at 5pm. It offers either cheap fast food – noodles, curry rice and so forth – or an inexpensive dining room upstairs, with sets at under ¥1000.

## Kirishima Jingū

The small town of **KIRISHIMA JINGŪ**, built on the southern slopes of Takachiho-no-mine, makes a possible alternative base to Ebino Kōgen. The top end of town, partly enveloped in cedar forests and focused round a cheerful, red-lacquer bridge, has an appealing, village atmosphere. It also boasts a number of reasonable accommodation options and a couple of mildly interesting sights.

The first of these is a small **craft village** (daily 9am–5/5.30pm; free) immediately south of the lacquered bridge. Though it's a mite touristy, some of the demonstrations are worth a look and there's also a short, riverside walk. Heading over the bridge, walk under the bright vermilion *torii* and up a steep flight of steps to the shrine, **Kirishima-jingū**, after which the town is named. A surprisingly imposing complex, it's dedicated to Ninigi-no-mikoto and his fellow gods who first set foot in Kirishima at the dawn of Japan's creation. Although there are fine views of Kagoshima Bay from the shrine, they're better from the summit of **Takachiho-no-mine** (1574m) itself, roughly three hours' walk to the northeast. With your own transport you can halve the walking time by driving 7km up the road to **Takachiho-gawara**. It's then a steady climb on a well-marked path, ending in a short scramble on scree to the crater rim where a replica of Ninigi's sacred sword points skywards. Takachiho last erupted in 1913, and now only faint wisps of steam indicate that it's still active.

As well as a **Visitor's Centre** (daily 8.30am–5pm), Takachiho-gawara also has a good **campsite** (☎0995/57-0996; [1]) just south of the road. Otherwise, if you're looking for **places to stay**, try one of the cluster of minshuku at the top end of Kirishima Jingū village. Among these, the friendly *Minshuku Kirishima-ji* (☎0995/57-0272; [4]–[5]), beside the bridge, and *Minshuku Kirishima Shimizu-sō* (☎0995/57-0111; [4]–[5]), a few doors further down, are both pleasant places with just four rooms apiece. Take the road east in front of the *Kirishima-ji* for *Kirishima Jingū-mae Youth Hostel* (☎ & fax 0995/57-1188; [1]). It's basic, but pretty relaxed and the food's plentiful and tasty. All these places have their own hot-spring baths and offer rooms without meals. There are small **restaurants** and convenience stores on the main square, where you'll also find a **post office** and bus stops for services down to Kirishima Jingū Station or on up to Hayashida Onsen.

# Miyazaki and around

A breezy, semi-tropical city on the southeast coast of Kyūshū, **MIYAZAKI** claims the longest sunshine hours in Japan. Its brightly coloured blooms and phoenix palms, the city's emblems, giving the streets a relaxed, summery feel. The city's sights are a little thin on the ground – a historic shrine, municipal park and the world's largest indoor beach – but Miyazaki makes a good base for exploring the **Nichinan coast**. A short train ride south, the island of **Aoshima** is a natural, sub-tropical garden ringed by platforms of heavily scored rocks, while further along the coast **Udo-jingū**'s main shrine nestles in a sacred cave. From here you can continue down the peninsula to **Cape Toi**, or turn inland to circle round via **Obi**, an attractive castle town with a passable collection of museums and old houses.

Miyazaki's **festivals** are launched on January 15 with a dip in the sea off Aoshima to pray for the coming year. While north Japan is still wrapped in snow, in mid-March the city's flower festival announces the arrival of spring, but the most important event is autumn's Miyazaki-jingū Taisai (last weekend in Oct). This takes the form of a costume parade in honour of Emperor Jimmu, Japan's first emperor, featuring women dressed in gorgeous wedding kimono.

## Orientation, arrival, information and city transport

The bulk of Miyazaki lies on the north bank of the Ōyodo-gawa, crooked in a bend of the river just before it empties into the Hyūga Sea. The city centre consists of a cluster of department stores around the junction of its two main thoroughfares,

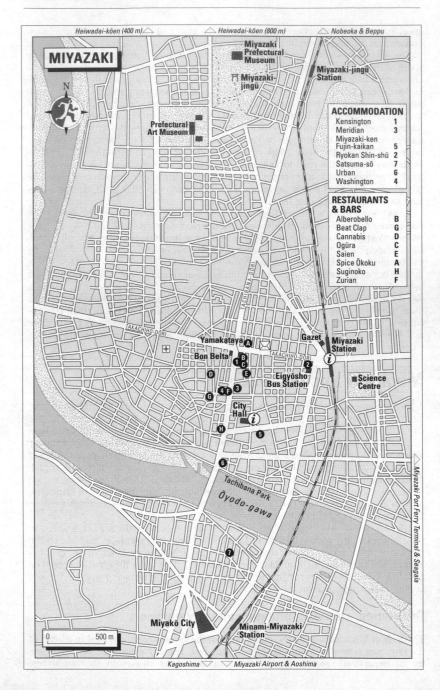

Heiwadai-kōen (400 m)    Heiwadai-kōen (800 m)    Nobeoka & Beppu

# MIYAZAKI

N

Miyazaki
Prefectural
Museum

Miyazaki-
jingū

Miyazaki-jingū
Station

Prefectural
Art Museum

## ACCOMMODATION
| | |
|---|---|
| Kensington | 1 |
| Meridian | 3 |
| Miyazaki-ken Fujin-kaikan | 5 |
| Ryokan Shin-shū | 2 |
| Satsuma-sō | 7 |
| Urban | 6 |
| Washington | 4 |

## RESTAURANTS & BARS
| | |
|---|---|
| Alberobello | B |
| Beat Clap | G |
| Cannabis | D |
| Ogūra | C |
| Saien | E |
| Spice Ōkoku | A |
| Suginoko | H |
| Zurian | F |

TACHIBANA-DŌRI

TAKACHIHO-DŌRI

Yamakataya

Bon Belta

Gazet    Miyazaki
Station

TAKACHIHO-DŌRI

Eigyōsho
Bus Station

Science
Centre

City
Hall

Tachibana Park

Ōyodo-gawa

Miyazaki Port Ferry Terminal & Seagaia

Miyakō City

Minami-Miyazaki
Station

0    500 m

Kagoshima    Miyazaki Airport & Aoshima

**Tachibana-dōri** and **Takachiho-dōri**. The latter ends 800m further west at Miyazaki Station, while Tachibana-dōri leads north to the city's two main sights, Miyazaki-jingū and Heiwadai-kōen, and south across the river to **Minami-Miyazaki**. This southern district is home to **Miyakō City**, consistency of a vast Daiei shopping mall and the city's principal bus centre.

**Arriving** in Miyazaki by **long-distance bus**, you end up at Miyakō City Bus Centre, though most services also call at Miyazaki Station or the central crossroads on their way through town. Likewise, **trains** stop at both Miyazaki Station and southerly Minami-Miyazaki Station, three minutes' walk east of Miyakō City. The **airport** also lies on the south side of town, just 5km from the city centre. It's connected by both train (1–3 hourly; 10min; ¥330) and limousine bus (every 20min; 25min; ¥360) to Miyazaki Station via Minami-Miyazaki. Finally, **ferries** from Kawasaki, Naha, Ōsaka and Yakushima dock at Miyazaki Port Ferry Terminal, east of the city centre. You'll find buses waiting outside the terminal buildings to bring you to Miyazaki Station or Miyakō City (15–20min; ¥290).

Miyazaki is well provided with English-language information. Both the main **tourist information office** (daily 9am–5pm; ☎0985/22-6469) inside Miyazaki Station, and the airport desk (daily 7am–8.30pm; ☎0985/51-5111) have English-speaking staff. There's also a telephone **helpline** (☎0985/52-4754) for assistance outside office hours. The Prefectural International Centre, 6F Higashi-Bekkan, 1-6 Miyata-chō (Mon–Fri 8.30am–5.15pm; ☎0985/32-8457), beside the City Hall, is another useful resource, aimed primarily at long-term residents.

Look out for two publications, *Discovering Miyazaki* and *Miyazaki Relax and Enjoy*, which contain helpful tips about using **local buses**. Though most services depart from Miyakō City, a few use the Miyazaki Eigyōsho terminus, opposite Miyazaki Station's west entrance, or depart from the station concourse. However, almost all buses call at stops around the city's central crossroads, so the best thing is to head for this junction and ask which stop you need; getting off here, ask for Depāto-mae. Destinations are shown on the front of the bus in *kanji*; take a numbered ticket as you board and pay the driver on exit according to the fare on the display panel.

## Accommodation

If you're looking for **accommodation** in Miyazaki, the best option is to head for Tachibana-dōri south of the central crossroads, where you'll find a sprinkling of mid-range business hotels. Cheaper places cluster round Miyazaki Station and in Minami-Miyazaki, while the local youth hostel is a bit of a hike from the station, but within walking distance of Tachibana-dōri.

**Hotel Kensington**, 3-4-4 Tachibana-dōri Higashi (☎0985/20-5500, fax 32-7700). "Nostalgic days of England" are promised at this smartish business hotel south of Miyazaki's central crossroads. Cheaper rooms lack windows, but they're all equipped with phone, TV and en-suite bath. ⑤.

**Hotel Meridian**, 3-1-11 Tachibana-dōri Higashi (☎0985/26-6666, fax 26-8992). Sleek, professional business hotel south of the *Kensington*. It offers comfortable, airy rooms, a business centre and choice of restaurants. ⑤.

**Miyazaki-ken Fujin-Kaikan**, 1-3-10 Asahi (☎0985/24-5785). Miyazaki's youth hostel is about fifteen minutes' walk southwest of the station, across from the Prefectural Office. The accommodation consists of *tatami* rooms in the Prefectural Women's Centre – though men are welcome – and there's a 9.30pm curfew. Cheap café downstairs and bike rental (around ¥1000 per day). ①.

**Satsuma-sō**, 3-6-9 Ota (☎0985/51-4488). One of the nicest places to stay in Minami-Miyazaki, in a residential area ten minutes' walk north of Miyakō City (near the Nakamura 1-chōme bus stop). It's bright, clean and friendly with *tatami* rooms, shared bathrooms and optional meals. ④–⑤.

**Ryokan Shin-shū**, 2-12-24 Hiroshima-dōri (☎0985/24-4008, fax 29-6561). Cheap, homely ryokan on an arcade opposite Miyazaki Station. The rooms are all Japanese style, some with bath, and rates are available with or without meals. ④–⑤.

## MIYAZAKI AND AROUND

| | | |
|---|---|---|
| Miyazaki | *Miyazaki* | 宮崎 |
| Heiwadai-kōen | *Heiwadai-kōen* | 平和台公園 |
| Minami-Miyazaki | *Minami-Miyazaki* | 南宮崎 |
| Miyakō City | *Miyakō Shitii* | 宮交シティー |
| Miyazaki-jingū | *Miyazaki-jingū* | 宮崎神宮 |
| Miyazaki Prefectural Museum | *Miyazaki-kenritsu Sōgō Hakubutsukan* | 宮崎県立総合博物館 |
| Miyazaki Port Ferry Terminal | *Miyazaki-kō Ferii Tāminaru* | 宮崎港フェリーターミナル |
| Prefectural Art Museum | *Miyazaki-kenritsu Bijutsukan* | 宮崎県立美術館 |
| Science Centre | *Kagaku Gijutsukan* | 科学技術館 |
| Seagaia | *Shiigaia* | シーガイア |

| ACCOMMODATION | | |
|---|---|---|
| Hotel Kensington | *Hoteru Kenjinton* | ホテルケンジントン |
| Hotel Meridian | *Hoteru Meridian* | ホテルメリディアン |
| Miyazaki-ken Fujin-Kaikan | *Miyazaki-ken Fujin-Kaikan* | 宮崎県婦人会館 |
| Satsuma-sō | *Satsuma-sō* | さつま荘 |
| Ryokan Shin-shū | *Ryokan Shin-shū* | 旅館新洲 |
| Urban Hotel | *Āban Hoteru* | アーバンホテル |
| Washington Hotel | *Washinton Hoteru* | ワシントンホテル |

| RESTAURANTS | | |
|---|---|---|
| Ogūra | *Ogūra* | おぐうら |
| Saien | *Saien* | 菜苑 |
| Spice Ōkoku | *Supaisu Ōkoku* | スパイス王国 |
| Suginoko | *Suginoko* | 杉の子 |
| Zurian | *Zurian* | 寿里庵 |

| AROUND MIYAZAKI | | |
|---|---|---|
| Aoshima | *Aoshima* | 青島 |
| Cactus Garden | *Saboten Hābu-en* | サボテンハーブ園 |
| Obi | *Obi* | 飫肥 |
| Obi-jō | *Obi-jō* | 飫肥城 |
| Obi-ten Chaya | *Obi-ten Chaya* | おび天茶屋 |
| Udo-jingū | *Udo-jingū* | 鵜戸神宮 |

**Urban Hotel**, 1-5-8 Tachibana-dōri Higashi (☎0985/26-7411, fax 26-7532). Just east of the Tachibana bridge, this odd-looking, turreted business hotel hides a few well-priced rooms. They're simple but spacious and all are en suite. ④–⑤.

**Washington Hotel**, 3-1-1 Tachibana-dōri Nishi (☎0985/28-9111, fax 22-6222). Oldish member of the *Washington* chain on the main drag, with boxy but perfectly adequate rooms, and in-house bars and restaurants. ⑤.

## The City

Central Miyazaki's wide boulevards and colourful shopping arcades, as well as its compact, boisterous entertainment district, make it an appealing stop on the tour round Kyūshū. Though they won't appear on anyone's must-see list, the city's sights are sufficiently interesting to fill a leisurely day, particularly if you're keen to relax on its tropical indoor beach, the Ocean Dome at **Seagaia**. If this doesn't appeal, there's a clutch of more conventional sights scattered around the city. In the northern suburbs,

**Heiwadai-kōen** is a hill-top park with a delightful collection of clay *haniwa* figurines – replicas of statues found in ancient burial mounds. The grounds of nearby **Miyazaki-jingū**, the city's foremost shrine, contain a good **municipal museum** and there's a sleek new **art museum** nearby, while the station area boasts the entertaining **Miyazaki Science Centre**. Much is made of the riverside **Tachibana park**; by day it's just a narrow strip of green with a few tables and chairs, but comes into its own at dusk, when the palm trees glitter with fairy lights.

## The northern districts

Low hills rise to the north of Miyazaki, where the rather Stalinist "Tower of Peace" dominates a large public park, **Heiwadai-kōen**. To reach the park take a #8 bus from Miyakō City or the Depāto-mae stop outside Bon Belta department store (10–20min; ¥240). The 37-metre-high tower was built in 1940 – the name was coined after the war – using stones presented from around the world. The only reason to visit the tower, however, is for its odd acoustic effects; stand on the hexagonal stone in front and clap. Further into the park you'll find the **Haniwa Garden** where dozens of clay statues of houses, animals and people populate a mossy wood. Look out for the charming warriors with elaborate uniforms and the pop-eyed, open-mouthed dancers. These are copies of the *haniwa* figures discovered in fourth-century burial mounds at nearby Saitobaru; it's believed the statues were used to "protect" aristocratic tombs. You can buy smaller versions in the park shop, though they make rather fragile souvenirs.

Around 1km southeast of Heiwadai-kōen, **Miyazaki Prefectural Museum** (Tues–Sun 9am–4.30pm; ¥200) gives a good overview of local history, including the *haniwa* figurines, with much information in English. The same complex includes an archeological centre, where you can watch people patiently glueing together pottery shards, and the **Minka-en** (daily 10am–5pm; free), a slightly unkempt collection of four thatched farmhouses from around the area. Don't miss the two traditional, stone and clay baths at the end of the path; the water was heated by lighting a fire underneath, like giant cauldrons. These museums stand in the extensive woodlands surrounding **Miyazaki-jingū**, a shrine dedicated to Japan's first emperor, Jimmu Tennō. An unusually large shrine at the end of an imposing avenue, the sanctuary itself is typically understated, though if you're lucky you'll catch a festive ceremony, or at least spot some of the colourful, semi-wild chickens scurrying round the raked-gravel compound.

Art lovers should walk five minutes west to a new complex of public buildings, including a concert hall, theatre and library, in the aptly named Culture Park. Here, the monumental **Prefectural Art Museum** (Tues–Sun 10am–6pm; ¥300) hosts temporary exhibitions alongside its permanent collection of twentieth-century painting and Italian sculptures. To get back into central Miyazaki you can catch a bus from the main road east of the Culture Park, or from the southern entrance to Miyazaki-jingū.

## Miyazaki Science Centre and Seagaia

Immediately behind Miyazaki's jolly, blue-and-yellow station, a forty-metre-high satellite launcher pinpoints the city's excellent **Science Centre** (Tues–Sun 9am–4.30pm; ¥510, or ¥710 including planetarium). Using examples from Kyūshū, the museum covers everything from micro-organisms, wind power and pulleys to robots and satellite imagery. Most of the displays are interactive and huge fun – ask for a copy of their very thorough English-language brochure. The museum also boasts the world's largest **planetarium** – 27m in diameter – which is well worth the extra expense. There are three shows daily Monday to Saturday and five on Sundays, giving you a superb, fifty-minute ride through the heavens.

The last sight in Miyazaki city is the **Seagaia** resort, a short bus ride to the northeast. Buses run roughly every twenty minutes from Miyazaki Station or every thirty from Miyakō City (20–40min; ¥430). The complex contains a golf course, zoo, luxury hotels and a man-made, indoor beach just a few hundred metres from the coast. Bizarre though it might be, **Ocean Dome** (daily 9.30am–10pm; closed occasionally on Tues or Wed; ☎0985/21-1114) attracts plenty of holiday-makers to its "paradise island", complete with unsalted water at a constant 28°C, balmy, tropical air at 30°C and a white beach of crushed stones. The whole lot is topped with the world's largest retractable roof – so, at least the sunshine's real.

If you just want to have a look, "View" **tickets** (¥1200) allow entry to the second-floor promenade, but to use the beach you'll need a one-day ticket (¥4200); you can upgrade from the View ticket inside. There are also a number of attractions, mostly water slides and rapid riders, which cost an extra ¥600 a go, or you can buy an "Attraction Free Band" (¥1200) allowing access to all attractions for the day. At regular intervals a wave machine creates 3.5-metre-high breakers for a none-too-spectacular surfing display, but afterwards you can have a go, if you don't mind forking out ¥1000 rental for a body board (2hr).

## Eating, drinking and entertainment

Beef, wild boar, *ayu* (sweet fish) and *shiitake* mushrooms from the mountains, clams, flying fish and citrus fruits – Miyazaki has a good spread of edible delicacies. There's also the local sushi – *retasu-maki* – containing shrimp, lettuce and mayonnaise, and *chicken Namban*, deep-fried, succulent chicken morsels with tartar sauce. The best choice of **restaurants** is in the streets either side of Tachibana-dōri, but the Gazet building, outside Miyazaki Station, also has an interesting selection. The city's energetic **nightlife** district is squeezed into the backstreets west of Tachibana-dōri, behind the Bon Belta department store and south to the *Washington Hotel*.

**Alberobello**, 3-4-26 Tachibana-dōri Higashi. Cheerful, jazz-playing pizza parlour down an alley one block south of Yamakataya department store. Choose from a list of imaginative toppings on their English menu, with pizzas from ¥1000 and slightly cheaper pasta dishes. Daily except Tues 11.30am–9pm.

**Beat Clap**, Tachibana-dōri Nishi. Approaching this large, downbeat disco in a car park behind the *Washington Hotel*, look out for their old, graffiti sign with an unfortunate misspelling. Inside you'll find the biggest dance floor in Miyazaki. ¥1000 cover charge including one drink. Sat only, from 9.30pm.

**Cannabis**, Tachibana-dōri Nishi. No cover charge – and no cannabis – at this very relaxed reggae bar in the midst of Miyazaki's entertainment district. Daily 9am–5/6am.

**Ogūra**, Tachibana-dōri Higashi. A café-style restaurant offering good, cheap food, but no atmosphere, tucked down an alley behind the Yamakataya store. The house special is *chicken Namban* (¥900), or they do burgers, fried pork cutlets, curry-rice and other comfort food in generous portions. Daily 10am–8.30pm.

**Saien**, Tachibana-dōri Higashi. Vegetarian haven on a back-alley east of Tachibana-dōri, with well-priced lunch deals (¥700), fresh juice, brown rice and tofu burgers. Service can be slow. Daily 11.30am–2.30pm & 5–9pm.

**Spice Ōkoku**, 4-6-23 Tachibana-dōri Higashi. Popular Indian serving Miyazaki's spiciest curries – let them know if you like it fiery – and plumpest nan breads. The daily lunch is a steal at ¥580, or they do sets from ¥1200. Daily 11am–9.30pm. Closed 2nd and 4th Mon.

**Suginoko**, 2-1-4 Tachibana-dōri Nishi. One of the city's most famous restaurants, at the south end of Tachibana-dōri, serving tasty country cooking in elegant surroundings. Try their lunchtime *Kuroshio teishoku* (¥1000) or *bentō* sampler (¥1600). Evening meals start at ¥4000. Mon–Sat 11.30–2pm & 4–11pm.

**Zurian**, 3-1-3 Tachibana-dōri Nishi. Underneath the *Washington Hotel*, this popular, modern *izakaya* specializes in seafood straight from the tank. There's a huge picture menu to choose from, with *yakiniku*, fries, salads and other standard *izakaya* fare. You can eat well for around ¥2000. Daily 5pm–midnight.

# Listings

**Airlines** Air Nippon Company (☎0985/23-5101); ANA (☎0120–029222); JAS & Japan Air Commuter (☎0120–511283).

**Airport information** ☎0985/51-5114.

**Banks and exchange** Miyazaki Bank, Ōita Bank and Fukuoka Bank all have foreign exchange desks. You'll find them on Tachibana-dōri, with branches of Miyazaki Bank also near Miyazaki Station and in the Miyakō City complex.

**Buses** Most long-distance buses start from the Miyakō City Bus Centre and call either at Miyazaki Station or the Depāto-mae stops in the city centre. A few services start at the station, but then travel via Miyakō City.

**Car rental** Eki Rent-a-car (☎0985/24-7206); Nippon Rent-a-car (☎0985/51-1861); Toyota Rent-a-car (☎0985/26-0100).

**Emergencies** For English-language assistance call the SOS telephone helpline on ☎0985/52-4754. Emergency numbers are listed in Basics on p.70.

**Ferries** Marine Express (☎0985/29-8311) has services to Ōsaka (daily; 12hr 30min; from ¥8230) and Kawasaki (every other day; 20hr 30min; from ¥17,710) departing from Miyazaki-kō Ferry Terminal, a short bus ride east of central Miyazaki (15–20min; ¥290). Also from this terminal, Ōshima Transport (☎0985/22-8895) operates weekly sailings to Naha (24hr; from ¥12,770), while Toppy jetfoils (Kagoshima Shōsen; ☎0985/28-2277) use the neighbouring terminal for their services to Yakushima (daily; 3hr; ¥10,000; reservations required). You can buy tickets for all these ferries at local travel agents (see below).

**Hospitals and medical care** The Prefectural Hospital, 5-30 Kita-takamatsu-chō (☎0985/24-4181), is on Takachiho-dori, west of the central crossroads. The International Centre (see p.733) has information about English-speaking doctors.

**Post office** Miyazaki Central Post Office, 1-1-34 Takachiho-dōri, is on the main road east of the Tachibana junction. They accept poste restante and operate a 24hr service for express mail.

**Travel agents** For domestic travel arrangements, try JTB (☎0985/29-2111), or Joy Road (☎0985/24-2626) in Miyazaki Station.

# Around Miyazaki

South of Miyazaki, the hills close in as road and railway follow the coast down to **Aoshima**. This low, oval island lying just offshore is best known for the surrounding platforms of "devil's washboard" rocks, scored into deep grooves as if by a giant's comb. In fact these rock formations stretch over several kilometres south to **Udo-jingū**, an eye-catching shrine halfway up the cliffs. Even here, as in much of Japan, the cliffs are plastered with great swathes of concrete, but as you head down the Nichinan coast to Cape Toi there are more sandy coves and picturesque islands. Apart from the scenery, the only specific sights along here are the castle ruins and old *samurai* houses of **Obi**, a small, attractive town lying 6km inland. Both Aoshima and Obi are stops on the JR Nichinan Line from Miyazaki to Shibushi, but the best way to explore the coast is by road. With a careful eye on the timetables, you can travel from Aoshima to Obi by public bus and then pick up a train for the return trip to Miyazaki.

## Aoshima

Five kilometres south of Miyazaki, the tiny island of **AOSHIMA**, just 1500m in circumference, is little more than a heap of sand capped by a dense forest of betel palms and other sub-tropical plants. It's best at low tide when you can explore the rock pools trapped on the surrounding shelf of washboard rocks. After that the only other thing to do is walk round the island – it takes all of fifteen minutes – and drop in at its small shrine. Swathed in tropical creepers, **Aoshima-jinja** is dedicated to Yamasachi Hiko, a god of mountain products. Each year he's honoured with a couple of lively **festivals**: on June 17 portable shrines are paraded round the island on boats and then manhandled back to Aoshima, while mid-January sees men rushing semi-naked into the sea to welcome the god back as part of the New Year celebrations.

The island is accessible via a causeway from the neighbouring town, also known as Aoshima, which is a stop on the JR Nichinan line **from Miyazaki**. Trains leave Miyazaki Station (25min; ¥310) every hour or so, stopping also at Minami-Miyazaki (23min; ¥230); the island's a six-minute walk east from Aoshima Station. The alternative is a bus from Miyazaki Station (45min; ¥600) via the Miyakō City Bus Centre (30min; ¥480); buses run roughly every fifteen minutes and drop you on the main road (Route 220) just behind Aoshima beach. You can pick up sketch maps at the small **tourist information** kiosk (daily 9am–6pm) outside Aoshima Station, and there are touristy **restaurants** on the main road and lining the approach to the causeway.

## Udo-jingū

South of Aoshima, the road climbs over the **Horikiri Pass**, along an attractive stretch of coast fringed with heavily ridged rocks, where fishermen and cormorants try their luck. On the way you might like to stop at the **Cactus Garden** (daily 9am–5/5.30pm; ¥670), home to over one million cacti of five hundred different species. They mostly bloom in early summer (April–June), but at any time of year you can sample vitamin-packed cactus ice cream and cactus steaks at the garden's restaurant.

Eight kilometres further down the road, a cleft in the rock hides one of this area's most famous sights, **Udo-jingū** (free). The main shrine fills the mouth of a large, low cave halfway down the cliff face, its striking, vermilion *torii* and arched bridges vivid against the dark rock. According to legend, Udo-jingū was founded in the first century BC and marks the spot where Emperor Jimmu's father was born. The rounded boulders in front of the cave are said to represent his mother's breasts – expectant women come here to pray for an easy pregnancy and newly weds for a happy marriage.

The shrine is protected to the rear by a wooded hill, where you'll find various other sanctuaries, but first you have to run the gauntlet of souvenir stalls clustering round the entrance. Arriving by **bus** from Miyazaki's Miyakō City (1–2 hourly; 1hr 20min; ¥1340) or Aoshima (1–2 hourly; 40min; ¥930), drivers generally let you off at the turning to the shrine, to save a steep climb up from the village. You can then cut through a tunnel from the car parks, but it's nicer to follow the old, mossy steps over the hill-top, to rejoin the crowds by the shrine's distinctly Buddhist entrance gate. When you've finished, walk south along the coast to Udo village (roughly 15min) to catch the bus back to Miyazaki or onwards to Obi; note that there are three buses from Udo to Obi in the late morning, another around 2pm and then nothing until 7pm.

## Obi

The JR Nichinan line sweeps inland round the Udo headland, passing through **OBI**, an old **castle town** about 50km south of Miyazaki. It's a pristine little place with a number of *samurai* houses and a fine collection of traditional whitewashed warehouses, many of them immaculately restored, clustered under the castle walls. Obi's heyday was under the Itō family, who were granted the fiefdom in 1588 and then spent much of their time feuding with the neighbouring Shimazu clan of Kagoshima. Only the walls of their once formidable castle remain, though the main gate and lord's residence have been rebuilt in the original style.

Central Obi lies in a loop of the Sakatani-gawa, with its historic core concentrated north of the main east–west highway. Here you'll find a few streets of **samurai houses** and the castle, **Obi-jō** (daily 9.30am–5pm; ¥510, including Yoshōkan and Komura Memorial Hall), on the low hill behind. Walking north up Ōte-mon-dōri, under the great southern gate, you reach a white-walled history museum full of Itō family heirlooms. Beyond is the Matsu-no-maru, an exact replica of the sprawling, Edo-period buildings where the lords once lived, including the reception rooms, women's quarters, tea-ceremony room and a lovely "cooling-off" tower, where the lord could catch the summer breezes after his steam bath.

The rest of the castle grounds are now just grass and trees, but on the way out take a quick look at Obi's largest *samurai* house, the **Yoshōkan** (same ticket and hours), immediately west of Ōte-mon gate. When the Meiji reforms abolished feudal holdings in the late-nineteenth century, the Itō family moved to this more modest villa which had previously belonged to their chief retainer. Though you can't go in, the house is a lovely, airy building surrounded by a spacious garden that's looking a bit worse for wear. On the opposite side of Ōte-mon from the Yoshōkan, the **Komura Memorial Hall** (same ticket and hours) commemorates a famous Meiji-era diplomat who was born in Obi in 1855. He's best remembered for his part in concluding the 1905 peace treaty following the Russo-Japanese War; the museum's most interesting material, much of it in English, revolves around this period.

*PRACTICALITIES*

The quickest way to reach Obi is a **train** on the JR Nichinan line from Miyazaki via Aoshima (1–2 hourly; 1hr 15min; ¥800). Obi Station lies on the east side of town, about fifteen minutes' walk across the river from the castle. Alternatively, **buses** from Aoshima and Udo-jingū (10 daily; 40min; ¥750) terminate a short walk west of Ōte-mon-dōri. Though Obi is small enough to tackle on foot, you can **rent bikes** at the station kiosk (daily 9am–6pm; ¥300 for 3hr) for scooting into town.

Obi has its own **speciality food**, *Obi-ten*, which consists of minced flying-fish mixed with tofu, miso and sugar, rolled into a leaf shape and deep fried. *Obi-ten Chaya*, a nicely rustic **restaurant** on Ōte-mon-dōri south of the Komura Memorial Hall, serves a good-value *teishoku*, including rice, soup and salad for ¥900.

## travel details

**Trains**

The trains between the major cities listed below are the fastest, direct services. There are also frequent slower services, run by JR and several private companies, covering the same destinations. It is usually possible, especially on long-distance routes, to get there faster by changing between services.

**Aso** to: Beppu (3 daily; 2hr); Kumamoto (hourly; 1hr–1hr 30min); Miyaji (hourly; 6min); Tateno (hourly; 25 min).

**Beppu** to: Aso (3 daily; 2hr); Fukuoka (1–3 hourly; 2hr–3hr); Kita-Kyūshū (2 hourly; 1hr 20min); Kumamoto (3 daily; 3hr); Miyazaki (hourly; 3hr 30min); Nobeoka (hourly; 2hr 30min); Ōita (frequent; 15min).

**Fukuoka (Hakata Station)** to: Arita (hourly; 1hr 20min); Beppu (1–3 hourly; 2hr–3hr); Dazaifu (2 hourly; 40min); Futsukaichi (6 hourly; 10–20min); Hiroshima (5 hourly; 1hr 10min–1hr 50min); Huis ten Bosch (hourly; 1hr 40min); Kagoshima (hourly; 3hr 50min); Kita-Kyūshū (frequent; 20min–1hr 30min); Kumamoto (2 hourly; 1hr

20min); Kyoto (2 hourly; 2hr 50min–3hr 40min); Miyazaki (hourly; 6hr); Nagasaki (1–2 hourly; 2hr 10min); Ōsaka (3–5 hourly; 2hr 30min–4hr 30min); Takeo (hourly; 1hr 10min), Tokyo (2 hourly; 5hr–6hr 15min).

**Isahaya** to: Shimabara (hourly; 1hr 10min).

**Kagoshima** to: Fukuoka (hourly; 3hr 50min); Ibusuki (1–2 hourly; 50min–1hr 20min); Kirishima Jingū (every 20min; 40–50min); Kumamoto (hourly; 2hr 30min); Miyazaki (6 daily; 2hr); Nagasaki (hourly; 5–6hr).

**Kita-Kyūshū (Kokura)** to: Beppu (2 hourly; 1hr 20min); Fukuoka (frequent; 20min–1hr 30min); Hiroshima (3–5hourly; 50min–1hr 20min); Kyoto (2 hourly; 2hr 30min–3hr 15min); Miyazaki (hourly; 5hr); Ōsaka (3–5hourly; 2hr 15min–4hr); Tokyo (2 hourly; 4hr 45min–6hr); Yahata (3 hourly; 15min).

**Kita-Kyūshū (Yahata)** to: Fukuoka (3 hourly; 50min); Kokura (frequent; 15min).

**Kumamoto** to: Aso (hourly; 1hr–1hr 30min); Beppu (3 daily; 3hr); Fukuoka (2 hourly; 1hr 20min); Kagoshima (hourly; 2hr 30min); Misumi (hourly;

50min); Miyazaki (3 daily; 5hr); Nagasaki (2 hourly; 3hr).

**Misumi** to: Kumamoto (hourly; 50mins).

**Miyazaki** to: Aoshima (hourly; 25min); Beppu (hourly; 3hr 30min); Fukuoka (hourly; 6hr); Kagoshima (6 daily; 2hr 10min); Kobayashi (3 daily; 1hr 30min); Kita-Kyūshū (hourly; 5hr); Kumamoto (3 daily; 4hr 20min); Nobeoka (hourly; 1hr 30min); Obi (1–2 hourly; 1hr 15min); Ōsaka (1 daily; 13hr 20min); Tokyo (1 daily; 20hr 30min).

**Nagasaki** to: Fukuoka (1–2 hourly; 2hr 10min); Huis ten Bosch (hourly; 1hr 30min); Isahaya (frequent; 20min); Kagoshima (hourly; 5–6hr); Kumamoto (2 hourly; 3hr).

**Takachiho** to: Nobeoka (hourly; 1hr 30min).

**Tateno** to: Takamori (hourly; 30min).

**Buses**

The buses listed below are mainly long-distance services – often travelling overnight – between the major cities, and local services where there is no alternative means of transport. For shorter journeys, however, trains are almost invariably quicker and often no more expensive.

**Aso** to: Beppu (4 daily; 2hr 40min); Kumamoto (hourly; 1hr 30min); Kurokawa Onsen (1 daily; 1hr); Senomoto Kōgen (4 daily; 45min).

**Beppu** to: Aso (4 daily; 2hr 40min); Fukuoka (1–2 hourly; 2hr–2hr 20min); Kumamoto (4 daily; 4hr–7hr); Nagasaki (7 daily; 3hr 30min); Nagoya (daily; 10hr 35min); Ōita (frequent; 20min).

**Ebino Kōgen** to: Hayashida Onsen Hotel (3 daily; 20min); Kagoshima (3 daily; 1hr 35min–3hr 10min); Kobayashi (4 daily; 1hr); Miyazaki (4 daily; 2hr 15min–3hr 15min).

**Fukuoka** to: Beppu (1–3 hourly; 2hr 15min–3hr 20min); Huis Ten Bosch (3 daily; 2hr); Kagoshima (1–2 hourly; 4hr); Kita-Kyūshū (frequent; 1hr 40min); Kumamoto (frequent; 1hr 45min–2hr 25min); Kyoto (daily; 9hr 30min); Miyazaki (1–2 hourly; 4hr 30min); Nagasaki (2–3 hourly; 2hr 30min–3hr 10min); Ōsaka (2 daily; 9–9hr 45min); Tokyo (2 daily; 14hr 35min).

**Isahaya** to: Unzen (1–3 hourly; 1hr 20min).

**Kagoshima** to: Chiran (10–12 daily; 1hr 20min); Ebino Kōgen (3 daily; 1hr 45min–3hr); Fukuoka (1–2 hourly; 4hr); Ibusuki (3 hourly; 1hr 30min); Kumamoto (10 daily; 3hr 30min); Kyoto (daily; 13hr 20min); Miyazaki (hourly; 2hr 30min); Nagoya (daily; 14hr 20min); Ōsaka (3 daily; 12hr 35min).

**Kirishima Jingū Station** to: Hayashida Onsen Hotel (10 daily; 35min); Kirishima Jingū-mae (10 daily; 15min).

**Kita-Kyūshū (Kokura)** to: Fukuoka (frequent; 1hr 40min); Kumamoto (9 daily; 2hr 35min); Nagasaki (9 daily; 3hr).

**Kumamoto** to: Aso (hourly; 1hr 30min); Aso-san Nishi-guchi (2 daily; 2hr); Beppu (4 daily; 4hr–7hr); Fukuoka (frequent; 1hr 45min–2hr 25min); Kagoshima (10 daily; 3hr 30min); Kumamoto Shin-kō (hourly; 35min); Miyazaki (10 daily; 2hr 10min–3hr 30min); Nagasaki (10 daily; 3hr).

**Miyazaki** to: Aoshima (every 10–20min; 30–45min); Ebino Kōgen (3–4 daily; 2hr 15min); Fukuoka (1–2 hourly; 4hr 15min); Kagoshima (10 daily; 2hr 30min); Kumamoto (hourly; 3hr–3hr 30min); Ōsaka (daily; 12hr 30min); Udo-jingū (1–2 hourly; 1hr 20min).

**Nagasaki** to: Beppu (7 daily; 3hr 30min); Huis Ten Bosch (2 hourly; 1hr); Kumamoto (10 daily; 3hr); Unzen (1–2 hourly; 1hr 40min–2hr 20min).

**Takamori** to: Takachiho (5 daily; 1hr 30min).

**Unzen** to: Shimabara (8 daily; 45min).

**Ferries**

**Beppu** to: Hiroshima (1 daily; 5hr); Kōbe (2 daily; 11hr 35min–12hr 30min); Matsuyama (daily; 3hr 40min); Misaki (4 daily; 2hr 10min); Ōsaka (2 daily; 14hr); Uwajima (1 daily; 3hr); Yawatahama (5 daily; 2hr 45min).

**Fukuoka** to: Naha (1–2 weekly; 25hr); Pusan (South Korea) by hydrofoil (1 daily; 2hr 55min), by ferry (3 weekly; 15hr 40min).

**Ibusuki** to: Kagoshima (1 daily; 40min); Yakushima (1 daily; 1hr 15min).

**Kagoshima** to: Ibusuki (1 daily; 40min); Naha (4–6 weekly; 18hr 30min–24hr); Yakushima (5 daily; 2hr–3hr 45min).

**Kita-Kyūshū (Kokura)** to: Matsuyama (1 daily; 6hr 30min).

**Kita-Kyūshū (Shin-Moji-kō)** to: Kōbe (1 daily; 12hr 30min); Ōsaka (1 daily; 13hr); Tokushima (1 daily; 17hr).

**Kumamoto** to: Nagasaki (1 daily; 1hr 45min); Shimabara (hourly; 1hr).

**Miyazaki** to: Kawasaki (4 weekly; 20hr 30min); Naha (1–2 weekly; 24hr); Ōsaka (1 daily; 12hr 30min); Yakushima (1 daily; 3hr).

**Nagasaki** to: Kumamoto (1 daily; 1hr 45min).

**Shimabara** to: Kumamoto (hourly; 1hr); Misumi (6 daily; 1hr).

**Yakushima** to: Ibusuki (1 daily; 2hr); Kagoshima (5 daily; 2hr–3hr 45min); Miyazaki (1 daily; 3hr 10min).

**Flights**

**Fukuoka** to: Auckland (1 weekly; 15hr 45min); Bangkok (3 weekly; 3hr 35min); Beijing (1 daily; 1hr 30min); Hong Kong (1 daily; 3hr); Jakarta (3 weekly; 7hr 15min); Kansai International (6–7 daily; 1hr); Kuala Lumpur (3 weekly; 5hr 25min–7hr 20min); Melbourne (2 weekly; 14hr 20min); Naha (8 daily; 1hr 40min); Ōsaka (Itami; 5 daily; 1hr); Sapporo (4 daily; 2hr 10min); Seoul (1 daily; 1hr 20min); Tokyo (1–3 hourly; 1hr 30min).

**Kagoshima** to: Hong Kong (2 weekly; 1hr 55min); Kansai International (2 daily; 1hr 10min); Nagoya (4 daily; 1hr 25min); Naha (3 daily; 1hr 20min); Ōsaka (Itami; 9 daily; 1hr 10min); Sapporo (1 daily; 2hr 25min); Seoul (3 weekly; 1hr 35min); Tokyo (9 daily; 1hr 50min); Yakushima (4–5 daily; 40min).

**Kumamoto** to: Kansai International (2 daily; 1hr 5min); Naha (1 daily; 1hr 35min); Ōsaka (Itami; 6 daily; 1hr 5min); Seoul (2 weekly; 1hr 30min); Tokyo (8 daily; 1hr 30min).

**Miyazaki** to: Fukuoka (7 daily; 45min); Kansai International (2 daily; 1hr); Nagoya (3 daily; 1hr 10min); Naha (1 daily; 1hr 35min); Ōsaka (Itami; 8 daily; 1hr); Sapporo (3 weekly; 2hr 30min); Tokyo (7 daily; 1hr 30min).

**Nagasaki** to: Kansai International (2–3 daily; 1hr 5min); Naha (1 daily; 1hr 35min); Ōsaka (Itami; 6–7daily; 1hr 10min); Sapporo (2 daily; 2hr 20min); Seoul (2 weekly; 1hr 30min); Shanghai (2 weekly; 40min); Tokyo (9 daily; 1hr 35min).

**Ōita** to: Kansai International (2–3 daily; 1hr); Naha (1 daily; 1hr 35min); Ōsaka (Itami; 5 daily; 50min); Tokyo (8 daily; 1hr 30min).

CHAPTER TEN

# OKINAWA

The prefecture of **Okinawa** comprises more than one hundred islands, stretching over 700km of ocean from Kyūshū southwest to Yonaguni-jima, almost within sight of Taiwan. Collectively known as the **Ryūkyū Shotō**, this chain of sub-tropical islands, with their lush vegetation, paradise beaches and superb coral reefs, has become a popular destination for Japanese holidaymakers and foreign residents alike. Few other tourists make it down here, partly because of the time and cost involved, but if you've had your fill of shrines and temples, or simply fancy a spot of winter sun, then Okinawa is well worth considering.

The largest island in the group, **Okinawa-Hontō**, usually referred to simply as Okinawa, is the region's transport hub and home to its prefectural capital, **Naha**. It's also the most heavily populated and developed of the Ryūkyū chain, thanks largely to the controversial presence of **American military bases.** While it's the remoter islands that are worth concentrating on, Okinawa-Hontō boasts a number of historical sights, many of them associated with the **Battle of Okinawa** at the end of the Pacific War (see p.744). But the island has more to offer, particularly in its northern region, where the old way of life still survives among the isolated villages.

To see the best the region has to offer, you have to hop on a plane or ferry and explore the dozens of **outer islands**, many of which are uninhabited. Even quite close to Naha, you'll find idyllic beaches and fantastic dive spots around the **Kerama islands**, just 30km off the main island. Beach connoisseurs will want to visit **Miyako-jima** and **Ishigaki-jima**, way down the Ryūkyū chain, where the sand consists of gorgeous, star-shaped shells left by tiny sea creatures. **Iriomote-jima** is also known for its wildlife, notably the elusive Iriomote lynx, as well as thick groves of mangrove, palms and steamy rainforest.

It's on these outer islands that you'll also find the strongest evidence of the much-vaunted **Ryūkyū culture**, born of contact with Taiwan and China, as well as Japan. The most obvious features are a vibrant use of colour, and bold, tropical patterns, while the Chinese influence is clearly visible in the architecture and traditional dress. There's also a Ryūkyū dialect, with dozens of variations between the different islands, unique musical instruments, and a distinctive musical style which has recently captured an international

### ACCOMMODATION PRICE CODES

All accommodation in this book has been graded according to the following price codes, which refer to the cheapest double or twin room available for most of the year, and include taxes. Note that rates may increase during peak holiday periods, in particular around Christmas and New Year, the Golden Week (April 28–May 6) and Obon (the week around August 15), when accommodation is very difficult to get without an advance reservation. In the case of hostels providing dormitory accommodation, the code refers to the charge per bed. See p.36 for more details on accommodation.

| | | |
|---|---|---|
| ① under ¥3000 | ④ ¥7000–10,000 | ⑦ ¥20,000–30,000 |
| ② ¥3000–5000 | ⑤ ¥10,000–15,000 | ⑧ ¥30,000–40,000 |
| ③ ¥5000–7000 | ⑥ ¥15,000–20,000 | ⑨ over ¥40,000 |

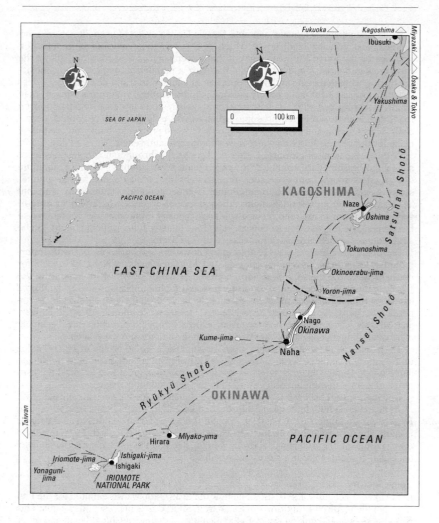

audience. If you're lucky, you'll stumble on a local festival, such as wrestling giant ropes or dragon-boat races, while the biggest annual event is the *Eisa* festival (15th of the sixth lunar month) when everyone downs tools and dances to the incessant rhythms.

Less fertile than mainland Japan, Ryūkyū **cuisine** focuses on sweet potato, pork and bitter melon, with a good helping of fish, of course. Similarly, the **crafts** are less sophisticated than elsewhere in Japan, with the exception of the beautiful *Bingata* textiles. Originally reserved for court ladies, *Bingata* fabrics are hand-dyed with natural pigments from hibiscus flowers and various vegetables, in simple but striking patterns. Ceramics are thought to have been introduced to the region from Spain and Portugal in the fifteenth century, but Ryūkyū potters concentrated on roof tiles and fairly rustic utensils. Nowdays, they churn out thousands of sake flasks and *shiisā* – the ferocious lion figures that glare down at you from every roof top.

Besides Hokkaidō, Okinawa contains Japan's largest areas of unspoilt natural environment and greatest biodiversity. Much of this wealth of **wildlife** is underwater, spawned by the warm Kuroshio current that sweeps up the east coast and allows the coral reefs to flourish. But on land, too, there are a number of unique species, including turtles, a crested eagle and a woodpecker, in addition to Iriomote's wild cat. A less welcome local resident is the highly poisonous **habu snake**. It measures around 2m in length, is dark green with a yellow head, and usually lurks in dense vegetation or on roadsides, though rarely ventures into urban areas. As long as you're careful – especially during spring and autumn – you should have no problems, but if you are bitten, make for the nearest hospital where they should have anti-venom.

With its sub-tropical **climate**, Okinawa stays warm throughout the year. Average annual temperatures are around 23°C, with a winter average of 17°C and a minimum of 10°C. Winter lasts from December through February, while the hot, humid summer starts in April and continues into September. Temperatures at this time hover around 34°C and the sun can be pretty intense, though the sea breezes help. The **best time to visit** is in spring or autumn, roughly March to early May and late September to December. The rainy season lasts from early May to early June, while typhoons can be a problem in July and August, and occasionally into October.

One of the more unusual ways of **getting to Okinawa** – and Japan – is to take the **international ferry** from Taiwan via Ishigaki and Miyako islands to Naha (see p.746 for details). By far the majority of visitors, however, arrive by plane. Most come from the Japanese mainland, though there are **international flights** to Naha from Taiwan, Korea and Hong Kong. **Domestic airlines** operate between Naha and Tokyo, Ōsaka and a number of other Japanese cities (see "travel details", p.766), while a few fly direct to Ishigaki and Miyako. Though flying may seem an expensive option, discounts are becoming increasingly common, so it's always worth asking the airlines and travel agents.

The other option is a **local ferry** from Tokyo, Ōsaka, Kōbe or one of several cities on Kyūshū. All of these services stop in Naha, from where some continue to Miyako and Ishigaki (see p.763 for details). These ferries can be a great way to travel if you're not in a hurry – though horribly crowded in the peak summer season.

**Getting around** between islands presents a similar choice between air and sea, with Naha as the main hub. Inter-island **flights** are operated by Japan Transocean Air (JTA), Ryūkyū Air Commuter (RAC) and Air Nippon (ANK), with connections to all the major islands. The **ferry** network, on the other hand, fans out from Naha's three terminals to every corner of the prefecture, allowing you to island-hop at your leisure. See individual island accounts for more about these sailings.

### Some history

In the fifteenth century, the islands that now make up Okinawa were united for the first time into the **Ryūkyū kingdom**, governed from Shuri Castle in present-day Naha. This period is seen as the golden era of Ryūkyū culture. Trade with China, Japan and other Southeast Asian countries flourished, while the traditionally non-militarized kingdom maintained its independence by paying **tribute to China**. But then, in 1609, the **Shimazu** clan of Kagoshima (southern Kyūshū) invaded. The Ryūkyū kings became **vassals** to the Shimazu, who imposed punitive taxes and ruled with an iron hand for the next two hundred years, using the islands as a gateway for trade with China when such contact was technically outlawed. When the Japanese feudal system was abolished in the 1870s, the islands were simply annexed to the mainland as **Okinawa Prefecture**. Against much local opposition, the Meiji government established a military base and tried to eradicate local culture by forcing people to speak Japanese and swear allegiance to the emperor, forbidding schools to teach Ryūkyū history.

By the early twentieth century, Okinawa had been fairly successfully absorbed into Japan and became a key pawn in Japan's last line of defence during the **Pacific War**.

Following the battle of Iwō-jima in March 1945, the American fleet advanced on Okinawa and, after an extensive preliminary bombardment, referred to locally as a "typhoon of steel", the Americans invaded on **April 1, 1945**. It then took nearly three months of bitter fighting before General Ushijima, the Japanese commander, committed suicide on June 23 and the island surrendered. The **Battle of Okinawa** left 12,500 American troops dead (plus 37,000 casualties) and an estimated 250,000 on the Japanese side, nearly half of whom were local civilians.

It's estimated that one third of the population of Okinawa died in the war, many in **mass suicides** that preceded the surrender, and others from disease and starvation. But the islanders' subsequent anger has been directed at the Japanese government rather than America. Most people feel that Okinawa was **sacrificed** to save the mainland – this was the only major battle fought on Japanese soil – and that they were misled by Japanese assurances that they were luring the American fleet into a trap. Compounding this was the behaviour of Japanese troops, who are accused of denying locals shelter and medical treatment, and ultimately of abandoning them to the Americans.

By comparison, the American invaders were a welcome relief, despite the islanders' worst fears. They brought in much-needed food supplies – Spam was an instant hit in this pork-loving country – and gradually helped restore the local economy. This wasn't wholly altruistic, of course, since Okinawa was ideally placed for monitoring events in Southeast Asia. As the 1950s Korean War merged into the Vietnam War, so the **American bases** became a permanent feature of the Okinawa landscape (see box, p.757). In fact, Okinawa remained under **American jurisdiction** until 1972, when local protests forced them to return it to **Japanese sovereignty**. Since then, the two governments have colluded to maintain an American military presence on the island despite growing opposition, which reached a peak when three American servicemen were found guilty of raping a 12-year-old school-girl in 1995. In response to this and other incidents, local leader **Governor Ota** has made increasingly vociferous demands for a complete withdrawal of the military by 2015.

# Okinawa-Hontō

Once the centre of the Ryūkyū kingdom, **Okinawa-Hontō**, or Okinawa Main Island, is a strangely ambivalent place. Locals are fiercely proud of their Ryūkyū heritage and yet the competing cultures of Japan and America are far more prevalent. It was these two countries – both of whom invaded and occupied Okinawa – who fought it out on the island's middle and southern reaches in 1945. To some extent, the island still feels like occupied territory, especially central Okinawa, where the **American bases** and the nearby "American" towns, with their drive-ins and shopping malls, have become a bizarre tourist attraction for mainland Japanese come to soak up a bit of American culture.

Fascinating though all this is, it doesn't make Okinawa the most obvious holiday destination. However, if you're drawn by the more appealing outer islands (see p.760), the chances are you'll spend some time on the main island waiting for plane or ferry connections. Okinawa's chief city and the former Ryūkyū capital is **Naha**, whose prime attraction is its reconstructed castle, **Shuri-jō**. There are also some interesting market streets and a pottery village to explore, and you'll want to take advantage of its banks – not to mention its excellent bars and restaurants – before heading off to remoter regions.

Southern Okinawa saw the worst fighting in 1945, and the scrubby hills are littered with **war memorials**, particularly around Mabuni Hill, where the final battles took place. North of Naha, the island's central district has little to recommend it, but beyond Kadena the buildings start to thin out. Here you'll find one of the better "Ryūkyū culture villages", **Ryūkyū-mura**, and the island's best beaches. The largest settlement in northern Okinawa, **Nago** is a more appealing town which provides a base for exploring

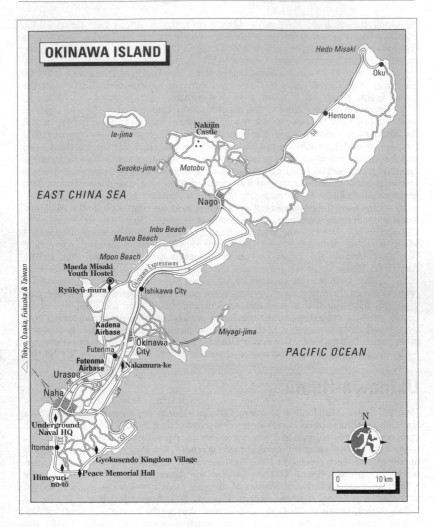

**OKINAWA ISLAND**

Hedo Misaki

Oku

Hentona

Ie-jima

Nakijin
Castle

Sesoko-jima    Motobu

EAST CHINA SEA

Nago

Inbu Beach
Manza Beach

Moon Beach

Maeda Misaki
Youth Hostel

Okinawa Expressway

Ryūkyū-mura    Ishikawa City

Kadena
Airbase

Miyagi-jima

Futenma

Futenma
Airbase    Okinawa
City

Urasoe    Nakamura-ke

PACIFIC OCEAN

Naha

Underground
Naval HQ

Itoman

Gyokusendo Kingdom Village

Himeyuri-
no-tō    Peace Memorial Hall

N

0    10 km

*Tokyo, Osaka, Fukuoka & Taiwan*

this empty, mountainous region. Again there are few specific sights, though the
scenery improves dramatically towards **Hedo Misaki**, Okinawa's north cape.

Long and thin, Okinawa measures just 135km from tip to toe, so you can drive the
whole length in a matter of hours. The best way to get around is to rent your own car,
particularly if you want to explore the northern hills, but most places are accessible by
local bus – eventually.

## Naha

Most people find themselves passing through **NAHA** at some time on their visit to
these islands. It's not a particularly attractive city, a mix of municipal blocks and

parades of tacky souvenir shops catering to the constant stream of Japanese holiday-makers, but while you're waiting for onward transport there a couple of sights to aim for. For more than four centuries Naha was the capital of the Ryūkyū kingdom, and makes much of its royal heritage. Thanks to the war, virtually no relics survive, but the beautifully reconstructed **Shuri-jō**, the king's small, solid castle, constitutes the city's major attraction. The Shuri area also contains a moderately informative Prefectural Museum, as well as some original royal graves and stone-paved lanes. After exploring the central **Tsuboya** pottery district, however, there's not a lot else to detain you.

## Arrival, information and city transport

Naha **airport** occupies a promontory some 3km southwest of the city centre. Of the three terminals, Terminal 1 handles domestic flights from mainland Japan; Terminal 2 flights from Okinawa's outer islands, and Terminal 3 international carriers. From the airport you can either take a taxi (15min; around ¥800) into central Naha, or one of the local buses (#7, #24, #120, #111 and #102) departing from outside the terminal buildings (20min; ¥190).

The new **ferry port**, Naha Shin-kō, lies north of the city. Most ferries, including those from Fukuoka, Ōsaka, Kōbe, Nagoya, Tokyo and Taiwan, dock here, while slow boats from Kagoshima and Fukuoka pull in further south at the old Naha Port. Naha Shin-kō is on the #101 bus route into central Naha (1–3 hourly; 25min; ¥190), while Naha Port is more conveniently located only about fifteen minutes' walk from the main Naha Bus Terminal (see below).

Naha's **tourist information** services comprise a desk in Terminal 1 of the airport (daily 9am–9pm; ☎098/857-6884), and a quieter office on the ground floor of the Palette Kumoji department store (daily 9am–6pm; ☎098/866-7515), at the south end of the city's main shopping street, Kokusai-dōri. Both offices have English-speaking staff, plentiful maps and brochures, and can help with hotel reservations and car rental.

Apart from taxis, the only way to get around Naha is by **local bus**, since the city is sufficiently spread out to make walking impractical. The bus system is pretty comprehensive, with frequent services on the main routes, but traffic often grid-locks at peak times, so don't expect to zip around. Nearly all buses, including long-distance services, start from or pass by Naha Bus Terminal, on the south side of the city. Although there's no information in English, buses show the route number on the front, with the destination in *kanji*. Lines #1 to 17 operate within the city, while #20 and above go further afield. One of the most useful city routes is #7, running from Naha airport to Naha Bus Terminal and then north along Kokusai-dōri to terminate at Shuri-jō. Payment is straightforward as there's a flat fare of ¥190 within the city. Pay this to the driver as you get on city buses (routes #1–17), but on other buses take a numbered ticket on entry and pay at your destination. If you're going to be using the buses a lot, it's worth picking up the island-wide timetable from the bus terminal.

## Accommodation

Naha has a fair number of smart tour-group **hotels**, but isn't particularly blessed with good-value rooms at the middle and lower end of the market. Rooms are hard to come by in the peak holiday seasons – Golden Week, August and New Year – when rates may rise by up to forty percent. That said, Naha does possess one of Japan's plushest youth hostels, and one or two other reasonable options which are detailed below.

**Capsule Inn Okinawa**, Asato, Kokusai-dōri (☎098/867-6017). Capsule hotel for both men and women, at the north end of Kokusai-dōri. Men have the choice of standard or deluxe capsules. Check in from 3pm. ②.

**Harumi Youth Hostel**, 2-22-10 Tomari (☎098/867-3218). The older, smaller and marginally cheaper of Naha's two youth hostels, on the northwest edge of town near the Tomari ferry port, though still a good hike from the centre. It's on bus route #24 from the airport, #101 from Naha Shin-kō and #3 from Naha Port; get off at the Tomari Takahashi stop. ①.

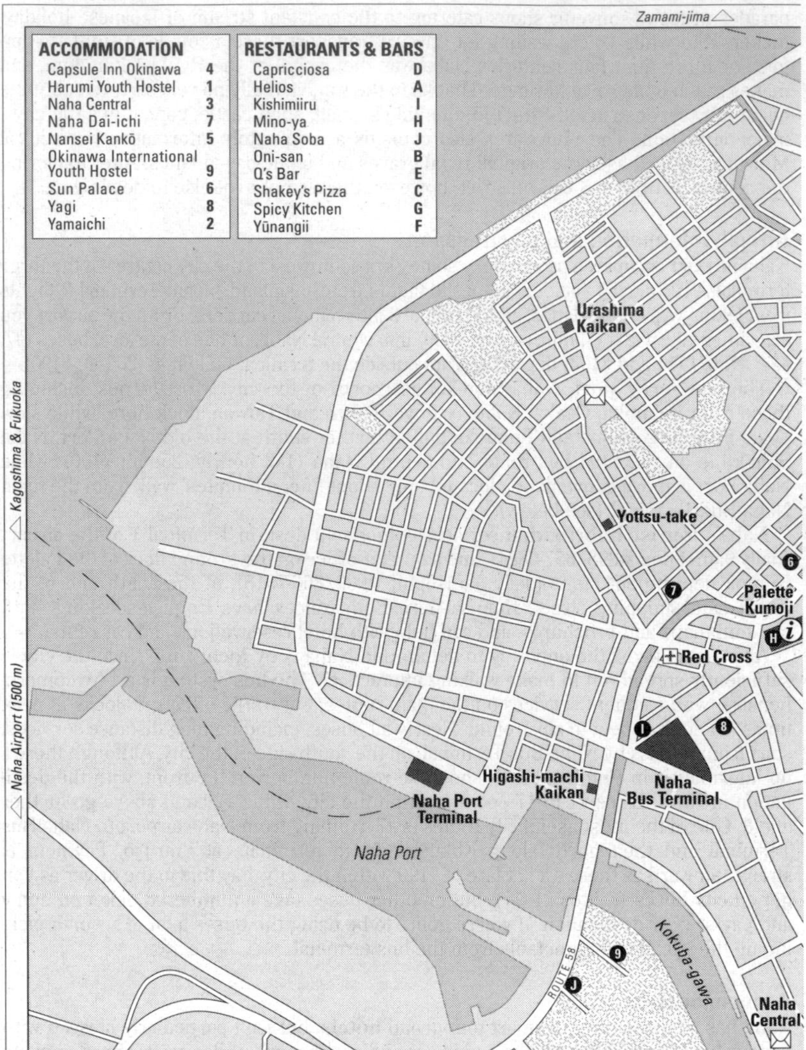

ACCOMMODATION
Capsule Inn Okinawa 4
Harumi Youth Hostel 1
Naha Central 3
Naha Dai-ichi 7
Nansei Kankō 5
Okinawa International Youth Hostel 9
Sun Palace 6
Yagi 8
Yamaichi 2
RESTAURANTS & BARS
Capricciosa D
Helios A
Kishimiiru I
Mino-ya H
Naha Soba J
Oni-san B
Q's Bar E
Shakey's Pizza C
Spicy Kitchen G
Yūnangii F
Zamami-jima
Kagoshima & Fukuoka
Naha Airport (1500 m)
Itoman
Urashima Kaikan
Yottsu-take
Palette Kumoji
Red Cross
Naha Bus Terminal
Higashi-machi Kaikan
Naha Port Terminal
Naha Port
Route 58
Kokuba-gawa
Naha Central


**Naha Central Hotel**, 2-16-36 Makishi (☎098/862-6070, fax 862-6109). This good-value hotel lies just off Kokusai-dōri behind Mitsukoshi department store. Rooms are on the small side, but nicely decorated and a notch above the competition. ⑤.

**Naha Dai-ichi Hotel**, 2-2-7 Kume (☎098/868-0111, fax 868-0555). One of the cheaper options in central Naha, this no-frills business hotel with boxy, en-suite rooms gets booked up. It's on Highway 58, west of the Palette store. ④–⑤.

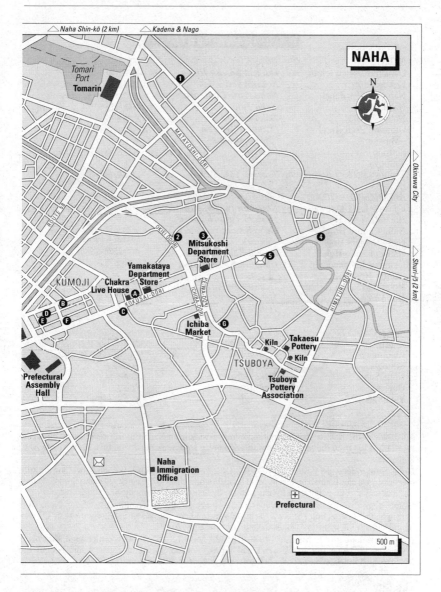

**Nansei Kankō Hotel**, 3-13-23 Makishi (☎098/862-7144, fax 862-7110). Another decent, mid-range hotel towards the north end of Kokusai-dōri, boasting bright, comfortable rooms with TV, phone and bath as standard. ⑨.

**Okinawa International Youth Hostel**, 51 Ōnoyama (☎098/857-0073, fax 859-3567). Naha's swish new hostel offers bunk-bed dorms, each with its own TV, sofa and wash basin. They also have a sauna, small shop and coin laundry and can arrange diving trips and bike rental. The hostel's on the

## OKINAWA-HONTŌ

| | | |
|---|---|---|
| Naha | *Naha* | 那覇 |
| Dai-ichi Kōsetsu Ichiba | *Dai-ichi Kōsetsu Ichiba* | 第一公設市場 |
| Kokusai-dōri | *Kokusai-dōri* | 国際通り |
| Naha Bus Terminal | *Naha Basu Tāminaru* | 那覇バスターミナル |
| Naha Port | *Naha Futō* | 那覇埠頭 |
| Naha Shin-kō | *Naha Shin-kō* | 那覇新港 |
| Okinawa Prefectural | *Okinawa Kenritsu* | 沖縄県立博物館 |
| Museum | *Hakubutsukan* | |
| Shuri-jō | *Shuri-jō* | 首里城 |
| Tsuboya | *Tsuboya* | 壺屋 |
| Tsuboya Pottery Association | *Tsuboya Tōki Kaikan* | 壺屋陶器会館 |

*ACCOMMODATION*

| | | |
|---|---|---|
| Capsule Inn Okinawa | *Kapuseru In Okinawa* | カプセルイン沖縄 |
| Harumi Youth Hostel | *Harumi Yūsu Hosuteru* | 春海ユースホステル |
| Naha Central Hotel | *Naha Sentoraru Hoteru* | 那覇セントラルホテル |
| Naha Dai-ichi Hotel | *Naha Dai-ichi Hoteru* | 那覇第一ホテル |
| Nansei Kankō Hotel | *Nansei Kankō Hoteru* | 南西観光ホテル |
| Okinawa International | *Okinawa Kokusai Yūsu* | 沖縄国際ユースホステル |
| Youth Hostel | *Hosuteru* | |
| Hotel Sun Palace | *Hoteru San Paresu* | ホテルサンパレス |
| Hotel Yagi | *Hoteru Yagi* | ホテルやぎ |
| Hotel Yamaichi | *Hoteru Yamaichi* | ホテル山市 |

*RESTAURANTS*

| | | |
|---|---|---|
| Capricciosa | *Kapurichōza* | カプリチョーザ |
| Kishimiiru | *Kishimiiru* | きしみーる |
| Mino-ya | *Mino-ya* | みの屋 |
| Naha Soba | *Naha Soba* | 那覇そば |
| Oni-san | *Oni-san* | 鬼さん |
| Yūnangii | *Yūnangii* | ゆうなんぎい |

south side of the Kokuba-gawa, about ten minutes' walk from Naha Bus Terminal, or on bus route #7, #24 or #102 from the airport. From the Kōen-mae stop, walk north and turn right beside *KFC*. ②.

**Hotel Sun Palace**, 2-5-1 Kumoji (☎098/863-4181, fax 861-1313). Small balconies overflowing with greenery are a nice flourish on this pleasant hotel, beside a canal to the north of Palette Kumoji. Rooms are light and airy, though it's worth upgrading to the more spacious double or standard twin. ⑤.

**Hotel Yagi**, 1-16-10 Izumizaki (☎098/862-3008, fax 862-3028). Handily placed for Naha Bus Terminal, this budget hotel offers a warm welcome and cheery Western-style rooms with TV, telephone and a small bathroom. Rates include breakfast. ④–⑤.

**Hotel Yamaichi**, 2-16-13 Makishi (☎098/866-5421, fax 867-3713). Though rather aged, the rooms in this small, family-run hotel aren't bad for the location, west of Kokusai-dōri behind the Mitsukoshi store. There's a choice of Western or *tatami* rooms, some with bathroom. ④.

## The City

Central Naha is bordered to the south by the Kokuba-gawa which flows into Naha Port, and to the west by Highway 58. About 500m north of the river, **Kokusai-dōri** cuts northeast from the highway, past the Palette Kumoji department store and Prefectural Assembly Hall. The city's main thoroughfare, nearly 2km long, it's lined with a strange mix of classy boutiques, souvenir stalls and army-surplus outlets. Follow the road northeast and it eventually leads to **Shuri-jō**, where the castle's vivid palaces lie hidden

**Southern Okinawa**

| | | |
|---|---|---|
| Gyokusendo Kingdom Village | *Gyokusendō Ōkoku-mura* | 玉泉洞王国村 |
| Himeyuri-no-tō | *Himeyuri-no-tō* | ひめゆりの塔 |
| Mabuni Hill | *Mabuni-no-oka* | 摩文仁の丘 |
| Underground Naval Headquarters | *Kyū Kaigun Shireibugō* | 旧海軍司令部壕 |

**Central Okinawa**

| | | |
|---|---|---|
| Hotel City Plaza | *Hoteru Shitii Puraza* | ホテルシティープラザ |
| Maeda Misaki Youth Hostel | *Maeda Misaki Yūsu Hosuteru* | 真栄田岬ユースホステル |
| Nakamura-ke | *Nakamura-ke* | 中村家 |
| Nakagusuku-jō ruins | *Nakagusuku-jō-seki* | 中城城跡 |
| Okinawa City | *Okinawa-shi* | 沖縄市 |
| Ryūkyū-mura | *Ryūkyū-mura* | 琉球村 |
| Sunrise Hotel | *Sanraizu Hoteru* | サンライズホテル |

**Northern Okinawa**

| | | |
|---|---|---|
| **Nago** | *Nago* | 名護 |
| Akachōchin | *Akachōchin* | あかちょうちん |
| Nago Museum | *Nago Hakubutsukan* | 名護博物館 |
| Hotel Shiroyama | *Hoteru Shiroyama* | ホテル城山 |
| Hotel Tōwa | *Hoteru Tōwa* | ホテル東和 |
| Yamabuki | *Yamabuki* | 山吹 |
| Yamada-sō | *Yamada-sō* | 山田荘 |

| | | |
|---|---|---|
| Hedo Misaki | *Hedo Misaki* | 辺戸岬 |
| Hentona | *Hentona* | 辺土名 |
| Minshuku Miyagi | *Minshuku Miyagi* | 民宿みやざ |
| Nakijin-jō ruins | *Nakijin-jō-seki* | 今帰仁城跡 |
| Oku | *Oku* | 奥 |

behind stout walls. Alternatively, head east from Kokusai-dōri through the backstreets to the **Tsuboya** district. Famous for its pottery kilns, Tsuboya is a pleasing, compact area of little workshops and dusty galleries.

## SHURI-JŌ AND AROUND

Perched on a hill to the northeast of central Naha, **Shuri-jō** (daily 9am–5.30/6pm; ¥800) served as the royal residence of the Ryūkyū kings from the early fifteenth century until 1879. Elaborate ceremonies took place in the castle's opulent throne room, on occasion attended by envoys from China and, later, from Kyūshū. The present buildings date from the early 1990s, painstakingly restored in the original style, and are mainly of interest for their distinctive blend of Chinese and Japanese architecture. To reach the castle, take bus #7 from Naha Bus Terminal or Kokusai-dōri (every 15–20min; 30min). It terminates underneath the modern **Suimuikan** information and shopping centre, where you can get a fairly sketchy English-language map of the area. It's also worth popping into the small exhibition room for the short video about Shuri-jō and Ryūkyū culture (every 20min; free).

The castle's main entrance lies across the road from the Suimuikan, through the decorative **Shurei-mon**. This outer gate is a popular spot for group photos, but the inner **Kankai-mon** is a far more impressive structure, its no-nonsense guard tower flanked by sun-baked limestone walls. Inside there's yet another defensive wall and no less than three more gates – the last now housing the ticket office – before you reach the central courtyard. Pride of place goes to the **Seiden**, a double-roofed palace with an immense, colourful porch and two throne halls. From the more elaborate, upper throne room, the king, surrounded by gilded dragons writhing against lustrous red and black lacquer, would review his troops or watch ceremonies in the courtyard below. Other buildings house remnants of the dynasty and details of the restoration work, but no English explanations to bring them alive.

Exiting Shuri-jō, a quiet park featuring a stone-walled pond and old trees lies across the road. The pond's pretty, island pavilion once belonged to **Enkaku-ji**, which was built in 1492 as the local headquarters of the Rinzai sect; it was said to have been the most impressive structure in the kingdom. Nowdays only a few shell-pocked walls remain of the original temple, east of the pond. Heading northwest, along the banks of an elongated lake, you soon reach the **Okinawa Prefectural Museum** (Tues–Sun 9am–5pm; ¥200) which provides a good overview of local history and culture.

Buses back into central Naha (#1, #12, #13 and #17) stop outside the museum. If you've got time to kill, walk back to the main road west of Shuri-jō, where the sixteenth-century **mausoleum** of King Sho En still survives in a walled compound known as the **Tama-udōn** (daily 9am–5.30pm; ¥200). More like a fortress than a grave, the burial chambers stand across a dirt forecourt, with the easternmost reserved for the kings; unfortunately, you can't go inside. Instead, you can continue downhill (west) from the mausoleum and take the next lane left, working your way round to the south of the castle through an attractive residential area, **Kinjō-chō**. These **stone-paved lanes** were laid in 1522 to link Naha town with its castle. You can follow them all the way down and catch a bus at the bottom, but services are few and far between; it's better to hike back up to the castle bus stops.

## *ICHIBA-DŌRI AND TSUBOYA*

Roughly halfway up central Naha's Kokusai-dōri, near Mitsukoshi department store, look out for the **Ichiba-dōri** and **Heiwa-dōri** shopping arcades. Among the souvenir stalls and discount outlets, these streets host a number of lively **markets**, of which the best is Ichiba's food market, **Dai-ichi Kōsetsu Ichiba** – its narrow entrance is marked by festive international flags. The ground-floor stalls are piled high with sweet-smelling tropical fruits, ice-packed arrays of multicoloured fish and mysterious, spiny crabs. You'll see fishmongers deftly slicing sashimi, some of it destined for the **food stalls** upstairs (10am–8pm). If you're a sashimi fan, then this is a good place to fill up – prices are reasonable and the fish doesn't come much fresher.

From the market, walk north onto Heiwa-dōri and follow it east. After a few minutes you'll emerge in the pottery village of **Tsuboya**. This compact area has been the centre of local pottery production since 1682, when the government gathered a number of workshops together, of which around ten are still in operation. Traditionally they produced large jars for storing the local liquor (*awamori*) and miso paste, but nowdays concentrate on smaller items for the tourist market, typically half-moon-shaped sake flasks and snarling *shiisā* lions. As you walk along the main road, keep an eye out on your left for a traditional climbing kiln up on the embankment; constructed in the 1680s, this is one of very few original kilns still intact. There are also a number of **showrooms** along the main road, of which the biggest is the Tsuboya Pottery Association (daily 9am–6pm), at the far east end, displaying a range of different styles.

Wander the back lanes and you'll also stumble across working **potteries**. Take the lane heading north in front of the Pottery Association shop, for example, turn right at the next junction and then into what looks like a private gateway immediately on your left; to the right of the lovely old house you'll see a tumble-down, 300-year-old climbing kiln. Back at the junction, follow the lane north and then west, past the **Takaesu**

**Pottery**, and keep going along the hillside for an attractive route looping back down to the main street.

## Eating, drinking and entertainment

As you would expect, **Okinawa cuisine** blends Chinese and Japanese cooking styles, with a good dose of tropical ingredients and fresh seafood. Among the most common dishes, *Okinawa soba* is a filling bowl of thick noodles and pork chunks, while *chanpuru* combines stir-fried vegetables in a thicker stew. It comes in many varieties, depending on the principal ingredient; look out for *chanpuru* made with sponge gourd (*nabera*), bitter melon (*goya*), wheat gluten (*fu*) and wheat noodle (*sōmen*).

You can try these dishes in the Ichiba-dōri market (see opposite) and also at several of the **restaurants** listed below. Kokusai-dōri is probably the best single area to trawl for eating places, particularly in the Kumoji district, north of the Palette Kumoji building, which is full of atmospheric bars, restaurants and *izakaya*. Palette itself has a decent choice of outlets on the ninth floor, plus a decent basement food hall, though not as good as the Mitsukoshi department store.

In recent years, **Okinawa music** has experienced something of a revival, with bands such as NeNe's, Diamantes and Champloose winning international acclaim. You can hear local bands most nights at the Chakra Live House on Kokusai-dōri (7pm–2am; ¥1500–3000; ☎098/869-0283). Naha is also a good place to catch performances of traditional **Ryūkyū court dance**, particularly if you coincide with the weekly show in the Higashi-machi Kaikan, just north of the Kokuba-gawa. Performances are usually on Tuesday evening (8pm; ¥2500), but check with the tourist office for the current schedule, and note that there's ¥500 discount on advance tickets. The alternative is a more expensive dinner show where you'll pay from around ¥3000–5000 up for a meal, sometimes including *tōndā-bun* – beautifully presented royal hors d'oeuvres. Two of the best-known venues are *Yottsu-take*, 2-22-1 Kume (☎098/866-3333), and *Urashima Kaikan*, 1-14-8 Wakasa (☎098/861-1769), both in the backstreets west of Highway 58.

### BARS AND RESTAURANTS

**Capricciosa**, 3-11-22 Kumoji. The popular Italian chain has been an instant success in Naha. Prices look expensive, but most dishes are enough for two. Daily 11am–10.30pm.

**Helios**, Matsuo 2-chōme, Kokusai-dōri. This stylish "craft beer pub", south of the Yamakataya store, belongs to a micro brewery offering three types of home brew – Pale Ale, Weizen and Pilsner. Bar snacks till 5pm. Daily 11am–midnight.

**Kishimiiru**, 1-22-1 Izumizaki. Relaxed reggae *izakaya*, with wooden tables, the inevitable Bob Marley posters and a range of tasty dishes. You'll eat well for under ¥2000 a head. Mon–Sat 6pm–5am, Sun 6pm–1am.

**Mino-ya**, 9F, Palette Kumoji, 1-1-1 Kumoji. Café-style restaurant that's low on atmosphere but serves well-rated local cuisine at a good price. Try their *Minoya soba*, or one of the *chanpuru* dishes.

**Naha Soba**, Highway 331, Ōnoyama. No prizes for guessing the house speciality at this rustic noodle house near the *International Youth Hostel*. Naha soba is laced with pork, ginger and spring onion, and they also offer a variety of reasonably priced set meals. From the hostel turning, walk south along the highway, then turn left just before the footbridge. Daily 10am–9.30pm.

**Oni-san**, B1, 3-12-4 Kumoji. Large, upbeat *izakaya* with a goofy devil on the *noren* curtain. The food's good and prices are reasonable. Daily 5pm–1am.

**Q's Bar**, B1, 3-9-3 Kumoji. Cool jazz bar on the corner southwest of *Capricciosa* (see above), decked out with primitive art, mellow fabrics and big vats of *awamori*. Cover charge ¥300. Daily 6pm–1am.

**Shakey's Pizza**, Matsuo 2-chōme, Kokusai-dōri. *Shakey's* is infamous for its lunchtime feeding frenzy when they lay on an eat-all-you-can pasta and pizza buffet (10am–3pm; ¥600). Daily 11am–11pm.

**Spicy Kitchen**, Sakurazaka-dōri, Makishi 3-chōme. Look out for the chilli-pepper mural on this cheery Indian restaurant up a lane near the east end of Heiwa-dōri. The simple menu includes chicken, mutton and seafood curries from ¥1000, plus a range of vegetarian dishes and a good lunch deal for ¥700. Daily except Wed noon–4pm & 6–9.30pm.

**Suimui**, Suimuikan, Shuri-jō. Surprisingly good garden-view restaurant in the Shuri-jō information centre (see p.751), serving Okinawa dishes as well as mainstream Japanese and Western meals. Not to be confused with the noisy snack bar. Daily 9am–5.30/6pm.

**Yūnangii**, 3-3-3 Kumoji. Country-style restaurant with a warm welcome serving Okinawa cuisine, including *Okinawa soba, chanpuru* and various pork dishes. Set meals from around ¥1300, with free rice refills. Mon–Sat noon–3pm & 5.30–10.30pm.

## Listings

**Airlines** ANK (☎0120–029222); Asiana Airlines (☎098/869-7701); China Airlines (☎098/863-1013); JAL (domestic ☎0120–255971; international ☎0120–255931); Japan Asia Airlines (☎098/861-1261); JTA (☎0120–255971); Ryūkyū Air Commuter (☎098/858-3291).

**Airport information** ☎098/857-6856.

**Banks and exchange** The Ryūkyū Bank branch in the airport arrival lobby (Mon–Fri 9am–3pm) only exchanges dollars (cash or travellers' cheques); when they're closed the central information counter can change up to $50 cash. In Naha itself, banks along Kokusai-dōri have foreign exchange desks, or try the main branch of the Okinawa Bank (north of Palette Kumoji), or the Ryūkyū Bank (west on the same road). Naha Central Post Office (see below) also handles foreign exchange, from 9am–4pm on weekdays only. Note that no ATM machines in Naha accept foreign-issued credit cards. To withdraw cash on a Visa card apply to the Ryūkyū Bank or Okinawa Bank; Kaihō Bank handles Mastercard transactions.

**Car and bike rental** Nippon Rent-a-car (☎098/868-4554), Japaren (☎0120–413900), Toyota (☎098/857-0100) and Hertz (☎098/867-0082) all have representatives in both Naha airport and the city centre. You can rent motorbikes at Helmet Shop SEA, 3-15-50 Makishi (☎098/864-5116), west of Kokusai-dōri, while the *International Youth Hostel* has mountain bikes at ¥1600 per day.

**Consulates** Korea, 2-15-3 Kumoji (☎098/867-6940); United States, 2564 Nishihara, Urasoe City (☎098/876-4211).

**Emergencies** In addition to the usual emergency number (see Basics, p.70), you can also call an ambulance on ☎098/938-1726 for help anywhere on the island.

**Ferries** The RKK Line (☎098/868-1126) operates ferries to Ōsaka, Fukuoka and Kagoshima. "A" Line, also known as Ōshima Unyu (☎098/861-1886), sails to Tokyo, Ōsaka, Kōbe, Miyazaki, Kagoshima and islands in the Satsunan chain. Marix Line (☎098/862-8774) specializes in slow boats through the Satsunan islands to Kagoshima. Arimura Sangyō (☎098/860-1980) boats stop in Naha on their way from Ōsaka to Taiwan, and also call at Miyako and Ishigaki. Most of these ferries depart from Naha Shin-kō, north of town on the #101 bus route, but a few use Naha Port (bus #24), so check when you buy your tickets. For details of ferries to other Okinawa islands, see the individual accounts later in this chapter.

**Festivals** Shuri-jō is the venue for traditional Ryūkyū New Year celebrations (Jan 2–3) and the Shuri-jō Festival (Nov 1–3), featuring a parade of Ryūkyū-dynasty clothing, dance displays and other performing arts.

**Hospitals and medical care** In central Naha, there's the Red Cross Hospital, 1-3-8 Kumoji (☎098/853-3134). If you need an English-speaking doctor, however, your best bet is the Adventist Medical Centre (☎098/946-2833), on Route 29 northeast of Naha.

**Immigration office** To renew your visa apply to the Naha Immigration Office, 1-15-15 Higawa (☎098/832-4185), on Route 221 southeast of Kokusai-dōri.

**Police** 1-2-9 Izumuzaki (☎098/836-0110)

**Post offices** Naha Central Post Office, inconveniently located on the south side of town, accepts poste restante. For ordinary services, you'll find a sub-post office in Palette Kumoji and another at the north end of Kokusai-dōri beside the *Nansei Kankō Hotel*.

**Shopping** Kokusai-dōri and the Ichiba-dōri arcades are the places to trawl for souvenirs. Shops specializing in local crafts include the high-quality Okinawa Busan Centre (daily 9am–7pm), northeast of Palette Kumoji, and the smaller Okinawa Craft Shop (daily 10am–8pm), behind Mitsukoshi. Shuri-jō's Suimuikan also has a decent craft shop. Kokusai-dōri's Tower Records stocks the biggest range of English-language books and magazines.

**Taxis** If you give a couple of days' notice, Okinawa-ken Taxi Association (☎098/868-1344) can arrange English-speaking drivers.

**Travel agents** For domestic travel, phone JTB on ☎098/864-1321 or Okinawa Tourist ☎098/933-1152. The latter can also help with international tickets, as can International Travel on ☎098/933-0690.

# Southern Okinawa

During the long-drawn-out Battle of Okinawa (see p.745), it was the area **south of Naha** that saw the worst fighting and received the heaviest bombardment. Not only was the **Japanese Navy Headquarters** dug deep into the hills here, but also the region's many limestone caves provided shelter for hundreds of Japanese troops and local civilians, many of whom committed suicide rather than be taken prisoner. One of these caves has been preserved as a memorial to the young **Himeyuri** nurses who died there, and the area is dotted with peace parks and prayer halls. It's not completely devoted to war sights, however. **Gyokusendo Kingdom Village**, over on the southeast coast, combines a stalactite-filled cave with a rather dubious tourist village dedicated to Ryūkyū culture.

By far the best way of **getting around** this area is by car, allowing you the freedom to explore some of the coves and beaches on the east coast. Exploring by bus, on the other hand, involves a lot of waiting for connections. The alternative is to join one of the organized bus tours out of Naha, which pack a lot into a short time and at a reasonable price. Four companies offer almost identical southern tours, of which Naha Kōtsū (☎098/868-3750) has the widest choice, running full-day and half-day tours from the Tomarin Building in northwest Naha. Both cost ¥4800 and cover the same sights, though on the one-day tour you also visit Naha's Shuri-jō (see p.751; entrance ticket extra) and stop for lunch (included in the price). You can buy tickets on the first floor of the Tomarin Building, or ask at Naha's tourist information offices (see p.747).

## Underground Naval Headquarters

For centuries, Tomishiro-jō has stood on the low hills looking north over Naha. During the Pacific War the spot was chosen for the headquarters of the Japanese navy, but, instead of using the old fortifications, they tunnelled 20m down into the soft limestone. The complex, consisting of Rear Admiral Ota's command room and various operations rooms, is now preserved as the **Underground Naval Headquarters** (daily 8.30am–5pm; ¥410). If you're travelling by bus, take route #33 from central Naha to the Tomishiro-jiroshi-kōen stop (1–2 hourly; 25min; ¥220), from where it's a ten-minute walk uphill to the ticket gate. Inside, there are a few photos of the 1945 battle, but little else to see beyond holes gouged in the plaster walls; they're said to be grim reminders of where Ota and 175 of his men killed themselves with hand grenades on June 13 as the Americans closed in. Beside the tunnel entrance there's a small museum and a monument to the 4000 Japanese troops who died in this area.

## Himeyuri-no-tō

Heading south down the coast, Highway 331 passes through **ITOMAN** town and then cuts inland across the peninsula to **Himeyuri-no-tō** (9am–5pm; ¥300). From the naval headquarters, bus #33 continues to Itoman (1–2 hourly; 40min; ¥370), where you might have to wait a while for the #108, which runs mostly in the morning and late afternoon (20min; ¥200). Himeyuri-no-tō is another war memorial, this time dedicated to more than two hundred schoolgirls and their teachers who committed suicide here in a shallow cave. The nearby **museum** (daily 9am–5pm; ¥300) describes how the highschool students, like many others on Okinawa, were conscripted as trainee nurses by the Japanese army in the spring of 1945. As the fighting became more desperate the girls were sent to a Field Hospital, gradually retreating south from cave to cave, and were then abandoned altogether as the Japanese army disintegrated. Terrified that they would be raped and tortured by the Americans, the women and girls killed themselves rather than be captured.

## Mabuni hill and Gyokusendo Kingdom Village

The final battle for Okinawa took place on **Mabuni hill**, on the island's southeast coast. The site is now occupied by a grassy park and the **Peace Memorial Hall** (daily 9am–5/5.30pm; ¥520), its distinctive white tower sheltering a large, lacquered Buddha. Around the park there are various other monuments to the more than 200,000 troops – both Japanese and American – and civilians who died on Okinawa. The entrance to the park lies on bus route #82 from Itoman (9 daily; 30min; ¥220); the same bus will then take you on to **Gyokusendo Kingdom Village** (daily 9am–5/5.30pm; ¥1050, or ¥1470 including Habu Park). The recently created "village" is a showcase of local crafts and culture, including *Bingata* dyeing, *awamori* brewing and performances of Eisa dances (11.30am & 1pm). It's built over a 900-metre-long cave with an impressive array of rock formations along an underground river, but the most popular attraction is the Habu Park. Here you can mug for the cameras with a python and watch a dopey cobra being dispatched by a mongoose. Afterwards, bus #83 will take you back to central Naha in around one hour (8 daily; ¥490).

# Central Okinawa

North of Naha, traffic on Highway 58 crawls up the coast of **central Okinawa** between a strip of McDonald's, Shakey's Pizza and used car lots on one side, and neat rows of artillery on the other. This is army country, where huge tracts of land are occupied by the **American military** (see box opposite). Kinser, Hoster and Lester camps, and the vast Kadena Airbase extend along the coast as far north as the Maeda peninsula, where beach resorts take over. You can avoid the coastal strip by taking the expressway or Highway 330 up the island's less crowded centre past **Okinawa City**. A bizarre mix of American and Japanese life, Okinawa City is the region's main urban centre, but even here there's little reason to stop unless you're looking for accommodation. If you do want a break on the journey north, there are a couple of moderately interesting sights in the area. Though it's difficult to get to, **Nakamura-ke** is one of the few genuinely old buildings on Okinawa still standing, and the nearby ruins of **Nakagusuku Castle** offer commanding views. Then on the district's northern fringes, there's **Ryūkyū-mura**, a quieter, more interesting culture village than Gyokusendo (see above).

## Kita-Nakagusuku

About 10km north of Naha, Highway 330 skirts east of Futenma Airbase before hitting a major junction. A little further north, a road cuts east through the hills to **KITA-NAKAGUSUKU** village where, in the early fifteenth century, Nakamura Gashi served as a teacher to Lord Gosamaru. In the early eighteenth century, after a rocky patch, one of Gashi's descendants was appointed village leader and started building his family's large, beautifully solid residence, **Nakamura-ke** (daily 9.30am–5pm; ¥300). Protected by limestone walls, a thick belt of trees and a growling *shiisā* perched on the red-tile roof, the house is typical of a wealthy landowner's residence, with its barns, a lovely grain store and the inevitable rows of pig sties. Inside, there are a few family heirlooms, and the enterprising owners have set up a small shop and restaurant next door.

To reach Nakamura-ke by public transport, take one of the many buses from Naha north to Okinawa City (#23, #25, #31 and #90 are all fairly frequent) for the hour's ride to the Futenma junction. Then hop on the next #59 bus heading north (hourly; 15min; ¥140) and ask the driver to let you off at the Nakamura-ke turning, from where it's a 1500-metre walk uphill. Alternatively, a taxi from Futenma costs about ¥700 one way.

While you're up here, it's worth walking five minutes west to where the limestone cliffs merge into the crumbling walls of **Nakagusuku-jō** (Tues–Sun 8.30am–5pm; ¥300). These impressive fortifications, consisting of six citadels on a spectacular promontory, were originally built in the early fifteenth century by a local lord, Gosamaru. They weren't enough to withstand his rival, Lord Amawari, however, who ransacked the castle in 1458 and then abandoned the site. Nowadays you can walk through the grassy, tree-filled park and scramble among the ruins to admire the views clear across the island. Taxis usually hang around the castle entrance to whisk visitors back down to Futenma.

## Okinawa City

Local tourist literature makes much of the international feel of **OKINAWA CITY**, roughly 20km north of Naha. With the Kadena Base just up the road, it's not surprising that the streets are full of American adverts, chain restaurants and 24-hour shops. But it's all rather tacky and, apart from its hotels and restaurants, the city doesn't really have anything to offer the majority of tourists.

The city centre is the **Goya crossroads**, where Highway 330 and Kūkō-dōri meet. There's an **information centre** (daily 9am–5pm; ☎098/932-8735) southeast of this junction, and a branch of Ryūkyū Bank on its northwest corner. If you need a place to stay, try one of the **hotels** just south on the highway. Of these, the friendly *Sunrise Hotel* (☎098/933-0170, fax 932-6221; ④) offers the cheapest rooms, but is still comfortably

---

### THE AMERICAN QUESTION

Twenty percent of Okinawa-Hontō and a small number of outer islands are covered by American military bases, employing more than 20,000 American personnel. This in itself has fuelled local anger, but what rankles most is that Okinawa makes up less than one percent of the Japanese land mass, yet contains 75 percent of the country's American bases.

Most of the bases are concentrated in central and south Okinawa, on land that was seized in the 1950s. Nowdays the land is leased from the owners by the Japanese government who sublet it to the US military under the Security Treaty. Though the leases are renewed every five years, the landowners have no choice in the matter, since the governor of Okinawa is authorized to sign on behalf of anyone who objects. This worked reasonably well until Governor Ota Masahide was voted in to power in 1995 – the year the schoolgirl was raped (see p.745) – on a pledge to end the American military occupation. His refusal to co-operate on the leases was eventually overruled by Japan's supreme court, but not before he'd won agreement to relocate a number of artillery ranges and Futenma Airbase away from the main urban areas; the current proposal is for Futenma to be replaced with a floating heliport off Nago in north Okinawa, though the locals are predictably opposed.

The question of the American bases is a thorny one for the islanders, since the Americans contribute vast sums to the local economy and the bases provide thousands of jobs. Despite that, Okinawa is the poorest of Japan's prefectures, with unemployment twice the national average, and people are beginning to argue for more investment in local industry. Governor Ota has proposed a free trade zone and other measures to reduce Okinawa's reliance on the bases, though the current economic downturn in Asia makes this a far more difficult task.

In recent years, public opinion has gradually hardened against the bases, though not against Americans as such. A 1995 poll revealed a majority in favour of a continued American presence but with a more even distribution throughout Japan. At that time, only twenty percent of the population wanted a complete withdrawal, but by 1996 the figure had increased to a convincing ninety percent, and Governor Ota was demanding that all bases be removed by 2015. Whether this is a serious threat or a mere bargaining ploy remains to be seen, but in the meantime it's likely that more bases will be closed or at least relocated.

furnished with TV, fridge and large bathrooms. The next-door *Hotel City Plaza* (☎098/933-5599, fax 932-5944; ⑤), on the other hand, is a more modern establishment that's only a touch more expensive. **Eating** options are more limited. Across the highway from the hotels, the Nakanomachi nightlife district has a number of snack bars and steak houses. There's more of the same on the city's main shopping street, Chūō Park Avenue, to the left of Highway 330 a few blocks north from the Goya crossing.

### Ryūkyū-mura

The final sight in Okinawa's central region lies on the west coast, where **Ryūkyū-mura** (daily 8.30am–5.30pm; ¥600) preserves several old Okinawa farmhouses and the remnants of Ryūkyū culture. Though some will find it too touristy, the village provides a hint of what Okinawa might have been like before the war. In addition to performances of Eisa dances and traditional music, you can see people weaving, dyeing textiles and milling sugar cane for molasses – try the freshly fried local doughnuts. In the less-appealing Habu Centre (¥400) a mongoose is brought out at regular intervals to make quick work of poisonous habu snakes. Ryūkyū-mura occupies a wooded hillside west of Highway 58 some 30km north of Naha. Bus #20 takes you right to the door (every 15–20min; 1hr 20min; ¥970); coming from Okinawa City, take bus #62 to Kadena (every 15–30min; 30min; ¥400), then change to the #20 northbound.

Fifteen minutes' walk northwest of Ryūkyū-mura, in Onna village, the *Maeda Misaki Youth Hostel* (☎ & fax 098/964-2497; closed early Feb; ①) is a great place to stay. It's in a lovely quiet location, with walks along the cliffs and down to the white, sweeping curve of Moon beach. You can rent bikes (¥1000 per day) at the hostel and they also offer windsurfing and diving courses, as well as excellent meals. The nearest bus stop is Kuraha, on bus route #20, from where the hostel is a signed ten minutes' walk northwest.

## Northern Okinawa

North of Okinawa's pinched waist, the scenery begins to improve as classy resort hotels line the western beaches. Bleached-white, coral-fringed Moon beach merges into Tiger beach and then there's the rocky, wild Onna promontory before you rejoin the sands at Manza. Beyond this strip, **northern Okinawa**'s only major settlement, **Nago**, sits at the base of the knobbly **Motobu peninsula**. A generally quiet, workaday place, there's not a lot to see in Nago, but the small city makes a good base for exploring Okinawa's mountainous north. The district boasts the island's most attractive scenery, particularly around **Hedo Misaki**, the northern cape, and on through sleepy **Oku** village down the rugged northeast coast. It's possible to travel up the west coast by slow local bus, but you're on your own after Oku.

### Nago

Apart from weekends, when off-duty soldiers come up from the bases, **NAGO** sees few foreigners. If the proposed heliport goes ahead (see box, on previous page) all this will change, but for the moment Nago is a slow-moving, fairly pleasant city – more a large town – best-known for its tree population, including a huge banyan and a spectacular display of spring cherry blossoms. Its other sights consist of a marginally interesting local museum and views from the former castle hill.

Nago curves round a south-facing bay. Highway 58 runs along the seafront and then turns north again on the west side of town, while behind the harbour a road strikes inland to the central **Nago crossroads**, where it cuts across the city's main shopping street. A short walk east along this street, across a river and past a three-hundred-year-old **banyan tree** in the middle of the road, you'll come to the small **Nago Museum** (Tues–Sun 10am–6pm; closed fourth Thurs of the month; ¥150). It's worth a quick look, though the displays of rice-planting, farming and whale-hunting are aimed primarily at showing local youngsters a disappearing way of life. Perhaps more appealing is the next-door **Orion Brewery** (☎0980/52-2137) – phone to arrange a free factory tour and tasting of Okinawa's very drinkable homebrew. Finally, there's **Nago Castle Hill**; follow the road northeast from the brewery, along the river and up a long flight of stairs. Nothing remains of the castle, but turn left at the top for an attractively landscaped children's park and views over Nago bay.

*PRACTICALITIES*
Arriving by bus, most services stop near Nago's central crossing before terminating at the **bus terminal** on the main highway to the west of town. However, some stop on the seafront, notably the Express Bus from Naha airport, via Naha Bus Terminal (hourly; 1hr 40min; ¥2000), which ends up outside Nago's Lego-block City Hall, roughly 500m from the centre. You'll find the **tourist information office** (Mon–Fri 8.30am–5.30pm, Sat 8.30am–noon; ☎0980/53-7755) in the covered market immediately southwest of the Nago crossroads; staff here speak a modicum of English. The Ryūkyū Bank, just north of the central junction, can **exchange** dollar and sterling cash and travellers' cheques, and there's a small post office a couple of blocks to the west.

Two of the best **places to stay** in Nago are the *Hotel Tōwa* (☎0980/52-3793; ③) and the *Yamada-sō* (☎0980/52-2272; ④), opposite each other in the backstreets northeast of Nago crossroads; you'll find them by walking east along the main street and taking the second left. They're both clean and friendly, but the *Hotel Tōwa* wins out for slightly bigger rooms and lower prices. If these are full, try the more aged *Hotel Shiroyama* (☎ & fax 0980/52-3111; ④), on the east side of town near the banyan tree.

The *Hotel Shiroyama* also has a popular **restaurant** serving fresh seafood and set menus from around ¥1200 (daily 5pm–midnight). Going more upmarket, *Yamabuki* (Mon–Sat 11am–10pm; ☎0980/52-2143) is in a grey, modern building one block northeast of *Hotel Tōwa*, where they serve an Okinawa set meal, *chanpuru* and other local dishes. Prices are reasonable and there's a selective picture menu, but you need to get there before 7.30pm, or make a reservation. Head down towards the harbour from *Hotel Tōwa* and you can't miss the cheerful red lanterns of *Akachōchin* (daily 5pm–1am), a lively *izakaya* offering cheap, filling food on the far side of the shopping street. *Bar 77* (daily noon–4pm & 7pm–3am), on the main drag east of Nago crossroads, is the place to go for a nightcap. They've got a billiards table (¥100) and a small, dark dance floor which gets pretty busy at weekends.

## Hedo Misaki and the Motobu peninsula

North of Nago, Highway 58 hugs the mountainside as the cliffs rise higher and the only settlements are a few weather-beaten villages in sheltered coves. The biggest of these is **Hentona**, from where it's another 20km to Okinawa's northern cape, **Hedo Misaki**. Ignoring the unsightly restaurant block and cigarette butts, this is a good spot to stretch your legs, wandering over the headland's dimpled limestone rocks while the waves pound the cliffs below. On clear days you can see northerly Yoron-jima, the first island in Kagoshima Prefecture, and lumpy Iheya-jima to the west, over a churning sea where the currents sweeping round Okinawa collide. If you're travelling by **bus**, take #67 from a stop near central Nago's Ryūkyū Bank to Hentona (1–2 hourly; 1hr; ¥880), then change to #69 for the last leg to Hedo Misaki iriguchi (8 daily; 45min; ¥670); it's a twenty-minute walk out to the point from where the bus drops you.

Six kilometres east of Hedo Misaki, the bus terminates in a large fishing village, **OKU** (15min; ¥330), with an attractive array of traditional Okinawa houses skulking under their low, tiled roofs. A quiet, seemingly deserted place, there's nothing to do but wander the lanes and peer at the neat, walled gardens protected to seaward by thick stands of trees. In early spring (Jan & Feb) the surrounding hills are clothed in bright cherry blossoms – and in early April you can feast on the ripened fruit. Most of Oku's inhabitants are elderly, but one young couple have recently opened the delightful *Minshuku Miyagi* (☎ & fax 0980/41-8383; [5] including two meals) beside the river mouth; there are only three rooms, two *tatami* and one Western, so make sure you book early. From the bus terminus, outside the wonderful village shop, the minshuku's red roof is clearly visible beside the bridge, a few minutes' walk down a sandy track.

If you've still got time to spare in Nago, head out west to the hilly, mushroom-shaped **Motobu peninsula**. The best thing is to take a loop round the coast or drive over the hills to the **Nakijin-jō ruins** (daily 8.30am–6pm; ¥150), overlooking the north coast. Though even more gutted than Nakagusuku (see p.756), the castle's outer walls are slowly being rebuilt, and it's a lovely, peaceful spot with good views north to Hentona and Iheya. Buses #65 and #66 circle Motobu clockwise and anticlockwise respectively in roughly two hours, with departures every hour or so from central Nago. These buses stop on the main highway, from where the castle's a gentle one-kilometre climb up a quiet, country road.

# The outer islands

The beaches on Okinawa's main island can't compare with the gems lying offshore among the dozens of **outer islands** that make up the rest of the prefecture. Here, you'll find not only superb, white sands and limpid water, but also magnificent diving – both skin and scuba – which is among the best in Asia. Most of these islands also escaped damage during the battles of 1945, so you'll see much more evidence of Ryūkyū culture and the old traditions. Not that they're completely unspoilt; even here the paradise image is punctured by eyesore developments and a good deal of rubbish along the shore, while summer brings plane-loads of holidaymakers to the islands.

Fortunately, there's plenty of choice and, outside the main holiday season, few tourists. One of the most accessible islands is **Zamami-jima**, just a short ferry ride west of Naha, which offers great beaches, great diving and has recently become a centre for whale-watching. For a real sense of escape, however, you need to head further south, to **Miyako-jima** and the emptier, more mountainous **Ishigaki-jima**, while nearby **Iriomote-jima** is often described as Japan's last wilderness. In all these islands, it's the scenery and water sports that provide the main attractions, but Iriomote has the added distinction of its unique wildlife population and lush, almost tropical rainforest.

## The Kerama Islands

Lying some 30km offshore, the **Kerama Islands** are the closest group to Naha. A knot of three large, inhabited islands and numerous pinpricks of sand and coral, the Keramas offer some of the most beautiful and unspoilt beaches in Okinawa and superb diving among the offshore reefs. **Tokashiki-jima**, the largest island and the closest to Naha, attracts the greatest number of tourists, but all the islands are surprisingly quiet outside the summer peak (July & Aug). The signs are that this won't last much longer. Already **Zamami-jima**, the most interesting of the group, and nearby **Aka-jima** are busy upgrading their ports, hotels and roads. Much of this has been spurred by the recent boom in **whale-watching** during the winter months.

Historically **whaling** was an important part of the local economy, but in the 1960s the whales simply disappeared and the industry died. Then, about ten years ago, the humpbacks started coming back to their winter breeding grounds – which the locals have been quick to exploit, though this time for tourism rather than hunting. Several decades earlier, the islanders were faced with less welcome arrivals, when the **US Navy** chose these deep, sheltered waters as a base for attacking Okinawa Island. Here,

## THE OUTER ISLANDS

| The Kerama Islands | | |
|---|---|---|
| Pension Hoshizuna | *Penshon Hoshizuna* | ペンション星砂 |
| Joy Joy | *Joi Joi* | ジョイジョイ |
| Kerama airport | *Kerama kūkō* | ケラマ空港 |
| Marumiya | *Marumiya* | まるみや |
| Minshuku Sendoran | *Minshuku Sendoran* | 民宿船頭殿 |
| Shirahama Islands Resort | *Shirahama Airanzu Rizōto* | シラハマアイランズリゾート |
| Tokashiki-jima | *Tokashiki-jima* | 渡嘉敷島 |
| Urizun | *Urizun* | うりずん |
| Zamami-jima | *Zamami-jima* | 座間味島 |

| The Southern Islands | | |
|---|---|---|
| **Miyako-jima** | *Miyako-jima* | 宮古島 |
| Hirara | *Hirara* | 平良 |
| Higashi Henna Misaki | *Higashi Henna Misaki* | 東平安名岬 |
| Hotel Kyōwa | *Hoteru Kyōwa* | ホテル共和 |
| Maehama Beach | *Maehama Biichi* | 前浜ビーチ |
| Miyako-jima Tōkyū Resort | *Miyako-jima Tōkyū Rizōto* | 宮古島東急リゾート |
| Miyako-jima Youth Hostel | *Miyako-jima Yūsu Hosuteru* | 宮古島ユースホステル |
| Sunayama Beach | *Sunayama Biichi* | 砂山ビーチ |
| Hotel Urizun | *Hoteru Urizun* | ホテルうりずん |

| **Ishigaki-jima** | *Ishigaki-jima* | 石垣島 |
|---|---|---|
| Minshuku Ishigaki-jima | *Minshuku Ishigaki-jima* | 民宿石垣島 |
| Kabira Bay | *Kabira-wan* | 川平湾 |
| Hotel Miyahara | *Hoteru Miyahara* | ホテルミヤハラ |
| Miyara Donchi | *Miyara Donchi* | 宮良殿内 |
| Sukuji Beach | *Sukuji Biichi* | 底地ビーチ |
| Taketomi-jima | *Taketomi-jima* | 竹富島 |
| Takana Ryokan | *Takana Ryokan* | 高那旅館 |
| Torin-ji | *Torin-ji* | 桃林寺 |
| Trek Ishigaki-jima Youth Hostel | *Torekku Ishigaki-jima Yūsu Hosuteru* | トレック石垣島ユースホステル |
| Yaeyama Museum | *Yaeyama Hakubutsukan* | 八重山博物館 |
| Minshuku Yaeyama-sō | *Minshuku Yaeyama-sō* | 民宿八重山荘 |
| Yashima Ryokan Youth Hostel | *Yashima Ryokan Yūsu Hosuteru* | 八洲旅館ユースホステル |

| **Iriomote-jima** | *Iriomote-jima* | 西表島 |
|---|---|---|
| Funaura | *Funaura* | 船浦 |
| Irumote-sō Youth Hostel | *Irumote-sō Yūsu Hosuteru* | いるもて荘ユースホステル |
| Iriomote-jima Midori-sō Youth Hostel | *Iriomote-jima Midori-sō Yūsu Hosuteru* | 西表島みどり荘ユースホステル |
| Ōhara | *Ōhara* | 大原 |
| Shirahama | *Shirahama* | 白浜 |

as on Okinawa, there were several mass suicides, including Zamami-jima's whole town council. However, most young Japanese associate the Keramas not with the war but with a cutesy 1970s **film** called *I Want to See Marilyn*. Based on a true story, it tells of a romance between two dogs on neighbouring islands: Shiro on Aka-jima, and Marilyn some 3km away on Zamami. They met when Shiro travelled to Zamami in his owner's boat, but the passion was such that he started swimming over every day to rendezvous with Marilyn on Zamami's Ama beach – or so the story goes.

Fortunately, there are other ways of **getting to the islands**. They're served by **Kerama airport**, on southerly Fukazi-jima, with daily flights from Naha by Ryūkyū Air Commuter (4–7 daily; 15min; ¥7000, or ¥12,600 return); boats wait to shuttle passengers from the airport to the islands (¥510–¥820). The alternative is a **ferry** from Naha's Tomari Port. The high-speed *Queen Zamami* departs twice daily for Zamami, calling at Aka-jima either on the outward or return journey (55min–1hr 15min; ¥2630, or ¥5090 return; ☎098/868-4567). Or there's the slower, cheaper *Zamami-maru* (daily; 2hr 15min; ¥1750, or ¥3330 return; same phone number). For Tokashiki-jima, there's just one daily ferry from Tomari Port (1hr 10min; ¥1340, or ¥2540 return; ☎098/868-7541).

## Zamami-jima

A frolicking whale statue greets ferries pulling in to **Zamami-jima's** grand, new harbour, behind which **ZAMAMI village** is expanding on the back of the tourist boom. This is the only settlement of any size on the island, with 500 inhabitants out of a total population of 650, who speak their own dialect and maintain a fierce rivalry with the much larger Tokashiki-jima a couple of kilometres away to the east. Despite the rash of building plots, Zamami-jima is still a good place to get away from it all. It has spectacular **beaches**, both on the island itself or a short boat ride away. You can **dive** year round, but the best time to visit is in autumn, when most tourists have gone and while the water is still warm enough for swimming and snorkelling.

From late January through March, Zamami is the main centre for **whale-watching**. The Whale-Watching Association (☎098/987-2277) arranges **boat trips** from Zamami port every day at 10.30am depending on the weather (2hr; ¥5000). Note that reservations are essential, and that you should bring rain gear and a wind-breaker as you'll be out in the open sea.

With a good pair of binos you can often spot humpbacks spouting and cavorting off Zamami's north coast. There's a special **whale observatory** about 3.5km northwest of Zamami village, one of several look-out points scattered round the cliffs and on the island's highest peak, **Takatsuki-yama**. Even allowing for stops it only takes a couple of hours to explore every road on Zamami, after which there's nothing for it but to head to the beach. Roughly 1km southeast of the village, **Furuzamami beach** is the best on the island, with excellent coral and troops of multicoloured fish. In season, you can rent snorkels at the small shop and there's also a restaurant and showers. However, the beaches get even better on the tiny, **offshore islands**, such as Gahi-jima and Agenashiku-jima, just south of Zamami. In summer (June–mid-Sept) small boats take day-trippers out to these islands for a small fee, but out of season you'll have to charter your own boat from either the information office or village office (see below).

### PRACTICALITIES

Zamami village faces southwest and is ringed by low hills. Its main street heads inland from the harbour jetty, across a small river to the **Village Office** (☎098/987-2311) and **post office**. Coming off the ferry, the first building on the left – yellowish-brown, with a pitch roof – contains the **tourist information office** (Mon–Fri 8.30am–5pm; ☎098/987-2311), ferry booking office and the Whale-Watching Association office.

There's one **car rental** outlet, Zamami Rent-a-car (daily 9am–6/7pm; ☎098/987-3250), in the sandy lanes on the village's eastern edge. Prices start at ¥3000 for an hour, or ¥8000 per day, but they only have five vehicles, so it's a good idea to reserve. You can rent **motorbikes** (¥3000 per day) and **pedal bikes** (¥1000–2000) at a shop on the road to the Village Office. There are dozens of places offering **diving** trips and courses, but *Joy Joy* (see opposite) and Diving Noi (☎098/987-3262), north of the Village Office, are recommended for their friendly, reliable service.

As yet there are no big **hotels** on Zamami, instead a reasonable choice of family-run minshuku with a few simple Japanese- and Western-style rooms. It's wise to book ahead at any time of year, particularly if you want to stay at the popular *Pension Hoshizuna* (☎098/987-2253; [5]) or *Minshuku Sendoran* (☎098/987-2016; [4]), both offering clean, bright rooms on the main street. *Joy Joy* (☎098/987-2445; [5] including two meals), on the northwest edge of the village, has a handful of decent rooms and a small garden. If you get stuck, try the grandly named *Shirahama Islands Resort* (098/987-3111, fax 987-2655; [5]), on the road out to Furuzamami; this is Zamami's biggest, smartest hotel, but not overly welcoming. Finally, there's a good **campsite** (☎098/987-3259) behind Ama beach, twenty minutes' walk east along the coast road. You can rent tents (¥500) and other equipment, and there are also six-berth cabins (¥21,000).

It's best to arrange **meals** at your accommodation, though Zamami does have one decent restaurant, the *Marumiya* (closed Wed), next door to *Joy Joy*, which does a ¥650 lunch special and reasonable evening meals. The only alternative is a cheap cafeteria upstairs in the information office building, serving basic noodle and rice dishes. Afterwards, you can repair to the friendly *Urison* bar, opposite the *Shirayama Islands Resort*.

## The southern islands

There's a gap of nearly 300km between Okinawa-Hontō and the next link in the chain, the **Miyako Islands** centred around **Miyako-jima**. Then, a further 100km southwest, there's a cluster of coral reefs and forested mountains which make up the **Yaeyama Islands**. The main base for exploring this group is **Ishigaki-jima**, though you can also stay on nearby **Iriomote-jima**, famous for its wild, wooded interior and unique wildlife population. Stuck out on its own, around 100km west of Ishikagi-jima, **Yonaguni-jima** marks Japan's most westerly point, from where it's only another 125km to Taiwan.

None of these isolated, impoverished islands suffered damage during the Pacific War and here, more than anywhere else in Okinawa, there's still a strong flavour of the distinctive **Ryūkyū culture** and style of **architecture**. But the main attractions are the islands' spectacular white **beaches** lapped by crystal-clear, emerald green waters and fringed by stunning coral reefs. Naturally, this hasn't gone unnoticed and all these islands are now popular tourist destinations for mainland Japanese, particularly during the July/August summer break.

There are even direct **flights** to Ishigaki and Miyako from Tokyo and Ōsaka's Kansai International Airport, though the major jumping-off point is Naha (see p.747). Japan Transocean Air (JTA; ☎0120–255971) and Air Nippon (ANK; ☎0120–029222) both have several departures daily from Naha to Miyako and Ishigaki (around ¥12,000 and ¥15,000 respectively in peak season), while JTA also flies between Miyako and Ishigaki (¥6820). **Ferries** are, of course, a cheaper option. Arimura Sangyō (☎098/860-1980) and RKK Line (☎098/868-1126) run two to three services a week between them from Naha's Shin-kō or Naha Port to Miyako (from ¥3810 one way) and Ishigaki (from ¥5250 one way) – Arimura Sangyō boats continue to Taiwan (see pp.13 & 754). Note that all these ferries sail overnight and that you need to reserve at least two weeks in advance in July and August. Though they cost the same, Arimura Sangyō boats tend to be quicker and more comfortable.

### Miyako-jima

The largest in the Miyako group, **Miyako-jima** is a low-lying triangular-shaped island roughly 35km from tip to tip and just 12km at its widest point. **HIRARA**, the main town, lies on the island's northwest coast, from where roads fan out across a plain of sugarcane fields. In late April, you'll find Miyako swarming with swarthy athletes competing in the Japanese Triathlon, a combination of swimming, cycling and running, but otherwise the prime attraction is the coastal scenery.

Miyako's most interesting historical sight is **Nintō-zei-seki**, a crumbling, 1.4m-high pinnacle of stone on the coast road north of Hirara. It stands as a monument to the heavy burden of taxes imposed when Kagoshima's Shimazu clan ruled Okinawa (see p.744), when it was used as a crude measuring device – tax was levied on anyone taller than the stone. Continue north along the coast and you'll eventually reach **Sunayama beach**, one of the nicest near Hirara, but Miyako's best swimming spot is on the island's southwest coast, where **Maehama beach** stretches over 4km of gleaming white sand. The island's two skinny promontories also make good excursions, particularly the two-kilometre-long, southeastern **Higashi Henna Misaki** which is renowned for its wild flowers and panoramic views; look down and you should also be able to see shoals of fish darting among the coral.

*PRACTICALITIES*

**Hirara** faces northwest towards its harbour and **ferry terminal**, where you'll find the **tourist information office** (Mon–Fri 9am–5.30pm; ☎09807/3-1881) on the terminal's second floor. **Miyako airport** lies just 3km from central Hirara, making it feasible to walk, while a taxi costs about ¥630 for the ten-minute ride; Miyako Taxi (☎09807/2-4123) has a number of English-speaking drivers. **Buses** round the island depart from beside the harbour, or you can rent your own transport. There are several **bike** and **motorbike rental** outlets in Hirara, with rates at around ¥1500 per day for pedal bikes and from ¥3000 for motorbikes. Cars are available through Nippon (☎09807/2-0919) and Toyota Rent-a-car (☎09807/2-0100).

There are a number of **hotels** and plenty of cheap minshuku in Hirara, with prices starting at around ¥4000 without meals. Overlooking the harbour, *Hotel Kyowa* (☎09807/3-2288, fax 3-2285; ⑤), is one of the larger hotels, with a range of decent, Western-style rooms. For something slightly cheaper, try *Hotel Urizun* (☎ & fax 09807/2-4410; ⑤), buried in the backstreets inland from the ferry pier. *Miyako-jima Youth Hostel* (☎09807/3-7700; ②) is five minutes' walk from the airport on the road into town. At the other extreme, the island's top resort is down at Maehama beach, where the *Miyako-jima Tōkyū Resort* (☎09807/6-2109, fax 6-6781; ⑥–⑦) sits among tropical gardens.

The best place to look for **restaurants** is in the streets immediately inland from the harbour, particularly Nishizato-dōri which runs parallel to the main road, Highway 390, but two blocks west. Here you'll find several good local restaurants, including an area of foodstalls which stays open till late. There's also a fairly wild **nightlife** area, Iizato, inland from the harbour, with dozens of expensive hostess bars as well as more reasonable establishments; *Jammin'* reggae bar gets lots of recommendations.

## Ishigaki-jima and Taketomi-jima

The southernmost islands in Okinawa Prefecture are the **Yaeyama Islands**, lying just north of the Tropic of Cancer. Their main base is the northerly **Ishigaki-jima**, home to the prefecture's tallest peak, Omoto-dake (526m), as well as a fringe of stunning **beaches**. It's main town, **ISHIKAGI**, is located on the island's southwest coast, where you'll find most of the tourist facilities. Just six kilometres off the coast, the tiny, low-slung island of **Taketomi-jima**, with its traditional architecture and "star-sand" beaches, makes a popular day-trip or a possible overnight stop.

Ishigaki town boasts a number of minor sights. The first of these lies ten minutes' walk inland from the harbour, where the small **Yaeyama Museum** (Tues–Sun 9am–4.30pm; ¥100) contains a moderately interesting collection of local artifacts. A bit further away to the northwest, **Miyara Donchi** (daily except Tues 9am–5pm; ¥100) was built by a *samurai* in 1819; it's surrounded by an attractive, coral rock garden, though the whole place is badly in need of attention. On the town's northwest outskirts, **Torin-ji**, a Zen temple where they still practice meditation, was founded in 1614. Its two guardian kings are now worshipped as the island's protectors.

Around Ishigaki island, the most gorgeous beaches are on the north coast at **Kabira Bay**, about forty minutes by bus from Ishigaki town (¥570). The bay, which is also the centre of Ishigaki's black-pearl industry, is dotted with pristine islets, with views north to the long, lumpy Hirakubo peninsula. Fifteen minutes' walk northwest from Kabira across a headland, **Sukuji beach** also has fine sands and crystal-clear water, though you have to walk out a long way to swim.

When you've had your fill, hop on a ferry from Ishigaki port across to nearby **Taketomi-jima** (every 15min; 10min; ¥570). Only 1500m across at its widest point, the island is perched on a bed of coral and ringed with beaches known for their "sand" of minuscule star-shaped shells. The star-sand beaches are mostly round the south coast, particularly the southeast side, while midway up the west coast, **Kondoi beach** provides the island's best swimming spot. **Taketomi village**, with a population of just 260, comprises a cluster of traditional, red-tiled houses surrounded by coral walls, bright tropical flowers and huge butterflies. It stands in the middle of the island, while the ferry port lies on the north coast, from where a sandy lane leads past the post office and youth hostel (see below) to the village centre. The only way of getting round the island is by bike (around ¥1000 per day) or tourist buffalo cart (¥1000 per person for 50min). It's also possible to walk, but as there's no coast road, you have to keep coming back to the centre.

*PRACTICALITIES*

Oriented southwest, Ishigaki is a reasonably compact town with most tourist facilities located within easy walking distance of the **ferry pier**. The **airport** is a few kilometres east, from where you'll have to take a taxi (10min; around ¥740). There's an **information office** (Mon–Fri 8.30am–5pm; ☎09808/2-2809) in the Hamasaki district, to the west of the ferry terminal behind the *Hotel Miyahira*. Since bus services are fairly erratic, it's best to rent your own transport. **Bikes** and **motorbikes** are available at roughly the same rates as on Miyako (see opposite), and you can arrange **car rental** through the Nissan (☎09808/3-0024), Toyota (☎09808/2-0100) and Nippon (☎09808/2-3629) agencies. If you'd rather go by **taxi**, call Tokai Kōtsū (☎09808/2-3585) or Shirayuri Kōtsū (☎09808/3-1688), both of which have some English-speaking drivers.

Looking out to sea from a block of reclaimed land west of the ferry pier, *Hotel Miyahira* (☎09808/2-6111, fax 3-3236; ⑤–⑥) is central Ishigaki's top **hotel**, with reasonably comfortable, mostly Western-style twin rooms. Moving down a few notches, *Minshuku Yaeyama-sō* (☎09808/2-3231, fax 2-6806; ④–⑤), and *Minshuku Ishigaki-jima* (☎09808/2-6066; ④–⑤), are worth seeking out. The former is located on the main road, about 800m northeast from the harbour, while the latter is to the north of this road, a little closer to the sea.

There are also two **youth hostels** on Ishigaki-jima and one on Taketomi-jima. The first of these is the rather aged *Yashima Ryokan Youth Hostel* (☎09808/2-3157; ①), in the backstreets of Ishigaki town, behind the Yaeyama Museum. The more modern *Trek Ishigaki-jima Youth Hostel* (☎09808/6-8257; closed at New Year; ①) is in Hoshino village over on the island's east coast; take a bus from Ishigaki port to Hoshino (30min), then walk down behind the village shop to find the hostel by the sea. Finally, Taketomi-jima's youth hostel is in *Takana Ryokan* (☎09808/5-2151; dorm ①, room ⑤ including meals); it's about ten minutes' walk south from the port, opposite the post office.

Ishigaki town is poorly served with **restaurants**, so you're best off taking meals in your accommodation or buying your own supplies in the public market, west of the Yaeyama Museum, or local supermarkets.

## Iriomote-jima

Some 20km west of Ishigaki, **Iriomote-jima** rises out of the ocean. Its uncharted, mountainous interior, covered with dense sub-tropical rainforest, harbours a unique population of wildlife including one of the world's rarest species, the **Iriomote lynx**.

There's little chance of encountering this nocturnal, cat-like animal, but the island and its surrounding waters are also home to a splendid array of mangrove swamps, Yaeyama palms and coral reefs shimmering with tropical fish. Much of the area is protected under the **Iriomote National Park** but there are plenty of opportunities for swimming, diving and walking through the rainforest.

Iriomote's main town is **FUNAURA**, on the north coast. Most **ferries** from Ishigaki (8 daily; 45min; ¥1800) arrive here, but some cross to **Ōhara** village on the island's southeast tip (9 daily; 35–45min; ¥1500, or ¥2060 for a highspeed ferry). Iriomote's only road runs along the coast from Ōhara via Funaura to **Shirahama** in the west; all these villages are linked by infrequent buses which take roughly an hour to complete the journey (¥1050).

Iriomote's main **information office** (daily 8am–6pm; ☎09808/2-9836) is in Funaura near the ferry terminal. You can **rent bikes** in both Funaura and Ōhara; count on around ¥1500 per day for a pedal bike and ¥3000 for a motorbike. Most people visit Iriomote on a day-trip from Ishigaki but, if you've got the time, it's worth **staying** at least one night on the island. There are dozens of minshuku – ask at the tourist office – and a couple of youth hostels. In Funaura itself, you'll find the attractive *Irumote-sō Youth Hostel* (☎09808/5-6255, fax 5-6076; ①), ten minutes' walk west from the port, with excellent meals, bikes and scooters for rent and a dive club. If they're full, try the *Iriomote-jima Midori-sō Youth Hostel* (☎09808/5-6526; ①), twenty minutes' walk further along the coast, or five minutes by bus.

## travel details

### Ferries
**Naha** to: Fukuoka (1–2 weekly; 25hr); Ishigaki-jima (2–3 weekly; 12–18hr); Kagoshima (3–4 weekly; 19–25hr); Kōbe (2 weekly; 39–43hr); Miyako-jima (2–3 weekly; 8–10hr 30min); Miyazaki (1–2 weekly; 24hr); Nagoya (2 weekly; 43hr); Ōsaka (5 weekly; 29–41hr); Taiwan (1 weekly; 22hr); Tokyo (1–2 weekly; 45hr); Zamami-jima (3 daily; 55min–2hr 15min).

### Flights
**Ishigaki** to: Fukuoka (1 daily; 2hr); Kansai International (1 daily; 2hr 15min); Miyako (3 daily; 30min); Tokyo (1 daily; 3hr 15min).

**Miyako** to: Kansai International (1 daily; 1hr 55min); Tokyo (1 daily; 2hr 35min).

**Naha** to: Fukuoka (7–9 daily; 1hr 35min); Hiroshima (1 daily; 1hr 45min); Hong Kong (2 weekly; 3hr 10min); Ishigaki (11 daily; 1hr); Kagoshima (3 daily; 1hr 20min); Kansai International (6 daily; 2hr); Kerama (4–7 daily; 15min); Kumamoto (1 daily; 1hr 25min); Miyako (9–11 daily; 45min); Miyazaki (1 daily; 1hr 25min); Nagasaki (1 daily; 1hr 30min); Nagoya (7 daily; 2hr 10min); Niigata (1 daily; 2hr 40min); Sapporo (1 daily; 3hr 35min); Sendai (1 daily; 2hr 55min); Seoul (2 weekly; 2hr 15min); Taipei (2–3 daily; 30min); Tokyo (10 daily; 2hr 30min).

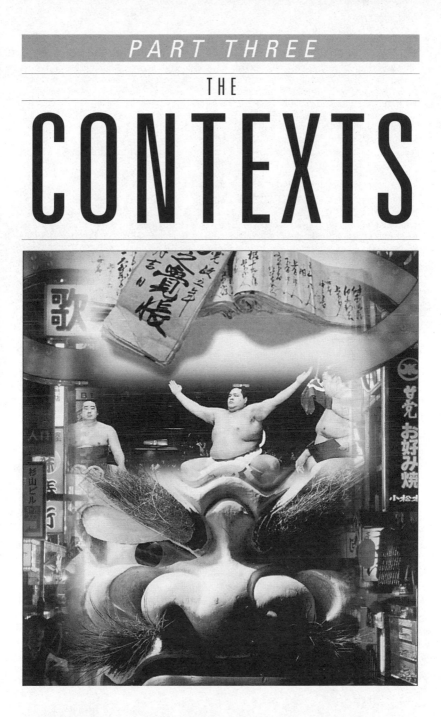

# HISTORY

Thanks largely to its geographical isolation and social cohesion, Japan numbers among the world's most enduring and stable nations. Though the country has certainly had its share of violent civil wars, coups and one revolution, albeit fairly gentle, Japan has rarely been invaded and never truly colonized. Indeed, it boasts the longest-reigning dynasty in the world, with the present monarch, Emperor Akihito, 125th in an unbroken line stretching back to the first century BC.

During the seventeenth century, Japan cut itself off almost completely from outside influence for a period of more than two hundred years. It then did an about-turn, embraced Western technology and in no time possessed one of the world's most powerful economies. As a result, modern Japan initially seems like so many other developed, industrial countries, but scratch the surface and you'll find a society

deeply layered in ancient legends and a vibrant history.

## THE BEGINNINGS

It is believed that the Japanese people are descended from immigrants from mainland Asia and possibly Polynesians who moved north along the east Asian coast. This migration is estimated to have taken place over a period prior to 10,000BC, from when pottery remains have been found. The earliest wave of migrants, known as the **Ainu**, were gradually pushed north by succeeding groups, until today only a few remain in the interior of Hokkaidō (see p.298).

The first migrants lived as fishers and hunters in what is now known as the **Jōmon** era (10,000BC–300BC), named after the rope markings on pottery made at that time (see p.790). The **Yayoi** era which followed saw the development of wet-rice cultivation, which gives the countryside of Japan its characteristic appearance today, and the use of bronze and iron implements. Then came the **Kofun** era (300AD–710AD), whose main legacy is many thousands of burial mounds mainly in central and western Japan.

It is not surprising that much of this early history is the stuff of myth and legend, first recorded in the **Kojiki**, "Record of Ancient Matters" and the **Nihon-shoki**, "Chronicles of Japan". These are Japan's oldest surviving historical documents, completed in 681AD and 720AD respectively. Though they don't always agree, the accounts tell of a land peopled by semi-gods engaged in fabulous adventures. One of these was the Sun Goddess Amaterasu, from whom all Japan's emperors are supposedly descended, starting with her great-great-grandson, **Emperor Jimmu**.

According to common belief, Jimmu founded the dynasty about 660BC and died at well over

| THE MAJOR HISTORICAL ERAS | | | |
|---|---|---|---|
| Jōmon | 10,000BC–300BC | Momoyama | 1573–1600 |
| Yayoi | 300BC–300AD | Edo (or Tokugawa) | 1600–1868 |
| Kofun | 300–710 | Meiji | 1868–1912 |
| Nara | 710–784 | Taishō | 1912–1926 |
| Heian | 794–1185 | Shōwa | 1926–1989 |
| Kamakura | 1185–1333 | Heisei | 1989–present day |
| Muromachi | 1333–1573 | | |

100 years of age. The reality is that he probably lived about six hundred years later, and was no more than a successful local chieftain. He established his capital at Kashiwabara, between present-day Ōsaka and Nara, and gave the name Yamato to what is now Japan. The country's subsequent political history up to the modern era is the story of the rise and fall of a succession of powerful clans who preserved the monarchy largely as mere figureheads.

## RELATIONS WITH KOREA AND CHINA

From the earliest days of reliable history, Japan has made incursions into **Korea**. In 200AD Empress Jingō led an invasion force, and the Japanese maintained a presence on the peninsula until the middle of the sixth century, reaching as far north as Pyongyang in 391. It was thus Korean scholars who, in 405, first introduced the **Chinese script** to Japan, which until then had no written language of its own. Then, in 552 the King of Paekche sent an image of Buddha and some Buddhist scriptures to Japan, extolling the virtues of the new belief. By the mid-sixth century the first of Japan's non-imperial ruling dynasties, the Soga clan, had risen to power and taken **Buddhism** to heart. At the same time one of the most revered names of Japanese history appeared on the scene. This was **Prince Shōtoku**, who was installed as heir apparent and regent to Empress Suiko around 592AD. A zealous Buddhist and great patron of the arts and sciences, Shōtoku also fostered an exchange of scholars with China and Korea, framed a legal code and was responsible for introducing the Chinese calendar.

As the Soga became increasingly arrogant and high handed during the seventh century, so their power gradually waned. In 645 the Nakatomi clan staged a successful coup, and then, having changed their name to **Fujiwara**, rose to become the most influential and aristocratic family in Japan's history. In the late seventh century, Emperor Mommu chose a Fujiwara lady as his consort, starting a trend that continued until the reign of Emperor Taishō in 1921.

As early as 646, the Fujiwara introduced a series of reforms, the **Taika**, or Great Reforms, reorganizing the government on Chinese lines in order to strengthen the throne. The Chinese system of land tenure and taxation was adopted, and an attempt was made to decentralize the government, though this was hampered by Japan's difficult, mountainous terrain. In 702 further reforms saw the nationalization of land and the founding of a university to teach Chinese history and philosophy. Confucian principles, which espoused filial piety and the subordination of women, were encouraged. For a while it also became the custom to relocate the royal palace after the death of each emperor, until Japan's first would-be permanent capital, **Nara**, was founded in 710.

## THE HEIAN ERA 794–1185

Nara, however, only survived as the capital until 784, when the Fujiwara decided they needed to escape from the monks and priests who were meddling too much in politics. After a short spell in nearby Nagaoka, the court eventually moved to **Heian-kyō** (Capital of Peace) in 794. Later known as Kyoto, the city remained the official, if not the de facto, capital of Japan until 1869. Thus commenced one of the most stable and long-lasting epochs in Japan's history, an era in which the political influence of the Fujiwara flourished, at least initially, and which saw a blossoming of religion, literature, and other artistic pursuits.

In 760 the **Manyōshū**, the first great anthology of Japanese **poetry**, was written in a transliterated form of Chinese. Towards the end of the eighth century Dengyō Daishi, who had spent some years in China, founded the **Tendai sect** of Buddhism, and a few years later, Kōbō Daishi established the **Shingon sect**. According to tradition, it was Kōbō Daishi who developed the simplified *hiragana* syllabary, which Lady Murasaki later used to write the world's first novel, **The Tale of Genji** (see p.792), some time around 1000AD. Another work from this period which is still popular today is *The Pillow Book*, a diary of often acid observations on court life by a lady-in-waiting, Sei Shōnagon.

For a while the Fujiwara steadily increased their grip on power. In 866 Fujiwara Yoshifusa was the first person of non-royal blood to be appointed regent, to rule on behalf of the emperor, and his successors held this position virtually continuously for the next three hundred years. The clan's power reached its zenith under **Regent Fujiwara Michinaga**, who held control for thirty years after 967 AD, partly by marrying his daughters to four successive emperors.

## THE GENPEI WARS

During the eleventh century, Buddhist monks were again meddling in secular affairs. The Fujiwara, whose lives were now dedicated to courtly pursuits, had no option but to invite more militaristic clans, such as the **Minamoto** and **Taira** (also known as the Genji and Heike respectively), to act on their behalf. These clans naturally used the opportunity to advance their own status and thus began the great struggle for power which culminated in the **Genpei Wars** (1180–1185).

The Taira were the first to gain the upper hand, under the leadership of Lord Kiyomori, whose great mistake was to spare the lives of the Minamoto brothers **Yoritomo** and **Yoshitsune**. This pair have achieved an almost legendary status in Japanese history, Yoritomo as the great statesman – despite an unpleasant degree of cruelty and paranoia – and Yoshitsune as the dashing young general. With Yoshitsune commanding the Minamoto fleet, the Taira were finally defeated at the **Battle of Dannoura** (1185), in the straits of Shimonoseki between Honshū and Kyūshū, in one of the most decisive moments of Japanese history.

Dannoura was not to be the end of conflict, however. Yoritomo feared his brother might stage a coup, and this suspicion sparked off a period of internecine strife. A popular story, portrayed in a later Kabuki drama, is that of Yoshitsune defeating a common soldier, Benkei, in single combat. Subsequently Benkei became the most loyal of Yoshitsune's retainers and the two heroes died together near Hiraizumi in 1189, outnumbered by Yoritomo's superior forces.

## THE KAMAKURA ERA 1185-1333

Yoritomo established his *Bakufu*, or "tent government", at **Kamakura** (near present-day Yokohama), in 1192. The term tent government was symbolic of the spartan, military character of the new regime. Yoritomo styled himself Sei-i Tai Shogun, the "Barbarian-subduing Great General", a title which had previously been used on appropriate occasions but which now became permanent.

To drive home the martial emphasis of the new government, military governors were appointed to work alongside the civil administrators, and taxes were levied to cover military expenditure. More generally, Japan settled in to a period of **semi-feudalism**, with the peasants being allowed tenure of land in return for service to their local lord.

The Kamakura *Bakufu* did not survive long after the death of Yoritomo in 1199, since his successors lacked his strong character and organizational skills. During the latter part of his administration he had been ably and loyally supported by **Hōjō Tokimasa** who, in partnership with Yoritomo's widow Masa, now took the helm. Tokimasa quickly assumed the combined roles of military and civil governor, ushering in the century-long era of the **Hōjō regents**. By the late thirteenth century, therefore, the government had evolved into a multi-layered entity. A cloistered retired emperor presided over his successor in Kyoto, who had ceded power to the shogun in Kamakura, who in turn had been rendered powerless by the Hōjō regent, who by then had also handed over power to a new generation of front men.

The thirteenth and fourteenth centuries saw the **rise of the merchant class**. Trade and commerce were encouraged by monks travelling to China and Korea, and by a demand for military supplies. The ports of **Hyōgo** (now Kōbe) and **Ōsaka** developed to handle this trade, while towns and markets grew under the patronage of feudal lords and monasteries. On the political front, Regent Yasutoki formulated the **Jōei Code** in 1232, which provided guidelines on behaviour for the *samurai* class (see box on p.773) as well as rules on land tenure and the maintenance of religious buildings. It was during this period that the class distinctions were demarcated: warriors at the top, then farmers, artisans and, finally, merchants.

This fairly stable state of affairs was shattered in 1268 when the great Mongol leader, **Kublai Khan**, sent six envoys to demand that Japan pay tribute to China. Japan's rejection provoked the Khan to invade in 1274, when the **Mongol army** landed at Hakata (north Kyūshū), but had to withdraw when a storm threatened their fleet. After the Japanese executed further envoys, in 1281 the Khan dispatched a huge punitive expedition, believed to number about 100,000 men. The invaders gained a foothold and fought fiercely for seven weeks, but their fleet was again scattered by a typhoon. The grateful Japanese dubbed it the **kamikaze**, or

"Divine Wind", a name which later reappeared during the Pacific War (see p.776).

## THE MUROMACHI ERA 1333–1573

The demands of war, a generally deteriorating economy and an ineffectual government, eventually led to the collapse of the Hōjō in 1333. This coincided with the accession to the throne of the **Emperor Go-Daigo**, who, being older than earlier incumbents, was less easy to manipulate. After Go-Daigo's commander defeated the Hōjō, the Kamakura *Bakufu* dispatched **Ashikaga Takauji** to bring Go-Daigo to heel. Seeing his chance to seize power, the wily Takauji switched allegiance to the emperor. When Go-Daigo uncovered Takauji's plot, the two sides clashed briefly before the emperor was forced to retreat to the mountains of Yoshino. Takauji set up a rival emperor in Kyoto and for sixty years Japan had two courts, until they were reconciled in 1392. By this time, the **Ashikaga Shogunate** had established its headquarters in Kyoto's **Muromachi** district, from where they ruled for more than two centuries.

Over the years, the Ashikaga, too, began to lose their grip on power due to a combination of mismanagement and circumstances. The shoguns and their retinues were inclined to lives of extravagance. It was during this period that **Kinkaku-ji** and **Ginkaku-ji** (Kyoto's Gold and Silver pavilions) were built, while the decorative arts reached new heights of perfection and Nō theatre was developed. The result of such profligacy was, predictably, increasing exactions on the peasants, and a spate of **peasant revolts**. At the same time, local power bases were re-consolidating, so that by the end of the fifteenth century virtually all central authority had disappeared. In the absence of a strong government, festering inter-clan enmities culminated in the **Ōnin Wars** (1467–78), which took place mainly in and around Kyoto. These marked the start of a period of civil wars which lasted until the early seventeenth century.

In 1549, towards the end of the Muromachi era, the Portuguese missionary **Saint Francis Xavier** arrived on the shores of Kyūshū. Initially the **Christian** newcomers were treated with tolerance, partly out of curiosity but mainly because they carried valuable new technology. Not surprisingly in a country embroiled in civil war, the Europeans' **firearms** attracted much envious attention. Japan's warlords were quick to master the new weapons and eventually developed tactical use of massed musketry unsurpassed even in Europe.

At the same time, this eastward advancement of the Europeans was counteracted by explorations to the west by **Japanese seafarers**, many of whom were privateers, if not actually pirates. They reached as far as the Indian Ocean, and it is one of the interesting conundrums of history as to what would have happened if these adventurers had not been recalled by the somewhat paranoid Tokugawa regime.

## REUNIFICATION

The civil wars ended with the **reunification of Japan** under a triumvirate of generals of outstanding ability. The first, **Oda Nobunaga**, had the initial advantage of hailing from Owari, one of Japan's strategically placed central districts. Having achieved dominance of the Kyoto region, however, he was promptly assassinated. His successor was **Toyotomi Hideyoshi**, who had risen from obscurity to be one of Nobunaga's most trusted generals. Hideyoshi avenged Nobunaga's death and managed to outmanoeuvre all rivals with a shrewd mix of force and diplomacy. Success went to his head, however, and he embarked on costly excursions into Korea, which eventually had to be abandoned.

Shortly before his death in 1598, Hideyoshi persuaded **Tokugawa Ieyasu**, now an ally after a period of circumspect confrontation, to support the succession of his son **Hideyori**. This trust was misplaced. After defeating the remaining western clans at the **Battle of Sekigahara** in 1600, the ambitious Ieyasu decided to seize power, and sacked Ōsaka castle, Hideyori's stronghold, in 1615. The western clans retreated to their fiefdoms to brood on their grievances for the next 250 years, when they emerged to exact a sort of revenge against the Tokugawa Shogunate (see p.774).

## THE TOKUGAWA SHOGUNATE 1600–1868

Ieyasu established his administrative capital at **Edo**, now Tokyo, and set about guaranteeing the security of the **Tokugawa Shogunate**. The three Tokugawa-related clans were given estates in the most strategically important areas, followed by the lords who had fought on the Tokugawa side. Last came the "outside lords", whose loyalty was questionable; they were allocated fiefdoms in the remotest regions. To keep all these *daimyō* in check they were required to reside part of the year in Edo, thus forcing them into expensive, time-consuming journeys, and to surrender family hostages who lived permanently under the eyes of the authorities in Edo Castle. A sophisticated network of inspectors and spies was set up, and any significant rebuilding of local castles had to be reported.

In its early years, the Tokugawa Shogunate exhibited a high degree of ambivalence towards the European arrivals. As **Christianity** increasingly appeared to threaten state security, more and more strictures were placed on all foreigners and harsh **persecutions** were conducted against the missionaries and Christian converts.

By 1638, the year of final exclusion of foreigners, an estimated 250,000 Japanese Christians had been executed, imprisoned or forced to apostatize. The final stand took place in 1637 at **Shimabara**, near Nagasaki, when a Christian-led rebel army was annihilated (see box, p.689). Thus began the period of *sakoku*, or the **closed country**, which lasted more-or-less continuously until 1853. The only legitimate exceptions to the edicts were a handful of Dutch and Chinese traders allowed to operate out of Nagasaki.

The long period of stability under the Tokugawa, interrupted only by a few peasant rebellions, brought steady **economic development**. Several towns grew to a considerable size, and by the late eighteenth century Edo had become the world's largest city, with a population of roughly one million. The arts also flourished, especially during the Genroku Period (1688–1703), which saw the first mention of

## THE RISE AND FALL OF THE SAMURAI

The origins of the **samurai**, Japan's warrior caste, go back to the ninth century, when the feudal lords began to maintain regular forces. Gradually, they evolved into an elite group of hereditary warriors, their lives governed by an unwritten code of behaviour which came to be known as *bushidō*, **the way of the warrior**. Though practice was often far from the ideal, *bushidō* encouraged rigorous self-discipline, the observance of strict laws of etiquette and, most importantly, unquestioning loyalty.

According to this code, the *samurai*, his wife and children were expected to die willingly to protect the life and honour of their feudal lord. If they failed in this duty, or were about to be taken prisoner on a battlefield, then suicide was the only fitting response. The traditional, and excruciatingly painful, method of **ritual suicide** (*seppuku*, or *hara-kiri*) was disembowelment with a sword or dagger, though in later years an accomplice would stand by to cut off the victim's head. However, there were many variations on the theme; one particularly gruesome legend tells of a warrior who had himself buried alive, in full armour, astride his poor horse.

The *samurai* creed reached full bloom in the early Tokugawa era (see opposite), when class distinctions were officially delineated. The *samurai* were deemed "the masters of the four classes" – above farmers, artisans and merchants – and they alone were permitted to carry swords. They even had the right to kill any member of the lower

orders for disrespectful behaviour – real or imagined. This privilege was graphically known as *kirisute-gomen*, literally "cut, throw away, pardon".

During the more peaceful seventeenth and eighteenth centuries, many *samurai* found themselves out of work as their lords were dispossessed and fiefdoms redistributed. Many became **rōnin**, or masterless *samurai*, whose lives were romanticized in such films as *The Seven Samurai* (see p.803). Among the most celebrated were the 47 *rōnin* (see p.138) and an individual called Musashi, who reputedly prevailed in 66 sword fights, several against heavy odds, and then went to live in a cave since there was no one else worthy of the challenge.

As their fighting skills were no longer required, the *samurai* grew increasingly impoverished and demoralized. Some found alternative ways to earn a living, while others were encouraged to study and later proved invaluable administrators in the post-1868 Meiji administration. At the same time the government formally abolished the **samurai** system, and only allowed members of the new imperial army to wear swords. All this was too much for some of the old guard, the most famous of which was Saigō Takamori. A larger-than-life hero, Saigō led a rebellion against the Meiji government in 1877 (see p.775) and died on the battlefield in true *samurai* spirit, fighting to the end against desperate odds.

*ukiyo*, the **"floating world"** of fleeting plea-sures. Artists churned out **woodblock prints** (*ukiyo-e*) popularizing the puppet plays of Chikamatsu (see p.797) and novels of Saikaku; **Hokusai** alone is said to have produced 35,000 paintings and illustrated 437 volumes (see p.794).

## A CHINK IN THE DOOR

During Japan's period of seclusion a small num-ber of Westerners managed to breach the barri-ers. Of these, perhaps the most famous were two academics: **Kaempfer**, a Dutchman who wrote the first European-language history of Japan in the late seventeenth century, and the German physician **Siebold** who arrived in 1823. Somewhat surprisingly, Japan also became briefly embroiled in the Napoleonic Wars, when Captain Pellew of the British Royal Navy pursued two Dutch merchantmen, then the enemy, into Nagasaki harbour in 1808. Various British survey vessels and Russian envoys also visited Japan in the early nineteenth century, but the greatest pressure came from **America**, whose trading and whaling routes passed to the south of the country.

The American government's initial aim was merely to secure victualling stations and guar-anteed protection for shipwrecked sailors. With this in mind, **Commodore Matthew Perry** was sent with a small fleet to persuade the Japanese to open at least some ports to for-eigners. On his first visit in 1853 he outlined his requirements and promised he would return after the authorities had been given due time to consider them. He also made it clear that refusal was not an option.

His visit threw Japan into turmoil. The Shogunate was already fearful of foreign incur-sions following the British defeat of China in the Opium Wars. Lines were quickly drawn between those for and against acceding to Perry's demands, while the weakness of the Shogunate was thrown into clear relief when the emperor demanded that the foreigners be rebuffed – Japan's military was no longer up to the task.

There followed a decade of jockeying for power between the Japanese factions, and for influence by the foreign envoys. The first of these was the American **Townsend Harris** (see p.194), who managed to extract concessions in the form of the pioneering **Treaty of Commerce and Navigation** in 1858. This was followed by a flurry of similar agreements with other Western countries, which were known locally as the **"unequal treaties"**. They opened the **treaty ports** of Yokohama, Hakodate, Nagasaki and, later, Kōbe and Ōsaka to trade, forbade the Japanese to impose protective tariffs and allowed foreigners the right of residence and cer-tain judicial rights in the enclaves. Opponents of such shameful appeasement by the Shogunate, took up the slogan "Revere the Emperor! Expel the barbarians!". Other, less reactionary factions could see that Japan was in no state to do this, and their only hope of remaining independent was to learn from the more powerful nations.

During the 1860s there were several murder-ous attacks on foreign residents, but these paled into insignificance compared to the opposing forces now gathering among the Japanese fac-tions. The great **western clans**, the Satsuma, Chōshū, Tosa and Hizen, lately at each other's throats, combined under the banner of the **emperor** to exact revenge against the Tokugawa, whom they had seen as usurpers of the throne ever since Sekigahara (see p.772). Evidence of the shift in power came in 1863 when the emperor ordered Shogun Iemochi to Kyoto to explain his conciliatory actions – it was the first visit by a shogun to the imperial capital since 1634. To add to the humiliation, he could muster a mere 3,000 retainers, compared with the 300,000 who accompanied Ieyasu to Kyoto on that earlier occasion.

In 1866, seeing the writing on the wall, the fifteenth and final shogun, **Tokugawa Yoshinobu**, formally applied to the emperor to have imperial power restored, and in January 1867 the Shogunate was terminated. In December of the same year the **Imperial Restoration** was formally proclaimed and the fifteen-year-old Mutsuhito acceded to the throne, ushering in a period optimistically dubbed **Meiji** or "enlightened rule". In 1869, the young emperor shifted his court from Kyoto to Edo, and renamed it **Tokyo** (Eastern Capital), the first official, administrative and commercial capital of Japan.

## THE MEIJI ERA 1868–1912

The reign of **Emperor Meiji**, as Mutsuhito was posthumously known, saw vast changes taking place in Japan. A policy of **modernization**, termed *fukoku kyohei* (enrich the country, strengthen the military), was adopted.

Railways were built, compulsory education and military service introduced, the solar calendar adopted and the feudal fiefs and the class system abolished. Such rapid changes were bound to create resistance and in 1877, **Saigō Takamori**, a hero of the restoration, led an army of 40,000 in the **Satsuma Rebellion** (named after the area of Kyūshū in which it erupted), see box on p.710.

In the 1880s, even more changes were rubber stamped by the ruling oligarchy of Meiji Restoration leaders, who imported thousands of foreign advisors (*yatoi*) for assistance. As a craze for Japanese *objets d'art* swept Europe, Western architecture, fashions, food (such as beef, referred to as "mountain whale") and pastimes were *de rigueur* in Japan. But as Japan adopted a Western-style constitution in 1889, drawn up by the emperor's trusted advisor **Itō Hirobumi**, the seeds of the country's later troubles were being sown.

The **Meiji Constitution**, modelled after Germany's, created a weak parliament (the Diet), the lower house of which less than twenty percent of the population were entitled to vote for. In effect the oligarchy, and in particular the military, was still in charge, a situation enforced with the Imperial Rescript on Education in 1890, which enshrined almost as law loyalty to the emperor, family and state. Shinto, which emphasized emperor-worship became the state religion, while Buddhism, associated too closely with the previous order, was disestablished.

Having taken their lead from the West in terms of material change, Japan's rulers began to copy their territorial ambitions. The island of Hokkaidō, previously left pretty much to the native Ainu (see box, p.298), was actively colonized, partly to ward off a rival take over by Russia. Territorial spats with the ailing empire of China developed into the **Sino-Japanese War** in 1894, over the Chinese tributary state of Korea. The fighting lasted less than a year, with a treaty being signed in Shimonoseki in 1895 which granted Korea independence and indemnities, economic concessions and territory to Japan, including Taiwan, then called Formosa.

This unexpected victory brought Japan into conflict with the colony-hungry Western powers, and in particular Russia who had her eye on China's Liaodong peninsula for a naval base at Port Arthur. After cordial relations with Britain were cemented in the 1902 Anglo-Japanese Alliance, Japan felt bold enough to launch her navy on a successful rout of the Russian fleet in February 1904. The land battles of the **Russo-Japanese War** were less decisive, but in a US-mediated treaty in September 1905, Russia was forced to make many territorial concessions to Japan.

In 1909, the assassination of Itō Hirobumi, the newly appointed "resident general" of Korea, gave Japan the excuse it was seeking to fully annex the country the following year. With the military in control, and a plot against the emperor's life uncovered in 1911, any domestic left-wing dissent was quashed. Meanwhile, the Western powers' admiration of plucky Japan, which less than half a century before had been a medieval country, tempered any qualms they might have had about its increasingly aggressive territorial behaviour.

## TAISHŌ ERA 1912–1926

The sudden death of Emperor Meiji in 1912 ushered in the relatively brief **Taishō** (Great Righteousness) **era**. Meiji's son Yoshihito, the only surviving male out of his fourteen children, suffered hereditary mental illness and by 1921 was so incapacitated that his own son Hirohito was declared regent.

Britain had sent 500 sailors from the Royal Navy to march in Emperor Meiji's funeral parade and when **World War I** broke out two years later, this was the country Japan chose to ally itself with. Despite gaining more territory in Asia after the war and being one of the "Big Five" at the Paris Peace Conference and a founder member of the League of Nations in 1920, Japan was frustrated by Australia, Britain and the US in its attempts to get a declaration of racial equality inserted as part of the Charter of the League.

This snub didn't stand in the way of continued friendly relations between Japan and the West, though. In 1921 Crown Prince Hirohito was a guest of King George V at Buckingham Palace, while the following year the Prince of Wales spent a month touring Japan.

In many ways, the Roaring Twenties were no different in Japan (at least in the cities) than anywhere else in the industrialized world. Jazz, Marxism, modern arts and café society all caught on. Levelling Yokohama and much of Tokyo, and leaving 140,000 dead or missing, the

1923 **Great Kantō Earthquake** was a significant blow, but the country was quickly back on its feet and celebrating the inauguration of **Emperor Hirohito**, in 1926, who chose the name **Shōwa** (Enlightened Peace) for his reign.

## THE SLIDE TO WAR

Sadly, peace is the last thing that Hirohito's reign is remembered for. Economic and political turmoil in the early 1930s provided the military with the opportunity it needed to seize full control. Japan's politicians stood by helplessly during the **Manchurian Incident** of 1931, when army officers unilaterally cooked up an excuse for attacking and occupying the Manchurian region of northern China. Japan installed **P'u Yi**, the last emperor of China's Manchu dynasty, as the head of their puppet state, Manchukuo, and responded to Western condemnation of its actions by pulling out of the League of Nations.

At home, the military increased its grip on power in the wake of **assassinations** in 1932 of both the finance and prime ministers, and a confused, short-lived **coup** by 1400 dissident army officers in February 1936. At the same time, **rapid industrialization** was laying the foundations for some of the most famous Japanese firms of the twentieth century, including the automobile makers Mazda, Toyota, Nissan, the film company Fuji and the electronics giant Matsushita.

In 1936, Japan nailed its colours to the mast by joining with Nazi Germany and Fascist Italy in the **Anti-Comintern Pact**, and the following year launched a full-scale invasion of China. In December 1937, the infamous **Rape of Nanking** occurred when appalling atrocities and massacres were committed against hundreds of thousands of unarmed Chinese soldiers and civilians.

As **World War II** began in Europe, Japan initially held off attacking Allied colonies in the Far East, but when France and Holland fell to Germany their qualms disappeared. Sanctions were imposed by Britain and the US as Japan's army moved into Indo-China, threatening Malaya and the East Indies. War between the Allies and Japan was becoming inevitable.

## THE PACIFIC WAR

On December 7, 1941, the Japanese launched a surprise attack on the US naval base at Hawaii's **Pearl Harbour**, starting the **Pacific War**. In rapid succession, the Philippines, Indonesia, Malaya and Burma fell to the seemingly unstoppable Japanese forces. However, the tide was stemmed in New Guinea and, in June 1942, the US navy won a decisive victory at the **Battle of Midway**, by sinking four Japanese aircraft carriers.

Although Japan had launched her campaign to secure the "Greater East Asia Co-Prosperity Sphere", in which she would free her neighbours from colonization and help them develop like the West, the brutal, racist and exploitative reality of Japanese occupation meant there was no support from these potential Southeast Asian allies. Nor was there a likelihood of military co-operation between Japan and Germany, who both eyed each other suspiciously despite their pact.

By 1944, with the US capture of the Pacific island of Saipan, Japan was clearly heading for **defeat**. The country was now within range of US heavy bombers, but there was a determination to fight to the bitter end, as exemplified by suicidal kamikaze pilots (see pp.722–723) and the defending forces on the islands of Iwō-jima and Okinawa who fought to the last man.

In March 1945, Tokyo was in ashes and 100,000 were dead following three days of fire bombings. The government insisted that the emperor-system remain inviolate when they put down arms, but no such assurances were offered in July 1945 when the allies called for Japan's unconditional surrender in the Potsdam Declaration. Japan failed to respond, providing the allies with the excuse they needed to drop the **Atomic bomb** on **Hiroshima** on August 6 (see p.549). Two days later, the USSR declared war on Japan, while the next day, the second A-bomb exploded over **Nagasaki**.

With millions homeless and starving, and the country brought to its knees, it was a breathtaking understatement for Emperor Hirohito to broadcast, on August 15, 1945, that the war had "developed not necessarily to Japan's advantage". For his subjects, gathered at wireless sets around the country, the realization of defeat was tempered by their amazement at hearing, for the first time, the voice of a living god.

## THE AMERICAN OCCUPATION 1945–1952

Having never lost a war, let alone been occupied, Japan little knew what to expect from the arrival of the "American Shogun" **General Douglas MacArthur**, designated the Supreme

Commander of the Allied Forces (SCAP). Some 500 soldiers committed suicide, but for the rest of the population the **Occupation** was a welcome relief from the privations of war and an opportunity to start again, under the guidance of the world's most successful nation.

MacArthur wasted no time in instituting **political and social reform**. The country was demilitarized, the bureaucracy purged of military supporters and war trials held, resulting in seven hangings, including that of the ex-prime minister, Tōjō Hideki. The emperor, whose support for the new regime was seen as crucial, was spared although he had to publicly renounce his divinity to become a symbolic head of state.

In 1946, the Americans took a week to draft a **new constitution**, which, ironically, proclaimed sovereignty resided in the Japanese people, and contained the unique provision renouncing war and "the threat or use of force as a means of settling international disputes". Land and educational reform followed.

The **peace treaty** signed in San Francisco on September 8, 1951, resolved all issues with the Allies, leaving only the USSR as a threatening Communist force. The outbreak of the **Korean War** in 1950 gave a further boost to Japan's economy as the country became the main supplier of food and arms for the US forces.

The Occupation officially ended on April 28, 1952, but with the Korean War continuing and the **Treaty of Mutual Co-operation and Security** guaranteeing the US the right to maintain bases on Japanese soil, a strong American presence remained for many years to come. The island of Okinawa was, in fact, only returned to Japan in 1972.

## THE 1960S ECONOMIC MIRACLE

In 1955, in the face of rising left-wing antagonism to the continued security pact with the US, America's CIA provided funding for the right-wing Liberal and Democrat parties to join forces. The **Liberal Democratic Party** (LDP), a tight coalition of power-hungry factions, governed Japan uninterrupted for close on the next forty years, creating the stable political conditions for an incredible economic recovery. The term **Japan Inc** was coined for the close co-operation that developed between government, bureaucracy and business, with the civil service

bodies such as the Ministry for Intenational Trade and Industry (MITI) calling many of the shots.

In 1959, **Crown Prince Akihito** married Shoda Michiko, a commoner he'd met on the tennis courts of the summer resort Karuizawa, a far cry from the marriage of his own father, arranged by the court without Hirohito even setting eyes on his prospective bride. As the decade closed, the economy had grown at twice the rate expected, and during the 1960s, under a ten-year plan drawn up by **Prime Minister Ikeda Hayato**, it continued to boom. A key year was 1964: Japan joined the rich nations "club", the Organization for Economic Co-operation and Development, inaugurated the high-speed bullet train and hosted the Summer Olympic Games.

As families across the country worked to buy a refrigerator, television and washing machine (the "three sacred treasures"), the growing consumer economy around the world provided the main outlet for Japan's highly desirable industrial and technical goods. Japanese **exports** grew twice as fast as world trade, an incredible reversal of events for a country whose products, only a couple of decades earlier, had been the last word in unreliability. At the same time, Japan protected its home markets by subjecting imports to quotas, a mass of regulations or outright bans.

Although Japan notably didn't suffer the kind of social breakdown (increased crime, use of drugs) associated with growing affluence in the West, it didn't escape entirely from paying for its economic miracle. Not only did rapid industrialization physically scar the country, **pollution** wrecked lives, particularly in the Kyūshū fishing village of Minamata, where mercury poisoning caused the horrific Minamata disease (see p.696). In 1971, Tokyo's metropolitan government officially declared that the capital's residents breathed polluted air, drank contaminated water and were "subjected to noise levels that strain the nerves".

By the 1970s, the ingrained **corruption** festering at the heart of Japanese politics was also becoming clear. The conservative LDP had continued to hold power partly by astutely hijacking its rivals' policies, but mainly by entering into cosy financial relationships with supporters in industry and commerce. Prime Minister **Tanaka Kakuei**, a self-made politician from Niigata, had already attracted criticism for pushing through the needless construction of a Shinkansen line to his home town, when his abuse of party funds in the Upper House elections of July 1974 caused fellow LDP grandees to quit the Cabinet in protest. Takeda rode the scandal out, but couldn't survive the bribery charges, brought in February 1976, in connection with the purchase of aircraft from America's Lockheed Corporation.

## THE OIL SHOCK

Attention was swiftly diverted from other problems, however, by the **Middle East oil embargo** of 1973. Three-quarters of Japan's energy needs were met by imported fuel, so the overnight quadrupling of oil prices was a severe shock to the country, which rapidly had to introduce measures to tackle inflation, reduce energy consumption and stem growth. The economy suffered, but, as ever, Japan learnt lessons, improved its processes and emerged in the next decade fitter and more vigorous than ever.

A buzzword of the booming 1980s was **kokusaika** (internationalization), even if nobody seemed to know quite what it meant. Yet, at the same time as the Japanese were being urged to take a global view, the world was increasingly complaining about Japan's insular ways. The country's huge **balance of payments surplus** and restrictive trade practices set it at odds with the international community and particularly the US. The tense situation wasn't eased as cash-rich Japanese companies snapped up American firms and assets, such as the Rockefeller Center in New York, and the trade surplus with the US totalled over $30 billion.

Despite the factional infighting and jockeying for power that continued within the LDP, the party clung on to power largely by providing voters with a continually rising standard of living. Opposition parties, such as the Japan Socialist Party, were too weak and espoused unrealistic policies. The country, however, ran through a succession of **scandal-prone prime ministers**, who slipped quickly in and out of office in the wake of bribery allegations and sexual shenanigans. Even the dapper Nakasone Yasuhiro, who became the first fluent English-speaking prime minister in 1982, was not immune, offending the US by saying that it lagged behind Japan because it was hampered by ethnic minorities.

In the meantime, Japan's **booming economy** and soaring rise in real estate values fed into a decade of unprecedented wealth and spending. Families now aspired to the "3 Vs" – video, villa and vacation abroad. Construction, long the bedrock of the economy, continued apace with skyscrapers shooting up across the country along with mammoth engineering projects, such as the Seto Ōhashi, the bridge linking the main island of Honshū and Shikoku.

The decade wasn't all conspicuous domestic consumption, though. By the time of the death of Emperor Hirohito in January 1989, Japan was the world's second largest donor of **overseas aid**. But as the Shōwa era came to an end, ushering in the **Heisei** (Accomplished Peace) **era**, the omens for the country were far from auspicious as the overheated "bubble economy" reached bursting point.

## THE 1990S: A DECADE OF UNCERTAINTY

The 1990s kicked off with the coronation of Emperor Akihito and a political crisis surrounding the **Gulf War**. Japan's command of its economy had long been sure footed, but its management of defence issues, constrained by the anti-war constitution and security alliances with the US, was less certain. Now it was under pressure to send its Self Defence Forces (SDF) overseas, something expressly forbidden by the constitution.

As a member of the United Nations and an aspirant for a seat on the Security Council, Japan knew it had to respond to the international call to arms. The compromise of $17.3 billion in financial aid satisfied no one, not least the more hawkish factions of the splintering LDP. In 1992, after protracted debate and amid public demonstrations, the Diet passed a controversial bill allowing Japanese troops to join **UN peace-keeping missions** abroad.

The main reason for a continued squeamishness about an overseas military role is the haunting presence of Japan's actions during World War II. The San Francisco treaty did little to satisfy those who had experienced first-hand brutal treatment by the Japanese army during the war, not least the former colonies in Southeast Asia. Old wounds were re-opened as the covered-up issue of forced prostitution, or "comfort women" as it was euphemistically dubbed, was blasted across the media in the early 1990s.

Some light relief was supplied in 1993 when Crown Prince Naruhito married Owada Masako, a high-flying career diplomat. But even this happy occasion was marred for some by the fact that Owada, a shining symbol of improved opportunities for women in what remains a highly sexist country, appeared to have been pressured into the deeply conservative role of empress-in-waiting.

Despite a growing recognition that the boom years were well and truly over, the mass of the population continued to enjoy the affluent good life. Particularly noticeable were Princess Masako's less-fettered contemporaries, the army of **office ladies** (OLs) who with their spending power kick-started many a fashion fad, from a taste for the Italian sweet Tiramisu to the G-string panties favoured by podium dancers at mega discos, such as Tokyo's Juliannas.

As the recession gripped and fashions changed, it also seemed that the days of the ruling LDP were finally numbered. By the time the crusty power broker **Kanamaru Shin** locked himself away at home and played mah-jong rather than answer police questions about yet another bribery scandal, the public had had their fill of corrupt politicians. More importantly, rival factions within the LDP decided to make independent bids for power rather than brokering yet more deals in smoke-filled rooms.

Leading the most influential faction was **Ozawa Ichiro**, one of Japan's powerful politicians, as much loathed for his outspoken views as admired for his radical policies. A successful no-confidence motion in June 1993 forced Prime Minister Miyazawa Kiichi's shaky government into a hasty **general election**. Although the LDP actually gained one seat, the overall balance of power passed to a coalition of opposition parties, who formed the first non-LDP government in 38 years under leadership of the populist, reforming politician **Hosokawa Morihiro**.

However, hopes of a new beginning for Japanese politics faded as the charismatic Hosokawa, who'd stood on an anti-corruption ticket and had relied on Ozawa's support to become prime minister, lasted less than a year. A plan to double the hated consumption tax went down like a lead balloon and when a story broke about Hosokawa's less than white past with regard to election funding, it was

clear he had to go. His successor **Hata Tsumoto**, another ally of Ozawa, saw the Socialists walk on the coalition on his first day of office, and his premiership went down in history as the shortest since World War II, at just four months.

The Socialists, already decimated in numbers at the last election, did themselves no favours by siding with their old foes, the LDP, to form the next government. This cynical alliance put the LDP back in the control seat, just over a year since it had lost power and forced new premier **Murayama Tomiichi**, a Socialist elder statesman to have his party drop long-held pacifist policies (much to the disgust of voters).

The political paralysis at the heart of the LDP/Socialist coalition became all too apparent in the sluggish response to the massive **Great Hanshin Earthquake** of January 1995 which devastated Kōbe (see p.506). Immediate offers of foreign help were rebuffed and the local *yakuza* further shamed the government by organizing food supplies to the thousands of homeless. The nation's self-confidence took a further battering less than a couple of months later when members of a religious cult, **AUM Shinrikyō** (see p.788), killed 12 and poisoned 5500 when they released Sarin nerve gas on the Tokyo subway. Japan went into introspective shock.

The voters' disillusion with the traditional political parties was underlined by the elections in 1995 of former popular TV performers (*tarento*) as mayors of Tokyo and Ōsaka, and the success of the squeaky-clean Communist Party in the local election of 1996. The same year, however, in the Diet, the Socialists crumbled and the LDP returned to full power, under the leadership of **Hashimoto Ryutaro** who made a name for himself as a tough-talking, slick trade negotiator with the US.

Although at first a popular choice, Hashimoto's premiership was incapable of withstanding the continued onslaught of economic problems. In November 1997 the image of the sobbing president of the failed major brokerage firm, Yamaichi Securities Co, summed up the end of the era of Japan Inc. No longer were Japan's government and bureaucrats willing – or able – to support enterprises, especially those like Yamaichi with billions of yen of bad debts spawned by the dubious financial practices of the previous decade. The dead hand of the market had finally caught up with Japan, and the one-time wonder economy that had been the envy of the world appeared on the brink of collapse.

## INTO THE MILLENNIUM

The official announcement of **recession** in June 1998 coupled with the plummeting value of the yen and rising unemployment, saw the LDP take a drubbing in the August 1998 upper house **elections**, when the party didn't win a single seat in the major metropolitan districts. Hashimoto resigned and was replaced by the Obuchi Keizo, a genial but lacklustre politician who many believe is only holding the fort until **Kan Naoto**, the charismatic leader of the opposition Democratic Party, can garner enough votes at the next lower house elections to finally topple the LDP.

In the meantime, the rest of the world is looking on nervously as each month brings worsening reports of Japan's economic health. However, amid all the doom and gloom, it's worth bearing in mind that Japan is still an enormously wealthy country and that it has bounced back from similarly dire straits many a time before. In what could come to be seen as a pivotal moment, the nation was gripped, at the end of 1998, by the saga of Japan's first legal sex-change operation, turning a woman into a man. Perhaps there's time yet for Japan to reinvent itself for the new Millennium.

Ron Clough and Simon Richmond

# RELIGION, BELIEF AND RITUAL

The indigenous religion of Japan is Shinto, and all Japanese people belong to it by default. From a population of roughly 126 million, 96 million people are also Buddhist and around 1.5 million Christian. The idea of combining religions may seem strange, but a mixture of philosophy, politics and a bit of creative interpretation has, over time, enabled this to happen.

The most important factor that allowed faiths to combine is that Shinto, a naturalistic religion, does not possess one all-powerful deity, sacred scriptures or a particular philosophy or moral code. It states that its followers must live their lives according to the way of mind of the **kami** (gods), and that the *kami* favour harmony and co-operation. Therefore, Shinto tolerates its worshippers following other religions, and they find it an easy step to combine Shinto's nature worship with the worship of an almighty deity, such as that in Christianity, or with the philosophical moral code of Buddhism.

Religion still has great relevance to the Japanese, even though many people do not involve themselves with it regularly until their later years. The relationship between people and their tutelary *kami* is like that between parent and child. Generations have been born and lived under the protection of the *kami*. When they die, the Japanese become *kami*, so not only are their ancestors *kami*, but they themselves will become so, creating, in theory, an inherent and unbreakable relationship with religion. Festivals are a common sight and many ancient Shinto customs are still manifest in everyday life.

## SHINTO

**Shinto**, or "the way of the gods", only received its name in the sixth century to distinguish it from the newly arrived Buddhism. Gods are felt to be present in natural phenomena, for example mountains, trees, waterfalls, strangely shaped rocks, even in sounds. But Shinto is more than just a nature-worshipping faith; it is an amalgam of attitudes, ideas and ways of doing things that for more than 2000 years has become an integral part of what it is to be Japanese. Shinto is a personal faith in the *kami*, a communal way of life in accordance with the mind of the *kami* and a spiritual life attained through worship of and communion with the *kami*. People believe that

## THE BIRTH OF JAPAN

Japan's **mythological origins** could have come from the pen of J R R Tolkien. According to the oldest written records, the **Kojiki** and the **Nihonshoki** (see p.769), the god Izanagi-no-Mikoto and goddess Izanami-no-Mikoto leant down from the Floating Bridge of Heaven and stirred the ocean with a jewelled spear. Drops of brine falling from the spear created the first island of Japan, Onogoro-jima, where the couple gave birth to an "eight island country", complete with *kami*. **Amaterasu**, the **Sun Goddess** and ultimate ancestress of the imperial family, was created out of a bronze mirror held in Izanagi's left hand and sent to rule the heavens. Her younger brother, **Susano-ō**, was put in charge of the earth. Unhappy with this situation, he started causing turmoil in the heavens, and so upset Amaterasu that she hid herself in a celestial cave, plunging the world into darkness.

The other gods banished Susano-ō to the underworld. Then, in an effort to coax Amaterasu out of the cave, they performed a comical dance involving a spear. Upon hearing the somewhat ribald laughter, Amaterasu's curiosity got the better of her and she poked her head out to see the fun. Enticed out a little further by a beautiful jewel, Amaterasu was then captivated by a bronze mirror. While she was preoccupied, the gods quickly sealed the cave entrance and sunlight returned to the world.

In time, Amaterasu's grandson, **Ninigi**, was sent down to rule Japan. She gave him three gifts which were to be his **imperial regalia**: a bronze mirror, a sword and a curved jewel. Here myth finally merges into proto-history, when **Jimmu**, said to be Ninigi's great grandson, became the **first emperor** of Japan on the first day of spring 660 BC.

they are the children of both their parents and *kami* and therefore owe their lives to both society and nature. In return for the love and protection they receive, they are obliged to treat both of them with loyalty and honesty, and to continue the family line showing kindness and guidance to their descendants.

Throughout most of Japanese history, Shinto did not play a particularly important role in state politics. This all changed, however, after the **Meiji Restoration** of 1868 when Shinto was revived as the dominant religion, largely to reestablish the cult of the emperor, while Buddhism was suppressed. Thus started the most sinister episode of Japan's religious and political life: **State Shinto**.

State Shinto ushered in a period of **extreme nationalism** which lasted from around 1890 to 1945. During this period, Japan's mythological origins (see box on previous page) were taught as historical fact and people were encouraged to believe that all Japanese were descended from the imperial line. At the same time, the traditional values of loyalty, inner strength and self-denial expressed in *bushidō* (the way of the warrior) were promoted as desirable personal qualities. Such sentiments were milked by the 1930s military regime to foster a national sense of superiority. Ultimately, this potent cocktail created a highly dedicated nation on the eve of World War II. After the war, Emperor Hirohito was forced to renounce his divinity, to became a merely titular head of state, and the State branch of Shinto was abolished.

### SHINTO SHRINES

Shinto shrines are called **jinja** (*kami*-dwelling), although you will also see the suffixes -*jingū* and -*gū*. These terms, and the *torii* gates (see below), are the easiest ways to distinguish between Shinto shrines and Buddhist temples (see p.785). The shrine provides a dwelling for the *kami*, which is felt to be present in the surrounding nature, and also a place to service and worship it. Though there are many styles of **shrine architecture**, they are traditionally built from unpainted cypress wood with a grass-thatch roof. Look out for the *chigi*, extensions of the end beams which form a cross at each end of the roof ridge, and *katsuogi*, short logs lying horizontally on top of the ridge. The best examples of such traditional architecture are the Grand Shrine of Ise, Izumo Taisha (near Matsue), and

Tokyo's Meiji-jingū. Later designs show Chinese or Korean influences, such as the use of red and white paint or other ornamentation.

Perhaps the most distinctive feature of a shrine is the **torii** which marks the gateway between the secular and the spiritual world. Traditionally, these were plain and simple wooden constructions consisting of two upright pillars and two crossbeams. Gradually various styles, such as the distinctive red paint, evolved on the same basic design until there were over twenty different types of *torii*. Nowadays, they are also made of stone, metal and concrete, in which case they tend to remain unpainted. Though the origins are obscure, *torii* means "bird perch" and they were a common form of secular gateway before 1884, after which their use was restricted to shrines.

Inside the compound, you often find pairs of human or animal **statues** on the approach to the shrine building: austere dignitaries in ancient court costume laden with weapons are the traditional Japanese guardians, though you'll also find lion-dogs (*koma-inu*), or large, ferocious-looking *Niō* borrowed from Buddhist temples. Others may be animal-messengers of the *kami*, such as the fox-messenger of Inari, the deity of good harvests.

Somewhere in the compound you'll often see a **sacred tree**, denoted by a twisted straw rope, *shimenawa*, sporting zigzags of white paper, tied around it. In the past these trees were believed to be the special abode of some *kami*. Now they're just an expression of divine consciousness which, like other aspects of the surrounding nature, help to bring people's minds out of the mundane world and enter into that of the *kami*.

Finally, you come to the **shrine building** itself. At the entrance there's a slotted box for donations and a rope with a bell or gong at the top. Some say the bell is rung as a purification rite to ward off evil spirits, others that it's to attract the *kami*'s attention. You'll also notice another *shimenawa* delineating the *kami*'s sacred dwelling place. Inside each shrine there's an **inner chamber** containing the *shintai* (divine body). This is a sacred object which symbolizes the presence of the *kami* and is kept under lock and key – if ever seen, it loses its religious power. The sacred objects of some shrines are known to be mirrors (see below). In front of the chamber an **offering table** holds the *gohei*, a symbolic offering consisting of a stick with more white-paper zigzags attached, and the purification wand (*haraigushi*). This is either a wand of thin paper strips and flax, or a sprig of the sacred *sakaki*, an evergreen tree. Sometimes there's also a **mirror** between the table and the inner chamber. The mirror is of great mythological and religious importance since it symbolizes not only the stainless mind of the *kami*, but also the fidelity of the worshipper since it reflects everything truthfully. In some cases the mirror itself can be the sacred object; for example, the mirror that Amaterasu gave Ninigi is supposedly held in the inner chamber of Ise-jingū – Japan's most sacred shrine.

A large shrine may also comprise many other buildings, such as subordinate shrines, an oratory, ablution pavilion, offering hall, shrine office and shop, priests' living quarters, treasure house and sometimes even a platform for sacred dances, a *Nō* drama stage or a sumo arena.

## SHINTO RITES AND FESTIVALS

The Japanese pray at shrines for many different reasons, and this may determine which shrine they go to. It may be just to offer thanks to their local or clan *kami* for their protection and blessing, or it may be to pray for something special, for example a successful child birth. *Kami* are sometimes specialists in a certain type of blessing, so it's no use going to a *kami* who specialises in health if you want to pray for success in a forthcoming exam.

When **visiting a shrine** you should try to fulfil at least three of the four elements of worship. Of these, **purification** is perhaps the most important as it indicates respect for the *kami*. Traditionally, anyone suffering from an illness or open wound, menstruating women or those in mourning are considered impure and are not supposed to enter the shrine. At the ablution pavilion (a water trough near the entrance), ladle some water over your finger tips and then pour a little into your cupped hand and rinse your mouth with it; afterwards, spit the water out into the gutter below. Now purified, you can proceed to the shrine itself and the **offering**. This normally consists of throwing a coin in the box – a five yen coin is considered luckiest – though a special service warrants a larger sum wrapped in formal paper. Depending on the occasion, food, drink, material goods or even sacred dances (*kagura*, performed by

female shrine attendants) or sumo contests are offered to the *kami*.

The third element is **prayer**. Pull the rope to ring the bell, bow slightly once, then deeply twice, pray, bow deeply two more times, clap your hands twice at chest level and end with two last bows, deep and then slight. The final element of worship is the **sacred feast**, which usually only follows a special service or a festival. It sometimes takes the form of consuming the food or drink offered to the *kami* – once the *kami's* had its symbolic share. The feast starts with a formal toast of sake and often ends up in great merriment and karaoke.

At the shrine shop you can buy charms (*omamori*) against all manner of ills, fortune papers (*omikuji*), which people then twist round tree branches to make them come true, and wooden votive tablets (*ema*) – write your wishes on the tablet and tie it up alongside the others.

Perhaps the most interesting aspect of Shinto for the visitor is its lively and colourful **festivals**. All shrines have at least one annual festival which are well worth hunting out. During the festival, the *kami* is symbolically transferred from the inner chamber to an ornate palanquin. This is its temporary home while young men hurtle around the local area with it so that the *kami* can bless the homes of the faithful. The passion with which they run, turning it this way and that, jostling it up and down shouting "*wassho, wassho*" has to be seen to be believed, especially in rural towns where festivals are usually conducted with more gusto. All this frantic action is said to make the *kami* happy, and it is highly contagious: long after the palanquin has returned to the shrine the merriment continues with the help of copious amounts of alcohol and the odd karaoke machine or two.

## BUDDHISM

The vast majority of Japanese people are followers of **Buddhism** as well as Shinto. Buddhism originated in India with a wealthy Hindu prince called **Siddhartha Gautama** who, dissatisfied with Hinduism's explanation of worldly suffering, rejected asceticism as the way to spiritual realization and turned instead to meditation. After several nomadic years he achieved enlightenment (*nirvana*) while meditating one night under a *bodhi* tree, and devoted the rest of his life to teaching that "right thoughts" and "right actions" must be followed to reduce all material and emotional attachments in order to increase awareness and ultimately to attain *nirvana*.

The **Mahayana** (Greater Vehicle) school of Buddhism, which believes in salvation for all beings jointly rather than the individual pursuit of *nirvana*, was introduced to Japan from China in the mid-sixth century. As with many things, Japan adapted this foreign import to suit its own culture and values. Buddha was accepted as a *kami* and, over the years, certain religious aspects were dropped or played down, for example celibacy and the emphasis on private contemplation.

But Buddhism did not travel alone to Japan; it brought with it Chinese culture. Over the next two centuries, monks, artists and scholars went to China to study religion, art, music, literature and politics, all of which brought great advances to Japanese culture. As a result, Buddhism became embroiled in the **political struggles** of the Nara and Heian eras, when weak emperors used Buddhist and Chinese culture to enhance their own power and level of cultural sophistication, and to reduce the influence of their Shintoist rivals. The balance of power between buddhas and *kami* also shifted: *kami* were regarded as being prone to rebirth, from which they could be released by Buddhist sutras. To this end, Buddhist temples were built next to Shinto shrines, and statues and regalia placed on Shinto altars to help raise the *kami* to the level of buddhas. Eventually, some *kami* became the guardians of temples, while buddhas were regarded as the prime spiritual beings.

Up until the end of the twelfth century, Japanese Buddhism was largely restricted to a small, generally aristocratic minority who had been initiated into the faith. However, at this time the dominant sect, **Tendai**, split into various **new sects**, notably Jōdo, Jōdo Shinshū, Nichiren and Zen Buddhism, which each appealed to different sections of the population. The first two in particular were simple forms of the faith which enabled Buddhism to evolve from a religion of the elite to one which also appealed to the population en masse. The Nichiren sect had a more scholastic approach, while Zen's concern for ritual, form and practice attracted the *samurai* classes and had a great influence on Japan's traditional arts. Almost all contemporary Japanese Buddhism developed

from these sects, which are still very much in existence today (see below for more on their basic tenets).

From the fifteenth century, however, Shinto started making a comeback. In reaction to the absorption of the indigenous faith into this foreign religion, various Shinto sects revived the ascendancy of *kami* over buddhas, ending the idea that they were merely Japanese manifestations of buddhas. This process came to a head after the 1868 Meiji Restoration, when Shinto was declared the national faith. Most Buddhist elements were removed from Shinto shrines and destroyed, and Buddhism was suppressed until the end of World War II when religious freedom returned to Japan. Nowadays Buddhism and Shinto co-exist peaceably once again and share the vast majority of their followers.

### THE PRINCIPAL BUDDHIST SECTS

The Tendai and Shingon sects were founded in the early ninth century, and were both based on Chinese esoteric Buddhism. Involving meditation and tantric rituals, they were established on mountains and had some similarities to the Shugendō faith of mountain asceticism (see p.786). The **Tendai** (Heavenly Terrace) sect was founded by the monk **Saichō** (767–822) on Hiei-zan near Kyoto (see p.469), where it is still very much alive. Based on the supremacy of the "Lotus Sutra", which expresses the Buddha's ultimate truth, Tendai recognized other beliefs – including Shinto – as different aspects of the one universal force. Similarly, the **Shingon** (True Word) sect, founded by **Kōbō Daishi** (774–835) and based on Kōya-san, south of Nara (see p.493), sought to reconcile various faiths around the central image of Dainichi Nyorai, the Cosmic Buddha who embodies the essence of the universe. Shingon emphasizes the idea of mutual interdependence as expressed by mandala (graphic representations of the Buddhist universe), and asserts that enlightenment can be achieved in one lifetime through chanting and meditation. For centuries, followers of Shingon have also been seeking spiritual purification by completing the 88-temple pilgrimage around Shikoku (see p.599).

**Jōdoshū**, the Pure Land sect, was founded in 1133 by the monk **Hōnen** during a period of famine, treachery and clan warfare. He asserted that the world was inherently evil and that, as it was impossible to achieve Buddhahood in this life, people should concentrate on salvation in the after-life. Faith in Amida Buddha (the Buddha of the Western Paradise) would lead to bliss in the next world. Scholastic study and religious ritual were unnecessary, making this sect popular with the uneducated masses. Instead, all that was necessary was daily prayer to Amida, often by chanting the *nembutsu*, "*Namu Amida Butsu*" (Praise to Amida Buddha). To set the pace, Hōnen would sometimes recite the *nembutsu* 60,000 times a day.

The **Jōdo Shinshū**, "True Pure Land" sect, was founded around 1224 when the monk **Shinran** broke away from the Jōdo sect. He believed that salvation was not just limited to the after-life, but that by praying to Amida one could be saved in the present life, too. He rejected all religious ritual except prayer and held that saying the *nembutsu* just once was enough if said with sufficient sincerity. He also enraged the monks of other sects by dropping celibacy and meat-eating laws. This inevitably made Jōdo Shinshū even more popular among ordinary folk, and it is one of the biggest Buddhist sects in Japan today.

By contrast, the **Nichiren** sect, named after its founder, had a very scholastic approach. Nichiren (1222–82) believed that truth, enlightenment and salvation can only come from studying Buddhist scriptures, particularly the "Lotus Sutra". He considered all other teachings and sects to be heretical. With their battlecry "*Namu Myōhō Renge Kyō*" (Hail to the Lotus of Divine Law), his fanatical followers crusaded their cause almost to the point of violence. Nichiren, however, was also an astute observer of the political situation in mainland Asia. With masterful timing, he warned that unless people repented their sins and followed his sect they would suffer the wrath of the heavens in the form of a foreign invasion – the Mongol hordes attacked soon after (see History, p.771). Never one to go quietly, Nichiren upset too many people with his fanatical preaching and was exiled on several occasions. At one point he was even sentenced to execution but, according to legend, won a reprieve – no doubt due to divine intervention – when the sword shattered on his neck.

More elaborate than its rivals, **Zen Buddhism** is far more concerned with ritual, form and practice than scholastic study. Instead, enlightenment and salvation can only come from within, and followers of the Sōtō school of Zen try to achieve this by meditating in the lotus position (*zazen*), attempting to empty the mind of all worldly thoughts and desires. Alternatively, followers of the Rinzai school try to achieve this by meditating on enigmatic riddles (*kōan*), whose only answer is enlightenment; perhaps the most famous *kōan* is "What is the sound of one hand?". Both methods serve the same purpose of taking the believer out of the material world and onto a higher plane where they can learn the nature of the Buddha.

Zen was first imported from China in the seventh century, though it didn't really get going until after 1192 when it was reintroduced by the monk **Eisai**. This time it was found more success among the new military rulers, now based in Kamakura. Zen's austere practices, demanding individual action, strong self-discipline and a spartan lifestyle, struck a chord with the *samurai*, who supported the great Zen temples of Kamakura and, later, Kyoto. Zen's minimalist approach to life, coupled with Shinto's appreciation of nature, had a profound influence on Japan's traditional arts (see p.792) and gardens. The **Zen rock gardens**, consisting of rocks placed in a "sea" of white rippled gravel, are designed to aid contemplation about everything and nothing: the whole universe and the tiny grain of sand that is an insignificant part of it. Although the individual rocks sometimes symbolize specific things – a tiger, tortoise, mountain or a crane, for example – Zen rock gardens are meant to be viewed many times without lending themselves to any one particular meaning. (See p.789 below for more about Japanese gardens.)

## BUDDHIST TEMPLES AND WORSHIP

As with Shinto shrines, **Buddhist temples** (called -*tera*, -*dera* or -*ji*) come in many different styles, depending on the sect and the date they were built, but the foremost architectural influences are Chinese and Korean. The temple's **main hall** is called the *kon-dō* or *hon-dō*; this is where you will find the principal image of Buddha and a table for offerings. Sometimes the entry **gate** (*San-mon*) is as imposing as the temple itself, consisting of a two-storey wooden structure with perhaps a pair of brightly coloured, fearsome guardians called *Niō*, or *Kongo Rikishi*. Despite their looks, the *Niō* are actually quite kind natured – except to evil spirits.

Some temples also have a **pagoda** in their compound. Pagodas are usually either three or five stories high with a roof dividing each storey and a metal spire on top. They are Chinese versions of stupas, the Indian structures built to enshrine a relic of the Buddha, and historically used to be the main focus of Buddhist worship. Depending on the temple's size, you might also see other buildings such as a study hall (*kō-dō*), scripture or treasure houses, living quarters and a temple shop. Zen temples, especially the colourful temples of Kyoto, are also famous for their stunningly beautiful rock and landscape gardens which are designed to aid meditation (see previous page).

Buddhism has no festivals or rites to match Shinto, preferring instead simple prayer and chants, the unforgettable smell of smouldering incense, and offerings of food, flowers or money. Its mystic forte are the Zen monks meditating in a lotus position, breathing slowly, emptying their minds and being periodically hit with bamboo sticks to stop them from falling asleep – for which they thank their aggressors.

The most important occasion in Japan's Buddhist calendar is **Obon** (late July to mid-August) when spirits return to earth and families traditionally gather to welcome them back to the ancestral home. *O-higan*, which falls on the spring and autumn equinox (usually March 21 and Sept 23), is again a time to visit ancestors' graves. But probably the biggest celebration is **Shōgatsu** (New Year), though it's as much a Shinto event as a Buddhist one. A long public holiday enables plenty of time for merriment and sake drinking, though remember to remain sober enough to visit the local temple or shrine to pray for good fortune in the coming year.

## SHUGENDŌ

**Shugendō** is a colourful blend of Buddhist esoteric and tantric concepts, Chinese Taoist magic and Shinto shamanism. Based on mountain asceticism, the religion was formalized in the eighth century by the monk **En-no-Gyōja**, who was famous for his mystic powers.

Following Shinto practice, Shugendō's mountain priests, **yamabushi**, believe that the mountains are centres of sacred power. They go through elaborate initiation rites, austerities and self-denial to acquire this sacred power which they can then use to heal and bless common people. Their practices include meditation, mountain hiking, chanting under freezing water falls, sitting in smoke-filled rooms, sumo wrestling, and partial denial of food, sleep and daily ablutions. These are designed to train both body and spirit, and are a metaphor for the soul's uncomfortable journey from death to rebirth.

Shugendō was quite popular until the 1868 Meiji Restoration when it, along with other forms of Buddhism, was suppressed. Nevertheless, pockets of this mysterious faith can still be found, notably on **Dewa-sanzan** in north Honshū (see p.278) where some of the ancient practices survive. One of the most lively events is the **Shōreisai** (Pine Festival), held on the night of New Year's eve. Two groups of priests hurl abuse at each other (made all the more colourful by large quantities of sake) and engage in various contests to divine whether the coming year will bring good harvests.

## FOLK RELIGION

Japanese **folk religion** draws on ideas from Shinto, Buddhism and Chinese Taoism, which added shamanism, spirit possession and magico-religious practices to the pot. The "holy men" (or women) of folk religion may be specialists in, among other things, geomancy, divination, healing, exorcism and communicating with the gods. They offer various rites and advice, for example explaining why misfortunes have occurred or recommending auspicious times for weddings, long journeys and other important events.

One manifestation of such beliefs is the **six day calendar** (sometimes incorporated into normal calendars) in which one day is considered good for all endeavours, another day is considered bad, and the other days are either good or bad at certain times for certain things. Similar notions govern the **naming of children**. Not only the time and place of birth affects the character and destiny of a person, but also their name. Before deciding on a given name, therefore, parents may consult a *hiriji* (holy man, or priest) about the number of pen strokes required to write the chosen characters. A bad combination of name, time and place of birth may result in a life of persistent misfortune.

There is also a more mythological side to Japanese folk religion involving a whole host of **gods**, **guardians** and **demons**. The ones to have on your side are the **Seven Lucky Gods**, *Shichi Fuku-jin*, often seen sailing in a boat on New Year greetings cards to wish good fortune for the coming year. Of these, the best-loved are **Ebisu**, the god of prosperity, identified by his fishing rod and sea-bream; **Daikoku**, the god of wealth, carries a treasure-sack over one shoulder and a lucky hammer; the squat **Fukurokuju**, god of longevity, is marked by a bald, egg-shaped head; while the jovial god of happiness, **Hotei**, sports a generous belly and a beaming smile.

Characters to avoid, on the other hand, are the **oni**, a general term for demons and ogres, though *oni* aren't always bad. At *Setsubun* (Feb 3 or 4) children can be seen running round throwing soya beans all over the place, shouting *"oni wa soto, suku wa uchi"*, meaning "out with the demons, in with good luck". **Tengu** are mischievous mountain goblins with red faces and very long noses, while **kappa** are a bit like a small troll and live under bridges. If anything goes missing while you're hiking, you can probably blame one of these as they both like to steal things, including animals and children. If it's your liver that's missing, however, it will definitely be a *kappa*; he likes to extract them from people's bodies through the anus, so watch out.

## CHRISTIANITY

Shipwrecked Portuguese traders were the first Christians to set foot in Japan, in Tanagcshima, an island off Kyūshū, in 1543. As far as **Christianity** is concerned though, it was not until **Saint Francis Xavier** and his **Jesuit** missionaries landed in Kagoshima, southwest Kyūshū, in 1549 that things really took off. Initially, the local *daimyō* were eager to convert, largely in order to acquire firearms and other advanced European technologies, while often also maintaining their original religious belief and practices. It wasn't only about trade, though; many feudal lords were also attracted by Jesuit austerity, which accorded with their *bushidō* values, while the poor were attracted by social programmes which helped raise their standard of living.

The port of **Nagasaki** was created in 1571 to trade with the Portuguese. It soon became a centre of Jesuit missionary activity, from where Catholicism spread rapidly throughout Kyūshū. At first, the converts were tolerated by the authorities, and in the late 1570s the then ruler

of Japan, the great, unifying general **Oda Nobunaga**, used Christianity, with all its material benefits, to win over his remaining influential opponents against the troublesome Buddhists. In 1582 he was succeeded by **Toyotomi Hideyoshi** who completed the unification of Japan. To Hideyoshi's mind the Christians had now served their purpose, and their increasing stranglehold on trade, coupled with a growing influence in secular affairs, was beginning to pose a threat. **Persecution** began in 1587 when Hideyoshi ordered the expulsion of all missionaries, though there was little immediate action; in fact the number of foreign missionaries increased temporarily with the arrival of Spanish Franciscan friars. In 1597, however, Hideyoshi struck again: six Franciscan priests and twenty local converts were crucified upside-down in Nagasaki.

Shogun Tokugawa Ieyasu succeeded Hideyoshi in 1598. Though generally more tolerant of the Christian Europeans – principally in the interests of maintaining good trade relations – Ieyasu passed several edicts prohibiting Christianity after 1612. It was a short reprieve. Ieyasu's son, **Hidetada**, turned persecution into an art form when he came to power in 1618. Suspected Christians were forced to trample on pictures of Christ or the Virgin Mary to prove their innocence. If they refused, they were tortured, burnt at the stake or thrown into boiling sulphur; over 3,000 local converts were martyred between 1597 and 1660. Things came to a head with the **Battle of Shimabara** in 1637, when a Christian-led army rebelled against the local *daimyō* (see box, p.689). Japan had been gradually closing itself off from the world during the 1620s, but this was the final straw. Christian worship in Japan was forbidden and the edicts were only finally repealed in the late nineteenth century. Amazingly, a sizeable number of converts in Kyūshū continued to uphold their faith, disguised as *onando buppo* "back room Buddhism", throughout this time. When foreign missionaries again appeared in Nagasaki in the mid-1860s, they were astonished to discover some 20,000 of these "hidden Christians" (see p.682).

Today, Christians represent less than two percent of Japan's population. Though churches can be found even in small rural towns, **Christmas** is only celebrated as a brief commercial fling. Christianity – however superficially – has also had an impact on Japanese **weddings**. It is currently fashionable to get married in Western-style chapels, created solely for that purpose, partly because it appears exotic, and partly because it's less complex than the traditional Shinto ceremony.

## THE NEW RELIGIONS

Several **new religions** appeared in Japan during the nineteenth and twentieth centuries, many of them off-shoots of Nichiren Buddhism. Their basic beliefs and practices are generally a mix of Shinto, Buddhism and Confucianism, incorporating loyalty to work and the family with teachings of karma, reincarnation and the coming of a new age. Most tend to have charismatic leaders, often of a shamanistic tradition, and grand headquarters. They also tend to appeal to the poorer classes, to whom they offer sympathy, a sense of belonging and importance, and help in adjusting to modern life. Considering the extremely rapid modernization of Japan during the last two centuries, the success of these organizations is perhaps not so surprising.

The biggest such organization is **Sōka Gakkai** (Value Creation Society). It was founded in 1937 by schoolteacher Makiguchi Tsunesaburo, who emphasized the importance of educational philosophy alongside the day-to-day benefits of religion. Under the umbrella of Nichiren Buddhism, Sōka Gakkai's structure was formalized after World War II, focusing on tightly knit groups engaged in educational work, social activities and large-scale jamborees aimed at finding fulfilment in the present. With its proselytizing mission and broad appeal to people of all ages and classes, Sōka Gakkai now claims around twenty million members. The movement also has a nominally independent political branch, the Komeito or "Clean Government Party" founded in 1964. Created as a backlash to corruption in Japanese politics, Komeito are a significant group within Japan's opposition parties.

At the other end of the scale, **AUM Shinrikyō** (AUM Supreme Truth) was founded in 1986 by a blind yoga teacher, **Asahara Shoko**. Claiming to be a Buddhist sect, adherents believed that the world would end in 1997 and that only AUM members would survive. At its height, the cult boasted 10,000 members in Japan and 30,000 abroad, mainly in Russia. Little-known to most of his followers, however, Asahara's prime goal was world domination, but the truth started to emerge after the 1995 Sarin gas attack on the Tokyo subway. Fortunately, the police stopped AUM before Asahara could carry out his plans, but the group's activities stunned the Japanese population and raised fears that Japan may no longer be the safe and harmonious country it once was. (See p.806 for more about AUM.)

## RELIGION, RITUAL AND CULTURE

It's often said that Shinto and Buddhism have given the Japanese a unique appreciation for ritual, nature and art. Various aspects of Japanese culture have developed from **religious ritual** and values, such as the **Nō** drama which evolved out of Shinto's ancient sacred dances (see p.796 for more on Nō). In addition, sumo wrestling, traditional gardens, the tea ceremony and flower arranging all stem from ritualistic aspects of Japanese religions.

### SUMO

Japanese mythology teaches that the gods used to wrestle each other. This was adopted in ancient times as a form of divination, and became an important part of New Year festivals to predict the fortunes of the coming year. **Sumo** became a spectator sport as early as the sixth century and is probably the most popular sport in Japan today.

Sumo's connections to its religious past are easy to see. For example, the referee's elaborate **costume** is strikingly similar to that worn by Shinto priests, while the wrestlers' *mawashi* belt, with its tassels reminiscent of Shinto's purification wand, developed from the loincloth, *fundoshi*, worn at Shinto festivals. **The bout** itself is almost all ritual ceremony, with the actual wrestling often lasting only a matter of seconds. As soon as they enter the ring, the wrestlers (*dohyō*) purify themselves by rinsing their mouths with water, in the Shinto manner, and throwing salt into the ring to ward off evil. They usually do the latter three or four times, stamping their feet on the floor and psyching each other out in-between. Sumo wrestlers are highly respected in Japan and are expected to behave with the decorum befitting a religious event. So, despite the evil looks they exchange before lunging at each other, it's very bad form for a wrestler to display emotions of anger or frustration at loosing – the gods may still be watching.

## GARDENS

Japanese **gardens** developed out of the sacred grounds surrounding Shinto shrines and imperial palaces. The earliest gardens, dating from the Nara and Heian eras (eighth to twelfth centuries), took the form of a **pond and island** representing the mythical land of the gods, Tokoyo. Both the turtle and crane, animals symbolizing longevity, were associated with Tokoyo and appear frequently in garden design, usually in the form of islands or rock groupings.

Later the rocks, ponds and islands largely lost their religious symbolism, but were used instead to evoke famous Japanese beauty spots or scenes from literary masterpieces. At first these gardens provided the venue for elegant boating parties as depicted in *The Tale of Genji* (see p.792) but, as the gardens and their ponds became smaller, evolved into the classic **stroll-gardens**. Designed to be appreciated on foot, these secular, Edo-period gardens comprise various tableaux which unfold as the viewer progresses through the garden, and often "borrow" the surrounding scenery to enlarge the space. Many superb stroll-gardens still exist in Japan, but among the most stunning are Takamatsu's **Ritsurin-kōen**, **Suizenji-kōen** in Kumamoto and **Kōraku-en** near Okayama.

Back in the ninth century, Shingon Esoteric Buddhism (see p.785 above) promoted the idea that paradise could be achieved on earth, by the grace of Amida Buddha. Thus were **paradise gardens** born, in which temples strove to create their own version of Amida's Pure Land, or Jōdo, featuring a pond, islands and rocks in a completely manufactured "natural" setting, such as Uji's magnificent **Byōdō-in**. By contrast, in the fifteenth century the severe precepts of Zen Buddhism favoured highly austere "**dry gardens**" (*kare-sansui*), in which the entire universe is reduced to a few rocks, white-rippled gravel and one or two judiciously placed shrubs (see p.785). Kyoto's **Daisen-in** and **Ryōan-ji** are magnificent examples of this type of garden, which were designed solely to facilitate meditation and lead the viewer to enlightenment.

## THE TEA CEREMONY

Tea was introduced to Japan from China in the ninth century. Tea drinking, however, didn't really catch on until after the twelfth century, particularly among Zen Buddhists who appreciated the tea's caffeine kick during their long meditation sessions. Zen Buddhists believe that all actions have a religious significance and the very act of tea-making gradually evolved into part of the meditation process. The highly ritualistic **tea ceremony**, *cha-no-yu*, however, didn't develop until the late sixteenth century under a gifted tea master, *samurai* and garden designer called **Sen no Rikyū** (1521–1591).

Influenced by the culture of the *samurai* and *Nō*, the most important aspect of the tea ceremony is the **etiquette** with which it is performed. Central to this is the selfless manner in which the host serves the tea and the humble manner in which the guests accept it. Indeed, the inner spirit of the participants during the ceremony is considered more important than its ritual form. Guests are expected to admire the hanging scroll and flower arrangement decorating the tea room, and the cup from which they drink – all are valued for the skill of the craftsmen and their seasonal note or rustic simplicity. Today, the tea ceremony is popular mostly among young women; as with *ikebana*, it's deemed a desirable quality for a woman of marriageable age to acquire.

## IKEBANA

**Ikebana**, or the art of flower arranging, also has its roots in ancient Shinto rituals, Buddhist practice and a Japanese aesthetic that balances three components to create a dynamic image. Again, however, *ikebana* reached its peak in the sixteenth century, largely on the coat tails of the tea ceremony, when several distinct schools emerged.

Originally, the emphasis was on presenting materials and forms in ways which imitated their natural state. While the materials remained natural, the **ideology** evolved to employ three leading sprays which signify the sky, earth and humankind; the sprays are arranged to express the harmonic balance of these elements in nature. The four main **styles** of *ikebana* are the self-explanatory *shōkai* (living flowers), the formal *rikka* (standing flowers), *noribana* (heaped flowers), and the more naturalistic *nage-ire* (thrown in). Within each of these there are many **schools**, such as Ikenobō in Kyoto and Tokyo's Sōgetsu, as well as avant-garde groups which use non-natural materials (iron, glass etc) to the same harmonious effect.

**Peter Grimshaw**

# ART AND ARCHITECTURE

In the mid-nineteenth century an exotic array of pictures, crafts and curios came flooding out of Japan as this virtually unknown country re-established trade with the outside world. Western collectors eagerly snapped up exquisite ink-painted landscapes, boldly colourful ukiyo-e (pictures of the floating world), samurai swords, porcelain, inlaid lacquerware, bamboo utensils and ivory carvings – even artists such as Van Gogh and Whistler were influenced by the contemporary vogue for things Japanese. From these collections came our first detailed knowledge of the diversity of Japanese arts, ranging from expressions of the most refined spiritual sensibilities to the bric-a-brac of ordinary life.

This enormous wealth of artistic expression reflects the wide variety of sources of **inspiration** and **patronage** over the centuries. Periods of aristocratic rule, military supremacy and merchant wealth all left their mark on Japanese arts, building on a rich legacy of religious art, folk traditions and the assimilated cultural influences of China and Korea. More recently, the West became a model for artists seeking to join the ranks of the avant-garde. Today it's difficult to speak of prevailing tendencies, as Japanese artists both draw on traditional sources and take their place amongst international trends.

What does span the centuries, however, is a love of nature, respect for the highest standards of craftsmanship and the potential for finding beauty in the simplest of things. These qualities pervade the visual arts of Japan but are also reflected in aspects of the performing arts where the actor's craft, costume and make-up combine with the stage setting to unique dramatic effect. The official designation of valued objects and individuals as "National Treasures" and "Living National Treasures" acknowledges the extent to which the arts and artists of Japan are revered.

One of the joys of visiting Japan, however, is in experiencing the ordinary ways in which the Japanese aesthetic enters into everyday life. The presentation of food, a window display or the simplest flower arrangement can convey, beyond the walls of any museum, the essential nature of Japanese art.

## THE BEGINNINGS

The earliest artefacts excavated in Japan date back to 10,000 BC when the **Jōmon culture** (10,000–300BC), a society of hunters, fishers and gatherers, inhabited small settlements throughout the country. The name Jōmon, meaning "cord pattern", refers to the impression made by twisted cord on the surface of clay. Early Jōmon pots were built up from coils of clay pressed together, to which cord markings were applied as a form of decoration, and shells added for further embellishment. Increasingly elaborate variations in the size and type of Jōmon pottery suggest its religious or ceremonial significance. Certainly, by the Middle Jōmon, the production of female pottery figurines and stone phalli point to the association of such items with basic fertility rites. Fired-clay *dogū* are typical of Late Jōmon sculpture; these stiffly posed figures with female attributes, staring out of large oval eyes, mainly occur in sites in eastern Japan.

The more sophisticated **Yayoi culture** (300BC–300AD), which displaced the Jōmon, is characterized by a finer-quality, reddish-brown wheel-turned pottery, which was first discovered at Yayoi, near today's Tokyo. Their pots were more diverse in shape and function but simpler in decoration, with the incision of straight, curved and zig-zagged lines and combed wave patterns. Yayoi also saw the introduction of iron and bronze to Japan, which led to the production of iron tools, while bronze was reserved for ritual objects. The most distinctive Yayoi bronze objects are the *dōtaku* or straight-sided bells which have been linked with agricultural rituals and burial practices.

The following **Kofun era** (300–710AD) is defined by the number of huge burial mounds (*kofun*) built during the period. The tombs were generally bordered by a series of low-fired clay cylinders, or *haniwa*, topped with delightful representations of animals, people, boats and houses. Though probably related to ancient Chinese burial practices, the *haniwa* show a distinctively Japanese artistic form.

## THE RELIGIOUS INFLUENCE

Shinto and Buddhism, Japan's two core religions, have both made vital contributions to the art and architecture of Japan. In the case of **Shinto**, the influence is extremely subtle and difficult to define, but is apparent in the Japanese love of simplicity, understatement and a deep affinity with the natural environment. The architecture of Shinto **shrines** captures the essence of these ideals, as well as expressing the sense of awe and mystery which is central to the religion. Their plain wooden surfaces, together with their very human scale, gradually evolved into a native approach to architectural design in which buildings, even important religious edifices, strove to be in harmony with their surroundings. (See p.782 for more about Shinto shrines.)

The introduction of **Buddhism** into Japan from China in the sixth century had a profound effect on Japanese arts. The process of transmitting this foreign religion to Japan led to the copying of Buddhist sutras, the construction of temples as places of worship and of study, and the production of Buddhist paintings and sculptures. The **temples** themselves, with their red-lacquered exteriors, tiled roofs supported by elaborate bracketing and tall pagodas, were in stark stylistic contrast to the architecture of Shinto. They represented visually the superimposition upon Japan's native traditions of a different set of beliefs and values.

Some of Japan's earliest **Buddhist sculptures** can be found at **Hōryū-ji** (near Nara) and take their inspiration from Chinese and Korean sculpture of an earlier period. Though many statues have been moved to Tokyo's National Museum, the temple is still a magnificent museum of early Buddhist art. Its bronze Shaka (the Historic Buddha) Triad by Tori Bushii, a Korean-Chinese immigrant, dates back to 623

and reflects the stiff frontal poses, archaic smiles and waterfall drapery patterns of fourth-century Chinese sculpture. At the same time, Hōryū-ji's standing wooden Kudara Kannon, depicting the most compassionate of the boddhisattvas, is delicately and sensitively carved to emphasize its spirituality. Another contemporary example of Buddhist sculpture, possibly also by a Korean immigrant, is the seated Miroku Bosatsu (Future Buddha) at Chūgū-ji, within the Hōryū-ji complex. With one leg crossed and his head resting pensively on one hand, it is a model of the grace and serenity associated with Asuka-era (552–650) sculpture.

As with Christian art, Buddhist **iconography** draws on a wealth of historic and symbolic references. The legends associated with Buddhism and the attributes of buddhahood are represented in the *mudra*, the hand gestures of the Buddha, his poses and in the objects he holds. Similarly, as with the heightened spirituality of the boddhisattvas which often flank the Buddha and the exaggerated realism of the fearsome-looking guardian figures at the entrance to the temple compound, the style in which such sculptures are rendered is frequently an aspect of their function. While the sweetness and calm of the bodhisattvas may direct thoughts 'heaven'-wards, the bulging eyes, tensed muscles and aggressive poses of the guardian figures are intended to ward off evil and to protect both the Buddha and the temple.

During the early years of Buddhism in Japan and the periods of closest contact with China (the seventh to tenth centuries), Japanese styles of Buddhist art mimicked those current in China or from her recent past. However, a gradual process of assimilation took place in both painting and sculpture until during the Kamakura era (see below) the adaptation of a distinctly Japanese model can be observed in Buddhist art.

## THE HEIAN ERA 794–1185

In 794 the Japanese capital was moved from Nara to Heian-kyō (present-day Kyoto), heralding the start of the **Heian era**. A more significant transitional date, however, is 898 when the Japanese stopped sending embassies to the Chinese T'ang court. The abrupt ending of centuries of close relations with China was to have a significant impact upon artistic developments in Japan. Gradually the cloistered and leisured lifestyle of the Heian aristocracy, combined with a diminishing Chinese influence, spawned a uniquely Japanese cultural identity.

**Court life** in Heian Japan revolved around worldly pleasures and aesthetic pastimes, and the period is renowned for its artistic and cultural innovation. *Kana,* or the phonetic syllabary, was developed during this time and was employed in the composition of one of Japan's greatest literary masterpieces, **The Tale of Genji**, or *Genji Monogatari.* Lady Murasaki's portrayal of the effeteness and insularity of the Heian-court nobility eloquently described the artistic pursuits which dominated their daily life. The poetry and incense competitions, the arts of painting, calligraphy and gardening, and the elaborate rituals of court dress were all aspects of Heian aesthetic refinement.

A new painting format, the *emaki* or **picture scroll**, also evolved during the Heian era. The narrative handscroll allowed for the picture and story to unfold as the viewer unrolled and observed its contents. *Emaki* depicted romances, legends and historical tales, of which the most famous is an illustrated edition of *The Tale of Genji*, published around 1130. The painting technique used, known as *Yamato-e*, employs flat blocks of colour with a strong linear focus and boldness of style which was uniquely Japanese. At the same time, the **decorative arts** reached a similarly high level of sophistication. Inlaid lacquerware, using the *maki-e* technique (sprinkling the surface with gold or silver powder) and finely crafted bronze mirrors employed surface designs to equally dramatic effect.

The lavishness of Heian taste is reflected in **Buddhist painting** and **sculpture** of this period. New sects of Buddhism gave rise to the diagrammatic *mandala*, schematic depictions of the Buddhist universe, while religious sculpture became more graceful and sensual, with gilded, delicately featured deities marking the transition to an aristocratic form of Buddhist art. The large, gilded wooden image of Amida in Uji's **Byōdō-in** (near Kyoto) is a representative example. Here the serene, seated Buddha is set against a backdrop of elaborate openwork carving with gilded angels and swirling cloud patterns animating the scene. The overall effect is one of splendid sumptuousness.

## SAMURAI CULTURE

Japan's medieval age began in 1185 with the establishment of the Kamakura Shogunate.

While Kyoto remained the imperial capital and the cultural heartland of Japan, the rise to power of a **military elite** generated an alternative artistic taste. *Bushidō*, "the way of the warrior", was the guiding spirit of the *samurai* class. This spirit gave rise to a demand for art forms that were more in keeping with the simplicity, discipline and rigour of the military lifestyle.

This new realism made itself felt in the portrait painting and picture scrolls of the **Kamakura era** (1185–1333), most graphically in the *Handbook on Hungry Ghosts*, now held in Tokyo's National Museum. Highly individualized portraits of military figures and Zen masters also became popular, as did lively narrative tales focusing on the cult of war and Buddhist legends. Kamakura sculpture similarly combined a high degree of realism with a dynamic energy, reflecting the emergence of popular Buddhist sects which appealed more directly to the common people. The two giant guardian figures at Nara's Tōdai-ji, fashioned by the sculptors Unkei and Kaikei in 1203, are outstanding examples of this vigorous new style.

However, *samurai* culture had a more direct impact on the development of the decorative arts. Military armour was made in quantity during the Kamakura era and the **art of the sword** became an important area of artistic production for centuries to follow. The long and short sword of the *samurai*, the sword guard (*tsuba*), scabbard and elaborate fittings and ornaments are all considered achievements of Japanese metalwork design. While sword production in the fifteenth and sixteenth centuries was concentrated in the provinces of Bizen and Mino (today's Okayama and Gifu), by the Edo era (1600-1868), Edo and Ōsaka had become leading centres of swordmaking. Swordsmiths were noted for their skill in forging and for the meticulousness of finish which they applied to the blades. Through the peaceful years of the Edo era, however, swordfittings came to be associated with the decorative rather than the practical. Sword furniture from this time might be either simple and abstract, or draw on representational themes from nature, religion and everyday life.

## THE ARTS OF ZEN

With the spread of **Zen Buddhism** in the thirteenth century, the arts of Japan took on a new focus. Here was a religion which cultivated self-discipline and austerity as the path to enlightenment. Not surprisingly, it was taken up with enthusiasm by the *samurai* class. Meditation is at the centre of Zen practice and many Zen art forms can be seen as vehicles for inward reflection or as visualizations of the sudden and spontaneous nature of enlightenment.

Monochromatic **ink painting**, known as *suiboku-ga* or *sumi-e*, portrayed meditative landscapes and other subjects in a variety of formats including screens, hanging scrolls and handscrolls, with a free and expressive style of brushwork that was both speedily and skilfully rendered. *Haboku*, or "flung-ink" landscapes, took this technique to its logical extreme by building up (barely) recognizable imagery from the arbitrary patterns formed by wet ink splashed onto highly absorbent paper. **Sesshū** (1420–1506), a Zen priest, was Japan's foremost practitioner of this technique.

Zen **calligraphy** similarly moved beyond the descriptive to emphasize spontaneity of expression in a style of writing that captured the essence of its subject matter, frequently based on poems and Zen sayings. Calligraphy of this type can be so expressively rendered as to be almost unreadable except to the practised eye. One of the most striking examples, by the monk **Ryōkan Daigu** (1757–1831), is a hanging scroll with the intertwined symbols for heaven and earth. Ryōkan's bold brushwork dramatically links the symbols of these two aspects of the cosmos to portray them as one sweeping and continuous force. Both the symbolism of this literal union and the unconventionality of the style in which the characters are rendered encapsulate the spirit of Zen.

A **love of nature** also lies at the very core of Zen. The qualities of abstraction and suggestion which characterized *suiboku-ga* were fittingly applied to the design of **Zen gardens**. Japanese gardens employ artifice to create an environment that appears more natural than nature itself. Trees and bushes are carefully pruned, colour is restricted and water channelled to convey, in one setting, the essence of the natural landscape. The word for landscape in Japanese is *sansui*, meaning "mountain and water". In Zen-inspired *kare-sansui* or "dry landscape" gardens, such as that of **Ryōan-ji** in Kyoto, these two elements are symbolically combined. *Kare-sansui* gardens consist only of carefully selected and positioned rocks in a bed of sand or gravel which is raked into water-like

patterns. As vehicles for contemplation, such gardens convey the vastness of nature through the power of suggestion.

*Cha-no-yu*, or "the way of tea", also evolved out of Zen meditation techniques, and draws on the love of nature in its architectural setting and utensils. The spirit of *wabi*, sometimes described as "rustic simplicity", pervades the Japanese **tea ceremony**. The traditional teahouse is positioned in a suitably understated garden, and naturalness is emphasized in all aspects of its architecture; in the unpainted wooden surfaces, the thatched roof, *tatami*-covered floors and the sliding-screen doors (*fusuma*) which open directly out onto a rustic scene. As with the garden itself, colour and ostentation are avoided. Instead, the corner alcove, or *tokonoma*, becomes the focal point for a single object of adornment, a simple flower arrangement or a seasonal hanging scroll.

Tea ceremony **utensils** contribute to the mood of this refined ritual. Raku, Shino and many other varieties of roughcast tea bowls are admired for the accidental effects produced by the firing of the pottery. Water containers, tea caddies and bamboo ladles and whisks complement the tea wares and are themselves much prized for their natural qualities. The guiding light behind all this mannered simplicity was the great tea-master **Sen no Rikyū** (1521–91), whose "worship of the imperfect" had a long-lasting influence on Japanese artistic tastes.

## FEUDAL ARTS AND ARCHITECTURE

Zen arts flourished during the **Muromachi era** (1333–1573) and close links with China once again dominated cultural life. The Ashikaga shoguns, now headquartered in Kyoto alongside the imperial court, indulged their love of the arts and landscape gardening in grand style. While many of Kyoto's Muromachi palaces and temples were destroyed during the late-fifteenth-century Ōnin Wars, two magnificent monuments still survive in the **Kinkaku-ji** and **Gingaku-ji**, the Golden and Silver pavilions. Built as country villas for the shoguns, both these buildings are modest in scale and combine simplicity of design with luxuriousness of finish – particularly the gold-leaf exterior of Kinkaku-ji. The Japanese style of domestic architecture was thus adapted to the requirements and tastes of the military elite.

Some of the most notable emblems of the power and wealth of the feudal lords (*daimyō*) were their **castles**. These reached their apogee in the sixteenth century as the warlords jockeyed for power. The castles were large in scale, surrounded by moats and elaborate defence works, and were constructed of wood on top of monumental stone foundations. Though obviously built for defence, their uncompromising solidity is offset by multi-storey watchtowers looking like so many layers of an elaborate wedding cake with their fanciful, multiple roofs. **Himeji-jō** (White Egret Castle), west of Ōsaka, is an outstanding example of Japan's unique style of castle architecture.

Under the patronage of the feudal hierarchy, Japanese art reached its most opulent during the **Momoyama era** (1573–1600). The scale of feudal architecture created a new demand for decorative **screen paintings**, which were used to adorn every storey and were either fixed on walls, *fusuma* or folding screens (*byōbu*). From the late sixteenth century, the Kyoto-based **Kanō School** of artists came to dominate official taste. Their screens combined the bright colours and decorative boldness of *Yamato-e* with the more subtle compositional features of *suiboku-ga*. Subjects were mainly drawn from nature and from Japanese history and legend, while the extensive use of gold leaf added a shimmering brightness to the dark interior spaces of the great Momoyama castles, palaces and temples. **Kanō Eitoku** and his grandson, **Kanō Tanyū**, were the school's most famous exponents and their works can still be seen in Kyoto's Daitoku-ji and **Nijō-jō**. This latter is the only surviving palace from the Momoyama era. Originally part of a castle complex, its sweeping roof lines and intricately carved and ornamented gables show a lavishness and boldness of style appropriate to its subsequent use as the Tokugawa shoguns' Kyoto base.

## THE EDO ERA 1600–1868

After 1603, the Tokugawa Shogunate was established at **Edo** (modern-day Tokyo) where it remained in power for the next 250 years. These were years of peace and stability in Japan, marked by isolation from the outside world, the growth of cities, economic development and social mobility. To begin with, the **merchant class** were at the bottom of the feudal social ladder while the *samurai* remained the ruling elite.

As their wealth increased, however, the position and influence of the merchants rose accordingly.

Edo-era arts flourished under these new patrons. In **painting**, while the Kanō school continued to receive official support from the shoguns, other schools explored different styles and found different masters. Artists such as **Tawaraya Sōtatsu** (died around 1643) and **Ōgata Kōrin** (1658–1716) stand out for reviving aspects of the *Yamato-e* tradition and injecting new decorative life into Japanese painting. Sōtatsu's famous golden screen paintings based on *The Tale of Genji* dramatically adapt the subject matter and style of Heian-era *emaki* to this larger format. Kōrin's most noted works include the "Irises" screens, now held in Tokyo's Nezu Museum, which take an episode from a Heian-era novel, *The Tale of Ise*, and reduce its content to the striking patterns of flatly conceived blue irises and green leaves against a shimmering gold background.

In patronizing the arts, merchants sought not only reflections of their own affluence but also of their lifestyle. Paintings which depicted the often bawdy **pleasures of city life** came into vogue. The lively entertainment districts of Edo, Ōsaka and Kyoto, with their brothels, teahouses and Kabuki theatres, were depicted in painted screens and scrolls. This new genre of painting, **ukiyo-e**, or "pictures of the floating world", devoted itself to the hedonistic pastimes of the new rich. By the early eighteenth century, *ukiyo-e* were most commonly produced as hand-coloured woodblock prints which became gradually more sophisticated in their subtle use of line and colour as mass-printing techniques developed.

Catering to popular taste, late-eighteenth-century artists such as Harunobu, Utamaro and Sharaku portrayed famous beauties of the day and Kabuki actors in dramatic poses. Explicitly erotic prints known as *shunga*, (spring pictures), were also big sellers, as were humorous scenes of daily life (*manga*), the forerunners of today's comics. **Hokusai** (1760–1849), perhaps the most internationally famous *ukiyo-e* artist, was originally known for his *manga*, but went on to create one of the most enduring images of Japan, *The Great Wave*, as part of his series the *Thirty-Six Views of Mount Fuji*. Followed by the equally popular *Fifty-Three Stages of the Tōkaidō*, by **Hiroshige** (1797–1858), these later landscape prints were instantly popular at a time when travel was both difficult and restricted.

The **decorative arts** reached new heights of elegance and craftsmanship during the Edo era. Varieties of Imari- and Kutani-ware **porcelain** (from Kyūshū and Ishikawa-ken) were made in large quantities for domestic consumption and later for export. Inlaid **lacquerware** was executed in bold and simple designs. Honami Kōetsu (1558–1637) and Ōgata Kōrin (1658–1716) were leading lacquer artists of the period, as well as celebrated painters and calligraphers – their design skills translated readily across different materials and craft forms. One of Kōetsu's most famous lacquer works, an inkstone box in the Tokyo National Museum, reflects these combined talents with its inlaid-lead bridge and silver calligraphy forming integral parts of the overall design. Kōrin carried on this tradition with his own black-lacquer, inkstone box; its jagged, lead and silver bridge across a bed of inlaid gold and shell irises translates his earlier "Irises" screens (see opposite) into a three-dimensional format.

**Textile** production, meanwhile, was centred in the Nishijin district of Kyoto where silk cloth was made both for the Shogunate and the imperial court. Luxurious effects were achieved using elaborate embroidery and weaving techniques, which became works of art in themselves. Paste-resistant **yūzen** dyeing developed in Kyoto in the late seventeenth century. This complicated process involved multiple applications of rice-starch paste and dyes by hand to capture subtle, multi-colour painted effects. The resulting patterns were often embellished with embroidery or gold and silver foil. Fine examples of kimono of the period can be seen in Japan's museums but *ukiyo-e* provide numerous illustrations of this aspect of "the floating world".

## WESTERN INFLUENCES

Episodes of **Western contact** prior to the Edo era resulted in some specific examples of artistic exchange. The *Namban* (southern barbarian) golden-screen paintings of the Momoyama era show Portuguese merchants and missionaries at Nagasaki before they were expelled. The continued Dutch presence similarly gave rise to paintings and prints which portrayed the Dutch settlement at Nagasaki's Dejima. Later, this was also the route for stylistic change generated by imported Western art.

The **re-opening of Japan** by Commodore Perry in 1854 and the fall of the Tokugawa Shogunate in 1867 launched a period of massive social and cultural change. With the restoration of the Emperor Meiji to power and a new government in place in Tokyo from 1868, a process of modernization and **Westernization** was embarked upon which transformed the face of Japan and of the visual arts.

The opening of the treaty ports furnished a **new subject matter** for woodblock print artists who produced marvellous portraits of big-nosed Westerners in Yokohama and other ports. Meiji modernization provided additional themes as the opening of the first railway, spinning factory and many other advances were recorded for posterity. Western advisers assisted in the design and construction of **European-style buildings**, some of which can still be found scattered around Japanese cities, while others have been relocated to the Meiji Mura Open-Air Museum near Nagoya.

In the early years of the Meiji era (1868–1912), traditional Japanese and Chinese styles of painting were rejected by many artists in favour of Western styles and techniques. Artists such as **Kuroda Seiki** (1866–1924) and **Fujishima Takeji** (1867–1943) studied in Paris and returned to become leaders of **Western-style painting** (*Yōga*) in Japan. Realism, Impressionism and other Western art movements were directly transplanted to the Tokyo art scene. More conservative painters, such as **Yokoyama Taikan** (1868–1958) worked to establish **Nihon-ga**, a modern style of Japanese painting, drawing on a mixture of Chinese, Japanese and Western techniques.

Western influence on the arts expanded greatly in the Taishō era (1912–1926) with **sculpture**, as well as painting, closely following current trends. In the postwar period, Japanese artists looked again to Europe and America but more selectively took their inspiration from a range of avant-garde developments in the West. Art in Japan today can be seen as a blend of Japanese and international currents. Sources of tradition can no longer be identified purely with the East or the West.

## MINGEI: THE FOLK CRAFT TRADITION

It is in the area of the **folk crafts** that Japan has maintained a distinctive tradition and one that delights in the simplicity and utilitarian aspects of ordinary everyday objects. **Mingei** really is "people's art", the works of unknown craftsmen from all regions of Japan that are revered for their natural and unpretentious qualities.

While Japanese folk crafts flourished during the Edo era, the mass production techniques of the machine age led to a fall in the quality of textiles, ceramics, lacquer and other craft forms. The art critic and philosopher **Yanagi Sōetsu** (1889–1961), worked from the 1920s to stem this tide and to preserve the craft products of the pre-industrial age. Yanagi established the Mingei-kan, or Japanese Folk Crafts Museum, in Tokyo's Meguro district in 1936 to display Japanese folk crafts of every description. But the revival of the *mingei* tradition also celebrated works by living artist-craftsmen as well as regional differences in style and technique. The potters **Hamada Shōji** (1894–1978) and the Englishman **Bernard Leach** (1887–1979) were most famously associated with the *mingei* movement, as was the woodblock print artist, **Munakata Shikō** (1903–1975).

A wide range of traditional handicrafts are still being produced today all over Japan. *Yūzen*-style kimono dyeing and *kumihimo* braid craft are associated with Kyoto; *shuri* weaving techniques with Okinawa; *Hakata ningyō*, or earthenware dolls, with Fukuoka; and Kumano brushes with Hiroshima. Pottery, lacquerware, wood, bamboo and handmade paper products of every description continue to preserve the spirit of *mingei* in contemporary Japan.

## THE PERFORMING ARTS

The traditional theatre arts evolved in the context of broader cultural developments during different periods of Japan's history. **Nō** (or Noh) is the classic theatre of Japan, a form of masked drama which has its roots in sacred Shinto dances, but was formalized 600 years ago under the patronage of the Ashikaga shoguns and the aesthetic influence of Zen. The bare wooden stage with its painted backdrop of an ancient pine tree, the actors' stylized robes and the elusive expressions of the finely crafted masks create an atmosphere that is both understated and refined. The dramatic contrasts of stillness and sudden rushes of movement, and of periods of silence punctuated by sound, conjure up the essence of the Zen aesthetic. The *kyōgen* interludes inject an element of comic relief into this otherwise stately ceremonial entertainment.

The 240 plays of the **Nō repertoire** are divided into five categories. *Waki-nō* (or *kami-nō*) depict deities in stories of rejoicing; *shura-mono* portray famous warriors in tales of suffering and torment; and *kazura-mono* depict young and beautiful women in a gentle setting. The fourth group comprises *kyojo-mono* (mad-women pieces) and *genzai-mono*, depicting mad men or obsessed women. In the final category, *kiri-nō* are fast-paced plays featuring supernatural beings, gods or demons. Though a traditional programme contains a selection from each group, with three or four *kyōgen* interludes, most programmes nowadays consist of only two Nō plays and one *kyōgen*.

The principal character in Nō plays is known as the *shite*, and may be either a ghost, mad person, or a superhuman or animal creature. The secondary character, the *waki*, on the other hand always represent people living in the present. *Shite* characters generally wear a mask, of male, female or demon type, which conceals the actor's presence and allows the characterization to dominate. The actor's skill lies in transcending the conventions of archaic language, mask and formalized costume to convey the dramatic tensions inherent in the play. Dance elements and musical effects aid directly in this process and draw on the folk entertainment tradition from which Nō is derived. Famously inaccessible to some, Nō is capable of achieving tremendously subtle and evocative effects.

By comparison, the **kyōgen** interludes primarily aim at amusement and providing a counterpoint to the Nō drama. As with Nō, *kyōgen* performers are all male and assume a variety of roles, some of which are completely independent of the Nō play, while others comment on the development of the main story. The language used is colloquial (though of sixteenth-century origin) and compared to the esoteric poetry of Nō, far more accessible to a contemporary audience. There is a greater emphasis on realistic portrayal in *kyōgen* and the actors only occasionally wear masks. Humour is achieved through exaggerated speech and formalized acting techniques and movements. Essentially a dialogue play between two characters or groups of actors, *kyōgen* makes use of wit and satire to balance the mood of Nō.

While Nō is classical and restrained, **Kabuki**, Japan's popular theatre, is colourful, exuberant and full of larger-than-life characters, a highly stylized theatrical form which delights in flamboyant gestures and elaborate costumes, make-up and staging effects. While the language may still be incomprehensible, the plots themselves deal with easily understandable, often tragic themes of love and betrayal, commonly taken from famous historical episodes.

Kabuki originated in the early 1600s as rather risqué dances performed by all-female troupes. The shogun eventually banned women because of Kabuki's association with prostitution, but their replacement – young men – was no more successful and in the end Kabuki actors were predominantly older men, some of whom specialize in female roles. It developed as a more serious form of theatre in the late sixteenth century when Kabuki was cultivated chiefly by the merchant class. It gave theatrical expression to the vitality of city life and to the class tensions between *samurai*, merchants and peasants which informed the plots of so many plays. As an indication of the popularity of Kabuki, powerful images of famous actors were a favourite theme of Edo-era *ukiyo-e* prints.

**Bunraku**, Japan's puppet theatre, was another product of Edo-era culture and exerted a strong influence on Kabuki, even providing many of its plots. Bunraku developed out of the *jōruri* story-telling tradition, in which travelling minstrels recited popular tales of famous heroes and legends, accompanied by the *biwa* (Japanese lute) or *shamisen* (three-stringed guitar). Adapted to the stage in the early seventeenth century, Bunraku made use of stylized puppets, one-half to one-third the size of humans, to enact the various roles. The great Ōsaka playwright **Chikamatsu Monzaemon** (1653–1724), often referred to as "the Shakespeare of Japan", is responsible for around one hundred Bunraku plays, many of which are still performed in Japan today. The most famous plays in the Bunraku repertoire include Chikamatsu's *Sonezaki Shinjū* (The Love Suicides at Sonezaki), based on a true story, and *Kokusenya Kassen* (The Battles of Coxinga), about a legendary pirate.

Three operators take part in a **Bunraku performance**, while a chanter, using a varied vocal range, tells the story to the accompaniment of *shamisen* music. The main puppeteer is in full view of the audience and uses his left hand to manipulate the face and head, with his right controlling the puppet's right arm. One assistant operates the left arm while another moves the puppet's legs; both dressed in black, these moving shadows simply disappear into the background. The skill of the puppeteers – the result of lengthy apprenticeships – contributes to the high degree of realism in the performance, and the stylized movements can result in great drama. Indeed, Kabuki actors employed some puppet-like gestures from Bunraku to enhance and enliven their own acting techniques.

## CONTEMPORARY THEATRE

As with the visual arts, there are many different types of **contemporary theatre** in Japan. **Shingeki** (meaning "new theatre") is the term applied to a type of modern theatre which first developed during the Meiji era. Essentially a theatre of realism, it arose through the influence of Shakespeare and the European naturalists and plays in this representational genre continue to be produced. *Shingeki* is very much the literary product of a playwright and can therefore be distinguished from more spectacle-orientated, home-grown drama forms.

The contemporary theatre scene also embraces the diverse spectacles of **Takarazuka**, a Rockettes-like all-female musical review company originating from Ōsaka in the early 1900s (see box, p.423), and **Butō** (or Butoh), the abstract and improvisational dance form established in the 1950s. Butō developed from the work of dancers Hijikata Tatsumi and Ōno Kazuo and jolted the establishment with the performers' stark, white make-up and the spectacle of aggressive eroticism borne of instinctive gestures and movements.

Formerly known as *angura* (underground theatre), the **experimental theatre** of the 1960s has had an ongoing impact through the wide range of *shōgekijō-engeki* (small-theatre drama) companies which cater to the interests and tastes of Japan's younger generation. Drama students from the University of Tokyo formed *Yume no Yumin-sha* in 1976, while their counterparts at Waseda University established *Daisan Butai* in 1981. Both young theatre groups focus on the preoccupations and social problems of the *shin-jinrui*, Japan's materially privileged postwar generation. Outside of Tokyo, another more experimental group, *Dumb Type*, was founded in 1984 by Fine Art students from Kyoto City University of Arts. Their multimedia performances make use of installations and video and computer art to explore aspects of human behaviour.

In addition to these, there are many other theatre groups in Japan creating original works, neo-Kabuki productions and adaptations of Western musicals. At the same time, the more mainstream work of the director **Ninagawa Yukio** has won a considerable following outside Japan. Ninagawa has directed both traditional Japanese plays and Western productions at home and abroad, and in a sense bridges the theatrical conventions of East and West.

**Marie Conte-Helm**

# FILM

If you thought Godzilla and samurai flicks are all there is to Japanese film, think again. The history of cinema in Japan extends over a century, with the first Western-made moving images being shown to rapt audiences in 1896. Within a couple of years, the Japanese had imported equipment and established their own movie industry, which flourished with all things Western in the early decades of the century. Recovering quickly after World War II, Japanese film burst onto the international scene with the innovative Rashōmon, directed by Kurosawa Akira, who along with Ozu Yasujirō, director of the highly respected Tokyo Monogatari (Tokyo Story), is the country's best-known cinema auteur.

Apart from the scandal surrounding Oshima Nagisa's explicit Ai-no-Corrida, the movie scene generally languished during the 1970s, while in the 1980s, Japanese corporations were more intent on ploughing bubble-era profits and investment into Hollywood production companies rather than home-grown product. The 1990s has seen a minor resurgence with the international popularity of the films of Itami Jūzō, Takeshi Kitano and runaway success of Suo Masayuki's Shall We Dance?, which has become the sixth highest-earning foreign-language film ever at the American box office.

## PRE-WORLD WAR II

Japan got its first taste of cinema at Kōbe's **Shinko Club** in 1896, and by the end of the following year, the Crown Prince had put in an appearance at Tokyo's Kabuki-za theatre to be entertained by the latest Western wonder. From the very beginning, **theatrical embellishments** were considered a vital part of the cinema experience; one theatre had a mock up of a valley in front of the screen, complete with fish-filled ponds, rocks and fan-generated breeze, to increase the sense of realism. Additionally, the story and dialogue were acted out to the audience by a *benshi*, playing a similar role to the theatrical interpreters in traditional Japanese performing arts. Thus when "talkies" arrived in Japan in the 1930s, they were less of a sensation because sound had been part of the movie experience from the very beginning.

The **earliest Japanese films** also looked towards the traditional performing arts, such as classical dance and Kabuki, for their subject matter, although in 1905 cameras were sent to the Asian mainland to record the Russo-Japanese War. By the outbreak of World War I in Europe, there were nine film-production companies in Japan, the largest being Nikkatsu which released fourteen films a month from its two studios. Western ways of filmaking were catching on and it became increasingly common for actresses to take roles previously played by *oyama* (female impersonators).

The contemporary landscape of **Tokyo** was a popular choice for films which adopted modern, realistic themes (**gendaigeki**). However, the Great Kantō Earthquake of 1923 shifted movie production for a time to **Kyoto**, which with its old architecture was the perfect backdrop for **jidaigeki**, or period dramas. Both forms were in turn influenced by the art of Western filmmaking, in particular German expressionism, while at the same time retaining a quintessential Japanese style.

The **1930s** were the boom years for early Japanese cinema with some five hundred features being churned out a year, second only in production to the United States. One of the era's top directors, who would not gain international recognition until the mid-1950s, was **Mizoguchi Kenji** (1898–1956). His initial speciality was the *jidaigeki* melodramas, based in Meiji-era Japan, but he is best known in the West for his later lyrical medieval *samurai* dramas, such as Ugetsu Monogatari (1954). During the 1920s and 1930s, however, Mizoguchi also turned his hand to detective, expressionist, war, ghost and comedy films, becoming the best-known director of realist *gendaigeki*. As Japan fell deeper into the ugliness of nationalism and war, Mizoguchi embraced traditional concepts of stylized beauty in films such as 1939's *Zangiku Monogatari* (*The Story of the Last Chrysanthemums*).

Also developing his reputation during the pre-World War II period was perhaps Japan's greatest film director **Ozu Yasujirō**, whose *Tokyo Monogatari* (*Tokyo Story*) is a permanent fixture on many critic's best film lists. In the 1930s, Ozu was taking his cues from the West, making films such as *Dragnet Girl*, about rebellious youths. By the time he made his first talking film *The Only Son* in 1936 – the story of a country woman who visits her feckless son in Tokyo – Ozu was considered one of Japan's leading directors.

## THE 1950S AND 1960S

Japanese cinema undoubtedly suffered in the authoritarian years surrounding World War II. In 1945 only 26 films were made and the future didn't look any brighter when the Allied Occupation Forces took over, drew up a list of thirteen banned subjects for films, including "feudal loyalty", and burned movies considered unsuitable. However, the Occupation authorities were more than happy to encourage "American-style" *gendaigeki*, which led to the Japan's first screen kiss, a previously taboo activity, in 1946.

Local talent broke through in 1950 when **Kurosawa Akira's** brilliant **Rashōmon** hit the screen, subsequently garnering a Golden Lion at the following year's Venice Film Festival and an honorary Oscar. This story of a rape and murder told from four different points of view – including most ingeniously from the dead nobleman, via a medium – made a star of lead actor Mifune Toshiro and ushered in a decade considered to be the golden age of Japanese film.

In 1954 Kurosawa again teamed up with Mifune to make the classic **Shichinin-no-Samurai** (*The Seven Samurai*), about a band of *rōnin* (masterless *samurai*) coming to the rescue of a village community plagued by bandits. If the story sounds familiar that's because it was copied by Hollywood in *The Magnificent Seven* (1960), just as another of Kurosawa's *samurai* drama's, **Yōjimbō** (1961), was the basis for Sergio Leone's *A Fistful of Dollars*. The story snatching was not all one way. Kurosawa borrowed themes and plots from Dostoevsky, Gorky

and Shakespeare; **Throne of Blood** (1957) being based on the Bard's Macbeth and **Ran** (1985) on King Lear.

Ozu's masterpiece **Tokyo Monogatari** was another highlight of the 1950s. This simply told, yet quietly emotional tale of an elderly couple's visit to Tokyo to see their grown-up children and the cold reception they receive from everyone except their widowed daughter-in-law, has become a classic of world cinema.

At the other end of the artistic spectrum, the 1950s saw the birth of one of Japan's best known cinema icons, **Godzilla**, or *Gojira* as he was known on initial release in 1954. The giant mutant, whose Japanese name combined gorilla (*gorira*) and whale (*kujira*), was very much a product of fears surrounding nuclear proliferation, rather than the camp monster mega-star he would later become. At ¥60 million *Gojira* was one of the most expensive films of its time, with an all-star cast headed by Shimura Takeshi, who went on to star in Kurosawa's *Shichinin-no-Samurai*. Despite the monster being killed off in the grand finale, the movie's success led to an American release, with added footage, in 1956 under the title *Godzilla, King of the Monsters*. Over the next four decades Godzilla kept on returning to do battle with, among others, King Kong, giant shrimps, cockroaches and moths, and a smog monster.

Gangster movies also gained popularity in the 1960s as Japanese studios began pumping out violent, yet highly romaticized films about the **yakuza**. Known as *ninkyo eiga* (chivalry films), these movies were usually played like modern-day *samurai* sagas, the tough, fair *yakuza* being driven by a code of loyalty or honour. One of the major actors to emerge from these movies is **Takakura Ken**, who has since starred in Western films including Ridley Scott's *Black Rain*.

## THE 1970S AND 1980S

The most successful movie development of the next two decades was the **Tora-san** series, which began with *Otoko wa Tsurai Yo* (*It's Tough Being a Man*) at the tail end of the 1960s. Tora-san, or Torajiro Kuruma, a lovable itinerant peddler from Tokyo's Shitamachi, was played by Atsumi Kiyoshi in 48 films up until the actor's death in 1996, making it the most prolific movie series in the world. The format of the films is invariably the same; Tora-san chasing after his latest love, or "madonna", in various scenic areas of Japan, before returning to his exasperated family.

Tora-san was only a hit in Japan, but **Ai-no-Corrida** (*In the Realm of the Senses*; 1976) by rebel film-maker **Oshima Nagisa** created an international stir with its explicit sex scenes and violent content. Based on a true story, the film was about the intense sexual relationship between a woman servant and her master, that results in murder and a chopped-off penis. The censor demanded other kinds of cuts, which forced the director into a lengthy and ultimately unsuccessful legal battle. This was all the more galling for Oshima, whose film gathered critical plaudits abroad, but remained unseen in its full version at home, at the same time as the major Japanese studios made their money from increasingly violent films and soft-core porn, called *roman poruno*.

By the late 1970s, Japanese cinema was in the doldrums. Entrance fees at the cinema were the highest in the world (they're still expensive), leaving the public less willing to try out off-beat local movies when they could see sure-fire Hollywood hits instead. The art-house film-maker Oshima turned in the prisoner of war drama **Merry Christmas Mr Lawrence** in 1983 and the decidedly quirky **Max Mon Amour**, three years later before retiring, content to build his reputation as TV pundit. Instead of investing money at home, Japanese companies, like Sony, went on a spending spree in Hollywood, buying up major American studios and film rights, thus securing software for video releases.

By the end of the 1980s, the one light on the horizon was **Itami Jūzō**, an actor who turned director with the mildly satirical **Ososhiki** (*The Funeral*) in 1984. His follow up **Tampopo** (1986), a comedy about the attempts of a proprietress of a noodle bar to serve up the perfect bowl of ramen, set against the background of Japan's gourmet boom, was an international success, as was his **Marusa no Onna** (*A Taxing Woman*) in 1988. The female star of all Itami's movies, which poke gentle fun at Japanese behaviour and society, was his wife, the comic actress **Miyamoto Nobuko**.

## THE 1990S

Itami's success was consolidated by a string of hits in the 1990s, but his satirical approach went too far for some with 1992's **Minbo-no-Onna** (*The Gentle Art of Japanese Extortion*), which sent up the *yakuza*. Soon after its release, Itami was severly wounded in a knife attack by mob thugs. Undaunted, he recovered and went on to direct more challenging comedies, such as **Daibyōin** (1993), about the way cancer is treated in Japanese hospitals, and **Sūpā-no-Onna** (1995), which revealed the shady practices of supermarkets. Itami's career ended abruptly in 1997, when he committed suicide in the wake of a planned exposé of his love life in a scandal magazine.

Stepping into Itami's shoes as the darling of Japan's contemporary cinema scene is **Takeshi Kitano**, better known at home as Beat Takeshi, after his old comedy double act with Beat Kiyoshi in the Two Beats. Takeshi had already taken on a serious role in Oshima's *Merry Christmas Mr Lawrence* when he starred in and also directed **Sono Otoko, Kyobo ni Tsuki** (*Violent Cop*) in 1989. His next film **3-4 x 10 Gatsu** (*Boiling Point*) was an equally bloody outing, but it was his more reflective and comic **Sonatine** (1993), about a gang war in sunny Okinawa, that had foreign critics hailing him as Japan's Quentin Tarantino.

Surviving a near fatal motorbike accident in 1994, Takeshi has gone on to broaden his movie range with the badly received comedy **Minna Yatteruka** (*Getting Any?*) and **Kid's Return**, a sober film about high-school dropouts. Given his still numerous TV appearances, it's amazing Takeshi has time to make movies, but 1997's **Hanabi** saw him back on form directing himself as a troubled cop pushed to breaking point.

*Hanabi* scooped up a Golden Lion at the Venice Festival in 1997, just as Kurosawa's *Rashōmon* had done nearly fifty years previously. The legendary director, whose historical epics *Kagemusha* and *Ran* had blazed onto the screen in the 1980s, received a lifetime achievement Academy Award in 1990, the same year as he teamed up with George Lucas and Steven Spielberg to make the semi-autobiographical **Yume** (*Dreams*). His anti-war film **Hachigatsu-no-Kyoshikyoku** (*Rhapsody in August*; 1991), however, attracted ctristicism abroad for its somewhat one-sided treatment of the subject. Referred to respectfully as "Sensei" (teacher) by all in the industry, Kurosawa's final film before his death, aged 88 on September 6, 1998, was the low-key drama **Madadayo** (1993) about an elderly academic.

The 1990s have also seen the continued success of **animated films** (*anime*). From their beginnings with the "god of manga" Tezuka

Osamu's *Astroboy* and *Kimba, the White Lion*, in the 1960s, and continuing with the dark sci-fi fantasy *Akira* in the 1988, more animated films are now released each year in Japan than in the US and Europe. Miyazaki Hayao, who created the charming Casper-like ghost character Tottoro, runs **Studio Ghibli**, which has regularly beaten Walt Disney's high-profile animated releases at the Japanese box office. The studio scored its biggest hit in 1997 with **Mononoke-hime** (*Princess Mononoke*), the gutsy tale of a warrior princess with a strong environmental message.

**Independent film makers** are also making their mark with more daring subject matter. **Tsukamoto Shinya** had an art-house hit with the sci-fi horror movie **Tetsuo**, about a man turning into a machine, while **Yazaki Hitoshi** took a cool look at incest in **Sangatsu-no-Rion** (*March Comes in Like a Lion*). Two notable films focusing on ethnic minorities are **Nakata Toichi**'s **Ōsaka Story** (1994), charting the experiences of a gay Korean-Japanese film student returning from London to his family, and **Masato Harada**'s **Kamikaze Taxi**, a gangster flick also about ethnic Japanese who grew up in Brazil and Peru returning to Japan. These films, plus the stylish futuristic drama **Swallowtail Butterfly**, by hot young talent **Iwai Shunji**, have attracted favourable attention on the international circuit.

There's likely to be a less than rapturous overseas reception, however, for **Pride, the Fateful Moment**, the *cause-célèbre* film of 1998. A critique of the war crime trials held in Tokyo after World War II, this homegrown *Judgement at Nuremburg* has sparked controversy because of its sympathetic portrayal of the Japanese and boorish depiction of the American occupiers. Police were stationed outside many theatres when it was first released in Japan. Despite the touchiness of the subject, the producers hope it will also be shown in the US, an important market for Japanese film since the cross-over success of **Shall We Dance?**. Director **Suo Masayuki**'s charming ballroom dancing comedy/drama swept up all thirteen of Japan's Academy Awards in 1996 and is the most profitable Japanese film ever released in America.

## FILMS TO LOOK OUT FOR

*JAPANESE CLASSICS*

**Ai-no-Corrida** (*In the Realm of the Senses*; Oshima Nagisa; 1976). Judge for yourself whether this *cause-célèbre* film is art or pornography. Based on the true story of servant girl Sada Abe and her intensely violent sexual relationship with her master Kichi. A sex game results in Kichi's death and Sada slices off his penis as a keepsake. The real Sada was shown pity and spent just six years in prison. Oshima followed this film up with the equally erotic *Ai-no-Borei* (*Empire of Passion*), which won him best director award at the 1979 Cannes Film Festival.

**Black Rain** (Imamura Shohei; 1989). Not to be confused with the US *yakuza* flick, this serious drama traces the strains put on family life in a country village after the Bomb is dropped on Hiroshima.

**Godzilla, King of the Monsters** (1956). Originally released two years earlier in Japan as *Gojira*, the giant mutant lizard, born after a US hydrogen bomb test in the Bikini Atoll, was such a hit that extract footage was added for the American market. Raymond Burr plays the journalist telling in flashback the event that led to Godzilla running amok in Tokyo. Over twenty more tackily enjoyable Godzilla films followed, only for the whole series to be overshadowed by the overkill of the 1998 US remake.

**Nijūshi-no-Hitomi** (*Twenty Four Eyes*; Kinoshita Keisuke; 1954). One of Japan's most-loved films about the events leading up to, during and after World War II, as seen through the eyes of a first-grade female teacher and pacifist on the island of Shōdo-shima. The twelve cute children in Oishi-san's class make up the 24 eyes. Shamefully sentimental most of the time, the film is ultimately touching and memorable for the luminous performance of Takahime Hideko as the teacher.

**Tōkyō Monogatari** (*Tokyo Story*; Ozu Yasujirō; 1954). The most popular of Ozu Yasujirō's films, although it will appear laborious to audiences brought up on fast-moving MTV images. An elderly couple travel to Tokyo from their seaside home in Western Japan to visit their children and grandchildren. The only person who has any time for them is Noriko, the widow of their son Shoji killed in the war. On their return, the mother falls ill and dies. Ozu's themes of loneliness and the breakdown of tradition are grim, but his simple approach and the sincerity of the acting make the film a genuine classic.

## THE FILMS OF KUROSAWA AKIRA

**Kagemusha** (1980). Nominated for an Academy Award and co-winner of the Grand Prize at Cannes, Kurosawa showed he was still on form with this sweeping historical epic. A poor actor is recruited to impersonate a powerful warlord who has inconveniently died mid-campaign. The ruse is eventually discovered, but not before many a colourful battle.

**Ran** (1985). This much-lauded, loose adaption of King Lear is a true epic with thousands of extras and giant battle scenes. The daughters become sons, although the Regan and Goneril characters survive in the form of the gleefully vengeful wives Lady Kaede and Lady Sue.

**Rhapsody in August** (*Hachigatsu-no-Kyoshikyoku*, 1991). One of Kurosawa's more recent films is notable for an unlikely performance by Richard Gere as a Japanese-American visiting relations in Nagasaki and feeling sorry for the Atomic bombing.

**Rashōmon** (1950). The film that established Kurosawa as an exceptional director in the West and brought Japanese cinema to worldwide attention. A notorious bandit, the wife he perhaps rapes, the man he perhaps murders and the woodcutter who perhaps witnesses the events each tell their different story of what happened in the woods. Fascinatingly open-ended narrative and a memorably physical performance by Mifune Toshiro as the restless bandit make this a must-see movie.

**The Seven Samurai** (*Shichinin-no-Samurai*, 1954). A small village in sixteenth-century Japan is fed up of being raided each year by bandits so it hires a band of *samurai* warriors for protection. There's little else to the plot of Kurosawa's entertaining period drama, later remade in Hollywood as *The Magnificent Seven.*

**Yōjimbō** (1961). Mifune Toshiro stars in one of Kurosawa's best-known *samurai* sagas as a *rōnin* who arrives in a dusty town, is greeted by a dog carrying a human hand, and discovers he's walked in on a bloody feud. The *rōnin* pits both sides against each other, kills off the bad guys and restores peace to the town.

## MODERN JAPANESE CINEMA

**Hanabi** (Takeshi Kitano; 1997). Revealingly introspective Venice Festival winner with the all-round talent directing himself as a detective pushed to breaking point by a stake-out that went wrong, a seriously ill wife and outstanding loans to the *yakuza*. The artwork that appears in the film was also painted by Takeshi.

**Kamikaze Taxi** (Masato Harada; 1995). This realistic gangster story is unusual in that, amongst the violence and double crossing, it deals with the issue of ethnic Japanese returning to Japan from South America and being discriminated against as foreigners.

**Kid's Story** (Takeshi Kitano; 1996). In a quieter mode, Takeshi Kitano turns his attention to a couple of high-school dropouts in Tokyo, one of whom becomes a boxer while the other joins the *yakuza*. Although it supposedly has autobiographical elements, Kitano remains behind the camera for this one.

**Merry Christmas Mr Lawrence** (Oshima Nagisa; 1982). Pop stars David Bowie and Sakamoto Ryuichi, as well as thesps Tom Conti and Jack Thompson, star in this powerful POW drama based on Sir Laurens van der Post's book *The Seed and the Sower*. The art-house version of *Bridge on the River Kwai* just about sums it up. Look out for Takeshi Kitano in his first major role as a brutal camp sergeant.

**Minbo-no-Onna** (*The Gentle Art of Japanese Extortion*; Itami Jūzō; 1992). A grand Tokyo hotel, hoping to host an international summit meeting, has to deal with the *yakuza* first. Enter the director's wife, Miyamoto Nobuko, playing a feisty lawyer, who's more than a match for the preening gangsters.

**Murasa-no Onna** (*A Taxing Woman*; Itami Jūzō; 1988). Fascinating comedy about the battle of wills and wiles between a scrupulous tax collector (Miyamoto Nobuko) and her quarry, a love-hotel owner with two sets of books. The follow up *Murasa-no-Onna II* (A Taxing Woman's Return) is a darker, more prescient tale of the links between politicians, developers and a creepy religous cult.

**Ōsaka Story** (Nakata Toichi; 1994). Nakata Toichi ticks off many difficult contemporary issues in his film which follows the homecoming of a gay, Korean-Japanese film student to his Ōsaka-based family. His staunchly Korean father expects him to take over the business and get married, but the son has other ideas.

**Ososhiki** (*The Funeral*; Itami Jūzō; 1984). Itami's first film as a director is a wry comedy about a grieving family bumbling their way through the obscure conventions of a proper Japanese funeral. The young couple learn the "rules" by watching a video and the Buddhist priest turns up in a white Rolls Royce. Like most of his films, *Ososhiki* springs from Itami's personal experience and is all the funnier and more telling for that.

**Shall We Dance?** (Suo Masayuki; 1996). More than just a Japanese version of the Aussie hit *Strictly Ballroom*, Suo's film is firmly set in the reality of everyday lives. Yakusho Koji plays a quietly frustrated middle-aged salaryman whose spark returns when he takes up ballroom dancing. He has to keep it secret from his family and work colleagues, though, because of the social stigma attached. At turns touching and hilarious, *Shall We Dance?* also makes Blackpool, the ballroom dancer's far off mecca, appear glamorous.

**Sonatine** (Takeshi Kitano; 1993). An accomplished film seeing the director playing a tired gangster, high tailing it to the sunny isles of Okinawa and getting mixed up in more mob fueds, before blowing his brains out on the beach. The mixture of quirky comedy and violence had Western critics lining up to compare him to Quentin Tarantino.

**Swallowtail Butterfly** (Iwai Shunji; 1997). In this chic sci-fi thriller, Chinese prostitute/pop star Glico and her lover Hyou, a Shanghai immigrant, are set adrift in "yen town" a futuristic *gaijin* ghetto in Tokyo.

**Tampopo** (Itami Jūzō; 1985). Tampopo, the proprietress of a noodle bar, is taught how to prepare ramen that has both sincerity and guts, in this comedy about Japan's gourmet boom. From the old woman squishing fruit in a supermarket to the gangster and his moll passing a raw egg sexily between their mouths, this is a film packed with memorable scenes guaranteed to get the tummy rumbling.

**Violent Cop** (Takeshi Kitano; 1989). Takeshi Kitano's first film as a director sees him starring as a cop in the Dirty Harry mould, bent on revenge. As its title indicates, this is not a film that pulls its punches in the violence department.

## FOREIGN FILMS FEATURING JAPAN AND THE JAPANESE

**Black Rain** (Ridley Scott ; 1989). Gruff Michael Douglas and younger sidekick Andy Garcia team up with stoic local policeman Takakura Ken to deal with the *yakuza*. Notable in that it's set in Ōsaka, providing a slightly different cityscape from Tokyo.

**Bladerunner** (Ridley Scott; 1982). Although it's set in the Los Angeles of the future rather than Tokyo, this seminal sci-fi thriller takes its cues directly from contemporary Japan; the sets are practically indistinguishable from a rainy night in Shinjuku's Kabukichō, from the blazing neon to the giant video screens.

**Bridge On The River Kwai** (David Lean; 1957). Famous prisoner of war movie with army major Alec Guinness going bonkers as the Japanese extract blood, sweat and tears from the plucky Brits building a bridge in Thailand's jungle.

**Empire of the Sun** (Stephen Spielberg;1987). Based on the J. Ballard book, Spielberg's serious film explores the Japanese occupation of Shanghai through the eyes of a young boy. An impressive cast, including John Malkovich and Miranda Richardson, only partly distract from the leaden story telling.

**Mishima** (Paul Schrader; 1985). Art-house take on the bizarre and fascinating life of Japan's contemporary literary giant Mishima Yukio, who committed ritual suicide after leading a failed military coup in 1970.

**Paradise Road** (Bruce Beresford; 1997). Respectable addition to the POW drama genre, this time told from the female point of view. A starry cast, including Glen Close, Pauline Collins, Kate Blanchett and Julianna Margoiles, form a vocal orchestra to keep their flagging spirits up in the face of mulitple indignities. Based on a true story.

**The Pillow Book** (Peter Greenaway; 1996). In this dazzling high-tech adaption of the Sei Shōnagon classic, the action is updated to contemporary Hong Kong. The beautiful images capture the essence of the book, even if the story of a woman who gets her kicks by writing on the bodies of her lovers flags at times.

**Rising Sun** (Peter Kaufman; 1993). Based on Michael Crichton's rabble-rousing book about murder and corporate skullduggery, this slick thriller has its moments, most of which involve Sean Connery as the Zen-like detective teamed up with Wesley Snipes' LA cop to crack the case of the dead blonde on the boardroom table. Ultimately simplistic tale of Japanese business practices and manners.

**Until the End of the World** (Wim Wenders; 1993). Rambling Millennium angst road movie with an interesting premise, but gets bogged down during its Australian Outback section. The Japan scenes, contrasting frantic Tokyo and the soothing countryside, are among the best. Also stars the great actor Ryu Chishu, who played the father in Ozu's *Tokyo Story.*

**The Yakuza** (Michael Hamilburg; 1975). Robert Mitchum takes on the Japanese mafia after a friend's daughter is kidnapped in this Hollywood attempt to cash in on the popularity at the time of martial arts and violence.

**You Only Live Twice** (Lewis Gilbert; 1967). Sean Connery's fifth outing as 007 has Bondo-san grappling with arch enemy Blofeld and sundry Oriental villains in Tokyo and the countryside. Fun escapism, packed with glamourous girls and cool gadgets, including a mini-helicopter in a suitcase (with rocket launchers, of course).

# POP CULTURE

**Relatively few Japanese will be able to recommend a Nō play or tell you how to create an ikebana flower display. Ask them again to name their favourite comedian or karaoke song and the response will be instant. Popular culture rules in Japan and with 126 million avid consumers to draw upon, its products and buzzwords are all pervasive.**

The West's familiarity with contemporary Japan – Muji's chic "no-brand" products, Sony's electronic gadgets, Godzilla movies, Yoko Ono – is very slender compared to the thousands of other goods, cultural phenomena and people that are unknown and totally mystifying to the average *nama-gaijin* (raw foreigner). The following is a general A to Z primer for the visitor who would like to appear clued up. More serious students should avail themselves of the wit and wisdom in Mark Schilling's illuminating *The Encyclopedia of Japanese Pop Culture* (Weatherhill).

## A: *AUM SHINRIKYŌ*

On March 20, 1995, the New Age cult **AUM Shinrikyō**, burst into the news when its members planted bags of the deadly nerve gas Sarin on the Tokyo subway. Twelve people died and 5500 others were injured in Japan's worst terrorist attack.

The cult's leader, a virtually blind guru, **Asahara Shoko**, was born Matsumoto Chizuo, and began the "Supreme Truth" cult in the late 1980s – a period dubbed "rush hour of the gods" because of the proliferation of new religions in Japan at the time. At its height in the early 1990s, AUM had 40,000 members in several countries and nearly a billion dollars in assets, earned from, among other things, one-million-yen fees for rituals involving potions made of Asahara's dirty bathwater (called Miracle Pond), his blood, and even his beard clippings.

When AUM failed to get its members elected to the Diet in 1990, Asahara began to use his wealth and power for far more sinister aims. Suspicion had long been mounting against AUM before the tragic events of March 1995, but even after the Tokyo attack it took the authorities nearly three months to arrest the elusive

Asahara. In the meantime, the National Police Agency chief was the victim of an attempted assassination, in broad daylight, by an AUM member who escaped on a bicycle. Most of AUM's top dogs were eventually arrested, several immediately confessing their part in the terrorist attack. When the cult's compound near Mount Fuji was raided, a vast arsenal of weapons and chemicals was discovered, as well as Asahara calmly meditating in his pyjamas.

Asahara's trial began in 1996 and will run for years. There are only four hearings a month (twice the usual number) and proceedings have been further slowed by the guru's rambling in-court outbursts and his refusal to enter a plea. Over 100 cases of lesser AUM members have already gone through the courts, most of the defendants pleading guilty. The only question is whether Asahara's possible insanity will save him from the death penalty. "It's always at the back of my mind that he might be insane," said Osamu Watanabe, Asahara's court-appointed lawyer in March 1997, "but we haven't firmly made up our minds about this yet."

## B: THE BUBBLE ECONOMY

The **Bubble Economy** began in the mid-1980s when low interest rates fuelled booming land prices and a runaway stock market. It was believed by many that the stock market, which at its height was worth over forty percent of all the world's other stocks added together, would never fall. Of course it did, but rather than suffering a cataclysmic blowout, the economy has taken eight years to run down to an all-out recession, the equivalent of a slow puncture.

Many small investors were encouraged to plough their savings into the market, the most notorious being **Onoue Nui**, who became known as the "Bubble Woman". At one point, Onoue was, on paper, one of the richest people in the world, her share holdings, financed by stupendous loans, worth ¥1.13 trillion. Even more incredible than the fact that the banks were happy to lend such large amounts to a small-time restaurant owner, were the midnight seances Onoue held with brokers to choose her stocks.

By 1990, the unthinkable was happening. Stocks were devaluing and the extent of brokerages' perfidy – including dealings with gangsters and guarantees of no losses to major clients – was becoming clear. Onoue was one of the first to come a cropper, going bankrupt and standing trial for fraud in 1992. The fallout from bad debts racked up by the banks has since brought several seemingly impregnable financial institutions down and continues to threaten several more.

## C: COMEDY

Spend one night watching Japanese television and you'll realize that the stereotype view of the locals being a dour, unfunny lot is rubbish. The Japanese love a laugh and have long enjoyed the skilfully told monologues of *rakugoka*, traditional **comedy** peformers. Even more popular is the contemporary format *manzai* – a two-man team of comic (*boke*) and foil (*tsukkomi*).

The Kansai area around Ōsaka has traditionally produced the nation's best comics and has even had an ex-comedian, "Knock" Yokoyama, as mayor of the city since 1996. Internationally famous now for his movies is "Beat" **Takeshi Kitano** (see Film, p.801), one half of the old *manzai* act The Two Beats, and still a regular host and guest on quiz and light entertainment shows. The current top performers are Matsumoto Hitoshi and Hamada Masatoshi, a comedy duo known as **Downtown**, who have won a loyal following for their dazzling improvisational show *Gaki no Tsukai ya Arahende!!* (This Is No Job For Kids!!). Other funny guys you'll find hard to avoid on prime-time telly are Ishibashi Taka-aki and Kinashi Noritake, aka the Tunnels, and U-chan and Nan-chan.

## D: DORAEMON AND DANGO

One of Japan's most famous cartoon characters is **Doraemon**, a time-travelling blue robot cat, and Nobita, his ten-year-old pal from suburban Tokyo, both born in December 1969 in a series of educational magazines. Nobita is always getting into scrapes and it's Doraemon who helps him out, usually by producing a twenty-first-century gadget, such as a helicopter hat to help them fly around, or the *doko-de-mo* door, a pink wood gateway to "anywhere" in the world. Doraemon has since gone on to star in many a comic book (*manga*), a TV series, a string of animated film (*anime*) and feature on a host of products.

Construction is one of Japan's biggest businesses and has become a major tool in economic planning since World War II, supervised by the Ministry of Construction. So much public money is available for work that the practice of

**dango**, or bid rigging, is rife. Contracts are often carved up within the industry with bribes to smooth the way. Even though the Fair Trade Commission has tried on many occasions to stop the practice, there have been very few prosecutions.

## E: ENJO KOSAI

Subsidized dating, or **enjo kosai**, is the catch-phrase that has been coined for the worrying phenomena of teenage prostitution, whereby high-school girls date older men for financial compensation. Held up as an example of declining moral values in Japan, *enjo kosai* has been fuelled by the increase in "telephone clubs" where men pay to wait in a cubicle for a call from a potential date. Female callers ring in on the free-dial numbers often advertised on the free packs of tissues distributed outside stations and on busy streets. The extent of the problem is probably nowhere near as large as reported in the media, although there's certainly more to it than the hoo-ha from a few years back over schoolgirls selling their used underwear to sex shops.

## F: FOCUS, FRIDAY AND FLASH

The death of Diana, Princess of Wales, saw Japanese media rip into foreign *paparazzi*, somewhat rich considering the weekly, high-gloss scandal-mongering and intrusive behaviour of the best-selling magazines **Focus**, **Friday** and **Flash**. A combination of *News of the World* and *Life*, these magazines are the antithesis of *Hello*, but equally addictive, offering a regular menu of candid shots of the famous and not so famous.

Although they kowtow to Japan's prudery when it comes to photographs of naked bodies, masking over pubic hair, other shots generally leave nothing to the imagination. There's certainly no squeamishness about shots of dead bodies, or parts of them, as one famous photograph of a railway employee carrying the head of a suicide victim away from the tracks, showed. *Flash* claimed its own victim in 1997 when film director Itami Jūzō committed suicide when he heard the magazine was planning an exposé of his love life.

## G: GAMES

**Golf** was the sport of the boom decade, but is in the bunker now that recession is biting and casual players can no longer afford the ultra-expensive membership and green fees. When Japan's corporate warriors retire, as often as not they can be found down at the neighbourhood park, mallet in hand, enjoying a round of **gateball**, a form of croquet and a favourite pastime of OAPs.

Japan's most popular game is **baseball** (see p.66). While you'll hear a lot about Ō Sadaharu, the Yomuri Giants player who broke the home-run record of America's Hank Aaron, it's his old team mate **Nagashima Shigeo** who still hogs the limelight and has earned the nickname "Mr Giants". Nagashima had clocked up seventeen years as a star player by the time he retired in 1974; he has since made his mark as the Giants' manager, a sports commentator and all round media personality.

## H: HELLO KITTY AND HANAKO

The Japanese have a fatal attraction for cuteness, which manifests itself in a menagerie of cuddly toys and cartoon characters on everything from bank cards to the side of jumbo jets. One design that has made an impact on overseas markets is **Hello Kitty**, a white kitten with a jaunty red hair ribbon. According to the official biography, concocted by parent company Sanrio, Kitty was born in London, where she lives with her parents and twin sister Mimi. The cartoon character, who graces stationery and lunch boxes, also has her own theme park, Sanrio Puroland, in the suburbs of Tokyo.

More trendy than cute is **Hanako**, the phenomenally successful style bible magazine of young urban women. The popularity of the Australian pop artist Ken Donne in Japan is almost exclusively down to his work being featured regularly on the cover of *Hanako*, whose articles have whipped up a storm for many a consumer product or passing fashion.

## I: IDOLS

Japanese **idols** (*aidoru*) are a polymorphous bunch, switching between singing, acting and modelling careers, regardless of where they got their start. An idol's time in the sun is usually brief but blazing, their image staring down from a multitude of billboards as well as out from countless magazines and a range of other media. Not to be confused with TV personalities (*tarento*), idols are usually picked for their looks rather than talent, although the best of them do have both.

One of the hottest idols currently is **Amuro Namie**, a slinky Okinawan pop star whose CDs have sold in the millions and whose look – layered long brown hair, micro-skirt, white nails and lips – has inspired an army of teenage wannabes. The top male heart throb is **Takuya Kimura**, a fresh-faced member of the boy-band SMAP, who has gone on to star in many a *trendy drama* (see p.811). The one true idol-survivor is **Matsuda Seiko**, a pop star of the 1980s who refused to give up her career when she married and has since survived a high-profile divorce, becoming a role model for many downtrodden housewives.

## J: JUKU

Japan has one of the most highly educated populations in the world, but its educational system is not without its faults. The pressure-cooker atmosphere created by the need to get good grades to attend the best schools and colleges has led to the development of a parallel education system of *juku* or "cram schools".

It's estimated that some forty percent of children go to *juku* at some stage, with attendance pretty much compulsory for those who wish to get into the country's top universities. Kids start as young as five years old at these cram schools, prepping for the "examination hell" to be endured at each stage of their education until they reach university, where they can finally relax (degree study is often treated like a three-year holiday between school and career).

The pressure put on kids to get good results and to fit into the homogenized society nurtured by the education system has led to the disturbing phenomena of *ijime*, or bullying, which results in several deaths a year, often from suicide. There's also been a sharp increase in incidents of violence at schools, and although the figures are low compared to other industrialized countries, they're worrying enough for the government to have made educational reform, emphasizing creativity and respect for the individual, a priority.

## K: KARAOKE

The Japanese were partial to a good singsong long before **karaoke**, literally meaning "empty orchestra", was invented, possibly by an Ōsaka record store manager in the early 1970s. The machines, originally clunky eight-track tape players with a heavy duty microphone, have come a long way since and are now linked up to videos, screening the lyrics crooned along to, and featuring a range of effects to flatter the singer into thinking their catarwauling is harmonious. Not for nothing have karaoke machines been dubbed the "electronic *geisha*".

In the mid-1980s, the whole industry, which earns ¥1 trillion a year, was boosted by the debut of the **karaoke box**, a booth kitted out with a karaoke system and rented out by groups or individuals wanting to brush up on their singing technique. These boxes have proved particularly popular with youngsters, women and families who shied away from the smoky small bars frequented by salarymen that were the original preserve of karaoke. Amazingly, research has shown that the introduction of karaoke has coincided with a significant drop in the number of drunks taken into protective custody by the police, salarymen drinking less, rather than more, as they relax over a rousing rendition of *My Way*.

### L: LOVE HOTELS

There are around 35,000 **love hotels** (see Basics, p.38) in Japan, which rent rooms by the hour to couples, often married, seeking a little privacy. Once called *tsurekomi ryokan* (drag her/him in hotels), there's now a trend to call them fashion hotels, in acknowledgement of the fact that it's usually the more discerning, trend-conscious woman who makes the room choice. All kinds of tastes can be indulged at love hotels, with rotating beds in mirror-lined rooms being almost passé in comparison to some of the fantasy creations on offer. Some rooms even come equipped with video cameras so you can take home a souvenir of your stay.

### M: MANGA AND MUJI

All types of drawn cartoons, from comic strips to magazines, are known as **manga**, and together they constitute a multi-billion yen business that accounts for around a third of all published material in Japan. The best seller is *Shukan Shōnen Jump*, a weekly comic for boys (but read by all ages and sexes), that regularly shifts five million copies, but there are hundreds of other titles, not to mention the popular daily strips in newspapers such as *Chibi Maruko-chan*, about the daily life of school girl Maruko and her family.

Although there are plenty of *manga* that cater to less wholesome tastes, with sexual violence

against women being top of the perversions list, comic books are frequently used to explain complicated current affairs topics, such as trade friction problems between the US and Japan, and to teach high-school subjects. *Manga* are targeted at all age groups and it's common to see a cross-section of society reading them.

More than big business, *manga* have become a recognized art form, many incorporating a startling quasi cinematic style of close ups and jump cuts. Top artists are respected the world over. The "god of manga" was **Tezuka Osamu** (see p.423), creator of Astro Boy and Kimba, the White Lion in the 1960s, who went on to pen more challenging fare such as the adventures of the mysterious renegade surgeon Black Jack and the epic war-time saga *Adorufu no Tsugu* (*Tell Adolf*). Successful *manga* artists, such as **Miyazaki Hayao**, have also helped boost the enormous popularity of animated movies (*anime*). Miyazaki's biggest hit has been *Nausicaä*, a sci-fi series set in a post-nuclear holocaust world.

One of Japan's top retail success stories is **Muji**, short for Mujirushi Ryohin (No-brand quality goods), an offshoot of the giant Seiyu supermarket group, with branches now around the world. Launched in 1980, the stores, which stock practical household goods, clothes and foods in simple packaging and monotone colours, prospered from the backlash against the designer-label craze that gripped Japan during the boom years of the 1980s. The irony is that the starker economic realities of the following decade have made Muji's goods desirable commodities in their own right.

### N: NIHONJINRON

**Nihonjinron** is a bizarre nationwide phenomenon in which the study of the specialness of Japan has been elevated to a high art. It has led to a host of ludicrous pronouncements that wouldn't be given the time of day anywhere else in the world, such as politicians justifying import bans for certain foods and skis because Japanese intestines and snow are, apparently, uniquely different. The fad for books analysing Japan was sparked in the 1970s by a slim volume *The Japanese and The Jews*, written by a local scholar under the pseudonym Isaiah Ben Dassan. Since then, real *gaijin* experts have climbed on the bandwagon of telling the Japanese about themselves and some, who've taken the trouble to master the language, have made TV *tarento* careers out of it.

## O: OTAKU AND OLS

Nerdish characters who become obsessive about a particular subject are known as **otaku** and Japan has millions of them, highly knowledgeable about their chosen field, be it a particular cartoon character or computer game. Mostly harmless, *otaku* were tarnished by the brutal child murders perpetrated in 1988 by Miyazaki Tsutomua, a young printer whose cruel behaviour had been fed by his vast collection of porn *manga* and videos.

**OL** is short for office lady, the female clerical workers considered "flowers of the workplace" by their sexist bosses, who need them around to make tea and generally brighten the place up for dull salarymen. If unmarried by the age of 25 and not safely tucked up at home, then an OL is like a Christmas cake, useless after the holiday. It's not quite as grim as this for career-minded women today, but the recession has not helped increase their chances of promotion as businesses have chopped back on hiring females in the first place.

## P: PACHINKO AND PURIKURA

One of Japan's top pastimes and major industries, raking in a staggering ¥26.3 trillion a year, is **pachinko**, a pinball game of limited skill. It's not difficult to spot *pachinko* parlours – they look like mini Las Vegas casinos on steroids, all flashing lights and big neon signs. Inside, the atmosphere is no less in your face. The noise of thousands of steel balls clattering through the upright electronic bagatelles is deafening, yet rows of players sit mesmerized as they control the speed with which the balls fall through the machine.

The aim of pachinko is for the balls to fall into the right holes so more balls can be won These are traded in for prizes, such as cigarette lighters and calculators. Although it's illegal for the parlours to pay out cash, there's always a cubby hole close by where prizes can be exchanged for money, a charade that the authorities have long turned a blind eye to. The initial cost of indulging in this mechanized mayhem can be as little as ¥100 for 25 ball bearings; just remember to take your earplugs, too.

One of the latest consumer crazes that is firmly headed for *pachinko*-like success are **purikura** (print club), digital photo booths which combine your mug shot with a vast selection of designs on a sheet of sixteen mini-stickers. Launched by Sega Corp in 1995, there are now well over 20,000 booths around Japan, and no self respecting teenager is without their album of swapped stickers, with many adults getting in on the act, too, jazzing up their business cards with the personalized *purikura*. The machines, found in all major shopping areas, are well worth searching out; for a couple of hundred yen you'll have a neat pop-art souvenir of Japan.

## Q: QUIZ SHOWS

The combined travel and general knowledge quiz show *Naruhodo za Warudo* (I Understand the World), which began on Fuji TV in October 1981, revolutionized the **quiz show** genre in Japan, with its lively presentation and use of celebrity contestants rather than the general public. Although the show was laid to rest after fifteen seasons in 1996, it has since set the format for a host of copy-cat quizzes packed with bantering celebrities.

## R: RŪSU SOKKUSU

One of the more noticeable fashions of high-school girls is their preference for **rūsu sokkusu** (loose socks), baggy white legwarmer socks, worn as only the most dishevelled granny would do. The socks, which are held up by special glue, are believed to present plump calves in a more flattering light. What they're actually about is a form of rebellion from the strict uniform rules that students must keep to at school.

## S: SALARYMEN AND SOAPLANDS

The dark-suited **salaryman** is generally a clerical office worker, although the term is applied to many other types of jobs. Guaranteed lifetime employment and steady promotion, Japan's corporate warriors during the boom years of the 1960s through to the 1980s only had to watch out for *karoshi*: death from overwork. Nowadays, the fear is more of their company announcing a "restructuring", a polite way of saying there will be redundancies.

Although it's perhaps not discussed as openly in Japan as in the West, sex generally comes with less hang-ups for the Japanese. One place a frisky salaryman might turn for relief is a **soapland**, or massage parlour where the rubbing and other services are carried out by women under the guise of a Turkish bath. Soaplands were once call Turkish baths until the Turkish embassy complained that this was insulting to their wholly honourable bathing practices.

## T: TAIGA AND TRENDY DRAMAS

Long-running soap operas are very unusual in Japan, the exception being the public broadcaster NHK's **taiga dramas**. These epic historical sagas, which screen every Sunday night for a year, began in 1963 and have fallen in and out of popularity ever since. Usually concerning some great warrior figure of the past (1997's was about the warlord Mōri Motanari), *taiga* dramas are pretty much a national institution.

The antithesis of these *samurai* epics is the even more popular **trendy drama**, which run for a strict twelve-week season and concern themselves with contemporary issues, such as the trials and tribulations of modern career women or the risky (for Japan) topic of single mothers. One of the most daring and popular, racking up a third of the viewing audience when screened in 1992, was *I Have Been in Love With You For a Long Time*, whose plot revolved around the complex emotional triangle between uptight yuppie Fuyuhiko, his overbearing mother and Fuyuhiko's arranged-marriage (yes, these still happen) bride Miwa.

## U: UYOKU

The loud-speaker-mounted trucks of the **uyoku**, or ultra nationalists, are an inescapable and noisy feature on the streets of every Japanese city. These mobile ghetto blasters, decorated with Rising Sun flags and screaming slogans, blare out distasteful right-wing messages or stop outside large companies and banks, broadcasting embarrassing statements about them.

There are estimated to be around a thousand such ultra-nationalist groups in Japan, and to a startling extent, the police turn a blind eye (and deaf ear) to their activities. Politicians and the media who openly criticize the ideals and institutions they hold dear, such as the imperial household, set themselves up for some kind of nasty retribution. To most people, though, *uyoku* are an embarrassment best ignored.

## V: VIRTUAL PETS AND POP STARS

The virtual pet game **Tamagochi** is one of the most successful gizmos of recent years, selling some twenty million units worldwide. Meaning "lovable egg", the pocket game is an egg-shaped key ring with an LCD screen. The aim is to hatch the chick that appears on the screen, feed and nurture it – just like a real pet – over its life span of thirty days so that it rises to heaven and turns into an angel. The Tamagochi, invented by housewife Maita Aki, has been so successful that advice books on how to care for the virtual pet have become best sellers and bereavement counselling has been offered to kids whose pets have died before reaching heaven.

Death or aging is not something that Japan's first **virtual pop star**, Date Kyoko, has to worry about. The computer-animated character was created in 1996 to fit a precise marketing profile and had an instant hit with her first CD. Although no more enduring than other bubblegum pop singers, Date's "talents" are an ironic comment on her flesh and blood counterparts whose voices are as electronically altered and images as carefully packaged as those of the cyber songstress.

## W: WORLDS

The length of Japan it's possible to visit many other **worlds** than the one you're actually travelling in. These theme park facsimiles of other countries range from Canada World in Hokkaidō through to Huis ten Bosch in Kyūshū, a painstakingly accurate replica of the Netherlands. Along the way, you can also discover many other mini nations, including theme parks of old Japan, such as Meiji Mura near Nagoya. The popularity of these parks lies in the safely packaged exotic escape they provide from home without the inconvenience of long-distance travel, language barriers and nasty shocks, such as crime and disease.

## Y: YAKUZA

With membership estimated at around 80,000, the **yakuza** is believed to be a far bigger criminal organization than America's Mafia. Organized crime in Japan is exactly that, a highly stratified, efficient and surprisingly tolerated everyday operation, raking in trillions of yen from extortion, protection rackets, prostitution, gambling and drug peddling.

Part of the reason that the seven major *yakuza* syndicates (who keep offices, like regular companies) have prospered is that they have acted as an alternative police force, containing petty crime and keeping violence within their own ranks. Favours, financial and otherwise, granted to high-ranking politicians and businesses, have also gained the *yakuza* protection and their romantic, *samurai*-value image has been boosted by countless movies.

It's highly unlikely that your path will cross with a *yakuza*, unless you take to hanging out in the dodgier areas of cities like Tokyo and Ōsaka. Younger gang members, called *chimpira*, can often be spotted by their tight perm hairdos, dark glasses and appalling dress sense. Other giveaway signs to look for are missing digits (amputation of fingers, joint by joint, is traditional form of punishment for breaking the *yakuza* code) and full body tattoos.

## Z: ZOKU

Prior to the mid-1980s, Japan's media often reported the latest youth subculture sweeping the country under the tag line of **zoku** (tribe).The most enduring of these labels is the **bosozoku** (wild speed tribe) of the 1970s, originally a mild version of the Hell's Angels, greased-hair bikers out for a loud time. Now, the term is more commonly used for rebel teenagers.

# BOOKS

The one thing the world is not short of is books about Japan. Virtually every foreign writer and journalist who has passed through the country has felt compelled to commit to paper their thoughts and experiences. Many of these accounts are hopelessly out of date (or just plain hopeless), but we've picked out a personal selection of the best that provide a deeper understanding of what is too easily assumed to be the world's most enigmatic country. As throughout this guide, for Japanese names we have given the family name first. This may not always be the order in which it is printed on an English translation.

Drawing on over a thousand years of literature and navel-gazing, the Japanese also love writing about their own country and culture. The vast bulk of translated works widely available in the Britain and the US are novels, spanning from the courtly elegance of *Genji Monogatari* (*The Tale of Genji*) to the contemporary fiction of Nobel Prize winner Ōe Kenzaburō and the Generation-Y author Yoshimoto Banana. Such books are often released by Kodansha, one of the world's biggest publishers, and Charles E Tuttle, a long-established imprint for specialist books on Japan. Both these publishers have an excellent range of reference and coffee-table books on all aspects of Japanese culture, from architecture and gardens to food and martial arts, which are best bought at major bookstores in Japan, such as Kinokuniya and Maruzen. Look out also for the series of pocket-size booklets by JTB on many different aspects of Japanese culture. Books published by Kodansha, Tuttle and JTB are usually cheaper in

Japan, but other books won't be, so buy them before your journey.

## HISTORY

**Pat Barr** *The Coming of the Barbarians* (Penguin). Entertaining and very readable tales of how Japan opened up to the West at the beginning of the Meiji Restoration.

**Ian Buruma** *The Wages of Guilt* (Random House). Buruma's skilful comparison and explanation of how and why Germany and Japan have come to terms so differently with their roles in World War II.

**John Hersey** *Hiroshima* (Penguin). Classic account of the devastation and suffering wrought by the first A-bomb to be used in war.

**George Hicks** *The Comfort Women* (Souvenir Press). The story of one of the more shameful episodes of World War II, when the Japanese forced women to become prostitutes (euphimistically known as "comfort women") for the army, that was only officially admitted by the government in the 1990s.

**Richard Hughes** *Foreign Devil* (Century). The veteran Australian journalist arrived in Japan in 1940, eighteen months before Pearl Harbour, and came back in 1945 to turn his enormous talent (and wit) to commenting on postwar Japan and the Far East. Goes behind the scenes with Fleming-san to research *You Only Live Twice* (see p.819).

**Mishima Akio** *Bitter Sea* (Kosei). The Kyūshū port of Minamata is now a byword in Japan for the devastating impact of industrial pollution. This dramatic account of the poisoning of Minamata's citizens and their long, painful battle for compensation, was penned by a former journalist, turned environmentalist.

**Sir George Samson** *Japan: A Short Cultural History* (Tuttle). Condensed from the former diplomat's scholarly three-volume epic – but by no means concise – this is one of the standard texts on Japan's past.

**Edward Seidensticker** *Low City, High City* (Tuttle) and *Tokyo Rising: The City Since the Great Earthquake* (Tuttle). Seidensticker, a top translator of Japanese literature, tackles Tokyo's history from its humble beginnings to the Great Kantō quake of 1923 in the first book and follows up well with a second volume focusing on the capital's postwar experiences.

**Oliver Statler** *Japanese Inn* and *Japanese Pilgrimage* (Tuttle). In the first book, a ryokan on the Tōkaidō road provides the focus for an entertaining account of over four hundred years of Japanese history. In *Japanese Pilgrimage*, Statler applies his talents to bringing alive the history of the 88-temple hike around Shikoku.

**Richard Storry** *A History of Modern Japan* (Penguin). Ideal primer for basics and themes of Japanese history.

**Kenneth Strong** *Ox Against the Storm* (Japan Library). The revealing story of one man's fight against the Meiji Government on behalf of peasants affected by copper pollution. A larger-than-life character, Tanaka Shozo was a fierce champion of democracy and people's rights, as well as one of Japan's first conservationists.

**Richard Tames** *A Traveller's History of Japan* (Windrush Press). This clearly written and succinct volume romps through Japan's history and provides useful cultural descriptions and essays.

**Marvin Tokayer and Mary Swartz** *The Fugu Plan* (Weatherhill). Semi-fictionalized tale, based on incredible true-life events, which saw over 5000 Jews being allowed into Japan during World War II and protected first in Kōbe and later in Japanese-occupied Shanghai.

**Paul Waley** *Tokyo: City of Stories* (Weatherill). An intimate, anecdotal history of the capital, which delves into Tokyo's neighbourhoods uncovering some fascinating stories in the process.

## BUSINESS, ECONOMICS AND POLITICS

**Peter Hadfield** *Sixty Seconds That Will Change The World* (Sidgwick & Jackson). The main theme – the terrible threat hanging over Tokyo and the world by a coming earthquake – allows Hadfield to reveal much about Japanese attitudes, bureaucracy and politics.

**Robert M March** *Working for a Japanese Company* (Kodansha). One of the best studies on what it's really like inside Japan's corporate powerhouses by an Aussie management consultant who's done thorough research.

**Miyamoto Masao** *Straitjacket Society* (Kodansha). As the subtitle hints, this "insider's irreverent view of bureaucratic Japan" is quite an eye-opener. Unsurprisingly, Miyamoto was

fired from the Ministry of Health and Welfare, but his book sold over 400,000 copies.

**Ōmae Kenichi** *The Borderless World* (Fontana). One of Japan's top management consultants airs his free-market theories of how national economic borders are melting away in the wake of multinational business success. A useful insight into the thoughts of a man whose views have influenced many important businesses and political leaders.

**Jacob M Schlesinger** *Shadow Shoguns* (Simon & Schuster). Cracking crash course in Japan's political scene, scandals and all, from Wall Street Journal reporter Schlesinger, who spent five years at the newspaper's Tokyo bureau and whose wife was an aide to current top politician Ozawa Ichiro.

**Peter Tasker** *Inside Japan* (Penguin). First published in 1987, at the height of the boom years, but still recommended reading. This is a highly readable and intelligent examination of Japanese business and society, by a British financial analyst who has made Japan his home since 1977.

**Karel Van Wolferen** *The Enigma of Japanese Power* (Macmillan/Tuttle). The 1993 version is the most recent edition of what has become a standard text on the triad of Japan's bureaucracy, politicians and business, and the power gulf between them. A weighty, thought-provoking tome, worth wading through.

## ARTS, CULTURE AND SOCIETY

**Ruth Benedict** *The Chrysanthemum and the Sword* (Tuttle). This classic study of the hierachical order of Japanese society, first published in 1946, is still relevant now for its intriguing insight into the psychology of a nation that had just suffered defeat in World War II.

**Ian Buruma** *A Japanese Mirror* and *The Missionary and the Libertine* (Faber). The first book is an intelligent, erudite examination of Japan's popular culture, while the *The Missionary and the Libertine* collects together a range of the author's essays, including pieces on Japan-bashing, Hiroshima, Pearl Harbour, the authors Mishima Yukio, Tanizaki Junichirō and Yoshimoto Banana and the film director Oshima Nagisa.

**Nicholas Bornoff** *Pink Samurai* (HarperCollins). Everything you ever wanted to know about the history and current practices and mores of sex in Japan, plus – at seven hundred-odd pages – plenty you'd rather not have known.

**Kittredge Cherry** *Womansword* (Kodansha). Slightly dated but fascinating portrait of women in Japanese society as revealed through language. From "Christmas cake" (an unmarried woman) to "giant garbage" (a retired husband), *Womansword* makes linguistics both fun and thought provoking.

**Mark Coutts-Smith** *Children of the Drum* (Lightworks Press). The life of Sado Island's kodo drummers capture in powerful black-and-white images by a photographer who spent five years studying and working with the group.

**Lesley Downer** *The Brothers* (Chatto & Windus). The Tsutsumi family are the Kennedys of Japan and their saga of wealth, illegitimacy and the fabled hatred of the two half brothers is made gripping reading by Downer. Also look out for *On the Narrow Road to the Deep North*, her book following in the footsteps of the poet Bashō.

**Bruce S Feiler** *Learning to Bow* (Ticknor & Fields). An enlightening and entertaining read, especially for anyone contemplating teaching English in Japan. This book recounts the experiences of a young American on the JET programme, plonked into a high school in rural Tochigi-ken.

**Norma Field** *In the Realm of a Dying Emperor* (Pantheon). Field paints a vivid alternative portrait of contemporary Japan, as seen through the experiences of three people who broke ranks: Chibana Shoichi, who hauled down the Rising Sun flag in Okinawa; Nakaya Yasuko, a housewife who tried to stop the burial of her husband, a former Self Defence Forces member, at a Shinto shrine; and Motoshima Hitoshi, ex-mayor of Nagasaki, who criticized Emperor Hirohito's role during World War II.

**Gunji Masakatsu** *Kabuki* (Kodansha). Excellent, highly readable introduction to Kabuki by one of the leading conoisseurs of Japanese drama. Illustrated with copious annotated photos of the great actors and most dramatic moments in Kabuki theatre.

**Joe Joseph** *The Japanese* (Penguin). Former *Times* correspondent sets down some thoughts on the nation, mainly gathered during the madly extravagant and unrepresentative bubble years of the late 1980s.

**David Kaplan & Andrew Marshall** *The Cult at the End of the World* (Arrow). Chilling account of the nerve gas attack on the Tokyo subway by the AUM cult in 1995. The gripping, pulp-fiction-like prose belies formidable research by the authors into the shocking history of this killer cult and their crazed leader Asahara Shoko.

**Donald Keene** *The Blue-Eyed Tarōkaja* (Columbia University Press). Wide-ranging anthology of literary essays, interviews and travel pieces by Donald Keene, one of the foremost authorities on Japanese literature.

**Alex Kerr** *Lost Japan* (Lonely Planet). Although it's part of the usually tedious "Japan's not what it once was" school of writing, this book won a prestigious literature prize when first published in Japanese, and the translation is just as worthy of praise. Kerr, the son of a US naval officer, first came to Japan as a child in the 1960s and has been fascinated by it ever since. This beautifully written and thoughtfully observed set of essays covers aspects of his life and passions, including Kabuki, art collecting and cities such as Kyoto and Ōsaka.

**Richard McGregor** *Japan Swings* (Allen & Unwin/Yen). One of the more intelligent books penned by a former Tokyo correspondent. McGregor sets politics, culture and sex in 1990s post-bubble Japan in his sights, revealing a fascinating world of ingrained money politics and shifting sexual attitudes.

**Brian Moeran** *Ōkubo Diary* (Stanford University Press). An affectionate though far from rose-tinted view into the daily life of a Japanese village by a cultural anthropologist. Moeran spent four years with his family in a community of potters in deepest Kyūshū, before their dreams were shattered in a totally unexpected and harrowing way.

**John K Nelson** *A Year in the Life of a Shinto Shrine* (University of Washington Press). Fascinating insight into Japan's native animist religion based on this American ethnologist's research at Suwa-jinja in Nagasaki. Amid all the detail, Nelson also catches gossipy asides such as a trainee priest being told to be "careful not to fart during the ritual".

**Gunter Nitschke** *Japanese Gardens* (Taschen). A far less lavish book on gardens than Itoh Teiji's seminal work (see p.817), but nonetheless informative, wide-ranging and beautifully illustrated.

**Donald Richie** *Public People, Private People*

(Kodansha), *A Lateral View* (Japan Times) and *Partial Views* (Japan Times). These three books, all collections of essays by a man whose love affair with Japan began when he arrived with the US occupying forces in 1947, set the standard other expat commentators can only aspire to. *Public People* is a set of sketches of famous and unknown Japanese, including profiles of novelist Mishima and the actor Mifune Toshiro. In *A Lateral View* and *Partial Views*, Richie tackles Tokyo style, avant-garde theatre, *pachinko*, the Japanese kiss and the Zen rock garden at Kyoto's Ryōan-ji temple, among many other things.

**Mark Schilling** *The Encyclopedia of Japanese Pop Culture* (Weatherhill). Forget sumo, *samurai* and *ikebana*. Godzilla, pop idols and instant ramen are really where Japan's culture's at. Schilling's book is an indispensible, spot-on guide to late twentieth-century Japan. Don't leave home without it.

**Frederik L Schodt** *Dreamland Japan: Writings on Modern Manga* (SBP). In the sequel to his *Manga! Manga! The World of Japanese Comics*, Schodt pens a series of entertaining and informative essays on the art of Japanese comic books, profiling the top publications, artists, animated films and English-language *manga*.

**Joan Stanley-Baker** *Japanese Art* (Thames and Hudson). Highly readable introduction to the broad range of Japan's artistic traditions (though excluding theatre and music), tracing their development from prehistoric to modern times.

**David Suzuki & Oiwa Keibo** *The Japan We Never Knew* (Allen & Unwin). Canadian broadcaster and writer Suzuki teamed up with half-Japanese anthropologist Oiwa to tour the country and interview an extraordinary range of people, from the Ainu of Hokkaidō to descendants of the "untouchable" caste, the Burakumin. The result is an excellent riposte to the idea of a mono-cultural, conformist Japan.

**Rey Ventura** *Underground in Japan* (Cape). The non-Caucasian *gaijin* experience in Japan is brilliantly essayed by Ventura, who lived and worked with fellow Filipino illegal immigrants in the dockyards of Yokohama.

## TRAVEL WRITING

**Dave Barry** *Dave Barry Does Japan* (Random House). Hilarious spoof travel book by top American satirist.

**Isabella Bird** *Unbeaten Tracks in Japan* (Virago). After a brief stop in Meiji-era Tokyo, intrepid Victorian adventurer Bird is determined to reach parts of Japan not trampled by tourists. She heads north to Hokkaidō, taking the time to make acute, vivid observations along the way.

**Alan Booth** *The Roads to Sata* (Penguin) and *Looking for the Lost* (Kodansha). Two classics by one of the most insightful and entertaining modern writers on Japan, whose talents were tragically cut short by his death in 1993. The first book sees Booth, an avid long-distance walker, hike (with the aid of many a beer) from the far north of Hokkaidō to the southern tip of Kyūshū, while *Looking for the Lost*, a trio of walking tales, is by turns hilarious and heartbreakingly poignant.

**Sir Alfred East** *A British Artist in Meiji Japan* (In Print). The short journal of a slightly pompous British landscape painter who was among the first foreigners to travel around Japan after 1868. His artist's eye and curiosity make for some perceptive and fascinating insights, alongside the inevitable cultural misconceptions.

**Pico Iyer** *Video Nights in Katmandu* and *The Lady and the Monk* (Black Swan). The first book, by this former *Time* correspondent, has a brilliant essay on baseball and the incongruities of modern Japan. Iyer obviously fell in love with Japan, a fact reflected in the beautifully written *The Lady and the Monk*, devoted to a year he spent studying Zen Buddhism and dallying with a married woman in Kyoto. A rose-tinted, dreamy view of the country.

**Donald Richie** *The Inland Sea* (Kodansha) and *Lafcadio Hearn's Japan* (Tuttle). The first is Richie's writing at its very best. A subtle, elegiac travelogue, in the form of a diary, first published in 1971, that totally captures the timeless beauty of the island-studded Inland Sea. The latter is an anthology, edited by Richie, of one of the best-known and respected foreign writers who lived in Japan in the late nineteenth century. Includes sections from the classic *Glimpses of Unfamiliar Japan*, among Hearn's other works.

## GUIDES AND REFERENCE BOOKS

**Jude Band** *Tokyo Night City* (Tuttle). Hip, streetwise guide to the capital's hot nightspots, although it's somewhat superseded by her more recent contributions to the *TokyoQ* Web site, penned under the *nom de plume* Sister Chill.

**Jan Brown** *Exploring Tōhoku* (Weatherhill). Detailed and well-written guide to Japan's backcountry by a long-term resident and obvious enthusiast. Provides plenty of historical and cultural information as well as practical snippets.

**John Carroll** *Trails of Two Cities* (Kodansha). Enjoyable and informative walking guide to Yokohama and Kamakura by a long-time resident. Full of fascinating historical detail and local insights.

**Judith Clancy** *Exploring Kyoto* (Weatherhill). One of the better Kyoto guides, whose thirty well-researched walking tours (each with an accompanying map) cover both the famous sights and the less well-known by-ways of this ancient city.

**Diane Durston** *Old Kyoto* (Kodansha) and *Kyoto: Seven Paths to the Heart of the City* (Mitsumura Suko Shoin). Few people can get under the skin of this enigmatic city as well as Diane Durston. In *Old Kyoto* she seeks out the best traditional craft shops, restaurants and ryokan, while her more recent book explores seven neighbourhoods where Kyoto's special magic still survives.

**Enbutsu Sumiko** *Old Tokyo: Walks in the City of the Shogun* (Kodansha). Tokyo's old Shitamachi area is best explored on foot and Enbutsu's guide, illustrated with characterful block prints, helps bring the city's history alive.

**Harry Guest** *Traveller's Literary Companion to Japan* (In Print). Explore Japan in the company of the country's literary greats and a host of foreign writers. Regional essays with selected extracts are backed up by author bios, booklists and a brief romp through the historical and cultural background. The essential travel accessory.

**Brian Harrel ed** *Cycling Japan* (Kodansha). Harrel also edits the biking newsletter *Oikaze* and this highly practical guide tells you everything you need to know for a biking trip around the country, with plenty of personal accounts. If nothing else, try the Yamanote Countryside Ride, a 45-kilometre loop around Tokyo, which is guaranteed to reveal many of the city's forgotten gems.

**Anne Hotta with Ishiguro Yoko** *A Guide to Japanese Hot Springs* (Kodansha). Over 160

onsen, including 25 within easy reach of Tokyo, are detailed in this indispensable guide for bath lovers, as well as the cultural history of natural hot water pursuits in Japan.

**Paul Hunt** *Hiking in Japan* (Kodansha). Hunt demonstrates there's far more to mountain climbing in Japan than scaling Fuji-san. His detailed hikes cover all the top destinations from Kirishima in Kyūshū to Daisetsu-zan in Hokkaidō, by way of the fabulous Japan Alps.

**Itoh Teiji** *The Gardens of Japan* (Kodansha). Huge coffee-table book covering all the great historical gardens, including many not generally open to the public, as well as contemporary design. A comprehensive overview with splendid photos.

**Thomas F Judge and Tomita Hiroyuki** *Edo Craftsmen* (Weatherhill). Beautifully produced portraits of some of Shitamachi's traditional craftsmen still working in the backstreets of Tokyo. A timely insight into a disappearing world.

**Rick Kennedy** *Good Tokyo Restaurants* (Kodansha). By an author who's sampled thousands of restaurants during his many years in Tokyo, so he knows what he's talking about. Not as wide ranging as other guides, but very reliable.

**John Kennerdell** *Tokyo Journal's Tokyo Restaurant Guide* (Yohan). Over 300 recommendations is this excellent bi-lingual guide, covering the full gamut of Tokyo's multi-national cuisines. Spot-on maps ensure you won't get lost on the way to your chosen restaurant.

**John and Phyllis Martin** *Tokyo: A Cultural Guide to Japan's Capital City, Kyoto: A Cultural Guide to Japan's Ancient Imperial City* and *Nara: A Cultural Guide to Japan's Ancient Capital* (Tuttle). Three excellent books designed around walking tours of Japan's most historic cities, which go well beyond the usual sights.

**Ed Readicker-Henderson** *The Traveller's Guide to Japanese Pilgrimages* (Weatherhill). A practical guide to Japan's top three pilgrim routes: Hiei-zan (near Kyoto); the 33 Kannon of Saigoku (a broad sweep from the Kii peninsula to Lake Biwa); and following the steps of Kōbō Daishi round Shikoku's 88 temples.

**T R Reid** *Ski Japan!* (Kodansha). If you're planning a ski trip in Japan, don't leave without having first read through this witty and informative guide that profiles 93 of the best resorts in the country. Understandably, ski-mad Reid prefers to be on rather than off the slopes, so don't expect much in the way of accommodation or apres-ski recommendations.

**Robb Satterwhite** *What's What in Japanese Restaurants* (Kodansha). Handy guide to all things culinary you'll encounter during your adventures in Japanese food and drink. Written by a Tokyo-based epicure who also manages the excellent *Tokyo Food Page* on the Web. The menus annoted with Japanese characters are particularly useful.

**Marc Treib & Ron Herman** *A Guide to the Gardens of Kyoto* (Shufunotomo). Handy, pocket-sized guide to more than fifty of the city's gardens, with concise historical details and step-by-step descriptions of each garden.

**Gary D'A Walters** *Day Walks Near Tokyo* (Kodansha). Slim volume of strolls and hikes all within easy reach of the capital to help get you off the beaten tourist path. The maps are clear, as are the practical details and directions.

**Diane Wiltshire Kanagawa & Jeanne Huey Erickson** *Japan for Kids* (Kodansha). Immensely practical guide covering everything from vocabulary for the labour ward, to where to rent a Santa. Aimed mainly at expat parents living in Tokyo, but also full of practical tips and recommendations for visitors with kids.

## LITERATURE

### CLASSICS

**Bashō Matsuo** *The Narrow Road to the Deep North* (Penguin). The seventeenth-century haiku poetry master chronicles his journey through northern Japan, pausing to compose his thoughts along the way.

**Kawabata Yasunari** *Snow Country, The Izu Dancer*, etc (Tuttle). Japan's first Nobel Prize winner for fiction, writes intense tales of passion usually about a sophisticated urban man falling for a simple country girl.

**Murasaki Shikibu** *The Tale of Genji* (Penguin/Tuttle). Claimed as the world's first novel, a lyrical epic of the lives and loves of a nobleman spun by a lady of the Heian court around 1000 AD.

**Sei Shōnagon** *The Pillow Book* (Penguin). Fascinating insight into the daily life and artful thoughts of a tenth-century noblewoman, translated by Ivan Morris.

**Sōseki Natsume** *Botchan* and *I am a Cat* (Tuttle). In his comic novel *Botchan*, Sōseki draws on his own experiences as an English teacher in turn-of-the-century Matsuyama. The three volumes of his classic *I am a Cat* sees the humorist adopting a wry feline point of view on the world.

**Tajima Noriyuki** *Tokyo: A Guide to Recent Architecture* (Ellipsis). Compact, expertly written and nicely illustrated book, that's an essential accompaniment on any modern architectural tour of the capital.

**Tanizaki Jun'ichirō** *Some Prefer Nettles* and *The Makioka Sisters* (Tuttle). One of the great stylists of Japanese prose, Tanizaki's finest book is often considered to be *Some Prefer Nettles*, about a romantic liaison between a Japanese man and a Eurasian woman. However, there's an epic sweep to *The Makioka Sisters* which documents the decline of a wealthy merchant family in Ōsaka.

### CONTEMPORARY FICTION

**Alfred Birnbaum ed** *Monkey Brain Sushi* (Kodansha). Eleven often quirky short stories by contemporary Japanese authors. A good introduction to modern prose writers.

**Ishiguro Kazuo** *An Artist of the Floating World* (Faber) and *A Pale View of the Hills* (Faber). Nagasaki-born author who's lived in Britain since 1960. *A Pale View*, his first novel, is a haunting tale set in Nagasaki which unravels the vaguely expressed horrors of the atomic bombing against the backdrop of a dislocated postwar society. *An Artist of the Floating World* takes a look at the rise of Japanese militarism in this century through the eyes of an aging painter. It won the Whibread Book of the Year for 1986.

**Maruya Saiichi** *Singular Rebellion* (Kodansha). Comedy of manners about a middle-aged salaryman who shacks up with a bimbo model, only to find himself also sharing house with granny, just out of jail for murder.

**Mishima Yukio** *After the Banquet, Confessions of Mask, Forbidden Colours, The Sea of Fertility* (all Penguin/Kodansha). Novelist Mishima sealed his notoriety by committing ritual suicide after leading a failed military coup in

1970. He left behind a highly respectable, if at times melodramatic, body of literature, including some of Japan's finest postwar novels. Themes of tradition, sexuality and militarism run though many of his works.

**Miyabe Miyuki** *All She Was Worth* (Kodansha). When a young man's fiancé goes missing, a trail of credit-card debts and worse turns up. There's more to this clever who-dunnit set in contemporary Tokyo than immediately meets the eye.

**Murakami Haruki** *A Wild Sheep Chase, Dance Dance Dance* (Penguin/Kodansha) and *The Wind-Up Bird Chronicle* (Harvill). Hailed as a postwar successor to the great novelists Mishima, Kawabata and Tanizaki, Murakami is an inventive and compulsive writer. *A Wild Sheep Chase* and its follow up *Dance, Dance, Dance* are funky, funny and ultimately disturbing modern-day fables, dressed up as detective novels. *The Wind-Up Bird Chronicle* is his most ambitious book yet, mixing an intriguing cast of characters into a dreamy cocktail of mystery, war reportage and philosophy.

**Murakami Ryu** *Almost Transparent Blue, Sixty-nine* and *Coin Locker Babies* (Kodansha). Murakami burst onto Japan's literary scene in the mid-1980s with *Almost Transparent Blue*, a hip tale of student life mixing reality and fantasy. *Sixty-nine* is his semi-autobiographical account of a 17-year-old stirred by the rebellious passions of the late 1960s, set in Sasebo, Kyūshū; while *Coin Locker Babies* is his most ambitious work, spinning a revenger's tragedy about the lives of two boys dumped in adjacent coin lockers as babies.

**Ōe Kenzaburō** *Nip the Buds Shoot the Kids* (Kodansha), *A Personal Matter* (Tuttle) and *A Healing Family* (Kodansha). Ōe won Japan's second Nobel Prize for literature in 1994 and is a writer who aims, in his own words, to "push back the rising tide of conformity". *Nip the Buds*, his first full-length novel published in 1958, is a tale of lost innocence concerning fifteen reformatory school boys evacuated in wartime to a remote mountain village and left to fend for themselves when a threatening plague frightens away the villagers. *A Personal Matter* sees Ōe tackling the trauma of his handicapped son Hikari's birth, while *A Healing Family* catches up with Hikari thirty years later documenting his trials and tri-umphs. Never an easy read, but always startlingly honest.

**Yoshimoto Banana** *Kitchen, Lizard* and *Amrita* (Faber). Trendy thirty-something novelist whose quirky, lyrical style and odd stories have struck a chord with modern Japanese youth and overseas readers.

### JAPAN IN FOREIGN FICTION

**Alan Brown** *Audrey Hepburn's Neck* (Sceptre). Beneath this rib-tickling, acutely observed tale of a young guy from the sticks adrift in big-city Tokyo, Brown weaves several important themes, including the continuing impact of World War II and the confused relationships between the Japanese and *gaijin*. An evocative, enchanting fable of contemporary Japan.

**James Clavell** *Shogun* (Dell). Blockbuster fictionalized account of Englishman Will Adams' life in seventeenth-century Japan as an advisor to Shogun Tokugawa Ieyasu.

**Ian Fleming** *You Only Live Twice* (Pan). Bondo-san on the trail of arch-enemy Blofeld in trendy mid-sixties Tokyo and the wilds of Kyūshū, assisted by Tiger Tanaka and Kissy Suzuki.

**William Gibson** *Idoru* (Penguin). Love in the age of the computer chip. Cyberpunk novelist Gibson's sci-fi vision of Tokyo's high-tech future – a world of non-intrusive DNA checks at airports and computerized pop icons (the *idoru* of the title) – rings disturbingly true.

**Arthur Golden** *Memoirs of a Geisha* (Vintage). Rags to riches potboiler following the progress of Chiyo from her humble beginnings in a Japanese fishing village through training as a *geisha* in Kyoto to setting up her own tea house in New York. Full of accurate details and colourful characters.

**Steven Heighton** *Flightpaths of the Emperor* (Granta). Entertaining and thought-provoking collection of short stories by a young award-winning Canadian writer, most based in downtown Ōsaka where Heighton once taught English like the character in some of the tales.

**Gavin Kramer** *Shopping* (Fourth Estate). British lawyer Kramer's zippy first novel is on the bleak side, but captures the turn-of-Millennium zeitgeist of Tokyo, where schoolgirls trade sex for designer labels and *gaijin* flounder in a sea of misunderstanding.

**John David Morley** *Pictures from the Water Trade* (Flamingo). The sub-title, *An Englishman in Japan*, says it all as Morley's alter-ego, Boon, crashes headlong into an intense relationship with demure, yet sultry Mariko in an oh-so-foreign world. Along the way, some imaginative observations and descriptions are made.

**Peter Tasker** *Silent Thunder* (Orion/Tuttle). Top British financial analyst Tasker's first stab at fiction is a fun, throwaway thriller, with Bond-like set pieces and some lively Japanese characters, especially Mori, his down-at-heel gumshoe. Much better than the follow-up *Buddha Kiss*.

# LANGUAGE

**First the good news. Picking up a few words of Japanese, even managing a sentence or two, is not difficult. Pronunciation is simple and standard and there are few exceptions to the straightforward grammar rules. With a couple of weeks' effort you should be able to read the words spelled out in hiragana and katakana, Japanese phonetic characters, even if you can't understand them. And, any time spent learning Japanese will be amply rewarded by the thrilled response you'll elicit from the locals, who'll always politely comment on your fine linguistic ability.**

The bad news is that it takes a very great effort indeed to become halfway proficient in Japanese, let alone master the language. One of the main stumbling blocks is the thousands of *kanji* characters that need to be memorized, most of which have at least two pronunciations, depending on the sentence and their combination with other characters. Another major difference is the multiple levels of politeness embodied in Japanese, married with different sets of words used by men and women (although this is less of a problem). Finally, as you move around Japan there are different dialects to deal with, such as Ōsaka-ben the dialect of the Kansai area, involving whole new vocabularies.

## JAPANESE CHARACTERS

The exact origins of Japanese are a mystery, and until the sixth century it only existed in the spoken form. Once the Japanese imported Chinese characters, known as *kanji*, they began to develop their own forms of written language.

Japanese is now written in a combination of three systems. The most difficult of the three to master is **kanji** (Chinese ideograms), which originally developed as mini-pictures of the word they stand for. To be able to read a newspaper or a book, you'll need to know around 2000 *kanji*, much more difficult than it sounds since what each one means varies with its context.

The easier writing systems to pick up are the phonetic syllabaries, **hiragana** and **katakana**. Both have 45 regular characters (see box, p.829) and can be learned within a couple of weeks. *Hiragana* is used for Japanese words, while *katakana*, with the squarer characters, is used mainly for loan words from Western languages (especially English) and technical names. Increasingly, **romaji** (see p.828), the roman script used to spell out Japanese words, is also used in advertisements and magazines. Good places to practice reading *hiragana* and *katakana* are on the advertisements plastered in train carriages and on restaurant menus

The first five letters in *hiragana* and *katakana* (**a**, **i**, **u**, **e**, **o**) are the vowel sounds (see Pronunciation, p.828). The remainder are a combination of a consonant and a vowel (eg. **ka**, **ki**, **ku**, **ke**, **ko**), with the exception of **n**, the only consonant that exists on its own. While *hiragana* provide an exact phonetic reading of all Japanese words, it's a mistake to think that *katakana* does the same for foreign loan words. Often words are shortened, hence television becomes *terebi* and sexual harrassment *sekuhara*. Sometimes, they become almost unrecognizable, as with *kakuteru*, which is cocktail.

Traditionally, Japanese is written in vertical columns and read right to left. However, the Western way of writing from left to right, horizontally from top to bottom is increasingly being used. In the media and on signs you'll see a mixture of the two ways of writing.

## GRAMMAR

There are several signficant **grammar** differences between Japanese and European languages. **Verbs** do not change according to the person or number, so that *ikimasu* can mean "I go", "he/she/it goes", or "we/they go". **Pronouns**, such as I and they, are usually omitted, since it's clear from the context who or what the speaker is referring to. There are no

## COMMON WORDS AND PHRASES IN JAPANESE

### Personal pronouns

| | | |
|---|---|---|
| I | *watashi* | 私 |
| I (familiar, men only) | *boku* | ぼく |
| I (polite) | *watakushi* | わたくし |
| You | *anata* | あなた |
| You (familiar) | *kimi* | きみ |
| He | *kare* | 彼 |
| She | *kanojo* | 彼女 |
| We | *watashitachi* | わたしたち |
| You (plural) | *anatatachi* | あなたたち |
| They (male/female) | *karera/kanojotachi* | かれら／かのじょたち |
| They (objects) | *sorera* | それら |

### Basics

| | | |
|---|---|---|
| Yes | *hai* | はい |
| No | *iie/chigaimasu* | いいえ／違います |
| OK | *daijōbu/ōkē* | だいじょうぶ／オーケー |
| Well...(as in making things less definite) | *chotto* | ちょっと |
| Please (offering something) | *dōzo* | どうぞ |
| Please (asking for something) | *onegai shimasu* | お願いします |
| Excuse me | *sumimasen/shitsurei shimasu* | すみません／失礼します |
| I'm sorry | *gomen nasai/sumimasen* | ごめんなさい／すみません |
| Thanks (informal) | *dōmo* | どうも |
| Thank you | *dōmo arigatō* | どうもありがとう |
| Thank you very much | *dōmo arigatō gozaimasu* | どうもありがとうございます |
| What? | *nani?* | なに？ |
| When? | *itsu?* | いつ？ |
| Where? | *doko?* | どこ？ |
| Who? | *dare?* | だれ？ |
| This | *kore* | これ |
| That | *sore* | それ |
| That (over there) | *are* | あれ |
| How many? | *ikutsu?* | いくつ？ |
| How much? | *ikura?* | いくら？ |
| I want (x) | *Watashi wa (x) ga hoshii desu* | 私は（x）がほしいです |
| I don't want (x) | *Watashi wa (x) ga irimasen* | 私は（x）がいりません |
| Is it possible...? | *... koto ga dekimasu ka* | 。。。ことができますか |
| It is not possible | *... koto ga dekimasen* | 。。。ことができません |
| Is it ...? | *... desu ka* | 。。。ですか |
| Can you please help me | *Tetsudatte kuremasen ka* | 手伝ってくれませんか |

### Communicating

| | | |
|---|---|---|
| I don't speak Japanese | *Nihongo wa hanashimasen* | 日本語は話しません |
| I don't read Japanese | *Nihongo wa yomimasen* | 日本語は読みません |
| Can you speak English? | *Eigo ga dekimasu ka* | 英語ができますか |
| Is there someone who can interpret? | *Tsūyaku wa imasu ka* | 通訳はいますか |
| Could you please speak slowly | *Motto yukkuri hanashite kuremasen ka* | もっとゆっくり話してくれませんか |
| Please say that again | *Mō ichido itte kuremasen ka* | もう一度言ってくれませんか |
| I understand/I see | *Wakarimasu/Naruhodo* | わかります／なるほど |
| I don't understand | *Wakarimasen* | わかりません |
| What does this mean? | *Imi wa nan desu ka* | 意味は何ですか |

| How do you say (x) in Japanese? | Nihongo de (x) o nan-te iimasu ka | 日本語で（x）を何て言いますか |
| What's this called? | Kore wa nan-to iimasu ka | これは何と言いますか |
| How do you pronounce this character? | Kono kanji wa nan-te iimasu ka | この漢字は何て言いますか |
| Please write in English/Japanese | Eigo/Nihongo de kaite kudasai | 英語／日本語で書いてください |

## Greetings and basic courtesies

| Hello/Good day | Konnichiwa | こんにちは |
| Good morning | Ohayō gozaimasu | おはようございます |
| Good evening | Konbanwa | こんばんは |
| Good night (when leaving) | Osaki ni | お先に |
| Good night (when going to bed) | Oyasuminasai | おやすみなさい |
| How are you? | O-genki desu ka | お元気ですか |
| I'm fine (informal) | Genki desu | 元気です |
| I'm fine, thanks | Okagesama de | おかげさまで |
| How do you do/Nice to meet you | Hajimemashite | はじめまして |
| Don't mention it/you're welcome | Dō itashimashite | どういたしまして |
| I'm sorry | Gomen nasai | ごめんなさい |
| Just a minute please | Chotto matte kudasai | ちょっと待ってください |
| Goodbye | Sayonara | さよなら |
| Goodbye (informal) | Dewa mata/Jā ne | では又／じゃあね |

## Chitchat

| What's your name? | Shitsurei desu ga o-namae wa | 失礼ですがお名前は |
| My name is (x) | Watashi no namae wa (x) desu | 私の名前は（x）です |
| Where are you from? | O-kuni wa doko desu ka | おくにはどこですか |
| Britain | Eikoku | 英国 |
| British | Igirisu | イギリス |
| Ireland | Airurando | アイルランド |
| America | Amerika | アメリカ |
| Australia | Ōsutoraria | オーストラリア |
| Canada | Kanada | カナダ |
| France | Furansu | フランス |
| Germany | Doitsu | ドイツ |
| Japan | Nihon | 日本 |
| Outside Japan | Gaikoku | 外国 |
| New Zealand | Nyū Jiirando | ニュージーランド |
| How old are you? | Ikutsu desu ka | いくつですか |
| I am (age) | (age) sai desu | （age）才です |
| Are you married? | Kekkon shite imasu ka | 結婚していますか |
| I am married/not married | Kekkon shite imasu/imasen | 結婚しています／いません |
| Do you like...? | ... suki desu ka | 。。。好きですか |
| I do like | ... suki desu | 。。。好きです |
| I don't like | ... suki dewa arimasen | 。。。好きではありません |
| What's your job? | O-shigoto wa nan desu ka | お仕事は何ですか |
| I'm a student | Gakusei desu | 学生です |
| I'm a teacher | Sensei desu | 先生です |
| I work for a company | Kaishain desu | 会社員です |
| I'm a tourist | Kankō kyaku desu | 観光客です |
| Really? | hontō | 本当？ |
| That's a shame | zannen desu | 残念です |
| It can't be helped | shikata ga nai/shō ga nai (informal) | 仕方がない／しょうがない |

continued overleaf

## COMMON WORDS AND PHRASES IN JAPANESE contd

### Adjectives

| | | |
|---|---|---|
| Clean/dirty | *kirei/kitanai* | きれい／きたない |
| Hot/cold | *atsui/samui* | あつい／さむい |
| Fast/slow | *hayai/osoi* | はやい／おそい |
| Pretty/ugly | *kirei/minikui* | きれい／みにくい |
| Interesting/boring | *omoshiroi/tsumaranai* | おもしろい／つまらない |

### Numbers

There are special ways of counting different things in Japanese. The safest option is to stick to the most common first translation, used when counting time and quantities and measurements, with added qualifiers such as minutes (*pun/fun*) or yen (*en*). The second translations are sometimes used for counting objects, as in *biiru futatsu, onegai shimasu* (two beers please). Above ten, there is only one set of numbers. For four, seven and nine there are alternatives to the first translation used in some circumstances.

| | | | | |
|---|---|---|---|---|
| Zero | *zero* | | | ゼロ |
| One | *ichi* | *hitotsu* | 一 | ひとつ |
| Two | *ni* | *futatsu* | 二 | ふたつ |
| Three | *san* | *mittsu* | 三 | みっつ |
| Four | *yon/shi* | *yottsu* | 四 | よっつ |
| Five | *go* | *itsutsu* | 五 | いつつ |
| Six | *roku* | *muttsu* | 六 | むっつ |
| Seven | *shichi/nana* | *nanatsu* | 七 | ななつ |
| Eight | *hachi* | *yattsu* | 八 | やっつ |
| Nine | *ku/kyū* | *kokonotsu* | 九 | ここのつ |
| Ten | *jū* | *tō* | 十 | とう |
| Eleven | *jū-ichi* | | 十一 | |
| Twelve | *jū-ni* | | 十二 | |
| Twenty | *ni-jū* | | 二十 | |
| Twenty one | *ni-jū-ichi* | | 二十一 | |
| Thirty | *san-jū* | | 三十 | |
| One hundred | *hyaku* | | 百 | |
| Two hundred | *ni-hyaku* | | 二百 | |
| Thousand | *sen* | | 千 | |
| Ten Thousand | *ichi-man* | | 一万 | |
| One hundred thousand | *jū-man* | | 十万 | |
| One million | *hyaku-man* | | 百万 | |
| One hundred million | *ichi-oku* | | 一億 | |

### Time and dates

| | | |
|---|---|---|
| Now | *ima* | 今 |
| Today | *kyō* | 今日 |
| Morning | *asa* | 朝 |
| Evening | *yūgata* | 夕方 |
| Night | *yoru* | 夜 |
| Tomorrow | *ashita* | 明日 |
| The day after tomorrow | *asatte* | あさって |
| Yesterday | *kinō* | 昨日 |
| Week | *shūkan* | 週間 |
| Month | *gatsu* | 月 |
| Year | *nen/toshi* | 年 |
| Monday | *Getsuyōbi* | 月曜日 |
| Tuesday | *Kayōbi* | 火曜日 |
| Wednesday | *Suiyōbi* | 水曜日 |

| Thursday | *Mokuyōbi* | 木曜日 |
| Friday | *Kinyōbi* | 金曜日 |
| Saturday | *Doyōbi* | 土曜日 |
| Sunday | *Nichiyōbi* | 日曜日 |

| What time is it? | *Ima nan-ji desu ka* | 今何時ですか |
| It's 10 o'clock | *Jū-ji desu* | 十時です |
| 10.20 | *Jū-ji ni-juppun* | 十時二十分 |
| 10.30 | *Jū-ji han* | 十時半 |
| 10.50 | *Jū-ichi-ji juppun mae* | 十一時十分前 |
| AM | *gozen* | 午前 |
| PM | *gogo* | 午後 |

| January | *Ichigatsu* | 一月 |
| February | *Nigatsu* | 二月 |
| March | *Sangatsu* | 三月 |
| April | *Shigatsu* | 四月 |
| May | *Gogatsu* | 五月 |
| June | *Rokugatsu* | 六月 |
| July | *Shichigatsu* | 七月 |
| August | *Hachigatsu* | 八月 |
| September | *Kugatsu* | 九月 |
| October | *Jūgatsu* | 十月 |
| November | *Jūichigatsu* | 十一月 |
| December | *Jūnigatsu* | 十二月 |

| 1st (day) | *tsuitachi* | 一日 |
| 2nd (day) | *futsuka* | 二日 |
| 3rd (day) | *mikka* | 三日 |
| 4th (day) | *yokka* | 四日 |
| 5th (day) | *itsuka* | 五日 |
| 6th (day) | *muika* | 六日 |
| 7th (day) | *nanoka* | 七日 |
| 8th (day) | *yōka* | 八日 |
| 9th (day) | *kokonoka* | 九日 |
| 10th (day) | *tōka* | 十日 |
| 11th (day) | *jū-ichi-nichi* | 十一日 |
| 12th (day) | *jū-ni-nichi* | 十二日 |
| 20th (day) | *hatsuka* | 二十日 |
| 21st (day) | *ni-jū-ichi nichi* | 二十一日 |
| 30th (day) | *san-jū-nichi* | 三十日 |

### Transport and travelling

| Airplane | *hikōki* | 飛行機 |
| Airport | *kūkō* | 空港 |
| Bus | *basu* | バス |
| Long-distance bus | *chōkyori basu* | 長距離バス |
| Bus stop | *basu tei* | バス亭 |
| Train | *densha* | 電車 |
| Station | *eki* | 駅 |
| Subway | *chikatetsu* | 地下鉄 |
| Ferry | *ferii* | フェリー |
| Left luggage office | *ichiji azukarijo* | 一時預かり所 |
| Coin locker | *koin rokkā* | コインロッカー |

*continued overleaf*

## COMMON WORDS AND PHRASES IN JAPANESE contd

| | | |
|---|---|---|
| Ticket office | *kippu uriba* | 切符売り場 |
| Ticket | *kippu* | 切符 |
| One-way | *kata-michi* | 片道 |
| Return | *ōfuku* | 往復 |
| Non-smoking seat | *kin'en seki* | 禁煙席 |
| Window seat | *mado-gawa no seki* | 窓側の席 |
| Platform | *hōmu* | ホーム |
| Bicycle | *jitensha* | 自転車 |
| Taxi | *takushii* | タクシー |

**Directions and general places**

| | | |
|---|---|---|
| Map | *chizu* | 地図 |
| Where is (x)? | *(x) wa doko desu ka* | （x）はどこですか |
| Straight ahead | *massugu* | まっすぐ |
| In front of | *mae* | 前 |
| Right | *migi* | 右 |
| Left | *hidari* | 左 |
| North | *kita* | 北 |
| South | *minami* | 南 |
| East | *higashi* | 東 |
| West | *nishi* | 西 |
| Temple | *otera/odera/-ji/-in* | お寺／一寺／一院 |
| Shrine | *jinja/jingū/-gū/taisha* | 神社／神宮／一宮／大社 |
| Castle | *-jō* | 一城 |
| Park | *kōen* | 公園 |
| River | *kawa/gawa* | 川 |
| Bridge | *hashi/bashi* | 橋 |
| Museum | *hakubutsukan* | 博物館 |
| Art gallery | *bijutsukan* | 美術館 |
| Zoo | *dōbutsuen* | 動物園 |
| Garden | *niwa/teien/-en* | 庭／庭園／一園 |
| Island | *shima/jima/tō* | 島 |
| Slope | *saka/zaka* | 坂 |
| Hill | *oka* | 岡 |
| Mountain | *yama/-san/-take* | 山／岳 |
| Hot spring spa | *onsen* | 温泉 |
| Lake | *-ko* | 一湖 |
| Bay | *-wan* | 一湾 |
| Peninsula | *hantō* | 半島 |
| Cape | *misaki/saki* | 岬 |
| Sea | *umi/kai/nada* | 海／灘 |
| Gorge | *kyō* | 峡 |
| Plateau | *kōgen* | 高原 |
| Train line | *sen* | 線 |
| Prefecture | *-ken/-fu* | 一県／一府 |
| Ward | *-ku* | 一区 |
| Exit | *deguchi/-guchi* | 出口／一口 |
| Street | *tōri/dōri/michi* | 通り／道 |
| Highway | *kaidō* | 街道 |
| Shop | *mise/-ya/-ten* | 店／屋 |

**Accommodation**

| | | |
|---|---|---|
| Hotel | *hoteru* | ホテル |
| Traditional-style inn | *ryokan* | 旅館 |

| | | |
|---|---|---|
| Guesthouse | *minshuku* | 民宿 |
| Youth hostel | *yūsu hosuteru* | ユースホステル |
| Single room | *shinguru rūmu* | シングルルーム |
| Double room | *daburu rūmu* | ダブルルーム |
| Twin room | *tsuin rūmu* | ツインルーム |
| Dormitory | *kyōdō/ōbeya* | 共同／大部屋 |
| Japanese-style room | *washitsu* | 和室 |
| Western-style room | *yōshitsu* | 洋室 |
| Western-style bed | *beddo* | ベッド |
| Bath | *o-furo* | お風呂 |

| | | |
|---|---|---|
| Do you have any vacancies? | *Aita heya wa arimasu ka* | 空いた部屋はありますか |
| I'd like to make a reservation | *Yoyaku o shitai no desu ga* | 予約をしたいのですが |
| I have a reservation | *Yoyaku shimashita* | 予約しました |
| I don't have a reservation | *Yoyaku shimasen deshita* | 予約しませんでした |
| How much is it per person? | *Hitori ikura desu ka* | 一人いくらですか？ |
| Does that include meals? | *Shokuji wa tsuite imasu ka* | 食事はついていますか |
| I would like to stay one night/ two nights | *Hitoban/futaban tomarimasu* | 一晩／二晩泊まります |
| I would like to see the room | *Heya o misete kudasaimasen ka* | 部屋を見せてくださいませんか |
| Key | *kagi* | 鍵 |
| Passport | *pasupōto* | パスポート |

**Shopping, money and banks**

| | | |
|---|---|---|
| How much is it? | *Kore wa ikura desu ka* | これはいくらですか |
| It's too expensive | *Taka-sugimasu* | 高すぎます |
| Is there anything cheaper? | *Mō sukoshi yasui mono wa arimasu ka* | もう少し安いものはありますか |
| Do you accept credit cards? | *Kurejitto kādo wa tsukaemasu ka* | クレジットカードは使えますか |
| I'm just looking | *Miru dake desu* | 見るだけです |
| Yen | *Yen/-en* | 円 |
| UK pounds | *pondo* | ポンド |
| Dollars | *doru* | ドル |
| Foreign exchange | *gaikoku kawase* | 外国為替 |
| Bank | *ginkō* | 銀行 |
| Travellers' cheque | *toraberāzu chekku* | トラベラーズチェック |

**Post and telephones**

| | | |
|---|---|---|
| Post office | *yūbinkyoku* | 郵便局 |
| Envelope | *fūtō* | 封筒 |
| Letter | *tegami* | 手紙 |
| Postcard | *hagaki* | 葉書 |
| Stamp | *kitte* | 切手 |
| Airmail | *kōkūbin* | 航空便 |
| Surface mail | *sarubin* | サル便 |
| Sea mail | *funabin* | 船便 |
| Post restante | *tomeoki* | 留置 |
| Telephone | *denwa* | 電話 |
| International telephone call | *kokusai-denwa* | 国際電話 |
| Reverse charge/collect call | *Korekuto-kōru* | コレクトコール |
| Fax | *Fakkusu* | ファックス |
| Telephone card | *Terefon kādo* | テレフォンカード |
| I would like to call (place) | (place) *e denwa o kaketai no desu* | （place）へ電話をかけたいのです |
| I would like to send a fax to (place) | (place) *e fakkusu shitai no desu* | （place）へファックスしたいのです |

*continued overleaf*

## COMMON WORDS AND PHRASES IN JAPANESE contd

**Health**

| | | |
|---|---|---|
| Hospital | *byōin* | 病院 |
| Pharmacy | *yakkyoku* | 薬局 |
| Medicine | *kusuri* | 薬 |
| Doctor | *isha* | 医者 |
| Dentist | *haisha* | 歯医者 |
| Diarrhoea | *geri* | 下痢 |
| Nausea | *hakike* | はきけ |
| Fever | *netsu* | 熱 |
| Food poisoning | *shoku chūdoku* | 食中毒 |
| I'm ill | *byōki desu* | 病気です |
| I've got a cold/flu | *kaze o hikimashita* | 風邪をひきました |
| I'm allergic to (x) | *(x) arerugii desu* | （x）アレルギーです |
| Antibiotics | *kōsei busshitsu* | 抗生物質 |
| Antiseptic | *shōdoku* | 消毒 |
| Condom | *kondōmu* | コンドーム |
| Mosquito repellent | *kayoke-supurē* | 蚊よけスプレー |

**definite articles**, and **nouns** stay the same whether they refer to singular or plural words.

From the point of view of English grammar, Japanese **sentences** are structured back to front. An English speaker would say "I am going to Tokyo" which in Japanese would translate directly as "Tokyo to going". Placing the sound "ka" at the end of a verb indicates a **question**, hence *Tokyo e ikimasu-ka* means "Are you going to Tokyo?". There are also levels of **politeness** to contend with, which alter the way the verb is conjugated, and sometimes changes the word entirely. For the most part, stick to the polite -**masu** form of verbs and you'll be fine.

If you want to learn more about the language and have a wider range of expressions and vocabulary at your command than those listed here, invest in a **phrasebook** or dictionary. *Japanese: A Rough Guide Phrasebook* is user-friendly and combines essential phrases and expressions with a dictionary section and menu reader. The phonetic translations in this phrasebook are rendered slightly differently from the standard way *romaji* is written in this book, as an aid to pronunciation. One of the best books for learning Japanese more thoroughly is *Japanese For Busy People* (Kodansha), which comes in three parts and is often used as a set text in Japanese-language classes. A worthy alternative, although more difficult to buy outside of Japan, is *Communicative Japanese for Time Pressed People* (Aratake Publishing).

## PRONUNCIATION

Throughout this book, Japanese words have been transliterated into the standard Hepburn system of romanization, called **romaji**. Pronunciation is as follows:

**a** as in r**a**ther
**i** as in macaron**i**, or **ee**
**u** as in p**u**t, or **oo**
**e** as in b**e**d; e is always pronounced, even at the end of a word
**o** as in n**o**t
**ae** as in the two separate sounds, **ah-eh**
**ai** as in Th**ai**
**ei** as in w**ei**ght
**ie** as in two separate sounds, **ee-eh**
**ue** as in two seperate sounds, **oo-eh**
**g**, a hard sound as in **g**irl
**s** as in ma**ss** (never z)
**y** as in **y**et

A bar over a vowel or "ii" means that the vowel sound is twice as long as a vowel without a bar. Only where words are well known in English, such as Tokyo, Kyoto, judo and shogun, have we not used a bar to indicate long vowel sounds. Sometimes, vowel sounds are shortened or softened, for example, the verb *desu* sounds more like *des* when pronounced, and *sukiyaki* like *skiyaki*. Apart from this, all syllables in Japanese words are evenly stressed and pronounced in full. For example, Nagano is Na-ga-no, not Na-GA-no.

## HIRAGANA AND KATAKANA

The Japanese script consists of **hiragana**, **katakana** and ideograms based on Chinese characters (*kanji*). *Hiragana* and *katakana* are two phonetic syllabaries represented by the characters shown below. *Katakana*, the squarer characters on the left of each column, are used for writing foreign "loan words". The rounder characters on the right, *hiragana*, are used for Japanese words, in combination with, or as substitues for, *kanji*.

| a | ア | あ | i | イ | い | u | ウ | う | e | エ | え | o | オ | お |
|---|---|---|---|---|---|---|---|---|---|---|---|---|---|---|
| ka | カ | か | ki | キ | き | ku | ク | く | ke | ケ | け | ko | コ | こ |
| sa | サ | さ | shi | シ | し | su | ス | す | se | セ | せ | so | ソ | そ |
| ta | タ | た | chi | チ | ち | tsu | ツ | つ | te | テ | て | to | ト | と |
| na | ナ | な | ni | ニ | に | nu | ヌ | ぬ | ne | ネ | ね | no | ノ | の |
| ha | ハ | は | hi | ヒ | ひ | fu | フ | ふ | he | ヘ | へ | ho | ホ | ほ |
| ma | マ | ま | mi | ミ | み | mu | ム | む | me | メ | め | mo | モ | も |
| ya | ヤ | や | | | | yu | ユ | ゆ | | | | yo | ヨ | よ |
| ra | ラ | ら | ri | リ | り | ru | ル | る | re | レ | れ | ro | ロ | ろ |
| wa | ワ | わ | | | | | | | | | | | | |
| n | ン | ん | | | | | | | | | | | | |

# GLOSSARY OF JAPANESE TERMS

(For food and restaurant terms, see p.47–49.)

## GENERAL TERMS

**aikido** "The way of harmonious spirit". A form of self-defence performed without weapons, now recognized as a sport.

**Amida Nyorai** Amida Buddha will lead worthy souls to the Western Paradise (the Pure Land).

**banzai** The traditional Japanese cheer, meaning "10,000 years".

**basho** Sumo tournament

**Benten** or **Benzai-ten**. One of the most popular folk-goddesses, usually associated with water.

**bodhisattva** or **bosatsu**. A Buddhist intermediary who has forsaken *nirvana* to work for the salvation of all humanity.

**Bunraku** Traditional puppet theatre.

**Butō** Highly expressive contemporary performance art.

**cha-no-yu** or **chadō** The tea ceremony. Ritual tea drinking raised to an art form.

**chō** or *machi* Subdivision of the city, smaller than a -*ku*.

**chōme** Area of the city consisting of a few blocks.

**daimyō** Feudal lords.

**-dake** Mountain peak, usually volcanic.

**Dainichi Nyorai** or **Rushana Butsu** The Cosmic Buddha in whom all buddhas are unified.

**donjon** Castle keep.

**dōri** Main road.

**Edo** Pre-1868 name for Tokyo.

**ema** Small wooden boards found at shrines, on which people write their wishes or thanks.

**fusuma** Paper-covered sliding doors, more substantial than *shōji*, used to separate rooms or for cupboards.

**futon** Padded quilt used for bedding.

**gagaku** Ancient Japanese music, now performed mostly in the imperial court.

**gaijin** Foreigner.

**geisha** Traditional female entertainer accomplished in the arts.

**genkan** Foyer or entrance hall of a house, ryokan and so forth, for changing from outdoor shoes into slippers.

**geta** Traditional wooden sandals.

**haiku** Seventeen-syllable verse form, arranged in three lines of five, seven and five syllables.

**hanami** "Flower-viewing", most commonly associated with spring outings to admire the cherry blossom.

**hashi**, or **bashi** Bridge.

**hiragana** Phonetic script used for writing Japanese in combination with *kanji*.

**ijinkan** Western-style brick and clapboard houses.

**ikebana** Traditional art of flower arranging.

**Inari** Shinto god of harvests, often represented by his fox-messenger.

**-ji** Buddhist temple.

**jigoku** The word for Buddhist "hell", also applied to volcanic mud pools and steam vents.

**-jinja** or **-jingū** Shinto shrine.

**Jizō** Buddhist protector of children, travellers and the dead.

**-jō** Castle.

**Kabuki** Popular theatre of the Edo period.

**Kami** Shinto deities residing in trees, rocks and other natural phenomena.

**kamikaze** The "Divine Wind" which saved Japan from the Mongol invaders (see p.771–772). During World War II the name was applied to Japan's suicide bombers.

**kanji** Japanese script derived from Chinese characters.

**Kannon** Buddhist goddess of mercy. A bodhisattva who appears in many different forms.

**katakana** Phonetic script used mainly for writing foreign words in Japanese.

**kawa** or **gawa** River.

**ken** Prefecture. The principal administrative region, similar to a state or county.

**kendo** The "way of the sword". Japan's oldest martial art, using wooden staves, with its roots in *samurai* training exercises.

**kimono** Literally "clothes", though usually referring to women's traditional dress.

**-ko** Lake.

**kōban** Neighbourhood police box.

**kōen**, or gyoen Public park.

**Kōgen** Plateau.

**ku** Principle administrative division of the city, usually translated as "ward".

**kura** Traditional storehouse built with thick mud-walls as protection against fire, for keeping produce and family treasures.

**kyōgen** Short, satirical plays, providing comic interludes in Nô drama.

**machi** Town or area of a city.

**maiko** Apprentice geisha.

**manga** Japanese comics.

**matcha** Powdered green tea used in the tea ceremony.

**matsuri** Festival.

**Meiji** Period named after Emperor Meiji (1868–1912), meaning "enlightened rule".

**Meiji Restoration** The Restoration (1868) marked the end of the Tokugawa Shogunate, when power was fully restored to the emperor.

**mikoshi** Portable shrine used in festivals.

**minshuku** Family-run lodgings, similar to bed-and-breakfast, which are cheaper than ryokan.

**mon** Gate, usually to a castle, temple or palace.

**mura** Village.

**netsuke** Small, intricately carved toggles for fastening the cords of cloth bags.

**ningyō** Japanese doll.

**Niō**, or **Kongo Rikishi** Two muscular, fearsome Buddhist kings (*ten*) who stand guard at temple gates, usually one open-mouthed and one closed.

**Nō** Highly stylized dance-drama, using masks and elaborate costumes.

**noren** Split curtain hanging in shop and restaurant doorways to indicate they're open.

**Notemburo** Outdoor hot-spring pool, usually in natural surroundings.

**obi** Wide sash worn with kimono.

**odori** Traditional dances performed in the streets during the summer Obon festival. The most famous is Tokushima's Awa Odori (see p.615).

**onsen** Hot spring, generally developed for bathing.

**pachinko** Vertical pinball machines.

**pond-garden** Classic form of garden design focused around a pond.

**romaji** System of transliterating Japanese words using the roman alphabet.

**rōnin** Masterless *samurai* (see p.773).

**rotemburo** Outdoor hot-spring pool, often in the grounds of a ryokan.

**ryokan** Traditional Japanese inn.

**salarymen** The thousands of suited office-workers who keep Japan's companies and ministries ticking over.

**samurai** Warrior class who were retainers of the *daimyō*.

**san**, or **-zan** Mountain.

**sentō** Neighbourhood public bath.

**seppuku** Ritual suicide by disembowelment, commonly known as *hara-kiri*.

**Shaka Nyorai** The historical Buddha, Sakyamuni.

**shamisen** Traditional, three-stringed instrument played with a plectrum.

**-shima**, or **-jima** Island.

**Shinkansen** Bullet train.

**Shinto** Japan's indigenous religion, based on the premise that gods inhabit all natural things, both animate and inanimate.

**Shitamachi** Low-lying, working-class districts of east Tokyo, nowadays usually referring to Asakusa and Ueno.

**shōji** Paper-covered sliding screens used to divide rooms or cover windows.

**shogun** The military rulers of Japan before 1868, nominally subordinate to the emperor.

**shukubō** Temple lodgings.

**soaplands** Euphemistic name for bathhouses offering massages and, frequently, sexual services.

**stroll-garden** Style of garden design popular in the Edo-period (1600–1868), comprising a series of tableaux which unfold as the viewer walks through the garden.

**sumi-e** Ink paintings, traditionally using black ink.

**sumo** Japan's national sport, a form of heavyweight wrestling which evolved from ancient Shinto divination rites.

**taiko** Drums.

**tatami** Rice-straw matting, the traditional covering for floors.

**-tera**, or **-dera** Buddhist temple.

**tokonoma** Alcove in a room where flowers or a scroll are displayed.

**torii** Gate to a Shinto shrine.

**ukiyo-e** Colourful woodblock prints or paintings which became particularly popular in the late eighteenth century.

**waka** Thirty-one syllable poem, arranged in five lines of five, seven, five, seven and seven syllables.

**washi** Traditional, handmade paper.

**Yakushi Nyorai** The Buddha in charge of physical and spiritual healing.

**yakuza** Professional criminal gangs, somewhat akin to the Mafia.

**yama** Mountain.

**yamabushi** Ascetic mountain priests.

**yukata** Loose cotton robe worn as a dressing gown in ryokan.

## ORGANIZATIONS

**ANA** All Nippon Airways

**JAL** Japan Airlines

**JAS** Japan Air System

**JNTO** Japan National Tourist Organization, the government's overseas tourist office.

**JR** Japan Railways.

**JTB** Japan Travel Bureau.

**SDF** (Self Defence Forces) Japan's army, navy and airforce, established in 1954 purely for national defence, though now also used for international peace-keeping operations.

**TIC** Tourist Information Centre, with English-speaking staff.

# INDEX

# Stay in touch with us!

**ROUGH***NEWS* **is Rough Guides' free newsletter. In three issues a year we give you news, travel issues, music reviews, readers' letters and the latest dispatches from authors on the road.**

I would like to receive ROUGH*NEWS*: please put me on your free mailing list.

NAME . . . . . . . . . . . . . . . . . . . . . . . . . . . . . . . . . . . . . . . . . . . . . . . . . . . . . . . . . . . . . . . . . . . . .

ADDRESS . . . . . . . . . . . . . . . . . . . . . . . . . . . . . . . . . . . . . . . . . . . . . . . . . . . . . . . . . . . . . . . . . . .

Please clip or photocopy and send to: Rough Guides, 62–70 Shorts Gardens, London WC2H 9AB, England or Rough Guides, 375 Hudson Street, New York, NY 10014, USA.

# Introducing Tekware.
## (What to wear when your biggest fashion concern is hypothermia.)

Lynn Hill climbing Three Sisters,
Photo: Clint Clemens

Made from advanced synthetic fabrics, **TEKWARE®** is clothing that dries faster, lasts longer and maintains overall comfort better than cotton. Its design combines the experience of world-class outdoor athletes and the expertise of our research and development teams. The result is a line of technologically superior outdoor equipment that makes cotton obsolete. For the dealer nearest you or to receive a free catalogue call: First Ascent, Units 2-5, Limetree Business Park, Matlock, Derbyshire, England DE4 3EJ, Freephone: 0800 146034.

**NEVER STOP EXPLORING**